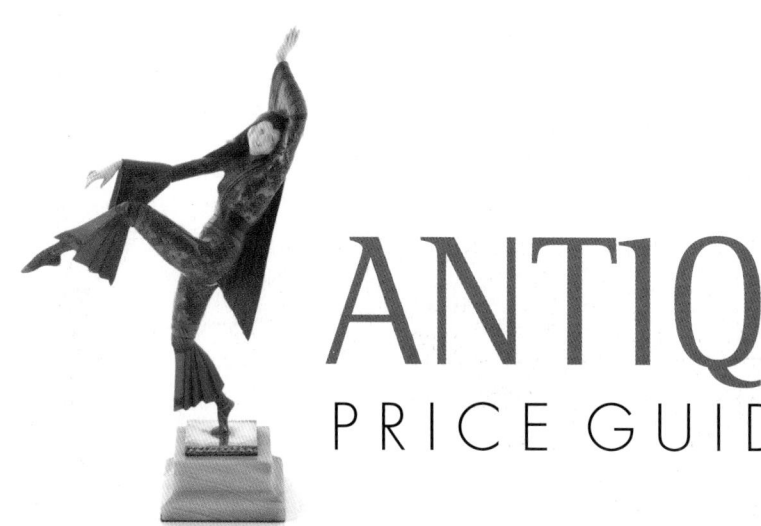

ANTIQUES

PRICE GUIDE 2007

ANTIQUES
PRICE GUIDE 2007

Judith Miller

TED SMART

LONDON, NEW YORK,
MELBOURNE, MUNICH, DELHI

A joint production from Dorling Kindersley
and The Price Guide Company

THE PRICE GUIDE COMPANY LIMITED

Publisher Judith Miller
Publishing Manager Julie Brooke
Senior Managing Editor Carolyn Madden
European Consultant Martina Franke
Editor Jessica Bishop
Sub-editors Dan Dunlavey, Sandra Lange, Karen Morden
Digital Image Co-ordinator Ellen Sinclair
Editorial Assistant Carolyn Malarkey
Design & DTP Tim & Ali Scrivens, TJ Graphics
Photographers Graham Rae, John McKenzie, Andy Johnson, Byron Slater, Heike Löwenstein, Adam Gault, Bruce Boyajian, Ellen McDermott
Indexer Hilary Bird
Workflow Consultant Bob Bousfield
Publishing Advisor Nick Croydon

DORLING KINDERSLEY LIMITED

Publishing Director Jackie Douglas
Managing Art Editor Christine Keilty
Managing Editor Julie Oughton
DTP Designer Adam Walker
Production Elizabeth Warman
Production Manager Sarah Coltman

First published in 2006 by
Dorling Kindersley Limited
80 Strand, London WC2R 0RL

Penguin Group

The Price Guide Company (UK) Ltd
Studio 21, Waterside
44–48 Wharf Road
London N1 7UX
info@thepriceguidecompany.com

2 4 6 8 10 9 7 5 3 1

A CIP catalogue record for this book is available from the British Library.

This edition produced for The Book People Ltd, Hall Wood Avenue,
Haydock, St Helens WA119UL

ISBN-13: 978 1 4053 1571 5
ISBN-10: 1 4053 1571 7

Printed and bound by MOHN media and Mohndruck GmbH, Germany

Discover more at
www.dk.com

CONTENTS

LIST OF CONSULTANTS

Ceramics

John Axford
Woolley & Wallis
51-61 Castle Street
Salisbury Wiltshire SP1 3SU

Clocks

Paul Archard
Derek Roberts Fine Antique Clocks
25 Shipbourne Road
Tonbridge Kent TN10 3DN

Gavin Strang
Gavin Strang
Lyon & Turnbull Ltd
33 Broughton Place
Edinburgh EH1 3RR

Decorative Arts

Michael James
The Silver Fund
1 Duke of York Street
London SW1Y 6JP

Michael Jeffery
Woolley & Wallis
51-61 Castle Street
Salisbury Wiltshire SP1 3SU

John Mackie
Lyon & Turnbull Ltd
33 Broughton Place
Edinburgh EH1 3RR

Furniture

Paul Roberts
Lyon & Turnbull Ltd
33 Broughton Place
Edinburgh EH1 3RR

Matthew Smith
Christie's
8 King Street, St. James's
London SW1Y 6QT

Glass

Jeanette Hayhurst
Jeanette Hayhurst Fine Glass
32a Kensington Church Street
London W8 4HA

Oriental

Clive Stewart Lockhart
Dreweatt Neate
Donnington Priory Salerooms
Newbury Berkshire RG14 2JE

Robert McPherson
R & G McPherson Antiques
40 Kensington Church Street
London W8 4BX

Paintings

Nick Curnow
Lyon & Turnbull Ltd
33 Broughton Place
Edinburgh EH1 3RR

Silver

Trevor Kyle
Lyon & Turnbull Ltd
33 Broughton Place
Edinburgh EH1 3RR

Toys

Glenn Butler
Wallis & Wallis
West Street Auction Galleries
Lewes
East Sussex BN7 2NJ

Tribal Art

Philip Keith

20th Century

Mark Hill
The Price Guide Company (UK) Ltd

HOW TO USE THIS BOOK

Running head – Indicates the sub-category of the main heading.

The introduction – The key facts about a factory, maker or style are given, along with stylistic identification points, value tips and advice on fakes.

Caption – The description of the item illustrated, including, when relevant, the period, the maker or factory, medium, the year it was made, dimensions and condition. Many captions have **footnotes** which explain terminology or give identification or valuation information.

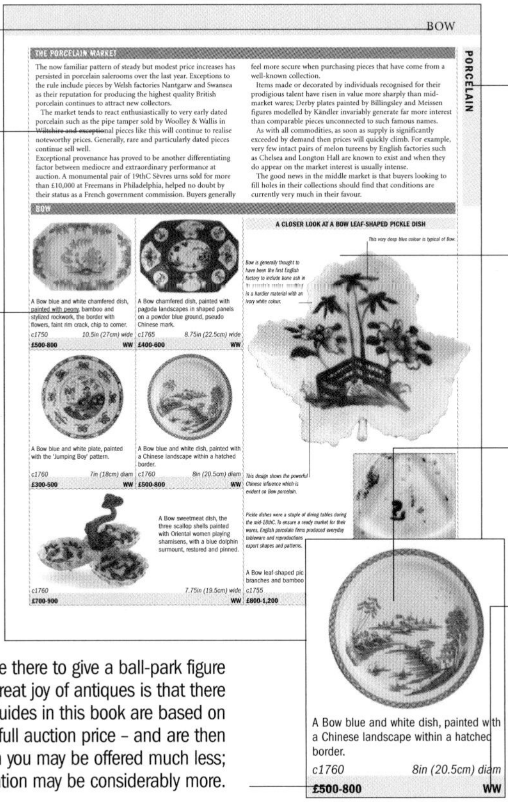

Page tab – This device appears on every spread and identifies the main category heading as indicated in the Contents List on pp.5–6.

A closer look at – Does exactly that. This is where we show identifying aspects of a factory or maker, point out rare colours or shapes and explain why a particular piece is so desirable.

The object – The antiques are shown in full colour. This is a vital aid to identification and valuation. With many objects, a slight colour variation can signify a large price differential.

The source code – Every item in *Antiques Price Guide 2007* has been specially photographed at an auction house, a dealer, an antiques market or a private collection. These are credited by the code at the end of the caption, and can be checked against the Key to Illustrations on pages 724–6.

The price guide – The price ranges in the Guide are there to give a ball-park figure of what you should pay for a similar item. The great joy of antiques is that there is not a recommended retail price. The prices guides in this book are based on actual prices – either what a dealer will take or the full auction price – and are then checked by consultants. If you wish to sell an item you may be offered much less; if you want to insure your items the insurance valuation may be considerably more.

WHAT'S HOT?

The generally accepted definition of the word "antique" was devised by US customs officials during the 1930s. Deciding to place the chronological cut-off point at around 1830, when mass production had forever changed the nature of consumer goods, they determined that an antique is something that is more than 100 years old. Why, then, have I allotted so much space in this book to objects made far more recently than 1907? It is my contention that the definition laid down by those excise men all that time ago no longer holds water and we need to ask the question again: what exactly is an antique?

An early 18thC walnut bureau bookcase, worth **£50,000-60,000 RGA**

THE CURRENT MARKET

Many of the areas that once made up the bedrock of the antiques trade have languished in relative neglect for years now. The bear market in "brown furniture" is well documented, but other fields have suffered a similarly unenviable fate. People who have accrued collections of 18th-century European porcelain – myself among them – have seen the value of their assets take a dive since the heady days of the early 1990s. Items at the top end of the market have been protected from this downturn to a certain extent by virtue of their extreme rarity, uncommon beauty, rock solid provenance, or a combination of these factors.

Elsewhere, however, prices have been falling and in many cases these falls have been dramatic. The antiques market is as susceptible as any commercial arena to the normal ups and downs of the economic cycle, but that doesn't explain our current predicament as the economic outlook at the moment is fairly rosy, albeit a little cautious.

The fact is that people are still buying furniture and decorative arts on the secondary market, but they are spending more and more of their money on "new antiques".

THE NEW SUPERSTARS

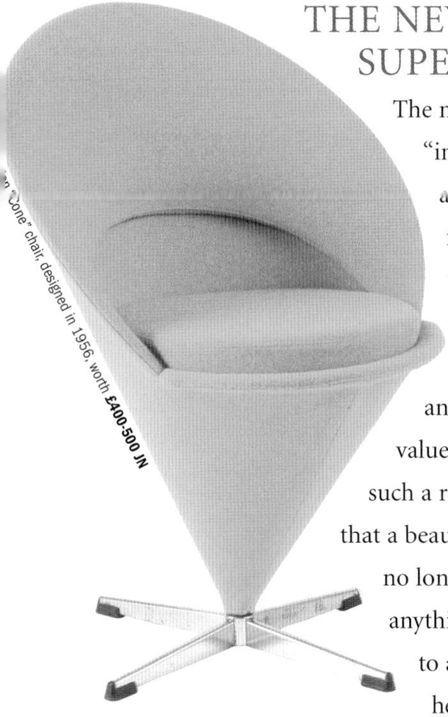

"Cone" chair, designed in 1956, worth **£400-500 JN**

The notion of the "instant classic" is a reflection of the fast pace of life as we live it in the 21st century. The best art and design accrues value and kudos at such a rate these days that a beautiful artefact no longer requires anything like 100 years to attain treasured heirloom status.

The cream of mid-20th century design is already well established; its aesthetic as well as its financial value is widely recognized by enthusiasts and casual observers alike. Verner Panton's "Cone" chair – a metal frame upholstered in brightly coloured felt – is now worth much more than the average 19th-century carved mahogany dining chair. Greater demand is pushing up prices. Similarly, Murano glass made during the great renaissance of creativity that took place on the island during the 1950s now occupies a higher rung on the secondary art market ladder than, say, an 18th-century air-twist wine glass. Dino Martens brought a painter's eye to the "Oriente" range he designed for Aureliano Toso between c.1948–55. By mixing different decorative techniques within the same piece he created glass tapestries with huge visual appeal that make a very bold statement. Even artefacts with a more immediately obvious "antique" appeal, such as leaded glass lampshades by Tiffany & Co., do not necessarily pass the 100 year test. Some of the finest Tiffany glass on the market today dates from the 1940s.

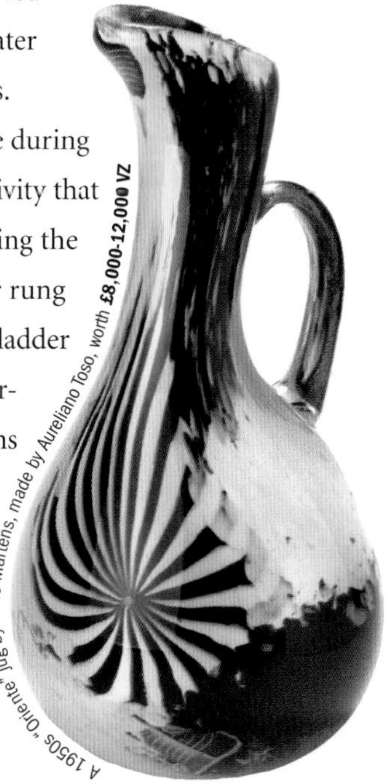

A 1950s "Oriente" jug by Dino Martens, made by Aureliano Toso, worth **£8,000-12,000 VZ**

A 1940s hydrangea cone shade, by Tiffany Studios, signed, worth **£60,000-100,000 SK**

TRIBAL COLOURS

An 1870s Cayeuse blanket strip, from the Plateau area, worth **£20,000-40,000 D&G**

There is currently a reaction against minimalist interiors and plain walls painted in off-white shades. Many people are looking for distinctive items to act as the focal point in a room – what decorators refer to as an "accent". Modern design is ideal for providing this kind of effect, but it can also come from more unexpected sources.

Another area of the antiques market presently enjoying a boom is Tribal Art, which shares many characteristics with modern design, including extensive stylization and use of geometric forms. As well as providing that all-important decorative accent, Tribal Art often has an extraordinary history. Artefacts that were made for use within tribal ceremonies or daily life are generally more important and so more valuable, but even pieces made for trade are attracting legions of collectors. People like to hear about the cultural significance of a particular artefact – it becomes a talking point. This is especially true in North America and Australia, where many collectors value art made by

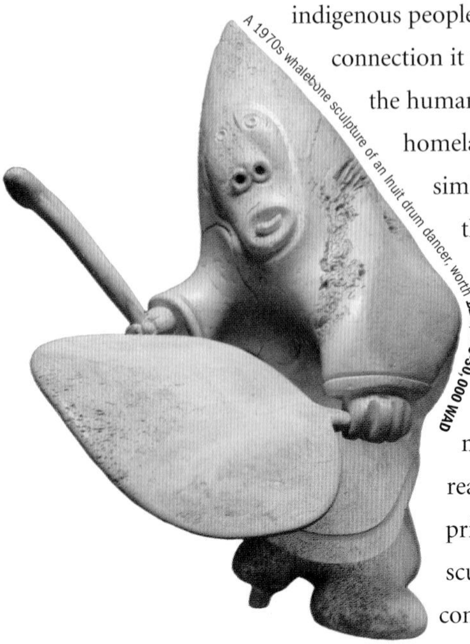

A 1970s whalebone sculpture of an Inuit drum dancer, worth **£25,000-30,000 WAD**

indigenous people for the connection it represents to the human history of their homeland. Another similarity between the Tribal Art market and the modern classics phenomenon is that even very new pieces can realize fantastic prices. Soapstone sculptures by the best contemporary Inuit artists are valued at tens of thousands of pounds today when they would have changed hands for very little just 20 or 30 years ago.

DIFFERENT STROKES FOR DIFFERENT FOLKS

Folk art is also basking in new popularity thanks to the strong sense of time and place that it imparts. In an increasingly uprooted society people seem to cherish the nostalgic value of folk art, viewing it as a link back to an imagined idyllic past. The key characteristic of folk art is that it is crafted by people with no academic artistic training, lending it a naivety of design that blends well with the pared-down modern interior. A well-chosen piece can provide a strong decorative focal point in any room, leavening the Spartan aspect of all that clean, empty space in the same way that a tribal artefact can. This sector of the market is area-specific to a greater extent than any other – collectors tend to value items that come from their immediate vicinity above all others. Folk art is an especially hot prospect around sites of early colonization along the east coast of America, but every country has its own folk art tradition and its own devotees of the genre. Provenance is extremely important in the folk art market – collectors invariably like to know where a piece was made and, if at all possible, who made it before they will think about spending very large sums. Good decorative folk art with a fully traceable provenance is quite capable of breaking auction room records in the current climate.

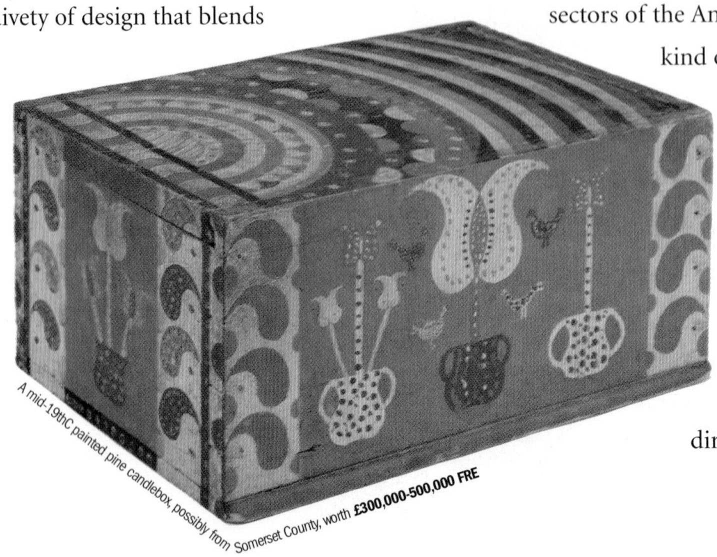

A mid-19thC painted pine candlebox, possibly from Somerset County, worth **£300,000-500,000 FRE**

PICTURE PERFECT

At the other end of the artistic spectrum, there have been interesting developments in the world of fine art. The Pennsylvania Impressionist school first started attracting increased attention from collectors priced out of the American Impressionist market in the 1980s. Now the cycle is complete, as Pennsylvania Impressionism is itself one of the hottest sectors of the American art market. This kind of "value by association" is something that has happened time and again – the market continually grows and evolves, adding new names and styles to the established canon. The trick, of course, is to work out in which direction it is headed next.

"The Old Stone Bridge", by Fern Isabel Coppedge (American 1888-1951), oil on canvas, worth **£30,000-40,000 FRE**

"Easter Eggs", by Edward Atkinson Hornel (1864-1933), oil on canvas, dated 1905, worth **£80,000-120,000 L&T**

Other recent successes on the fine art market include the sale of the Drambuie collection, assembled by the Mackinnon family, purveyors of that fine Scottish liqueur. Realizing more than £2.5 million, this sale proved that the increased press attention that accompanies prolific auctions can have a marked effect on the bottom line.

RISING IN THE EAST

The areas I have mentioned above are among the fastest growing on the market despite being worlds apart from the Louis XIV commodes and Staffordshire figures that spring to mind when we hear the word "antique". There are, of course, exceptions to this trend towards the new and the naive and the most prominent of these is Chinese porcelain, the market for which is currently booming. This is due in no small part to the huge changes sweeping modern China – a country where much of the population is enjoying more wealth and freedom than it has for generations.

Many of the best examples of Chinese porcelain to appear at auction in the last few years have been bought by Chinese collectors eager to acquire a piece of their own cultural heritage. Record-breaking prices in the last year for Yuan vases have shown that this state of affairs is set to continue. I was lucky enough to have the chance to view and handle this exquisite blue and white double gourd vase (*below*) sold at Woolley & Wallis in Salisbury, Wiltshire, during the summer. The vibrancy of the blue pigment and the way the painted decoration of gourd fruits complement the shape of this vase combine to make it a masterpiece of decorative art. The quality of the porcelain is also exceptional – in short, this is an incredibly sophisticated piece and I was not at all surprised to see it smash the record for the highest hammer price ever achieved by an English auction house outside of London. This vase dates from the Yuan dynasty, the period starting in the late 13th century when blue and white decoration was first extensively practiced in China.

The Alexander Vase, a very rare large Yuan Dynasty mid-14thC Chinese double gourd vase, worth **over £2.5 million WW**

Pieces from the Ming and early Qing dynasties – representing a wide timeframe stretching from the 14th century through to the 18th century – have enjoyed a similar upsurge in popularity over recent years and are just as capable of fetching eye-popping prices. More specifically it is blue and white porcelain from the Transitional period and the reign of the Emperor Kangxi that tends to garner the most attention. Demand is at such a pitch that even the values of damaged and restored articles have been rising quickly – something that is nigh-on unheard of in the world of antiques.

A Martin Brothers stoneware triple bird group, by Robert Wallace Martin, worth £40,000-50,000 WW

THE OLD GUARD

Despite these seismic changes it would be a mistake to assume that the traditional antiques market is in terminal decline. The adverse effects of the sea-change in collector's mores are being felt above all in the middle market. Rare and exceptional items from tiny snuffboxes up to and including massive longcase clocks continue to attract noteworthy bids and, despite their perennial protestations to the contrary, dealers who take care to source the very best examples in their field are doing good business. Rare lots in popular fields will always do well, no matter how depressed the market may appear. Martin Brothers pottery has been very popular on both sides of the Atlantic for generations – their bird figures in particular have many devoted collectors. When a very rare triple bird group came up for sale last year it easily reached its estimate price of £40,000.

Another sale I visited last year included an early porcelain pipe tamper in the form of a naval bust that sold for £4,400. A combination of factors made this piece an irresistible proposition. Firstly, it was absolutely unique: no other example is known, although a mould for a pipe tamper with a female bust was unearthed in excavations at the site of the Lowestoft factory, leading experts to believe that this one was made by the same firm. Secondly, it was dated – early ceramics and glass carrying such inscriptions inevitably attract more interest in an auction room than comparable undated examples. The fact that the pipe tamper was damaged and restored did not deter bidders in the least – with no chance of a perfect example appearing for sale, enthusiasts are quite prepared to spend money even on a heavily restored piece.

Our notion of what constitutes an "antique" has certainly changed. More specifically, it has broadened – it still encompasses things like gutta percha golf balls and pairs of Staffordshire dogs, but 20th-century decorative arts, folk art, and tribal artefacts are becoming increasingly important. Even modern design can now share saleroom space with the most venerable and dusty old antiques. Finally, don't be disheartened if you were hoping to realize the capital tied up in your collection of Staffordshire figures – bearish market trends can quickly reverse and resume an upward trajectory, so there may well be life in the old dogs yet!

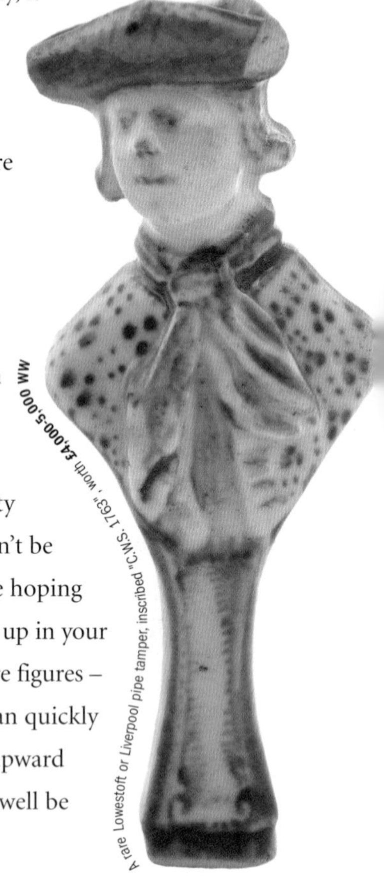

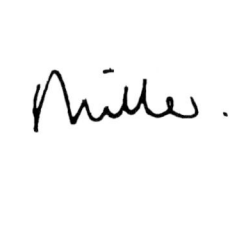

A rare Lowestoft or Liverpool pipe tamper, inscribed "C.W.S. 1763", worth £4,000-5,000 WW

Judith Miller.

THE PORCELAIN MARKET

The now familiar pattern of steady but modest price increases has persisted in porcelain salerooms over the last year. Exceptions to the rule include pieces by Welsh factories Nantgarw and Swansea as their reputation for producing the highest quality British porcelain continues to attract new collectors.

The market tends to react enthusiastically to very early dated porcelain such as the pipe tamper sold by Woolley & Wallis in Wiltshire and exceptional pieces like this will continue to realise noteworthy prices. Generally, rare and particularly dated pieces continue to sell well.

Exceptional provenance has proved to be another differentiating factor between mediocre and extraordinary performance at auction. A monumental pair of 19thC Sèvres urns sold for more than £10,000 at Freemans in Philadelphia, helped no doubt by their status as a French government commission. Buyers generally feel more secure when purchasing pieces that have come from a well-known collection.

Items made or decorated by individuals recognised for their prodigious talent have risen in value more sharply than mid-market wares; Derby plates painted by Billingsley and Meissen figures modelled by Kändler invariably generate far more interest than comparable pieces unconnected to such famous names.

As with all commodities, as soon as supply is significantly exceeded by demand then prices will quickly climb. For example, very few intact pairs of melon tureens by English factories such as Chelsea and Longton Hall are known to exist and when they do appear on the market interest is usually intense.

The good news in the middle market is that buyers looking to fill holes in their collections should find that conditions are currently very much in their favour.

BOW

A Bow blue and white chamfered dish, painted with peony, bamboo and stylized rockwork, the border with flowers, faint rim crack, chip to corner.

c1750 *10.5in (27cm) wide*

£500-800 **WW**

A Bow chamfered dish, painted with pagoda landscapes in shaped panels on a powder blue ground, pseudo Chinese mark.

c1765 *8.75in (22.5cm) wide*

£400-600 **WW**

A Bow blue and white plate, painted with the 'Jumping Boy' pattern.

c1760 *7in (18cm) diam*

£300-500 **WW**

A Bow blue and white dish, painted with a Chinese landscape within a hatched border.

c1760 *8in (20.5cm) diam*

£500-800 **WW**

A Bow sweetmeat dish, the three scallop shells painted with Oriental women playing shamisens, with a blue dolphin surmount, restored and pinned.

c1760 *7.75in (19.5cm) wide*

£700-900 **WW**

A CLOSER LOOK AT A BOW LEAF-SHAPED PICKLE DISH

This very deep blue colour is typical of Bow.

Bow is generally thought to have been the first English factory to include bone ash in its porcelain recipe, resulting in a hardier material with an ivory white colour.

This design shows the powerful Chinese influence which is evident on Bow porcelain.

Pickle dishes were a staple of dining tables during the mid-18thC. To ensure a ready market for their wares, English porcelain firms produced everyday tableware and reproductions of popular Oriental export shapes and patterns.

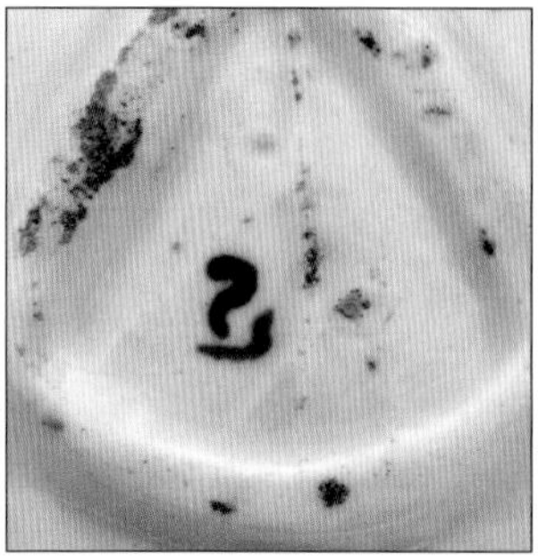

A Bow leaf-shaped pickle dish, painted in underglaze blue with a fence, flowering branches and bamboo in the Chinese style, workman's numeral "27" in blue.

c1755 *4in (10cm) wide*

£800-1,200 **LFA**

A Bow candlestick group of musicians before floral bocage, with double bass and lute, with two scroll-moulded sconces and pierced base, decorated in coloured enamels and gilt, with red anchor and dagger mark.

c1765 *11in (28cm) high*

£6,000-8,000 **AA**

A pair of Bow figures of 'Dutch Dancers', decorated in enamels, the scroll-moulded bases applied with flowers, red anchor and dagger marks in imitation of Chelsea.

c1770 *6.25in (16cm) high*

£3,000-4,000 **AA**

A Bow model of a lion, finely shaded in brown, on a pale green glazed mound base, unmarked.

c1750 *3.75in (9.5cm) high*

£3,000-4,000 **AA**

THE BOW FACTORY

- Thomas Frye and Edward Heylen patented a porcelain formula in 1744. However it is unlikely that the first pieces, made at a factory at Bow in London, went on sale before 1748.
- By 1750, the factory was producing everyday wares heavily influenced by Chinese and Japanese porcelain and these became known as 'New Canton'.
- Bow's tableware tended to stain brown after repeated use because of the burnt bone ash in the mix. To avoid this problem, Bow began to produce ornamental wares that would not come into contact with food or require washing.
- Typified by the 'Muse Modeller', Bow figures were often clumsy copies of sophisticated figures by Meissen and Chelsea. Their rustic appeal suited the Rococo style fashionable at the time.
- The colourful figures sold well until fashion swung towards Neo-classicism and the factory was forced to close in 1770.

A Bow chamber candlestick, in the form of birds and a nest in branches, decorated in enamels, a dog and a lamb at the base, the scroll-moulded sconce with a tole peint stem, on a pierced mound base, some old restoration.

c1760 *9.5in (24cm) high*

£800-1,200 **LFA**

A Bow mug, with a grooved loop handle, painted with two Chinese figures, beneath a floral leafy border, painter's mark inside the foot rim, chipped.

c1760 *3.5in (9cm) high*

£300-500 **WW**

A small Bow model of a bird of prey, the stump base painted in green and iron red with a flower spray, unmarked.

c1760 *3in (7.5cm) high*

£5,000-7,000 **AA**

A Bow coffee can, brightly painted with three Chinese figures.

c1760 *2.25in (6cm) high*

£300-500 **WW**

A Bow baluster-shaped sparrow beak milk jug, with loop handle, painted in enamels with flowers and leaves, brown line rim, two rim chips.

c1760 *3.5in (9cm) high*

£350-400 **LFA**

A rare Caughley miniature cylindrical mug, with loop handle, painted in underglaze blue with the 'Island' pattern.

Thomas Turner established the Caughley factory in Staffordshire c1772, producing painted and transfer-printed blue and white wares in competition with Worcester. The factory closed c1799.

c1780 *1.5in (3.5cm) high*

£1,000-1,500 **LFA**

A rare Caughley small cylindrical mug, with loop handle, printed in underglaze blue with the 'Parrot Pecking Fruit' pattern.

1780 *3.25in (8.5cm) high*

£800-1,200 **LFA**

A rare Caughley miniature baluster-shaped sparrow beak jug, with loop handle, painted in underglaze blue with the 'Island' pattern.

c1780 *2in (5cm) high*

£800-1,200 **LFA**

A Caughley blue and white punch bowl, painted with a version of the 'Rock Strata' pattern, after Worcester, open crescent mark, some surface scratches.

c1780 *9.75in (24.5cm) diam*

£200-300 **DN**

A Caughley lobed sauce tureen, cover and ladle, the cover with loop knop, painted in underglaze blue with the 'Weir' pattern, gilded key fret and diaper panelled borders, tureen cracked.

c1785 *5.5in (14cm) wide*

£500-700 **LFA**

An 18thC Caughley blue and white mask jug, printed with 'The Fisherman' pattern on the leaf-moulded body, "S" mark.

The "S" mark stands for Salop, the county in which Caughley was based. These wares are sometimes referred to as 'Salopian'. Pieces marked "C" date from c1775-1795.

9.25in (23.5cm) high

£350-400 **CHEF**

A pair of 18thC Caughley asparagus servers, later over-painted with flowers and printed in blue with 'The Fishermen' pattern, "S" marks.

2.75in (7cm) long

£180-220 **CHEF**

A Caughley small oval creamboat, with C-scroll handle, painted in coloured enamels with two flowersprays within gadrooned borders, with gilt rim.

c1790 *4.25in (11cm) long*

£500-800 **LFA**

A Caughley teapot and cover, with loop handle and ball knop, painted in enamels with the 'Back to Back Roses' pattern, within gilt line borders.

5.75in (14.5cm) high

£700-900 **LFA**

A rare Caughley faceted tea bowl and saucer, in the famille rose palette with baskets of flowers and leaves within puce and iron red dot and line borders.

No comparable Caughley pieces appear to have been recorded with this New Hall style of decoration.

c1790

£300-500 **LFA**

A rare Caughley miniature lobed round dish, decorated in underglaze blue and gilt with looped bands, impressed Salopian mark.

c1790 *2.5in (6.5cm) diam*

£800-1,200 **LFA**

A Chelsea leaf-shaped dish, with puce veining and a green border.

c1755 *8in (20.5cm) wide*

£700-900 **WW**

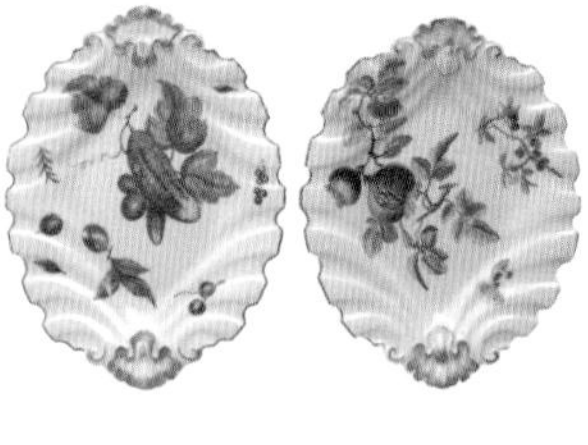

A pair of Chelsea fluted dishes, of 'silver' shape, painted in enamels with fruit, handles picked out in puce and gilt, within a brown line rim, brown anchor marks.

c1760 *9.75in (25cm) wide*

£7,000-9,000 **AA**

A Chelsea 'silver' shape dish, painted in enamels with insects.

9.25in (23.5cm) wide

£3,000-4,000 **AA**

An unusual Chelsea lobed dish, painted in the famille rose palette, with flower sprays and butterflies around a central flowerhead.

c1750 *8.5in (21.5cm) wide*

£300-500 **WW**

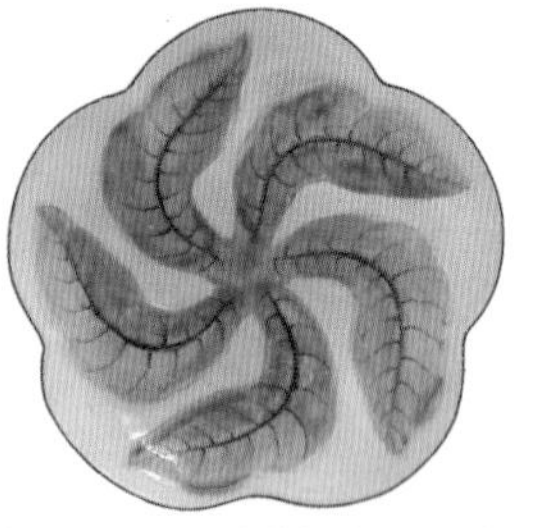

A Chelsea moulded dish, decorated with spiralling green hart's tongue fern leaves, brown line rim, red anchor mark.

c1755 *7in (18cm) wide*

£1,500-2,000 **WW**

A Chelsea plate, painted in enamels with a spray of flowers and leaves, the lobed rim painted with exotic birds, alternating with wave-moulded panels, within a brown line rim, red anchor mark.

c1755 *8.5in (21.5cm) diam*

£250-300 **LFA**

A CLOSER LOOK AT A CHELSEA DISH

Chelsea based this design on Japanese Kakiemon porcelain, which remained popular with the English market. The floral patterns of Vincennes and Meissen were also a major influence.

Chelsea porcelain from this period is creamy white and sometimes has 'moons' - bubbles trapped in the paste - and impurities. Tin oxide added to the glaze made it more opaque and lent it a silky feel.

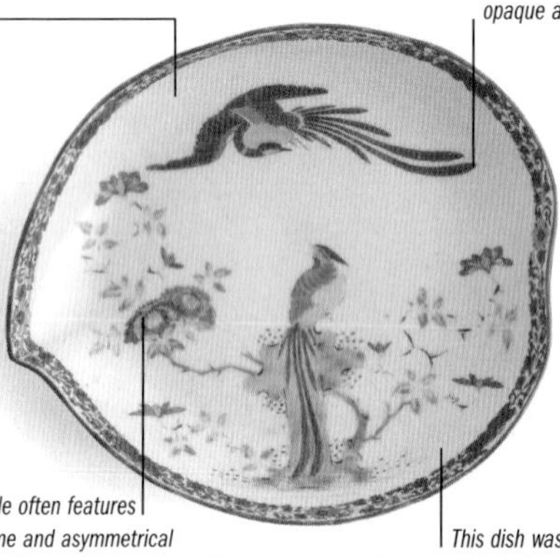

The Kakiemon style often features delicate polychrome and asymmetrical clusters of delicate flowers, birds and spindly branches used sparingly against a white ground, although designs vary a great deal.

This dish was produced during the red anchor period which dated from c1753-6 and is named for the mark found on the base of Chelsea porcelain made at this time.

A Chelsea peach-shaped dish, painted in the Kakiemon style with a bird perched on a rock beneath a bird in flight, red anchor mark, restored.

c1755 *8in (20.5cm) wide*

£1,500-2,000 **WW**

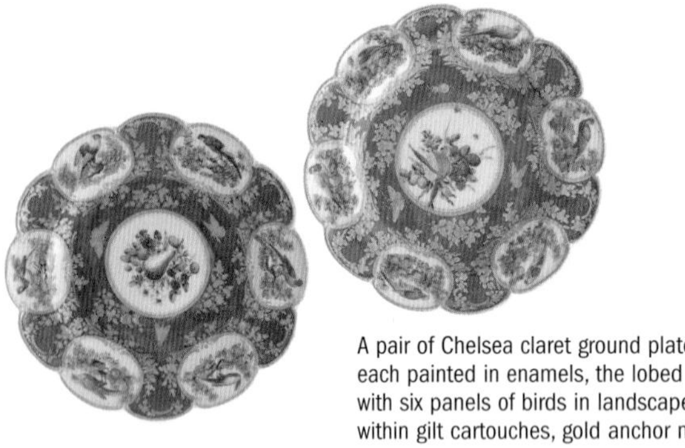

A pair of Chelsea claret ground plates, each painted in enamels, the lobed rims with six panels of birds in landscapes, within gilt cartouches, gold anchor marks.

c1760 *8.75in (22cm) diam*

£8,000-10,000 **AA**

A pair of Chelsea plates, of Mecklenburg-Strelitz type, painted in enamels with exotic birds, the borders with flowers and blue ground panels, decorated in gilt with insects, gold anchor marks.

In 1763, George III commissioned a table service for his new bride Charlotte Mecklenburg-Strelitz and their new home in Buckingham House, providing a boost to the Chelsea factory.

c1765 *8.75in (22cm) diam*

£2,500-3,500 **AA**

A Chelsea plate, painted in enamels with two flowering stems, feather-moulded border, brown anchor mark.

c1760 *8.25in (21cm) diam*

£380-420 **LFA**

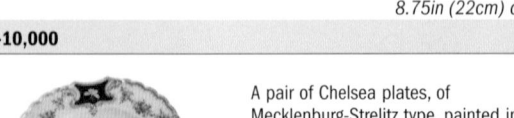

A Chelsea blue and white lobed dish, decorated in blue and white, two small restored rim chips.

c1755 *8.25in (21cm) diam*

£400-600 **WW**

THE CHELSEA FACTORY

- Established c1744 at Chelsea by Huguenot immigrant Nicolas Sprimont, production at Chelsea falls into four distinct periods.
- Wares from the Triangle period (1744-49) generally have a glassy white body with little decoration to show off the pale body. Shapes were copied from British Rococo silver. Early porcelain was hard to fire so pieces were small.
- The Raised Anchor period (1749-52) saw improvements to the texture and look of the glaze. The body was made more robust and decoration focussed on copies of Japanese Kakiemon and landscapes in the style of Meissen and Vincennes. Scenes from Aesop's Fables became a Chelsea speciality.
- During the Red Anchor period (1752-56) the focus shifted to dessert table settings, especially in the form of fruit, vegetables and animals. 'Hans Sloane wares', named for the patron of Chelsea Physic Garden, were decorated with botanical designs. 'Toy' perfume bottles and seals were shaped as humans, animals or fruit. Figures became important as Chelsea began to utilise the skills of Flemish modeller Josef Willems (1715-66).
- The Gold Anchor period (1756-69) was characterised by the use of gilding, Rococo shapes and coloured grounds inspired by Vincennes and Sèvres. Figures became more elaborate, incorporating bocage backgrounds.
- The Chelsea factory closed in 1769. Heath and Duesbury, owners of the Derby factory, bought the works in 1770 and ran both premises. The company finally ceased operations in 1784.

A rare Chelsea figure of Dr Boloardo, after the Commedia dell'Arte series modelled by J.J. Kändler and P. Reinicke for Meissen, red anchor mark to the back of the base, restored.

c1755 6in (15cm) high

£3,000-5,000 WW

A Chelsea model of a musician, playing a pipe and tambourine, amid flowers and foliage, some chipping and body cracks.

c1760 10.75in (27cm) high

£600-800 WW

A pair of large Chelsea figures of the Imperial Shepherd and Shepherdess, before floral bocage, the flower-applied scroll-moulded bases picked out in gilt, gold anchor marks and incised "R".

c1765 13in (33cm) high

£8,000-10,000 AA

A pair of Chelsea sweetmeat figures of Turks, after the Meissen models by J.J. Kändler, each seated on rockwork and holding a flower painted shell, red anchor marks.

c1755 6in (15cm) high

£6,000-8,000 AA

A rare Chelsea white-glazed tawny owl, perched on a rocky mound, triangle or raised anchor period.

Only a small number of Chelsea models of owls are known, all of which are white glazed. Similar models from Staffordshire in white saltglazed stoneware, usually polychrome decorated and less naturalistic, are also known.

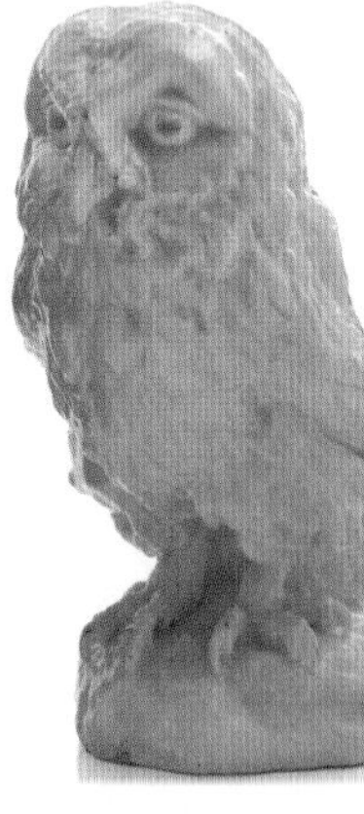

c1750 7.75in (19.5cm) high

£20,000-25,000 WW

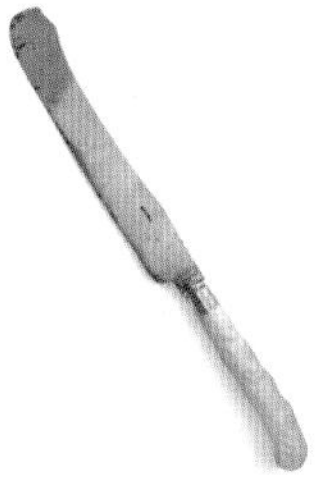

A Chelsea pistol-grip knife haft, in the white, moulded in bold relief with trailing teaplants, later mounted as a knife.

c1750

£180-220 LFA

A Chelsea pistol-grip knife haft, in the white, moulded in bold relief with entwined flowers and leaves, later mounted as a spoon.

c1755

£150-200 LFA

A Chelsea etui, formed as an Ionic column, the top inset with a seal and inscribed "Libre et Constant", gilt metal mounts.

c1760 4.25in (11cm) high

£1,200-1,800 WW

A Chelsea rose box and cover, the stalk loop knop with single bud terminal, unmarked.

Rose buds are recorded in the 1755 Chelsea Sale Catalogue, lot 80: "Four fine roses and four leaves to ditto for desart".

c1755 3.5in (9cm) high

£2,000-2,500 AA

A large Chelsea sauceboat, with scroll handle, painted in enamels with exotic birds in landscapes, flowers and leaves, beneath a gilt feuille-de-choux border, scroll feet, the interior painted with a flower spray, unmarked.

c1760 9in (23cm) wide

£2,500-3,500 AA

A Coalport jug, of baluster shape, painted with flowers flanking gilt initials "WH", dated 1835.

8in (20.5cm) high

£120-180 CHEF

A 19thC Daniel's Coalport jug, of baluster shape, painted with flowers below gilt gadrooned rim.

8.75in (22cm) high

£200-300 CHEF

A CLOSER LOOK AT A PAIR OF COALPORT IMARI ICE PAILS

John Rose founded the factory in c1796 and quickly built up a hugely successful business. By the time of his death in 1841 the company employed more than 400 people. These ice pails date from his era.

Coalport can be difficult to identify as pieces were often decorated by a number of independent artists, resulting in a huge variety of styles. Other factories also copied Coalport shapes.

Coalport was influenced by Oriental decoration from the outset. In the early 1800s polychrome and gilded wares succeeded Chinese-style blue and white patterns and from c1815 Neo-classicism became more fashionable.

Bone china replaced hybrid hard-paste porcelain from c1820.

A pair of bone china Imari palette twin-handled ice pails, with lids and liners, probably John Rose, Coalport, decorated with urns of peony and flowers.

The Coalport factory in Shropshire began by manufacturing everyday teasets decorated by studios such as Baxter in London. From c1830 it produced Rococo Revival-style 'Coalbrookdale' ware. Key decorators included bird artist John Randall (active 1835-80) and floral artist William Cook (active 1843-76). The company still operates in Stoke-on-Trent.

9.5in (24cm) diam

£5,000-8,000 L&T

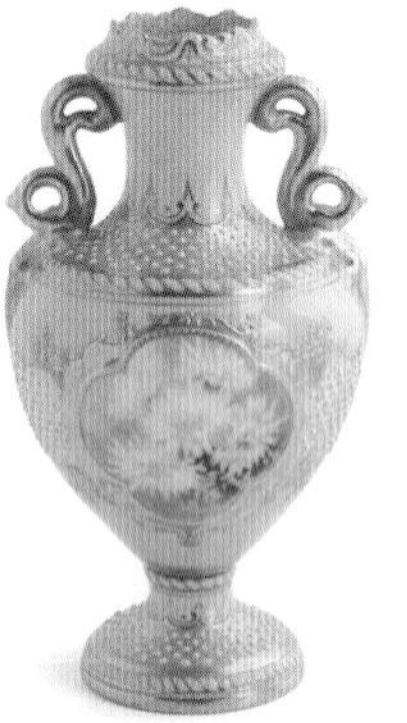

A jewelled Coalport vase, painted with two panels, one with chrysanthemums, on a green and gold ground.

c1900 6in (15cm) high

£400-600 WW

A pair of Coalport ovoid vases and covers, painted in enamels by J. Keeling, each with a Classical figure within a raised gilt cartouche, signed, titled in red "The Boquet", with printed marks in green and pattern number, minor restoration.

11.75in (30cm) high

£1,000-1,500 LFA

A Coalport plate, painted with a flower spray within a gilt border.

c1810 8.5in (21.5cm) diam

£300-500 WW

A Coalport Etruscan shape teacup and saucer, printed with flowers and leaves, within gilt cartouches, on a gilt cell diaper ground, marked "830" in gilt.

c1815

£50-70 LFA

Part of a Coalport 49-piece dessert service, with borders of scrolling foliage, comprising two ice buckets, covers and liners, a centrepiece, two tureens, cover and stands, 12 shaped serving dishes and 24 plates, some pieces marked with numeral "2".

c1815

£8,000-10,000 set WW

A Coalport cabaret tray, with a painted panel depicting a lady being rescued by a knight, by R.F. Abrahams, lilac surround with gilt detail, signed, restored.

17in (43cm) wide

£800-1,200 BRI

A pair of Coalport candlesticks, in the form of bronzed seated lions, sconces modelled as Prince of Wales feathers, decorated in blue and gilt.

c1800 7.75in (19.5cm) high

£2,500-3,500 AA

EARLY DERBY FIGURES

- The earliest Derby porcelain dates from c1750 when the modeller Andrew Planché arrived from France.
- William Duesbury and John Heath acquired the factory shortly after Planché's departure in 1756.
- The Rococo figural style of the 1750s and 1760s was influenced by Meissen, with wide scroll bases, backed with intricate bocage.
- During Derby's transitional phase (1755-56) the glaze became whiter and pieces were decorated with delicate enamels, earning figural groups from this period the name 'The Pale Family'.
- Derby porcelain is unmarked before 1770. After this time a model number is often scratched into the base. Meissen marks were sometimes also used.
- From c1770, Derby began to produce figures in the fashionable Neoclassical style, employing modellers from Europe to improve quality and inspire new subjects. The company developed a speciality in biscuit figures and the fine detailing of its unique Chinoiserie figure groups is best seen in the white.
- Figures may have 'patch marks' where bases were supported on pads to prevent them sticking to the kiln. The glaze tended to run during firing so the bases were wiped, creating a 'dry edge'.

A rare Derby white glazed dry-edge figure of 'Winter', depicted as a child warming his hands above a fire.

c1755 *4.25in (10.5cm) high*

£1,500-2,000 **WW**

A Derby figure of a child harlequin, holding a slapstick, decorated with bright enamels, the mound base applied with flowerheads and leaves, unmarked.

c1760 *4.5in (11.5cm) high*

£2,000-2,500 **AA**

A large pair of Derby figures of musicians, each seated on a flower bordered arbour, surmounted by a birdcage, the scroll-moulded bases with pierced trellis panels, unmarked.

c1770 *14.75in (37.5cm) high*

£5,000-7,000 **AA**

A pair of Derby figures of a shepherd and shepherdess, decorated in enamels, the flower-applied and scroll-moulded bases picked out in green and gilt, damaged.

c1770

£1,500-2,000 **LFA**

A late 18thC Derby figure representing 'Justice', standing on a pink and green rocaille base and holding a sword in one hand.

13.25in (33.5cm) high

£250-300 **CHEF**

A pair of Derby porcelain figures, with a cat and a dog.

c1780 *6in (15cm) high*

£1,500-2,000 **AA**

A Derby porcelain group, depicting four figures around a central obelisk.

c1780 *9.5in (24cm) high*

£2,500-3,000 **AA**

A Derby model of a ram, the mound base applied with flowers and leaves, horns restored.

c1760 *4.5in (11.5cm) wide*

£700-900 **LFA**

A small Derby model of a lamb, on a green glazed oval mound base, unmarked.

c1765 *1.5in (4cm) high*

£400-600 **AA**

A pair of Derby models of a ewe and a ram, each sparsely picked out in puce and black, on oval mound bases.

c1765 *1.5in (4cm) high*

£1,200-1,500 **AA**

A pair of Derby models of a stag and doe, the oval mound bases applied with flowers and leaves, unmarked.

c1755 *4.25in (11cm) high*

£4,000-6,000 **AA**

A large pair of Derby models of recumbent stags, before floral bocage, the oval mound bases with applied flowers and leaves, unmarked.

c1760 *7.25in (18.5cm) high*

£2,500-3,000 **AA**

A near pair of Derby cow and calf groups, standing before bocage of flowering trees, restored.

c1770 *4.5in (11.5cm) high*

£500-700 **WW**

A small Derby model of a boar, decorated in brown and black, the oval mound base with green and pale yellow washed bands, unmarked.

c1755 *2.5in (6.5cm) high*

£4,000-4,500 **AA**

A Derby-type model of a squirrel, decorated in iron red on a green glazed mound base, painted number "22" in black on base.

3.5in (9cm) high

£600-900 **LFA**

A Derby model of an owl, naturistically decorated in enamels, on a tree stump, applied with flowers and leaves.

c1760 *2.5in (6.5cm) high*

£4,000-6,000 **AA**

A Derby plate, with thick gilt border, painted with flowers, inscribed to rear "Tawny Day, Lily, Restharrow and Clustered Bell Flower", painted red crown mark.

8.75in (22cm) diam

£6,000-8,000 **AA**

A Derby plate, painted with flowers, gilt and yellow painted border and crimped edge, inscribed to reverse "Iris Versicalor Patricoloured Iris", with crown mark and "216".

8.75in (22cm) diam

£1,000-1,200 **AA**

A Derby plate, painted with flowers, gilt border and crimped edge, inscribed to reverse "Iris Persica Persian Iris", with crown mark and "216".

8.75in (22cm) diam

£1,000-1,200 **AA**

A Derby plate, with black and gilt border, inscribed "Houstonia Coccinea Scarlet Houstonia" to reverse, with Derby mark and "315".

10in (25.5cm) diam

£200-300 **AA**

A Derby oval dish, from the Duke of Hamilton service, painted in enamels with the arms of James, 8th Duke of Hamilton, crowned crossed batons and "D" mark in puce.

This is part of the service ordered by the 8th Duke to replace the Chinese export service ordered by his grandfather in 1738.

c1785 *14.5in (37cm) wide*

£3,000-4,000 **AA**

A Derby wide lobed Powys porcelain dish, painted with flowers, inscribed "Jacob's Ladder" and "Butterfly Orchus", with crossed swords and crown mark and "D139".

c1790 *11.5in (29cm) wide*

£2,000-3,000 **AA**

A Derby sauce tureen and cover, the pink rose knop with leaf terminals, painted with cherries, nuts, butterflies and insects, crowned crossed "D" mark in puce.

This form of Derby sauce tureen appears to be unrecorded.

c1785 *4.75in (12cm) high*

£2,000-2,500 **AA**

A Derby oval botanical sauce tureen and cover, painted with "Yellow Flax", "Winged Leav-ed Sposnaa" and "Venuss Looking Glass", titled in English and Latin, pattern number 115, crowned crossed batons mark in blue.

c1795 *8in (20.5cm) wide*

£700-900 **LFA**

A Derby basket, the interior painted with cherries and insects, double rope-twist handles, the exterior with applied flowers, on a yellow rope-twist foot.

c1760 *6.75in (17cm) diam*

£2,800-3,200 **WW**

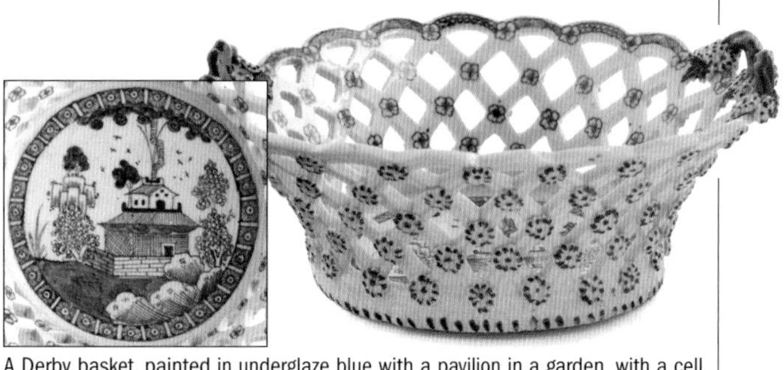

A Derby basket, painted in underglaze blue with a pavilion in a garden, with a cell diaper band, pierced sides applied to the exterior with flowerheads, and similarly painted to the interior, unmarked.

c1765 *7.5in (19cm) diam*

£1,500-2,000 **AA**

A Christian's Liverpool blue and white saucer dish, painted with an insect and a bird perched amid stylized flowers.

c1765 *7.75in (19.5cm) diam*

£500-800 **WW**

A Liverpool round bowl, by James Pennington's factory, decorated in underglaze blue, the interior inscribed "Ionathan Eplett 1785", the exterior with a fisherman, unmarked.

c1785 *7in (18cm) diam*

£4,000-6,000 **AA**

A blue and white saucer, probably Liverpool, with the 'Jumping Boy' pattern.

5in (12.5cm) diam

£2,000-2,500 **AA**

A Liverpool blue and white mug, by the Richard Chaffers factory, printed with flowers, bamboo and rockwork, beneath a cell diaper border.

Several porcelain factories operated in Liverpool during the 1750s. Chaffers and Christian were the most successful.

c1765 *6.25in (16cm) high*

£500-600 **WW**

A small Liverpool baluster-shaped coffee pot and domed cover, by the Richard Chaffers factory, painted in underglaze blue in Chinese style with the 'Jumping Boy' pattern, unmarked.

c1760 *7.75in (19.5cm) high*

£6,000-8,000 **AA**

A rare Liverpool armorial teapot and cover, by the Richard Chaffers factory, each side painted with the arms of Brougham and Lamplugh, cracked.

c1765 *7.75in (19.5cm) high*

£600-900 **WW**

A Liverpool ovoid teapot and cover, by Philip Christian & Co., painted with Chinese figures and flowers within leaf-moulded arched bands, handle crack.

c1770 *7.25in (18.5cm) high*

£1,000-1,500 **LFA**

A Liverpool faceted tea bowl and saucer, by William Reid's factory, flower sprays alternating with radiating iron red diaper panels, with iron red line borders.

c1760

£400-600 **LFA**

A large cider jug, by the Richard Chaffers factory, decorated in the Imari palette with Chinese figures fishing in a pagoda landscape.

c1760 *9.25in (24cm) high*

£800-1,200 **WW**

A CLOSER LOOK AT A LIVERPOOL CREAM JUG

Of all the factories making porcelain in 18thC Liverpool, the Shaw's Brow Manufactory was the most celebrated. Founded in 1756 by Richard Chaffers, it was taken over by Philip Christian in 1765.

This jug is made from soapstone soft-paste porcelain. True hard-paste porcelain was made by only a very small number of English potters until the end of the 18thC.

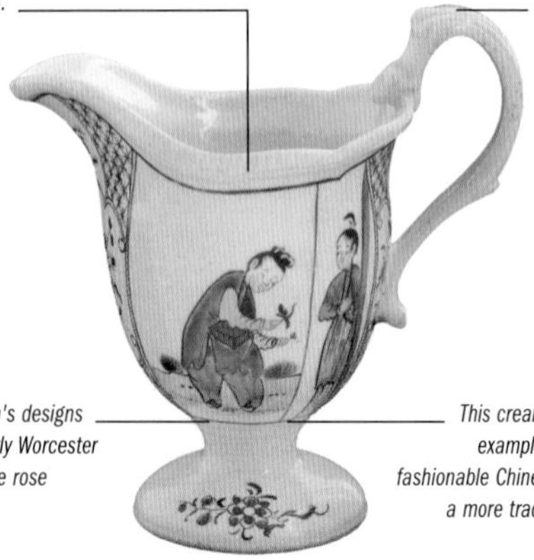

Many of Christian's designs are similar to early Worcester patterns in famille rose colours.

This cream jug is an archetypal example of the application of fashionable Chinese-style decoration to a more traditional English shape.

A rare Liverpool cream jug, by Philip Christian & Co., painted in famille rose palette with figures in gardens, alternating with iron red diaper bands, gadrooned rim, on round foot.

c1770 *3.75in (9.5cm) high*

£1,000-1,500 **LFA**

A Liverpool inverted baluster-shaped vase, by Philip Christian & Co., painted with exotic birds and panels of flowers and leaves, within gilt scroll cartouches on a blue ground, unmarked.

c1770 *9.75in (25cm) high*

£2,000-2,500 **AA**

One of a rare pair of Longton Hall leaf-shaped dishes, each painted with flowers, with puce veining.

c1755 *10.75in (27.5cm) wide*

£1,000-1,500 pair **WW**

A Longton Hall porcelain leaf dish, painted with exotic birds in a landscape.

c1755 *4.5in (11.5cm) wide*

£2,500-3,000 **AA**

A large Longton Hall leaf dish, with leaves and lilies.

c1755 *9in (23cm) wide*

£2,200-2,800 **AA**

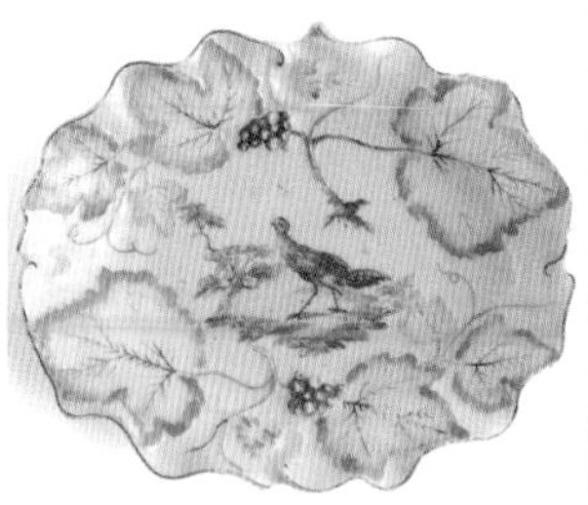

A Longton Hall dish with vines in relief, painted with a pheasant.

c1755 *8in (20.5cm) wide*

£1,200-1,800 **AA**

A Longton Hall dish, painted with a coastal settlement and a boat, by the 'Castle' painter.

c1755 *8in (20.5cm) diam*

£2,000-2,500 **AA**

A Longton Hall flared oval tea bowl, in the form of overlapping leaves, the interior painted in 'Trembly Rose' style, rim chip.

c1755 *5.5in (14cm) wide*

£1,200-1,800 **LFA**

A Longton Hall figure of 'Spring', modelled as a young man wearing a pink jacket sitting on a hod, raised on a scroll-moulded base.

c1755 *4.5in (11.5cm) high*

£400-600 **WW**

A Longton Hall blue and white mug, with a double scroll handle and painted with a pagoda landscape, "4" mark, restored.

c1755 *3.5in (9cm) high*

£800-1,200 **WW**

A pair of Longton Hall candlestick groups, each in the form of two putti and a goat, with tulip-shaped sconces and gilt detail, unmarked.

The Longton Hall factory was founded in 1749 by William Littler (1724-84), who perfected his glaze by 1752 to produce delicately moulded pieces. The factory went bankrupt c1760.

c1760 *9in (23cm) high*

£5,000-7,000 **AA**

A CLOSER LOOK AT A LONGTON HALL MELON TUREEN

Only two companies - Chelsea and Longton Hall - are known to have made melon tureens like this. Longton Hall was the only firm to make them this large and in three matching pieces.

The naturalistic painting is very well executed. Longton Hall porcelain was celebrated in its day for its fine polychrome decoration.

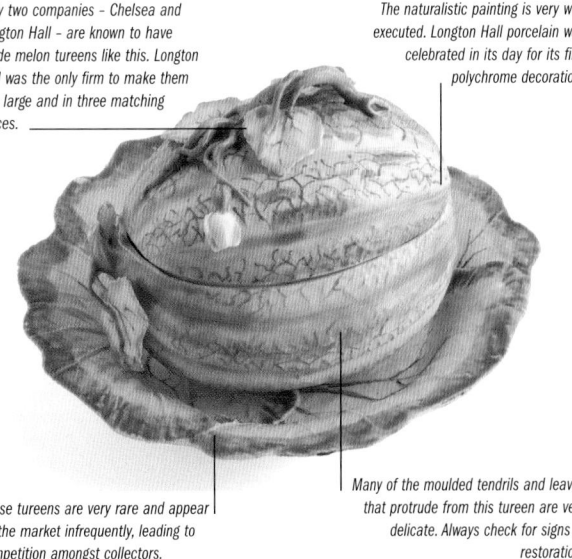

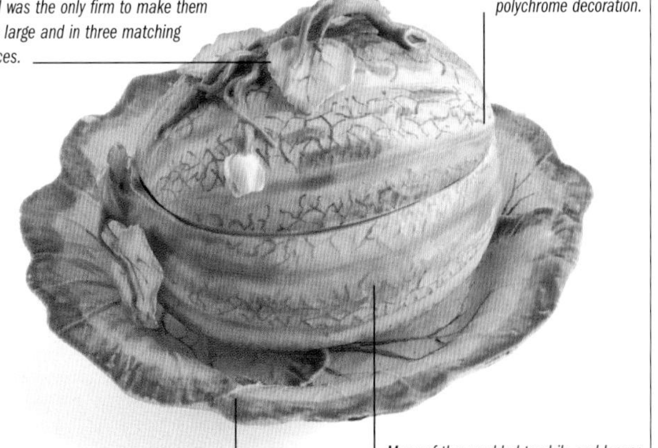

These tureens are very rare and appear on the market infrequently, leading to competition amongst collectors.

Many of the moulded tendrils and leaves that protrude from this tureen are very delicate. Always check for signs of restoration.

A Longton Hall lidded melon tureen on stand, decorated in relief with leaves and branches.

c1755 *stand 9.5in (24cm) wide*

£18,000-25,000 **AA**

A Lowestoft tea bowl and saucer, painted in underglaze blue with flowers and leaves, within wavy blue scale bands and blue line rim, chipped.

c1755

£700-1,000 **LFA**

A Lowestoft creamboat of Dolphin Ewer form, with Lamprey handle, painted in underglaze blue with flowers and leaves, the interior with a loop and dot band.

c1770 *2.5in (6.5cm) high*

£800-1,200 **LFA**

A CLOSER LOOK AT A LOWESTOFT PIPE TAMPER

The bust appears to be naval and may represent Rear-Admiral Rodney (1718-92). Rodney was the hero of the Seven Years War which ended in 1763 with the capture of Martinique, Greneda and Havana along with treasure worth £3 million. Rodney is one of the first personalities to appear on commemorative ceramics, usually wearing a tricorn hat.

Inscribed and dated pieces are highly prized amongst collectors. Early, naively painted pieces such as this are particularly desirable.

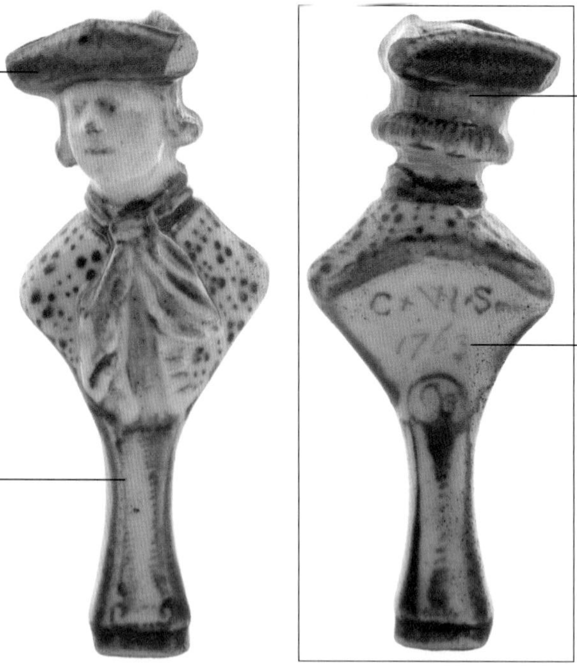

A mould for a pipe tamper with a female bust was found during excavations on the Lowestoft factory site but no models of this form are recorded.

The calligraphy of the date "1763" bears close similarities to a Lowestoft tea bowl inscribed "Ann Walker 1763" and the idiosyncratic "W" is very similar to that found on another Lowestoft fragment.

A rare dated and inscribed pipe tamper, Lowestoft or Liverpool, modelled as the bust of a man, detailed in cobalt blue, the reverse inscribed "C.W.S. 1763", restored.

2.75in (7cm) high

£5,000-7,000 **WW**

A Lowestoft teapot and cover, painted in iron red, blue and gilt with a Redgrave-type version of the 'Cannonball' pattern, damage and loss to spout.

'Redgrave type' is the name given to stylized Oriental designs thought to be the work of the Redgrave family, c1775-90, who had a long history as decorators with Lowestoft.

c1780 *6.75in (17cm) high*

£250-300 **DN**

A Lowestoft globular teapot and cover, painted in 'Tulip Painter' style, with flowers and leaves, within brown line borders, damaged.

c1780 *5.5in (14cm) high*

£700-1,000 **LFA**

A Lowestoft sparrow beak milk jug, painted with flowering branches, bamboo, rockwork and a fence, with gilt details, the interior with an iron red flower and leaf-panelled blue cell diaper band, tip of handle chipped.

c1780 *3.5in (9cm) high*

£300-500 **LFA**

A Lowestoft bowl, painted in polychrome with Chinese figures in a garden.

c1765 *6in (15cm) diam*

£300-500 **WW**

SPODE FACTORY

- Established c1776 in Stoke-on-Trent, Spode was known for fine painted and Imari pattern porcelain.
- It is thought that the first recipe for bone china, a mixture of ox bone, china clay and stone, was developed by the factory c1800.
- Spode bone china wares are pure white and smooth and often meticulously decorated.
- A number of services were 'bat-printed', a technique that involved applying tiny dots of oil to the surface of a piece using bats of glue and then dusting the oil with powdered colour.
- Blue-printed earthenware and stoneware were also produced and parian porcelain was introduced in the 1840s. It was popular for its semi-matte, non-glazed properties, making it suitable for finely moulded statuary.
- Before 1830, pieces were usually marked with a hand-painted "Spode", although some pieces from c1820 have printed marks.
- In 1833, the company was purchased by Copeland and Garrett. Wares were marked with their name in a circle, with "LATE SPODE" in the centre.
- The factory continues to operate today.

One of a rare pair of Spode chamber candlesticks, decorated in Imari style, on a blue and gilt flower and diaper panelled ground, red script marks.

c1815 *3in (7.5cm) high*

£1,000-1,500 pair **LFA**

A Spode 'New Shape' flared jardinière and stand, with dolphin loop handles, decorated in red and gilt, on a blue ground, pattern number 1029.

c1815 *4.5in (11.5cm) high*

£300-500 **LFA**

A fine Spode garniture of three 'Hollandais' vases, each with a separate base raised on four feet, decorated in the Imari palette with pattern number 967.

c1820 *7.5in (19cm) high*

£2,500-3,500 **WW**

A Spode pot pourri basket and pierced cover, the cover and interior decorated in Imari style with flowering branches, bamboo and rockwork, pattern number 967, red script marks.

c1820 *4.25in (11cm) wide*

£700-900 **LFA**

A rare Spode tulip-shaped cup, with loop handle, the exterior striped, the interior and the canted foot decorated in Imari style, pattern number 967, restored.

c1820 *2.5in (6.5cm) high*

£500-700 **LFA**

A Spode shoe-shaped inkwell, decorated in raised paste gilding with a bird, flowers and leaves, sgrafitto mark and pattern number 4054, cover missing.

c1820 *5.75in (14.5cm) wide*

£250-350 **LFA**

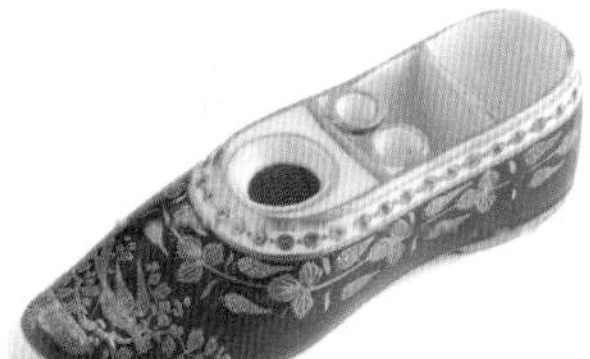

A Spode plate, painted in gilt and colours with a central roundel of flowers on a white ground, inscribed "3770".

8.5in (21.5cm) diam

£400-600 **AA**

A Spode Felspar 'cottage ornee' pastille burner, modelled with central chimney and flower-encrusted eaves, gables and base, cracked base.

c1825 *6.75in (17cm) high*

£200-300 **DN**

Part of an unusual Spode armorial part service, printed with a quartered shield, comprising a soup tureen, cover and stand, two sauce tureens, covers and stands, two meat plates and a strainer dish, printed and impressed marks and "B No108", damaged.

The arms on the service appear to be those of Robinson quartering Waldegrave.

c1825 *tureen stand 16.5in (42cm) wide*

£600-900 set **WW**

SWANSEA

- William Billingsley initially established a factory at Nantgarw in 1813, before moving production to Swansea the following year.
- Billingsley was largely responsible for the elegant, high quality painted porcelain produced in Wales during the early 19thC.
- Swansea pieces were made from highly translucent soft-paste porcelain. Three types have been identified – 'glassy', 'duck eggs' and 'trident'. The mixture suffered many firing problems and kiln loses were high.
- Many shapes and designs were in the fashionable French style. Talented painters, including Thomas Pardoe, William Pollard and David Evans, were employed to paint flowers. Thomas Baxter, who later worked for Worcester, painted landscapes and figures.
- Swansea received commissions from local dignitaries and members of the aristocracy.
- Billingsley abandoned the Swansea venture in 1817 and moved back to Nantgarw until his retirement in 1820. The factory survived until 1870.
- Some pieces bear a hand-painted "Swansea" mark.

A Swansea teacup and saucer, painted with flowers, leaves and bird's nests, within gilt flower panelled cell diaper bands, on a pink ground.

c1815

£800-1,200 **LFA**

A Swansea teacup, coffee cup and saucer, painted with sprays of flowers and leaves, within gilt 'C' scroll cartouches, on gilt diaper ground bands, stress crack.

c1815

£700-900 **LFA**

A Swansea coffee can and saucer, painted with flower sprays, with gilt line borders, unmarked.

c1820

£1,000-1,500 **WW**

A Swansea plate, probably painted by David Evans, with a spray of flowers and leaves, within a gilt line rim, red stencilled mark.

Evans was one of several talented flower painters employed by William Billingsley at Swansea between 1814 and 1817.

c1815 *8.25in (21cm) diam*

£1,500-2,000 **LFA**

A Swansea lobed plate, painted with a basket of flowers and leaves, the rim with flowers within lobed gilt cartouches, on a gilt patera and flowerhead ground.

8.5in (21.5cm) diam

£1,500-2,000 **LFA**

A Swansea plate, painted in the manner of William Pollard, the border moulded with leaf scrolls and painted with flowers and a strawberry spray, within gilt and enamel leaf fronds, unmarked.

c1820 *9in (23cm) diam*

£1,500-2,500 **WW**

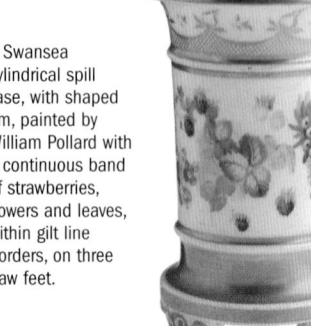

A Swansea cylindrical spill vase, with shaped rim, painted by William Pollard with a continuous band of strawberries, flowers and leaves, within gilt line borders, on three paw feet.

Pollard (1803-54) was one of the talented artists who helped to establish Swansea's reputation for exquisitely decorated floral porcelain.

c1815 *5in (12.5cm) high*

£500-800 **LFA**

A Swansea-style two-handled shaped comport, transfer-printed cuckoo pattern overpainted with flowers in famille rose palette, gilt rims, painted "SWANSEA" mark.

12in (30.5cm) wide

£500-800 **BRI**

A Worcester blue and white coffee can, painted with the 'Rock Warbler' pattern, workman's mark, glaze crack.

c1755 *2.5in (6.5cm) high*

£400-600 **WW**

A Worcester bell-shaped coffee cup, with wishbone handle, painted in underglaze blue with the 'Rock Warbler' pattern, the interior with a flower panelled diaper band, workman's mark,

c1760 *2.5in (6.5cm) high*

£400-600 **LFA**

A Worcester faceted coffee cup, with notched loop handle, painted in underglaze blue with the 'Prunus Root' pattern, workman's mark beneath the handle.

c1760 *2in (5cm) high*

£400-500 **LFA**

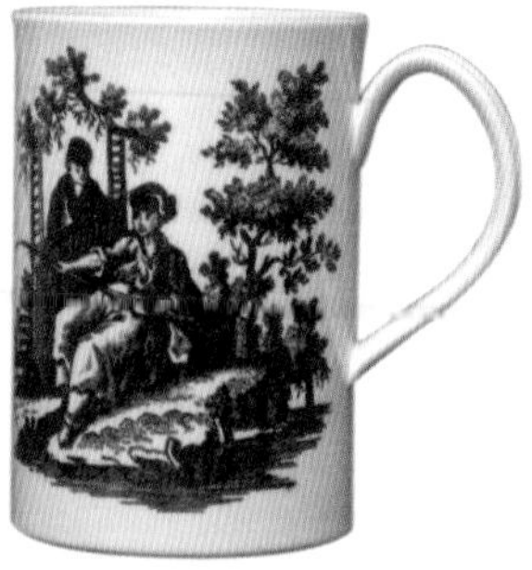

An early Worcester blue and white mug, printed with Chinoiserie figures in a landscape, crescent mark.

c1775 *4.5in (11.5cm) high*

£350-450 **BRI**

A Worcester miniature tea bowl and saucer, painted in underglaze blue with the 'Prunus Root' pattern, crescent and workman's marks.

c1760

£500-800 **LFA**

A rare Worcester tea bowl and saucer, printed in underglaze blue with clusters and sprays of narcissus and other flowers, within blue ground oval panelled bands, blue crescent mark.

This pattern is not recorded in Branyan, French and Sandon's "Worcester Blue and White Porcelain 1751-1790".

c1780

£2,500-3,000 **LFA**

A Worcester saucer, painted in underglaze blue with the 'Rock Warbler' pattern, crescent mark, tiny rim nick.

c1760 *5in (12.5cm) diam*

£500-700 **LFA**

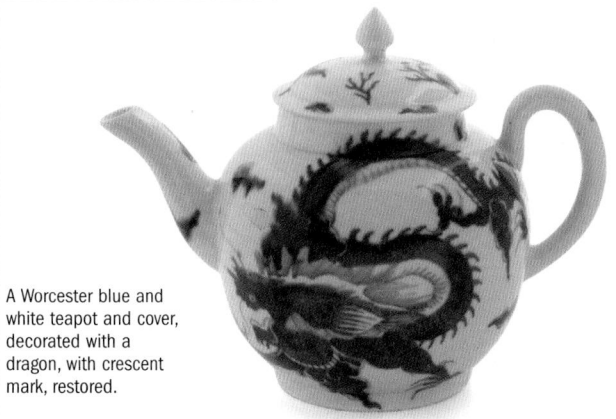

A Worcester blue and white teapot and cover, decorated with a dragon, with crescent mark, restored.

c1760 *7.5in (19cm) wide*

£800-1,200 **WW**

A Worcester blue and white sparrowbeak jug, painted with the 'Cannonball' pattern, some small footrim chips, open crescent mark.

c1775 *4.25in (11cm) high*

£250-300 **DN**

A first period Worcester jug of ovoid form with relief leaf and face mask decoration, underglaze blue transfer print of roses, blue crescent mark to base.

7.5in (19cm) high

£400-600 **MAX**

WORCESTER TRANSFER PRINTING

- Several names can be linked to the development of the transfer printing process at Worcester c1756-8. Foremost among them are engraver Robert Hancock, who first applied the method to porcelain, and the Holdship brothers.
- The process involved ink being transferred from a design engraved on a copper sheet to unglazed porcelain, using a sheet of tissue. The cross-hatching made by the engraving tools can often be seen in transfer-printed decoration. The pattern could be reproduced identically on every piece, much more cheaply than hand-painting.
- Worcester used transfer printing extensively for overglaze black enamel and underglaze blue printed pieces.
- Demand for blue and white wares was enormous from the mid-18thC and most English factories began mass-producing transfer-printed wares in the 1770s. Worcester and Caughley were the most successful.
- Some firms later applied transfer printing methods to earthenware, which was cheaper than porcelain. By the end of the 18thC, transfer-printed earthenware was common across Europe.

A Worcester feather-moulded coffee cup, with everted barbed rim and C-scroll handle, transfer-printed in black with a finch on a branch and birds in flight, the interior border with a flower-panelled trellis band.

c1760 *2.5in (6.5cm) high*

£1,200-1,800 **AA**

A Worcester coffee cup and saucer, with notched loop handle, printed after Robert Hancock with 'The Tea Party' in black, within black line borders.

c1770

£300-500 **LFA**

A Worcester mug, with notched loop handle, transfer-printed in black with the 'Whitton Anglers' pattern, faint base crack.

c1770 *6in (15cm) high*

£700-1,000 **LFA**

A rare Worcester silver shape sauceboat, printed in black with Chinoiserie scenes, the interior with a print of 'Bubbles', scratched line mark, rim crack and footrim chip.

c1755 *7.75in (19.5cm) wide*

£800-1,200 **WW**

A large and rare Worcester leaf-moulded mask jug, inscribed "Success to the Crosby Hunt", transfer-printed in black with a continuous fox hunting scene, the neck with two vignettes, unmarked, repaired cracks.

c1770 *9in (23cm) high*

£800-1,200 **WW**

A Worcester transfer-printed and over-painted mug, printed en grisaille and in coloured enamels with vignettes of ruins, probably by Robert Hancock after Pannini, with gilt rim, cracked.

c1765 *4.75in (12cm) high*

£500-800 **DN**

A CLOSER LOOK AT A WORCESTER COFFEE CAN

Worcester was established in 1751, making this mid-1750s coffee can early and desirable.

Early wares show the influence of silver shapes used by the Lund factory in Bristol, which Worcester acquired in 1752.

Pieces from this period have a grey-blue cast and are fully glazed, including the foot-rims and the rims of lids.

The Chinese influence is evident in the design.

A Worcester coffee can, one side painted with two figures between rocks and trees, the reverse with the 'Stag Hunt' pattern, a jui band to the inner rim, with scratched cross mark.

c1755 *2.25in (6cm) high*

£4,000-5,000 **WW**

A Worcester coffee cup, with notched loop handle, painted with flowers and leaves, gilt details, within oval and rectangular panels, on an alternating iron red on blue and gilt trellis ground.

c1770 *2.5in (6.5cm) high*

£400-600 **LFA**

A Worcester coffee cup, painted in the famille rose style with figures in a garden, within a black and gilt line border.

c1775 *2.5in (6.5cm) high*

£350-450 **LFA**

A Worcester teacup, decorated in the atelier of James Giles with flowers, leaves and a fruit sprig, crossed swords and "9" marks, worn interior.

c1775

£500-800 **WW**

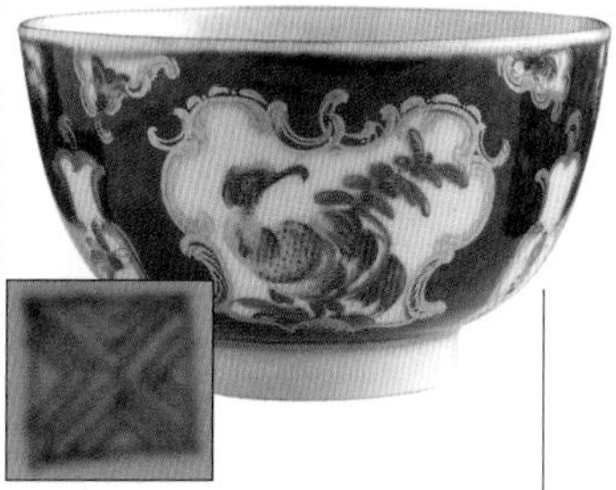

A Worcester tea bowl, painted with exotic birds in landscapes, butterflies and insects, within gilt cartouches, on a blue scale ground, blue fret mark.

c1770

£300-500 **LFA**

A Worcester teacup and saucer, painted with exotic birds, butterflies and insects, within gilt cartouches, on a blue scale ground, blue fret marks.

c1770

£500-700 **AA**

A Worcester fluted teacup and saucer, painted with swags of flowers, within gilt C-scrolls and shagreen and blue ground bands, decorated in gilt, the cup with script mark.

c1775

£700-1,000 **AA**

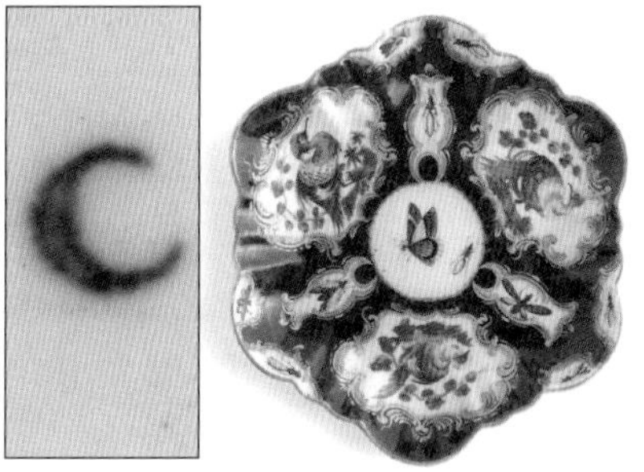

A hexagonal teapot stand, painted with exotic birds in wooded landscapes, butterflies and insects, within gilt cartouches, on a blue scale ground, blue crescent mark.

This piece looks like Worcester but is probably not. It may have been made as a replacement for a broken part of a service. The tea bowl above is a genuine Worcester piece in the same pattern.

c1850 *5.75in (14.5cm) wide*

£700-1,000 **LFA**

WORCESTER FACTORIES

- Established by Dr. John Wall and William Davis in 1752, the Worcester factory initially suffered heavy kiln losses until it acquired the Bristol factory and Lund's secret soapstone porcelain formula.
- During the 1750s-70s the factory specialized in durable tea and serving wares in the Rococo style.
- By 1770 the company was struggling. John Flight, whose father took over the factory in 1783, updated Worcester's wares in the fashionable French style and the company enjoyed a revival.
- When Martin Barr joined the company in 1792 the name was changed to Flight & Barr. This changed to Barr, Fight & Barr in 1804 when Martin Barr junior was brought in.
- A rival to the Flight Worcester company was set up c1786 by Humphrey Chamberlain and his son Robert, who had previously been in charge of decorating at Worcester. The two companies were finally united in 1840 as Chamberlain & Co.
- The name was changed to Kerr & Binns in 1852, finally becoming the Worcester Royal Porcelain Company in 1863.
- Royal Worcester is still in operation today, producing historical and contemporary forms.

A Worcester faceted teapot and cover, painted in the Kakiemon style with the 'Jabberwocky' pattern, with iron red diaper cartouches, blue fret mark, cover damaged.

c1770 *5.25in (13.5cm) high*

£300-500 **LFA**

A Worcester globular teapot, painted with bouquets and sprays of flowers in puce, green and iron red, the cover with a sprig handle.

c1770 *6in (15cm) wide*

£200-300 **GORL**

A Worcester miniature teapot and cover, with loop handle and ball knop, decorated in gilt with flowers and leaves, within gilt line borders.

c1780 *3.25in (8.5cm) high*

£400-600 **LFA**

A Worcester miniature coffee pot and domed cover, decorated in gilt with flowers and leaves, within gilt line borders, chips and repairs.

c1780 *3.75in (9.5cm) high*

£300-400 **LFA**

A Worcester faceted tea canister and domed cover, decorated in the famille verte palette with the 'Dragon in Compartments' pattern, blue fret mark, small chips.

c1770 *5.5in (14cm) high*

£800-1,200 **LFA**

A Worcester oval sauceboat, of silver shape, painted in the famille rose palette with a woman in a Chinese river landscape, within leaf and C-scroll cartouches, interior painted with flowers, damage.

c1755 *7.5in (19cm) wide*

£700-1,000 **LFA**

A Worcester silver shape sauceboat, painted with birds beside vases of flowers and leaves, small rim chip and crack.

c1760 *7.5in (19cm) wide*

£350-450 **WW**

A Worcester sauce boat, painted with Chinoiserie figures within foliate and scroll-moulded cartouches, damage.

7.5in (19cm) wide

£180-220 **BRI**

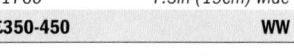

A first period Worcester sauce boat, moulded as a cos lettuce, the upper leaves painted with insects and the stalk forming the handle, bears label for "J Wickes".

9.75in (25cm) wide

£250-350 **CHEF**

A Worcester high Chelsea ewer, painted with a butterfly, flowers and sprigs and with purple camaieu sunbursts to the inner border.

c1760 *3.25in (8.5cm) high*

£700-1,000 **WW**

A small Worcester dolphin ewer, with lamprey handle, shell-moulded body and twin dolphins beneath the spout.

c1760 *3.75in (9.5cm) wide*

£1,200-1,500 **WW**

A rare Worcester wine taster, of peach form, the twig loop handle extends to form the foot, the exterior naturalistically decorated, on a basket moulded ground, the interior painted in the famille verte palette with flowers and leaves.

c1765 *3.5in (9cm) wide*

£3,000-4,000 **LFA**

A Worcester Flight barbed plate, painted in underglaze blue and gilt with the Prince of Wales feathers, within a roundel and leaf scroll band, the leaf border with garlands, blue crescent mark.

c1790 *8.5in (21.5cm) diam*

£800-1,200 **AA**

A pair of plates from a Worcester Barr, Flight & Barr tea and coffee service, probably painted by George Davis, with 'fancy' birds, butterflies and insects, within gilt scroll cartouches, on a blue and gilt scale ground, impressed marks.

c1810 *7.75in (19.5cm) diam*

£1,800-2,200 **AA**

A Worcester Flight, Barr & Barr claret-ground dessert plate, painted with a view of a church, within a C-scroll border with insects and gilt gadrooned rim, printed and impressed marks, entitled "Beauchief Abbey, Derbyshire".

c1815 *9in (22.5cm) diam*

£180-220 **DN**

A Worcester Barr, Flight & Barr twin-handled porcelain cup and saucer, painted with feathers, inscribed "Barr Flight & Barr Worcester", with crown mark.

4.25in (11cm) high

£1,800-2,200 **AA**

A Worcester Flight, Barr & Barr flared bowl and stand, the bowl with three gilt ball and claw feet, painted with feathers, within gilt gadrooned borders, marked in red.

c1820 *4.5in (11.5cm) diam*

£1,800-2,200 **AA**

A pair of Worcester Flight, Barr & Barr sauce tureens and covers, with flame finials and eagle and ring lifts, decorated with stylized flowers and gilding, impressed marks to the covers.

c1815 *6.25in (16cm) high*

£1,200-1,800 **WW**

A pair of Worcester Flight, Barr & Barr wine coolers, painted with oval panels of flowers and wide pink bands, with gilding, impressed marks.

c1815 *8.5in (21.5cm) wide*

£4,000-6,000 **WW**

A Worcester Flight, Barr & Barr vase and cover, with a flame finial and eagle lifts, painted with a panel of seashells, together with two Flight, Barr & Barr vases, painted and with impressed marks, damaged.

c1820 *6.75in (17cm) high*

£1,200-1,800 **WW**

A Davenport 'Etruscan Shape' teacup, coffee cup and saucer, painted with flowers and leaves, within border of cabbage roses and gilt leaves, brown printed marks.

c1820

£200-250 **LFA**

Part of a Davenport floral painted fruit service, comprising 12 circular plates, a pair of twin-handled serving dishes and four shaped dishes, with scalloped and pierced Rococo borders, puce printed marks and painted pattern number "584".

£800-1,200 set **L&T**

A CLOSER LOOK AT A LIMEHOUSE BLUE & WHITE FIGURE

The subject, 'The Old Vice-Roy of Kanton', is copied from an engraving from John Nieuhof's "An Embassy From The East India Company", published in Dutch in 1655 and English in 1669.

Two creamware Whieldon models copied from the same print are known, and this subject also appears moulded in relief on a saltglazed stoneware teapot in the Weldon collection in Canada.

Demand for blue and white porcelain in the Oriental style was high in the 18thC. English porcelain lacked the transparency and crispness of Chinese hard-paste porcelain.

Other than a seated cat and a number of small dogs, no Limehouse figure has previously been recorded.

A Limehouse porcelain blue and white figure, 'The Old Vice-Roy of Kanton', wearing a fur-trimmed head dress, on a moulded rectangular plinth decorated with a chequer design and a band of scrolls, unmarked, restored.

Joseph Wilson established the Limehouse factory in 1746, producing blue and white Chinoiserie-decorated porcelain dishes, teapots and sauceboats. It was undocumented until 1989 when the site was excavated and shards matching a type of porcelain previously ascribed to William Reid in Liverpool were found. The factory closed in 1748.

1746-8 *4.25in (10.5cm) high*

£25,000-30,000 **WW**

A Keys & Mountford parian bust of Sir Robert Peel, modelled in the Classical style on a socle base, inscribed "Pubd. by J. Hogarth 5 Haymarket London Oct. 1st 1850 S KEYS & MOUNTFORD".

1850 *9.75in (25cm) high*

£150-200 **DN**

One of a rare pair of Mason's campana-shaped wine coolers, decorated in gilt, puce and iron red with lanterns, rams' heads, cornucopia and leaf scrolls, the interior painted in iron red and gilt with a leaf scroll band, damaged.

c1815 *8in (20.5cm) high*

£1,500-2,000 pair **LFA**

A pair of English porcelain blue-ground campana vases, decorated with shaded gilding with figures and a dog, unmarked, possibly Mason's.

c1820 *6in (15.5cm) high*

£1,000-1,500 **WW**

A pair of Minton miniature jugs, each with glazed loop handle and applied with flowers and leaves beneath a gilt scroll band.

c1840 *2in (5cm) high*

£220-280 **LFA**

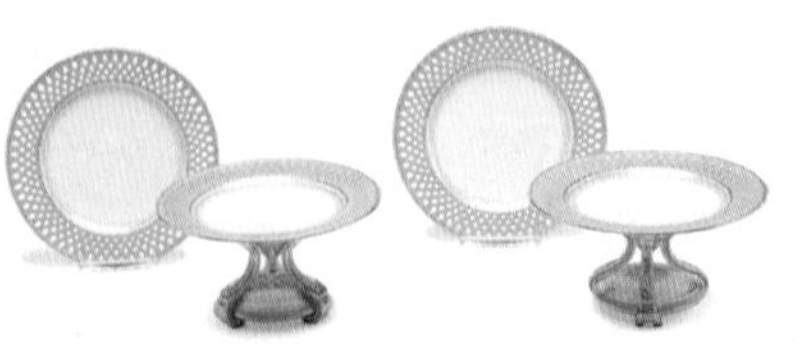

Part of a Minton porcelain dessert service, comprising two tazza and nine plates, retailed by T. Goode & Co. of London, one plate with Paris Exhibition 1878 printed mark, crowned globe printed mark.

c1880 *9.75in (25cm) diam*

£500-800 set **FRE**

A fine Minton pâte-sur-pâte peacock-blue pilgrim bottle, decorated with a copper lustre medallion depicting a river god, the reverse with a cameo depicting an angel in a pâte-sur-pâte frame, slight damage.

c1880 *10.25in (26cm) high*

£1,500-2,000 **FRE**

A Limoges Theodore Haviland porcelain coffee cup, saucer and side plate, designed by Suzanne Lalique, printed marks.

plate 6in (16cm) diam

£60-90 **DRA**

A set of six Limoges Theodore Haviland porcelain dessert plates, designed by Suzanne Lalique, printed marks.

With factory running costs escalating in Paris, Limoges became a cheaper alternative after the completion of a Paris-Limoges railway link in 1857. Limoges factories supplied Paris with blanks identical to the Paris models, while following an eclectic blend of decorative styles. Amongst others, Haviland & Co. adopted Japanese designs reflecting the fashion for the exotic.

7in (17.5cm) diam

£150-200 **DRA**

A Limoges Haviland pillow vase, painted in barbotine by 'JHL', with branches of blossoms on white and grey ground, hairlines and small chips to rim, stamped "H & Co. L."

10.5in (26.5cm) high

£600-900 **DRA**

Part of an early 20thC Limoges porcelain service, each painted with a different fish within vine borders, comprising platter, sauce boat and underplate and 12 plates, printed marks.

platter 23in (58.5cm) wide

£1,200-1,800 set **FRE**

A 19thC Limoges pâte-sur-pâte plaque, by A. Riffaterre, depicting a nymph taking a drink from a spring, signed lower right "A. Riffaterre, Limoges", framed.

20in (50cm) high

£800-1,200 **FRE**

SAMSON

A pair of Samson porcelain figures, modelled as a shepherd and shepherdess, on moulded Rococo bases, losses and restoration.

11in (28cm) high

£500-800 **SWO**

A pair of Samson Derby-style bocage figure groups, modelled as a flowerseller and male companion, on Rococo plinths.

11in (28cm) high

£400-600 **L&T**

A pair of Samson Turkish figures, in the style of Derby gold anchor, impressed number marks.

9.5in (24cm) high

£1,000-1,500 **L&T**

A late 19thC Continental porcelain figure of a street vendor, modelled after the Meissen original 'The Ironmonger' by J.J. Kändler, possibly Samson, mark ground out.

7.5in (19cm) high

£120-180 **DN**

A Samson porcelain group, depicting a seated gentleman awaiting his companion, on an oval Rococo scroll base, blue underglaze mark.

c1905 9.5in (24cm) wide

£400-600 **FRE**

A pair of large Samson famille rose baluster vases, with pink cellular ground, peony panels, decorated with scroll friezes filled with chrysanthemums, gilt pendants and peony sprays and butterflies.

Edmé Samson & Cie was founded in 1845 and soon began reproducing copies of European and Chinese porcelain, in the style of Meissen, Höchst, Chelsea and Worcester, but marked with the Samson mark. The factory closed in 1970.

25.5in (65cm) high

£1,200-1,800 **L&T**

THE SÈVRES FACTORY

- In 1756 the Vincennes porcelain factory moved to Sèvres and changed its name.
- Louis XV patronised the factory, issuing laws to protect its output.
- Deposits of kaolin, found at Limoges in 1768, enabled the factory to produce hard-paste porcelain. Sculptors and goldsmiths became more ambitious, creating larger, purely decorative pieces.
- After 1751, Etienne-Maurice Falconet (1716-91) utilised biscuit porcelain for his fine sentimental groups.
- In the late 1770s, the fashionable Neoclassical style was adopted at Sèvres.
- Sculptor Louis-Simon Boizot became head of modelling and by 1780 figural subjects were based on Classical and mythological forms, in preference to pastoral themes.
- The factory was taken over by the post-Revolution state in 1793 and focussed on Neoclassical pieces, also selling many undecorated blanks.
- During the 19thC, Sèvres' output moved towards the Empire style and was influenced by Egyptian and Oriental designs.
- The Rococo Revival in the mid-19thC saw the reintroduction of landscape panels and figures in the style of Rococo artists Watteau and Boucher. The white wares sold off earlier were often later decorated in the Rococo Revival style. These pieces are frequently called 'Sèvres' or 'Sèvres-style' today. Sèvres marks were widely copied.
- 20thC Sèvres output includes Art Deco pieces and copies of earlier work. 1940s Sèvres is highly sought-after today.
- The factory is still in operation and remains the property of the French State.

A pair of 19thC Sèvres-style ormolu-mounted vases, the painted panels depicting children, birds and flowers, outlined in red jewelling, each with elaborate gilding on a bleu celeste ground.

12.75in (32.5cm) high

£4,000-6,000 **WW**

A pair of 19thC Sèvres-style cache pots, with painted panels after Boucher, showing figures in an Arcadian landscape, on a bleu celeste ground, one signed with painted entrelac mark with letter "L".

9.25in (23cm) diam

£500-800 **L&T**

A CLOSER LOOK AT A PAIR OF SÈVRES URNS

The urns are finely painted with figural and landscape scenes, demonstrating continuity with the Sèvres tradition of treating porcelain as a medium for painting.

The large dimensions allow the painted decoration to be exhibited to its best advantage, as well as creating imposing display pieces suitable for a grand setting.

During the late 19thC, the Sèvres factory largely produced ornamental pieces, such as these urns, particularly for government buildings and embassies.

During this period, pieces were influenced by a variety of styles. The shape is Neoclassical in origin, whilst the painted panels feature 18thC-style figures.

A pair of late 19thC Sèvres porcelain and gilt-metal mounted urns, painted on one side with courting figures and on the other with mountain landscapes, wear.

41.5in (104cm) high

£15,000-20,000 **FRE**

A pair of late 19thC Sèvres-style vases and covers, with acorn knop gilt finials, the tapering turquoise bodies with opposing cartouche panels, one side depicting flowers, the other figures, on turned columns and indented square bases, with blue painted marks.

18in (45cm) high

£800-1,200 **L&T**

A 19thC Sèvres-style tête-à-tête, the finials modelled as flowers, painted with garlands beneath gilt and turquoise scrolling bands, interlaced "L"s enclosing "T".

£1,500-2,000 **WW**

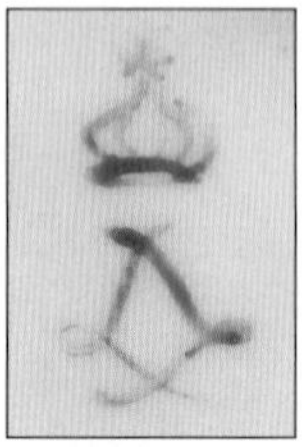

One of a pair of Sèvres salts, with oval Rococo-moulded bodies, raised on four feet and detailed with gilding, crowned interlaced "L" marks.

c1770 *3.25in (8cm) wide*

£600-800 pair **WW**

A Chantilly white glazed bouquetière figure, of a woman holding a pierced basket, unmarked.

c1735 *9.75in (25cm) high*

£3,000-5,000 **WW**

A mid-18thC Chantilly quatrefoil sucrier, cover and stand, painted with scattered floral sprays, with iron red hunting horn marks, finial restored.

£1,000-1,500 **DN**

A Mennecy snuff box, formed as a monkey's head, naturalistically coloured in pinks, brown and black, unmarked.

c1755 *2.25in (5.5cm) wide*

£250-300 **WW**

A pair of Feuillet fruit coolers, covers and liners, with knops in the form of clusters of feathers, painted with fruits to one side and flowers and a bumble bee to the reverse, within gilt line borders, script marks in gilt "Feuillet a Paris".

Jean-Pierre Feuillet (1777-1840) learned to paint at a school founded by the Prince de Condé in Chantilly. Around 1814 he established a workshop at Paris' rue de la Paix under the Prince's protection. Decorating blanks from Nast, Sèvres and Darte Frères, Feuillet gained a reputation as one of the best porcelain painters in the city.

c1820 *11in (28cm) high*

£6,000-8,000 **AA**

A Paris porcelain bourdaloue, with a loop handle, painted with flowers and leaves, within gilt stiff leaf borders, marked in blue.

c1820 *8.75in (22cm) wide*

£300-500 **LFA**

One of a set of three Paris porcelain plaques, painted with a still life of flowers in a basket, on a stone ledge, in original giltwood frame.

c1830 *10in (25.5cm) wide*

£6,000-8,000 set **AA**

A CLOSER LOOK AT A PARIS CABINET CUP

This opulent Empire cabinet cup dates from the 1790s-1820s heyday of Paris porcelain. Note the high quality gilding in mint condition.

The La Courtille factory had a reputation for producing outstanding hard-paste porcelain in the Meissen style, and its wares were exported throughout Europe.

The striking, delicate and finely realised shape of this display piece, as well as the female bust found to the handle, contribute to the value.

The cup is marked with two crossed torches. The factory's founder, Jean Baptiste Locré was granted the use of this mark in 1793.

A Paris porcelain cabinet cup and saucer by La Courtille, in the Empire style, painted with flowers and leaves, within gilt scroll, dot and dentil borders, blue crossed torches mark.

c1820 *4.75in (12cm) high*

£600-900 **AA**

A mid-18thC St Cloud box, modelled as a cat, moulded with flowers and leaves, painted in the Kakiemon palette with scattered insects and flower sprays, cover missing.

2.75in (7cm) wide

£800-1,200 **WW**

An 18thC French white-glazed porcelain model of a gardener, holding a sack, chipped.

6in (15cm) high

£500-800 **WW**

A late 19thC French 'Pagoda' figure of a Chinaman, with nodding head and wagging tongue and wrists, the robe painted with flowers and leaves, with "JR" monogram in underglaze blue.

11.5in (29cm) high

£1,500-2,000 **GORL**

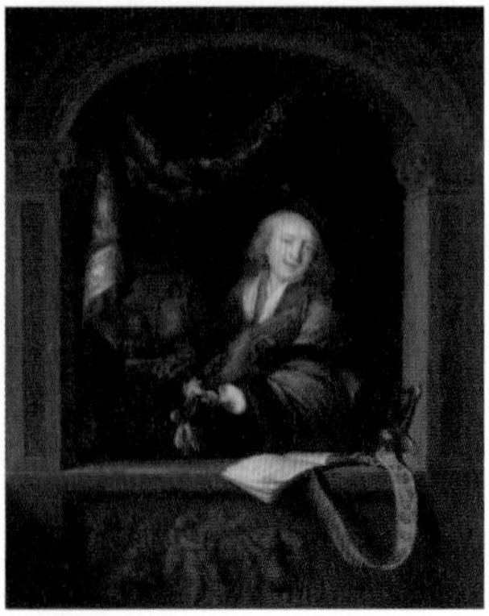

A 19thC Berlin KPM porcelain plaque, after Gerrit Dou, painted with a violin player at a window, impressed KPM sceptre mark, framed.

12in (30.5cm) wide

£7,000-10,000 **FRE**

A 19thC Berlin KPM porcelain plaque, depicting a figural marine scene, possibly Columbus discovering the New World, impressed KPM sceptre mark, framed, minor damage and losses.

The Berlin factory was founded in 1752 by Wilhelm Kaspar Wegely, and initially produced Meissen copies and fine, moulded work. It closed in 1757 but was bought in 1763 by Frederick the Great, becoming known as the Königliche Porzellan-Manufaktur (KPM). It is still operating today as the Staatliche Porzellan Manufaktur.

16.25in (41.5cm) wide

£7,000-10,000 **FRE**

A 19thC Berlin KPM porcelain plaque, depicting Napoleon Bonaparte, after Francois Gerard, signed "Wagner", impressed KPM sceptre mark, in modern giltwood frame.

6.25in (16cm) wide

£4,000-6,000 **FRE**

A 19thC Berlin KPM porcelain plaque, depicting Ruth, in a carved wood and velvet frame, printed black beehive mark, signed "Meyer".

6in (15cm) wide

£1,800-2,200 **FRE**

A 19thC Berlin KPM porcelain oval plaque, depicting Princess Louise, within an ornate openwork Rococo giltwood frame, signed "Lien".

7in (18cm) wide

£2,000-3,000 **FRE**

A Berlin KPM plaque, painted with a three-quarter length portrait of Yum-Yum, mounted in an elaborate gilt frame within a glazed case, impressed KPM sceptre marks.

c1880 9.5in (24cm) high

£4,000-5,000 **WW**

A late 19thC Berlin KPM porcelain plaque, after Gainsborough, depicting a lady with a feathered hat, impressed "18".

7in (17.5cm) high

£1,800-2,200 **FRE**

A late 19thC Berlin KPM porcelain plaque, painted with a woman in a wooded garden, impressed KPM sceptre mark, with "Franz Xavier Thallmaier, Munich" label.

6.25in (16cm) wide

£3,000-5,000 **FRE**

A 20thC Berlin KPM porcelain plaque, painted with a maid beside a wall fountain, signed indistinctly, impressed KPM sceptre mark, framed.

8.5in (21.5cm) high

£1,500-2,000 **FRE**

MEISSEN

- Established c1709 in eastern Germany, Meissen initially produced hard, finely textured stoneware.
- Meissen became the first European factory to discover the secret of hard paste porcelain and by the early 1720s it was producing a creamy white porcelain known as 'Böttger' porcelain.
- After 1723 the factory used a cross swords mark based on the arms of Saxony, sometimes with letters or a Roman numeral.
- During the 1730s, Meissen became the pre-eminent porcelain factory in Europe, producing figures and fashionable services. Pieces were widely copied throughout Europe.
- From 1733, Johann Joachim Kändler was responsible for modelling some of the factory's finest figures, including characters from the Italian Commedia dell'Arte theatre tradition and London street vendors.
- Later 18thC Meissen figures were produced in the lighter Rococo style. Bases were unglazed and often featured scrolls and gilding.
- During the 19thC mass-production increased and new decoration techniques and materials were used. Styles were diverse and included Biedermeier, Empire, Gothic Revival and Rococo Revival. Glazes from this period are hard and glassy.

A Meissen model of a putto, modelled contrapposto with a garland of flowers, seated on a later wooden seat, chips.

c1760 *5in (13cm) high*

£150-200 **DN**

A late 18thC Meissen allegorical figure of 'Peace', modelled as Minerva, seated upon two cannons beneath an obelisk inscribed "PAX", underglaze blue crossed swords, asterisk and two dashes, inscribed "1660".

6.5in (16.5cm) high

£500-800 **ROS**

A pair of 19thC Meissen figural table candlesticks, modelled as a man and woman, on Rococo plinths, blue painted crossed swords marks and impressed numbers.

8in (20cm) high

£1,800-2,200 **L&T**

A pair of 19thC Meissen figures of Turkish musicians, carrying stringed instruments, painted blue crossed swords marks and impressed number marks "1560", "1576" and "85".

7in (18cm) high

£800-1,200 **L&T**

A 19thC Meissen model of a 'Lady of the Mops', with a crinoline dress and two pug dogs, raised on a flared plinth, crossed swords mark, chipped.

10.75in (27.5cm) high

£2,000-3,000 **WW**

A 19thC Meissen group of two cherubs, each with a drum and one with a cornucopia, crossed swords mark and incised "2344", restored.

6.75in (17cm) wide

£2,000-2,500 **WW**

A 19thC Meissen group of romantic lovers, with a bouquet of flowers, crossed swords mark, incised "N704".

10.25in (26cm) high

£2,200-2,800 **WW**

A 19thC Meissen figural salt, modelled as a seated woman in exotic dress, holding a shell dish, crossed swords mark, chip to bowl.

6.75in (17cm) high

£1,500-2,000 **ROS**

A 19thC Meissen porcelain figure of 'Autumn', on four rocaille feet, a garland of corn in her hair, underglaze blue crossed swords mark, one finger missing, sickle broken.

11in (27.5cm) high

£700-1,000 **KAU**

A Meissen porcelain figure of a woman, with a sheep and an open birdcage, designed by Acier, a letter in her left hand, blue swords mark, model number "F.73".

7.5in (19cm) high

£300-400 **KAU**

A late 19thC Meissen porcelain figure of a woman, with fruits in her apron, underglaze blue swords mark, numbered "131" and "A22".

5.25in (13cm) high

£400-600 **KAU**

A Meissen porcelain figure, 'Winter Delight', the boy standing in front of a sleigh, throwing a snowball, underglaze blue swords mark.

c1900 *5.5in (13.5cm) high*

£800-1,200 **KAU**

An early 20thC Meissen harlequin, on an oval base, blue crossed swords and incised number.

6in (15cm) high

£1,000-1,500 **SWO**

A 20thC Meissen figure group, modelled as a man and woman in 18thC dress, with a dog, underglaze blue crossed swords mark, impressed and incised numbers.

6in (15cm) high

£400-600 **ROS**

A Meissen porcelain figure of a flower girl, painted and gilded, underglaze blue swords mark with dot, numbered "52" and "29".

c1930 *5.25in (13cm) high*

£350-450 **KAU**

A Meissen porcelain figure of a woman carrying flowers, underglaze blue swords mark with dot, numbered "110" and "1889".

c1930 *4in (10cm) high*

£250-300 **KAU**

A Meissen porcelain figure of a boy, leaning against a basket of grapes and holding a wine pitcher, underglaze blue swords mark with dot, numbered "121" and "A6".

c1930 *5.25in (13cm) high*

£300-500 **KAU**

A pair of Meissen pagoda figures, modelled as a seated Chinese man and woman, each with nodding heads and rocking hands, crossed swords marks.

7.25in (18.5cm) high

£5,000-7,000 **WW**

A Meissen model of an Oriental woman, modelled holding a parasol, blue crossed swords mark, incised "2676", restored.

7in (18cm) high

£250-300 **DN**

A Meissen-style pot pourri, with a figure of Diana, a putto and a hound, decorated with flowers and puce scroll-moulded borders, impressed numbers, minor chips, cover missing.

8.25in (21cm) high

£600-900 **LFA**

An unusual Meissen biscuit porcelain figure of a muse, by J.C. Jücht, raised on a square plinth, painted and incised crossed swords marks and "L66", minor faults.

c1790 *10.5in (26.5cm) high*

£800-1,200 **WW**

Two Meissen white glazed figures, modelled by Alexander Struck, one modelled as a jester seated on a pile of books, an owl on his shoulder, the other as a Chinese tailor with fabric draped over his knee.

c1955 *tailor 9in (23cm) high*

£600-800 **ROS**

An early 18thC Meissen plate, the rim with relief basket decoration, painted with flowers and insects, gilded rim, underglaze blue swords mark.

9in (22.5cm) diam

£200-250 **KAU**

An early 18thC Meissen plate, the rim with relief decoration and gilding, painted with flowers, underglaze blue swords mark.

9.5in (24cm) diam

£150-200 **KAU**

An early 18thC Meissen plate, the rim with relief decoration and gilding, painted with flowers, underglaze blue mark.

9.75in (24.5cm) diam

£70-100 **KAU**

An early 18thC Meissen plate, with floral relief rim, depicting a river scene flanked by a tit and a robin, underglaze blue swords mark.

10in (25.5cm) diam

£120-180 **KAU**

An early Meissen saucer, painted in the manner of Aufenwerth, with a Chinoiserie figure carrying a quiver of arrows, a dog to his side, wear to gilding.

c1730 *5in (12.5cm) diam*

£600-900 **WW**

A late 18thC Meissen plate, decorated with an Oriental floral pattern and gilt, underglaze blue swords mark.

8.75in (22cm) diam

£250-300 **KAU**

A Meissen charger, with gilt rims, painted with floral decoration to the centre and flower swags to the border, blue underglaze swords mark.

c1780 *15in (38cm) wide*

£220-280 **KAU**

A late 19thC Meissen oval tray, painted with peacocks and distant buildings, with a floral and insect border.

16.5in (42cm) diam

£280-320 **BRI**

A late 19thC Meissen quatrefoil dish, painted with scattered floral sprays, blue crossed swords mark, some wear to gilding.

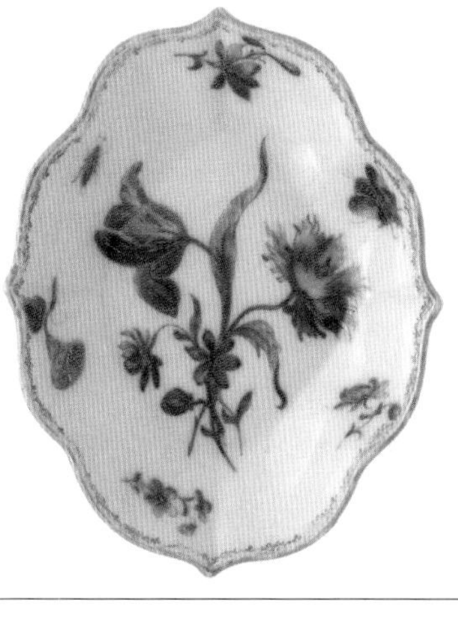

7in (18cm) wide

£80-120 **DN**

A small Meissen double gourd-shaped vase, painted in the Kakiemon style with a tiger, bamboo and prunus, blue crossed swords mark.

c1740 *3.5in (9cm) high*

£800-1,200 **AA**

A Meissen porcelain vase, decorated with flower bouquets, the handles formed as scrolling snakes, underglaze blue swords mark.

c1900 *16in (40cm) high*

£700-1,000 **KAU**

A Meissen-style three-piece garniture, decorated in relief with acanthus leaves and ribbon tied tassels on a gilded turquoise ground, one supported by two mermaids and the others by cherubs, pseudo-Meissen marks.

24in (61cm) high

£2,000-3,000 **FRE**

A CLOSER LOOK AT A MEISSEN PARTRIDGE TUREEN

The wide range of decorative techniques used on this tureen - including moulding, painting and gilding - are testament to the technical virtuosity of Meissen craftsmen during the 18thC.

The naturalistic painting of the partridge finial and the flowers on this tureen are very accomplished.

With its naturalistic colours, asymmetrical composition and florid decoration, this tureen is an excellent example of German Rococo at its height.

Sir Gawaine Baillie of Leeds Castle was well known in philatelic circles for his important collection of stamps. The provenance increases the appeal of this piece.

A large Meissen ogee-shaped soup tureen and cover, surmounted by a partridge, on four gilt-decorated scroll feet, blue crossed swords mark.

Provenance: Sir Gawaine Baillie of Leeds Castle.

c1750 *17in (43cm) wide*

£5,000-7,000 **AA**

A Meissen porcelain vase, with a flower cartouche, the handles formed as scrolling snakes, underglaze blue swords mark.

c1930 *15.5in (38.5cm) high*

£800-1,200 **KAU**

A rare early 18thC Meissen pot pourri vase and cover, formed as a gourd resting on a leaf, moulded with flowers, three impressed marks, probably for Albrecht.

6.75in (17cm) high

£1,500-2,500 **WW**

A Meissen Marcolini tureen and cover, in the form of a bundle of asparagus, tied with a ribbon.

c1800 *9in (23cm) wide*

£3,000-4,000 **AA**

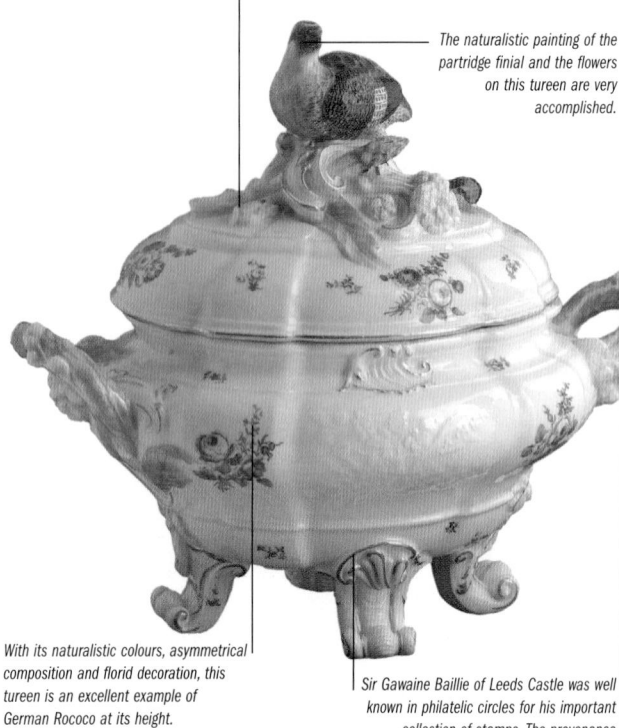

A set of four 18thC Meissen trencher salts, the anthemion-moulded cavetto sides painted with flowers, the bowls with nuts, flowers, fruit and spring onions, crossed swords marks.

4.25in (11cm) wide

£1,500-2,000 **CHEF**

A Frankenthal porcelain plate, with painted floral decoration and gilded rim, marked in blue with lions.

9.5in (24cm) diam

£150-200 **KAU**

A Frankenthal butter dish, moulded as a barrel, the lid with cow knop, painted with flower bouquets and gilded, underglaze lions mark.

c1760 *5.5in (14cm) diam*

£500-800 **MTZ**

A German porcelain gilt-metal mounted snuff box and hinged cover, possibly Furstenberg, painted with panels of putti within relief-moulded borders modelled en rocaille with C-scrolls, gilt interior, wear.

c1770

£3,000-5,000 **DN**

A Höchst coffee can and saucer, painted with alternating vertical bands of flowers, dots and zig-zags, within gilt line borders, painted marks in blue.

c1780

£280-320 **LFA**

A late 18thC German Ludwigsburg teacup and saucer, decorated with an initial "F" formed in flowers, underglaze blue crown and interlaced Cs.

2.75in (7cm) high

£150-200 **ROS**

A late 18thC Ludwigsburg allegorical figure of 'Plenty', modelled as a female in Classical dress, holding a cornucopia and bowl, underglaze blue crown and interlaced "C" mark over an "S", restored.

11in (28cm) high

£220-280 **ROS**

A Nymphenburg hunter on horseback figure, on a flat scrolled base with two hunting dogs on each side, stamped mark and model no. "382.7".

c1865 *7.5in (19cm) high*

£300-500 **KAU**

A late 19thC Thuringian Sitzendorf porcelain figure, 'The Flower Lover', on a naturalistic base, maker's mark.

5.5in (14cm) high

£50-80 **KAU**

A Thuringian Volkstedt-Rudolstadt porcelain figure of a girl with a lyre, on a naturalistic base, maker's mark and number "34".

c1900 *6.75in (17cm) high*

£50-80 **KAU**

A German porcelain model of a parrot, perched on a stump, Chelsea-style gold anchor mark.

£150-200 **DN**

THE VIENNA FACTORY

- The Vienna factory was established by Claudius Innocentius Du Paquier c1719. Early wares were similar to those produced by Meissen, based on Baroque silver shapes, and were decorated with Oriental-inspired floral scenes.
- During the 1730s, Vienna became the first factory to introduce European flower decoration. Early European flower designs featured precise botanical representations, but from the 1740s the flowers were freely painted and more scattered.
- Due to financial difficulties, the factory was sold to the state c1744 and wares were gradually updated in the fashionable Rococo style.
- A wide variety of figures were also introduced at this time. Johann Josef Niedermayer's figures, usually left in the white or painted in pale colours, are particularly highly regarded.
- Conrad Sörgel von Sorgenthal took over as director in 1784 and introduced Neoclassical wares with rich decoration and heavy gilding.
- From c1830, the quality of the output went into decline and the factory closed in 1864.
- Many post-1744 wares are marked with a blue shield. From 1783, digits for the year can also be found.

An early 19thC Vienna Biedermeier porcelain cup and saucer, gilded, with leaf borders and forget-me-nots, underglaze blue shield mark.

saucer 5.5in (14cm) diam

£120-180 **KAU**

An early 19thC Vienna porcelain Biedermeier cup and saucer, with golden leaf border, depicting a butterfly, signed "So bin ich nicht" ("That's not how I am"), underglaze blue shield mark.

saucer 5.5in (14cm) diam

£100-150 **KAU**

A Vienna porcelain coffee jug, probably 19thC, the lid with a bell-shaped knop, decorated with a bouquet of flowers, and flower sprays, underglaze blue shield mark.

8in (20cm) high

£60-90 **KAU**

A late 18thC Vienna porcelain lidded bowl, the lid with a pear-shaped knop, decorated with flowers, blue shield mark.

5.75in (14.5cm) wide

£70-100 **KAU**

A pair of 19thC Vienna porcelain cups and saucers, with scrolled branch handles, decorated with a floral design and scattered flowers, underglaze blue shield mark.

saucers 5.5in (14cm) diam

£100-150 **KAU**

Two late 18thC Vienna porcelain coffee jugs, decorated with bouquets of flowers, the lid of the larger with a pear-shaped knop, underglaze blue shield marks.

larger 8.75in (22cm) high

£150-200 **KAU**

LEFT: An early 20thC Vienna cabinet plate, with gilt border moulded with stylized flowers, painted with a woman in Classical dress, signed "K Bauer", blue painted beehive mark and gilt painted "Tanz Bajadere, D11".

Die Bajadere (The Yankee Princess) is an operetta by the Hungarian composer Emmerich Kalman with a libretto by J. Brammer and A. Grunwald. It premiered in Vienna on 23rd December 1921.

9.5in (24cm) diam

£500-800 **L&T**

RIGHT: An early 20thC Vienna cabinet plate, with a gilt border moulded with stylized flowers, painted with a woman in Middle Eastern dress, signed "Bork", blue painted beehive mark and red painted "Tochter d Kalifen, D10".

9.5in (24cm) diam

£500-800 **L&T**

A Vienna porcelain bowl with saucer, partially gilded, the front with cartouches of Oriental landscapes, the back of the cup with an insect, underglaze blue mark.

c1800 *saucer 6in (15cm) diam*

£70-100 **KAU**

A mid-19thC Austrian Vienna 'Gure Nacht' porcelain plate, with a lady holding a chamber stick, the Paris blue border with rich gilt over-painted decoration.

11in (28cm) diam

£300-500 **BIG**

THE POTTERY MARKET

The pottery market is characterized by extremes. Whereas the rare appearance in a saleroom of a complete Mason's Ironstone dinner service or a large pearlware cow creamer will have collectors clamouring to bid, more common items will struggle to generate similar interest.

Staffordshire figures have enjoyed mixed fortunes - while some of the dogs and more unusual animals have fared well, demand for British political figures and commemorative wares has, to an extent, dwindled.

The market for German stoneware jugs is similarly polarized, with prices for Mettlach steins remaining relatively flat while early Cruessen pieces continue to accrue value.

A general rule is that the most exceptional pieces in terms of form, decoration or provenance are most likely to appreciate more quickly.

Early lead-glazed ceramics, particularly Delftware, have paradoxically reaped the benefits of the art market's enduring affair with modern and minimalist design. Collectors attracted to the sparse and naïve designs on these pieces have pushed up values in recent months and this trend looks set to continue in the near future.

Some of the highest prices have been reserved for polychrome Berlin faience and English delft. As with most other areas of the market, truly exceptional pieces with good provenance will continue to attract record bids, especially if they are dated. Even if damaged, these items at the very top end of the market are really the only ones that can be relied upon to appreciate significantly over the next year.

CREAMWARE

A creamware jug, printed in black, one side with figures in a farmyard, the reverse with dancing figures, inscribed "Sarah Chadwick, nod, 1791", cracked and restored.

9.25in (23.5cm) high

£400-600 **WW**

A Staffordshire creamware Liverpool-printed commemorative dated jug, transfer-printed in black with a three-masted ship flying a red ensign, the reverse with a Classical maiden emblematic of Hope, inscribed oval cartouche, dated.

Developed by Wedgwood and others c1760, creamware typically has a lightweight, thin, cream-coloured body covered in a smooth lead glaze that lends itself well to underglaze blue decoration, overglaze enamelling and printing.

1802 *10.75in (27cm) high*

£800-1,200 **DN**

An early 19thC creamware jug, painted with a hunting scene on one side and the 'Farmer's Arms' on the other, the initials "JG" above, dated "1806".

8.5in (21cm) high

£600-900 **CHEF**

A Continental creamware puzzle jug, with scrolled handle, pierced border and brown sponge decoration, damaged.

c1800 *9.5in (24cm) high*

£400-600 **SWO**

A creamware teapot and cover, printed with Harlequin, Columbine and Pierrot, the reverse with sheep and a cottage.

c1765 *7.25in (18.5cm) high*

£600-900 **WW**

A rare creamware mug, commemorating the life of George Washington, inscribed "Sacred to the memory Washington 14 Dec 1799 AE68", restored.

c1800 *6in (15.5cm) high*

£1,500-2,000 **WW**

An early 19thC Dixon and Co. pink lustre creamware mug, printed in black and overpainted with the 'Grand Union Odd Fellow's Arms', printed marks.

First used in the Middle East in the 7thC, lustre decoration involves painting metal oxides dissolved in acid onto a glazed body before firing. Staffordshire was one of the major centres for lustre ware.

4.75in (12cm) high

£250-300 **CHEF**

A rare Staffordshire creamware coffee cup and saucer, of Whieldon type, the cup with everted rim and angular loop handle.

c1770

£1,200-1,800 **LFA**

An unusual Whieldon-type creamware bowl, decorated with a speckled manganese brown glaze, centred with a green and yellow mottled patch, restored.

c1760 *11in (28cm) diam*

£500-600 **WW**

An Elijah Mayer creamware oval basket and stand, decorated with painted bands, impressed marks, some restoration.

c1800 *2.75in (7cm) wide*

£150-200 **LFA**

A creamware two-handled bowl and cover, probably Staffordshire, enamelled with sprays of roses and other flowers, the entwined handles with foliate terminals, small chips.

c1780 *6.25in (16cm) wide*

£300-500 **DN**

A CLOSER LOOK AT A PAIR OF SWANSEA PLATES

William Weston Young was a prolific and accomplished decorator of Welsh pottery. He worked at Nantgarw as well as Swansea.

Weston was particularly famed for his depictions of scenes local to his hometown of Neath.

This creamware is similar in quality to that made by Wedgwood.

The gilt vines and borders on these plates are remarkably free of rubbing.

A pair of Swansea creamware plates, probably painted by William Weston Young, part of a set with a matching oval dish and shallow bowl, each with a sepia landscape within a border of fruiting vines in brown and gilt, impressed Swansea marks and titled, damage.

c1805 *9.5in (24.5cm) diam*

£7,000-10,000 set **WW**

A Leeds creamware round tureen and cover, of lobed form, with two rope-twist handles and foliate terminal, restored.

c1800

£500-800 **DN**

A rare creamware jelly comb, possibly Neale, painted with an English three-masted vessel, the other three sides with military trophies, the pierced canted base with green line rim.

c1785 *10.25in (26cm) wide*

£3,000-4,000 **LFA**

An unusual early 19thC creamware spirit barrel, the removable lid modelled as Silenus the satyr, the barrel moulded with fruiting vine, raised on a detachable flared foot, restored.

16.75in (42.5cm) high

£1,000-1,500 **WW**

A pair of early 20thC creamware cats, the pink lustre splashed animals with green glass eyes and matching plinths.

10.5in (26.5cm) high

£800-1,200 **CHEF**

BRITISH DELFTWARE

- British potters made the first 'white' pottery by applying a tin glaze in the mid-16thC. The tin glaze gives the earthenware an off-white opaque finish that provided a good ground for further decoration.
- The centres of British delftware production included Lambeth, Norwich, Bristol, Liverpool and Wincanton. Glasgow and Dublin also had their own factories.
- As was the fashion at the time, early delftware was decorated after the Chinese fashion in blue and white, or copied the Dutch manganese, yellow and green palette.
- As well as chargers and smaller plates and bowls, delftware potters produced flower bricks, tankards, puzzle jugs and commemorative pieces.
- Delftware tiles were also very popular. Popular decorative motifs included landscapes and flowers, with smaller designs in each corner.
- By the mid-18thC British delft was increasingly overlooked by the buying public in favour of creamware and, eventually, porcelain.

A Bristol delftware tile, with a figure in a landscape in an unusual shade of manganese.

c1735 *5in (12.5cm) wide*

£60-90 **STE**

A Bristol blue and white delftware tile, with a landscape scene.

c1750

£100-150 **STE**

A Bristol manganese delftware tile, with a landscape and buildings.

Manganese is a mineral used since Egyptian times to stain glazes and bodies. The colour varies depending on the glaze. Lead glazes give it a purple-brown colour, whereas manganese mixed with iron in an alkaline glaze creates a rich black tone.

c1760

£60-90 **STE**

A Bristol polychrome delftware tile, decorated with a bird, crack to glaze.

Bristol produced some boldly decorated pieces that contrasted with the predominately delicate decoration favoured by other factories after c1720.

c1750

£250-350 **STE**

A Bristol manganese delftware tile, with a landscape scene.

c1760

£80-120 **STE**

A Bristol manganese delftware tile, with decoration of a figure in a landscape.

c1760

£60-90 **STE**

A Bristol blue and manganese delftware tile, with Rococo cartouche.

c1760

£80-120 **STE**

A Bristol blue and white delftware tile, with a woman in a landscape.

c1760

£80-120 **STE**

A Bristol blue and white delftware tile, with Chinoiserie landscape, stud borders and Michaelmas daisy corners.

c1760

£60-90 **STE**

A Bristol blue and white delftware tile, with a flower and unusual stylized floral corners.

c1770

£70-100 **STE**

A Liverpool delftware tile, decorated with a bird, with leaf corners.

c1770 *5in (12.5cm) wide*

£250-300 **STE**

An English delftware water-bottle or guglet, probably Liverpool, painted in blue with stylized Oriental flowers, beneath lappet bands, the neck with a diaper band, some chips, foot rim crack.

c1760 *9in (23cm) high*

£220-280 **DN**

A Liverpool polychrome delftware plate, with floral designs, chipped and small crack.

10in (25.5cm) diam

£100-150 **BRI**

A Liverpool delftware tile, decorated with a bird, with stylized floral corners.

c1770 *5in (12.5cm) wide*

£400-500 **STE**

An unusual 18thC delftware wall pocket, probably Liverpool, relief-moulded with scrolls and a face mask on a blue ground, cracked and repaired.

8.25in (21cm) high

£700-900 **WW**

A rare Liverpool Fazackerly delftware tile, depicting flowers in a delftware flower bowl.

c1770 *5in (12.5cm) wide*

£400-500 **STE**

A Liverpool delftware baluster-shaped puzzle jug, with loop handle, the neck with nozzles and pierced hearts and flowerheads, inscribed with a verse "Gentlemen come and try your skill...", rim glued.

c1760 *7.25in (18.5cm) high*

£700-900 **LFA**

A London delftware tile, decorated with a figure, ships and a castle.

c1770

£80-120 STE

A London delftware tile, with blue and white decoration of buildings.

c1770

£80-120 STE

A London delftware tile, decorated with a man in a rowing boat.

c1780

£80-120 STE

A London delftware tile, with manganese decoration of an unusual flower basket, with cherub corners.

c1755

£60-90 STE

An English delftware blue dash 'Adam and Eve' charger, probably London, painted with 'The Temptation', within a blue dash border.

c1680 *13in (33cm) diam*

£3,000-5,000 DN

An English delftware Chinoiserie plate, possibly London, painted with a pagoda in a landscape and two birds, foliate band border, rim chips.

c1740 *8.75in (22.5cm) diam*

£300-500 DN

A delftware plate, probably Lambeth, painted with a galleon, cracked.

c1750 *8.75in (22.5cm) diam*

£300-500 WW

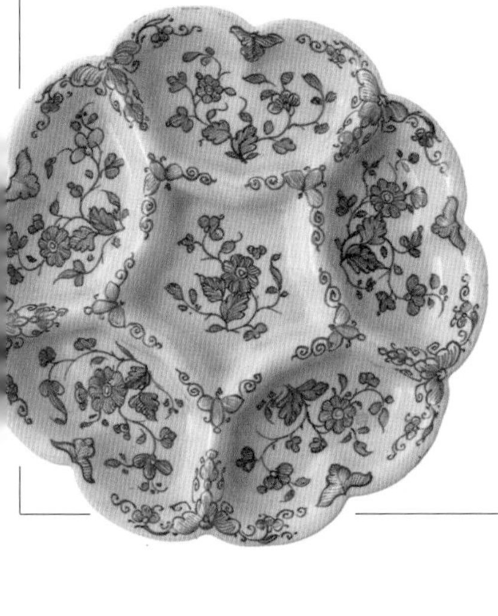

A London delftware sweetmeat dish, with a lobed rim, moulded with six segments painted with flowers and leaves.

c1760 *9in (22cm) high*

£800-1,200 WW

An English delftware posset pot, probably London, painted in the Kraak manner with Chinese figures in a landscape, lacking cover, one handle glued.

c1680

£800-1,200 DN

A large 18thC delftware dish, painted with a bird perched on a branch issuing from rockwork.

13.5in (34cm) diam

£450-500 **WW**

An 18thC English delftware plate, painted with a figure fishing and further figures in boats before a group of cottages.

12.75in (32.5cm) diam

£300-500 **WW**

An 18thC delftware lobed dish, painted with a stylized landscape, chipped.

8.75in (22cm) diam

£100-200 **WW**

An English delftware charger, boldly painted in underglaze blue with a dragon and flaming pearls in Chinese style, minor rim chips.

c1760 *12in (30.5cm) diam*

£700-1,000 **LFA**

A CLOSER LOOK AT A BLUE-DASH CHARGER

'Blue dash' chargers are named for the border. This motif is thought to have been used since 1600 on decorative polychrome dishes.

Although not marked with a specific date, the age of this charger can be deduced to within a few years because Anne's reign (1702-1714) was relatively short.

Early designs included fruit and flowers but royalty and biblical stories began to appear from 1614. The earliest monarch represented was Charles I, dated 1653.

The reverse was often glazed with a thick yellow lead glaze in order to save on the more costly tin glaze.

An English delftware royal commemorative blue-dash charger, painted with a portrait of Queen Anne standing holding an orb and sceptre with the initials "AR", flanked by sponged trees, restored.

c1710 *13.5in (34cm) diam*

£6,000-9,000 **WW**

An English delftware charger, painted with an Oriental flowering shrub within a diaper band border, minor rim chips.

c1760 *13.75in (35cm) diam*

£300-500 **DN**

An 18thC delftware plate, with stylized foliate decoration, chipped.

9in (23cm) diam

£150-200 **BRI**

DUTCH DELFT

- Dutch ceramicists were imitating tin-glazed maiolica – originally from Spain and Italy – as early as the 16thC.
- During the 17thC supply line problems with the Orient disrupted the flow of Chinese porcelain into Holland. Dutch ceramicists, concentrated in the southern town of Delft, began to emulate Chinese designs to fill the gap in the market.
- Many of the early blue and white wares were very similar in style to Chinese ceramics, including such details as Dog of Fo finials.
- Factories in other Dutch towns became involved in the manufacture of Delft ware. Other centres of production included Amsterdam, Delftshaven, Gouda and Haarlem.
- In time, Dutch Delft developed a style of its own. Overglaze colours of manganese, yellow and green were added to the original blue and the range of themes expanded to include local landscapes and stylized flowers.
- By the middle of the 18thC many of the Dutch Delft factories had gone out of business.

An 18thC Delft dish, decorated in the Kraak style with a central panel of a bowl of flowers, with stylized border panels.

13.75in (35cm) diam

£200-300 **WW**

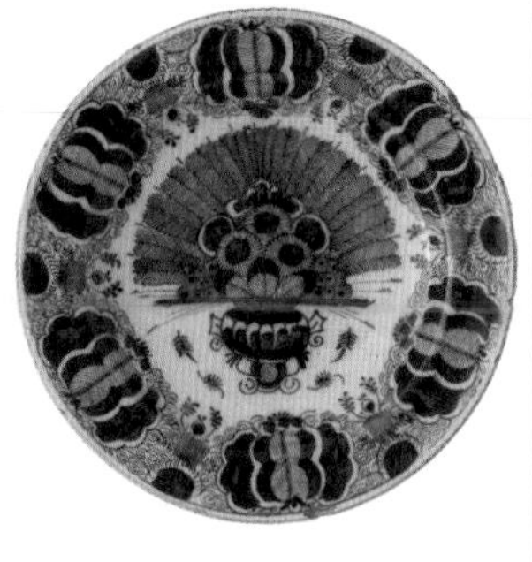

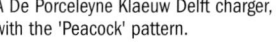

A De Porceleyne Klaeuw Delft charger, with the 'Peacock' pattern.

De Porceleyne Klaeuw (The Porcelain Claw) was in production from 1662 to 1840.

c1760

£150-200 **DN**

A De Porceleyne Bijl Delft charger, painted with stylized flowers within an ochre rim, rim chips.

13.75in (35cm) diam

£50-80 **DN**

A Delft plate, painted with a central flowerhead within a foliate band, painted "De 3 Vergulde Astonnekens" type mark, small rim chips.

9.5in (24cm) diam

£180-220 **DN**

A Delft panel of six tiles, painted with a rustic scene of a figure and a cow beneath a tree.

15.25in (39cm) high

£150-200 **H&L**

An 18thC Delft posset pot, of circular bellied form with scrolled handles, painted with birds perched amongst foliage, damaged.

5.5in (14cm) high

£700-1,000 **SWO**

A Delft sugar caster, probably 18thC, with a screw thread cover, painted with formal bands of flowers, foliage and scrolls, marked "400" to the foot.

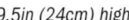

9.5in (24cm) high

£250-350 **WW**

A garniture of three late 18thC Dutch Delft vases, the central flared hexagonal vase painted with flowerheads and tendrils, with a pair of hexagonal baluster vases and covers with Dog of Fo finials.

c1790 *13.25in (33cm) high*

£800-1,200 **L&T**

A Mason's Patent Ironstone China blue ground bowl, decorated in coloured enamels and gilt with butterflies, within gilt bands.

c1815 *9.75in (25cm) diam*

£220-280 **LFA**

A Mason's Patent Ironstone China flared pot, decorated in Imari style with a bowl of flowers, leaves and trailing flowers, rim chip.

c1815 *2in (5cm) high*

£40-60 **LFA**

A Mason's Patent Ironstone China punch bowl, decorated with the 'Mogul' pattern, blue-printed crown and drape mark with no maker's name, some wear and chips.

c1820 *11.75in (30cm) diam*

£250-300 **DN**

Part of a mid-19thC Mason's Patent Ironstone China dinner service, comprising a pair of terrines and covers, a pair of sauce terrines with covers and stands, 16 meat plates, nine fish plates, 11 side plates, 10 dessert plates, brown printed mark, pattern number "2802".

£1,200-1,800 set **L&T**

Part of a mid-19thC Mason's Patent Ironstone China dinner service, possibly by Ashworth, comprising a soup tureen with cover and stand, a sauce tureen and cover, three vegetable dishes, six meat dishes, 24 dinner plates, five soup plates, 14 dessert plates, and 10 tea plates, printed crown and drape marks, repairs.

£1,000-1,500 set **DN**

Part of a 19thC Ironstone Imari dinner service, printed and painted with a vase and flowerheads, comprising six oval serving dishes, a tureen and cover, two sauce boats, nine side plates, ten fish plates, 28 dinner plates, 19 dessert bowls and 10 soup bowls, printed mark "Stone China 66", 10 plates with additional impressed mark "Ashworth real ironstone china".

largest 22in (56cm) wide

£1,200-1,800 set **L&T**

A Minton stone china footbath, printed with vases of flowering shrubs, impressed "BB" and "New Stone".

c1840 *18.75in (48cm) wide*

£280-320 **SWO**

An early 19thC earthenware pot pourri vase and pierced cover, possibly Ridgway, with printed and overpainted decoration, painted "N2300" mark, cover damaged.

13in (33cm) high

£150-200 **SWO**

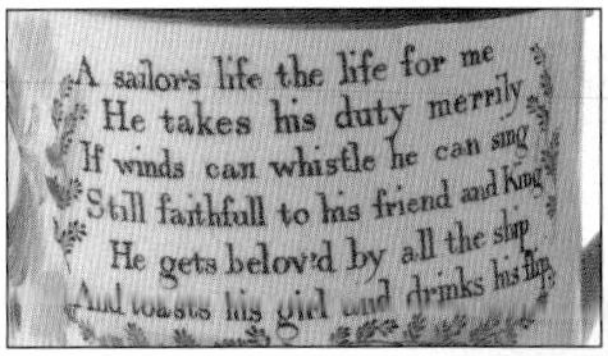

An early 19thC Sunderland pink splash lustre frog mug, printed with verses to sailors and trade, between yellow bands.

4.5in (11.5cm) high

£400-600 **CHEF**

A late 19thC orange lustre frog mug, printed in black and coloured enamels, one side with a three-masted sailing ship, the other with a verse "Now safe returned from dangers past ...", the interior with a brown-painted moulded frog, unmarked.

4.75in (12cm) high

£100-150 **DN**

A 19thC 'Gaudy Welsh' lustre octagonal jug, painted with forget-me-not pattern, moulded serpent handle.

'Gaudy Welsh' is a generic name for pottery and porcelain produced primarily in Staffordshire which is brightly decorated and sometimes lustred or gilded. The patterns are similar to 'Gaudy Dutch' wares and probably developed from Imari styles c1820.

7.5in (19cm) high

£50-80 **BRI**

An early 19thC pair of puce-printed and pink lustre earthenware jugs, with pineapple-moulded spouts, puce rural scenes of deer in reserves and pink lustre frames and details, unmarked, rim nick.

5.75in (14.5cm) high

£280-320 **DN**

A 19thC pink lustre jug, moulded with two portraits, entitled "H. Brougham Esq. MP" and "T. Denham Esq. MP", chipped spout.

£250-300 **WW**

A mid-19thC Sunderland lustre plaque, probably by John Carr of North Shields, with pink lustre border and inscription, unmarked.

9.5in (24cm) wide

£100-150 **DN**

A pink lustreware cow creamer and cover, on a moulded base, the horns chipped.

c1825 *6.75in (17cm) wide*

£250-300 **WW**

EARTHENWARE

- Earthenware is made from clay fired at a temperature that is insufficiently hot to vitrify, or fuse, the component ingredients. This results in a porous, or non-watertight, pottery.
- Stone china and Ironstone, manufactured by companies such as Minton and Mason, are types of earthenware with a very pale grey or blue tinge.
- Ironstone was celebrated in its day for its similarity to Oriental porcelain, although it is generally thicker and rougher.
- In its natural state most earthenware is the same colour as the clay it is made from – red or brown or somewhere in between.
- Most earthenwares are glazed to give them a non-porous surface suitable for eating from or for storing liquids.
- Lustre ware was popular during the 19thC. Metallic compounds are painted onto tin-glazed earthenware, which is then re-fired in a reduction kiln to bring out the colours.

A Llanethly earthenware round dish, painted in coloured enamels with a cockerel in a landscape, within an underglaze blue scroll border.

10.25in (26cm) diam

£300-500 **LFA**

A set of eight 19thC sponge-decorated whiteware soup plates, each decorated with geometric bands featuring floral devices.

c1850 *10in (25.5cm) diam*

£300-500 **FRE**

A Minton earthenware boat-shaped toast rack, with pierced divisions printed in underglaze blue with flowers and leaves, the central division with a ring handle.

c1830 *10.25in (26cm) wide*

£500-700 **LFA**

A mid-19thC earthenware cow creamer, with a milkmaid mounted on a shaped base, with speckled brown glaze and cream patches, chips.

8in (20cm) wide

£180-220 **DN**

A yellow-printed brown earthenware jug, of Dutch shape with white slip interior, decorated with a Chinoiserie scene and border, unmarked.

c1815 *5in (13cm) high*

£60-90 **DN**

An early 19thC buff earthenware oval cradle, the basket-moulded ground splashed in brown.

3.75in (9cm) wide

£200-300 **LFA**

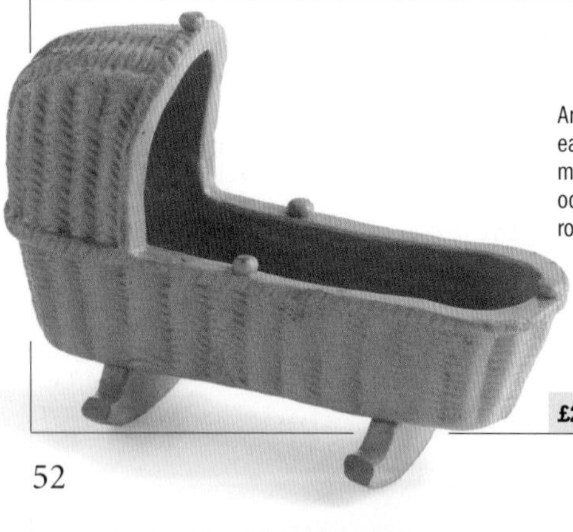

An early 18thC earthenware basket-moulded cradle, with an ochre glaze, tips of rockers chipped.

8in (20.5cm) wide

£200-250 **LFA**

A 17thC stove tile, the brick clay applied with moulded reliefs of a lady and a gentleman, possibly Charles II and Catherine of Braganza.

Catherine of Braganza (1638-1705) was the Catholic wife of Charles II and the daughter of the King of Portugal.

8.25in (21cm) high

£300-500 **WW**

PEARLWARE

- A number of potters in Staffordshire, Yorkshire and Wales manufactured pearlware during the late 18th and early 19thC. One of the most successful was Josiah Wedgwood, who coined the name 'Pearl White'.
- The key factor in the manufacture of pearlware is the application of a cobalt glaze to the earthenware body, resulting in an almost perfectly white body.
- Pearlware was far more suited than creamware to underglaze blue decoration. One of the most popular underglaze patterns for pearlware was 'Chinese House', which was used until at least 1800.
- Other underglaze colours found on pearlware include yellow, green, brown, purple and black.
- As well as tablewares, potters produced decorative pearlware shapes including figures, puzzle jugs and flower horns. Pipes and wall brackets can also be found.
- During the early 19thC, decoration was expanded to include Classical and English landscape designs.

A pearlware figure, depicting 'Peace Setting Fire to the Implements of War', unmarked, small chip to back of cloak.

c1795 *8in (20.5cm) high*

£120-180 **DN**

A pearlware group of Ralph Wood type, 'Roman Charity', picked out in green, blue and brown on a rocky mound base.

c1780 *7.5in (19cm) high*

£400-600 **LFA**

A Staffordshire pearlware group, "The Vicar and Moses", possibly by Ralph Wood of Burslem, the front with impressed title, with gilt details, impressed model number "62", firing crack in back of pulpit.

c1795 *9.5in (24cm) high*

£1,200-1,800 **DN**

A pair of small pearlware figures of Flora and Apollo, wearing crowns, he holding a lyre and an hour glass and she a cornucopia of flowers, on square bordered mound bases, adapted from a watchstand, chips.

c1800 *5in (13cm) high*

£300-400 **LFA**

A pearlware figure of the Virgin and Child, on a square base simulated to represent black marble, unmarked, faults to foot and corner of base coloured over during manufacture.

c1805 *13.5in (34.5cm) high*

£500-800 **DN**

A pearlware Cleric character jug, holding a jug and a glass, decorated in coloured enamels, on a marbled base, damage.

c1820 *8in (20.5cm) high*

£600-900 **LFA**

A rare pearlware bust of the Duke of York, the tapering socle moulded with the Prince of Wales feathers and "GR" cipher, the reverse impressed "Duke of York", socle glued.

c1820 *5.75in (14.5cm) high*

£400-600 **LFA**

A large Staffordshire pearlware bust of Sir Frances Burdett, the base inscribed "S.F.B.", restored.

Sir Frances Burdett, 1770-1844, was an MP from 1807-37 and was attacked for his radical views. He was imprisoned in 1810 and again in 1820 for speaking out against war with France, political corruption and flogging in the army.

c1820 *16.5in (42cm) diam*

£2,000-2,500 **WW**

A large Staffordshire pearlware figure of a seated woman, possibly the cobbler's wife, pouring drink and smoking a clay pipe, on a square base, pipe probably a replacement, unmarked, head re-attached.

c1820 *12.5in (31.5cm) high*

£80-120 **DN**

An early 19thC Staffordshire pearlware pastoral group, of a young man and woman sitting on a rocky outcrop, chipped.

9.75in (25cm) high

£200-300 **WW**

A CLOSER LOOK AT A COW CREAMER

Cow creamers of this large size are extremely rare. Most were designed to hold around a quarter of a pint and would be around half this size.

The naturalistic colours on this animal and its base are uncommon. Pieces like this were frequently painted in bright colours or with landscape scenes.

Cow creamers were difficult to clean and almost certainly led to cases of salmonella poisoning. After the cholera epidemics of the mid-19thC they fell out of favour with a newly health-conscious society.

As many Staffordshire firms made pearlware and cow creamers it is extremely hard to say with any certainty which factory manufactured this particular item.

A large early 19thC pearlware cow creamer, unmarked, repairs.

c1820 *13.5in (34.5cm) long*

£6,000-8,000 **DN**

A 19thC pearlware Toby jug and cover, probably Scottish, decorated in blue, green, yellow, pink and black, sitting holding his beer jug.

9.75in (25cm) high

£400-600 **WW**

A pearlware 'Jolly Traveller' group, with a mule and a dog, decorated in coloured enamels, the mound base titled on a yellow ground cartouche, some damage.

c1820 *6.75in (17cm) high*

£500-800 **LFA**

A rare pearlware model of a horse, on a green sponged oval mound base.

c1800 *3in (7.5cm) high*

£250-300 **LFA**

A pearlware model of an eagle, decorated in yellow, green and brown, the yellow glazed rocky mound base modelled with a flowerhead.

c1800 *7in (18cm) high*

£500-700 **LFA**

A late 18thC pearlware jug, possibly Caughley, moulded with leaves and detailed in blue and black.

8.5in (21.5cm) high

£150-200 **CHEF**

A pearlware Bacchanalian jug, modelled as Bacchus and a fawn on a barrel with sponged decoration, damage and restoration.

c1790 *12.5in (32cm) high*

£100-200 **SWO**

A pearlware jug, commemorating Lord Nelson, printed in yellow with a portrait and with HMS Victory on a brown ground, minor damage.

c1805 *6in (15cm) high*

£800-1,200 **WW**

A pearlware pierced disc-shaped puzzle jug, with loop handle, applied with a figure of Andromache weeping at Hector's ashes, painted in coloured enamels with flowers and leaves, within brown line borders, on a spreading round foot, rim reduced.

c1820 *9.75in (25cm) high*

£300-400 **LFA**

An early 19thC pearlware jug, decorated with a panel depicting men drinking, initialled, restored.

7in (17.5cm) high

£150-250 **WW**

A pearlware jug, inscribed "J. Cordal, 1832", in a heart beneath the spout, each side decorated with flowers.

10in (25.5cm) high

£300-500 **WW**

A Staffordshire pearlware Imari pattern baluster coffee pot and cover, painted and gilt with pagodas in a landscape, flowerhead finial, chips, restored rim.

c1790 *9.75in (25cm) high*

£600-800 **DN**

A Newcastle Pottery cylindrical pearlware mug, commemorating Lord Viscount Nelson, with figures flanking a memorial, cracked and stained.

c1805 *4.75in (12cm) high*

£800-1,200 **WW**

A 19thC pearlware mug, with loop handle, decorated with a blue-and-white transfer print of a pavilion scene.

6in (15cm) high

£50-80 **BRI**

Part of a pearlware tea service, printed in sepia with a sheet floral design in enamels, comprising a slop bowl, a sugar bowl and six Bute-shape teacups and saucers, unmarked, minor damage.

c1815

£280-320 set **DN**

A Swansea Pottery pearlware commemorative plate, named for "Wm, Lukey 1788" between floral sprays, within a blue edge feuille de chou rim, minor chip.

1788

£1,500-2,000 **DN**

A pair of Swansea pearlware botanical dishes, painted in coloured enamels in the Pardoe style, with silver lustre line borders, titled in iron red on the reverse "Scarlett Buzurra Carnation" and "Athaca Fruitet".

c1815 *8.25in (21cm) wide*

£1,000-1,500 **LFA**

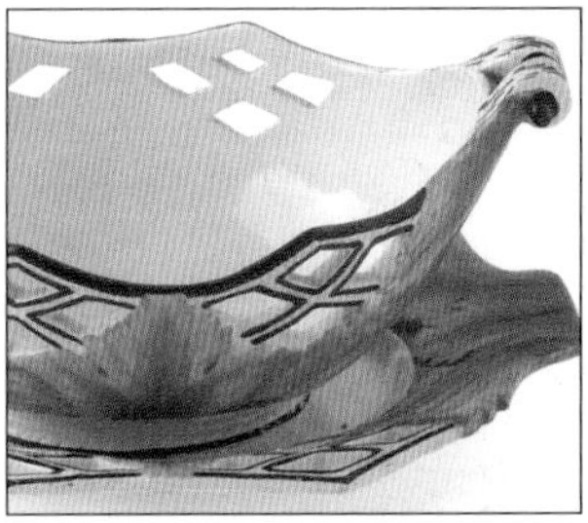

An unusual pair of pearlware boat-shaped baskets and stands, moulded with leaves, restored.

c1800 *8.5in (21.5cm) wide*

£1,000-1,500 **WW**

THE STAFFORDSHIRE POTTERIES

- 'The Potteries' are the five Staffordshire towns – Stoke, Burslem, Hanley, Longton and Tunstall – that became home to over 1,000 pottery and porcelain factories in the 19thC.
- Natural resources of clay and coal provided the materials for the industry to expand from farmer-potters producing butter pots (and digging 'potholes' in the roads to obtain clay) into a vast industry which is still operating today.
- Designers and potters moved between factories, so many similar shapes and patterns emerged. Pottery dealers discouraged the use of factory marks to engender customer loyalty to their own shops rather than particular makers, making it difficult to ascribe work to individual factories.
- Many of the larger, more successful factories, such as Wedgwood, Spode and Ridgway, produced a range of wares, subsidising their top-quality, finely decorated porcelain with more cheaply produced, transfer-printed earthenware.
- The development of the canals and, in 1848, the railway to Stoke, allowed wares to be transported across England. The port at Liverpool made export trade with America and India possible, turning Staffordshire pottery into a worldwide phenomenon.

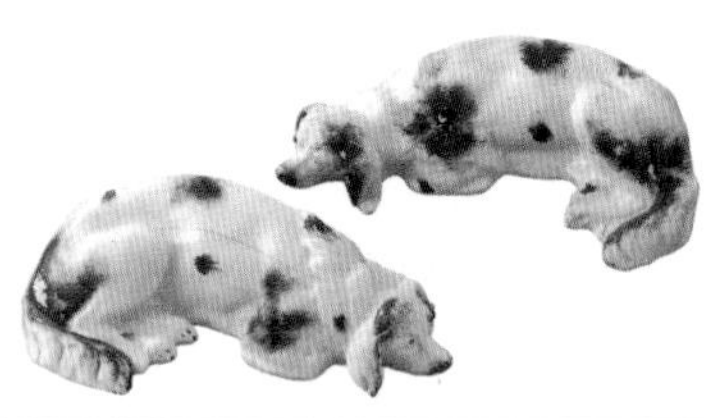

A pair of mid- to late 19thC Staffordshire hounds, lying with heads outstretched, some damage.

larger 9.25in (23.5cm) wide

£1,000-1,500 **DN**

A Staffordshire pottery group of two spaniels, one seated on a barrel, on a gilt banded oval base.

c1855 *8.5in (21.5cm) high*

£120-180 **LFA**

A pair of Staffordshire spaniels with flower baskets in their mouths, with Disraeli-type fringes, the flower baskets with gilding and coloured enamels, damaged.

British prime minister Benjamin Disraeli became caricatured for the curling fringe on his forehead.

c1860 *8in (20cm) high*

£1,200-1,800 **DN**

A pair of Staffordshire spaniels, standing on arched cushion bases decorated with moulded leaves, one with crack to rear, unmarked.

c1860 *9.75in (25cm) high*

£3,000-5,000 **DN**

A mid-19thC Staffordshire Dalmatian, modelled seated on an oval underglaze blue and gilt-lined base, unmarked.

7.25in (18.5cm) high

£250-300 **DN**

A mid-19thC pair of Staffordshire bull mastiff spill vases, modelled against bocage tree trunks forming the spill vases, unmarked, some chipping to bocages, one restored.

6in (15cm) high

£500-800 **DN**

A Staffordshire pottery model of a seated spaniel, with yellow glaze.

c1860 *4.5in (11.5cm) high*

£80-120 **LFA**

A pair of late 19thC Staffordshire models of Dalmatians, seated on blue bases.

5in (13cm) high

£200-300 **CHEF**

An 18thC Whieldon-type cow creamer and cover, decorated with manganese patches, standing on a green base, old restorations.

7.5in (19cm) high

£600-900 **WW**

A Staffordshire creamware model of a recumbent lion, picked out in brown, on a green glazed oval mound base, some restoration.

c1780 *2.75in (7cm) high*

£200-300 **LFA**

A pair of Ralph Salt bocage figures of a sheep and a ram, each with a lamb, impressed "SALT" on a moulded scroll on the back of each figure, the ram broken and glued.

Staffordshire figures tend to be unmarked but figures by Ralph Salt and John Walton, both of whom worked in the early 19thC, often have impressed names on the back or base of their work.

c1825 *6in (15.5cm) high*

£300-500 **DN**

A mid-Victorian Staffordshire pottery hen tureen and cover, rough tip to beak, unmarked.

c1865 *8.75in (22cm) wide*

£400-600 **DN**

An early 19thC Squire Toby jug, of typical form, decorated with green patches, restored.

10.75in (27cm) high

£600-900 **WW**

A Staffordshire pottery Toby jug, holding a jug of ale, handle repaired.

c1840 *9.75in (25cm) high*

£250-300 **SWO**

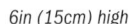

A pair of late 19thC Staffordshire Toby condiment figures, holding mugs, on hollow bases.

6in (15cm) high

£280-320 **H&L**

A 19thC Staffordshire box, modelled as the Duke of Wellington, his hat forming the cover.

7.5in (19cm) high

£200-300 **WW**

A pair of mid-19thC Staffordshire equestrian models, depicting Sir George Brown and Havelock, damaged.

9in (23cm) high

£250-350 **WW**

A pair of mid-19thC Staffordshire equestrian models, of the Prince and Princess of Wales, titled to the bases.

10.75in (27cm) high

£280-320 **WW**

Two mid-19thC matched Staffordshire figures of sailors, each next to a barrel on coils of rope, one probably a British tar, the other possibly Turkish, decorated with coloured enamels, unmarked.

An abbreviation from tarpaulin, 'tar' is an old colloquial name for a sailor, famously used in Gilbert & Sullivan's operetta HMS Pinafore, 1878.

11.5in (29cm) high

£300-500 **DN**

A pair of mid-19thC Staffordshire figures, of a soldier and sailor from the Crimean war, standing holding flags.

13.25in (33.5cm) high

£1,500-2,000 **WW**

An early 19thC Prattware figure of a young man, standing beside a flowering bush with a small dog at his feet, restored.

Prattware is similar to pearlware but is characterised by a strong palette of blues, greens and yellow. From the 1840s to the 1880s the factory specialised in polychrome transfer-printing for tablewares.

9.5in (24cm) high

£500-700 **WW**

A rare early 19thC Prattware model of Marat, the revolutionary sits on a stump, decorated in blue, ochre, green and brown glazes.

8in (20.5cm) high

£500-800 **WW**

A Prattware model of a sheep, with green and brown glazes.

3in (7.5cm) high

£150-200 **BRI**

A 19thC Prattware bear jug and cover, clutching a monkey representative of Napoleon Bonaparte forming the spout, his hat inscribed 'LONEY', with naturalistic scroll handle, in brown, blue and orange glaze, some damage.

10.5in (25.5cm) high

£1,000-1,500 **FRE**

A Prattware jug, commemorating Admiral Nelson and Captain Berry, each side moulded with a profile portrait.

c1805 *5.25in (13.5cm) high*

£400-600 **WW**

A Prattware plaque, moulded with three huntsmen, a barmaid, a horse and a hound outside an inn, a short hairline and factory fault.

There is another plaque from the same mould in the Royal Pavilion Art Gallery and Museum, Brighton.

c1790 *9in (23cm) wide*

£2,500-3,000 **WW**

STAFFORDSHIRE SALTGLAZED WARE

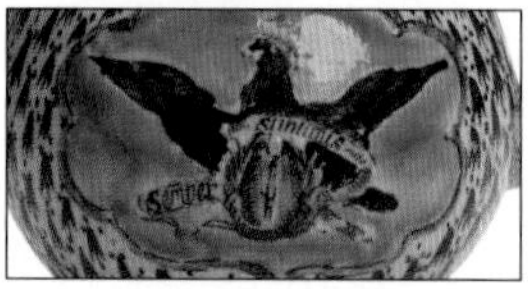

A rare mid-18thC English saltglazed Staffordshire teapot and cover, with a panel depicting Frederick the Great, inscribed "Fred.Prussia Rex", the reverse with a cartouche with crowned Prussian eagle and motto "Semper Sublimis", imitation ermine ground.

3.75in (9.5cm) high

£1,500-2,000 **L&T**

A Staffordshire saltglazed stoneware tureen, with handles and cover.

c1865 *13in (35.5cm) wide*

£2,200-2,800 **JHOR**

A Mortlake saltglazed stoneware silver-mounted jug, the ground with hunting subjects, the mounts hallmarked for London 1808, damage to the hinge of mounts.

The Mortlake, Fulham and later Doulton factories produced this type of vessel, decorated with sporting or drinking scenes, in the 18th and 19thC. The silver mounts indicate that these were treasured items.

8.75in (22cm) high

£1,000-1,500 **DN**

A CLOSER LOOK AT A SALTGLAZED BEAR

The delicate chain and painted detail indicate a finely wrought piece. Thinly potted off-white Staffordshire stoneware lends itself to detailed work.

Bear-baiting was a popular pastime in Georgian England and the subject was often depicted in wares from the Potteries.

The orange peel texture of salt-glazed ware is enhanced with tiny clay parings, to simulate fur.

The head is detachable and often doubled as a cup.

A Staffordshire saltglazed stoneware bear baiting jug and cover, his snout pierced with four chain links, details in brown.

c1760 *9.5in (24cm) wide*

£3,000-5,000 **WW**

A 19thC Pennsylvania redware charger, with yellow slip wavy line decoration.

12in (30cm) diam

£350-400 **POOK**

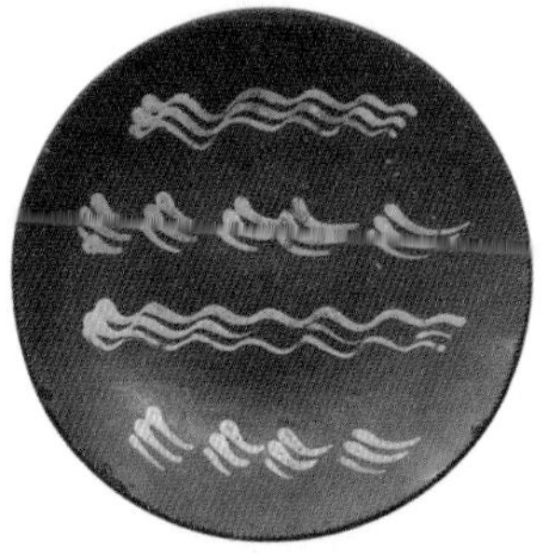

A 19thC Pennsylvania redware charger, with yellow slip wavy line decoration.

14.25in (36cm) diam

£350-400 **POOK**

A 19thC Pennsylvania redware charger, with yellow slip decoration in waves and spirals.

14in (35.5cm) diam

£500-800 **POOK**

A 19thC Pennsylvania redware charger, with slip decoration in loops and floral devices.

14in (35.5cm) diam

£2,200-2,800 **FRE**

A redware plate, attributed to the Smith Pottery in Norwalk, Connecticut, with coggled rim and yellow slip inscription reading: "Norwalk feb'y the 13 1854", restored.

1854 *12.25in (31cm) diam*

£12,000-18,000 **SK**

A Canadian redware storage jar, in the German style, from Western Ontario.

c1885 *8.25in (21cm) high*

£80-120 **RAON**

A 19thC Shenandoah Valley redware figure of a dog, with patchy green and yellow glaze.

The slip glaze decoration completely covers the red body of this piece.

9in (22.5cm) high

£35,000-40,000 **POOK**

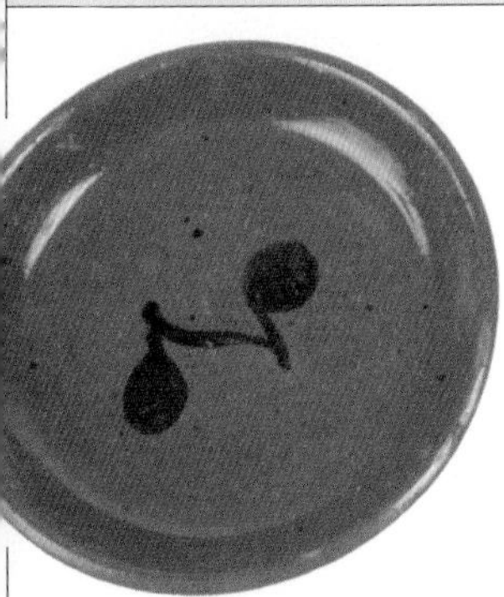

A Canadian redware plate by William Eby, decorated with cherries in brown slip.

9in (22.5cm) diam

£800-1,200 **WAD**

A Canadian redware jug, with mottled brown-red glaze, from Ontario.

c1875 *9.75in (25cm) high*

£150-200 **RAON**

A Canadian stoneware crock, painted with a stylized bunch of flowers, from Cornwall, Ontario, indistinct maker's name.

c1880 *10.75in (27.5cm) high*

£200-300 **RAON**

A Canadian stoneware crock, with painted bird motif, from Cornwall Ontario, indistinct maker's mark.

10.75in (27.5cm) high

£320-380 **ING**

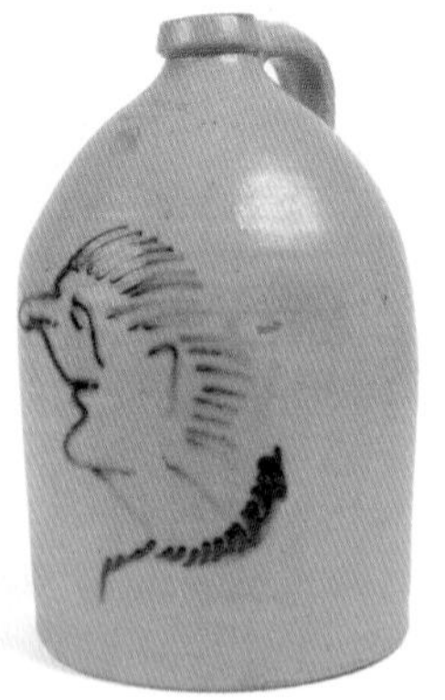

A Canadian two gallon stoneware jug, decorated in blue with a face in profile, marked "WARNER & CO. TORONTO."

13.5in (34cm) high

£2,800-3,200 **WAD**

A Canadian one gallon stoneware jug, decorated with a blue butterfly, marked "PICTON C.W."

7in (18.5cm) high

£250-300 **WAD**

A rare 19thC Pennsylvania stoneware harvest jug, with overall floral decoration, impressed "George Renerbel".

12in (30cm) high

£12,000-18,000 **POOK**

A set of stoneware jugs by Absalom Stedman and Frederick Seymour of New Haven, Connecticut, comprising four conjoined ovoid vessels with applied reeded strap handle, with cobalt blue decoration, impressed "STEDMAN & SEYMOUR" and "NEW HAVEN", hairline cracks.

c1825 *9.5in (24cm) high*

£6,000-9,000 **SK**

A Canadian three gallon stoneware jug, decorated with a blue bird, marked "G.I. LAZIER PICTON, C.W."

14.5in (37cm) high

£1,000-1,500 **WAD**

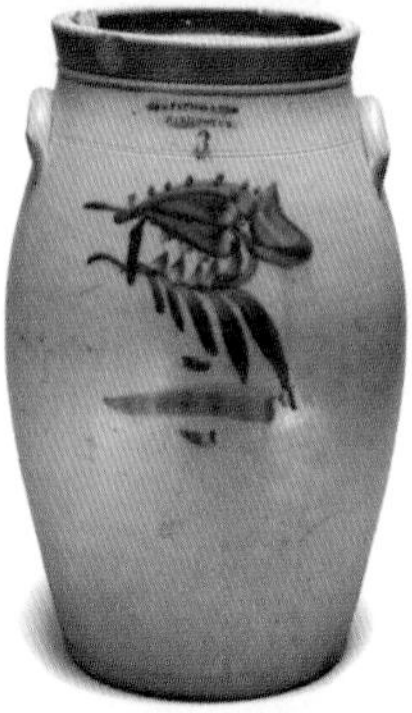

A Canadian six gallon stoneware churn, with blue stylized bee decoration, marked "S.G PATTON & CO. HAMILTON C.W."

19.5in (49.5cm) high

£400-600 **WAD**

A stoneware inkwell, attributed to the Remmey family, with large central filling hole and three small dipping holes, decorated with incised cobalt bell flowers and incised line-glazed inscriptions, dated 1797.

The Remmey family of potters worked in close proximity to the Crolius Pottery on Potter's Hill, Manhattan.

3.75in (9.5cm) diam

£15,000-20,000 **SK**

A Canadian moulded stoneware picture frame, of oval form with turquoise and cream mottled glaze, marked "G Beech Maker Brantford 1863".

13in (33cm) high

£3,500-4,500 **WAD**

A Dion Pottery hexagonal storage jar, with replaced carved pine handle to lid.

c1880 *9.75in (25cm) high*

£100-150 **RAON**

A Dion Pottery oval bowl.

The Dion Pottery was based in Quebec. It has a slightly lighter tone than similar products made at the Brantford Pottery.

c1880 *13.25in (33.5cm) wide*

£120-180 **RAON**

A Brantford Pottery platter, with brown mottled glaze on a beige ground.

c1885 *11.25in (28.5cm) diam*

£120-180 **RAON**

A Royal Opaque China 'Canada' moulded platter, with white glaze and impressed registered design diamond to reverse.

c1880 *18in (46cm) long*

£150-200 **RAON**

An early 20thC white Canadian ironstone chamber pot and cover, with embossed beaver and squirrel decoration, the cover with beaver finial, hairline crack.

8.5in (22cm) high

£300-400 **WAD**

A panelled pitcher and wash bowl set, with purple and blue rainbow spatter glaze.

bowl 12in (30cm) diam

£1,500-2,000 **POOK**

A Portneuf mug, with a sponge-decorated deer in red, green and brown.

4.5in (11.5cm) high

£700-1,000 **WAD**

A 19thC copy of the Portland vase, modelled in white stoneware with Classical figures brought into relief by deep blue glaze.

The Portland vase was an important ancient glass piece which provided inspiration for Wedgwood's jasperware. The Wedgwood factory, amongst others, made several copies.

10.5in (26.5cm) high

£300-500 **CHEF**

A large 19thC Wedgwood blue Jasper-dip campana vase, with pierced cover, applied with Classical scenes, impressed mark, repaired stem.

16.5in (42cm) high

£500-800 **WW**

A 19thC Wedgwood Jasperware campana vase, decorated with flowers and leaves in green, mauve and white, impressed "Wedgwood" mark.

7.25in (18.5cm) high

£400-600 **WW**

An unusual pair of early 19thC Wedgwood pot pourri vases and covers, moulded with acanthus leaves and guilloche bands, impressed "Wedgwood" mark, restored.

7.25in (18.5cm) high

£1,000-1,500 **WW**

An early 20thC Wedgwood Jasperware bowl and cover, decorated with a dice pattern in blue, green and white, impressed "Wedgwood England" mark.

4.25in (10.5cm) high

£400-600 **WW**

A late 19thC Wedgwood biscuit barrel and plated cover, sprigged in white with classical figures beneath a floral swag band on a sage-green ground, between two lilac ground bands, impressed mark, with handle, chips.

8in (20.5cm) high

£200-300 **DN**

A mid-19thC Wedgwood sage-dip jasper coffee can and saucer, sprigged in white relief with a band of dancers, the saucer with a stiff leaf band, impressed marks.

£500-800 **DN**

A late 19thC Wedgwood sage-green jasper-dip plaque, sprigged in white relief with a Classical maiden holding a ewer, impressed mark.

7.5in (19cm) high

£70-100 **DN**

A rare Wedgwood & Bentley creamware jardinière and stand, decorated with bands sponged black on orange, impressed "Wedgwood & Bentley", restored.

c1775 *10.5in (26.5cm) diam*

£1,000-1,500 **WW**

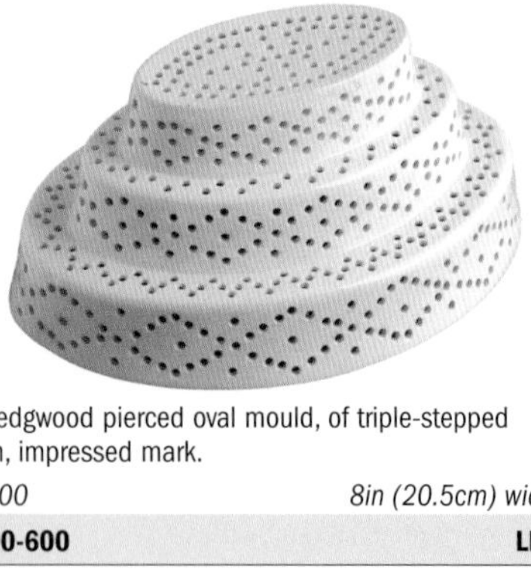

A Wedgwood pierced oval mould, of triple-stepped form, impressed mark.

c1800 *8in (20.5cm) wide*

£400-600 **LFA**

A rare Wedgwood pearlware shell-shaped wall pocket and pierced cover, with 'Moonlit Lustre' glaze, impressed mark.

c1815 *10.25in (26cm) wide*

£400-600 **LFA**

A pair of early 19thC Wedgwood pearlware tureens and covers, with matching quatrelobed dishes, decorated with Greek vases, impressed marks.

8.75in (22cm) wide

£500-800 **WW**

A Liverpool pottery commemorative jug, the rim inscribed to the memory of General Lafayette, with portraits of Lafayette and George Washington, a coat of arms maker's mark for "Ric'd Hall & Son", chips, crazing.

1824 *5in (12.5cm) high*

£500-700 **SWO**

A blue and white jug, printed with a portrait titled "The Late Sir Robert Peel Bart.", the reverse with a depiction of Drayton Church, chipped spout.

c1830 *5in (12.5cm) high*

£150-200 **WW**

A Royal commemorative mug, printed in black with William IV and Queen Adelaide, printed stone china mark.

c1835 *3.25in (8cm) high*

£500-800 **WW**

A Wedgwood Queensware King George IV coronation mug, designed by Eric Ravilious, printed factory mark.

4in (10cm) high

£700-1,000 **DN**

A Wedgwood Queensware Edward VIII 1937 Coronation mug, designed by Eric Ravilious, printed factory mark.

4in (10cm) high

£800-1,200 **DN**

A CLOSER LOOK AT A COMMEMORATIVE TYG

This tyg has cross appeal for collectors of royal commemoratives and Victoriana and for war memorabilia collectors, which, along with its scarcity and excellent condition, increases its value.

The fine moulding, well-printed images and gilding would have contributed to the initial cost of making this piece but also increased its exclusivity and perceived value to the subscriber.

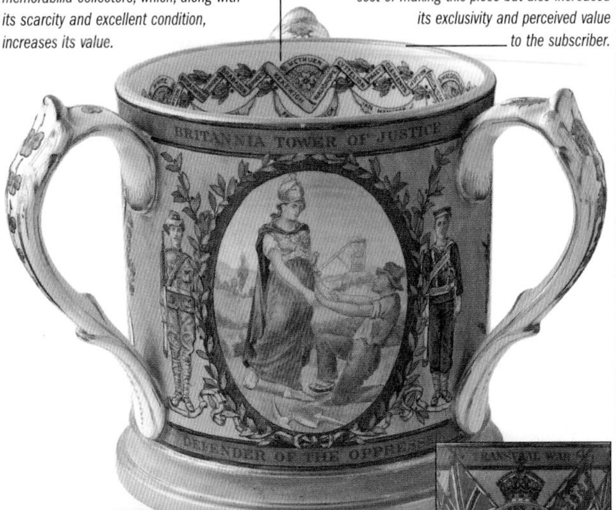

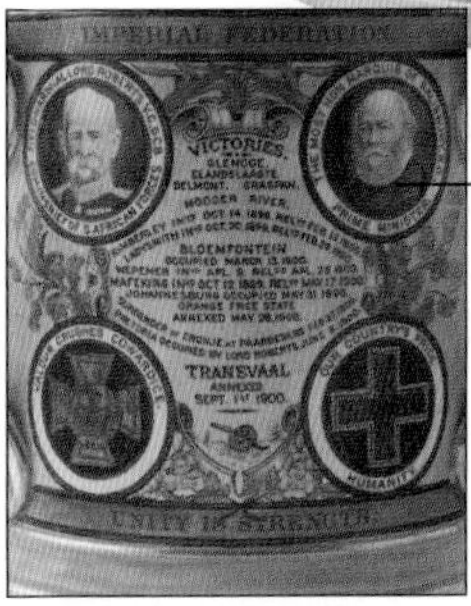

As Spode's first London retailers, Copeland & Garrett were very aware of the competition they faced when they took over the Spode factory in 1833. They moved production towards more fashionable designs, such as commemorative ware.

Pieces such as this were intended for display rather than everyday use, which explains its good condition

A Copeland 1899-1900 Transvaal War subscriber's copy three-handled tyg, printed with a portrait of Queen Victoria, a vignette of "Britannia - Tower of Justice", and details of the war, with black-printed marks for maker and London retailer Thomas Goode & Co., impressed "Spode".

c1900 *5.5in (14cm) high*

£800-1,200 **DN**

A Wedgwood Queensware mug, by Keith Murray, printed in puce with view of the Barlaston estate, a view of the factory verso, designed by Victor Skellern to commemorate the first firing of the Brown Boveri electrically fired tunnel oven, Summer 1940, with special backstamp.

5in (12.5cm) high

£100-150 **DN**

Two Wedgwood pottery coronation mugs, by Eric Ravilious, inscribed "To Commemorate the Coronation of Her Majesty Queen Elizabeth II 1953", printed marks.

4in (10cm) high

£250-300 **DN**

An early 19thC brown stoneware jug, modelled as Napoleon, with small impressed "W" mark, chipped.

13.5in (34.5cm) high

£400-600 **WW**

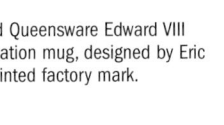

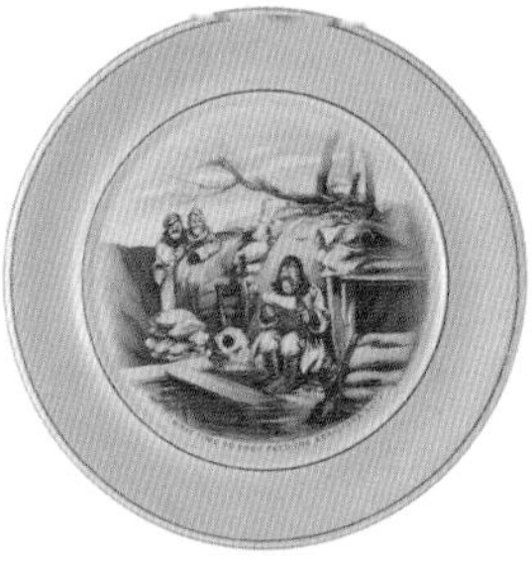

A Grimwades Bruce Bainsfather wall plate, printed with a cartoon "What time do they feed the sea-lions, Alf?", gilt lined rim, printed mark with inscription "Made by the girls of Staffordshire during the winter of 1917 when the boys were in the trenches fighting for liberty and civilisation".

9.75in (25cm) diam

£30-50 **DN**

SPODE & TRANSFER PRINTING

- Staffordshire potters adopted the transfer printing technique from Worcester and other porcelain factories. This enabled them to mass-produce inexpensive blue and white earthenwares.
- Established c1776 in Stoke-on-Trent, Josiah Spode's factory was the largest producer of blue and white ware, using the bat printing technique. Its transfer-printed ware was produced to a very high standard, which, along with the collectability of the patterns, makes it avidly sought after today.
- In order to compete with Chinese imports, Chinese-style patterns influenced early production. When the imports were suspended c1800 in an attempt by British manufacturers to reduce competition from abroad, demand for English pottery increased.
- Gradually, new designs were introduced, including scenes of British stately homes and, for the export market, Indian, American and Canadian scenes. Spode's 'Caramanian' and 'Indian Sporting' series are highly sought after.
- In 1833 Spode was taken over and renamed by Copeland & Garrett. Having reverted to the name 'Spode' in 1970, the company is still operating today.

An 'Oriental Sporting' series well-and-tree meat dish, printed in blue with a copy of the Spode scene 'Dooreahs Leading Out Dogs', printed series title mark.

c1825 *19in (48cm) wide*

£800-1,200 **DN**

A Copeland 'Caramanian' series meat dish, printed in blue with the 'Antique Fragments at Limisso' scene, with border from Spode's 'Italian' pattern, printed "SPODE" mark and impressed Copeland "Spode's Impl." mark, indistinct date code.

14.5in (37cm) diam

£200-300 **DN**

A 'Greek' series dish, attributed to Spode, printed in blue with a scene known as 'Artemis Drawn by a Griffin and a Lynx' within a border of vases and Classical figural panels, unmarked.

c1815 *18.5in (47cm) wide*

£250-300 **DN**

A Spode 'Union Wreath Third' pattern meat dish, printed in blue with the floral spray centre and usual floral border, printed and impressed upper-case marks.

c1825 *16.5in (42cm) wide*

£150-200 **DN**

A Copeland & Garrett 'Botanical' series meat dish, printed in blue with a floral spray and border, printed and impressed circular "Copeland & Garrett late Spode" marks.

c1840 *17in (43cm) wide*

£250-300 **DN**

A Spode 'Aesop's Fables' series soup plate, printed in blue with 'The Lion in Love' within a border of flowers and scrolls, printed title mark with "SPODE" and impressed upper-case mark.

c1820 *10in (25.5cm) diam*

£180-220 **DN**

A Spode 'Indian Sporting' series well-and-tree meat dish, printed in blue with 'Hunting a Leopard' within the series border, printed title mark, printed and impressed upper-case maker's marks.

c1820 *23.25in (59cm) wide*

£300-500 **DN**

A Copeland & Garrett 'Floral' series meat dish, printed in blue with a floral spray, panelled floral border, printed title cartouche and printed and impressed circular "Copeland & Garrett late Spode" marks.

c1840 *20.25in (51.5cm) wide*

£300-500 **DN**

A Spode 'Indian Sporting' series dinner plate, printed in blue with the 'Death of the Bear', printed title and printed and impressed upper-case marks.

c1820 *9.75in (25cm) diam*

£180-220 **DN**

A large Copeland 'Aesop's Fables' series washbowl, printed in blue with 'The Fox and the Sick Lion' within the usual floral scroll border, printed "Copeland late Spode" seal mark and impressed "COPELAND" crown mark with indistinct date code, possibly for 1912.

14.75in (37.5cm) diam

£40-60 **DN**

An Adams 'Lions' pattern meat dish, printed in blue with animal scene and floral border, unmarked.

c1825 *17.75in (45cm) wide*

£1,200-1,800 **DN**

A William Adams 'Regent's Park' series dessert plate, printed in blue with a villa identified as the residence of the Marquis of Hertford, within a foliate border, printed title mark, impressed crown mark with maker's name, rim chip.

c1825 *9in (22.5cm) diam*

£30-50 **DN**

A Ralph & James Clews 'Romantic Ruins' pattern dinner plate, printed in blue with a Classical scene and foliage border, unmarked, tiny nick on rim.

c1825 *9.75in (25cm) diam*

£80-120 **DN**

A Donovan 'Fisherman' pattern dessert plate, probably by Davenport, printed in blue with a Chinoiserie scene of fishermen by a temple, impressed "DONOVAN", chips and fault.

c1805 *8.25in (21cm) diam*

£150-200 **DN**

A Davenport Chinoiserie 'Bridgeless' pattern meat dish, printed in blue with a landscape scene and border, with impressed maker's anchor mark.

c1810 *18in (46cm) wide*

£60-90 **DN**

A set of nine Davenport 'Broseley' pattern stone china tea plates, printed in blue with a Chinoiserie pattern and border, gilt rims and band, printed maker's anchor mark, arch mark and red-painted pattern number "142", one cracked.

c1815 *7.5in (19cm) diam*

£70-100 **DN**

A Davenport 'Mosque and Fishermen' pattern soup tureen stand, printed in blue with the Eastern scene and floral border, impressed maker's anchor mark, crack in rim.

c1825 *13.5in (34.5cm) wide*

£60-90 **DN**

A Davenport stone china meat platter, printed in blue with cattle in a parkland setting before a country mansion, within an exotic floral border.

c1880 *18in (46cm) diam*

£300-500 **ROS**

A Don Pottery 'Named Italian Views' series meat dish, printed in blue with the 'Cascade at Isola' scene within a border of flowers and flying putti, unmarked.

The Don Pottery was established by John Green, the founder of the Leeds Pottery, in 1801 on the Don canal in Yorkshire. High quality wares bore a strong Leeds influence. The factory was declared bankrupt in 1834 and patterns and moulds were sold to other local potteries.

c1825 *17in (43cm) wide*

£300-500 **DN**

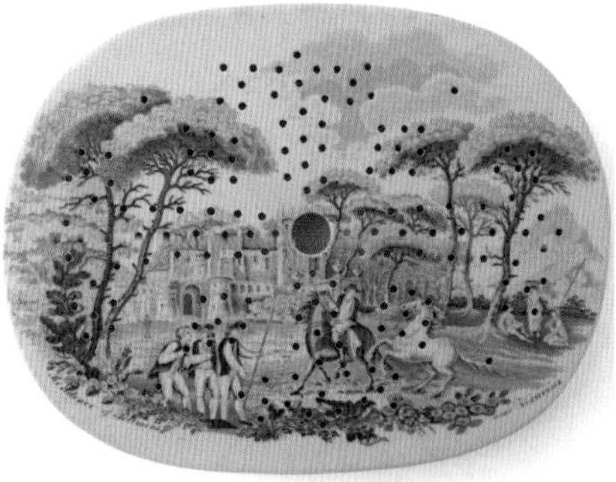

An early 19thC Don Pottery 'Named Italian Views' series oval drainer, printed in blue with the 'Residence of Solimenes Near Vesuvius' pattern, unmarked.

12.5in (32cm) wide

£300-400 **DN**

A Thomas & Benjamin Godwin 'Genevese' pattern meat dish.

£60-90 **DN**

A Thomas & Benjamin Godwin 'Asiatic Pheasants' pattern circular vegetable dish.

£30-40 DN

A Ralph Hall 'Pain's Hill, Surrey' dinner plate from the 'Select Views' series, printed in blue with the titled view in a scroll frame within the series border of fruit and flowers, printed title mark with maker's name and "Stone China".

Developed by John Turner c1800, stone china is a type of stoneware with qualities similar to porcelain. Turner sold the patent to Spode who used the formula to make tableware.

c1825 *10in (25.5cm) diam*

£70-100 DN

A late 18thC blue and white coffee pot, possibly by Joshua Heath, printed with Buddhist objects and flowers.

Joshua Heath was a Staffordshire potter working c1780-1800.

c1790 *7.5in (19cm) high*

£100-150 CHEF

A small 'Rock' pattern cream jug, of Hollins type, with sparrow beak spout, printed in blue with the 'Rock' pattern, the reverse with detail of a summer house, beneath a Chinoiserie border, printed leaf spray mark.

c1795 *5.25in (13.5cm) high*

£50-80 DN

A Jones & Son 'British History' series sauce tureen, cover and stand, printed in blue with 'Canute Reproving His Courtiers', printed title mark on stand, repairs.

c1825 *stand 8.25in (21cm) wide*

£80-120 DN

A Leeds Pottery barrel-shaped blue and-white mug, printed with cattle in a landscape, impressed mark.

The Leeds Pottery was established in 1760 by the Green brothers. It produced fine creamware, often sent to external decorators to be enamelled, and pierced goods. The factory closed c1880.

4.25in (11cm) high

£120-180 BRI

A Minton 'Monk's Rock' series cake or cheese stand, printed in blue with a rural scene featuring travellers passing a thatched gatehouse, floral borders, unmarked.

c1820 *10.5in (27cm) diam*

£250-300 DN

A 'Monk's Rock' series well-and-tree meat dish, attributed to Minton, printed in blue with a scene identified as Beeston Castle in Cheshire, within a floral border, unmarked, chip to rim.

c1825 *20.75in (52.5cm) wide*

£220-280 DN

A 'Monk's Rock' series meat dish, attributed to Minton, printed in blue with an unidentified scene featuring a riverside cottage, within floral border, unmarked, filled chip in rim.

c1825 *16.5in (42cm) wide*

£120-180 DN

A 'Basket of Flowers' pattern soup tureen and cover, attributed to Minton, with lion's head handles and finial, printed in blue with the floral pattern and border, cracked, unmarked.

c1825 *14.5in (37cm) wide*

£80-120 DN

An Andrew Stevenson 'Faulkbourn Hall' pattern dinner plate from the 'Rose Border' series, printed in blue with the titled view and floral border, printed title mark and impressed maker's circular crown mark, rim glaze chip.

c1825 *10.25in (26cm) diam*

£80-120 **DN**

A Swansea 'Long Bridge' pattern well-and-tree meat dish, with ochre rim, printed in blue with a Chinoiserie scene and border, impressed "SWANSEA".

c1810 *17.5in (44.5cm) wide*

£250-300 **DN**

A CLOSER LOOK AT A STAFFORDSHIRE VEGETABLE DISH

This dish is from a series of thirteen called 'Arms of the American States' produced by T. Mayer of Staffordshire around 1830.

This series is in demand today, especially among US enthusiasts of transfer-printed ware.

Transfer-printed ceramics with American nationalist themes provided many Staffordshire potters with a steady export market.

The quality of transfer printing can vary considerably depending on the quality of the plate and the amount of ink used. This pattern is crisp and has a good colour.

A Staffordshire historical blue transfer-printed vegetable dish, by T. Mayer, with 'The Arms of Georgia' pattern.

c1830 *11.75in (30cm) wide*

£5,000-7,000 **FRE**

A 'Swans' pattern bowl, attributed to Swansea, decorated with a river scene and two swans, with a broad Chinoiserie border and two different scenes on the outer sides, unmarked, hair crack in rim.

c1795 *8.5in (21.5cm) diam*

£80-120 **DN**

A Swansea 'Catch of the Day' pattern posset cup, printed in blue with a temple, the reverse with a fisherman and a figure by a wall, with a geometric border with framed reserves of flower sprays inside the ochre rim, unmarked, restored.

c1805 *4.5in (11.5cm) high*

£200-300 **DN**

A Swansea 'Ladies of Llangollen' pattern meat dish, printed in blue with a country scene of two ladies riding, within a floral border, small impressed Prince of Wales' feathers mark.

This pattern was issued by both Swansea potteries.

c1820 *16in (40.5cm) wide*

£600-900 **DN**

A Swansea 'Pulteney Bridge' pattern punchbowl, printed in blue with a view of Bath and a broad floral border.

9.5in (24.5cm) diam

£80-120 **DN**

One of two 'Bird Fountain' pattern dessert plates, possibly by Toft & May, printed in blue with a Romantic scene and floral border, unmarked.

c1825 *8.5in (21.5cm) diam*

£40-60 pair **DN**

A 'Corsica' pattern oval meat dish, probably by Wood & Challinor, printed in blue with a Romantic scene within a border of four alternating scenic and floral vignettes, unmarked.

c1835 *19.25in (49cm) wide*

£80-120 **DN**

A 'Mandarin Opaque China' series pepper pot, printed in blue with a group of two figures, with a floral and vase section to the reverse, with borders around the rim and foot, unmarked.

c1830 *4.75in (12cm) high*

£300-500 **DN**

Part of a 'Floral Vases' pattern part tea set, printed in blue, with floral border, comprising a teapot and cover, footed bowl, covered sugar box and six London shape teacups and saucers, with printed "SEMI CHINA" seal marks.

c1830

£180-220 set **DN**

A 'Tendril' pattern pepper pot, decorated with a stylized floral sheet pattern and a Chinoiserie-style border, unmarked, repair to sprinkler section.

c1810 *4.75in (12cm) high*

£70-100 **DN**

An 'Italian Scenery' series sauce ladle, with moulded handle, printed inside the bowl with part of a shipping scene within a border of scrolls and seashells, unmarked.

c1830 *5.5in (14cm) wide*

£150-200 **DN**

CANADIAN TRANSFER-PRINTED WARE

A large brown transfer ware platter, from 'The World' series by M.B. & Co, showing a scene of the Parliament Building in Ottawa, with beehive-shaped trademark and registered number 7624.

15.5in (40cm) wide

£1,000-1,500 **TCF**

An F.T. Thomas platter, depicting a view of Quebec.

Pottery with Quebec landscapes and monuments was produced in the late 19thC by British potteries including the Britannia Pottery in Glasgow for the Quebec merchant F. T. Thomas.

c1875 *13.75in (35cm) wide*

£1,200-1,800 **TCF**

An F.T. Thomas brown transfer ware plate, showing a scene of St Louis Gate, Porte St Louis, with beavers in the rim, cracked.

This piece clearly shows the transfer overlap. Seams are often visible when the print does not quite fit.

9.5in (24.5cm) diam

£250-300 **TCF**

An F.T. Thomas teapot, depicting a scene of Lorette Falls.

8in (20cm) high

£1,200-1,800 **TCF**

A British 'America Pattern' platter, transfer printed in blue with a view of Kingston, Lake Ontario, hairlines and crazing.

15.5in (40cm) wide

£500-800 **WAD**

A 'Lake' pattern platter, transfer-printed in grey with a view of Hallowell.

19.5in (49.5cm) wide

£400-600 **WAD**

THE ORIENTAL MARKET

Committed collectors from East and West have helped auctions of Oriental art make history in the last year. Woolley & Wallis in Wiltshire smashed the British record for the most valuable lot ever sold outside London with a Yuan vase that sold for £2.6 million. Christie's in London claimed the record for the most valuable Oriental lot sold at auction with another vase from the same period that realised more than £14 million. A blue and white Meiping vase from the early Ming period outperformed its estimate by a factor of ten to sell at Sotheby's in New York for more than £2 million.

The importance of vibrant Asian markets is reinforced by figures that show overseas sales of Oriental antiques from the UK are up nine per cent on last year. Buyers in Asia are equally as important to auction houses and dealers in North America.

Many examples of Oriental art have quite a pared down, minimalist look and this is helping them sell in a market increasingly besotted with modern design. The most popular finishes at the moment are blue and white underglaze decoration and famille rose enamels, although period is far more important. Aside from Yuan ceramics, buyers in China have been keen to acquire good Kangxi and Transitional pieces. As pristine examples of the best porcelain from these periods dwindle in the face of overwhelming demand, prices for damaged artefacts continue to rise.

An awareness of international trends is increasingly important in the current climate. Law Fine Art in Berkshire, UK, achieved a price of almost £100,000 for a fine Gujarati casket, bought by a dealer with an eye on the Portuguese market where very high prices are paid for such items. Interest in Asian art is set to step up as we approach 2008 and the Beijing Olympics.

ANCIENT CHINESE CERAMICS

A Han dynasty painted figure, depicting a standing female drummer wearing a long dress.

206BC-AD220 *14in (35cm) high*

£1,000-1,500 **KAU**

A Tang dynasty unglazed pottery horse, depicted saddled and standing with one hoof raised, on a later base, restored.

AD600-1000 *24in (60cm) high*

£2,500-3,000 **SWO**

A Han dynasty pottery figure, depicting a kneeling maiden with her arms raised, decorated with earth pigments, on a wooden stand, restored.

This figure has a thermoluminescence analysis report to authenticate its age.

206BC-AD220 *13in (33cm) high*

£2,500-3,000 **WW**

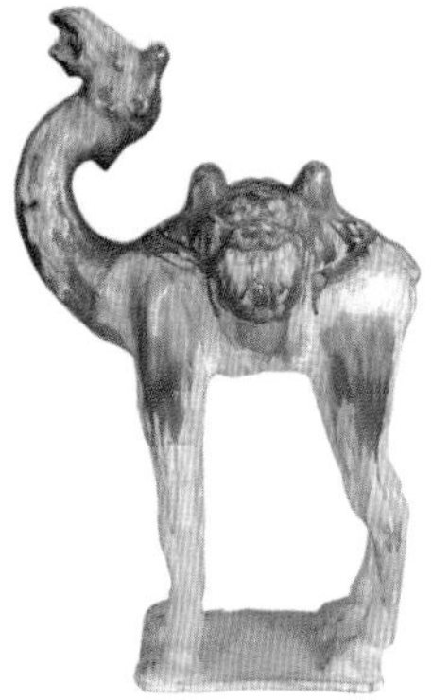

A Tang dynasty sancai glazed pottery camel, carrying a twin peaked saddle with a tigerskin saddle cloth, restored.

Sancai means 'three glazes'.

AD600-1000

£3,000-5,000 **SWO**

A celadon funerary vase, possibly Five Dynasties period, with frilled rim collar and lug handles, the slender neck applied with dignitary, attendant and sentinel figures.

18.75in (47.5cm) high

£300-500 **CHEF**

A Northern Song dynasty celadon bowl, the interior carved with a large peony head amidst scrolling foliage, the exterior with a wide band of ribs, on a small circular foot.

AD960-1127 *7.25in (18.5cm) wide*

£3,000-5,000 **WW**

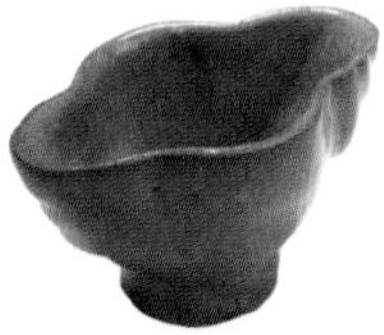

A Song dynasty lobed Jun ware bowl, of pale blue stoneware with moulded swag decoration at each end.

Jun ware has a thick glaze characterized by many tiny bubbles.

3.5in (9cm) wide

£800-1,200 **L&T**

CHINESE REIGN PERIODS AND MARKS

Imperial reign marks were adopted during the Ming dynasty, and some of the most common are reproduced here. Certain emperors forbade the use of their own reign mark, lest they should suffer the disrespect of a broken vessel bearing their name being thrown away. This is where the convention of using earlier reign marks comes from – a custom that was enthusiastically adopted by potters as a way of showing their respect for their predecessors. It is worth remembering that a great deal of Imperial porcelain is marked misleadingly and pieces bearing the reign mark for the period in which they were made are therefore especially sought after.

Early periods and dates

Xia Dynasty	*c2000 - 1500BC*	Northern and Southern Dynasties	*420 - 581*
Shang Dynasty	*1500 - 1028BC*	Sui Dynasty	*581 - 618*
Zhou Dynasty	*1028 - 221BC*	Tang Dynasty	*618 - 906*
Qin Dynasty	*221 - 206BC*	The Five Dynasties	*907 - 960*
Han Dynasty	*206BC - AD220*	Song Dynasty	*960 - 1279*
Three Kingdoms	*221 - 280*	Jin Dynasty	*1115 - 1234*
Jin Dynasty	*265 - 420*	Yuan Dynasty	*1260 - 1368*

Ming Dynasty Reigns

Hongwu	*1368 - 1398*	Jingtai	*1450 - 1457*
Jianwen	*1399 - 1402*	Tianshun	*1457 - 1464*
Yongle	*1403 - 1424*	Chenghua	*1465 - 1487*
Hongxi	*1425 - 1425*	Hongzhi	*1488 - 1505*
Xuande	*1426 - 1435*	Zhengde	*1506 - 1521*
Zhengtong	*1436 - 1449*		

Ming Dynasty Marks

大明嘉靖年製
Jiajing
1522 – 1566

大明隆慶年製
Longquing
1567 – 1572

大明萬曆年製
Wanli
1573 – 1619

大明天啟年製
Tianqi
1621 – 1627

崇禎年製
Chongzhen
1628 – 1644

Qing Dynasty Marks

大清順治年製
Shunzhi
1644 – 1661

大清康熙年製
Kangxi
1662 – 1722

大清雍正年製
Yongzheng
1723 – 1735

大清乾隆年製
Qianlong
1736 – 1795

嘉慶年製
Jiaqing
1796 – 1820

大清道光年製
Daoguang
1821 – 1850

大清咸豐年製
Xianfeng
1851 – 1861

大清同治年製
Tongzhi
1862 – 1874

大清光緒年製
Guangxu
1875 – 1908

大清宣統年製
Xuantong
1909 – 1911

Republic Period

崇禎年製
Hongxian (Yuan Shikai)
1915 – 1916

A rare 17thC blue and white dish, decorated with figures beneath a pine tree, from southern China.

7.5in (19cm) diam

£1,000-1,500 **WW**

A 17thC Swatow blue and white dish, painted with two deer beneath a pine branch, the border and the reverse decorated with stylized bands, with four-character mark.

7.75in (20cm) diam

£600-900 **WW**

LEFT: A late 18thC blue and white circular saucer dish, decorated with scrolling foliage, peony blossom and flower vases enclosed by a trellis work and floral border.

13.75in (35cm) diam

£200-300 **L&T**

RIGHT: A late 18thC blue and white saucer dish, decorated with trellis pattern, moulded foliate design and two further scrolling borders, with a peony sprig to the well.

13.75in (35cm) diam

£500-800 **L&T**

A Kangxi period provincial porcelain charger, decorated in underglaze blue with foliate motifs representing wealth, long life and happiness.

15.75in (40cm) diam

£150-200 **BIG**

A late 18thC blue and white soup tureen and cover, painted with fenced gardens, with beast mask handles.

14.5in (36cm) wide

£150-200 **CHEF**

An 18thC blue and white tureen, the lid with an applied fruit finial, the base with hare mask handles.

14.5in (36cm) wide

£500-600 **SWO**

A Kangxi period blue and white cylindrical brush pot, decorated with figures in an aquatic landscape, hair crack.

1662-1722 *7in (17.5cm) wide*

£1,800-2,200 **WW**

A Kangxi period blue and white cup, with an octagonal bowl and flared foot, painted with landscapes and birds in branches, with gold wax seal for the Duveens of Liverpool, small footrim chip.

1662-1722 *4.75in (12cm) diam*

£1,000-1,500 **WW**

A rare Qianlong period blue and white sweetmeat box and cover, formed as a flowerhead, the interior with seven segments, painted with scattered flowers, with six-character Qianlong seal mark.

1736-95 *6in (15cm) diam*

£1,800-2,200 **WW**

A rare Qianlong period blue and white stand for a jue vessel, with a central raised boss encircled by four cranes flying amid clouds, the reverse with a band of flowers and scrolls, raised on four panel feet, with four-character Qianlong seal mark.

A jue is a type of archaic Chinese wine cup.

1736-95 *6.25in (16cm) diam*

£3,500-4,500 **WW**

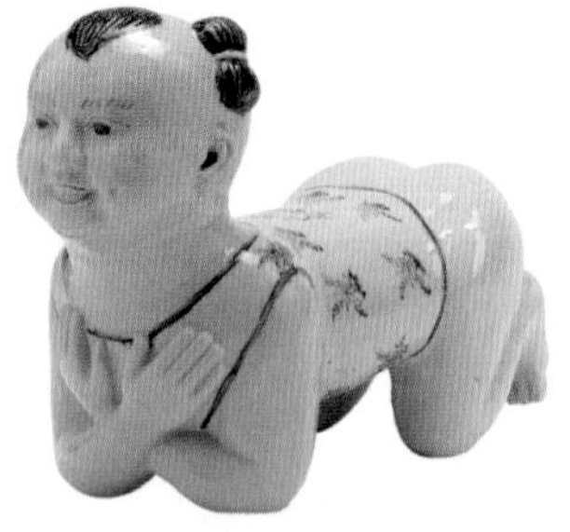

A 19thC porcelain head rest, glazed and partially painted in blue, in the form of a kneeling child.

13.5in (33.5cm) long

£120-180 **KAU**

A Transitional period vase, painted with a dragon and phoenix between rui heads and leaf borders.

c1650 *8.25in (20.5cm) high*

£500-700 **SWO**

A kendi, in the form of an elephant draped with a howdah in underglaze blue, the raised head with two pouring holes, the rim restored.

c1600 *7.25in (18.5cm) high*

£4,000-6,000 **DN**

A Kangxi period bottle, with a silver mount, the pear-shaped body painted with scrolls and flowers.

c1680 *7.5in (19cm) high*

£400-600 **SWO**

A near pair of Kangxi period triple gourd vases, with flared necks and splayed, raised feet, painted with large baskets of flowers, small footrim chips.

1662-1722 *9.75in (25cm) high*

£3,000-4,000 **WW**

A large Kangxi period vase, modelled after an archaic bronze vessel with vertical ribs, painted with stylized taotie masks, the base with an unusual mark.

1662-1722 *10.75in (27cm) high*

£3,500-4,500 **WW**

A large pair of Kangxi period blue and white vases, each with a flaring neck above a tapering shouldered body, decorated with a continuous frieze of figures in a landscape.

22.5in (57cm) high

£20,000-25,000 **L&T**

A blue and white archaic-style vase, probably 18thC, raised on four tall feet and decorated overall with lotus scrolls.

8.25in (21cm) high

£600-800 **WW**

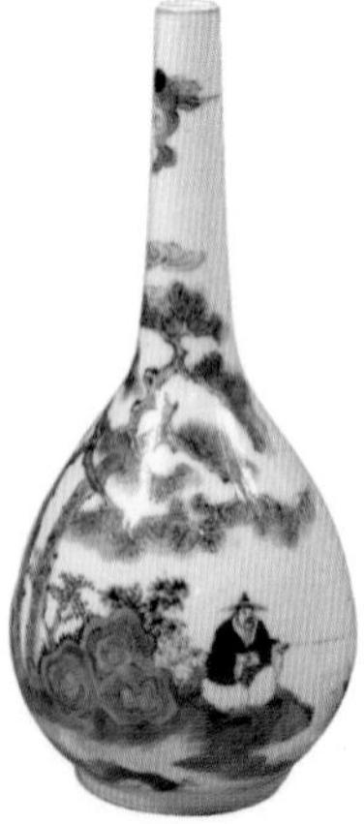

A 19thC blue and white bottle vase, painted in underglaze blue with a fisherman beneath a pine tree growing from rocks, with painted mark.

10in (25.5cm) high

£350-400 **SWO**

One of a pair of Chinese porcelain vases, decorated with chrysanthemums, damage to neck.

c1900 *30.5in (76cm) high*

£350-400 pair **SWO**

A CLOSER LOOK AT A YUAN DYNASTY BLUE & WHITE DOUBLE GOURD VASE

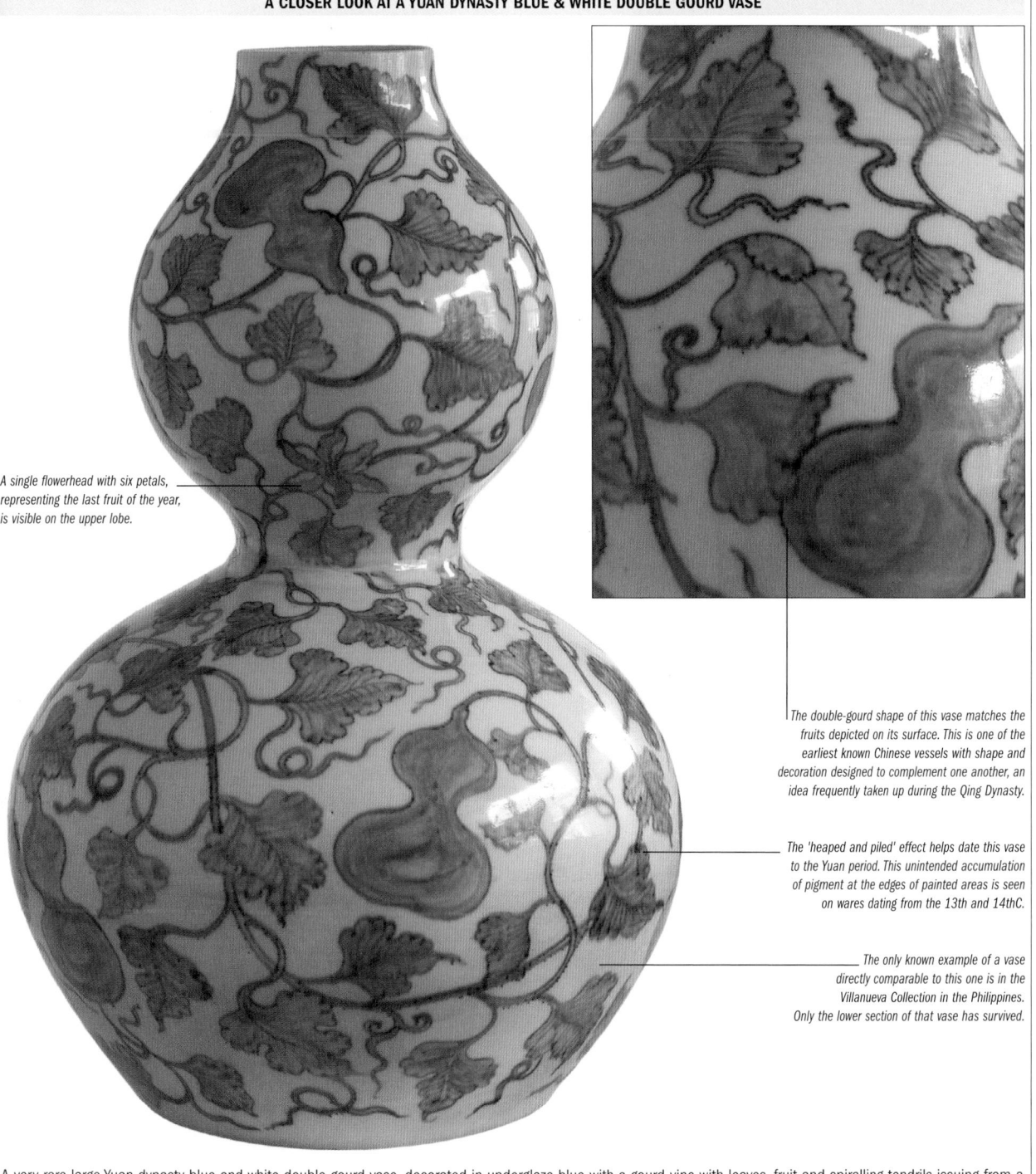

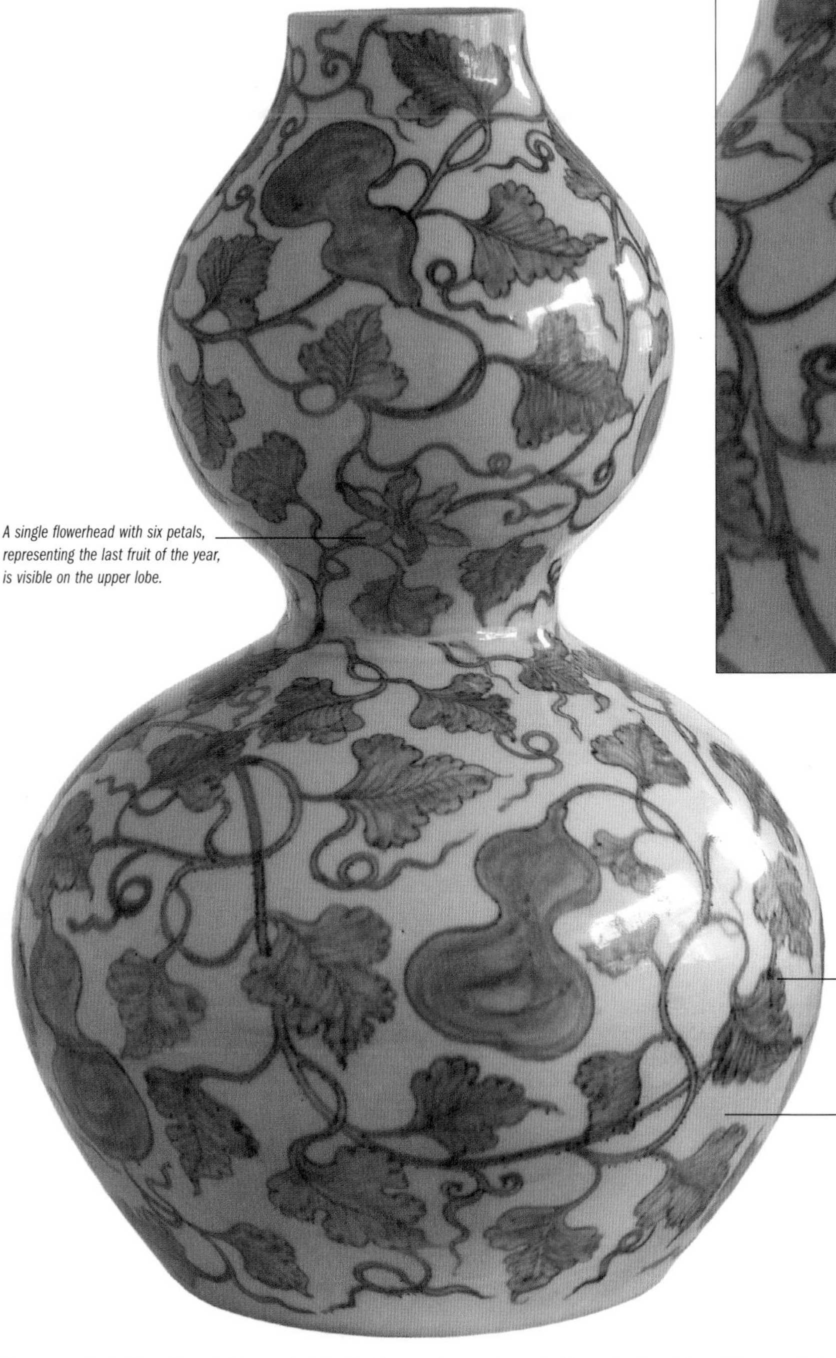

A single flowerhead with six petals, representing the last fruit of the year, is visible on the upper lobe.

The double-gourd shape of this vase matches the fruits depicted on its surface. This is one of the earliest known Chinese vessels with shape and decoration designed to complement one another, an idea frequently taken up during the Qing Dynasty.

The 'heaped and piled' effect helps date this vase to the Yuan period. This unintended accumulation of pigment at the edges of painted areas is seen on wares dating from the 13th and 14thC.

The only known example of a vase directly comparable to this one is in the Villanueva Collection in the Philippines. Only the lower section of that vase has survived.

A very rare large Yuan dynasty blue and white double gourd vase, decorated in underglaze blue with a gourd vine with leaves, fruit and spiralling tendrils issuing from a single continuous stem which grows from a root at the base of the vase and circles the body several times before terminating at the rim, with an unglazed base and shallow cut broad foot rim.

William Cleverley Alexander (1840-1916) was a member of the Burlington Fine Arts Club and was renowned for his taste in Oriental works of art. His notes suggest that he acquired this piece on 23rd May 1900 for £10. This particular piece was never published or exhibited by Alexander, perhaps because Yuan blue and white had not been identified at that time and the vase puzzled the great authorities of the day.

c1350 *18.75in (47.5cm) high*

£3,000,000+ **WW**

CHINESE ARMORIAL PORCELAIN

- During the 17thC, Chinese porcelain was a status symbol in the West. The ownership of an armorial dinner service – costing up to ten times as much as a comparable export service – was even more highly regarded.
- Armorial ceramics were commissioned and traded on a small scale rather than through organisations such as the East India Company, which controlled most commerce with the Orient.
- In England, only companies and families with Letters Patent from the College of Arms were entitled to own armorial ceramics. They were therefore exclusively available to the wealthiest and most established members of society.
- Armorial services were frequently given as wedding gifts, to celebrate the union of two families. They often depict the arms of one spouse impaling, or standing beside, those of the other.
- The prestige associated with armorial ceramics imported from the Orient declined once European makers began to produce high quality porcelain in the late 18thC.

An early Qianlong period armorial octagonal plate, painted in famille rose colours with the crest of the Stede family, surrounded by a floral wreath.

8.25in (21cm) wide

£350-400 **CHEF**

A mid-18thC armorial plate, painted with the arms of Count Tessin within a silver-shape rim, with gilded vines and blue bell flowers.

9.25in (23.5cm) diam

£400-600 **CHEF**

A mid-18thC armorial soup plate, decorated with arms within flowerhead and spearhead borders, damaged.

8.75in (22.5cm) diam

£320-380 **SWO**

A rare Chinese export armorial plate, painted with 'The Death of the Fox' and the arms of the May family of Rawmere in Sussex, damaged.

c1755 *9in (23cm) wide*

£800-1,200 **SWO**

A pair of Qianlong period armorial dishes, made for the French market.

c1780 *8.5in (21.5cm) diam*

£1,000-1,500 **R&GM**

An armorial bowl with shaped rim, decorated in famille rose enamels with "JJA" monogram beneath a crescent crest and motto "We Still Do Grow" on a pendant swagged with flowers and husks, the interior with a Fitzhugh-style band in underglaze blue.

c1800 *5.5in (14cm) diam*

£120-180 **DN**

Part of a late 18thC monogrammed dinner service, comprising a canted rectangular tureen and cover with boars' head handles and leaf finial, a large ashet, four small ashets, a pair of scalloped oval sauce boats and stands, two serving dishes, six dinner plates, four side plates and eight dessert bowls, decorated with opposed green and gilt swagged "JAW" monograms.

tureen 13.5in (34cm) wide

£1,000-1,500 set **L&T**

A Kangxi period famille verte saucer dish, painted with flowers and rockwork, the border with fruits within underglaze blue bands, with channelled footrim and flower mark, rim frits.

c1680 *13.25in (33.5cm) wide*

£600-800 **WW**

A rare Kangxi period famille verte dish, painted with figures bringing tribute to a dignitary in a pagoda, within a diaper border with six panels of mythical beasts, rim frits.

1662-1722 *14.75in (37.5cm) wide*

£2,500-3,000 **WW**

A large Kangxi period famille verte octagonal dish, painted with two birds beside a pine tree in a garden, the border with four phoenix amid flowers and foliage, minor damage.

1662-1722 *15.5in (39.5cm) wide*

£1,500-2,000 **WW**

One of a pair of 18thC famille verte dishes, painted with stylized leaf motifs and red flower heads, with a central blue flowerhead, within a diaper-type border, encircled leaf mark to base, one with restored rim.

10.5in (26.5cm) diam

£280-320 pair **H&L**

A pair of Kangxi-style famille verte plates, each painted with the eight horses of Mu Wang, within a diaper and flower border, with Fang mark, damaged.

Mu Wang was an ancient Chinese ruler who undertook an epic journey with eight fine horses.

8.5in (21.5cm) diam

£400-600 **SWO**

A pair of 19thC Cantonese famille verte baluster vases, with reserve panels decorated with domestic scenes, flowers, birds and insects.

17in (43cm) high

£400-600 **MAX**

A 19thC famille verte hexagonal section vase, with panels decorated with foliage and birds.

17.5in (44cm) high

£350-400 **SWO**

A pair of 19thC famille verte vases, each painted with He Xian-gu below a crane.

He Xian-gu is one of the eight Taoist Immortals.

8.25in (20.5cm) high

£200-250 **SWO**

A pair of late 19thC Cantonese covered tapering vases, decorated in the famille verte style, with circular feet and pierced inset lids.

13in (33cm) high

£180-220 **MAX**

An early 18thC famille verte bowl, the exterior painted with garden panels below a diaper band and overglaze blue framed vignettes.

13.25in (33.5cm) diam

£2,500-3,000 **CHEF**

A rare Wanli period wucai bowl, with a flared rim, the exterior brightly painted with four figures divided by lanterns, the rim with stylized flowers, with six-character Wanli mark within a double ring, some wear and faults.

A similar Wanli bowl in this pattern is exhibited at the National Palace Museum in Taiwan.

1573-1619 *6in (15cm) diam*

£12,000-18,000 **WW**

A Kangxi period famille verte biscuit figure of Guandi, seated on a throne holding his beard in his right hand, minor faults.

Guandi is the Taoist god of war.

1662-1722 *10in (25.5cm) high*

£10,000-12,000 **WW**

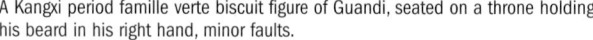

A Kangxi period famille verte rouleau vase, painted with seated dignitaries and their attendants before pine trees and distant mountains.

1662-1722 *17in (43cm) high*

£25,000-30,000 **WW**

One of a pair of Yongzheng period famille rose saucer dishes, painted with butterflies above lotus flowers and leaves, with six-character Yongzheng marks.

1723-35 *6in (15.5cm) diam*

£2,000-2,500 pair **WW**

A famille rose saucer dish, painted with a bird perched on a flowering branch above a large peony, one small glaze scratch, unmarked, probably Yongzheng period.

9.75in (25cm) diam

£800-1,200 **WW**

A Kangxi period famille rose dish, decorated with a flowering tree.

1662-1722 *10.75in (27.5cm) diam*

£220-280 **BEA**

A Qianlong period famille rose plate, of octagonal form, painted with two birds on rocks and flowering foliage.

c1740 *8.75in (22cm) wide*

£250-300 **SWO**

An 18thC famille rose circular plate, painted with two European figures in a landscape, the border with peony and summer flower sprays.

The painted scene is after an engraving by S. Le Clerc, from a 17thC French translation of Ovid's "Metamorphoses".

9in (23cm) diam

£1,500-2,000 **L&T**

A 19thC famille rose dish, with an unusual full length portrait of a man in a red robe.

9.75in (25cm) diam

£300-500 **R&GM**

A 19thC famille rose porcelain plate, depicting two female figures, a seated priest and two men with gifts of flowers, surrounded by floral decoration and insects, damaged.

10in (25.5cm) diam

£70-100 **KAU**

A rare pair of Qianlong period famille rose dishes, each painted with two figures holding fans and a third figure watching through a hole in the wall, the border with small panels of pink flower sprays and figures in landscapes, detailed in blue and gold, some wear to the gilding.

1736-95 *14.25in (36cm) wide*

£2,000-3,000 **WW**

A Xianfeng period famille rose canted square dish, painted with a dragon clutching a flaming pearl against a cloud ground, with Xianfeng seal mark.

£600-900 **CHEF**

A famille rose punch bowl, decorated with panels of figures in a landscape and sprays of flowers on a gilt and black ground, the interior with a spray of flowers and spear-head border.

10.5in (26.5cm) diam

£400-600 **DN**

An early 19thC Canton famille rose oval tureen and cover, brightly decorated with figures within borders of flowers, leaves, insects and fruit, the knop re-gilded.

13.75in (35cm) wide

£2,200-2,800 **WW**

An early 19thC Canton famille rose rectangular tureen and cover, brightly decorated inside and out with figures within borders of flowers, fruit, foliage and insects.

13in (33cm) wide

£1,000-1,500 **WW**

A Canton famille rose hot water serving dish, cover and stand, painted with exotic birds, butterflies and peonies on a celadon green ground, with gilt cowrie shell finial.

18in (45cm) wide

£300-500 **L&T**

A pair of famille rose rouleau vases, each brightly decorated with a phoenix standing on rockwork amidst flowers, with four-character Kangxi marks.

11.5in (29.5cm) high

£800-1,200 **WW**

A pair of 19thC Canton famille rose vases, mounted as table lamps with elaborate gilt brass bases, each painted with panels of figures, with later fittings.

15.75in (40cm) high

£1,000-1,500 **WW**

A CLOSER LOOK AT A FAMILLE ROSE VASE

This very unusual design imparts a sense of fun, thus generating extra interest with collectors.

This piece is in extremely fine condition with no chips or cracks.

The intricate floral decoration has been painted in a full famille rose palette and the colours remain extremely clear and bright.

This design was not fired in one piece and was therefore relatively costly to manufacture. Consequently, few were produced and it is a scarce shape today.

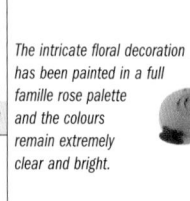

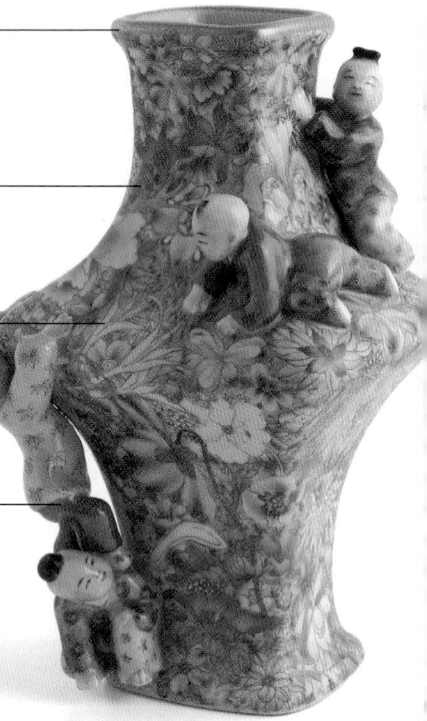

A famille rose square-section baluster-shaped vase, modelled with five clambering children, on a flower and leaf ground, with Qianlong seal in red.

7in (18cm) high

£3,500-4,500 **LFA**

A Yongzheng period famille rose hexagonal-section brush pot, each face brightly painted with a figure, raised on six bracket feet.

1723-35 *5.25in (13.5cm) high*

£4,000-6,000 **WW**

A late 18thC famille rose guglet and basin, painted with mandarins and their companions within underglaze blue coral diaper bands.

bowl 11in (28cm) diam

£700-1,000 **CHEF**

A mid-19thC Chinese famille rose jug, of barrel form, decorated with a band of flowers and butterflies over a court scene.

9in (23cm) high

£350-400 **ROS**

A famille rose wall pocket, in the form of a half-opened scroll, painted with an interior scene with figures.

5in (12.5cm) high

£400-600 **CHEF**

A 19thC export supper set contained in a lacquered box, with nine sectional supper dishes painted in gilt and famille rose colours with elders seated in a garden.

box 12.5in (32cm) diam

£400-600 **ROS**

A Ming dynasty celadon pear-shaped vase, incised with scrolling foliage below a reduced rim with a later metal mount.

8.5in (21.5cm) high

£150-200 **CHEF**

A Transitional period wucai baluster vase, brightly decorated with three dragons in pursuit of pearls amid stylized clouds, restored rim chip.

c1650 *13in (33cm) high*

£800-1,200 **WW**

A large mid-17thC Transitional period trumpet vase, of gu form, painted with women and boys playing, restored and converted as a lamp.

20.75in (52cm) high

£800-1,200 **SWO**

A large mid-17thC Transitional period wucai vase, with a flared neck, painted with a woman and attendants in a garden, restored.

15.25in (38.5cm) high

£3,500-4,500 **WW**

A mid-17thC Transitional period wucai baluster vase, the body decorated with small squirrels clambering over a fruiting vine issuing from green rockwork, with wooden cover and stand, some small rim frits.

11.75in (30cm) high

£4,000-6,000 **WW**

A Kangxi period celadon baluster vase, painted with birds and floral decoration.

18in (46cm) high

£1,000-1,500 **BLA**

A Kangxi period small double gourd vase, with a green, yellow and aubergine mottled 'egg and spinach' glaze, small rim chip.

1662-1722 *4.5in (11cm) high*

£220-280 **SWO**

A CLOSER LOOK AT A TRANSITIONAL PERIOD VASE

The Transitional period (c1620-50) is the phase in Chinese history marked by the progress from the Ming dynasty to the Qing dynasty. Prime Transitional period ceramics can exceed even the very best Ming pieces in quality.

The Taoist Immortals have been venerated in Chinese popular religion for many hundreds of years. This is a popular subject and has strong appeal for the Chinese market which is currently pushing prices for Transitional wares steadily higher.

Wucai is a Chinese word meaning 'five coloured'. A combination of overglaze and underglaze enamels in blue, green, orange yellow and red make up the design.

This flared, trumpet-like form is taken from a type of ancient Chinese vessel called a 'gu'. Bronze gu were used ceremonially as far back as the Shang dynasty (c1700-1000BC).

A large mid-17thC Transitional period trumpet vase, of gu form, painted in underglaze blue and enamels with a Taoist Immortal being offered precious objects by attendants above bands of peony and pomegranates.

17.25in (43cm) high

£6,000-8,000 **SWO**

An early 18thC baluster vase, with a sang de beouf-style glaze.

6.5in (16cm) high

£220-280 **SWO**

An unusual mid-18thC tea canister and cover, of ovoid form, painted with a European subject en grisaille with red details and applied scrolls, chipped.

5.25in (13cm) high

£350-450 **SWO**

A garniture of five Qianlong period vases, consisting of a pair with bulbous bodies and three baluster-shaped vases, all painted with figural panels within scroll reserves against a mandarin cell-pattern ground.

11.5in (29cm) high

£5,000-6,000 **GORL**

A blue glazed altar vase and cover, the oval body moulded with a key fret and stylized scrolls, each piece with a moulded Jiaqing mark, possibly of the period.

9.5in (24cm) wide

£3,500-4,500 **WW**

A 20thC lidded hexagonal-section vase, with short neck, depicting a landscape scene with a woman carrying a vase, fish and floral decoration.

13.5in (34cm) high

£10-20 **KAU**

A 19thC celadon vase, the rectangular panelled sides moulded with pairs of Taoist Immortals, with Qianlong seal mark.

11.5in (29cm) high

£150-200 **CHEF**

A pair of late 19thC Chinese celadon bottle vases, with tea-coloured rims above white interiors, the glaze lightly crackled.

11.75in (30cm) high

£250-300 **CHEF**

A pair of late 19thC Canton vases, each with two handles and reserved panels of warriors, within an allover floral ground, one handle restuck.

24in (61cm) high

£500-800 **SWO**

One of a large pair of Cantonese vases on later French bases, finely painted with figures, butterflies and flowers, standing on gilt ormolu scroll bases with acanthus.

27.75in (70.5cm) high

£3,000-4,000 pair **JN**

A rare Kangxi period blanc de Chine figure of Buddha, seated cross-legged, the hands in dhyana mudra.

Blanc de Chine was first made in Fujian province during the Song dynasty. Connoisseurs distinguish three types – the first, and best, with a very faint brown or ivory colour, the second with a delicate cream colour and the third with a slight blue tinge. The colour white has associations with death and mourning in Chinese culture, so blanc de Chine ceramics are most often seen with devotional themes.

1662-1722 *7in (18cm) high*

£2,800-3,200 **WW**

An 18thC blanc de Chine figure of Guanyin, seated with a child in her lap.

9.25in (23.5cm) high

£120-180 **CHEF**

A rare 19thC marked blanc de Chine figure of Guanyin, seated in repose, with impressed double gourd mark.

3.5in (9cm) high

£280-320 **SWO**

A 19thC blanc de Chine figure of Shou Lao, shown standing on a scrolled base, minor losses.

11.5in (29cm) high

£400-600 **SWO**

A 19thC blanc de Chine figure of Guanyin, seated on a kylin.

The kylin is one of the four sacred animals of China.

12in (30.5cm) high

£150-200 **SWO**

A blanc de Chine figure of a warrior on horseback, on a plinth base, minor damage.

c1935 *10.5in (26.5cm) high*

£200-250 **SWO**

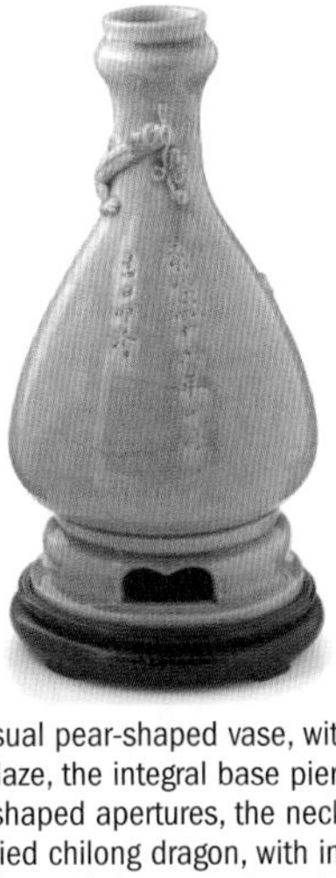

An unusual pear-shaped vase, with a green glaze, the integral base pierced with B-shaped apertures, the neck with an applied chilong dragon, with incised inscription and date, on a turned wooden stand.

1707 *10.75in (27.5cm) high*

£2,500-3,000 **WW**

An early 19thC cafe au lait glazed brush pot, moulded in relief in the style of Wang Ping Yung with a figure on a water buffalo losing his hat in a landscape of islands and mountains, with four-character mark.

6.25in (16cm) high

£220-280 **CHEF**

A terracotta figure of a mustachioed gentleman, seated on pillow, with painted decoration, restored.

12in (30.5cm) high

£3,000-4,000 **BRU**

SATSUMA

- Satsuma wares are named after a feudal province at the southern tip of the Japanese island of Kyushu. Close proximity to the Korean peninsula meant that Satsuma province benefited from an influx of Korean master potters following Japan's invasion of Korea in 1597.
- The first ceramics made in the Satsuma kilns were simple tea ceremony vessels decorated with a crackled yellow glaze on a cream ground.
- It was not until the end of the 18thC that potters from Satsuma learned sophisticated decorative techniques including enamelling and gilding from artists in Arita and Kyoto.
- Satsuma became a generic term for any Japanese pottery with a cream body that was exported to the West from the 19thC onwards.
- Typical Satsuma decorative motifs include figures, flowers and Japanese fauna. Many Satsuma designs use perspective to create complex multi-layered scenes.
- The quality of Satsuma pottery varies enormously between the oldest, most carefully decorated pieces and the gaudy items made for the export trade in more recent times.

A Satsuma vase, decorated with depictions of Buddha and the Immortals beneath a diaper and mon shoulder band, with character marks.

c1880 *9.5in (24cm) high*

£500-700 **SWO**

A Satsuma baluster vase, decorated by Matsumoto Hozan with a reserve panel of figures on each side, on a chocolate and gilt ground, with gilt marks.

Matsumoto Hozan was a celebrated Japanese artist active in the late 19thC.

c1880 *11in (28cm) high*

£1,200-1,800 **SWO**

A Meiji period Satsuma vase, painted with cockerels, hens and chicks walking and pecking in a bamboo grove, with impressed and gilt marks for Kinkozan.

The Kinkozan family workshop in Kyoto produced some of the finest Satsuma wares of the late 19thC.

1868-1912 *14.25in (36cm) high*

£3,500-4,500 **WW**

A Meiji period Satsuma vase, the slim ovoid body decorated with panels depicting figures in a landscape, and hens by a wheatsheaf, with four-character gilt signature.

1868-1912 *12.25in (31cm) high*

£1,500-2,000 **WW**

A large Meiji period Satsuma double gourd vase, decorated in silver and gold with birds flying amid wisteria and iris on a black ground, with gilt Kozan seal mark.

The Kozan dynasty operated the Makuzu kiln at Yokohama for four generations.

1868-1912 *15.75in (40cm) high*

£800-1,200 **WW**

A Meiji period Satsuma vase, with chrysanthemum handles, decorated with figures, animals, fans and musical instruments beneath a band of migrating cranes, with red painted mark.

1868-1912 *4.25in (11cm) high*

£400-600 **WW**

A pair of Hododa Satsuma vases, each of trumpet form, moulded in relief and painted with Lohan on a black and gilt ground, with gilt Hododa marks.

Lohan are disciples of Buddha.

c1890 *9.25in (23.5cm) high*

£350-400 **SWO**

A pair of Satsuma vases, of square section, decorated with figures on a diaper ground.

c1900 *9.5in (24cm) high*

£180-220 **SWO**

A 20thC Satsuma vase, of shouldered form with everted rim, painted with panels depicting figures watching captive apes, an exotic bird amid flowers and a woodsman bowing towards a group of females, within diaper borders, with nine-character black seal mark to base.

6.75in (17cm) high

£2,800-3,200 **ROS**

A Satsuma vase, of bucket form, reserved with a panel of fowl and a landscape on the reverse, on a gilt and coloured flowerhead ground, with gilt mark, restored.

c1900 *5in (12cm) high*

£250-300 **SWO**

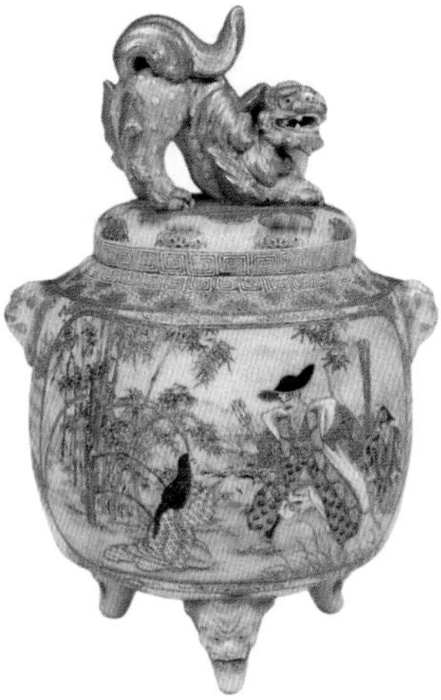

A Satsuma koro, decorated with two enamelled and gilded panels depicting warriors and a maiden at a lakeside pavilion, with shi shi mask feet, handles and knop, signed, small chips.

c1875 *6.75in (17cm) high*

£320-380 **SWO**

A Satsuma koro, in the form of a garden lantern, surmounted with a karashishi with a dragon below the rim, decorated by Choshuzan in enamel and gilt, on a hardwood stand, signed.

c1890 *7in (18.5cm) high*

£150-200 **SWO**

A small Satsuma koro, of hexagonal section.

c1890 *3in (8cm) high*

£1,200-1,800 **SWO**

A Meiji period Satsuma koro, with a finial in the form of a dog of Fo holding a pierced ball, surrounded by a band of ornamental fans, painted with a processional scene, on three short legs, with gilt character marks, both handles restuck.

4.5in (11cm) high

£1,000-1,500 **SWO**

A Meiji period Satsuma compressed circular koro, with a reticulated metal cover, standing on three feet, with overglaze blue Satsuma mon and signature in iron red, some wear.

1868-1912 *7.5in (19cm) high*

£500-800 **WW**

A Meiji period Satsuma koro, decorated with women and children viewing an aquarium, the reverse with two women beneath a tree beside a lake, some wear to gilding.

1868-1912 *5.5in (14cm) high*

£400-600 **WW**

A Meiji period Satsuma koro, decorated with panels containing many figures on a complex floral ground, with four-character mark, the knop missing.

1868-1912 *14.5cm (37cm) high*

£500-800 **WW**

A pair of Meiji period Kinkozan Satsuma plates, each decorated with a female in a garden within a blue ground border heightened with gilding, with impressed and gilt character marks.

7.25in (18cm) diam

£500-800 **SWO**

A 20thC Satsuma plate, decorated with chrysanthemums and other flowers, signed.

9.5in (25cm) diam

£80-120 **SWO**

One of a pair of 19thC Imari porcelain vases.

First made during the late 17thC, Japanese Imari porcelain uses a palette of underglaze blue with iron red and gilt. It was widely copied in China and Europe.

5.5in (14cm) high

£80-120 pair **MAX**

A large Zoshuntai Sanpo Imari vase, of slender baluster shape with a flared neck, decorated with exotic birds amid flowers, painted signature, chips to rim.

c1880 *26.5in (67cm) high*

£220-280 **SWO**

A late 19thC Imari baluster vase, decorated in underglaze blue and burnt orange with flowers and birds.

£120-180 **MAX**

A rare early 18thC export plate, painted in the Imari palette with a parrot, a dragonfly and peony, rim chips.

9.25in (23cm) diam

£100-150 **SWO**

A pair of late 19thC Imari dishes, painted in underglaze blue with rocks, trellis and peony, within panelled borders.

13in (33cm) diam

£500-600 **SWO**

An unusual early 18thC armorial teapot, decorated in the Imari palette with a Continental coat of arms, the cover missing and spout re-glued.

6.5in (16.5cm) wide

£220-280 **WW**

A pair of Kakiemon dishes, with foliate rims, each painted in bright enamels with a blue butterfly and a chrysanthemum spray, unmarked.

c1680 *8.25in (21cm) diam*

£2,500-3,000 **WW**

A CLOSER LOOK AT A KAKIEMON DISH

Nigoshide, identifiable from its milky white colour, is the finest quality Japanese porcelain and is associated with the very best Kakiemon wares.

The well-spaced asymmetric decoration, with extensive areas left in the white, is characteristic of Kakiemon painting at its best.

This dish was made during the time of the second Kakiemon Sakaida - an illustrious family line that has been at the forefront of the Japanese ceramic tradition for almost 400 years.

The Kakiemon palette of red, blue, turquoise and yellow evolved over time. This is an early example to feature the full range of colours.

A late 17thC Kakiemon dish, the nigoshide body painted in iron red, blue, turquoise and yellow with a tiger beneath a prunus spray growing from colourful rockwork, the border with a flower and leaf scroll with gilded details and a brown line rim.

8.75in (22cm) wide

£10,000-12,000 **WW**

A late 17thC Arita tapering ovoid vase, decorated in underglaze blue with three panels of peonies amid grasses, the panels divided by bands of stylized flowers, the shoulders with bands of lappets and asa-no-ha.

Asa-no-ha is a repeating geometric design that resembles the hemp leaf.

10in (25.5cm) high

£1,000-1,500 **DN**

An early 18thC Arita blue and white charger, decorated with floral panels, with hairline cracks.

16.25in (40.5cm) diam

£500-700 **SWO**

An early 19thC Arita blue and white vase, on a hardwood stand, with crazing and cracks.

11.75in (30cm) high

£220-280 **SWO**

A 19thC monochrome vase, with a flared neck and ovoid body, decorated with a deep sky blue crackle glaze.

11.5in (29cm) high

£500-800 **CHEF**

A Koransha porcelain vase, the globular body painted in underglaze blue and gilding with cranes flying across Mount Fuji between large chrysanthemums, the reverse with carp and butterflies, spray mark.

'Koransha' translates as 'The company of the scented orchid'. It was founded in 1875.

c1880 *12in (30.5cm) high*

£800-1,200 **SWO**

A near pair of early 20thC bottle vases, of octagonal section with tall cylindrical necks, painted with sparrows over blue and white floral sprays.

10.25in (26cm) high

£350-450 **ROS**

An unusual 19thC kinrande wine cup, by Eiraku Hozen, decorated with gilt leaves and scrolls above breaking waves on an iron-red ground, with six-character mark, with wooden presentation box.

Eiraku Hozen (1795-1854) was the 11th generation of his family to make tea ceremony wares. Kinrande is gold leaf applied with lacquer.

2.75in (7cm) high

£300-500 **WW**

A 10-piece Kutani coffee set, painted in enamel and gilding with millefleur, the cup interiors with long inscriptions, the saucers marked "Kutani", one cup damaged.

c1890

£220-280 **SWO**

A Fukagawa-style platter modelled as a fish, with blue and gilt decoration to the head, tail and fins, the scales with rouge de fer and gilt repeat decoration, the underside painted in blue with stylized waves, with six-character painted mark.

20.75in (52cm) wide

£800-1,200 **L&T**

A 19thC Persian polychrome pottery tile, with moulded relief decoration depicting a warrior on horseback, restored.

9.5in (24cm) high

£400-600 **SWO**

A Kashan tortoise pottery oil lamp, probably 13thC, the hemispherical reservoir pinched into a beak-shaped spout above the dished circular foot.

2.5in (6cm) high

£80-120 **CHEF**

A 15thC Thai box and cover, unglazed with a rough appearance, the design incised and coloured with iron oxide, on a later stand.

Although pieces like this do not attract very high prices, fakes abound.

4in (10cm) wide

£100-150 **R&GM**

A discarded Thai pot, damaged in the kiln.

Although this piece would have been regarded as worthless when it was made, it has value today as an eccentric curiosity.

c1350-1500 *4.25in (11cm) high*

£80-120 **R&GM**

A Tibetan stone Buddha's head, modelled with eyes cast down, partially gilded.

9.25in (23cm) high

£180-220 **KAU**

A Tibetan stone Buddha's head, modelled with eyes cast down and lines scored into the hair, partially painted in blue.

12.75in (32cm) high

£180-220 **KAU**

A Tibetan stone Buddha, painted and partially gilded, standing on a lotus blossom, with one outstretched palm.

40in (100cm) high

£700-1,000 **KAU**

A Japanese Meiji period ivory okimono, by Ikkosai, depicting Hotei seated beside his bag of treasures which is inhabited by a pack of rats, engraved "Ikkosai", damaged.

c1870 *2.25in (5.5cm) high*

£220-280 **SWO**

A Japanese Meiji period ivory okimono, by Masakazu, depicting two entertainers, one dancing in fear, the other crouching with a tzuzumi, a bag behind engraved "Masakazu", two fingers chipped.

A tzuzumi is a kind of Japanese hand drum.

c1870 *4in (10cm) high*

£500-800 **SWO**

A Japanese Meiji period ivory group, depicting Hotei, Benten, Diakoku and Bishamon, four of the seven gods of good fortune.

c1870 *2.25in (5.5cm) high*

£350-400 **SWO**

A Japanese Meiji period ivory okimono, by Isshisai, depicting a father peeling a fruit for his son, signed "Isshisai" on a lacquer reserve, chipped.

c1890 *5.25in (13.5cm) high*

£250-300 **SWO**

A Japanese Meiji period ivory group, by Munenobu, of a grandmother seated on a bench with her granddaughter while her grandson feeds birds on the rootstock base, engraved "Munenobu" and "Nobu" on a lacquer reserve, small losses.

c1890 *5in (13cm) high*

£1,800-2,200 **SWO**

A Japanese Meiji period carved ivory okimono, modelled as an actor wearing a noh mask and holding a fan.

c1890 *2.5in (6.5cm) high*

£100-150 **SWO**

A Japanese Meiji period carved ivory figure of a sage, holding a staff and a fan, a netsuke and inro carved to his back, on a wooden plinth.

10.5in (26.5cm) high

£400-600 **GORL**

A Japanese Meiji period ivory figure of an elder, with a long beard, wearing a loose robe and holding a staff, on a wooden plinth.

6.25in (16cm) high

£400-600 **GORL**

A Japanese Meiji period carved ivory figure, by Shizuyuki, depicting a woman holding a scythe and carrying a basket of flowers on her back, her loose-fitting robe engraved and inlaid with mother-of-pearl, on a circular base, signed.

7.25in (18.5cm) high

£700-1,000 **GORL**

A Japanese Meiji period carved ivory okimono, depicting a farmer feeding chickens, with a basket strapped around his shoulder and chickens by his feet, on an oval plinth, with red seal mark to base.

Okimono are sculptures, usually of ivory, made to stand inside alcoves within a house.

6in (15cm) high

£600-900 **DNT**

A Japanese Meiji period ivory fisherman, by Toshitsuki, depicted standing and holding a fish with a crab crawling over his shoulder, signed "Toshitsuki", some damage.

c1900 *7.75in (19.5cm) high*

£350-400 **SWO**

A Japanese Meiji period ivory figure of a bijin and a miniature kodansu chest, decorated with lacquered water plants, some losses.

c1900 *6in (15cm) high*

£180-220 **SWO**

A Japanese late Meiji period ivory figure of a young lady with an infant on her back, mounted upon a later turned hardwood stand.

£180-220 **BIG**

A 20thC Japanese carved ivory okimono, depicting two Buddhist monks, stained green, signed.

2.75in (7cm) high

£100-150 **SWO**

A mid-19thC Japanese ivory netsuke, by Senko of Hannya, in the form of a grimacing face with devil's horns, engraved "Senko".

1.5in (4cm) high

£220-280 **SWO**

A Japanese ivory model of a cockerel, carved with very fine detail, inset with glass eyes.

c1910 *5.5in (14cm) high*

£800-1,200 **ROS**

A mid-19thC Japanese ivory netsuke, depicting an octopus clutching a straw tray, a tobacco pouch and a pipe, signed.

2in (5cm) high

£500-800 **SWO**

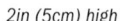

A Chinese carved ivory crouching lion dog, the head turned sinister, raised on a rectangular base, probably Kangxi period.

2.75in (7cm) wide

£1,000-1,500 **WW**

A Japanese carved ivory model of a goose, inset with glass eyes, with two-character signature to the base in red.

c1910 *7.5in (19cm) high*

£600-900 **ROS**

An early 20thC Chinese carved ivory model of a crab, raised on an elaborate wooden stand.

5in (13cm) wide

£700-1,000 **WW**

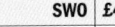

A Canton oval ivory vase, carved with figures and temples.

c1850　　　　　*4in (10cm) high*

£280-320　　　　　　　**SWO**

A pair of 19thC Chinese carved ivory vases, on pierced stands.

4in (10cm) high

£400-600　　　　　　　**SWO**

A CLOSER LOOK AT A PAIR OF TUSK VASES

The distinctive curve of these vases is due to the fact that they have each been carved from a single piece of elephant tusk.

It is important to check the authenticity of ivory by looking for the striations that form as the tusk grows.

The intricate shibayama decoration on these vases uses expensive materials and signifies good quality.

The wooden stands are well carved with delicate pierced decoration and complement the vases, adding to their overall aesthetic appeal.

A pair of ivory tusk vases, each carved with scenes depicting the planting and harvesting of rice and a monkey entertainer, on fixed red and black lacquer stands.

c1880　　　　　*9.5in (24cm) high*

£1,800-2,200　　　　　　**SWO**

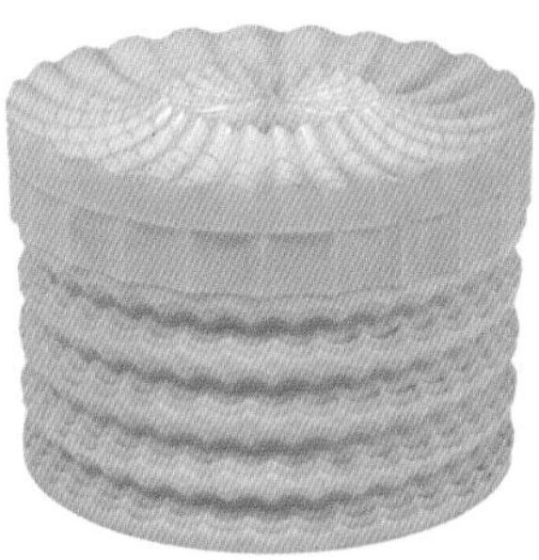

A Chinese ivory cylindrical box.

3.5in (9cm) diam

£150-200　　　　　　　**SWO**

A pair of Japanese Meiji period tusk vases, inlaid in mother-of-pearl, ivory and coloured stones, decorated in shibayama lacquer with birds perched in flowering trees and with butterflies above hibiscus, raised on elaborate carved wooden stands, some losses.

1868-1912　　　　　*16in (41cm) high*

£3,000-4,000　　　　　　**WW**

A late 19thC carved ivory box, depicting boys playing under a pine tree, with two boys sat on the lid, some damage.

3.5in (9cm) high

£350-400　　　　　　　**SWO**

An ivory tusk box and cover, carved with an old woman carrying a box on one side and a man opening it to reveal treasures on the reverse, all in a bamboo landscape, with figural knop, restored.

c1900　　　　　*7.5in (19cm) high*

£220-280　　　　　　　**SWO**

A 19thC Chinese ivory-mounted gourd cricket cage, the body decorated with figures in a mountainous landscape, the reticulated lid carved with two birds amid prunus.

4.5in (11.5cm) high

£1,000-1,500　　　　　　**WW**

An ivory card case, carved with flowers on a lattice ground, the reverse with two shaped figural cartouches.

4.25in (10.5cm) high

£220-280 **SWO**

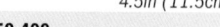

An ivory card case, carved with a cartouche containing figures bordered with flowers.

4.5in (11.5cm) high

£350-400 **SWO**

An ivory card case, profusely carved on both sides with figures amid buildings, the corners carved with dragons and bats.

3.75in (9.5cm) high

£320-380 **SWO**

An ivory card case, profusely carved on both sides with figures amid buildings and trees.

3.75in (9.5cm) high

£320-380 **SWO**

An ivory card case, of rectangular shape, profusely carved with figures amid buildings and trees.

4in (10cm) high

£350-400 **SWO**

An ivory card case, profusely carved on both sides with figures amid buildings and trees.

4.25in (10.5cm) high

£200-250 **SWO**

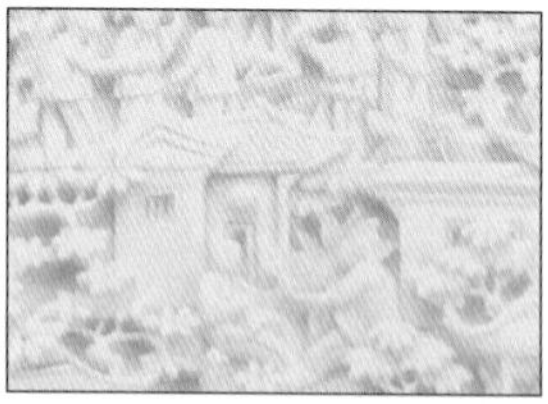

An ivory card case, carved profusely with figures amid trees and pagodas.

4.5in (11.5cm) high

£220-280 **SWO**

JADE

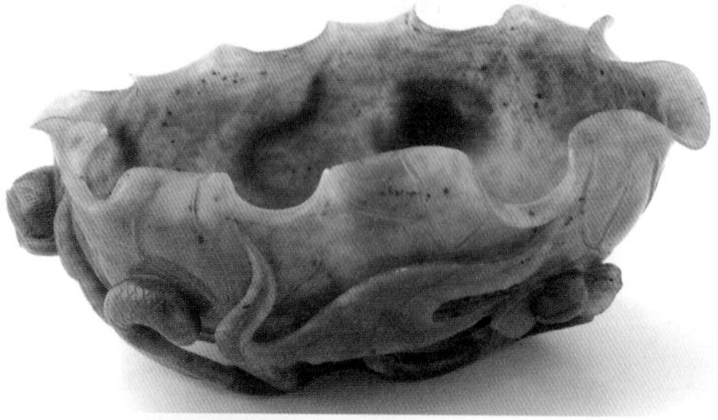

A Chinese nephrite jade bowl, in spinach green, carved as a lotus pad supported on a basket of buds, tendrils and leaves.

6in (15.5cm) wide

£500-800 **CHEF**

A Chinese nephrite jade bowl, in pale olive green with one purple corner, carved with three groups of lotus and two cranes.

6.5in (17cm) wide

£800-1,200 **CHEF**

A 19thC Chinese jade brush washer, carved in shallow relief with a scholar and a deer in a rocky landscape, with four-character mark.

4.5in (12cm) high

£1,000-1,500 **WW**

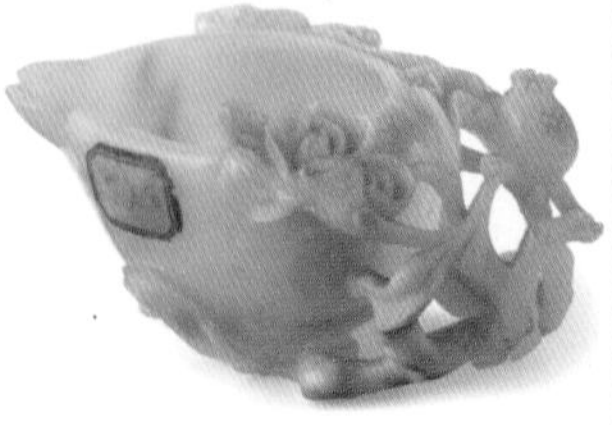

A Chinese white jade brush washer, probably 18thC, modelled as a pomegranate, the handle in the form of open leafy branches, a small fruit and a chilong dragon clinging to the side, the stone with pale beige inclusions.

4.5in (11cm) high

£2,800-3,200 **WW**

A Chinese jade double vase, probably 18thC, the pale green stone with brown inclusions, carved as a pair of finger citron growing from a single branch.

6.5in (16cm) high

£2,500-3,000 **WW**

A pair of Ginbari vases, decorated with goldfish against a green and orange ground, one struck to the underside.

Ginbari is a type of Japanese cloisonné enamel work.

c1890 9.75in (24.5cm) high

£400-600 SWO

A Japanese Meiji period cloisonné vase, decorated with two sparrows amid bamboo and other flowers, with key fret borders.

1868-1912 7in (18cm) high

£600-900 WW

A late 19thC cloisonné garniture, comprising a jardinière with winged handles mounted on a base with dog feet and a pair of vases, each similarly decorated with flower blossom and butterflies.

vases 10.5in (26cm) high

£500-800 SWO

A cloisonné vase and cover, of angular discus form, finely detailed with millefleur, birds and diaper bands, with chrysanthemum knop.

c1890 4.25in (11cm) high

£400-600 SWO

A pair of cloisonné vases, of hemispherical form with trumpet mouths, decorated with flag irises, the necks with wisteria and birds.

c1900 6in (15cm) high

£400-600 SWO

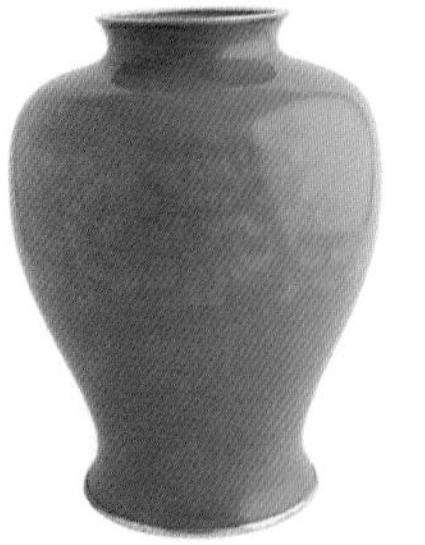

A Japanese cloisonné vase, of inverted baluster shape, decorated in white with a band of flowers and leaves on a bright green ground, the foot and rim with white metal bands, signed "Ando".

c1955 9.5in (24cm) high

£350-400 LFA

A 19thC cloisonné bowl, with applied dragon handles, supported upon three short legs, with Fang Ming mark.

9.25in (23cm) diam

£220-280 SWO

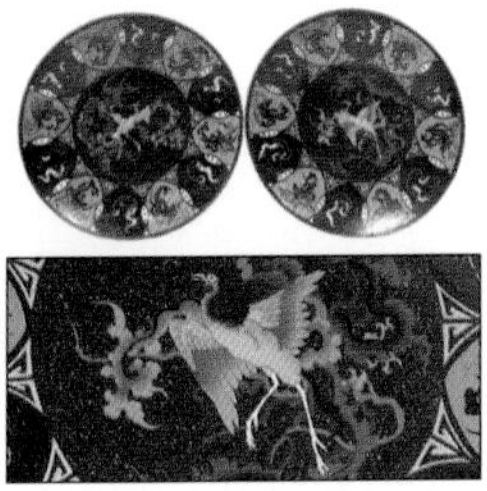

A pair of late 19thC cloisonné dishes, each with a central panel of a ho-ho on an aventurine ground, the rim with blade panels of ho-ho and dragons.

The ho-ho bird is a stylized depiction of a pheasant with the tail feathers of a peacock.

14.25in (36cm) wide

£220-280 SWO

A late 18thC cloisonné eating set sheath, of tapering cylindrical form, decorated with florets and scrolls on a turquoise ground, with gilt engraved mounts, containing ivory chopsticks.

£700-1,000 SWO

CLOISONNÉ

- Cloisonné is a specialist decorative technique whereby different coloured enamels are separated by thin strips of metal, usually copper wire.
- The technique originated in the Byzantine Empire and was certainly known in China by the time of the Yuan dynasty (1279-1368).
- During the mid-15thC Chinese craftsmen developed the deep blue enamel that has traditionally been favoured as a background colour for Oriental cloisonné.
- Some of the finest Chinese cloisonné dates from the Qianlong period (1736-95), when craftsmen were encouraged by the patronage of the emperor.
- Cloisonné was not known in Japan until the Edo period (1615-1868) and was not popularised until Kaji Tsunekichi perfected the technique c1850.
- Japanese craftsmen developed a delicate cloisonné technique known as 'Ginbari', whereby the copper wire divisions are substituted by a fine foil.

A pair of 19thC cloisonné eating set sheaths, decorated with flowers and landscapes, complete with implements.

£800-1,200 SWO

A late 18thC cloisonné scroll weight, of rectangular form, decorated with hooked linear patterns, some damage.

7in (17.5cm) long

£2,500-3,000 SWO

An 18thC cloisonné censer, of Fang Ding form, decorated with taotie masks, on cylindrical legs, with a later cover.

£800-1,200 SWO

An 18thC Chinese red lacquer quatrelobed vase, carved with four panels depicting figures beneath trees, the neck with stylized lappets, the foot with a flower scroll, damaged.

11in (28.5cm) high

£5,000-6,000 **WW**

A CLOSER LOOK AT A PAIR OF LACQUER VASES

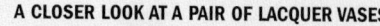

The shibayama lacquer technique was developed towards the end of the Edo period, primarily for the export market. It is most frequently associated with furniture.

The ground of gold lacquer is inset with precious metals and other expensive materials to create an object of outstanding opulence.

Vases like these would have been extremely expensive and were therefore produced in small numbers.

Objects like this, with high visual impact but of modest dimensions, are sought-after as they will blend with most types of interior decoration.

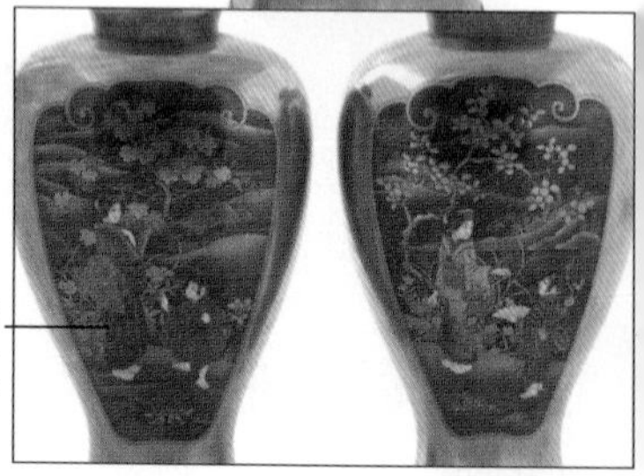

A fine pair of Japanese Meiji period shibayama vases, with silver-coloured metal mounts, inlaid with ivory, mother-of-pearl, coral and semi-precious stones, decorated with figures, birds in flight and paulownia scrolls.

6in (15cm) high

£6,000-8,000 **WW**

A Japanese shibayama vase, inlaid with silver and gold, with enamelled phoenix handles, decorated with flowering plants, some losses.

11.5in (29cm) high

£600-900 **GORL**

A 19thC Japanese shibayama lotus-shaped dish, with six gold lacquer panels set in a wirework frame, with two-character signature on a gold pad, some damage.

12in (31cm) wide

£800-1,200 **WW**

A mid-19thC Japanese lacquer bowl and cover, decorated with asa-no-ha, prunus and pine fronds on a mura-nashiji ground.

This piece was exhibited at the Great London Exposition of 1862. This was the first time that Japanese decorative arts were seen by a wide European audience and its effect on European arts and crafts was immense.

15.5in (39.5cm) diam

£600-900 **DN**

A 19thC Chinese lacquer box and cover, carved with Immortals in a landscape between peach and leaf borders.

5in (12.5cm) high

£600-900 **SWO**

An early 19thC red lacquer three-case inro, carved in relief with Buddhist precious objects.

3in (7.5cm) long

£400-600 **CHEF**

A mid-19thC Japanese lacquer five-case inro, decorated with butterflies in varying tones of gold lacquer.

3.25in (8cm) long

£280-320 **SWO**

A Japanese small rectangular lacquer tray, decorated in gilt with cranes in flight in a rocky landscape, on four short feet.

c1900 *6.5in (16.5cm) wide*

£300-400 **LFA**

A Japanese black lacquer screen, decorated in shibayama lacquer with figures, on a carved rosewood stand.

24in (61cm) wide

£700-1,000 **SWO**

A pair of late 19thC Japanese bronze vases, each with silver and gold coloured metal inlay, depicting cockerels on blossoming branches, signed.

8.5in (21cm) high

£500-800 **SWO**

A pair of late 19thC Japanese bronze vases, of elongated ovoid form, cast with eagles, cranes, birds and insects between mask and tongue handles.

19.25in (48cm) high

£280-320 **SWO**

A pair of Japanese bronze vases, each of bellied form, inlaid with flying egrets above rushes and engraved waves in silver, gold and shibuichi, signed marks for "Miyabe Atsuyoshi" and "Kakihan".

c1880 *6in (15cm) high*

£2,200-2,800 **SWO**

A large Japanese Meiji period Komai ware twin-handled bronze vase, of tapered ovoid form, decorated with panels of birds perching amid peony blossom, with a frieze of stylized bats and grotesque mask ring handles, on scroll bracket feet and a carved hardwood stand.

27.5in (70cm) high

£10,000-15,000 **L&T**

A pair of monumental 20thC Chinese silvered bronze vases, the flared necks and ovoid sides embossed with dragons, clouds and masks inlaid with coral, raised on turned wooden bases.

71in (180.5cm) high

£5,000-6,000 **FRE**

An early 20thC Japanese silver four-piece tea set, of baluster form, decorated in high relief with an iris swamp, comprising a teapot, sugar bowl, cream jug and slop bowl, with a similarly decorated tea caddy and coffee pot, with maker's marks in Japanese characters.

£3,000-4,000 **SWO**

A bronze figure of a girl, possibly by Miyao, modelled carrying her baby brother on her back.

c1890 *4in (10cm) high*

£220-280 **SWO**

A late 19thC Japanese bronze figure, by Gyoko, of a bijin wearing a peony-engraved kimono with dragons on the back knot, engraved "Gyoko", stand and fan missing.

11.5in (29cm) high

£500-800 **SWO**

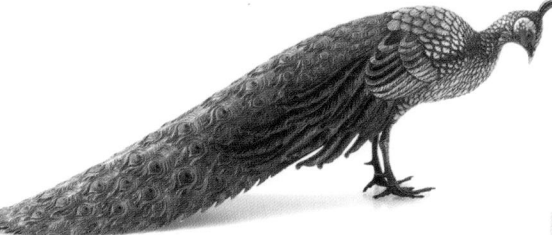

A Japanese Meiji period silver and enamel peacock, the wings detailed in copper and gold, the eyes of the tail feathers enamelled in blue, green and brown, with small character mark to breast.

12.75in (32.5cm) long

£5,000-6,000 **WW**

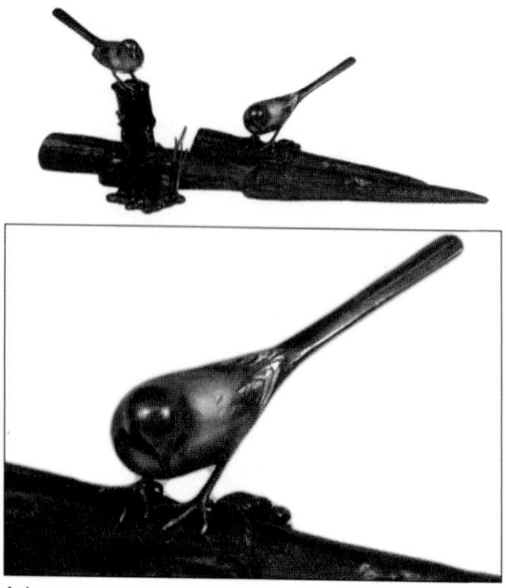

A Japanese cold-painted bronze group, depicting birds perched on logs, signed.

c1900

£220-280 SWO

A Japanese bronze elephant, with a raised trunk and ivory tusks, on a hardwood base.

13.5in (34cm) high

£200-250 SWO

A pair of Chinese Ming dynasty bronze censers and covers, cast as standing ducks with open beaks, with incised plumage and webbed feet, on rectangular stands.

9.75in (24.5cm) high

£2,000-2,500 L&T

A 17thC Chinese bronze incense burner, cast in the form of a fabulous animal with gilt highlights, on a later wooden stand, some damage.

9in (23cm) high

£500-700 WW

An 18thC iron soten tsuba, of circular form, with pierced and carved decoration, inlaid with silver and shakudo with gold nunome details depicting the demon of Rashomon, unsigned.

Shakudo is an alloy of gold and copper which has a deep purple patina.

2.75in (7cm) diam

£280-320 DN

A Japanese iron and gold inlay tsuba, inscribed with Japanese verse.

3in (7.5cm) diam

£80-120 ROS

A Chinese Shang dynasty copper helmet, with ornamental decoration in relief.

1766-1027BC *8.5in (21cm) high*

£800-1,200 KAU

A massive 19thC Chinese bronze water trough, cast with dragons amid waves above a reserve chased with inscriptions on both sides, resting on four demon feet, with green and grey patina.

There is a similar trough in the Palace Museum in Beijing that dates from the Warring States period (481-221BC).

51.75in (129.5cm) long

£3,000-5,000 SWO

A Sino-Tibetan bronze gilded Buddha, wrapped in an overlapping gown, the hands in bhumispara and ahyana mudra, seated on a lotus base.

5in (12.5cm) high

£100-150 CA

A Chinese Qianlong period ruby glass vase, carved with eight fluted facets, with incised four-character Qianlong mark.

1736-95 5.5in (14.5cm) high

£8,000-12,000 **WW**

A Chinese Qianlong period Peking lithyalin glass vase, the handles carved with scrolls surmounted by animal heads, with four-character Qianlong mark, restored.

1736-95 10in (25.5cm) high

£1,000-1,500 **WW**

A Chinese Qianlong period Peking glass vase, the ovoid body with a deep egg-yolk glaze, with four-character Qianlong mark to the base.

1736-95 4in (10cm) high

£4,000-5,000 **SWO**

A Chinese amethyst-coloured glass snuff bottle, probably 18thC, carved with squirrels climbing amid fruiting vines.

2in (5cm) high

£800-1,200 **WW**

A 19thC rock crystal snuff bottle, carved on one side with a bird and peony, the reverse with pine trees and bamboo.

2.5in (6.5cm) high

£300-400 **SWO**

A Peking yellow-tinted glass snuff bottle, with carved decoration depicting carp and a pagoda, beneath a ruyi head band, with a turquoise glass stopper.

3in (7.5cm) high

£300-400 **LFA**

A 19thC Peking red glass bowl, the exterior carved with a frieze of lotus.

6in (15.5cm) wide

£800-1,200 **WW**

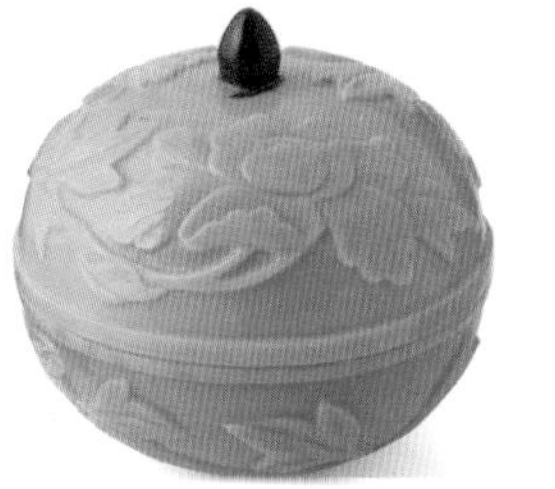

A 19thC Peking turquoise glass bowl and cover, carved with a flowering peony, the red glass knop re-glued.

4.5in (11cm) wide

£300-500 **WW**

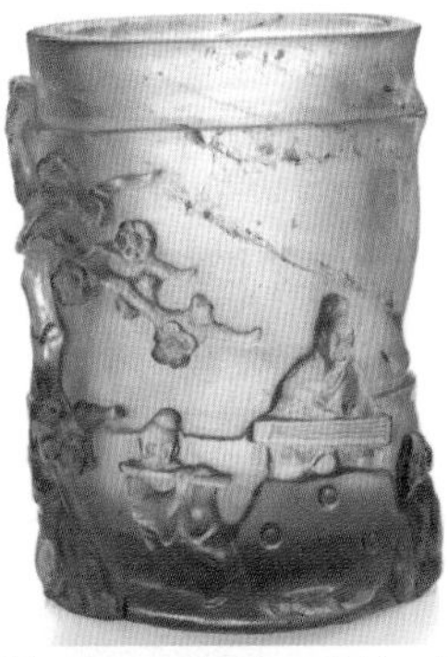

A Chinese carved rock crystal brush pot, probably 17thC, carved in relief with three figures seated around a rock, beneath a flowering prunus tree.

3.5in (9cm) high

£1,000-1,500 **WW**

A Peking cameo glass vase, overlaid in green with three cranes amid pine trees.

12in (30cm) high

£280-320 **WW**

A 19thC Peking cameo glass brush washer, the yellow ground overlaid in red and carved with shou characters, bats and endless knots.

Shou is a Chinese symbol for long life and luck.

4in (10cm) wide

£800-1,200 **WW**

A 20thC Peking cameo glass jar and cover, the green overlay etched and cut with birds amid lotus on a white ground.

6.5in (16.5cm) high

£180-220 **CHEF**

A 19thC bamboo figure of a Lohan, modelled seated holding a fly whisk and looking over his shoulder.

5.25in (13.5cm) high

£500-800 **CHEF**

A Chinese carved boxwood group, depicting a Sennin on top of a rock reaching for a three-legged toad in a pool below.

A Sennin is the mountain-dwelling spirit of a hermit.

5.75in (14.5cm) high

£220-280 **CHEF**

A CLOSER LOOK AT A BAMBOO RUYI SCEPTRE

The form of the ruyi sceptre evolved from early Chinese back scratchers, commonly called 'old man's joy'.
Ruyi translates as 'as you wish'. These sceptres were used ceremonially and given as auspicious gifts, particularly on birthdays because of their association with longevity.
The great skill of the craftsman who made this sceptre is evident in the very delicate and intricate carved decoration.
Ruyi sceptres were particularly prevalent during the Qianlong period, from when this example dates. Emperor Jiaqing, who succeeded Qianlong, apparently suppressed their use.

A Chinese Qianlong period carved bamboo ruyi sceptre, with an intricate reticulated stem decorated with lotus, peach and bamboo, the head with three peaches and a large seed pod.

1736-95 *17.25in (44cm) long*

£4,000-6,000 **WW**

A Chinese root carving, in the form of a man with a toad on his shoulder.

7in (18cm) high

£220-280 **LFA**

A rare mid-19thC Tamba School wooden netsuke, by Toyomasa, carved with sealife including a carp and crayfish, signed "Toyomasa".

This netsuke was probably by the elder Toyomasa (1773-1856), revered as a great master of netsuke carving.

2.25in (5.5cm) wide

£1,500-2,000 **SWO**

A 19thC carved wooden netsuke, depicting a recumbent cow.

2.5in (6cm) wide

£400-600 **SWO**

A Chinese hardwood cylindrical brush pot, probably 19thC, inset in soapstone with a sage seated beside a rock, inscribed with calligraphy.

6in (15.5cm) high

£400-600 **WW**

A 20thC Chinese hardwood brushpot, inlaid in jade, soapstone, mother-of-pearl and ivory with two birds perched amid flowering prunus.

6.25in (16cm) high

£400-600 **WW**

A 19thC Chinese bamboo vase, carved in relief with figures planting rice and working in fields beneath trees.

5.75in (14.5cm) high

£400-600 **WW**

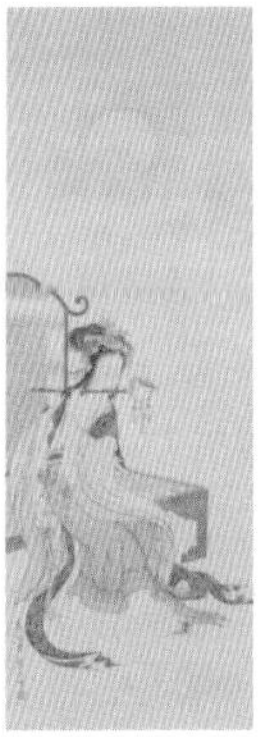

A 19thC Japanese painting of Yang Guifei on silk, mounted as a hanging scroll, attributed to Hosoda Eishi.

Yang Guifei (713-756) was the favourite concubine of the Tang dynasty emperor Xuanzong. Despised by the people, she was eventually forced to commit suicide.

33.75in (84.5cm) high

£500-700 **NAG**

Two panels of a Japanese Taisho period triptych on paper, mounted as hanging scroll, by Munenobu.

37.5in (94cm) high

£500-800 set **NAG**

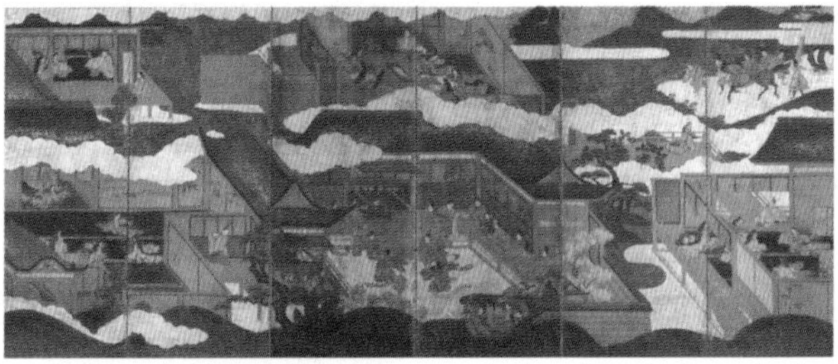

An early Edo period Japanese six-panel screen, in the style of the Tosa school.

49.5in (123.5cm) high

£12,000-15,000 **NAG**

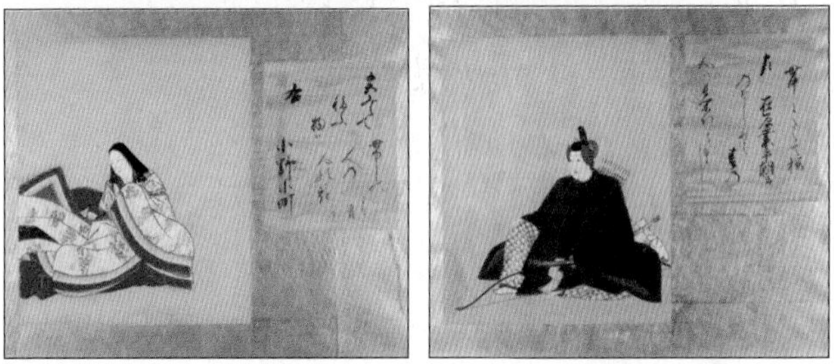

Three of a set of four 17thC Japanese Kano school paintings, anonymous, framed under glass.

£3,000-4,000 set **NAG**

A CLOSER LOOK AT A FAN PAINTING

These fan paintings are very unlikely to have survived had they not been mounted onto album pages, and so this treatment does not have a detrimental effect on their value.

The Heike Monogatari is an epic Japanese prose narrative, first transcribed in the 14thC from an earlier oral tradition.

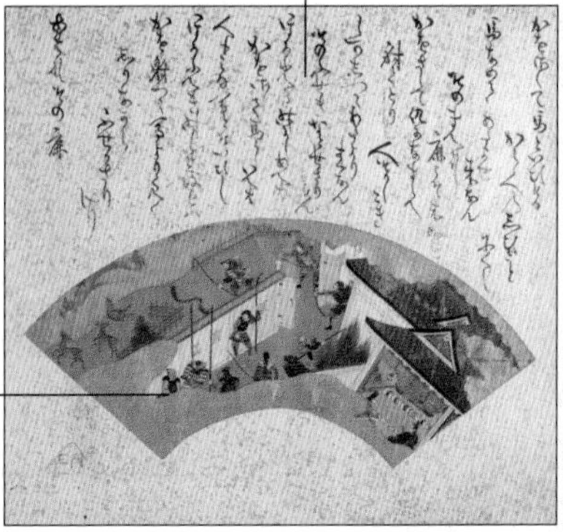

The great age and rarity of these paintings means that similar examples come to the market infrequently, therefore attracting great interest from collectors.

These paintings are very attractive artifacts. The figures in particular exhibit extremely fine detailing.

A rare pair of 17thC Japanese miniature fan paintings, depicting scenes from the Heike Monogatari, mounted on album pages.

9.5in (24cm) wide

£2,500-3,000 **NAG**

A pair of 18thC Japanese fragments of a paravent, depicting views of Kyoto, anonymous.

10.5in (26cm) wide

£1,200-1,800 **NAG**

A Japanese Meiji period carved wooden cabinet, with lacquer panels decorated in relief with ivory and mother-of-pearl flowers, urns, baskets and exotic birds, raised on a fret-pierced panelled base.

1868-1912 *49.5in (125.5cm) wide*

£1,500-2,000 **FRE**

An early 19thC Chinese black lacquered table cabinet, with a shaped crest over two panelled doors, enclosing six long drawers, decorated in gilt with flowers, figures and buildings.

26.75in (67cm) high

£500-700 **SWO**

A Chinese hardwood shrine cabinet, with carved and pierced panels and mouldings.

15.5in (39cm) high

£300-400 **SWO**

An Oriental-style stained wood side cabinet, with blind and pierced fretwork decoration and decorative panels with applied metal and ivory details, carved with dragons and flowers, on a plinth with scroll feet, stamped "V OPAVA".

40in (102cm) wide

£400-600 **L&T**

A Chinese lacquered cabinet on stand, with two panelled doors, decorated with birds in branches, buildings and figures, with engraved metal mounts and side carrying handles, the stand with scroll-carved apron, on short feet.

35in (89cm) wide

£350-400 **LFA**

A Chinese lacquer cabinet on stand, carved in relief with green and black highlights on a red ground, the crest pierced and carved with a dragon, above a row of reverse breakfront cupboards and open shelves, cupboards and drawers, on a shaped plinth, the stand with bulbous apron and scrolling legs.

52in (132cm) wide

£2,000-2,500 **L&T**

An early 20thC Japanese carved hardwood side cabinet on stand, fitted with an arrangement of pigeon holes, cupboards and drawers, with inlaid bone decoration.

57in (145cm) high

£1,800-2,200 **SWO**

A late 19thC Japanese shibayama lacquer screen, decorated with ho-ho birds, with fretwork and foliate decoration.

£400-600 **SWO**

A Chinese eight-fold draught screen, each rectangular fold painted with courtly figural scenes.

157.5in (400cm) wide

£600-900 **L&T**

A late 19thC Japanese lacquer four-fold screen, with carved and pierced borders.

£120-180 LFA

An early 20thC Japanese four-panel lacquer screen, decorated with depictions of samurai and inlaid with ivory.

70.5in (179cm) high

£350-400 SWO

An early 20thC Chinese carved rosewood and porcelain table screen.

30.25in (77cm) high

£700-1,000 SWO

An 18thC Chinese hardwood open armchair, the curved splat with a carved panel, with sectional curving frame, seat on conforming legs and peripheral stretchers, losses.

27.5in (70cm) wide

£1,000-1,500 WW

An 18thC Chinese miniature root chair.

30in (76cm) high

£2,000-2,500 B&I

A 19thC southern Chinese huang huali open armchair, with yoke toprail above solid splat and open outscrolled arms, inset rattan board seat and rounded square section legs joined by low stretchers and pierced apron.

Huang-huali is an especially prized type of Chinese rosewood.

£6,000-8,000 L&T

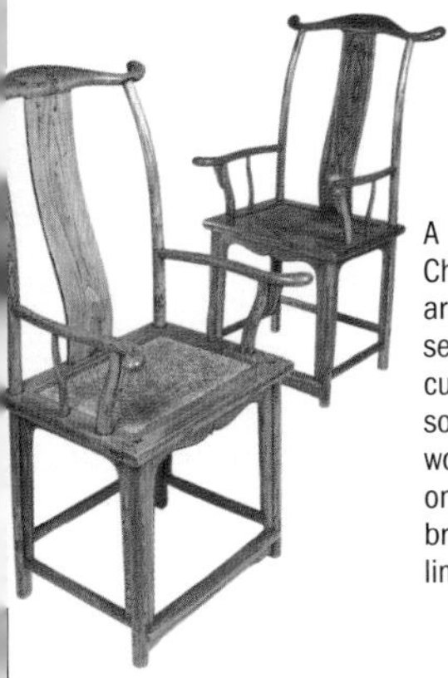

A pair of 19thC Chinese elm open armchairs, each with serpentine top rails, curved splats and solid seats with woven panels, raised on turned legs with bracket supports and linked by stretchers.

£800-1,200 L&T

An early 20thC Oriental hardwood desk, carved with dragons and fitted with shelves, cupboards, drawers and pigeon holes, on a table base with two frieze drawers and four cabriole legs.

47.25in (120cm) wide

£1,000-£1,500 SWO

A nest of four Chinese hardwood occasional tables.

19.25in (49cm) wide

£600-900 SWO

LACQUERWARE

- Lacquering involves applying layers of varnish made from the sap of a tree, Rhus vernicifera, onto wood, leather or fabric. When dry, the layers form a hard coating which can be carved.
- The technique was known in China and Japan from late Neolithic times and in Korea from c1000BC. Social and artistic exchange between Japan and China was sporadic, but Japanese lacquerware was influenced by Chinese techniques from the 8thC onwards, particularly in Buddhist sculpture.
- The most common colours are black, red, aubergine and cream.
- In the 16thC, lacquerware became very desirable in Europe and Oriental lacquerware boxes, screens and cabinets were imported. Pieces were often cut up to be reused in veneering.
- Imported lacquerware was costly, so by 17thC 'Japanning' became fashionable as a finish for furniture and smaller items. This technique involved dissolving shellac in alcohol but the finished effect was weak and water-permeable.
- High quality Japanese lacquer should be rich and lustrous with a clean, sharp design. Pieces may bear a signature, monogram or seal mark but this should not be used to date them as successive generations of artists may have used the same name.

A rare 16thC Japanese Momoyama lacquer writing box, decorated in gilt and inlaid in mother-of-pearl, with birds, flowers and leaves, detachable cover, fitted with a square inkwell and a sander, with gilt metal mounts, above two small drawers.

Lacquerware with mother-of-pearl inlay is called 'raden'. This is a very unusual size for this type of box – they are normally the size of a laptop computer.

9.5in (24cm) wide

£40,000-50,000 **LFA**

An early 17thC Gujarati casket, inlaid in mother-of-pearl with figures on horseback and scrolling flowering foliage, bound with iron and resting on shaped bracket feet.

These boxes were imported into Europe via Portugal and are still avidly collected there by enthusiasts of Oriental art who view them as something of a status symbol.

15.25in (38.5cm) wide

£100,000-120,000 **LFA**

THE FURNITURE MARKET

A period of renewed optimism has injected energy into the furniture market over the past 12 months replacing the caution that has affected the market over the last few years. The levelling of prices at the lower end of the market has attracted many new clients, and established buyers are returning to the market. Selling rates are up and concerns about the future of the furniture market and the global economy in general have subsided.

Trade experts have acknowledged the potential of a realistic approach to prices for months and these notions have now been transferred to buyers who have become aware of the many opportunities for picking up good quality bargains. Possibilities for wise purchasing exist particularly in dining room furniture, especially tables and sets of chairs. Although prices currently remain relatively low, it is likely that demand for dining sets will be ongoing, especially in light of the housing market recovery.

It remains the case that unusually fine pieces continue to perform well, with exceptional pieces in excellent condition selling for sums well in excess of auction house estimates. At the same time, buyers are continuing to shun low quality items. Pieces in need of major restoration are frequently ignored. Bookcases are also suffering, now selling for more realistic prices than the inflated levels of 3 or 4 years ago.

A greater knowledge of antiques amongst buyers, partially brought about by television and books, has also had an impact. The demand for ornate, gilt furniture has dipped as buyers become more sophisticated and seek out other types of antique furniture. Superb and rare ornate pieces do, however, continue to sell well. This trend is compounded by a change of fashion for a simpler style more in keeping with contemporary interiors.

– Paul Roberts, Lyon & Turnbull

A CLOSER LOOK AT GEORGE III BREAKFRONT BOOKCASE

The breakfront bookcase shape with its two side wings and glazed upper section became popular in the mid-18thC. The shallower glazed section and deeper base are typical of 18thC bookcases.

The astragal glazed doors help date the piece. Solid glazing bars retaining panes of glass were replaced c1750 by astragals (glazing bars with semi-circular profiles). Later 19thC bookcases often feature bars that have been simply laid on top of a single sheet of glass.

Mahogany was the favoured material for bookcases.

Bookcases were typically large in size to compliment the proportions of fashionable rooms, a style advocated by the architect Robert Adam (1728-92).

A George III mahogany breakfront bookcase, with dentil frieze and four astragal doors enclosing adjustable shelves, the base with four long drawers flanked by panelled doors enclosing shelves, raised on a plinth base.

96.5in (245cm) high

£10,000-15,000 **L&T**

A Regency mahogany breakfront bookcase cabinet, the cornice with moulded panels and applied roundels above twin astragal glazed doors with lancet arches, enclosing adjustable shelves flanked by two panelled doors inlaid with anthemion motifs.

98in (249cm) wide

£6,000-8,000 **L&T**

A late Regency reverse breakfront mahogany bookcase, with fiddleback veneers, the upper section with glazed doors enclosing adjustable shelves, the projecting lower section with panelled cupboard doors, on a plinth base.

97.75in (248cm) wide

£6,000-8,000 **L&T**

A William IV mahogany breakfront library bookcase, possibly Scottish, with moulded cornice above four astragal glazed doors enclosing adjustable shelves, flanked and divided by Doric-style pilasters surmounted by patera, raised on a plinth base.

c1835 *110in (279.5cm) wide*

£7,000-10,000 **FRE**

A 19thC mahogany breakfront bookcase, with projecting moulded cornice above four astragal glazed doors enclosing adjustable shelves, the base with four panelled cupboard doors, on plinth base.

117in (297cm) wide

£7,000-9,000 **L&T**

A Chippendale mahogany secretaire bookcase, the upper section with swan neck pediment and brokered inlaid plinth above two glazed doors, resting on a base with tiger maple drawers, above three long drawers supported by straight bracket feet.

39in (99cm) wide

£7,000-9,000 **POOK**

A George II burled walnut secretaire bookcase, with double dome top, fall front with amphitheatre interior and four drawers, supported by straight bracket feet.

82.5in (206cm) high

£7,000-10,000 **POOK**

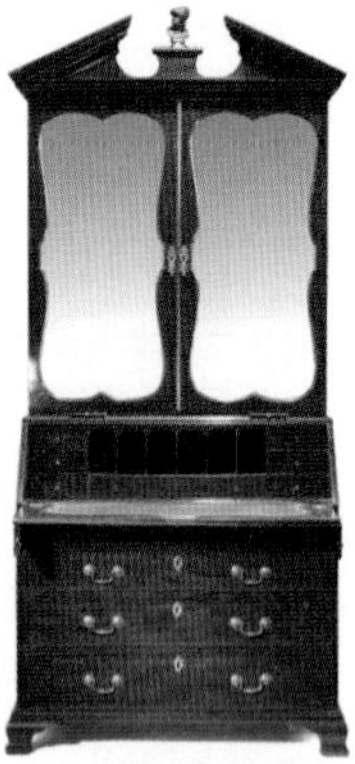

A George II mahogany bureau bookcase, with dentil-carved broken arch pediment centred by a later Grecian bust above a pair of mirrored panel doors and candle slides, the lower section with a fall front enclosing a fitted interior above graduated drawers, raised on ogee bracket feet.

c1755 *42in (106.5cm) wide*

£3,000-4,000 **FRE**

A George II-style adapted mahogany bureau bookcase, with scrolling leaf-carved swan neck pediment above astragal glazed doors and three drawers, with fold-over writing surface and ogee bracket feet.

43.25in (110cm) wide

£2,500-3,000 **L&T**

A Chippendale walnut secretaire bookcase, the upper section with broken arch bonnet centring an eagle finial over two panelled cupboard doors, resting on a lower section with fall front over four drawers flanked by fluted quarter columns, on ogee bracket feet.

c1775 *39.25in (99.5cm) wide*

£3,000-4,000 **POOK**

A George III mahogany bureau bookcase, with moulded cornice above two oval panelled and crossbanded cupboard doors enclosing shelves, the lower section with hinged sloping fall flap enclosing a fitted interior, above two short and three long graduated drawers, on bracket feet.

48in (122cm) wide

£1,200-1,800 **L&T**

A George III mahogany bureau bookcase, with dentil-carved swan neck pediment above astragal glazed doors enclosing adjustable shelves, raised on a bureau with fall front enclosing fitted interior, above graduated drawers and lopers, with shaped bracket feet.

91.25in (232cm) high

£2,500-3,000 **L&T**

A George III mahogany bookcase cabinet, the moulded cornice with Greek key frieze above twin astragal glazed doors enclosing shelves, the base with twin doors with fake drawer fronts, raised on bracket feet.

43.75in (111cm) wide

£2,000-3,000 **L&T**

A George III mahogany secretaire bookcase, with fall front concealing drawers and pigeon holes above three further drawers, on bracket feet.

40.5in (103cm) wide

£3,500-4,500 **SWO**

A George III mahogany and crossbanded double secretaire bookcase, with projecting cornice above two glazed doors, the base with two secretaire drawers each fitted with drawers and pigeonholes, above two panelled doors and a plinth base.

96.5in (245cm) high

£3,000-4,000 **L&T**

A George III strung mahogany secretaire bookcase, the later top with astragal glazed doors over fitted drawers, on bracket feet.

The chest was made for the cabin of Thomas Dance who was a Trinity House pilot between 1794 and 1833. It is believed that he had the glazed cabinet added on his retirement.

39in (99cm) wide

£800-1,200 **SWO**

A late 18thC George III mahogany secretaire bookcase, with dentil moulded cornice over two cupboard doors opening to a fitted interior, the lower section with a fall front over four long drawers, supported on straight bracket feet.

c1790 *36in (91.5cm) wide*

£2,200-2,800 **POOK**

A mid-Atlantic Federal walnut secretaire bookcase, with broken arch bonnet centring a fan-carved plinth above two arched glazed doors flanked by line-inlaid chamfered stiles, the lower section with three short over three long drawers.

c1805 99in (247.5cm) high

£3,500-4,500 **POOK**

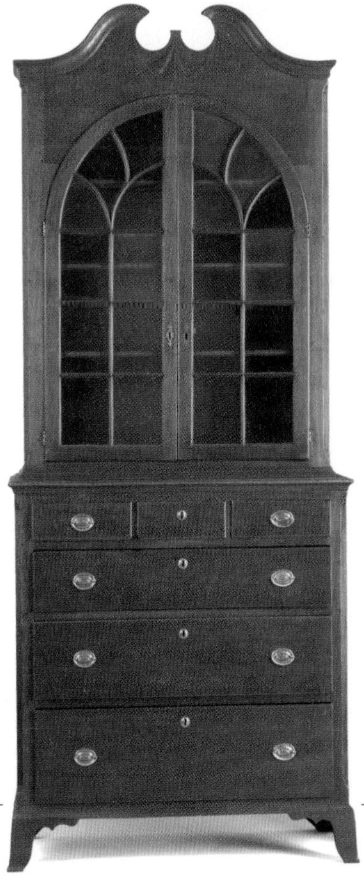

A Baltimore Federal mahogany secretaire bookcase, with moulded cornice over two glazed doors with inlaid mullions, the lower section with desk and three long drawers.

c1810 *101in (252.5cm) high*

£10,000-12,000 **POOK**

A Federal mahogany secretaire bookcase, probably Massachusetts, with moulded cornice, glazed doors with moulded mullions, compartmented interior, fold-out writing surface and three drawers flanked by fluted pilasters, on turned reeded tapering legs.

c1810 *50in (125cm) high*

£12,000-15,000 **SK**

A New Jersey Federal mahogany secretaire bookcase, with moulded swan's neck cresting centring on gilt-carved pineapple and acanthus-leaves, glazed doors enclosing shelves, pull-out tray drawer, cockbeaded short drawers, and cupboard doors opening to shelves, on carved acanthus leaf hairy paw feet.

c1830 *103.5in (259cm) high*

£4,000-6,000 **SK**

A 19thC New England Federal mahogany secretaire bookcase, with moulded cornice, latticed glazed doors, base with fold-out writing surface and drawer, on tapered legs.

68.75in (172cm) high

£1,800-2,200 **FRE**

A Regency mahogany secretaire bookcase, with scroll surmount, the upper section fitted with a pair of glazed astragal doors, the lower section with secretaire drawer and two panelled doors below on turned supports.

48in (122cm) wide

£3,000-4,000 **BRI**

An Irish Regency mahogany bowfront secretaire bookcase, with arched cornice and reeded mouldings above twin astragal glazed doors with four short drawers below, the base with secretaire drawer opening to reveal a fitted interior, above two panelled doors enclosing a kneehole and cellar drawers, raised on carved paw feet.

100.5in (255cm) high

£10,000-15,000 **L&T**

A 19thC mahogany secretaire bookcase, the upper section with a moulded cornice over a pair of astragal glazed doors, the lower section with three long graduated drawers, on bracket feet.

42.25in (107cm) wide

£1,000-1,500 **SWO**

A 19thC mahogany bureau bookcase, with glazed doors over a fall front, two short and two long drawers below, on bracket feet, associated.

38.25in (97cm) wide

£700-900 **SWO**

A Victorian mahogany bookcase, with a plain moulded cornice and rounded glazed doors, over canted corners, the base with a pair of panelled doors, on a plinth stand.

47.5in (121cm) wide

£1,500-2,000 **SWO**

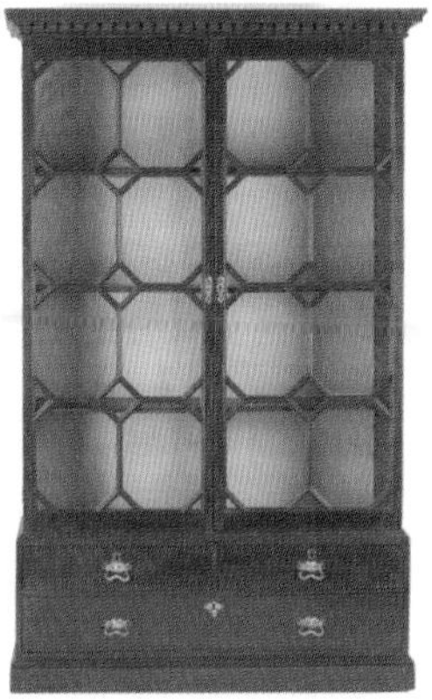

A George III mahogany bookcase, the upper section with a corbel-enhanced cornice above two lattice glazed doors, resting on a lower section with drawers, on a plinth base.

c1780 *54in (137cm) wide*

£4,000-6,000 **POOK**

A Regency mahogany and inlaid bookcase, attributed to Gillows, the upper section with open shelves, over brushing slide and two frieze drawers, the lower section with two grille panel doors flanked by reeded pilasters, raised on squat turned legs terminating in brass cappings and castors.

c1815 *49.5in (124cm) high*

£3,500-4,500 **FRE**

A mid-19thC kingwood bookcase chest, by Gillow & Co., with gilt metal mounts, the upper section with twin serpentine glazed doors enclosing shelves, the corresponding base with two short over two long drawers, raised on bracket feet with cast swing handles, stamped "Gillow & Co."

50.5in (128cm) wide

£8,000-10,000 **L&T**

A William IV mahogany open bookcase, with shaped top and frieze above two graduated shelves and a drawer, on bun feet.

28in (71cm) wide

£800-1,200 **DN**

A late Victorian oak bookcase, with arched and moulded cornice above cartouche with oak garlands, the three glazed doors enclosing shelves, the base with three frieze drawers and three panelled doors flanked by lion mask and leaf-carved brackets, raised on a plinth base.

109.75in (279cm) high

£3,000-4,000 **L&T**

An Edwardian mahogany and inlaid dwarf bookcase, with rectangular top over a central panelled door flanked by two astragal glazed panel doors enclosing shelves, raised on squat square tapered legs with spade feet.

c1910 *54in (135cm) wide*

£600-900 **FRE**

An Edwardian inlaid mahogany revolving bookcase, on castors.

33in (84cm) high

£800-1,200 **SWO**

A Louis XV-style kingwood open bookcase, with shaped marble top over two small drawers with kingwood and rosewood parquetry, the interior with a single fixed shelf, the base with gilt metal banding and shaped apron.

c1925 *44.25in (110.5cm) wide*

£1,000-1,500 **FRE**

A 19thC Biedermeier birch veneer bookcase, of architectural form, with a pediment cornice, two glazed doors and lower drawer, raised on short square tapering feet.

c1825 *41.5in (105.5cm) wide*

£1,000-1,500 **POOK**

A pair of Biedermeier-style mahogany bookcases, with stepped tops over glazed panel doors enclosing shelves, raised on plinth bases.

43in (109cm) wide

£1,500-2,000 **FRE**

A 19thC Italian carved walnut cupboard bookcase, with some earlier elements, the moulded cornice over chip carved panels and two grille panel doors, the lower section with two frieze drawers and two cupboard doors, on carved claw feet.

44.5in (113cm) wide

£1,500-2,000 **FRE**

An Italian Renaissance Revival walnut bookcase, carved with cherubs, masks, mythological beasts, exotic birds and scrolling foliage, the pierced cartouche-shaped pediments flanked by cherubs and surmounted by a crown, raised on a plinth base with acanthus carved block feet, impressed mark "G. Pizzati, Vicenza".

c1880 *87in (217.5cm) high*

£1,200-1,800 **FRE**

A late 18thC oak and mahogany crossbanded dresser, with moulded cornice above three plate racks, the lower section with three drawers and a shaped apron, raised on cabriole legs with pointed pad feet.

75.5in (92cm) wide

£2,000-3,000 L&T

A George III oak dresser, with mahogany crossbanding and ebony stringing, the plate rack with moulded cornice above shaped frieze, over one long shelf and two shorter shelves flanked by two cupboard doors, the base with drawers and shaped frieze, on cabriole front legs with pad feet.

73.5in (187cm) wide

£3,000-5,000 L&T

An 18thC oak dresser, with closed plate rack over six spice drawers, the lower section with three frieze drawers and two panelled doors.

116.25in (295cm) high

£4,000-6,000 SWO

A George III oak dresser, with moulded cornice over three drawers flanked by reeded sides, the base with three frieze drawers and three central drawers with panel doors either side, raised on bracket feet.

76.75in (195cm) wide

£5,000-6,000 SWO

A small early 19thC oak dresser, made in the Jacobean style, with bead mouldings, split balusters and geometric panels.

44in (112cm) wide

£800-1,200 SWO

A Canadian open dish dresser, with boldly scrolled frieze above two open shelves, the base with a pair of cupboard doors on a plinth base, painted red.

51in (129cm) wide

£1,500-2,000 WAD

An early 18thC oak and elm dresser base, with galleried top over three frieze drawers, flanked by cupboards either side of two central drawers, on a plinth base.

65.5in (164cm) wide

£1,000-1,500 SWO

An 18thC oak dresser base, with rectangular top above two drawers with panelled doors below, flanked by two banks of three short drawers, the whole enclosed by chip carved friezes and raised on bracket feet.

73.25in (186cm) wide

£1,500-2,000 **L&T**

A late 18thC oak dresser base, with later ledge back above rectangular top with moulded edge and three drawers, the shaped apron raised above cabriole legs terminating in pointed pad feet.

71.25in (181cm) wide

£600-900 **L&T**

A CLOSER LOOK AT AN OAK COURT CUPBOARD

Massive double-bodied cupboards, with an upper section that was narrower than the lower section, were popular during the 17thC. The upper section, typically used for the display of silver plate, is missing on this example.

This dresser base was situated in the Kings Drawing Room at Holyroodhouse in the 1930s. The association with a royal palace demonstrates the importance of the piece.

This piece is dated '1694'. If authenticated a date will add to the value.

Low-relief carved motifs were often used to decorate oak pieces, and the turned columns are also typical of the period. Later examples tended to have drawers to the base rather than cupboards.

A part 17thC oak court cupboard, with carved foliate frieze supported by boldly turned columns, enclosing two doors above a further carved frieze and twin panelled doors flanked by carved rosettes on side supports, carved with floral and geometric motifs, with Palace of Holyroodhouse numbers, carved with initials "LH" and date "1694".

74.75in (190cm) wide

£8,000-12,000 **L&T**

A Georgian oak dresser base, with two-plank top with carved leaf border, over a later carved front with gouged and foliate decoration and three drawers, raised on four squared tapered legs.

74.75in (190cm) wide

£500-700 **BIG**

A George III oak and mahogany crossbanded dresser base, the later ledge back above hinged rectangular top with moulded edge over banks of crossbanded drawers, enclosed by reeded angles and raised on ogee bracket feet.

72in (183cm) wide

£1,500-2,000 **L&T**

A George III and later oak dresser base, with moulded surround mounted on flat plank top with moulded edge over an arrangement of five drawers with later handles, raised on cabriole forelegs with a shaped carved apron and pad feet around a knee hole centre.

80in (200cm) wide

£4,000-6,000 **BIG**

A New York Chippendale walnut carved linen press, with flat moulded cornice above doors with recessed panels opening to shelves, flanked by lamb's tongue reeded corners, the lower section with drawers, on bracket feet.

c1775

£10,000-12,000 **SK**

A William IV mahogany linen press, surmounted with a scrolled pediment, with two arched panelled doors enclosing slides and flanked by pilaster columns, over three drawers, raised on bun feet.

94.5in (240cm) high

£1,800-2,200 **SWO**

An early 19thC mahogany linen press, the projecting cornice with architectural pediment above twin doors with lancet arch panels enclosing sliding shelves, the base with ogee-moulded frieze drawer and three long drawers, flanked by columns and raised on a plinth base.

94.5in (240cm) high

£1,500-2,000 **L&T**

A 19thC mahogany linen press, with blind fret-carved decoration, the two panelled doors enclosing four slides over two short and two long drawers.

£1,500-2,000 **SWO**

A 19thC mahogany linen press cupboard, with double doors above two short and one long drawer, raised on bracket feet.

50.5in (126cm) wide

£500-700 **SWO**

An 18thC fruitwood gentleman's press cupboard, the upper section with double panelled doors enclosing a fitted brass rail, the lower section with two short and one long drawer, on splayed bracket feet.

48in (122cm) wide

£1,800-2,200 **BRI**

A CLOSER LOOK AT A GILLOWS WARDROBE

This wardrobe is the work of the manufacturer Gillows. The company was founded by Robert Gillow (1704-1772) in Lancaster c1728 and was subsequently run by his son Richard. A London branch opened in 1770.

This wardrobe dates from the second-half of the 18thC - an important period for English furniture and the golden age of Gillows.

Lancaster was an important trading port during the period, meaning Gillows had easy access to mahogany from Jamaica and Cuba. As the popularity of the wood grew, Gillows became increasingly well known throughout Britain.

The company had a reputation for innovation, good traditional workmanship and value for money. The quality of the work is apparent in this fine wardrobe.

A George III mahogany breakfront wardrobe, by Gillows of Lancaster, with dentilled cornice above crossbanded frieze and four panelled doors divided by ring-turned and reeded columns, the central section with graduated drawers, on a plinth base, with "HAMILTON SUNDRUM" label.

101in (257cm) wide

£10,000-15,000 **L&T**

An early Victorian mahogany gentleman's wardrobe, the centre section with a pair of panelled doors enclosing sliding trays, with two drawers below, flanked by hanging cupboards.

89.25in (227cm) wide

£800-1,200 **SWO**

A Victorian mahogany gentleman's compactum, the lower centre section with seven drawers, flanked by two cupboards with arched panels.

90.5in (230cm) wide

£1,000-1,500 **SWO**

A Victorian mahogany breakfront wardrobe, with moulded cornice, panelled doors and plain plinth base.

£800-1,200 **SWO**

A late Victorian inlaid oak triple wardrobe, by Shapland & Petter, with a moulded cornice over two panelled doors and a mirrored door over two base drawers, inlaid with stylized foliage and birds, with hammered copper strap hinges and handles, the locks stamped "S & P B".

78.75in (200cm) wide

£1,800-2,200 **SWO**

An 18thC German Baroque wardrobe, veneered with walnut and walnut root, with two doors and iron handles, raised on on four ball feet.

95.5in (239cm) high

£1,200-1,800 **KAU**

A Swiss Renaissance pine wardrobe, with walnut veneer, the two doors flanked by fluted columns, with carved shell ornaments, complete with original mountings, locks and keys.

c1750 *105.5in (264cm) high*

£2,500-3,000 **KAU**

A German Biedermeier pine wardrobe, with walnut veneer, the two doors with bevelled corners, complete with original and mountings, lock and key.

c1825 *85.25in (213cm) high*

£1,200-1,800 **KAU**

A late 18thC Swiss Baroque pine wardrobe, with walnut veneer, raised on four ball feet, complete with original mountings, lock and keys.

85.5in (214cm) high

£1,000-1,500 **KAU**

A late 17thC lacquer cabinet on a gilt stand, decorated with Chinoiserie scenes, with a pair of doors enclosing eleven drawers and pierced and etched brass strap hinges, raised on associated contemporary gilt stand with deep carved and pierced apron and square section tapering legs.

36in (93cm) wide

£2,200-2,800 **L&T**

A Regency penwork collector's cabinet on stand, profusely decorated with flowering foliage on a stained ground, with rectangular hinged top above two panelled doors opening to reveal galleried shelves and a fitted interior, raised above a shaped apron on square cabriole legs linked by a lower platform.

53in (134.5cm) high

£10,000-15,000 **L&T**

A CLOSER LOOK AT A JAPANNED CABINET

Inspired by Oriental lacquering, the European technique of japanning involved dissolving shellac in alcohol then applying several layers to the surface of an object.

Gilt areas were raised with sawdust and gum arabic.

This cabinet is a fairly early example of the technique, popular from the mid-17thC.

Despite the delicate nature of japanning, this imposing piece is in remarkably good condition.

A late 17thC japanned cabinet, fitted with an arrangement of nine short and one long drawers with gilt metal ring handles, enclosed by two doors decorated with mounted huntsmen and deer in an extensive landscape, with pierced and engraved brass escutcheons, on a giltwood stand with gadrooned frieze above a pierced apron, carved in bold relief with flowers and leaves, the four flattened front legs each headed by a preening eagle, united by an X-stretcher with central vase stand, on tapering feet.

40.5in (103cm) wide

£6,000-8,000 **LFA**

An early 18thC Hudson Valley gumwood kasten, with moulded flat cornice above panelled doors opening to a shelved interior, set into a base with single drawer, the facade with central applied diamond panel flanked by shaped panels, on turned feet.

79in (197.5cm) high

£12,000-15,000 **SK**

A Hudson Valley cherry cupboard, with heavy moulded cornice, fluted pilasters, raised panel cupboard doors, fitted interior and thumb-moulded drawers on a scrolled skirt and curved legs ending in pad feet, restored.

c1755 *53in (134.5cm) wide*

£4,000-6,000 **SK**

A Philadelphia Chippendale walnut corner cupboard, with broken arch pediment and pierced fretwork above a dentil-moulded cornice, glazed doors flanked by fluted pilasters, on a base with recessed panel doors and ogee bracket feet.

c1775 *102in (255cm) high*

£6,000-9,000 **POOK**

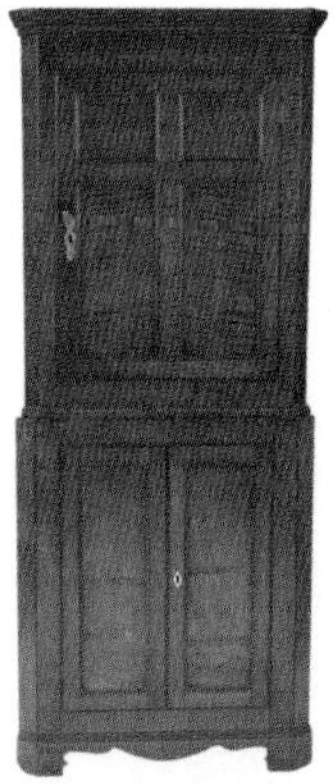

A George III oak corner cabinet, with moulded cornice above single panelled door, the lower section with twin panelled doors, raised on bracket feet.

32.75in (83cm) wide

£700-1,000 **L&T**

A George III mahogany two-part corner cupboard, with arched cornice over a bowfront case with two arched glazed doors, resting on a lower section with drawers and cupboards, raised on bracket feet.

c1790 *93.5in (234cm) high*

£3,000-4,000 **POOK**

A George III mahogany writing cabinet on stand, with moulded cornice above two panelled cupboard doors enclosing an arrangement of pigeonholes around a fall front secretaire, brass plaque inscribed "This cabinet was presented to John Gibson Junior Esq WS by Sir Walter Scott Bart, Abbotsford".

48.5in (123cm) wide

£4,000-6,000 **L&T**

A George III mahogany secretaire cabinet, the associated later top with swan neck pediment, pierced fretwork spandrels, frieze and astragal glazed doors enclosing shelves, the base fitted with a secretaire drawer above graduated drawers, on cut bracket feet.

39in (99cm) wide

£4,000-6,000 **L&T**

An early 19thC cherry stepback cupboard, from Chester county, with moulded cornice, glazed doors opening to shelves, lower case fitted with drawers and panelled doors, raised on ogee feet, restored.

53.5in (136cm) wide

£4,000-6,000 **FRE**

A Pennsylvania pine architectural corner cupboard, with moulded cornice over two arched and moulded cupboard doors and two recessed panel doors, flanked by reeded stiles, on a cutout bracket base and feet.

c1800 *84.5in (211cm) high*

£2,500-3,000 **POOK**

An early 19thC Pennsylvania poplar corner cupboard, with moulded cornice, glazed doors, interior with three scalloped shelves, one working and two faux short drawers, above recessed panel doors, on straight bracket feet.

90.5in (226cm) high

£2,000-2,500 **POOK**

An early 19thC Pennsylvania pine wall cupboard, with moulded cornice above recessed panel doors, over short drawers and cupboard doors supported by straight bracket feet, retains old blue painted finish.

81.5in (204cm) high

£1,800-2,200 **POOK**

A Montgomery County corner cupboard, with arched glazed door and single short drawer, on straight bracket feet, with later red and orange grain decoration with yellow highlights.

c1810 *93in (232.5cm) high*

£3,500-4,500 **POOK**

A Pennsylvania pine corner cupboard, with moulded cornice over a glazed door and raised panel doors, supported by ogee bracket feet, retains old blue finish with white mullions.

c1810 *86in (215cm) high*

£3,500-4,500 **POOK**

An early 19thC New Jersey pine corner cupboard, with moulded cornice over four raised panel cupboard doors, on bracket feet, with old grey and green finish.

92.5in (231cm) high

£1,800-2,200 **POOK**

An early 19thC Pennsylvania Federal pine cupboard, with matchstick moulded cornice over glazed doors on a lower section with two short drawers and raised panel doors, on bracket feet.

87.25in (218cm) high

£2,000-2,500 **POOK**

An early 19thC Pennsylvania pine corner cupboard, with moulded cornice over arched raised panel doors, flanked by reeded pilasters, above a lower section with cupboard doors supported by ogee bracket feet, with old ochre finish over red.

83in (211cm) high

£1,800-2,200 **POOK**

A Montgomery County corner cupboard, with glazed door and single short drawer over recessed panel doors, on straight bracket feet, with later red and orange grain decoration with yellow highlights.

c1810 *93in (232.5cm) high*

£5,000-7,000 **POOK**

An early 19thC faux tiger maple corner cupboard, with flat cove-moulded cornice with canted corners above a smoke-painted divided glazed door opening to shelves, the lower section with recessed panelled door.

88in (220cm) high

£7,000-10,000 **SK**

A Pennsylvania Dutch walnut cupboard, with moulded cornice over glazed doors and five candle drawers, the lower section with three short drawers over cupboard doors, on turned feet.

c1820 *87in (217.5cm) high*

£4,000-6,000 **POOK**

A Pennsylvania Dutch pine cupboard, with moulded cornice, glazed doors and four candle drawers, resting on a lower section with two short drawers and recessed panel cupboard doors flanked by turned half columns, on turned feet, with original red stained finish.

c1830 *81.5in (204cm) high*

£6,000-9,000 **POOK**

A Pennsylvania Dutch pine cupboard, with moulded cornice and glazed doors over a pie shelf, the lower section with three short drawers over raised panel doors, on straight bracket feet, with ochre grain decoration.

c1830 *83.5in (209cm) high*

£7,000-10,000 **POOK**

A 19thC stripped pine cupboard, with moulded cornice over arched opening with shelves and panelled doors.

£2,000-2,500 **SWO**

A 19thC simulated and parcel gilt Gothic cabinet, with a brass gallery above a top section containing six drawers enclosed by a pair of panel doors, the base with shelves enclosed by a pair of doors with applied named armorial shields for "Robert Glover", "Ralph Brook", "Edward Bushe" and "John Guillim", on a plinth moulded base.

Robert Glover and Ralph Brook were both Elizabethan officers of the College of Arms. John Guillim was the author of 'A Display of Hereldry' published 1610.

33.5in (85cm) wide

£1,500-2,000 **WW**

A pair of late Victorian mahogany cabinets, in the manner of Collinson and Lock, each with D-shaped top with fluted rim above anthemion and palmette panelled frieze, with flame-veneered panelled doors flanked by reeded and ribbon-tied inset columns with acanthus capitals, above engaged fluted columns, raised on stop fluted tapering feet.

£10,000-15,000 **L&T**

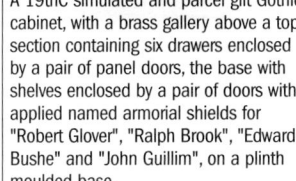

An early 19thC Dutch walnut and marquetry inlaid display cabinet on chest, with carved cartouche crest above twin astragal glazed doors enclosing shelves and flanked by glazed panels, the base of bombé outline, raised on carved paw feet.

65.75in (167cm) wide

£4,000-6,000 **L&T**

A Canadian pine corner cupboard, with double fielded panel doors, drawers and horizontal mouldings, retaining outstanding original painted finish of brown-black over vermillion.

63.5in (161cm) wide

£2,500-3,000 **WAD**

A German Biedermeier walnut veneered cabinet, the upper section with ebonized columns and gilded ends, inlaid with a coat of arms, raised on four partly ebonized feet, with original lock and key.

c1815 *74.5in (186cm) high*

£1,000-1,500 **KAU**

A 19thC Directoire secretaire à abattant, with rectangular marble top, pierced brass gallery, single panelled drawer and fall front enclosing a fitted interior above three further drawers, flanked by brass inlaid fluted columns.

£1,500-2,000 **L&T**

A German fruitwood cupboard, with dark brown patina, raised on three ball and two square feet, signed "Engelm Anno 1741".

85.5in (214cm) high

£1,000-1,500 **KAU**

A Renaissance Revival ebony and ivory inlaid curio cabinet, with moulded cornice surmounted by a broken arch pediment inlaid with penwork enhanced ivory foliate scrolls, the central ivory plaque with a landscape scene, the base with two doors over a moulded base, with block feet.

c1880 *84.75in (212cm) high*

£800-1,200 **FRE**

A 19thC Italian Renaissance Revival walnut court cupboard, the upper section with a moulded cornice over a series of small drawers surrounding a central prospect door, the lower section with two arched panel doors flanked by pilasters with Classical figures and lions.

82in (205cm) high

£3,500-4,500 **POOK**

A 19thC Italian ebonized and bone-inlaid cabinet on stand, with moulded top over three panelled cupboard doors, inlaid with hunting scenes, animals, figures, and mythical creatures, the stand with three inlaid drawers, raised on spiral turned legs joined by conforming stretchers.

62.25in (155.5cm) high

£1,500-2,000 **FRE**

An early Australian cedar chiffonier, with a three-quarter gallery supported by turned tapering columns, the base with figured cedar hooked matched drawer, the arched doors with flame cedar panels, banded with casuarina.

c1835 *43.5in (110cm) wide*

£1,800-2,200 **BONA**

A George III mahogany secretaire, the raised back with a shelf and brass supports over a fitted panelled drawer, with two panelled doors enclosing shelves, raised on turned feet, with brass label for "S. & H. Jewell, 131 High Holborn, London, W C".

36.5in (93cm) high

£1,200-1,500 **SWO**

A Regency rosewood chiffonier, with carved scroll top over a mirrored back supported by brass scrolls, breakfront marble top over a central pierced door flanked by columns and open shelves, on a plinth base.

50in (127cm) high

£1,200-1,800 **SWO**

An early 19thC mahogany chiffonier, with over-shelf and barleytwist side columns, the base with similar columns and two panelled doors, on a plinth base.

46.5in (118cm) wide

£400-600 **MAX**

A 19thC mahogany chiffonier, with a pierced brass gallery above waisted and reeded supports over a single drawer, two cupboard doors with pointed arched panels flanked by rounded pilasters, on a plinth base.

£400-600 **SWO**

A 19thC rosewood inverted breakfront chiffonier, with a mirror back and fretwork pediment, above a single glazed door flanked by pierced fretwork doors, on a plinth base.

42.25in (107cm) high

£800-1,200 **SWO**

A pair of Victorian walnut chiffoniers, by Holland & Sons, each with a broken arch cornice, mirrored panel and shelf, over a long frieze drawer with rosette and flute carving, above a pair of panelled doors between fluted pilasters, on a plinth base, the door tops stamped.

57.5in (146cm) high

£2,200-2,800 **SWO**

A 19thC ebonized D-front credenza, with ebony and boxwood line inlay and wide burr walnut cross-banding, ormolu beading and mounts, the central Sèvres panel depicting an 18thC female half portrait.

62in (157.5cm) wide

£800-1,200 **MAX**

A Victorian ebonized and amboyna breakfront credenza, with gilt-metal mounts, the shaped top over two glazed panel doors and a central mirrored panel door enclosing shelves, flanked and divided by fluted Corinthian pilasters, on a plinth base with turned bun feet.

c1880 *57in (142.5cm) wide*

£3,500-4,500 **FRE**

A Victorian ebonized credenza, with bowed glazed doors, strung and inlaid decoration and gilt bronze mounts.

60.25in (153cm) wide

£600-900 **SWO**

A Victorian walnut credenza, with marquetry inlay and marble top above arched panelled doors, on plinth base.

60in (152.5cm) wide

£1,200-1,800 **BRI**

A Victorian walnut and inlaid credenza, of semi-bowed form, the shaped top above floral and foliate inlaid frieze and central door with gilt metal banding and central marquetry urn issuing flowers, raised on a shaped plinth.

59.75in (152cm) wide

£3,000-4,000 **L&T**

An early 17thC northern Italian credenza, with oblong moulded edge top over two short drawers, flanking cherub heads over two lower doors with pilasters, raised on animal paw feet.

40.5in (103cm) wide

£4,000-5,000 **POOK**

A Victorian ebonized display cabinet, with burr walnut inlay and beadwork mounts, the glazed doors flanked with fluted columns.

48.5in (121cm) wide

£500-700 **SWO**

A Victorian burr walnut display cabinet, with arched glazed door and applied ormalu mounts.

30.5in (77.5cm) wide

£500-700 **MAX**

A Victorian mahogany cupboard, with panelled doors flanked with reeded and chamfered edges, on a plinth base.

48in (120cm) wide

£1,000-1,500 **SWO**

A fine 19thC Louis XVI-style mahogany side cabinet, with gilt bronze mounts, by Paul Sormani, with inverted breakfront marble top over two frieze drawers applied with bacchic figures and scrolls, two parquetry veneered cupboard doors centred by an open shelf and tambour doors, raised on square tapered legs ending in sabots, signed "P. Sormani, Paris, 10 Rue Charlot".

£8,000-10,000 **FRE**

A Napoleon III boullework ebonized side cabinet, with rough marble top over acanthus-cast frieze, with gilt bronze mounts and two glazed panel doors enclosing shelves, flanked by female figures, raised on a shaped plinth base.

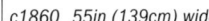

c1860 55in (139cm) wide

£2,500-3,000 **FRE**

A mid-19thC walnut and inlaid meuble d'appui, with gilt metal mounts and rectangular marble top above a parquetry frieze and single panel door, profusely inlaid with a marquetry panel of an urn issuing flowers within a floral and foliate border, flanked by turned and fluted columns, raised on turned feet.

44in (112cm) high

£1,800-2,200 **L&T**

A 19thC French kingwood and mahogany meuble d'appui, with panelled frieze with applied cast gilt metal foliate guilloche mounts, above a single drawer inlaid with marquetry oval panel of tulips, raised on turned legs.

41.75in (106cm) high

£1,000-1,500 **L&T**

CLOSER LOOK AT AN ITALIAN WALNUT SIDE CABINET

The 17thC was a prosperous time for parts of Italy and this lead to great developments in the arts and architecture. This side cabinet dates from this exciting period.
Walnut was a popular material for everyday Italian furniture of the period. Fruitwood was also a favoured option.
The simple design is typical of more ordinary furniture that contrasted greatly with the ornate gilded pieces produced for the state apartments.
Carving and inlaid designs were important decoration techniques during the period. Handles were usually drop-rings.

A 17thC Italian walnut and inlaid side cabinet, with moulded rectangular top over two frieze drawers flanked by three secret drawers, above two cupboard doors, raised on bracket feet, with "D E Mertz & Co. Antiques & Works of Art, Philadelphia, PA" label.

64in (162.5cm) wide

£14,000-18,000 **FRE**

A 19thC French kingwood side cabinet, with floral marquetry and marble top.

52.25in (133cm) wide

£2,200-2,800 **SWO**

A 17thC Italian walnut side cabinet, of canted rectangular form, with four drawers over two panelled doors, on carved claw feet.

61.5in (156cm) wide

£4,000-6,000 **FRE**

A 17thC Italian walnut serpentine side cabinet, with moulded hinged top enclosing a void well, above a plain frieze and two fielded panel doors enclosing shelves, flanked by fluted doric-form pilasters, raised on a moulded plinth base.

65.5in (166.5cm) wide

£15,000-20,000 **FRE**

A 17thC Italian carved walnut side cabinet, with moulded top over two frieze drawers and two paneled doors, flanked and divided by foliate carved panels and diamond motifs, with gadrooned apron and moulded plinth base.

64.5in (164cm) wide

£4,000-6,000 **FRE**

A 19thC German Baroque Revival carved walnut side cabinet, carved in high relief with satyrs, putti, grotesques, lion masks, fruit and scrolling foliage, with frieze drawers and two panelled doors, flanked by male figures, raised on a shell-carved base.

75in (187.5cm) high

£2,500-3,000 **FRE**

A Georgian inlaid mahogany bow front corner washstand, with hinged foldout splash back top, central cupboard and lower drawer.

27in (68.5cm) wide

£300-500 **MAX**

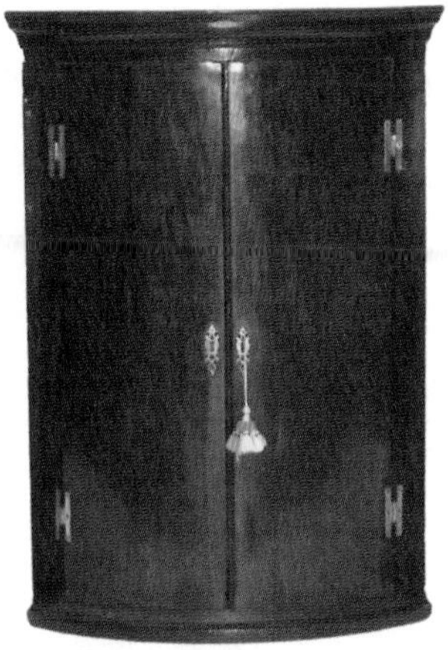

A George III mahogany bow front corner cupboard, with three internal shelves and two small drawers, enclosed by doors with brass hinges, surmounted by a moulded cornice.

29in (73.5cm) wide

£280-320 **MAX**

A George III mahogany bow front hanging corner cupboard, with a moulded cornice over two doors enclosing three shelves.

£500-700 **SWO**

A George III oak bow front corner cupboard, with moulded mahogany cornice and twin mahogany cross-banded doors, with brass hinges and ornate escutcheons, enclosing three shelves.

39.5in (100.5cm) high

£300-400 **MAX**

A George III oak bow front hanging corner cupboard.

38.5in (98cm) high

£400-600 **SWO**

A 19thC elm hanging corner cupboard, with a single panelled door.

£500-700 **SWO**

An early 20thC pine folk art hanging corner cupboard, the arched crest with a carved eagle flanked by stars, over a door enclosing shelves, embellished with applied and painted carved pine motifs, painted in shades of red, white, and blue.

16in (40.5cm) wide

£1,800-2,200 **SK**

An Edwardian demi-lune display cabinet, in the late Georgian manner, with moulded cornice and two glazed doors, the frieze and square tapering legs carved with drapery and harebells.

37in (95cm) wide

£800-1,200 **MAX**

An Edwardian strung mahogany demi-lune display cabinet, with inlaid and painted decoration, raised on square tapering legs with a decorated undertier.

40.25in (102cm) wide

£1,200-1,800 **SWO**

A CLOSER LOOK AT A LOUIS XVI-STYLE VITRINE

The Louis XVI style was first popular throughout Europe during the French king's reign of 1774-1792. Pieces had become more Neoclassical in design and, although luxurious, were characterised by restraint and simplicity. This display cabinet revisits the Louis XVI style.

Francois Linke (1855-1946) was one of the most important and influential French furniture makers of the Belle Epoque.

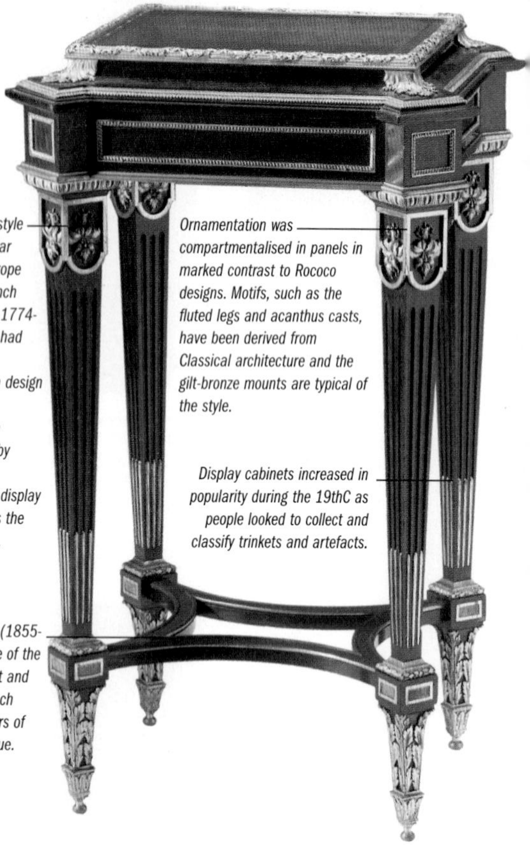

Ornamentation was compartmentalised in panels in marked contrast to Rococo designs. Motifs, such as the fluted legs and acanthus casts, have been derived from Classical architecture and the gilt-bronze mounts are typical of the style.

Display cabinets increased in popularity during the 19thC as people looked to collect and classify trinkets and artefacts.

A late 19thC Louis XVI-style mahogany and gilt bronze mounted vitrine, attributed to Francois Linke, with hinged bevelled glass top, ogee frieze with acanthus-cast corners, panelled sides raised on fluted square tapered legs joined by an open X-stretcher, terminating in acanthus cast toupie feet.

19in (48.5cm) wide

£5,000-8,000 **FRE**

An Edwardian inlaid mahogany sideboard, of serpentine shape, with two glazed doors flanking open shelves and mirrors, on slender cabriole legs.

48.5in (123cm) wide

£700-900 **SWO**

An Edwardian display cabinet, of small proportions, with three drawers below a glazed velvet lined interior.

22in (56cm) wide

£1,000-1,500 **SWO**

A pair of Louis XVI-style kingwood parquetry and brass inlaid vitrines, with white marble tops over breakfront friezes and glazed panel doors enclosing shelves, raised on square tapered legs united by wavy stretcher.

£1,000-1,500 **FRE**

A late 19thC pair of French mahogany and gilt bronze vitrines, with moulded marble tops over a panelled frieze applied with musical trophies and flowers, the glass panelled sides opening to reveal shelved interiors, flanked by fluted rounded corners, on square cabriole legs terminating in sabots.

17.25in (44cm) wide

£6,000-9,000 **FRE**

An early 20thC French rosewood vitrine, with serpentine-shaped front and sides enclosing velvet-lined shelves, with hand-painted panels and gilt metal mounts.

66.5in (169cm) high

£800-1,200 **SWO**

A French mahogany and gilt brass mounted vitrine, with serpentine glass panels and shelves, enclosed by a door with a shaped 'Vernis Martin' panel.

27.25in (69cm) wide

£1,200-1,500 **WW**

An early George III mahogany collector's cabinet, with crossbanded arched top above a door enclosing six short and four long drawers, on ebony-strung square section tapering legs.

17in (43cm) wide

£5,000-8,000 **L&T**

A Georgian mahogany tray top commode, with boxwood banding and ebony and box string inlay, with frieze drawer, double cupboard enclosed by oval figured panel door and square chamfered legs.

£220-200 **MAX**

A George III mahogany night commode, the square top with raised gallery above a door and drawer, on square tapering legs.

18in (46cm) wide

£400-600 **DN**

A 19thC mahogany bedside cupboard, with three-quarter gallery, on turned legs.

15.75in (39.5cm) high

£400-600 **SWO**

An Edwardian satinwood and crossbanded side table, the top with inlaid decoration over drawers with crossbanded satinwood fronts, raised on boxwood strung squared, splayed legs united by an X-frame stretcher.

£280-320 **BIG**

A small French Rococo-style commode, veneered with rose and other tropical woods, with marble top and bronze mountings, on cambered legs.

28.75in (73cm) high

£180-220 **KAU**

A pair of Italian walnut and inlaid commodes, surmounted by patera, with moulded rectangular tops over frieze drawers and cupboard doors, raised on turned fluted legs.

c1800 *30in (75cm) high*

£1,500-2,000 **FRE**

An early 19thC square mahogany commode chest, with a pair of doors over a deep drawer.

24.5in (61cm) wide

£320-380 **SWO**

A Victorian satinwood and inlaid pot cupboard, stamped "Lamb, Manchester".

15in (38.5cm) high

£220-280 **SWO**

A pair of walnut pot cupboards, converted from a Victorian washstand.

15.25in (38.5cm) high

£700-1,000 **SWO**

A pair of walnut pot cupboards, converted from a dressing table.

£800-1,200 **SWO**

A pair of mahogany pot cupboards, each with a bow front door, converted from a washstand.

£700-1,000 **SWO**

A Victorian cylindrical mahogany pot cupboard, with a grey marble top and a single door.

26.75in (68cm) high

£350-400 **SWO**

A pair of Edwardian inlaid mahogany pot cupboards, with marble tops, converted from a washstand.

£1,000-1,500 **SWO**

Two Victorian mahogany cylindrical pot cupboards, with inset marble tops over fluted sides, each with one cupboard door enclosing a shelf, raised on octagonal plinth bases.

c1880 *28.5in (71cm) high*

£700-1,000 **FRE**

A pair of Windsor fan-back armchairs, in elm, walnut and fruitwood, with traces of original paint.

c1770 *24.75in (63cm) wide*

£6,000-9,000 **RY**

A CLOSER LOOK AT AN ENGLISH WINDSOR CHAIR

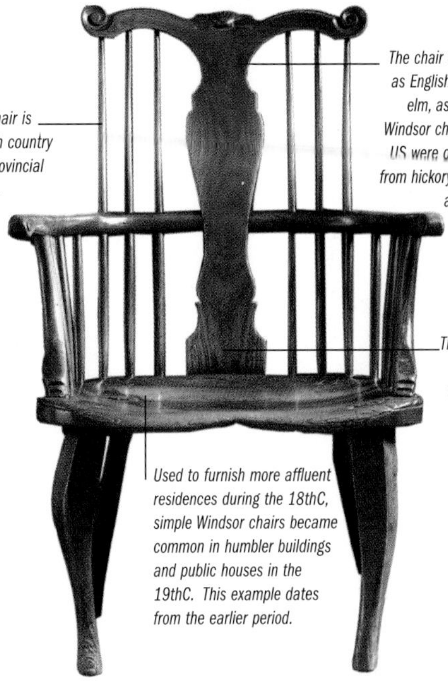

The Windsor chair is associated with country timbers and provincial manufacturers.
The chair can be identified as English from the use of elm, ash and fruitwood. Windsor chairs made in the US were often constructed from hickory, chestnut, pine, and other woods.
The presence of a splat is also typically English.
Used to furnish more affluent residences during the 18thC, simple Windsor chairs became common in humbler buildings and public houses in the 19thC. This example dates from the earlier period.

An early crooked leg English Windsor chair, with rams horn and shell-carved cresting, in fruitwood, ash and elm.

c1750 *26.25in (66.5cm) wide*

£4,000-4,500 **RY**

A George III ash and elm Windsor carver, with stick back, twin swept arms and sculpted seat, raised on turned legs united by 'H' stretcher.

£300-400 **BIG**

An early 19thC primitive ash and elm comb-back Windsor armchair.

£600-900 **SWO**

A pair of early 19thC North Country Windsor elbow chairs, with pierced splat backs and older seats, on turned supports and stretchers.

£500-700 **BRI**

A 19thC yew and elm Windsor armchair, with pierced splat and crinoline stretcher.

£600-900 **WW**

A pair of 19thC Windsor armchairs, in yew with elm seats, pierced splats and turned legs with crinoline stretchers.

£1,500-2,000 **BRI**

Two of a set of six 19thC elm low back Windsor armchairs, with pierced and shaped splats, solid seats, turned legs and crinoline stretchers, one stamped "F.Walker Rockley", another "J Spencer".

£2,200-2,800 set **MAX**

A 19thC yew Windsor armchair, with pierced splat and elm seat, with later ash back legs and stretcher.

23.5in (59.5cm) wide

£220-280 **WW**

A Philadelphia combback Windsor armchair, the arched crest with carved ears, with flaring arm supports and baluster-turned legs terminating in blunt arrow feet.

c1760

£1,500-2,000 **POOK**

A Lancaster County sackback Windsor armchair, with arched back and arms, shaped plank seat, baluster- and ring-turned legs with blunt arrow feet joined by H-stretcher, the red grained surface with yellow and green pinstriping.

c1765 *37in (92.5cm) high*

£6,000-8,000 **POOK**

A late 18thC continuous rail Windsor chair, with shaped saddle seat, on turned supports.

£1,800-2,200 **WAD**

A New England sackback Windsor armchair, with seven spindle back over oval seat supported by baluster-turned legs.

c1790

£700-1,000 **POOK**

A New England sackback Windsor armchair, with seven spindle back over oval seat, supported by baluster-turned legs.

c1790

£1,200-1,800 **POOK**

A late 18thC New England writing-arm Windsor chair, with shaped back crest and conforming drawer beneath writing surface, shaped saddle seat on splayed legs joined by stretchers, with dark green painted finish.

30.5in (76cm) high

£3,000-4,000 **SK**

A Philadelphia bowback Windsor armchair, with red painted finish and yellow pinstriping, branded "I.H." for Joseph Henzey.

c1800

£1,500-2,000 **POOK**

A set of six bowback Windsor side chairs, in hickory, yellow pine, and maple, each with a bowed crest, seven spindles, shaped seats and splayed bamboo-turned legs and stretchers, with old finish.

c1805 *38in (95cm) high*

£8,000-12,000 **SK**

A Connecticut Windsor combback armchair, with seven spindles, scalloped seat, and bamboo-turned legs joined by stretchers, stamped "E. Tracy".

£1,200-1,800 **POOK**

A small Windsor settee, with birdcage back and bamboo-turned legs joined by stretchers.

c1825 *47in (117.5cm) wide*

£3,000-4,000 **POOK**

A Massachusetts maple and ash great chair, with boldly turned finials, shaped splats and rush seat, linked by turned stretchers.

c1690s *42.75in (108.5cm) high*

£2,200-2,800 **SK**

A late 18thC Delaware Valley maple slatback armchair, with tapering turned stiles flanking five arched concave slats, with shaped arms continuing to legs and bulbous turned feet with wooden wheels, joined by ring-turned stretchers, with black-painted finish over salmon and green.

50in (127cm) high

£1,500-2,000 **SK**

An early 19thC Pennsylvanian ladderback armchair, with ball finials to stiles, five arched slats, shaped arms on turned posts with double turned stretchers and stained rush seat, refinished.

£800-1,200 **FRE**

Two of set of eight 19thC harlequin ash ladderback side chairs, with rush seats.

£1,200-1,800 set **WW**

Two of a set of eight 19thC Lancashire ash spindle back dining chairs, the shaped top rails with ears, with rush seats on turned club legs.

24.5in (62cm) wide

£1,500-2,000 set **WW**

Two of a set of six 19thC harlequin ash and alder side chairs, with shape top rails above spindles and rush seats with turned legs and stretchers.

18.5in (47cm) wide

£1,200-1,800 set **WW**

A Canadian pine rocking chair, with typical Quebec 'angel wing' back splats and cat gut seat.

Plain pine Canadian rockers like this are earlier and less common than painted examples, which were made during the 1870s and later.

c1850 *39.75in (101cm) high*

£400-600 **RAON**

A 17thC oak open armchair, with serpentine top rail above a twin fielded panel back, shaped arms, baluster-turned supports, planked seat and conforming legs with stretchers.

24.25in (61.5cm) wide

£1,000-1,500 **WW**

A late 17thC North Country high back chair, with arched top rail and back panel carved with a tulip, flowers and leaves, side columns with square pyramid finials, tray seat and turned legs.

£2,000-2,500 **MAX**

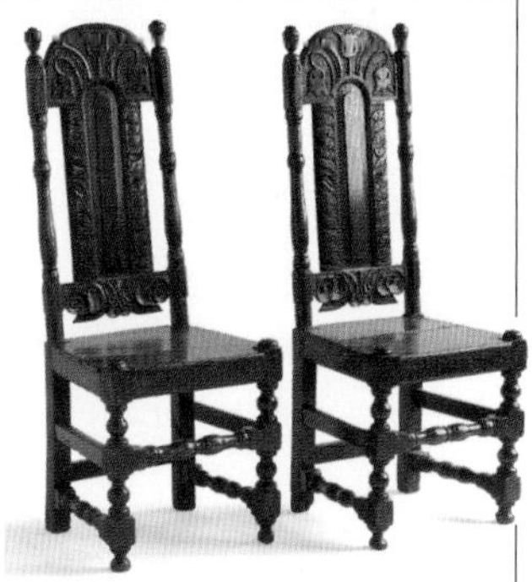

A pair of 18thC oak side chairs, with arched tulip-carved crests, panelled backs, turned supports and finials, wooden seats and turned legs with stretchers.

£4,000-6,000 **LFA**

A set of four New England Queen Anne side chairs, each with carved yoked crest rail over moulded stiles enclosing vaseiform splats, raised on vase- and block-turned legs joined by double stretchers.

£3,000-4,000 **FRE**

A set of six late 18thC Irish Queen Anne oak dining chairs, with shell-carved crests, solid splats, compass seats, and cabriole front legs with shell-carved knees terminating in pad feet and joined by serpentine stretchers.

£5,000-7,000 **POOK**

ENGLISH PATTERN BOOKS

- Published to attract wealthy clients and introduce new styles to the public, illustrated 18thC pattern books greatly influenced furniture design of the period.
- Thomas Chippendale's "The Gentleman and Cabinet-Maker's Director" (1754) was the first pattern book to concentrate solely on furniture. Chippendale chairs were widely emulated.
- George Hepplewhite's "The Cabinet-Maker and Upholsters Guide" (1788) was published posthumously. His fame is purely a result of his book and the surviving pieces made in his style: no furniture has been directly attributed to him.
- Thomas Sheraton's "The Cabinet Dictionary" (1803) was particularly detailed in its instructions and measurements.
- William Ince and John Mayhew's "The Universal System of Household Furniture" (1759-62) and Thomas Shearer's "The Cabinet-Maker's London Book of Prices" were also influential.
- Other cabinet-makers were encouraged to recreate and modify patterns found in these books, leading to the creation of furniture in the style of the author.

A Boston Queen Anne walnut side chair, with spooned crest rail above a vasiform splat and raked chamfered stiles, with balloon slip upholstered seat, on frontal cabriole legs ending in pad feet.

c1750 *40in (101.5cm) high*

£3,500-4,500 **SK**

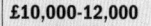

A pair of Pennsylvania Queen Anne walnut dining chairs, each with shell-carved Cupid's bow crest and vasiform splat, over trapezoidal slip seats supported by cabriole legs terminating in trifid feet.

c1760

£10,000-12,000 **POOK**

Two of a set of eight Queen Anne style walnut dining chairs, with scroll backs, burr walnut vase splats, drop-in leather squab seats and cabriole legs with pad feet, joined by turned and blocked H-stretchers .

£2,200-2,800 set **L&T**

Two of a set of five Victorian walnut Queen Anne-style dining chairs, with leaf-carved and pierced scrolling top rails above corresponding splats, stuffover seats, carved cabriole legs and pad feet.

£800-1,200 set **L&T**

A set of six early 20thC Queen Anne-style walnut dining chairs, including two armchairs, with vasiform splats and drop-in seats, raised on shell-carved cabriole legs terminating in claw and ball feet.

£1,500-2,000 **FRE**

A George III Chippendale design mahogany single chair, with carved vertical splat back and overstuffed seat.

£100-200 **SWO**

A Philadelphia Chippendale carved mahogany side chair, attributed to Daniel Trotter, with four pierced splats and central carved plume ornament, moulded chamfered legs with H-stretcher, restored.

Daniel Trotter (1747-1800) is the Philadelphia crafstman most closely associated with Chippendale-style chairs.

c1780

£2,500-3,000 **FRE**

A set of eight New England Chippendale cherry dining chairs, each with a serpentine crest, above pierced splats and trapezoidal slip seats supported by square moulded edge legs joined by stretchers.

c1780

£2,000-3,000 **POOK**

A pair of late 18thC Philadelphia Chippendale mahogany side chairs, with moulded serpentine crests carved with flowers and vines above tapering pierced splats, on moulded trapezoidal seats and straight moulded legs.

£500-700 FRE

LEFT: A late 18thC New York Chippendale mahogany side chair, with serpentine crest rail above pierced splat and moulded trapezoidal seat, shaped stretchers and cabriole legs ending in ball and claw feet.

£280-320 FRE

RIGHT: A late 18thC New York Chippendale mahogany side chair, with serpentine crest rail above pierced splat and trapezoidal seat, the cabriole legs ending in ball and claw feet, restored.

£350-400 FRE

A set of six late 18thC Massachusetts Chippendale side chairs, with serpentine crest rails above vasiform heart-pierced splats and raked stiles on trapezoidal rush seats and square beaded legs joined by stretchers, with brown grain-painted finish.

37.75in (94cm) high

£5,000-6,000 SK

Two of a set of eight Victorian Chippendale-style mahogany dining chairs, with yoked toprails centred by shell-carving above pierced vasiform splats, red leather upholstered seats and floral carved cabriole legs with dolphin's head feet.

£8,000-10,000 set L&T

A late 19thC Canadian birch side chair, in the Chippendale manner, with pierced vasiform back splat, trap seat and chamfered square supports.

£1,000-1,500 WAD

One of a set of six early 20thC Chippendale-style mahogany dining chairs, with carved Cupid's bow top rails, pierced vase splats, drop-in seats in brown hide, carved cabriole legs and hairy paw feet.

£700-1,000 set MAX

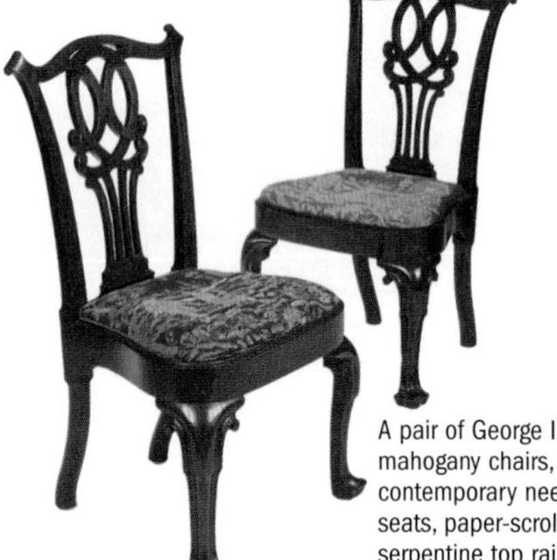

A pair of George II mahogany chairs, with contemporary needlework seats, paper-scrolled serpentine top rails, pierced interlaced splats, cabriole legs and shaped toes.

£4,000-6,000 L&T

A mid-18thC George III side chair, with pierced vasiform splat, stuffed overseat and acanthus-carved cabriole legs terminating in pad feet.

£400-600 FRE

A pair of George III mahogany dining chairs, with pierced vasiform splats, raised on cabriole legs.

£300-400 SWO

Two of a set of eight 19thC mahogany George III-style dining chairs, with quatrefoil pierced top rails, Gothic arched pierced splats, drop-in seats and square section chamfered legs joined by H-stretchers.

£2,000-3,000 set L&T

LEFT: One of a set of six 19thC George III-style mahogany dining chairs, with carved and pierced vasiform splats, drop-in seats, cabriole legs and ball and claw feet.

£5,000-7,000 set L&T

RIGHT: One of a set of six 19thC George III-style mahogany dining chairs, with pierced interlaced splats, stuffover seats and square section chamfered legs joined by H-stretchers.

£2,000-3,000 set L&T

Two of a set of 16 Edwardian mahogany dining chairs, in the mid-18thC style with drop-in seats and front cabriole legs.

These chairs are from the boardroom of the former office premises of The Scotsman newspaper, in Edinburgh.

£4,000-6,000 set L&T

Two of a set of 12 carved mahogany dining chairs, in mid-18thC style, with shell-carved and pierced splat backs with eagle's head top rails, stuff-over seats and acanthus-capped cabriole legs with claw and ball feet.

24.5in (62cm) wide

£2,500-3,000 set WW

Two of a set of six Hepplewhite-style mahogany dining chairs, with carved shield-shaped backs and moulded square tapering legs.

£600-900 set SWO

A set of six George III shield back dining chairs, with vasiform splats carved with wheatsheafs and drapery, serpentine seats and fluted square tapered legs.

c1780

£400-500 FRE

Two of a set of six oak Hepplewhite period dining chairs, with square backs, vertical reeded splats and drop-in seats, the legs united with H-stretchers.

£600-900 set SWO

Two of a set of 10 George III mahogany dining chairs, with later arms, curved spindle backs, upholstered serpentine seats and square tapering moulded legs linked by stretchers.

£2,000-3,000 set L&T

A set of eight Maryland Federal side chairs and two armchairs, the shield backs outlined with beaded edges above pierced splats with scrolling and ribbon devices, minor restoration.

c1795 *37.75in (96cm) high*

£12,000-18,000 SK

A set of six Philadelphia Federal mahogany shield back dining chairs, each with a pierced and fluted splat with central floral carved cartouche, above a slip seat, supported by square tapering moulded legs joined by stretchers.

c1800 *38.75in (97cm) high*

£5,000-7,000 POOK

A set of eight Federal cherry side chairs, probably Massachusetts, with moulded shield backs above over-upholstered seats with serpentine front rails, on moulded square tapering legs joined by H-stretchers.

c1800 *36.5in (91cm) high*

£7,000-10,000 SK

A set of three Federal mahogany side chairs, attributed to Thomas Seymour of Boston, the square backs inlaid with circles, with reeded stiles and carved leaves above the over-upholstered seats, on turned and tapering reeded legs.

c1810 *34.5in (87.5cm) high*

£25,000-30,000 SK

A set of eight mid-Atlantic Federal dining chairs, each with serpentine seat rails and square tapering moulded legs.

c1810

£6,000-9,000 POOK

A set of six Philadelphia Classical mahogany carved scrollback side chairs, with reeded and panelled crests above acanthus- and rosette-carved splats joining moulded stiles, on Grecian-style front legs.

c1815 *32in (80cm) high*

£1,800-2,200 **SK**

A set of six Massachusetts Federal mahogany dining chairs, in the manner of Samuel McIntire, each with straight crest above an acanthus-carved splat flanked by scrolled arms over a trapezoidal slip seat supported by turned and foliated carved legs, with overall line inlay.

c1825

£3,000-4,000 **POOK**

Two of a set of 16 19thC mahogany dining chairs, with shaped top rails carved with foliage, draped urn backs, bow front seats and square tapering legs terminating in spade feet.

These chairs come form the Dining Hall at Winchester College in Hampshire.

£6,000-9,000 set **WW**

Two of a set of 12 19thC mahogany dining chairs, with vertical bar backs inlaid with ebonized stringing, stuffover seats and reeded tapering legs, stamped "MB" and with ivorene labels for "Trapnell & Gane, 38-40 College Green Bristol".

£6,000-9,000 set **WW**

Two of a set of 14 Scottish mahogany brander back chairs, with moulded backs, stuffover horsehair seats and square section tapering legs joined by H-stretchers, some with label for "Hamilton Sundrum".

£6,000-8,000 set **L&T**

Two of a set of eight early 19thC mahogany dining chairs, the curved top rails with rosewood banding, with open bar backs, drop-in seats and sabre legs.

20.5in (52cm) wide

£2,500-3,000 set **WW**

Two of a set of eight Regency mahogany dining chairs, with bar backs, drop-in seats and turned and reeded front legs.

£1,500-£2,000 set **SWO**

Two of a set of six Regency mahogany dining chairs, possibly Colonial, with scroll-carved top rails above entablature panels and drop-in seats, on reeded sabre legs.

£5,000-7,000 set **L&T**

Two of a set of 10 Regency mahogany dining chairs, with acanthus-carved and gadrooned tablet toprails with central diamond lattice panels, similar horizontal splats and upholstered seats on spirally reeded and ring-turned tapering legs.

£5,000-8,000 set **L&T**

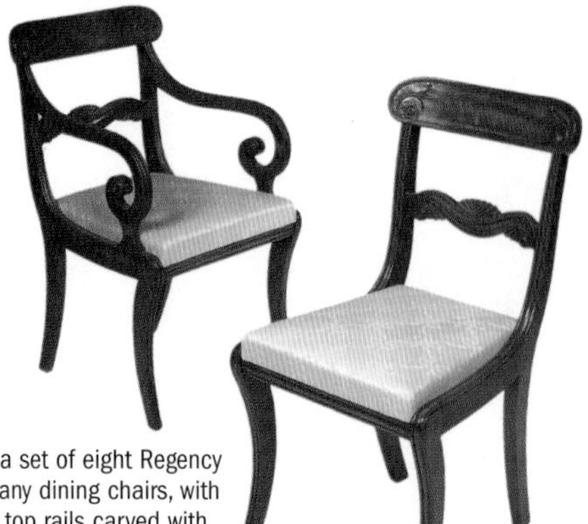

Two of a set of eight Regency mahogany dining chairs, with curved top rails carved with scrolling foliage, reeded uprights, scroll carved mid-rails and drop-in seats on moulded sabre legs.

£8,000-12,000 set **L&T**

Two of a set of eight Regency mahogany dining chairs, with scroll-carved panelled top rails, reeded uprights, shaped and gadrooned mid-rails and drop-in seats, on reeded sabre legs.

£8,000-12,000 set **L&T**

Two of a set of four Regency mahogany dining chairs, the top rails with gadrooned crestings, with carved leaf and flower bars, drop-in seats and sabre legs.

£400-600 set **SWO**

Two of a set of seven Regency mahogany dining chairs, with drapery-carved yokes, reeded mid-rails centred by tablets, drop-in seats and moulded sabre legs.

£1,000-1,500 set **L&T**

A set of four Irish Regency mahogany dining chairs, the top rails with gadrooned crestings, with carved leaf and flower bars, drop-in seats on sabre legs.

£400-600 **SWO**

Two of a set of six George IV simulated rosewood side chairs, inlaid with brass marquetry, with veneered bar backs, shaped and carved horizontal splats, caned seats and turned and ribbed tapering legs.

17.5in (44.5cm) wide

£1,000-1,500 set **WW**

One of a set of six Regency rosewood dining chairs, with carved foliate crest rail, moulded and scrolled uprights and splat and drop-in seat, raised on sabre forelegs.

£800-1,200 set **BIG**

A set of six Gillows oak chairs, after Pugin's design for the Houses of Parliament, re-upholstered in red leather, with chamfered frames, stamped "Gillows, Lancaster".

£3,000-5,000 **SWO**

Two of a set of six 19thC satinwood dining chairs, of Neo-classical style, with rosette- and leaf-carved top rails, Vitruvian scroll frieze and turned and fluted legs terminating in toupie feet.

£2,200-2,800 set **L&T**

One of a set of six Victorian walnut balloon back dining chairs, with carved pierced splat, over-stuffed seat of embossed red velvet and cabriole legs.

£700-1,000 set **MAX**

A set of six late 19thC Renaissance Revival carved walnut chairs, by Victor Aimone, with carved backs surmounted by grotesque mask motifs and centred by oval figural panels, raised on carved square tapered legs joined by H-stretchers and terminating in bun feet, signed "V. Aimone".

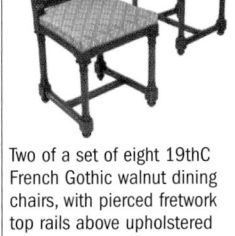

£1,500-2,000 **FRE**

Two of a set of eight 19thC French Gothic walnut dining chairs, with pierced fretwork top rails above upholstered panels and arcaded frieze, raised on turned legs with leaf-carved capitals terminating in turned and blocked feet.

£4,000-6,000 set **L&T**

A pair of 19thC Dutch mahogany and marquetry chairs, inlaid with scrolling foliage and feather banding, with padded square backs and stuffed overseats, raised on sabre legs.

£500-700 **FRE**

A matched pair of George II elm open armchairs, with straight top rails, pierced splats, outscrolled arms and stuffover nailed leather seats, on square section legs joined by stretchers.

£1,000-1,500 **L&T**

A George III mahogany umbrella-back armchair, in the French Hepplewhite taste, with a central floral medallion, crestrail carved with bellflowers, wide caned seat with cushion, the seat rail with centrally carved trophy, on cabriole legs terminating in trifid pad feet.

c1785 *36in (90cm) high*

£800-1,200 **FRE**

A George III mahogany spindle back open armchair, with pierced shaped top rail, scroll arms, stuffover seat and moulded square chamfered legs with scroll brackets.

26in (66cm) wide

£300-400 **WW**

A George III chestnut elbow chair, in the manner of Robert Manwaring, with shaped and pierced crest, five shaped upright rails, padded serpentine seat and straight legs with stretchers.

£1,500-2,000 **LFA**

One of a pair of George III mahogany elbow chairs, with leaf-carved crest, pierced splat and a drop-in seat, the shaped arms with reeded supports, on blind fret-carved legs.

24.5in (62cm) wide

£2,200-2,800 pair **DN**

A George III painted elbow chair, with pierced horizontal back splats and tapering legs.

£200-300 **SWO**

Two of a set of four Regency open armchairs, decorated in floral polychrome, with tablet top rails above pierced bars, caned bowfront seats and turned tapering legs.

21.5in (54.5cm) wide

£1,500-2,000 set **WW**

A Regency mahogany elbow chair, with carved top rail, scrolled splat and arms, raised on sabre legs.

£180-220 **SWO**

A walnut upholstered open armchair, in the Queen Anne style, on carved cabriole legs.

£350-400 **SWO**

A late 19thC Louis XV-style walnut swivel cane bergère, with curved back, padded scroll arms and loose cushion seat upholstered in green leather, raised on moulded cabriole legs.

£800-1,200 **FRE**

An early 20thC George I-style mahogany and leather upholstered cock-fighting chair, covered in studded red leather, with shapes arm rest, adjustable writing surface and balloon-shaped seat, raised on cabriole legs united by turned stretchers.

£1,200-1,800 **FRE**

A George II mahogany armchair, with rectangular upholstered stepped back, stuffover seat, open padded arms with fluted curved supports and cabriole legs with applied brass blocks and castors.

£1,800-2,200 **L&T**

A mahogany Gainsborough armchair, in the 18thC style, with carved scroll arms and cabriole legs.

£800-1,200 **SWO**

A George III mahogany Gainsborough chair, with floral upholstery, downswept arm supports, square legs and turned stretchers.

£500-800 **SWO**

A George III mahogany and upholstered open armchair, in the French Hepplewhite manner, with shaped back, padded scroll arms and stuffover seat upholstered in distressed gold fabric, raised on moulded cabriole legs.

c1785

£400-600 **FRE**

A George III-style Gainsborough open armchair, with outswept padded arms, on cabriole legs terminating in ball-and-claw feet.

£800-1,200 **SWO**

A pair of early 20thC George III-style mahogany and upholstered armchairs, with square backs, padded acanthus-carved outswept scroll arms, stuffed overseats and carved cabriole legs terminating in ball and claw feet.

£1,800-2,200 **FRE**

A Regency adjustable library armchair, with loose buttoned squab cushion, brass adjusters and pull-out upholstered footstool, raised on cross supports with pot castors.

£1,000-1,500 L&T

A Regency mahogany cane-sided bergère chair, with scroll tablet top rail and leather button cushion, on reeded front supports and castors.

£1,000-1,500 SWO

A CLOSER LOOK AT A PAIR OF REGENCY BERGÈRES

This style of armchair, with its caned back and seat, was introduced in the early 19thC and was often used in libraries.

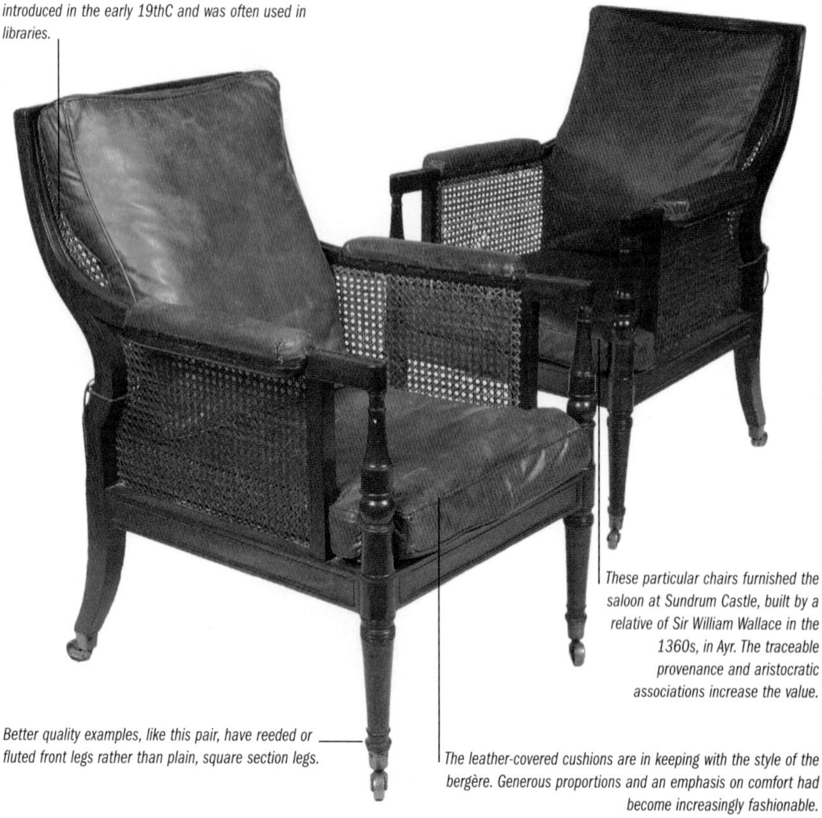

These particular chairs furnished the saloon at Sundrum Castle, built by a relative of Sir William Wallace in the 1360s, in Ayr. The traceable provenance and aristocratic associations increase the value.

Better quality examples, like this pair, have reeded or fluted front legs rather than plain, square section legs.

The leather-covered cushions are in keeping with the style of the bergère. Generous proportions and an emphasis on comfort had become increasingly fashionable.

A pair of Regency mahogany bergère armchairs, with caned backs and seats and turned terminals extending into legs, upholstered in leather.

£20,000-25,000 L&T

A Regency mahogany library chair, with plain frame and caned seat, back and sides, with baluster-turned details, on brass caps and castors.

£700-1,000 SWO

A Massachusetts Federal inlaid mahogany chair, the upholstered back with serpentine crest above serpentine arms on string-inlaid concave supports, with vase- and ring-turned tapering legs, restored.

c1805 *46in (115cm) high*

£7,000-10,000 SK

A 19thC French mahogany Empire armchair, the armrests carved with Egyptian sphinx, on two sabre legs and two square legs terminating in claw feet, upholstered in blue fabric.

35.25in (88cm) high

£1,000-1,500 KAU

A French Empire upholstered armchair, with carved back and scrolled arm fronts, on shaped profile legs.

£350-450 SWO

A 19thC carved gilt wood elbow chair, with cartouche-shaped back, velvet upholstery and scrolled front supports.

£500-700 **SWO**

A 19thC Continental ash open armchair, with scrolled arms, supports and stretchers.

£700-1,000 **SWO**

A William IV mahogany library chair, with padded and upholstered back, seat and arms.

£600-900 **SWO**

A William IV mahogany adjustable armchair, with upholstered scroll-over back, padded open scroll arms, hinged reclining and foot rest mechanisms, raised on turned front legs with leaf claspings and brass castors, stamped "G. Minter, 33 Garrard Street, Soho W.R. patent No. 672".

£700-1,000 **L&T**

A William IV mahogany library chair, with pierced and carved splat, upholstered in green buttoned leather.

£700-1,000 **SWO**

An early Victorian carved mahogany library armchair, with pierced and carved splat and later brass studded leather upholstery.

£300-400 **WW**

A Victorian mahogany and beech desk chair, with horseshoe arms, raised on turned and tapered carved and fluted forelegs with castors, upholstered in yellow velour.

£120-180 **BIG**

A Victorian mahogany Dawes patent reclining armchair, upholstered in red buttoned leather.

£1,500-2,000 **SWO**

A Victorian mahogany adjustable armchair, with two detachable wings, reclining action and pull-out foot stool, upholstered in brown leather.

£400-600 **SWO**

An early 18thC wing armchair, on walnut cabriole legs with pad feet, upholstered with verdure-type tapestry with a matching cushion.

£3,000-5,000 **LFA**

An American Queen Anne walnut easy chair, the straight cresting above shaped sides continuing to outward-scrolling arms, all on four cabriole legs with shaped knee returns, continuing to pad feet on platforms.

c1750 *49in (122.5cm) high*

£5,000-6,000 **SK**

A late 19thC Louis XV-style mahogany and gilt bronze mounted bergère, in the manner of Francois Linke, with shaped padded back and stuff-over seat, on square tapered legs terminating in sabots, upholstered in foliate green fabric.

£1,000-1,500 **FRE**

A walnut desk chair, profusely carved in the 18thC style, with cabriole front legs and ball and claw feet.

£600-900 **SWO**

A Regency library chair, with carved and turned mahogany arm supports and legs, with a pull-out foot rest.

£1,200-1,800 **SWO**

A George IV mahogany library armchair, with upholstered tub-shaped back, 'U'-shaped arm facings with roundels, panelled seat rail and ring-turned tapering legs, with brass terminals and castors.

38.25in (97cm) high

£800-1,200 **DN**

A George IV white painted and parcel-gilt armchair, in the manner of George Smith, the arm facings carved with stylized flowers, on turned, carved legs with brass terminals and castors.

35.75in (90.5cm) high

£2,200-2,800 **DN**

A pair of Howard & Sons club armchairs, with outscrolled back and lower arms, autograph lining fabric and loose covers by Colefax & Fowler.

£4,000-6,000 **L&T**

A Victorian rosewood library armchair, with scrolled carved arms, re-upholstered in red leather.

£400-600 **SWO**

A pair of 17thC Italian sgabello chairs, with elaborate shaped backs and supports.

£1,500-2,000 **FRE**

A pair of George III mahogany hall chairs, with shaped and moulded backs above carved seats with circular moulding, raised on scrolling cut-out supports linked by curved stretchers.

£1,500-2,000 **L&T**

A 19thC Micmac British wooden chair, decorated with porcupine quill work, from Nova Scotia, Canada.

17in (43cm) wide

£2,000-3,000 **WJT**

A matched pair of George III fruitwood and mahogany corner armchairs, with pierced splats and similar turned supports, with drop- in seats on square legs united by X-stretchers.

£1,000-1,500 **WW**

A pair of 19thC mahogany corner armchairs, with carved and moulded arms, above vasiform splats and turned and moulded uprights, the drop-in seats raised on moulded cabriole legs terminating in carved paw feet, linked by cross stretchers.

£1,000-1,500 **L&T**

An early 20thC George III-style hall porter's chair, with two apron cupboard doors, upholstered in buttoned red leather.

68in (179cm) high

£2,200-2,800 **FRE**

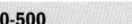

A 19thC child's mahogany lambing chair.

The lambing chair is an example of regional vernacular furniture popular in Lancashire and Yorkshire c1750-1850.

£300-500 **SWO**

An Edwardian walnut revolving desk chair, with cabriole legs terminating in ball feet and united by an X-stretcher.

£400-600 **SWO**

A Victorian rosewood harpists chair, with shaped back, shell- and scroll-carved splat and tripod base, upholstered in leather.

£300-350 **SWO**

A 19thC Moorish olive wood and bone Savonarola chair, inlaid with parquetry and chevron banding, with stylized foliage and a central fleur-de-lys motif.

£400-600 **FRE**

An early 20thC painted advertising bench, with shaped arms and front legs, the back rest pierced with inscription "Star Brand Shoes Are Better".

£320-380 FRE

A 20thC Black Forest bear bench, naturalistically carved with two bears depicted holding the seat.

60in (150cm) wide

£500-700 KAU

Part of a Louis XVI five-piece parlour suite, comprising a settee, a pair of fauteuils and a pair of single chairs, carved and gilt wood, surmounted by a flambeau and quiver, with acanthus-scrolled arms.

£800-1,200 set SWO

A Philadelphia or Baltimore Chippendale mahogany sofa, with arched back over scrolled arms and serpentine front seat supported by square legs joined by stretchers.

c1780 *92in (230cm) wide*

£2,500-3,000 POOK

An early Canadian Chippendale settee, with rolled arms and fluted square supports.

c1800 *82in (208.5cm) wide*

£2,800-3,200 WAD

A Massachusetts Federal mahogany inlaid sofa, with arched back, reeded handholds on vase- and ring-turned swelled and reeded supports and similar tapering legs.

c1810 *79in (197.5cm) wide*

£7,000-10,000 SK

A mid-Atlantic States Sheraton mahogany sofa, with straight crest over scrolled arms supported by turned and reeded legs.

c1825 *76in (190cm) wide*

£1,800-2,200 POOK

An Empire mahogany square sofa, with ogee-moulded crest rail continuing to scrolling arms with columnar supports, on tapering feet joined by ogee-moulded seat rail, damaged.

84in (213.5cm) wide

£2,000-2,500 FRE

A carved Philadelphia Classical mahogany sofa, with scrolled crest rail flanked with cornucopia above upholstered back and seat enclosed by carved arms, raised on claw feet with cornucopia supports.

c1830 *36in (91.5cm) high*

£600-800 FRE

A William IV rosewood show frame settee, carved with scrolling leaves, the 'S'-shaped arms headed with flowerhead paterae.

£600-900 **SWO**

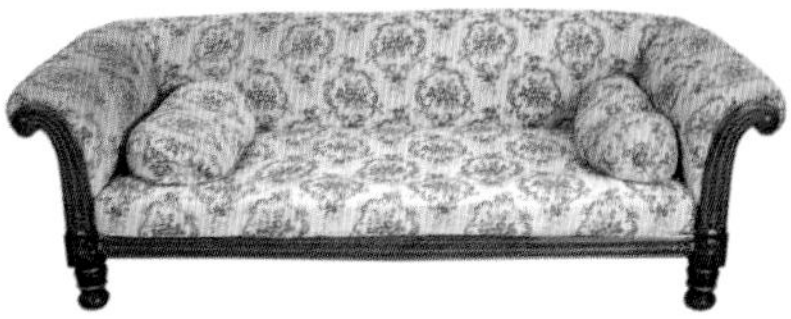

An early 19thC rosewood settee, with scroll ends, incised parcel gilt decoration and turned legs.

90.5in (226cm) wide

£3,000-4,000 **SWO**

A CLOSER LOOK AT A NEOCLASSICAL BRASS INLAID SETTEE

During the early 19thC Russia was experiencing a great recovery in economy and the arts. This sofa dates from this exciting time for the decorative arts.

Like other European countries, Russia was influenced by the French Empire style. The patera brass inlay and lyre-shaped arms are typical of the Russian interpretation of the style.

After 1820, revivalist styles such as Neo-Gothic and Rococo became fashionable. The influences of various design movements are evident in the shape of this sofa.

The sofa is in good condition.

A Neoclassical brass inlaid settee, probably Russian, with removable upholstered back, rosewood top rail with scroll and patera brass inlay, lyre-shaped arms faced with ebony and conforming foliate inlay, on brass and ebony inlaid conical feet.

c1830 *94in (239cm) wide*

£5,000-6,000 **FRE**

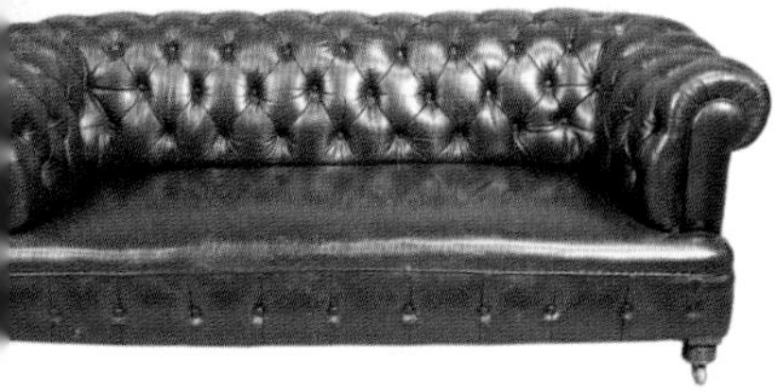

A Victorian Chesterfield sofa, upholstered in buttoned leather.

£500-700 **SWO**

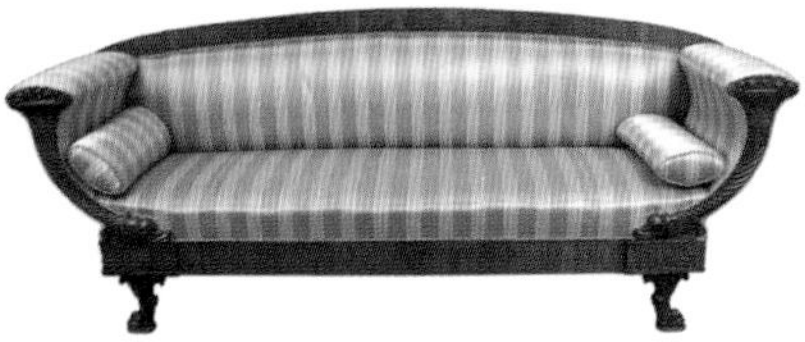

A 19thC Swedish walnut upholstered sofa, of large proportions, with caned scrolled arms, stuff-over seat and lion's paw feet.

96in (244cm) wide

£1,500-2,000 **SWO**

A late 19thC Hepplewhite-style triple chair back mahogany settee, the arched backs with bellflower carved pierced splats, with scroll arms and stuffover seat, raised on square splayed legs.

65in (165cm) wide

£1,000-1,500 **FRE**

An Edwardian inlaid mahogany settee.

48in (122cm) wide

£600-900 **SWO**

Part of a 19thC French Empire-style ameublement comprising four armchairs, a bench and a table, with mahogany veneer and upholstered seats and backs, decorated with female bronze busts.

table 32in (80cm) diam

£3,000-4,000 set **KAU**

A French walnut canapé sofa, with rectangular upholstered back, scrolled arms and curved square tapering legs.

72in (180cm) wide

£500-800 **SWO**

A Pennsylvania William & Mary cherry daybed, with scalloped crest rail over three vasiform splats and rush seat, supported by boldly turned ring and baluster legs and stretchers.

c1740 *67in (167.5cm) wide*

£1,800-2,200 **POOK**

A late Victorian Louis XV-style duchesse armchair, with moulded giltwood frame enclosing buttoned silk upholstery, raised on carved and moulded cabriole legs.

£2,000-3,000 **L&T**

A French Louis XVI walnut récamiere, on eight legs with upholstered seat.

c1790 *75.5in (189cm) wide*

£800-1,200 **KAU**

A Regency mahogany and brass inlaid chaise longue, decorated with scrolled motifs and raised on swept legs with brass caps and castors.

82in (205cm) wide

£2,800-3,200 **SWO**

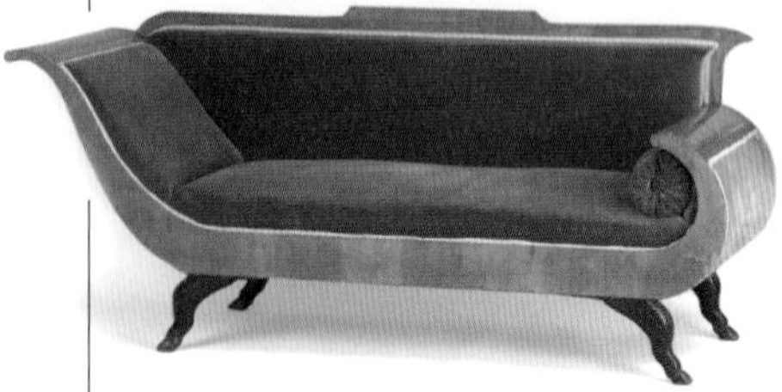

An early 19thC Biedermeier maple and burl veneer récamiere, with a stepped and arched crest, scrolling arms with burl panels, supported by ebonized animal-form legs terminating in hoof feet.

83in (210cm) wide

£500-700 **POOK**

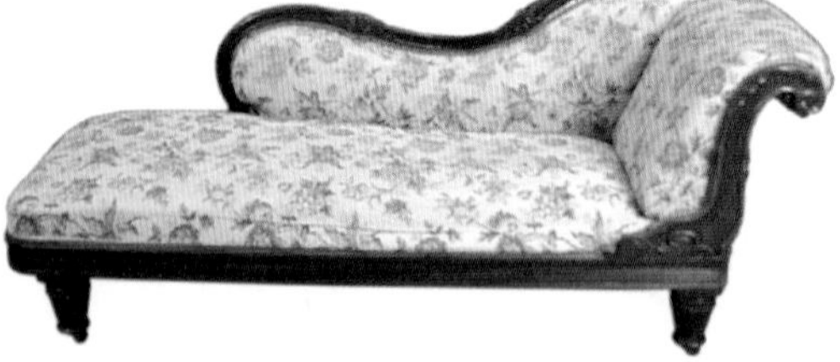

An early Victorian rosewood chaise longue, with shaped back and carved decoration on carved and turned legs.

£500-800 **SWO**

A Victorian oak framed day bed, with tan leather upholstery and fold down end.

£600-900 **SWO**

A George III mahogany window seat, with scrolled, reeded supports applied with roundels and padded seat and sides, on square tapering legs and block feet.

45.25in (115cm) wide

£1,200-1,800 **DN**

A pair of French Empire-style giltwood X-frame stools, with dog's head finials and striped and tasselled upholstery.

£1,200-1,800 **FRE**

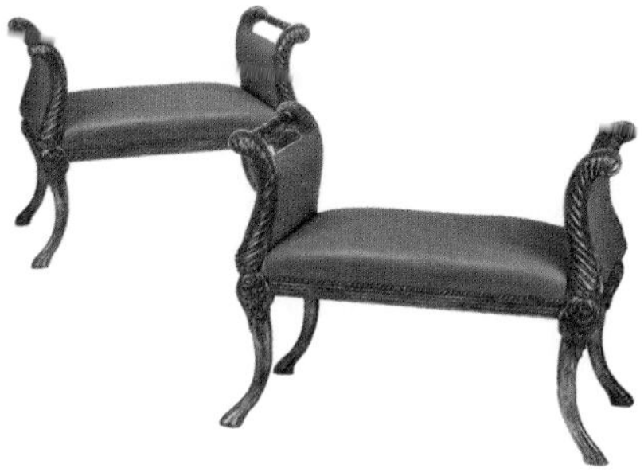

A pair of Neoclassical-style gilt wood stools, with rope-twist scroll arms and seat, raised on cabriole legs with claw feet, upholstered in beige leatherette

£700-1,000 **FRE**

A Classical mahogany carved window seat, possibly Pennsylvania, with vase- and ring-turned spiral-carved crest rails continuing to sabre legs, the horizontal splats with central shaped tablets flanked by scroll devices, and upholstered slip seat.

c1820 *41in (102.5cm) wide*

£3,000-4,000 **SK**

A set of three 19thC Italian Rococo-style carved giltwood stools, with openwork foliate scroll-carved friezes, raised on S-scroll legs united by ornate pierced shell- and scroll-carved stretchers.

36in (90om) wide

£6,000-8,000 **FRE**

A pair of New York mahogany carved Classical ottomans, the rectangular over-upholstered seats on beaded frames and Grecian cross-legs centred with carved rosettes.

c1820 *22.25in (55.5cm) wide*

£2,000-3,000 **SK**

A large Victorian walnut stool, raised on carved cabriole legs.

43.25in (110cm) high

£1,500-2,000 **SWO**

An Edwardian mahogany duet stool.

43.75in (111cm) wide

£500-700 **SWO**

An oak joined stool, with moulded edge seat, on turned legs.

£1,000-1,500 **SWO**

A Canadian carved birch miniature stool, possibly a gout stool.

c1890 *9.75in (25cm) wide*

£50-80 **ING**

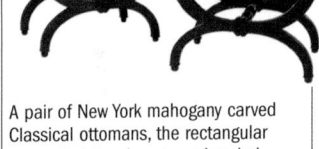

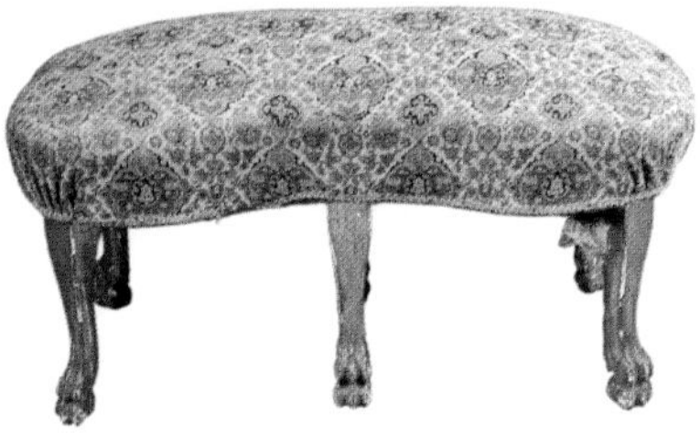

An early 20thC upholstered stool, with waisted seat on six gilt wood legs with carved hairy paw feet.

44.75in (112cm) long

£400-600 **SWO**

A small 17thC oak six plank coffer, with a carved front.

39.5in (99cm) wide

£500-700 **SWO**

A 17thC oak coffer, with a plain moulded lid over a two panel carved front.

38.25in (97cm) wide

£500-700 **SWO**

A 17thC oak coffer, with a carved three panel front.

£500-700 **SWO**

A late 17thC oak coffer, with a moulded edge over a carved frame and panels.

44in (112cm) wide

£500-700 **SWO**

A late 17thC oak coffer, the four panelled top over three carved panels.

50.5in (128cm) wide

£700-1,000 **SWO**

A late 17thC oak three panel coffer, with a carved and moulded frame.

46.75in (119cm) wide

£1,000-1,500 **SWO**

An 18thC oak panelled coffer, of narrow proportions, on high stile legs.

42in (106.5cm) wide

£600-900 **SWO**

A late 17thC Northern Italian walnut cassone, the lift-lid opening to a velvet lined insert, above a carved arcaded case with door, supported by animal paw feet.

52.5in (131cm) wide

£1,500-2,000 **POOK**

A Southern German pine model chest, painted, with five carved fields, with vases and fruiting vines, dated, original lock and key.

c1675 *18in (45cm) wide*

£600-900 **KAU**

A 17thC small Italian walnut cassone, the moulded hinged lid enclosing a void interior, over panelled sides over a gadrooned apron, raised on a plinth base with paw feet.

38in (96.5cm) wide

£700-1,000 **FRE**

A Connecticut River carved pine board chest, with moulded edges and original cleats overhanging crease-moulded nailed case, the sides with cut-out scalloped design, the front corners chip-carved, with original red finish.

c1700 *49in (124.5cm) wide*

£12,000-15,000 **SK**

A Pennsylvania or Virginia painted pine dower chest, the moulded lid with clover-shaped panels with tulips over a dovetail case, all on an ochre stippled ground supported by short bracket feet, inscribed "ANN 1772".

48.5in (121cm) wide

£7,000-10,000 **POOK**

A Pennsylvania blanket chest, with moulded rectangular hinged lid painted red and decorated with a shaped reserve enclosing birds and an urn with flowers in black, red and white, the base inscribed "Rosina Beutelmann 1788".

Rosina Beutelmann was born in 1756 in Springfield, Bucks County, the child of Elias and Anna Maria Beutelmann.

£4,000-5,000 **FRE**

A Pennsylvania dower chest, the front with a central cartouche surrounded by trailing vines and tulips, flanked by two arched panels with potted floral trees, the ends with similar panels, resting on straight bracket feet, inscribed "Magthalena Knaussin".

c1800 *48in (120cm) wide*

£12,000-15,000 **POOK**

A Pennsylvania painted pine dower chest, with moulded top over a case with central cartouche, resting on bold ogee bracket feet, inscribed "Veronica Detweiler 1806".

1806 *47in (117.5cm) wide*

£3,500-4,500 **POOK**

A Pennsylvania poplar blanket chest, the rectangular lid over a dovetailed case supported by straight bracket feet, with vibrant red and yellow grain finish.

c1820 *36in (90cm) wide*

£1,500-2,000 **POOK**

A Pennsylvania pine blanket chest, with sunken panel front over four drawers flanked by tiger maple stiles, supported by turned feet, with original salmon swirl decoration.

c1825 *48in (120cm) wide*

£2,800-3,200 **POOK**

An early 19thC Pennsylvania pine dower chest, with hinged lift top over a dovetail constructed moulded box on a base with turned feet, with original pinwheel and quarter-fan decoration in green, salmon and mustard.

44in (111.5cm) wide

£4,000-6,000 **SK**

A Pennsylvania trinket chest, by Joseph Lehn, with dovetailed case resting on four turned feet, decorated with appliqué die cuts of floral panels and busts of women on front, on a red ground bordered by salmon, green, red, and yellow bands.

13.5in (34cm) wide

£2,000-2,500 **POOK**

A Canadian cherry blanket chest, raised on bracket feet.

43.5in (110cm)

£400-600 **WAD**

CHESTS

- The chest was the most basic item of furniture in medieval Europe. The simplest form of the chest is the coffer, often constructed from six timber boards nailed together. The mule chest is a hybrid of a coffer and a chest of drawers.
- A single chest might be the only article of furniture in a poor household. The wealthy elite would own dozens of chests and fill them with clothes, coin and other trappings.
- Chests designed for the safe transportation of goods had curved lids to drain away rain water and were generally undecorated. Those that doubled as home furnishings had flat lids and might also have feet or even legs.
- When they were married young women were presented with linen and blankets in a wooden chest sometimes called a 'dower chest'. These were frequently carved with date of the marriage and initials of the bride and groom.

A late 17thC oak mule chest, the hinged moulded rectangular top above a frieze with two moulded octagonal panels between and flanked by pairs of turned demi-columns, the lower section with two similarly moulded long drawers, on stile feet.

37.5in (95cm) wide

£800-1,200 **L&T**

A late 17thC oak and fruitwood mule chest in two halves, the moulded edge cleated plank top revealing a deep lidded candle box to a recessed and raised panel front with applied split mouldings, the base with a pair of drawers, fitted brass drop handles and escutcheons, with spliced stile feet.

52.5in (133.5cm) wide

£4,000-6,000 **WW**

A George III oak mule chest, the rectangular hinged top above front with two over two false drawers with three drawers below, flanked by inset fluted angles and raised on ogee bracket feet.

49.5in (126cm) wide

£1,000-1,500 **L&T**

A George III oak mule chest, with a three-panel front over two single drawers.

55.5in (141cm) wide

£400-600 **SWO**

A George III mahogany mule chest, the moulded rectangular hinged lid above two short drawers, fitted with brass carry handles to the sides, the moulded stand with square legs.

48.75in (124cm) wide

£1,500-2,000 **L&T**

A large 18thC oak mule chest, with one cupboard door above two drawers.

56.75in (144cm) high

£500-700 **SWO**

A William IV bird's-eye maple Wellington chest, fitted with six graduated drawers, and an inverted marble top.

33.25in (84.5cm) high

£2,000-3,000 **SWO**

A 19thC French Empire satin walnut tall chest of drawers, the square moulded top over a shallow ogee-shaped drawer with long drawers beneath, flanked by ebonized Corinthian columns, terminating in block plinths and squared base.

45.5in (115.5cm) wide

£1,800-2,200 **FRE**

A 19thC Continental pollard oak, marquetry and parquetry secretaire à abattant, the marble top over a fall front, opening to reveal later sliding trays, below are three long drawers, on bun feet.

49in (124.5cm) high

£700-1,000 **FRE**

A Victorian Wellington chest, with seven graduated drawers.

41.25in (103cm) high

£550-600 **SWO**

A mid-19thC Dutch marquetry tall chest of drawers, the moulded top over a bombé frieze drawer surmounting five long drawers, inlaid with floral sprays, classical urns and exotic birds, on wide pedestal feet.

43in (109cm) wide

£2,200-2,800 **FRE**

A small Edwardian satinwood Wellington chest, with chevron-inlaid stringing and six drawers.

15.75in (40cm) wide

£400-600 **SWO**

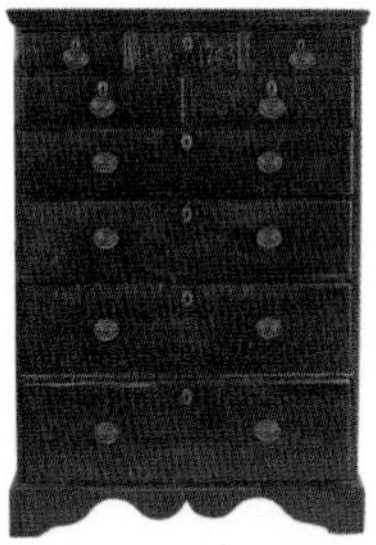

A Pennsylvania Queen Anne walnut tall chest, with moulded cornice over a configuration of drawers and a scalloped skirt supported by ogee bracket feet, dated and initialled "ID".

1743 *59.25in (148cm) high*

£4,000-6,000 **POOK**

A late 18thC New England Chippendale tiger maple and maple tall chest of drawers, with applied cornice moulding above a case of five scratch-beaded graduated drawers, all on tall dovetailed bracket feet.

51.25in (130cm) high

£1,800-2,200 **SK**

A late 18thC Pennsylvania Chippendale cherry tall chest, with flat cove-moulded cornice above a case of two thumb-moulded short drawers and five graduated long drawers, supported on dovetailed bracket feet.

58.5in (146cm) high

£1,500-2,000 **SK**

A late 18thC New England Chippendale tiger maple tall chest of drawers, with moulded cornice above a case of six graduated scratch-beaded drawers, on tall bracket feet.

61in (152.5cm) high

£8,000-12,000 **SK**

A Pennsylvania Federal walnut chest-on-chest, with dentil-moulded cornice over drawers with central tulip vine and heart inlay, the lower drawers flanked by chamfered stiles, above a scalloped skirt with similar tulip inlays supported by flaring French feet.

c1810 *68in (170cm) high*

£12,000-15,000 **POOK**

A Pennsylvania late Federal cherry and tiger maple tall chest, with moulded cornice over three short and five long drawers, flanked by panelled sides and supported on turned feet.

c1825 *66.5in (166cm) high*

£2,800-3,200 **POOK**

A William & Mary marquetry and walnut chest-on-stand, profusely inlaid with scrolling flowering foliage, the chest with three long drawers over a base with a single long drawer on bun feet, restored.

37.75in (96cm) wide

£3,500-4,000 **SWO**

A late 17thC small oak chest, the four drawers with geometric moulded decoration on later bun feet.

33.5in (85cm) wide

£1,000-1,500 **SWO**

A late 17thC small oak chest of drawers, with two short and two long drawers, within a double D-moulded carcass.

32in (80cm) wide

£1,000-1,500 **SWO**

A Queen Anne walnut chest of drawers, having a segmental veneered and feather-strung top over two short and three long drawers, with brass furniture on later bracket feet.

35.5in (90cm) high

£2,000-2,500 **SWO**

An early 18thC walnut chest, the crossbanded top over two short and three long drawers and an associated stand, with repairs and alterations.

39.75in (101cm) wide

£700-1,000 **SWO**

An early 18thC oyster walnut and boxwood-strung chest of two short and three long drawers, with brass drop handles and escutcheons, the walnut ends with a bold boxwood diamond design, on later bracket feet.

37.5in (95cm) wide

£3,000-4,000 **LFA**

An 18thC oyster veneered chest of drawers, with boxwood stringing, two short and three long drawers, within a D-moulded carcass and bun feet.

38.5in (96cm) wide

£3,000-4,000 **SWO**

A George III mahogany chest of four graduated drawers, on bracket feet.

37in (94cm) high

£700-1,000 **SWO**

A George III mahogany chest of drawers, with a brushing slide, on bracket feet.

31in (79cm) high

£1,800-2,200 **SWO**

An mid- to late 18thC George III mahogany serpentine chest, formerly with two cupboard doors, the moulded top over a brushing slide and four later graduated drawers, raised on bracket feet.

42.5in (108cm) wide

£700-1,000 **FRE**

A George III mahogany serpentine-shaped chest, with three long graduated drawers, flanked by canted corners, raised on square splayed legs.

c1800 *40in (100cm) wide*

£2,200-2,800 **FRE**

A George III mahogany serpentine chest, the moulded top above four long graduated drawers with boxwood stringing raised on bracket feet.

43.25in (110cm) wide

£1,200-1,800 **L&T**

A George III serpentine mahogany chest of drawers, the top with an oval panel, within crossbanded, strung and inlaid borders, over four long drawers with crossbanded borders, on bracket feet.

39.5in (99cm) wide

£3,000-4,000 **SWO**

A George III mahogany serpentine chest of drawers, the shaped rectangular top above three long graduated drawers flanked by blind fret pilasters, bracket feet.

46.75in (119cm) wide

£3,000-5,000 **L&T**

A George III mahogany bow front chest of four graduated drawers, repairs to back legs.

33.5in (84cm) wide

£1,000-1,500 **SWO**

A fine pair of George III bow front mahogany and satinwood-banded chest of drawers, each with a moulded top over a slide and three graduated long drawers, with boxwood and ebony stringing on tapered outward curved legs.

c1800 *39.5in (100.5cm) wide*

£4,000-5,000 **FRE**

A New England William and Mary maple chest of drawers, the rectangular top over three short and three long drawers, supported by turned bun feet.

c1730 *40in (100cm) high*

£4,000-6,000 **POOK**

A Pennsylvania Chippendale walnut chest of drawers, the rectangular top over four graduated drawers, flanked by fluted quarter columns supported by ogee bracket feet.

c1770 *39.75in (99cm) wide*

£2,200-2,800 **POOK**

A Pennsylvania Chippendale mahogany chest of drawers, with rectangular top over four graduated drawers, flanked by fluted quarter columns, supported by ogee bracket feet.

c1770 *38in (95cm) wide*

£2,500-3,000 **POOK**

A Philadelphia Chippendale mahogany chest of drawers, the rectangular top over a case with four drawers, flanked by fluted quarter columns supported by ogee bracket feet.

c1770 *39in (97.5cm) wide*

£2,200-2,800 **POOK**

A Massachusetts Chippendale birch carved serpentine chest of drawers, with overhanging moulded top and serpentine front above a cockbeaded case of four graduated drawers, on carved claw and ball feet.

c1770 *35.5in (89cm) wide*

£4,000-6,000 **SK**

A Massachusetts Chippendale mahogany serpentine chest of drawers, with overhanging moulded top and serpentine front above a cockbeaded conforming case of four graduated drawers, all on ogee bracket feet with shaped knee returns.

c1770 *32in (80cm) high*

£8,000-12,000 **SK**

A Massachusetts Chippendale mahogany block-front chest of drawers, with overhanging moulded top over a cockbeaded case of four graduated drawers, on later turned feet.

c1770 *32.5in (81cm) wide*

£15,000-20,000 **SK**

A New Hampshire Federal bow front bureau, the mahogany top with inlaid edge overhanging a case of drawers with flame birch-veneered panels interspersed with rosewood-veneered escutcheons, above a moulded base with flared front feet.

c1800 *41.25in (105cm) wide*

£8,000-12,000 **SK**

A New England Federal bow front chest of drawers, with rectangular top above a case of four graduated mahogany veneer drawers centring inlaid drapery and bellflowers, bordered by stringing and tiger maple crossbanding, on cut-out base and French feet.

c1800 *39in (97.5cm) wide*

£7,000-10,000 **SK**

An early 19thC New England pine chest over two drawers, with moulded lift-top above a case of two drawers and an arched cut-out base, painted with vigorous freehand black and white swirled designs over earlier salmon pink.

42in (105cm) wide

£16,000-20,000 **SK**

A early 19thC New England diminutive pine chest-over-drawer, with thumb-moulded hinged top above a case with single drawer resting on cutout feet, with blue-grey painted finish and white feather designs.

34in (86.5cm) high

£20,000-25,000 **SK**

A Massachusetts Federal mahogany and bird's-eye maple veneer inlaid bow front chest of drawers, with crossbanding and stringing on a base of four graduated drawers of bird's-eye maple panels bordered by mahogany crossbanding and stringing, old embossed American eagle brass pulls, refinished.

c1805 *39in (97.5cm) wide*

£4,000-6,000 **SK**

A Virginia or North Carolina Federal figured walnut chest on frame, with moulded top above two short over three long drawers, resting on a base with inlaid apron and cuffs with incised zig-zag decoration.

c1810 *45in (112cm) high*

£4,000-6,000 **POOK**

A Kentucky Federal cherry tall chest, with moulded top overhanging a narrow frieze of contrasting veneers and a case of six cockbeaded drawers with bone-inlaid escutcheons, supported on flaring French feet with spurs.

c1825 *52in (132cm) high*

£3,000-4,000 **SK**

A rare Australian cedar chest, raised on turned feet.

c1860

£1,800-2,200 **BONA**

A 19thC Australian cedar chest of drawers, with rectangular top and serpentine front above a hidden drawer and arrangement of further drawers, raised on turned feet.

48in (122cm) wide

£1,500-2,000 **BONA**

A Canadian pine chest of drawers, with original finish, ceramic knobs and lettered drawers corresponding to internal compartments.

c1930

£400-600 **RAON**

A Canadian pine stand-up desk on chest, with lift top above four drawers with fielded panel ends, raised on bracket feet, with original brown stain finish.

41.5in (105.5cm) wide

£1,000-1,500 **WAD**

A mid-18thC Louis XV bombé kingwood and rosewood crossbanded commode, by Jean Francois Lapie, with gilt bronze mounts, later serpentine moulded marble top, stamped "J. F. Lapie, JME".

51.5in (129cm) wide

£5,000-7,000 **FRE**

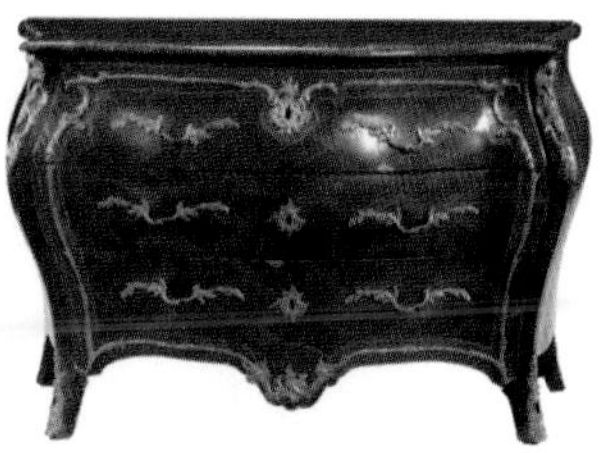

A Louis XV rosewood and parquetry bombé commode, with gilt bronze mounts and inlay, the cubic veneered serpentine shape top over three conforming drawers and sides, raised on outswept feet, ending in sabots.

c1760 *48in (120cm) wide*

£4,000-5,000 **FRE**

An early 20thC Louis XV-style bombé kingwood, marquetry and gilt bronze mounted commode, the moulded serpentine marble top over two long drawers inlaid with flowers, raised on square splayed legs, ending in sabots.

39.5in (99cm) wide

£3,000-4,000 **FRE**

A French Directoire mahogany marble top commode, the moulded top with outset corners, over three long drawers, raised on turned tapered legs ending in toupie feet.

c1800 *45in (112.5cm) wide*

£1,200-1,800 **FRE**

A CLOSER LOOK AT A GERMAN BOMBÉ COMMODE

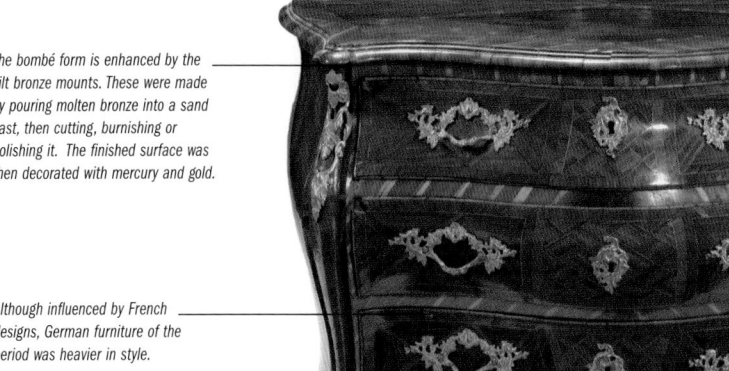

The bombé form is enhanced by the gilt bronze mounts. These were made by pouring molten bronze into a sand cast, then cutting, burnishing or polishing it. The finished surface was then decorated with mercury and gold.

Although influenced by French designs, German furniture of the period was heavier in style.

The commode evolved from the chest of drawers and became popular in the early 18thC. Like this example, they typically have a curved case described as bombé.

Pairs of commodes with pier glasses often flanked windows in fashionable homes. Pairs command a premium.

A German Baroque kingwood and sycamore, crossbanded and parquetry bombé commode, with gilt bronze mounts, the moulded top centred by a cubic veneered diamond reserve, with conforming veneered sides, over three long drawers, raised on outset scroll ending in sabots.

c1760 *46.5in (116cm) wide*

£10,000-15,000 **FRE**

A 19thC Italian walnut and inlaid commode, inlaid throughout with scrolling foliage, cherubs, exotic birds and mask motifs, the shaped top over three long drawers raised on cabriole legs.

56in (142cm) wide

£2,500-3,000 **FRE**

A 19thC Italian carved walnut commode, with some earlier elements, the rectangular top with a shell-carved edge, over two short and three long bead-moulded drawers, with male mask handles, raised on outset claw feet.

57in (142.5cm) wide

£2,000-3,000 **FRE**

A 19thC French walnut three-drawer commode, with a serpentine front and moulded corners and three drawers.

49.5in (126cm) high

£2,000-3,000 **SWO**

A Continental kingwood and marquetry bombé commode, with gilt-metal mounts inlaid throughout with scrolling foliage, two long drawers and two short drawers, the apron raised on outset bracket feet.

57.5in (146cm) wide

£1,200-1,800 **FRE**

An early 18thC walnut and seaweed marquetry chest-on-chest, with two long and three short moulded drawers, the lower section with three long graduated drawers, on bracket feet, adapted, with associated veneers.

39.75in (101cm) wide

£3,000-4,000 L&T

A George I walnut and crossbanded chest-on-chest, the cavetto moulded cornice over three short and three long graduated drawers, the lower section with two short and two further long drawers, raised on bracket feet.

c1720 *42in (106.5cm) wide*

£2,200-2,800 FRE

A George III mahogany secretaire chest-on-chest, the fall revealing a fitted interior with cedar-lined drawers, pigeonholes and a mirrored door, above two long drawers, all fitted with replaced brass handles, on bracket feet.

47in (119.5cm) wide

£4,000-6,000 WW

A George III mahogany tallboy, the broken pediment with Greek key moulding above three short and three long graduated drawers, the lower section with brushing slide above three further long drawers, on bracket feet.

45.75in (116cm) wide

£2,500-3,000 L&T

A George III mahogany chest-on-chest, the arched cornice with urn finials above two short and six long drawers, on splayed bracket feet.

42in (107cm) wide

£1,000-1,500 L&T

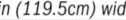

A George III mahogany chest-on-chest, with two short and three long drawers, the base with three long drawers and bracket feet, later brass handles.

43.25in (110cm) wide

£1,800-2,200 SWO

A George III mahogany chest-on-chest, the moulded and projecting cornice above a dentil and blind fretwork frieze and three short over three long graduated drawers, the base with brushing slide and three long graduated drawers, on shaped bracket feet.

44.5in (113cm) wide

£3,000-4,000 **L&T**

A George III oak and mahogany crossbanded chest-on-chest, on bracket feet.

43.75in (111cm) high

£2,000-3,000 **SWO**

A mid-Atlantic Chippendale walnut chest-on-chest, with broken arch bonnet over five short drawers and three long drawers flanked by fluted quarter columns on a lower section with three long drawers, supported by ogee bracket feet.

c1770 *90in (225cm) high*

£5,000-8,000 **POOK**

A late 18thC Chippendale cherry chest-on-chest, the upper section with three short drawers centred with a fan above four long drawers, the lower section with three long drawers, on a moulded base with ogee bracket feet.

38in (96.5cm) wide

£4,000-6,000 **FRE**

A Regency mahogany bow front chest-on-chest, the lambrequin decorated cornice over two short and six long drawers, on splayed feet.

43.75in (111cm) high

£1,200-1,800 **SWO**

A 19thC Colonial padouk cabinet-on-chest, the moulded cornice above two arched moulded panel doors with ornate brass hinges, enclosing variously sized drawers, the lower section with drawers, on bun feet.

40.25in (102cm) wide

£2,000-3,000 **L&T**

A mid-18thC Pennsylvania Queen Anne tiger maple highboy, with flat cover-moulded top, three small and four graduated lip-moulded wide drawers, the base with single wide drawer and carved apron on plain cabriole legs and stockinged webbed feet.

41in (104cm) wide

£20,000-30,000 **FRE**

An 18thC New Hampshire Queen Anne carved cherry highboy, with flaring cornice moulding above five graduated thumb-moulded drawers, above a blocked area and three flat-headed arches flanked by cabriole legs ending in pad feet.

36in (91.5cm) wide

£16,000-20,000 **SK**

A Connecticut Queen Anne maple high chest of drawers, with cove-moulded cornice above a case with an arrangement of drawers, above a valanced apron joining cabriole legs with scrolled carved knee returns ending in ball and claw feet.

c1750 *67in (170cm) high*

£5,000-6,000 **SK**

A Queen Anne mahogany highboy, possibly Bermuda, with moulded cornice over an arrangement of drawers supported by cabriole legs terminating in Spanish feet.

c1760 *69.5in (174cm) high*

£4,000-6,000 **POOK**

A Pennsylvania Chippendale walnut highboy, with moulded cornice over an arrangement of drawers, with elaborate scalloped skirt supported by cabriole legs ending in ball and claw feet.

c1770 *76.25in (193.5cm) high*

£4,000-6,000 **POOK**

A New Hampshire Queen Anne maple carved highboy, attributed to the Dunlap family, with flat moulded cornice above a case with an arrangement of drawers, the lowermost of which centres a carved fan, all on cabriole legs with shaped knee returns continuing to pad feet.

c1790 *76in (193cm) high*

£15,000-20,000 **SK**

A Connecticut Queen Anne cherry carved scroll-top highboy, the top section with scrolled cornice centring a turned finial, with central fan-carved short drawer flanked by thumb-moulded drawers below, on a valanced skirt joining cabriole legs ending in pad feet.

c1750 *37.75in (96cm) wide*

£5,000-6,000 **SK**

A Queen Anne carved mahogany highboy, the top section with scroll-moulded cornice centring a plinth and flanking drawers, set into a lower section with central fan-carved drawer and flanking drawers, all on cabriole legs ending in pad feet.

c1785 *42in (106.5cm) wide*

£12,000-18,000 **SK**

A George I cross and feather banded walnut bureau, with fall front revealing a fitted interior to a well, with two short and two long drawers fitted with later engraved brass plate handles, on bracket feet.

31.25in (79.5cm) wide

£6,000-7,000 **WW**

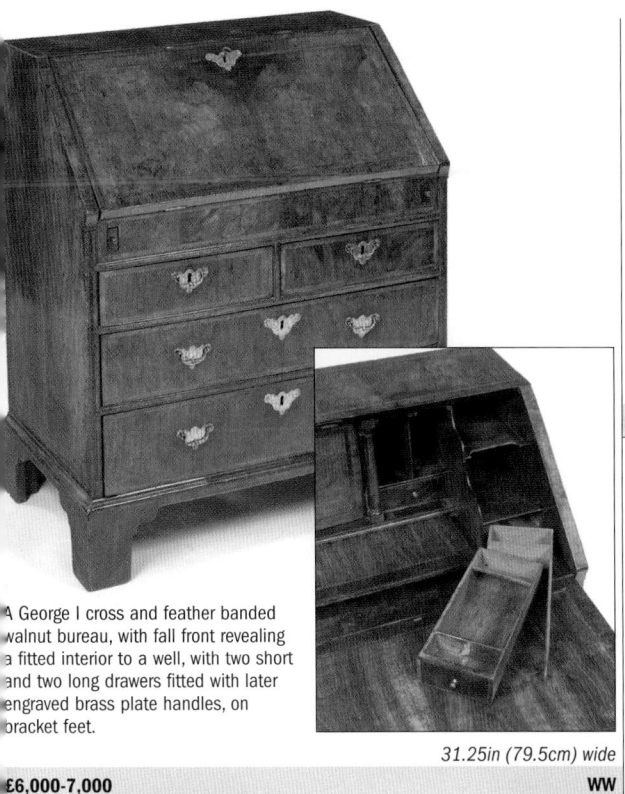

A George III elm small bureau, with fall front enclosing pigeonholes and small drawers, above three long drawers, with engraved brass handles and escutcheons, on bracket feet.

32.25in (82cm) wide

£1,200-1,800 **LFA**

A George III oak bureau, with a fitted interior over three long drawers.

35in (89cm) wide

£400-500 **SWO**

A George III mahogany bureau, with pigeonholes and drawers over four long drawers, raised on bracket feet.

36.75in (92cm) wide

£1,200-1,500 **SWO**

A late 18thC American Chippendale cherry desk, with fall front enclosing fitted interior above four long drawers, supported by ogee bracket feet.

c1780 *37in (94cm) wide*

£1,200-1,800 **POOK**

A Georgian country oak fall front bureau, with stepped and fitted interior, four long graduating drawers with brass swan-neck handles and pierced and shaped back plates, brass escutcheons and bracket feet.

36in (91.5cm) wide

£800-1,200 **MAX**

A mid-Victorian Gillow & Co. amboyna and ebonized wood secretaire chest, with raised shelf above a panelled fall front drawer enclosing pigeonholes and a central strong box, with two panelled doors flanked by turned and reeded pilasters, stamped "Gillow & Co. No. 5347".

45in (114cm) wide

£4,000-6,000 **LFA**

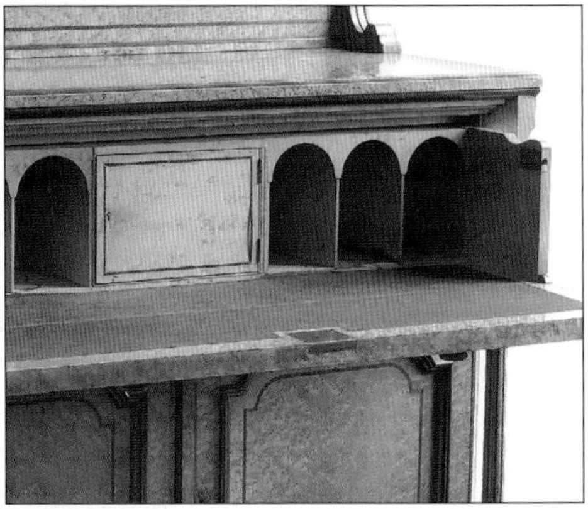

A 17thC Italian walnut secretaire, with hinged top enclosing secret compartment with two drawers, fall front enclosing fitted interior and two panelled doors flanked by fluted Doric-form pilasters, on bracket feet.

42in (106.5cm) wide

£1,500-2,000 **FRE**

An 18thC Italian walnut and marquetry serpentine bureau, inlaid with scrolling foliage, figures and mythological beasts, the fall front centred by a horse-drawn chariot, opening to reveal fitted stepped interior with covered well, raised on bracket feet.

42in (106.5cm) wide

£4,000-6,000 **FRE**

An 18thC Austrian birchwood bureau, with burr inset panels, strapwork decoration and crossbanding, the upper section with eight drawers and central cupboard, above fall front enclosing fitted interior with marble paper lining, flanked by two small drawers, raised on saucer feet.

48in (122cm) wide

£3,000-5,000 **L&T**

A 19thC Italian Baroque-style walnut and marquetry bureau, inlaid with figures, animals, mythological beasts and foliate scrolls, the fall front enclosing fitted interior with covered well, over three long drawers, raised on plinth base.

42in (106.5cm) wide

£3,000-5,000 **FRE**

An 18thC-style Dutch bureau, with fitted interior over a bombé front, with ball and claw feet.

33.5in (85cm) wide

£1,000-1,500 **SWO**

A 19thC Dutch walnut and floral marquetry bureau, with fitted interior above serpentine front with three long drawers, on carved bracket supports.

36in (91.5cm) wide

£2,800-3,200 **BRI**

A French Biedermeier mahogany veneered secretaire, with brass inlays, bevelled corners and ebonized half columns with gilt ends, the lower part with two doors, the upper part with drawers, inlaid with ebonized coat of arms.

c1820 *57.5in (144cm) high*

£1,500-2,000 **KAU**

A Swiss Biedermeier walnut veneer desk, with three drawers and hinged writing top, the interior with eight drawers, complete with original mountings, locks and keys.

c1850 *51.5in (129cm) high*

£600-900 **KAU**

A New England Queen Anne tiger maple bureau, the lid opening to a fitted interior above a fan-carved central drawer flanked by drawers, above a case of four thumb-moulded drawers, on a cut-out bracket base.

c1750 *42in (105cm) high*

£16,000-18,000 **SK**

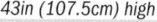

A mid-18thC New England Queen Anne maple bureau, the lid enclosing a fitted interior with cockbeaded surrounds, on a case of four thumb-moulded drawers, on bracket feet.

43in (107.5cm) high

£2,000-3,000 **SK**

A Pennsylvania Chippendale walnut bureau, the fall front enclosing a fitted interior with raised tombstone panel prospect door, over a case with drawers flanked by fluted quarter columns, supported by ogee bracket feet.

c1765 *43.75in (109cm) high*

£3,000-4,000 **POOK**

A Rhode Island Chippendale mahogany slant front desk, the fall front enclosing a shell-carved interior, above a case with four drawers supported by ogee bracket feet.

c1770 *41.5in (104cm) high*

£7,000-9,000 **POOK**

A Massachusetts Chippendale mahogany oxbow serpentine desk, probably Salem, with fitted interior flanked by four valanced compartments, above cockbeaded case of four graduated drawers all resting on carved ball and claw feet.

c1770 *44in (110cm) high*

£8,000-10,000 **SK**

A Connecticut Chippendale birch desk, with fall front enclosing a fitted interior, above an oxbow case with four drawers, supported by ogee bracket feet.

c1780 *44.5in (113cm) high*

£1,800-2,200 **POOK**

A Lancaster county, Pennsylvania, Chippendale walnut slant front desk, the line inlaid fall front enclosing a fitted interior with paterae inlaid prospect door, above drawers flanked by quarter columns, on bracket feet.

c1780 *43.5in (109cm) high*

£2,000-3,000 **POOK**

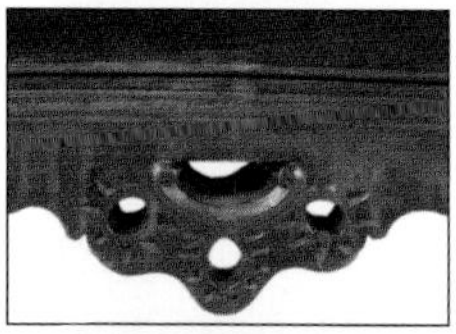

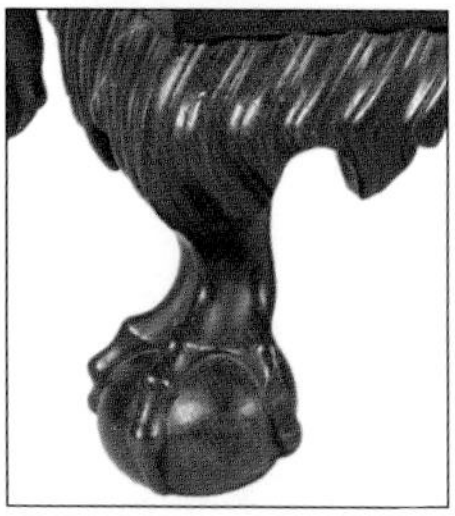

A Massachusetts Chippendale mahogany oxbow serpentine desk, attributed to William King of Salem, the lid enclosing a fitted interior, above a serpentine case of cockbeaded drawers, on gadroon-carved cabriole legs ending in ball and claw feet.

c1780 *44.75in (112cm) high*

£20,000-25,000 **SK**

A late 18thC American Chippendale maple slant-lid desk, the lid enclosing a fitted interior above a case of four thumb-moulded graduated drawers on bracket feet.

36in (91.5cm) wide

£2,000-3,000 **SK**

A late 18thC American Chippendale walnut desk, the slant lid enclosing a stepped fitted interior, over a case of graduated drawers with cockbeaded surrounds on a moulded bracket base, restored.

40in (101.5cm) wide

£2,500-3,000 **SK**

A late 18thC American Chippendale cherry desk, the slant lid enclosing a fitted interior over thumb-moulded graduated drawers on a moulded bracket base with central pendant.

38in (96.5cm) wide

£1,500-2,000 **SK**

A late 18thC New England Chippendale cherry desk, the lid enclosing a fitted interior, above four graduated cockbeaded drawers on ogee feet.

39in (99cm) wide

£3,000-3,500 **SK**

A late 18thC Massachusetts Chippendale tiger maple desk, the lid enclosing a fitted interior, on base of four thumb-moulded graduated drawers resting on bracket feet.

37in (94cm) wide

£8,000-10,000 **SK**

A Federal cherry and birch desk, the thumb-moulded lid enclosing a fitted interior, above a case of four graduated scratchbeaded drawers and flaring French feet, restored.

c1800 *41in (104cm) wide*

£800-1,200 **SK**

A Federal cherry inlaid desk, by Samuel S. Noyes, the thumb-moulded lid enclosing a fitted interior, above cockbeaded graduated drawers bordered by mahogany banding and stringing, on a tall inlaid cutout base, with label for "Samuel Noyse".

c1810 *39.75in (101cm) wide*

£1,800-2,200 **SK**

A Pennsylvania painted pine and poplar desk, with fall front enclosing a fitted interior, above four graduated drawers, over a scalloped skirt supported by straight bracket feet, with ochre grained finish.

c1810 *43in (107.5cm) high*

£1,500-2,000 **POOK**

A walnut and crossbanded bureau, in the Queen Anne style, with a hinged sloping writing surface, the base fitted with two long drawers, on shell-carved cabriole legs.

34.75in (88cm) high

£800-1,200 **SWO**

An Irish George II mahogany bureau, with hinged fall front enclosing a fitted interior above a frieze drawer and shell-carved apron, on cabriole legs with faceted pad feet.

39in (99cm) wide

£2,000-3,000 **L&T**

A Georgian-style walnut bureau, with crossbanded decoration and frieze drawer, on a later stand.

30.5in (76cm) wide

£500-700 **SWO**

A Georgian-style walnut and feather-strung open bureau, with slope front enclosing shaped shelves and pigeonholes over two drawers, on carved cabriole legs.

21in (53.5cm) high

£700-1,000 **SWO**

A mid-18thC Pennsylvania Chippendale walnut carved bureau on legs, the top section with slant lid enclosing a fitted interior, above a thumb-moulded drawer and valanced skirt joining cabriole legs terminating in ball and claw feet.

43.5in (109cm) high

£9,000-11,000 **SK**

A Howard & Sons maple veneer lady's writing desk, with crossbanded oval top above drawers and open voids, with gilt metal mounts and panelled frieze, raised on turned and tapering fluted legs with toupie feet, stamped "Howard & Son, Berner St".

43in (109cm) wide

£3,000-4,000 **L&T**

A CLOSER LOOK AT A LOUIS XV-STYLE BUREAU

Francois Linke (1855-1946) was one of the most important and influential French furniture makers of the Belle Epoque and the association with him emphasises the quality of the piece.

The influential Rococo style, prevalent during the reign of Louis XV, was characterised by curving lines, lightness and informality. Throughout the 19thC historic styles such as Rococo were revisited by furniture makers.

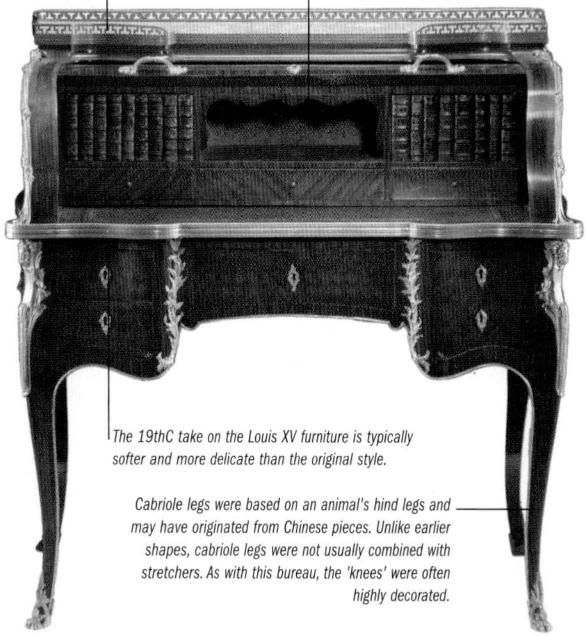

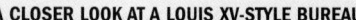

The 19thC take on the Louis XV furniture is typically softer and more delicate than the original style.

Cabriole legs were based on an animal's hind legs and may have originated from Chinese pieces. Unlike earlier shapes, cabriole legs were not usually combined with stretchers. As with this bureau, the 'knees' were often highly decorated.

A fine late 19thC Louis XV-style mahogany parquetry bureau à cylindre, in the manner of Francois Linke, with gilt bronze mounts, inverted breakfront marble top, crossbanded solid cylinder enclosing fitted interior with leather-lined writing slide, the sides with Bacchus masks cast with vines, on cabriole legs with gilt bronze ram mask heads and foliate cast clasps, terminating in scrolled sabots.

40.5in (103cm) wide

£7,000-10,000 **FRE**

A late Victorian tulipwood bureau plat, by Mellier & Co., of London, in the French transitional style, with gilt brass mounts, fitted with shelves and drawers, on square-section chamfered and panel-veneered cabriole legs with scrolling foliate terminals and sabots, stamped.

£4,000-6,000 **L&T**

A Louis XV-style burr walnut and tulipwood crossbanded bureau de dame, with gilt brass mounts, rosette cast edge and central glazed cupboard door flanked by tiers of three drawers, raised on square section cabriole legs with sabots.

49.25in (125cm) wide

£4,000-6,000 **L&T**

A 19thC Louis XV-style kingwood, rosewood and parquetry bureau de dame, with gilt metal mounts, fall front enclosing stepped fitted interior with drawers and pigeon holes, raised on square cabriole legs.

40in (100cm) high

£800-1,200 **FRE**

A 19thC Continental-style walnut and ebonized bonheur du jour, with frieze drawer, sliding writing surface, raised back with shelf and four short drawers, raised on cabriole legs.

39in (99cm) high

£500-800 **MAX**

A late 18thC Dutch walnut veneer cylinder desk, with marquetry and pewter-inlaid roll front above two drawers, supported by square tapering legs.

c1785 *45in (114.5cm) wide*

£1,800-2,200 **POOK**

A 19thC Dutch mahogany and marquetry bombé bureau, inlaid with scrolling foliage, with fall front centred by a flowering urn flanked by two exotic birds, raised on square cabriole legs.

38in (95cm) high

£2,000-3,000 **FRE**

A George III mahogany roll top desk, with rectangular moulded top, curved tambour fall enclosing fitted interior and slide-out writing surface, raised on moulded square tapering legs with spade feet.

42.5in (108cm) wide

£1,200-1,800 **L&T**

A William IV mahogany cylinder desk, with curved fall front enclosing fitted interior.

£1,000-1,500 **SWO**

A late 19thC walnut veneer bureau à cylindre, with gilt brass mounts, rectangular galleried top, curved fall front with applied ribbed veneers, applied leaf-cast mounts and moulded cabriole legs with floral and foliate cast mounts and sabots.

46in (117cm) wide

£3,000-4,000 **L&T**

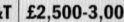

A Louis XV-style inlaid rosewood bureau à cylindre, with floral inlay, ormolu mounts, fitted interior, pull-out writing surface, frieze drawer and shaped legs united by X-stretcher.

35.5in (90cm) wide

£2,500-3,000 **SWO**

A 19thC Louis XV-style mahogany and parquetry bureau à cylindre, with gilt bronze mounts, shaped galleried top with inset marble, veneered fall front enclosing fitted interior with simulated and book end cupboards, raised on square cabriole legs terminating in sabots.

43.5in (109cm) wide

£3,000-4,000 **FRE**

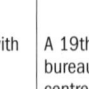

A Louis XVI-style mahogany bureau à cylindre, with rouge marble galleried top above drawers with painted floral and ribbon decoration, the lower drawer raised above turned and fluted legs.

45in (114cm) high

£1,000-1,500 **L&T**

A Victorian rosewood davenport, with brass gallery, satinwood veneered drawers and pigeon holes, hinged top with pull-out writing compartment, on ribbed flattened bun feet with brass castors.

22.5in (57cm) wide

£2,000-2,500 **WW**

A Victorian burr walnut davenport, with rising piano top concealing fret-cut letter rack, pull-out writing surface and door enclosing side drawers.

38.5in (97.5cm) high

£4,000-6,000 **SWO**

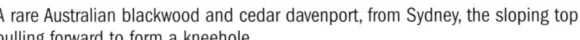

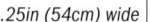

A rare Australian blackwood and cedar davenport, from Sydney, the sloping top pulling forward to form a kneehole.

c1845 *21.25in (54cm) wide*

£2,000-2,500 **BONA**

An Edwardian inlaid rosewood davenport, with red tooled leather writing surface.

£500-800 **SWO**

A CLOSER LOOK AT AN EDWARDIAN WRITING DESK

Although some early 20thC households embraced the cutting-edge Art Nouveau style, many others returned to designs of the past and the latest Classical revivals. This desk harks back to Neo-classical furniture designs.

However, contemporary influences are evident in the restrained adornment of the piece, which turns away from heavy Victorian forms.

The inlaid decoration is typically elaborate.

There was a large demand for desks during the period. Desks can vary in quality - this is a good example.

An Edwardian mahogany and marquetry inlaid kidney-shaped writing desk, the shaped top with inset leather skiver, above a central drawer flanked by two banks of four drawers, the whole profusely inlaid and raised on square tapering legs.

53.5in (133cm) wide

£5,000-7,000 **L&T**

A George III satinwood kneehole secretaire desk, with rosewood crossbanding, fitted writing surface, drawers and pigeonholes, small drawer and kneehole with recessed cupboard door, with marquetry urn inlay, on bracket feet.

33in (84cm) wide

£3,000-5,000 **L&T**

A George III mahogany kneehole desk, with moulded rectangular top and kneehole with recessed cupboard door, flanked on each side by three short drawers, on bracket feet.

40.25in (102cm) wide

£1,000-1,500 **L&T**

A George III mahogany crossbanded kneehole desk, with moulded edge above a single drawer and two banks of three drawers, with frieze drawer and cupboard, raised on bracket feet.

32.25in (82cm) wide

£2,500-3,000 **L&T**

A George III mahogany kneehole desk, with carved edge over a single frieze drawer and six drawers flanking a central well, on bracket feet.

30.75in (78cm) high

£1,500-2,000 **SWO**

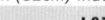

A 19thC mahogany kneehole desk, with tulipwood and boxwood stringing, with one long and six short drawers, brass handles, and bracket feet.

36.25 (92cm) wide

£700-1,000 **LFA**

A Victorian burl walnut and kingwood crossbanded kneehole desk, the rectangular top with an inset leather writing surface over three frieze drawers, the pedestal supports each with three further drawers on plinth bases.

c1880 *41.75in (106cm) wide*

£1,200-1,800 **FRE**

An early 19thC mahogany and boxwood-strung sideboard, the semi-bowed top above central drawer flanked by short drawers over doors and raised on square section tapering legs terminating in spade feet.

83.75in (213cm) wide

£1,000-1,500 **L&T**

A large early 19thC mahogany and inlaid serpentine sideboard, the shaped top above two central drawers over an inlaid apron and flanked by two cupboard doors with false drawer front, on lozenge section front legs inlaid with husk swags and terminating in spade feet.

96.5in (245cm) wide

£3,000-4,000 **L&T**

An early 19thC Scottish mahogany sideboard, with boxwood stringing, the stage back with two sliding doors enclosing infrastructure, the semi-bowed breakfront top above three frieze drawers with deep drawers below, on square tapering legs.

86.25in (219cm) wide

£1,000-2,000 **L&T**

A Maryland Hepplewhite mahogany sideboard, with an oblong top with ovolo corners, above a conforming case with three drawers above four doors with line inlays, supported by square tapering legs with bellflower inlays and banded cuffs.

c1795 *60in (150cm) wide*

£4,000-6,000 **POOK**

A New England Federal mahogany sideboard, the rectangular top on a case of two cockbeaded half drawers and recessed doors with flanking concave panels, on square tapering legs.

c1800 *69.5in (176.5cm) wide*

£5,000-6,000 **SK**

A Virginia walnut huntboard, with an oblong top overhanging a base with five drawers and pronounced scalloped skirt, supported by straight square legs.

c1800 *50in (125cm) wide*

£3,500-4,500 **POOK**

A New York Federal mahogany sideboard, with shaped top on a conforming case with drawers and cupboard doors, all joining square tapering legs, embellished throughout with contrasting inlaid stringing.

c1800 *67in (167.5cm) wide*

£4,000-6,000 **SK**

A Maryland Hepplewhite mahogany sideboard, with serpentine line-inlaid top with single drawer above two cupboard doors flanked by bottle drawers, supported by square tapering legs terminating in spade feet.

c1805 *72in (180cm) wide*

£8,000-12,000 **POOK**

A Maryland late Federal mahogany and tiger maple sideboard, the rectangular top over three drawers and four cupboard doors, flanked by reeded pilasters supported by turned feet.

c1820 *72.75in (182cm) wide*

£2,500-3,000 **POOK**

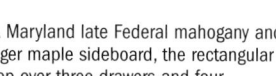

A New York Federal mahogany serpentine inlaid sideboard, with veneered shaped top above three drawers with a central cupboard flanked by end drawers, with bookend and quarter-fan inlays and lozenges, topped by pellets, on six legs.

c1800 *71.75in (179cm) wide*

£15,000-20,000 **SK**

A Charles II cedar centre table, the rectangular panelled moulded edge top above a frieze drawer fitted with a brass drop handle, on baluster, ring and acorn cover turned supports, on block feet.

35.25in (89.5cm) wide

£3,500-4,000 **WW**

A William & Mary walnut and laburnum oyster veneered and marquetry centre table, with reserve of flowers, frog and bird, corner spandrels with flowers, on later ebonized spiral-turned legs.

46in (117cm) wide

£3,000-4,000 **BR**

A William IV rosewood centre table, fitted with two short frieze drawers, on turned end supports, terminating in shell carved feet and brass castors.

54in (137cm) wide

£1,200-1,800 **SWO**

A William IV yew wood centre table, the rounded rectangular top raised on Corinthian capped octagonal columns, with a shaped stretcher, on shaped petal feet.

37in (94cm) high

£500-800 **SWO**

A Victorian rectangular walnut centre table, with marquetry inlay, on pierced and carved oval end supports with carved dome finials and turned stretcher, on knurled splay feet and later castors.

52in (132cm) wide

£3,000-4,000 **MAX**

A mahogany centre table, the matched rectangular top with rosewood crossbanding on a George III platform base with brass inlay reeded outswept legs and brass paw castors.

59.5in (151cm) wide

£700-900 **SWO**

An Italian Neo-classical painted and parcel gilt console table, the later faux marble top over a frieze carved with ram's masks, centred by a portrait medallion, on turned and fluted tapered legs, surmounted by patera.

c1800 *50.5in (126cm) wide*

£2,800-3,200 **FRE**

A 19thC Italian ebonized and ivory table, the top centred with an engraved image of 'Europa and the Bull' with attendants, above a frieze drawer on turned legs united by a shaped 'X' stretcher centred by an urn finial.

53.5in (136cm) wide

£1,200-1,800 **WW**

A 19thC Italian carved walnut Renaissance Revival library table, the top with a gadrooned edge, over a foliate scroll carved frieze with two drawers, on inverted urn shaped supports, on outset scroll feet and brass castors.

54in (137cm) wide

£1,200-1,800 **FRE**

A Regency oak drum table, the planked moulded circular top above a frieze fitted with drawers and false drawers above ropetwist moulding, on leaf-carved column and channelled legs, brass caps and castors.

51.25in (130cm) diam

£2,500-3,000 **L&T**

A Regency rosewood and brass inlaid breakfast table, the circular snap top with crossbanded frieze decorated with continuous flower tendrils, on tapered inlaid square section column, with shaped quadripartite base on scroll feet.

48in (122cm) wide

£2,500-4,000 **L&T**

A CLOSER LOOK AT A RENT TABLE

Tables with frieze drawers, known as drum, writing or library tables were popular from c1780-1820.

The leather writing surface, revolving top and turned pillar, with its inward curving legs, are typical of the style.

Rent tables, a type of drum table with neat and clearly labelled drawers, provided an organised filing system particularly popular with landlords and estate managers.

The decorative addition of rosewood banding and the fitted brass swan neck handles enhance the appeal of the table.

A George III mahogany rent table, the circular revolving top with a central covered well, inset gilt tooled green leather to rosewood banding, the frieze with eight drawers each with an inlaid and lettered cartouche, fitted brass swan neck handles, the baluster-turned stem on four inlaid splay legs to brass caps and castors, later spring to well, one leg repaired.

42in (106.5cm) diam

£8,000-12,000 **WW**

A Regency rosewood and brass inlaid pedestal centre table, on a bulbous stem and tripod base, brass lion paw feet, slight fading.

55in (140cm) diam

£3,500-4,000 **SWO**

A Regency strung mahogany drum table, with a later tooled leather top, over drawers and dummy drawers, a turned column and downswept reeded legs.

48.5in (123cm) diam

£2,800-3,200 **SWO**

A late Regency mahogany circular centre table, with a segmented top, raised on a triform pedestal and bun feet.

48.75in (124cm) diam

£1,000-1,500 **SWO**

A Scottish late Regency rosewood loo table, the circular top with bead and reel frieze raised on leaf-carved turned column and concave quadriform base with carved bun feet and sunk castors.

51.25in (130cm) diam

£1,000-2,000 **L&T**

A William IV mahogany drum table, the revolving top with wide rosewood and scroll marquetry inlay, four frieze drawers and four false fascias with turned wood handles, turned baluster column, quatrefoil base, paw feet and castors.

43in (109cm) diam

£600-1,000 **MAX**

A William IV octagonal centre table, the dish top with radiating veneers and a gadrooned edge, supported by a faceted ropetwist carved column and ending on four acanthus-carved downswept legs.

c1835 *38in (96.5cm) wide*

£1,500-2,000 **FRE**

A William IV rosewood circular top breakfast table, on an octagonal bulbous column and a circular base, on claw feet.

52in (130cm) diam

£700-1,000 **SWO**

A Victorian walnut loo table, the oval burred top with strung and inlaid decoration and a shaped frieze on a turned column and outswept legs.

58.25in (148cm) diam

£800-1,200 **SWO**

A 19thC Anglo-Indian hardwood centre table, the circular top with rouge marble inset and carved beaded edge above a plain frieze on boldly turned column with spreading base, profusely carved with fruiting and flowering foliage, raised on carved paw feet.

52.75in (134cm) diam

£8,000-12,000 **L&T**

A rare and important Australian blackwood circular centre table, from Melbourne, with moulded top supported by a turned and carved centre column and four carved and decorated feet.

c1870 *55in (140cm) diam*

£3,000-4,000 **BONA**

An Edwardian kingwood parquetry inlaid centre table, in the Louis XVI manner, the top with floral border above gilt-metal band and parquetry frieze with single drawer, on slender cabriole legs with central galleried vase stand.

35.5in (90cm) diam

£2,200-2,800 **L&T**

A late 18thC Continental Empire-style ebonized and carved giltwood centre table, the Sienna marble top above a carved frieze, raised on winged female term supports, ending in hairy hook feet.

32.5in (81cm) diam

£1,800-2,200 **FRE**

A late 19thC Italian walnut and marquetry centre table, from Sorrento, inlaid throughout with chariots, figures, mythological beasts and foliate scrolls, the tilt top raised on turned ebonized pilasters and column, on bun feet.

28.5in (72.5cm) wide

£2,000-3,000 **FRE**

A Classical carved mahogany and giltwood pier table, the rectangular top with gadrooned edge and cove-moulded apron, supported by tapering columnar front legs ending in acanthus-carved feet.

39in (99cm) wide

£1,200-1,800 **FRE**

An 18thC George III mahogany hall table, the plain rectangular top with boxwood stringing, above a similarly plain frieze, on square tapering legs and spade feet, restored.

61.25in (153cm) wide

£400-600 **FRE**

A New York Classical pier table, the white marble top on a conforming base with applied ebonized moulding and rosewood veneer frieze with brass gilt mounts showing Psyche and Cupid in a chariot drawn by peacocks, on frontal legs with gilt acanthus capitals and tapering white marble columns, all on gilt gesso and acanthus-carved legs ending in hairy paw feet.

c1825 *50.5in (126cm) wide*

£4,000-6,000 **SK**

A 19thC Anglo-Indian carved rosewood console table, the raised back with pierced foliage and a pineapple, to a demi-lune top, four leafage supports with lion's head terminals, on scroll beast feet.

58.5in (148.5cm) wide

£600-800 **WW**

A 19thC giltwood and gesso console table, with a shaped white marble top.

20.75in (52cm) wide

£500-700 **SWO**

A 19thC carved giltwood console table, with a shaped white marble top on a carved and scrolled front support.

36.25in (92cm) high

£350-550 **SWO**

A late 19thC pair of Louis XVI-style giltwood and gesso console tables, the later green marble tops over breakfront friezes, on stop-fluted turned and tapered legs, stretchers surmounted by urns and floral swags.

36in (90cm) high

£2,000-2,500 **FRE**

An 18thC Italian carved giltwood console table, the serpentine marble top over an ornate Rococo scroll- and shell-carved frieze, raised on conforming cabriole legs.

46in (117cm) wide

£5,000-7,000 **FRE**

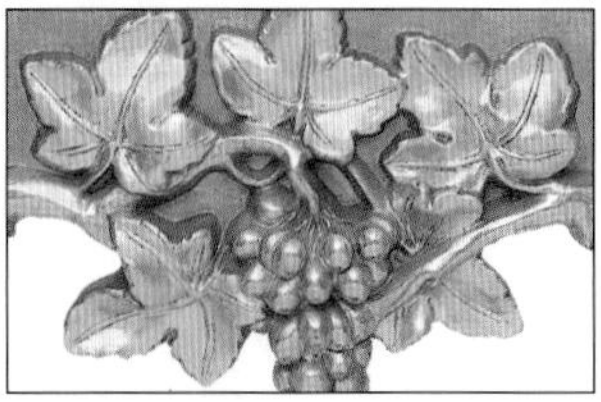

A late 19thC console table, in carved and gilded wood and stucco, on two cambered legs with stretcher, marble top, with vine and grape decoration.

Provenance: *Russian Court, Weimar.*

41.5in (104cm) wide

£1,500-2,000 **KAU**

GATELEG TABLES

- The gateleg table was first introduced in England during the late 16thC. Most early examples are made from oak.
- The top is generally constructed from two or three hinged boards. Pivoting legs swing out to support the outermost leaves when the table is in use.
- The legs are usually joined by stretchers at the top and bottom. Ornamental turning, and spiral designs in particular, are a common feature.

An English William and Mary turned and joined oak gateleg table.

c1690 *39in (99cm) diam*

£6,000-9,000 **RY**

A 17thC oak credence table, the planked D-shaped hinged top above an arched acanthus lunette and ropetwist carved frieze, on ring-turned legs joined by channelled rectangular stretchers, lacking hinged back leg.

37.5in (95cm) wide

£1,800-2,200 **L&T**

A mid-17thC oak altar table, with a plank top over a moulded and scratch-carved frieze on baluster-turned legs and plain stretchers.

49.25in (123cm) wide

£1,000-1,500 **SWO**

An 18thC oak and elm gateleg table, with a single drawer, on turned baluster supports.

53.5in (134cm) wide

£300-600 **SWO**

An 18thC oak side table, with a single frieze drawer over a shaped apron and square cabriole legs.

28in (70cm) wide

£500-700 **SWO**

A Pennsylvania walnut tavern table, with lift-off top, single drawer, and baluster-turned legs joined by stretchers.

c1760 *41in (102.5cm) wide*

£2,800-3,200 **POOK**

An early 19thC New England Shaker cherry and pine table, the rectangular overhanging top on block-turned tapering legs joined by beaded apron, with original painted finish.

48.75in (122cm) wide

£4,000-6,000 **SK**

A 17thC oak refectory table, the rectangular top above scroll-carved frieze on turned and blocked supports linked by stretchers, some replaced elements.

31in (78.5cm) wide

£700-1,000 **L&T**

A 17thC Italian walnut refectory table, the rectangular top raised on foliate carved urn shaped supports joined by a cross stretcher and ending in scroll feet, minor damage.

25in (63.5cm) wide

£12,000-18,000 **FRE**

A late 19thC French oak refectory table, on scroll-carved end supports, with scroll toes.

108in (274.5cm) wide

£1,500-2,000 **LFA**

A 17thC Italian walnut refectory table, the moulded rectangular top raised on twin square ovoid end supports, united by a stretcher and ending in scroll feet.

93.5in (237.5cm) wide

£10,000-15,000 **FRE**

An American Gothic Revival walnut refectory table, attributed to Rose Valley, the rectangular top above scalloped supports joined by a wrought iron scrolling trestle, attributed to Herbert Walton.

c1905 *133in (332.5cm) wide*

£8,000-12,000 **POOK**

A Regency mahogany breakfast table, with a reeded rectangular top and turned column, raised on a quadripartite base.

52.5in (131cm) wide

£700-1,000 **SWO**

A Victorian mahogany dining table, the rectangular top on a turned column, with three moulded cabriole legs and castors.

46in (117cm) wide

£400-600 **SWO**

A Regency mahogany supper table, the drop-leaf top with a reeded edge, one real and one dummy frieze drawer, turned baluster column, on four reeded downswept legs, terminating in brass cappings and castors.

c1820 *53in (132.5cm) wide*

£600-900 **FRE**

A 19thC mahogany rectangular tilt top supper table with rosewood crossbanding on turned column and four reeded legs.

60in (152.5cm) wide

£1,800-2,200 **MAX**

An early 19thC mahogany expanding dining table, the circular top with moulded edge and four removable curved leaves, above a plain frieze with beaded moulding on square tapering column and concave quadriform base, with reeded panelling and massive carved paw feet with acanthus brackets.

72.75in (185cm) diam

£15,000-20,000 **L&T**

An early 19thC rosewood veneered dining table, the circular top supported upon a column with stiff leaf carving, and foliate collar on a triform base with squat bun feet.

51.25in (130cm) diam

£600-800 **SWO**

A 19thC mahogany tilt-top breakfast table, the circular top on a vase-turned column and downswept quadripartite base.

43.25in (110cm) high

£100-150 **SWO**

A Victorian rosewood circular dining table, with a tilt top and beadwork edge, on a bulbous support and four downswept legs, terminating in castors.

54in (135cm) diam

£700-1,000 **SWO**

An early Victorian mahogany and parquetry breakfast table, inlaid with geometric decoration and dog tooth surround, raised upon a faceted column with triform base and lion's paw feet with castors.

48.75in (122cm) diam

£2,000-3,000 **BIG**

A George III mahogany pedestal dining table, comprising a pair of substantial D-ends and a single leaf on a pair of gun barrel stems, on splay quadripartite bases and castors, reduced.

86.5in (220cm) wide

£3,500-4,000 **SWO**

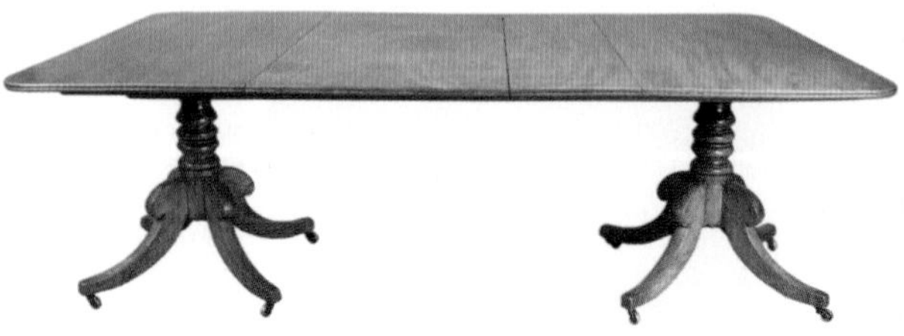

A Regency mahogany twin pedestal dining table, comprising two leaves with reeded edges over turned columns and outswept legs.

88in (220cm) wide

£3,000-4,000 **SWO**

A late 18thC Georgian mahogany triple pedestal dining table, each section with a reeded edge top over a baluster-turned standard, supported by downward curving reeded legs terminating in brass animal paw castors.

c1790 94in (239cm) wide

£3,000-4,000 **POOK**

A Regency triple pedestal mahogany dining table, crossbanded top, on three ring-turned tapering supports on quadruped base with four sabre legs, later inlaid, brass cast paw caps and castors.

118in (300cm) wide

£800-1,200 **L&T**

A Victorian mahogany extending dining table, with a single carved quatraform pedestal supporting five leaves, the D-shaped end leaves supported on turned and reeded drop down legs.

139.25in (248cm) wide

£4,000-5,000 **SWO**

A Regency-style mahogany triple pedestal dining table, the rectangular top raised on three pedestals, each with turned columns and four moulded cabriole legs terminating in cast brass paw caps and castors, includes two additional leaves.

50.5in (128cm) wide

£7,000-10,000 **L&T**

A Rhode Island Queen Anne mahogany dining table, with overhanging rectangular drop-leaf top above valanced apron joining four cabriole legs terminating in pad feet.

c1750 46.5in (116cm) wide

£6,000-9,000 **SK**

A Philadelphia Hepplewhite figured mahogany three-part dining table, the demi-lune ends with drop leaves flanking a rectangular centre section, each with line-inlaid skirt supported by square tapering legs.

c1795 158in (395cm) wide

£10,000-15,000 **POOK**

A CLOSER LOOK AT A PAIR OF DEMI-LUNE DINING TABLES

This table is thought to be from the Great Cabin of Nelson's flagship HMS Vanguard.

The line of provenance is strong. The table descended in the family of Sir Boscawen Savage, who served alongside Nelson at St. Vincent, the Nile and Copenhagen.

The 200th anniversary of Nelson's death in 1805 increased public interest in the Admiral.

The tables are made in a manner of construction which suggests the hand of a shipyard's carpenter.

A similar round table is shown in WM Craig's famous print of Lord Nelson explaining to the officers the plan of attack previous to the Battle of Trafalgar, published on the day of his funeral.

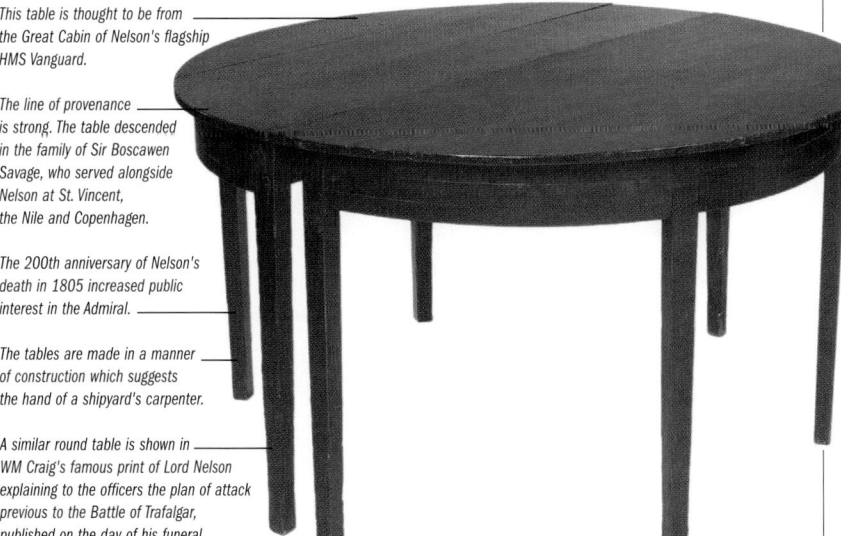

A pair of late 18thC oak demi-lune dining tables, by long tradition made for the Great Cabin of Admiral Nelson's flagship HMS Vanguard, of nautical construction, on square-section tapering legs.

50.5in (128cm) wide

£50,000-70,000 pair **L&T**

A Regency mahogany extending dining table, with a plain frieze moulding, three extra leaves, two original and one matched, raised on tapering reeded legs.

113.5in (288cm) wide

£3,000-4,000 **SWO**

A Pennsylvania Federal mahogany dining table, with two demi-lune ends with single, deep leaves supported by square tapering legs terminating in banded cuffs, stamped "T.H."

c1800 *85in (212.5cm) wide*

£700-1,000 **POOK**

A Pennsylvania Federal mahogany banquet table, with D-shaped ends above a conforming beaded apron joining five vase- and ring-turned and acanthus-carved reeded legs ending in tapering feet.

c1810 *96in (240cm) wide*

£1,000-1,500 **SK**

A New England Sheraton mahogany two-part dining table, each section with rectangular top and drop-leaf, over a frame with carved corners supported by rope-turned legs and brass castors.

c1825 *open 84.5in (211cm) wide*

£1,000-1,500 **POOK**

An early 19thC mahogany dining table, the rectangular top with rounded edge and angles above plain cockbeaded frieze, comprising central gateleg section with six legs and a pair of D-ends, the legs turned and reeded with brass caps and castors.

extended 123in (312cm) wide

£3,000-4,000 **L&T**

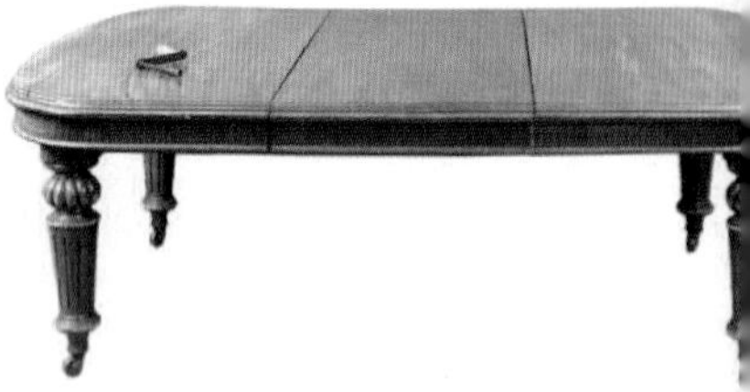

A Victorian mahogany extending dining table, with three leaves on reeded knop and fluted legs terminating in brass capped castors.

28.25in (72cm) high

£2,800-3,200 **SWO**

A large William IV mahogany extending dining table, including five extra leaves, each D-end with moulded edge above a concave frieze on turned tapering legs, with reeded feet resting on pot castors, with leaf holder.

187.75in (477cm) wide

£10,000-15,000 **L&T**

A Victorian mahogany extending dining table, with three leaves.

extended 122in (310 cm) wide

£2,000-3,000 **SWO**

A Victorian mahogany extending dining table and leaf stand, with four extra leaves, on carved bulbous turned legs.

128in (320cm) wide

£3,000-4,000 **SWO**

An early 18thC yew and burr walnut lowboy, the moulded rectangular top with wide burrwood crossbanding, above three short drawers over shaped frieze, on turned tapering legs with pad feet.

32in (81cm) wide

£800-1,200 **L&T**

A Georgian mahogany lowboy, with three frieze drawers and a shaped apron on square chamfered legs.

28.5in (72cm) wide

£800-1,200 **SWO**

A Georgian-style walnut lowboy, with shaped three-quarter gallery, the writing surface hinged to reveal a partitioned interior.

27.75in (70.5cm) wide

£400-600 **SWO**

A Massachusetts Queen Anne walnut veneer dressing table, the veneered top divided into quadrants with herringbone veneers in outline, over a skirt with a high central cut-out flanked by double arches, outlined in cockbeading, on cabriole legs ending in pad feet.

c1740 *33.5in (85cm) wide*

£3,000-4,000 **SK**

A mid-18thC Pennsylvania mahogany lowboy, the lip-moulded top with notched front corners above an arrangement of drawers and shaped apron on slender cabriole legs with shell knees and trifid feet.

34in (86.5cm) wide

£8,000-12,000 **FRE**

A Delaware Valley Queen Anne walnut dressing table, with rectangular moulded top over a case with drawers, above a scalloped skirt supported by squared cabriole legs with intaglio-carved knees terminating in crooked feet.

The unusual lappet- or intaglio-carved knees and crooked feet are often associated with the Savery School.

c1750 *30.25in (75.5cm) wide*

£12,000-18,000 **POOK**

A Delaware Valley Queen Anne walnut dressing table, with rectangular moulded top over a case with one long over two short drawers, above a scalloped apron with central 'fish tail', supported by cabriole legs terminating in stocking drake feet.

c1750 *31.5in (79cm) wide*

£12,000-18,000 **POOK**

A Philadelphia Chippendale carved walnut dressing table, attributed to Clifton, Carteret & Bernard, the top overhanging a case with an arrangement of drawers and Rococo flat carving, above a front skirt with pierced and reverse-carved elements.

Nicholas Bernard, a distinguished Philadelphia carver, probably trained under Samuel Harding.

34in (86.5cm) wide

£100,000-120,000 **SK**

A Virginia or North Carolina Chippendale walnut dressing table, the rectangular top over a frame with three short drawers with star and lattice inlay, supported by square moulded legs with pierced returns.

c1780 *36in (90cm) wide*

£3,000-4,000 **POOK**

A George III satinwood dressing table, the crossbanded rectangular top opening to reveal a hinged sliding mirror, the front with four drawers, on square tapering legs with brass caps and wooden castors.

42in (107cm) wide

£1,800-2,200 **L&T**

A George III mahogany dressing chest, the top above a drawer fitted with a baise lined slide over a divisioned interior fitted with various compartments around a hinged mirror, above three further long graduated drawers, on bracket feet.

38.25in (97cm) wide

£2,000-3,000 **L&T**

A George III mahogany and satinwood enclosed washstand, with ebony stringing, the hinged top revealing a mirror, two lidded compartments and two recesses, above dummy and real drawers, brass handles, on square tapering legs with castors, the legs probably replaced.

30.75in (77.5cm) wide

£700-1,000 **LFA**

A George III mahogany dressing table, the stepped rectangular top with hinged lids enclosing a fitted interior with mirror and various lidded compartments, the front with cupboard doors and drawers, on square tapering legs with brass castors.

39.75in (101cm) wide

£4,000-5,000 **L&T**

A Regency mahogany dressing table, by Gordon & Watson, Ayr, the mirror suspended between supports, later applied top concealing filled apertures, turned legs with brass caps and castors.

Provenance: *Sundrum Castle, Ayr*

45.25in (115cm) wide

£1,000-1,500 **L&T**

A 19thC Federal pine dressing table, the serpentine top on a conforming frieze with single drawer on square tapering legs, painted brown and decorated with Neo-classical swags and floral devices in red and yellow.

39in (99cm) wide

£1,800-2,200 **FRE**

A Victorian burl walnut dressing table, the breakfront top with an inset writing surface and rising mirror, over one central frieze drawer, flanked by ten further graduated drawers, on lobed bun feet.

c1880 *48in (122cm) wide*

£2,000-3,000 **FRE**

A 19thC French Empire mahogany gilt bronze mounted dressing table, with grey marble top and oval mirrored plate, the gilt metal mounted drawer opening to reveal a fitted interior with leather writing surface, stamp with crowned "EU".

54in (135cm) high

£2,000-3,000 **FRE**

A Scottish Regency plum pudding mahogany card table, by William Trotter of Edinburgh, the foldover top raised on four typical scrolls with applied rosettes, square section sabre legs, inscribed to the interior "Pitroddie".

35.75in (91cm) wide

£3,000-4,000 **L&T**

A Regency rosewood and brass inlaid foldover card table, on a shaped support, and four splayed legs with scrolled feet on brass castors.

£1,800-2,200 **SWO**

A pair of Regency rosewood and brass inlaid foldover card tables, each top enclosing baize lined interior above foliate frieze on a lozenge section support, concave quadrapartite base and carved paw feet.

36in (91.5cm) wide

£8,000-12,000 **L&T**

A Regency mahogany card table, with a canted top with ebony strung inlay, ebony decorated frieze, mounted upon a turned column with quadruped splayed legs and brass paw castor terminals.

36in (90cm) wide

£1,200-1,800 **BIG**

A Regency mahogany crossbanded fold-over card table, with twin ring-turned columns on a swept quadripartite base with brass caps and castors.

£800-1,000 **SWO**

A late 18thC English Chippendale games table, serpentine front with floral-carved corners, foldover top, rear legs to double size of table, blind lock in sliding panel to stabilize, damage and repairs.

36.5in (92.5cm) wide

£2,500-3,000 **BRU**

An early 19thC Sheraton Revival satinwood and rosewood crossbanded card table, with a demi-lune top with moulded edge over a deep frieze, baize-lined interior raised on four square, tapered and shaped legs.

36.75in (92cm) wide

£1,200-1,500 **BIG**

An early 19thC Hepplewhite mahogany demi-lune card table, the line inlaid top over a conforming frame supported by square tapering legs with floral inlaid capitals and banded cuffs.

c1805 *36in (91.5cm) wide*

£1,200-1,800 **POOK**

An early 19thC Hepplewhite mahogany card table, the demi-lune top with line-inlaid edge, over a conforming frame with barber's pole inlaid skirt supported by square tapering legs with herringbone inlaid capitals and diamond cuffs.

c1800 *36in (91.5cm) wide*

£1,200-1,800 **POOK**

An unusual walnut triangular card table, the folding top with cross and feather banding to a re-entrant front with an inset plush surface, hinging to a further plush surface and compartmented well, the plain frieze on slender square-shaped tapering legs.

24.5in (62cm) wide

£4,000-5,000 **WW**

A Victorian carved and gilt wood and gesso painted games table, attributed to Thomas Perfect Harding, the circular top game board painted with miniature portraits depicting English monarchs and nobility, tripod base.

c1860 *29in (73.5cm) diam*

£2,200-2,800 **FRE**

A Dutch 18thC walnut and marquetry inlaid fold-over card table, the shaped top with lobed angles, enclosing a baize-lined interior with candle stands inlaid with playing cards, single drawer, the pad feet carved as buckled shoes.

28.75in (73cm) high

£3,000-4,000 **L&T**

A 19thC Dutch mahogany and marquetry games table, inlaid throughout with foliage, opening to reveal two marquetry oval reserves and counter wells, inlaid with playing cards, frieze drawer, on cabriole legs, ending in ball and claw feet.

31.75in (79cm) wide

£3,000-4,000 **FRE**

A small 19thC burr walnut bureau plat, of Louis XV design, with inlaid chess board and marquetry musical cartouche panels, frieze drawer, on cabriole legs with cast gilt brass Rococo mounts and leaf-cast sabot feet.

38.25in (97cm) wide

£1,500-2,000 **L&T**

A French boullework fold-over card table, the shaped top over an ormolu-mounted frieze centred with a mask on cabriole legs.

c1880 *34in (86.5cm) high*

£1,200-1,800 **SWO**

A Massachusetts Chippendale carved mahogany games table, the serpentine top with moulded edges and rounded front corners, over a skirt with scribed edge and a shell-carved centre flanked by moulded tapering legs with inside chamfering.

c1770 *34.5in (86.5cm) wide*

£4,000-6,000 **SK**

A Federal mahogany and inlaid D-shaped games table, with satinwood banded fold-over top enclosing a later leather-inset playing surface, over a breakfront frieze, raised on reeded, turned and tapered legs.

c1810 *36in (90cm) wide*

£800-1,200 **FRE**

A New York Sheraton mahogany card table, with shaped top over a conforming frame with five turned and reeded legs terminating in brass ball feet.

c1825 *36in (90cm) wide*

£800-1,200 **POOK**

A pair of Massachusetts Federal mahogany inlaid card tables, the folding tops with serpentine fronts, half-serpentine sides, ovolo corners and inlaid edge, on conforming bases with bird's-eye maple panels.

c1810 *37in (92.5cm) wide*

£12,000-18,000 **SK**

A Massachusetts Hepplewhite mahogany card table, with serpentine top over a conforming frame with inlaid bird's-eye maple and satinwood panels and an arrow-inlaid apron, supported by square tapering legs with banded cuffs.

c1805 *36.25in (90.5cm) wide*

£5,000-6,000 **POOK**

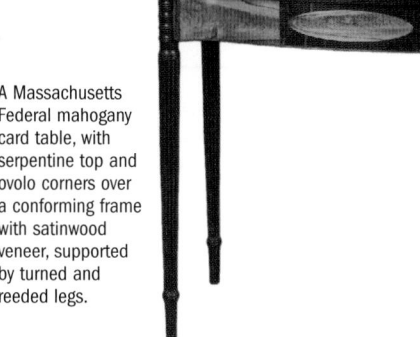

A Massachusetts Federal mahogany card table, with serpentine top and ovolo corners over a conforming frame with satinwood veneer, supported by turned and reeded legs.

c1810 *35.75in (89cm) wide*

£2,000-2,500 **POOK**

A New York Federal mahogany card table, with serpentine top supported by six turned and reeded legs, terminating in brass animal paw feet.

c1815 *36in (90cm) wide*

£8,000-12,000 **POOK**

LEFT: An American Chippendale cherry Pembroke table, with a drop-leaf top with pronounced scalloped leaves supported by straight square legs.

c1780 *30.5in (76cm) wide*

£1,000-1,500 **POOK**

RIGHT: A Delaware Valley mahogany Pembroke table, with an oblong top overhanging frame and single drawer supported by straight square tapering legs joined by cross stretchers.

29.5in (75cm) wide

£1,000-1,500 **POOK**

A George III-style oval mahogany Pembroke table.

29.25in (75cm) high

£250-300 **SWO**

A George III-style mahogany Pembroke table, with short drop-leaves over a frieze drawer, square chamfered legs and a shaped stretcher.

29.25in (75cm) high

£300-500 **SWO**

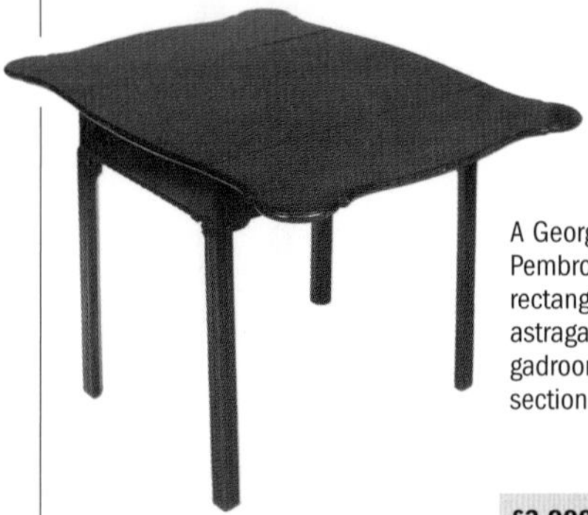

A George III mahogany shaped Pembroke table, the serpentine rectangular top with lobed corners and astragal edge above frieze with gadrooned border and moulded square-section chamfered legs.

39.75in (101cm) wide

£3,000-4,000 **L&T**

A George III mahogany Pembroke table, the rectangular top supporting two drop-leaves with floral carved edges, over a frame with single drawer supported by square legs terminating in Marlborough feet.

c1775 *27in (68.5cm) wide*

£2,800-3,200 **POOK**

A George III mahogany and satinwood banded oval Pembroke table, the drop-leaf top over one frieze drawer, raised on slender square tapered legs ending in spade feet.

c1800 *33in (84cm) wide*

£800-1,200 **FRE**

A George III rosewood and satinwood banded Pembroke table, the rounded rectangular top over one real and one dummy frieze drawer terminating in brass cappings and castors.

c1800 *32in (81.5cm) wide*

£1,500-2,000 **FRE**

A George III mahogany Pembroke table, with a single frieze drawer, on turned legs.

24.25in (61.5cm) wide

£400-600 **SWO**

A Regency mahogany Pembroke table, the top with a reeded edge and rounded corners, above a drawer opposing a false drawer, on a turned column and reeded sabre legs with brass paw terminals and castors.

44.5in (113cm) wide

£600-800 **DN**

A William IV mahogany Pembroke table, with rounded flaps, on reeded legs, brass caps and castors.

41in (104cm) high

£400-500 **SWO**

A CLOSER LOOK AT A GEORGE III PEMBROKE TABLE

William Linnell and his son were important 18thC London furniture makers. Although less well-known, some experts consider the Linnells alongside the likes of Chippendale.

Cabinet-makers took advantage of the increasing availability of exotic woods with a strong grain, such as the expensive satinwood, to create interesting veneers.

The lattice and trellis patterns were popular and reflected the desire for symmetrical designs.

Some of the finest cabinet-making of the period is seen in this type of table. Named after the Countess of Pembroke, the Pembroke table was produced in England from the mid-18thC. It was used for occasional pursuits such as playing cards, needlework and taking light meals.

A George III parquetry Pembroke table, in the manner of John Linnell, elaborately inlaid with satinwood and rosewood or olivewood, secret drawer to each end, on tapering legs also inlaid with wenge panels.

46in (117cm) wide

£40,000-60,000 **L&T**

A 19thC Continental rosewood Pembroke table, with a single drawer, on a curved and parquetry inlaid support and downswept legs, terminating in brass capped castors.

29in (73.5cm) wide

£700-1,000 **SWO**

A 19thC mahogany Pembroke table, on square tapering legs.

£280-320 **SWO**

An Edwardian inlaid mahogany Pembroke table.

£600-900 **SWO**

A Regency mahogany sofa table with satinwood and rosewood crossbanding and stringing, fitted with two real and two dummy drawers, on downswept legs with brass caps and castors.

extended 60in (152.5cm) wide

£2,800-3,200 **BRI**

A Regency mahogany sofa table, with satinwood crossbanding and boxwood stringing, two frieze drawers opposing two dummy drawers, on sabre legs with brass cap and castors.

60.5in (154cm) wide

£2,000-3,000 **L&T**

A Regency mahogany sofa table, the figured top with rosewood and mahogany crossbanding, panelled frieze with hidden drawers and beaded moulding, on ebony-strung square-section legs with brass paw cast caps and castors.

56.25in (143cm) wide

£800-1,200 **L&T**

A Regency mahogany sofa table, with a single frieze drawer.

33in (84cm) wide

£400-600 **SWO**

A Regency mahogany and ebony banded sofa table, the top with a reeded edge, over two real and two opposing dummy drawers, raised on twin end supports and four sabre legs terminating in brass cappings and castors.

c1815 59in (150cm) wide

£1,000-1,500 **FRE**

A Regency mahogany and satinwood-banded sofa table, the top with moulded edge above two drawers, each with ebony lines, opposed by two dummy drawers, with sabre legs terminating in brass caps and castors.

56.75in (144cm) wide

£2,000-3,000 **L&T**

A Regency period mahogany sofa table, the frieze with one real and one dummy drawer on each side, on rectangular end standards, each with a pair of reeded sabre legs and brass lions' paw castors.

45.25in (133cm) wide

£1,800-2,200 **SWO**

A Regency strung rosewood sofa table, the drop-leaf top over two frieze drawers with gilt bronze mounts on standard ends and sabre legs.

37.25in (93cm) wide

£1,800-2,200 **SWO**

A Regency rosewood sofa table, with drop-flap top over twin in-line frieze drawers with period ormolu applied motifs and knops, on four baluster and ringed supports, swept sabre legs.

£1,800-2,200 **BIG**

A Regency rosewood and tulipwood line-inlaid sofa table, with two drop-leaves and two frieze drawers to one side, on turned and leaf carved column and concave sided base, splayed legs and brass paw terminals.

61in (155cm) wide

£1,000-1,500 **LFA**

A William IV mahogany sofa table, the drop-leaf top over two frieze drawers, centred by a patera motif raised on twin acanthus-carved ogee end supports, on sabre legs.

c1835 64.5in (164cm) wide

£1,500-2,000 **FRE**

A 19thC oak lamp table, the circular top with later inlay and a frieze.

£500-700 **SWO**

A Victorian papier-mâché tilt-top table, the serpentine-shaped oval top painted with a floral bouquet and with mother-of-pearl inlaid decoration, on a baluster-turned column support, platform base with three outset feet.

c1860 *27.5in (69cm) high*

£300-400 **FRE**

A 19thC Victorian specimen marble and slate occasional table, the circular top inlaid with various marbles, supported by a semi-lobed turned vasiform column, ending in a triform base and squat bun feet.

29in (72.5cm) high

£1,500-2,000 **FRE**

A Victorian papier-mâché occasional table by Jennens & Bettridge, the tilt-top painted after Landseer and signed "Jennens & Bettridge", the block stamped "a crown, J&B patent 24", on a ribbed stem to a welled base with scroll feet.

27.75in (70.5cm) diam

£800-1,200 **WW**

A Victorian rosewood occasional table, the circular top on a column with carved leaf decoration, triform base and gardrooned feet.

17in (43cm) diam

£500-700 **SWO**

A Victorian papier mâché lobed round tip-up table, the top painted with flowers and leaves, inlaid with mother-of-pearl, on turned column and concave-sided triform base, with bun feet.

20in (51cm) diam

£200-300 **LFA**

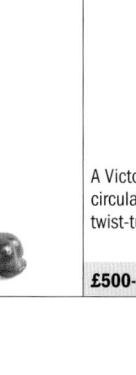

A Victorian walnut lamp table, the circular top inset with beadwork on a twist-turned column and platform base.

22in (56cm) diam

£500-700 **SWO**

A George III mahogany circular top tripod table.

25.5in (63.5cm) diam

£800-1,200 **SWO**

A George III mahogany tilt-top tripod table, formerly with a birdcage, the dish top supported by a fluted turned column, raised on three shell-carved cabriole legs terminating in egg and claw fee.

c1765 *28in (70cm) high*

£600-900 **FRE**

A George III mahogany tripod table, the dished circular top on a turned column.

20in (51cm) diam

£700-1,000 **SWO**

A George III mahogany dish top tripod table.

19.75in (50cm) diam

£700-1,000 **SWO**

A George III mahogany tripod table, with a circular snap-top on a gun barrel column and slender outswept legs.

32in (80cm) diam

£1,000-1,500 **SWO**

A George III mahogany occasional table, with figured plain top, candy-twist baluster column raised on tripod base with ball and talon feet.

£800-1,200 **BIG**

A George III mahogany tip-top occasional table, with Chippendale pie-crust top, mounted on a foliate-carved column raised on tripod cabriole legs with foliate-carved knees and plain pad feet.

30.75in (78cm) diam

£400-600 **BIG**

A George III mahogany snap-top occasional table, the square top with moulded edge above a birdcage and a turned column with spirally fluted knop, raised above a tripod base with cabriole legs terminating in pad feet.

28.5in (72.5cm) high

£2,000-3,000 **L&T**

A George III mahogany circular top tripod table.

28.25in (71.5cm) high

£500-700 **SWO**

A George III mahogany tripod table, the circular dished top on a turned column and three cabriole legs.

21.5in (54.5cm) diam

£500-700 **SWO**

A George III mahogany circular top tripod table.

21.75in (55cm) diam

£700-1,000 **SWO**

A George III yew wood tripod table, the circular plank top on a birdcage, baluster-turned column and outswept legs.

22in (56cm) high

£700-1,000 **SWO**

A Delaware Valley Chippendale mahogany candlestand, the circular pie crust top tilting over an urn-turned standard supported by cabriole legs and ball and claw feet.

c1770 *28.5in (71cm) high*

£2,000-2,500 **POOK**

A late 18thC Pennsylvania Queen Anne cherry tea table, with circular dished tilt-top on a baluster-turned birdcage platform and a bulbous vase- and ring-turned post continuing to tripod cabriole leg base ending in pad feet.

34in (85cm) diam

£4,000-6,000 **SK**

A late 18thC Massachusetts Chippendale mahogany tilt-top stand, with moulded serpentine top on vase- and ring-turned support and tripod cabriole leg base ending in padded feet on platforms.

26in (65cm) high

£3,000-4,000 **SK**

A Pennsylvania cherry candlestand, the circular dish top with central star inlay within two concentric circles, on a circular birdcage support, over a baluster-turned standard supported by cabriole legs terminating in pad feet.

c1800 *29.5in (74cm) high*

£3,000-4,000 **POOK**

A pair of English satinwood crossbanded oval tripod tables in the 18thC style, the tops with boxwood and ebony stringing, on green painted and parcel gilt bases, with three hipped legs carved with acanthus and paw feet.

19.25in (49cm) wide

£2,000-2,500 **DN**

A Regency rosewood tripod reading stand, having an adjustable slide with a hinged rest on a turned column and outswept reeded legs.

29.5in (74cm) high

£2,000-3,000 **SWO**

A Regency mahogany tripod table, with a rectangular top and ebony banding, on a ring-turned column base.

29.25in (74cm) high

£400-600 **SWO**

A 19thC mahogany tripod table, with a rectangular top and baluster-turned column.

30.5in (76cm) wide

£800-1,200 **SWO**

A 19thC mahogany occasional table, the circular tilt-top on a baluster-turned column and a tripod base.

32.75in (83cm) high

£300-500 **SWO**

A pair of 19thC painted tripod tables, the rectangular tops with canted corners, decorated with floral panels surrounded by leaf and baton borders, on ring-turned stems to scroll legs.

18in (45.5cm) wide

£2,000-3,000 **WW**

A pair of Victorian ebonized low tripod tables, each circular top with a painted river landscape with mother-of-pearl inlay on scrolled supports.

23.25in (58cm) high

£700-1,000 **SWO**

An Australian cedar wine table, the hexagonal top inlaid with Australian specimen timbers, supported by a turned shaped column and a tripod footed base.

c1880 *19.25in (49cm) wide*

£800-1,200 **BONA**

A 19thC elm tripod table, the sixteen-sided hinged top on a turned column and three stepped curved legs.

22in (57cm) wide

£700-1,000 **SWO**

A Victorian walnut tripod table, the snap top with geometric inlay on a turned column and fret cut outswept supports.

26.75in (67cm) diam

£600-900 **SWO**

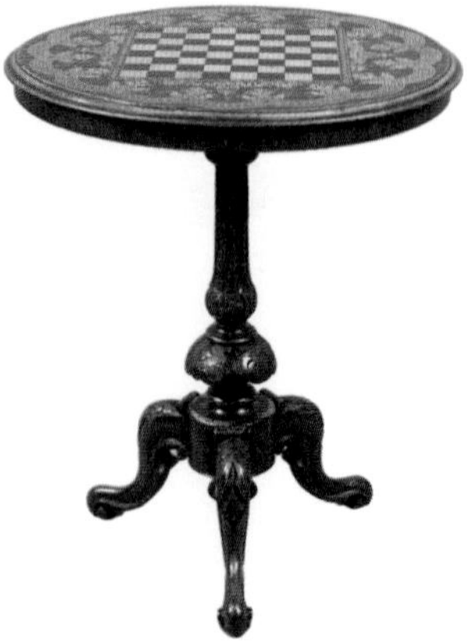

A Victorian walnut tripod table, inlaid with a chessboard, floral and strapwork border, on a carved baluster column.

24in (61cm) high

£700-1,000 **SWO**

A Chinese ebonized and shell-inlaid tripod table, inset with a bird, peonies and bamboo, on a turned base.

23.75in (60.5cm) wide

£400-600 **DN**

A George III mahogany and satinwood inlaid octagonal work table, the hinged lid opening to reveal lidded compartments, on square tapering legs and spade feet.

18.5in (47cm) wide

£700-1,000 **SWO**

A Regency mahogany work table, the rectangular top inlaid with specimen marble parquetry, above a frieze drawer and wool bin, the curved supports raised above square cabriole legs.

17in (43.5cm) wide

£2,000-3,000 **L&T**

A Regency period mahogany work table, the twin flap-top over two real and two dummy drawers and a pull silk box, on a U-frame and four sabre legs.

16.5in (42cm) wide

£700-900 **SWO**

A Regency mahogany sewing table, with a rectangular top, two drawers over a beadwork frieze, and a shaped column, on a quadripartite base.

30.5in (76cm) high

£1,000-1,500 **SWO**

A Regency rosewood worktable, the plain rectangular top with a frieze drawer, and carved lyre-shaped supports, united with a stretcher.

24in (61cm) high

£500-700 **SWO**

A Regency rosewood and boxwood-strung work table, with a fitted drawer and a wool bag, flat stretcher and sabre legs with paw feet.

26.5in (67cm) wide

£700-900 **DN**

A Regency faux rosewood and brass-strung work table, fitted with two true and two dummy drawers, on lyre-shaped supports and downswept legs.

23.25in (58cm) wide

£600-900 **SWO**

A William IV rosewood work table, with a single drawer above the slide, raised on a octagonal tapering column, on a quadripartite base.

19.5in (48.5cm) high

£800-1,200 **SWO**

A 19thC satinwood work table, with a central amboyna panel and rosewood crossbanding, partitioned lift-out tray and pleated bag.

18in (45.5cm) wide

£1,000-1,500 **WW**

A mid-19thC Chinese export lacquered work table, painted with figures and landscapes in gilt on a black ground, hinged to enclose recesses, lidded divisions and ivory fittings, lacking wool bag, damaged.

24.5in (62.5cm) wide

£600-900 **DN**

A 19thC Anglo-Indian rosewood work table, the top carved mouldings over a drawer and four pierced brackets, the sewing box and uprights with ornate pierced and carved bird and foliage decoration.

31.5in (80cm) wide

£300-500 **SWO**

A Victorian mahogany and rosewood crossbanded ladies work table, fitted with two true and two dummy drawers.

20.5in (52cm) wide

£500-700 **SWO**

A Victorian mahogany work table, on turned and carved supports, with brass capped ceramic castors.

£500-700 **SWO**

A Victorian inlaid walnut games and sewing table, the fold-over top with strung and inlaid decoration opening to reveal an inlaid chess board, backgammon board and cribbage board over a frieze drawer and basket on turned end supports.

27.25in (69cm) wide

£2,000-3,000 **SWO**

A Victorian rosewood serpentine-shaped work table, with a frieze drawer enclosing fabric lined fittings and a sliding bag, on a 'U' shaped support and four flower-carved cabriole legs, with recessed castors.

22.25in (56.5cm) wide

£1,200-1,800 **DN**

A Victorian shaped rectangular walnut work table, with hinged lid, mirror, and fitted interior, tapering well and shaped and moulded lyre end supports, scroll feet and castors.

21in (53.5cm) wide

£300-500 **MAX**

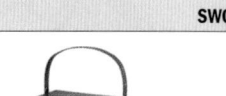

A late 19thC Sheraton Revival work table, with painted cartouches and floral sprays, supported on slender square tapering legs.

£400-600 **SWO**

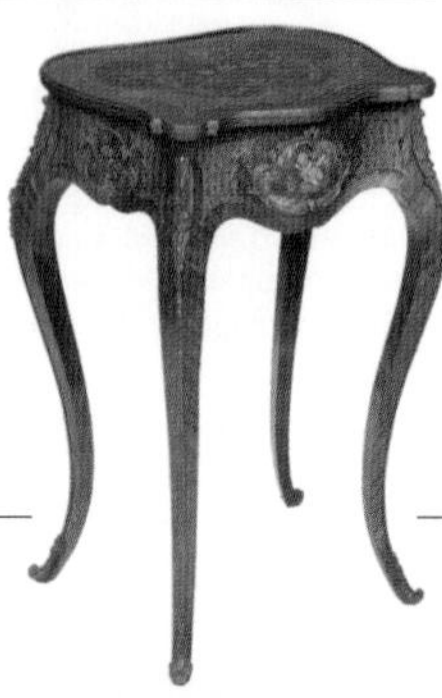

An Edwardian mahogany and marquetry inlaid work table, in the Louis XV style, the shaped hinged top inlaid enclosing a silk-lined interior, serpentine apron, on cabriole legs terminating in cast sabots.

17.75in (45cm) high

£1,000-1,500 **L&T**

FEDERAL STYLE

- American Federal style dates from the period leading up to and following the foundation of the first Federal government under George Washington in 1789.
- The American establishment took Classical Greece and Rome as its model. The Neoclassical style was therefore very popular in America until the mid-19thC.
- Patriotic emblems such as stars and stripes or American eagles clutching bundled fasces express the optimistic nationalism of the times.
- Furniture forms associated with the American Federal style include secretaire bookcases, cellarets, sofa tables and work tables.
- Cabinet-makers used mahogany, often accented with inlays of satinwood. Indigenous woods such as maple were also popular.
- Like European furniture of the period, American Federal furniture employs refined Classical proportions and symmetry. Slender turned legs and carved Classical motifs such as urns and scrolls provide decorative interest.
- Federal furniture is often classified by geographical area. Differences in construction, materials and decoration distinguish pieces made in different states, counties and even individual towns.

A Massachusetts Sheraton work table, attributed to the Seymor workshop, with satinwood and bird's-eye maple inlaid top with turned corners, above two satinwood inlaid drawers, supported by turned and reeded legs.

c1800 *27in (67.5cm) high*

£2,200-2,800 POOK

A Philadelphia Federal mahogany workstand, attributed to Henry Connelly, with two graduated cockbeaded drawers, on turned and acanthus-carved support with tapering legs terminating in brass paw caps with castors.

c1815 *19in (48.5cm) wide*

£2,000-2,500 FRE

A New York Federal mahogany workstand, with two drawers over an urn-turned standard, resting on four curved acanthus-carved legs terminating in brass animal paw feet and castors.

c1805 *28.25in (70.5cm) high*

£3,000-4,000 POOK

A Massachusetts Federal mahogany and satinwood veneer inlaid work table, probably Salem, the serpentine top with ovolo corners on a conforming frame with drawer and bag drawer below, joining vase- and ring-turned reeded legs.

c1805 *28.75in (72cm) high*

£25,000-30,000 SK

A Massachusetts Federal mahogany workstand, the rectangular top with rounded corners, over a case with three drawers flanked by half turned stiles, supported on turned legs.

c1810 *29in (72.5cm) high*

£1,000-1,500 POOK

A Massachusetts Federal mahogany and bird's-eye maple veneer work table, with ivory bosses above two cockbeaded drawers with embossed brass pulls and ivory escutcheons.

c1812 *28.75in (72cm) high*

£8,000-12,000 SK

A Massachusetts Federal mahogany sewing table, with a checkerboard inlaid edge, over a case with two drawers and a sewing bag supported by turned and reeded legs.

c1815 *29.75in (74cm) high*

£1,500-2,000 POOK

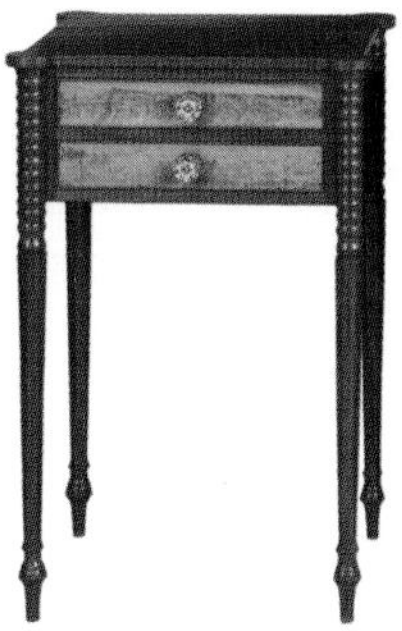

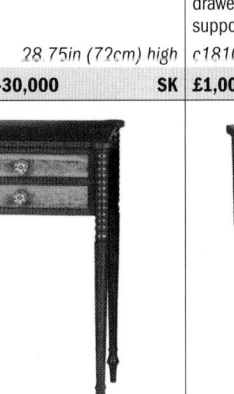

A Massachusetts Federal mahogany work table, the rectangular top over a case with two drawers supported by turned legs.

c1815 *30in (75cm) high*

£2,000-2,500 POOK

A tiger maple and bird's-eye maple work table, probably mid-Atlantic, with rectangular top above two drawers, on vase- and ring-turned swelled tapering legs.

c1830 *21in (53.5cm) wide*

£1,800-2,200 SK

A George III mahogany writing desk, with tooled inset skiver above six opposing frieze drawers, brass caps and castors.

48in (122cm) wide

£5,000-7,000 **L&T**

A Regency rosewood writing table, in the manner of Gillows & Co., with a single drawer with applied anthemion escutcheon, on turned tapering and reeded legs and brass caps and castors.

28.75in (73cm) high

£1,500-2,000 **L&T**

A Sheraton-style painted satinwood and rosewood crossbanded writing table, the top painted with a flowering vase and swags, over three frieze drawers, on acanthus carved fluted legs.

48in (122cm) wide

£2,500-3,000 **FRE**

A Regency mahogany writing table, inset with tooled leather writing surface above three opposing drawers, one with fitted interior, on turned and reeded tapering legs.

54in (137cm) wide

£1,200-1,800 **L&T**

A Regency-style mahogany library table, with a tooled leather top, fitted with short drawers, on splayed legs, terminating in brass cap castors.

51.5in (131cm) wide

£700-1,000 **SWO**

A George IV mahogany writing table, the tooled leather inset top over a pair of cockbeaded drawers with turned ebony handles, on flattened end supports, downswept legs, brass caps and castors.

38in (96.5cm) wide

£600-900 **SWO**

A fine George IV mahogany desk, by Gillows & Co., with an inset gilt embossed leather writing surface over three frieze drawers, impressed stamp "Gillows, Lancaster".

c1825 *46in (117cm) wide*

£3,000-4,000 **FRE**

A William IV mahogany library table, the moulded top over one frieze drawer, raised on carved X-form end supports united by a turned stretcher.

c1835 *45.5in (115.5cm) wide*

£1,800-2,200 **FRE**

A New Hampshire Federal mahogany carved tall post bed, with vase- and ring-turned, leaf-carved, and reeded foot posts continuing to square moulded legs joining red-painted tapering head posts and blue-painted arched headboard.

c1805 *51in (129.5cm) wide*

£3,500-4,500 **SK**

A New England Federal carved mahogany and maple tester bed, the four posts with leaf-carved capitals above reeding, joined at the arched headboard and square tapering head posts by a flat tester.

c1810 *97in (242.5cm) high*

£4,000-6,000 **SK**

A late mid-Atlantic Federal tiger maple tall post bed, with four vase- and ring-turned octagonal chamfered posts continuing to ring-turned tapering legs, joined by peaked recessed panelled headboard.

c1820 *54in (137cm) wide*

£2,200-2,800 **SK**

A 19thC French walnut double bed, with carved headboard.

58.75in (147cm) wide

£400-600 **SWO**

A four poster bed, with a pair of Victorian carved mahogany posts.

60in (152.5cm) wide

£1,200-1,800 **SWO**

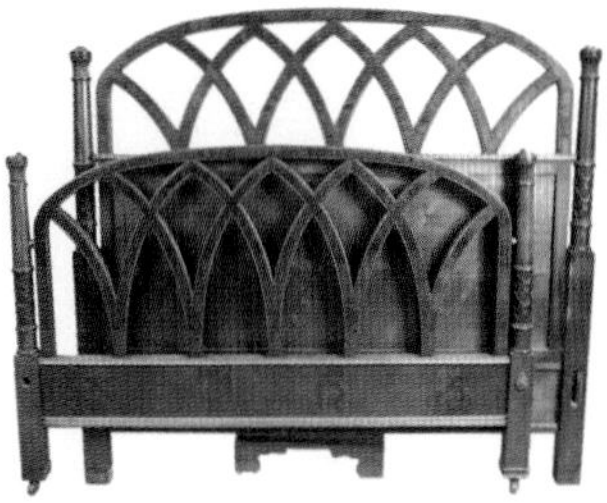

An Edwardian mahogany bed, with pierced trellis work ends flanked by carved columns.

60in (152.5cm) wide

£800-1,200 **SWO**

An Australian cedar and blackwood half tester double bedstead, Tasmania.

c1870

£2,500-3,000 **BONA**

A mid-Victorian mahogany half-tester bed, with cushion-moulded canopy and rail and ornate flame-veneered tailboard.

90.5in (230cm) high

£1,000-1,500 **BIG**

A Georgian mahogany four-tier whatnot, with baluster-turned supports, the bottom shelf fitted drawers, on turned taper supports and brass castors.

18in (45.5cm) wide

£700-1,000 **BRI**

A George IV mahogany three-tier whatnot, with ring--turned acorn finials, with a door and drawer, on turned legs with brass terminals and castors.

16in (41cm) wide

£600-900 **DN**

An Australian full cedar three-tier whatnot, Tasmania, in the style of Champion, the turned columns supporting full cedar shelves, on short turned feet with brass castors.

c1835 *53.5in (136cm) wide*

£4,000-5,000 **BONA**

A George IV mahogany whatnot, the ratcheted top with a removable book rest with replaced brass clips, central tier with a frieze drawer, on brass castors.

20in (51cm) wide

£800-1,200 **WW**

A 19thC mahogany whatnot, drawers to both the top and bottom tiers, with turned supports.

£800-1200 **BRI**

A Victorian mahogany three-tier buffet, on turned supports.

30in (76cm) wide

£700-1,000 **SWO**

A Victorian walnut three-tier whatnot.

20.75in (52cm) high

£300-500 **SWO**

A late Victorian whatnot, with an inlaid gallery top supported by barley-twist columns and a single drawer to base.

£300-400 **SWO**

A pair of 19thC mahogany étagères, of Louis XVI style, each with marble tops with pierced brass lattice galleries, inlaid with kingwood parquetry panels, on turned toupie feet.

13in (33cm) wide

£4,000-6,000 **L&T**

A 19thC mahogany and brass étagère, of three square tiers, each with brass gallery supported by turned columns with sphere finials, raised on brass castors.

30in (76cm) high

£1,500-2,000 **L&T**

A Victorian burr walnut two-tier étagère, with crossbanding and stringing, the upper section with brass edge, hinged fall-down front, the lower part with pierced gallery, on cheval frame.

29in (73.5cm) wide

£1,200-1,800 **BRI**

A Victorian amboyna two-tier étagère with ebonized banding and ormola beading, on three turned side columns, trestle base with splay feet and castors.

30in (76cm) wide

£700-1,000 **MAX**

An Edwardian inlaid mahogany kidney-shaped étagère.

22.75in (58cm) wide

£300-400 **SWO**

A George III mahogany dumb waiter, with three graduated dished tiers, on a tripod base and pad feet with brass castors.

45in (114cm) high

£600-900 **SWO**

A 19thC mahogany two-tier dumb waiter, with dished moulded tiers, inverted part-ribbed baluster stem and three reeded scroll legs to brass sabots and castors.

23.5in (59.5cm) diam

£500-700 **WW**

A 19thC carved dumb waiter, in the form of a monkey standing on a rockwork base, holding an engraved brass dish.

55in (140cm) high

£1,500-1,800 **SWO**

A French kingwood and parquetry two-tier guiridon, in Louis XVI style, with inset marble top and pierced gilt metal galleries, on reeded column, three splayed legs and gilt metal leaf-cast sabots.

31.75in (81.5cm) high

£1,000-1,500 **LFA**

A Regency pollard oak teapoy, the caddy top opening to reveal two lidded compartments, flanking a central lidded tin box, on a column stem, quadripartite base and splayed legs with brass cap castors.

£1,500-2,000 **SWO**

A rectangular Regency rosewood teapoy, of waisted form with hinged lid, fitted interior, baluster-turned column, quatrefoil base and pad feet.

16.5in (42cm) wide

£400-600 **MAX**

A rare early 19thC figured maple teapoy, of sarcophagus form, with fitted interior, on turned pedestals and scrolled played supports with brass caps and castors.

33in (84cm) high

£2,800-3,200 **WAD**

A George IV rosewood and brass line-inlaid teapoy, in the manner of Gillow's, the later hinged top with two bowl recesses and two lidded canisters, on scroll legs to brass sabots and castors.

17in (43cm) wide

£1,000-1,500 **WW**

An early Victorian ebonized coromandel teapoy, ornately carved overall with flowers, leaves and fruit, the hinged lip opening to reveal a plain interior, raised on a carved floral trailing spiral column.

18.75in (47.5cm) wide

£600-£800 **SWO**

A Victorian rosewood teapoy, the top section fitted with three boxes, on an octagonal tapering column and a platform base, with four bun feet.

33.5in (85cm) high

£600-900 **SWO**

A mahogany jardinière, raised on splayed legs.

34.75in (87cm) high

£200-300 **SWO**

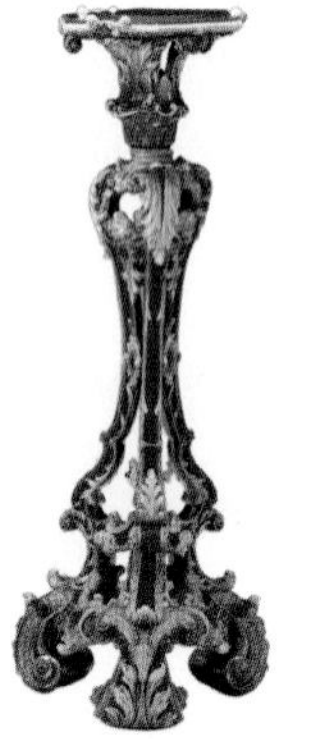

A late 19thC Continental majolica jardinière stand, in red and green glaze enriched with gilt, the hexagonal top raised on an ornate Rococo scroll openwork triform support.

46.5in (116cm) high

£400-600 **FRE**

A Napoleon III mahogany marquetry and parquetry jardinière, the removable top with a musical trophy, the frieze inset with two faience panels decorated with figures, on splayed legs headed by a ram's mask.

£1,200-1,800 **FRE**

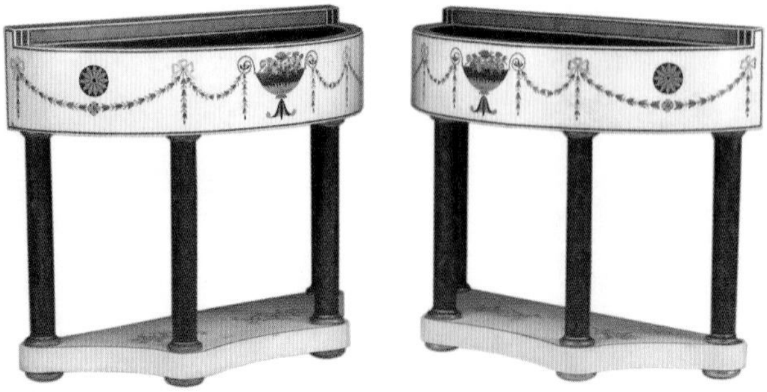

A pair of Continental Neoclassical-style veneered marble demi-lune jardinières, the ornate pietra dura friezes centred by a fruiting urns with ribbon tied bellflower swags, on four column supports and platform bases.

49in (124.5cm) wide

£6,000-8,000 **FRE**

A Victorian kingwood veneered jardinière stand, in the Louis XV style, with zinc liner and pierced gilt metal gallery, the apron set with opposed Sèvres-style panels.

29.5in (75cm) wide

£1,500-2,000 **L&T**

A Federal pine stand, the rectangular top with apron drawer on rakish square tapering legs.

c1800 *28.5in (71cm) high*

£350-400 **FRE**

An early 19thC Pennsylvania Federal walnut table, the square overhanging top with chamfered underside, on square tapering splayed legs, joined by a beaded skirt containing a drawer.

20in (51cm) wide

£6,000-9,000 **SK**

An Australian blackwood hallstand, with shaped arms, the base with umbrella stand.

c1870 *54.5in (138cm) high*

£1,200-1,800 **BONA**

A Pennsylvania Classical tiger maple chamber stand, the top flanked by a scrolled splashboard above single drawer and turned tapering legs, with a concave shaped medial shelf.

c1830s *31in (78.5cm) wide*

£3,500-4,500 **SK**

An Ontario pine lamp table with drawer, with tapered legs.

c1880 *25.5in (65cm) high*

£200-300 **RAON**

A painted stand, with rectangular overhanging top above a scratchbeaded drawer and straight skirt.

15.75in (40cm) wide

£400-600 **SK**

An Edwardian mahogany three-tier cake stand, with boxwood inlay, tiers held within squared uprights with matching boxwood inlaid decoration and a central handle.

£180-220 **BIG**

An early 18thC giltwood wall mirror, the shaped rectangular plate with elaborate carved frame with scrolling foliage and pendants of flowers and fruits.

66.5in (169cm) high

£5,000-7,000 **L&T**

A George II gilt mirror, the shaped rectangular plate within C-scroll and pierced rocaille work frame.

29.25in (74cm) wide

£6,000-9,000 **L&T**

A mid-18thC large George II burlwood veneer looking glass, with scrolled crest over a moulded frame and scrolled base.

c1750 *27.5in (70cm) wide*

£1,500-2,000 **POOK**

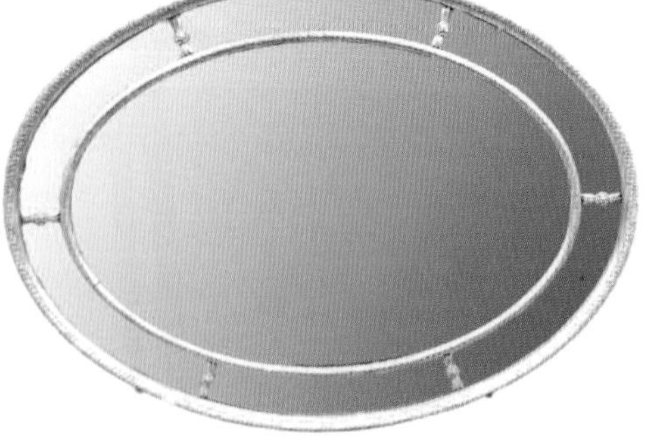

A George III oval gilt wood wall mirror, the central glass with a six-piece sectional border.

39.25in (100cm) wide

£700-1,000 **SWO**

An early 19thC giltwood pier glass, in the Rococo manner, with a an elaborate Rococo frame carved with C-scrolls, rocaille work and foliage and enclosing a border of multiple plates.

99.5in (253cm) high

£6,000-8,000 **L&T**

A late 18thC carved and pierced gilt wood wall mirror with rectangular 20thC plate, contained in a leaf-bordered frame with scrolls and wave motifs.

30.5in (76cm) high

£2,000-3,000 **BIG**

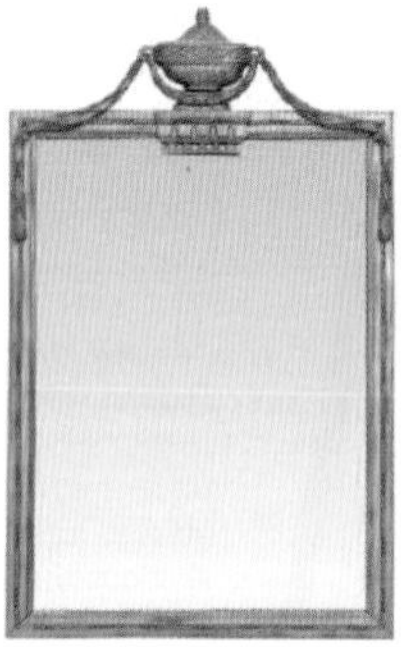

A late 18thC German Louis XVI-style mirror, in carved and gilded wood, with a vase and festoon to the top, original glass, with label of a Freiburg noble house.

48.75in (112cm) high

£1,000-1,500 **KAU**

A Regency carved gilt wood convex wall mirror, surmounted by an eagle on rockwork with leaf scrolling to the sides, snake and acorn decoration beneath the plate glass.

35in (89cm) high

£1,000-1,500 **SWO**

A 19thC Masonic gilt pier glass, with an architectural pediment over split Corinthian columns and Masonic motifs.

29.5in (75cm) high

£200-300 **SWO**

A 19thC carved pine and gilt gesso framed wall mirror, the rectangular plate within a scrolled surround.

57.75in (147cm) wide

£800-1200 **SWO**

A 19thC German harvest mirror, with stucco and gilded vine and grape decoration, the lower corners with figures holding baskets and a grape picker.

Provenance: *The Russian Court, Weimar, Germany.*

105.5in (264cm) high

£1,000-1,500 **KAU**

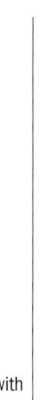

A George III mahogany cheval mirror, with a satinwood, purple heart and kingwood-banded frame with a shaped surmount, on square supports, scroll legs and brass castors.

27.25in (69cm) wide

£1,200-1,800 **WW**

A Regency mahogany cheval mirror, with an ebonized reeded slip and crossbanded rise and fall frame, with brass handle, on reeded sabre legs, brass caps and castors.

28.25in (72cm) wide

£2,500-3,000 **L&T**

An Edwardian mahogany cheval mirror, with a fret-cut crest and carved frame, on scrolled feet.

£2,500-3,000 **SWO**

A tortoiseshell-veneered and ivory-mounted swing mirror, with bevel edge glass.

c1930 *16.75in (42cm) high*

£700-1,000 **SWO**

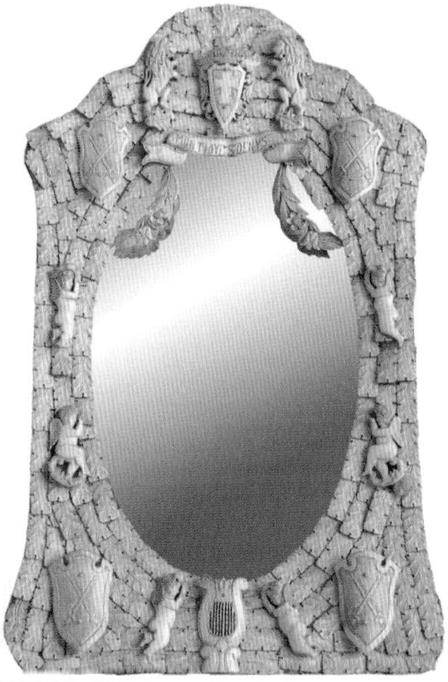

A 19thC Dieppe bone-framed wall mirror, applied with armorial shields, putti and flower garlands, and the motto "Montioyl S Denys".

32in (81cm) high

£2,000-3,000 **LFA**

A Dieppe bone-framed mirror, with a shaped surmount, applied with a basket, a coat of arms, winged putti and plumed festoons, enclosing a bevelled oval glass.

32.75in (82cm) high

£800-1,200 **SWO**

A late 18thC American Chippendale mahogany and gilt wood looking glass, with an eagle with outstretched wings centred by foliate scrolls on swan-neck pediment, label of John Elliott, Philadelphia, regilded.

59in (150cm) high

£4,000-5,000 **FRE**

A Federal carved gilt wood convex mirror, the round frame with ball ornaments, surmounted by an ebonized spread-winged eagle perched on a wreath and flanked by two arms, above an oak leaf and grape cluster lower pendant.

c1800 *41in (102.5cm) high*

£5,000-8,000 **POOK**

A CLOSER LOOK AT AN AMERICAN CONVEX MIRROR

The spread-winged eagle was a favourite motif during the Federal period. The patriotic sentiment expressed here remains popular to this day.

Check that mirror glass has not been replaced by placing a coin against it. Glass dating from c1800 and earlier is thin, so the gap between the coin and its reflection should be no more than a couple of mm.

Round, convex mirrors like this, with highly decorative gilded frames are typical of the American Federal style. Details such as the carved shell are also hallmarks of the style.

Convex 'bull's-eye' glass was a by-product from the manufacture of sheet glass. A great deal of it was shipped to America as ballast.

A Federal carved gilt wood convex mirror, with ornate round frame surmounted by a spread-winged eagle, flanked by foliate appliqués, above a shell-carved pendant.

c1800 *48in (120cm) high*

£6,000-9,000 **POOK**

A massive Federal mahogany looking glass, the broken arch pediment with swan-neck mouldings centring a carved giltwood urn, over a leaf and acorn inlaid frieze and plate with gilt liner, scalloped base.

c1800 *68in (170cm) high*

£3,000-4,000 **POOK**

A pair of Massachusetts Federal gilt wood and gesso mirrors, with moulded cornices with bands of floral devices and grapevine and ropetwist borders, flanked by spiral-engaged columns on square plinths.

c1820 *25in (63.5cm) wide*

£4,000-6,000 **SK**

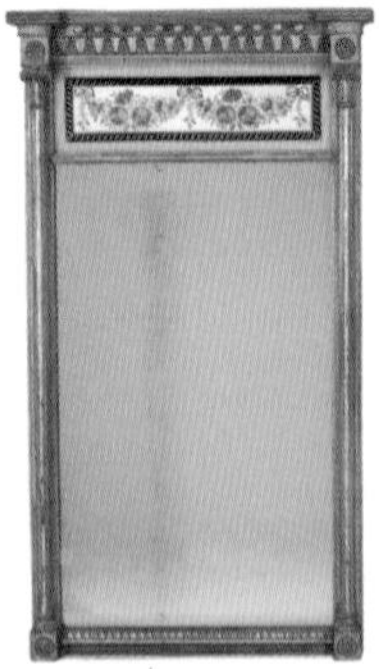

A Federal gilt wood mirror, with moulded cornice over an eglomise panel and rectangular looking glass flanked by reeded columns.

c1815 *49.5in (124cm) high*

£1,200-1,800 **POOK**

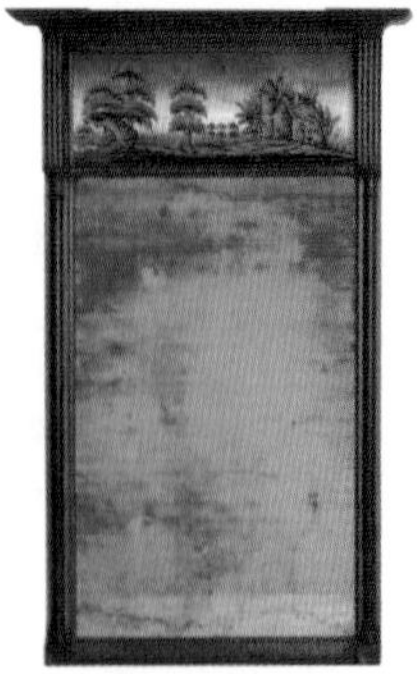

A large Pennsylvania Federal tiger maple and walnut mirror, with moulded and blocked cornice over fluted matchstick frieze and eglomise panel depicting a landscape and cottage, flanked by half-turned stiles.

c1820 *54in (135cm) high*

£1,800-2,200 **POOK**

A New York Classical mahogany cheval mirror, with rectangular swiveling mirror, turned supports and ormolu capitals, on formed feet.

c1825 *71.5in (179cm) high*

£800-1,200 **POOK**

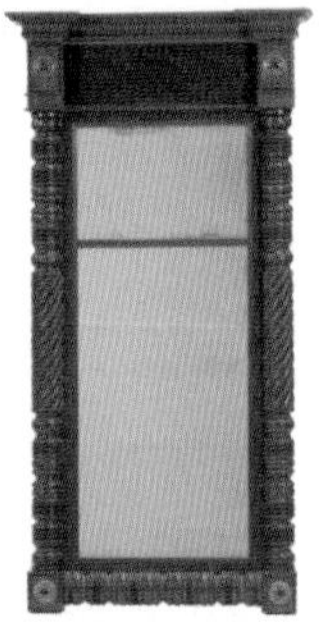

A mahogany pier mirror, with stepped cornice above conforming entablature with brass and wood bosses supported by turned split balusters enclosing mirror plate.

c1830 *28in (71cm) wide*

£350-450 **FRE**

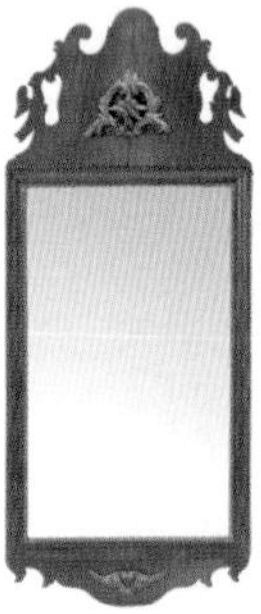

A 19thC Chippendale-style mahogany and giltwood looking glass, with shaped and arched pediment with applied giltwood floral device, above moulded frame with beaded gilt liner.

45in (114.5cm) high

£220-280 **FRE**

A 19thC Chippendale-style mahogany and carved gilt wood looking glass, carved with gilt phoenix and scroll ornamented shaped pediment above the moulded frame flanked by shaped ears and gilt trailing vine, restored.

54in (137cm) high

£350-450 **FRE**

A 19thC Pennsylvania carved and painted frame with mirror, with blocked corners with yellow bird decoration.

19in (47.5cm) high

£800-1,200 **POOK**

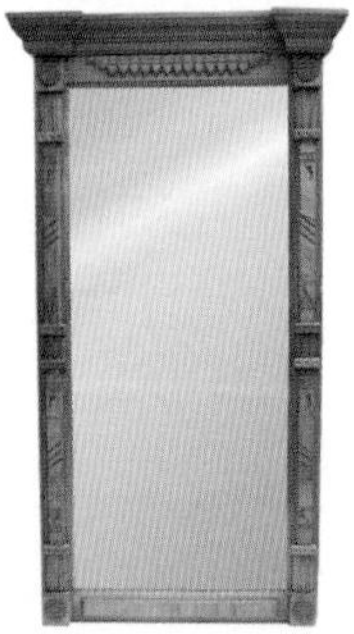

An Ontario carved mirror frame, from Niagara.

Pieces from Niagara are scarce. They tend to be fairly formal in style.

c1880 *47.25in (120cm) high*

£350-400 **RAON**

A Canadian mirror, carved from a single piece of wood, with duck's head designs.

c1880 *17.75in (45cm) high*

£150-200 **RAON**

An Ontario carved pine mirror frame, with original colour and finish.

c1880 *18.5in (47cm) high*

£100-150 **RAON**

A Canadian deep-carved and varnished pine frame, from the Germain Masse in Quebec.

c1980 *27.75in (70.5cm) wide*

£180-220 **RAON**

A late 18thC George III mahogany cellaret, the body of hexagonal form, the base with wavy moulding, on three reeded square legs with castors, the interior with lead liner.

16in (40.5cm) wide

£1,200-1,800 **FRE**

A late 18thC mahogany and white pine cellaret, brass straps, tin-lined sectioned interior.

19in (48.5cm) wide

£3,500-4,000 **SK**

A George III octagonal mahogany and brass-bound wine cooler, with side carrying handles, the hinged lid enclosing a lead lined interior, the stand on square legs with brass castors.

c1780 *18in (45.5cm) wide*

£1,500-2,000 **FRE**

A George III satinwood cellaret, with kingwood crossbanding, the hinged lid centred by a fan medallion enclosing later fitted interior with baize-lined bottle apertures.

29.25in (74cm) high

£2,000-3,000 **L&T**

A George III mahogany and inlaid cellaret, with lion-mask and loop handles, the hinged lid and front centred by a fan motif, on ring-turned tapered legs.

c1790 *16.5in (42cm) wide*

£1,500-2,000 **FRE**

A George III mahogany cellaret, for four bottles, with boxwood strung edges, turned ivory knop handle and a shaped brass escutcheon, upon short square tapering legs and brass castors.

c1810 *20.25in (51.5cm) high*

£400-600 **SWO**

A George III mahogany cellaret, of pointed arch form with drop-down door enclosing six baize-lined compartments, on square-section tapered legs with brass caps and castors.

15in (38cm) wide

£6,000-9,000 **L&T**

A George IV mahogany, crossbanded and boxwood-strung cellaret, the hinged domed top enclosing divisions for bottles, on turned legs with brass terminals and castors.

17.25in (44cm) wide

£700-1,000 **DN**

A William IV mahogany cellaret, of sarcophagus shape, with applied and carved decoration, stamped "James Winter & Son, 101 Wardour St, Soho, London".

30.5in (76cm) wide

£800-1,200 **SWO**

An Edwardian inlaid mahogany cellaret, with a dome top, raised on square tapering legs, and a shaped X-stretcher.

19.5in (48.5cm) high

£400-500 **SWO**

A late Regency mahogany three-division canterbury with X-framed dividers and circular carved mount, having base drawer, turned bun feet and brass castors.

22in (56cm) wide

£500-800 **MAX**

An early Victorian rosewood canterbury, the X-frame joined by turned supports with stylized wreaths to front and back, panelled drawer and turned feet with brass caps and castors.

21.25in (54cm) wide

£1,000-1,500 **L&T**

A Victorian walnut canterbury, with three divisions, over a drawer.

22in (56cm) high

£600-900 **SWO**

A 19thC mahogany small canterbury, the dipped divisions to a frieze drawer fitted with embossed lion mask brass handles, on ring turned tapering legs to brass castors.

16in (40.5cm) wide

£600-800 **WW**

A Victorian walnut canterbury, with four fret cut divisions, and a single drawer below.

20in (50cm) wide

£500-700 **SWO**

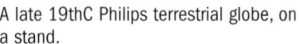

A J. & W. Newton terrestrial 12 inch globe, with brass meridian ring, four curved moulded supports, rotating on associated George II mahogany tripod base, dated.

1810 *18.25in (46cm) diam*

£8,000-12,000 **L&T**

A pair of 19thC Wilson's New American 13 inch terrestrial and celestial globes.

James Wilson (1763-1855) was America's first globe maker.

c1835 *19in (48cm) high*

£8,000-12,000 **FRE**

A pair of Newton's "New and Improved" 12 inch terrestrial and celestial globes, each raised on mahogany stand with four astragal moulded quadrant supports, turned pedestal and tripod stand with square section sabre legs with roundels at the terminals and ebonized bun feet.

39.75in (101cm) high

£12,000-18,000 **L&T**

A late 19thC Philips terrestrial globe, on a stand.

14in (35cm) diam

£200-300 **SWO**

A pair of nine-inch terrestrial and celestial table globes, by John Lothian, St Andrews Square, Edinburgh, each raised on three ebonized Doric columns and a concave mahogany veneered triform base with ebonized ball feet.

c1830 *13.5in (34cm) high*

£12,000-18,000 **L&T**

A pair of 19thC Continental 'blackamoor' figures, each modelled as a man in 18thC costume holding a flaming torch and standing on a pillow, raised on square bases terminating in carved paw feet, some losses.

71.75in (182cm) high

£5,000-7,000 **FRE**

A Victorian four-fold rosewood screen, with pierced strapwork cresting and panels of needlework and tapestry.

each fold 93.75in (238cm) wide

£3,000-4,000 **L&T**

A George III mahogany cellaret, of stepped form with eight lead-lined pigeonholes, on splayed feet.

13in (33cm) wide

£7,000-10,000 **L&T**

A 19thC painted leather four-fold draught screen, decorated with a hunting scene above musical trophies.

66.5in (169cm) high

£2,200-2,800 **L&T**

A 19thC Dutch four panel screen, each panel with a reeded and arched gilt wood frame and oil on board painting depicting elaborate floral bouquets and drapery, with views to distant landscapes.

79in (197.5cm) high

£3,000-4,000 **FRE**

An embossed four-fold draught screen, each arched fold of rectangular outline, embossed and painted with scenes from Canterbury Tales.

88.5in (225cm) high

£1,200-1,800 **L&T**

A George III oval papier mâché tray, the centre painted with a Claudesque scene, the border decorated in gilt with acorns and leaves, impressed clay patent.

28.5in (72.5cm) wide

£1,200-1,800 **SWO**

A Victorian papier-mâché serpentine tray, painted in polychrome with a spray of roses and flowers within a border of gilt scrolls and flowers, stamped "Jennens & Bettridge".

31in (79cm) wide

£800-1,200 **DN**

A 19thC toleware serving tray, of rectangular form with pierced carrying handles, painted with a panoramic scene of the city of Edinburgh from Calton Hill, within gilded foliate border, painted marks verso "G.w. 85 29688".

31.5in (80cm) wide

£2,000-3,000 **L&T**

A Canadian hand-painted and stencilled toleware tray, from Ontario, with flowering tulip design and hand-painted border.

c1880 *14.25in (36cm) wide*

£80-120 **RAON**

A Canadian hand-painted toleware tray, from Ontario, with floral design.

c1900 *17.5in (44.5cm) wide*

£50-70 **RAON**

An Edwardian inlaid mahogany drinks tray, with wavy gallery and brass handles.

22.5in (56.5cm) wide

£220-280 **SWO**

An Ontario Indian-made rack, with incised design of a chief.

c1910 *17.25in (44cm) wide*

£50-80 **RAON**

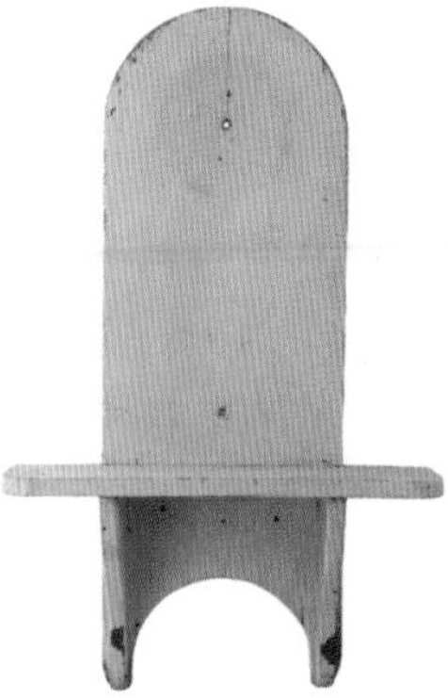

A 19thC Canadian painted pine clock shelf, with original light green paint.

34.75in (88cm) high

£100-150 **ING**

An Ontario varnished pine sewing shelf.

c1930 *21.25in (54cm) high*

£100-150 **RAON**

A Canadian walnut whatnot, with turned uprights and finials.

c1880 *52in (132cm) high*

£350-400 **RAON**

An unusual early 19thC New Brunswick tiger maple adjustable table, the shaped rectangular top on a baluster pedestal, with splayed and scrolled tripod supports and ball feet.

24in (61cm) wide

£3,500-4,500 **WAD**

An Ontario pine and tin butter churn, with revolving paddle inside, the tin painted black.

c1880 *31in (79cm) high*

£100-150 **RAON**

A Canadian pine dough box, from Quebec.

c1860 *41in (104cm) wide*

£300-350 **RAON**

A Canadian pine washstand, from Quebec, with original painted finish.

c1860 *33.75in (86cm) high*

£300-500 **RAON**

One of a set of four Canadian arrowback chairs, from Quebec, with turned legs.

Arrowback chairs are typical of Quebec.

c1870 *32.75in (83cm) high*

£500-800 set **RAON**

A late 19thC Black Forest carved wood tobacco pot, modelled as two owls and three owlets all with glass inset eyes.

13in (33cm) high

£1,200-1,800 **SWO**

A late 19thC Black Forest inkwell, carved as an owl's head with glass eyes.

4.25in (10.5cm) high

£200-300 **SWO**

A late 19thC Black Forest carved wood standing bear, holding a hollow tree trunk.

10.25in (26cm) high

£250-300 **SWO**

An early 20thC Bavarian carved softwood model of a standing bear.

10.25in (26cm) wide

£300-500 **BIG**

A Bavarian carved wood tobacco box, in the form of a begging Mastiff with glass inset eyes, hinged at the rear of the neck, with apertures to the front for unused and spent matches, damage.

10in (25.5cm) wide

£500-700 **SWO**

A 17thC wooden Maria Immaculata, carved and painted, on a naturalistic socle, wearing a red dress and a blue-red coat, stepping on a snake with her left foot, wearing an aureole on her head, chipped.

43.25in (108cm) high

£4,000-5,000 **KAU**

An early 17thC Italian carved fruitwood figure of a bishop, with outstretched arm and staff, standing on a plinth with the Medici coat of arms.

27in (67.5cm) high

£5,000-7,000 **POOK**

A late 18thC German carved soft stone figure of St. Michael slaying the dragon, with a crown, shield, and sword standing on top of a human form beast, resting on a shield and scroll carved plinth, losses.

23in (57.5cm) high

£4,000-5,000 **POOK**

A pair of 18thC carved and gilt wooden cherub heads and wings, each stamped "Montague Guest".

23.25in (59cm) high

£600-900 **SWO**

A pair of 19thC Italian wooden putti, carved and gilded details, chipped.

16.75in (42cm) high

£700-1,000 **KAU**

A George III tortoiseshell tea caddy, the front inlaid with flowers in mother-of-pearl, containing a pair of covered canisters, on ball feet.

7.5in (19cm) wide

£800-1,200 **GORL**

A Regency blonde tortoiseshell two-division tea caddy, with silver inlay, the shaped top with gilt metal ball finial enclosing lidded divisions with ivory handles, on ball feet.

6.5in (16.5cm) wide

£600-800 **GORL**

An early 19thC blonde tortoiseshell tea caddy, with ivory stringing, inlaid to the top with mother-of-pearl floral sprays, the interior with two tortoiseshell-veneered lidded compartments with turned ivory knobs.

7.5in (19cm) wide

£800-1,200 **SWO**

An early Victorian tortoiseshell tea caddy, the casket-shaped top with silver tableau, enclosing twin lidded compartments with ivory finials, decorated with mother-of-pearl floral inlay, raised on later brass feet.

7in (18cm) wide

£1,200-1,800 **BIG**

An early 19thC tortoiseshell and ivory tea caddy, with silver medallion, escutcheon plate and feet, the silver ball finial opening to reveal a twin compartment interior with ivory knops.

6.75in (17cm) high

£1,800-2,200 **FRE**

A 19thC tortoiseshell tea caddy with two interior lidded divisions on turned ivory feet.

7in (18cm) wide

£700-1,000 **BRI**

LEFT: A George III fruitwood tea caddy, in the form of a melon, the lobed body with stalk and green tinged patination, shaped escutcheon.

5in (12.5cm) high

£3,000-4,000 **L&T**

RIGHT: A 19thC fruitwood tea caddy, formed in the shape of a pear, the hinged lid with applied stalk raised above bulbous body with ivory escutcheon.

6.75in (17cm) high

£600-900 **L&T**

An early 19thC fruitwood tea caddy, in the form of a melon.

5.5in (14cm) high

£2,000-3,000 **SWO**

A George III rolled paperwork tea caddy, lozenge-shape with two painted silk ovals and chequer banding.

7.5in (19cm) wide

£700-1,000 **GORL**

A CLOSER LOOK AT A TEA CADDY

From the 1730s, caddies were often stored in decorative wooden cases, kept locked to protect the expensive contents. Later the caddies themselves had locks.

The aesthetic appeal and good condition of the set, as well as the known maker, contribute to the value.

Following a period of ornate decoration, silver forms became simpler in the middle of the 18thC. This clean style is evident in these two caddies.

Caddies from this period were typically produced in pairs to hold black and green tea, or tea and sugar.

A George III silver tea caddy and matching sugar box, by Daniel Smith & Robert Sharp, of London, contained in original mahogany case, date mark, 14.4oz.

1761

case 8in (20.5cm) wide

£4,000-5,000 **CHEF**

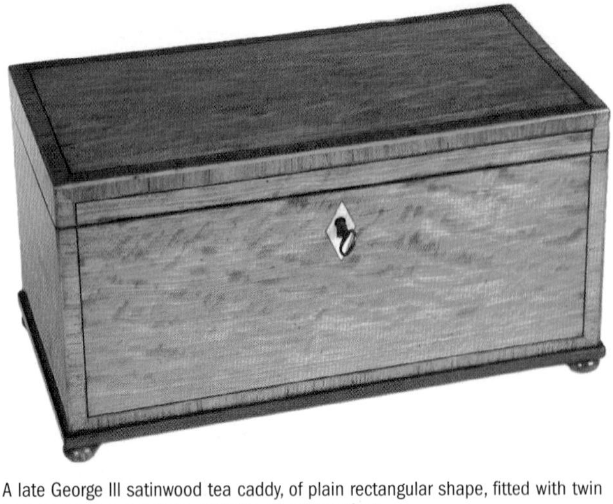

A late George III satinwood tea caddy, of plain rectangular shape, fitted with twin canisters and a cut glass mixing bowl, on bun feet.

12in (30.5cm) wide

£1,500-2,000 **SWO**

A George III harewood tea caddy, the lid and front panel inlaid with patera within tulipwood crossbanding.

7.5in (19cm) wide

£300-400 **DNT**

A George III mahogany tea caddy, the hinged lid with patera inlay, the front panels with acorns between two pateras, all with boxwood and rosewood crossbanding, some faults.

£300-400 **DNT**

A George III chinoiserie tea caddy, with hinged cover with a brass handle, the interior formerly fitted, on bracket feet.

9in (23cm) wide

£300-400 **WW**

A George III shellwork tea caddy, of hexagonal shape with a hinged lid, bears paper label to the front.

6.75in (17cm) wide

£1,800-2,200 **SWO**

A late Regency amboyna and ebonized sarcophagus-shaped tea chest, with a pair of hinged canisters, one later, and a cut glass footed bowl, the sides with brass lion-mask ring handles, on turned feet.

14in (35.5cm) wide

£400-600 **WW**

An early 19thC tiger maple box, with parquetry top, ogee bracket feet, brass handle and escutcheon.

8in (20.5cm) wide

£1,500-2,000 **WAD**

A 19thC burr yew wood tea caddy, with two compartments.

8in (20.5cm) wide

£200-300 **SWO**

A 19thC French kingwood and walnut bombé two-division tea caddy, with lozenge parquetry decoration and spring-loaded base drawer.

13in (33cm) wide

£600-900 **GORL**

A 19thC Indian camphorwood tea chest, fitted with two lidded caddies, the interior and exterior finely carved with animals amid scrolling flowers and leaves, within ivory ground parquetry borders.

9.5in (24cm) wide

£180-220 **LFA**

A Regency burr maple workbox, with tapering sides, a pair of brass ring handles and a base drawer.

13in (33cm) wide

£200-300 **SWO**

A William IV brass-bound rosewood work box.

c1835 *9.75in (25cm) wide*

£100-150 **MB**

A William IV rosewood work box.

c1830 *9in (23cm) wide*

£100-150 **MB**

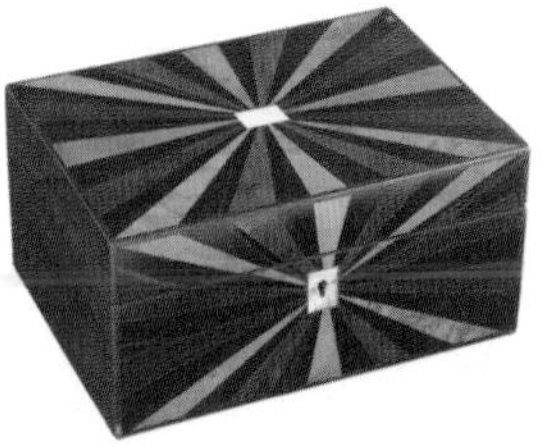

A William IV rosewood work box, the top and front inlaid with a radial design in ebony, yew and maple woods, interior with fitted tray.

10in (25.5cm) wide

£180-220 **GORL**

An early Victorian pewter glove box.

1841 *9.5in (24cm) wide*

£80-120 **MB**

An early 19thC Prisoner of War straw work box, with hinged barrelled lid enclosing a fitted interior and painted lozenge depicting a tall ship and a mermaid.

11in (28cm) wide

£400-600 **GORL**

A 19thC Killarney arbitus wood marquetry inlaid work box, of sarcophagus form, the hinged cover inlaid with a harp, scrolling leaves, shamrock, thistles and dog roses, enclosing an interior with fitted tray, above conforming side panels, on bun feet.

14.25in (36cm) wide

£180-220 **DNT**

An Edwardian tortoiseshell sewing case, of scalloped form, with a caddy top.

6.5in (16.5cm) wide

£500-700 **SWO**

A 19thC boullework box, with hinged lid and front and brass scroll inlay on red tortoiseshell ground.

11.5in (29cm) wide

£150-200 **BRI**

An Edwardian mounted wooden box, with embossed corners and a central cartouche flanked by an owl, the interior lined, marked for "J.A.R.S." of Birmingham.

1904 *8.5in (22cm) wide*

£120-180 **WW**

An American Chippendale cherry document box, the moulded top with mirrored insert edge over a dovetailed case, on ogee bracket feet.

c1780 *14.5in (36cm) wide*

£3,000-4,000 POOK

A Regency satinwood writing slope, the top with a painted oval panel within floral swags and a penwork border.

9.25in (23cm) wide

£300-400 SWO

A William IV rosewood and brass-inlaid writing slope, the top decorated with a central motif of two deer and a shield within a border.

14in (35.5cm) wide

£250-300 GORL

A late 19thC parquetry desk stand, with a tortoiseshell mounted to the top, and carved tortoise features, opening to reveal a well inside, with a drawer below.

14.75in (37cm) wide

£600-800 SWO

Part of a Victorian tortoiseshell and silver-mounted three-piece desk set, by William Comyns, London, comprising an inkstand with two square cut glass inkwells, a stationery casket with a red Morocco leather fitted interior and a rectangular blotter, date marks.

1892 *casket 11.75in (30cm) wide*

£1,500-2,000 set DNT

A 19thC Indian ebony, bone and porcupine quill desk top stationery box, with rising letter rack flanked by two urn-shaped inkwells, the front fitted with a drawer, above shaped apron and bracket feet.

16in (41cm) wide

£600-900 L&T

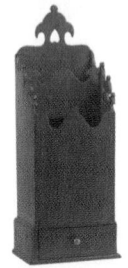

A Pennsylvania mahogany pipe box, with pierced and scalloped crest over a double pocket case with scalloped sides and single drawer.

c1780 *19.25in (49cm) high*

£2,000-2,500 POOK

A Federal mahogany hanging pipe box, with scalloped crest over a herringbone-inlaid slide lid and case.

c1790 *18in (45cm) high*

£1,200-1,800 POOK

An early 19thC cherry pipe box, with pierced shaped backboard, thumb-moulded front panel, lower single drawer and brass pull, containing five clay pipes.

22in (56cm) high

£2,800-3,200 SK

A Victorian oak brass-bound cedar smoker's box.

13.25in (33.5cm) wide

£150-200 MB

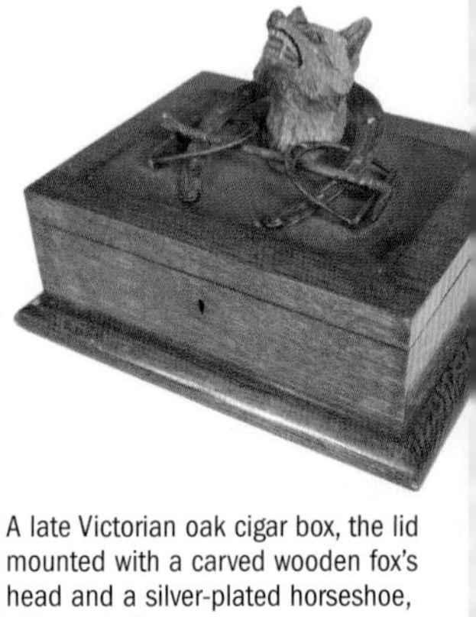

A late Victorian oak cigar box, the lid mounted with a carved wooden fox's head and a silver-plated horseshoe, whip and stirrups.

11.75in (30cm) wide

£400-600 SW

A Victorian brass-bound coromandel wood metamorphic toilet box, by Jenner & Knewstub, with detachable mirror to lid, brass Gothic tracery, two drawers and lower compartment over a base drawer, thirteen accessories remaining.

13.5in (34.5cm) wide

£800-1,200 **GORL**

A mid-Victorian walnut veneered vanity box, with figured top with brass inset tablet, opening to a complete array of silver capped lead crystal boxes and jars and a full set of manicure items, fall flap with twin drawers below.

12in (30cm) wide

£500-700 **BIG**

A 19thC French wood, leather and tortoiseshell travel manicure case, by Audot, with von Glaubitz and Altengabel family coat-of-arms, the interior with a manicure set, shaving set and other boxes and flacons.

Provenance: *Baron von Glaubitz and Altgabel.*

13.5in (33.5cm) wide

£700-1,000 **KAU**

A French papier mâché make-up box.

5.25in (13.5cm)wide

£50-70 **MB**

A George III mahogany, crossbanded and string inlaid serpentine knife box, with fitted interior.

8.75in (22cm) high

£200-300 **GORL**

A burr walnut decanter travelling box, of square shape, with brass-bound corners and handles, the cover inset with engraved plaque "Be Merry & Wise", inside fitted with four matching cut glass decanters and stoppers.

c1850 *10.75in (27cm) high*

£300-500 **ROS**

A Regency mahogany tantalus, the cushion-shaped lid with marquetry inlaid decoration and surround, the hinged opening revealing a period four-bottle lined interior.

£200-300 **BIG**

A pair of George III mahogany knife boxes, with chequer stringing, inlaid with rosette patera, enclosing interior fitted for cutlery.

12.5in (32cm) high

£3,000-4,000 **L&T**

A George III mahogany knife box, later painted allover with Neoclassical decoration, the hinged lid enclosing an interior later fitted for stationery.

15in (38cm) high

£500-800 **L&T**

A late Victorian blonde tortoiseshell games box.

9.25in (23.5cm) wide

£300-500 **SWO**

An early 18thC iron and bronze money box, with handles to the sides, the lid with four bolting devices, key.

11.75in (29.5cm) wide

£1,000-1,500 **KAU**

A George III partridge wood and hare wood box, edged with boxwood.

c1815 *9in (23cm) wide*

£200-300 **MB**

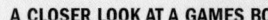

A CLOSER LOOK AT A GAMES BOX

The interior of the box is neatly fitted with trays and compartments and the box retains several mother-of-pearl counters making this an attractive piece.

The courtly scenes are stunningly realized and the crest suggests that this box was specially made for a wealthy client, indicating this is a high quality piece.

During the early 19thC, exotic design became popular and chinoiserie enjoyed a revival. This games box is a fine example from the period.

Lacquering was a favoured form of decoration used on furniture and smaller items like this box. Numerous layers of varnish made from the sap of the Rhus vernicifera tree were applied to the wood to form a hard crust that can be carved with decoration.

An early 19thC Anglo-Chinese lacquered games box, decorated with courtly scenes, Watson armorial crest and inscription "ESTO QUOD ESSE VIDERIS" framing initials 'J.W.', the interior fitted with 12 counter trays and seven lidded boxes, with various mother-of-pearl counters.

15in (38cm) wide

£4,000-5,000 **L&T**

A George III walnut box in the form of a townhouse, with pitched roof, three mirrored windows, concealed drawer to one side, plain interior.

13in (33cm) wide

£2,000-3,000 **GORL**

An 18thC Italian walnut and inlaid box, the hinged lid with checker banding, with baluster-turned split pilasters, on a plinth base, later bun feet.

27.75in (69cm) wide

£800-1,200 **FRE**

An early 19thC ebony and pietra dura box, depicting a brightly coloured parrot eating berries, opening to reveal a red plush interior, on gilt bronze hairy feet.

13.75in (34cm) wide

£4,000-5,000 **FRE**

A late 19thC Killarney marquetry inlaid jewellery box, inlaid with a view of Muckross Abbey, the back panel inlaid with a stag.

11in (28cm) wide

£700-1,000 **DNT**

A 19thC Italian ebonised and ivory-inlaid table cabinet, the cupboard doors enclosing drawers, all inlaid with ivory panels depicting biblical scenes.

22in (56cm) wide

£1,500-2,000 **FRE**

A fine 19thC German rosewood and ivory-inlaid table cabinet, inlaid throughout with mythical figures and scrolling foliage, panelled doors, bun feet.

£2,500-3,000 **FRE**

An Indian Vizagapatam padouk table cabinet, decorated with a deity and attendants, the interior with a Moorish arched alcove.

6.5in (16.5cm) wide

£250-300 **GORL**

A 19thC Viennese ebonized table cabinet, with inverted bell top with gilt metal birds and amorini, faux enamel panels with Classical figures.

14.5in (36cm) wide

£2,200-2,800 **BIG**

A late 18thC Pennsylvania Bucher box, decorated with a building in a landscape within red, green, and yellow tulip decoration and the initials "ID".

9.5in (24cm) wide

£1,500-2,000 **POOK**

An early 19thC Pennsylvania turned canister and cover, with overall vibrant yellow and ochre grain painted decoration.

6in (15cm) wide

£2,000-3,000 **POOK**

A 19thC bride's box, of oval form with polychrome painted decoration including flowering vines and floral sprigs enclosing figures of a man and woman, with German inscription, paint wear.

18.25in (46.5cm) long

£300-400 **FRE**

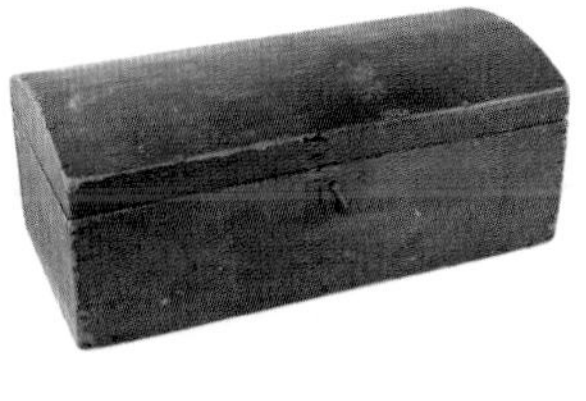

A Canadian dome top pine box, with geometric carving to lid, from Quebec.

c1840 *24.5in (62cm) long*

£150-200 **RAON**

A CLOSER LOOK AT A PAINTED PINE CANDLEBOX

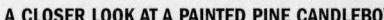

This candlebox sold for many times its initial estimate, highlighting the market tendency to pay exceptionally high prices for the very best examples in any collecting field.

Crucially, every side of this box is painted with a different design, to an extremely high standard. The repeated tulip motif and colour scheme provides decorative unity.

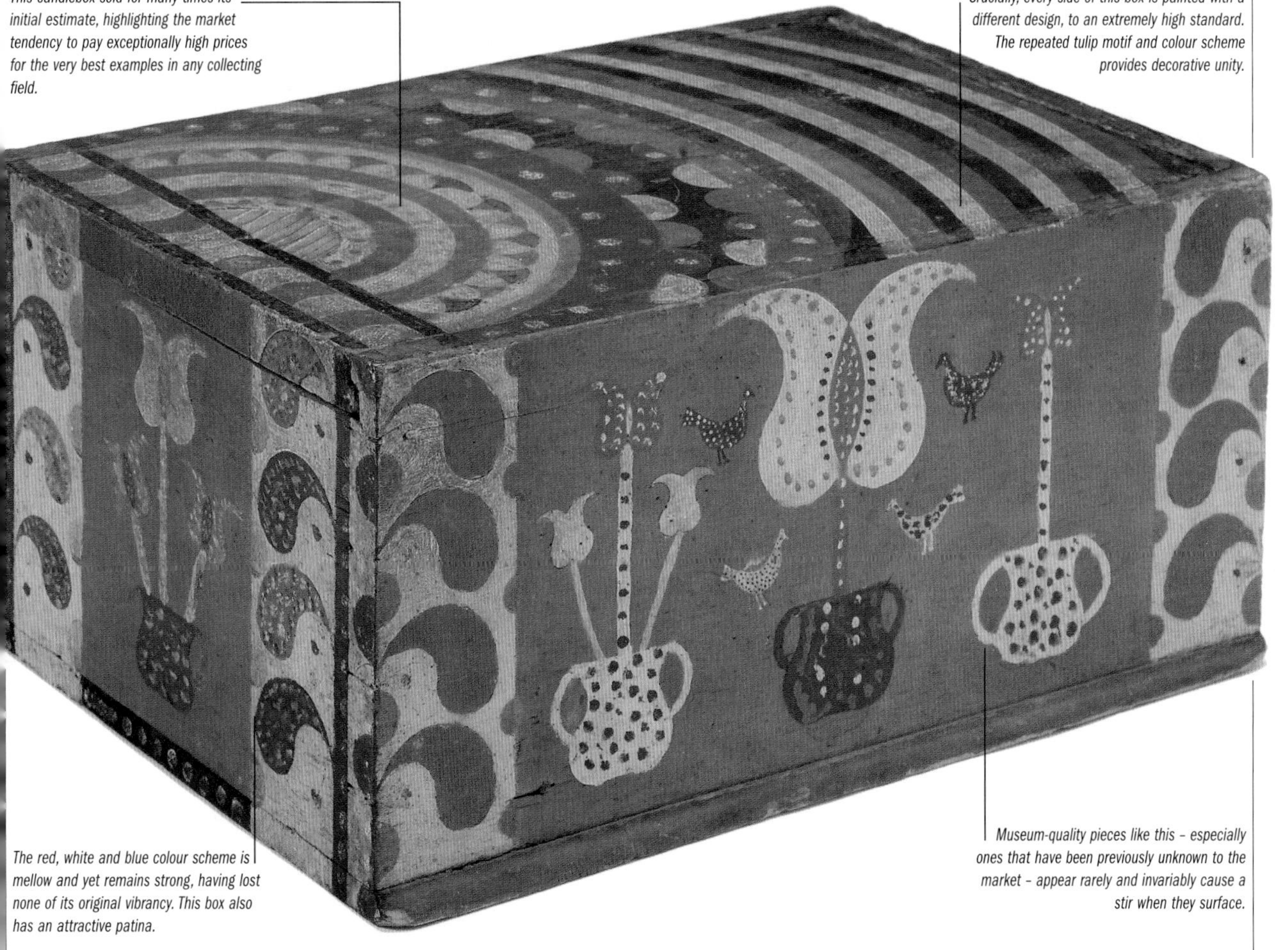

The red, white and blue colour scheme is mellow and yet remains strong, having lost none of its original vibrancy. This box also has an attractive patina.

Museum-quality pieces like this - especially ones that have been previously unknown to the market - appear rarely and invariably cause a stir when they surface.

A pine candlebox, possibly from Somerset County, Pennsylvania, of rectangular form with sliding lid, with incised and painted decoration in red, white and blue, the lid with demi-lune rainbow banding, the sides with potted tulips, chickens and paisley corners, on a moulded base.

This box is pictured in "The Flowering of American Folk Art".

c1840 *12.25in (31cm) long.*

£400,000-600,000 **FRE**

An 18thC papier-mâché painted table snuff box.

3.25in (8.5cm) wide

£300-350 **MB**

An early 19thC papier-mâché snuff box, bearing a black print on the straw yellow top of a man looking on a sleeping lady, titled "A Danger".

3.5in (9cm) diam

£120-180 **CHEF**

An early 19thC papier-mâché snuff box, the bedroom scene on the top titled "Les Jets D'Eau" and the erotic scene inside titled "Hercule Et Omphale".

3.5in (9cm) diam

£150-250 **CHEF**

A 19thC rose-coloured metal snuff box, with a hardwood base, embossed and inlaid in gold and silver with doves of peace and trophies of war.

2.75in (7cm) diam

£200-300 **DNT**

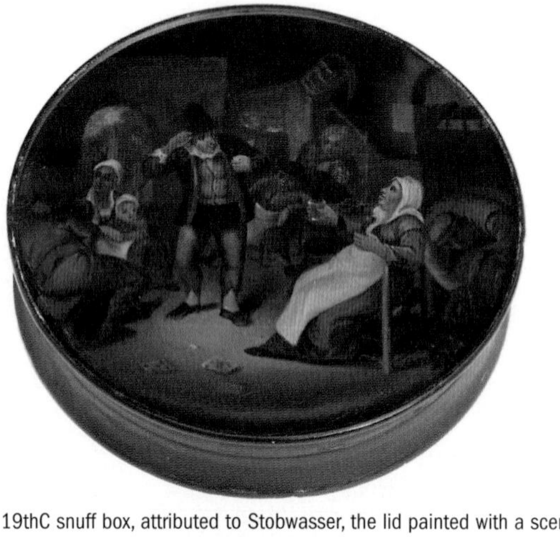

An early 19thC snuff box, attributed to Stobwasser, the lid painted with a scene after Teniers of drinkers discussing an upset in playing cards, the gilding on the interior probably obscuring inscriptions.

£500-700 **CHEF**

A 19thC boxwood snuff box, the hinged lid enclosing a tortoiseshell-lined interior.

4in (10cm) high

£250-300 **SWO**

A late 19thC papier-mâché snuff shoe, the hinged cover decorated with a lady, with inlaid pewter decoration.

3.25in (8.5cm) wide

£100-150 **WW**

A 19thC French mahogany piano etui, with keyboard inlay to a part fitted interior, replaced musical movement.

11.75in (30cm) wide

£300-400 **WW**

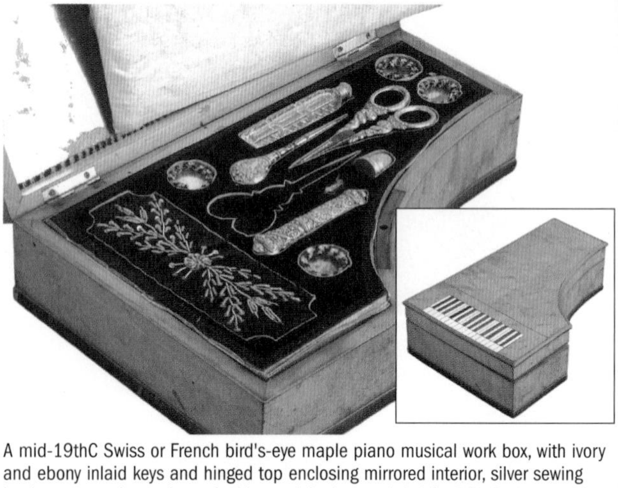

A mid-19thC Swiss or French bird's-eye maple piano musical work box, with ivory and ebony inlaid keys and hinged top enclosing mirrored interior, silver sewing implements and two air musical box, original paper label for P&L Gotheimer of London, feet missing.

11.5in (29cm) wide

£500-700 **GORL**

An early 19thC Canadian burl bowl, with open handles.

17.5in (45cm) diam

£3,000-4,000 **WAD**

A treen chalice, the turned bowl above a knopped stem and pedestal base.

8in (20.5cm) high

£200-300 **BRI**

An Aberdeen mounted coconut cup, the globular cup carved with a stylized pineapple, palm tree, rose, shamrock and thistle, with plain collar, stamped "ABD".

4.5in (11cm) high

£500-700 **L&T**

A Victorian Scottish mounted wooden quaich, the circular wooden bowl with mounted rim and handles, also applied with three hoops, with central circular plaque engraved with the monogram of the 5th Earl of Rosebery, marks for Edinburgh, maker's mark rubbed.

1884 *8.5in (21cm) wide*

£500-700 **L&T**

Two rare 19thC solid wood measuring cups, stamped "VR" on the inside.

larger 6in (15cm) high

£60-90 **MUR**

An 18thC carved mahogany adjustable swift, retaining its original period tube case.

20.75in (53cm) high

£600-900 **POOK**

A Victorian woolwinder, with a painted cast iron tripod base.

21.25in (54cm) high

£100-200 **SWO**

A mid-19thC carved maple, rosewood and ivory wool winder, the four adjustable arms with acorn finials around a turned wood and ivory standard, over a circular carved ring of flowers and turned base, resting on three ivory-inlaid ball feet.

c1840 *16in (40.5cm) high*

£1,500-2,000 **POOK**

A 19thC mahogany cotton reel stand, with two circular tiers, a baluster-turned column, the dished top with a pin cushion on a turned circular base.

11.5in (29cm) high

£200-£300 **SWO**

A 19thC turned wooden plate stand.

11.5in (29cm) high

£80-120 **SWO**

An 18thC carved coquilla nut pomander, the turned base with two screw threads, to a conical body carved with a depiction of Christ, to a leaf finial with screw thread.

3.5in (9cm) high

£400-600 **WW**

A 19thC wooden bulto of Nuestra Senora de la Rosario, from New Mexico, with pinned movable arms and flaring skirt painted in red, green and umber, on a rectangular base.

18in (45.5cm) high

£4,000-6,000 **FRE**

A late 19thC carved mahogany figure of an Irish setter, in pointer position, with red-brown varnished surface, mounted on a rectangular plinth.

30in (75cm) long

£4,000-6,000 **SK**

A pair of Rose Valley carved and painted cat and dog figures, by John Maene.

c1905 *37.5in (94cm) high*

£10,000-12,000 **POOK**

A carved figure of a bird, attributed to 'Schtockschnitzler' Simmons of Berks County, Pennsylvania, with wire legs on a cylindrical base, painted and inscribed "Aunt Mae's Bird".

c1890 *7in (18cm) high*

£3,500-4,500 **FRE**

A Canadian folk art carving of a bird, by Edmond Chatigny of Quebec, painted with red and white spots.

c1965 *9.75in (25cm) long*

£120-180 **RAON**

A Canadian reddened pine pestle and mortar, with turned design of concentric rings, from Quebec.

c1880 *7.75in (20cm) high*

£70-100 **RAON**

A Canadian mortar, carved from a silver birch log, with remnants of original silver birch bark, possibly of Indian manufacture.

c1900 *19in (48cm) high*

£70-100 **RAON**

A Lehnware lidded saffron cup, with floral and stencil decoration on a tan ground, inscribed to base "Made by Joseph H. Lehn in his 93rd year March 24 1890".

Joseph Lehn was a Pennsylvania farmer and woodworker who started to turn and decorate wooden ware in his 70s.

1890 *5.5in (14cm) high*

£700-1,000 **POOK**

One of a set of three hand-painted and carved plates, with floral and fruiting scenes, from Ontario.

c1900 *16in (40.5cm) diam*

£80-120 set **RAON**

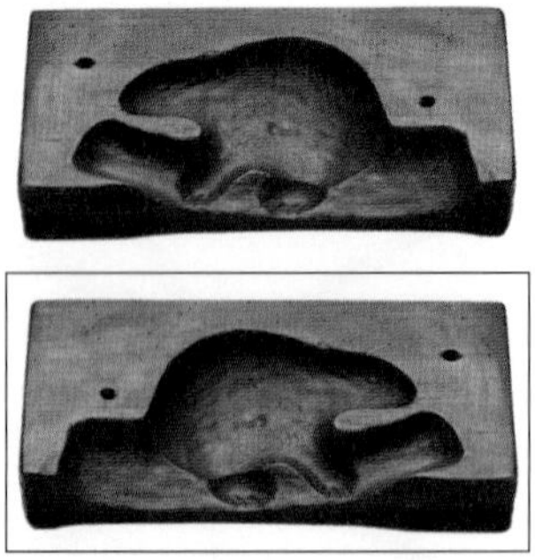

A Canadian wooden maple sugar mould, in the form of a beaver.

12.5in (32cm) long

£120-180 **WAD**

A double-sided painted trade sign, depicting a landscape and inscribed "D. N. Adams 1839", painted in black, gold and green, with wrought iron hardware.

1839 *39in (101cm) wide*

£1,800-2,200 **FRE**

A 19thC carved and gilded wooden sea serpent figural medallion, from Nahant, Massachusetts, carved in high relief and mounted on a round wooden plaque, impressed "R.C. WILSON".

This medallion was once mounted at "Witch House", named after a nearby cave which was rumoured to have sheltered witches escaping persecution in Salem.

31in (78.5cm) diam

£4,000-6,000 **SK**

An early 19thC Canadian prisoner of war straw-work marquetry picture, depicting the view from the Citadel of Quebec.

31.5in (80cm) wide

£10,000-12,000 **WAD**

A painted wooden and metal model of the steam tug Philadelphia, inscribed "Presented to John H. Starin of New York by Neafie and Levy Penn Works, Phila. 1875", inside a gilt metal and glass case.

c1875

£5,000-7,000 **FRE**

An early Tunbridgeware rosewood jewellery cabinet, the hinged sloping lid with a lozenge-shaped specimen perspective cube panels with chequer stringing, the three drawers retained by a pair of doors with oval white ground mosaic panels within half square mosaic banding.

10.75in (27cm) high

£700-1,000 **DNT**

A Tunbridgeware games box, the chequerboard top framed by inlaid Tunbridgeware flowers and with an inlaid backgammon board interior, hinged at the centre with dark satinwood veneer finish.

18in (46cm) square

£400-600 **SWO**

A Tunbridgeware rosewood playing card box, the lid with specimen perspective cube panel within narrow tesserae mosaic banding.

4.5in (11.5cm) wide

£90-140 **DNT**

An early 19thC Tunbridgeware rosewood work box, the sarcophagus-shaped body with van dyke and dog tooth banded lid, over similarly decorated sides on gilt brass ball feet, the blue papered interior with a single removable tray.

9.5in (24cm) wide

£400-600 **DNT**

A Tunbridgeware rosewood table snuff box, the hinged lid with tesserae mosaic of a dog, the walls with stylized flower banding, the zinc interior housing fifteen novelty fish gaming counters.

4.25in (11cm) wide

£280-320 **DNT**

An early Tunbridgeware rosewood box, the lid with specimen wood perspective cube panel within chequer stringing and the sides with half square mosaic within chequer stringing.

3.5in (9cm) wide

£180-220 **DNT**

A Tunbridgeware rosewood stationery box, the domed lid with tesserae view of Battle Abbey within van dyke cross banding, the swept sides with broadband of tesserae flowers.

10.25in (26cm) wide

£500-600 **DNT**

A Tunbridgeware rosewood collar box, the hinged lid with flower spray on a dark ground, within light ground tesserae border, the side with running leaf banding.

6in (15cm) wide

£250-300 **DNT**

A goliath Tunbridgeware glove box, by Edmund Nye, the domed cover with rose repeat tesserae panel within running rose border, the sides with running oak leaf border, with torn label to base, cracks.

16.5in (42cm) wide

£180-220 **DNT**

A large Tunbridgeware rosewood tea caddy with tesserae view of Warwick Castle, the interior with rare block of two mice, probably the work of Henry Hollamby, interior with a pair of lidded canisters.

12.25in (31cm) wide

£1,200-1,800 **DNT**

A Tunbridgeware circular yew wood box and cover by T. Barton, the lid with eight point star, the interior with paper label, and another smaller box and cover, the lid with eight point star.

1.75in (4.5cm) diam

£150-200 **DNT**

An unusual Tunbridgeware rosewood book stand, possibly by Wise, with tesserae bird panel within half square mosaic banding and marbled wood shaving banding, the three quarter gallery with half square mosaic and the single drawer with a tesserae and chequer front.

15in (38.5cm) wide

£800-1,200 **DNT**

A Tunbridgeware tesserae view of Great Malvern Priory .

6.25in (16cm) wide

£80-120 **DNT**

A Tunbridgeware octagonal basket, the well with perspective cube panel, the convex sides with tesserae flower band, the swing handle with one replacement stickware mount.

8.75in (22cm) diam

£250-300 **DNT**

Two Tunbridgeware thread wheels and a thread cross, the two thread wheels with eight point star centres and the thread cross missing two tips.

£300-400 **DNT**

A CLOSER LOOK AT A TUNBRIDGEWARE PLAQUE

The complexity of the image of the castle suggests that the production of this piece was extremely labour intensive.

The central panel is a masterpiece of gauge work produced by William Harris junior while he was working for the famous Tunbridgeware maker George Wise in the 1830s and 1840s.

Many Tunbridgeware designs were made by gluing strips of coloured wood together to form a block which was then sliced into thin veneers. These multicoloured veneers were laid flat on the surface of a wooden object to give the impression of an inlaid mosaic. The border is a fine example.

Finely realised landscape and architecture views are typical of high quality pieces made for the top end of the market.

A rare Victorian green Morocco leather album with Tunbridgeware gauge work view of the State Apartments, Windsor Castle, the leather embellished with gilt tooling to include a Royal coronet and Prince of Wales' feathers.

14.75in (37.5cm) wide

£1,200-1,800 **DNT**

A Tunbridgeware sealing wax outfit, possibly by Nye Barton, the octagonal stem with tesserae bands, the top with ebony sconce, the threaded base with match strike, the threaded circular plinth with match strike base.

6in (15cm) high

£280-320 **DNT**

A Tunbridgeware Cleopatra's Needle thermometer stand, the rosewood body with tesserae flower and perspective cube panels, the lower section of the plinth base warped.

7.75in (20cm) high

£150-200 **DNT**

A Mauchlineware fob watch case, decorated with a view of the Petit Trianon at Versailles.

3.5in (9cm) wide

£30-40 **GORL**

A Mauchlineware box, decorated with a view of the Bareges Etablissement Thermal.

£12-18 **GORL**

A Mauchlineware stamp or coin box, decorated with a view of Uriage-les-Bains.

£18-25 **GORL**

A Mauchlineware jewellery box, decorated with views of Dunkerque, Roesendael and Place Jean Bart, with mirror to interior of lid.

6.5in (16.5cm) wide

£60-90 **GORL**

A Mauchlineware twin scent bottle case, the slanted lid decorated with a view of St Germain en Haye, and Chapelle du Chateau, housing two Baccarat scent bottles and stoppers.

3in (7.5cm) wide

£130-180 **GORL**

A Mauchlineware box, decorated with three views of Windermere.

£18-22 **GORL**

A Mauchlineware pill box, decorated with a view of Etal Castle.

2.25in (6cm) diam

£30-40 **GORL**

A Mauchlineware pill box, decorated with a view of Marine Terrace, Silloth.

£30-40 **GORL**

A Mauchlineware pill box, decorated with a view of Old London Road, Hastings.

£30-40 **GORL**

A heart-shaped Mauchlineware pin cushion, decorated with a view of Malo-les-Bains.

2.25in (6cm) wide

£70-100 **GORL**

A circular Mauchlineware pin cushion, decorated with a view of Ross Church.

£50-70 **GORL**

A circular Mauchlineware pin cushion, decorated with a view of the church at La Delivrande.

£50-70 **GORL**

A Mauchlineware necessaire, decorated with a view of la Place de la Concorde, retaining three tools.

3.5in (9cm) wide

£90-120 **GORL**

A Mauchlineware necessaire, decorated with a view of Cayeux, lacking contents.

2in (5cm) wide

£60-90 **GORL**

A small Mauchlineware purse, decorated with a view of Mont St. Michel.

£30-40 **GORL**

A Mauchlineware paper knife, decorated with a view of Lourdes.

8.75in (22cm) long

£25-40 **GORL**

A Mauchlineware blotter, decorated with a street view of Lydd, Kent.

7.5in (19cm) high

£70-100 **GORL**

A Mauchlineware bookmarker, decorated with a view of Orleans, Place du Martray.

8.75in (22cm) long

£25-40 **GORL**

A Mauchlineware bookmarker, decorated with a view of Lyon-Sur-Mer.

8.75in (22cm) long

£25-40 **GORL**

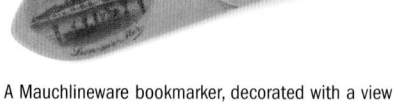

A Mauchlineware paper knife, decorated with a view of the jetty at Le Harve.

8.75in (22cm) long

£25-40 **GORL**

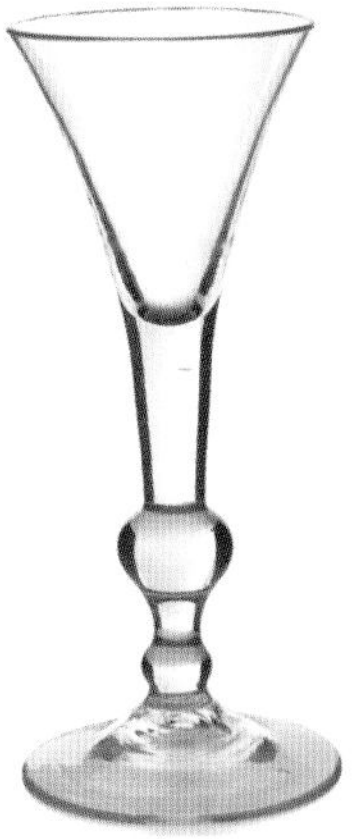

A baluster wine glass of 'Kit-cat' type, of drawn trumpet form, with plain section on an inverted baluster and basal knop, on a conical foot.

c1730 *7in (17.5cm) high*

£700-1,000 **DN**

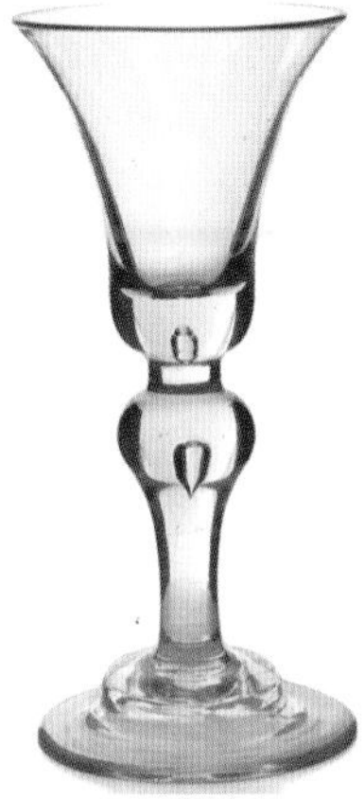

A baluster wine glass, the bell bowl with a solid lower section with bead inclusion, on an inverted baluster stem with tear inclusion, on a domed foot.

c1730 *6.25in (15.5cm) high*

£800-1,200 **DN**

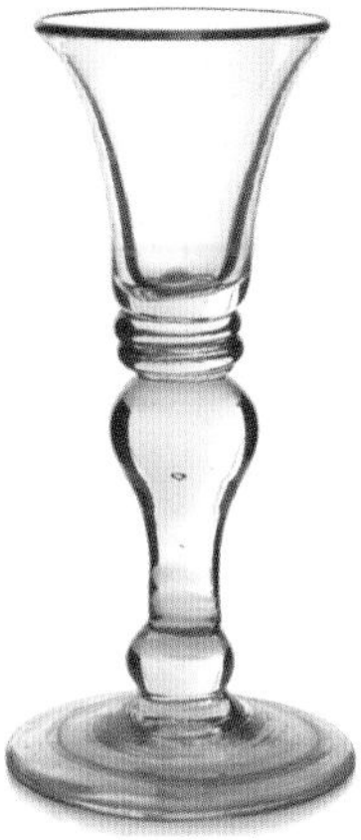

A baluster gin glass, the bell bowl on a double-knopped stem with an inverted baluster section, on a folded conical foot.

c1740 *5in (12.5cm) high*

£500-800 **DN**

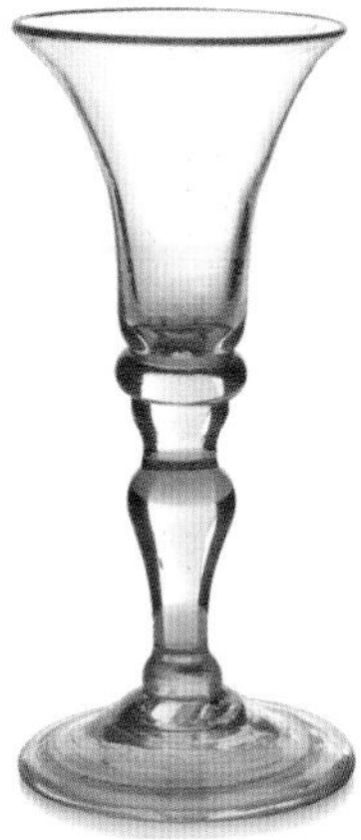

An 18thC gin glass, with a flared bowl on a baluster stem and folded foot.

5in (12.5cm) high

£300-500 **WW**

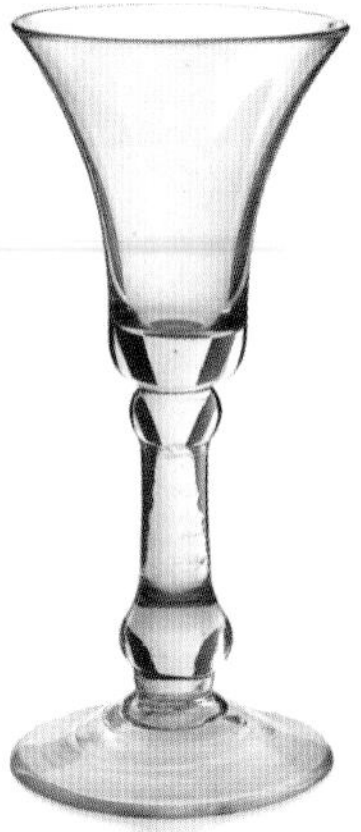

A baluster wine glass, with a trumpet bowl on a knopped stem.

c1725 *6.75in (17cm) high*

£500-800 **WW**

A light baluster wine glass, the funnel bowl engraved with foliate swags, on a multi-knopped stem with tear inclusion of 'Newcastle light' type, and a central inverted baluster section with bead inclusions, on a conical foot.

c1750 *7in (18cm) high*

£1,800-2,200 **DN**

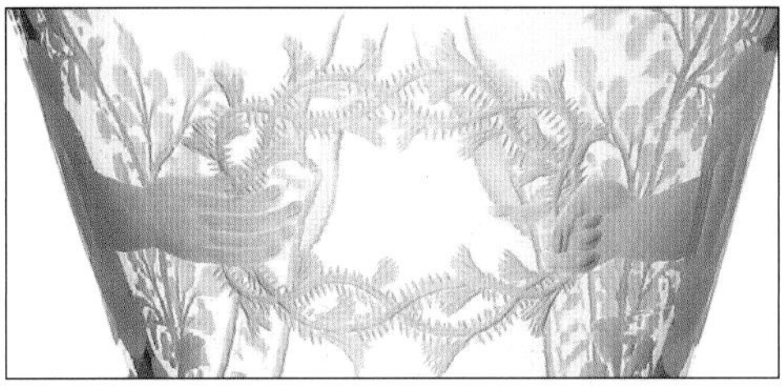

A Dutch engraved marriage or friendship goblet, the funnel bowl with a wreath, inscribed "PLUTOT MOURIR QUE MANQUER DEFOY", on a multi-knopped stem with inverted baluster section, and a conical foot.

c1750 *7in (17.5cm) high*

£1,500-2,000 **DN**

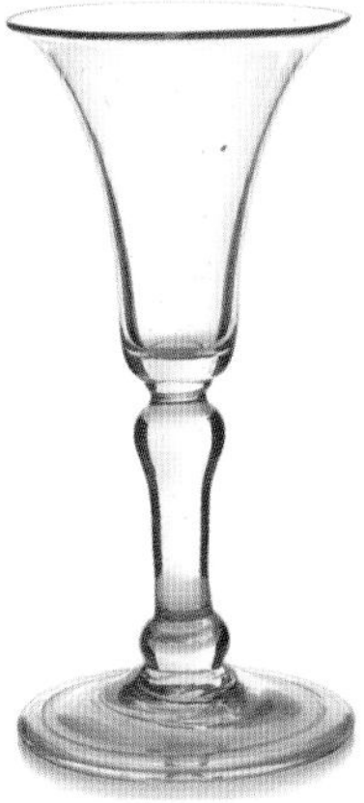

A balustroid wine or gin glass, the bell bowl supported on a double-knopped stem with an inverted baluster section, on a folded conical foot.

c1740 *5.25in (13.5cm) high*

£250-300 **DN**

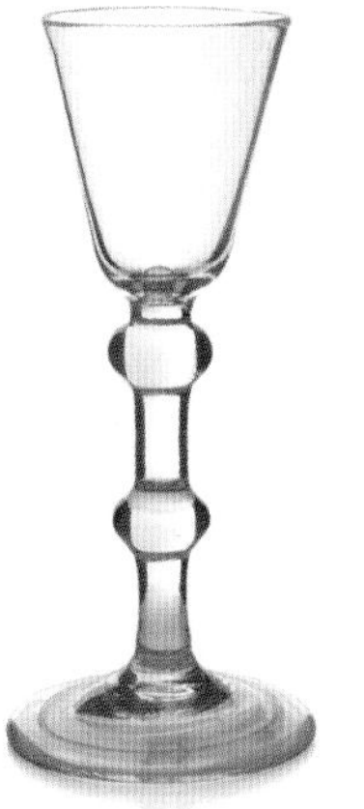

A balustroid wine glass, the round funnel bowl supported on a double-knopped stem and folded conical foot.

c1740 *6in (15cm) high*

£300-500 **DN**

A balustroid wine glass, the round funnel bowl on a triple-knopped stem, with a central knop above a hollow section, on a conical foot.

c1750 *5in (13cm) high*

£220-280 **DN**

A composite stemmed wine glass, the bell bowl engraved with a flower and a moth, on a stem of spiral threads, above an inverted baluster plain section with bead inclusions, on a conical foot.

c1750 *6.5in (16.5cm) high*

£800-1,200 **DN**

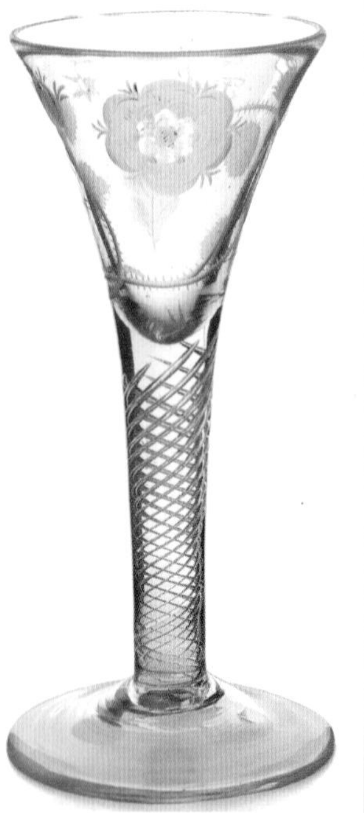

A mid-18thC air-twist wine glass, of Jacobite significance, of drawn trumpet form, the bowl engraved with a rosebud and foliage, inscribed "Fiat", the stem filled with spiral threads, on a conical foot.

6.5in (16.5cm) high

£800-1,200 **DN**

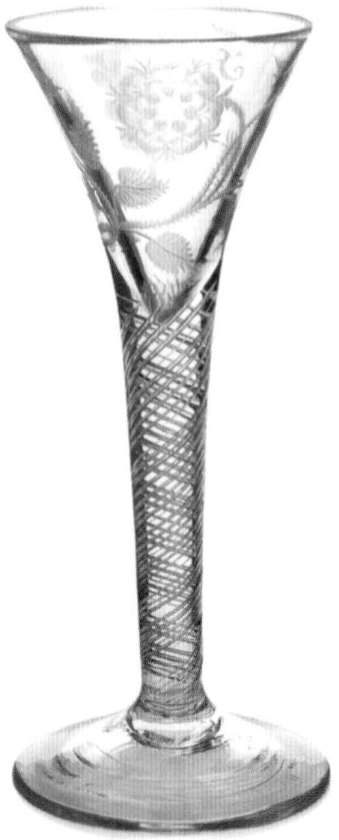

An air-twist wine glass, of Jacobite significance, of drawn trumpet form, engraved with a rose, rose buds, oakleaf and inscribed "Fiat", the stem filled with spiral threads, on a conical foot.

c1760 *6.75in (18cm) high*

£800-1,200 **DN**

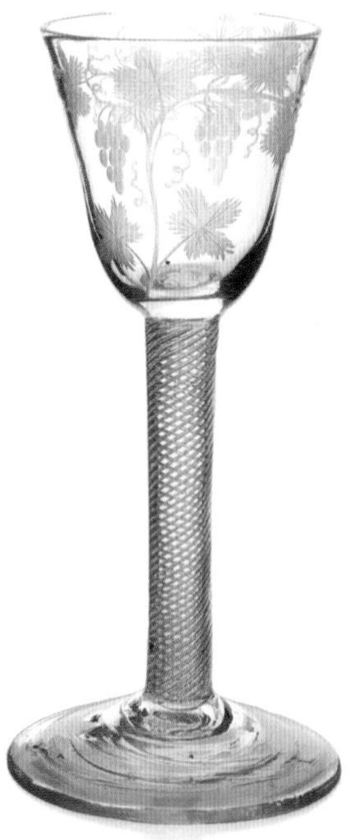

An air-twist wine glass, the round funnel bowl engraved with a band of fruiting vine.

c1750 *7.25in (18.5cm) high*

£300-500 **DN**

An 18thC Jacobite-style wine glass, engraved with a rose, two buds and a thistle to the reverse, raised on a knopped air-twist stem.

6.25in (16cm) high

£1,200-1,800 **WW**

A composite stemmed wine glass, the round funnel bowl on an annular knop above an opaque-twist double-knopped section, on a conical foot.

c1770 *7in (17.5cm) high*

£1,500-2,000 **DN**

A mid-18thC cordial glass, with a U-shaped bowl raised on an air-twist stem.

6.25in (16cm) high

£700-1,000 **WW**

An air-twist cordial glass, the ogee bowl supported on a double-series stem with spiral cable within multi-ply spiral threads, on a conical foot.

c1750 *6.5in (16.5cm) high*

£700-900 **DN**

A pair of 18thC cordial glasses, each with an ogee bowl engraved with chinoiserie figures in a landscape, set on opaque-twist stems.

5.5in (14cm) high

£700-1,000 **ROS**

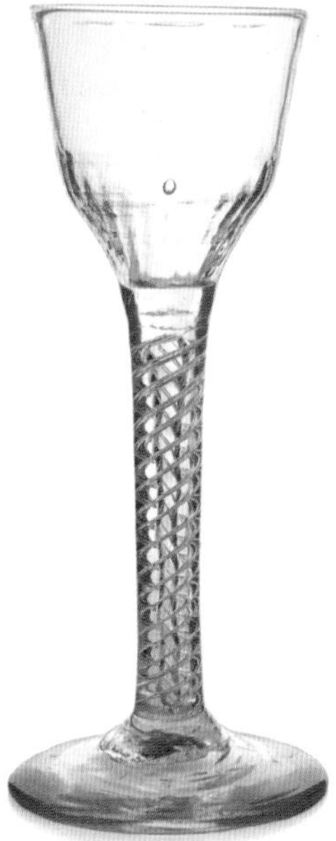

A wine glass, the part-moulded ogee bowl on a hollow mercury-twist stem.

c1760 *6in (15cm) high*

£250-300 **WW**

An engraved opaque-twist cider glass, the round funnel bowl with fruiting apple, supported on a double-series stem, and a conical foot.

c1760 *7.5in (19cm) high*

£2,000-3,000 **DN**

An opaque-twist wine glass, the slender funnel bowl with everted rim, on a double-knopped stem, with a gauze cable within spiral tapes, conical foot.

c1760 *7.75in (19.5cm) high*

£600-900 **DN**

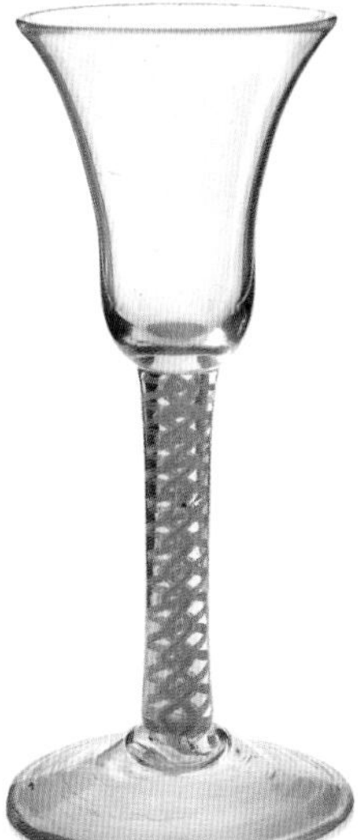

A wine glass, with a bell-shaped bowl, raised on a double-series opaque-twist stem.

c1770 *7in (17.5cm) high*

£300-500 **WW**

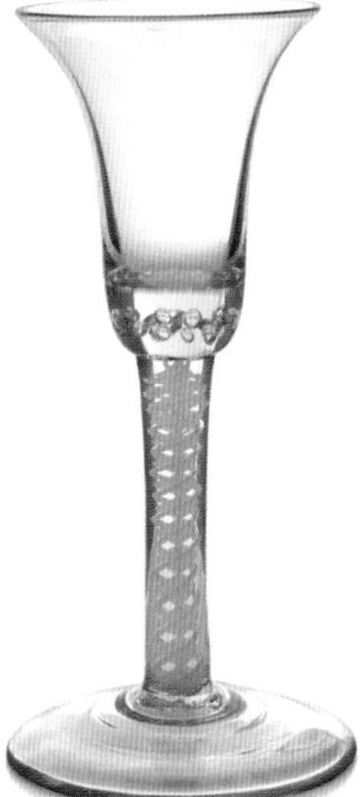

A wine glass, the bell bowl with bubbles in the base, raised on an opaque-twist stem.

c1770 *6.75in (17cm) high*

£250-300 **WW**

An engraved opaque-twist goblet, the bucket bowl with everted rim decorated with a band of fruiting vine, on a stem with a pair of entwined gauze cables, and a conical foot.

c1770 *7.5in (19cm) high*

£500-800 **DN**

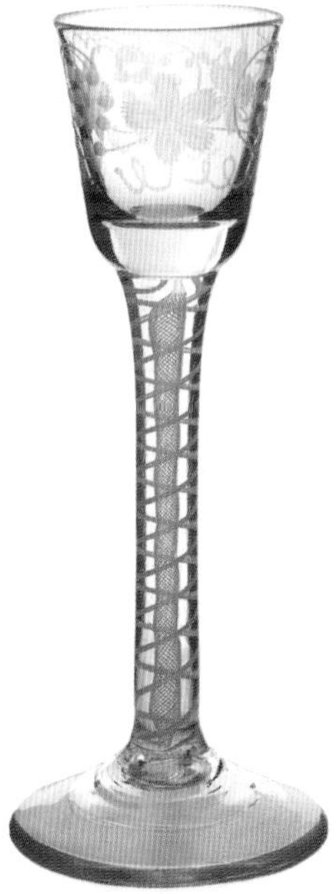

An engraved opaque-twist cordial glass, the round funnel bowl decorated with fruiting vine, the stem with a central gauze cable within a pair of spiralling tapes, on a conical foot.

c1770 *6.75in (17cm) high*

£800-1,200 **DN**

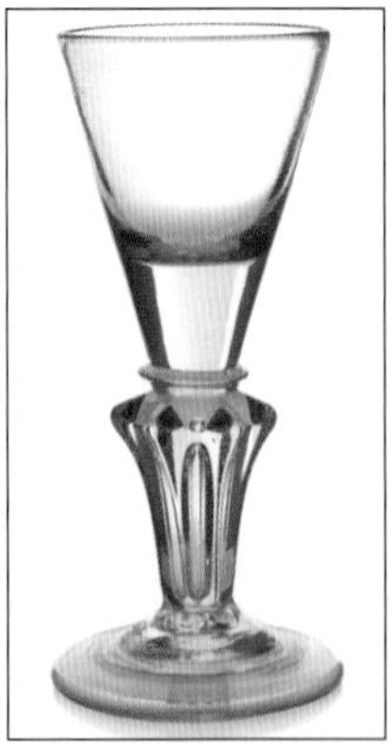

An early 18thC wine glass, with a conical bowl on a hexagonal moulded stem and folded foot.

6in (15cm) high

£800-1,200 **WW**

A plain-stemmed toasting glass, of Jacobite significance, of drawn trumpet form, the bowl engraved with a rose and an insect, on a conical foot.

c1750 *7in (18cm) high*

£400-600 **DN**

A late 18thC ale glass, with an engraved bowl and faceted stem.

6.25in (16cm) high

£300-500 **WW**

An 18thC goblet, with a bell-shaped body, raised on an octagonal moulded stem and domed folded foot.

7.5in (19cm) high

£500-800 **WW**

A Sunderland Bridge rummer, engraved with a brig sailing beneath the bridge, above the inscription "SUNDERLAND BRIDGE", the reverse with monogram "JB & B", on a capstan stem and conical foot.

c1820 *5.5in (14cm) high*

£300-500 **DN**

An engraved commemorative goblet, the bucket bowl decorated with a sail-and-steam paddle ship, inscribed "Great Liverpool Steam Pakket (sic)" and with initials "JSB" and dated 1839, on a capstan stem, chip to rim.

Launched under the name of 'Liverpool' in 1838 for the Transatlantic Steamship Company, this ship was sold to P&O who renamed her 'Great Liverpool'. She was wrecked off Cape Finisterre, Spain, in 1846.

6.25in (16cm) high

£100-150 **DN**

A large 19thC glass goblet, engraved with huntsmen and hounds in pursuit of a fox.

9.5in (24cm) high

£400-600 **WW**

A pair of early 19thC large rummers, each with a broad, fluted bowl, knopped stem and plain foot.

7.25in (18.5cm) high

£300-400 **ROS**

A large 18thC sweetmeat glass, with an ogee bowl, raised on a hollow moulded stem and domed foot.

6.75in (17cm) high

£300-500 **WW**

An 18thC sweetmeat glass, with a ribbed bowl and knopped stem, on a moulded foot.

5.5in (14cm) high

£400-600 **WW**

A George III sweetmeat glass, the diamond-cut shallow bowl with shaped rim, on silesian stem with collar, and massive beaded knop, on domed scalloped foot.

Fashionable in the Georgian era, a silesian stem is a many-sided moulded stem.

6.5in (16.5cm) high

£120-180 **LFA**

JEANETTE HAYHURST

FINE GLASS

32A Kensington Church St. London W8 4HA. 0207 938 1539

A group of rare 18th Century drinking glasses.

We specialise in glass of all ages including Roman vessels, 17th, 18th, 19th century drinking glasses, cut, coloured and engraved glass for the table.

Open: Monday-Friday 10AM-5PM
Saturday 12PM-5PM

MEMBER OF THE BRITISH ANTIQUE DEALERS ASSOCIATION

A mid-19thC miniature Baccarat weight, set with a purple clematis and five green star leaves, with a star-cut base.

1.5in (4cm) diam

£400-600 **WW**

A mid-19thC Baccarat anemone weight, with a large blue and white flower set upon a leafy stem, with a star-cut base.

2.75in (7cm) diam

£600-800 **WW**

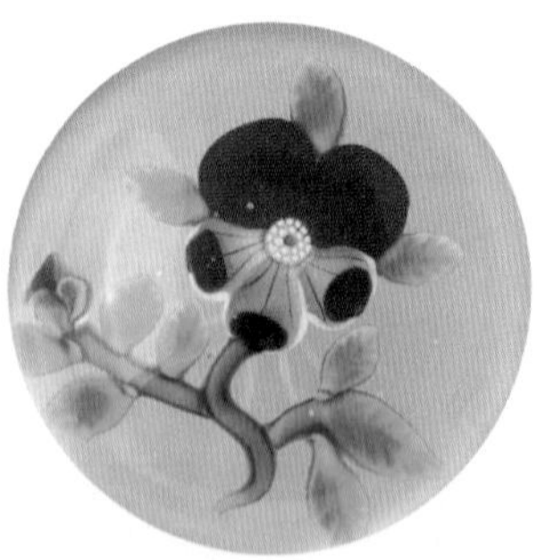

A 19thC Baccarat pansy paperweight, with a purple, yellow and white flower and a single bud growing from leafy stems, with a star-cut base.

3in (7.5cm) diam

£300-500 **WW**

A Baccarat paperweight, containing a pansy and a bud and leaves, on a star-cut ground.

2.25in (6cm) diam

£500-700 **LFA**

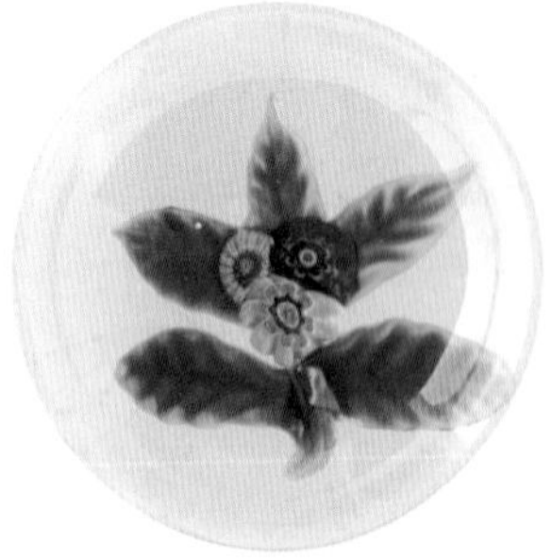

A Clichy small glass paperweight, containing three flowerheads and leaves.

2in (5cm) diam

£500-700 **LFA**

A good Clichy blue-ground paperweight, set with coloured canes.

c1845 *3in (7.5cm) diam*

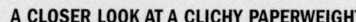

£700-1,000 **WW**

A small mid-19thC faceted Clichy paperweight, set with coloured canes on a lace ground, bruised foot-rim.

2.25in (5.5cm) diam

£400-600 **WW**

A St. Louis paperweight, with scrambled aventurine, millefiori and latticino canes.

2.75in (7cm) diam

£500-700 **LFA**

A St. Louis paperweight, with a blue clematis and two leaves, on a pink jasper ground.

2.5in (6.5cm) diam

£1,000-1,500 **LFA**

A CLOSER LOOK AT A CLICHY PAPERWEIGHT

Founded in 1838, Clichy-la-Garenne was one of the three most influential crystalleries in the golden age of paperweight manufacture from 1845-55, along with Baccarat and St Louis. Clichy weights are dateable to 1849. They exhibited at Crystal Palace in 1851 and at the 1853 New York Exhibition. Retail records of the time indicate that demand outstripped supply.

Despite the damage, the densely clustered canes, the skilled use of cog canes and the major manufacturer contribute to the value of this weight.

Clichy used a rose as its signature, in white, pale pink or yellow. This cane demonstrated the great skill of Clichy artists in creating the petal effect in molten glass.

Clichy also used initial canes to identify its work as did rival company St Louis, although full signatures are rare.

A Clichy scrambled paperweight, the canes including a white rose, and inscribed 'LICH', tiny chip to side.

c1845 *3in (7.5cm) diam*

£1,800-2,200 **WW**

19THC BOHEMIAN GLASS INNOVATIONS

- The 19thC saw a new era of experimentation in glass-making, often by chemists who developed new colours, techniques and effects.
- **Hyalith**
  Inspired by Wedgwood's black basalt wares, Count Georg von Buquoy (1781-1851) produced hyalith, a dense opaque glass in red or black, usually gilded, in 1819.
- **Lithyalin**
  Friedrich Egermann (1777-1864) patented 'Lithyalin' glass at his factory at Novy Bor, Bohemia. It was designed to represent polished hardstones by mixing together glass of differing colours and brushing the surface with metal oxides to create a striated effect.
- **Stained glass**
  Egermann also invented staining glass which inexpensively produced a solid, even colour over clear glass. This was often cut through to show the clear glass below. Egermann developed the yellow stain in 1818, using silver chloride, and a red in 1832 using gold chloride mixed with copper oxide.
- **Flashed glass**
  Egermann's technique involved dipping a glass piece into glass of a different colour. The effect is similar to overlaid glass, except that flashed glass is thinner and produces a hard line between the two colours.

An 18thC Bohemian beaker, painted in red with sitting birds flanking an oval cartouche.

4.5in (11cm) high

£100-150 KAU

An early 19thC armorial beaker, painted with the coat of arms of von Roggenbach, white floral decoration, the rim with red and yellow stripe.

5.25in (13cm) high

£400-600 KAU

A 19thC Bohemian glass beaker, with brown monochrome decoration of a huntsman and female companion, coursing within their country grounds.

5in (12.5cm) high

£150-250 SWO

A faceted beaker, possibly Friedrich Egermann, Blottendorf, in blue-purple marbled glass, on a faceted foot.

c1835 *4.5in (11.5cm) high*

£600-900 KAU

A faceted beaker, possibly by Friedrich Egermann, Blottendorf, in dark blue, yellow and green marbled glass, on a faceted foot.

c1835 *4.75in (12cm) high*

£400-600 KAU

A faceted beaker, possibly by Friedrich Egermann, Blottendorf, with blue, yellow and green marbled glass.

c1835 *4.5in (11cm) high*

£600-900 KAU

A Friedrich Egermann, Blottendorf, faceted beaker, in brown-green marbled glass.

c1835 *4.75in (12cm) high*

£600-900 KAU

A rare faceted cup, possibly Friedrich Egermann, Blottendorf, in red-beige marbled glass, with baluster knop.

c1835 12.25in (30.5cm) high

£500-700 **KAU**

A Bohemian lidded cup, in clear glass, gilded and with an enamel overlay, the lid with a faceted knob and oval cartouche with floral bouquet.

c1840 12.5in (31cm) high

£180-220 **KAU**

A late 19thC Bohemian ruby-cut glass goblet and cover, decorated with scrollwork, a hunting lodge, a figure and animals.

9.75in (24.5cm) high

£300-500 **SWO**

A set of four Bohemian facet-cut amethyst goblets, decorated with gilt figures.

c1925 6.5in (16.5cm) high

£280-320 **SWO**

An 18thC Bohemian decanter, clear glass, painted in red with vine leaves, with a spinner-shaped stopper.

10.5in (26cm) high

£100-150 **KAU**

A German flacon and bonbonnière, painted and gilded, decorated with blossom and tendril pattern with coloured glass pearls in light red and green, some pearls missing.

c1880 flacon 7in (17.5cm) high

£30-50 **KAU**

One of a pair of 20thC Bohemian pink flash vases, engraved with buildings, animals, foliage and shells.

4.75in (12cm) high

£120-180 pair **SWO**

A pair of Bohemian vases, black glass with white opaque painting and gilding, depicting a guardian angel with a child and an angel holding a torch and a child, gilded rim.

c1890 12.75in (32cm) high

£150-200 **KAU**

A French white-to-clear overlay box, the hinged lid above a conforming base, decorated overall with chinoiserie figural reserves within scrolling surrounds.

c1820 *4in (10cm) wide*

£250-300 **FRE**

An early 19thC French cut glass and gilt brass mounted box, the hinged cover to floral decorated mounts, shell lifts to the sides.

5in (12.5cm) wide

£300-400 **WW**

A 19thC amethyst glass box, with canted corners, the hinged lid etched with a central star, above a conforming base etched with foliage.

6.25in (15.5cm) wide

£300-500 **FRE**

A Bristol blue glass hinged box, the lid with rounded corners above a conforming base, mounted with brass band and locking mechanism complete with key.

c1920

£500-800 **FRE**

A pair of 19thC ruby-flashed and overlaid table lustres, painted with floral panels and with scrolling gilt, slight wear.

11.5in (29cm) high

£1,200-1,800 **WW**

A large pair of 19thC ruby-flashed and white overlaid table lustres, decorated with floral panels and gilt.

12.75in (32.5cm) high

£1,200-1,800 **WW**

A pair of Victorian table lustres, the columns and tops with overlay gilt and coloured flower decoration, each with ten lustre drops.

12in (30.5cm) high

£1,200-1,800 **SWO**

An 18thC green tinted glass 'globe and shaft' wine bottle, with an old label inscribed "Washed up by sea at Scarborough".

7.5in (19cm) high

£1,500-2,000 **LFA**

Part of a set of nine 19thC amethyst glass pharmacist's bottles and stoppers, each of globular form with elongated neck, some with labels.

13in (33cm) high

£1,200-1,800 set **L&T**

A large Victorian green glass dump weight.

8.5in (22cm) high

£400-600 **SWO**

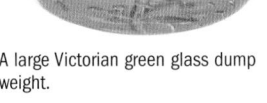

A 19thC French Empire bronze and ormolu cut glass table centre, the bowl supported on four leaves and four black sphinxes on stand and paw feet.

9in (23cm) high

£500-800 **GORL**

MOUNT WASHINGTON GLASS

- Established in 1837 in South Boston by William Libbey, the early output of Mount Washington was utilitarian glassware.
- William Libbey moved the factory to New Bedford in 1870 and began producing American art glass, including hand-painted white opal glass and Amberina and Burmese ranges.
- Amberina glass was developed by Frederick Shirley at Mount Washington in 1884 and also at the New England Glass Company. Following a failed lawsuit, Mount Washington used the name 'Rose Amber'. It is difficult to distinguish between pieces from these two factories unless they are applied with wishbones or rigaree, both Mount Washington innovations.
- Burmese glass was patented in 1885. This heat-sensitive glass, also developed by Shirley, was produced with either a shiny or a more popular satin finish.
- Decorators Alfred and Harry Smith came to Mount Washington from the Sandwich Glass Company in 1871, but by 1874 had established their own workshop, decorating Mount Washington blanks.
- Mount Washington supplied glass to the Pairpoint Manufacturing Company to create silver-plate mounted pieces, such as pickle castors, from 1880 to 1894. The two companies then merged.

A Mount Washington Crown Milano rose bowl, shape number 620, with hand-painted decoration.

Mount Washington had a large dedicated decorating shop and the quality of the painting on its glass is extremely high.

c1895 *2.75in (7cm) high*

£200-300 **BRK**

A Mount Washington Crown Milano rose bowl, shape number 619.

c1895 *3.5in (9cm) high*

£200-300 **BRK**

A Mount Washington Crown Milano rose bowl, shape number 618, with carnation decoration.

c1895 *4.5in (11.5cm) high*

£200-300 **BRK**

A Mount Washington Crown Milano glass vase.

c1895 *5in (12.5cm) high*

£400-600 **BRK**

A Mount Washington Crown Milano glass bowl.

First patented in 1886, Crown Milano was originally called 'Albertine' after the Prince Consort, but did not sell well under that name. Intended to imitate English porcelain such as Royal Worcester, it later became popular and was made well into the 1890s.

c1895 *9in (23cm) diam*

£700-1,000 **BRK**

A Mount Washington Crown Milano glass vase, with roses painted in a solution of gold.

c1895 *7in (18cm) diam*

£500-700 **BRK**

A Mount Washington Crown Milano sugar shaker.

c1895 *5.25in (13.5cm) diam*

£200-300 **BRK**

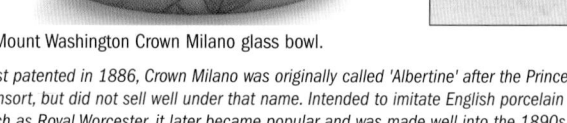

A Mount Washington Crown Milano egg-shaped glass sugar shaker.

Sugar shakers in this style were made by many different companies. They are very popular collectables, and Mount Washington is the most sought-after maker.

c1895 *4.5in (11.5cm) high*

£200-250 **BRK**

A Mount Washington Royal Flemish vase, with silver-plated mount, stained glass decoration and gold piping.

Royal Flemish glass was patented in 1894 and was one of the most ambitious ranges issued by Mount Washington, boasting a variety of complex shapes. This decorated camphor glass was often divided into panels with heavy gold lines and elaborately decorated. Some pieces are marked with the RF monogram.

c1890 *7.25in (18.5cm) high*

£1,000-1,500 **BRK**

A Mount Washington Royal Flemish vase, with separate ropetwist handle.

c1890 *18in (45.5cm) high*

£5,000-7,000 **BRK**

A Mount Washington Burmese glass pitcher.

c1890 *7.5in (19cm) high*

£400-600 **BRK**

A Mount Washington Burmese glass milk jug.

Thomas Webb in England secured a licence to manufacture Burmese glass and did so until 1915.

c1890 *6in (15cm) high*

£300-400 **BRK**

A Mount Washington Burmese glass creamer, with applied 'wishbone' feet and raspberry prunt over the pontil.

Over 300 different shapes were produced in the Burmese range.

c1890 *4.75in (12cm) long*

£500-700 **BRK**

A Mount Washington Burmese glass sugar bowl and creamer, of petticoat shape, with piecrust rim.

c1890 *5.5in (14cm) high*

£300-500 **BRK**

A Mount Washington Burmese glass cup and saucer.

The peach colour of Burmese glass comes from a second firing in the glory hole. The base of the glass stays cooler and retains more of the yellow colour. Areas at the very top of the vessel are heated to such an extent that the peach colour reverts back to yellow.

c1890 *saucer 4.75in (12cm) diam*

£300-400 **BRK**

A CLOSER LOOK AT A BURMESE VASE

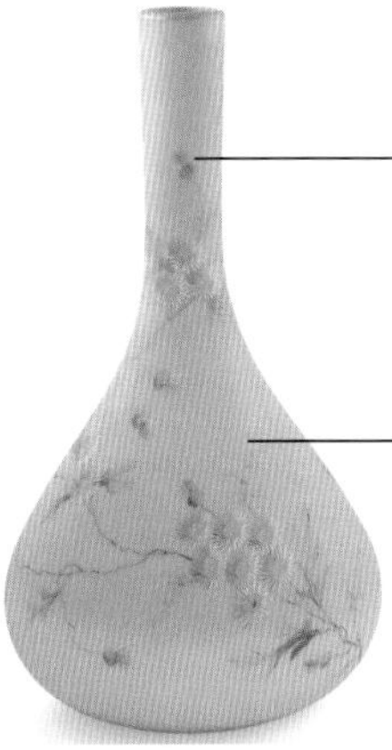

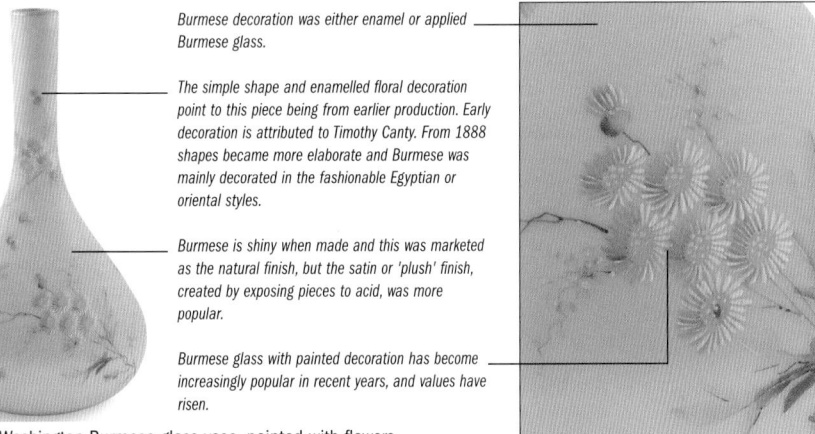

Burmese decoration was either enamel or applied Burmese glass.

The simple shape and enamelled floral decoration point to this piece being from earlier production. Early decoration is attributed to Timothy Canty. From 1888 shapes became more elaborate and Burmese was mainly decorated in the fashionable Egyptian or oriental styles.

Burmese is shiny when made and this was marketed as the natural finish, but the satin or 'plush' finish, created by exposing pieces to acid, was more popular.

Burmese glass with painted decoration has become increasingly popular in recent years, and values have risen.

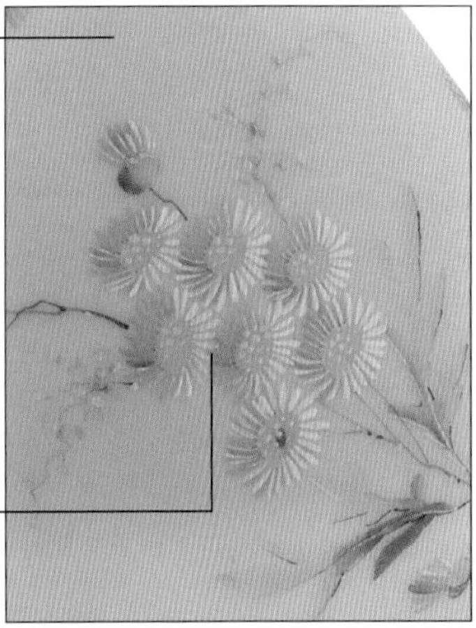

A Mount Washington Burmese glass vase, painted with flowers.

c1885 *11.75in (30cm) high*

£800-1,200 **BRK**

A Mount Washington Mother-of-pearl Satin glass vase, with polka dot airtrap pattern.

8.75in (22cm) high

£200-300 **BRK**

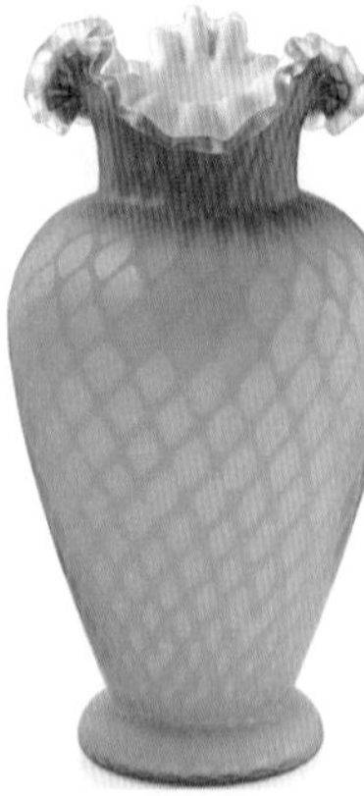

A Mount Washington Mother-of-pearl Satin glass vase, of deep rose shading to pink, with diamond quilted airtrap pattern and typical ruffled top.

11in (28cm) high

£300-400 **BRK**

A Mount Washington Mother-of-pearl Satin glass vase, with muslin airtrap pattern.

Mount Washington produced more than 50 different airtrap patterns in this range. Mother-of-pearl glass, often opal, was mould-blown, with a second layer of coloured glass blown over it, forming a pattern in the glass. This glassware was so popular that Mount Washington issued a licence to Phoenix Glass company to produce it.

8in (20.5cm) high

£200-250 **BRK**

A Mount Washington Mother-of-pearl Satin glass vase, with snowflake airtrap pattern and coralene decoration.

The airtrap pattern was achieved by using wires to trap air between multiple layers of glass.

7.5in (19cm) high

£300-500 **BRK**

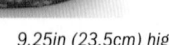

A Mount Washington Mother-of-pearl Satin glass vase, with diamond quilted airtrap pattern and coralene decoration.

Coralene decoration consists of reflective glass beads applied to the surface of the glass.

9.25in (23.5cm) high

£400-600 **BRK**

A Mount Washington Peachblow glass vase.

c1890 *5in (12.5cm) high*

£1,200-1,800 **BRK**

A Mount Washington Peachblow glass vase.

In 1886 Shirley patented Peachblow, sometimes called 'Peachskin'. This was not a great commercial success and the factory ceased marketing it in 1888.

c1890 *8in (20.5cm) high*

£700-1,000 **BRK**

A Mount Washington Peachblow glass finger bowl.

c1890 *4.5in (11.5cm) diam*

£700-1,000 **BRK**

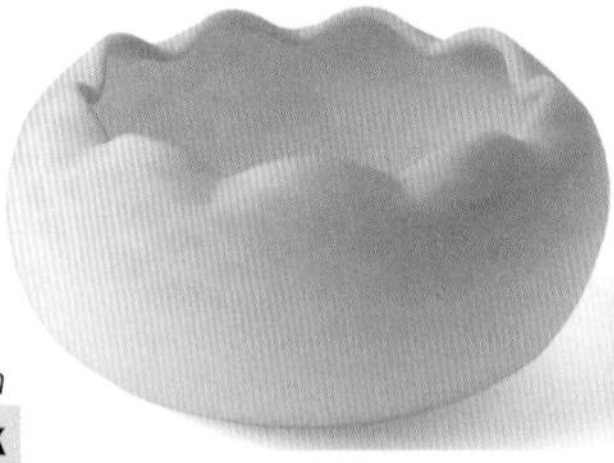

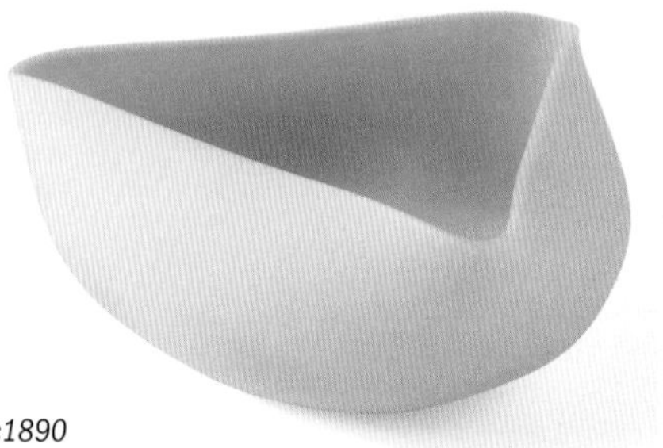

A Mount Washington Peachblow triangular glass bowl.

c1890 *4.5in (11.5cm) wide*

£700-1,000 **BRK**

A Mount Washington Amberina wine glass.

4in (10cm) high

£180-220 **BRK**

A Mount Washington Amberina glass cordial.

4.5in (11.5cm) high

£120-180 **BRK**

A Mount Washington Amberina glass epergne.

Amberina was the name given to a new type of heat-sensitive glass, developed by Frederick Shirley from 1884. When gold was added in production, the glass shaded from amber to red.

9in (23cm) high

£2,000-2,500 **BRK**

A Mount Washington Amberina glass cheese dish.

8.25in (21cm) diam

£1,800-2,200 **BRK**

A Mount Washington Rose Amber Amberina glass wishbone creamer and sugar bowl.

5in (12.5cm) high

£1,800-2,200 **BRK**

A rare Mount Washington glass tazza, with diamond-cut bowl and paperweight base.

7in (18cm) diam

£1,000-1,500 **BRK**

A Mount Washington Lava glass vase, made with lava from Mount Etna.

This is one of only a few true black glasses ever made. Rare Lava glass, also known as Sicilian ware, used basalt-based glass embedded in the surface. Usually black with gold decoration, it can be found in pink and cobalt with a shiny, sometimes iridized finish.

1878 *6.25in (16cm) high*

£500-700 **BRK**

A Mount Washington acid-etched cameo glass vase.

c1890 *8.75in (22cm) high*

£2,000-3,000 **BRK**

A New England Glass Company Wild Rose Peachblow glass jug, with matt finish.

c1885 7in (18cm) high

£800-1,200 **BRK**

A New England Glass Company Wild Rose Peachblow glass creamer, with matt finish.

This is an unusual shape.

c1885 4.5in (11.5cm) wide

£500-800 **BRK**

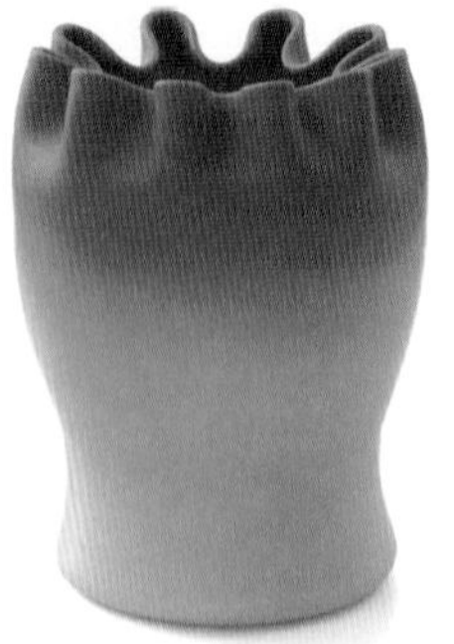

A New England Glass Company Wild Rose Peachblow glass spooner, with matt finish.

The New England Glass Company was founded in 1818 in East Cambridge, Massachusetts. It closed in 1890.

c1885 4.5in (11.5cm) high

£300-500 **BRK**

A New England Glass Company Wild Rose Peachblow glass gourd vase, with gloss finish.

Gloss finish Peachblow is rarer and less popular among collectors.

c1885 8.75in (22cm) high

£500-700 **BRK**

A New England Glass Company pressed Amberina glass stork vase, designed by Joseph Locke.

Pressed Amberina glass is scarce.

4.5in (11.5cm) high

£1,200-1,800 **BRK**

A New England Glass Company Amberina glass vase.

6.5in (16.5cm) high

£400-600 **BRK**

A New England Glass Company Amberina glass carafe.

8.25in (21cm) high

£400-600 **BRK**

A New England Glass Company Amberina glass milk pitcher, with crimped edge.

5.5in (14cm) high

£1,200-1,800 **BRK**

A New England Glass Company Amberina lemonade glass, originally part of a set with a pitcher.

4in (10cm) high

£120-180 **BRK**

A New England Glass Company Amberina glass goblet.

Amberina stemware is relatively hard to find.

6.75in (17cm) high

£300-400 **BRK**

A New England Glass Company sugar bowl and creamer, of green opaque glass with agate staining.

c1880 5.5in (14cm) wide

£800-1,200 **BRK**

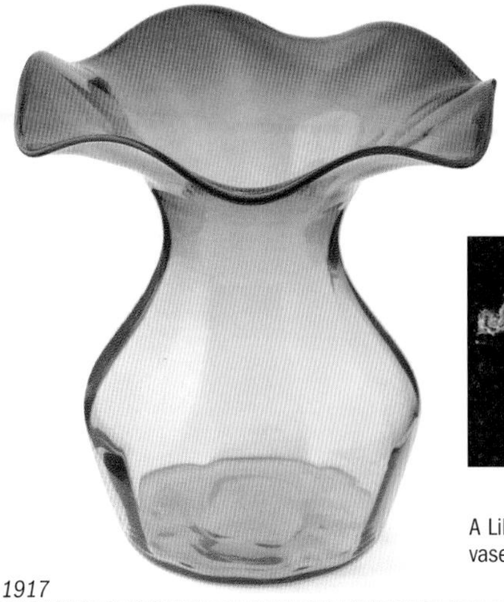

A Libbey Amberina glass vase.

1917 6in (15cm) high

£300-500 **BRK**

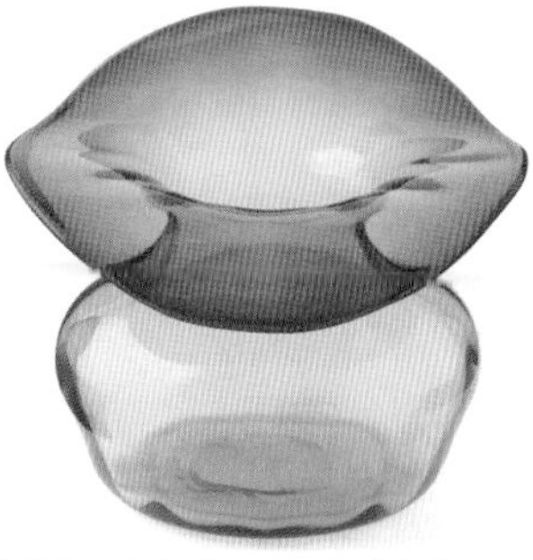

A Libbey Amberina glass jack-in-the-pulpit vase.

The Libbey Glass Company was founded in 1888 in Ohio. English glassmaker Joseph Locke worked there for a time, creating fine cameo and innovative coloured glassware.

1917 5in (12.5cm) high

£500-700 **BRK**

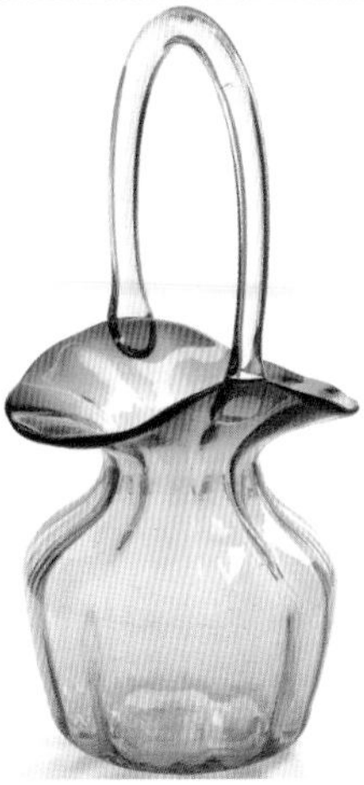

A Libbey Amberina glass vase, with handle.

8in (20.5cm) high

£1,500-2,000 **BRK**

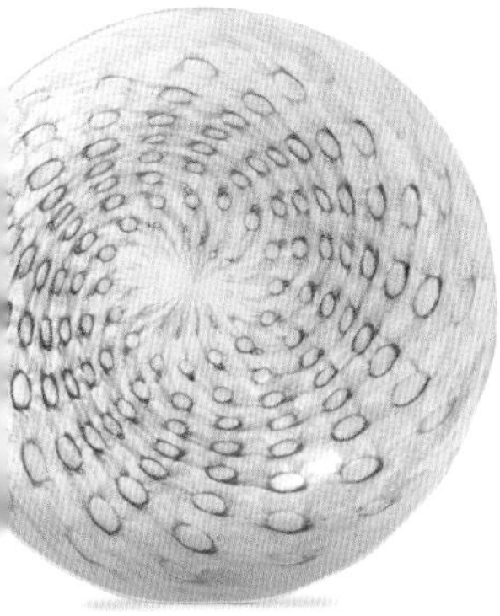

A Libbey Clutha glass bowl, with air bubble inclusions.

c1930 11in (28cm) diam

£200-250 **BRK**

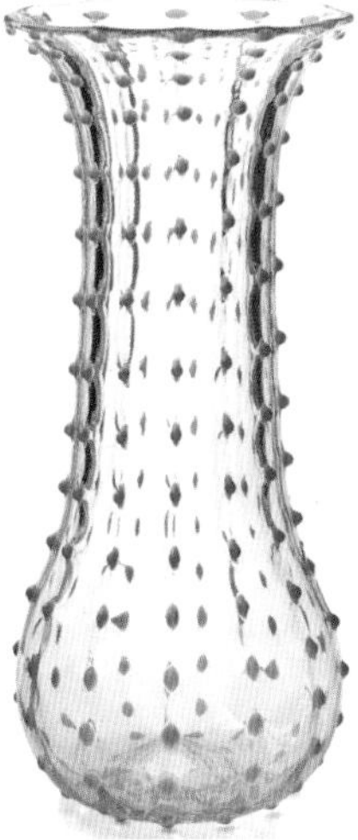

A Libbey glass vase.

A. Douglas Nash had previously worked for Tiffany and ran his own business before he went into partnership with Libbey in 1930.

c1930 10in (25.5cm) high

£150-200 **BRK**

MONROE

A C.F. Munroe Co. Wave Crest glass cracker jar, with silver-plated mount.

c1900 7.75in (19.5cm) high

£300-400 **BRK**

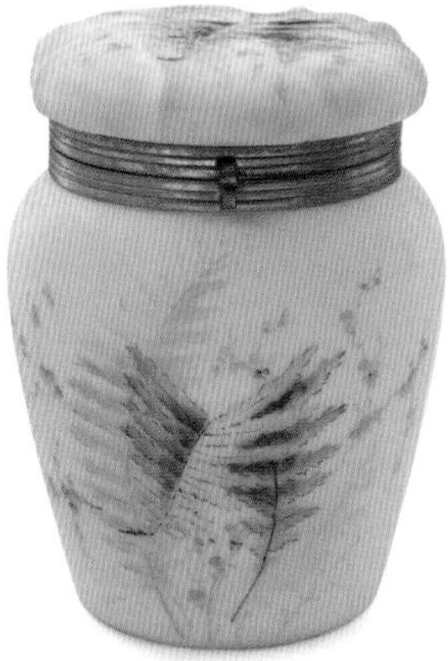

A C.F. Munroe Co. Wave Crest glass tobacco jar, with Helmschmidt swirl pattern and hand-painted decoration.

c1900 7.5in (19cm) high

£300-500 **BRK**

A C.F. Munroe Co. Nakara glass jewel box.

c1900 4.5in (11.5cm) wide

£300-400 **BRK**

A C.F. Munroe Co. Wave Crest glass jewel box, with Helmschmidt swirl pattern.

c1900 8in (20.5cm) wide

£300-500 **BRK**

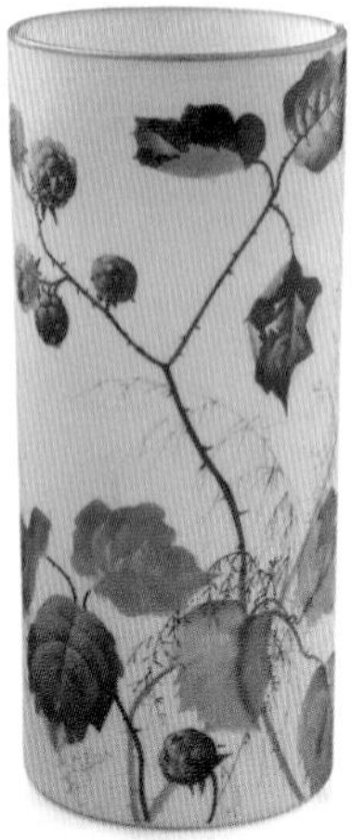

A Smith Bros. decorated glass cylinder vase.

c1885 *8in (20.5cm) high*

£300-500 **BRK**

A Smith Bros. decorated melon-shaped glass vase.

Smith Bros. was a decorating company that bought in made-to-order shapes from glassmakers including Mount Washington.

c1885 *8.5in (21.5cm) high*

£700-1,000 **BRK**

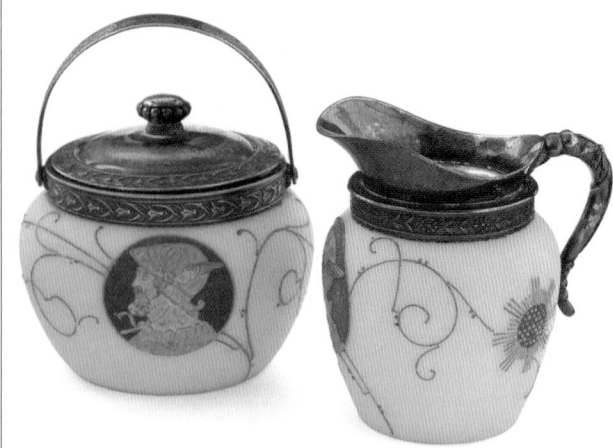

A Smith Bros. glass sugar bowl and creamer, with silver-plated mount.

c1885 *3.5in (9cm) wide*

£200-300 **BRK**

A Hobbs Amberina glass window-hanging boat.

8.5in (21.5cm) high

£200-250 **BRK**

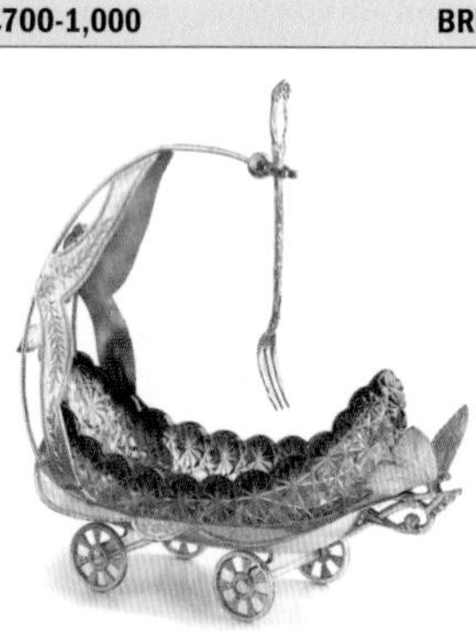

A Hobbs Amberina glass pickle dish, with silver carriage and hanging fork.

The silverware was made by another company.

3in (7.5cm) long

£1,200-1,800 **BRK**

A Hobbs Amberina toothpick holder.

3in (7.5cm) high

£250-350 **BRK**

A Phoenix Glass Company Peachblow glass hobnail pitcher.

c1885 *4.5in (11.5cm) high*

£200-250 **BRK**

A Phoenix Glass Company apricot glass vase, with airtrap decoration.

Phoenix airtrap glass has a slightly coarser finish than Mount Washington.

c1885 *8.25in (21cm) high*

£200-300 **BRK**

A Phoenix Glass Company glass bowl, with crescent pattern airtrap decoration.

4.5in (11.5cm) wide

£100-150 **BRK**

A Fry mould-blown glass vase.

c1925 *7.5in (19cm) high*

£300-500 **BRK**

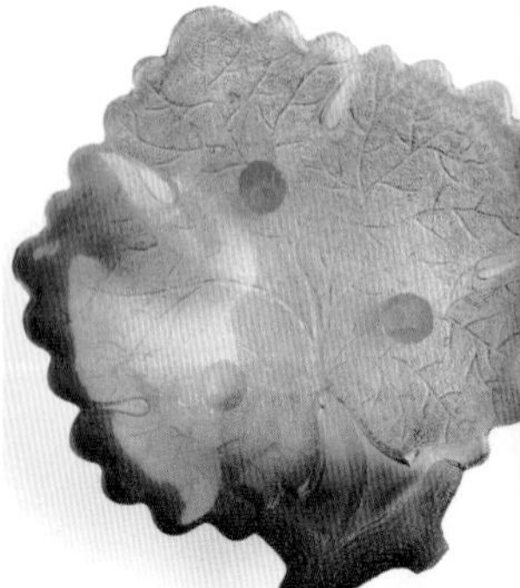

A Gillinder & Co. Amberina pressed glass dish, originally part of a larger set.

Gillinder & Co. dealt mostly in frosted glass.

c1885 *5.5in (14cm) wide*

£100-150 **BRK**

THE SILVER & METALWARE MARKET

Silver and metalware buyers tend to be knowledgeable and selective about what they buy. Items at the lower end of the market such as mass-produced 20thC tea sets and salvers are becoming increasingly difficult to sell. Attractive or unusual pieces, and 20thC pieces of good quality or design are holding their value. Highly regarded 19thC makers including Hennell, Hunt Roskell and Storr have also held their appeal. Georgian cutlery sets, Victorian novelty boxes, vinaigrettes and caddy spoons are popular. Condition is also becoming increasingly more important to buyers.

The Scottish silver market remains healthy, and Irish silver has become highly sought after as demand outstrips supply. Lyon & Turnbull in Edinburgh recently sold a pair of Irish silver table candlesticks from the 1740s for around £9,000 – more than three times the average selling price of a pair of London candlesticks from the same period. Irish silver can be difficult to date as hallmarks are often unclear, so consult an expert if in doubt.

Traditionally, silver with engraved inscriptions has attracted little interest, but buyers, increasingly fascinated by provenance, now intentionally seek out original examples. Pre-1800 pewter remains in demand, though buyers are choosy about condition.

A recent trend is silver incorporating enamel work, such as napkin rings and boxes. Hunting and shooting designs featured on the enamel are popular. Internationally, Russian pieces such as Fabergé kovschs attract a lot of interest. Unusual bold colourways on the enamel can increase the value dramatically.

Those buying to use can take advantage of current low prices to obtain bargains: a standard 20thC silver cutlery set with some age is substantially less expensive than buying antique or new.

– Trevor Kyle, Director, Lyon & Turnbull

SILVER

A George III silver swing-handled cake basket, by Thomas Daniel, with pierced scrolling foliage to basket and foot, London hallmarks for 1782.

14in (35.5cm) wide

£700-1,000 **SWO**

A George IV sterling silver cake basket, by J. & T. Settle Gunn & Co., Sheffield, with a swing handle and embossed and chased decoration.

12in (30cm) diam

£500-700 **FRE**

A 19thC Dutch silver pierced basket, with a swing handle, on four bracket feet.

7.5in (19cm) diam

£200-300 **FRE**

A late 19thC Russian silver trompe-l'oeil basket, simulating basketweave, with an applied 'napkin'.

10.75in (27cm) wide

£1,200-1,800 **FRE**

A silver basket, by Charles Steward, London, of shaped oval outline, with engraved swags and pierced decoration.

1895 *7.5in (18.5cm) wide*

£400-600 **SWO**

A silver Regency-style bonbon dish, with a swing handle, Dublin 1908.

8.25in (21cm) high

£300-400 **ROS**

A George III colonial silver bleeding bowl, sterling standard, engraved "Dr Miller" to the rim, two pairs of marks, duty mark.

£400-600 **L&T**

An 18th to 19thC French silver bowl, decorated with couples, stamped.

Provenance: *Baron von Glaubitz und Altengabel.*

8in (20cm) diam

£400-600 **KAU**

An Edwardian silver swing-handled basket, by Goldsmiths & Silversmiths Co. Ltd, with marks for London 1909.

13in (33cm) wide

£1,200-1,800 **L&T**

A Russian Sazikov silver strawberry dish, with gilt interior, St Petersburg.

1870 *10in (25.5cm) diam*

£300-400 **ROS**

A late 19thC Dutch silver bowl, with foliate pierced sides and shell and scroll cast rim.

6.5in (16cm) diam

£600-900 **FRE**

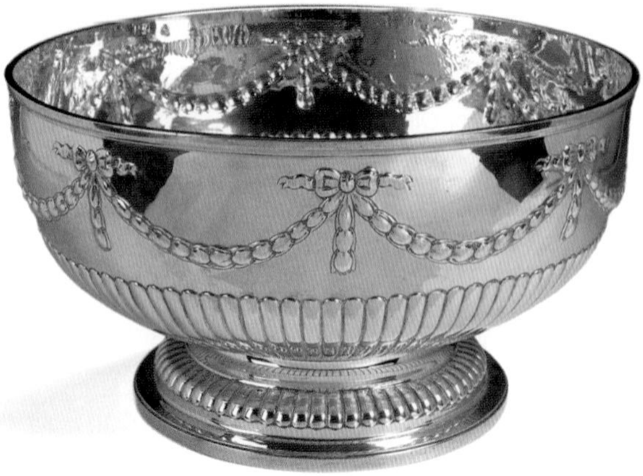

A large silver punch bowl, with ribbon and swag border, marks for London 1946, maker's mark indistinct.

1946 *14in (36cm) diam*

£2,500-3,000 **L&T**

An American silver limited-edition bowl, engraved with the 'Four Seasons' pattern, by S. Kirk & Son Inc. of Baltimore.

This bowl was originally projected as a limited edition of 500 that was probably uncompleted. This example is not numbered.

c1970 *9in (23cm) diam*

£250-300 **IHB**

A silver flower bowl, by James Dixon & Sons, with bright-cut garland motif, Sheffield hallmarks for 1936.

9.5in (24cm) diam

£300-400 **BIG**

A 20thC American silver small bowl, of hemispherical form, on a short beaded pedestal, by the Randahl Shop of Chicago, IL.

5in (12.5cm) diam

£80-120 **IHB**

A 19thC Irish silver monteith, by West & Son, in late 17thC style, crested, Dublin hallmarks for 1882.

9.75in (24.5cm) diam

£800-1,000 **SWO**

A late Victorian shaped oval dish, with pierced flower, scroll and shell cast edge and clear glass liner, marks for London, maker's mark "HE Ltd".

1901 *13.25in (33cm) wide*

£700-1,000 **L&T**

An American silver double vegetable dish, by the Gorham Manufacturing Co. of Providence, RI, and retailed by J.E. Caldwell & Co. of Philadelphia, engraved "MMcM Xmas 1902".

7.75in (19.5cm) wide

£700-1,000 **IHB**

A pair of silver 'Warwick Vases', by Goldsmiths & Silversmiths Co. Ltd., with cast classical decoration, marks for London 1909 and 1911.

8.5in (21.5cm) high

£3,500-4,000 **L&T**

An early 20thC Russian silver kovsch, with inscribed border, profusely decorated with foliate scrolls and mythical birds, possibly commemorating a regimental dinner.

The Cyrillic inscription, which is in the old orthography usually dated pre-1917, toasts: "The glory of carousing friends, The bosom-pal of fun and pleasure".

9.75in (25cm) high

£2,000-3,000 **L&T**

A CLOSER LOOK AT A PRESENTATION WINE COOLER

The coolers are complete with original removable liner and inner rim.

The provenance is strong. Descending through the Hinds family, who were among the earliest English settlers in Barbados, the pair include papers and documents relating to the wine coolers and the family.

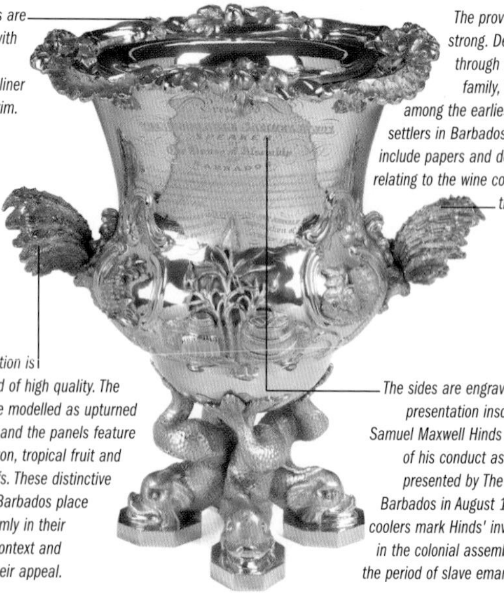

The decoration is profuse and of high quality. The handles are modelled as upturned clamshells and the panels feature coffee, cotton, tropical fruit and sugar motifs. These distinctive images of Barbados place this pair firmly in their historical context and increase their appeal.

The sides are engraved with a presentation inscription to Samuel Maxwell Hinds in tribute of his conduct as Speaker, presented by The House of Barbados in August 1839. The coolers mark Hinds' involvement in the colonial assembly during the period of slave emancipation.

One of a pair of important silver presentation wine coolers, engraved with the two coats of arms of the Island of Barbados and other crests and mottos of Samuel Maxwell Hinds, with marks for London 1842 and J. E. Terrey & Co.

Provenance: *By family descent, includes papers and documents relating to the wine coolers and the Hind family.*

1842 *13.75in (35cm) high*

£40,000-50,000 pair **L&T**

An early 19thC Scottish silver and horn vinaigrette, embossed with thistles, unmarked.

2in (5cm) wide

£300-400 **LFA**

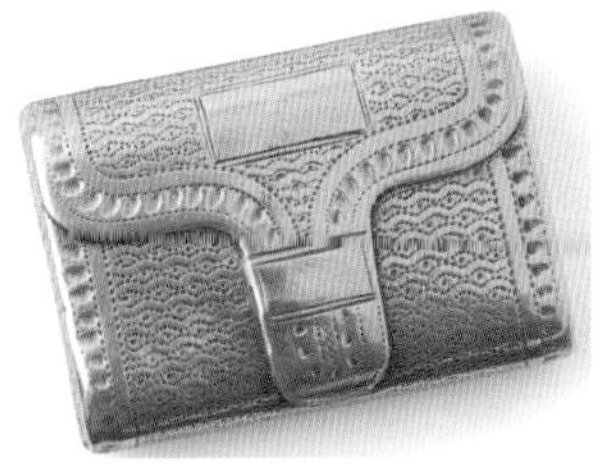

A George III silver vinaigrette, by John Shaw, of 'satchel' shape with wriggle- and bright-cut engraving, Birmingham 1816.

0.25in (0.5cm) wide

£250-300 **CHEF**

A Victorian 'castletop' silver vinaigrette, by C.H. Cheshire of Birmingham.

1878 *1.75in (4.5cm) wide*

£1,800-2,200 **WW**

A rare William and Mary silver nutmeg grater, initialled "MA", maker's mark "IA", unascribed.

c1690 *3in (7.5cm) high*

£6,000-8,000 **WW**

A rare William and Mary silver tubular nutmeg grater, initialled "TF" over "GL", maker's mark "IA", unascribed.

c1690 *2.5in (6cm) high*

£2,000-2,500 **WW**

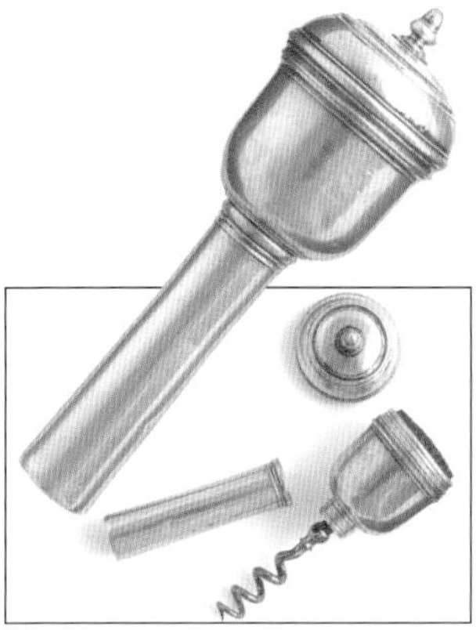

An English 18thC silver combined nutmeg grater and corkscrew, of mace form with acorn finial.

3in (7.75cm) high

£2,000-2,500 **ROS**

A George III silver nutmeg grater, William Sutton, London 1788, bright-cut decorated and initialled.

0.25in (0.5cm) wide

£400-600 **CHEF**

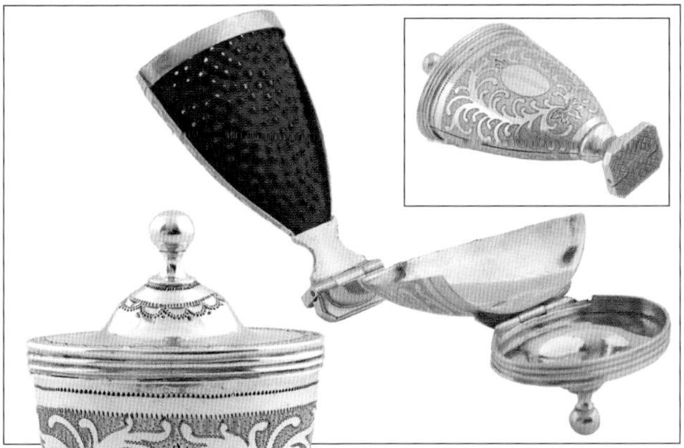

A fine George III engraved silver nutmeg grater, by Thomas Phipps and Edward Robinson of London, in the form of a covered vase with blued steel grater.

1804 *2.75in (7cm) high*

£7,000-10,000 **WW**

A George III silver nutmeg grater, probably John Robbins, London 1807.

0.25in (0.5cm) wide

£400-600 **CHEF**

A George III silver tea caddy, by T.B. Pratt and Arthur Humphreys, with a key, maker's mark and marks for London 1780.

1780 *5in (13cm) wide*

£700-1,000 **L&T**

A French early 19thC gold snuff box, inscribed "To Capt Ross 92nd Reg from Chas Grant of Jamaica."

James Kerr Ross received the Military General Service medal 1793-1814, the Portuguese War Cross for six engagements, and the Waterloo Medal in 1815. It is likely that a Charles Grant of the parish of St Andrews gave Ross this gold box in 1819.

2.75in (7cm) diam

£1,200-1,800 **L&T**

A William IV silver snuff box, by Nathaniel Mills, with Masonic presentation engraving, gilded interior and engine-turned surround, red leather box, Birmingham hallmarks for 1832.

£500-700 **BIG**

A Victorian silver card case, by Nathaniel Mills, with a view of Winchester Cathedral, in original case, Birmingham 1844.

4in (10cm) high

£2,800-3,200 **LFA**

A Victorian 'castletop' silver cigarette case, by George Unite of Birmingham, depicting Warwick Castle, inscribed "MA Proctor".

1865 *4in (10cm) high*

£1,200-1,800 **WW**

A pair of Edwardian novelty silver cigarette boxes, by Samuel Jacob, each modelled as a ship's lantern, inscribed "PORT" and "STARBOARD", with marks for London 1901.

5.5in (13.5cm) high

£1,800-2,200 **L&T**

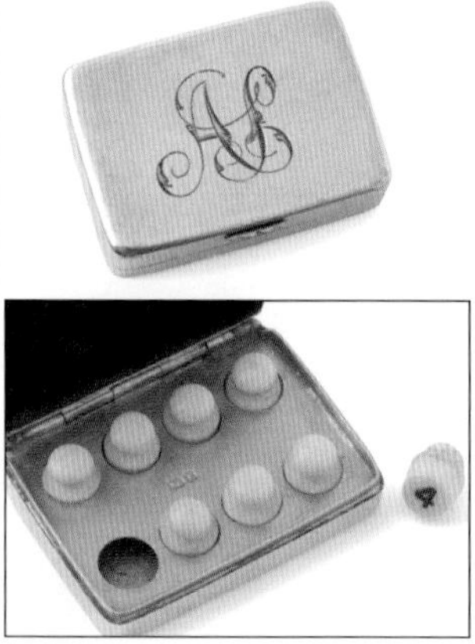

A silver shooting place finder case, by Sampson Mordan & Co, with eight numbered ivory peg markers, Chester 1905, engraved "AS".

1.5in (4cm) wide

£2,200-2,800 **CHEF**

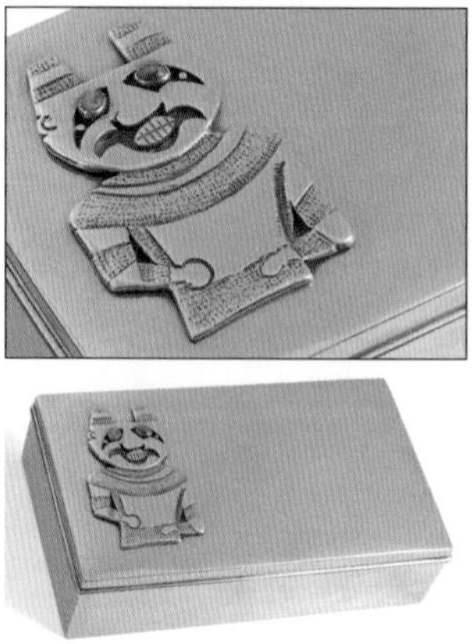

An American silver cigarette box, by John Chattellier of Newark, NJ, with ancient Indian-style applied decoration, lined with wood.

c1925 *5.75in (14.5cm) wide*

£100-150 **IHB**

An early 20thC silver cigarette case, by Docker & Burn Limited, later enamelled with a Spitfire, Birmingham hallmarks for 1926, together with the photograph from which the enamel was taken.

£800-1,200 **SWO**

A silver box with a Grecian scene, hallmarked with a lion and "O".

2.5in (6.5cm) wide

£300-350 **MB**

A pair of George I silver octagonal candlesticks, by Mathew Cooper, London, Britannia standard marks for 1717.

7.25in (18.5cm) high

£7,000-10,000 **LFA**

A pair of George I cast silver candlesticks, by Henry Jay of London, with engraved coat of arms, scratchweight "22-17".

1719 *7in (17.5cm) high*

£8,000-12,000 **WW**

A pair of George II candlesticks, by J. Gould, crested, detachable sconces, crested, marks for London.

1747 *7.5in (19cm) high*

£2,200-2,800 **L&T**

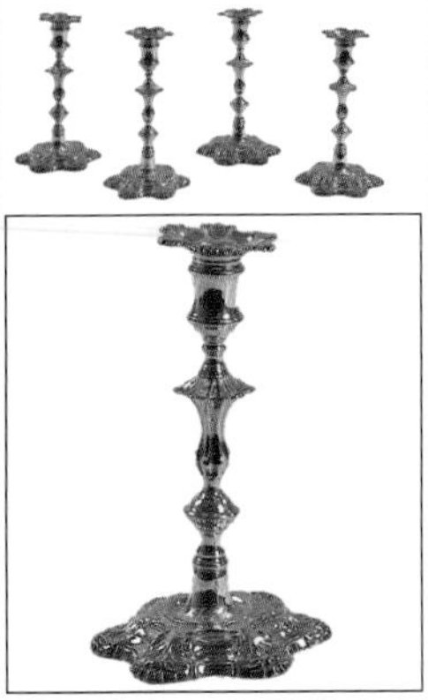

A set of four George III Rococo sterling silver candlesticks, with shell motifs and petal-form bases.

1752 *8.75in (22cm) high*

£6,000-9,000 **SK**

An early George III silver figural candlestick, by John Schuppe, London, modelled as a draped female on a repoussé base.

1764 *5.5in (14cm) high*

£700-1,000 **SWO**

A pair of George III tapersticks, with detachable sockets, marks for London, maker's mark "IC".

1767 *6.75in (17cm) high*

£2,200-2,800 **L&T**

A pair of George III silver candlesticks, by John Green & Co, with marks for Sheffield, loaded.

1802 *12.5in (32cm) high*

£1,200-1,800 **L&T**

A pair of American silver candlesticks, with bulbous nozzles, made by Jenkins & Jenkins of Baltimore, MD, 1908-23.

10in (25.5cm) high

£1,000-1,500 **IHB**

Two of a set of four American silver weighted candlesticks, by the Gorham Manufacturing Company of Providence, RI.

1911 *10.5in (26.5cm) high*

£1,200-1,800 set **IHB**

A 19thC pair of Louis XV-style silver candelabra, of ornate Rococo scroll form with scroll branches.

10.5in (27cm) wide

£2,800-3,200 **FRE**

A pair of German or Austrian candlesticks, with a winged putto holding the arms and crowned "L" for the princedom Liechtenstein, "HD" mark.

c1890 *11.5in (29cm) high*

£1,000-1,500 **KAU**

A pair of three-light candelabra, each of hexagonal outline with three scroll-form branches, marks for London, maker "RC".

1964 *11.25in (28cm) high*

£1,200-1,800 **L&T**

A pair of silver chambersticks and original snuffers, all engraved with a crest, London 1904.

4.25in (11cm) high

£600-900 **ROS**

A Victorian silver-gilt plated 'Medallion' epergne, with three lion masks and cut-glass circular bowls.

c1870 *19.25in (48cm) high*

£800-1,200 **FRE**

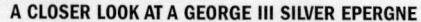

A CLOSER LOOK AT A GEORGE III SILVER EPERGNE

The ornate design helps fulfil the epergne's role as an attractive table decoration and as a striking centrepiece that would indicate the wealth and standing of the owner.

Reflecting the fashions of the time, this epergne was wider than mid-18thC versions and the form is simpler, exhibiting clean Neo-Classical elements rather than extensive Rococo embellishments. Silver baskets were largely replaced with cut-glass bowls from the Regency period.

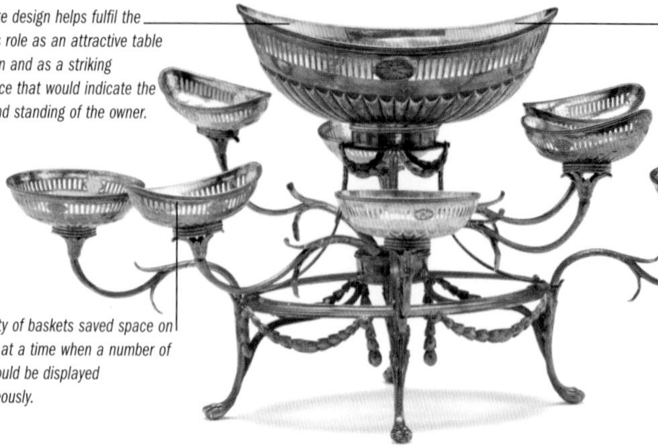

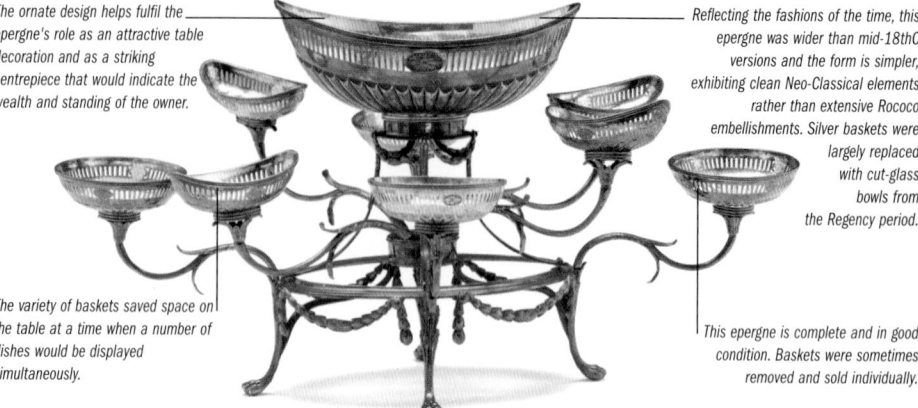

The variety of baskets saved space on the table at a time when a number of dishes would be displayed simultaneously.

This epergne is complete and in good condition. Baskets were sometimes removed and sold individually.

A George III silver epergne, possibly John Plimmer, London, with acanthus-decorated scroll branches and circular baskets.

c1804 *13.25in (33.5cm) high*

£12,000-18,000 **FRE**

A French silver three-section table de surtout, with applied foliate scroll decoration.

c1880 *47.5in (119cm) wide*

£4,000-6,000 **FRE**

A late Victorian silver footed circular dish, by Richard Martin & Ebenezer Hall, with marks for Sheffield 1894.

11.5in (29cm) diam

£400-600 **L&T**

A German silver and glass centrepiece, with openwork rim, German stamp.

c1900 *8.75in (22cm) high*

£700-1,000 **KAU**

SILVER CONDIMENTS

A William III silver lighthouse caster, with a knop finial and a moulded girdle, by an unascribed maker "MH" of London.

1696 *6.25in (16cm) high*

£1,200-1,800 **WW**

A Queen Anne pear-shaped silver sugar caster, by Charles Adams of London, with a bayonet fitting cover, piercing and a ball finial.

1712 *7.75in (20cm) high*

£800-1,200 **WW**

A George I silver kitchen pepper, by James Godwin of London, with the initials "IK".

1719 *3in (7.5cm) high*

£700-1,000 **WW**

Two pairs of American silver casters and salt cellars, by the Gorham Manufacturing Co. of Providence, RI.

1878 *2.75in (7cm) high*

£60-90 SET **IHB**

Two pairs of American silver pepper casters and salt cellars, by Tiffany & Co. of NY, of reproduction baluster form, "JMD" monogram.

c1950 *4in (10cm) high*

£200-250 **IHB**

A pair of American silver casters, by an unknown Baltimore silversmith, with monogram "R".

c1950 *4.75in (12cm) high*

£200-250 **IHB**

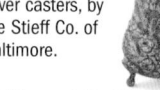

A pair of American silver casters, by the Stieff Co. of Baltimore.

1955 *4.5in (11.5cm) high*

£180-220 **IHB**

A George III sterling silver and four-bottle cruet, by Robert & Samuel Hennell, London, fitted with four cut glass silver-mounted condiment bottles.

1808 *8.25in (20.5cm) wide*

£280-320 **FRE**

A Georgian silver cruet, by Charles Chesterman, London, the eight cut glass bottles with silver mounts, in a stand.

1809 *10in (25.5cm) high*

£800-1,200 **SWO**

A George III oval cruet, by Robert Hennell, London, holding six cut glass and silver mounted bottles, one replaced.

1825

£400-600 **SWO**

A pair of Queen Anne Britannia Standard trencher salts, by Robert Kempton, each of canted rectangular outline, crested, marks for London.

1713 *2.5in (6.5cm) wide*

£700-1,000 **L&T**

A pair of American silver salt cellars, by the Towle Mfg. Co of Newburyport, MA, with gilt bowls.

c1885 *1.75in (4.5cm) wide*

£40-60 **IHB**

An Edwardian set of four silver Scottish open salts, by Hamilton & Inche, of torus form, with marks for Edinburgh 1904.

3in (7.5cm) diam

£400-600 **L&T**

A pair of George II cast silver circular salts, by Peter Archambo I, with anthemion band decoration, date marks rubbed.

3.5in (9cm) wide

£4,000-6,000 **GORL**

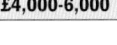

A George II silver cream pail, by Edward Aldridge of London, with a lattice work handle.

1752 *2in (5cm) high*

£300-400 **WW**

A rare George IV Scottish silver cream scoop, by W.P. Cunningham of Edinburgh, of plain semi-circular form with a rim running down the back and a turned wooden handle, crested.

1823 *11in (28cm) wide*

£400-500 **WW**

A 19thC Scottish silver mustard pot, Edinburgh, the hinged lid and body with embossed flower decoration, on three hoof feet, marks rubbed.

£150-250 **SWO**

A George IV silver drum mustard pot, by Charles Fox of London, with a shell thumbpiece and a gadrooned border, blue glass liner.

1862 *2.5in (6.5cm) wide*

£400-600 **WW**

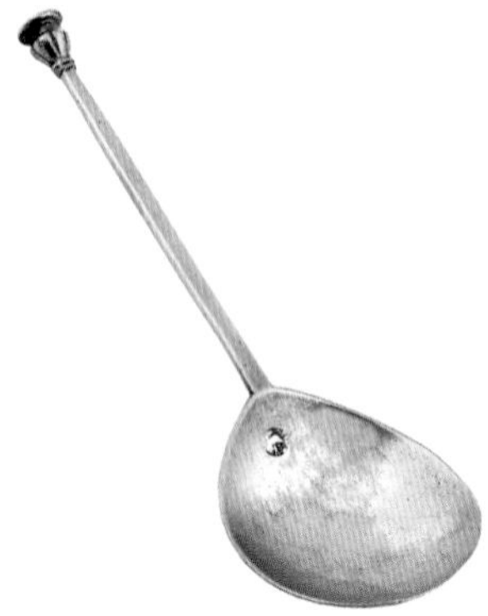

A James I Cornish sealtop silver spoon, by John Parnell of Truro, with later initials, maker's mark "PARN" and 'silver ship of Truro'.

c1620 *6.5in (16.5cm) long*

£1,500-2,000 **WW**

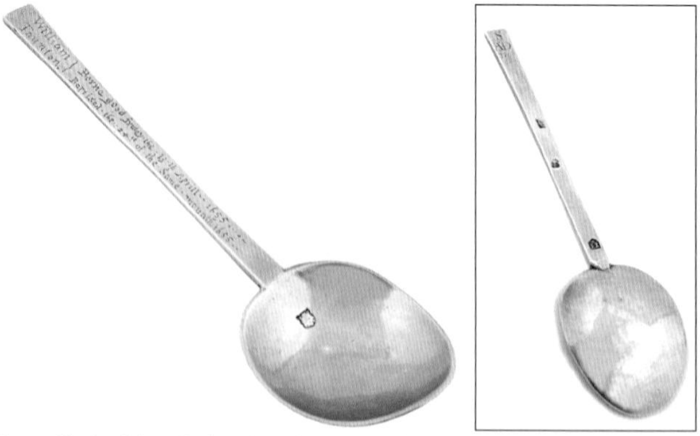

A rare Charles II inscribed puritan silver spoon, by Jeremy Johnson of London, inscribed for birth of "William Taunton" and dated "1665", scratched "S","AD" and "1708".

1662 *7.5in (19cm) long*

£3,000-5,000 **WW**

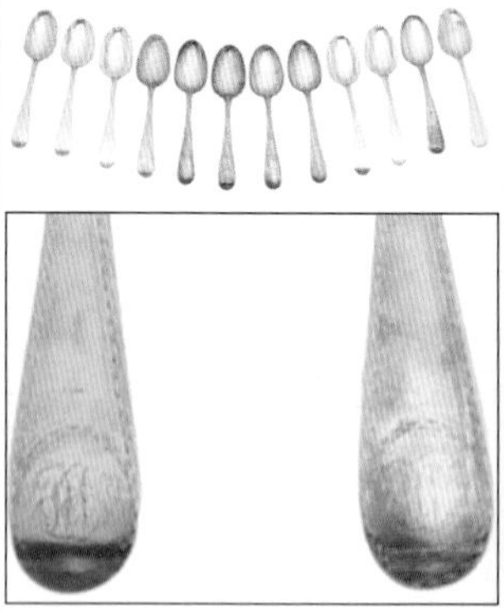

A set of twelve silver tablespoons, by Joseph Nathaniel Richardson, Philadelphia, with monograms in oval bright-cut wreath.

c1795

£1,200-1,800 **FRE**

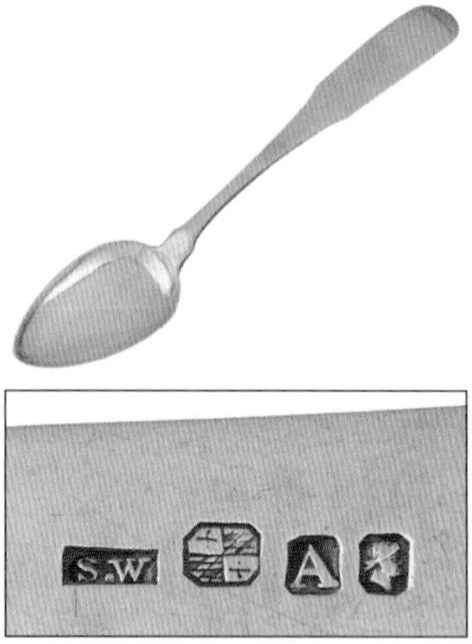

One of a set of six American silver dessert spoons, in the 'Fiddle' pattern, by Simon Wedge Sr., struck with the Baltimore assay marks used by Thomas Warner in 1815.

7.25in (18.5cm) long

£200-250 set **IHB**

An American silver sugar sifter, in the 'Kings' pattern, marked for Bennett & Caldwell of Philadelphia, engraved "Mrs Bevan".

1843-48 *7in (18cm) long*

£80-120 **IHB**

A pair of American silver-gilt serving spoons, by Krider & Biddle of Philadelphia, engraved "Clara".

c1865 *7.25in (18.5cm) long*

£80-120 **IHB**

An American silver olive spoon, by the Gorham Mfg. Co. of Providence, in a variation of the 'Medallion' pattern, retailed by Crosby & Morse of Boston.

1864 *6.75in (17cm) long*

£100-150 **IHB**

An American silver candy dish, by the Gorham Mfg. Co. of Providence, RI, erased monogram, 1895-1915.

7in (18cm) long

£150-200 **IHB**

An American Arts and Crafts silver pitcher spoon, by Charles W. Brown, in the 'Pointed End' pattern, with ovoid bowl.

Charles W. Brown was a spoonmaker, working between 1912-37, for Arthur Stone in Gardner, MA.

12in (30.5cm) long

£80-120 **IHB**

An American silver soup ladle, in the 'Fiddle' pattern, marked "RC" probably for Robert Campbell of Baltimore, with "ESS" monogram.

13.25in (33.5cm) long

£200-250 **IHB**

A George II silver Old English pattern soup ladle, by Jeremiah King of London.

1736 *13in (33cm) long*

£180-220 **GORL**

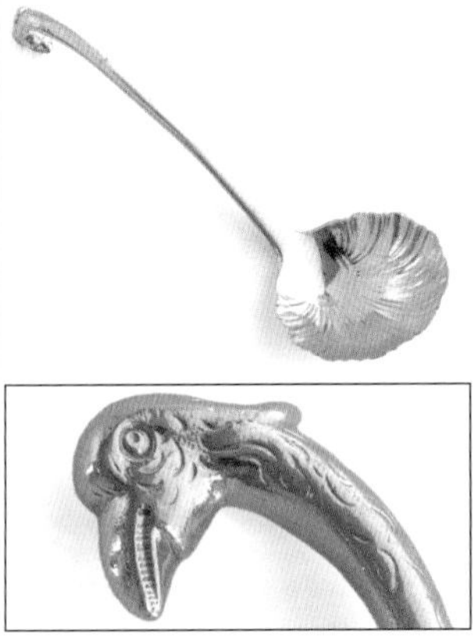

A rare George II Scottish silver shell bowl sauce ladle, with eagle head terminal, Edinburgh.

c1750

£700-900 **LFA**

An American silver soup ladle, in the 'Double Swell Fiddle' pattern, marked for Gabriel Duval Clark of Baltimore, with "AS" monogram, 1840-60.

12.75in (32.5cm) long

£150-200 **IHB**

A 'Queens' pattern silver ladle, by Williams Theobalds and Robert Atkinson, London.

13.5in (33.5cm) long

£200-300 **SWO**

A pair of American silver large salad servers, by Jacobi & Jenkins of Baltimore, with "MSW" monogram.

1896-1907 *10in (25.5cm) long*

£250-300 **IHB**

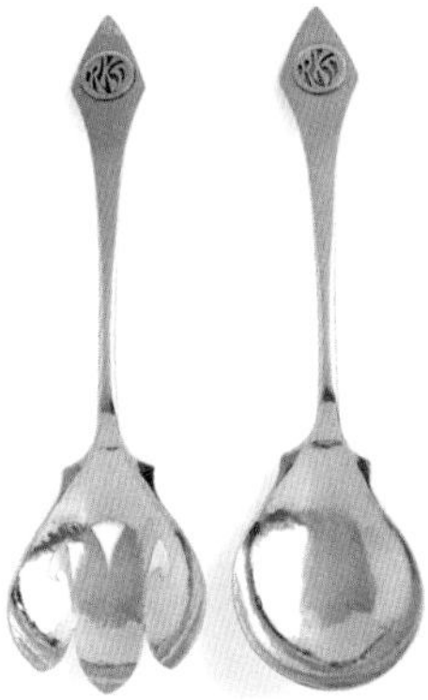

A pair of American Arts and Crafts silver salad servers, with pointed handles and ovoid bowls in a hammered pattern, marked for the T.C. Shop of Chicago, with "RKD" monogram, 1910-23.

9.75in (25cm) long

£200-250 **IHB**

An American silver dessert server, in the 'Mayflower' pattern, by William Gale & Son of NY, with "LHW" monogram, 1850-65.

10.25in (26cm) long

£120-180 **IHB**

An American silver fish slice, by James S. Vancourt of New York, with landscape-decorated pierced blade.

1852-55 *11.75in (30cm) long*

£120-180 **IHB**

An American silver ice cream set, in the 'Medallion' pattern with gilt bowls, "HRW" monogram.

c1863 *9.75in (25cm) long*

£300-500 **IHB**

A set of sterling silver Birks cutlery, with hallmarks for 1900.

It is unusual to find such a set complete and with a box.

knife 8.25in (21cm) long

£1,000-1,500 **TFR**

A CLOSER LOOK AT A MYER MYERS SILVER SALVER

Myer Myers (1723-1795), was one of the most talented and productive silversmiths working in pre-industrial America, making this an important and desirable piece.

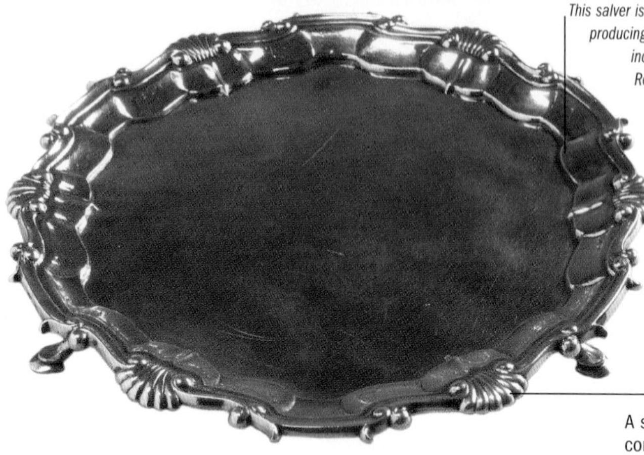

This salver is of extremely high quality - Myers specialized in producing outstanding custom order work for rich clients, including New York's elite, in the years prior to the Revolutionary war, as well as more modest forms.

His pieces have historical significance. Myers registered as a 'goldsmith' in 1746, becoming the first native Jew within the British Empire to establish himself as a retail silversmith since the foundation of the Worshipful Company of Goldsmiths in 1327.

The curves, shells and C-scroll decoration reflect Myers position as a leading proponent of US Rococo.

A silver salver, by Myer Myers, New York City, with applied moulded edge consisting of cyma recta-cyma reversa curves with six shells and C-scrolls, on short cabriole legs, marked "Myers", struck twice.

8.25in (20.5cm) diam

£60,000-90,000 **SK**

An early 18thC Irish provincial silver tazza, by William Martin, Cork, overscratched initials and scratch weight, possibly with later unmarked foot.

c1725 *8.25in (21cm) diam*

£8,000-12,000 **SWO**

A George II silver salver, maker's mark overstruck with that of Edward Pocock, London, later engine-turned and engraved.

1732 *12.25in (31cm) diam*

£400-600 **CHEF**

A silver footed salver, by Thomas Cooke II and Richard Gurney, inscribed "Left by ye Will of Mrs Phillippa Stanley..." and "1750", London.

1751 *9in (23cm) wide*

£800-1,200 **ROS**

A George II large silver salver, possibly by William Bond, with marks for London, with engraved armorial for "NORREYS" of "SPEKE", Lancashire, further inscriptions.

1752 *21in (53cm) diam*

£1,200-1,800 **L&T**

A silver salver, by William Peaston, with shell and scroll rim on three scroll feet, London.

1755 *12.5in (31.5cm) diam*

£600-900 **ROS**

An early George III silver salver, by "EC", with lozenge for Mrs Atkinson of Angerton, Northumberland, with marks for London.

1763 *14in (36cm) diam*

£500-700 **L&T**

A silver salver, by John Schofield, with ownership initials "IP" to base, London.

£600-900 **ROS**

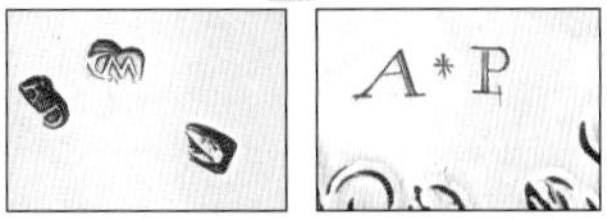

A George III colonial silver waiter, with crest to the centre and marks for Jamaica, marked with alligator's head, "WD" and "AD".

£800-1,200 **L&T**

A silver mirrored plateau, by John W. Faulkner, New York, with egg and dart mirror surround, original mahogany underside, impressed maker's mark.

c1835 *25in (62.5cm) wide*

£12,000-18,000 **SK**

A large Victorian silver salver, by Robert Garrard, with marks for London.

1845 *21.5in (55cm) diam*

£1,200-1,800 **L&T**

A pair of silver comports, by Robert Garrard, London, each with a pierced and chased dish, marked RG".

1800 *8.5in (21cm) high*

£1,200-1,800 **SWO**

An American silver small waiter, by Charters, Cann & Dunn and retailed by Ball, Tompkins & Black of New York, with "CAWS" monogram.

c1850 *6.5in (16.5cm) wide*

£200-300 **IHB**

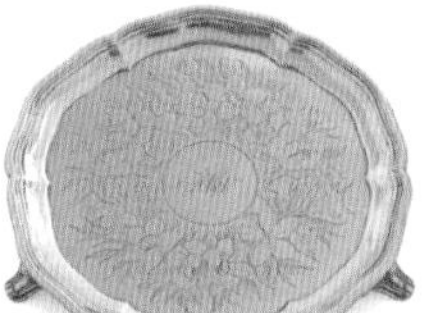

A silver platter, by Hunt and Roskell, Late Storr and Mortimer, engraved with crest of Sir Richard Arkwright, London.

1853 *18.5in (47cm) diam*

£600-900 **ROS**

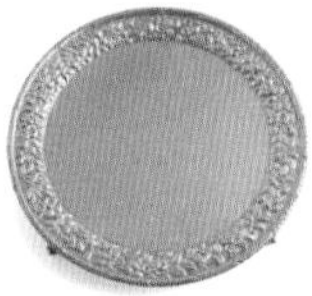

An American silver waiter, by S. Kirk & Son of Baltimore, engraved with 'snowflake' diaperwork around a foliate wreath, "HRW" monogram.

c1880 *13in (33cm) diam*

£800-1,200 **IHB**

A large Victorian silver tray, by Thomas Bradbury & Sons, engraved "B" within a Rococo scroll cartouche.

1893 *30in (76.5cm) wide*

£1,800-2,200 **SWO**

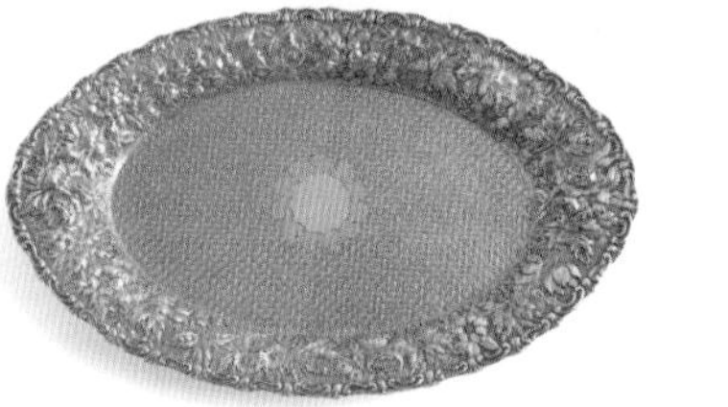

One of a pair of American silver bread trays, by A. Jacobi & Co., retailed by James R. Armiger of Baltimore.

1893-95 *14in (35.5cm) wide*

£1,500-2,000 pair **IHB**

A Thomas Bradbury & Sons silver drinks tray, with twin integral handles, Sheffield hallmarks.

1895

£1,000-1,500 **BIG**

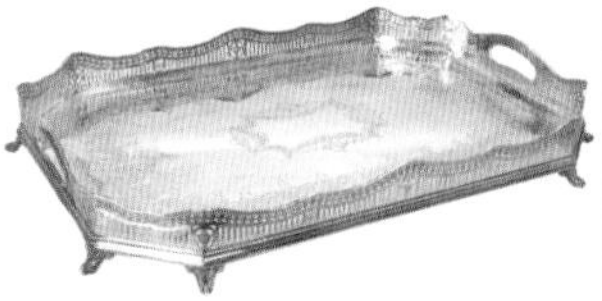

A set of six silver plates, with crests of a lion rampant couped and a dragon, London.

1907 *9.75in (25cm) diam*

£700-1,000 **ROS**

A Birks sterling silver repoussé tray, with marks commemorating the first silver mined in Canada.

Provenance: *From the collection of Thomas George Shaughnessy, first president of the Canadian Pacific Railway (1853-1923)*

13.75in (35cm) wide

£1,000-1,500 **TCF**

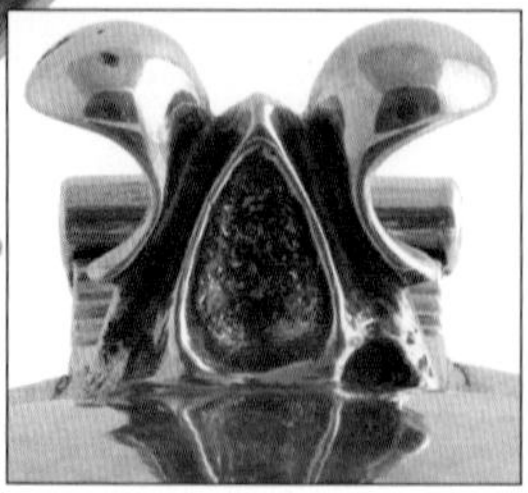

A Charles II silver tankard, possibly by John Sutton of London, engraved with an armorial, maker's mark for "IS".

The arms show two lions passant guardant. Prominent amongst those using this design in late 17thC London were the Ducie family of Gloucestershire. The family descended from Sir Robert Ducie who was created a Baronet in 1629, became Lord Mayor of London 1630-31 and was a banker to Charles I.

1674 *6.25in (16cm) high*

£7,000-10,000 **GORL**

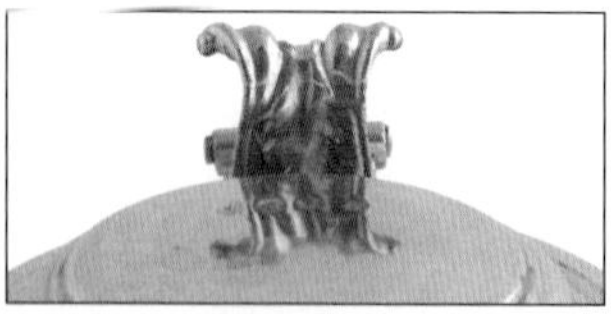

A Queen Anne Britannia standard silver tankard, by John Fawdrey of London, with a bifurcated scroll thumbpiece.

1706 *7.25in (18.5cm) high*

£3,000-5,000 **GORL**

A Queen Anne Britannia standard silver tankard, by Richard Green of London, with engraved armorial.

The arms are those of the Kemp family of Gissing Hall in Norfolk, possibly engraved for one of the sons of Sir Robert Kemp (1627-1710), Baronet and MP for Norfolk and Dunwich.

1707 *7.25in (18.5cm) high*

£4,000-6,000 **GORL**

A George II tankard, probably by John Berthellot, with heart-shaped kick, initialled, marks for London.

1753 *6.75in (17cm) high*

£1,500-2,000 **L&T**

A George III silver tankard, by William Shaw, inset with Queen Anne crown, later decoration and inscription dated "1859", marks for London.

1762 *4.5in (11.5cm) high*

£700-900 **L&T**

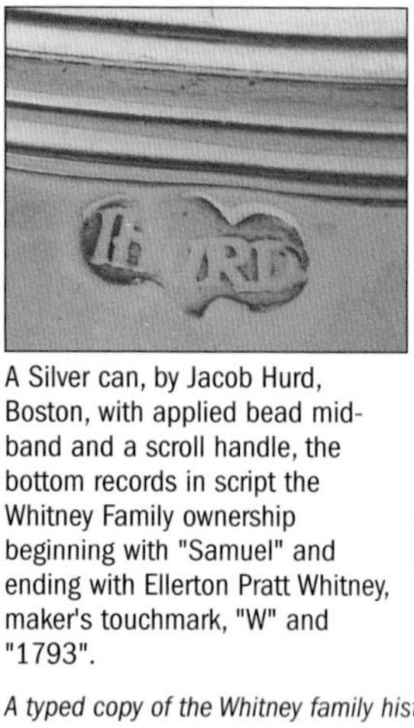
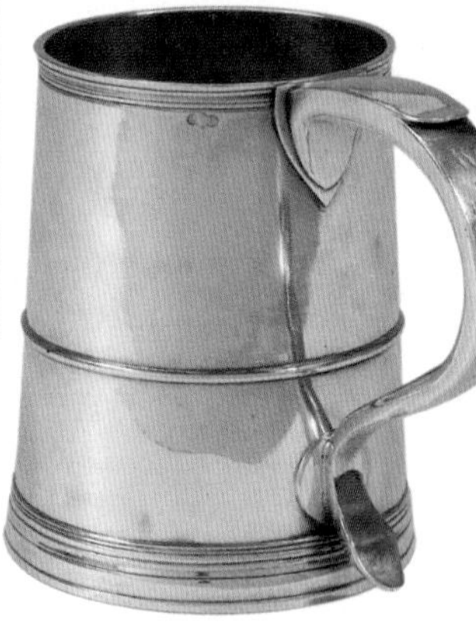

A Silver can, by Jacob Hurd, Boston, with applied bead mid-band and a scroll handle, the bottom records in script the Whitney Family ownership beginning with "Samuel" and ending with Ellerton Pratt Whitney, maker's touchmark, "W" and "1793".

A typed copy of the Whitney family history accompanies this can.

c1730 *4.75in (12cm) high*

£12,000-18,000 **SK**

A German silver tankard, in the late 17thC style, inset with a coin inscribed "Wilhelm IV" and "1598-1662" maker's mark "KR".

£600-900 **CHEF**

A George I silver tapering mug, by William Pearson of London, with a large scroll handle.

1716 *4.75in (12cm) high*

£1,000-1,500 **WW**

A mid-18thC bellied silver mug, by Pierre Amiraux of Jersey, with a tucked-in base, scratched underneath with "EBD" and "EBT", maker's mark struck thrice.

c1755 *4.75in (12cm) high*

£5,000-7,000 **WW**

A William IV silver pint mug, by John and Joseph Angell of London, inscribed "Toll taken off Bewdley Bridge March 25 1834", and "To T. Marson Esq" with an accompanying reform medal and badge.

1835 *4.5in (11.5cm) high*

£600-900 **WW**

An American silver cup, by Samuel Kirk of Baltimore, MD, with cast and chased double-scroll handle and floral and landscape decoration, 1835-46.

3.5in (9cm) high

£400-600 **IHB**

A Victorian embossed silver christening mug, by C. Reilly and G. Storer of London, decorated with a Scottish archer and his companion, gilt interior.

1839 *4in (10cm) high*

£500-700 **WW**

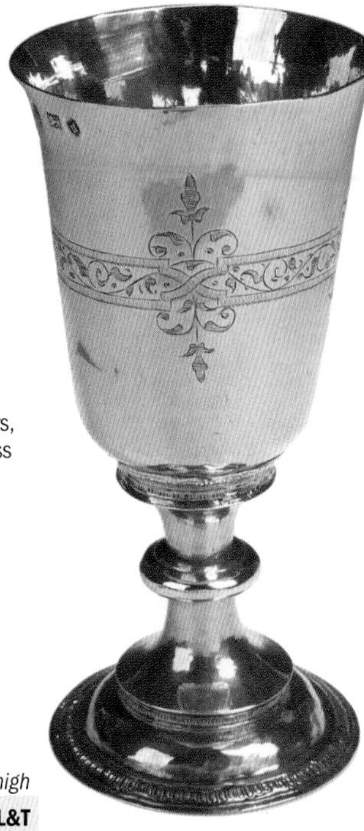

An Elizabeth I communion cup, with scrollwork engraved band, ovolo and narrow milled borders, marks for London, orb-and-cross maker's mark.

1577 *7.25in (18cm) high*

£6,000-9,000 **L&T**

An early 19thC silver cup, inscribed "Lauter sei die Labung wie Dein Walten", and with two dates in roman numerals "MDCCCXXXXII" and "MDCCCXVII", maker's mark.

8.75in (22cm) high

£80-120 **KAU**

A fine 19thC French silver gilt chalice, with chased and embossed figures from the life of Christ, with maker's mark "M. D.", possibly for Martin et Dejean, Paris.

12.25in (31cm) high

£1,200-1,800 **FRE**

A Victorian silver stirrup cup, in the form of a boar's head, with maker's mark "CT & GF", London.

1856 *4.75in (12cm) high*

£2,200-2,800 **FRE**

A sterling silver goblet, by Savage, Lyman & Co., Montreal, with holly leaves and "TRIA JUNCTA IN UNO" motto, date marks.

1856 *6.25in (16cm) high*

£1,000-1,500 **TCF**

A late Victorian enamelled trophy cup, by James Ramsey, decorated with enamels, inscribed "Presented by A.J. Ramsey to Newport Boating Club...", also with recipients' names, maker's mark and marks for London.

1895 *9.5in (24cm) high*

£800-1,200 **L&T**

Two of a set of 12 American silver wine cups, by the Schofield Company of Baltimore, with "ALS" monogram, 1925-50.

5in (12.5cm) high

£200-250 set **IHB**

Two of a set of six American silver water goblets, by S. Kirk & Son of Baltimore, chased all over with floral repoussé decoration, 1935-50.

6.75in (17cm) high

£3,000-4,000 set **IHB**

An early 18thC silver sauce boat, by Peter Archambo, crested, marks for London, no date letter.

4.25in (10.5cm) wide

£2,000-3,000 **L&T**

A cast George II silver sauce boat, by Peter Archambo, with mask and shell knees, floral and scroll cartouches, marks for London.

1744 *9in (23cm) high*

£2,500-3,000 **L&T**

A late 18thC French silver saucière, with relief floral decoration and cartouches, stamped.

Provenance: *Baron von Glaubitz und Altengabel.*

9in (23cm) wide

£300-500 **KAU**

A pair of Chippendale-style silver sauce boats, by Barraclough & Sons, Leeds, with acanthus scrolled handle and foliate cast knees.

1898

£200-250 **BIG**

A Chippendale-style silver sauce boat, by Charles Stuart Harris & Sons, with upscrolled handle, raised on four hoof feet, London hallmarks.

1915

£100-150 **BIG**

A Walker & Hall silver sauceboat, with up-scrolled handle and reeded wire rim, Sheffield hallmarks.

1932

£40-60 **BIG**

An American silver sauceboat, of reproduction helmet form, marked for Ensko of New York, engraved "KEM" and dated "April 6th 1940".

7.5in (19cm) long

£120-180 **IHB**

A George III silver pedestal cream jug, by Walter Brind, London, with a bright-cut and punch-decorated border and cast applied bead wire decoration.

1787 *5.5in (14cm) high*

£120-180 **BIG**

A late 18thC silver creamer, by Joseph Richardson Jr., Philadelphia, with thread mould rim, monogrammed "J.T.", stamped to bottom.

4.75in (12cm) high

£400-600 **FRE**

A London George III silver pedestal cream jug, with upswept drawn wire handle, bright-cut cartouche and tooled motifs.

1795

£200-250 **BIG**

An early 19thC sterling silver water pitcher, by Anthony Rasch, Philadelphia, with bands of anthemion leaves.

13.25in (33.5cm) high

£5,000-7,000 **SK**

An American silver cream pot, with hollow S-scroll handle and applied milled bands, marks for William Mitchell Jr. of Richmond, VA, 1825-45.

5.75in (14.5cm) high

£2,200-2,800 **IHB**

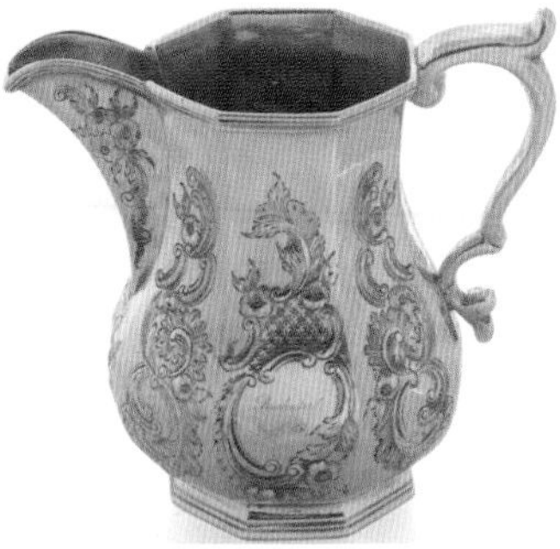

An American small silver pitcher, of octagonal baluster form, by William Gale & Son of New York, engraved "Presented to C.J. Woods by his Friends Rochester May 1 1851".

5.75in (14.5cm) high

£300-500 **IHB**

An American silver water pitcher, by James Armiger Co. of Baltimore, chased with floral repoussé decoration, "JH" monogram, 1900-1925.

8.5in (21.5cm) high

£1,200-1,800 **IHB**

An American silver water pitcher, by James Armiger Co. of Baltimore, chased with floral repoussé decoration, "JH" monogram, 1900-1925.

8.5in (21.5cm) high

£1,200-1,800 **IHB**

A Birks sterling silver cocktail shaker, with handle, marked with Gothic "u" for 1935.

8.75in (22cm) high

£600-800 **TCF**

An American silver water pitcher, by the Poole Silver Co. of Taunton, MA, a reproduction of the 'Liverpool' design used by Paul Revere, 1950-75.

7.25in (18.5cm) high

£280-320 **IHB**

An American silver syrup pitcher, by Frank M. Whiting & Co. of North Attleboro, MA, with hinged cover and scroll handle, 1950-75.

5.75in (14.5cm) high

£80-120 **IHB**

An American silver cocktail pitcher, of tapering cylindrical form, marked "Schroth" and "Hand made".

9in (23cm) high

£200-250 **IHB**

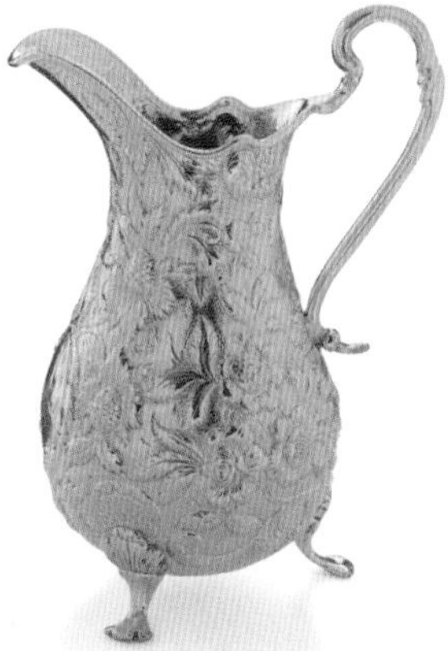

An American silver cream pot, of baluster form, by Samuel Kirk of Baltimore, inscribed "Dr. Bigelow 1939 from Mrs Francis C. Lowell".

6.25in (16cm) high

£400-600 **IHB**

A scarce teapot, probably by Richard Watts, engraved with the arms of "ATKINSON" of Newcastle, with marks for London 1718, on later stand by Robert (I) & David (II) Hennell with marks for London 1798.

teapot 6.5in (16.5cm) high

£15,000-20,000 **L&T**

A late George II silver teapot, with a gadrooned border and a coat of arms, mark for London, maker's mark partially defaced.

1758 *5in (12.5cm) high*

£1,000-1,500 **WW**

A silver teapot, of fluted oval design with pricked decoration to shoulder and cover, makers mark "M.P.", London.

1794 *6in (15cm) high*

£250-300 **ROS**

A George III silver bullet teapot, probably by John Mewburn of London, with a Cape rim, inscribed "Bequeathed by Capt. Robert Dalrymple... 1809".

1808

£800-1,200 **WW**

A Victorian silver melon-shaped teapot, by Martin Hall & Co. and the Goldsmiths and Silversmiths Company, London, with repoussé floral decoration.

1895

£320-380 **BIG**

A George II silver coffee pot, by J. Kirkup of Newcastle, with domed lid and acorn finial, engraved with an armorial.

The arms are those of the Howard family descended from Thomas Howard, 2nd Duke of Norfolk (1444-1524).

1728 *9.5in (24cm) high*

£2,000-3,000 **GORL**

A George III silver hot water pot, by Thomas Whipman and Charles Wright, London, later whipped handle and monogrammed.

1767

£400-600 **BIG**

An American silver coffee pot, in the Empire style, with acorn finial, struck with eagle's head, flowerette marks and marked for Amable Brasier of Philadelphia, 1810-30.

11.25in (28.5cm) high

£1,500-2,000 **IHB**

A mid-19thC sterling silver coffee pot by Dominic & Haff, with acorn finial and bright-cut decoration, inscribed "1841 14th April 1866".

12.25in (31cm) high

£200-300 **FRE**

An Edwardian silver hot water jug, by George Perkins, of baluster form with gadrooned borders engraved with crest, London hallmarks.

1901 *11in (28cm) high*

£250-300 **SWO**

A matched Queen Anne-style silver part coffee set, by Charles Stuart Harris and another, London hallmarks for 1932 and Birmingham hallmarks.

1933

£200-250 **BIG**

An American silver three-piece tea set, by Charters, Cann & Dunn and retailed by Ball, Tompkins & Black both of NY, with pheasant finials, "CAWS" monogram, 1848-51.

largest 9.5in (42.5cm) high

£1,200-1,800 **IHB**

A 19thC Continental sterling silver six-piece tea and coffee service, in the Neo-classical style, with scroll wood handles and eagles' mask spout.

tray 22in (55cm) wide

£1,000-1,500 **FRE**

A Boston coin silver four-piece tea service, bearing the touch of Jones, Ball & Poor, the creamer by Harris, Stonewood, & Co.

c1850 *kettle 10in (25.5cm) high*

£800-1,000 **POOK**

An American sliver six-piece silver tea and coffee set, with foliate repoussé chased bands, grapevine decoration and cast bud finials, marked for James E. Caldwell & Co. of Philadelphia, PA, 1860-80.

largest 11.5in (29cm) high

£3,000-4,000 **IHB**

A late 19thC Indian three-piece silver tea set, Cutch, decorated with scrolling foliage.

c1880

£700-1,000 **SWO**

A late 19thC Victorian sterling silver four-piece tea and coffee service, with repoussé decoration.

8in (20cm) high

£800-1,200 **FRE**

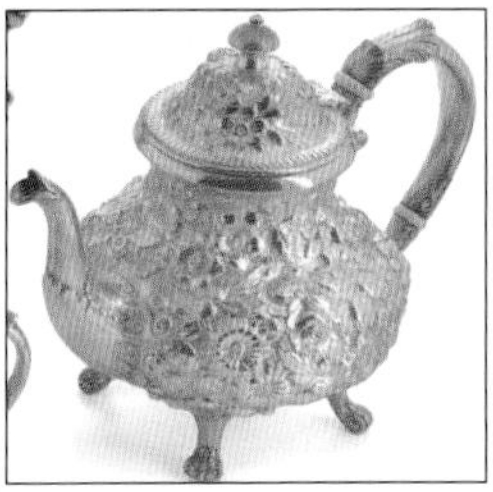

An American silver five-piece tea and coffee set, by Jenkins & Jenkins of Baltimore, chased with floral repoussé decoration, 1908-23.

largest 9.5in (24cm) high

£2,200-2,800 **IHB**

A Reed & Barton sterling silver seven-piece tea service, in the Francis I pattern, comprising two kettles on stands, coffee pot, teapot, covered sugar, creamer, waste bowl and tray.

c1937 *tray 30.75in (77cm) wide*

£12,000-18,000 **POOK**

A Reed & Barton sterling silver seven-piece tea service.

1951 *tray 24.25in (60.5cm) wide*

£1,500-2,000 **POOK**

A Reed & Barton coin silver four-piece tea service in a floral repoussé pattern.

kettle 17in (42.5cm) high

£1,500-2,000 **POOK**

A Tiffany & Co. sterling silver eight-piece tea service, in an acanthus and bellflower design.

tray 24.5in (61cm) wide

£6,000-9,000 **POOK**

An American silver sugar bowl and creamer, by the Gorham Manufacturing Co. of Providence, RI, with intertwined "HRW" monogram.

1870 *largest 4.5in (11.5cm) high*

£150-200 **IHB**

An American silver sugar bowl, by Tiffany & Co. of New York, 1882-91.

4.75in (12cm) diam

£180-220 **IHB**

An American silver cream pot and sugar bowl, by Lebkeucher & Co. of Newark, NJ, with "MMP" monogram, 1900-30.

5in (12.5cm) high

£70-100 **IHB**

An American silver creamer and sugar bowl, by Reed & Barton of Taunton, MA.

Reed & Barton was established c1840 in Taunton, Massachusetts, and is still producing silverware today.

1948 *tray 9.75in (25cm) long*

£100-150 **IHB**

A George III silver hot water urn, London, with a flame finial and an ivory tap, maker's mark indistinct, later lid.

1766 *19in (48.5cm) high*

£2,000-2,500 **FRE**

A CLOSER LOOK AT A QUEEN ANNE SILVER KETTLE

The kettle was engraved for Isaac Borrow (1673-1745) of Gray's Inn, who descended from John Borrow of Derby, sometimes High Sheriff of the county. The family feature in Burke's 'Landed Gentry' (1937).

Tea-kettles were developed in the early 18thC as a means of replenishing the small teapots of the period with hot water. Their popularity had declined by c1760. This is an early example.

The Queen Anne shape is popular with silver collectors. As with other early 18thC examples, the kettle has a swing handle and wooden grip. It is fairly plain, while later kettles are often chased and embellished.

Tea kettles are fairly rare as they were often melted down.

A Queen Anne silver kettle and stand, by Isaac Deighton and J. Rand of London, with engraved armorial and swing handle, burner and stand with turned wooden handle.

1705 *13in (33cm) high*

£10,000-15,000 **GORL**

A George III tea caddy, with bright-engraved decoration and mounted pineapple-carved ivory finial, marks for London, maker's mark indistinct.

1788 *6.25in (15.5cm) high*

£1,200-1,800 **L&T**

A William IV claret jug, probably by William Eley I, with caryatid cast handle, inscribed "From Major Sir Walter Scott, Charles Scott & C. Sophia Lockhart, to Robert Ferguson M.D.", with marks for London.

1830 *15in (37.5cm) high*

£4,000-6,000 **L&T**

A 19thC Indian silver hot water jug, probably Cutch, decorated with exotic hunting scenes, monogrammed, unmarked.

c1880

£250-300 **SWO**

An American silver hot water kettle on burner stand, by Currier & Roby of New York, in the Queen Anne plain baluster style, 1900-35.

11in (28cm) high

£500-700 **IHB**

A pair of George III silver-gilt sweetmeat dishes, by Orlando Jackson of London, with collet feet, maker's mark and lion passant.

c1770 *6.5in (16.5cm)*

£500-700 **WW**

LEFT: A late 18thC Scottish carved horn and mounted snuff mull, of large size, the seal's head with a humorous expression, with a chain and part spoon.

5.5in (14cm) wide

£400-600 **L&T**

RIGHT: A 19th century carved horn snuff mull, of curved form with simple blank cartouche to the lid, the terminal carved as a seal's head.

4.5in (11.5cm) wide

£400-600 **L&T**

A pair of George III silver shell dishes, of scallop shape and on three dolphin feet, London.

1808 *6in (15cm) wide*

£1,000-1,500 **L&T**

A pair of George III silver bottle coasters, by Alexander Goodman & Co., with spiral fluted sides, marks for Sheffield.

1808 *5.5in (14cm) diam*

£1,000-1,500 **L&T**

A George III silver soup tureen and associated cover, the base with marks for London, bearing sponsor's mark of Paul Storr.

1812 *12in (30.5cm) high*

£3,000-5,000 **L&T**

A William IV gothic silver toast rack, by Benjamin Reece Dexter of London, with cast foliate handle.

1836 *6.5in (16cm) wide*

£400-600 **WW**

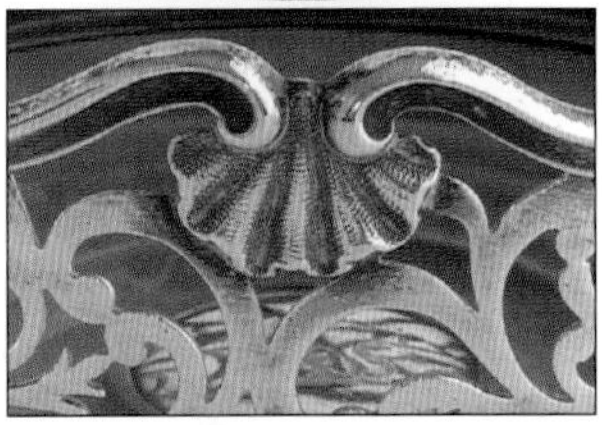

A William IV silver round coaster, with shell and scroll cast rim, pierced with leaf scrolls, London.

1836 *5.75in (14.5cm) diam*

£400-600 **LFA**

A set of four Victorian Scottish silver menu holders, in the form of stags' heads, with alternating hardstones, unmarked.

1.5in (4cm) high

£1,000-1,500 **LFA**

A Victorian twin-handled silver desk stand, by Charles Thomas Fox & George Fox, with presentation inscription, crested, London.

1846 *12.25in (31cm) wide*

£800-1,200 **L&T**

An unusual Victorian cast silver cream jug, by E.H. Stockwell of London, in the form of a swimming swan with textured plumage and a gilt interior.

1872 *5.25in (13cm) wide*

£800-1,200 **WW**

A Victorian silver-gilt rectangular inkstand, by George Fox, with two oval wells, London.

1886 *9in (23cm) wide*

£800-1,200 **LFA**

A late 19thC to early 20thC Continental silver-gilt figure, depicting Cupid and a lion, on a rectangular base, unmarked.

10in (25.5cm) wide

£3,000-4,000 **FRE**

A pair of late Victorian Irish silver dish rings, by J. Wakeley and F.C. Wheeler of Dublin, pierced with chinoiserie figures, clear glass liners.

1895 *6in (15.5cm) diam*

£1,500-2,000 **WW**

A late Victorian novelty silver paper-knife, by S. Moran & Co. of London, in the form of an officer's sword with scabbard.

1897 *5.5in (14cm) long*

£400-600 **WW**

A pair of novelty silver scissors, by James Dudley of London, in the form of a bearded gentleman holding two bunches of flowers.

1898 *3in (7.5cm) long*

£400-500 **WW**

An American silver mounted flask, by the Alvin-Beiderhase Co. of Sag Harbor, NY, with openwork foliate scroll decoration, engraved "MMR" and dated "1900".

5in (12.5cm) high

£200-250 **IHB**

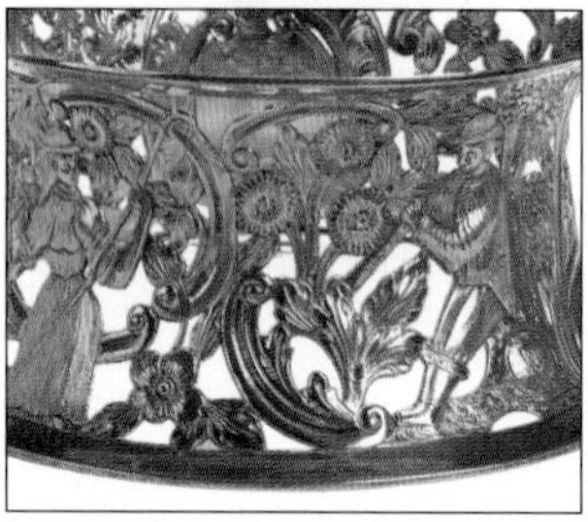

An Edwardian Irish silver dish ring, by JW & FCW, decorated with pastoral figures and foliage, with central vacant cartouche, marks for Dublin.

1908 *7in (18cm) diam*

£700-1,000 **L&T**

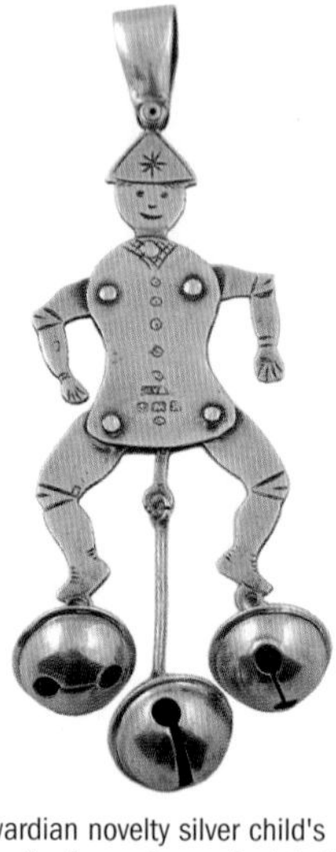

An Edwardian novelty silver child's rattle, in the form of an articulated figure with bells, maker's mark "WVS" of Birmingham.

1909 *3.5in (9cm) high*

£300-400 **WW**

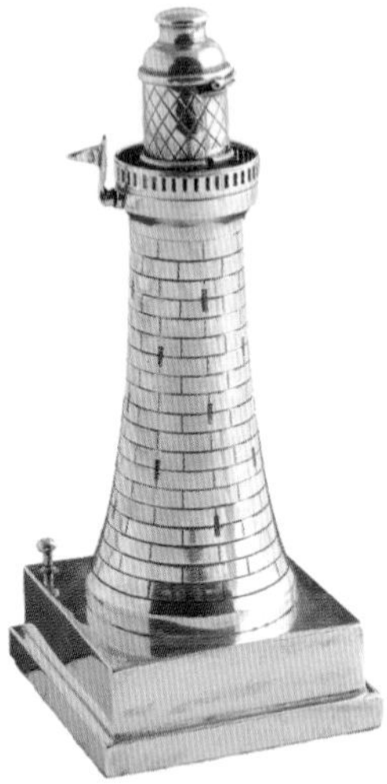

An English silver novelty lighthouse lighter, by S&M, stamped marks for Birmingham.

1931 *7.75in (20cm) high*

£600-800 **WW**

A Russian silver mounted easel back mirror, of rectangular outline with beaded border.

16in (40cm) wide

£800-1,200 **L&T**

A Marius Hammer Norwegian silver kasa, with horse head handles and plique-à-jour enamelling, signed and numbered "930S".

4.5in (11cm) wide

£700-1,000 **L&T**

A Victorian silver-plated spirit kettle, on stand.

£100-150 SWO

A pair of Victorian silver-plated salts, in the form of dolphins and shells, with glass liners.

5.5in (14cm) high

£180-220 SWO

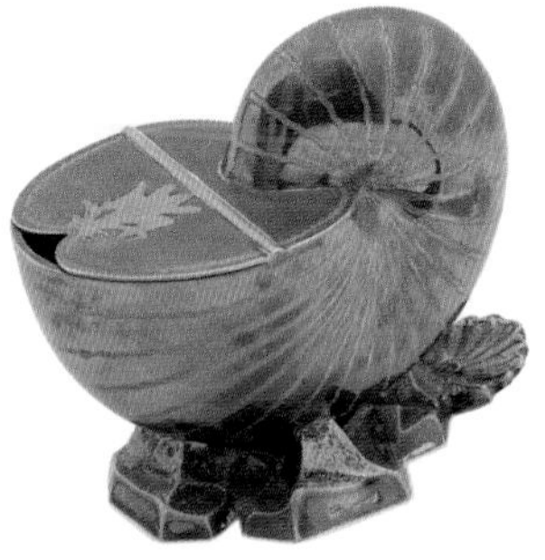

A Victorian silver-plated novelty silver spoon warmer, by H. Wilkinson & Co., in the form of a nautilus shell.

c1870 *5.5in (14cm) high*

£150-200 WW

A WMF silver-plated water jug, with an ebonized wood scroll handle, signed "Vom Turnverein zu Weihnachten 1885", WMF mark.

1885 *14.5in (36cm) high*

£80-120 KAU

A late 19thC pair of silver-plated wine coolers, by Elkington & Co., of flared urn form, applied with fruiting vines.

11.5in (29cm) high

£2,000-2,500 FRE

A silver-plated kettle on a stand, with a melon-shaped body on a base inset with a burner, hallmarks for Sheffield.

1902 *11in (28cm) high*

£180-320 ROW

A pair of electroplated five-light candelabra, with fluted columns and leaf-capped branches, loaded.

20in (51cm) high

£600-800 L&T

A pair of Old Sheffield Plate three-light candelabra, each with two reeded scroll branches.

20.5in (51.5cm) high

£400-600 L&T

A silver-plate-mounted Moorcroft Hazeldene pattern dish, decorated with a tree against a sunset, factory mark, "Made in England" and numbered "114".

4in (10cm) wide

£400-600 ROW

A Continental articulated fish, unmarked, with movable fins and gem-set eyes.

4.75in (12cm) wide

£150-200 CHEF

An electroplate-mounted double ram's horn inkwell, with two cylindrical wells.

17.5in (44cm) wide

£600-900 L&T

A pair of George III brass candlesticks, each with a turned and canted column and a domed foot.

8in (20cm) high

£800-1,200 **DN**

An early 19thC French brass candlestick, engraved overall with lozenges and flowers, on a square canted foot.

6in (15cm) high

£300-400 **DN**

A pair of 19thC French Rococo-style brass candlesticks, each cast and engraved with foliate scrolls and flowers on a shaped, moulded base.

11.5in (29cm) high

£250-300 **DN**

A George III brass and copper tobacco box, by Henry Giese, commemorating the death of George II, engraved with the Royal Coat of Arms, busts of George II and III and inscription.

6.5in (16.5cm) wide

£300-400 **DN**

A 18thC Dutch brass tobacco box, engraved with Christ carrying the cross, the base depicting the crucifixion.

7in (17.5cm) wide

£400-600 **SWO**

A Victorian brass perpetual calendar.

8.75in (22cm) high

£70-100 **GAZE**

A brass filigree picture frame, with C-scroll and figural decoration.

12in (30.5cm) high

£70-100 **AAC**

A pair of gilt metal post office scales, with fretwork and engraved scrolling decoration.

8.25in (21cm) high

£250-£300 **SWO**

A brass signal cannon, with turned raised bands on the barrel, on hardwood carriage.

8.25in (71cm) wide

£1,200-1,800 **L&T**

A German gothic pewter libation cup, with gothic inscription and three animal-form embellishments to base.

Little early pewter householdware survives as it was often discarded or melted down and re-cast into more fashionable styles.

c1450 *7in (17.5cm) high*

£7,000-10,000 **POOK**

An important Charles II pewter Restoration charger, with tulip vine and rose decoration surrounding a cartouche of an archer, the well with a Stuart coat of arms, pewter marks "B.H." and pseudo hallmarks.

c1665 *18.25in (45.5cm) diam*

£15,000-20,000 **POOK**

A CLOSER LOOK AT A PEWTER FLAGON

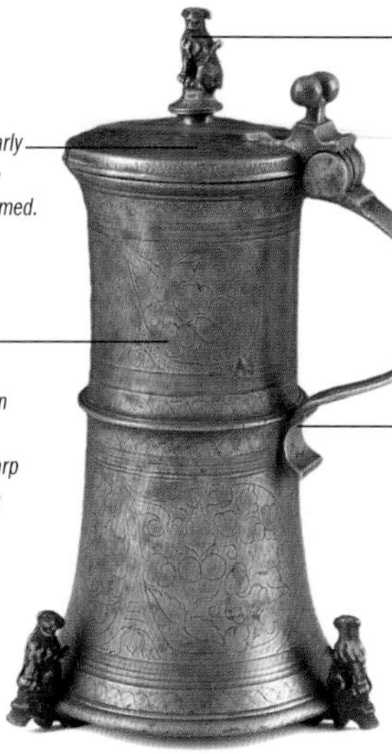

The flat lid reflects the early date. From the end of the 18thC, lids were often domed.

Pewter is often plain and unadorned. Pieces with wrigglework decoration, an engraving technique that involves zig-zagging a sharp tool across a surface, are desirable.

Following the Black Death, European drinking vessels often had lids to keep out the flies that were thought to cause disease. The introduction of lids gave guilds a further decoration opportunity, as is apparent in this lion finial.

This flagon is marked with its place of origin. Early traceable pewter items can command a premium.

A rare Viennese pewter guild flagon, with wrigglework decoration and a lion finial, on three lion-form feet, initials "M.S." and "Wien" mark.

c1575 *17in (42.5cm) high*

£30,000-40,000 **POOK**

A late 18thC rare Philadelphia William Will pewter tankard, with a domed lid, impressed inside base "Wm. Will".

7.75in (19cm) high

£22,000-28,000 **POOK**

An 18th to 19thC pewter baluster measure, the domed cover engraved "WB AG".

9.25in (23cm) high

£1,000-1,500 **SWO**

A Viennese 'Imperial' Nebien pewter beaker, presented by Emperor F. Joseph.

1863 *5.75in (14cm) high*

£4,000-5,000 **POOK**

COPPER

A 17thC copper token, issued by Henry Woodley of Newport Pond, now Newport, Essex.

During the reigns of James I and Charles I, various nobles were licensed to produce copper coins. These coins were demonetized with the abolition of the monarchy and traders all over England issued their own tokens to combat the shortage of small change.

1657

£70-100 **SWO**

A Regency copper and case samovar, with ebonized handles and brass tap.

20.5in (52cm) high

£120-180 **SWO**

A Victorian copper and brass samovar.

17.25in (44cm) high

£120-180 **SWO**

A Siebe Gorman copper six-bolt diver's helmet, serial number "16060".

19.5in (48.5cm) high

£2,800-3,200 **SWO**

An 18thC painted tin clay-pipe stand and smoker's companion, with crown finial, missing rear foot.

14.25in (36cm) wide

£700-1,000 **L&T**

An 18thC white metal inkwell, of circular shape, together with a pen, with crest for the Earl of Leicester.

£250-300 **SWO**

A 19thC wrought iron double-plate trivet, with geometric piercings and a floriform handle.

15in (38cm) high

£180-220 **FRE**

A 19thC wrought iron devil's face.

13.25in (34cm) high

£180-220 **FRE**

A Victorian iron bell in the shape of a pig, the nose and tail activating the clockwork bell.

5.5in (14cm) wide

£500-700 **SWO**

An early 19thC waffle iron, one side decorated with tulips and geometric devices, the other side with overall diamond pattern.

29.5in (75cm) long

£100-150 **FRE**

A late 19thC iron group of two dogs flushing out a partridge, after Mene.

8.75in (22cm) high

£300-500 **SWO**

An Elkington and Co. castle cigar lighter, the central lighter flanked by four castellated towers with removable flags, struck "Elkington & Co", and "8127".

4.25in (10.5cm) high

£300-500 **SWO**

A 19thC red toleware coffee pot, with strap handle and gooseneck spout, decorated with and green and yellow flowers.

10.5in (26cm) high

£2,000-2,500 **POOK**

A mid-19thC Pennsylvania toleware coffee pot, with floral decoration on a black ground, the domed lid and flaring base with yellow swags.

11in (27.5cm) high

£2,500-3,000 **POOK**

An early 19thC tin document trunk, possibly by Oliver Filley of Bloomfield, Connecticut, with dome top and hinged lid, decorated with a bird perched on a branch surrounded by flowers in red, green and yellow, minor paint loss.

9.5in (24cm) wide

£2,500-3,000 **SK**

A 1789 George Washington Commemorative Inaugural Button, with a sunburst above a spreadwing eagle and American shield, surrounded by the inscription "MARCH THE FOURTH 1789 MEMORABLE ERA".

This button was sold as a souvenir to commemorate the second inauguration of George Washington as President in 1789.

1789 *1.75in (4.5cm) diam*

£500-800 **SK**

A pair of 19thC cast iron hitching posts, with horse head finials, inscribed "Wm Adams Phila".

61in (125.5cm) high

£1,500-2,000 **POOK**

A Philadelphia cast iron 'Star Mill #20' coffee grinder.

1885 *73in (182.5cm) high*

£2,000-2,500 **POOK**

A late 19thC cast iron buck and doe, attributed to Fiske, mounted on rectangular plinths.

larger 62in (155cm) high

£5,000-8,000 **POOK**

A 20thC sheet iron silhouette of a cat and dog, mounted on a stand, with weathered surface, losses.

24in (61cm) wide

£350-450 **FRE**

A late 19thC cast iron relief of a buffalo's head.

25in (62.5cm) high

£4,000-6,000 **POOK**

A Canadian cast iron money bank, in the form of a cottage, impressed "OLD QUEBEC".

6in (15cm) long

£2,200-2,800 **WAD**

THE CLOCK MARKET

Like furniture, antique clocks have generally had a good year. Demand for all types of clock with fine and interesting mechanisms has remained consistently strong.

The highest prices are achieved for rare, early and exceptional examples and an attractive and elegant case or striking design can also help to increase value. At the same time, clocks at the lower end of the market, particularly examples in poor condition or pieces in need of major restoration, are taking longer to sell and are achieving more modest sums. These lower prices have, however, opened up the market to new buyers, injecting much needed life into the field.

Unusual clocks from the 'golden age' of British clockmaking, dating from c1670-1730, remain very appealing, and pieces by the likes of Tompion and Knibb rarely fail to attract attention. Good British bracket clocks have also continued to perform well, particularly examples dating from before 1700.

British clocks originating from London and Edinburgh, cities known for high quality clockmaking, often prove to be good investments. Eighteenth century London clocks for the export market are also appealing, and signed pieces by known makers can command astonishing sums.

Eighteenth century American clocks and pieces by well-known 19th century American makers such as Eli Terry and Aaron Willard are also selling well. American pieces dating from before 1840 often attract a great deal of interest.

As with other clocks, condition and the quality of the mechanism are crucial in determining the price of longcase clocks. Fine dials, marquetry cases and high quality movements push up value. Additional elements, such as moon phases, automatons and other dials and instruments add appeal.

The value of a clock can be reduced by as much as three-quarters if it shows unsympathetic restoration. Mass-produced pieces and poor 'marriages' should also generally be avoided, although attractive longcases with contemporary married elements can realize very healthy prices.

– Gavin Strang, Lyon & Turnbull

LONGCASE CLOCKS

An early 18thC lacquer longcase clock, the eight-day movement striking on a bell to a square brass dial, with silvered chapter ring and subsidiary seconds dial and date aperture, engraved with a Tudor rose and with gilt Chinoiserie decoration.

81in (205.5cm) high

£2,000-2,500 **WW**

An early 18thC oak longcase clock, by William Cockey, Yeovil, the brass dial with a calendar aperture and pierced brass work, 30-hour movement.

81.5in (207cm) high

£1,000-2,000 **SWO**

An early 18thC oak longcase clock, with an associated movement, the silvered dial inscribed "Tho. Brewer, Darlistone", 30-hour striking movement on a new seat board, extensive alterations to movement.

86in (218cm) high

£1,000-1,500 **SWO**

An early 18thC longcase clock, the square brass dial with subsidiary seconds dial and date aperture, eight-day movement, the dial inscribed "Langley Bradley, London", later pine case.

£1,500-2,000 **SWO**

An early 18thC mahogany eight-day longcase clock, inscribed 'John Davies Wollampton' with day and date mechanisms and an eight-day striking movement.

87.75in (223cm) high

£1,500-2,000 **SWO**

An early 18thC oak eight-day longcase clock, the twin-train movement with anchor escapement, the square train dial with silvered chapter ring enclosing subsidiary seconds dial and date aperture.

33.5in (225cm) high

£2,000-3,000 **L&T**

An 18thC oak longcase clock, with long pendulum door, the 30-hour movement with square brass dial by Richard Evans, Oswestry.

£800-1,200 **MAX**

A rare 18thC quarter repeating oak longcase clock, arched brass dial, Father Time automaton in the arch, penny moon, date dial, and centre sweep seconds, two-train eight-day rack striking movement with dead beat escapement, pull quarter repeat and hour strike on two bells.

Moon phases and automatons can add considerable value to longcase clocks. Moon phases were often called penny moons because of their size.

81.5in (207cm) high

£4,000-6,000 **MAX**

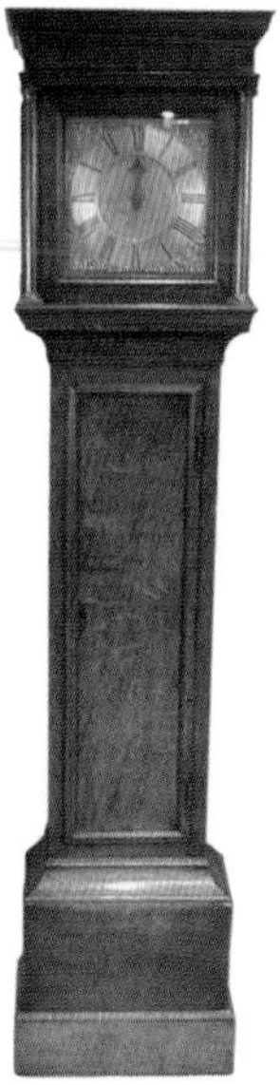

An 18thC oak longcase clock, by James Smyth, Saxmundham, the square brass dial with a single hand supporting a 30-hour striking movement dial.

£800-1,200 **SWO**

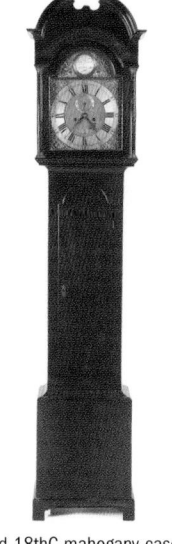

An 18thC George III burl walnut tall case clock, the brass dial signed "Sam.J. Hollyer, London", blind fret-carved hood and crossbanded case.

92in (233.5cm) high

£2,000-3,000 **FRE**

A mid-18thC mahogany cased eight-day longcase clock, by James Niccoll, Canongate, the twin train movement with anchor escapement, the brass arched dial with silvered chapter ring, cast spandrels, enclosing subsidiary seconds dial and date aperture.

86.75in (220cm) high

£2,000-3,000 **L&T**

A CLOSER LOOK AT A LONGCASE CLOCK

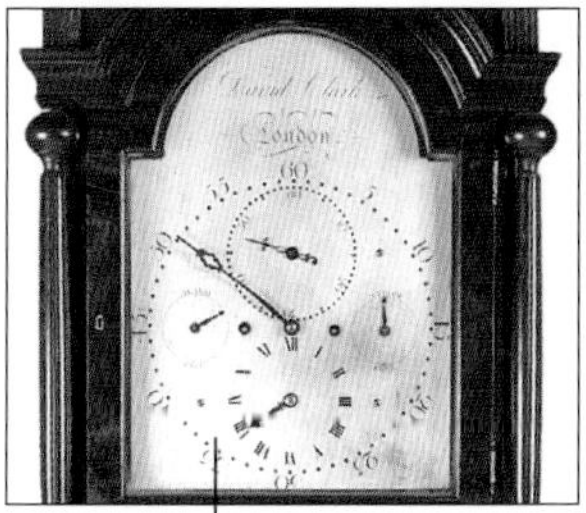

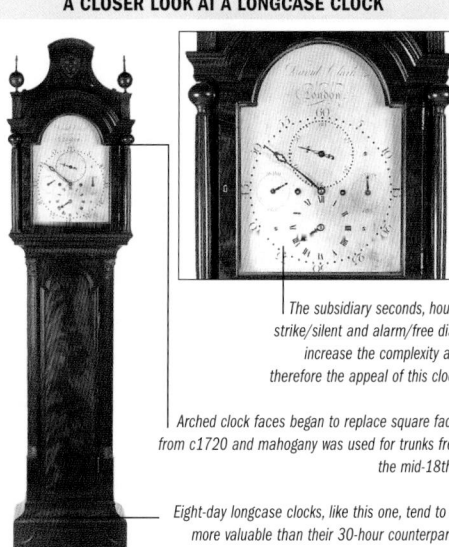

The subsidiary seconds, hours, strike/silent and alarm/free dials increase the complexity and therefore the appeal of this clock.

Arched clock faces began to replace square faces from c1720 and mahogany was used for trunks from the mid-18thC.

Eight-day longcase clocks, like this one, tend to be more valuable than their 30-hour counterparts.

Clocks made in London during this period tended to be of higher quality than the work of many provincial makers.

An 18thC mahogany cased eight-day longcase clock, by David Clark, London, the twin-train movement with anchor escapement, the arched silvered dial with subsidiary seconds, hours, strike/silent and alarm/free dials.

93.25in (237cm) high

£8,000-12,000 **L&T**

A Chippendale walnut tall case clock, with a brass face and 30-hour works, inscribed "Anthony Ward Philadelphia 1772".

91.5in (232.5cm) high

£2,500-3,500 **POOK**

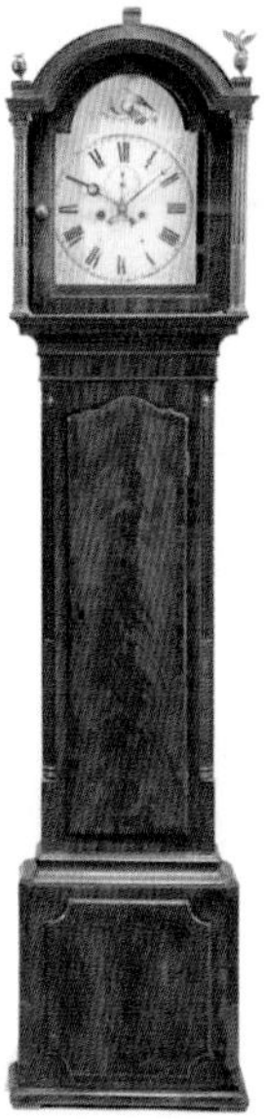

A George III mahogany and crossbanded longcase clock, the painted dial with a subsidiary second dial and date aperture.

c1780 88in (223.5cm) high

£1,200-1,800 FRE

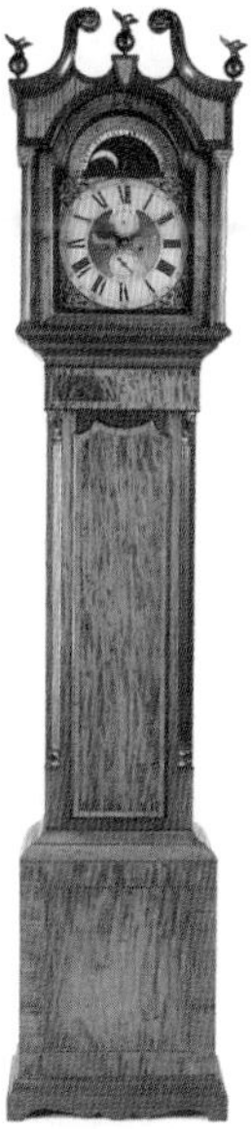

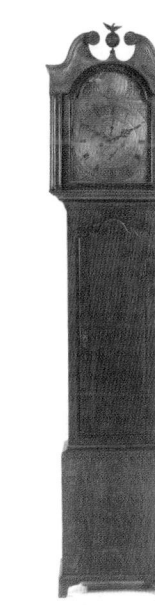

A monumental late 18thC mahogany eight-day longcase clock, by Charles Graham, Edinburgh, with moon phase to the arch.

109.75in (279cm) high

£1,000-1,500 L&T

A late 18thC oak eight-day longcase clock, by William Robb, Montrose, the twin-train movement with anchor escapement, the brass dial with subsidiary seconds and date dials.

83.75in (213cm) high

£1,000-1,500 L&T

A late 18thC oak eight-day longcase clock, by James Peddie, Stirling, the twin-train movement with anchor escapement, the brass dial with subsidiary seconds dial and date aperture.

86.25in (219cm) high

£800-1,200 L&T

A George III oak cased eight-day longcase clock, brass dial, with a silvered chapter ring, pierced brass spandrels and a subsidiary minutes dial, surmounted by a moon phase.

£1,800-2,200 SWO

A George III mahogany longcase clock, the case in the style of Gollows, eight-day movement, arched moon phase dial inscribed "Robert Douglas, Bolton", the spandrels painted with courting couples, subsidiary seconds dial.

The moon phase was introduced to track the cycle of the moon. Knowing the date of the next full moon was useful to anyone wishing to travel at night.

94.5in (240cm) high

£4,000-5,000 SWO

A George III oak longcase clock, the arched painted dial with a calendar aperture, inscribed, "Fordham Braintree", below a strike/silent dial, supporting an eight-day striking movement.

dial 11.5in (29.5cm) diam

£1,200-1,800 SWO

An early 19thC Scottish mahogany eight-day longcase clock, the dial painted with "Burns and Highland Mary", the spandrels as England, Ireland, Scotland and Wales, inscribed "Thomson, Kilmarnock".

92in (230cm) high

£1,500-2,000 SWO

A late George III oak and mahogany crossbanded eight-day longcase clock, the twin train movement with an anchor escapement, striking on a bell.

86.5in (220cm) high

£1,200-1,800 SWO

CLOCK TERMINOLOGY

- Automata: Decorative moving part depicting a figure or animal. The first known example was the crowing cock on the 14thC Strasbourg clock. Automata clocks are sought after today.
- Chapter ring: The circular dial marked with the hours.
- Count Wheel: A slotted wheel that controls the number of strikes.
- Eight-day Clock: A clock with an eight-day movement. Longcase clocks usually have eight-day or 30-hour movements.
- Escapment: The mechanism that controls the speed at which the clock runs.
- Moon Phase: A dial that shows the phases of the lunar cycle. First introduced on some longcase clocks in the early 18thC, moon phases can increase the value.
- Perpetual Clock: A clock that works for long periods.
- Thirty-hour Clock: A clock that must be wound every 30 hours. They are typically less sought after, with many exceptions, than clocks that can work for longer periods.
- Train: The system of gears and levers that control the escarpment.

An early 19thC provincial oak longcase clock, with arched long pendulum door, the eight-day movement with arched painted dial, by Thos Wignal, Ormskirk.

£800-1,200 **MAX**

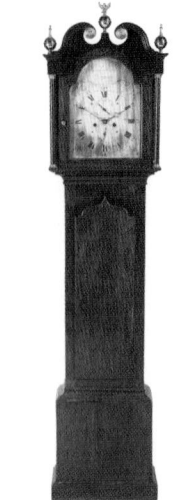

An early 19thC stained oak eight-day longcase clock, by George Dunbar, Turriff, the twin-train movement with anchor escapement, strike/silent switch.

83.75in (213cm) high

£800-1,200 **L&T**

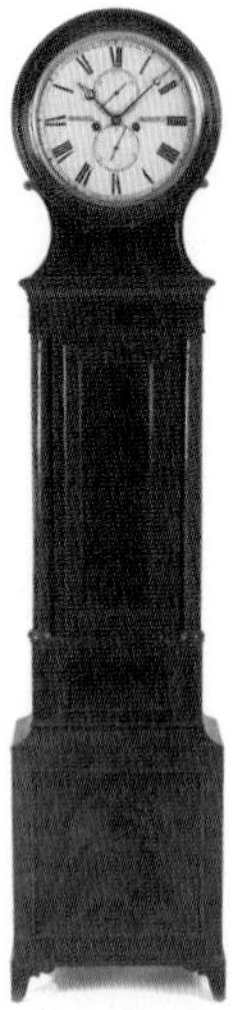

An early 19thC mahogany eight-day longcase clock, by Andrew Smith, Tranent, the twin-train movement with anchor escapement, drum hood.

81in (206cm) high

£1,000-1,500 **L&T**

An early 19thC mahogany eight-day longcase clock, by Duncan Robertson, Blairgowrie, the twin-train movement with anchor escapement, the arched painted dial with subsidiary seconds and date dials, painted to the arch with a maiden.

84.75in (215cm) high

£1,500-2,000 **L&T**

An early 19thC mahogany cased eight-day longcase clock, by John Boyle, Liverpool, the signed painted dial with moon phase, painted spandrels and subsidiary seconds dial, the twin-train movement with an anchor escapement striking on a bell.

94in (239cm) high

£2,000-3,000 **SWO**

An early 19thC mahogany eight-day longcase clock, by George Bain, Brechin, the twin-train movement with anchor escapement, the painted dial with subsidiary seconds and date dials, with Scotsmen and castles.

84.75in (215cm) high

£1,800-2,200 **L&T**

An early 19thC mahogany eight-day longcase clock, by J. Little, Annan, the twin-train movement with anchor escapement, the arch fitted with a moon phase and the spandrels painted with castles.

88.5in (225cm) high

£1,200-1,800 **L&T**

An early 19thC mahogany longcase clock, the case with inlaid stringing, crossbanding and applied roundels, arched dial, revolving moon phase disc, inscribed "A Riley, Bromley", with an eight-day striking movement.

91.25in (232cm) high

£1,200-1,800 **SWO**

An early 19thC mahogany longcase clock, the hood and trunk with two pairs of twist-turned columns, the arched dial painted with rustic scenes, with a striking eight-day movement.

88.25in (224cm) high

£1,200-1,800 **SWO**

An early 19thC mahogany cased eight-day longcase clock, by John Boyle, Liverpool, the signed painted dial with moon phase, the twin-train movement with an anchor escapement striking on a bell.

94in (239cm) high

£1,500-2,000 **SWO**

An early 19thC mahogany longcase clock, the square painted dial with working dog spandrels, inscribed "Illingsworth, Near Meadowlane Bar, Leeds", with an eight-day striking movement.

90.5in (230cm) high

£800-1,200 **SWO**

A mid-19thC mahogany eight-day longcase clock, by Jason & Andrew Kelley, Glasgow, the twin train movement with anchor escapement, the white enamel circular dial with subsidiary seconds dial.

82in (208cm) high

£1,200-1,800 **L&T**

A rare 19thC Australian mahogany and cedar longcase regulator by James Robertson, Sydney, silvered dial, signed, the movement with a dead beat escapement and mecurial pendulum.

78in (198cm) high

£20,000-25,000 **SHA**

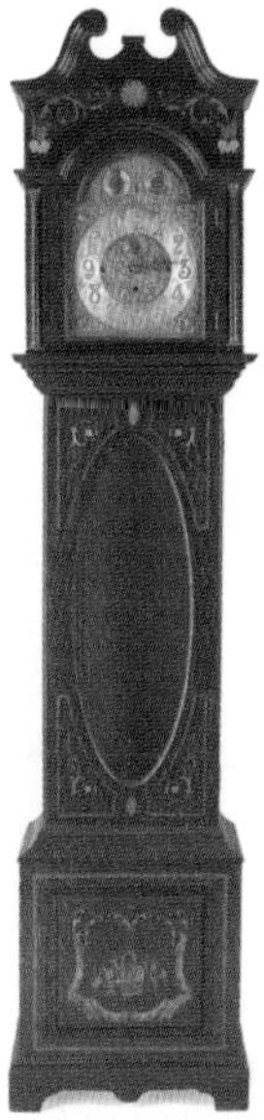

A late Victorian mahogany longcase clock, with a brass face works with Westminster chimes, overall floral marquetry inlay.

c1900 *96.5in (245cm) high*

£3,000-4,000 **POOK**

An early 20thC mahogany eight-day longcase clock, moon phase mechanism over a subsidiary seconds dial and calendar aperture, inscribed "Chas Monks Prescott".

£1,800-2,200 **SWO**

A mahogany longcase clock, the twin-barrel movement striking on a bell, subsidiary seconds dial and date aperture, subsidiary month dial, inscribed "Jno Jordan, Bristol".

89in (226cm) high

£2,000-3,000 **WW**

An eight-day longcase clock, the brass dial with ringed winding holes and cherub spandrels supporting a striking and repeating movement, now housed in a black lacquered and chinoiserie case.

80in (200cm) high

£700-1,000 **SWO**

A mahogany and inlaid longcase clock, the arched painted dial with an eight-day movement and subsidiary seconds dial and date aperture inscribed "Jacob Moseley, Neath".

£1,200-1,800 **SWO**

A Philadelphia Chippendale walnut longcase clock, with broken arch bonnet over a tombstone door enclosing brass eight-day works, inscribed "Jacob Gotshalk", with arched windows and foliate mullion, over a recessed panel base with ogee bracket feet.

c1775 93.5in (234cm) high

£30,000-40,000 **POOK**

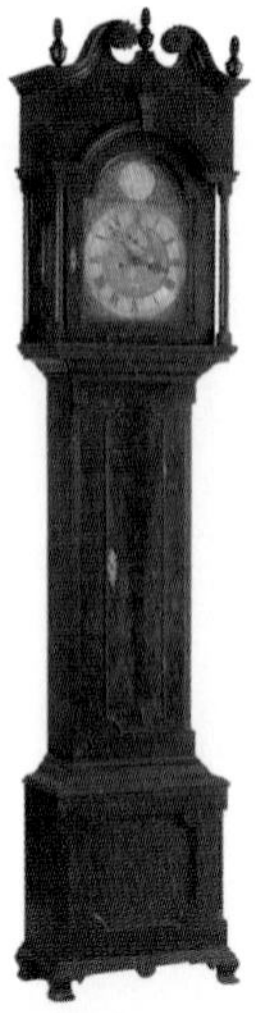

A Pennsylvania Chippendale walnut longcase clock, attributed to Isaac Thomas, the broken arch bonnet with carved floral rosettes, over a glazed tombstone door enclosing eight-day works, inscribed "James Warne London", on a panelled base with ogee bracket feet.

c1775 97.25in (243cm) high

£12,000-18,000 **POOK**

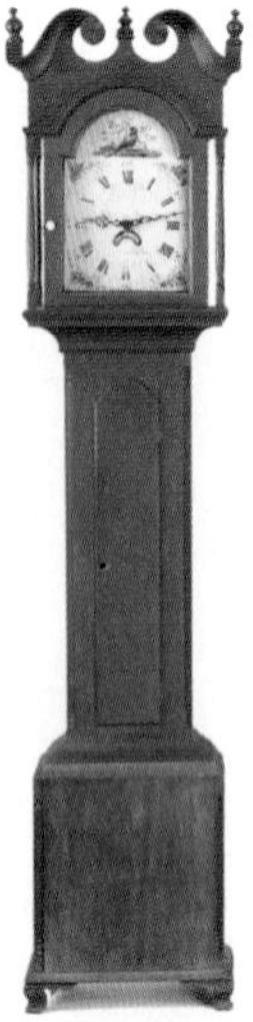

A Pennsylvania Chippendale cherry longcase clock, the broken arch bonnet with carved rosettes enclosing a white painted face with 30-hour works, inscribed "David Seip Northampton Town", over a rectangular base with ogee bracket feet.

c1780 91.5in (229cm) high

£2,800-3,200 **POOK**

A Pennsylvania Chippendale walnut longcase clock, the broken arch bonnet with carved floral rosettes, above a glazed tombstone door enclosing eight-day works, signed "Jacob Gorgas near Ephrata", with straight bracket feet.

c1785 98in (249cm) high

£8,000-12,000 **POOK**

A late 18thC mahogany inlaid longcase clock, by Isaac Brokaw of New Jersey, the silvered brass dial with moon phase indicator, with brass eight-day weight-driven movement, the waist inlaid with a conch shell and stringing, on ogee bracket feet, restored.

98in (249cm) high

£6,000-9,000 **SK**

A Pennsylvania Chippendale cherry longcase clock, with carved pineapple finial, dentil mouldings and turned rosettes enclosing a painted dial inscribed "Solomon Parke, Philadelphia", above a waist with wall of Troy moulding and fluted quarter columns, on ogee bracket feet.

c1795 92.5in (231cm) high

£10,000-15,000 **POOK**

A CLOSER LOOK AT A NEW JERSEY FEDERAL LONGCASE CLOCK

William Dawes was a successful clockmaker who emigrated to America during the War of Independence. He married into the family of Aaron Miller, the most famous clockmaker of the Colonial period.

The case bears many hallmarks of American Empire furniture, including the broken arch and the intricate inlays.

European clocks generally had brass dials but the metal was very hard to come by in America. Clockmakers instead used iron, which they painted white.

Most of the value of this clock lies in the exceptional quality of the case, and the fact that it is attributable to a known cabinet maker.

A New Jersey Federal mahogany longcase clock, the broken arch bonnet with pinwheel inlaid rosettes over a glazed tombstone door, enclosing an eight-day works and white painted dial inscribed "William Dawes, Hackensack", the case elaborately inlaid with conch shell, oval, and barber's pole inlays, on bracket feet.

William Dawes (1746-1811) worked in Elizabethtown. The exceptional case of this clock may be attributed to the workshop of Olive Parsell of New Brunswick.

c1800 94.5in (236cm) high

£18,000-22,000 **POOK**

A Philadelphia Federal cherry longcase clock, the broken arch bonnet over a glazed tombstone door enclosing an eight-day works with painted face, signed "Solomon Parke Philad.", over a case with chamfered and fluted stiles, on ogee bracket feet.

c1805 *91in (227.5cm) high*

£4,000-6,000 POOK

A New Jersey Federal mahogany longcase clock, the broken arch bonnet with brass floral rosettes, above a glazed tombstone door enclosing a painted face and eight-day works, over a straight base with scalloped apron supported by flaring French feet, with overall line inlay.

c1810 *93.5in (234cm) high*

£4,000-5,000 POOK

A New Jersey Federal walnut longcase clock, the broken arch bonnet enclosing a painted face and eight-day works, inscribed "Josh Budd Pemberton NJ", over a case with chamfered stiles and panelled base, on turned feet.

c1810 *91in (227.5cm) high*

£3,500-4,500 POOK

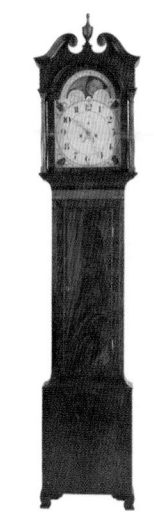

A Pennsylvania Federal mahogany longcase clock, the broken arch bonnet enclosing a painted face and eight-day works, above a case with chamfered stiles supported by ogee bracket feet.

c1810 *103in (257.5cm) high*

£4,000-6,000 POOK

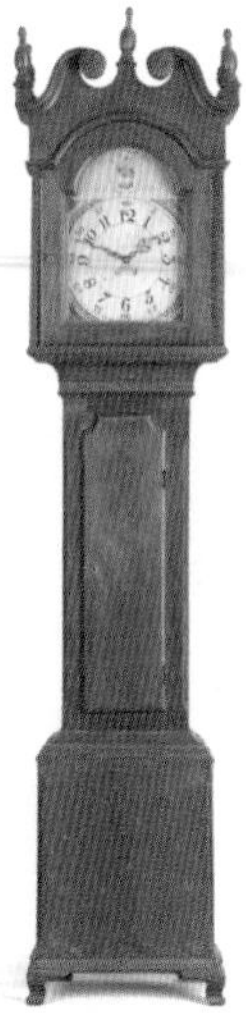

A Pennsylvania painted pine longcase clock, attributed to Peter Miller, the broken arch bonnet carved with rosettes, above a glazed tombstone door enclosing a painted face and 30-hour works, over a waist with matchstick moulding and chamfered stiles, on ogee bracket feet, with original finish.

c1815 *95in (237.5cm) high*

£6,000-8,000 POOK

A New Jersey Federal mahogany eight-day longcase clock, signed "Kennedy Miller Eliz:town".

Kennedy Miller was the grandson of Aaron Miller, the renowned New Jersey clock maker.

c1815 *94in (235cm) high*

£7,000-10,000 POOK

A Pennsylvania Federal cherry longcase clock, the arched pediment over a glazed tombstone door enclosing a painted face and eight-day works, over a case with chamfered sides, supported by straight bracket feet.

c1815 *93in (236cm) high*

£1,800-2,200 POOK

A Pennsylvania Federal cherry longcase clock, the moulded cornice over a glazed tombstone door enclosing an eight-day works with painted face, over a case with chamfered stiles and recessed panel base on turned feet.

c1815 *85.5in (214cm) high*

£1,000-1,500 POOK

A Federal cherry longcase clock, by Riley Whiting of Connecticut, the hood with pierced fretwork and brass urn finials, above a glazed tombstone door covering a painted and gilt wooden dial, with thirty-hour weight-driven movement, painted with simulated ebonized stringing, spread-wing eagle and American flag, signed.

c1820 *93in (236cm) high*

£2,500-3,000 SK

An early 19thC Canadian longcase clock, by James Hanna of Quebec, the eight-day movement fronted by an arched painted dial, contained in an inlaid mahogany case.

James Hanna was a British-born clockmaker who worked in Quebec c1763-1807.

80in (203cm) high

£6,000-9,000 **WAD**

A Pennsylvania Federal mahogany longcase clock, the broken arch bonnet over a glazed tombstone door enclosing a brass face and eight-day works, above a case with turned columns and scalloped skirt, supported by straight bracket feet.

c1820 *90in (225cm) high*

£1,800-2,200 **POOK**

A Pennsylvania late Federal mahogany longcase clock, the scrolled crest enclosing a white-painted face and eight-day works, over a case with half-turned and grain-painted stiles.

c1835 *78.75in (197cm) high*

£2,000-3,000 **POOK**

A mahogany longcase clock, by Bailey, Banks, & Biddle, the broken arch bonnet enclosing a brass face and musical works, above a shell-carved case, supported by animal paw feet.

c1900 *103in (257.5cm) high*

£2,500-3,000 **POOK**

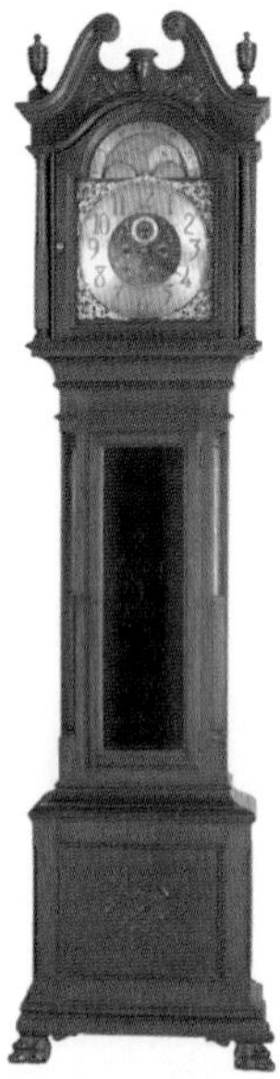

An early 20thC mahogany longcase clock, by J.E. Caldwell, the broken arch bonnet enclosing a brass face and works with moon phase, above a case with smooth quarter columns, on animal paw feet.

94.75in (237cm) high

£1,200-1,800 **POOK**

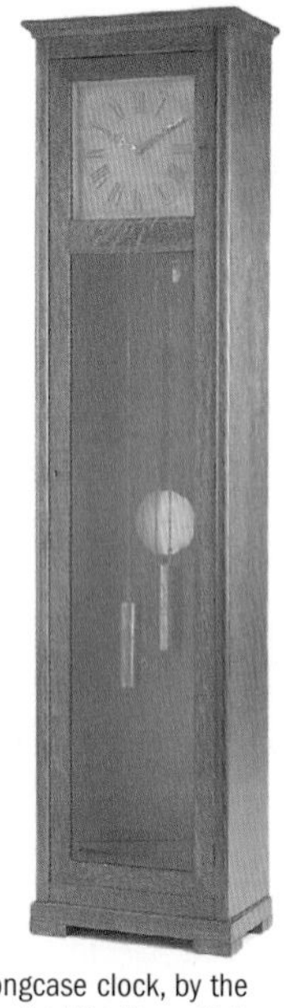

A longcase clock, by the Colonial Mfg. Co., with brass face and bevelled glass door, with original finish, decal to the interior and paper label on back.

77.5in (194cm) high

£600-900 **DRA**

A late 17thC ebony bracket clock, with repeat, the twin-fusee five-pillar movement striking on four bells, the foliage engraved backplate inscribed "Nicolas Masey A Londres", the brass dial with silvered chapter ring, the matt centre with date aperture to cast foliage silvered spandrels.

15.25in (38.5cm) high

£8,000-12,000 **WW**

A late 17thC boulle bracket clock, by Jacques Hory, Paris, with gilt brass mounts, the triple train movement striking on two steel bells, the circular stamped gilt dial with enamelled Roman chapters above cast figural scene enclosed behind glazed door.

27.5in (70cm) high

£3,000-5,000 **L&T**

A ebony veneered striking table clock, John Beeckman, Pall Mall, London, the twin train fusee five pillar movement with verge escapement, striking on a bell with lacking pull repeat, count wheel, inscription "John Beeckman in ye Pall Mall".

c1700 *14.5in (37cm) high*

£8,000-12,000 **L&T**

A George III mahogany and gilt brass mounted chiming bracket clock, the triple-fusee quarter-repeating on eight bells, backplate inscribed "Spencer & Perkins London", subsidiary calendar dial.

26in (66cm) high

£3,000-5,000 **WW**

A George III ebonized bracket clock, with silvered chapter ring and moon phase aperture, with 19thC French movement.

19.5in (49.5cm) high

£1,000-1,500 **GORL**

An 18thC ebonized bracket clock, by Marmaduke Storr, London the twin-train fusee movement with silvered chapter ring and Roman numerals, enclosing date aperture and with strike/silent dial to the arch.

18.5in (47cm) high

£1,200-1,800 **L&T**

An 18thC mahogany cased bracket clock, by Joseph Wrigley, London the twin-train fusee movement with silvered chapter ring, date aperture and strike/silent dial to the arch.

19in (48cm) high

£3,000-5,000 **L&T**

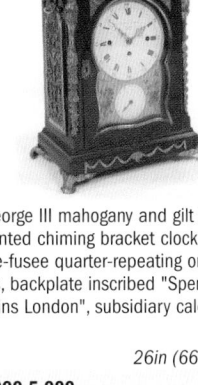

A Regency rosewood bracket clock, the caddy top with a gilt metal pineapple finial, the circular enamel dial with eight-day movement and Roman numerals, the sides with brass grilles.

20.5in (52cm) high

£1,200-1,800 **SWO**

A Regency mahogany bracket clock, the arabesque arched case enclosing a dial painted with Roman numerals, on bun feet.

£600-800 **SWO**

An early 19thC mahogany bracket clock, the twin-train fusee movement striking on a bell, the circular overpainted enamelled dial within arched case with ball finial.

15.75in (40cm) high

£1,000-1,500 **L&T**

A CLOSER LOOK AT A GEORGE III BRACKET CLOCK

Matthew and Thomas were respected late 18thC makers. They trained under their father and his partner, the eminent clockmakers William Dutton and Thomas Mudge.

A finely moulded case, evident in this bracket clock, is a hallmark of the Duttons.

The brothers produced clocks for a very short period, between 1799 and 1804, making their work rare and desirable.

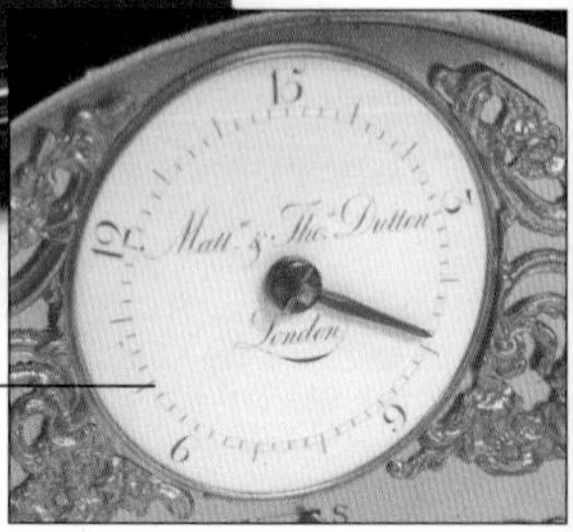

The more complex the clock and the more functions it offers, the more desirable it tends to be. The subsidiary dial adds interest.

A George III ebony bracket clock by Matthew & Thomas Dutton, Fleet Street, London, number 279, the twin-fusee movement striking on a bell, to a circular enamel dial, strike/silent lever below, inscribed.

17in (43cm) high

£15,000-20,000 **WW**

An early 19thC mahogany bracket clock by Brockbanks & Atkins, London, the twin-fusee movement striking on a bell, circular enamelled dial.

16.25in (41cm) high

£1,000-1,500 **L&T**

A walnut cased bracket clock, the twin-fusee movement striking on a ball to a square brass dial with silvered chapter ring inscribed "Thomas Elliott".

16.5in (42cm) high

£1,000-1,500 **WW**

MANTEL CLOCKS

A French gilded bronze Louis-XVI clock, with a man playing the lyre, bronze clockface with enamelled Roman number ring, Breguet hands.

Abraham Louis Breguet (1747-1823) designed this type of hand, with its off-centre hollowed-out points.

c1780 *20.5in (51cm) high*

£1,500-2,000 **KAU**

A Swiss mantel clock, white marble and gilded bronze, white enamel clock face with Roman numerals and Arabic minute ring, brass hands.

c1785 *15.25in (38cm) high*

£800-1,200 **KAU**

A French Louis XVI mantel clock, white marble and bronze, gilded, clockface with Roman numerals, blued Breguet hands, signed "Gentilhomme Palais à Paris".

c1790 *21.25in (53cm) high*

£2,000-3,000 **KAU**

A French white marble and bronze clock, with gilding, the clock held by Greek gods and a putto, white clockface with Arabic numerals.

c1800 *14in (35cm) wide*

£2,000-3,000 **KAU**

A French Louis XVI mantel clock, white marble and bronze, gilded, engraved bronze clockface with enamelled Roman number ring, Breguet hands.

c1800 *19.25in (48cm) high*

£1,000-1,500 **KAU**

A 19thC French Empire-style lyre form gilt bronze and Sienna marble clock, the gilt embossed dial with a white enamel chapter ring, surmounted by a female bust and lion's-masks.

21in (53.5cm) high

£1,500-2,000 **FRE**

An early 19thC ebonized bracket clock, the silvered dial inscribed "Marshall, 5 King Square, London" with a double fusee movement, striking on a bell.

15in (38cm) high

£800-1,000 **SWO**

A Vienna wooden mantel clock, ebonized, bronze and white marble, clock held by two fish, white enamel clockface with date ring, blackened hands, key.

c1820 *19.75in (49.5cm) high*

£1,200-1,800 **KAU**

A 19thC pendule d'officier, the twin-train movement with circular enamelled dial, bears retailers mark "Howell and James Ltd".

20in (51cm) high

£2,000-3,000 **L&T**

A 19thC French ormolu mantel clock, eight-day movement striking on bell, inscribed "Hy Marc, Paris, No 12751", the drum case with figure of Napoleon.

14in (35.5cm) wide

£1,000-1,500 **BRI**

A 19thC French mantel clock by Marti & Cie, with eight-day striking movement, visible anchor escapement, mercury-filled pendulum.

14in (35.5cm) high

£800-1,200 **BRI**

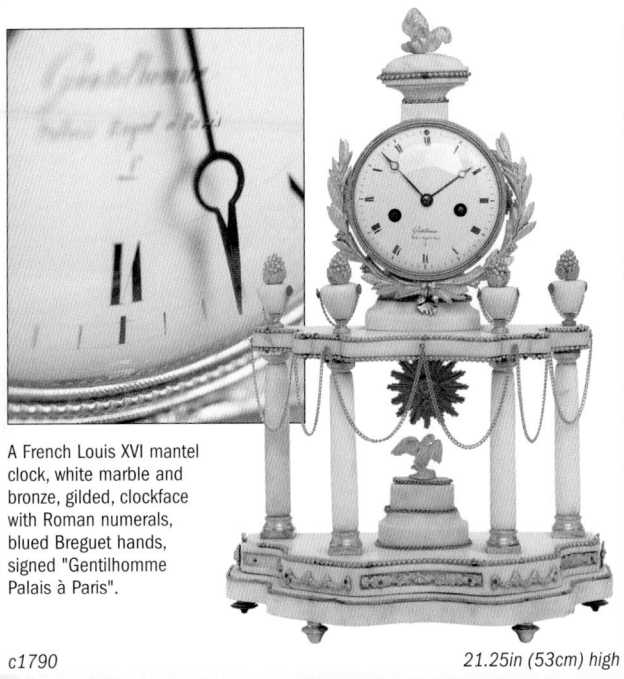

A 19thC spelter figural mantel clock, with brass and enamel dial, inscribed "Time is Money", twin-train movement striking on a bell.

26.5in (67cm) high

£800-1,200 **SWO**

A 19thC French brass mantel clock, the pierced scrolled case supporting a seated bronze figure within a portico, the white enamel dial signed "De E Vizzot", the twin-train movement striking on a bell.

24in (61cm) high

£600-800 **SWO**

A 19thC French ormolu and porcelain applied mantel clock, mounted with a lady and two cherubs, on disc feet.

12in (30.5cm) high

£1,500-2,000 **GORL**

A 19thC gilt bronze mantel clock, decorated with hunting trophies and stags heads, the enamelled dial with Roman numerals and strike/silent over a painted porcelain plaque, depicting a wild boar hunt.

15.75in (40cm) high

£1,200-1,800 **SWO**

A 19thC French Sienna marble and gilt bronze mantel clock, the engine-turned gilt dial signed "Galle Rue Richelieu No. 95", the glazed door with a serpent frame, surmounted by a bronze bust of a scholar.

17in (43cm) high

£800-1,200 **FRE**

A 19thC French gilt and silvered bronze clock, the silvered engine turned dial signed "La Gache A Boulogne", surmounted by an Arab on horseback, raised on an ornate base.

20in (51cm) high

£500-700 **FRE**

A mid-19thC French porcelain mantel clock, Rococo style, movement striking on a bell, on giltwood and gesso plinth, the enamelled dial signed "Aubert Klaftemberger Paris".

19.5in (49.5cm) high

£1,500-2,000 **GORL**

A 19thC French clock, gilded bronze, lion's head handles, flaming oil lamp with festoons, white enamel clockface with black Arabic and blue Roman numerals, gilded rocaille hands.

16in (40cm) high

£500-700 **KAU**

A CLOSER LOOK AT A MANTEL CLOCK

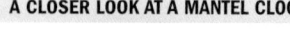

The revived fortunes of Meissen from the 1840s led to over 40 other German factories imitating their successful rival. Sitzendorf is one of the most notable and widely collected of these companies.

Clock cases, as well as figures and vases, were typical of the output from German factories during the mid-19thC.

The figural subject and large size make this clock unusual and appealing.

Figures were often dressed in 18thC costume, but 19thC colours were more garish than the ones used on pieces from the earlier era.

A 19thC German porcelain mantel clock, possibly Sitzendorf, signed "R & G Drummond Paris", raised on a shaped base, painted with a river scene.

27in (68.5cm) high

£5,000-7,000 **FRE**

A 19thC French gilt bronze mantel clock, the painted enamel dial inscribed "Planch Palais Royal".

15in (38cm) high

£600-900 **SWO**

A Victorian bronze easel clock, cast as an owl and rat perched on a branch.

6.25in (16cm) high

£200-300 **SWO**

A French gilded bronze clock, with a girl holding a letter, white enamel clockface with Roman numerals, blackened Breguet hands, signed "Cachette".

c1860 *15.25in (38cm) high*

£400-600 **KAU**

A French ormolu and porcelain mounted mantel clock, the twin train movement striking on a bell, contained under a glass dome.

c1870 *14.5in (36cm) high*

£700-1,000 **SWO**

A Grecian revival gilt and patinated bronze mantel clock, the black slate case with a gilt dial, surmounted by a patinated bronze group depicting a knight slaying a warrior.

c1880 *28.5in (71cm) high*

£2,000-3,000 **FRE**

A Louis XVI-style lyre-shaped mantel clock, retailed by Tiffany & Co., the frame in green onyx, convex enamelled dial, French movement striking on a bell, signed "Tiffany & Co."

19.25in (49cm) high

£1,800-2,200 **GORL**

A late 19thC French ormolu-mounted alabaster mantel clock, with urn finial on rectangular platform surmounted by dolphins and cherubs.

14.5in (37cm) high

£600-800 **GORL**

A late 19thC Neuenburg console clock, Lenzkirch, wood, painted and gilded, white enamel clock face with Roman numerals.

13.75in (34.5cm) wide

£500-700 **KAU**

A late 19thC French Odobey tower clock, wood, iron, patinated in black-gold, brass, with open-work sides holding the movement, white enamel clock face with Roman numerals, blackened hands.

60.75in (152cm) high

£1,500-2,000 **KAU**

A rare pillar and scroll shelf clock, with brass finial and original eglomise panel, with label for "Mark Leavenworth, Waterbury Connecticut".

c1780 *22.5in (56cm) high*

£3,500-4,500 **POOK**

A Plymouth, Connecticut Federal mahogany pillar and scroll clock, by E. Terry & Sons, with broken arch pediment, white painted face and eglomise panel depicting an estate, supported by bracket feet.

28.5in (71cm) high

£600-900 **POOK**

A Federal mahogany mantel clock, by Eli and Samuel Terry of Plymouth, Connecticut, the scrolled cresting with inlaid plinths and brass urn finials above a glazed door flanked by urns and willow trees, opening to a white and gilt decorated dial and thirty-hour wooden weight-driven movement, original paint.

c1825 *31.5in (80cm) high*

£4,000-6,000 **SK**

A Louis XVI-style ormolu and marble globe clock, the bell-striking movement contained within a spherical case with revolving dial, supported by three ormolu female nudes.

24in (61cm) high

£5,000-7,000 **GORL**

A Gothic mahogany 'Candlestick' shelf clock, by Birge & Fuller of Bristol, Connecticut, with painted zinc dial and eight-day time and strike movement, above tablets depicting a honey bee and beehive, inscribed "BY INDUSTRY WE THRIVE", restored.

c1845 *25.5in (65cm) high*

£4,000-6,000 **SK**

A Tiffany Furnaces parcel-gilt acid-etched mantel clock, with enamelled accents, replaced hinge pin on back door, stamped "LOUIS C. TIFFANY FURNACES INC. 651".

7.5in (19cm) high

£1,500-2,000 **DRA**

A 19thC French assembled gilt bronze and marble clock garniture, the white enamel dial signed "Raingo Fres Paris", the candelabra with later associated silvered bronze candelabra.

19.75in (50cm) high

£3,000-4,000 **FRE**

A Victorian brass and painted porcelain clock garniture, the clock with movement striking on a bell, with twin-handled baluster urns

clock 16.5in (42cm) high

£1,000-2,000 **L&T**

A late 19thC French Avalon white marble and bronze mantel clock with candlesticks, white clockface with Arabic numerals and festoons, gilded Rococo hands, signed.

clock 12.75in (32cm) high

£400-600 **KAU**

A late 19thC St. Etienne marble clock with a pair of vases, green marble and bronze, white enamel face with Arabic numerals and festoons, gilded Rococo hands, signed.

clock 22.5in (56cm) high

£1,000-1,500 **KAU**

A late 19thC red marble and bronze mantel clock with a pair of vases, white enamel face with Arabic numerals and festoons, gilded Rococo hands.

clock 17.5in (44cm) high

£400-600 **KAU**

A Louis XVI-style ormolu-mounted five-piece clock garniture, count-wheel movement clock striking on a bell, with a pair of cassolettes and a pair of four-sconce candelabra, all in 'bleu-du-roi' porcelain with Classical ormolu mounts.

clock 18in (45.5cm) high

£3,000-5,000 **GORL**

A Louis XVI-style porcelain and ormolu-mounted clock garniture, the clock with Sèvres-style dial signed "Ernest Miroy Paris", movement striking on a bell, with a pair of ewers.

clock 18.5in (47cm) high

£3,000-5,000 **GORL**

A 19thC Reinholdt & Son carriage clock, Karlsruhe, white enamel clockface with Roman numerals, blackened hands.

7in (17.5cm) high

£500-700 **KAU**

A Victorian gilt brass carriage timepiece, the cylinder escapement with a numbered regulator, to a silver circular dial inscribed "O. SOWTER, OXFORD", within foliage, back with shuttered winding holes.

5.25in (13.5cm) high

£1,200-1,800 **WW**

A late 19thC French brass carriage clock, the case with Corinthian columns, striking on a gong.

6.75in (17cm) high

£300-400 **SWO**

A late 19thC French brass cased carriage clock, with repeat, the later platform lever escapement striking on a gong, to a brass dial having a pierced centre boss, arched column face.

French carriage clocks are more common than British examples.

7.5in (19cm) high

£500-700 **WW**

A 20thC French brass carriage clock, the case with bowed sides, the repeating movement striking on a gong.

7.5in (19cm) high

£400-600 **SWO**

A gilt-mounted tortoiseshell travelling clock, the white enamel dial with black Arabic numerals and hands, signed "Edward, Glasgow", with French movement, marks for London 1921, maker's mark "C&RC".

1921 *4.5in (11.5cm) high*

£500-800 **L&T**

A modern French brass gorge-cased carriage clock, with repeat, the lever escapement striking on a gong, white enamel dial, inscribed "L'Epee Fondee en 1839, Sainte-Luxanne, France" with subsidiary dials for day, alarm and date.

7.25in (18.5cm) high

£700-1,000 **WW**

A miniature brass carriage clock, with a white porcelain dial, under a glass dome.

3.75in (9.5cm) high

£300-500 **SWO**

A brass carriage clock, with repeating mechanism, enamel face, and leather carrying case.

5.5in (14cm) high

£300-400 **SWO**

A French gilt brass quarter-repeating carriage clock, with foliate capped columns and a silvered Roman dial.

7.5in (19cm) high

£1,800-2,200 **GORL**

A 19thC brass skeleton clock, the pierced silvered chapter ring with Roman hours, the single-train movement with an anchor escapement, contained under a glass dome.

£700-1,000 **SWO**

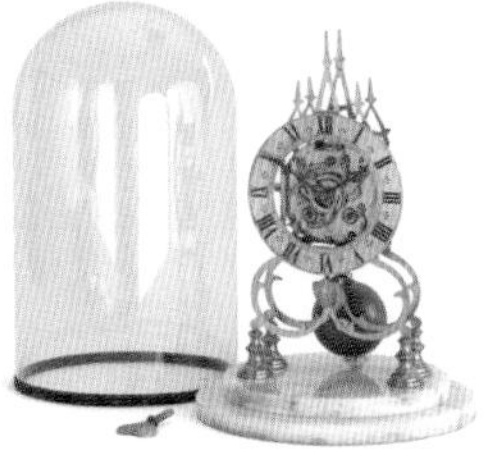

A brass 'Gothic' skeleton clock, the later movement with a lever escapement and striking on a bell, to a silver chapter ring, on a circular onyx stepped base and under a glass dome.

13in (33cm) high

£400-500 **WW**

A 19thC lacquered brass skeleton clock, the frame of typical form, centred by a bell, the silvered and pierced Roman chapter ring having a twin-fusee movement, glass dome.

17.75in (45cm) high

£1,200-1,800 **SWO**

A Victorian brass skeleton clock with single-train fusee movement, anchor escapement, ebonized plinth with glass dome.

18in (46cm) high

£700-1,000 **BRI**

A Victorian brass skeleton clock, with a silvered dial and painted with Roman numerals on a white marble base, reconditioned and with a glass case.

£500-700 **SWO**

WALL CLOCKS

An 18thC overpainted wall timepiece, the single-train movement with painted dial having Roman chapters, painted harbour scene, gilded and overpainted case.

39.75in (101cm) high

£6,000-8,000 **L&T**

A CLOSER LOOK AT A HANGING WATCH CASE

This is a very rare type of watch case. It was probably used for the safekeeping of a very valuable pocket watch when it was not being worn. It may well have been made as a bespoke commission.

The case resembles the hood of a fine longcase clock. It was designed to hang from a wall.

The use of burr walnut and the shape of the mouldings on this case indicate that it was made in the early 18thC. It is probably English, although the marquetry work indicates that it may have been made in Holland.

This knob at the foot of the case would activate the watch's striking mechanism when it was pulled and released.

A rare early 18thC walnut and burr walnut carved hanging watch case, watch aperture, with inlaid marquetry frieze.

5.5in (14cm) wide

£12,000-18,000 **WW**

A late Regency period mahogany drop dial wall clock, the eight-inch painted dial with a single-fusee movement, pendulum not original.

£1,000-1,500 **SWO**

An early 19thC wall clock, enamel dial, inscribed "H. Linsell, Hadham", within a convex bezel and a mahogany frame supporting a single-fusee movement.

£600-900 **SWO**

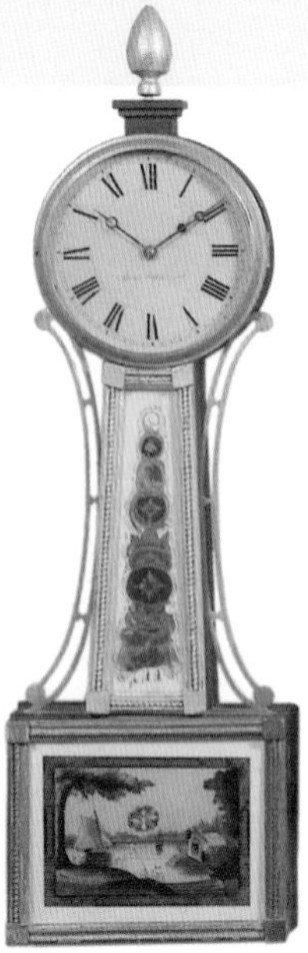

An early 19thC Federal mahogany and gilt gesso presentation banjo wall clock, probably Massachusetts, with moulded brass bezel, painted and inscribed metal dial, brass eight-day weight-driven movement and pendulum box bordered by gilt spiral mouldings, flanked by pierced brass side pieces, restored.

33.5in (85cm) high

£700-1,000 **SK**

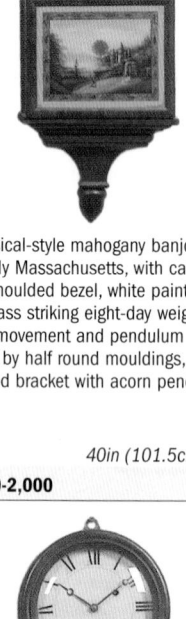

A Classical-style mahogany banjo clock, probably Massachusetts, with carved finial, moulded bezel, white painted iron dial, brass striking eight-day weight-driven movement and pendulum box framed by half round mouldings, all on moulded bracket with acorn pendant.

c1830 *40in (101.5cm) high*

£1,500-2,000 **SK**

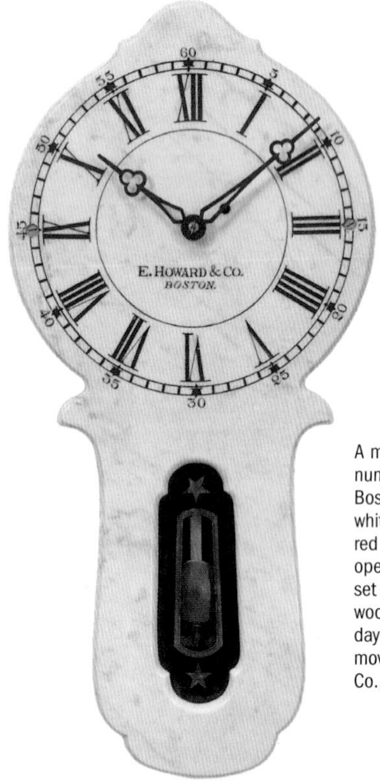

A marble wall clock, model number 27 by E. Howard & Co. of Boston, the shaped and moulded white marble front with black and red painted dial above an opening with an eglomise panel, set on a shaped white-painted wooden case housing an eight-day brass weight-driven movement, marked "E. Howard & Co., Boston".

c1875 *30in (76cm) high*

£2,500-3,000 **SK**

A Classical-style mahogany lyre wall clock, probably by Enoch J. Titcomb of Boston, with moulded brass bezel door, painted and inscribed iron dial and eight-day weight-driven brass movement, the rectangular pendulum box with rounded frame joining corner blocks, restored.

c1830 *36in (91.5cm) high*

£2,500-3,000 **SK**

A mahogany banjo clock, retailed by J.J. Beal & Son of Boston, with moulded bezel, inscribed and painted metal dial, brass eight-day weight-driven movement and shaped pendulum box, framed by half round mouldings.

c1860 *30in (76cm) high*

£600-900 **SK**

An early 19thC American brass watch safe, with spread-winged eagle crest over a swag base.

6in (15cm) high

£320-380 **POOK**

A George III Thomas Hunter pocket watch, the verge quarter-repeating movement with a single bell enclosed within a fretted case, signed "Hunter 160", silvered regulation dial, dust cover, chased allegorical scene, the chain with shepherd's hook and dog clip fittings.

c1790

£3,000-4,000 **HAMG**

A George III 18ct gold open-faced pocket watch, the engine turned dial with Roman numerals and black hands, with fusée movement and engine-turned case, with key.

£400-500 **L&T**

A William IV 18ct gold open-faced key wind pocket watch, with subsidiary seconds dial and fusée movement, later white dial, inscribed "Given by His Majesty King William 4th to William Henry Kennedy Erskine of Dun, July 1st 1836", with engine-turned outer case and key, contained in a fitted box.

£1,200-1,800 **L&T**

A Swiss ladies' giltmetal open pocket watch, by Patek Philippe & Co., Geneve, with an engine-turned case and Geneva bar mechanism with cylinder escapement faced by mixed Arabic and Roman enamel dial, case number "41613", with leather carry case.

1872

£400-600 **BIG**

A CLOSER LOOK AT A HALF HUNTER POCKET WATCH

Pieces by the respected maker Jaeger-LeCoultre are very desirable to collectors. The company was established in Switzerland in 1833 by Antoine le Coultre, who pioneered the keyless winding system and invented the milionmeter. It is still in production today.

Switzerland became the leading watchmaking country in the 19thC, taking over from England and France.

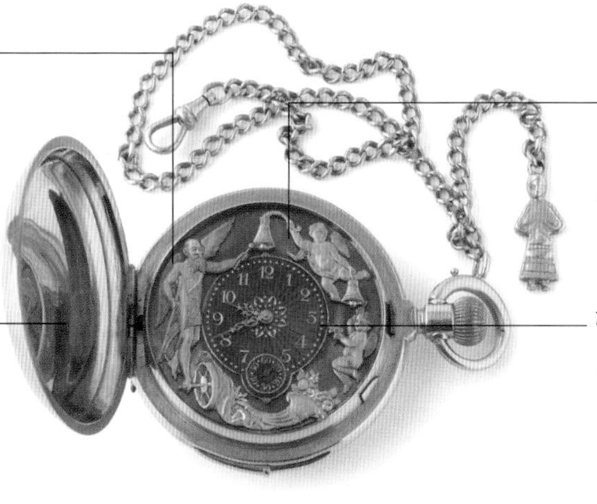

The watch is marked "ligne droite spiral Breguet". The Breguet spiral, invented by important watchmaker Abraham-Louis Breguet in the late 18thC, is still used in quality watches today.

The dial is in blue enamel and ornately decorated with cherubs, which contributes to the precious feel of this pocket watch.

A late 19thC Jaeger-LeCoultre gold full hunter quarter repeating automaton pocket watch, with subsidiary seconds dial and Father Time automaton, the 32 jewelled lever movement quarter-repeating on two hammers.

£3,000-4,000 **HAMG**

A late Victorian 18ct gold gentleman's demi-hunter pocket watch, by W. Ehrhardt, Hockley, English part-jewelled keyless lever mechanism with compensation balance faced by calibrated dial with subsidiary seconds, on a 9ct gold lightweight Albert with vesta case attached.

£300-400 **BIG**

A Swiss ladies' silver pocket watch, remains of old gilding, enamelled in emerald-green, the back with filigree decoration, enamel clockface with Arabian numerals, gilded movement.

c1900 *1.25in (3cm) diam*

£70-100 **KAU**

An Ulysse Nardin 18ct slimline open-faced keyless wind pocket watch, silvered dial, inscribed "Ulysee Nardin, Locle & Geneve", subsidiary seconds dial, the lever movement also inscribed, engine-turned rear case, with monogram, in a fitted leather case.

£600-800 **L&T**

A gentleman's keyless wind 18ct cased pocket watch with stopwatch action, in full hunter case, the enamel dial with sweep central second hand, subsidiary seconds and hour elapsed dial and an up/down dial.

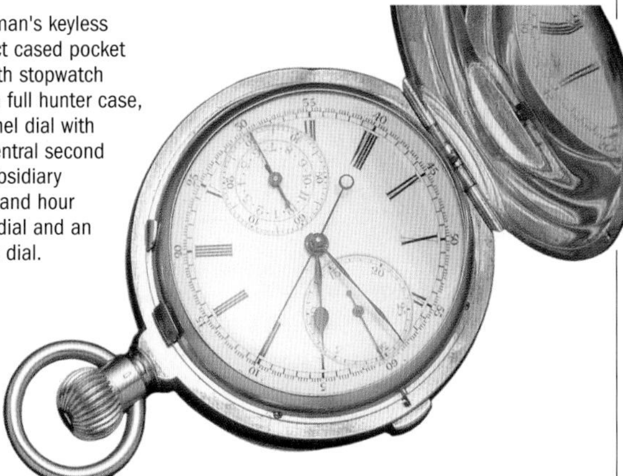

£800-1,200 **L&T**

A lady's diamond and 18ct gold wrist watch, set with 22 old brilliant-cut diamonds, approximately 1.10ct total, border of rose-cut diamonds, 15 jewelled lever movement, hallmarked London import 1914 and numbered "2939589".

£400-600 **HAMG**

A 1940s Swiss IWC gentleman's wristwatch, yellow and red gold, cream-coloured clockface with Arabic numerals, seconds at number six, Cartier leather bracelet, buckle with single diamond.

1.25in (3cm) diam

£500-700 **KAU**

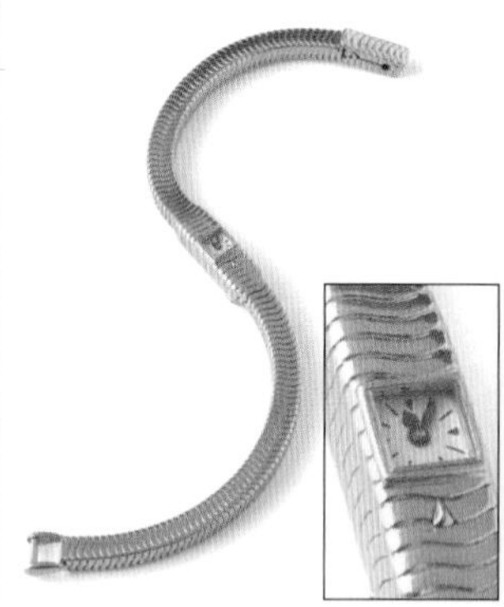

A Jaeger-LeCoultre ladies' slimline cocktail watch, with baton numerals, serpentine link bracelet, 15-jewelled calibre 101 backwound movement signed "Swiss fab" and "Jaeger le Coultre", Swiss control marks and numbered "701866".

£1,200-1,800 **HAMG**

A 1960s Genève Baume & Mercier gentleman's wristwatch, gold, matte rounded, silver-plated clockface, date at number three, dealer's signature "Van Cleef & Arpels", automatic movement, leather bracelet.

1.25in (3cm) wide

£400-600 **KAU**

A 1960s Swiss Bucherer Chronometer gentleman's wristwatch, gold, silver-plated clockface, Dauphine hands, date at number three, original bracelet, original box, in working order.

1.5in (3.5cm) diam

£400-600 **KAU**

A 1970s Swiss Jaeger-LeCoultre gentleman's wristwatch, gold, rounded corners, gilded, partly matted clockface with Roman and Point numerals, date at number three, quartz movement, leather bracelet.

1.25in (3cm) wide

£300-400 **KAU**

A late 20thC Swiss Cyprus platinum ladies' wristwatch, with open-work chain decoration and 92 diamonds, mother-of-pearl clockface with Arabic numerals, blued modern hands, in working order.

1in (2.5cm) long

£500-700 **KAU**

A 1980s Swiss Omega Seamaster-Cosmic gentleman's wristwatch, stainless steel, silver clockface.

During World War I, wristwatches were issued in the military for convenience. Returning veterans brought home the new fashion and a new market emerged.

1.25in (3cm) diam

£200-300 **KAU**

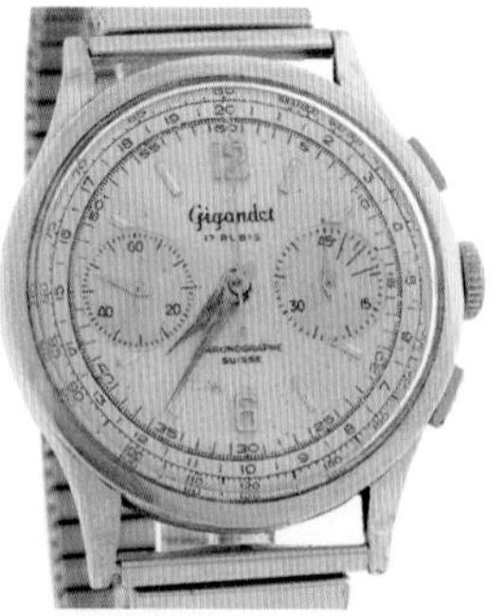

A 1980s Swiss Gigandet Chronographe gentleman's wristwatch, gold, gilded clockface with Arabic numerals, Dauphine hands, decentral second at number nine, central chronograph, elastic bracelet.

1.5in (4cm) diam

£200-300 **KAU**

A Rolex Oyster gentleman's wristwatch, perpetual day-date movement, 18ct yellow gold flexible bracelet.

£6,000-8,000 **FRE**

A gentleman's 14ct yellow gold case wristwatch, by Audemars Piguet, case no. 8765, including an 18ct yellow gold wide mesh flexible bracelet.

£5,000-7,000 **FRE**

A George III mahogany inlaid mahogany barometer, with a silvered dial, inscribed to the level Pawsey & Hawke Warranted.

£500-700 **SWO**

A George III mahogany banjo barometer, inscribed to level "I Harris & Sons, London".

42.5in (108cm) high

£500-700 **SWO**

An early 19thC mahogany barometer, with hygrometer, thermometer, silvered scale and level, by J. Alibini, London.

39in (99cm) high

£200-300 **MAX**

A 19thC rosewood-cased barometer, with a silvered dial and thermometer.

38in (95cm) high

£100-200 **SWO**

An early Victorian mahogany double banjo barometer, by Taglia**, 11 Brook Street, Hoban.

38.5in (98cm) high

£300-400 **BIG**

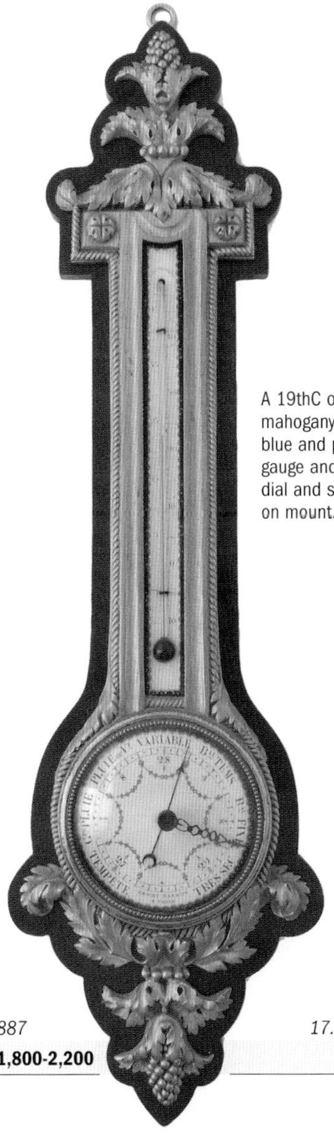

A 19thC ormolu-mounted mahogany barometer, with blue and parcel gilt enamel gauge and dial, signed on dial and signed and dated on mount.

1887 *17.5in (44.5cm) high*

£1,800-2,200 **GORL**

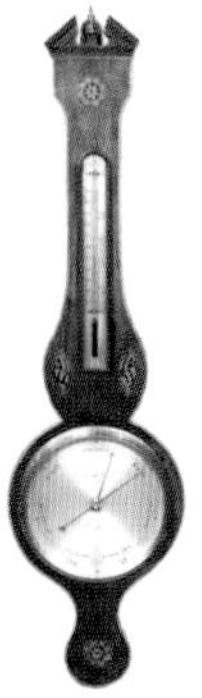

A Victorian inlaid mahogany wheel barometer, the silvered dial inscribed Cattelli & Co, Hereford.

40in (102cm) high

£500-700 **SWO**

A Victorian walnut mercury column banjo barometer, with spirit thermometer.

36in (91.5cm) high

£200-300 **MAX**

A Victorian rosewood wheel barometer, silvered hygrometer, thermometer, level and dial, inscribed "H Hughes, 120 Fenchurch Street, London".

£300-500 **SWO**

A Victorian rosewood wheel barometer, inlaid with mother of pearl, with a hygrometer, thermometer and level dial, inscribed 'Wenham, 62 Paddington Street, London',

43.5in (110cm) high

£500-700 **SWO**

A barometer, by Mathieson & Son, Edinburgh, lacking a small piece of moulding.

£200-400 **MUR**

A late 18thC George III Chippendale mahogany stick barometer, the elaborately engraved face inscribed "Pelegrino fecit London".

43in (109cm) high

£3,000-4,000 **POOK**

A George III mahogany cased stick barometer, by J. Lowe, the engraved brass dial with glass mercury tube, enclosed within case with oval reservoir cover.

37.75in (96cm) high

£800-1,200 **L&T**

A George III birds'-eye maple cased stick barometer, by J. & J. Gardner, Glasgow, with ivory scales and later glass mercury tube.

39in (99cm) high

£800-1,200 **L&T**

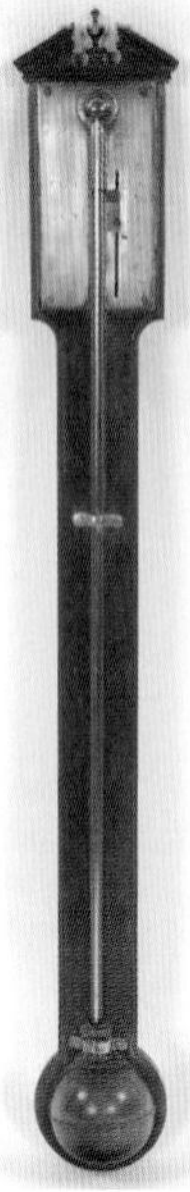

A late George III mahogany stick barometer, the broken arch pediment with a brass urn finial, to a brass dial inscribed "Wm Watkins, St James's Street, London".

38in (96.5cm) high

£2,000-3,000 **W**

A Regency mahogany bow-fronted stick barometer, with urn-shaped cistern cover and silvered scale signed "Cary London".

38in (96.5cm) high

£3,000-4,000 **GORL**

An early 19thC mahogany stick barometer, brass dial with vernier scale and thermometer, inscribed "Cattelly, London", the case with chequer stringing.

39in (99cm) high

£1,200-1,800 **WW**

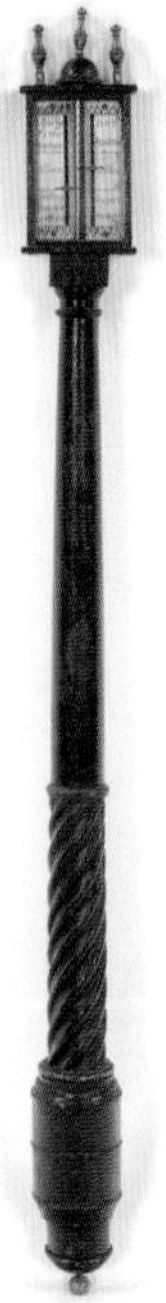

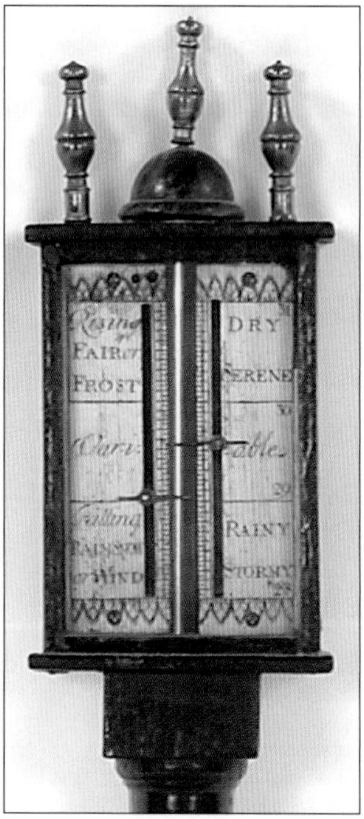

An early 18thC japanned stick barometer, silvered dial, turned tapering and spiral ribbed body, decorated with birds and foliage.

37in (94cm) high

£5,000-6,000 **WW**

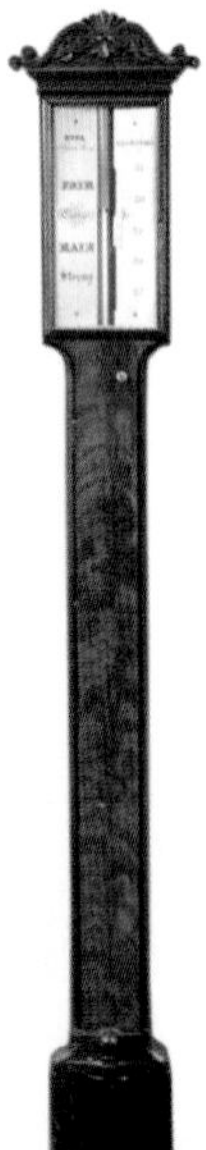

An early 19thC mahogany stick barometer, inscribed "Ross, 53 Wigmore St., Cavendish Square", thermometer missing.

40.5in (103cm) high

£800-1,200 **SWO**

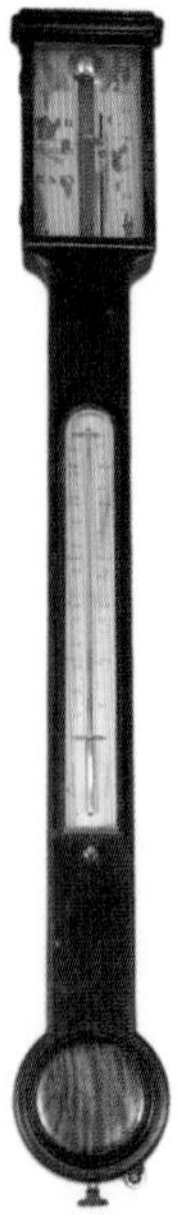

A 19thC mahogany stick barometer, by Dolland of London, with a silvered register and thermometer, silvering worn.

37.75in (96cm) high

£1,800-2,200 **SWO**

A Victorian Scottish walnut bow-front marine stick barometer and gimbal, ivory dials with vernier scales, inscribed "P.A. Feathers, 26 Dock Strt, Dundee", above two bone adjusters.

Dundee was an important whaling port during the 19thC. Peter Airth Feathers was at 26 Dock Street from 1853-63.

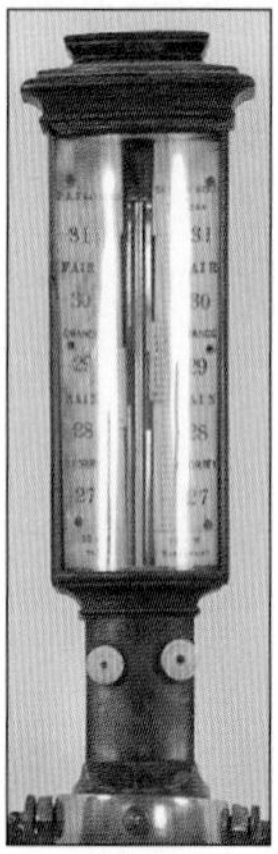

37in (94cm) high

£2,000-3,000 **WW**

A combined pocket barometer, thermometer and compass, inscribed "J.H. Steward, 406 Strand, London", in a plush travel case.

£200-300 **SWO**

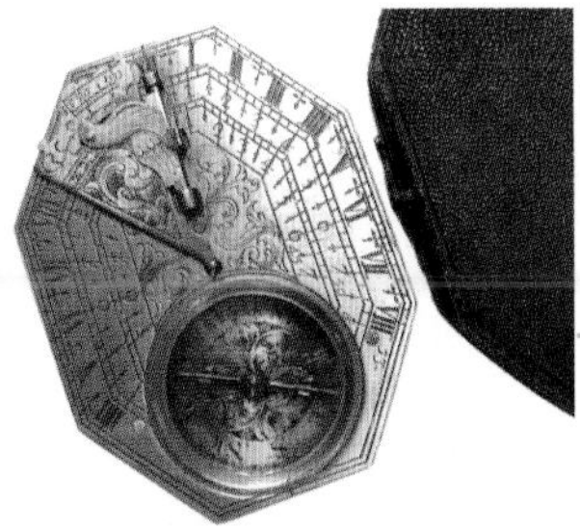

An 18thC Butterfield-type sundial compass, the bird gnomon engraved with latitude scale of 45-60 degrees, the compass with blued iron needle, the underside engraved with the latitudes of 16 English and Irish cities and towns, contained in original fish skin case.

2.5in (6.5cm) diam

£800-1,200 **SWO**

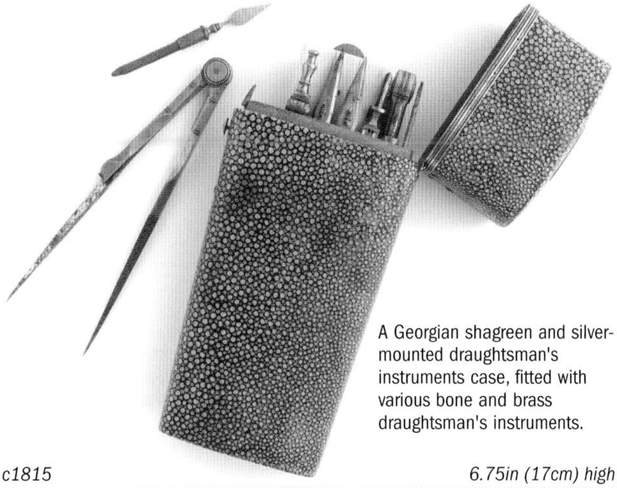

A Georgian shagreen and silver-mounted draughtsman's instruments case, fitted with various bone and brass draughtsman's instruments.

c1815 *6.75in (17cm) high*

£700-1,000 **ROS**

A late 19thC barograph, in oak-framed case with leaf-carved frieze, turned columns and bevelled glass panels.

A barograph records atmospheric pressure over time.

17.5in (44.5cm) wide

£1,000-1,500 **BRI**

A late Victorian mahogany barograph, having five-glass detachable cover, original lacquered brass action and drum and ink bottle on a moulded drawerless plinth.

14.5in (37cm) wide

£400-600 **BIG**

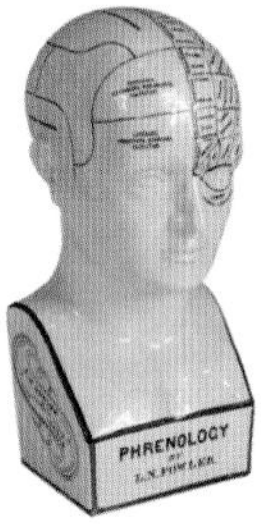

A Staffordshire earthenware L. N. Fowler phrenology head, with black printed script and blue painted borders.

12.5in (31.5cm) high

£300-500 **SWO**

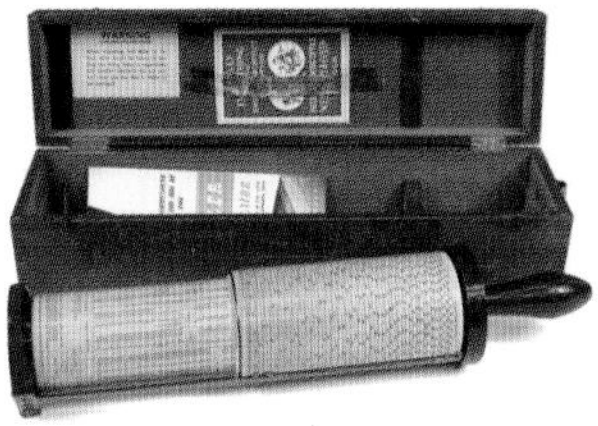

A Fuller's calculator, by W. F. Stanley & Co., with Bakelite fittings, instructions and mounting bracket.

£220-280 **SWO**

A lacquer brass barograph, the six-tier vacuum with turned supports and a glass ink bottle, ivorene label for "HARRODS LTD LONDON", in mahogany case with a chart drawers.

10.5in (26.5cm) wide

£800-1,200 **WW**

A Negretti and Zambra barograph, seismograph, humidity dial, barograph clockwork mechanism and altometer with combined thermometer and spirit level.

£500-700 **SWO**

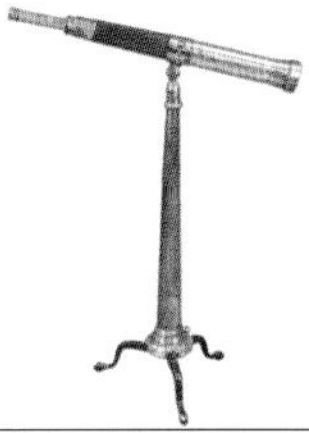

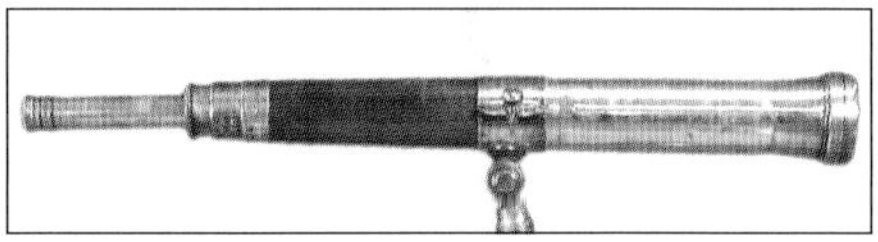

A brass and mahogany telescope, by Troughton, on a copper tripod stand.

£250-300 **SWO**

A double-sided pocket barometer, the silvered dial inscribed "D. Norris, Rio de Janeiro" and "C.F. Casella & Co. Ltd., London S.W., No. 9916" with a rotating outer altitude scale and thermometer verso, double-hinged leather case.

£300-400 **SWO**

A double sided barometer, the silvered dial inscribed "E.R. Watts & Son, London, No.1113", mother-of-pearl compass, and a stop level verso, leather case with shoulder strap.

dial 2.5in (6.5cm) diam

£400-600 **SWO**

A Belle Epoque pearl, diamond and enamel brooch, with rose-cut and old brilliant-cut diamonds above a golden guilloche enamel surmount, French poinçon control marks.

c1890

£700-1,000 **HAMG**

A late Victorian diamond cluster stick pin, the central cushion-shaped old brilliant-cut diamond claw set above a surround of ten similar smaller diamonds, 1.20 cts.

c1890

£800-1,200 **HAMG**

A late 19thC pearl and diamond brooch, with a cluster of cushion-shaped old brilliant-cut diamonds, mounted in gold-backed silver, 2.40 cts.

£700-1,000 **HAMG**

A Russian Belle Epoque diamond brooch, with old brilliant- and eight-cut diamonds, stamped with 56 kokoshnik marks, St Peterburg.

c1910

£800-1,200 **HAMG**

An early 20thC ruby, emerald and diamond naval crown brooch, pavé-set with old brilliant- and rose-cut diamonds, ruby highlights, set in platinum-flashed gold.

c1910

£500-800 **HAMG**

An early 19thC Neoclassical enamel mourning brooch, with seed pearls, gold wirework and clipped hair, bright-cut frame, 14ct rose gold mount, inscribed, red leather box.

1.75in (4.5cm) diam

£2,200-2,800 **SK**

An emerald and diamond heart, with pendeloque-cut emerald millegrain set to a border of old cut diamonds.

c1920

£1,000-1,500 **HAMG**

A late Victorian Essex crystal brooch, depicting a terrier, in a rub over mount stamped "18".

c1900

£1,200-1,800 **HAMG**

A large oval shell cameo brooch, carved with a Classical female portrait, within a shaped oval gold surround.

2.25in (6cm) long

£600-900 **L&T**

A Regency gold and gem set 'regard' locket, the ruby, emerald, garnet, amethyst, ruby and diamond spelling "regard", interior compartment.

c1825

£1,200-1,800 **HAMG**

A late Victorian diamond swan pendant, set with old brilliant- and rose-cut diamonds, with a cabochon ruby eye, mounted in gold-backed silver, trace link chain, diamonds 5 cts.

c1890

£1,500-2,000 **HAMG**

An Edwardian diamond and velvet pansy pendant, in rose-cut diamonds with an old brilliant-cut diamond and lilac velvet petals, mounted in platinum-flashed gold, on fancy link chain.

c1905

£1,000-1,500 **HAMG**

An historically important gold, enamel and gem-set presentation medallion pendant, commemorating the 1904 state visit of French president Emile Loubet to Italy, with enamel portrait of Loubet, diamond-set enamelled French and Italian coats-of-arms, a pavé-set emerald, diamond and ruby stylized circlet, with a gold and gem-set plaque, on a later cable twist chain.

£3,000-5,000 **HAMG**

A cased pair of Swiss canton bracelets, with enamel plaques of women in regional costume, mountainous lake scenes and the names of cantons, set with gemstones to three-colour gold scrollwork and beadwork on a granulated ground.

c1830 *6.5in (16.5cm) long*

£8,000-10,000 **WW**

A mid-Victorian gold and coral bracelet, set at the centre with three coral cabochons to an embossed stylized knot motif, applied to a flexible gold mesh bracelet.

c1850

£800-1,200 **HAMG**

A mid-Victorian gold bangle, with blue enamel plaques set with rose-cut diamond quatrefoil motifs and half-pearl spacer bars, old brilliant-cut diamond highlights, on a bloomed gold hinged bangle.

£800-1,200 **HAMG**

A pair of 19thC gold Etruscan work bangles, of bloomed gold appliqué with Etruscan wirework decoration, engraved "pat'd. feb.25 1879 oct.14.79", in an original fitted case.

c1880

£1,800-2,200 **HAMG**

A French diamond bracelet, with brilliant-cut diamonds pavé set in flexible honeycomb mounts, box snap clasp, numbered "49909", French pioncon assay marks, maker's mark "C.H", diamonds 11 cts.

c1950

£4,000-6,000 **HAMG**

A Georgian tortoiseshell cameo ring, the blonde tortoiseshell carved to depict two Classical figures and Venus and Cupid, in a rub over gold mount to a plain gold shank, finger size N.

c1780

£500-800 **HAMG**

A Victorian emerald and diamond ring, the square-cut emerald claw set in a cut-down collet to a surround of old brilliant-cut diamonds, mounted in gold backed silver, finger size K.

c1860

£800-1,200 **HAMG**

A late Victorian diamond cluster ring, the central old brilliant-cut diamond set above two tiers of further old brilliant-cut diamonds, 4.15 cts, mounted in gold backed silver, finger size O.

c1880

£1,800-2,200 **HAMG**

A late Victorian navette diamond cluster ring, pavé-set throughout with old brilliant-cut diamonds, 2.20 cts, to trifurcated shoulders, stamped "18ct", finger size N.

c1900

£800-1,200 **HAMG**

A late Victorian ruby and diamond three stone ring, the central hexagonal-cut ruby claw set with an old brilliant cut diamond to either side, diamonds 0.50 cts, finger size O.

c1900

£2,000-2,500 **HAMG**

A pair of mid-Victorian blue enamel and diamond earrings, the blue guilloche enamel ground highlighted with a web of rose-cut diamonds, suspended from a blue enamel and rose-cut diamond terminal.

c1860

£1,200-1,800 **HAMG**

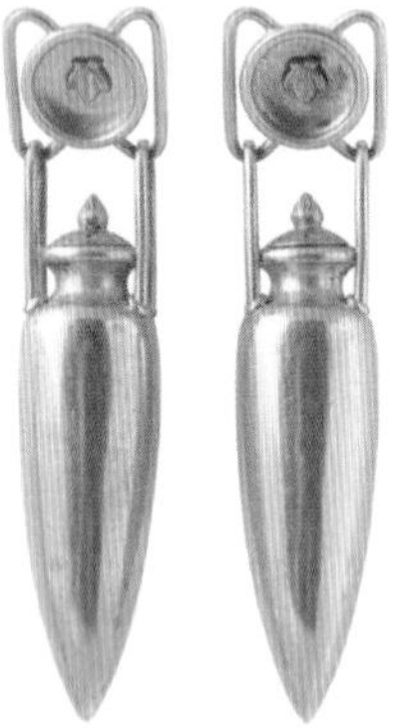

A pair of mid-Victorian Classical Revival gold ear pendants, by Robert Phillips, designed as amphora drops with opening hinged tops, suspended from disc terminals, signed "RP" to the reverse and stamped "18".

c1860

£1,500-2,000 **HAMG**

A CLOSER LOOK AT A CARTIER CORSAGE JEWEL

The Cartier name makes this piece instantly attractive and desirable. The company was established c1850 in Paris and by the turn of the century, Louis Cartier, the grandson of the founder, was internationally known for his precious jewellery.

The diamond and platinum combination exemplifies Cartier garland jewellery of the period. The platinum is woven extremely finely to maximize the sparkle from the diamonds.

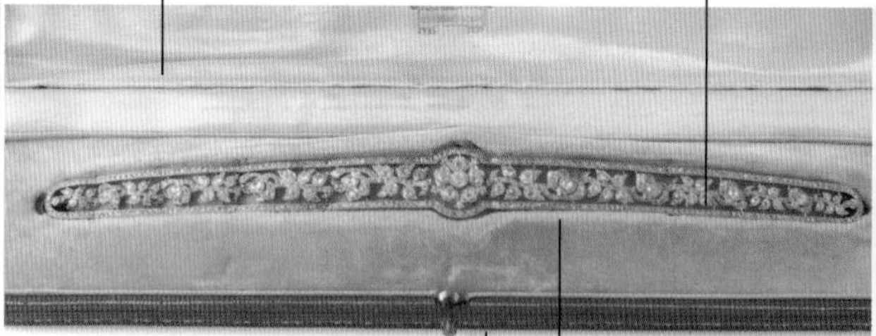

The fitted pink leather and gold tooled case, dating from between 1909 and 1917, adds to the appeal.

The piece oozes elegance, luxury and prestige and has been finely worked.

A Cartier garland-style diamond and platinum bandeau and corsage jewel, set with old brilliant-cut diamonds, with a border of millegrain-set rose-cut diamonds, with fittings for use as a corsage jewel, in a leather box, marked "Cartier London, Paris and New York".

c1910

£30,000-35,000 **HAMG**

A pair of mid-Victorian coral ear pendants, the carved coral drops suspended from similarly carved terminals in gold wire work mounts.

c1870

£500-800 **HAMG**

A pair of Victorian diamond cluster earrings, the central old brilliant-cut diamonds set above a surround of ten smaller old brilliant-cut diamonds, 2.60 cts, mounted in gold backed silver.

c1890

£2,000-2,500 **HAMG**

A silver gilt and red enamel and half-pearl belt buckle, by Michael Perchin for Carl Fabergé, signed "Faberge" in Cyrillic, Cyrillic mark "M.P." for Michael Perchin, 88 kokoshnik assay marks for St. Petersburg 1899-1908, assay master "Ja.L." for Jakov Ljapunov.

Provenance: *Accompanied by a letter of authenticity from Wartski dated 26th October 1965.*

3in (7.5cm) wide

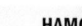

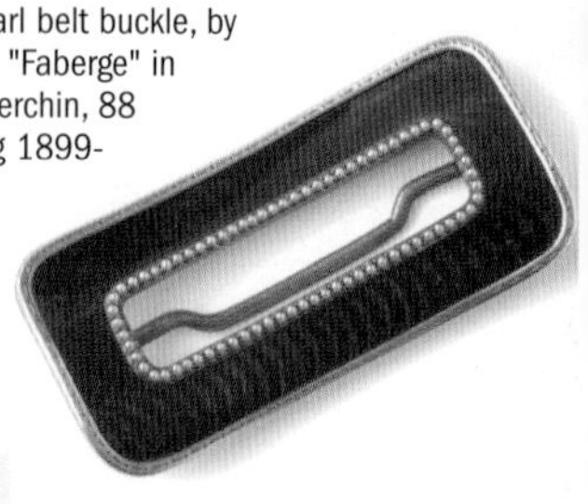

£5,000-8,000 **HAMG**

CARL POUL PETERSEN

- Carl Poul Petersen was born in Denmark in 1895.
- He was apprenticed to Georg Jensen in Copenhagen. His workmanship, learned from Jensen, is of high quality. Based on traditional techniques, the simplicity and modernism of his forms are highlighted with areas of naturalistic ornamentation.
- In 1929 Petersen emigrated to Montreal, Canada. He was employed by Henry Birks & Son but soon opened his own studio 'C. P. Petersen and Sons', which with the help of his sons Arno, John Paul and Ole, remained in operation until 1975. Demand for his solid silver tea and dessert services, plates, bar accessories, serving platters and chandeliers as wedding gifts was huge.
- Scandinavian design was particularly fashionable in Canada during the 1950s and 1960s.
- All Petersen pieces are sought after today. Larger pieces such as tazzas or serving bowls command prices in the range of £1,000-2,000 ($1,500-3,000), depending on size and design.
- The ongoing comparison with Georg Jensen makes Petersen's smaller pieces, especially jewellery, sell for far less than the equivalent Jensen type.
- Petersen died in 1977 in Montreal, Canada.

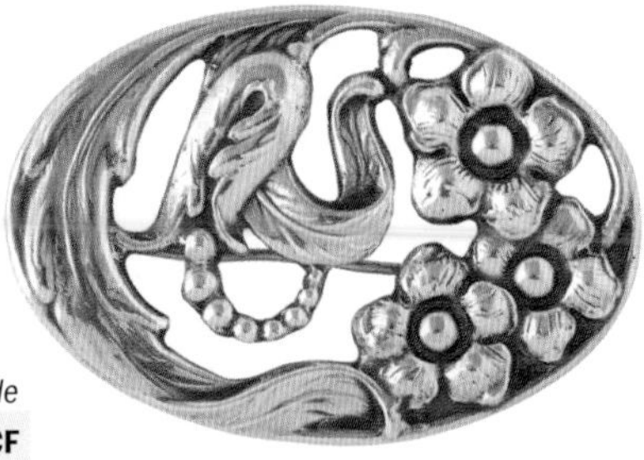

A Petersen pin, with three flowers and a curling leaf.

3.25in (8cm) wide

£220-280 **TCF**

A Petersen pin, with curling fish.

2.5in (6cm) wide

£120-180 **TCF**

An oval Petersen pin of two leaves with berries.

1.5in (4cm) wide

£120-180 **TCF**

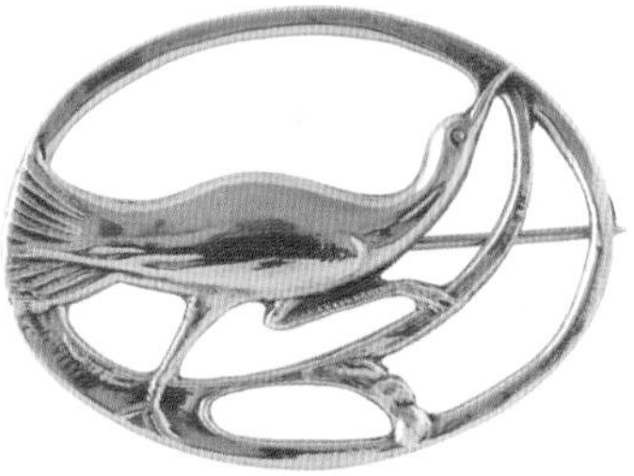

A Petersen of Montreal Handmade Sterling pin, of a leaping bird with raised head, stamped with monogram mark and "HANDMADE STERLING" on the back.

2.5in (6cm) wide

£200-250 **TCF**

A Petersen pin of a swordfish leaping out of the sea.

2.25in (5.5cm) diam

£200-250 **TCF**

A Petersen pin, with moulded floral and foliate decoration.

2in (5cm) diam

£120-180 **TCF**

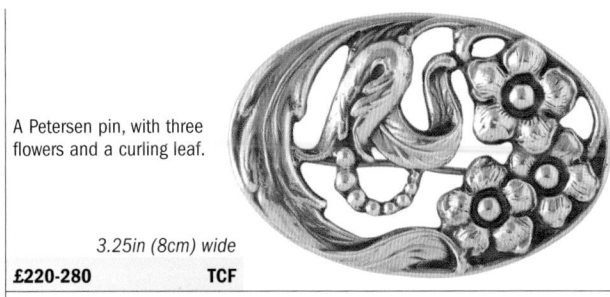

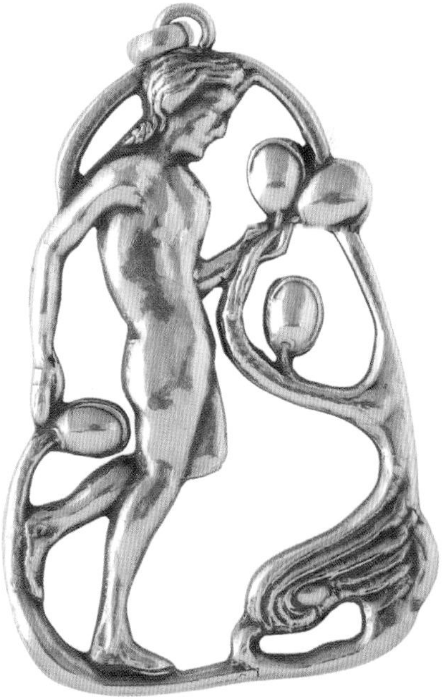

A Petersen pendant, depicting a lady near a stylized tree.

This piece is unusual for Petersen as it depicts a figure rather than a foliate design.

2.5in (6cm) high

£300-350 **TCF**

A Georg Jensen silver brooch with Art Nouveau floral patterns, with malachite cabochons and a coral drop pendant.

c1905 *2.5in (6.5cm) high*

£5,000-8,000 **SF**

A Georg Jensen designed silver brooch with a drop pendant in the form of an acorn in amber.

c1905 *4.5in (11.5cm) high*

£7,000-10,000 **SF**

A Georg Jensen silver brooch with three oval onyx panels and an onyx drop pendant.

c1910 *2in (5cm) wide*

£3,000-5,000 **SF**

A Georg Jensen silver brooch, with three drop pendants in the form of acorns.

c1940 *4in (10cm) high*

£11,000-13,000 **SF**

A Child & Child enamelled butterfly brooch, decorated in enamel, with maker's trade mark, contained in a fitted case stamped "Child & Child..."

2.25in (6cm) wide

£400-600 **L&T**

A 20thC butterfly pin, gold, open-work brooch in the shape of a butterfly, with ten cabochons and 88 diamonds.

1.5in (4cm) wide

£500-800 **KAU**

An Art Nouveau brooch, formed as two grotesque dolphins with enamel decoration, with cut diamonds and small diamond eyes, with fitted case by Lavender.

1.5in (4cm) wide

£1,800-2,200 **WW**

An enamelled pendant, by Charles Horner, in two shades of lilac to a trace link chain, marked "C.H." and hallmarked for Chester.

1912 *1.5in (4cm) high*

£400-600 **WW**

A Tiffany Studios leaded glass dragonfly pendant, the filigreed wings with panels of fractured glass, suspended from original metal chain, unmarked.

pendant 10in (25.5cm) wide

£2,000-3,000 **DRA**

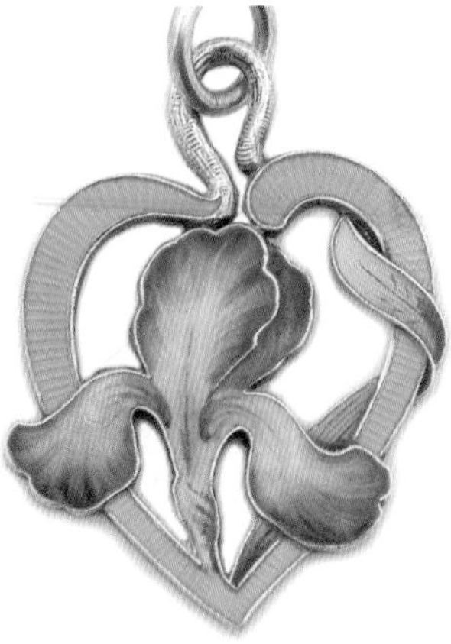

An Art Nouveau enamelled pendant, in the form of an iris in a blue heart surround, unmarked.

1.5in (4cm) high

£300-500 **WW**

An Art Nouveau pendant, of foliate scroll form, set overall with graduated circular- and rose-cut diamonds on silver and gold, centred with an emerald and suspending a pearl.

1.75in (4.5cm) wide

£600-900 **WW**

A Georg Jensen 'Pansy' necklace, with hollow green cabochons, fastening clip to the largest cabochon.

£2,500-3,000 **SF**

A Georg Jensen 18ct gold necklace with pearl cabochons, repoussé-moulded with lily and fan shapes, stamped "750".

7.75in (20cm) diam

£3,000-4,000 **SF**

A French Art Nouveau necklace, cast gold and chased, and carved with roses and set with pearls.

c1900 *1in (2.5cm) drop*

£1,000-1,500 **NBLM**

A French Art Nouveau necklace set with pearls.

c1900 *1in (2.5cm) drop*

£1,500-2,000 **NBLM**

An Art Nouveau nurse's buckle, with a gilt metal back, the front inlaid with enamels, fashioned as two flowers and foliage within a turquoise cartouche.

£15-30 **BIG**

An Art Nouveau emerald and diamond ring, with trap-cut emerald claw set with an old brilliant-cut diamond and carving depicting Adam and Eve, with old cut diamond accents, finger size P.

£1,500-2,000 **HAMG**

A ruby and diamond Royal Welsh Fusiliers regimental brooch, of the rampant dragon, set with calibre-cut ruby wings and body, with old cut diamond spine details.

The rampant dragon was the regimental emblem of the Royal Welsh Fusiliers. This brooch was commissioned from Messrs Tessiers, 26 New Bond Street, London, with a second example given to Queen Mary. This brooch was a gift from Sir Charles Dobell to his wife, on his appointment as colonel of the the Royal Welsh Fusiliers in 1926. The second example is thought to be still in the Royal Collection.

1926

£7,000-10,000 **HAMG**

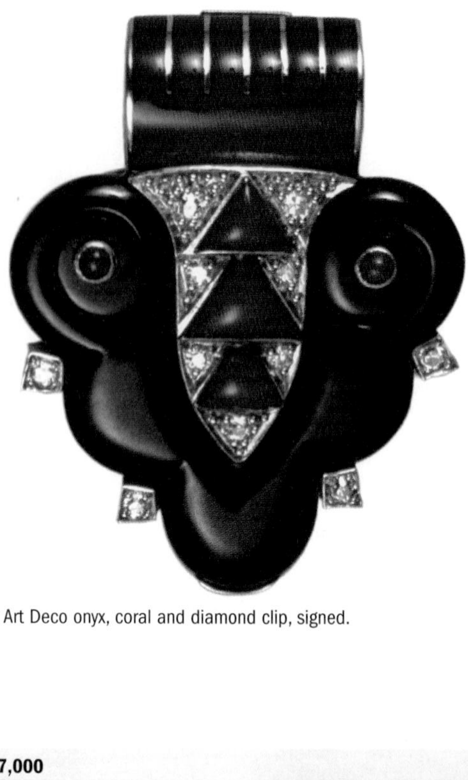

A Cartier Art Deco onyx, coral and diamond clip, signed.

£5,000-7,000 **JES**

An Art Deco diamond-set clip, set overall with circular-cut diamonds in platinum, fitted case by Mappin & Webb.

1.25in (3cm) long

£1,200-1,800 **WW**

An Art Deco diamond and sapphire scroll brooch, set with graduated circular-cut diamonds with baguette, circular and tapered baguette sapphires, millegrain set in platinum.

2in (5cm) high

£1,800-2,200 **WW**

An Art Deco jadeite and diamond brooch, the jadeite plaque carved to depict flowerheads and foliage to palmette terminals set with old brilliant- and eight-cut diamonds.

c1930

£500-800 **HAMG**

A 1940s ruby and diamond clip brooch, designed as an abstract tied ribbon, with a central scroll of pavé-set old brilliant-cut diamonds and calibre-cut ruby accents, one ruby missing.

£700-1,000 **HAMG**

A 1950s diamond ear clip by Boucheron, designed as a four petal flower with a central band of eight-cut diamonds, signed "Boucheron Paris" and numbered "96?310" with French pioncon assay marks.

£200-300 **HAMG**

An abstract flower brooch by Hermes of Paris, with textured petals and stem, signed "Hermes Paris" with French pioncon control marks.

c1960

£500-800 **HAMG**

An Art Deco Marcel Boucher retro bird brooch, in rose gold wash over sterling, with ruby stones across wings and pavé accents, old "MB" mark.

c1935 *4in (10cm) wide*

£300-400 **DD**

A late 1930s Art Deco Marcel Boucher sterling retro bird brooch, in gold wash, with slight wear, clear pavé accents on wing and head flume, emerald stones across wings, old "MB" mark.

3.75in (9.5cm) high

£300-400 **DD**

A 1930s Art Deco Marcel Boucher retro sterling brooch, with blue topaz emerald -cut centre stone and clear pavé accents, old "MB" mark.

3in (7.5cm) high

£300-400 **DD**

A late 1930s American Art Deco Boucher sterling floral brooch, gold washed with citrine baguette rhinestones, in a rhodium setting with clear pavé accents, signed.

2.5in (6.5cm) high

£300-400 **DD**

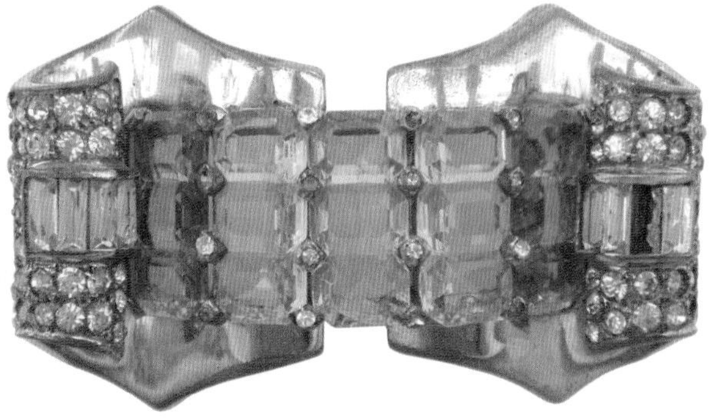

A late 1930s Art Deco Marcel Boucher sterling retro brooch, with blue topaz-coloured stones, and pavé clear rhinestone accents, old "MB" mark.

2.25in (5.5cm) wide

£300-400 **DD**

A very rare late 1930s Marcel Boucher sterling silver retro duette brooch, separating into two fur clips, with emerald rhinestones and clear accents, old MB mark.

Marcel Boucher (1937-72) started his career at Cartier and moved into costume jewellery after the Wall Street Crash of 1929 reduced demand for expensive jewellery.

3.5in (9cm) wide

£700-1,000 **DD**

A 1930s Boucher Art Deco dangle fur clip, in a gold washed fan design with snake chain dangles, rhodium setting with clear pavé accents, signed "MB".

3.5in (9cm) high

£150-200 **DD**

A late 1930s Art Deco Boucher fur clip, with invisible set sapphire rhinestones and clear pavé accents, in rhodium setting, old "MB" mark.

1.5in (4cm) wide

£600-800 **DD**

A late 1930s Art Deco Boucher retro fur clip and earring set, with invisible set ruby rhinestones and clear pavé accents in a rhodium setting, signed and old "MB" marks.

brooch 1.5in (4cm) high

£600-800 **DD**

An American Pennino Art Deco watch brooch, with pavé set clear rhinestones set in sterling, signed "Pennino".

c1935

£400-600 **DD**

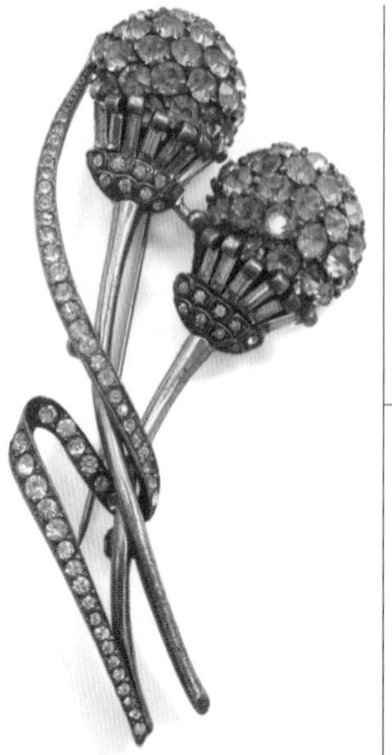

An American Pennino Art Deco dandelion brooch, with a rose goldwash, blue flower rhinestones, clear accents, signed "Pennino, sterling".

c1945 *4in (10cm) high*

£400-600 **DD**

An American Pennino Art Deco floral brooch, with bright silver finish and blue topaz-coloured flower rhinestones, invisible settings, signed "Pennino, sterling".

1940s *3.75in (9.5cm) high*

£400-600 **DD**

An American Pennino Art Deco floral brooch and clip earring set, blue topaz coloured floral stones set with ruby and clear accents in a highly polished sterling setting, signed "Pennino, sterling".

c1945 *brooch 3.35in (9.5cm) high*

£280-320 **DD**

An Art Deco Nettie Rosenstein retro ballerina fur clip, in rose goldwash over sterling with clear pavé rhinestones, double prong fur clip back, signed "Nettie Rosenstein, Sterling".

c1945 *3.25 (8.5cm) high*

£220-280 **DD**

An Art Deco Nettie Rosenstein butterfly fur clip, enamel and rose goldwash over sterling, signed "Nettie Rosenstein, Sterling".

c1945 *4in (10cm) wide*

£600-900 **DD**

An Art Deco Nettie Rosenstein octopus brooch, sterling with rose goldwash, emerald rhinestones and moonstone head.

c1945 *3.35in (8.5cm) wide*

£600-800 **DD**

An Art Deco Nettie Rosenstein retro cuff bracelet and shoulder brooch, in rose goldwash over sterling, with pavé accents over dimensional feathers, signed "Nettie Rosenstein, Sterling".

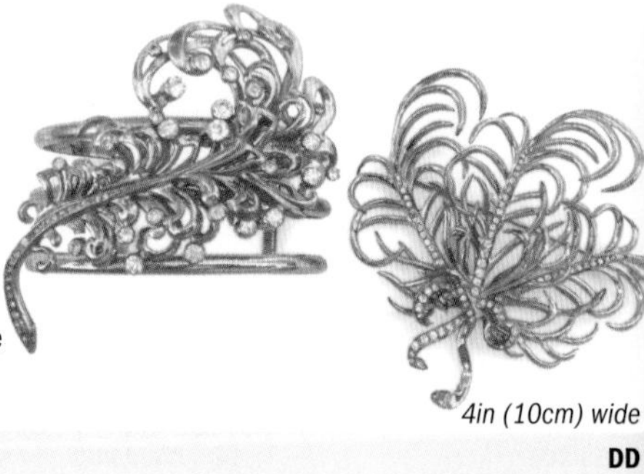

c1945 *4in (10cm) wide*

£500-700 **DD**

A 1930s Art Deco Trifari moonstone brooch, with small sapphires and pavé set in Rhodium, unsigned.

1930s *2in (5cm) high*

£700-1,000 **DD**

A 1930s Art Deco Trifari flower basket brooch, with all clear rhinestones in rhodium setting, signed "Trifari".

£220-280 **DD**

A CLOSER LOOK AT A TRIFARI JELLY BELLY POODLE BROOCH

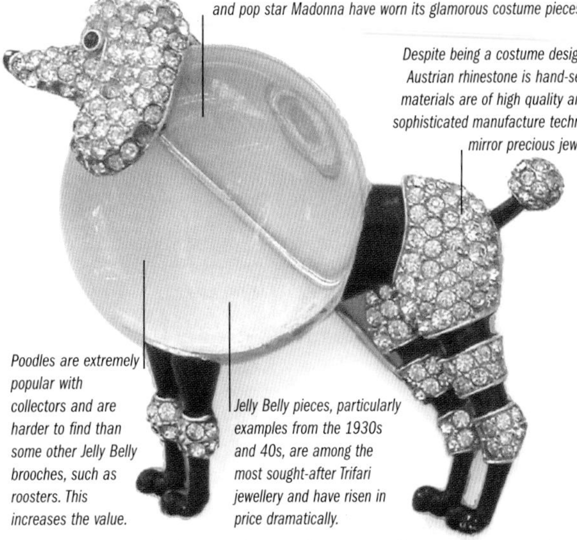

Trifari jewellery is extremely popular and since the company's foundation c1910, celebrities such as First Lady Mamie Eisenhower and pop star Madonna have worn its glamorous costume pieces.

Despite being a costume design, the Austrian rhinestone is hand-set, the materials are of high quality and the sophisticated manufacture techniques mirror precious jewellery.

Poodles are extremely popular with collectors and are harder to find than some other Jelly Belly brooches, such as roosters. This increases the value.

Jelly Belly pieces, particularly examples from the 1930s and 40s, are among the most sought-after Trifari jewellery and have risen in price dramatically.

A 1930s Art Deco Trifari poodle brooch, designed by Alfred Philippe, with lucite jelly belly, rhodium plated with enamel and rhinestones, signed.

2.25in (5.5cm) wide

£1,200-1,800 **DD**

A 1930s Trifari Art Deco bow brooch, in stylized floral design within bow, all clear stones, unsigned.

3in (7.5cm) wide

£180-220 **DD**

A 1940s Trifari Art Deco small poodle brooch, with various shaped clear rhinestones, signed.

1.75in (4.5cm) wide

£70-100 **DD**

A 1940s Art Deco Trifari small poodle brooch, with large round red ruby rhinestone belly, sterling setting, signed.

1.75in (4.5cm) wide

£70-100 **DD**

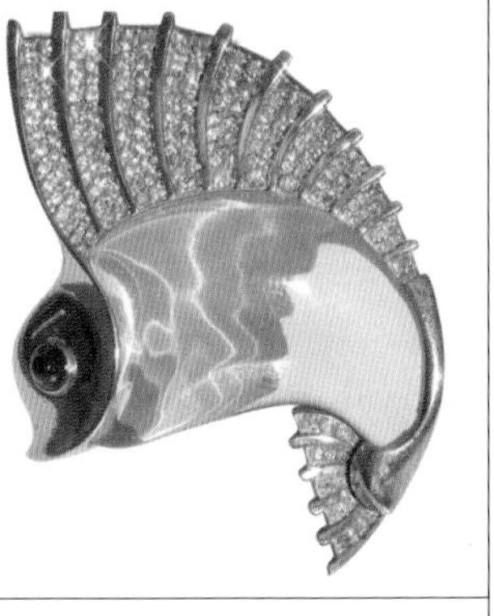

An Art Deco Trifari Jelly belly fur clip, by Bel Geddes, goldwashed with pavé rhinestones, cabochon eye and lucite jelly belly, signed with patent.

This is the only piece of jewellery industrial designer Norman Bel Geddes ever designed.

1941 *3.75in (9.5cm) high*

£1,000-1,500 **DD**

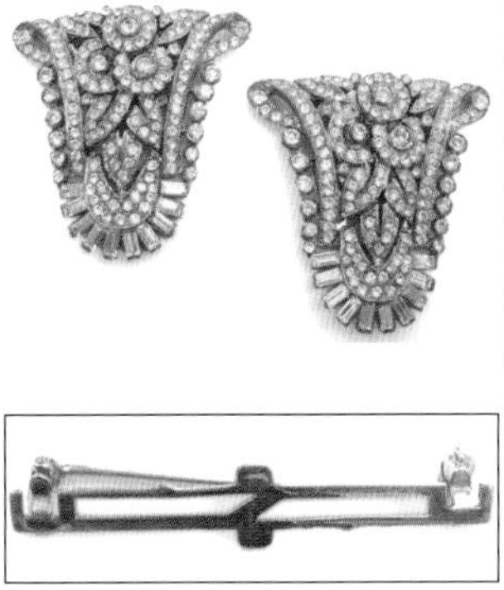

A 1930s Art Deco Trifari stylized floral duette pair of clips/brooch, with rhodium set clear rhinestones, signed "Trifari Clipmates".

1930s *3in (7.5cm) wide*

£500-700 **DD**

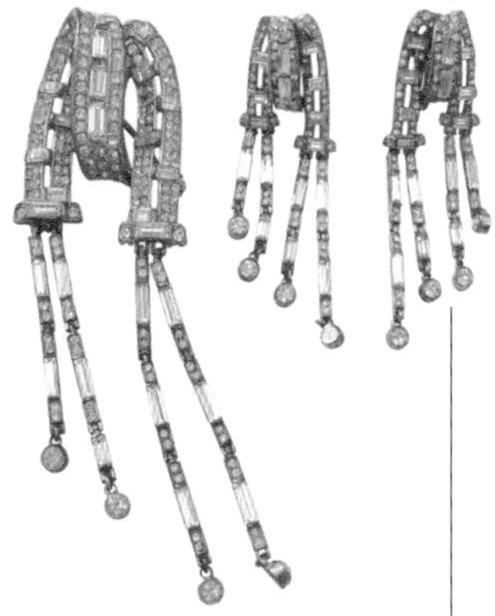

An Art Deco Trifari dangle-style brooch and earrings set, with clear rhinestones set in Sterling silver, the earrings with screw backs, signed "TRIFARI, STERLING".

c1930 *brooch 3.5in (9cm) high*

£300-500 **DD**

A 1930s Art Deco Trifari duette pair of clips/brooch, in moonstone and clear rhinestones, signed "Trifari Clipmates".

3.5in (9cm) wide

£600-800 **DD**

A rare 1930s early Chanel palm tree brooch, in enamel with rhinestone baguettes set in gold-plated pot metal, signed with the early 'Chanel' script signature on back.

c1935 *3in (7.5cm) high*

£1,800-2,200 **DD**

A rare 1930s early Chanel poured glass brooch, with Gripoix stones set with rhinestones in pot metal, signed.

2.25in (5.5cm) wide

£1,000-1,500 **DD**

An Art Deco Corocraft gold-plated poodle pin, in gold over sterling with pavé rhinestones, signed.

c1945 *2.5in (6.5cm) wide*

£120-180 **DD**

A late 1930s Art Deco DeRosa brooch, in enamel with rhinestones, over gold-plated pot metal, signed 'Derosa'.

5in (12.5cm) high

£1,200-1,800 **DD**

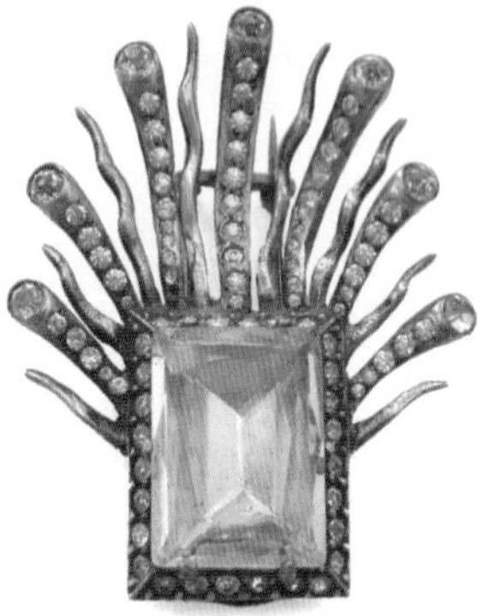

A 1930s Art Deco Eisenberg Original sterling double prong fur clip, of sunburst style with large emerald cut aquamarine stone, signed "Eisenberg Original".

2.25in (5.5cm) high

£300-400 **DD**

A rare 1930s Art Deco early Hobe cuff bracelet, brooch and ring set, with hand-wired brass filigree setting and sapphire and clear rhinestones.

brooch 2.25in (5.5cm) wide

£1,200-1,800 **DD**

A 1940s Art Deco Joseff of Hollywood tassel brooch, with pear shaped sapphire rhinestones in a matte brass setting.

6in (15cm) high

£300-400 **DD**

A late 1930s Art Deco Sandor floral shoulder brooch, in goldwash over pot metal, with enamel and rhinestones, signed "Sandor".

4.25in (11cm) high

£300-500 **DD**

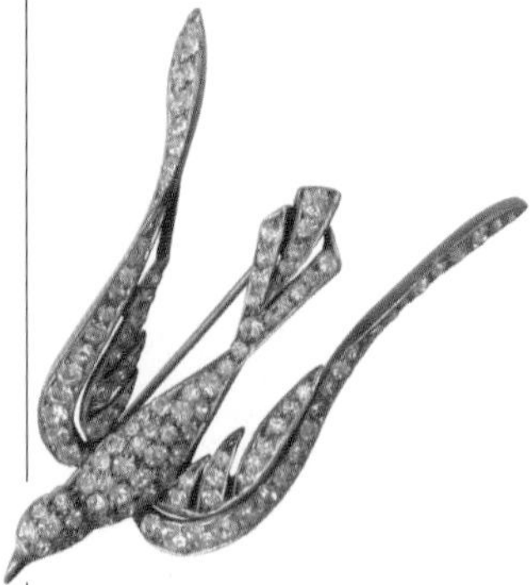

A 1920s French Art Deco paste stylized bird brooch, in sterling.

2.5in (6.5cm) wide

£300-400 **DD**

A 1930s Art Deco figural dancer brooch, in style of Josephine Baker with her famous banana skirt, with rhinestones and enamel over gold-plated pot metal, unsigned, probably French.

3.25in (8.5cm) wide

£600-800 **DD**

A 1930s French Egyptian-style Art Deco figural brooch, with Phoenix, Pharoah and Cleopatra, in silver over brass, with faceted ruby rhinestones, clear rhinestones and turquoise cabochon stones, enamel details.

4.75in (12cm) high

£700-1,000 **DD**

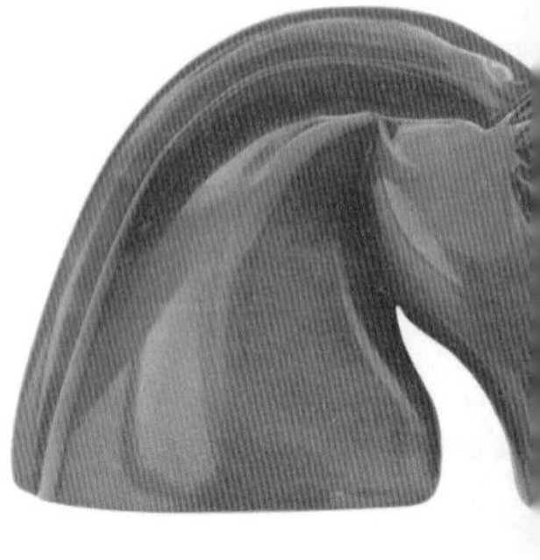

A 1930s early American Art Deco bakelite horse brooch, highly polished, glued on a pin back.

2.25in (5.5cm) high

£200-300 **DD**

WILLIAM SPRATLING

- Spratling (1900-1967) is known as 'The Father of Mexican Silver'.
- Born in New York, Spratling trained as an architect before becoming a lecturer and writer. He moved in artistic circles and was friends with contemporaries such as William Faulkner.
- In 1929, Spratling relocated to Mexico and in 1931 he began to design jewellery and other decorative items, near the site of silver mines in Taxco. He soon employed a number of trained silversmiths to produce his work.
- Pre-Columbian Mexican design inspired early forms.
- His Taxco company ceased to trade in 1946. After working on a project with Alaskan artists in the late 1940s, pieces became influenced by Alaskan design.
- During the 1960s, Spratling developed his interests in archaeology and these forms began to inspire his work.
- From c1933, pieces were often signed with a stylized "WS".
- He died in an accident in 1967.

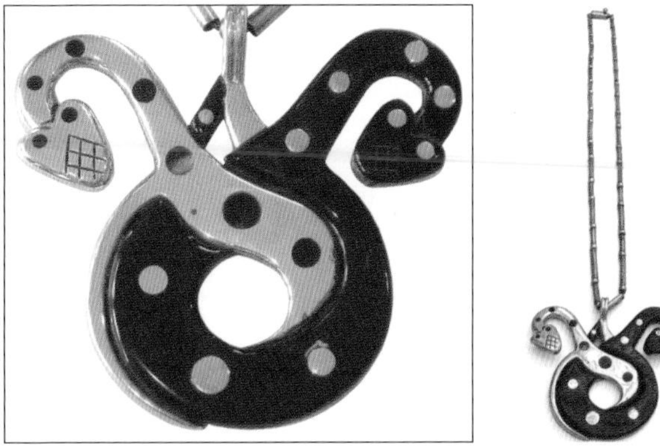

A 1940s Art Deco William Spratling circular serpent necklace, in tortoiseshell and sterling silver, signed.

1940s *2.75in (7cm) wide*

£5,000-7,000 **DD**

A 1940s Art Deco William Spratling twisted serpent necklace, in tortoiseshell and sterling silver, signed.

3in (7.5cm) long

£5,000-7,000 **DD**

A rare Art Deco/Modernist William Spratling necklace, of alternating tortoiseshell and silver domed disc design.

18in (45.5cm) long

£4,000-6,000 **DD**

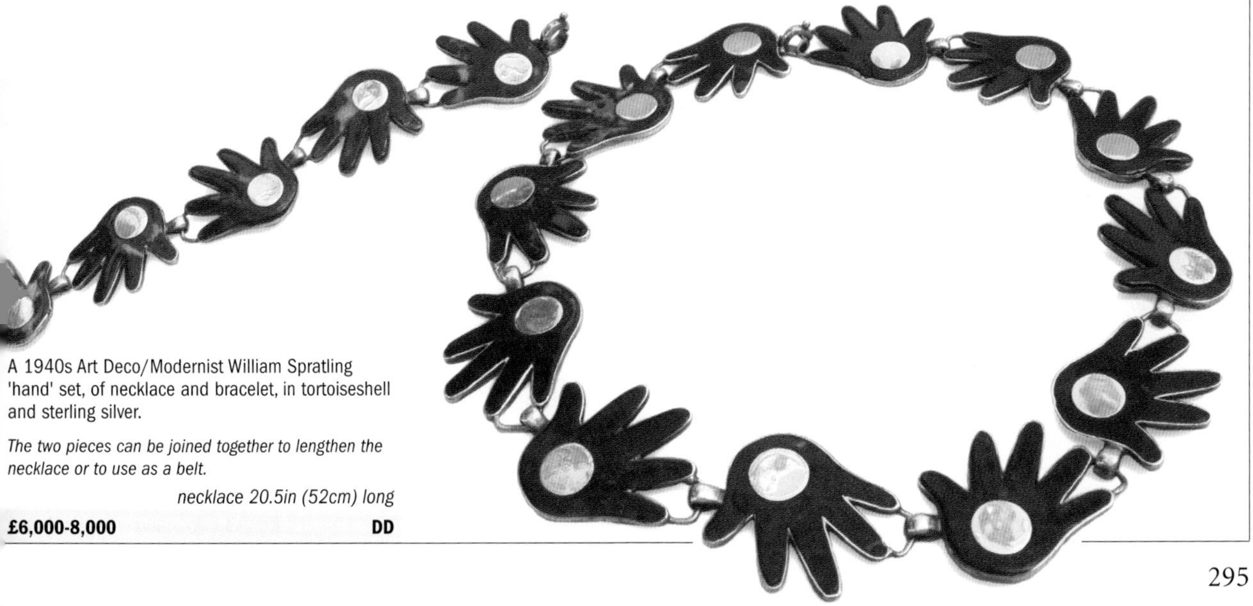

A 1940s Art Deco/Modernist William Spratling 'hand' set, of necklace and bracelet, in tortoiseshell and sterling silver.

The two pieces can be joined together to lengthen the necklace or to use as a belt.

necklace 20.5in (52cm) long

£6,000-8,000 **DD**

A 1940s Art Deco Marcel Boucher set, comprising necklace, bracelet and clip earrings, in peridot green and clear rhinestones set in rhodium, all pieces signed.

1940s *bracelet 6.75in (17cm)*

£700-1,000 **DD**

A rare 1940s Art Deco Miriam Haskell choker, with gilt plated half moons covered in rhinestones and baroque pearl dangles, signed.

15in (38cm) long

£1,000-1,500 **DD**

A French Art Deco Lacloche Freres enamelled minaudiere, in the form of a caricature of Enrico Caruso, signed "Lacloche Freres Paris" with facsimile of Caruso's signature.

The term 'minaudiere' refers to a small, hard-bodied purse. Born in Naples, Italy, Enrico Caruso (1873-1921) was one of the most famous tenors in the history of opera.

c1925 *4.5in (12cm) high*

£3,000-£4,000 **JES**

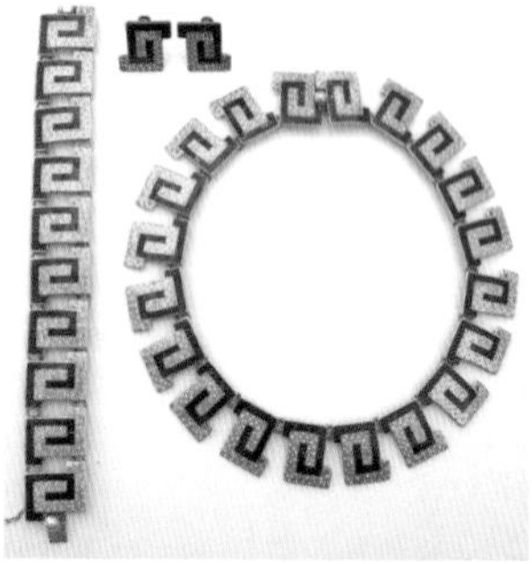

A 1940s Art Deco Margot Greek key demi-parure, comprising necklace, bracelet and earrings, in mosaic enamel over sterling, made in Mexico.

1940s *necklace 15in (38cm) long*

£1,800-2,200 **DD**

A 1940s Art Deco Margot trapezoid demi-parure, comprising necklace, bracelet and earrings, white enamel over sterling, made in Mexico.

necklace 15in (38cm) long

£1,800-2,200 **DD**

A Canadian Sherman parure, comprising necklace, earrings and bracelet, with ice blue rhinestones and glass beads.

Bracelet 2.75in (7cm) diam

£400-500 **TCF**

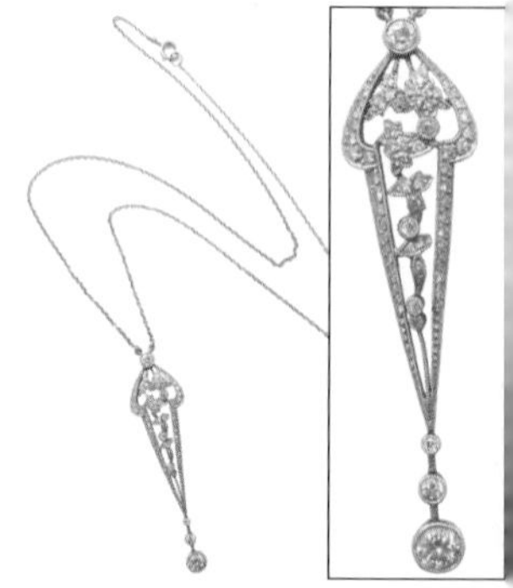

A 1920s American Art Deco lavalliere necklace, in platinum with diamonds.

16in (10.5cm) long

£1,800-2,200 **DD**

A 1920s French Art Deco sautoir, strung on black silk, with a variety of shaped luminous green art glass panels, black jet beads and a tassel.

1920s *32in (81cm) long*

£1,000-1,500 **DD**

An Art Deco pendant, with coral set to a lozenge mount of twenty four old cut diamonds, on an onyx disc with an old cut diamond suspensory loop, attached to a fine link chain.

c1925

£1,500-2,000 **HAMG**

A French Art Deco/Machine Age geometric necklace, with black and lipstick red faceted glass, set in sterling with geometric links, French markings.

c1930 *24in (61cm) long*

£1,000-1,500 **DD**

An Art Deco necklace, with a bold zig-zagging green and black design.

14.25in (36cm) long

£150-250 **PC**

A 1940s French Art Deco glass tassel choker, with tiny luminous amethyst glass beads, opalescent pale white-blue glass beads and opalescent lavender glass beads, rose-gold coloured findings.

necklace 14in (35.5cm) long

£1,000-1,500 **DD**

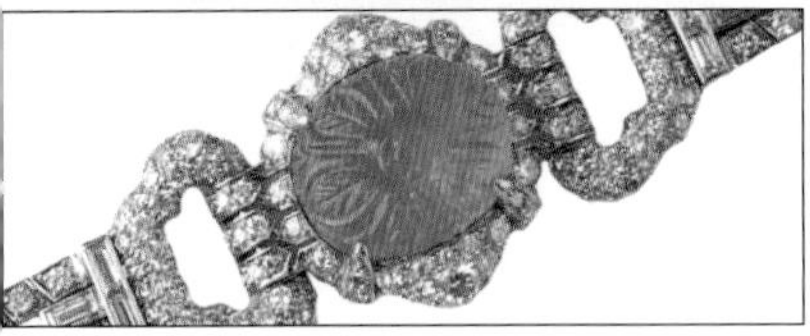

A 1920s to 1930s Birks platinum and 11 carat cut emerald bracelet, with 212 diamonds equalling 6.56 carats, in original box.

£10,000-15,000 **TCF**

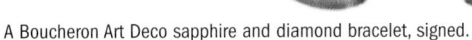

A Boucheron Art Deco sapphire and diamond bracelet, signed.

The Boucheron company was founded in Paris in 1858.

c1930

£20,000-25,000 **JES**

A 1920s American gold-mounted diamond bracelet, with later rhodium finish, comprising seven tableau, each with a large pendeloque brilliant bordered by an Art Deco frame, detachable oval clasp, cased.

£7,000-9,000 **BIG**

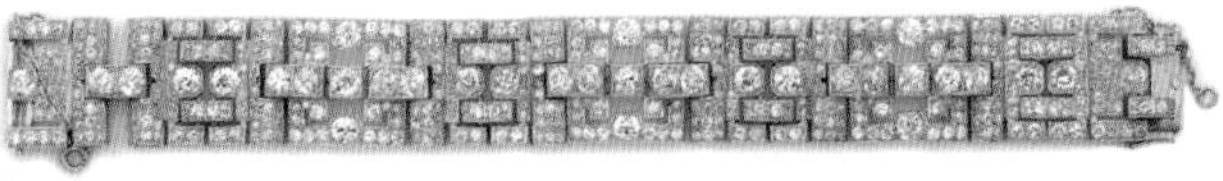

A French Art Deco diamond bracelet, set overall with graduated circular cut diamonds, in platinum, with associated case.

7.25in (18.5cm) long

£8,000-12,000 **WW**

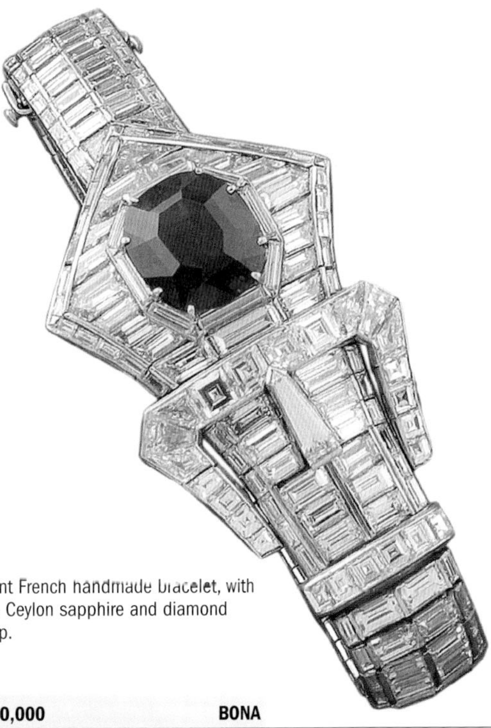

An important French handmade bracelet, with a platinum, Ceylon sapphire and diamond cluster strap.

£30,000-40,000 **BONA**

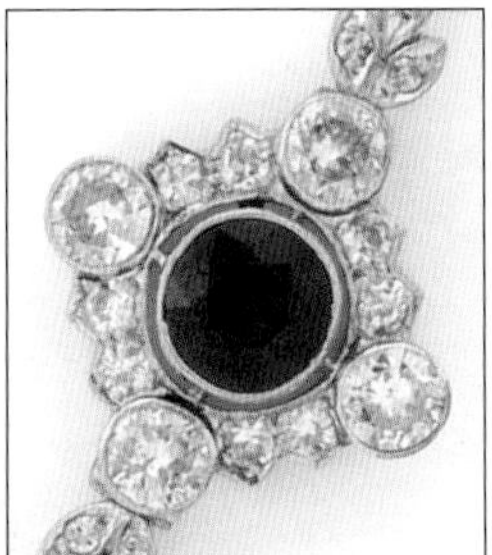

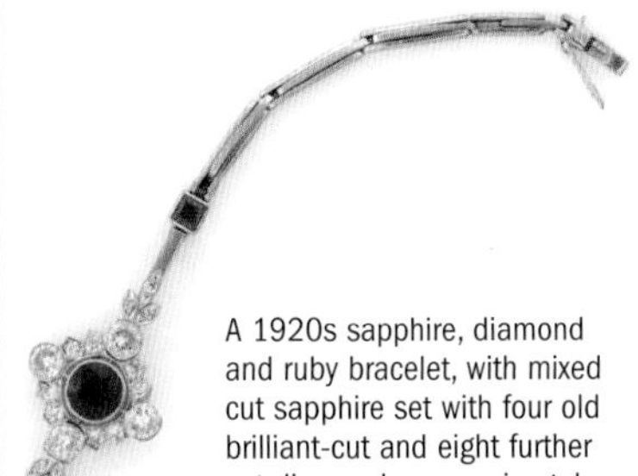

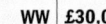

A 1920s sapphire, diamond and ruby bracelet, with mixed cut sapphire set with four old brilliant-cut and eight further cut diamonds, approximately 1.20 cts total, two cut ruby accents, stamped '18ct'.

£800-1,200 **HAMG**

An Art Deco diamond bracelet, with articulated architectonic panels of old brilliant, baguette and eight cut diamonds, approximately 32 carats total, box snap clasp.

c1930 *7in (18cm) long*

£10,000-15,000 **HAMG**

A French Art Deco Auguste Bonaz bracelet, in celluloid, signed.

c1925

£100-150 **JES**

A French Art Deco Auguste Bonaz bracelet, in celluloid.

c1925 *3in (7.5cm) high*

£150-200 **JES**

A French Art Deco Jean Despres geometric bracelet, in black onyx, blue sodalite flat cut stones and French paste rhinestones, set in a silver frame, hallmarked.

1930 *7in (18cm) long*

£1,800-2,200 **DD**

A 1930s Swedish Art Deco Wiwen Nilsson rock crystal and onyx bracelet, set in silver, signed "Wiwen Nilsson", made for Anders Nilsson of Lund Sweden.

2.5in (6cm) diam

£3,000-3,500 **JES**

A 1940s Art Deco Nettie Rosenstein sunburst cuff bracelet, in rose goldwash over sterling, with sapphire cabochon, rose gold snowflake and pavé clear rhinestones, signed "Nettie Rosenstein, Sterling".

2.5in (6.5cm) wide

£300-500 **DD**

An Art Deco Gerard Sandoz bracelet, inlaid with black, grey and red enamels and lacquer, signed "G Rogers Sandoz".

Gerard Sandoz created handmade luxury items, often with geometric Cubist elements.

c1925 *2.25in (5.5cm) wide*

£20,000-25,000 **JES**

A 1940s Art Deco William Spratling silver and tortoiseshell Modernist hinged cuff bracelet, a rare and bold asymmetrical unisex design.

3in (7.5cm) wide.

£5,000-7,000 **DD**

A 1930s Tillander Art Deco Finnish bracelet, in silver with a jade centrepiece, marked "A. Tillander".

2.5in (6.5cm) diam

£3,000-3,500 **JES**

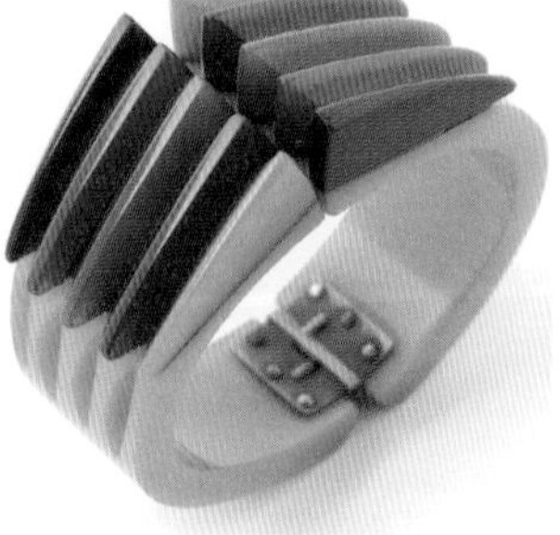

A 1930s American Art Deco bakelite hinged bracelet, in red, green black and orange, known as 'the Philadelphia'.

1930s *1.5in (3.5cm) wide*

£800-1,200 **JES**

A 1930s French Art Deco bakelite hinged cuff bracelet, highly polished with brass decorative disc featuring an oriental symbol.

2.25in (5.5cm) wide

£300-400 **DD**

A 1930s American Art Deco bracelet, with clear pavé, baguettes and ruby oval stones set in rhodium, signed "KTF".

7in (2.75cm) long

£500-700 **DD**

A 1920s American Art Deco ring, mine-cut diamonds set in platinum.

0.75in (2cm) wide

£400-600 **DD**

A 1930s Art Deco platinum diamond cluster ring, mount carved with 3ct diamond J VS2.

0.5in (1.5cm) wide

£20,000-25,000 **NBLM**

An Art Deco diamond ring, with three old brilliant-cut diamonds, approximately 0.60ct total, to a pierced surmount of eight- and rose-cut diamonds, Austrian control marks, finger size L.

c1925

£400-600 **HAMG**

A flawless emerald-cut diamond ring, 3.09ct, D colour.

£40,000-60,000 **BONA**

An Art Deco chrysoberyl catseye and diamond cluster ring, with a border of twenty-eight square-cut diamonds, finger size P.

c1930

£1,200-1,800 **HAMG**

An Art Deco diamond and black onyx ring, set with graduated circular-cut diamonds and a section of black onyx in gold.

0.75in (2cm) high

£400-600 **WW**

ART DECO COSTUME RINGS

A 1940s Art Deco/Modernist William Spratling tortoise and sterling ring, with a sweeping tortoise band held on with four silver rivets as design details, Mexico.

1in (2.5cm) diam

£800-1,200 **DD**

An American Art Deco ring, in marcasite set in sterling with rhinestones and jade.

1.25in (3cm) wide

£60-80 **DD**

A 1930s American Art Deco Modernist ring, in bezel set coral and black onyx with diamonds in 14ct gold setting.

1in (2.5cm) high

£1,000-1,500 **DD**

A late 1930s American Art Deco retro ring, citrine set high in a simple rose gold setting.

1in (2.5cm) wide

£300-500 **DD**

An Art Deco-style pair of earrings, with black jade, 1.50ct diamonds, South Sea pearls and an 18ct white gold setting, for pierced ears.

2in (5cm) high

£4,000-6,000 **DD**

A pair of French Art Deco diamond and black jade earrings, with 1ct diamonds set in white gold.

c1930 *1.25in (3cm) high*

£800-1,200 **DD**

A pair of blue chalcedony and diamond ear studs, the blue chalcedony sugar loaf cabochons set to a border of rose-cut diamonds

£500-700 **HAMG**

A pair of Art Deco diamond earclips, set throughout with marquise, brilliant and eight cut diamonds with baguette cut diamond highlights, approximately 2.50ct in total.

c1935

£2,200-2,800 **HAMG**

A pair of 1940s ruby and diamond earclips, set with a line of calibre cut rubies, flanked by pavé set eight cut diamond accents, set in two colour mounts.

£400-600 **HAMG**

ART DECO WATCHES

A Ladies Art Deco Hamilton watch, with 22 jewel movement, in platinum and diamonds, 1ct total weight.

c1930 *6in (15cm) long*

£2,000-2,500 **DD**

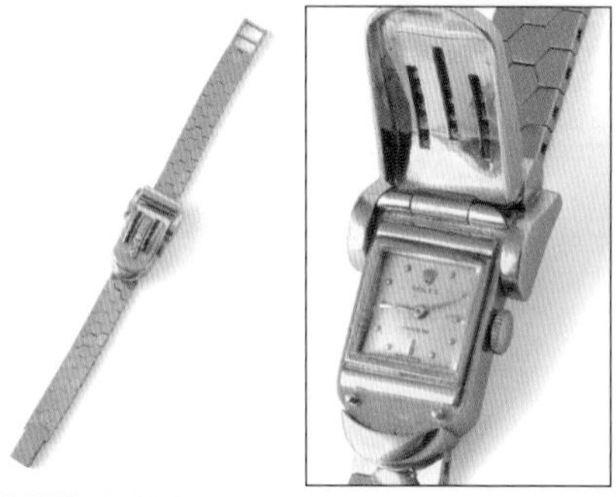

A 1940s lady's Rolex ruby and diamond cocktail watch, with calibre cut rubies and eight cut diamonds, an integral hexacomb 'ludo' style bracelet, dial and jewelled lever movement signed "Rolex", Swiss control marks stamped "0.750-18k", numbered "827".

£1,200-1,800 **HAMG**

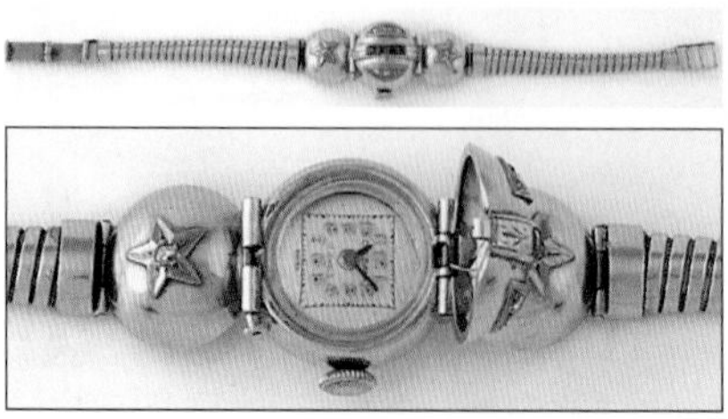

A 1940s 18ct gold ruby cabochon and diamond flip-top watch.

7.75in (19cm) long

£700-900 **SSP**

An Art Deco lady's platinum and diamond canted wristwatch, with eight-cut diamond single line bezel and Swiss 15 jewel tonneau shaped movement, stamped "999 Platinum", on an associated Milanese strap.

£250-300 **DN**

A 1930s American Art Deco compact, in silver with geometric enamel decoration.

2in (5cm) diam

£50-70 **DD**

A German Art Deco compact, decorated with an abstract scene in sterling silver and enamel.

1925 *2.5in (6.5cm) diam*

£400-500 **JES**

A 1930s Art Deco compact, with red and cream zig-zag design, probably German.

3.5in (9cm) diam

£150-200 **JES**

A 1930s Art Deco enamel on aluminium elephant compact, with black details, probably French.

3.5in (9cm) wide

£200-300 **JES**

A 1920s French Art Deco purse set, comprising a compact, perfume atomizer and pill box, in brass with celluloid geometric decoration, signed.

atomizer 2.5in (6.5cm) high

£500-700 **DD**

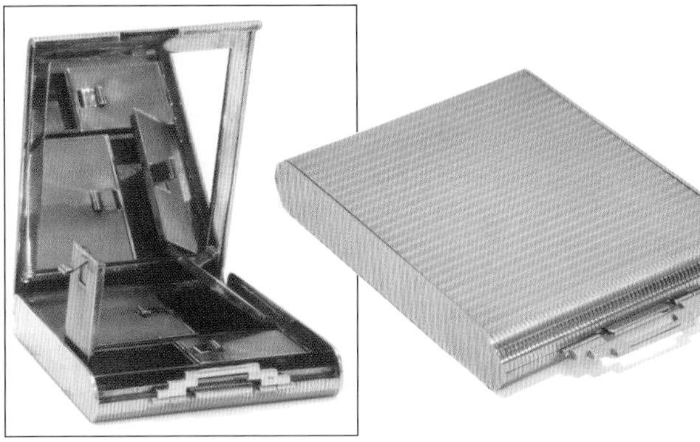

An American Art Deco vanity case, engine turned, in sterling and 14kt gold wash, with stepped clasp and multiple compartments and mirror inside, hallmarked.

c1940 *6in (15cm) high*

£1,200-1,800 **DD**

ART DECO CIGARETTE CASES

An Art Deco Boucheron nephrite box, with enamelled hinges and a diamond single stone catch, signed "Boucheron Paris" with French pioncon assay marks, maker's mark "F B" for Frederic Boucheron.

c1925

£4,000-6,000 **HAMG**

An Art Deco Ramsden and Roed enamel cigarette case, with London hallmark 1931.

7in (18cm) high

£2,000-2,500 **JES**

A Gustave Roger Sandoz and Gerard Sandoz cigarette case, in parcel-silver gilt, lacquer and eggshell lacquer, with a Cubist Parisian street scene, signed, punch marks.

5in (13cm) high

£3,000-4,000 **ISA**

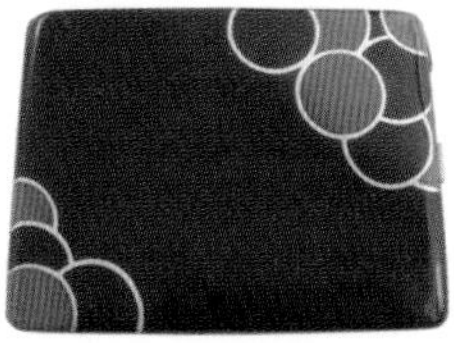

A 1930s French Art Deco cigarette case, with enamel geometric decoration over silver.

4.25in (11cm) wide

£600-800 **DD**

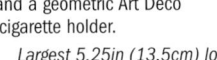

A 1930s American Art Deco red bakelite and rhinestone cigarette holder, and a geometric Art Deco sterling cigarette holder.

Largest 5.25in (13.5cm) long

£50-70 **DD**

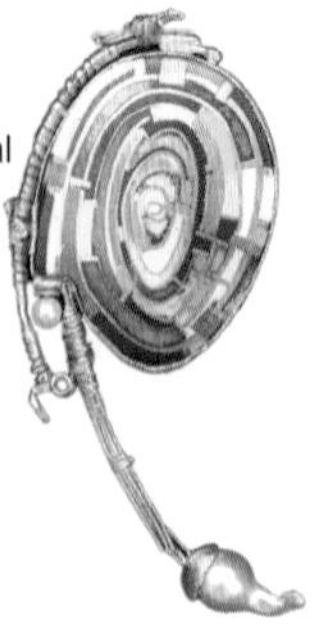

A large William Harper 'Faberge's Seed #5' sculptural brooch, in 14K rose and yellow gold and sterling, with spherical golden pearl and massive baroque pearl, in shaded and polychrome cloisonne, signed, titled and dated.

1992 *5in (12.5cm) high*

£6,000-9,000 **SDR**

A Georg Jensen stylized silver and green enamel frog brooch, by Henning Koppel, with loop to rear, possibly for use as a pendant.

2.25in (6cm) wide

£600-900 **SF**

A large William Harper 'The Firebird' sculptural brooch, in 14ct rose and yellow gold and sterling, with baroque pearl and polychrome cloisonne, with gold cloisons, signed, titled and dated.

American designer William Harper (b.1944) is known for his distinctive and unusual sculptural jewellery. His work has featured in many major exhibitions.

1994 *5in (12.5cm) wide*

£7,000-10,000 **SDR**

A Georg Jensen abstract silver pin, by Henning Koppel, with blue enamel decoration, back stamped "HK".

c1945 *2in (5cm) wide*

£400-500 **SF**

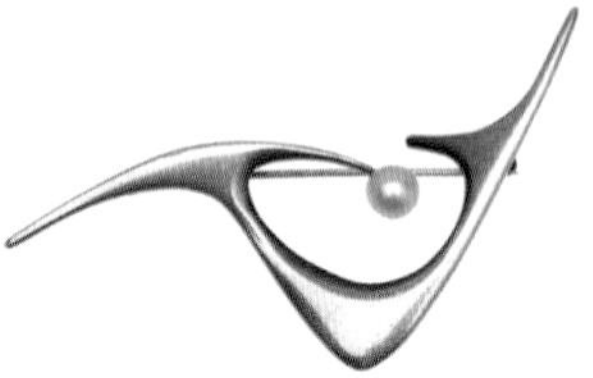

An Ed Wiener biomorphic brooch, in sterling with pearl, stamped "Ed Wiener".

3in (7.5cm) wide

£500-700 **SDR**

MODERNIST NECKLACES

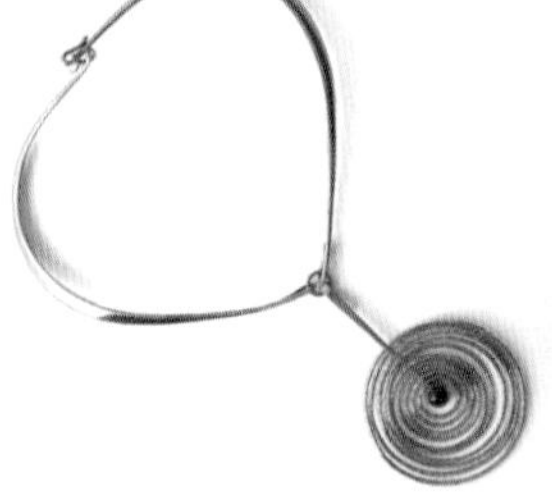

A Georg Jensen silver necklace with pendant, by Nana Dietzel, stamped.

Pendant 2.75in (7cm) wide

£2,500-3,000 **SF**

A 1960s Georg Jensen silver 'Torun' necklace and pendant, stamped "Torun" with angel hair resinous stone.

6in (15cm) wide

£3,000-3,500 **SF**

MODERNIST GEORG JENSEN

- Georg Jensen (1866-1935) founded his silver company in Copenhagen in 1904. He soon became known for his simple, modern and beautifully crafted household objects and jewellery. Significantly influencing modern design, his forward-looking older pieces are very valuable today.
- The Georg Jensen company continued to produce well-made and understated pieces beyond Jensen's death. Modern pieces continued the Jensen tradition of simple, organic forms in high quality silver.
- Many celebrated modern designers, such as Harald Nielsen and Arne Jacobsen, have worked for the firm over the years.
- Henning Koppel (1918-1981) produced a wide variety of designs for Georg Jensen. Known as a radical Modernist, his pieces were typically biomorphic and unadorned.
- The company continues to produce fine silver jewellery and other objects today.

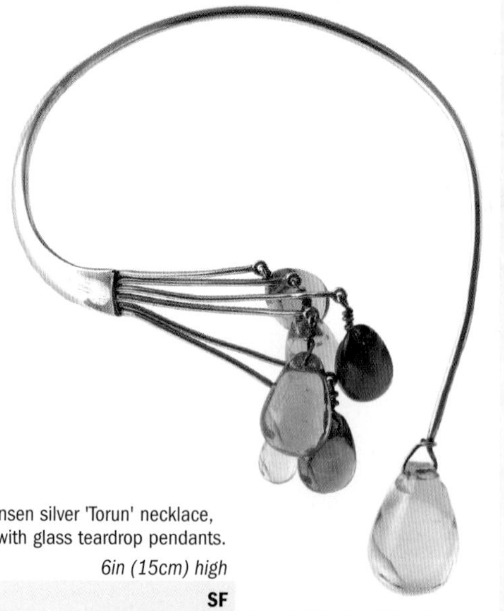

A 1960s Georg Jensen silver 'Torun' necklace, stamped "Torun", with glass teardrop pendants.

1960s *6in (15cm) high*

£4,000-5,000 **SF**

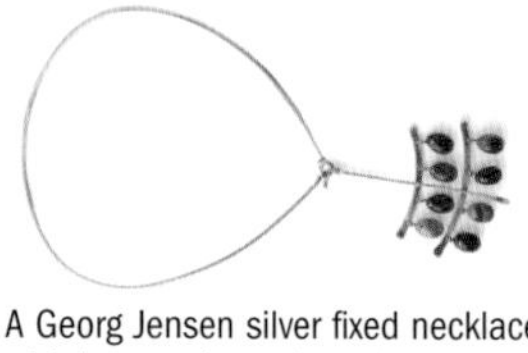

A Georg Jensen silver fixed necklace, with bars and amethyst drop pendant.

10.25in (26cm) high

£3,000-4,000 **SF**

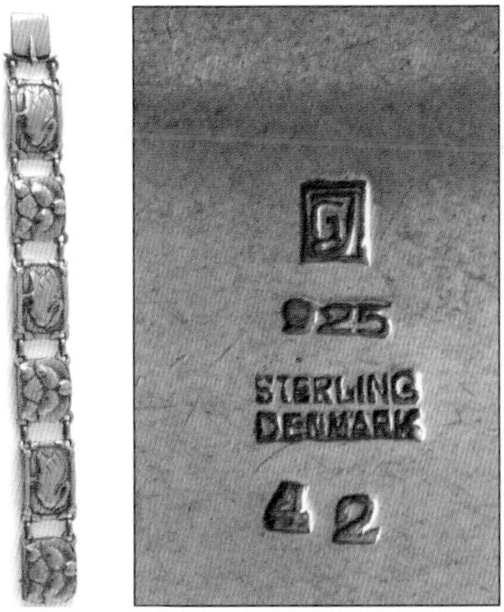

A 1930s Georg Jensen rectangular silver bracelet, with alternate repoussé decoration of swans and leaves, with stylized Georg Jensen mark.

c1935 *7.25in (18.5cm) long*

£1,200-1,800 **SF**

A 1950s Georg Jensen silver curving bracelet, by Henning Koppel, with large green cabochons.

7.25in (18.5cm) long

£2,000-2,500 **SF**

A 1960s Georg Jensen curved semi-circular bracelet, with stylized stamp, London import marks "K".

7.25in (18.5cm) diam

£4,000-5,000 **SF**

A 1960s Georg Jensen silver bracelet, with moulded stylized omega symbol.

7.75in (19.5cm) long

£2,500-3,000 **SF**

A 1960s Georg Jensen silver articulated bracelet, constructed of hollow bulbous and rounded squares.

7.5in (19cm) long

£2,000-2,500 **SF**

A Georg Jensen 'slave' bracelet, manufactured from individual segments of hollow silver pinned together.

7.75in (19.5cm) long

£2,500-3,000 **SF**

A Georg Jensen silver articulated bracelet, of curving oval form, possible import marks.

8.5in (21.5cm) long

£1,000-1,500 **SF**

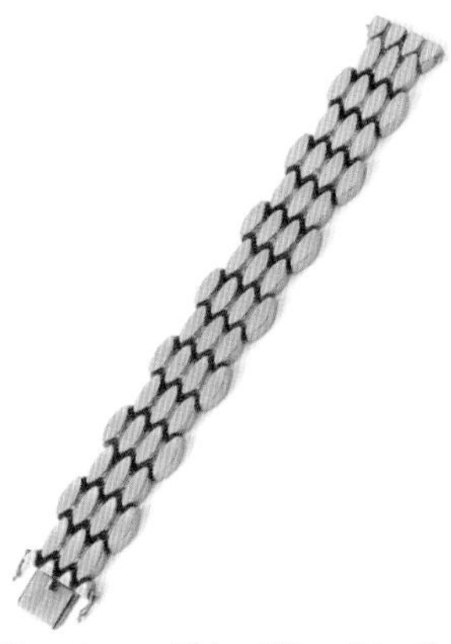

A Georg Jensen 18ct gold bracelet, with truncated curved ovals, stamped "750".

7.5in (19cm) long

£4,000-5,000 **SF**

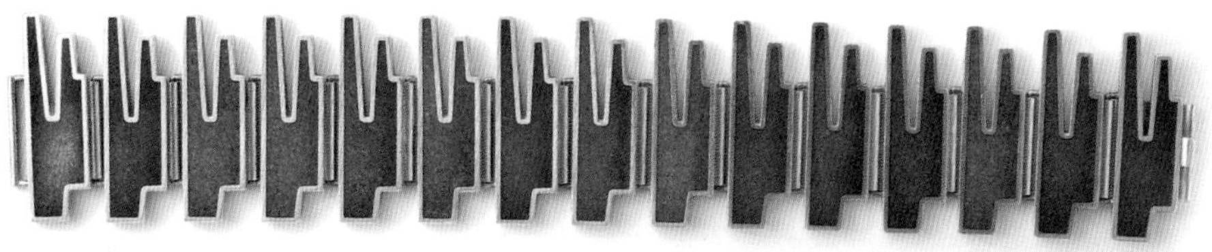

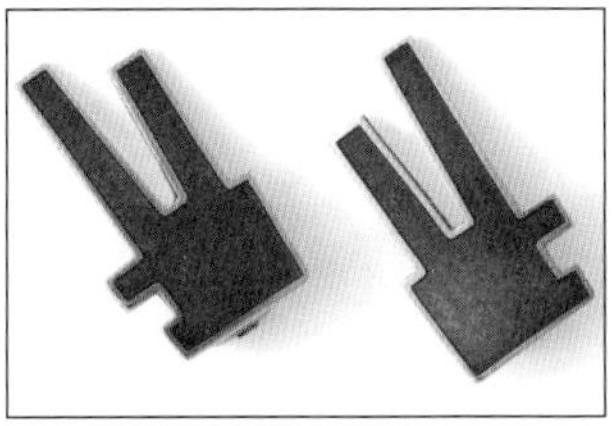

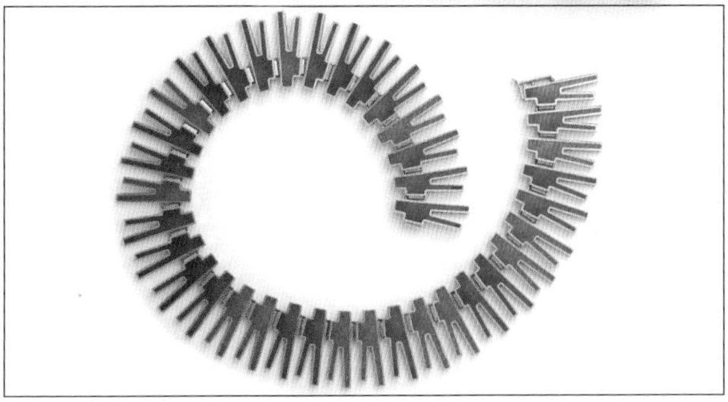

A Georg Jensen silver and blue enamel geometric set, comprising necklace, bracelet and earrings.

7.5in (19cm) diam

£5,000-6,000 set **SF**

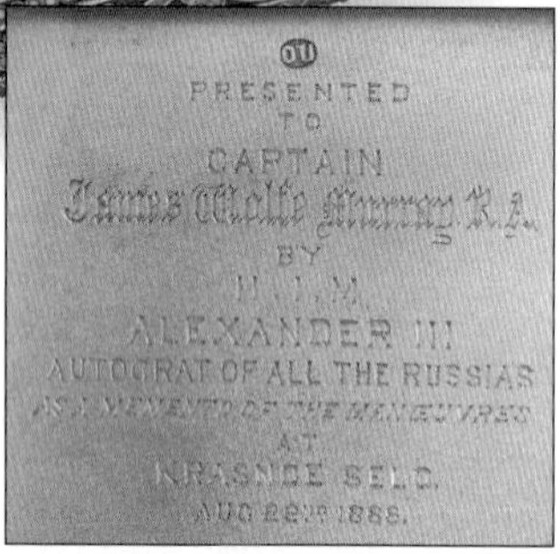

A Russian silver and cloisonné enamel Imperial presentation cigarette box, by Pavel Ovchinnikov, engraved "Presented to Captain James Wolfe Murray RA by H.I.M. Alexander III...", signed, Imperial eagle warrant, maker's mark of Cyrillic 'PO', with 88 zolotnik assay mark for Moscow pre-1899.

£4,000-5,000 **HAMG**

Twelve late 19thC Russian champlevé enamel salts and spoons, comprising a set of five with maker's mark rubbed, a set of six, maker's mark "GK 1892" and a single, maker's mark "GK 1891".

1891

£1,500-2,000 **FRE**

A early 20thC Russian silver and enamel vodka beaker, of cylindrical form, enriched with stylized floral and foliate motifs.

2.5in (6cm) high

£280-320 **ROS**

A 20thC Russian silver and enamel cordial set, comprising a decanter, six glasses and tray stamped "925".

tray 9.5in (24cm) wide

£600-900 **FRE**

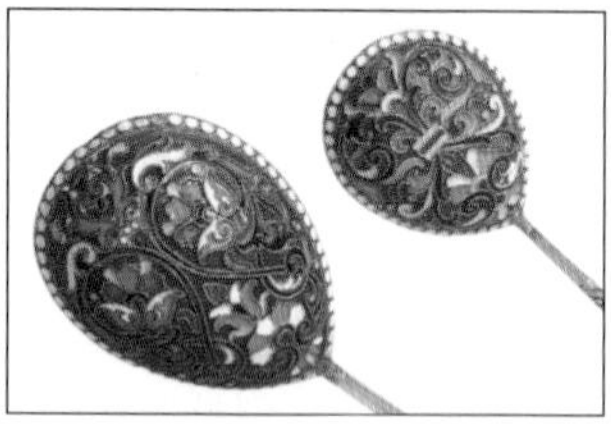

Two Russian silver gilt and enamel presentation spoons, each with ornately decorated backs.

£400-600 **BIG**

FRENCH ENAMEL

A 17thC Limoges triptych enamel plaque depicting 'The Crucifixion', 'The House of Loretto' and 'The Descent from the Cross', bears old paper label verso for Christie's sale, "bought by Sir T.W. Booyd, on 7th March 1866 for 5 guinnies".

each panel 4.75in (12cm) wide

£2,800-3,200 **FRE**

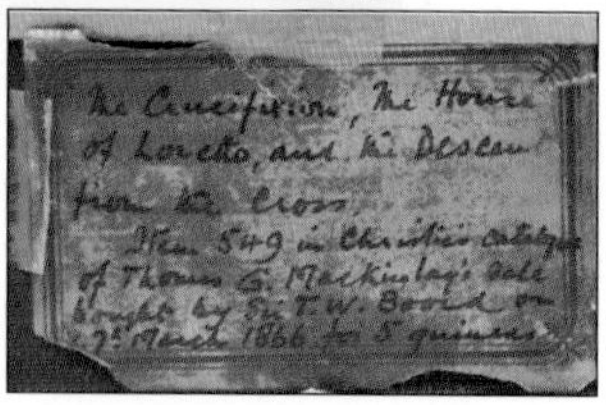

An 18thC French tortoiseshell and gold pique cylindrical box and cover, with an oval enamel panel.

2in (5cm) diam

£3,000-4,000 **LFA**

A late 18thC to early 19thC French gold-mounted agate necessaire, inscribed "L'Amour Surmonte Tout Obstacle" to an enamelled ground, containing two mounted glass bottles, an ivory notecard, tweezers, a pencil, a bodkin and a small folding knife.

1.75in (4.2cm) wide

£4,000-5,000 **L&T**

A 19thC French Limoges small enamel box, with a female portrait in reserve, the sides decorated with grotesque masks.

4.5in (11cm) wide

£220-280 **FRE**

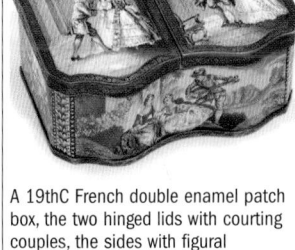

A 19thC French double enamel patch box, the two hinged lids with courting couples, the sides with figural landscapes.

3.75in (9cm) wide

£1,200-1,800 **FRE**

A French champlevé enamel and alabaster centrepiece, with enamel-decorated brass stand and winged dragon-head twin handles.

26in (66cm) wide

£400-600 **ROS**

OTHER ENAMEL

An 18thC set of four Battersea enamel candlesticks, with painted and gilt floral sprays on a white ground, with scalloped circular sconce on knopped stem.

9.75in (25cm) high

£4,000-6,000 **L&T**

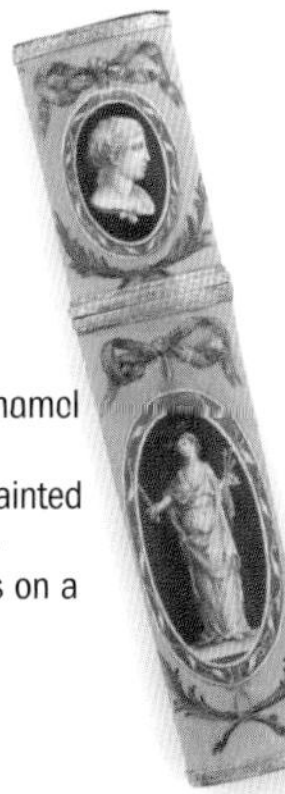

A Staffordshire enamel bodkin case, decorated with painted busts and figures within cartouches on a pink ground.

4.5in (11.5cm) long

£600-800 **AA**

A 19thC Continental silver-gilt and white enamel snuff box, with oval carnelian-inset top bordered by foiled pink stones, rim inscribed "Emma Lyon Hamilton 1799", in fitted case.

£700-1,000 **GORL**

A 19thC German enamel erotic patch box, opening to reveal an interior painted with architectural ruins and an erotic scene.

2.5in (6cm) diam

£1,800-2,200 **FRE**

A late 19thC to early 20thC erotic enamelled alpacca cigarette case, with a semi-nude seated woman drinking tea, some chips.

3.25in (8.5cm) high

£400-600 **ROS**

A Continental silver enamelled compact, with decoration to the hinged cover depicting a courting couple in a pastoral landscape, stamped "800".

3.75in (9.5cm) wide

£300-400 **L&T**

An early 20thC Fabergé silver and cloisonné enamelled kovsch, the exterior decorated with a bold pattern of stylized floral, geometric and scroll designs, gilt interior, scratch inventory number of the base, marks for the Fabergé workshop, Moscow, 1907-1918.

14.75in (37cm) wide

£40,000-60,000 **L&T**

A small gold Fabergé kovsh, set with a pear-shaped cabochon sapphire, an emerald-cut diamond and an oval cabochon ruby, fluted gold geometric band, signed "MP" in Cyrillic for Michael Perchin of St. Petersburg, scratched inventory number "37996", in a fitted wooden box.

3.25in (8.5cm) wide

£9,000-12,000 **WW**

A CLOSER LOOK AT A FABERGÉ BOX

Since the young Carl Fabergé created the first traditional Easter egg for Tsar Alexander III in the spring of 1885, the House of Fabergé employed the finest enamellers, painters and jewellers available to create luxury items. The Fabergé name makes a piece valuable and sought after.

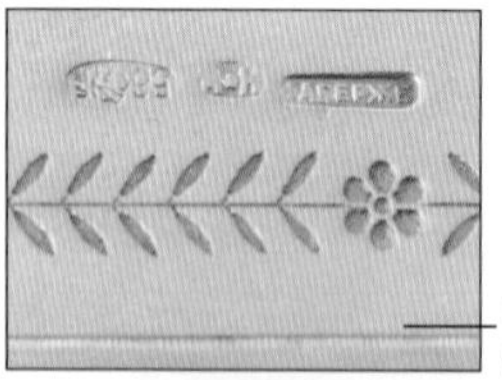

Workman's marks relating to a master, like August Hollming or Feodor Afanasiev, increase the value.

The value of Fabergé pieces is often enhanced by a grand provenance, such as a dedication to a historical figure. This one is for His Imperial Highness, Grand Duke Sergei Alexandrovich.

The forty-six cushion-shaped old brilliant-cut diamonds increase the desirability.

An important gold and diamond Imperial presentation box by Peter Carl Fabergé, work master August Frederick Hollming, the hinged box with laurel leaf engraved decoration highlighted with arrows, the front cover containing a miniature by Johannes Zehngraf, the inner lid inscribed in Russian "Presented by His Imperial Highness Prince Sergei Alexandrovich To cadet of the Imperial Court Prince Andrei Alexandrovich Shirinsky Shachmatov Moscow 31st October 1901".

£120,000-180,000 **HAMG**

A Fabergé carved kalgan jasper elephant, with rose-cut diamond eyes.

c1910 *2.75in (7cm) wide*

£9,000-12,000 **HAMG**

A Fabergé carved nephrite elephant, with rose-cut diamond eyes.

2in (5cm) wide

£5,000-7,000 **HAMG**

A Fabergé miniature carved nephrite elephant, with rose-cut diamond eyes.

c1910 *1in (2.5cm) wide*

£7,000-10,000 **HAMG**

A rare late 19thC Fabergé beaker, in green malachite glass, painted in silver, the faceted bowl with four semi-precious cabochons, stamped and master's mark.

5.25in (13cm) high

£1,000-1,500 **KAU**

A Fabergé silver and blue guilloche enamel frame, by Anders Johan Nevalainen, with beaded silver frame and chased acanthus leaf border, signed "K Faberge" in Cyrillic, maker's mark 'A.N' for Anders Nevalainen, with 91 kokoshnik mark for St Petersburg 1899-1908.

4.5in (11.5cm) high

£9,000-13,000 **HAMG**

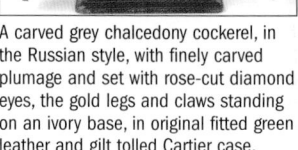

A carved grey chalcedony cockerel, in the Russian style, with finely carved plumage and set with rose-cut diamond eyes, the gold legs and claws standing on an ivory base, in original fitted green leather and gilt tolled Cartier case, dated 1906-1909.

£6,000-9,000 **HAMG**

A Russian icon, in tempera and wood, with a three-handed Mary with Christ on her arm, signed.

c1800 *18in (45cm) high*

£600-900 **KAU**

A 19thC Russian icon, in tempera and wood, depicting the descent into hell and the resurrection of Christ, bordered by twelve images of the main holidays of the orthodox church.

21.25in (53cm) high

£600-900 **KAU**

A 19thC Russian enamel icon, the richly painted convex panel depicting a group of male and female saints, set in a gilt metal lobed frame with applied mounts in the form of cherubim.

9.5in (24cm) high

£2,000-2,500 **FRE**

A 19thC Russian icon, in tempera and wood, with John the Evangelis and the Holy Eudokia, flanked by the Holy Antipius and John Chrysostomos.

14in (35cm) high

£300-500 **KAU**

A 19thC Russian holiday icon, in tempera and wood, depicting the descent into hell and the resurrection of Christ, bordered by twelve images of the main holidays of the orthodox church, signed.

18.75in (47cm) high

£1,000-1,500 **KAU**

A late 19thC Russian icon, in tempera, wood and silver, depicting Christ Pantokrator, the silver oklad with golden aura, stamped.

10.5in (26.5cm) high

£200-300 **KAU**

A Russian icon, depicting the Archangel Michael flanked by an Angel Guardian and St. John the Warrior, with St. Paul and St. Martyr Agrippina, with extensive gold hatchings, painted against a gold ground on a wood panel.

14in (35cm) high

£1,500-2,000 **FRE**

A Russian 'The Dormition' icon, depicting Mary in the company of the Holy Spirit and orders of angels, with saints attending and other onlookers, on wood panel.

12.25in (30.5cm) high

£500-700 **FRE**

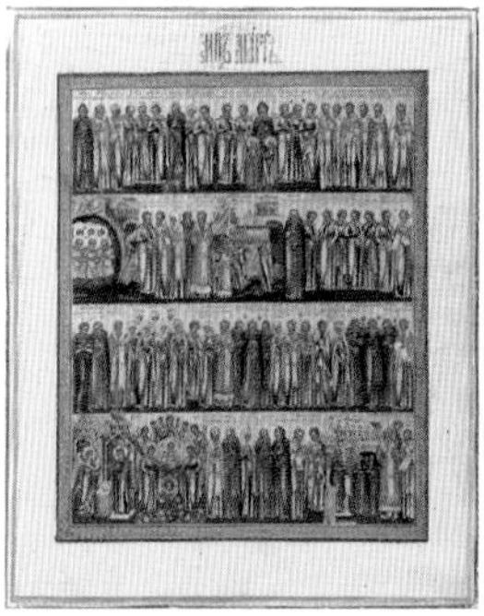

A Menological icon for the month of March, painted with four registers with depictions of saints, on a wood panel with gilt enhancements.

12in (30cm) high

£1,500-2,000 **FRE**

A Russian 'Queen of Heavenly Peace' icon, depicting Mary with the child Christ seated on her arm, on a blue over gold ground, flanked by angels ministering to the destitute, on a wood panel with gilt enhancements.

12.25in (30.5cm) high

£700-1,000 **FRE**

A Russian 'St. Mary of Egypt' icon, the saint depicted holding a scroll in a rocky landscape within an ochre border, on a wood panel.

12in (30cm) high

£3,000-4,000 **FRE**

A Russian 'Saint George slaying the dragon' icon, depicted on a grey charger piercing the dragon with a lance while crowds overlook from a stylized fortress.

14in (35cm) high

£2,500-3,000 **FRE**

A rare late 17thC French set of four ivory gaming boxes, each with a raised dial numbered one to nine, representing a separate card suit, inscribed "Marialual Le Jeune a Paris Fecit".

3.25in (8.5cm) wide

£1,800-2,200 **SWO**

An 18thC Continental carved ivory and gilt metal-mounted covered cup, the lid surmounted by a male head finial, the side carved in relief with naked figures.

10in (25cm) high

£1,200-1,800 **FRE**

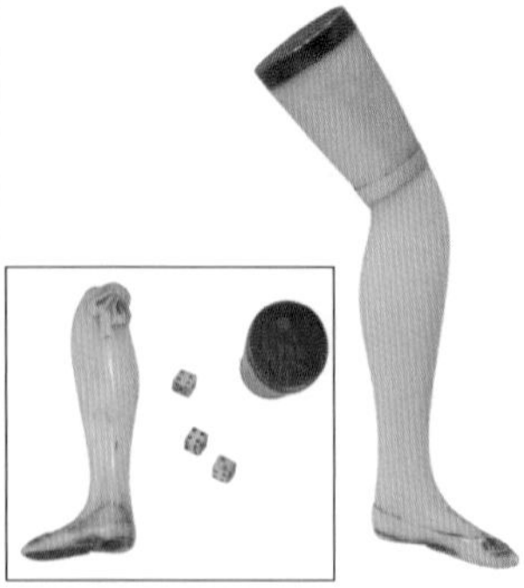

A Georgian ivory dice holder/seal, fashioned as a gartered lady's leg with carved integral shoe, with monogrammed silver end, revealing three period miniature dice.

£500-700 **BIG**

An 18th to 19thC Continental carved ivory figure of Christ, possibly German, depicting Christ chained to a post, chain lacking, mounted on a later wood base.

7in (17.5cm) high

£800-1,200 **FRE**

A 19thC gold mounted ivory and lapis lazuli desk seal, the hand wearing a ruby-set ring and clenching a baton, carnelian and bloodstone matrices to each seal end, all matrices blank.

2.5in (6cm) high

£2,800-3,200 **DNT**

A 19thC marine ivory scrimshaw, decorated with a three-masted sailing ship 'Ann Alexander' flying the stars and stripes and inscribed verso "Ann Alexander, Sunk by a Whale, 1851".

6in (15cm) long

£600-900 **SWO**

A 19thc French carved ivory 'Napoleon Bonaparte' figure, modelled in full military dress standing cross armed, mounted on square plinth base.

4.75in (12cm) high

£280-320 **ROS**

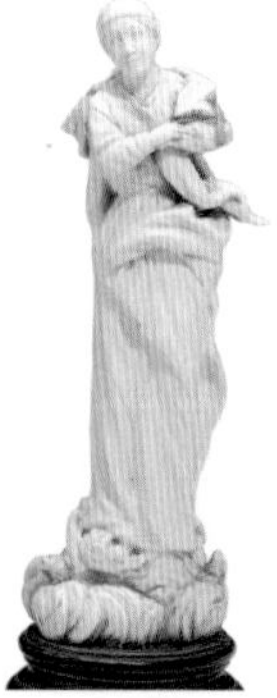

A 19thC Continental ivory figure of a saint, depicting the standing figure wearing a head scarf and voluminous robe, on a naturalistic base.

9.25in (23cm) high

£500-700 **FRE**

A 19thC carved ivory crucifix, mounted on a bronze cross, minor losses.

15.25in (39cm) high

£350-400 **SWO**

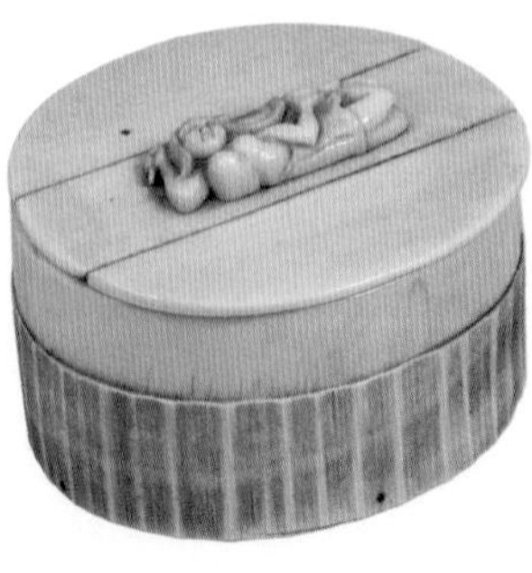

A late 19thC oval ivory pot and cover, the oval tusk section with a pine base, the lid applied with a reclining female.

4.25in (11cm) high

£220-280 **SWO**

A medieval-style baline tooth miniature casket, mounted with white metal straps and lock.

2.5in (6.5cm) wide

£1,500-2,000 **CHEF**

An early 19thC scrimshaw whale's tooth, engraved on one side with a dancing couple and inscribed "FASHIONABLE AMUSE'T" above an oval reserve depicting a portrait of a gentleman with the inscription "DAPPER PEER", the reverse with a gentleman leaning on a chair and inscribed "A WELL SPENT DAY" above an oval reserve with a portrait of a fashionably dressed lady with the inscription "OBSCURE BEAUTY".

6.5in (16cm) high

£10,000-12,000 **SK**

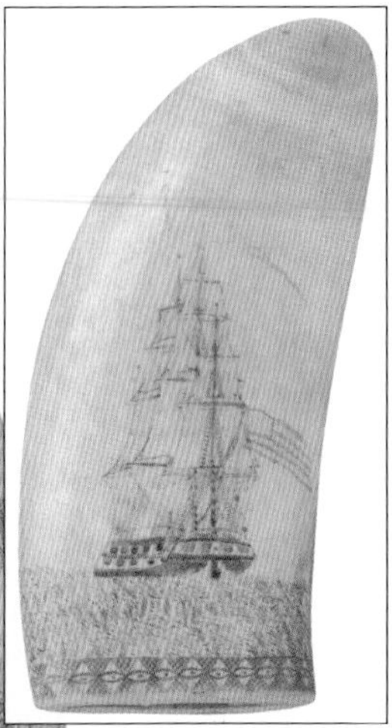

A scrimshaw whale's tooth, one side engraved with a ship in full sail flying an American flag, the reverse with a ship within a tombstone reserve above a woman, her left arm resting on an anchor.

c1835 *5.25in (13cm) long*

£10,000-12,000 **SK**

A large mid-19thC scrimshaw whale's tooth, engraved with a whaling bark and three long boats pursuing whales and inscribed "South Sea Fishery", the reverse centred with a ship in harbour flying a British flag and inscribed "Port Owharre, Huahene", with a sperm whale to the bottom of the tooth, portions filled with red and black sealing wax.

Huahine is the easternmost of the Leeward Islands, part of French Polynesia in the South Pacific. It is most notable as the last stop of the HMS Bounty before the 1789 mutiny.

8.25in (20.5cm) long

£40,000-50,000 **SK**

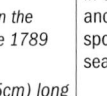

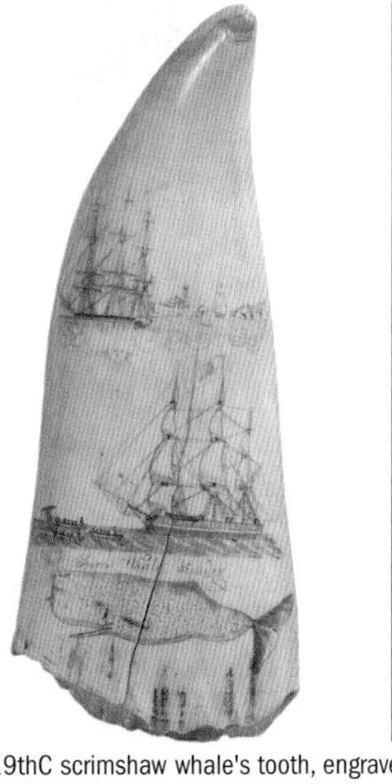

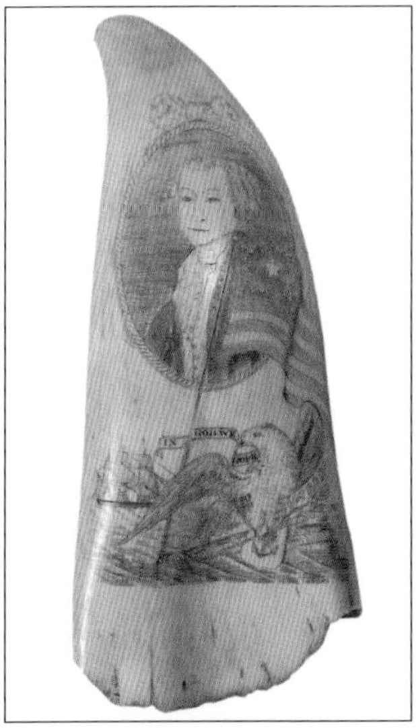

A 19thC scrimshaw whale's tooth, engraved with a portrait of George Washington in an oval reserve over an American flag and a spread-wing eagle grasping an anchor and an olive branch, inscribed "IN GOD WE HOPE", the reverse with a spouting whale and inscribed "Sperm Whale Fishery", filled with red and blue sealing wax, imperfections.

7.5in (19cm) long

£15,000-20,000 **SK**

A miniature portrait of William Hull, possibly by Anson Dickinson, with the sitter's name inscribed on a piece of paper in an oval copper case, with a lock of plaited brown hair, unsigned.

c1810 *2.5in (6.5cm) high*

£4,000-5,000 **SK**

Two miniature portraits of Captain John Page and Mrs. John Page, attributed to Joseph Dunkerley, in watercolour on ivory, one signed with the initials "ID", with gilt copper oval cases.

Provenance: *By family descent. Joseph Dunkerley arrived in America with the British Army, but deserted soon after to serve as a lieutenant in a Massachusetts artillery regiment and become a citizen. He rented a house from silversmith Paul Revere, who probably made many of his miniature cases.*

1in (2.5cm) high

£5,000-7,000 **SK**

A 19thC American School hollow-cut silhouette of Katherine L. Hamblen, in watercolour and ink on paper, backed with fabric, sitter identified on reverse of frame, Maine.

sight 4.5in (11.5cm) high

£250-300 **FRE**

A 19thC American School hollow-cut silhouette of a lady, backed with white silk, the bodice in white paper heightened with graphite and ink wash, on a black ground, framed.

4.25in (11cm) high

£350-300 **FRE**

A 19thC American School miniature hollow-cut and printed silhouette of a lady, backed with fabric, stamped brass frame, creases.

4.25in (11cm) high

£180-220 **FRE**

A 19thC American School silhouette of a girl, in mixed media including paint, hair, gilt metal and fabric on paper, framed, discolouration, unsigned.

sight 6.75in (17cm) high

£150-200 **FRE**

A 19thC American School miniature portrait, watercolour on paper, inscription on the reverse reads "Moses Waterhouse Esq. Scarbro Me. Jan. 20 1839" in a period, white dotted pine frame, foxing, toning, stain, creases.

4.5in (11.5cm) high

£5,000-7,000 **SK**

An Edward Shrosbree & Thomas Penn carved tiger's eye dog walking cane, with glass eyes, with foliate scroll-engraved silver collar, with marks for Birmingham.

1886 *34.5in (86cm) long*

£400-600 **L&T**

A hardwood cane, the handle in the form of a dog's head, with silver buckled collar, the shaft carved with vine leaves in high relief, the gilt metal ferrule with steel tip.

34.25in (87cm) long

£300-400 **L&T**

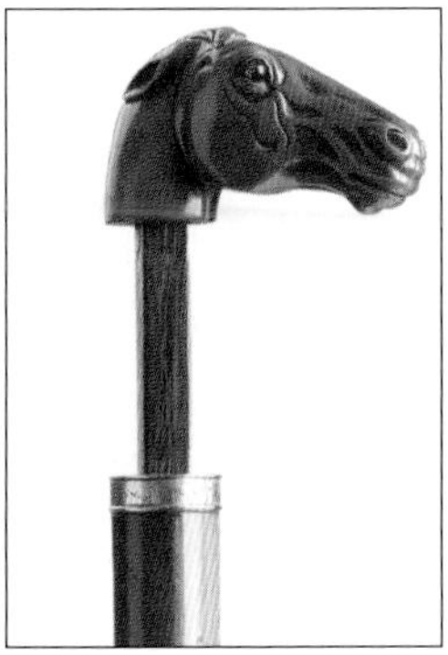

A boxwood and malacca horse measuring cane, the handle in the form of a horse's head, pulling to reveal a measuring stick inside the shaft.

38.5in (98cm) long

£300-400 **L&T**

An American dogwood traveller's cane, the handle in the form of a monkey biting the head of a serpent, the shaft carved with mystical beasts, with steel ferrule.

34.75in (88cm) long

£120-180 **L&T**

A Scottish thornwood crook, the handle inscribed "Mr Willm. Falchinor", carved allover with thistles, the Royal coat-of-arms, and highland animals, Celtic strapwork, with reduced giltmetal ferrule.

34.25in (87cm) long

£220-280 **L&T**

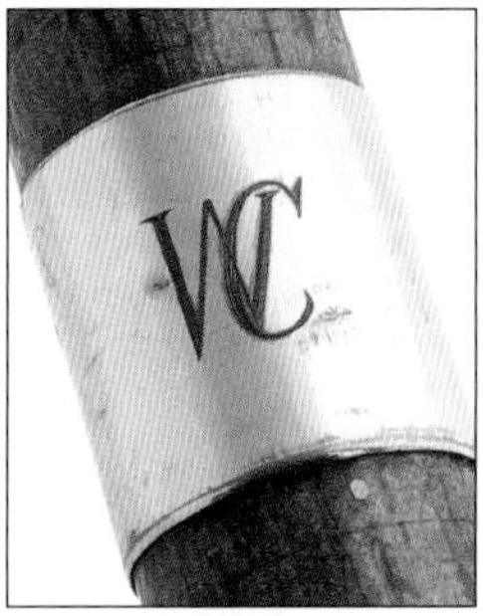

A walking stick, owned by Sir Winston Churchill, with a gold-plated collar inscribed "WC", with two related letters.

This stick was given to the vendor as a gift while he was working for Churchill as a temporary secretary.

36.5in (92.5cm) high

£3,000-4,000 **CA**

A Scottish hardwood cane, the handle in the form of a clenched fist holding a removable corked bottle, the knotted shaft with a pair of entwined adders and giltmetal ferrule with steel tip.

37in (94cm) long

£150-200 **L&T**

A Scottish laburnum topped rootwood cane, the handle in the form of a clenched fist holding a bar, the gnarled shaft with pewter band and giltmetal ferrule with steel tip.

34.25in (87cm) long

£120-180 **L&T**

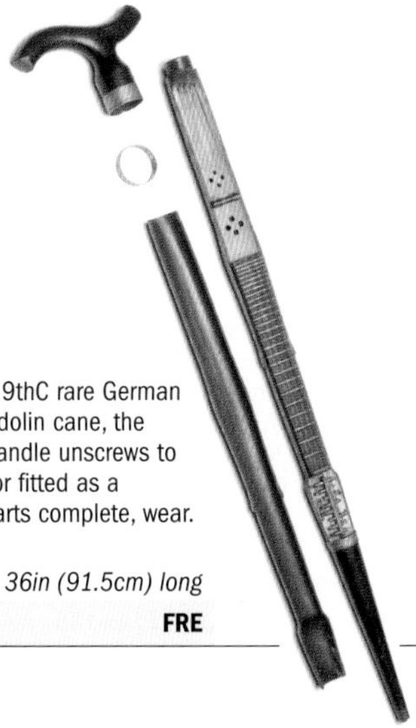

A second half 19thC rare German mahogany mandolin cane, the 'tau'- shaped handle unscrews to reveal an interior fitted as a mandolin, all parts complete, wear.

36in (91.5cm) long

£3,000-5,000 **FRE**

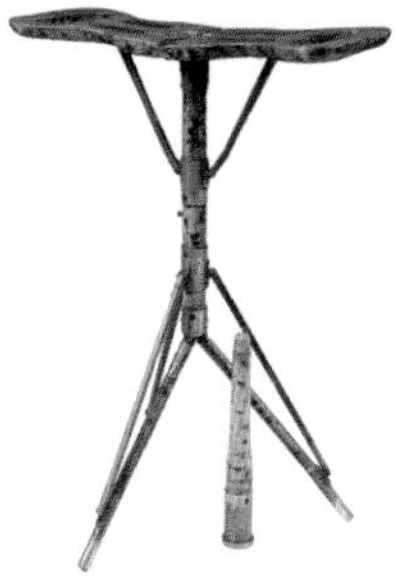

An Edwardian bamboo shooting stick, with a detachable end and folding tripod support.

£250-300 **SWO**

A cane with a silver erotic handle, probably designed by Garnier for the manufacture Antoine.

c1850

£1,500-2,000 **SEG**

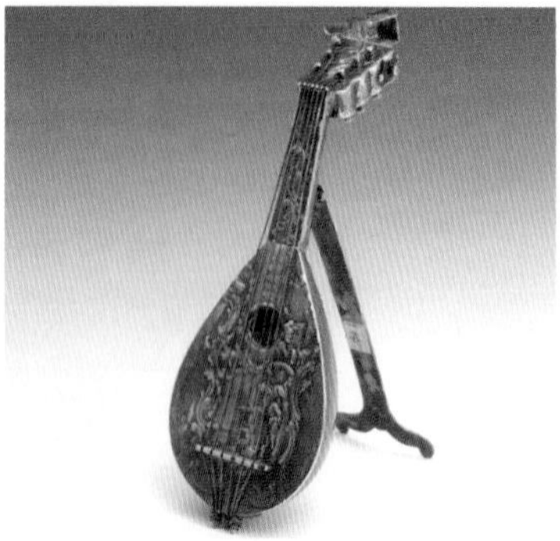

A rare silver perfume bottle, Amsterdam, probably 18thC, shaped as a lute, decorated with the image of a town, with floral motifs, several coats of arms, three stars and monogram "N".

6.75in (17cm) high

£300-400 **WDL**

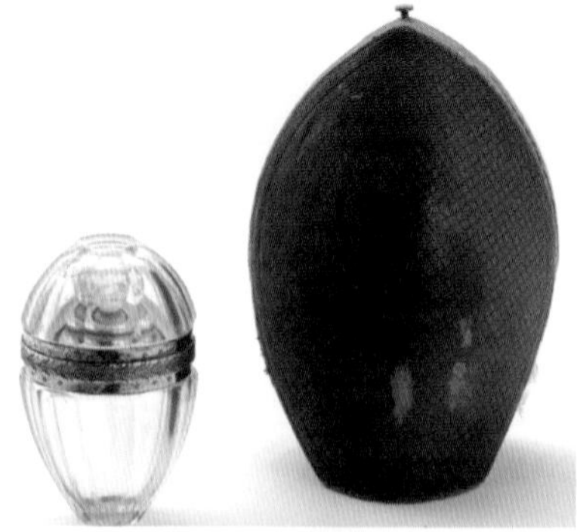

An early 19thC Continental silver-gilt-mounted clear glass scent, with a bright-engraved mount, hinging open to reveal a faceted stopper, unmarked, probably French, contained in original fitted case.

2.5in (6.5cm) high

£600-900 **WW**

A 19thC clear glass Oxford lavender bottle with green enamelling, probably Bohemian.

7.5in (19cm) long

£100-150 **TRIO**

A 19thC clear glass Oxford lavender bottle, decorated with flowers, probably Bohemian.

7.75in (19.5cm) long

£80-120 **TRIO**

A late 19thC Dutch miniature scent bottle, with a raffia-overlaid body and silver-gilt mounts.

c1860 *1in (2.5cm) high*

£120-180 **WW**

A 19thC continental silver-gilt-mounted agate scent flask, with embossed hinged cap and stopper, probably Dutch.

c1880 *2in (5cm) high*

£120-180 **WW**

An English Victorian red double-ended bottle, with silver tops.

c1885 *4.75in (12cm) high*

£180-220 **TRIO**

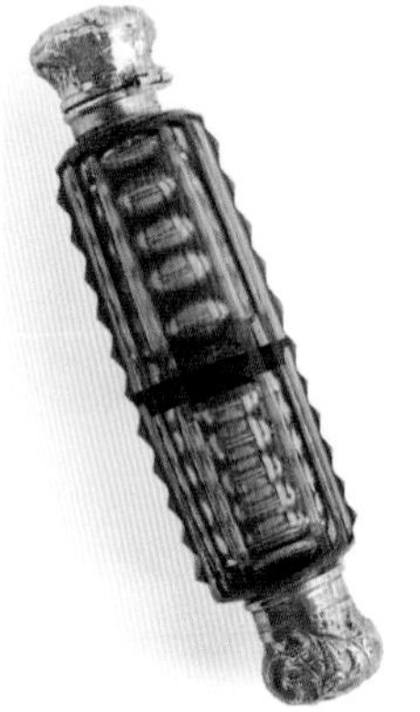

An English Victorian clear glass double-ended bottle, for perfume and salts, with ruby enamelling, silver tops.

c1885 *4.75in (12cm) high*

£220-280 **TRIO**

A Victorian gold-mounted and gem-set double-ended scent bottle, the covers with applied turquoise, seed pearl and coral inlaid monograms, inscribed "Thomas, Oxford Street", contained in a fitted velvet case.

With accompanying note from the Duchess of St Albans.

£1,800-2,200 **L&T**

A French silvergilt-mounted glass scent bottle, of faceted ovoid form, opening to reveal a mounted inner stopper, with cast seated cupid surmount, contained in a fitted red leather covered case.

3in (7.5cm) high

£800-1,200 **L&T**

A Bohemian glass scent bottle, with a silver-coloured metal top hinging to a clear stopper on a cranberry overlaid body, engraved to the centre with a monogram.

3.75in (9.5cm) high

£120-180 **SWO**

A Royal Vienna perfume bottle, featuring a maiden with purple drapes, the stopper with applied rose and leaves, blue beehive mark.

4in (10cm) high

£400-600 **JDJ**

RÉNÉ LALIQUE

- René Lalique (1860-1945) originally trained as a jeweller and began working with glass in 1893. He established his first glass shop in Paris in 1905.
- By the 1920s, he had three factories making an ever-growing range of pressed and moulded glass items, including decorative vases and perfume bottles. Over the years, the company has produced glamorous bottles for over 60 fashionable perfumers, from Coty to Nina Ricci.
- Technical developments allowed Lalique to combine outstanding craftsmanship with mass-production.
- Some early bottles feature flowing lines and floral, foliate and figural etching.
- The majority of Lalique's designs were modern and stylized, most being representative of the Art Deco era. Bottles were bold in shape and sometimes feature oversized decorative stoppers.
- After his death in 1945, no genuine pieces were marked with his initial 'R' before his surname. The company still exists, producing new and old designs. Pieces with a small 'registered mark' of an 'R' in a circle were manufactured recently.
- Original packaging adds considerably to the value.

A perfume sample tester box for Coty, in wood and bronze, with twelve glass bottles by Depinoix, the paper labels and plaque design by Lalique, plaque signed "R. LALIQUE", lacking two labels.

c1910 *2.25in (5.5cm) high*

£2,200-2,800 **RDL**

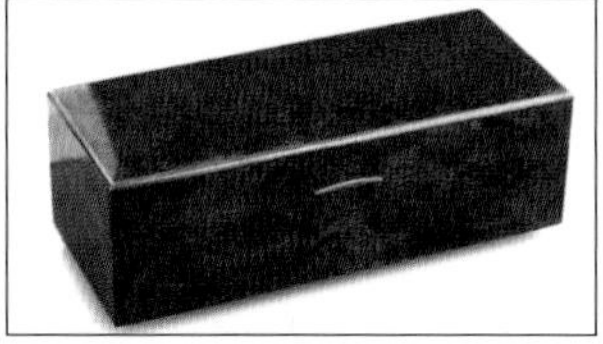

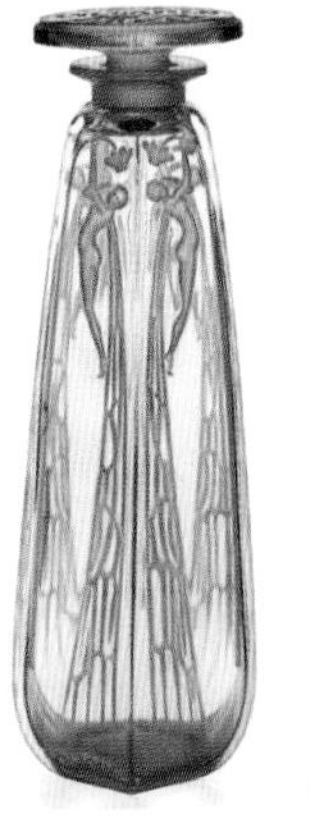

A Lalique 'Cyclamen' perfume bottle for Coty, in clear and frosted glass with sage green patina, moulded "LALIQUE", stopper moulded "COTY CYCLAMEN PARIS".

c1910 *5.5in (14cm) high*

£1,500-2,000 **RDL**

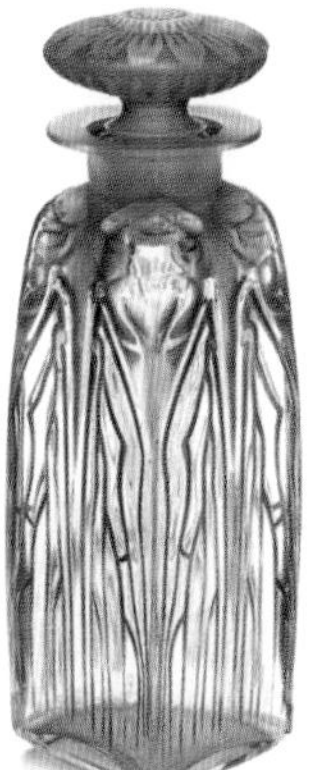

A Lalique 'Quatre Cigales' perfume bottle, in clear and frosted glass with grey patina, engraved "R. Lalique".

c1910 *5.5in (14cm) high*

£1,000-1,500 **RDL**

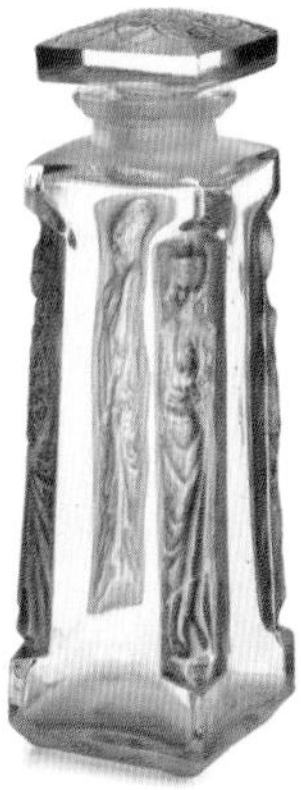

A Lalique 'Ambre' perfume bottle for D'Orsay, in clear and frosted glass with sepia patina, with moulded "LALIQUE" mark, frozen stopper.

c1910 *5in (13cm) high*

£500-700 **RDL**

A Lalique 'La Phalene' perfume bottle for D'Heraud, in deep amber glass, moulded "R. LALIQUE" and "PHALENE" and bears unidentified gilt label for "Mona Lisa".

c1925 *3.5in (8.5cm) high*

£3,000-4,000 **RDL**

A Lalique 'Dans la Nuit' perfume bottle for Worth, in clear glass with blue enamel, with moulded "R. LALIQUE" mark.

c1924 *5.75in (14.5cm) high*

£400-600 **RDL**

A Lalique 'Le Baiser du Faune' perfume bottle for Molinard, in clear and frosted glass, moulded "R. LALIQUE", with engraved "Molinard France".

c1930 *5.5in (14.5cm) high*

£1,200-1,800 **RDL**

PERSIAN RUGS & CARPETS

- From the mid-19thC there was a revival of interest in Persian weaving, largely generated by the Western fashion for 'exotic' Eastern design and materials.
- The main centres of production were Tabriz, Mashad, Isfahan, Kashan, Kirman, Heriz and Senneh.
- The most significant carpet-producing Persian tribes were the Ashfar, the Kashgai and the Khamseh.
- Towns concentrated on the production of carpets and rugs, typically finely woven with wool on cotton or occasionally silk on silk. Patterns were curvilinear and featured flowers and foliage.
- Villages and tribal regions produced mainly rugs and smaller items, such as bags, in wool on wool. Carpets are fairly rare. Designs, produced from memory, are individual and often geometric and stylized.
- Fine tribal rugs dating from before c1900 are especially sought after by enthusiasts.

A Persian Heriz carpet, ends nearly intact, some wear with cotton foundation showing.

Heriz carpets are from a district west of Tabriz in Northwest Iran.

c1920 *220x135in (559x343cm)*

£8,000-12,000 **FRE**

A Persian Heriz carpet, with cotton warp and weft and woollen pile, with stylized geometrical flowers and branches on brownish-red ground, dark blue main border with two green side borders, woollen fringe.

c1940 *136x94.8in (340x237cm)*

£200-250 **KAU**

A Persian Heriz rug, with eight-point star medallion in shades of cinnabar and brown on an ivory ground within multiple borders.

c1975 *94x127in (239x322.5cm)*

£700-1,000 **DRA**

A Persian Heriz carpet, with areas of wear, tinting and some moth damage.

215x140in (546x355.5cm)

£6,000-9,000 **FRE**

A Persian Heriz rug, with multiple star medallions and spandrels in shades of red, brown and ivory on a crimson gróund.

96x125in (244x317.5cm)

£600-900 **DRA**

KASHAN

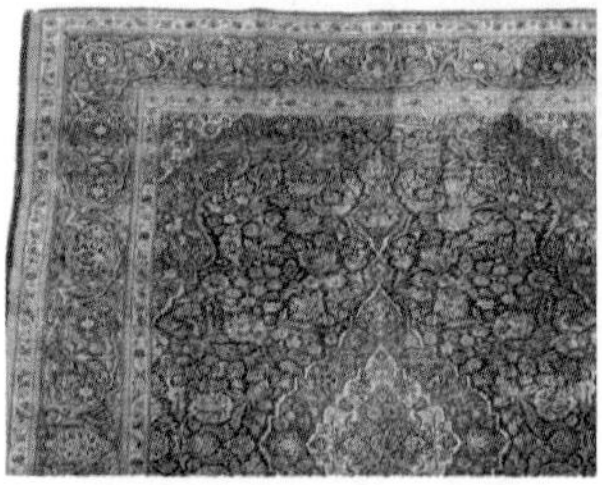

An early 20thC silk Kashan rug, one end largely intact, other end with losses, wear, dryness.

78x51in (198x129.5cm)

£1,500-2,000 **FRE**

A Kashan woollen rug, with cotton fringe, asymmetrical knots, central field with palmettes, rosettes and floral designs with a dark-blue border.

The town of of Kashan is situated between Tehran and Isfahan.

c1960 *85.6x53.6in (214x134 cm)*

£400-600 **KAU**

A Kashan Rug, with scalloped diamond centre medallion in shades of blue and ivory on a crimson ground within multiple blue borders.

c1960 *98x146in (249x371cm)*

£1,200-1,800 **DRA**

A Kashan pictorial rug, the red field with central entwined floral tree of life pattern, within indigo palmette and scrolling vine border between bands.

80.75x56.25in (205cmx143cm)

£700-1,000 **L&T**

A large Kashan carpet.

193in (490cm) wide

£800-1,200 **SWO**

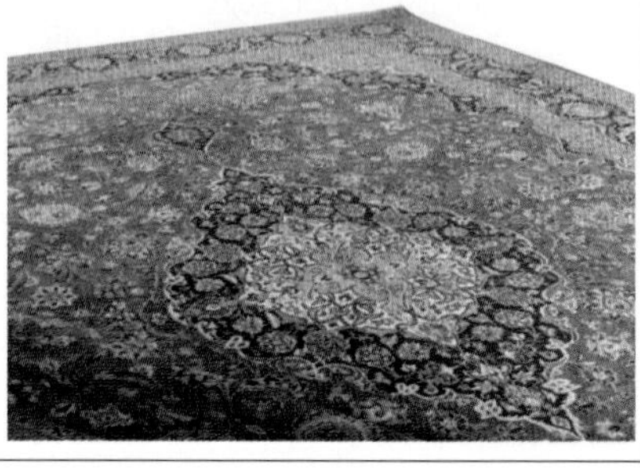

A Kashan room-size rug, with cobalt, ivory and crimson central medallions, surrounded by blue and ivory vinescroll borders.

156in (390cm) wide

£600-900 **DRA**

A late 19thC Sarouk Fereghan carpet, missing some rows of knots at each end, numerous places where carpet is threadbare down to foundation, areas of habrash toward each end.

118x77in (299.5x195.5cm)

£1,000-1,500 **FRE**

A Sarouk Fereghan pictorial rug, with a low pile clip, no threadbare areas, losses.

c1900 *78x55in (198x139.5cm)*

£2,500-3,000 **FRE**

An early 20thC Sarouk Fereghan carpet, each end missing part of flowerhead cream border, with generally minor habrash in places, small repiled areas, crease wear.

118x87in (299.5x221cm)

£1,800-2,200 **FRE**

An early 20thC Sarouk Fereghan rug.

78x48in (198x122cm)

£1,000-1,500 **FRE**

A Sarough rug, in cotton and wool, a central medallion on a blue ground, fringes.

c1970 *153.25in (383cm) long*

£600-900 **KAU**

A Sarouk carpet, the blue, cream and rust ground with a central scrolling leaf medallion.

76.25inx132in (194cmx335cm)

£1,800-2,200 **SWO**

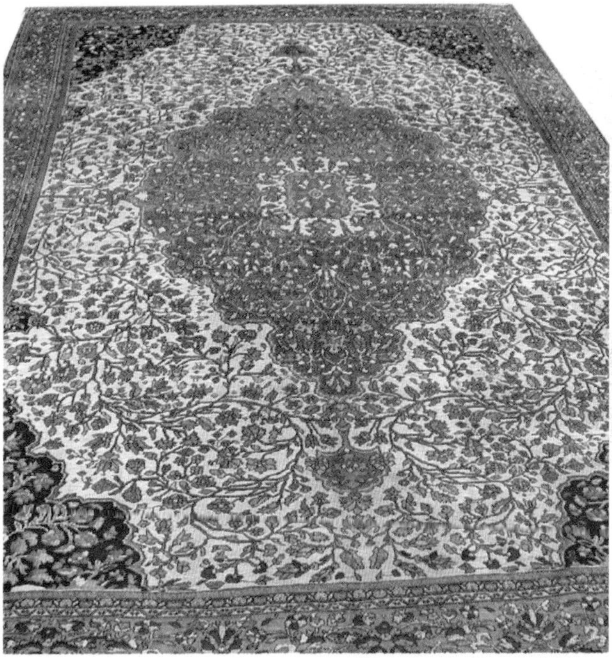

A Persian carpet, of Sarouk design with floral motifs on a red and cream field.

20inx134.25in (51x341cm)

£3,500-£4,500 **SWO**

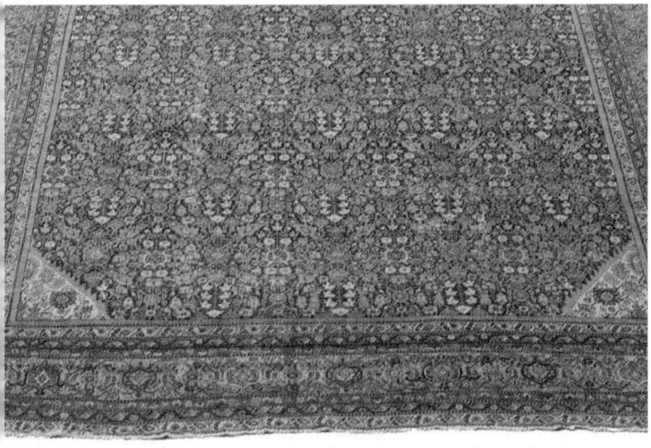

A Fereghan carpet, thin throughout, threadbare down to the foundation in many places, repairs, visible tinting and colour bleeding.

199x160in (505.5x406.5cm)

£2,200-2,800 **FRE**

A Sarouk carpet, decorated with floral motifs on a red field.

204.75in (520cm) wide

£1,500-2,000 **SWO**

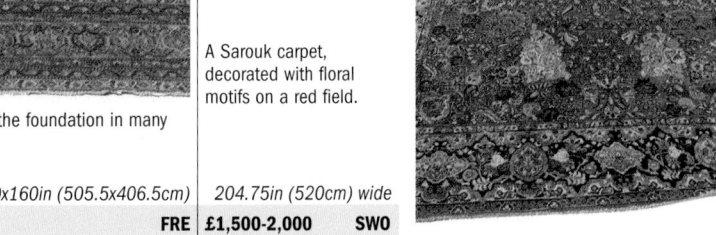

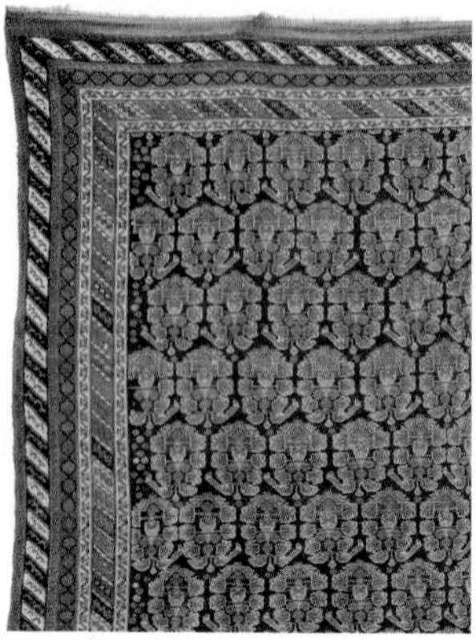

A late 19thC Afshar carpet.

151in (377.5cm) long

£1,200-1,800 **FRE**

An Afshar bag face, selvage intact, top end with khilim strip.

11x19in (28x48.5cm)

£800-1,200 **FRE**

A Persian Garden Bakhtiari rug with tiles of stylized trees and flora in polychrome on an ivory ground.

63x116in (160x294.5cm)

£200-250 **DRA**

A Persian Garden Bakhtiari area rug, with teal, cobalt, ochre and orange in varying foliate patterns within a polychromatic border.

114in (285cm) long

£800-1,200 **DRA**

A late 19thC Bidjar carpet, from north west Persia, the navy outer border with palmettes, cut and reduced in length, repairs, wear.

296x154in (752x391cm)

£5,000-7,000 **FRE**

A Bidjar carpet, from north west Persia, generally low pile throughout, losses, old glue residue.

c1900 *141x91in (358x231cm)*

£2,000-2,500 **FRE**

A Bidjar carpet, with extensive stylized flowerheads within a scrolling leaf and flowerhead triple border.

69.25ix132in (176x335cm)

£400-600 **SWO**

A Bidjar runner, the rust, blue and cream ground with stylized flowers and boteh.

39.25x122in (100x310cm)

£400-600 **SWO**

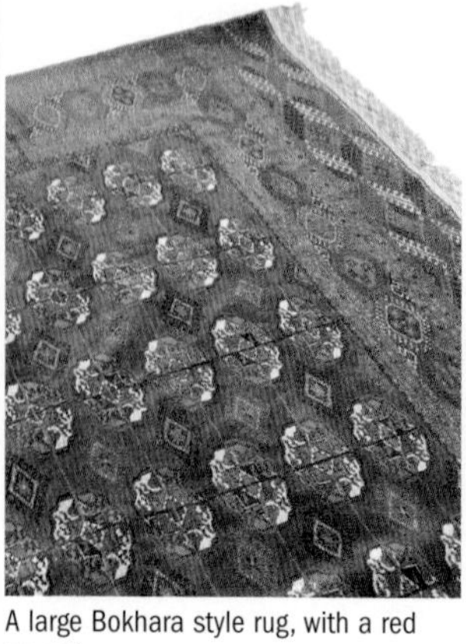

A large Bokhara style rug, with a red ground.

93x153.5in (236x390cm)

£400-600 **SWO**

An Iranian Ghom rug, in cotton and wool, with a central medallion on red field, fringes.

c1960 *50.5in (126cm) wide*

£70-100 **KAU**

A Hamadan rug, in cotton and wool, on brown fond.

c1960 *78in (195cm) long*

£70-100 **KAU**

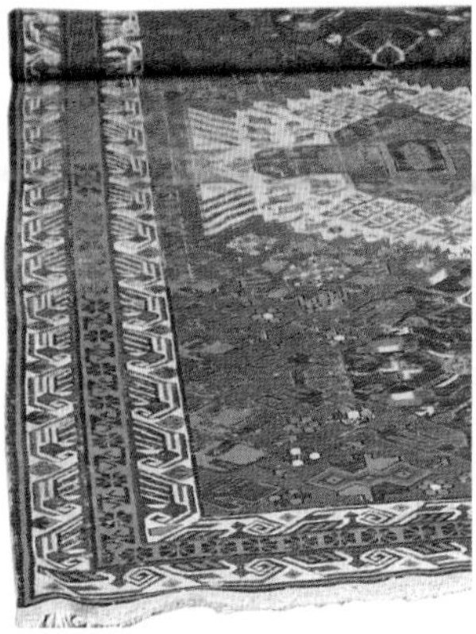

A Hamadan rug, with geometric motifs.

132in (330cm) long

£200-250 **SWO**

A Lavar Kerman carpet, from south west Persia, reduced in width, red wool wrapped single cord selvage, wear.

c1925 *262x133in (665.5x338cm)*

£800-1,200 **FRE**

A Kirman Lavar carpet, the cream field with central scrolling raspberry and blue medallion pendants, indigo and raspberry spandrels, within cream scrolling vine and palmette border between similar indigo and cream bands.

169.25x130in (430x330cm)

£3,000-5,000 **L&T**

A Kerman carpet, from south east Persia, with full lustrous pile.

c1940 *166x120in (421.5x305cm)*

£6,000-9,000 **FRE**

A Persian Kurdish Rug with lozenge medallions and cruciform panels in crimson and ivory on a black-brown ground within multiple borders.

51x110 (129.5x279.5cm)

£400-600 **DRA**

A Mahal carpet, from west Persia, one end with plain flatweave strip, other end missing some rows of knots in one area, thin, fleecy clip throughout, minor repairs, scattered thin areas, damage.

c1920. *151X104in (383.5x264cm)*

£1,500-2,000 **FRE**

A room-sized Mahal, with overall floral pattern on a red field wth blue border.

c1930 *136in (340cm) long*

£400-600 **POOK**

A Mashad carpet, from north east Persia.

c1940 *147in (367.5cm) long*

£1,500-2,000 **FRE**

A mid-20thC Qashqai carpet, from south west Persia, with barber pole selvages intact, one end with plain flatweave khilim strip with brocaded fringes, the outer end with outer guard border and no khilim strip.

117x81in (297x205.5cm)

£800-1,200 **FRE**

A late 19thC Kazak prayer rug.

63x38in (160x96.5cm)

£800-1,200 **FRE**

A late 19thC Moghan Kazak rug.

82x54in (208.5x137cm)

£800-1,200 **FRE**

A late 19thC Kazak Rug.

87x46in (221x117cm)

£1,000-1,500 **FRE**

A late 19thC Kazak rug

.

90in (225cm) long

£800-1,200 **FRE**

An early 20thC Karchapf Kazak, with central ivory medallions on a tomato field with navy border.

c1900 *86x67in (218.5x170cm)*

£2,500-3,000 **POOK**

An early 20thC Kazak runner, with overall geometric design on a blue field with ivory border.

c1910 *100x33in (254x84cm)*

£800-1,200 **POOK**

A Kazak cotton runner, with symmetrical knots, richly decorated central field with star motifs on dark blue ground, border with hexagons, sewed around the edges.

c1920 *165x44in (413x110cm)*

£400-600 **KAU**

A Kazak rug, the red field with three indigo and camel hooked lozenge medallions, within ivory hooked border between blue and camel bands.

79.5x53in (202x135cm)

£1,000-1,500 **L&T**

A Caucasian Kazak runner, with centre panel of overall polygons in ivory and polychrome on midnight blue ground.

38x112in (96.5x284.5cm)

£400-500 **DRA**

A Uzbek Kazak Rug, with cruciform medallion and symmetrical stylized forms in blue and ivory on a cinnabar ground.

55x79in (139.5x200.5cm)

£300-500 **DRA**

A Uzbek Kazak rug, with cinnabar diamonds and half diamonds on a Persian blue ground.

78x94in (198x239cm)

£300-500 **DRA**

A Beloutsch rug, from Afghanistan, wool, Mirhab motif, fringes.

c1970 *46in (115cm) long*

£150-200 **KAU**

A Beloutsch rug, from Afghanistan, wool, with Mirhab motif, fringes, spots.

c1970 *54.75in (137cm) long*

£150-200 **KAU**

A second half of the 19thC Chelaberd rug, from south Caucasus.

73x48in (186x122cm)

£700-1,000 **FRE**

A Orduz Kubo, from Russia, woollen, asymmetrical knots, with three octagonal medallions on dark blue ground with star motifs and four-fold border, with short woollen fringe, some faults.

c1920 *63x48.5in (157x121cm)*

£400-500 **KAU**

An early 20thC Shirvan throw rug, with three medallions on a navy field and multiple border.

c1910 *71x44in (180x112cm)*

£800-1,200 **POOK**

A Shirvan throw rug, with overall floral design on a red field with navy and ivory borders.

c1910 *64in (160cm) long*

£400-600 **POOK**

A second half 19thC Soumac carpet, from east Caucasus, losses, tear, wear.

120x76in (305x193cm)

£800-1,200 **FRE**

A Soumak flat weave rug with green, red and ochre motif on ochre and gold-toned ground.

103in (257.5cm) wide

£600-900 **DRA**

A Sumak runner, the cream and plum ground with medallions within a blue ground border.

124x50in (315x127cm)

£400-600 **SWO**

A Yomud carpet, from Russia, made from cotton, asymmetrical knots, decorated gallery with Yomud guls and added border above and below, woollen fringe.

c1965 *119.5x31in (299x77cm)*

£100-150 **KAU**

A throw rug, from Caucasia, with three medallions on a red field with ivory border.

c1910 *61in (152.5cm) long*

£700-1,000 **POOK**

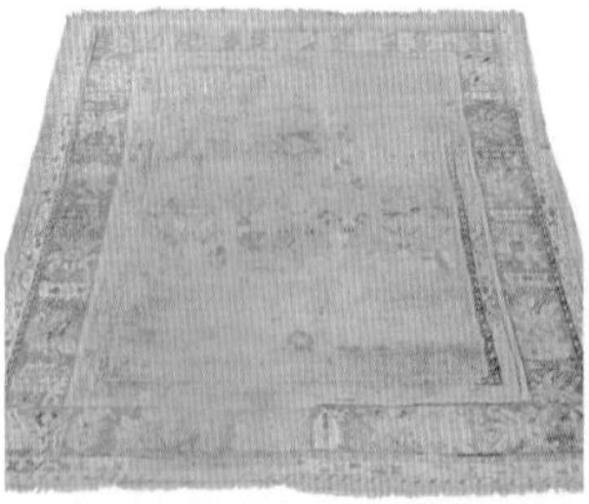

An early 20thC West Anatolia Oushak carpet.

164in (410cm) long

£1,800-2,200 **FRE**

A Tekke Turkoman carpet, the red ground with ivory medallions, within multiple borders.

94.5x137.75in (240x350cm)

£500-700 **SWO**

A Turkoman Rug, with centre panel of polygons and stars in blue and brown on a cinnabar ground.

c1920 81x87in (205.5x221cm)

£700-1,000 **DRA**

A 1920s Ushak carpet, with an allover pattern on a green ground, within multiple borders.

142.5x185in (362x470cm)

£2,800-3,200 **SWO**

A large Ushak carpet, the rose field with allover pattern of large palmettes and cruciform motifs in greens and yellows, within green rosette and floral spray border between various bands.

228.5x132in (580x335cm)

£4,000-6,000 **L&T**

A large Ushak carpet, the turquoise field with allover pattern of large salmon pink palmettes, scrolling vine border between bands.

238x173.25in (605cmx440cm)

£6,000-9,000 **L&T**

A 19thC susani, worked in threads to a pieced linen ground, the field designed with a series of palmettes to a foliate lattice ground, probably Bakhara, some damage.

59x39.5in (150x100cm)

£1,800-2,200 **L&T**

A mid-19thC susani, worked in silks to a linen ground, merchant's ink stamps, "Messrs Ramzan Khan & Co, Shawl, Silk and Skin Merchants, Anar Kali .....", probably Bakhara.

59x39.5in (150x100cm)

£1,500-2,000 **L&T**

A CLOSER LOOK AT AN AGRA RUG

High quality and luxurious carpets were made by prisoners in Agra and other Indian cities. These are extremely sought-after today.

White and ivory grounds are harder to come by than carpets with red or blue grounds, and as a result can attract a premium.

Rectangular carpets like this tend to attract higher prices than square ones.

Agra carpets are among the most valuable of all Indian carpets.

An Agra carpet, the ivory field with allover lattice of palmettes, within similarly decorated emerald green border, and claret guard bands.

231.5x136.25in (588x346cm)

£35,000-45,000 **L&T**

An Indian Serapi Rug, with unusual radiating polygon medallion in ivory and crimson on a midnight blue ground within multiple borders.

72x106in (183x269cm)

£400-600 **DRA**

A second quarter 20thC Indo-Tabriz carpet, repairs.

225x142in (571.5x360cm)

£5,000-7,000 **FRE**

A Grenfell hooked rug, depicting a polar bear with seagulls, with label and tag.

41.5in (105cm) high

£500-800 **WAD**

A Grenfell hooked rug, depicting a polar bear with an iceberg in the distance, with label.

11.5in (29.5cm) wide

£350-400 **WAD**

A Grenfell hooked rug, depicting four mallard ducks in flight, with label.

53in (134cm) high

£1,200-1,800 **WAD**

A Grenfell hooked rug, depicting a hunter and dog, with label.

The women of Labrador and Newfoundland had always made hooked rugs. From 1906 an English medical missionary, Dr. Wilfred T. Grenfell, helped develop the rug hooking into a cottage industry. By 1916 there were 16 mission picture mats, many designed by Grenfell himself.

11.5in (29cm) wide

£500-800 **WAD**

A Grenfell hooked rug depicting a map of Newfoundland with boats and whales, with label.

21.75in (54cm) high

£700-1,000 **POOK**

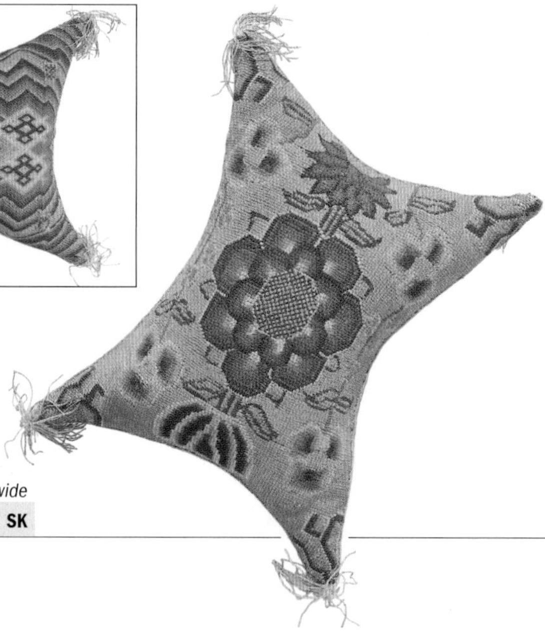

A canvaswork pincushion, probably from Chester County, Pennsylvania, worked in Irish stitch with waves of graded colours around a geometric diamond design, the corner blocks stitched with the initials "M E" and dated "1768".

7.5in (19cm) wide

£12,000-15,000 **SK**

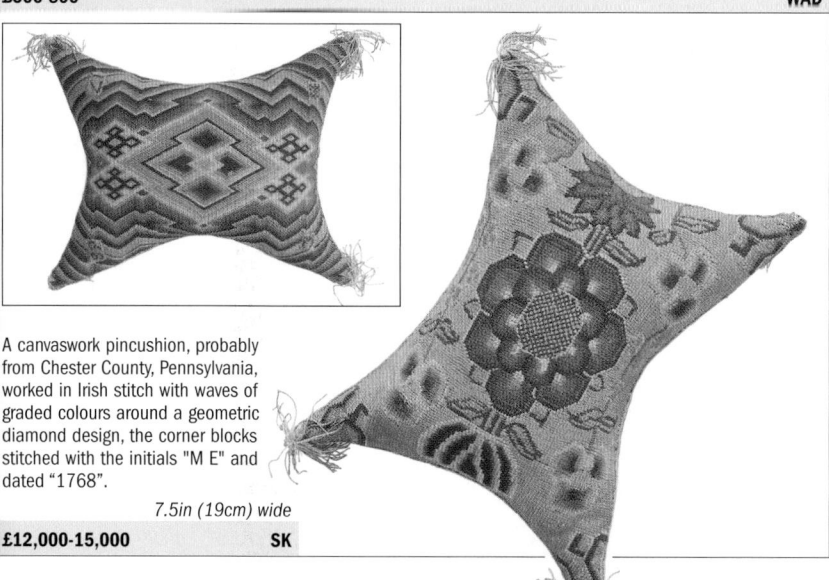

A crewelwork pillow cover, by Lydia Hoopes of Chester County, Pennsylvania, depicting elaborate flowering vines, butterflies and birds, dated.

1771 *30in (75cm) high*

£7,000-10,000 **POOK**

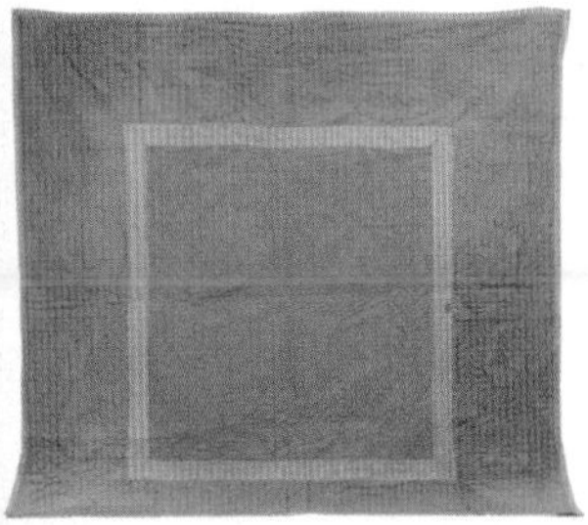

A 19thC Lancaster County Amish pieced wool quilt, with geometric pattern in brown, olive green and bronze wool heightened with feather, cable, floral and star patterns, the blue glazed cotton reverse with "Cambric Cloth" label.

78in (198cm) wide

£3,500-4,500 **FRE**

An early 20thC Lancaster County Amish pieced quilt, with diamond and square pattern in blue, brick red, purple and cherry red polished cotton, with diamond, feather band, arc, and star quilting, the reverse in blue and brick red stripes.

84in (213.5cm) wide

£2,800-3,200 **FRE**

An early 20thC Lancaster County Amish 'Sunshine and Shadow' pieced woollen quilt, in purple, burgundy, blue, brown and green wool heightened with feather, diamond and rope quilting, the reverse with grey cotton.

80in (203cm) wide

£3,500-4,500 **FRE**

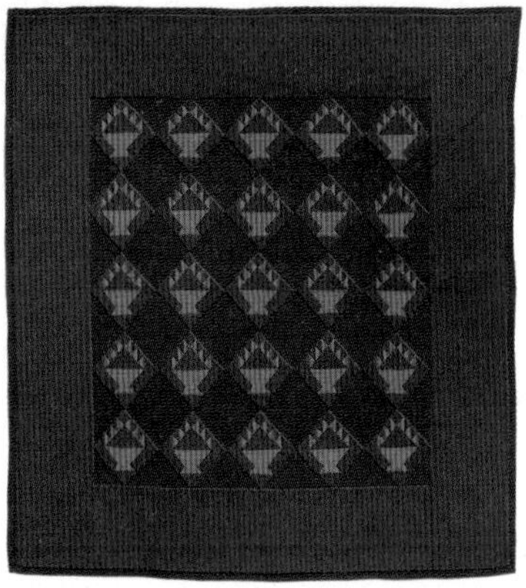

An Amish pieced quilt, with basket and diamond pattern.

c1940 *82in (205cm) wide*

£320-380 **POOK**

A mid-20thC Amish crib quilt, in a tumbling block pattern.

38in (95cm) wide

£1,000-1,500 **POOK**

A mid-20thC Amish pieced crib quilt, with a diamond and block pattern.

35in (87.5cm) wide

£320-380 **POOK**

An appliqué cotton 'Mariner's Compass Signature' quilt, from Philadelphia or New Jersey area, composed of 32 blocks in red, blue, and brown printed cotton with calico mariner's compass motifs, on a white ground, each block signed in ink with the names and dates, with white cotton binding and backing.

1842 *101in (254.5cm) high*

£800-1,200 **SK**

A appliqué cotton quilt from Baltimore, with patterned chintz and printed calicos on a white cotton ground, central design of a six-point star surrounded by cut-out floral, urn, and vine chintz designs, stuffed and appliquéd to the white background, with white cotton backing.

c1840 *134in (340.5cm) wide*

£12,000-15,000 **SK**

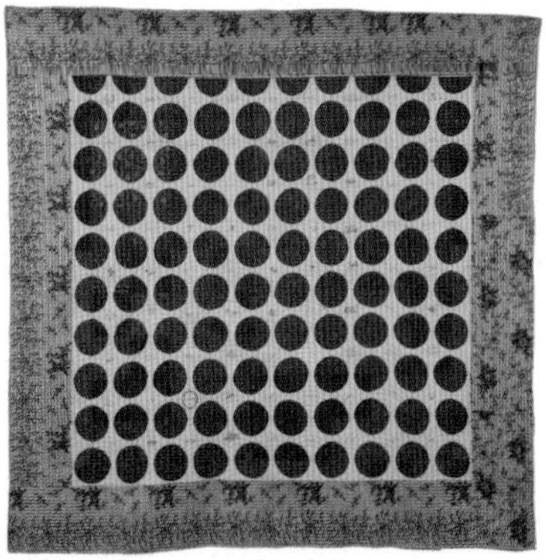

A pieced cotton and chintz friendship quilt from Port of Philadelphia, Pennsylvania, with white cotton squares and pieced and appliquéd red calico printed corners, each centred with a pen and ink signature and motifs including clasped hands, sailing vessels, musical instruments and flowers, edged in white twill, with white cotton backing.

1842 *96in (240cm) wide*

£1,200-1,800 **SK**

A pieced and appliquéd cotton Mariner's Compass quilt, from Pennsylvania or New Jersey, composed of blocks with Mariner's Compass motifs in printed red, green, yellow, and blue cotton fabrics, with red and white sawtooth sashing and oak leaf corners, red binding and matching backing.

c1845 *107in (272cm) high*

£8,000-12,000 **SK**

A Pennsylvania jacquard coverlet, inscribed "Henry Keemer Womelsdorf 1847 T. Werner".

1847 *94in (235cm) long*

£280-320 **POOK**

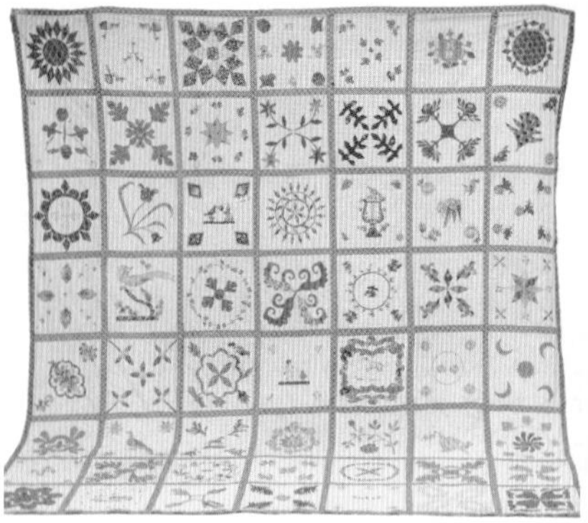

A 19thC appliqué spread from Pennsylvania, comprising squares, each with a different device including figures, animals, stars, flowers and other stylized elements in printed chintz and printed cotton patches.

100in (254cm) wide

£800-1,200 **FRE**

A 19thC 'Drunkards Path Quilt' from Pennsylvania, with orange and red cotton patches within a sawtooth border, with conforming flowerhead and cable quilting.

£1,500-2,000 **FRE**

An appliqué cotton Quaker album quilt, from Delaware or Chester County, Pennsylvania, comprising blocks of printed calico motifs including farm implements, tableware and geometric designs, framed by blue sashing, with brown glazed cotton backing.

c1850 *88in (223.5cm) high*

£8,000-12,000 **SK**

A President's Wreath friendship quilt, from Lancaster County, Pennsylvania, comprising blocks appliquéd with flowering circlets in printed calico on a white ground, each block centred with an ink signature, bound with white cotton tape.

1850 *88in (223.5cm) wide*

£700-1,000 **SK**

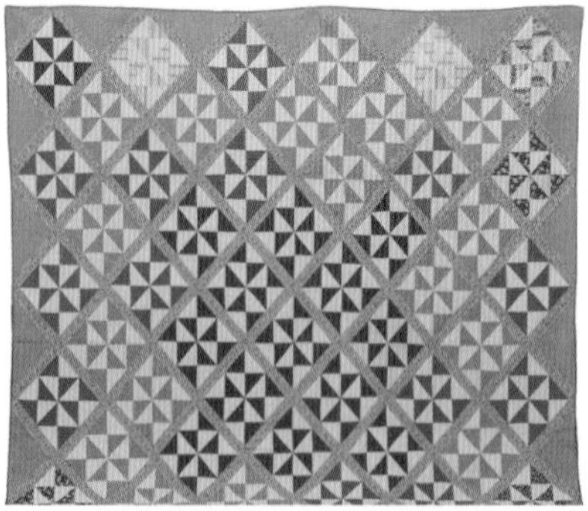

A patchwork quilt by Mary Jane Slack of Pennsylvania, comprising printed cotton patches arranged in a variation of the 'Cross Bar' pattern, with orange outer border, inscribed in ink to reverse "Mary Jane Slack's quilt fourth month 11, 1852".

88in (223.5cm) high

£500-800 **FRE**

A Civil War era pieced and appliquéd cotton presentation album quilt, comprising white cotton blocks with embroidery, trapunto, and reverse appliqué embellishments, a spread-winged eagle over an anchor to the centre, with other patriotic and floral motifs, with signatures of friends, family and makers, white cotton backing.

1863 *82in (208cm) high*

£15,000-20,000 **SK**

A six point star-form pincushion, of ribbed cream silk, inset with a central circular mirrored glass panel and mirrors to each point, with metal threads and glass beads, with display case.

This was reputedly worked by Mary Queen of Scots.

8.75in (22cm) wide

£800-1,200 **L&T**

A 17thC English needlework crib cover, with 35 slips and initialled "H.E.", by Honor Elliot, daughter of Vice Admiral of Devon Coast John Elliot, with animals and flowers worked in various silk threads, with many varieties of stitching and stumpwork.

44.5in (113cm) wide

£18,000-22,000 **POOK**

A pair of Elizabethan needlework pictures, with lions in the forest and birds perched in trees, worked in wool and silk thread.

c1680 *8.5in (21.5cm) wide*

£2,200-2,800 pair **POOK**

A late 17th to early 18thC English silk on silk needlework picture, depicting a country scene with shepherd, shepherdess and flock.

This piece is a predecessor to the 'Fishing Lady' needlework of America.

14.5in (37cm) wide

£4,000-5,000 **POOK**

A rare late 17th to early 18thC English needlepoint picture, by "Rebecca at the Well", worked in coloured silks, stumpwork, moss work with silver gilt thread outlines and sequin borders, with animals and floral sprays.

15in (38cm) wide

£12,000-18,000 **POOK**

An English silk on linen needlework picture, wrought by Mary Ann Oddey with alphabet over potted flowers and verse within a floral border, dated

1822 *17.5in (44.5cm) high*

£600-900 **POOK**

A 19thC silkwork picture, depicting medieval figures in an interior.

28.25in (72cm) wide

£220-280 **SWO**

Two pairs of 17thC crewelwork curtains, the wool serge ground with stylized forest and stag scene, sprigged chintz cotton lining, with pelmet.

larger pair 82x93in (208x236cm)

£6,000-8,000 set **L&T**

A 17thC stumpwork panel, having a central oval panel depicting two ladies in a landscape, flanked by a deer, unicorn and other animals and flowers.

16.5in (41cm) wide

£4,000-6,000 **SWO**

An early 18thC stumpwork picture of two figures before a castle, surrounded by animals, birds and insects, in a shaped oak frame.

35cm (13.75in) wide

£600-800 **SWO**

An early 19thC embroidered picture on paper, depicting deer, birds and insects amongst flowers.

16.5in (42cm) high

£400-600 **SWO**

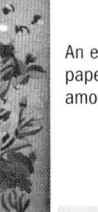

An 18thC English beadwork mirror, decorated with a floral and figural scene of a lion and a unicorn, the back mounted with velvet, possibly once an easel mirror, later glass plate, label verso "W Boswell & Sons, Experts & Purchasers of Works of Art, 48 London Street, Norwich, est. 1725".

1725 *57.5cm (22.5in) high*

£8,000-12,000 **SWO**

A rare English linen spot sampler, with geometric and figurative patterns worked in coloured silk and silver gilt thread in various stitches, initialled "ML" and dated "1611".

11.5in (29cm) high

£8,000-12,000 **POOK**

A fine English silk on linen needlework sampler, inscribed "Elizabeth Emes made this sampler November 23, 1720", with bands of alphabet and 'Elijah and the Ravens', coat of arms.

13.5in (34cm) high

£3,000-4,000 **POOK**

A George III sampler, by Charlotte Turnock, "aged 10 years", with two horses and the inscription reading "Blessed with joy of innocence".

14.5in (36.5cm) high

£600-900 **SWO**

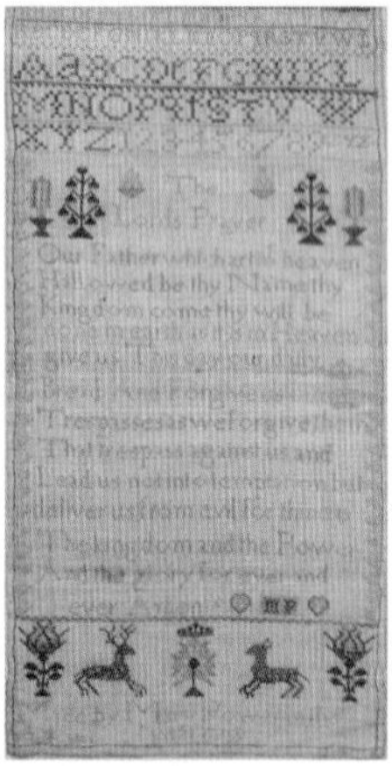

A George III Lord's Prayer sampler, by Mary Powerinthe.

1789 *17in (43cm) high*

£500-700 **SWO**

A George III sampler, by Jane Cullimore, who "finished this sampler in the tenth year of her age July the 22 in the year of our Lord 1795".

12in (30cm)high

£500-700 **SWO**

A Scottish silk on silk needlework sampler, inscribed "Isabel Simpson sewed this sampler in the year 1801", with alphabets and a strawberry border.

17in (43cm) high

£1,000-1,500 **POOK**

A Regency sampler, by Jean McDonald, aged 14, worked in coloured silks with a verse and Georgian house, later glazed and framed.

16.75in (42.5cm) wide

£2,200-2,800 **L&T**

A needlework sampler, the verse above a country house with a raised silkwork hedge and a pair of deer, "By Caroline Milne(?) January 1830".

18in (45cm) high

£500-700 **SWO**

An English silk on linen needlework sampler, by Elizabeth White, with central verse surrounded by potted flowers and birds, vine border, dated 1837.

16in (40.5cm) wide

£800-1,200 **POOK**

A late 18thC to early 19thC alphabet sampler, by Margaret Scotland, aged 11, worked in coloured silks and cottons, with verse, later glazed frame.

17.25in (43.5cm) high

£1,500-2,000 **L&T**

A framed sampler, by Isabella Kinloch, worked in coloured silks to a fine wool ground, with alphabets and a Georgian house between trees, glazed and framed.

13in (33cm) wide

£2,000-2,500 **L&T**

A late 18thC needlework sampler by Elizabeth Crandell, with alphabet, pious verse and inscription "Elizabeth Crandell is my name at 10 years old I work the same", losses, discolouration.

13.5in (34.5cm) high

£600-800 **FRE**

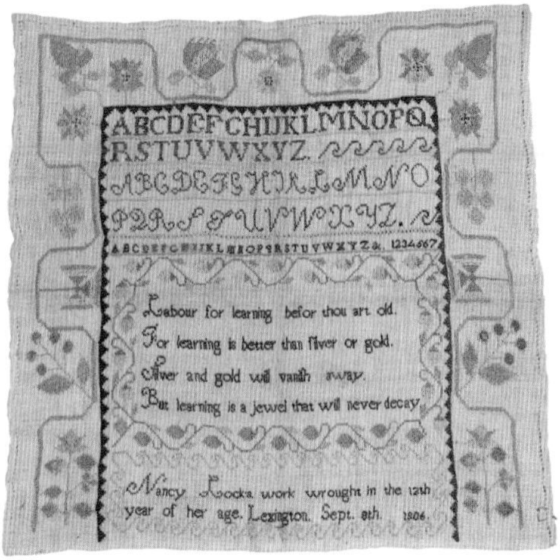

A needlework sampler, "Nancy Lock's work wrought in the 12th year of her age. Lexington. Sept. 8th.1806." in silk threads with three alphabet panels and verse "Labour for learning befor thou art old".

17in (4343cm) wide

£4,000-6,000 **SK**

A silk on gauze needlework sampler, wrought by "Susannah Higgins Her Work Aged 7 Years 1810," the central panel with strawberry vines, house and verse.

c1810 *16.5in (42cm) high*

£2,500-3,000 **POOK**

A needlework sampler, by "Eliza W. Gale at M. Tufts school Charlestown, 1813 AE. 12YRS," with rows of alphabet, a sentimental verse and inscription, worked in silk threads, fading.

21.5in (54.5cm) high

£4,000-5,000 **FRE**

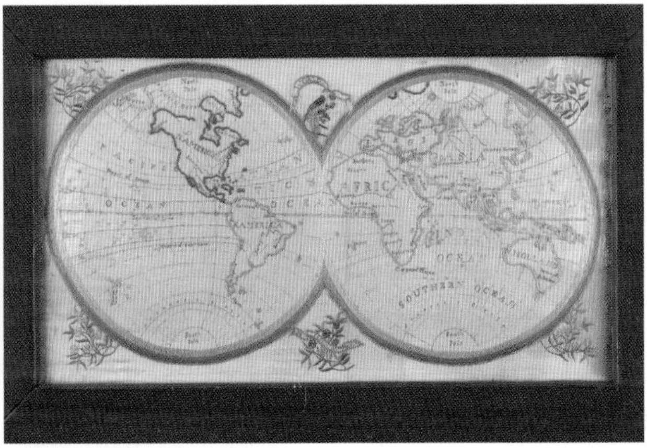

A rare American silk on silk map sampler, depicting a world map wrought by M. Skinner.

1819 *17.5in (44cm) wide*

£2,200-2,800 **POOK**

A New Jersey needlework sampler, with alphabet and inscription "Georgina Stubbs her work March 10 1827", in wool yarns on a linen ground, framed.

9.75in (25cm) high

£800-1,200 **FRE**

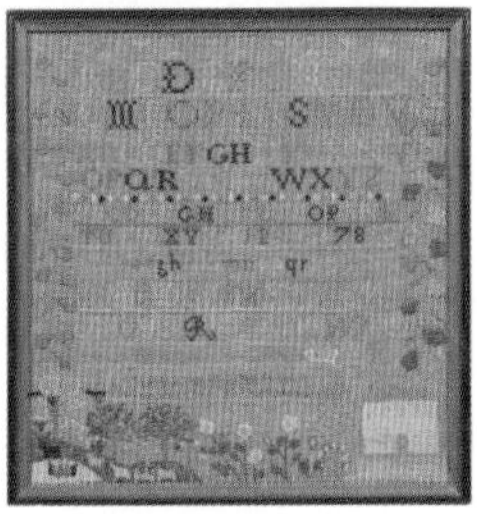

A needlework sampler, by "Abigail Clark Cilley AE 11 A.D. 1829", probably New Hampshire, silk threads on a linen ground with alphabet panels and verse "Let piety thy thoughts direct", fading.

A genealogy search revealed a record for an Abigail C. Cilley, born May, 1818. She went on to have nine children and lived in New Hampton, New Hampshire.

18.5in (47cm) wide

£2,000-2,500 **SK**

An American polychrome cross stitch sampler, with house and trees, and the legend "Create in me a clean heart O God and renew a right spirit within me, Margaret Holloway's Work Aged 10 years", discolouration.

18in (45.5cm) high

£400-600 **TA**

A Canadian sampler, by Mary Bray Robins, probably from Niagara Peninsula, with a large area of devices.

1827 *21in (53cm) high*

£1,000-1,500 **TFR**

A Canadian woven sampler, from Woodstock, either in New Brunswick, or Ontario, framed and glazed.

1862 *15.75in (40cm) high*

£800-1,200 **TFR**

A rare 18thC gilt tooled Morocco document purse, the case with ornately engraved white metal clasp, one side stamped "Abraham Aguilar, Kingston, Jamaica" and dated.

1787 *11.5in (29cm) wide*

£350-450 **ROW**

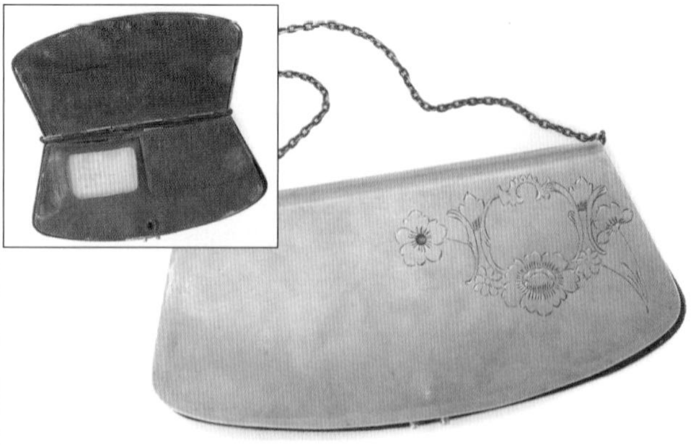

A Russian metal evening handbag, one of a kind, by Ivan Brietling.

1884 *8in (20.5cm) wide*

£150-200 **CHA**

A French 18ct gold purse, set with three rubies and a diamond in a leaf design.

c1900

£3,200-3,800 **JP**

A Whiting & Davis Art Deco mesh purse, with enamel geometric decoration, signed.

c1925 *7in (18cm) high wide*

£300-500 **DD**

A French Art Deco 'Flapper' handbag, rhinestone mesh purse, brass frame and decorative tassel.

c1925 *8.5in (21.5cm) high*

£300-500 **DD**

A Van Cleef & Arpels black Art Deco handbag, in silk, enamel, diamond and gold.

1925 *7.5in (19cm) wide*

£2,000-2,500 **JES**

An Art Deco handbag, in black suede with sterling, marcasite and enamel geometric decoration.

9in (23cm) wide

£300-500 **DD**

A 1930s black calfskin handbag by Nettie Rosenstein, with Art Nouveau-style clasp.

c1935 *8.75in (22cm) wide*

£300-500 **MGL**

A French Art Deco clutch handbag, in suede with cut crystal and rhinestone decorative clasp and frame.

c1935 *8in (20.5cm) wide*

£600-800 **DD**

A French Art Deco clutch handbag, suede with sterling, marcasite and onyx decorative clasp and frame.

c1935 *8in (20.5cm) wide*

£600-800 **DD**

BOX BAGS

- Practical and hardwearing box bags became popular in the 1950s.
- Wilardy of New York was particularly influential in the development of box bags. Will Hardy joined his father's handbag firm in 1948 and started to produce fashionable and hardwearing Lucite bags. Shapes were radical and boldly geometric, with gently curved lines and lollipop handles.
- Striking colourways, attractive shapes and additional decoration in materials such as Bakelite, glitter or metal can add value, as can maker's labels.
- Pale blue, yellow and green box bags are fairly rare, while white, greys and browns are more common.
- Rhinestones, glass and filigree work finish increased the level of exclusivity, making the bags popular with society ladies and celebrities of the time.
- Although a manmade material, the use of the plastic made early box bags expensive, as each example was hand cast and soldered.
- The invention of injection moulding in the 1950s allowed the cheap manufacture of plastic items opening the market to inferior mass-produced box bags. Quality declined and Lucite box bags eventually fell out of fashion.
- Check for cracks, decay and other damage that could affect the price.

A 1950s turquoise Lucite handbag by Charles Kahn with clear lid and handles.

This is a rare colour.

8in (20.5cm) wide

£700-1,000 **DJI**

A 1950s Lucite handbag, by Myles Original, butterscotch coloured.

9in (23cm) wide

£250-350 **DJI**

A 1950s tortoiseshell Lucite handbag, by Tyrolean, with pearls and metal lid.

8in (20.5cm) wide

£220-280 **DJI**

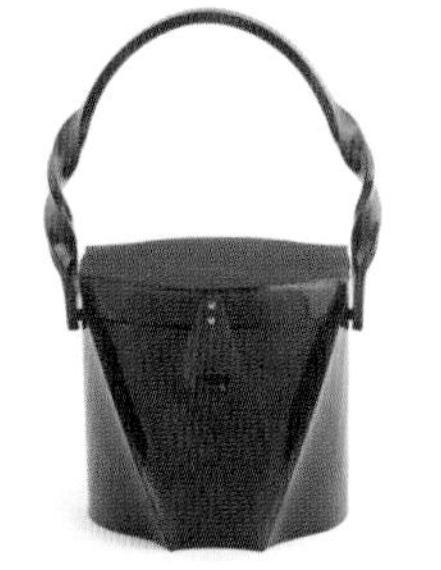

A 1950s caramel-coloured Lucite handbag, by Wilardy.

This won an International Fashion Institute design award in 1954.

6in (15cm) wide

£300-500 **DJI**

A 1950s pink fabric Lucite handbag, by Wilardy with rhinestone design.

8in (20.5cm) wide

£120-180 **DJI**

A 1950s Lucite handbag, by Wilardy caramel coloured, oval shaped with gold-coloured etched overlay.

7.25in (18.5cm) wide

£120-180 **DJI**

A 1950s Lucite handbag, by Wilardy, caramel coloured with triple-decker design.

5.5in (14cm) wide

£300-500 **DJI**

A rare 1950s to 1960s turquoise alligator box handbag, by Nettie Rosenstein, with restored clasp and mirror, made in Florence, Italy.

c1955 *9in (23cm) wide*

£1,000-1,500 **MGL**

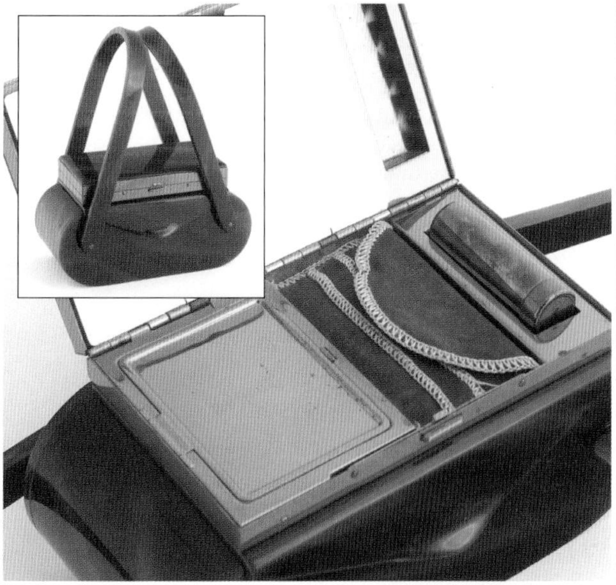

A 1950s caramel-coloured Lucite handbag, by Wilardy, with fitted compact.

7in (18cm) wide

£300-400 **DJI**

An early French tinplate fire vehicle, with mudguards and running boards, with front hinged roof, lithographed details and "SP9" registration, the tinplate tyres marked "Dunlop", clockwork mechanism.

6.5in (16.5cm) long

£180-220 **W&W**

A rare early 20thC Distler tinplate open-style fire escape engine, with yellow two-piece escape ladder with tilt mechanism and locking lever, three seated fireman figures, automatic bell and clockwork mechanism.

11in (28cm) long

£250-300 **W&W**

A Wells-Brimtoy 'Mickey Mouse' handcar, with composition figures of Mickey and Minnie and two card buildings marked "Mickey Mouse, his house" and "Station" and ten track sections, in original fitted box.

c1935

£600-900 **SWO**

A Gunthermann tinplate 'Autobahn Kurier' car, with cream and red paintwork.

11.5in (29cm) wide

£280-320 **ROS**

DINKY

DINKY VEHICLES

- Originally introduced in 1931 by the makers Meccano, the first Dinky vehicles were designed as accessories for Hornby '0'-gauge trains. By 1935 there were over 200 models to choose from.
- Output slowed during the war, but in 1947 the popular 'Supertoys' range of slightly smaller scale vehicles was introduced, followed later on by 'Speedwheels' in the 1970s.
- Production ceased in 1979, but the brand was revived between 1988 and 2001 by Matchbox, who released special editions for collectors.
- Pre-war vehicles fetch a premium, but early post-war reissues are also valuable and can be identified by wider wheels, black base plates and dull colours.
- Early trucks are popular, especially 1950s Foden flatbed trucks. Series 25 lorries and Series 28 delivery vans are also desirable.
- Models with advertising transfers from the 1950s and 60s are rapidly growing in popularity as are 1970s cult film and TV show models.
- Post-war examples should be supplied with original packaging, preferably in good condition.
- Rare colourways are sought-after across the board.

A Dinky Toys cars gift set no. 4, comprising a 23G Cooper-Bristol, 23F Alfa Romeo, 23H Ferrari, 23JHMW and a 23N Maserati, boxed.

1953-54

£400-600 **SWO**

A Dinky 161 Austin Somerset saloon car, in two-tone cream over black with cream hubs, boxed, with factory blemish.

1954-59 *3.5in (9cm) long*

£150-200 **W&W**

A Dinky 151 Triumph 1800 saloon car, in dark blue with light blue hubs, boxed.

1954-59 *3.5in (9cm) wide*

£120-180 **W&W**

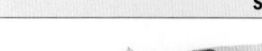

A Dinky 131 Cadillac Eldorado, in yellow with red interior, with cream hubs and driver figure, boxed, some wear.

A version with spun aluminium hubs, made from 1962-3, can be worth slightly more.

1956-61 *4.75in (12cm) wide*

£100-150 **W&W**

A Dinky 452 Trojan van, in green with green hubs and "Chivers Jellies" signing, complete with original box.

1954-57 *3.25in (8.5cm) wide*

£120-180 **W&W**

A Dinky 942 Foden tanker, with blue second-type cab, red wheels and tank with off-white centre line and "Regent" decals to sides, complete with blue and white striped box.

1955-57 *7in (18cm) wide*

£150-200 **W&W**

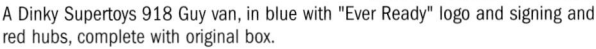

A Dinky Supertoys 918 Guy van, in blue with "Ever Ready" logo and signing and red hubs, complete with original box.

1955-58 *5.25in (13.5cm) wide*

£280-320 **W&W**

A Dinky military vehicles gift set 699, comprising a 674 Austin Champ, 641 cargo truck, 676 armoured personnel carrier and 621 heavy wagon, complete with inner stand and blue and white striped box.

1955-58 *Box 15.75in (40cm) wide*

£180-220 **W&W**

A Dinky 260 Royal Mail van, in red with matt black roof, boxed.

1955-61 *3in (7.5cm) long*

£120-180 **W&W**

A Dinky 917 Guy van, with red first-type cab, cream body and "Spratt's Bonio, Ovals and Dog Cakes" signs to sides, in original blue stripe box

1968-74 *5.25in (13.5cm) wide*

£200-250 **W&W**

An Arnold clockwork tinplate No.2500 USA Military Police Jeep,with dashboard mounted semaphore, rear plastic jerry can and two policemen figures, includes key and card box.

£350-450 **VEC**

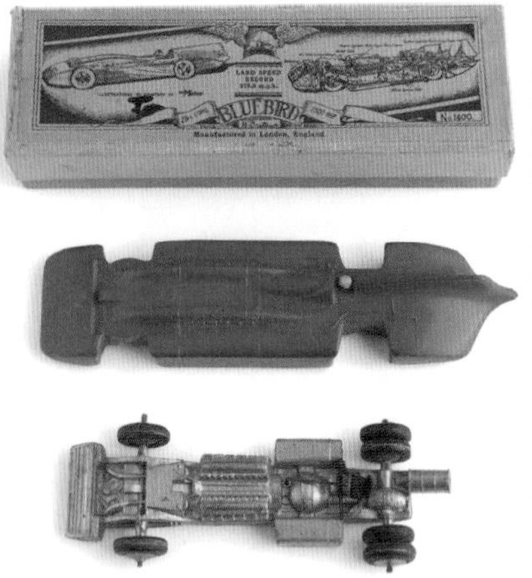

A rare Britains 1400 Bluebird land speed record car, with Campbell blue body that lifts to reveal detailed chassis, with twin rear wheels and rubber tyres, complete with original labelled box.

6.5in (16.5cm) wide

£200-250 **W&W**

A scarce Britains plastic 'Wild West' series 7615 Concord stage coach, containing a traditional Western-style coach with two crew, passengers and luggage, pulled by four horses, in a large cellophane window box, minor wear.

c1970 *14.75in (37.5cm) wide*

£100-150 **W&W**

A Britains 1433 covered military wagon, of caterpillar type with hinged tailboard, later-style cab with driver, finished in khaki with light brown tinplate cover and tow hook, in original box.

6in (15cm) wide

£150-200 **W&W**

A Corgi gift set 19, comprising a Land Rover in Chipperfield's Circus livery, with elephant and cage mounted on a trailer, in original box with inner display sleeve and packing.

1962-68. *8in (20.5cm) wide*

£200-250 **W&W**

A San Marusan Toys tinplate 'Smoky Joe' car, with battery-operated "Mystery Action Drive", finished in red with various trim colours, driver holds pipe, complete with original box, some wear.

8.5in (21.5cm) wide

£100-150 **W&W**

A Tri-Ang Spot-On 161 LWB Land Rover, finished in grey with white roof and interior, spare wheel mounted on bonnet and rear door, in original box, minor wear, possibly ex-factory.

4.5in (11.5cm) wide

£100-150 **W&W**

A rare Shackleton toys 'David Brown' Trackmaster 30 tractor, of heavy tinplate and diecast construction, with rubber tracks and clockwork mechanism.

Shackleton operated from 1939-52. Only 50 of these tractors are known to exist.

1952 *8.5in (21.5cm) wide*

£1,500-2,000 **W&W**

A Shackleton Toys clockwork tipping Foden lorry, in pale grey with red wings, complete with key and spanner, some losses and damage.

10.5in (26.5cm) wide

£500-700 **W&W**

A German Heinrich Handwerck bisque-head doll, with a jointed composite body, the head marked for Heirich Handwerck and Simon & Halbig.

head 1.75in (4.5cm) high

£280-320 **SWO**

An Ernst Heubach bisque doll, mould number 342, with sleeping eyes, open mouth and jointed wood and composition body, wearing gown and bonnet.

22in (56cm) high

£200-300 **GORL**

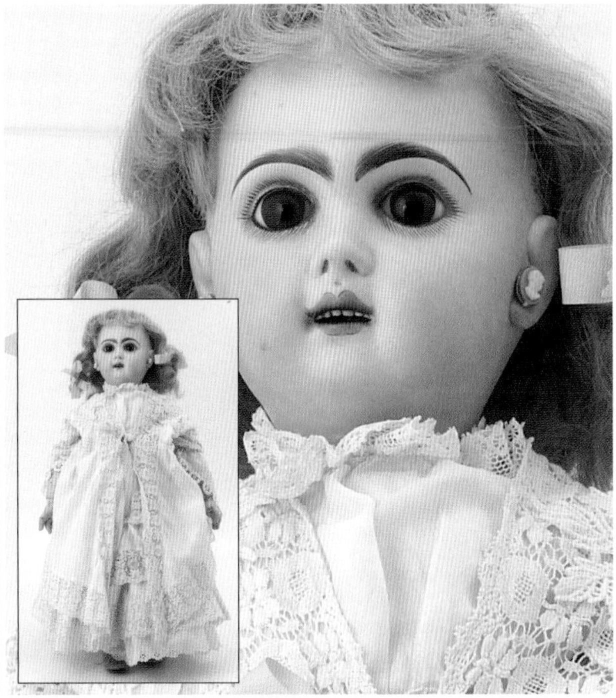

A Jumeau bisque doll, with fixed glass paperweight eyes, open mouth and pierced ears, on fully clothed jointed composition body with original shoes, back printed 'Paris Bebe Depose'.

c1880 *19.5in (49cm) high*

£800-1,200 **GORL**

A Kämmer & Reinhardt bisque character doll, with an open mouth, teeth and tongue, brown sleeping eyes, five-part body, in original brown mohair wig, silent voice.

16.75in (42cm) high

£200-250 **WDL**

A tall Kestner 'Franz' character boy, with a bisque head, brown sleeping eyes and painted lashes, open mouth with teeth, dimples, mohair wig, unmarked 17-piece body, head marked "P 19 made in Germany J.D.K. 247".

29.25in (73cm) high

£1,500-2,000 **WDL**

An Armand Marseille bisque doll, mould number 390, with open mouth and sleeping eyes, on jointed wood and composition body, wearing a cream dress with undergarments and bonnet.

17in (43cm) high

£100-150 **GORL**

A bisque head Parisienne with kid body and composition limbs.

£180-220 **ROS**

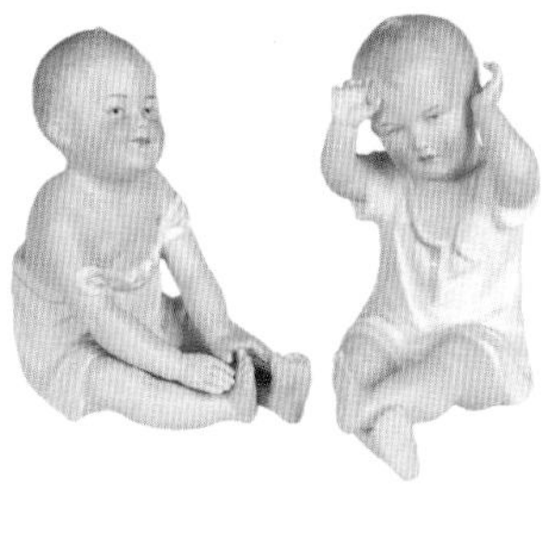

A pair of late 19thC Gebruder Heubach biscuit porcelain piano babies.

15cm (6in) high

£200-250 **SWO**

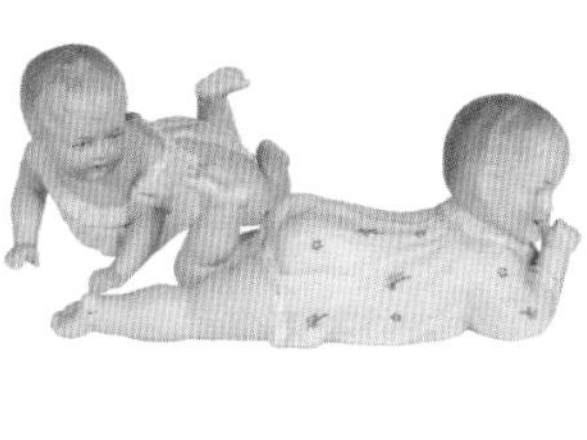

A pair of late 19thC German biscuit porcelain piano babies.

20cm (8in) long

£150-200 **SWO**

A bisque head 'Alice in Wonderland' doll, with painted head and head band, the fabric body with bisque forearms, original dress, underwear and socks and shoes.

11.25in (28cm) high

£300-500 **WDL**

A rare Biedermeier doll, with painted papier-mâché head and a leather body, open mouth and fixed eyes, painted lashes and hair, with an old real hair wig with plaits and one original leather shoe.

20.75in (52cm) high

£700-1,000 **WDL**

A late 19thC American doll, with painted papier-mâché head, fabric body and leather arms, wearing original underwear, feet missing, wear.

24.5in (61cm) high

£150-200 **WDL**

An early Kämmer & Reinhardt doll, with a celluloid shoulder head and a leather body, with modelled and painted eye brows, open mouth with teeth and a blonde wig with plaits, marked "K & R 255 SoR".

18in (45cm) high

£70-100 **WDL**

A British National Dolls doll, with open mouth, sleeping eyes and bent-limb composition body.

British National Dolls (BND) was established in the 1930s and closed in the 1960s.

14in (35.5cm) high

£150-200 **GORL**

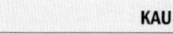

A Chinese 'Royal Doll', the head with modelled and painted eyes and red lips, the body in cardboard and metal, wearing an embroidered robe with a golden cardboard helmet and painted wooden shoes.

c1920 *11.25in (28cm) high*

£60-90 **WDL**

An Eastern Asian doll, possibly from China, the painted papier-mâché head with dark eyes and a black wig, fabric body, wooden feet, wearing a richly embroidered blue jacket, stamped on the inside of the jacket.

16in (40cm) high

£150-200 **WDL**

A 20thC wooden and plastic doll's house, with over 30 items figures and pieces of furniture, in an ebonized frame.

25.75in (64.5cm) wide

£70-100 **KAU**

A Canadian red painted doll's rocking chair, found in Waterloo county, probably from Quebec, original paint.

c1910 *14.5in (37cm) high*

£40-60 **ING**

A 20thC doll's kitchen, with stove, sink and detailed accessories including a porcelain service, baking pans and candlesticks, with a celluloid doll and bisque head doll.

37.25in (93cm) wide

£600-800 **KAU**

A Bing 1-gauge 'Münchner Kindl' carriage, with tinplate wheels, chromolithographed, one roof replaced, wear.

6in (15cm) long

£150-200 **LAN**

A Lionel 390E engine and tender, with a pair of 337 passenger cars and 338 observation car, together with a 219 crane.

overall 60in (150cm) long

£600-900 **POOK**

A Hornby O-gauge Princess Elizabeth electric locomotive and tender, in L.M.S livery, number "6201", contained in original blue cloth covered box, lid interior with printed details.

locomotive 14.25in (36cm) wide

£1,200-1,800 **ROS**

A scarce Wrenn 4-6-2 Dartmoor locomotive W2296, finished in British Rail green and black, number "34021", with tender, complete with original box and instructions, minor rubbing.

11in (28cm) long

£320-380 **W&W**

A scarce Wrenn 4-6-2 Blue Star locomotive W2297, finished in British Rail green and black, number "35010", with tender, complete with original box and instructions, minor rubbing and fading to name plate.

11.25in (28.5cm) long

£350-450 **W&W**

An Ives 'Grand Central Station', with lithographed detail.

Edward R. Ives founded his toy company in 1868 in Massachusetts. It was taken over by Lionel Corporation c1928.

22in (55cm) high

£600-900 **POOK**

A scratch-built live model steam traction engine.

24in (61cm) wide

£1,200-1,800 **SWO**

A 19thC carved wood and painted gesso rocking horse, with applied leather saddlery, horsehair mane and tail, upholstered seat, raised on rocking pine base.

61.25in (153cm) long

£800-1,200 **L&T**

A second half 19thC carved and painted rocking horse, retains elements of original tack.

63.5in (160cm) long

£300-500 **FRE**

A late Victorian carved wooden rocking horse, with glass eyes, the head turned slightly to the right, on a safety stand, with a brass coat of arms and a "Hamleys" label.

37.75in (96cm) high

£400-600 **SWO**

A late 19thC large carved and painted dappled rocking horse, with horsehair tail and mane.

88in (220cm) wide

£1,500-2,000 **POOK**

An early 20thC Ayres-type rocking horse, with a turned head, on a pine base.

42.75in (107cm) high

£700-1,000 **SWO**

A 20thC dapple grey rocking horse on a wooden stand.

43.5in (110cm) wide

£600-900 **SWO**

A CLOSER LOOK AT A ROCKING HORSE

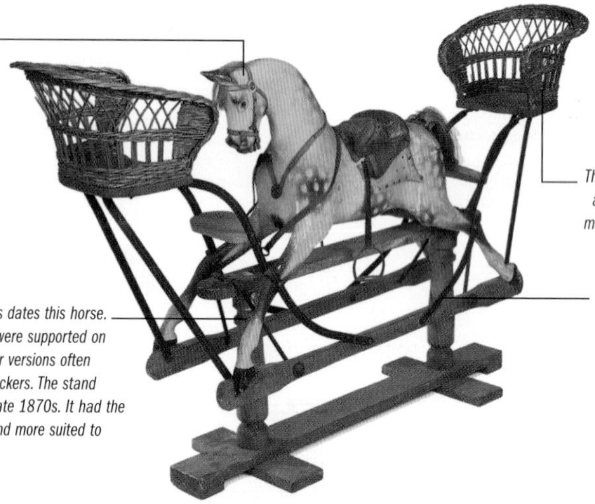

Horses were carved from single large blocks of wood, making each one slightly different.
The wicker seats are an appealing addition and would have enabled more children to be entertained at a time.
Dapple grey is the most popular colour. Earlier horses often have more pronounced dappling.
The swing mechanism helps dates this horse. Whilst early 19thC horses were supported on sharply bowed rockers, later versions often featured much shallower rockers. The stand became popular from the late 1870s. It had the advantage of being safer and more suited to modestly sized rooms.

A rare Edwardian nursery rocking horse, by G. and J. Lines, with saddle, tack, pommels for side-saddle riding, wicker seats to either end, on pedestal supports with cruciform base.

George and Joseph Lines established their toy company in the 19thC, primarily making rocking horses and other toys. Their three sons went on to found Tri-Ang.

78.75in (200cm) wide

£6,000-9,000 **L&T**

SOFT TOYS

An early Steiff cinnamon plush teddy bear, with button in left ear, boot-button eyes and stitched snout, hump-back, growler inoperative, repairs.

c1910 *13in (33cm) high*

£1,500-2,000 **GORL**

An early 20thC yes/no teddy bear, with a golden mohair body, amber glass eyes, four stitched claws to paws and feet, working growl box and with mechanical yes/no lever to rear.

15.75in (40cm) high

£200-250 **SWO**

Two British blonde mohair rabbits, each unjointed and with a stitched nose, wear and damage.

c1925 *largest 11in (28cm) high*

£50-70 **VEC**

A Robin Rive Mawley limited edition teddy bear, no.4 of 200, created to celebrate the 1999 4th Rugby World Cup, wool plush, wearing rugby shirt embroidered with country emblems.

21in (53cm) high

£80-120 **VEC**

A 19thC painted pine model of a butcher's shop.

14.75in (37cm) wide

£220-280 **SWO**

An architectural model of a house, with centre turret, painted mustard yellow and brown.

c1910 *23in (57.5cm) high*

£1,800-2,200 **POOK**

An early 20thC elaborate motorized circus diorama, with carved and polychrome figures, animals and tents, with 21 animals and 36 figures.

49in (122.5cm) wide

£1,800-2,200 **POOK**

An early to mid-20thC carved and painted farmhouse model, with outbuilding.

24.25in (60.5cm) wide

£800-1,200 **POOK**

A Continental Noah's Ark, with carved and painted animals.

19.75in (50cm) wide

£600-900 **SWO**

An oversized Dent cast iron hose reel wagon, with standing fireman and seated driver, horses and an open bench with attached spoke wheels.

21.5in (54cm) long

£2,800-3,200 **POOK**

An early cast iron hook and ladder truck, Harris or Hubley, with a nickel plated back end and three finely detailed horses, the driver, axes and fire bucket intact.

30in (75cm) wide

£1,200-1,800 **POOK**

An Ives 'Phoenix' cast iron fire patrol truck, with six seated fireman and two hanging onto rear platform.

20in (50cm) wide

£1,000-1,500 **POOK**

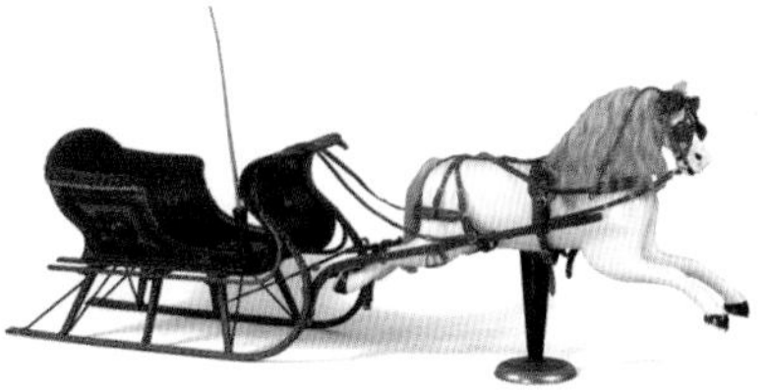

A child's carved and painted horse and sleigh, the sleigh with black chassis with floral highlights and red runners, the horse with horsehair mane and tail and white body.

c1900 *88in (220cm) long*

£800-1,200 **POOK**

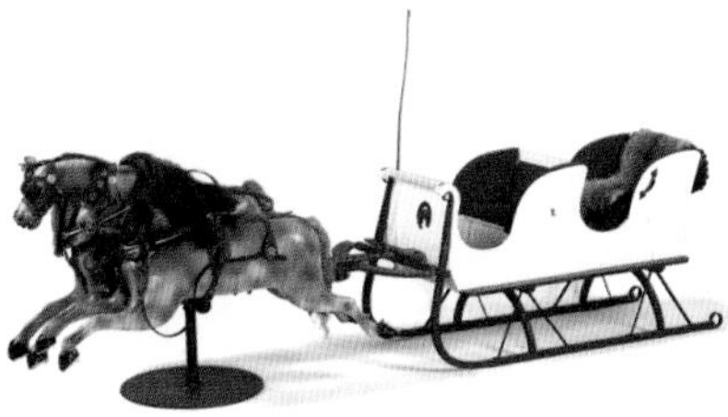

An early 20thC carved and painted two-seat sleigh, together with two polychrome hobby horses.

£300-500 **POOK**

An early 20thC Buddy-L pressed steel hook and truck.

25in (62.5cm) wide

£600-900 **POOK**

An early 20thC Buddy-L pressed steel hook and ladder truck.

25in (62.5cm) wide

£300-500 **POOK**

A Meccano construction kit, assembled, with pilot and original box.

18.75in (47cm) wide

£200-250 **LAN**

A mid-19thC mechanical weight-operated shooting gallery target, the complex mechanism concealed behind a depiction of four blacksmiths at a forge.

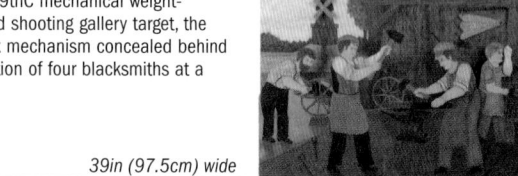

39in (97.5cm) wide

£500-700 **POOK**

A rare François Gaultier 'Tamer' automaton, of a standing boy in bisque porcelain holding a conductor's baton, the ducks of papier-mâché, marked "FG3".

c1895 *16.5in (41cm) high*

£2,000-2,500 **KAU**

A Schuco 'Bigo-Fix' dancing mouse, movement working, some wear.

£150-200 **LAN**

A painted wooden figure of a dancing man, on a rectangular base.

18in (45cm) high

£300-500 **SWO**

An 'Alice in Wonderland' lithograph on wood set, comprising ten characters.

£1,500-2,000 **POOK**

A Japanese Yonezawa 'Friction Powered X-27 Explorer', in lithographed tinplate, mint condition.

8.5in (22cm) high

£1,500-2,000 **SWO**

A tinplate battery-operated 'Mr Atomic Thinking Robot', by Cragstan of Japan, of recent production, in a colourfully illustrated box.

£500-700 **VEC**

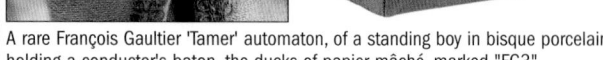

A 'Planet Robot', by Yosihiya of Japan, black tinplate construction, bright plated parts, red feet with red plastic hands, clockwork-operation, of recent production, box.

Black is the most common colourway. The olive clockwork version, and the blue remote-controlled battery-operated version are harder to find.

£300-500 **VEC**

THE TRIBAL ART MARKET

The higher end of the tribal art market has remained buoyant, while the lower to middle areas are attracting new buyers. The quality and provenance of a piece of tribal art are far more important factors than condition or area or tribe of origin.

Pieces that reach the highest prices are those that have not been seen on the market for twenty years or more, are unusual and of excellent quality, and that have sound provenance. Bonhams in London recently sold a small Kongo figure from the Democratic Republic of Congo that had not been on the market since 1950. The carving was exceptional and the piece was associated with a well-known dealer. It was of most unusual sculpture because it was a maternity figure – rare for a Kongo fetish figure. It sold for £24,000, ten times the high estimate.

Paris and Brussels, where the established BRUNEAF (Brussels Non European Art Fair) show is held, are the two main centres of the African tribal art market. There are many young and keen buyers at present, and several new dealers have also recently sprung up in Spain, Portugal and Italy.

The Pre-Colombian and Native American markets are traditionally rooted in the US and continue to thrive there. Mayan and Aztec items are popular. In Canada, the Inuit art market is still growing at a thrilling rate. Ethereal and abstract prints and carvings are sought after, and pieces by recognized artists such as Osuitok Ipeelee and Karoo Ashevak are fetching high prices.

In Australia and New Zealand the market for Oceanic art is healthy, and such items are also in demand in the northern hemisphere. Pieces of really high quality from Southeast Asia and Oceania tend to be rarer in the UK, and usually sell very well when they do appear.

Perhaps the most exciting recent development is the long-awaited opening in June 2006 of the new Quai Branly ethnographic museum in Paris, and with it the associated sales and events held by auction houses and dealers from around the world. This is expected to ignite 'tribal fever', which may significantly affect prices in the near future.

– Philip Keith

WEST AFRICA - IVORY COAST

A 19thC figurative gold measuring weight, from the Baule tribe.

1.25in (3cm) high

£50-80 **OHA**

A 19thC figurative gold measuring weight, from the Baule tribe.

1.25in (3cm) high

£50-80 **OHA**

A 19thC solid gold pendant, from the Baule tribe.

2.5in (6.5cm) high

£1,000-£1,500 **OHA**

A 19thC figurative gold measuring weight, from the Baule tribe.

1.25in (3cm) high

£40-60 **OHA**

A mid-20thC figurative hair comb, from the Baule tribe.

6.25in (16cm) high

£150-200 **OHA**

An early 20thC rice spoon, from the Dan tribe.

11.75in (30cm) high

£300-400 **OHA**

An early 20thC mask, from the Dan tribe.

The domed forehead and concave face are typical of Dan ceremonial masks.

8.25in (21cm) high

£1,000-1,500 **OHA**

An early 20thC ceremonial mask, from the Dan-We tribe.

8.25in (21cm) high

£300-500 **OHA**

An early 20thC passport mask, from the Dan-Guere tribe.

3.25in (8.5cm) high

£200-400 **OHA**

An early 20thC carved wooden mask, from the Senufo tribe, Ivory Coast.

£280-320 SK

A firespitter hardwood mask, from the Senufo tribe, carved as a zoomorphic head with curved horns surmounted by a bird holding a small animal in its beak.

36in (91.5cm) high

£700-1,000 AP

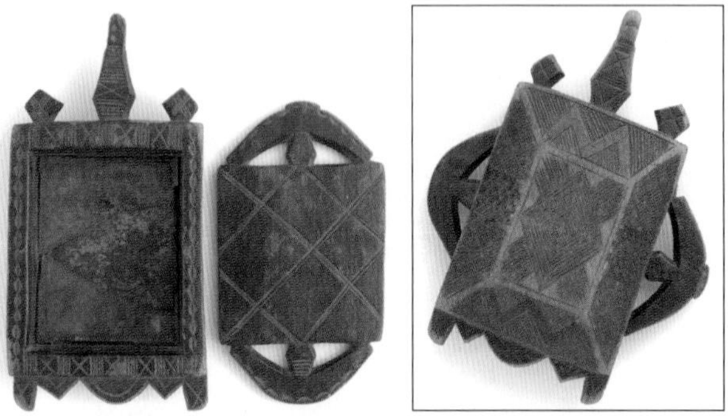

A 20thC mirror box, from the Senufo tribe, Ivory Coast, of zoomorphic alligator form, with removable cover.

7.75in (20cm) high

£400-600 PHK

A CLOSER LOOK AT A KPELIYE MASK

Kpeliye masks would be worn in Poro society ceremonies. They are identified by their oval faces, T-shaped noses, crests or wings and horns.
Although worn by men, the mask represents female beauty. Scarification marks are considered beautiful by the Senufo.
They usually have pierced eyes and are worn at an angle on the forehead so that the dancer can peer through the costume below the mask.
The flanges at the bottom of the mask refer to the hornbill, an important symbol to the Senufo and, according to legend, one of the first creatures on the earth. The hornbill symbolises smiths.

A carved wooden kpeliye mask, from the Senufo tribe, with linear decorated abstract flanges and coiffure, dark patina, old repairs, rodent damage.

Kpeliye masks are the most instantly recognizable of the Senufo masks.

c1920 *14.5in (37cm) high*

£4,000-6,000 SK

A carved wooden face mask, from the Guere Poro society, with typical features including open mouth with metal teeth and warthog horns, with original raffia and old worn cloth in the back and skin on the sides.

15in (38cm) high

£500-800 AP

A mid-20thC ceremonial persecution mask, from the Guere tribe, Ivory Coast.

13in (33cm) high

£300-400 OHA

An early 20thC Thil figure, from the Lobi tribe, Ivory Coast.

10.25in (26cm) high

£500-700 OHA

A Mende hardwood helmet mask, possibly carved by Mustafa Ado Dassama, the two small heads representing King George V and Queen Mary, to mark the 25th anniversary of King George's reign, from the Kenema District of Sierra Leone.

Mende carvers visited London for the Colonial Exposition, and came back inspired to use the images of the royal couple in various media, including carving and textile design.

This is the only documented use of masks by women in sub-Saharan Africa.

1936 *17in (43cm) high*

£1,800-2,200 AP

GHANAIAN TRIBAL ART

- The Asante, Ewe, Fante and Moba are the main tribes in Ghana. The colourful kente cloth, which is the Ghanaian national costume, reflects the vibrant vegetation in the area.
- Known in colonial times as the Gold Coast, gold is a major resource in the region. Portuguese sailors in the 15thC returned home with wild tales of kings adorned with gold.
- Gold weights, sculpted in brass, are highly collectable for their charm and diversity. Early ones (c1400-1720) are usually geometric in form, with notched edges. From c1720-1930, figurative designs became predominant, often depicting domestic activities or symbolic animals.
- The Asante are the dominant tribe. Their best known works are the akuaba figures – fertility dolls with disc-shaped heads.
- The Fante also carve these dolls, but they have rectangular heads and decorative details are scorched on to pale wood.

A 19thC Ashanti brass gold-weight, Ghana, in the form of a porcupine.

1.5in (4cm) wide

£40-60 **PHK**

An Ashanti brass gold-weight, Ghana, in the form of an antelope.

1.5in (4cm) wide

£40-60 **PHK**

A 19thC Ashanti brass gold-weight, Ghana, in the form of a pyramid of birds.

2.75in (7cm) high

£40-60 **PHK**

An Ashanti brass gold-weight, Ghana, in the form of a bird tray.

1in (2.5cm) high

£40-60 **PHK**

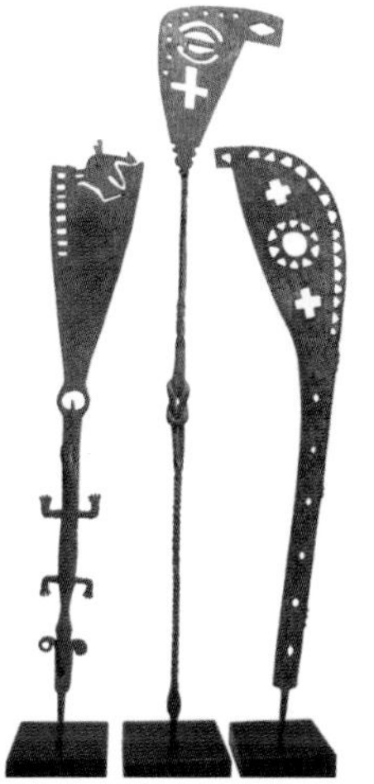

Three early 20thC prestige objects, Ashanti tribe, Ghana.

tallest 33.5in (85cm) high

£300-400 **OHA**

A 20thC Ashanti 'akua-ba' hardwood fertility doll, Ghana, the abstract female figure with a tiny glass beaded necklace, perforated cheeks for attached decorative elements.

Women tuck these disk-headed dolls into their skirts to aid fertility and health in pregnancy.

11in (28cm) high

£300-500 **AP**

An Ashanti Kente cloth, Ghana, with woven block of supplementary weft motifs.

The Kente cloth is the national costume of Ghana and is one of the most recognizable symbols of African heritage.

78in (198cm) wide

£400-600 **PHK**

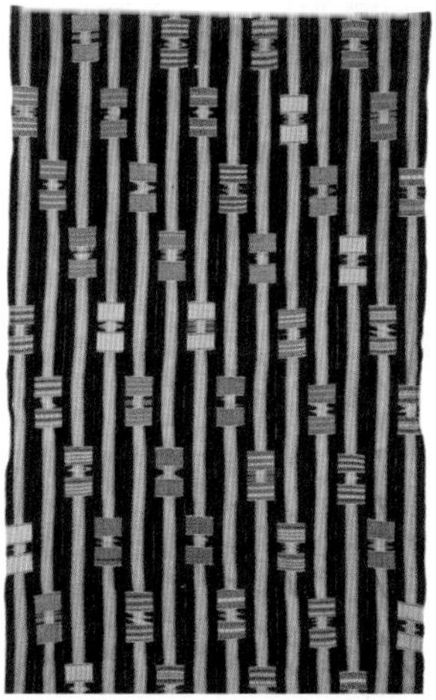

A mid-20thC woman's wrapper, Volta region, Ghana, the strip-woven cotton with spinning designs.

78in (198cm) high

£1,200-1,800 **EFI**

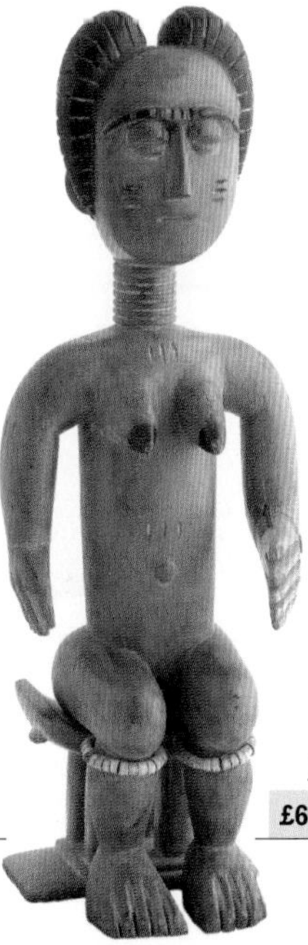

A 20thC Fante fertility figure, Ghana, seated on a typical stool.

17.75in (45cm) high

£600-800 **PHK**

An African carved wooden female figure, from the Bamana tribe, the large head with metal eyes, with geometric body decoration, old repairs.

The Bamana people are also known as the Bambara tribe.

25.5in (65cm) high

£180-220 **SK**

A mid-20thC door lock, from the Bamana tribe.

The significance of grain to the subsistence of Mali peoples is indicated by intricate decoration of granary doors and locks, which form a popular collecting area. Locks are often given as bridal gifts. Bamana locks are often male figures whereas Dogon locks tend to represent ancestors or horses.

11.75in (30cm) high

£250-350 **OHA**

An early carved wooden mask, from the Dogon tribe, with square pierced eyes and pointed top, surmounted by a standing female figure with scarification patterns, dark patina, restored.

35in (89cm) high

£400-600 **SK**

An Ireli antelope mask, from the Dogon tribe.

c1930 *19.5in (50cm) high*

£500-800 **PHK**

A carved wooden forehead mask, from the Dogon tribe, in the shape of an antelope, the long curved horns with zigzag devices, the human-like face with glass eyes, insect damage.

29in (73.5cm) high

£600-900 **SK**

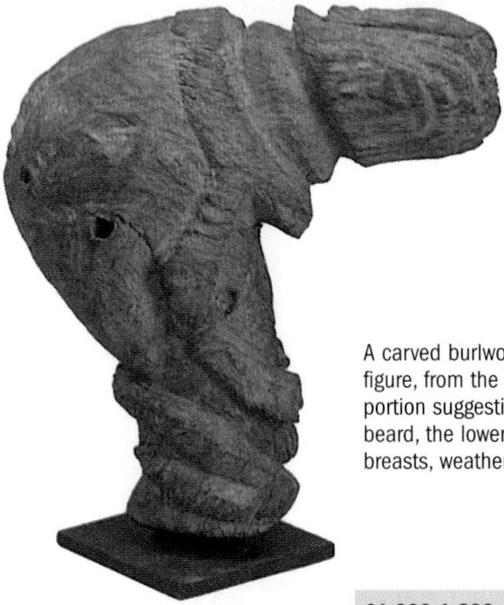

A carved burlwood hermaphrodite figure, from the Dogon tribe, the upper portion suggesting a male figure with a beard, the lower part female with breasts, weathered patina.

9.5in (24cm) high

£1,200-1,800 **SK**

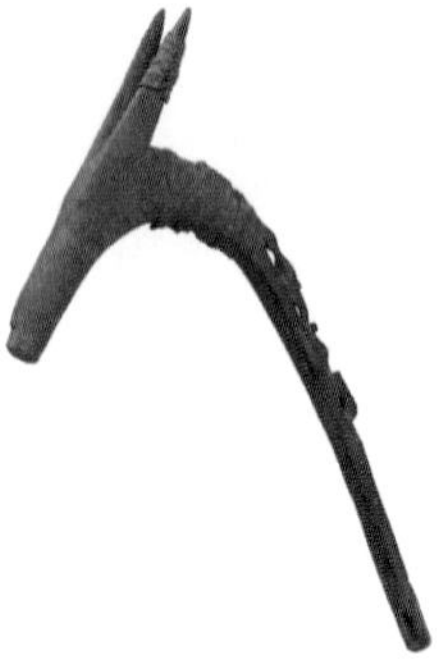

A wooden antelope staff, from the Dogon tribe, carved as an abstract antelope head, with incised geometric devices, the handle with abstract figures on the upper neck, dark patina, old hide repairs.

28.5in (72.5cm) long

£400-600 **SK**

A carved wooden granary door, from the Dogon tribe, with 16 stylized figures and traces of geometric design on one side, weathered patina, old forged iron repair.

13.5in (34cm) wide

£2,000-3,000 **SK**

A 20thC metal and stone 'hogon' priest's necklace, from the Dogon tribe, forged iron links with encased and perforated stone pendants, with patina.

21in (53.5cm) long

£250-300 **SK**

A metal and stone 'hogon' priest's necklace, from the Dogon tribe, forged and twisted iron links, with roughly cut carnelian attachments, single polished cylindrical stone pendant.

29in (73.5cm) long

£250-300 **SK**

A Benin bronze bracelet, decorated with a central band containing three relief human heads and three conical bells.

Dated by William Fagg, historian of Nigerian art, to the early 16thC.

4.5in (11.5cm) diam

£1,000-1,500 **AP**

A 19thC small Igbo mask.

8.25in (21cm) high

£500-800 **PHK**

A carved wooden Ikenga figure, from the Igbo tribe, the male figure holding a small head with stylized figure-eight horns, encrusted patina, insect damage.

Ikenga means 'cult of the hand', the figures are owned by the head of a household and kept for protection, strength and luck.

29.5in (75cm) high

£150-200 **SK**

A carved wooden male figure, from the Igbo tribe, the head with relief-carved scarification devices, wearing a hat, traces of pigment, weathered patina, wood loss, cracks.

27in (68.5cm) high

£300-400 **SK**

A mid-20thC Igbo Mami Wata headdress.

Mami Wata is a water spirit deity, physically similar to a mermaid, found throughout western coastal regions and believed to bring material wealth to her followers but also capable of inflicting infertility.

22.75in (58cm) high

£500-700 **OHA**

A pair of carved wooden Ibeji dolls, from the Yoruba tribe, the male and female forms with metal and hide attachments, traces of blue pigment, dark patina, wood loss.

An Ibeji doll represents a dead twin. The Yoruba have the highest rate of twins in the world (45 in 1000) with an infant mortality rate of 50 per cent. The Yoruba believe that the twins share a single soul so if one twin dies, a companion figure is carved and treated as if it were alive. They are honoured with libations and prayers because it is believed that they influence the life of the family.

12in (30.5cm) high

£300-500 **SK**

A pair of carved wooden Ibeji dolls, from the Yoruba tribe, the male and female forms with bold features and stylized coiffures, patina of use.

12in (30.5cm) high

£150-200 **SK**

A pair of carved wooden twin male Ibeji dolls, from the Yoruba tribe, with blue dyed coiffures, partially encrusted patinas, one with a trade bead necklace.

10.5in (27cm) high

£200-300 **SK**

NIGERIAN TRIBES

- Nigeria is Africa's largest coastal country with over 100 million people. Key tribes include the Yoruba, which accounts for 15 million people, and the Ibo, Edo and Dakakari.
- Yoruba traditions have spread to many countries, including Brazil, Cuba and Trinidad, due to the transportation of millions of slaves from the region.
- These traditions include the Ibeji twin cult, symbolized by the dolls, Ifa divination and Obgoni and Oshanyin metalwork cults.
- Benin became a major casting centre for copper and brass due to trade with Portugal between the 15th and 19thC, although the use of copper alloy in the region can be dated back to 1000BC.
- The Ibo people produced figurative brass plaques including the 'Benin bronzes' and royal altar heads. They are also known for their Ikenga figures with backward facing horns, symbolizing strength and courage.

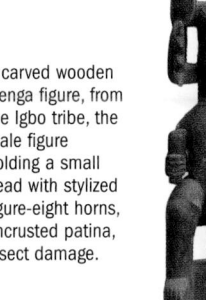

Two mid-20thC Yoruba carved wooden figures, by Thomas Ona Odulate, in Ijebu-Ode style.

Thomas Ona Odulate is a famous Yoruba artist who carved wooden figures for the tourist trade, often representing colonialists employed in daily activities.

£400-600 **SK**

A carved wooden helmet mask, from the Yoruba tribe, possibly carved by Agbonbiofe of Efon-Alaye, the janus-faced Epa mask surmounted by a male equestrian figure on a horse.

Epa masks are worn at funerals and rite of passage ceremonies, and stored in shrines, where libations are made to them. The form – a face topped by a standing figure – is typical.

£10,000-12,000 **SK**

An Oshe Shango staff finial, from the Yoruba tribe, Oyo region, termite damage.

An Oshe Shango is a dance wand used by women in Sango cult ceremonies. The double axe is a motif representing thunder in the cult.

15in (38cm) high

£1,800-2,200 **PHK**

A 1950s Yoruba Ifa divination bowl.

8.5in (22cm) high

£1,000-1,500 **PHK**

A Yoruba Ifa 'agere ifa' divination bowl.

Ifa priests use these bowls to communicate with Orunmila, the god of fate, in order to obtain insight into an individual's destiny.

9in (23cm) high

£5,000-7,000 **PHK**

A Yoruba stone head depicting an Oba, the tapered crown with a geometrically incised diadem, on an integral base.

An Oba is a Yoruban town leader.

8.75in (22cm) high

£200-300 **AP**

A Yoruba carved wooden container, the cover with a coiled snake biting an animal, two relief-carved stylized animals on the sides.

14in (35.5cm) diam

£600-900 **SK**

A Bini mask, from Benin city.

14.5in (37cm) high

£2,000-3,000 **PHK**

CAMEROON

A 20thC Babanki dignitaries' stool.

The continuous frieze of standing and squatting figures symbolizes the king's dynastic lineage, reinforcing his legitimacy to the throne.

33.75in (86cm) diam

£3,000-5,000 **PHK**

A rare Bamileke buffalo helmet mask.

Only the king is allowed to wear this mask.

28.25in (72cm) high

£1,500-2,500 **PHK**

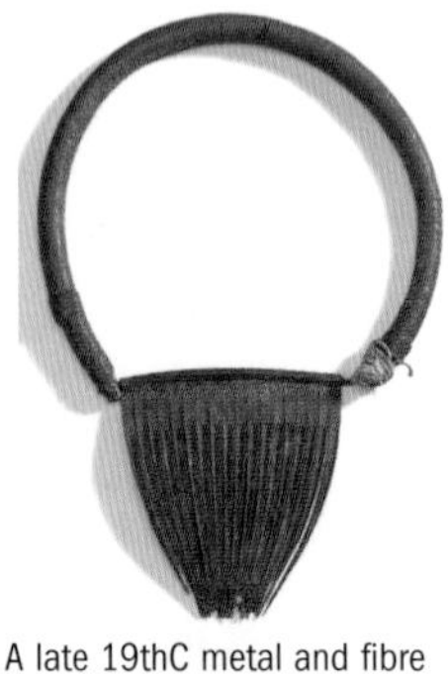

A late 19thC metal and fibre cache-sex.

6in (15.5cm) wide

£150-200 **SK**

A Grasslands horn drinking cup, ornamented with brass wire.

11.75in (30cm) long

£400-600 **PHK**

A Chokwe carved wooden staff, the grip with incised decoration and a relief-carved face with typical Chokwe features, the finial head wearing a fez, dark patina.

36in (91.5cm) long

£400-600 **SK**

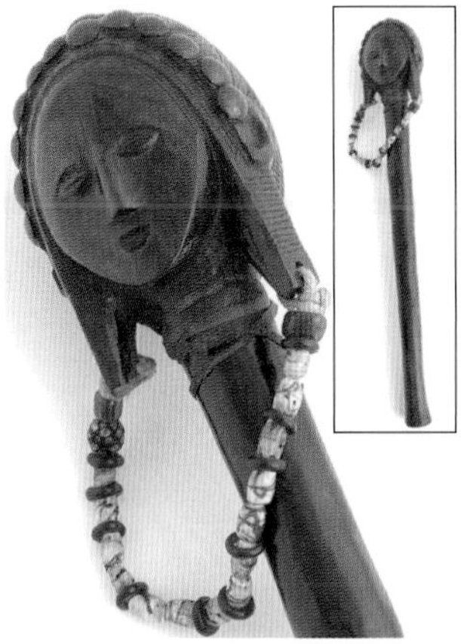

A Chokwe staff, Angola, Central Africa.

17.75in (45cm) high

£800-1,200 **PHK**

A early 20thC Hola statue, Democratic Republic of Congo.

6.75in (17cm) high

£500-700 **OHA**

A late 19thC Kongo carved wooden headrest, in the form of an elongated quadruped, the triangular head with incised details.

£250-300 **SK**

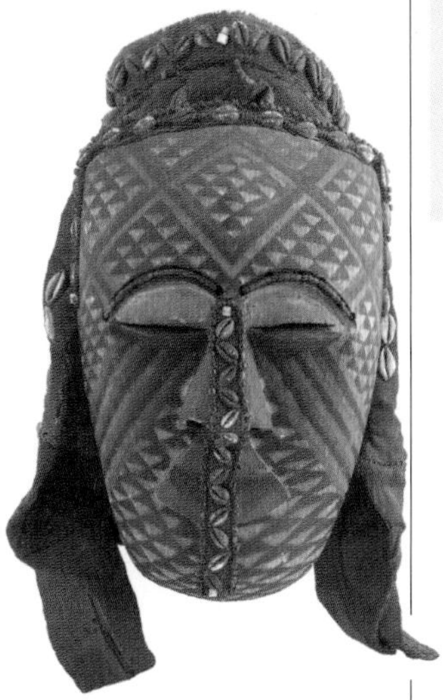

A Kuba mask, 'Ngady Mwaash', with woven raffia, beads and shells.

Ngady Mwaash is the personification of 'the Woman of Woot', one of three types of mask used by the Kuba in royal dances.

13.75in (35cm) high

£1,000-1,500 **PHK**

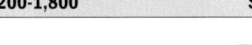

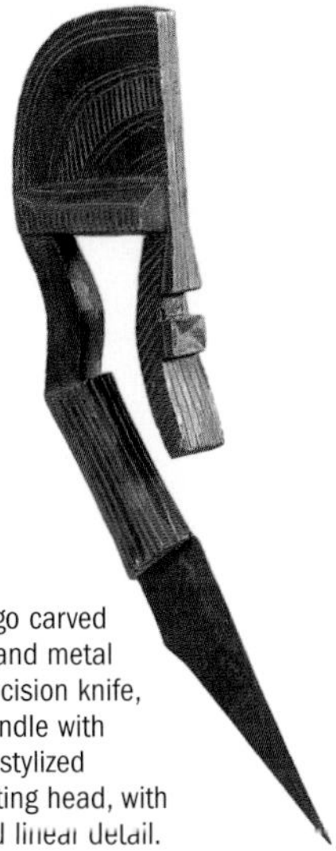

A Kongo carved wood and metal circumcision knife, the handle with highly stylized projecting head, with incised linear detail.

Spread along the Atlantic coast from Angola to Stanleypool, the Kongo tribes include the Vili, Woyo, Beembe and Yombe. They are known for their 'nkisi' or spirit receptacle ritual and ancestor sculptures.

£1,200-1,800 **SK**

A late 19thC Kongo carved ivory, the diminutive carving with six relief-carved figures, some wearing European clothing.

£1,200-1,800 **SK**

A Kongo bell rattle, Zaire river basin region, Central Africa.

8.75in (22cm) long

£400-600 **PHK**

A Mongo m'bili tribal knife, central Congo, broad double-edged blade with raised rib and expanded tip, copper-wound wooden hilt.

Mongo society is organized around lineage and covenants. Feuds are often settled through marriage and dowries, or 'm'bili'.

£30-50 **W&W**

A Ngombe m'pamba tribal knife, north-west Congo, broad blade to iron and brass wound hilt, inlaid with copper pellets, incised geometric decoration.

blade 16in (40.5cm) long

£100-150 **W&W**

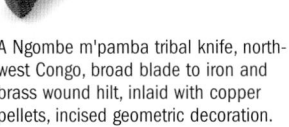

A Kuba helmet mask, Democratic Republic of Congo, carved hardwood male mask, with incised facial decoration, perforated lower rim for attachment and remains of a vegi-fibre netting.

14in (35.5cm) high

£1,000-1,500 **AP**

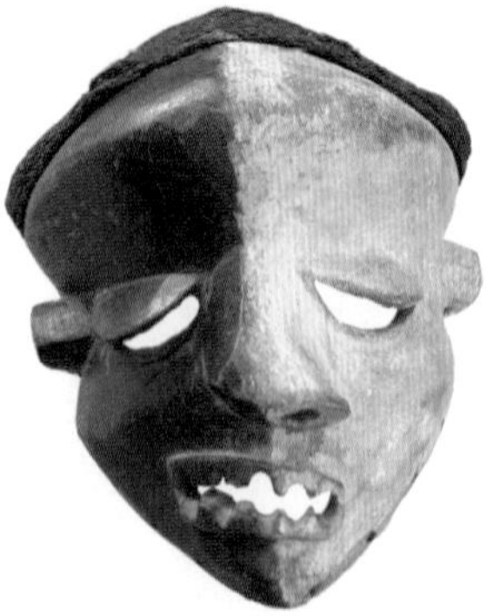

An early 20thC Pende sickness mask, Democratic Republic of Congo.

9in (23cm) high

£800-1,200 **OHA**

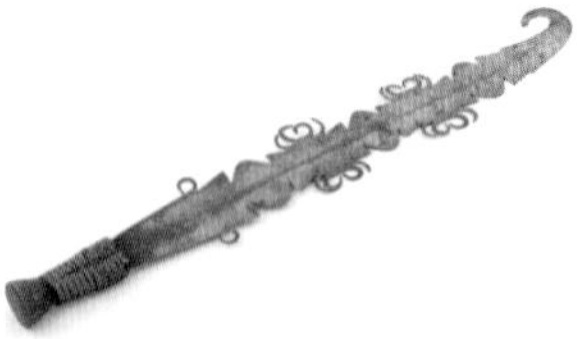

A Sengele maimai ndombe tribal knife, from south-west Congo, the blade cut in the form of scorpions in silhouette, with copper-wound wooden grip.

blade 16in (40.5cm) long

£220-280 **W&W**

A Zande mpoko kilo tribal war sword, from north-east Congo, curved single-edged blade, wooden grip.

blade 24in (61cm) long

£80-120 **W&W**

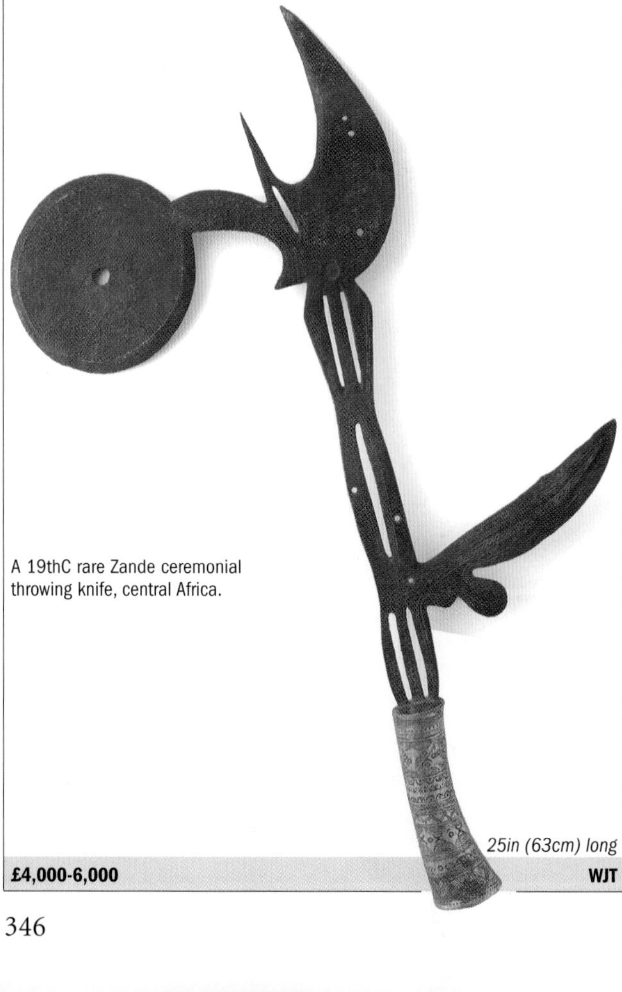

A 19thC rare Zande ceremonial throwing knife, central Africa.

25in (63cm) long

£4,000-6,000 **WJT**

A CLOSER LOOK AT A KUBA HELMET MASK

The Bushoong people founded the Kuba kingdom in 16thC, uniting 19 groups including the Kete and Ngeende. Each group is autonomous but pays tribute to the Nyim, or king, of the Bushoong clan.

Masks are carved for religious ceremonies, dances and initiations, although other figurative sculpture is rare.

Three major types of mask have been identified for use in royal dances. Moshambwooy or Woot is the founder of the Bushoong clan. The others are Ngady Mwaash or 'woman of Woot' and Bwoon, meaning 'pygmy'. Other masks, collectively known as Isheene Mwalu are used for dances and initiations.

Bushoong art typically uses cowrie shells, beads and geometric patterns using red or black pigment in its designs. Each tribe has its own characteristics but geometric design is common to all.

A large Kuba helmet mask, Democratic Republic of Congo, decorated with applied copper sheeting, cowrie shells and black glass beads, the black painted surface with white painted pigment on eyes, restored.

11in (28cm) high

£2,500-3,500 **AP**

A 19thC Zande woven shield, Democratic Republic of Congo.

65in (165cm) high

£2,000-2,500 **OHA**

A Tabwa staff, with double-headed detail, Zaire river basin region, central Africa.

41in (104cm) long

£2,000-3,000 **PHK**

An early 20thC Gurage leather shield, Ethiopia.

33.5in (85cm) high

£1,000-1,500 **OHA**

An early 20thC one-piece chair from Ethiopia, probably from the Gurage tribe.

41.25in (105cm) high

£1,000-1,500 **OHA**

An early 20thC one-piece chair, probably Gurage, from Ethiopia.

43.25in (110cm) high

£1,200-1,800 **OHA**

An early 20thC stool, from Jimma region of Ethiopia.

19.75in (50cm) high

£300-400 **OHA**

An early 20thC pair of Konso male and female grave post finials, with bone eyes and teeth, Ethiopia.

20.5in (52cm) high

£700-1,000 **PHK**

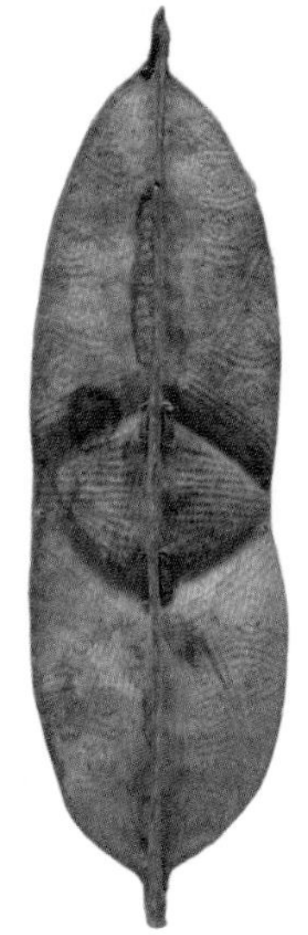

A 19th to early 20thC leather shield from the Konso Tribe of Ethiopia.

37in (94cm) high

£250-350 **OHA**

Two early 20thC room dividers from Ethiopia.

taller 59in (150cm) high

£500-800 **OHA**

An early 20thC classic one-piece chair from Ethiopia.

40in (101cm) high

£1,000-1,500 **OHA**

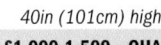

A mid-20thC Coptic painted chair from Ethiopia, with leather seat.

27in (70cm) high

£300-500 **OHA**

A mid-20thC mancala game board from Ethiopia.

19.75in (50cm) long

£200-400 **OHA**

A North Nguni beadwork and grass woven marriage belt.

85cm (33.5in) long

£400-600 **PHK**

A South Nguni beadwork waistband.

82cm (32.25in) long

£400-600 **PHK**

A North Nguni beadwork and gourd snuff container.

10cm (4in) high

£300-400 **PHK**

A 1940s North Nguni colonial staff, finial as a doctor.

85cm (33.5in) long

£1,000-1,500 **PHK**

A rare 19thC North Nguni Janus-headed staff, with wirework handle.

87cm (34.25in) long

£2,000-3,000 **PHK**

A rare late 19thC pair of North Nguni puppets, male and female, with jointed limbs.

22cm (8.5in) high

£1,500-2,000 **PHK**

A 19thC North Nguni wooden carved headrest.

14in (35.5cm) wide

£400-600 **WJT**

A North Nguni spoon.

40cm (15.75in) long

£200-300 **PHK**

A Shona knife, batakwa, Zimbabwe.

42cm (16.5in) high

£400-600 **PHK**

Mid-20thC Shona beer pot, Zimbabwe.

11.75in (30cm) high

£150-180 **OHA**

A late 19thC Sotho beadwork doll, with beaded string.

8cm (3in) long

£200-300 **PHK**

A Tsonga headrest, Mozambique, with banded cross bar.

15cm (6in) wide

£1,000-1,500 **PHK**

A 19thC Dayak ancestral figure, depicting the upper half of a woman holding a baby carved on both front and back.

30in (76cm) high

£2,000-3,000 **WJT**

A 19thC Dayak 'Hampatong' ancestral statue, the carved wood with inlaid porcelain eyes.

58in (147.5cm) high

£8,000-10,000 **WJT**

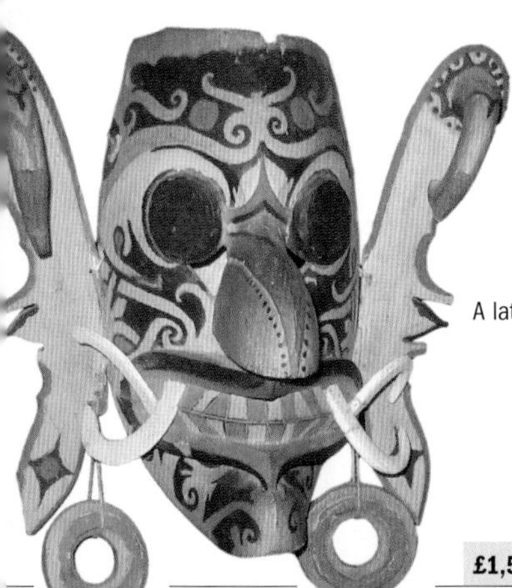

A late 19thC Dayak Hudoq mask.

13in (33cm) high

£1,500-2,000 **PHK**

A CLOSER LOOK AT A DAYAK MASK

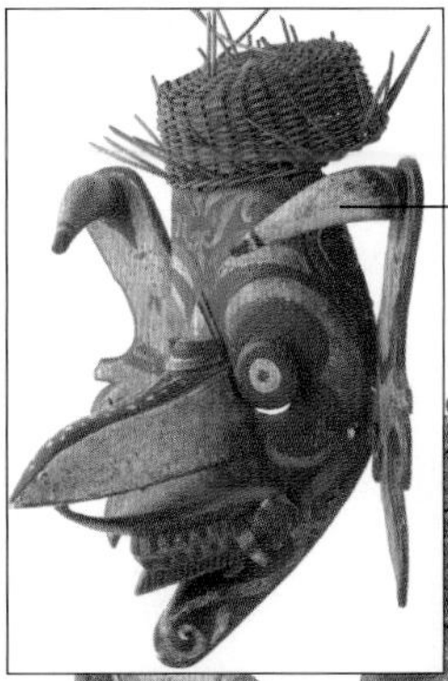

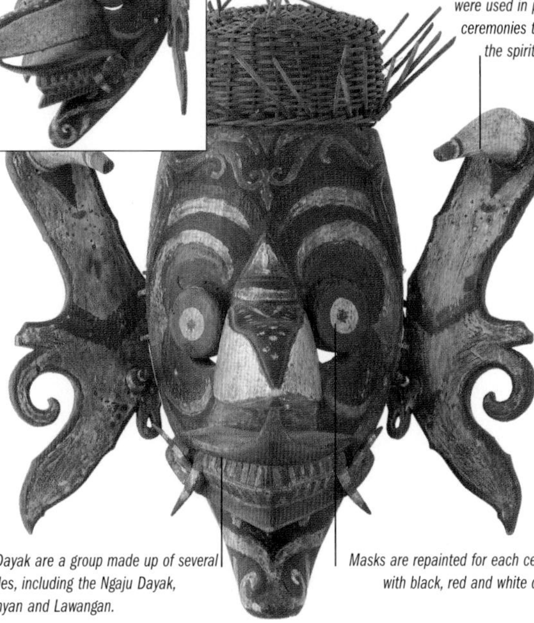

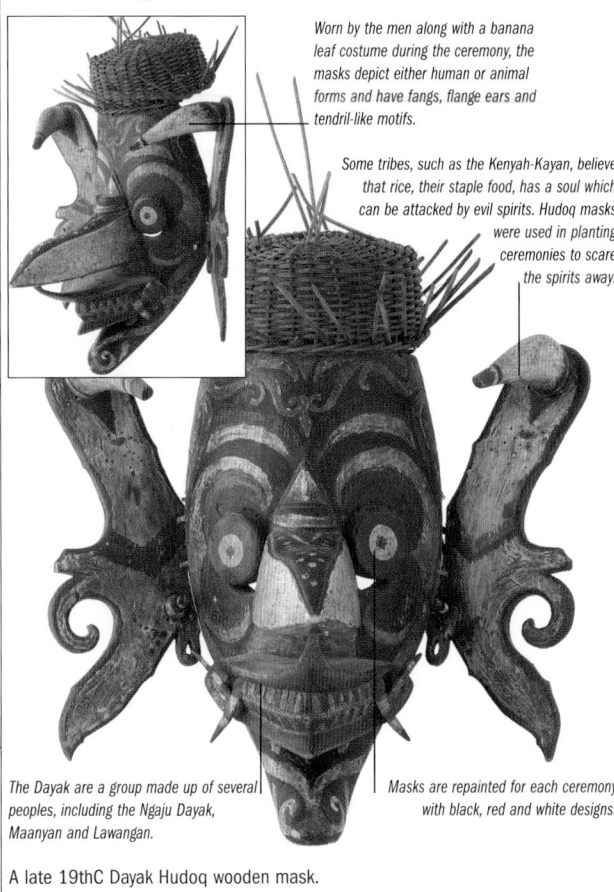

Worn by the men along with a banana leaf costume during the ceremony, the masks depict either human or animal forms and have fangs, flange ears and tendril-like motifs.

Some tribes, such as the Kenyah-Kayan, believe that rice, their staple food, has a soul which can be attacked by evil spirits. Hudoq masks were used in planting ceremonies to scare the spirits away.

The Dayak are a group made up of several peoples, including the Ngaju Dayak, Maanyan and Lawangan.

Masks are repainted for each ceremony with black, red and white designs.

A late 19thC Dayak Hudoq wooden mask.

20in (51cm) high

£5,000-8,000 **WJT**

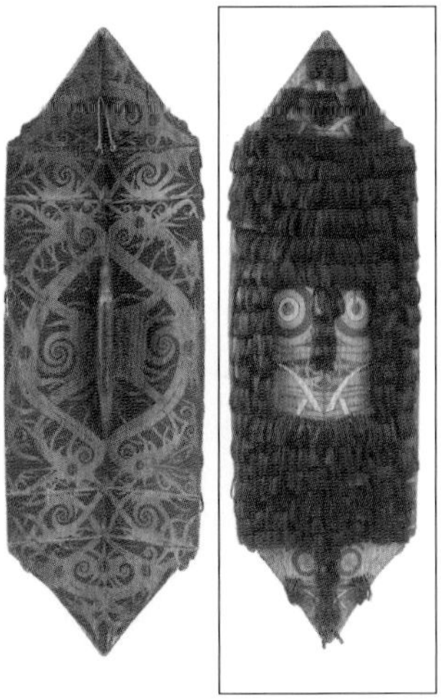

An early 20thC Dayak wood carved headhunter's shield, painted on both sides and decorated with inlaid human enemies' hair.

42in (107cm) high

£4,000-6,000 **WJT**

An early 20thC Dayak wood carved headhunter's shield, painted on front.

44in (112cm) high

£1,500-2,000 **WJT**

A mid-20thC Dayak canoe prow.

18in (45cm) long

£1,800-2,200 **WJT**

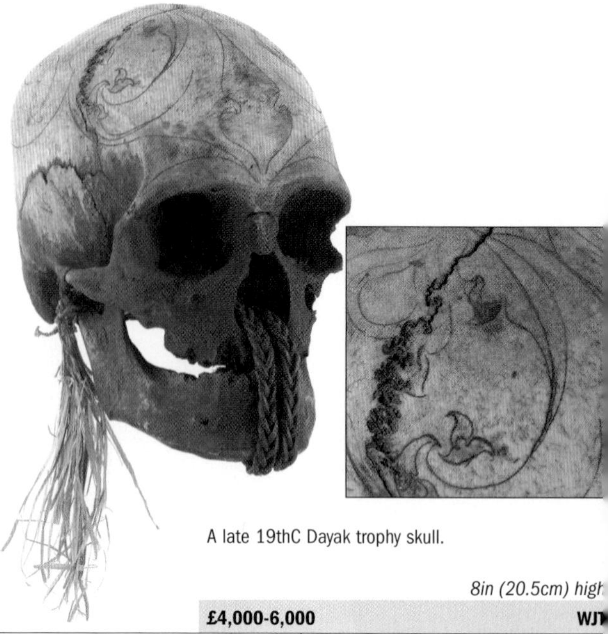

A late 19thC Dayak trophy skull.

8in (20.5cm) high

£4,000-6,000 **WJT**

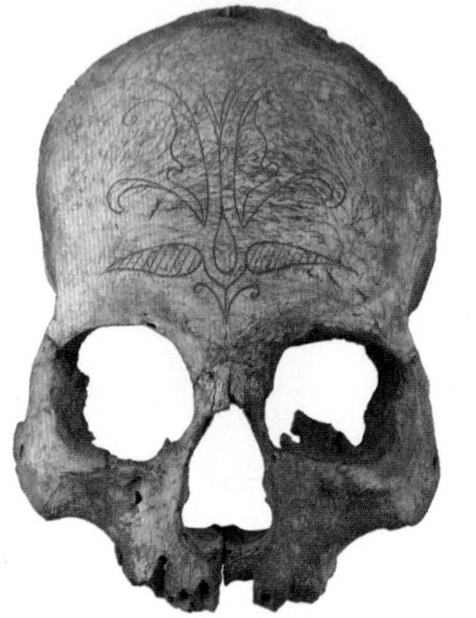

An early 20thC Dayak carved frontal trophy skull.

The back of the skull may have possibly been damaged during the taking of the head or in its preparation.

6.5in (16.5cm) high

£2,000-3,000 **WJT**

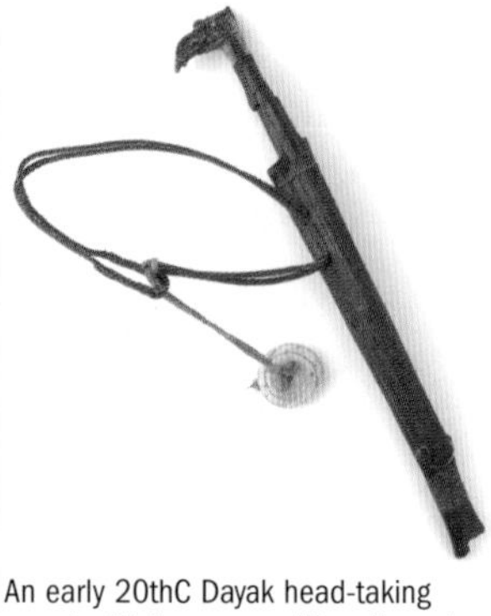

An early 20thC Dayak head-taking sword, with bone carved handle and wooden sheath.

knife 27in (68.5cm) long

£1,200-1,800 **WJT**

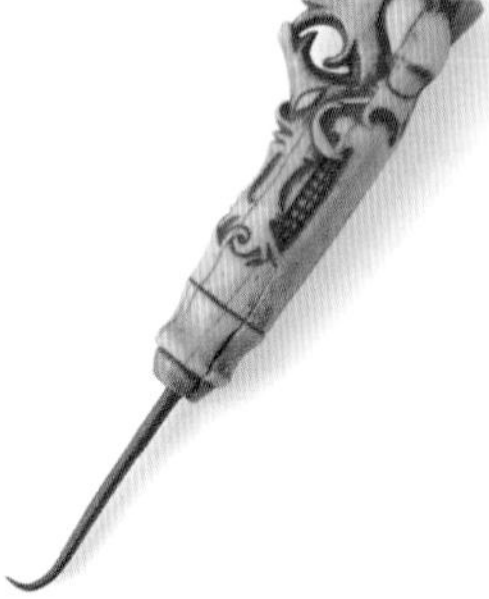

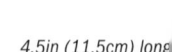

An early 20thC Dayak carved bone sewing needle.

4.5in (11.5cm) long

£350-550 **WJT**

An early 20thC Kayan trophy skull decorated on wood panel.

23in (58.5cm) high

£4,000-6,000 **WJT**

A 19thC 'Hampatong' ancestral statue, Modang Dayak Tribe, made of wood, iron and shell.

The Dayak erect Hampatong (ancestor poles) beside their longhouses. They are surmounted with stylized figures.

38in (96.5cm) high

£8,000-12,000 **WJT**

A 19thC wood ancestral figure, Timor.

35in (89cm) high

£4,000-7,000 **WJT**

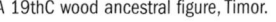

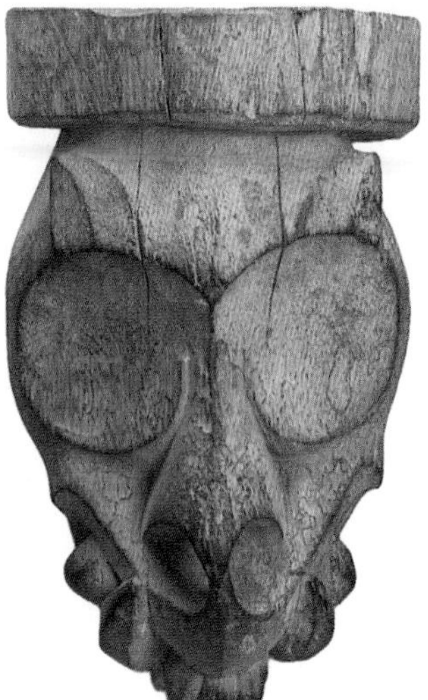

A late 19thC Indonesian carved wood coffin fragment, in the form of a stylized deity with large concave eyes, fangs, and protruding tongue.

9.5in (24cm) high

£700-1,000 **SK**

TOP: An abstract quadruped carved wood coconut grater, from the Caroline Islands, missing the shell blade, with patina.

BOTTOM: An Indonesian horse-shaped carved wood coconut grater, with separately carved and attached front legs, pierced tail and stylized head with metal blade protruding from the mouth, with patina.

largest 31.5in (80cm) wide

£250-400 each **SK**

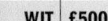

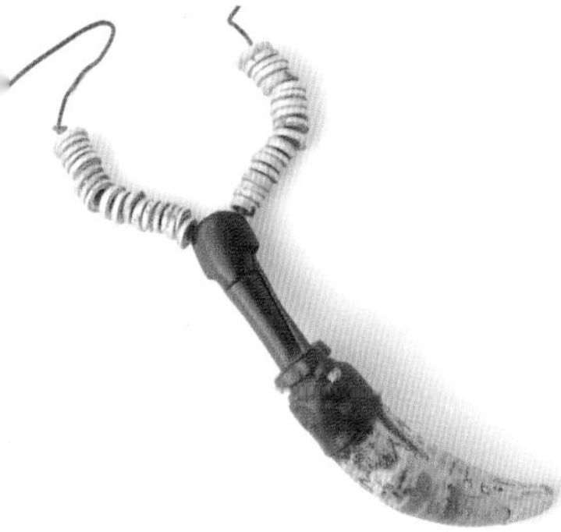

A late 19thC shaman's container, made from large, hollowed-out crocodile tooth, Batak tribe, Sumatra.

7in (18cm) long

£500-700 **WJT**

A late 19thC wooden Kris or knife handle, carved to depict a bird figure, Sumatra.

3.5in (9cm) high

£500-700 **WJT**

An early 20thC ivory Kris or knife handle, Sumatra.

3.5in (9cm) long

£500-700 **WJT**

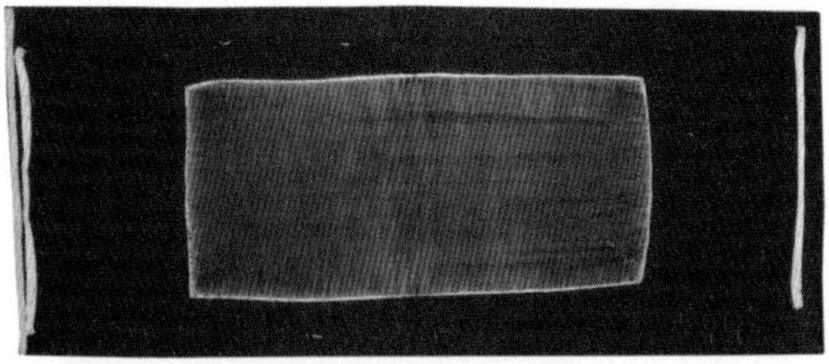

A mid-19thC orange handwoven silk lawon, or ceremonial cloth, from Palambang, Sumatra, with tritik process of resist dying on native silk.

78n (198cm) wide

£6,000-8,000 **EFI**

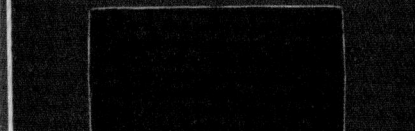

A mid-19thC purple handwoven silk lawon, or ceremonial cloth, from Palambang Sumatra, with tritik process of resist dying on native silk.

Information on this type of textile is largely anecdotal, but they are thought to be presented to wives at marriage and have a symbolic presence during house-raising.

83.5in (210cm) wide

£4,000-6,000 **EFI**

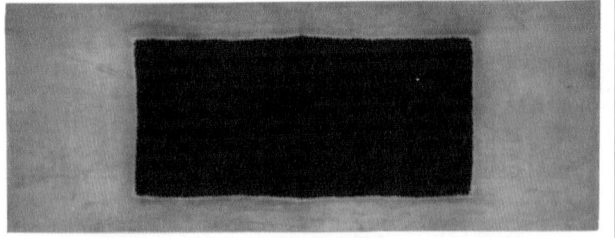

An early 20thC purple and moss handwoven silk lawon, or ceremonial cloth, Palambang, Sumatra, with tritik process of resist dying on Chinese silk.

66in (155cm) wide

£2,000-3,000 **EFI**

A ceremonial cloth, or 'Tampan', mounted, from the Lampung region of Indonesia.

c1900 *19.25in (49cm) wide*

£800-1,200 **PHK**

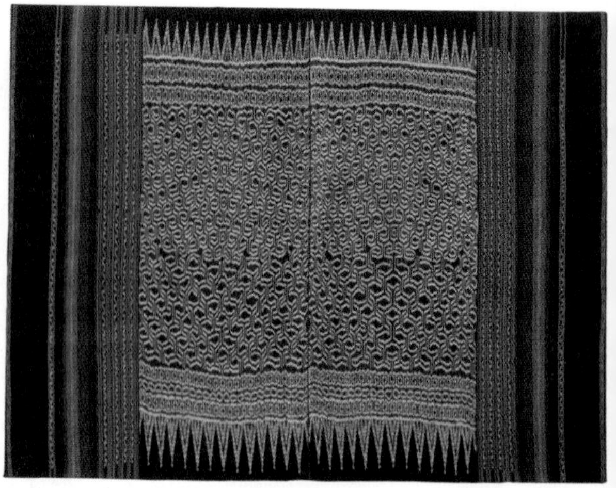

A late 19thC cotton warp Ikat Sekomandi or shroud, from Toraja, Central Celebes.

The central field is designed with connecting links, each representing an ancestor.

£5,000-10,000 **EF**

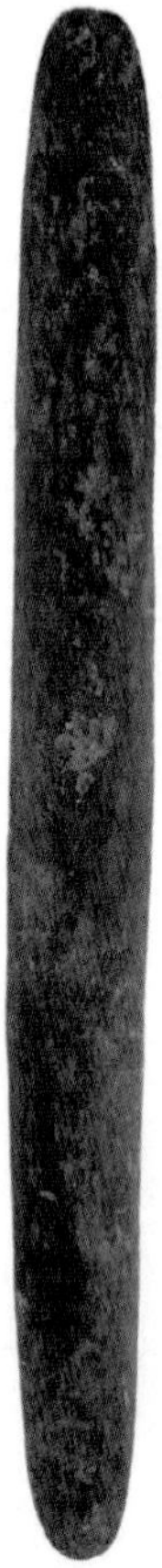

An Australian Leangle Club.

c1850 33in (83cm) wide

£1,200-1,800 **BONA**

An early south eastern Australian Parrying Shield.

£1,200-1,800 **BONA**

A western Australian hardwood shield.

£1,500-2,000 **BONA**

An Australian rainforest shield, North East Queensland.

93cm (36.5in) long

£15,000-20,000 **BONA**

A central Australia Aboriginal stone Churinga.

Churnigas are Aboriginal amulets, made of wood or stone.

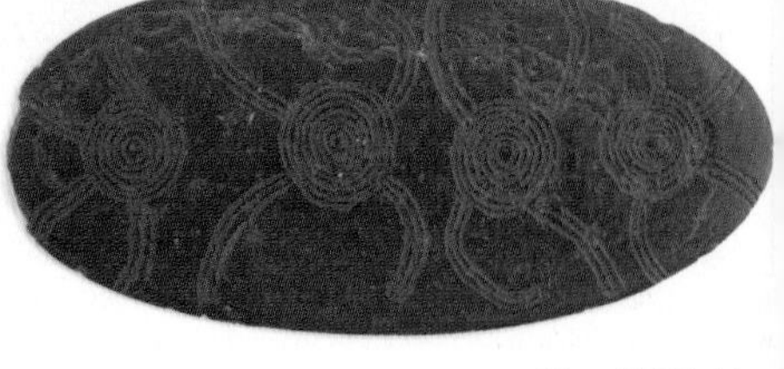

17cm (6.75in) long

£1,200-1,800 **PHK**

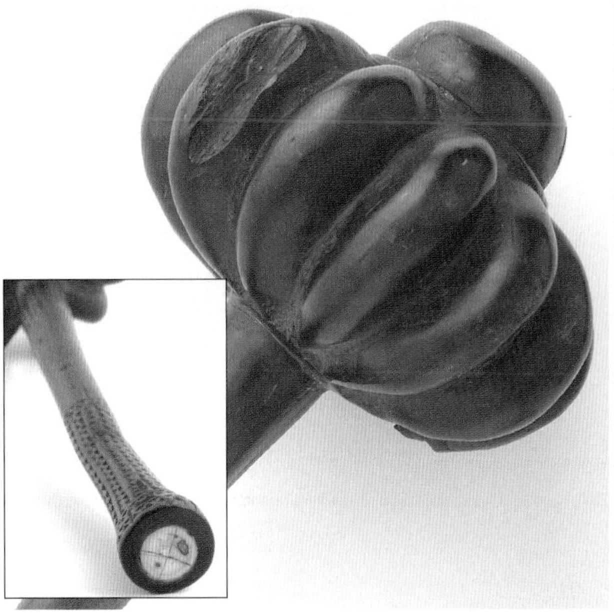

A 19thC Fijian throwing club, 'i ula tavatava', handle inset with whale ivory plug.

41cm (16in) long

£1,000-1,500 **PHK**

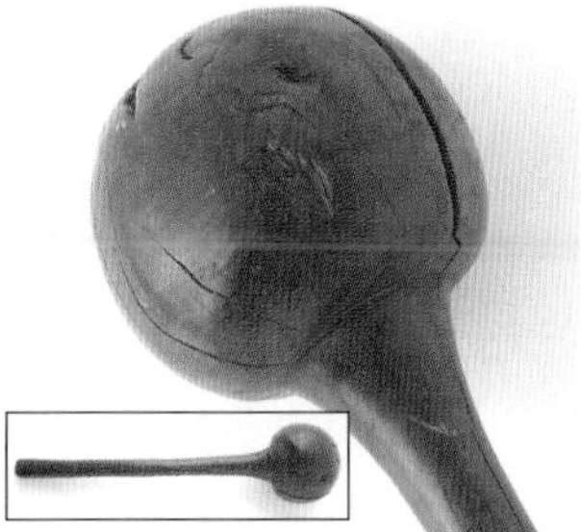

A 19thC Fijian 'i ula drisia' throwing club.

16in (40.5cm) long

£250-350 **WJT**

A 19thC Fijian wooden Sali club.

108cm (42.5in) high

£3,000-5,000 **PHK**

A 19thC Fijian kava bowl, carved as a stylized turtle, with remains of Kava inside.

Kava (or yaqona) is an intoxicating drink, consumed at rituals and before battles.

42cm (16.5in) diam

£4,000-6,000 **PHK**

MAORI

A Maori hei tiki nephrite jade pendant.

11cm (4.5in) high

£1,000-1,500 **PHK**

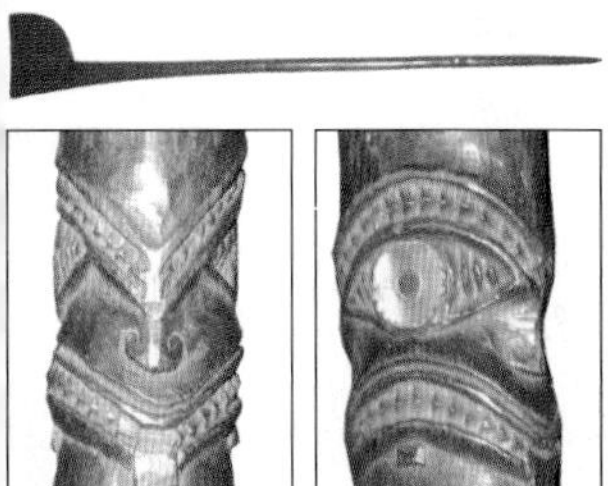

A Maori staff, or tewhatewha, carved with a collar depicting a tiki face.

98.5in (250cm) long

£2,000-3,000 **PHK**

A 19thC Maori gable mask or koruru, from a meeting house.

14.5in (37cm) high

£30,000-40,000 **KC**

A CLOSER LOOK AT A MAORI PENDANT

Hei tiki are pendants carved from nephrite jade, or pounamu, which is only found on New Zealand's South Island and is so hard it can take five months to carve using sandstone rasps and drills.

These pendants would be worn by high ranking men and women and passed on as heirlooms, increasing in mana, or prestige, over time. Each hei tiki would be given a name and addressed whenever it was removed from its box.

The tiki represents a family ancestor and is used as a motif on most objects.

Maori art is highly collectable: rare and finely carved or decorated objects command a premium.

A late 19thC Maori jade hei tiki pendant.

4in (10cm) high

£3,000-5,000 **SK**

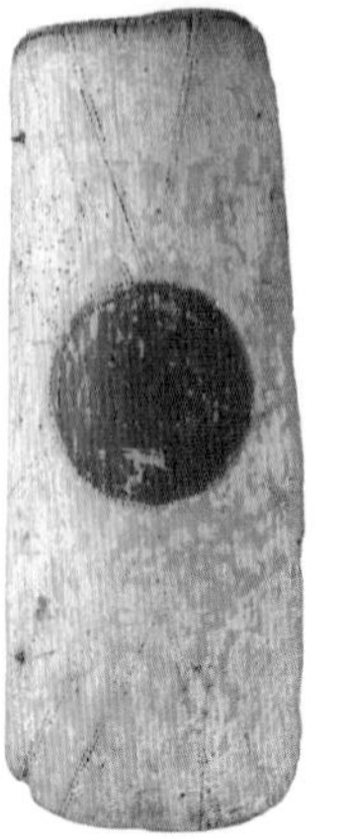

A mid-20thC wooden shield, Highlands, New Guinea.

The tribesmen viewed the Japanese Rising Sun, probably first seen on an aircraft, as a protective symbol. This particular shield has a shotgun blast located just to the left and top of the 'Rising Sun' symbol.

64in (162.5cm) high

£3,000-5,000 **WJT**

A mid-20thC wooden shield, Highlands, New Guinea, the top of the shield decorated with Cassowary feathers.

During WWII, American soldiers passed on 'Phantom' comic books to locals who painted the 'Phantom' image onto their shields as a form of protection.

34in (86.5cm) high

£3,000-5,000 **WJT**

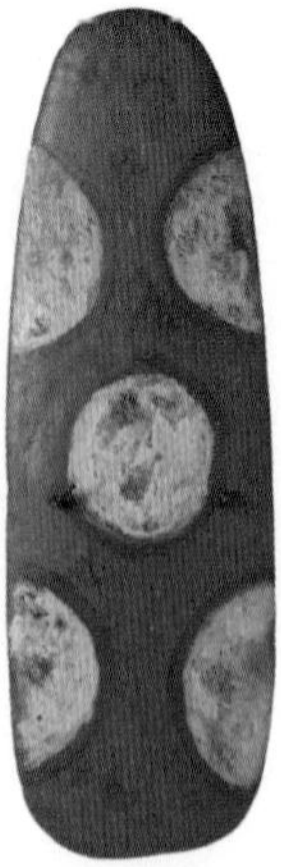

A mid-20thC painted wooden shield, Mendi culture, New Guinea.

Painted colours are derived from vegetable or mineral sources.

52in (134.5cm) high

£5,000-7,000 **WJT**

An early 20thC painted wood shield, Mendi culture, New Guinea.

Research suggests that red represents ancestors and descent, and is smeared on bones and on initiates' faces. Black, made from soot, indicates male solidarity and seniority and white indicates plenty.

48in (122cm) high

£5,000-7,000 **WJT**

A 19thC wood carved Simbai shield, New Guinea.

45in (114.5cm) high

£2,000-3,000 **WJT**

A 19thC wood carved Simbai shield, New Guinea.

37in (94cm) high

£1,500-2,500 **WJT**

A Ramu River spirit mask, Papua New Guinea.

43cm (17in) high

£6,000-8,000 **PHK**

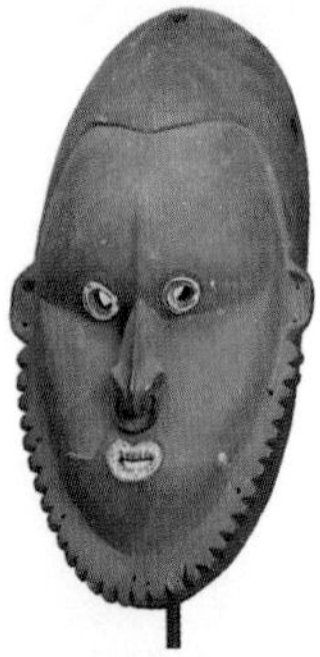

A carved wooden mask, Sepik River, New Guinea, with a stylized beard and upper rim pierced for suspensions, with flared nostrils and metal ring, inlaid round shell eyes, covered with red pigment, traces of kaolin.

14in (35.5cm) high

£1,000-1,500 **SK**

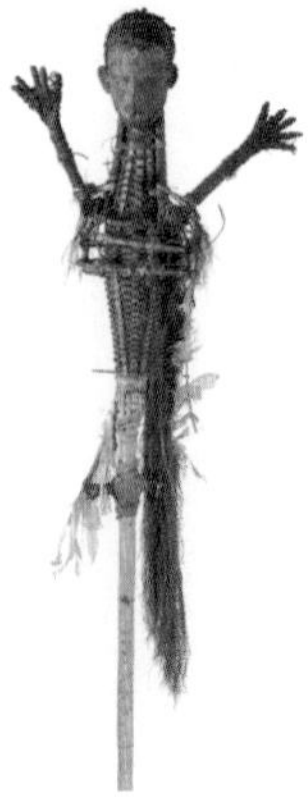

An early 20thC rattan and bone ancestral figure, Sepik River Area, New Guinea, with ancestor's skull covered in mud and clay with inlaid cowry shell eyes and human hair.

73in (185.5cm) high

£8,000-10,000 **WJT**

A CLOSER LOOK AT A GOPE BOARD

A 19thC wooden ancestral gope board, Papuan Gulf, New Guinea.

Tribal warriors were entitled to a gope board for each act of bravery they carried out. A board taken from the canoe of a vanquished enemy was particularly prized as it was believed that some of the previous owner's strength would be transferred to the victor in this way.

Gope boards were designed to house ancestors' spirits, with the belief that they would offer the tribe protection.

These boards were not designed for decoration, and most villagers would never see them as they were stored under the roof of the Men's house, the spiritual centre of the village.

The figure represents an ancestor spirit. The head is disproportionally large to provide a fitting receptacle for the spirit, which the tribes believed resided in the head.

Gope boards are highly collectable and not uncommon in western collections.

£1,500-2,000 **WJT**

OTHER MELANESIAN ISLANDS

An early 20thC ancestral decorated skull, Asmat, Irian Jaya.

14in (35.5cm) long

£5,000-8,000 **WJT**

A mid-19thC rattan and grass decorated 'jipae' funerary costume, Asmat Tribe, Irian Jaya.

The Jipae festival allows the recent dead to revisit the living, appearing in rope and grasswork costumes.

61in (155cm) high

£3,000-4,000 **WJT**

An early 20thC decorated ancestral cassowary bone dagger, Asmat tribe, Irian Jaya.

15in (38cm) high

£1,000-1,500 **WJT**

A mid-20thC wooden carved drum with lizard skin, Asmat tribe, Irian Jaya.

29in (73.5cm) high

£1,000-1,500 **WJT**

A wooden shield, Nakanai, West New Britain, with relief-carved abstract decoration consisting of twin opposing stylized faces, with painted surface and integral hand grip on reverse.

77in (195.5cm) high

£1,200-1,800 **AP**

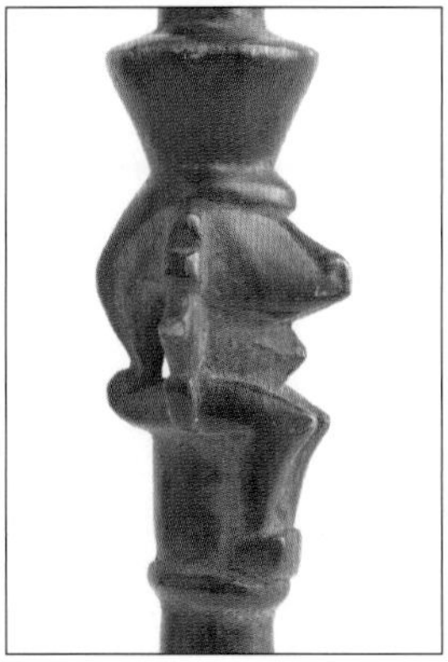

A 19thC parrying weapon, 'Roro Maraugi', San Cristobal, Solomon Islands.

53.5in (136cm) long

£4,000-7,000 **PHK**

A 19thC leaf-shaped club, Malaita Island, Solomon Islands.

80cm (31.5in) high

£2,000-3,500 **PHK**

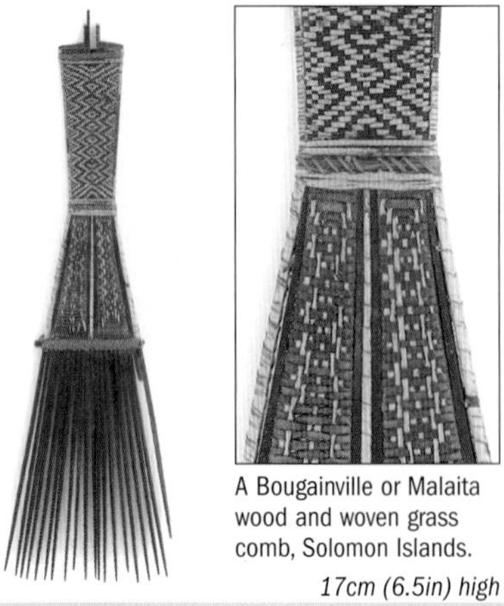

A Bougainville or Malaita wood and woven grass comb, Solomon Islands.

17cm (6.5in) high

£300-400 **PHK**

A 20thC fish lure, tortoise shell and clam shell, with bead spur, Solomon Islands.

7cm (2.75in) long

£200-300 **PHK**

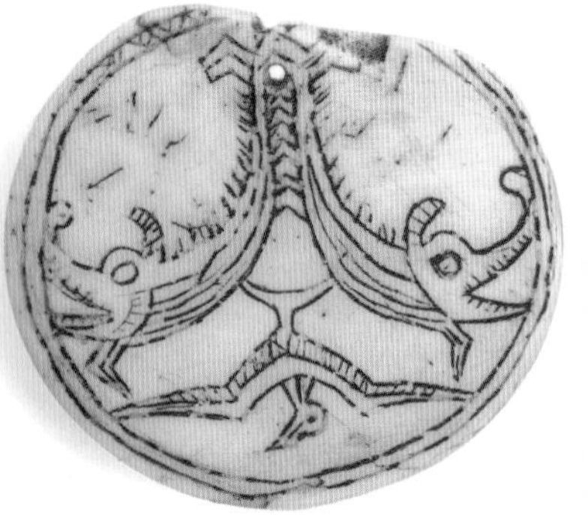

A late 19thC Malaita 'laoniasi' shell pendant, Solomon Islands, engraved with a fish and a frigate bird.

6cm (2.25in) wide

£100-150 **PHK**

A carved shell 'Kap Kap', Santa Cruz, Solomon Islands, with attached panel in the form of an abstract frigate bird, remnant of twisted fibre cord.

3.75in (9.5cm) diam

£500-800 **SK**

A Trobriand Islands lime spatula with ring handle.

Lime spatulas, part of the equipment required for chewing the stimulant betel-nut, are very collectable because of the huge range of handle designs available. This one 'claps' together, doubling as a musical instrument.

24cm (9.5in) long

£1,000-1,500 **PHK**

A 19thC wooden ancestral figure, Trobriand Islands.

16in (40.5cm) high

£2,500-3,500 **WJT**

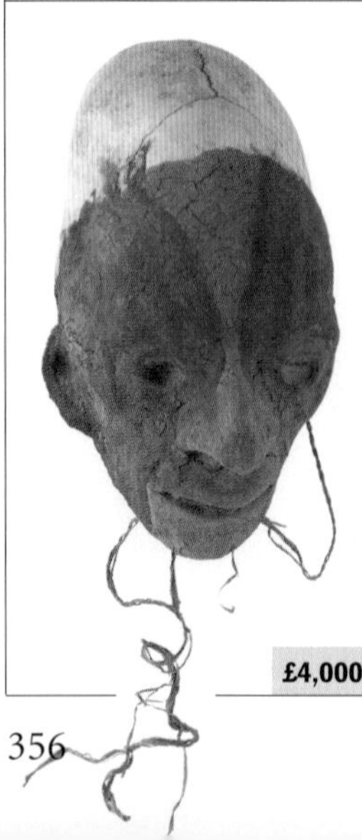

A 19thC elongated ancestral skull, Vanuatu, New Hebrides, South Pacific, cased in mud and clay.

9.5in (24cm) high

£4,000-6,000 **WJT**

A rare carved wood house post, New Caledonia, carved as a man in European clothing, possibly representing a missionary, traces of black and white pigment, losses.

34.5in (87.5cm) high

£1,200-1,800 **SK**

An 'hourglass' drum, D'Entrecastaux Islands.

37.75in (96cm) high

£500-800 **PHK**

THE NAVAJO

- The Navajo, or Diné as they called themselves, were descendants of the Athabascan race. Originally a nomadic tribe of hunters and raiders, the Navajo appeared in the Southwest around the 15thC and eventually began to settle, taking up many of the farming and artistic practices of the Pueblo people.
- Weaving and pottery, skills learned from the Pueblo, became the main artistic media of the Navajo. Simple striped blankets for wearing became more complex, with symmetrical geometric designs, in the 19thC.
- As the commercial market for their weaving grew, the Navajo began to incorporate animal, human and plant motifs into their rug designs, with representations of spirit figures, or yeis, and corn, birds, livestock and horses.
- Navajo silver work was also exceptional. Employing designs and techniques brought from Mexico, they developed the iconic squash blossom necklaces and horse ornaments.

A late 19thC south west Navajo weaving.

£1,500-2,000 **SK**

A late 19thC south west Navajo weaving.

£2,000-3,000 **SK**

A late 19thC Navajo weaving, from south west Germantown.

£5,000-8,000 **SK**

A Navajo Germantown weaving, pre-dyed Germantown wool on a cotton weft foundation.

c1890 *48in (122cm) high*

£500-800 **FS**

A late Navajo classic serape, tightly woven in hand spun and ravelled wool, the overall grid pattern with floating diamond devices over a variegated red ground, wool loss.

c1870 *68.5in (174m) high*

£15,000-20,000 **SK**

A Navajo serape, of cochineal and lac-dyed bayeta, with extensive use of deep indigo colour, from Arizona.

c1860 *76in (193cm) wide*

£60,000-65,000 **TB**

A Navajo silver and turquoise concho pin.

c1940 *2.25in (5.5cm) wide*

£50-70 **FS**

A Zuni silver and turquoise pin.

c1940 *2.25in (5.5cm) diam*

£150-200 **FS**

A Navajo silver and turquoise bracelet.

c1940 *2.75in (7cm) wide*

£200-250 **FS**

A Navajo silver bowl.

c1960 *2.25in (5.5cm) wide*

£30-50 **FS**

A Hopi Pueblo seed jar.
c1900 *6in (15cm) diam*
£4,000-6,000 **TB**

A Hopi clay pottery bowl, Arizona.
c1930 *7in (18cm) diam*
£250-350 **FS**

A Hopi pottery jar, with stylized bird frieze.
c1950 *6.5in (16.5cm) diam*
£250-350 **SK**

A Hopi coiled peach basket.
c1915 *13in (33cm) diam*
£2,200-2,800 **MSG**

A Hopi clay pottery vase, Arizona.
c1930 *10in (25.5cm) high*
£300-500 **FS**

A Hopi coiled storage basket, the pictographic design with full-body kachina motifs.

For thousands of years, the Hopi were subsistence farmers, living from the land atop arid mesas in the south west, entreating the gods through rituals to aid their meagre living. They violently resisted the 17th-18thC Spanish incursions, retaining their original culture.

c1935 *38in (96.5cm) high*
£4,000-6,000 **MSG**

An early 20thC Hopi carved wooden kachina, Masa-u, the cottonwood form with large case mask.
£400-600 **SK**

PUEBLO

A 19thC Pueblo human effigy figure with red pigment, abalone eyes and tar pitch, with leather carrying pouch.
5in (12.5cm) high
£4,000-6,000 **TB**

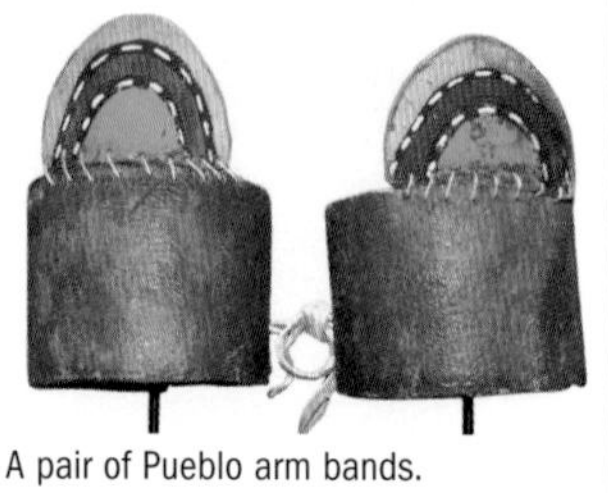

A pair of Pueblo arm bands.
c1920 *5in (12.5cm) high*
£1,500-2,000 **MSG**

A CLOSER LOOK AT A KACHINA DOLL

Kachinas represent helper deities. Most Zuni kachinas live at the bottom of the mythical Lake of the Dead, from where they emerge to participate in ceremonial dances.

Hututu, representing nature, takes his name from the cry he makes.

The Hopi and Zuni tribes carved kachina dolls to aid religious teaching for children. Zuni dolls are usually more slender and elongated with articulated arms.

Zuni dolls are dressed in cloth garments with leather moccasins and other tribal regalia.

A 19thC Zuni Pueblo kachina representing Hututu, wearing a case mask.
15in (38cm) high
£30,000-40,000 **D&G**

A Zuni olla, decorated with deer heartline design, from Pueblo, New Mexico.

c1890 *12.5in (32cm) diam*

£5,000-8,000 **D&G**

A Pueblo olla, from the Aguilar family of Santa Domingo, Pueblo.

c1910 *11in (28cm) wide*

£4,000-6,000 **TB**

A San Ildefonso pot with flaming sun motif, from Pueblo, New Mexico.

c1910 *10.5in (26.5cm)*

£3,000-5,000 **D&G**

A late 19thC painted pottery olla, Acoma Pueblo.

£12,000-15,000 **SK**

OTHER SOUTH WESTERN TRIBES

A large, early 20thC Apache coiled basketry olla.

21.5in (54.5cm) high

£7,000-10,000 **SK**

An Apache basket dish from Arizona, squaw huckleberry, devil's claw with a willow shoots foundation.

c1900 *16.5in (42cm) diam*

£400-600 **FS**

A Pima 'Man in the maze' basket, Arizona.

c1920 *15.5in (39.5cm) diam*

£1,500-2,000 **D&G**

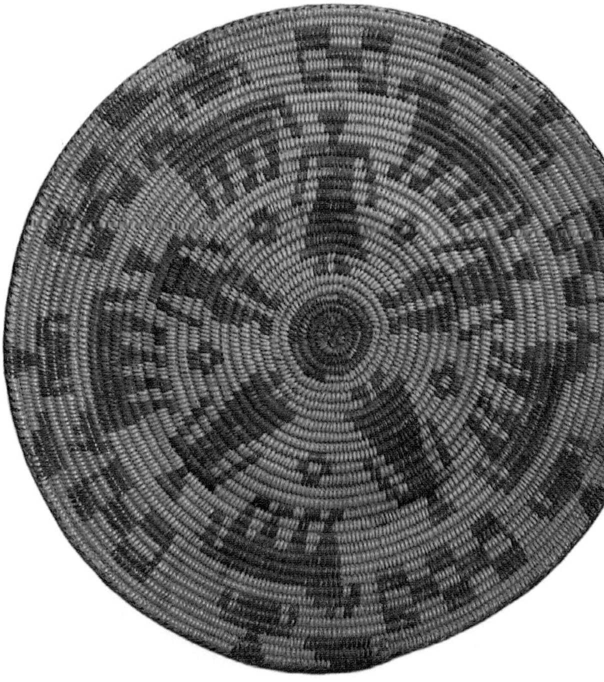

An early 20thC coiled basketry tray, Pima.

16.5in (42cm) diam

£1,500-2,000 **SK**

A Caddoan 'Means' engraved tripod bottle

Found in southern Arkansas in the Ouachita River area.

c1400 *9in (23cm) high*

£1,000-2,000 **RAM**

A Caddoan engraved giant whelk shell cup, Spiro Mound, Oklahoma.

c1300 *11.5in (29cm) high*

£3,000-5,000 **RAM**

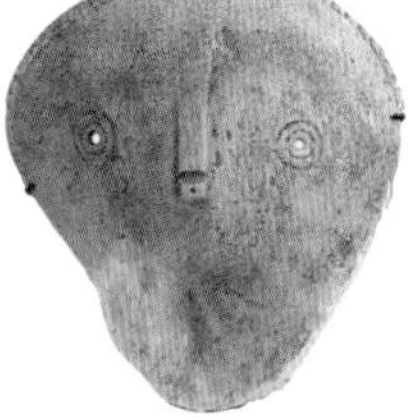

A Mississippian Chickamauga-style conch or whelk shell mask.

Such pieces show a similar distribution to that of the Buffalo-mask gorgets found along the upper Ohio River.

c1400 *8.5in (21.5cm) high*

£1,500-3,000 **RAM**

A Mississippian, Buffalo-style 'Weeping Eye' conch or whelk shell mask.

This represents the most widely distributed style of mask gorgets. They are found along the upper Tennessee River, the upper Ohio River and western tributaries of the Mississippi River.

8.5in (21.5cm) high

£1,500-3,000 **RAM**

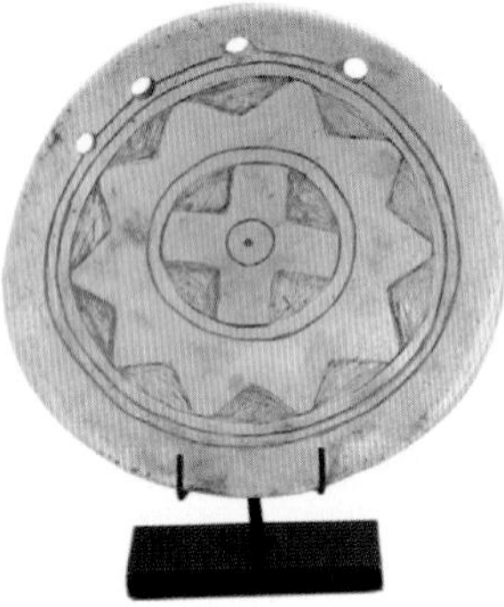

A Mississippian Tibbee Creek-style shell gorget.

Distribution is limited to the Moundville area and Tombigbee River of Alabama and Mississippi.

c1400 *4.5in (11.5cm) high*

£600-2,000 **RAM**

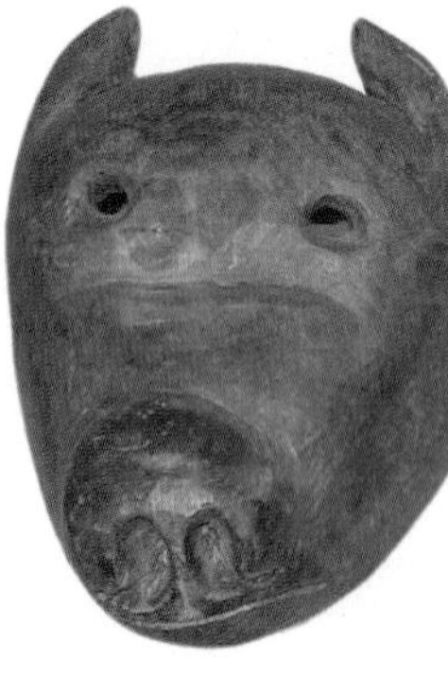

An early 20thC Cherokee Buffalo 'Booger' carved wooden dance mask, North Carolina.

11in (28cm) high

£1,500-2,500 **RAM**

A Chitimacha double-woven cane basket with feathers, 'Alligator Entrails' pattern, south east region.

c1890 *7.5in (19cm) diam*

£700-1,000 **D&G**

A twilled lidded Chitimacha basket, Louisiana, the lidded form with squares and rectangles over a two-colour striped diagonal background, damaged.

c1900 *5in (13cm) high*

£1,200-1,800 **SK**

A 20thC Coushatta tribe pinecone turkey, from southeast Louisiana.

13in (33cm) long

£300-400 **D&G**

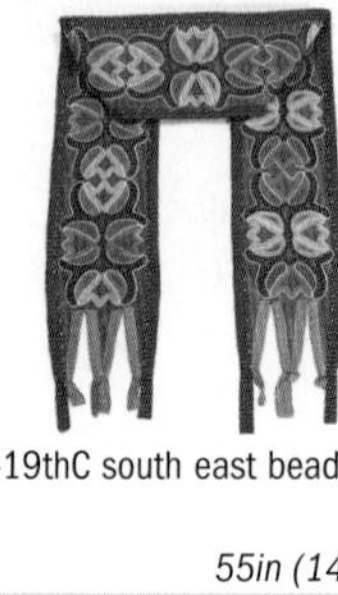

A mid-19thC south east beaded cloth sash.

55in (140cm) long

£4,000-6,000 **SK**

A south east Seminole bandolier bag.

c1870 *32in (81.5cm) long*

£20,000-25,000 **MSG**

A Huastec seated zoomorphic figure, depicted with a long tail spout and snout, on a white slip ground with black geometric surface decoration

cAD1000 *7.5in (19cm) high*

£300-500 **AP**

A pre-Columbian Mayan pottery warrior figure, Jaina.

cAD750 *6.5in (16.5cm) high*

£1,200-1,800 **SK**

A pre-Columbian Mayan pottery vessel.

cAD750 *6.75in (17cm) high*

£1,000-1,500 **SK**

A pre-Columbian Mayan carved pottery vessel, with a carved depiction of a seated ruler.

cAD750 *5in (13cm) high*

£500-800 **SK**

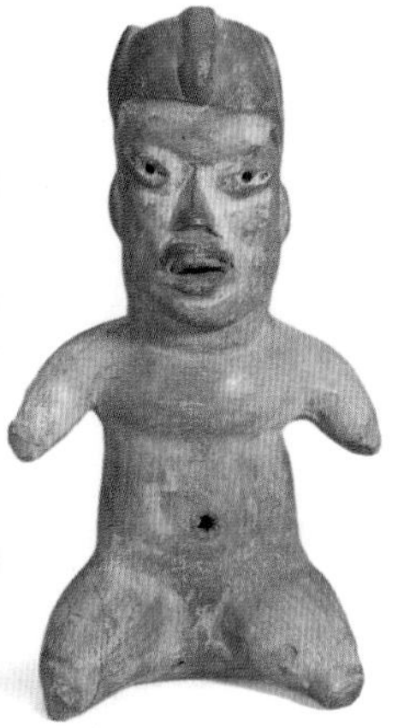

A pre-Columbian Olmec seated pottery figure.

c700BC *9.5in (24cm) high*

£250-300 **SK**

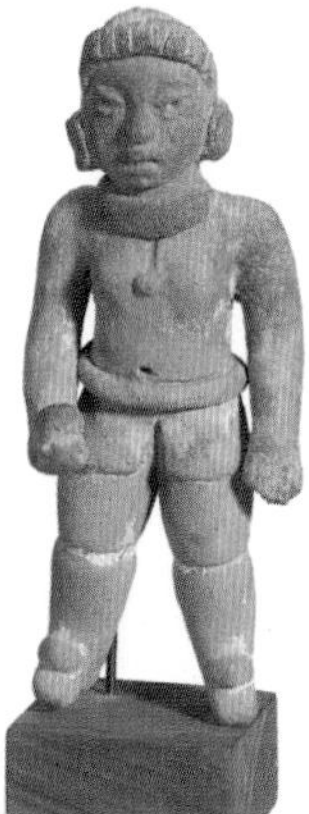

A pre-Columbian Olmec pottery ball player.

c600BC

£300-500 **SK**

A late Olmec jade flat monkey pendant, with open cut-out tail, Gulf Coast.

c450BC

£9,000-11,000 **TFA**

A pre-Columbian Vera Cruz pottery effigy figure, the seated Fire God with hands on his knees, wearing large ear decoration.

cAD600 *12in (31cm) high*

£500-800 **SK**

A large pre-Columbian Vera Cruz male figure, depicted standing and smiling figure with one upraised arm, the other hand raised.

Scholars speculate that the smiling faces found on Vera Cruz figures indicate drugged ecstasy.

cAD700 *19in (48.5cm) high*

£4,000-6,000 **SK**

A CLOSER LOOK AT AN OLMEC STONE MASK

The Olmec (c1500BC-300AD) are believed to have been the 'mother culture' of the region, developing a hierarchical elitist society which influenced the theology, aesthetics and commerce of the surrounding areas.

The down-turned lips are typical of Olmec art – the snarling open mouth is often compared to a jaguar's.

The Olmec influence spread across Mesoamerica without the use of force, indicating that missionary work was probably aided by hypnotically powerful masks such as this.

The heavily lidded, slanted, tapering eyes, pierced for the wearer to see, are another characteristic of Olmec art.

An Olmec stone mask with horizontal incisions, pierced eyes and earlobes, Gulf Coast.

c800BC *7.5in (19cm) high*

£200,000-220,000 **TFA**

A Huari wooden guardian figure, central coast, Peru.

cAD700 *34in (86.5cm) high*

£8,000-12,000 **WJT**

A Huari wooden burial mask, central coast, Peru.

cAD700 *12in (30.5cm) high*

£3,000-5,000 **WJT**

A Huari figural bottle, south coast, decorated as a standing human figure with four profile animal heads, relief nose and ears, intact.

cAD700 *6.75in (17cm) high*

£3,000-5,000 **AP**

A pre-Columbian Nazca pottery beaker.

cAD100 *6.75in (17cm) high*

£200-300 **SK**

A Nazca vessel, with a spout issuing from the headdress, depicting a male figure, flanked with smaller female figures and zoomorphic figures, restored.

c50BC *7in (18cm) high*

£2,000-3,000 **AP**

A 19thC Nazca trophy head, retaining the skin and hair of the enemy affixed to the skull, Peru.

The Nazca had a fascination with heads taken in battle which was reflected in their decorative art. Pottery and weaving both frequently used 'trophy' heads as decorative motifs, while the actual heads were preserved for display.

21in (53cm) high

£5,000-8,000 **WJT**

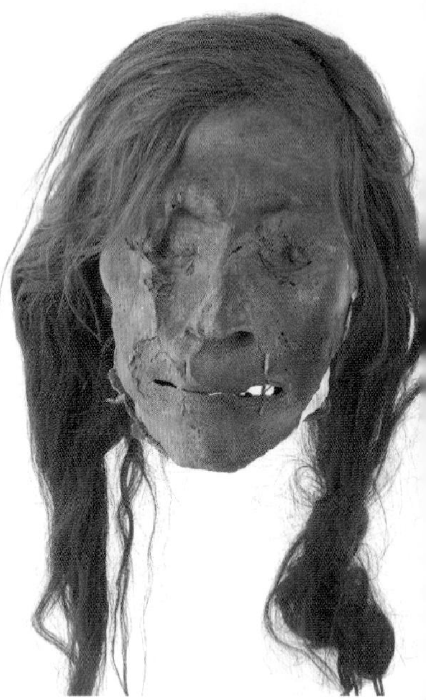

A trophy head, either Nazca or Huari, decorated with feathers, cotton fibre, gold and hair over a human skull, Peru.

cAD850 *12in (30.5cm) high*

£7,000-10,000 **WJT**

A Nazca cushma or tunic, Peru, camelid fibre woven in gauze, with complex interlocking warp weft technique, scaffold wefting.

cAD100 *86in (218cm) wide*

£15,000-25,000 **EFI**

A Paracas resin-painted vessel, with bridge spout, body decorated with smiling faces, with projecting noses, multi-circled eyes and triple-banded tattoos, stylized fish and red dots, painted in resin enamel, restored.

c250BC *6.25in (16cm) high*

£1,800-2,200 **AP**

An early 20thC Blackfoot beaded pouch.

£300-400 **SK**

A early 20thC Blackfoot beaded hide pouch and strap, the fringed strap beaded on one side.

22in (56cm) long

£1,200-1,800 **SK**

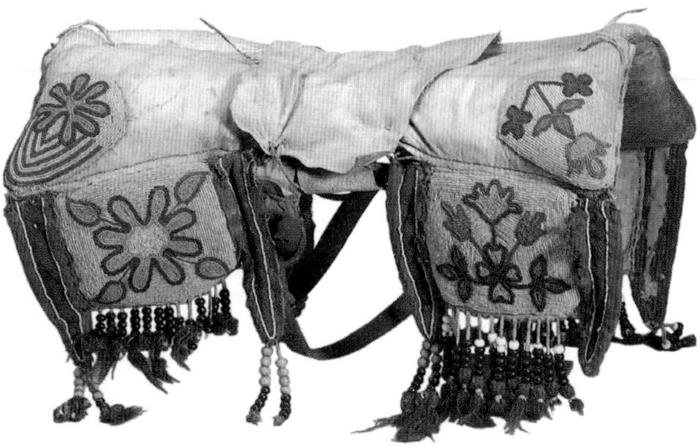

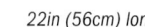

A Plains Cree beaded hide pad saddle.

22in (56cm) long

£1,800-2,200 **SK**

A pair of Crow buffalo hide moccasins, seed-beaded on red trade cloth.

c1865 *10in (25.5cm) long*

£5,000-7,000 **D&G**

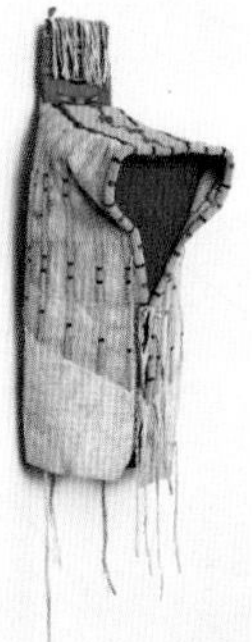

A late 19thC Sioux beaded infant papoose, glass seed beads sewn to hide with sinew.

24in (61cm) long

£3,000-5,000 **FS**

A late 19thC Sioux painted parfleche, Lakota.

£1,000-1,500 **SK**

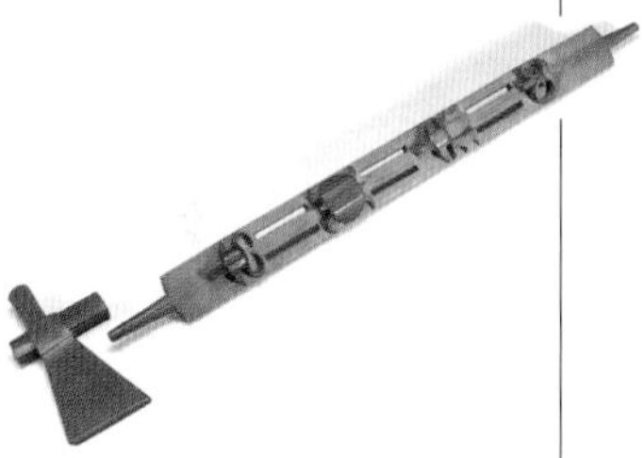

A late 19thC carved wooden and stone pipe, probably Sioux, Lakota.

£4,000-6,000 **SK**

CENTRAL & SOUTHERN PLAINS TRIBES

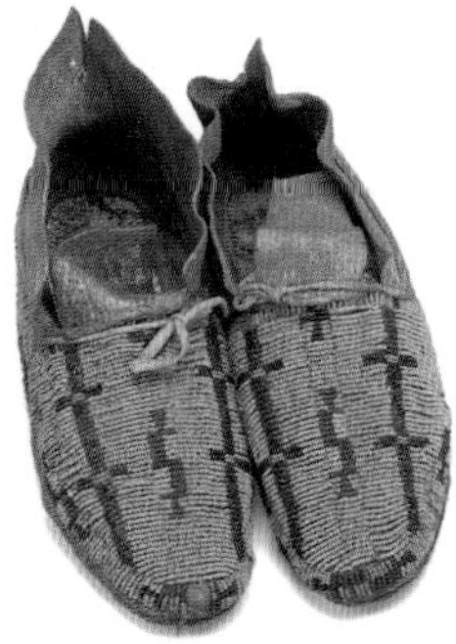

A pair of late 19thC Arapaho beaded hide moccasins.

£300-500 **SK**

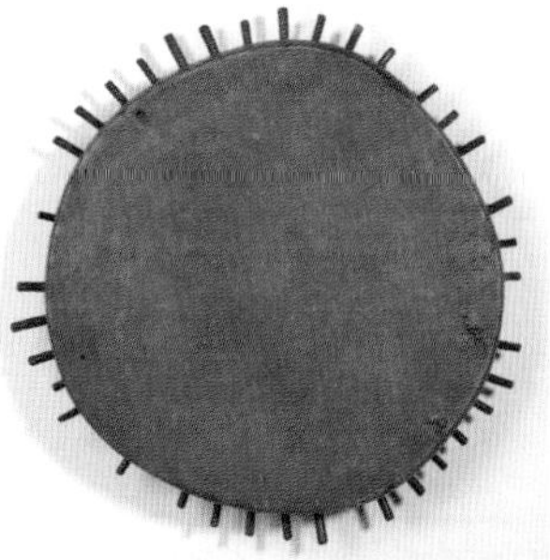

A Plains ceremonial drum, attributed to the Cheyenne.

c1860 *17.5in (44.5cm) diam*

£3,000-5,000 **TB**

A North Cheyenne war shirt, made of deerskin and natural dyed quill work, belonging to White Powder.

White Powder fought against Custer at the battle of Little Big Horn in 1876. The shirt was purchased off his back after he had his portrait painted by the famous American artist Joseph Scheuerle.

c1870

£70,000-80,000 **WJT**

A Cheyenne beaded hide bag, the soft rectangular form beaded on the front, sides and flap.

c1900

£1,500-2,000 **SK**

A very rare late 18thC Chumash coiled basketry tray, tightly woven with an unusual small pedestal bottom, brown chevron-filled expanding bands.

16.75in (42.5cm) diam

£25,000-30,000 **SK**

A very rare late 18thC Chumash coiled basketry bowl, of tightly woven flare-sided form with elaborate three-colour interconnected geometric devices, a band of hourglass devices near the rim, damaged.

18in (45.5cm) diam

£50,0000-60,000 **SK**

A Hupa Yurok basket bowl, northern California, of willow root, bear grass, woodwardia fern stem and maidenhair fern stem, with a willow shoot foundation.

c1920 *8.5in (21.5cm) diam*

£300-500 **FS**

A beaded Modoc basket, northern California.

c1920 *5in (13cm) high*

£3,000-4,000 **FS**

A Pomo oval basket, with negative design, California.

c1910 *5.5in (14cm) long*

£3,000-4,000 **D&G**

A western Mono bottleneck basket, with remnants of quail topknot feathers, California.

7.5in (19cm) wide

£3,000-5,000 **D&G**

A large Pomo basket, northern California, of split sedge root and dyed bulrush root on a willow shoot foundation with acorn woodpecker crest feathers, valley quail topknots, clamshell disks and glass seed beads applied with cotton thread.

16in (40.5cm) diam

£10,000-13,000 **FS**

A miniature beaded Pomo basket, northern California, with glass seed beads and split sedge root stitches on a willow shoot foundation.

c1930 *2.5in (6.5cm) diam*

£500-700 **FS**

A Wintum basket with quail topknots and shell discs, California.

c1900 *5in (12.5cm) diam*

£2,000-3,000 **D&G**

A Yurok woman's basket hat, northern California, of willow root, bear grass and maidenhair fern stem, with a willow shoot foundation.

c1910 *7in (18cm) diam*

£300-500 **FS**

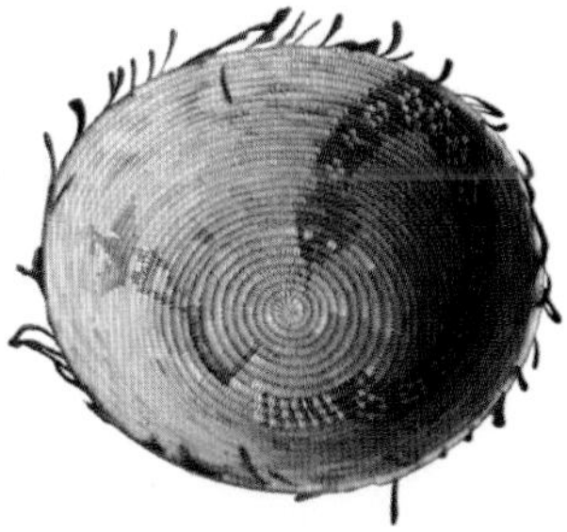

A Mission pictographic basketry bowl, with snake design, California.

c1900 *14in (35.5cm) diam*

£5,000-8,000 **MSG**

A Mission basketry bowl, with a long snake, California.

c1900 *14in (35.5cm) diam*

£5,000-8,000 **MSG**

A Mission basketry bowl, with a long snake, California.

c1900 *14in (35.5cm) diam*

£5,000-8,000 **MSG**

A late 19thC twined lidded basket, northern California.

£1,500-2,000 **SK**

A northern Californian basket, by Elizabeth Hickox, constructed from grass, porcupine quill and maidenhair fern.

Elizabeth Hickox was a renowned late 19thC north Californian weaver.

5in (12.5cm) diam

£18,000-22,000 **D&G**

PLATEAU TRIBES

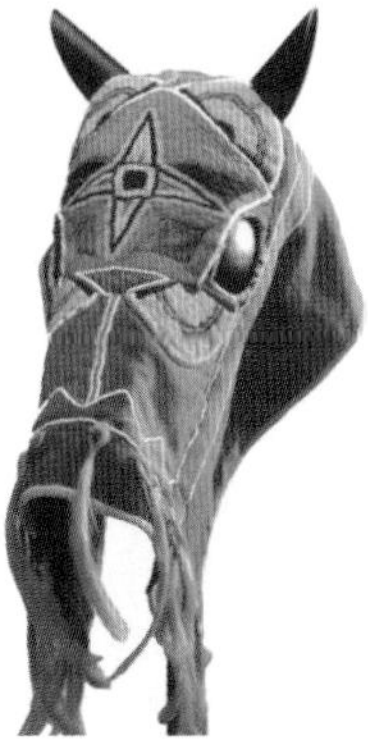

A Cayuse beaded horse mask.

c1890 *28in (71cm) long*

£4,500-5,500 **MSG**

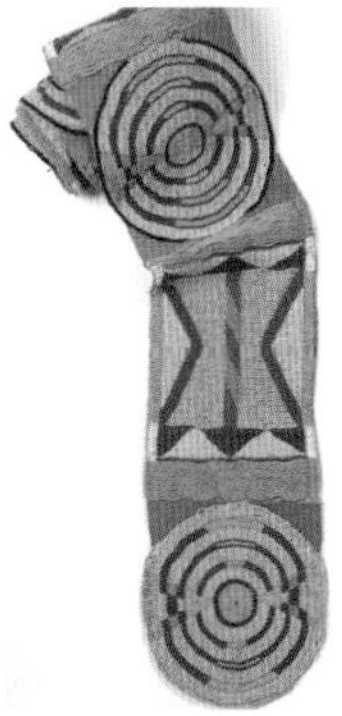

A Cayeuse blanket strip, from the Plateau area.

This would be sewn on to the skin side of a hide blanket as a sign of prestige.

c1870 *6in (15cm) long*

£24,000-26,000 **D&G**

A CLOSER LOOK AT AN INFANT CARRIER

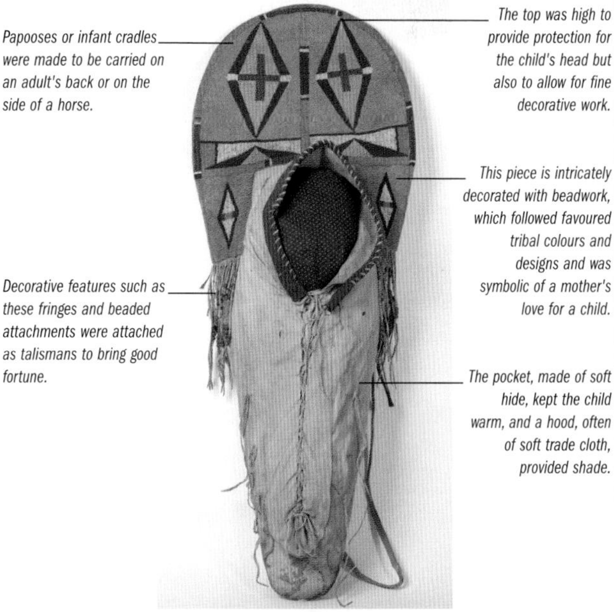

Papooses or infant cradles were made to be carried on an adult's back or on the side of a horse.
The top was high to provide protection for the child's head but also to allow for fine decorative work.
This piece is intricately decorated with beadwork, which followed favoured tribal colours and designs and was symbolic of a mother's love for a child.
Decorative features such as these fringes and beaded attachments were attached as talismans to bring good fortune.
The pocket, made of soft hide, kept the child warm, and a hood, often of soft trade cloth, provided shade.

A pair of Nez Perce hide moccasins, sewn with glass seed beads.

c1880 *10in (25.5cm) long*

£1,500-2,000 **FS**

A pair of Yakima beaded pictographic gauntlets.

c1925 *12in (30.5cm) long*

£2,500-3,500 **MSG**

A Nez Perce infant cradle, comprising a beaded panel attached to a board rimmed with red stroud cloth, deer hide construction, from the Plateau region.

c1870 *46in (117cm) long*

£35,000-40,000 **D&G**

A Kwakiutl wolf effigy face mask, from British Columbia.

c1910 *19in (48.5cm) long*

£18,000-22,000 **M&D**

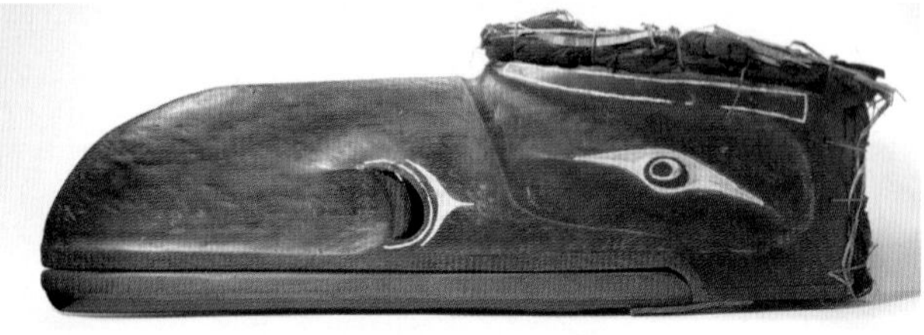

A Kwakiutl raven effigy face mask.

c1935 *30in (76cm) long*

£15,000-20,000 **M&D**

A Kwakiutl ceremonial wasp effigy mask, from British Columbia.

A similar mask is at the Museum of Natural History in Munich.

c1870 *10.5in (26.5cm) high*

£18,000-22,000 **M&D**

A Nootka mask, with round mouth.

c1880 *14in (35.5cm) high*

£15,000-20,000 **M&D**

OTHER NORTH WESTERN TRIBES

An Athabascan jacket, of native tanned hide with red trade cloth trim, partially beaded on the cloth with floral devices.

c1900 *29in (73.5cm) high*

£200-300 **SK**

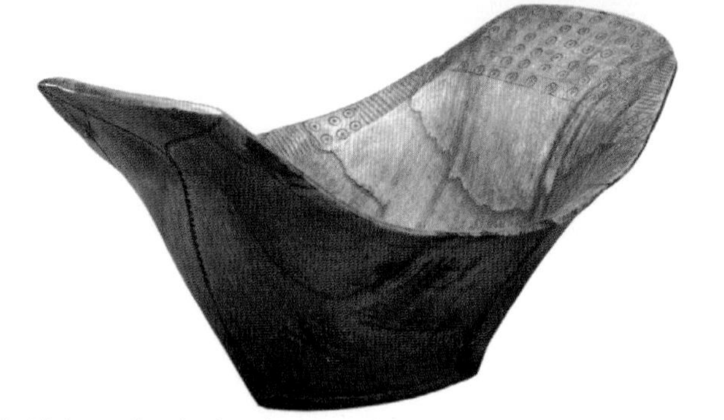

An Athabascan horn bowl, north west coast.

c1890 *7.5in (19cm) high*

£2,000-3,000 **MSG**

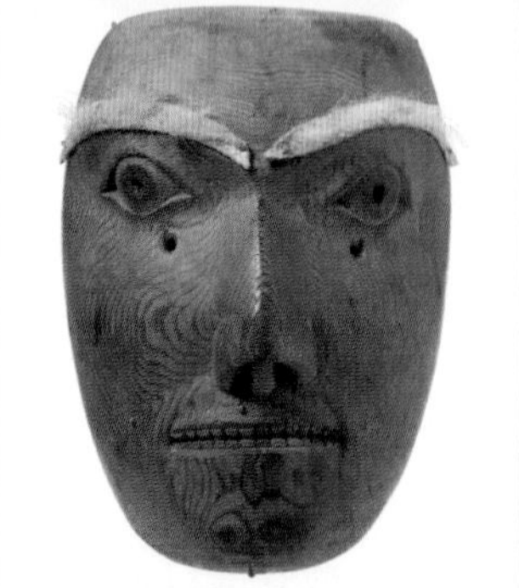

A Haida portrait mask, north west coast.

c1880 *9.5in (24cm) high*

£12,000-14,000 **M&D**

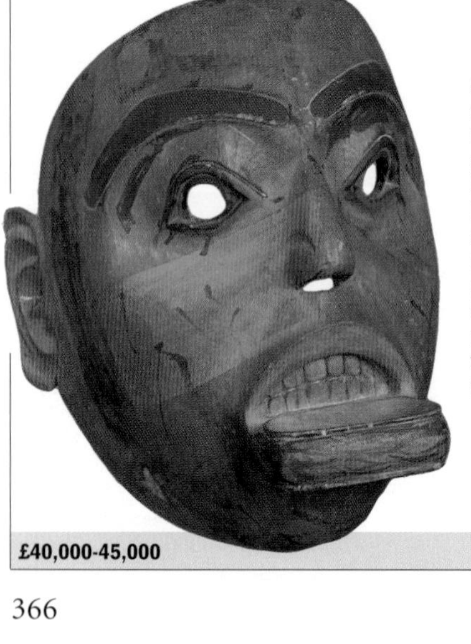

An early 19thC north west coast carved wooden mask, probably Haida, depicting a woman with a large labret in her lower lip, the eyes with incised detail and pierced at the centre, painted with red pigment, traces of black and green pigments, remnant paper label on the inside, patina of use, wood loss.

8.5in (21.5cm) high

£40,000-45,000 **SK**

A Haida carved effigy of a native female in Caucasian dress.

c1850 *3.5in (9cm) high*

£2,200-2,800 **M&D**

Two beaded cloth wall pockets, Tlingit, north west coast.

c1900

£200-300 **SK**

An Ojibwa beaded cloth bandolier bag, backed with commercial cloth, the strap and pouch beaded with a multi-coloured floral design.

European settlers traded glass beads with the peoples of the Great Lakes who skillfully decorated their clothing and accessories, developing tribal patterns and styles. The Ojibwa often represented floral sprays, whereas the Micmac developed lace-like designs.

c1900

£700-1,000 **SK**

An early 19thC Great Lakes finger-woven beaded wool sash, with interwoven zigzag and stacked diamond devices using white pony beads, long partially braided fringe, some with white pony bead trim.

72in (183cm) long

£5,000-8,000 **SK**

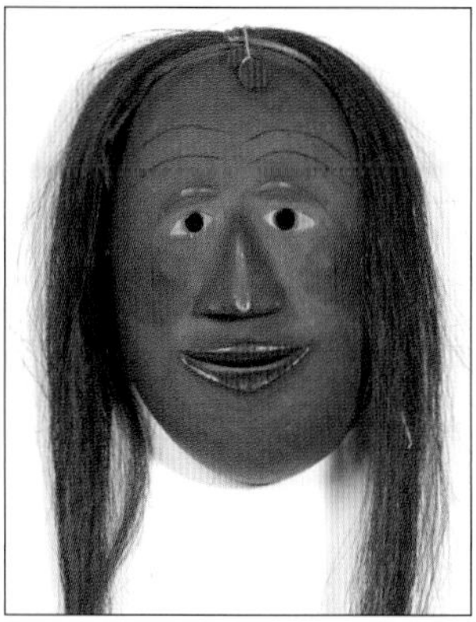

A pair of Iroquois male portrait masks, of basswood with horsehair, from the Brantford Iroquois Reserve in Ontario, Canada.

c1890 *8in (20.5cm) long*

£35,000-40,000 **TB**

A rare mid-19thC Great Lakes feathered cape.

£500-900 **SK**

A late 19thC Iroquois corn husk mask, from western New York state.

11in (28cm) long

£5,000-8,000 **TB**

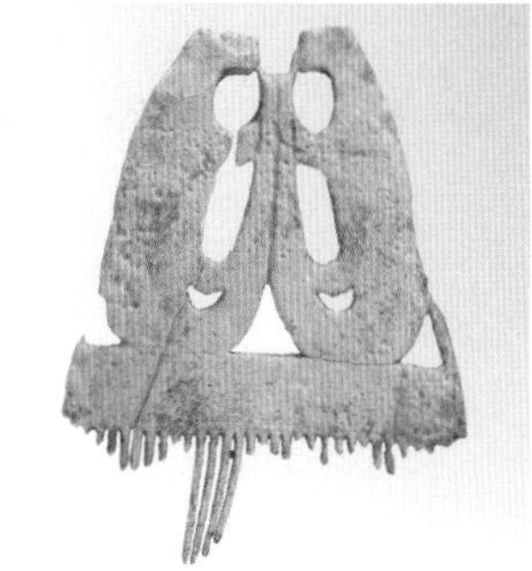

An Iroquois burial comb, decorated with confronting otters, from western New York state.

c1600 *3.25in (8.5cm) wide*

£4,000-7,000 **TB**

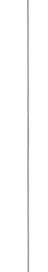

A mid-19thC Native American bird effigy ladle, with fine chip-carved details, from the eastern woodlands.

9in (23cm) wide

£4,000-6,000 **TB**

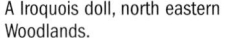

A Iroquois doll, north eastern Woodlands.

Iroquois dolls were designed to be faceless to prevent them from turning into the person they represent.

c1870 *7in (18cm) high*

£2,000-2,500 **MSG**

A Micmac presentation beaded cloth, on a navy blue wool ground, made to cover an early American candle stand, from New York.

c1850 *16in (40.5cm) wide*

£3,000-4,000 **D&G**

A mid-19thC Native American pipe, possibly Ojibwa, with brass wire native repair, on a stand.

9in (23cm) long

£1,800-2,200 **TB**

A Tlingit frog oil bowl, south eastern Alaska.

c1855 *8.5in (21.5cm) wide*

£6,000-8,000 **M&D**

A Tlingit basketry bowl, north west coast.

c1900

£1,500-2,000 **SK**

A late 19thC north west coast carved wooden totem pole, unusual form carved in the round, two opposing human figures with a highly stylized animal on top, with red, green, and black paint, paint loss.

17.75in (45cm) high

£2,500-3,500 **SK**

A 19thC Bella Bella painted wooden mask, with stylized upturned beak, relief-carved eyebrow, stylized painted details in green, red, black, and blue pigments, patina of use, restored.

8in (20.5cm) high

£45,000-50,000 **SK**

A carved and painted north western states portrait mask.

c1855 *8.5in (21.5cm) high*

£20,000-22,000 **D&G**

A late 19thC north west coast carved wooden bird.

£5,000-8,000 **SK**

An Alaskan Inuit lidded basket, with grass stitches on a coiled grass foundation and glass seed bead designs applied with cotton thread.

c1910 *10in (25.5cm) diam*

£500-700 **FS**

A 20thC north west coast button blanket, with cut-out animal forms of a spread eagle, turtle, and small birds, outlined and detailed with real and faux mother-of-pearl buttons.

North west coast art mainly depicts stylized animals, although floral and geometric patterns are also used. The representation of animal forms was believed to call forth their powers for human use.

69in (175cm) wide

£400-600 **SK**

INUIT ART

- Inuit people originally reserved decorative art for ritualistic purposes and personal adornment: tools and everyday objects were left undecorated.
- Inuit art roughly divides into three periods. Styles from 2000BC to around AD1700 represent pre-European contact, while pieces dating from c1700-1948, known as Historic Period Art, were adapted to European tastes. From 1949, the contemporary period began, with an exhibition of Inuit Art in Montreal organised by Toronto artist James Houston.
- Thanks to this exhibition, art-making became a viable alternative source of income for Inuit hunters. The Canadian government began to recognize the importance of Inuit art to national heritage and sought to promote this previously undervalued area.
- Inuit art covers a range of expression from realism and naturalism to abstraction. Sculpture is a key medium: stone, antler, ivory, driftwood and whalebone have traditionally been used by local artists. Printing and drawing, popular from the 1950s, are now also common media.

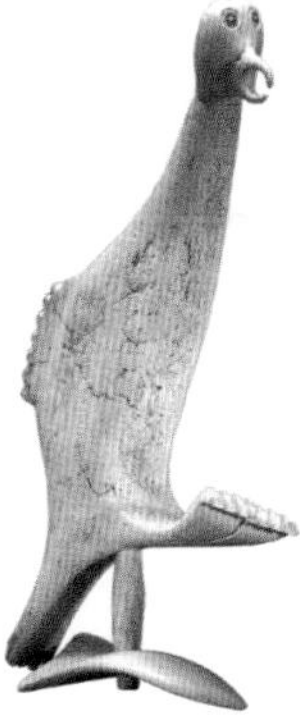

A whalebone sculpture of a spirit bird, by Karoo Ashevak, with inset eyes, mounted on a bone base, signed in syllabics.

21in (53.5cm) high

£12,000-15,000 **WAD**

A whalebone sculpture of a shaman, by Karoo Ashevak, carved with two faces, both with inset eyes, one with a sinew and bone suspension in the mouth, mounted to a bone base, signed in syllabics.

15in (38cm) high

£15,000-20,000 **WAD**

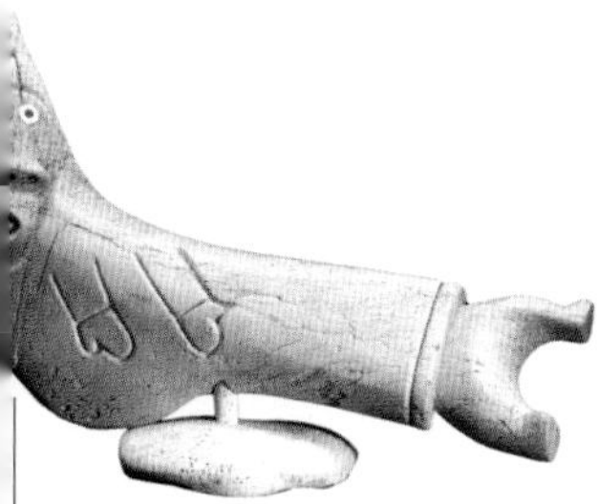

A whalebone sculpture of a flying shaman, by Karoo Ashevak, with inset eyes, mounted on a whalebone base, signed in syllabics.

22in (56cm) wide

£10,000-15,000 **WAD**

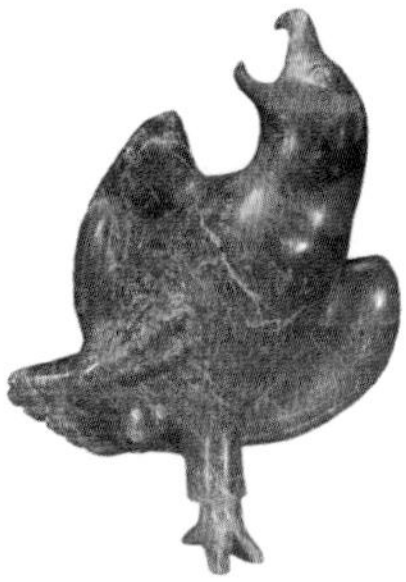

A mottled green soapstone sculpture, by Osuitok Ipeelee, depicting a threatened bird laying an egg.

c1975 *15.5in (39.5cm) high*

£9,000-12,000 **WAD**

A marbled green soapstone sculpture, by Osuitok Ipeelee, of Sedna swimming with a whale, signed in syllabics.

Sedna is the Inuit goddess of the sea.

16.5in (42cm) high

£10,000-12,000 **WAD**

A mottled green soapstone sculpture of an Inuk, by Osuitok Ipeelee, holding on to a running spirit caribou.

c1965 *12in (30.5cm) wide*

£3,000-5,000 **WAD**

A mottled green soapstone sculpture of a musk ox, by Ouitok Ipeelee, throwing an Inuit hunter into the air.

Ipeelee, formerly known as Oshaweetok B, is a sculptor and innovative print-maker from West Baffin Island. He comes from a long line of carvers and is known for his intimate knowledge of local carving stone and the intricate delicacy of his art.

c1970 *15in (38cm) high*

£12,000-18,000 **WAD**

A marbled green soapstone sculpture of a polar bear, by Joe Jaw, inset with ivory teeth, embracing its cub while holding a seal in its mouth.

c1970 *10.5in (26.5cm) high*

£6,000-9,000 **WAD**

An Inuit dark stone sculpture of a polar bear, by Joe Kowik.

8in (20cm) high

£400-600 **THG**

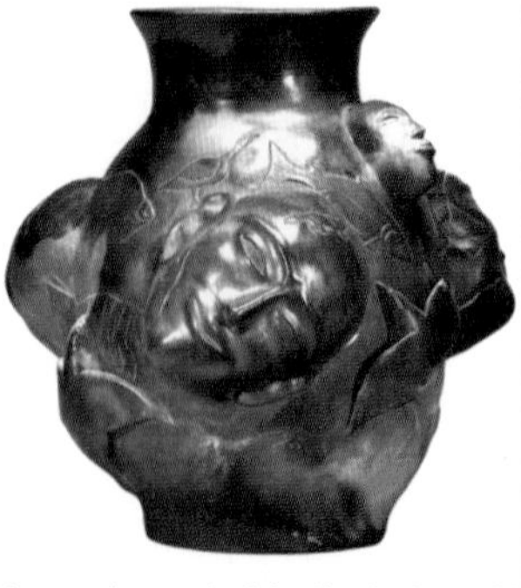

A ceramic vase by John Kurok, the ovoid body decorated in high relief with faces, birds and Arctic animals.

18in (45.5cm) high

£1,200-1,800 **WAD**

A ceramic vase, by Yvo Samgushak, the ovoid body decorated with Inuit figures, owls and whales, signed in syllabics and Roman script.

17in (43cm) high

£2,000-3,000 **WAD**

A mottled dark grey soapstone depiction of 'The Migration', by Joe Talirunili (1893-1976), the boat carved with figures, signed in Roman script.

11in (28cm) wide

£35,000-40,000 **WAD**

A mottled dark soapstone sculpture of a head, by Aisa Amaruali Tuluga, with inset ivory eyes and teeth.

c1950 *4.5in (11.5cm) high*

£2,000-3,000 **WAD**

A mottled green soapstone sculpture of a bird, standing with upswept wings.

c1970 *8in (20.5cm) high*

£4,000-6,000 **WAD**

A mottled dark soapstone transformation sculpture of a polar bear and shaman, with inset carved light stone face.

c1960 *8.5in (21.5cm) wide*

£10,000-12,000 **WAD**

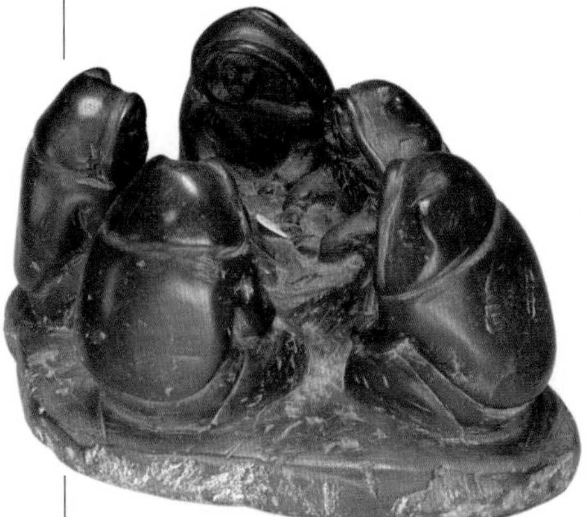

A mottled dark soapstone sculpture of crouching Inuit women preparing fish with an ivory ulu, disc number inscribed.

c1960

£9,000-11,000 **WAD**

An early Inuit doll, the seated mother with a green soapstone head and ivory hands holding a baby, both with inlaid ivory eyes and seated on a grass mat.

6in (15cm) high

£2,500-3,500 **WAD**

A scrimshaw tusk, depicting a walrus on floating ice, village in background, mounted on to a piece of argillite.

5.25in (13.5cm) high

£300-400 **TSG**

COALBROOKDALE

- Abraham Derby developed a method of using coke to smelt iron at his works in Coalbrookdale, Shropshire during the early 18thC.
- This new process made it possible to cast larger and more complex shapes in iron, and provided the basis for the Industrial Revolution.
- During the 19thC, the architectural use of cast iron became widespread. It was famously used to construct the magnificent Crystal Palace in 1851, where the Coalbrookdale Company exhibited a pair of ceremonial gates that were later installed in Hyde Park.
- Durable and rust-resistant, cast iron was ideally suited for use in the garden and the Coalbrookdale Company enjoyed great commercial success with its range of garden furniture.
- The Victorian taste for eclectic revival styles created a demand for cast iron garden furniture in ornate Gothic, Rococo and Classical forms.
- Many of the Coalbrookdale Company's most popular garden furniture designs are still in production today.

A 19thC garden chair, formed from bent rods and strips of sheet steel, painted black, with a brass button imprinted "Lalance and Grosjean 273 Pearl St. N.Y.".

c1865 *35in (89cm) high*

£400-600 **SK**

A pair of Coalbrookdale cast iron garden seats, the rectangular backs cast with Gothic-style tracery, with leaf-cast scrolling arms and legs, honeycomb pierced seat with pierced apron.

27.5in (70cm) wide

£800-1,200 pair **L&T**

A Coalbrookdale cast iron garden seat, with a Gothic-style design.

This design was registered in Coalbrookdale's 1875 catalogue.

c1875 *59.75in (152cm) long*

£800-1,200 **SWO**

A pair of Victorian cast iron garden benches, cast with a 'Lily of the Valley' pattern, one stamped "C B Dale" one repainted.

61.5in (156cm) wide

£3,500-4,500 pair **SWO**

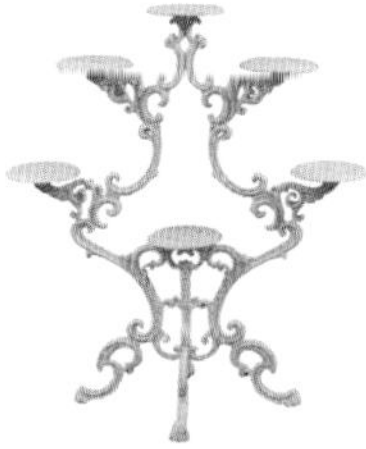

A Victorian cast iron six-branch plant stand.

40.5in (103cm) high

£250-300 **SWO**

A Victorian conservatory stand, by Parnall & Sons of London, with three marble shelves on a cast iron stand, numbered "238917".

36.25in (92cm) wide

£400-600 **SWO**

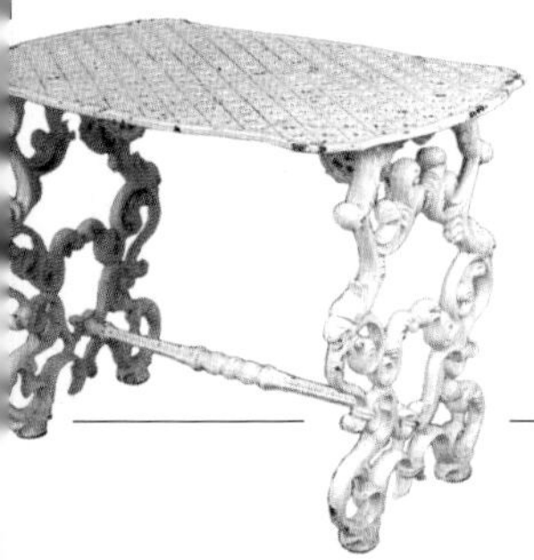

A Victorian cast iron garden table, with pierced trefoil pattern top and cast base.

35.75in (91cm) wide

£180-220 **SWO**

A pietra dura and white Carrara marble table, inlaid in the Neoclassical style with various marbles and hardstones, raised on twin supports carved with winged caryatids, mask motifs and fruit.

80in (203cm) wide

£4,000-6,000 **FRE**

A pair of marble obelisks, in the Neoclassical style, veneered and raised on bun feet, with square bases.

72.5in (184cm) high

£3,000-4,000 **FRE**

A 19thC French red and white marble column, comprising a square plinth, circular column and square plate to top.

26.5in (66cm) high

£180-220 **KAU**

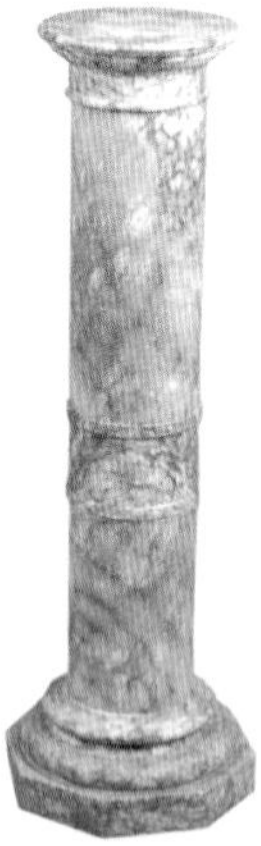

A late Victorian marble column, with a ring-turned column and octagonal base.

36in (90cm) high

£300-400 **SWO**

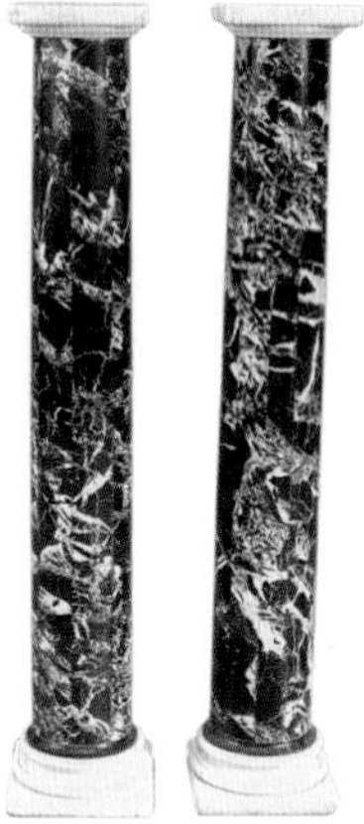

A pair of black and white veined marble columns.

55.5in (139cm) high

£1,000-1,500 **SWO**

A pair of Sienna marble pedestals, in the form of Doric pilasters, carved with guilloche and figures and raised on square bases, minor damage.

43.75in (111cm) high

£700-1,000 **FRE**

A pair of pink marble columns, with black marble capitals and bases.

45.25in (115cm) high

£700-1,000 **SWO**

A 20thC black marble fluted pedestal, on a square moulded plinth.

28.25in (70.5cm) high

£400-600 **KAU**

A pair of terracotta twin-handled garden urns on stands, each cast with a frieze of Classical figures and gadrooned bands, the square bases cast with rams' heads above Arabesque panels.

62.5in (159cm) high

£3,500-4,500 **L&T**

A pair of marble figures, in the 18thC Venetian style, depicting two males with full beards in antique robes, each holding a large shell bowl.

75.5in (189cm) high

£5,000-7,000 **KAU**

A set of four marble figures, comprising two atlantes and two caryatids, depicting the Four Seasons in the Neoclassical style.

largest 72in (183cm) high

£16,000-20,000 **FRE**

A white Carrara marble sculpture, in the Neoclassical style, depicting a semi-draped female with a basket on her back, supporting two angels, on a circular base.

48.5in (123cm) high

£3,000-4,000 **FRE**

One of a pair of marble sculptures, in the Neoclassical style, depicting two cherubs raised on a circular pedestal.

53in (135cm) high

£2,800-3,200 pair **FRE**

A Victorian marble bust of a young girl, her hair in a long plait, with a band of flowers below.

23.25in (59cm) high

£1,200-1,800 **SWO**

A Victorian white marble statue, by Benjamin Edward Spence, depicting a Scottish girl in a tartan shawl, the base signed "B.E. Spence Fl. Romae 1862", some restoration.

1862 *64in (160cm) high*

£2,500-3,000 **SWO**

A marble bust of a gentleman in Classical drapery, on a socle plinth, with indistinct signature.

1848 *28in (71cm) high*

£800-1,200 **L&T**

A fine 19thC marble sculpture, depicting a recumbant female on a chaise lounge holding a dish containing a posy and a string of pearls, raised on a moulded rectangular base, some damage.

37.5in (95.5cm) wide

£15,000-20,000 **FRE**

A 19thC Italian marble sculpture, depicting Beatrice Portinari, her hands and face sculpted in pure white with her body executed in variegated pink and black marble, with "BP" monogram and signed "Prof A. Petrilli Firenze".

85in (216cm) high

£16,000-20,000 **FRE**

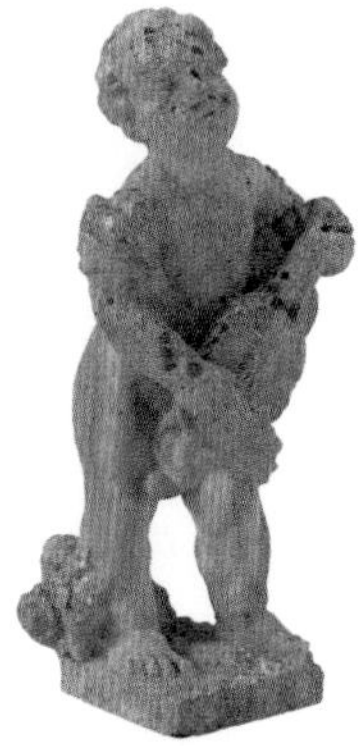

A 19thC stoneware putto, probably German, depicted holding a musical instrument, weather worn.

39.25in (98cm) high

£300-400 **KAU**

A white Carrara marble sculpture, depicting a seated dog on an oval base.

27in (68.5cm) high

£1,800-2,200 FRE

An early 19thC Russian marble tazza, of circular form, with turned stem and base on a grey veined column plinth with moulded cornice and base.

8.75in (22cm) high

£500-700 L&T

An early 20thC bird bath, in beige and cream marble, on a square stepped socle, with stylized leaf decoration and two pigeons sitting on the rim.

12in (30cm) diam

£180-220 KAU

A 20thC white marble bird bath, on a square socle, decorated with four pelicans and floral designs in relief, the bowl in the form of a shell.

35.25in (88cm) high

£800-1,200 KAU

A 20thC bird bath, in light pink marble, decorated with bay leaf festoons and winged men masks, raised on a circular foot.

19in (47.5cm) wide

£200-250 KAU

A pair of 19thC brown marble vases, the handles in the shape of swans and the lids with pine cone knops, decorated with cornucopias and raised on square socles.

23.5in (59cm) high

£700-1,000 KAU

A 20thC white marble fountain, depicting a horse prancing in waves, the rear with two horse heads and another horse.

48.75in (122cm) high

£1,800-2,200 KAU

A 20thC white marble pedestal and planter, on a stepped square plinth, with fluted foot and calyx bowl.

53.5in (134cm) high

£600-900 KAU

A pair of staddle stones.

Staddle stones have been used through the years for grinding corn and raising granary buildings above ground level. They are now valued for their decorative qualities.

£400-600 SWO

An 18thC fire surround, moulded in gesso with a pair of female heads and egg and butterfly mouldings.

82in (205cm) wide

£400-500 **SWO**

A Victorian white marble fire surround, with veined marble insets and anthemion decoration.

59.75in (152cm) wide

£350-400 **SWO**

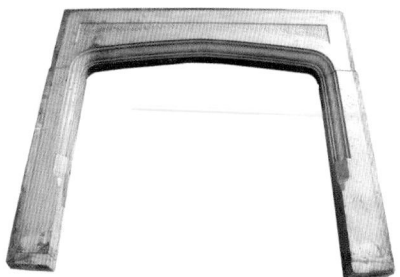

A stone fire surround, with a moulded arch mantel and jambs.

54in (137cm) wide

£70-100 **SWO**

A pair of late 18thC engraved brass andirons, with ball finials on beaded urns, supported on columns decorated with bellflower vines and engraved with eagle and shield and sunburst motifs.

£15,000-20,000 **SK**

A pair of Bradley & Hubbard andirons, with ball tops and swivelling backs, stamped "B&H 5950", some wear and rust.

22.5in (57cm) high

£220-280 **DRA**

An early 20thC cast iron Boston terrier andiron, the back moulded "121".

15in (38cm) high

£60-90 **ING**

A pair of cast iron andirons.

23.5in (60cm) high

£70-100 **SWO**

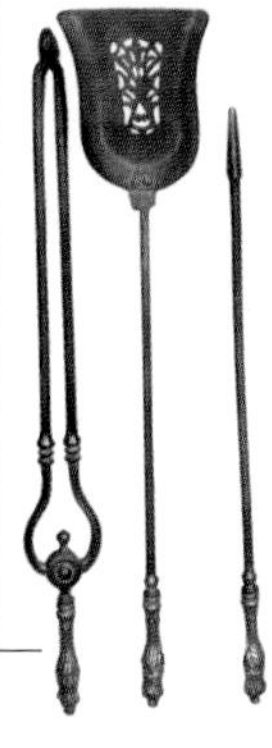

A set of three 19thC fireplace tools, with cast brass handles.

£280-320 **SWO**

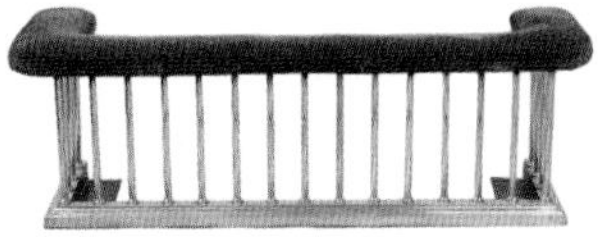

A brass club fender, with upholstered top rail.

68.5in (174cm) wide

£600-900 **SWO**

An early 19thC double-sided fireboard, one side painted with a hilly landscape with houses and figures, the other side showing a mountainous landscape, with a hunting scene, some paint wear.

37.75in (96cm) wide

£3,000-4,000 **SK**

A bronze fountain, in the Neoclassical style, with two graduated shell-form tiers surmounted by a merman blowing a horn, divided by four putti and raised on a circular base modelled as four dolphins.

47.5in (120.5cm) wide

£2,800-3,200 **FRE**

A bronze fountain, in the Neoclassical style, the shell-form bowl surmounted by a draped maiden holding an amphora and raised on four dolphin supports.

88in (223.5cm) high

£2,000-3,000 **FRE**

A rare German painted terracotta model of a gnome, the bearded figure with a pointed hat and brown tunic, standing holding a wicker basket.

20.5in (52cm) high

£2,500-3,500 **L&T**

A bronze fountain, in the Neoclassical style, modelled as a young boy blowing a horn, seated on three dolphins, with verdigris patina.

39in (99cm) high

£400-600 **FRE**

A bronze jardinière, in the Neoclassical style, modelled as two playful putti supporting cornucopia, on a naturalistic oval base.

43in (109cm) high

£1,000-1,500 **FRE**

A 19thC painted plaster tobacconist's figure, modelled as a Highland soldier playing the pipes, inscribed "Shout, Holborn".

c1815 12.25in (31cm) high

£1,800-2,200 **L&T**

A pair of 19thC painted and gilt cast iron doorstops, one depicting Highland Chieftain Cameron of Lochiel in full highland dress, the other Prince Charles Edward Stuart in similar dress.

15in (38cm) high

£4,000-5,000 **L&T**

A 19thC New England full-bodied running horse weathervane, with cast brass head.

31in (77.5cm) long

£4,000-6,000 **POOK**

A moulded copper and cast zinc running horse weathervane, attributed to A.L. Jewell & Co. of Waltham, Massachusetts, the mottled verdigris surface with traces of gilding.

c1860 *29in (74cm) long*

£7,000-10,000 **SK**

An early 20thC moulded copper weathervane, depicting Smuggler.

Smuggler was a famous racehorse. Many weathervanes depict racehorses, sometimes with their jockeys.

£1,500-2,000 **FRE**

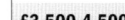

A moulded copper and cast lead centaur weathervane, attributed to A.L. Jewell & Co. of Waltham, Massachusetts, with vestiges of yellow sizing, gilt, verdigris, and black paint, restored.

c1860 *39.25in (99.5cm) long*

£30,000-35,000 **SK**

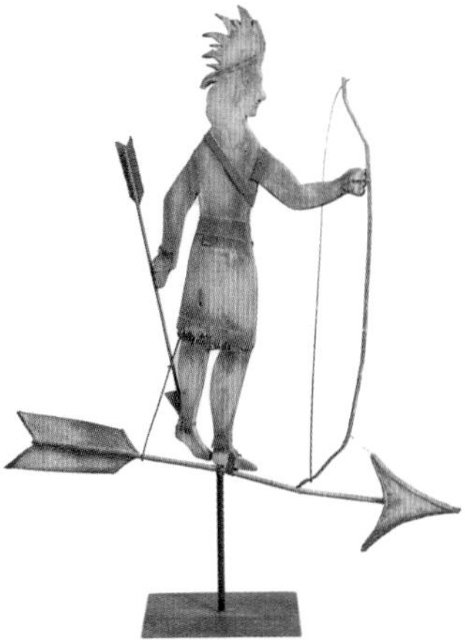

A large late 19thC iron and pine Indian weathervane, with headdress, shoulder strap, arm bands and belt, holding a bow and arrow and supported on another arrow, with iron tack eyes.

67in (170cm) high

£3,500-4,500 **SK**

A 19thC gilded sheet copper rooster weathervane, with weighted three-dimensional head and breast, the weathered gilded surface with verdigris.

23.5in (59cm) long

£4,000-6,000 **SK**

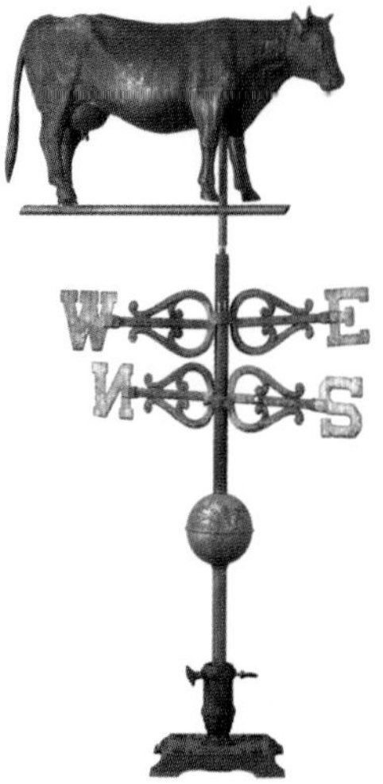

An American copper full body cow weathervane, with original solid brass directionals.

c1900 *29in (72.5in) long*

£6,000-8,000 **POOK**

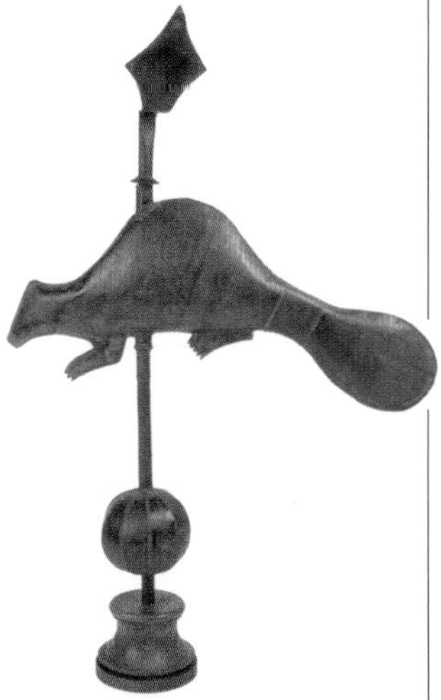

An early Canadian beaver weathervane, above a metal ball and a turned wooden base.

31in (78.5cm) high

£1,500-2,000 **WAD**

A late 19thC cast iron table top cigar store maiden, mounted on a later base, inscribed "CUT PLUG, SNUFF".

37in (92.5cm) high

£3,000-4,000 **POOK**

A late 19thC cast zinc and painted cigar store maiden, wearing a feathered headdress and red tunic, holding a basket of tobacco leaves and cigars, on a square plinth, inscribed "CONCHAS".

73in (182.5cm) high

£14,000-16,000 **POOK**

A late 19thC painted cast zinc cigar store maiden, attributed to Wm. Demuth & Co. of New York, holding three tobacco leaves, mounted on a later wooden plinth, inscribed "IMPORTED CIGARS".

79in (197.5cm) high

£10,000-12,000 **POOK**

A late 19thC cast zinc cigar store squaw, attributed to William Demuth & Co. of New York, with cigar in one hand, the other arm raised with a bundle of tobacco leaves, on a later wooden base, inscribed "NABOB 5¢ SEGARS".

81in (202.5cm) high

£15,000-20,000 **POOK**

A late 19thC cast zinc cigar store chief, attributed to Wm. Demuth & Co. of New York, with feather headdress and red cloak, standing over a mountain lion.

71in (177.5cm) high

£20,000-25,000 **POOK**

A painted cast zinc cigar store figure of a seated figure smoking a cigar, by Wm. Demuth & Co. of New York, mounted on a later wooden base, inscribed "FARGOS CIGARS" and "TOBACCO, SMOKERS ARTICLES".

54in (135cm) high

£20,000-22,000 **POOK**

A late 19thC cast zinc cigar store figure of Christopher Columbus, by W. Demuth & Co. of New York, on a later wooden base, inscribed "SNUFF, SEGARS, SNUFF".

67in (167.5cm) high

£8,000-12,000 **POOK**

A late 19thC cast metal tobacconist figure, in the form of a young man lighting a cigar standing over a frog, the base inscribed "MECCA".

25in (62.5cm) high

£1,800-2,200 **POOK**

A CLOSER LOOK AT A CIGAR STORE FIGURE

Cigar store figures were carved from wood and cast in zinc. Wooden examples are generally more valuable as each one is unique, whereas many zinc figures were cast from the same mould.

Although generally less expensive, metal figures are harder to find as many of them were melted down so the metal could be re-used.

Life-size figures like this one are more valuable than smaller examples. The dog is a most unusual addition and increases the appeal of this figure immensely.

Collectors value figures with original paint above all others. It is relatively easy to spot additional layers of paint using a magnifying glass.

There are a number of reproductions on the market today so care should be taken when buying.

A late 19thC cast zinc and painted warrior tobacconist figure, holding a hatchet and wearing a green beaded necklace and feather skirt, accompanied by a dog, mounted on a rocky and foliate base.

78in (195cm) high

£35,000-45,000 **POOK**

A Canadian galvanized iron and painted sign for a French Canadian tailor.

c1880 *39.25in (100cm) wide*

£200-250 **RAON**

A late 19thC painted tin and cast iron barber's pole, with louvred finial over a baluster-turned column and red and white candy stripe pole, flanked by four brass posts.

88in (220cm) high

£3,500-4,500 **POOK**

A late 19thC cast iron optician's trade sign, inscribed "J.B. SMITH EYEGLASSES".

58in (145cm) wide

£600-900 **POOK**

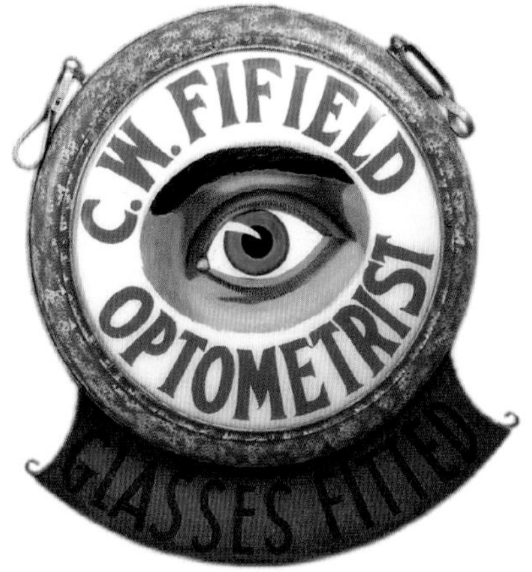

A cast metal optician's trade sign, with reverse-painted glass panels depicting an eye, inscribed "C.W. FIFIELD OPTOMETRIST, GLASSES FITTED".

c1900 *29in (72.5cm) high*

£1,200-1,800 **POOK**

An early 20thC painted tin and wrought iron trade sign, in the form of an anvil, inscribed "Bucks Livery".

41in (102.5cm) wide

£3,000-4,000 **POOK**

A 20thC two-sided painted tin shoe trade sign, from Millville, Pennsylvania, inscribed "We Rebuild Shoes Like New J.B. Ortwing".

52in (130cm) wide

£400-600 **POOK**

A early 20thC painted sheet metal Union Shield electric sign, painted red, white and blue and bordered with light bulbs, scattered paint wear.

49in (124.5cm) high

£3,000-4,000 **SK**

A sheet metal sign for the Coast Wrecking Company, in the shape of a horse, with weathered surface.

This insignia was devised as a tribute to the company agent who raced on horseback to the nearest telegraph to notify the Coast Wrecking Company of a vessel in distress.

26in (66cm) wide

£400-600 **FRE**

One of a pair of Regency bronze and ormolu figurine five-light candelabra, the stem modelled as a robed female, on an acanthus-scrolled plinth.

26.5in (67.5cm) high

£1,000-1,500 pair **GORL**

A pair of late 19thC bronze candelabra, with champlevé decoration, each with a putti supporting five sconces on a square plinth.

18.75in (47cm) high

£1,000-1,500 **SWO**

A CLOSER LOOK AT A PAIR OF CANDELABRA

The Belle Époque (1890-1914) was a period of conspicuous consumption in France. These candelabra are fashioned from gilt bronze, made to imitate solid gold.

Although in the Rococo style, these candelabra bear unmistakable marks of their period. The long, sinuous lines in particular are hallmarks of the Art Nouveau style.

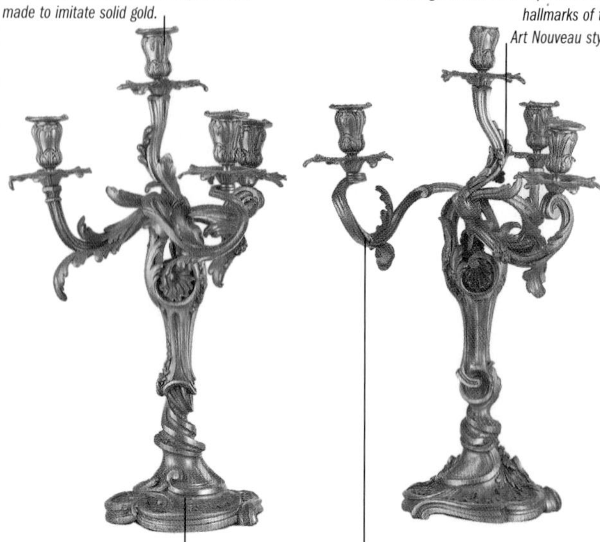

Henry Dasson was a renowned Parisian gilder in the late 19thC. He was especially adept at the mercurial gilding process used here.

The distinctive styling by an acknowledged master of his art makes these candelabra very valuable.

A pair of Belle Époque gilt-bronze five-light candelabra, by Henry Dasson et Cie, naturalistically modelled in the Rococo style with shell and acanthus motifs.

22in (56cm) high

£4,500-5,500 **ISA**

A pair of walnut and mahogany candlesticks, with brass engraved sconces and drip pans, attributed to Gimson & Barnsley, drilled for electricity.

20.25in (51.5cm) high

£2,000-2,500 **LFA**

A pair of wrought iron candelabra, with triform scroll bases, spiral twist stems and six branches terminating in flowerhead nozzles.

78in (198cm) high

£1,500-2,000 **FRE**

A Victorian oil lamp, the grey opaline conical base painted with herons amid bullrushes, the burner marked "Hink's Duplex Patent".

18in (45cm) high

£200-300 **SWO**

A Victorian ormolu oil lamp, with Rococo-style base, faceted clear glass reservoir and Hink's Duplex burner.

16.5in (41cm) high

£200-300 **SWO**

A gilt metal oil lamp, in the style of Dr Christopher Dresser, with amber glass reservoir and stylized fan and flowerhead motifs, the double burner marked "Hinks & Son Patent".

13.25in (33cm) high

£400-600 **SWO**

A Sheffield silver lamp, with a hobnail cut reservoir and a frilled etched glass shade, on a Corinthian column, with changeable electric and oil fittings.

1913

£350-400 **SWO**

A spelter lamp base, modelled as a boy with an outstretched arm.

c1890 *22in (56cm) high*

£500-700 **BEJ**

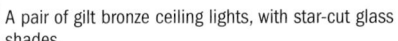

A cold-painted spelter lamp, cast as a Continental guardsman with a hound, on a shaped plinth base.

c1910 *53.25in (133cm) high*

£1,500-2,000 **SWO**

A cast metal standard lamp, finished in bronze, depicting a cherub holding a torch.

19in (48.5cm) high

£50-80 **MAX**

A pair of 19thC trumpet-shaped lustres, in clear glass overlaid in blue, painted in glit with leaf designs, with faceted drops.

11in (28cm) high

£700-1,000 **MAX**

A pair of Louis XV-style gilt brass two-branch sconces, with scrolling rocaille work branches.

17in (43cm) high

£300-400 **L&T**

A pair of 19thC ormolu three-branch wall candelabra, in the Rococo style, fitted for electricity.

19in (48.5cm) high

£350-450 **MAX**

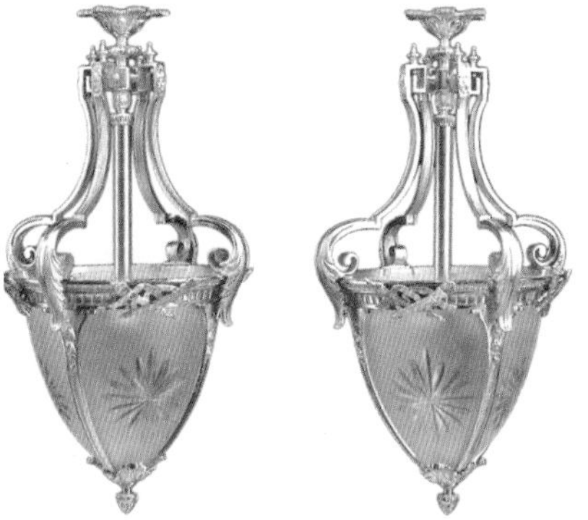

A pair of gilt bronze ceiling lights, with star-cut glass shades.

29in (73.5cm) high

£700-1,000 **FRE**

A pair of late Victorian hall lights, each surmounted with acanthus-scrolled crowns, the bases with acanthus drop finials, over four lobed shades, the glass missing.

37in (94cm) high

£600-900 **SWO**

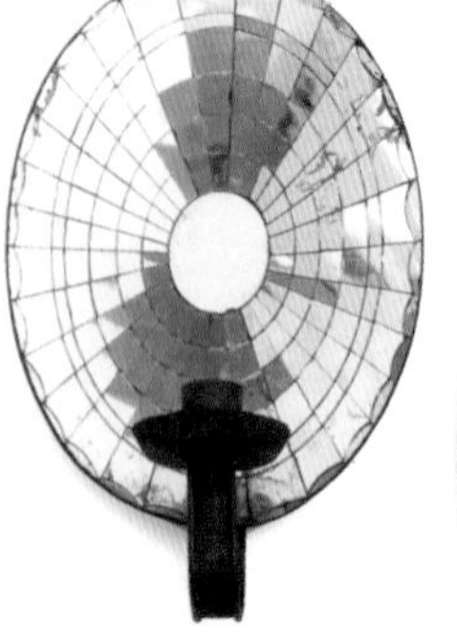

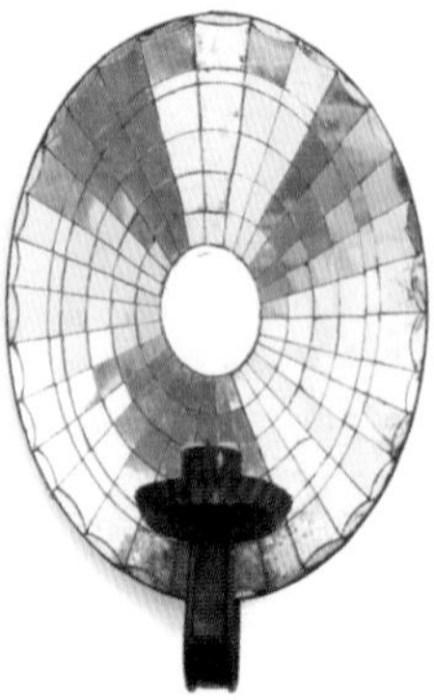

A pair of 19thC New England mirrored sconces, each with an oval concave back plate and crimped candlecup, some imperfections to mirror segments.

12.5in (32cm) high

£1,800-2,200 **FRE**

A pair of 20thC painted and mirrored tinware sconces, signed to rear "Made by Lucien Lyfron, Churchtown, Pa."

24.5in (62cm) high

£220-280 **FRE**

A 19thC bronze and alabaster ceiling light, with a large central shade and eight smaller shades on a cast column and ceiling rose.

35.5in (90cm) diam

£1,800-2,200 **SWO**

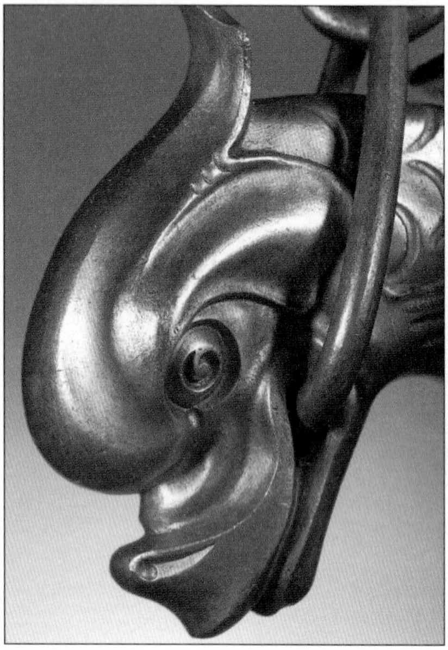

One of a pair of monumental Edwardian patinated and gilded bronze hanging lights, decorated with applied cast sealife forms.

These lights were hung in the Baltic Exchange in London, widely acknowledged as one of the finest Edwardian buildings in the City until it was damaged by an IRA bomb in 1992.

159.25in (398cm) high

£10,000-15,000 pair **L&T**

An early 20thC German metal ceiling lamp, with brass-coloured patination and crystal glass, with electrical candles and prisms.

28in (70cm) high

£220-280 **KAU**

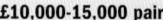

An early 20thC chandelier, in brass, bronze and crystal glass, electrified.

39.25in (98cm) high

£600-900 **KAU**

An early 20thC chandelier, in brass and crystal, electrified.

34in (85cm) high

£500-800 **KAU**

An early 20thC gilt bronze and lacquered metal oil lamp, in the Neoclassical style, with urn-shaped reservoir, fluted arrow sheath column, drapery swags and hoof feet.

65in (165cm) high

£1,800-2,200 **FRE**

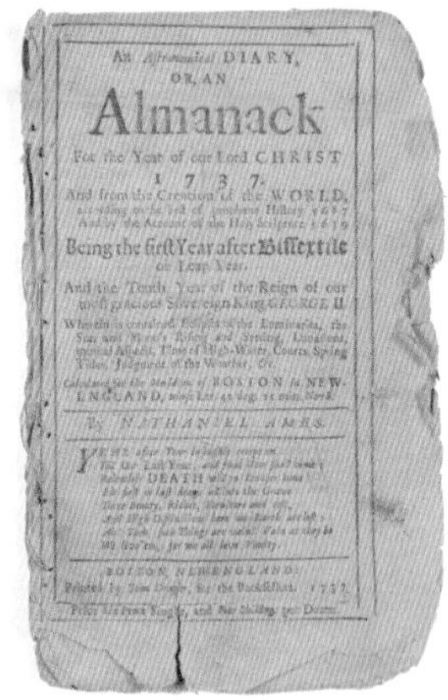

Ames, Nathaniel, "A Diary, or an Almanack for 1737", one of a set of 24 early American almanacs, 1737-1770.

£4,000-5,000 set FRE

Atkinson, John A. and Walker, James, "A Picturesque Representation of the Manners, Customs, and Amusements of the Russians", in three volumes, illustrated with 100 hand-coloured plates.

1803-04

£2,800-3,200 FRE

Austen, Jane, "Emma: a novel", first edition of three volumes, London, John Murray.

1816

£5,000-6,000 L&T

Burke, Edmund, "Reflections on the Revolution in France", first printing, uncut, with first state of title page.

1790

£3,000-4,000 FRE

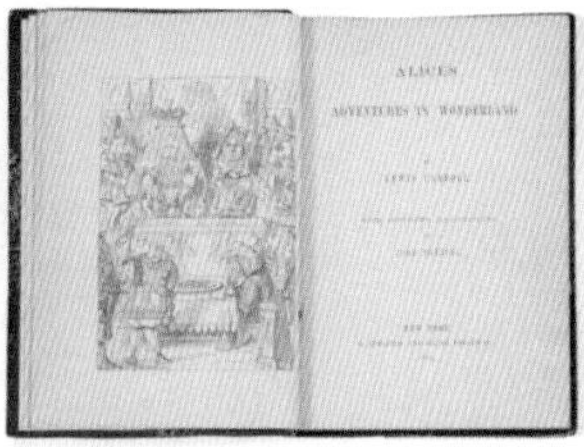

Carroll, Lewis, "Alice's Adventures in Wonderland", first American edition, New York, D. Appleton, illustrated by John Tenniel.

The first American edition was made up from the sheets of the suppressed first English edition with a cancel (a replacement leaf pasted onto the stub left by a removed leaf) title.

c1865

£2,500-3,000 FRE

Chaucer, Geoffrey, four volumes of "The Canterbury Tales", numbered 331 and 485 from an edition of 500, illustrated throughout with engravings by Eric Gill.

1929-31

£2,000-3,000 FRE

Curtis, William, "Flora Londinensis: or plates and descriptions of such plants as grow wild in the environs of London", first edition, three volumes, with six uncoloured and 217 hand-coloured plates.

Issued in 72 parts, the Flora Londinensis is much more comprehensive than its title might suggest, for it extends to most of the English flora, and could be regarded as the first colour-plate national flora.

£4,000-5,000 L&T

A CLOSER LOOK AT A 16THC NICOLAUS COPERNICUS FIRST EDITION

The publication of "On the Revolutions of the Celestial Spheres" in 1543 inaugurated the scientific revolution. It proposed that the sun, not the earth, was the centre of the cosmos and effectively destroyed the anthropocentric view of the universe. The great significance of the text adds to the value.

As an unrecorded copy, it is essential to establish its status. This copy has been examined by Dr. Owen Gingerich, author of "Annotated Census of Copernicus' De Revolutionibus", who found that the book is entirely new to him and is not one of the six copies known to be stolen or missing. It has also been examined by the Conservation Center of Philadelphia.

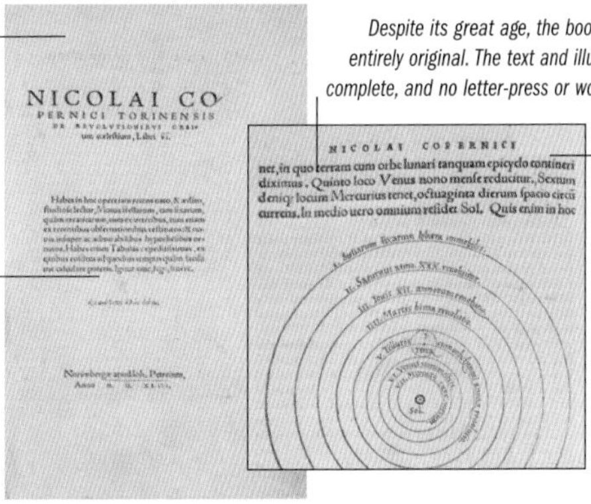

Despite its great age, the book and all of its leaves are entirely original. The text and illustrations are original and complete, and no letter-press or woodcut has been restored.

This book was so radical at the time of its release that the author delayed publication until he was in his last years so as to avoid the consequent controversy.

Copernicus, Nicolaus, "De revolutionibus orbium coelestium" ("On the revolutions of the celestial spheres"), first edition, illustrated with 149 woodcut diagrams.

1543 *11in (28cm) high*

£300,000-400,000 FRE

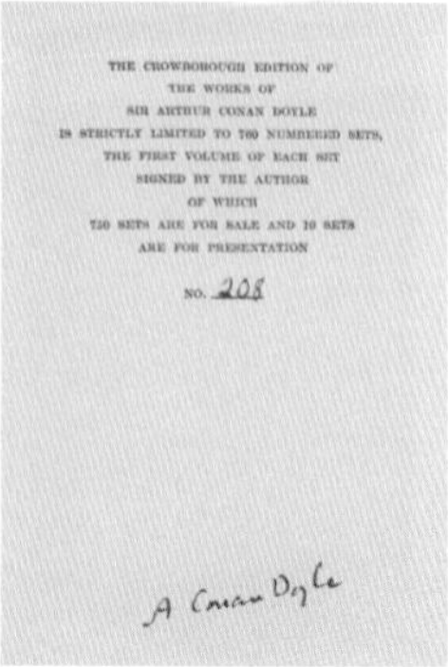
THE CROWBOROUGH EDITION OF
THE WORKS OF
SIR ARTHUR CONAN DOYLE
IS STRICTLY LIMITED TO 760 NUMBERED SETS,
THE FIRST VOLUME OF EACH SET
SIGNED BY THE AUTHOR
OF WHICH
750 SETS ARE FOR SALE AND 10 SETS
ARE FOR PRESENTATION
NO. 208
A Conan Doyle

Doyle, Sir Arthur Conan, "The Works", signed Crowborough edition, photogravure frontis.

£3,000-4,000 **FRE**

Forrest, Lieutenant-Colonel Charles Ramus, a volume of "Picturesque Tour along the River Ganges and Jumna", London, Ackermann, with 24 hand-coloured plates.

1824

£2,500-3,000 **FRE**

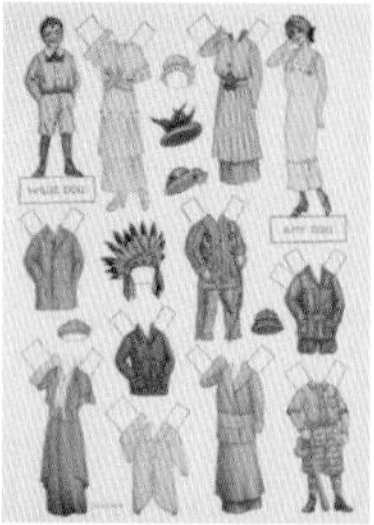

Fryer, Jane Eayre, "The Mary Frances Housekeeper; or Adventures Among the Doll People" with 18 plain plates of models for dolls and furniture with accompanying colour cut-out insert sheets, former owner's ink inscription.

c1915

£200-300 **FRE**

Havell, Robert, "A Series of Picturesque Views of Noblemen's & Gentlemen's Seats", with hand-coloured aquatint vignette title and 20 hand-coloured aquatint plates.

1823

£18,000-22,000 **FRE**

Kendall, Geo. Wilkins, "The War Between the United States and Mexico", with two maps and 12 colour lithographic plates.

1852

£15,000-20,000 **FRE**

Logan, James and Mclan, Robert Ronald, "The Clans of the Scottish Highlands", with 72 hand-coloured lithographic plates.

1845-1847

£4,000-5,000 **FRE**

Middleton, J.J., "Grecian Remains in Italy. A Description of Cyclopian Walls and Roman Antiquities", with two plain and 24 hand-coloured aquatint plates.

1812

£4,000-6,000 **FRE**

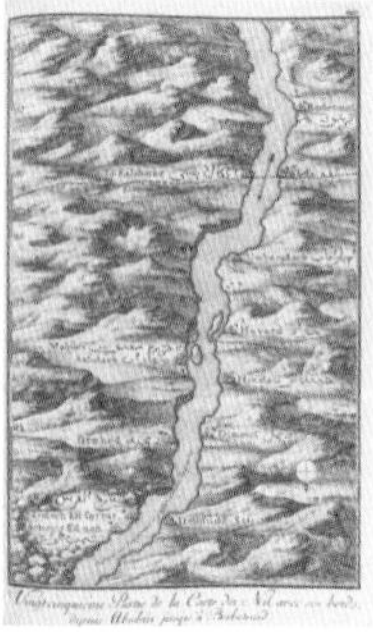

Norden, Friderik Ludwig, "Voyage d'Egypte et de Nubie", first edition, engraved portrait of the author and 159 engraved views and maps.

The first detailed description of Egypt. Norden surveyed the Nile and made detailed observations of the pyramids during a trip in 1737-38. Twenty-nine of the plates form a detailed map of the course of the Nile from the Delta to Aswan.

c1755

£4,000-6,000 **L&T**

Palladio, Andrea, "I Quattro Libri dell Architettura", Venice, Giambatista Pasquali, 1768, first edition of this version, with 218 copper engravings after the original woodcuts.

This edition of Palladio was largely financed by Joseph Smith, Honourary British Consul at Venice. Through Smith's association with Lord Burlington, himself a great proponent of Palladian architecture, this book helped form the English taste for Palladio's architectural style.

£2,800-3,200 **FRE**

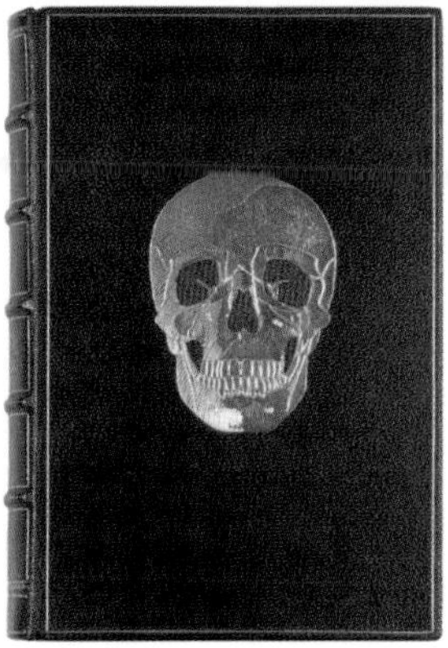

Poe, Edgar Allan, "The Works", ten volumes, New York, Scribner's, with silver skull motif with red morocco onlays on front covers.

1914

£2,000-3,000 **FRE**

Richardson Jr, Thomas Miles, "Richardson's Sketches on the Continent. A Series of Views in France, Italy, Switzerland, Germany, Holland", dedication page to the Duchess of Northumberland signed by Richardson, with 26 hand-coloured lithographic plates.

1837

£7,000-10,000 **FRE**

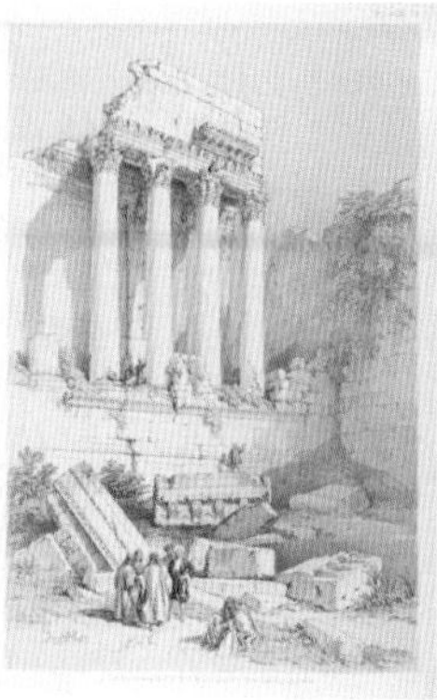

Roberts, David, "The Holy Land", after lithographs by Louis Hague, with 247 tinted lithographic plates and 2 maps, London, Day.

1855-56

£3,000-4,000 **L&T**

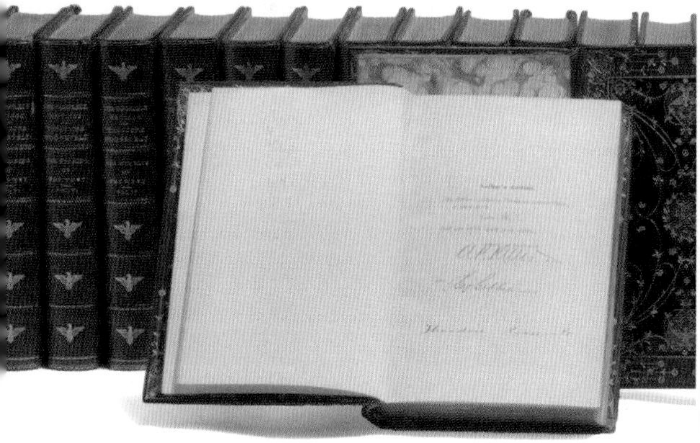

Roosevelt, Theodore, "The Complete Works", 22 volumes, author's edition signed by Roosevelt.

1902-03

£4,000-5,000 **FRE**

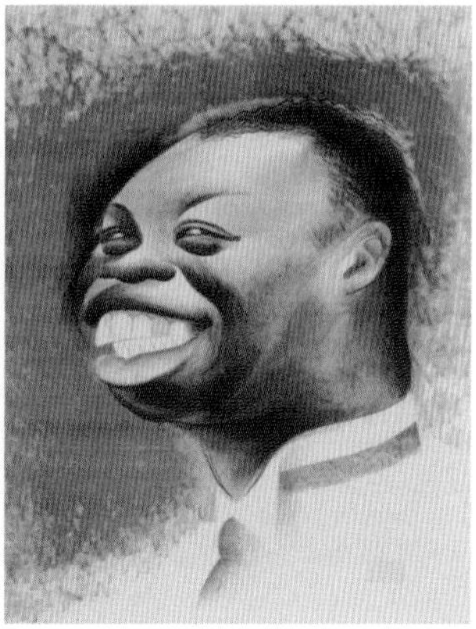

Saroyan, William, "Harlem as Seen by Hirschfeld", with 24 mounted lithographs by Hirschfeld.

c1940

£2,000-3,000 **FRE**

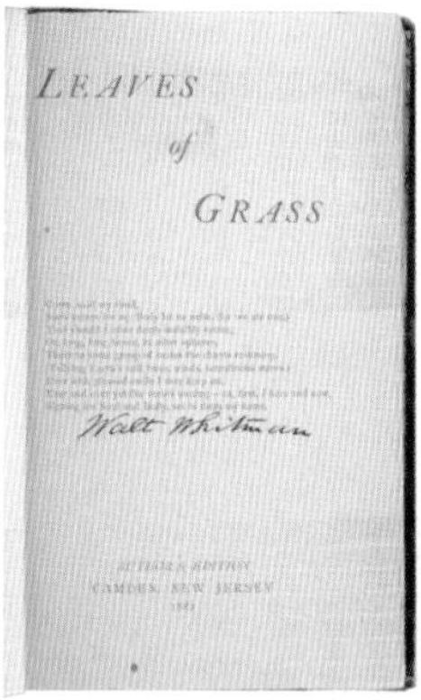

Whitman, Walt, "Leaves of Grass", signed author's edition, original green cloth, gilt-lettered spine, signed in ink on the title page by Walt Whitman.

1882

£2,500-3,000 **FRE**

"The Holy Bible Containing the Old and New Testaments", published by David Bryce & Son, Glasgow and Oxford, on a miniature wooden lectern.

1891

£500-700 **BLO**

"The Little Teacher, for Reading and Spelling Well, by a parent", first edition, published in Philadelphia by Jacob Johnson.

1802

£700-1,000 **FRE**

"The Naval Achievements of Great Britain from the Year 1793 to 1817", with 50 hand-coloured engraved plates.

1817

£3,000-4,000 **FRE**

"United States Journals of Congress" for 1779, bound, all title pages present.

£10,000-15,000 **FRE**

Baum, L. Frank, "Father Goose: His Book", Geo. M. Hill, Chicago, first edition, first printing, illustrated by W.W. Denslow.

1899

£2,200-2,800 **FRE**

Baum, L. Frank, "A New Wonderland", first edition, first printing, illustrated by Frank Verbeck, R.H. Russell, New York, scarce.

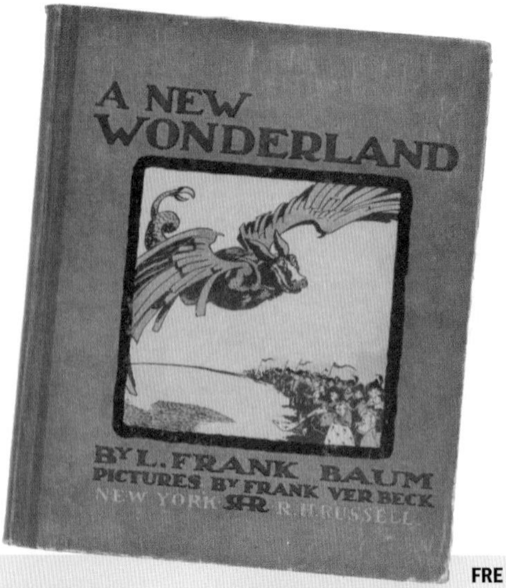

c1900

£4,000-6,000 **FRE**

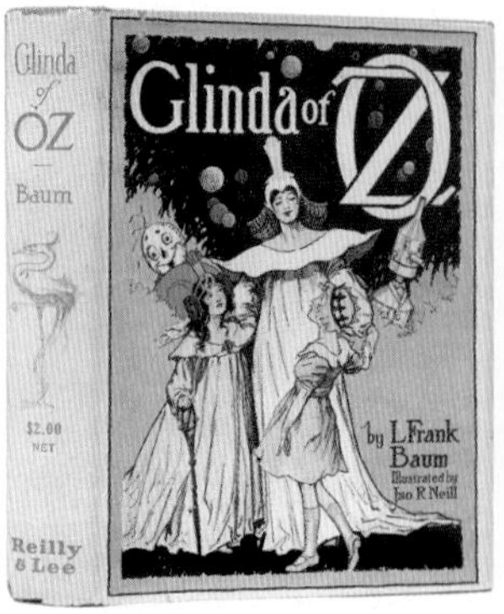

Baum, L. Frank, "Glinda of Oz", first edition, Reilly & Lee, Chicago, first state, illustrations by John R. Neill, owner's pencil inscription.

1920

£1,000-1,500 **FRE**

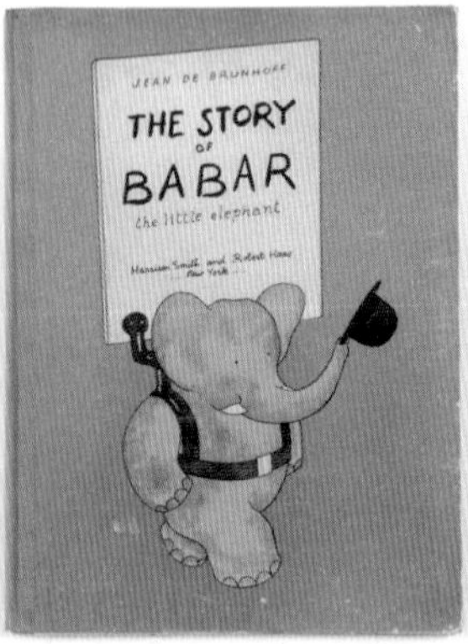

Brunhoff, Jean De, "The Story of Babar, the Little Elephant", first American edition, Harrison Smith & Robert Haas, New York.

1933

£250-300 **FRE**

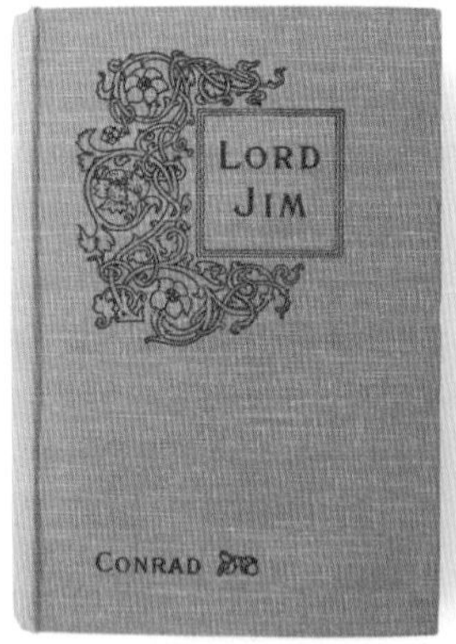

Conrad, Joseph, "Lord Jim", William Blackwood & Sons, Edinburgh and London.

1900

£3,500-4,000 **BRB**

Crane, Stephen, "War is Kind", first edition, illustrated and designed by Will Bradley, with 16 full page illustrations and 16 vignettes by Bradley.

1899

£200-300 **FRE**

Dick, Philip K., "The Man in the High Castle", first edition review copy, published by G. P. Putnam's Sons, New York, Hugo award winner.

1962

£1,000-1,500 **BRB**

Arthur Conan Doyle, "The Hound of the Baskervilles", first edition, first issue, published by George Newnes Ltd, London.

1902

£3,500-4,000 **BRB**

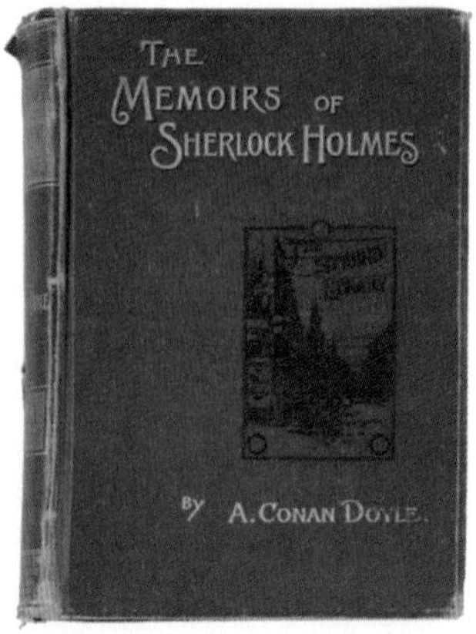

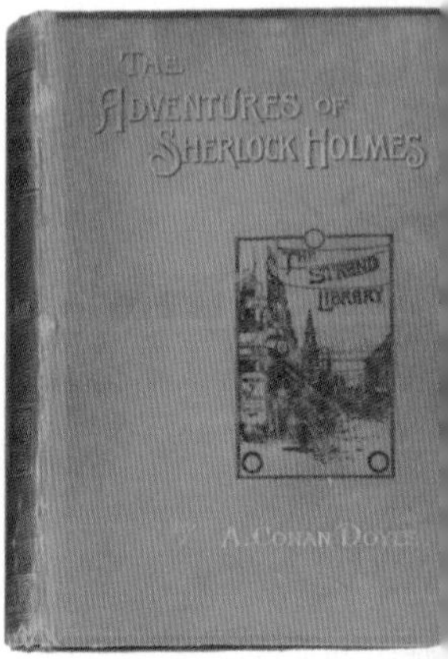

Doyle, Sir Arthur Conan, two volumes, "The Adventures of Sherlock Holmes", second edition, and "The Memoirs of Sherlock Holmes", first edition, illustrated by Sidney Pagent.

£400-500 **FRE**

Faulkner, William, "The Wild Palms", first edition, Random House, New York.

1939

£1,800-2,200 **BRB**

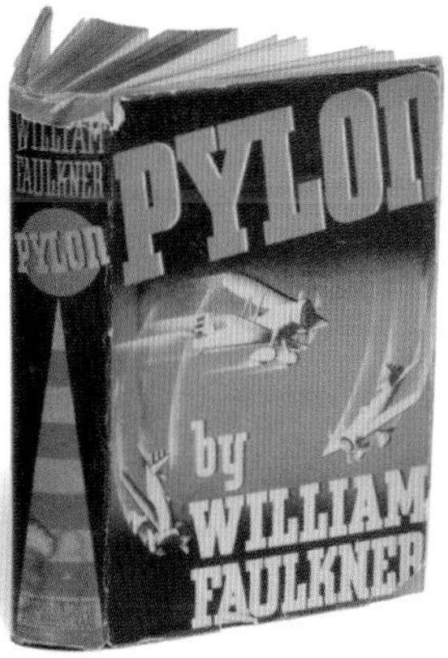

Faulkner, William, "Pylon", first edition, first printing.

1935

£150-200 **FRE**

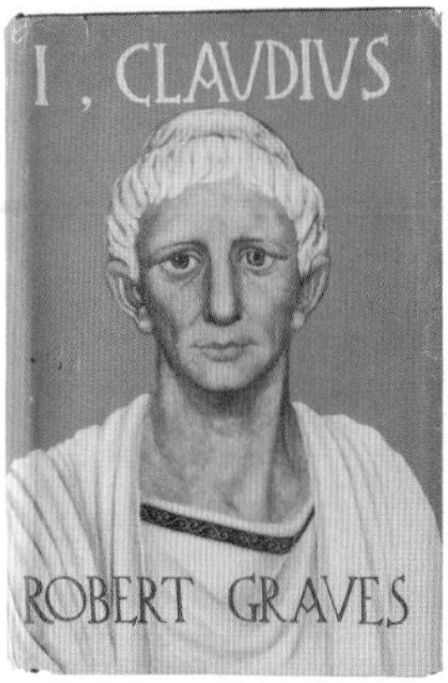

Graves, Robert, "I, Claudius" and "Claudius the God", first editions, Arthur Baker Ltd, London.

1934

£3,000-4,000 **BRB**

Harris, Joel Chandler, "Uncle Remus", first edition, first state, D. Appleton & Company, New York, with illustrations by Fredrick S. Church and James H. Moser.

1881

£2,500-3,000 **BRB**

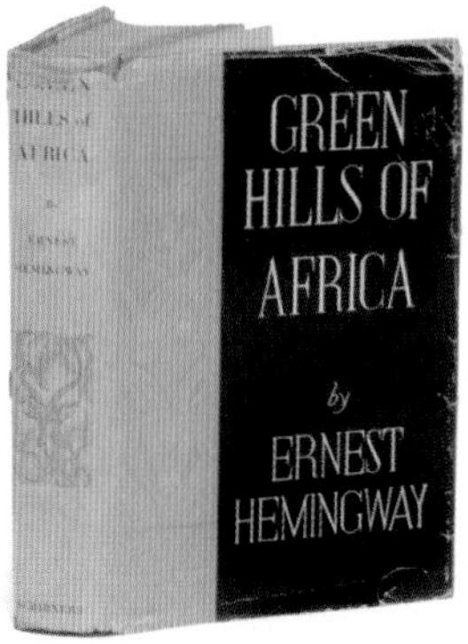

Hemingway, Ernest, "Green Hills of Africa" first edition, original green cloth.

1935

£200-300 **FRE**

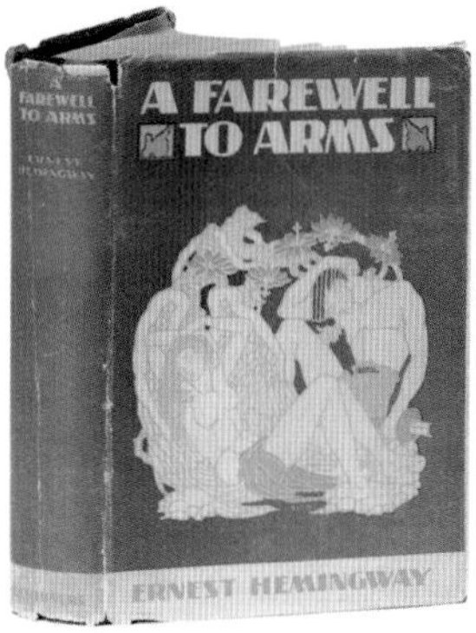

Hemingway, Ernest, "A Farewell to Arms", first trade edition, second printing, Scribner's, New York, signed by Hemingway on title page.

c1930

£3,000-4,000 **FRE**

Himes, Chester B., "If He Hollers Let Him Go", first edition, Doubleday, Doran & Co., New York.

1945

£400-500 **BRB**

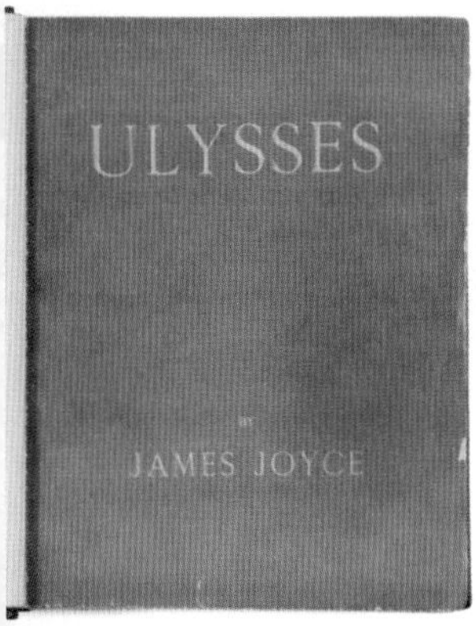

Joyce, James, "Ulysses", first edition, later flexible morocco, original white lettered blue wrappers.

9.5in (23.5cm) high

£6,000-8,000 **FRE**

A CLOSER LOOK AT A JAMES JOYCE FIRST EDITION

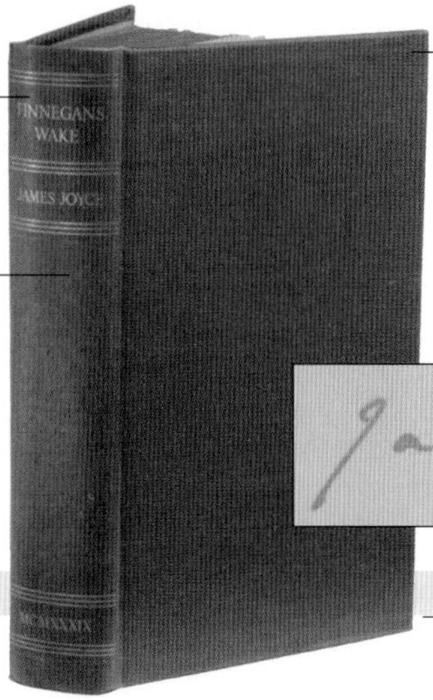

One of the most influential novelists of the 20thC, the great literary name of Irish writer James Joyce makes this book extremely attractive to booklovers and collectors.

The book is in its original slipcase and has only minor wear, increasing its desirability.

"Finnegan's Wake" is Joyce's most experimental work and it continues to intrigue scholars today.

This is one of a limited edition of 425 copies signed by the author. The signature contributes to the value of this book. An unsigned first edition copy can be worth considerably less - around £1,000-3,000, depending on condition.

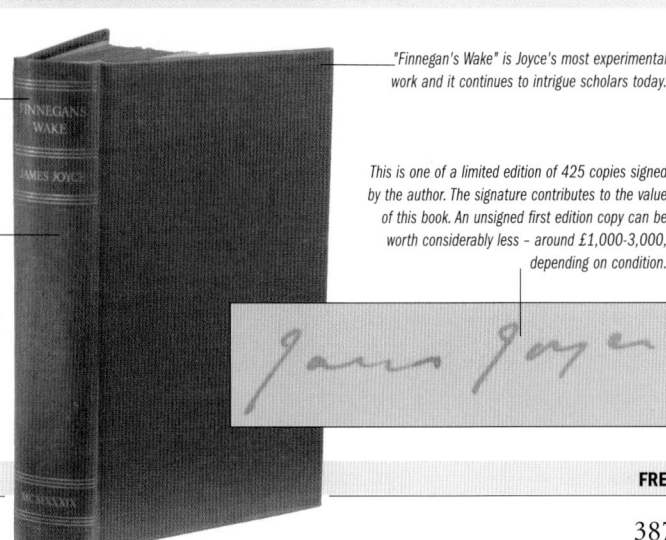

Joyce, James, "Finnegan's Wake" first edition, signed by James Joyce.

1939

£8,000-12,000 **FRE**

Juster, Norton, "The Phantom Tollbooth", first edition, Epstein & Carroll, New York, with illustrations by Jules Feiffer.

1961

£1,200-1,800 **BRB**

Knowles, John, "A Separate Peace", first edition, Secker & Warburg, London.

1959

£1,000-1,500 **BRB**

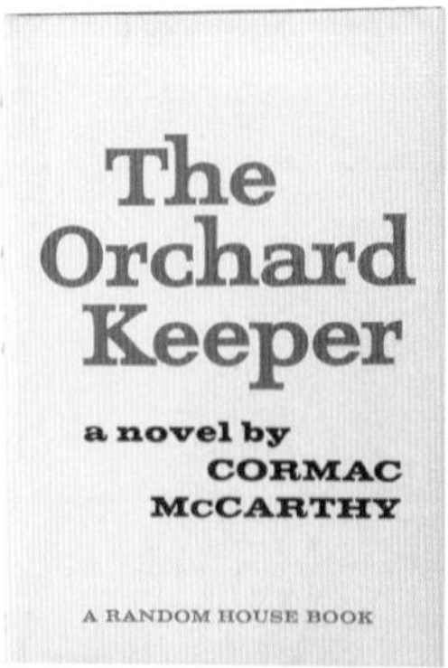

McCarthy, Cormac, "The Orchard Keeper", first edition, Random House, New York.

1965

£2,000-3,000 **BRB**

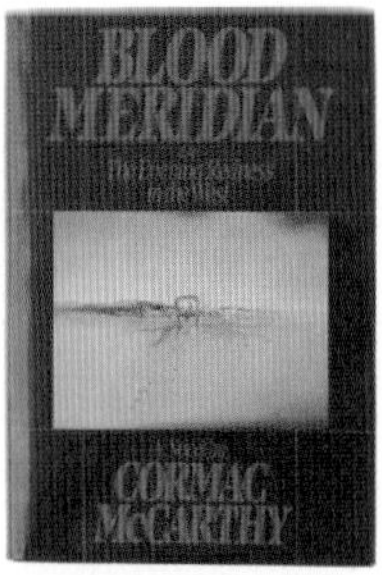

McCarthy, Cormac, "Blood Meridian or The Evening Redness in the West", first edition, Random House, New York.

This book was overlooked when first published and most copies were remaindered. This copy is unusual in that it bears no remainder mark.

1985

£1,500-2,000 **BRB**

McCullers, Carson, "The Heart is a Lonely Hunter", first edition, Houghton Mifflin, Boston.

1940

£1,000-1,500 **BRB**

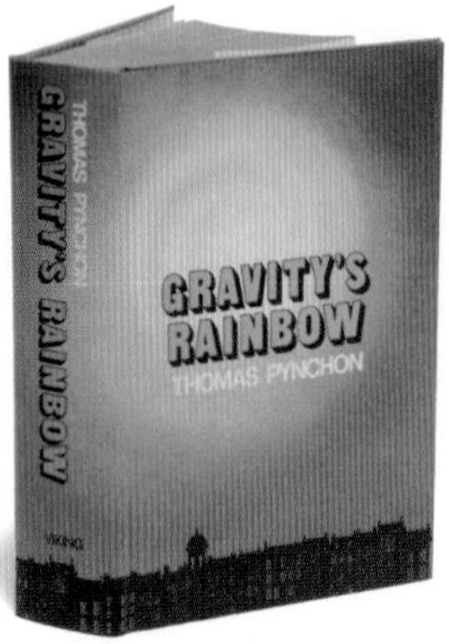

Pynchon, Thomas,"Gravity's Rainbow", first edition, original vermillion cloth.

£8,000-12,000 **FRE**

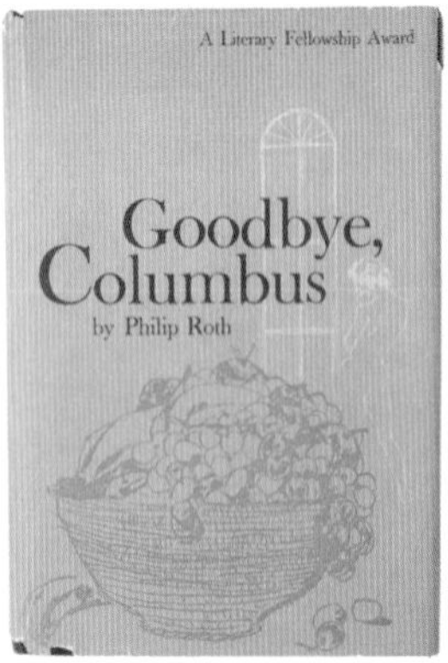

Roth, Philip, "Goodbye, Columbus", first edition, Houghton Mifflin, Boston, inscribed by the author.

1959

£1,500-2,000 **BRB**

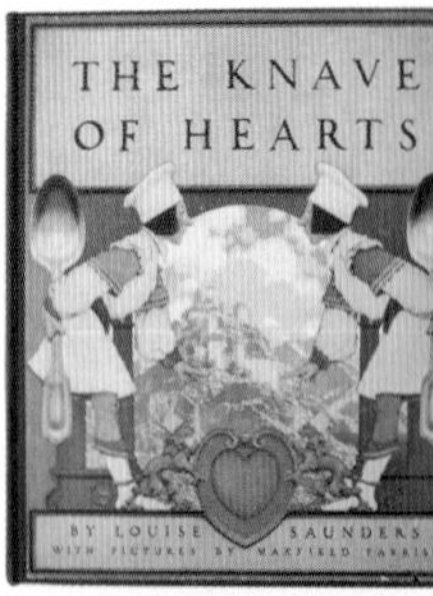

Saunders, Louise, "The Knave of Hearts", first edition, Charles Scribner's Sons, with illustrations by Maxfield Parrish, lacks original box.

This was the last book that Parrish illustrated.

1925

£3,000-4,000 **BRB**

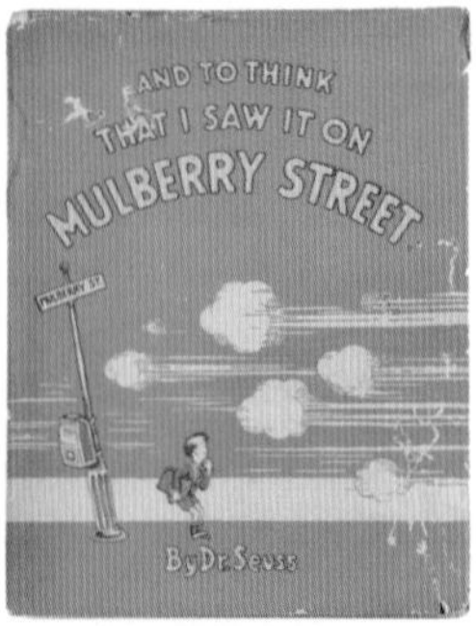

Dr. Seuss, "And To Think That I Saw It On Mulberry Street", first edition, Vanguard, New York, Younger & Hirsch.

Illustrated by Dr. Seuss, this was the author's first children's book.

c1935

£2,000-2,500 **FRE**

Smith, Jessie, "Mother Goose", first edition, illustrated and edited by the author, with 17 colour and plain plates, Dodd Mead, New York.

c1915

£300-400 **FRE**

Thompson, Kay, "Eloise in Paris", first edition, illustrated by Hilary Knight, Simon & Schuster, New York.

1957

£50-70 **FRE**

Tolkien, J.R.R., "The Fellowship of the Ring", first American edition, review copy, map near rear, with printed Houghton Mifflin review copy slip inserted.

1954

£1,500-2,000 **FRE**

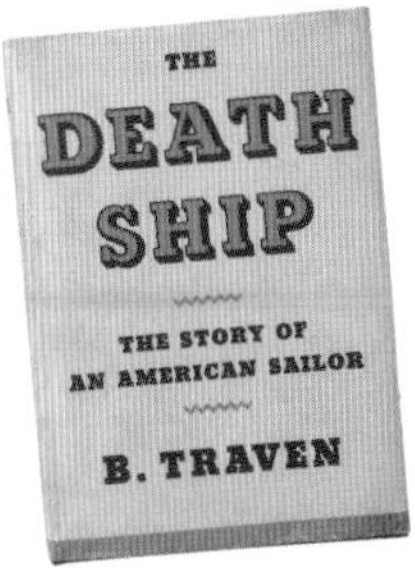

Traven, B., "The Death Ship", first American edition, Alfred A. Knopf, New York, in a custom tan cloth clamshell box.

Another translation of this novel was released by Eric Sutton in the same year, but this version is preferred as the translation from German was done by the author himself.

1934

£1,500-2,000 **BRB**

Twain, Mark, "Following the Equator: A Journey Around the World", first edition, first issue, American Publishing Company, Hartford.

1897

£500-700 **BRB**

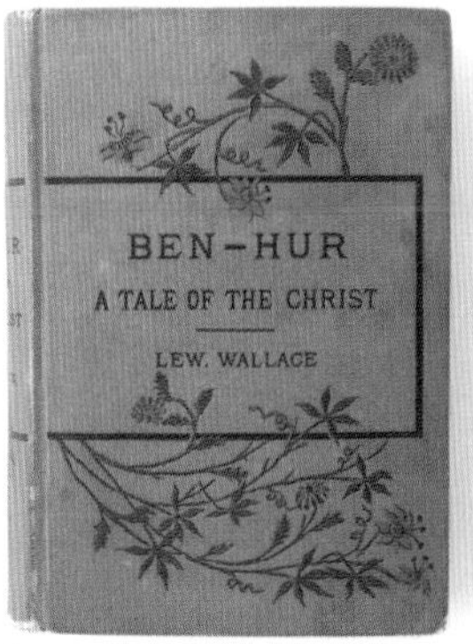

Wallace, Lew, "Ben-Hur - A Tale of the Christ", first edition, Harper & Brothers, New York.

1880

£1,000-1,500 **BRB**

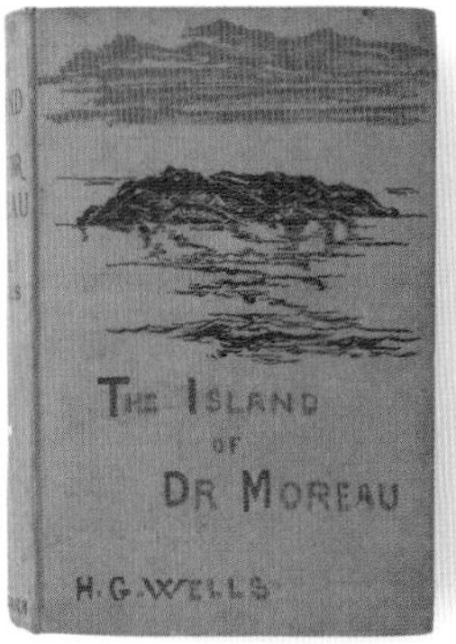

Wells, H.G. "The Island of Dr Moreau", first edition, first issue, William Heinemann, London.

1896

£1,500-2,000 **BRB**

Wells, H.G., "The Invisible Man", first edition, C. Arthur Pearson, London.

1897

£2,000-3,000 **BRB**

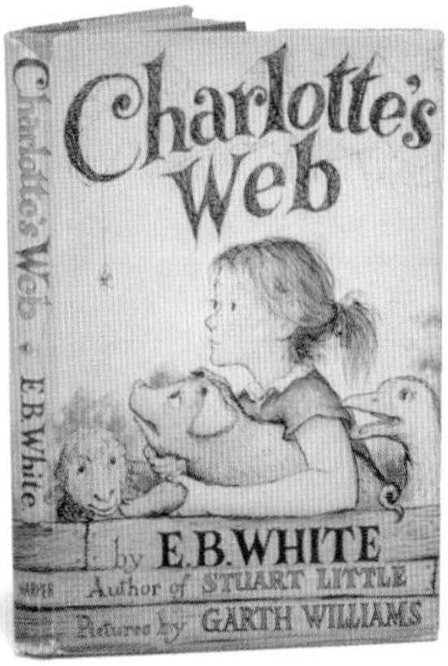

White, E.B, "Charlotte's Web", first edition, illustrated by Garth Williams, Harper, New York.

c1950

£300-400 **FRE**

Williams, Tennessee, "The Rose Tattoo", first edition, New Directions, New York.

1951

£300-400 **BRB**

Wilde, Oscar, "The Sphinx", limited edition, John Lane, London & New York, from an edition of 1,000 copies, with illustrations by Alastair.

1920

£1,200-1,800 **BRB**

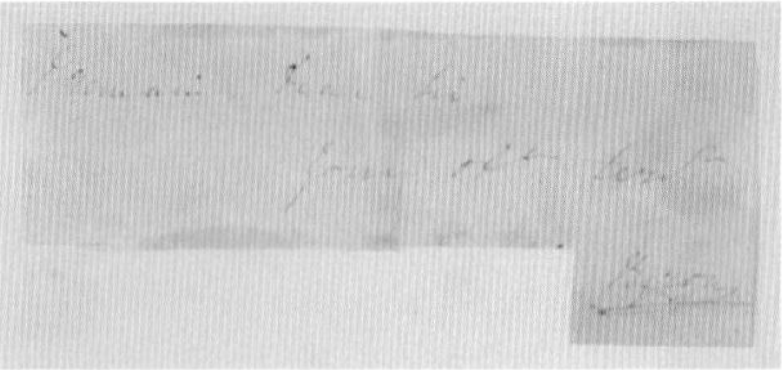

A cut signature by Lord Byron, closing letter, slightly faded.

£200-300 FRE

A signed autograph presentation by Howard Chandler Christy, with an original bust portrait of Helen Bardman, within a copy of 'The Keystone Perpetual Diary of Helen Bardman', dated September 1923.

£200-300 FRE

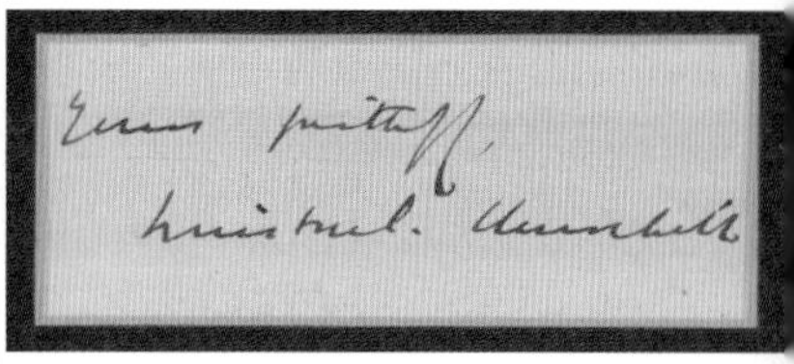

A cut signature by Winston S. Churchill, closing letter, mounted with half-tone photograph.

4in (10cm) wide

£400-500 FRE

A document signed by John Churchill, First Duke of Marlborough, July 15th 1710, a military commission appointing Edmund Naish as Ensign, executed in the field, minor wear, most of wax seal remains.

£300-400 FRE

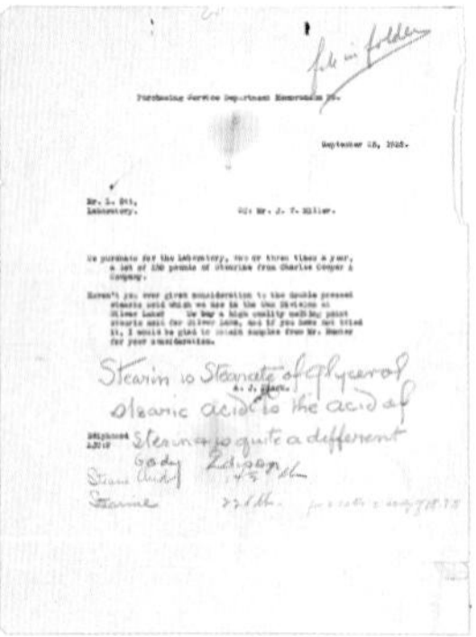

A document signed with autograph annotations by Thomas A. Edison, September 25th 1925, a purchasing memorandum document.

£300-400 FRE

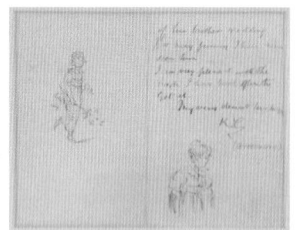

An autograph letter signed, 'KG' for Kate Greenaway, July 12th 1883, to Miss Metcalf, describing a letter from a correspondent who claims to be a long lost relative, "the Greenaways had always had long noses", embellished with original pen and ink drawings of young women by Greenaway.

£2,000-3,000 FRE

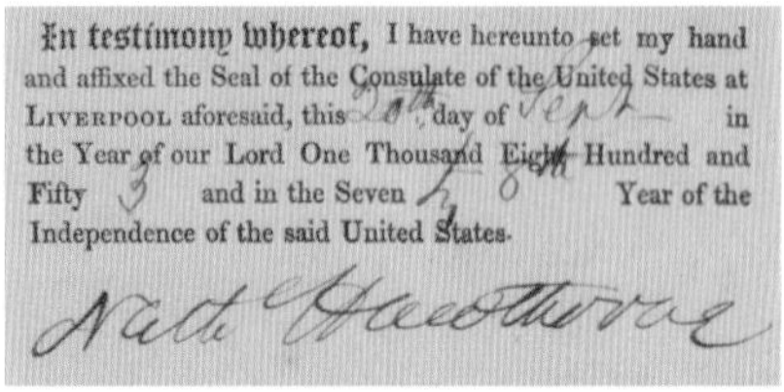

In testimony whereof, I have hereunto set my hand and affixed the Seal of the Consulate of the United States at Liverpool aforesaid, this 20th day of Sept in the Year of our Lord One Thousand Eight Hundred and Fifty 3 and in the Seven 78th Year of the Independence of the said United States.

Nath Hawthorne

A document signed by Nathaniel Hawthorne, ship's papers for the bark 'Undine' signed as United States Consul at Liverpool, September 20th 1853, with clearance papers for the ship.

1853

£400-600 FRE

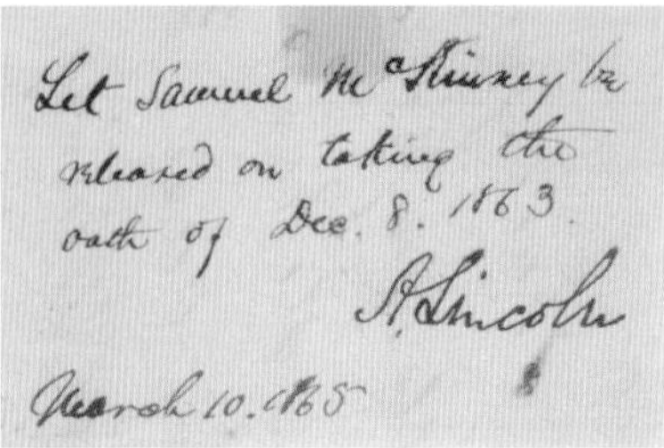

Let Samuel McKinney be released on taking the oath of Dec. 8. 1863.

A. Lincoln

March 10. 1865

A note signed by Abraham Lincoln, March 10th 1865, reading 'Let Samuel McKinney be released on taking the oath of Dec. 8, 1863', on cut slip.

3in (7.5cm) wide

£3,000-4,000 FRE

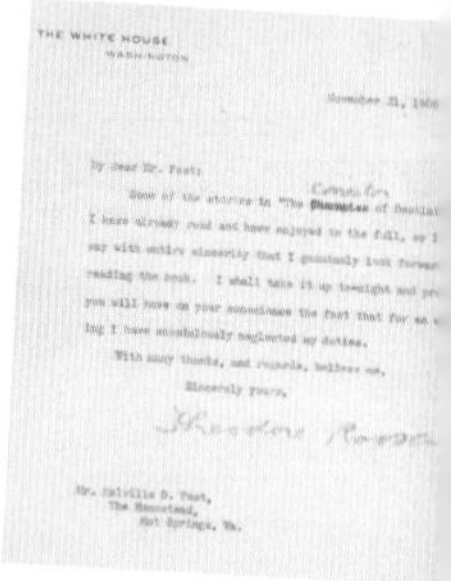

A typed letter signed by Theodore Roosevelt, Washington D.C. November 21st 1908, To Melville D. Post, regarding stories in 'The Corrector of Destinies', on White House letterhead in White House envelope.

Melville Davisson Post (1869-1930) was a successful American mystery writer. He was also a lawyer, active in judicial reform and local politics.

£500-700 FRE

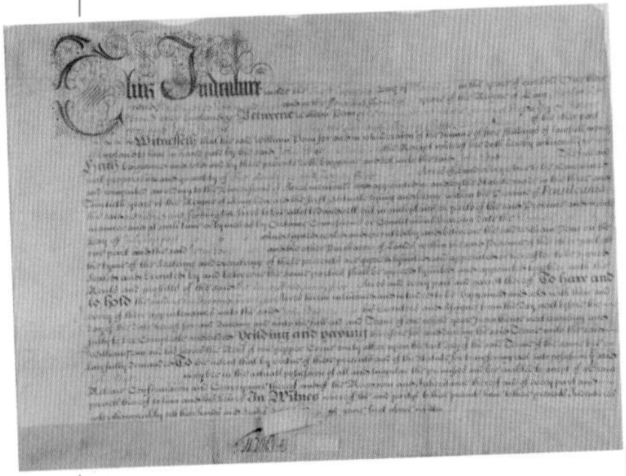

A document signed by William Penn, March 21 1681, a land patent to John Edge for 125 acres in New Providence, Chester County, Pennsylvania.

£2,000-3,000 FRE

A 19thC American printed advertising broadside, depicting "H.E. Hoyt & Co. Gift Book Store, No. 41 Baltimore St., Corner Frederick St., Baltimore, Md." 1855 with busy street.

40in (101.5cm) wide

£600-900 FRE

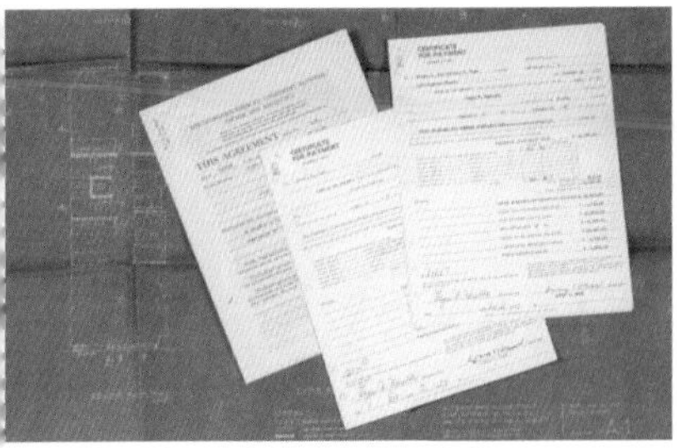

A file of architectural documents, relating to alterations and additions to the building at 2129 Cypress Street, Philadelphia, by the architect Louis I. Kahn, made for Isadore A. Shrager.

1957-59

£300-400 **FRE**

An Islamic manuscript, "Vignettes from Greek Philosophers for Young Men", with colour and gilt illuminated title leaves, text leaves with gilt and colour borders, scribed by Pamdit Sajram Kaul.

1953

£800-1,200 **FRE**

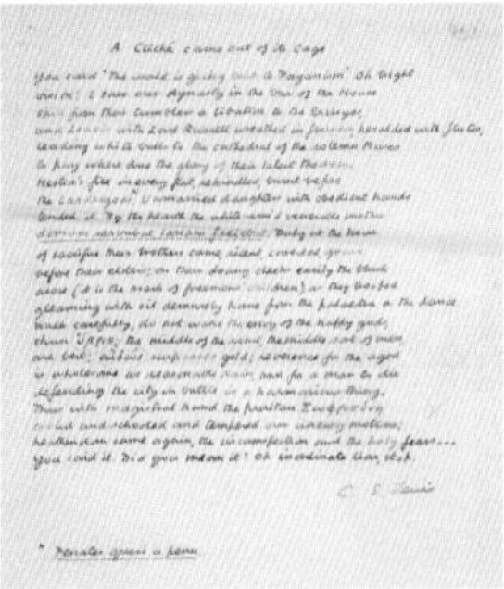

A manuscript poem, signed by C.S. Lewis, titled 'A Cliché Came Out of Its Cage'.

This early single stanza version of Lewis's verse attack on the 'New Paganism' as exemplified by F.R. Leavis and Bertrand Russell, was later expanded into two stanzas.

£5,000-7,000 **FRE**

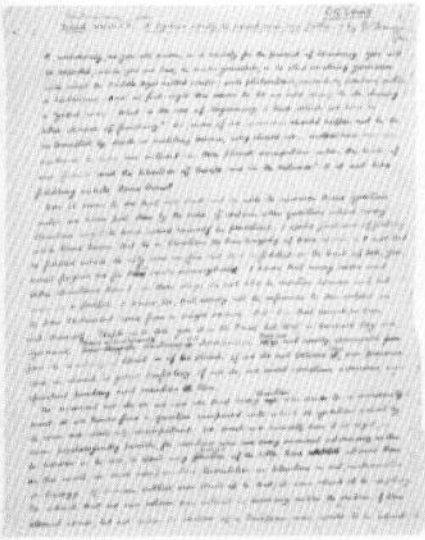

A manuscript sermon by C.S Lewis, titled 'Learning in War-Time', holograph in black ink with corrections and crossings out in ink & pencil.

This is apparently an early version of the sermon preached at the invitation of Canon Milford at Evensong in St. Mary the Virgin on October 22, 1939. It includes working corrections and revisions, and was further revised before its publication in 'The Weight of Glory'.

1949

£15,000-20,000 **FRE**

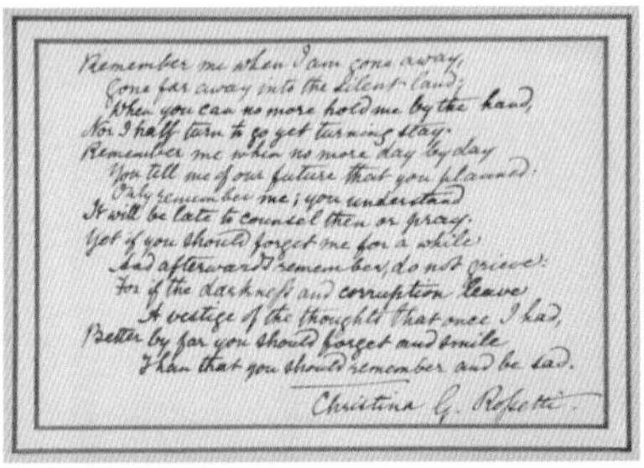

Remember me when I am gone away,
Gone far away into the silent land;
When you can no more hold me by the hand,
Nor I half turn to go yet turning stay.
Remember me when no more day by day
You tell me of our future that you planned:
Only remember me; you understand
It will be late to counsel then or pray.
Yet if you should forget me for a while
And afterwards remember, do not grieve:
For if the darkness and corruption leave
A vestige of the thoughts that once I had,
Better by far you should forget and smile
Than that you should remember and be sad.
Christina G. Rossetti

A signed manuscript poem by Christine Georgina Rossetti, titled 'Remember Me When I Am Gone Away', holograph sonnet signed by Rossetti.

£500-700 **FRE**

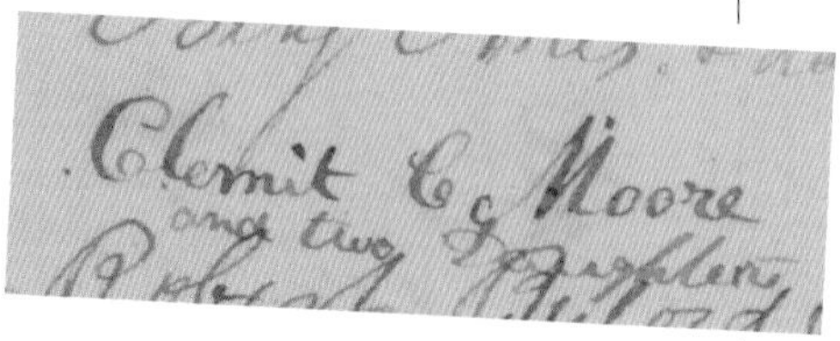

An American manuscript hotel ledger, from the Eagle Hotel in Bethlehem, Pennsylvania, 38 sheets with 1,200 signatures of prominent visitors.

This is among the earliest surviving American hotel registers.

c1930

£2,000-2,500 **FRE**

PHOTOGRAPHS

An original photograph by Hugo Brehme, hand-coloured silver print, titled 'Xochimilco' and signed by Brehme.

13.75in (33.5cm) high

£300-500 **FRE**

An original photograph signed by Ulysses Grant, a carte-de-visite portrait, depicting Grant at ease in military uniform, former owner's inscription on verso, dated 'Feb. 12, [18]66'.

£2,000-3,000 **FRE**

An original signed photograph of Albert Einstein, by Yousuf Karsh, gelatin silver print, signed in ink by Karsh, on original mount with Karsh's stamp verso and U.S. postage stamp, signed by Einstein.

8in (20.5cm) wide

£4,000-5,000 **FRE**

An original photograph by Barbara Morgan, 'Martha Graham, Letter to the World (Kick)', gelatin silver print, taken in 1940 and printed in 1980, signed and dated 1940 and 1980, framed.

18in (45.5cm) high

£2,000-3,000 **FRE**

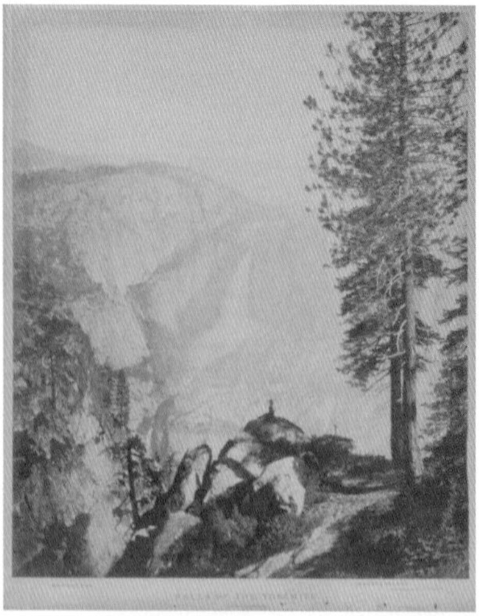

An original "Falls of Yosemite (2600 feet) from Glacier Point" photograph by Eadweard Muybridge, some fading to print, on original printed matter.

1872 *21in (54cm) high*

£3,500-4,000 **FRE**

An original signed and inscribed photograph of Theodore Roosevelt, on original mount, dated 'Aug. 7, 1907', photograph by Pack, New York, copyrighted 1904.

12in (30.5cm) high

£1,000-1,500 **FRE**

An original photograph of the Warren Athletic Association football team, silver print, contemporary frame.

1897 *16.5in (42cm) wide*

£180-220 **FRE**

A signed letter and photograph of Robert Baden-Powell, on South African Constabulary letter headed paper, dated 24/4/01.

In this letter, Baden Powell describes his interest in the news that the intended recipient, a 'Master Davis' had become a choir boy.

£180-220 **SWO**

An original photograph, signed by Charlie Chaplin.

c1925 *7in (18cm) high*

£180-220 **FRE**

A pair of Silver Jubilee commemorative glass vases, of square tapering form, with hand-tinted photograph portraits of H.M. King George V and H.M. Queen Mary, Emperor and Empress of India.

1935 *25cm (9.75in) high*

£100-£150 **SWO**

An original photograph signed by Henry Ford, shown with George Matthew Adams, founder of the George M. Adams News Service.

c1935 *8in (20cm) high*

£500-700 **FRE**

An original photograph signed 'Sergei Rachmaninoff'.

c1940

£600-800 **FRE**

A signed and inscribed original photograph of Dwight D. Eisenhower, silver print, inscribed 'To Lincoln Memorial University, Dwight D. Eisenhower, General, U.S. Army, Africa – 1943'.

13in (33cm) high

£600-800 **FRE**

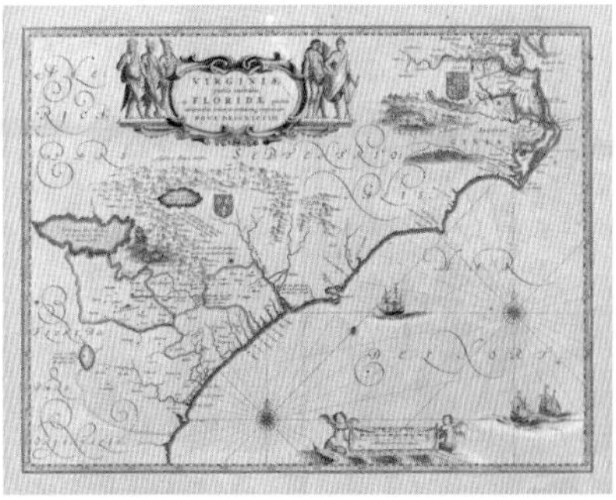

A William and Jean Blaeu hand-coloured engraved map, 'Virginae partis australis et Floridae partis orientalis,... Nova Descriptio', Amsterdam, second state, Latin text on verso.

The maps of the Blaeu family helped call into question the accuracy of the work of Abraham Ortelius.

1640 *19.75in (49cm) wide*

£600-900 **FRE**

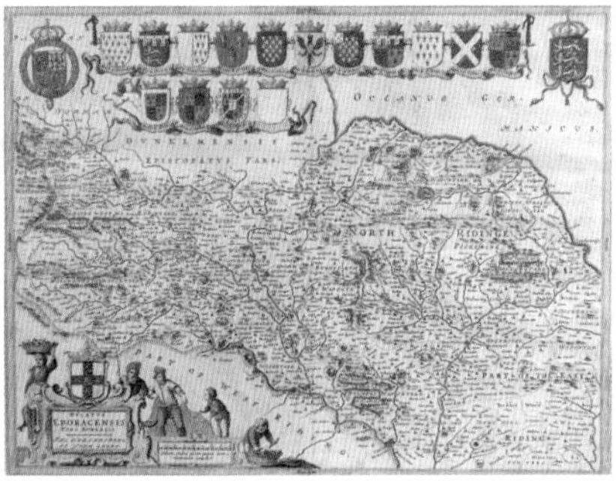

A William and Jean Blaeu engraved map, 'Ducatus Eboracensis pars Borealis, The North Riding of Yorkshire', hand-coloured in outline, with a historical and pictorial title cartouche, 13 coloured coats of arms and three uncoloured.

19.25in (49cm) wide

£180-220 **SWO**

A William Blaeu engraved map, 'Nova Virginia Tabula' of the state of Virginia, with an ornamental cartouche incorporating the scale, hand-coloured detail, mounted in a double glazed frame.

18.5in (48cm) wide

£1,000-1,500 **SWO**

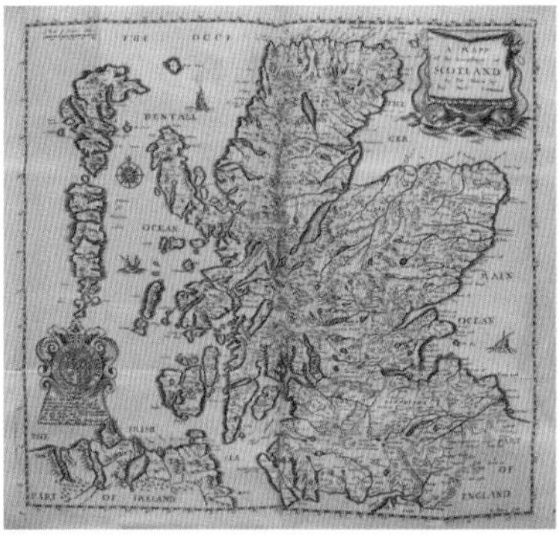

A Richard Blome 'Britannia: or, a geographical description of the Kingdoms of England, Scotland, and Ireland, with the isles and territories thereto belonging', first edition, comprising 49 of 50 maps, lacking that of the Isle of Wight, together with a plan of London and 24 plates illustrating 812 coats of arms, Roycroft, London.

Includes a chapter on the 'Isles and territories belonging to His Majesty in America' as well as brief chapter on 'Isles and territories ... in Africa, Asia, and the Indies'.

1673

£2,500-3,000 **L&T**

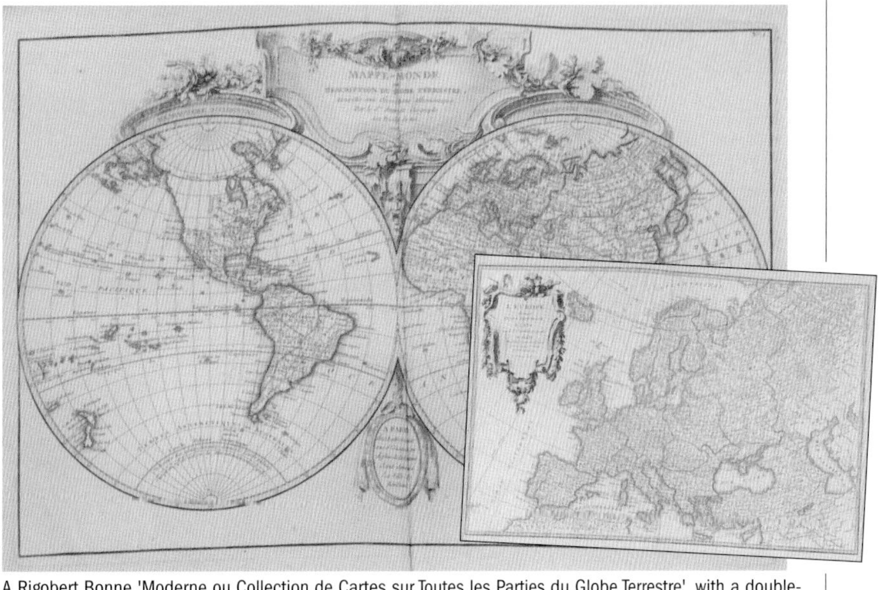

A Rigobert Bonne 'Moderne ou Collection de Cartes sur Toutes les Parties du Globe Terrestre', with a double-page plate and 36 double page engraved maps, hand-coloured in outline, damage.

£1,500-2,000 **FRE**

A Nicolas Sanson d'Abbeville 'Description de Tout l'Univer, en Plusieurs Cartes', including Luyt's 'Tables Geograpiques' and Bion's 'l'Usage des Globes', comprising 71 of 74 double-page, hand-coloured maps and 10 of 15 hand-coloured plates in Bion's supplement, damaged.

1700

£4,500-5,000 **FRE**

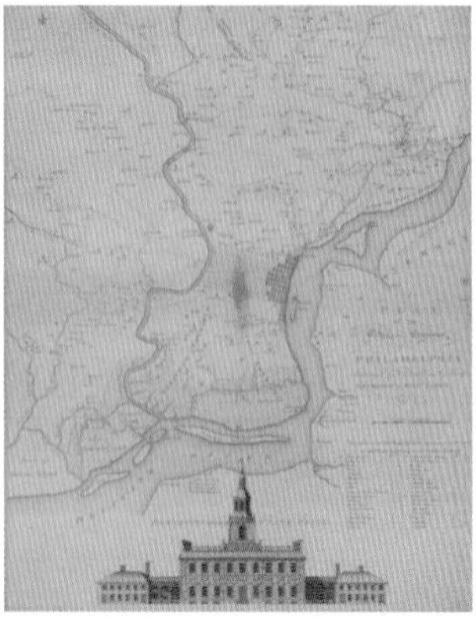

A William Faden 'Plan of the City and Environs of Philadelphia', engraved map, after N. Scull and G. Heap, G., London, first state.

1777

£300-400 FRE

A 'New Edinburgh General Atlas', revised by J. Lothian, with a hand-coloured comparative view of the principal mountains and rivers, 45 engraved maps, hand-coloured in outline, A.K. Newman & Co., London and J. Morrison, Glasgow.

c1850

£400-600 L&T

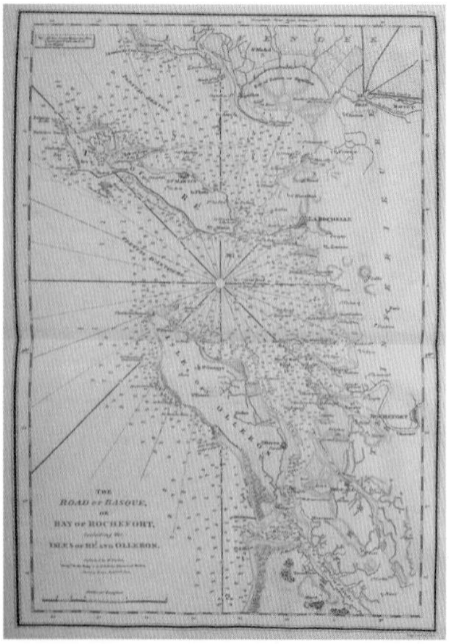

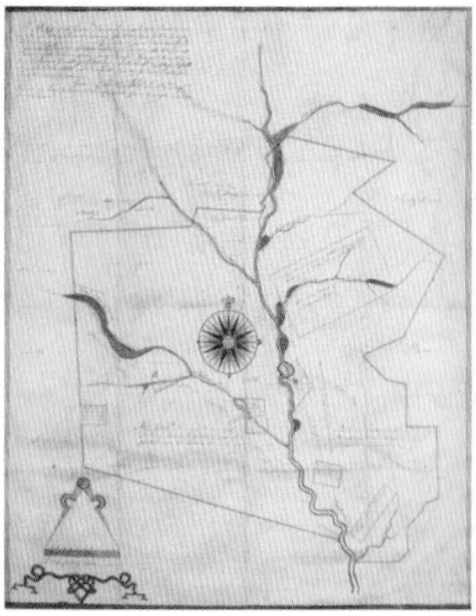

An Ebenezar Miller 'Map of the Hanour: Thomas Penn & Richard Penn Land at Prince Morris River...', begun in 1748 and completed in 1749, ink and watercolour.

25in (62.5cm) high

£1,500-2,000 POOK

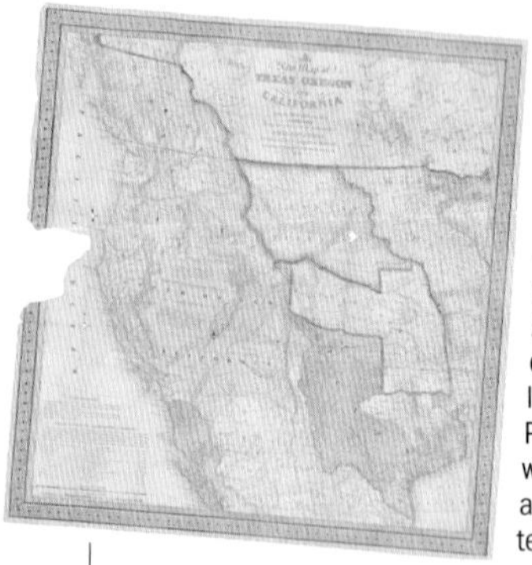

A Samuel Augustus Mitchell 'A New Map of Texas, Oregon and California, with the Regions Adjoining' hand-coloured lithographic map, Philadelphia, without the accompanying text, damaged.

This was one of the great pocket maps of the American West. Mitchell was among the first maps by a commercial cartographer to utilize recent technological developments.

c1845 *22.25in (56cm) wide*

£1,200-1,800 FRE

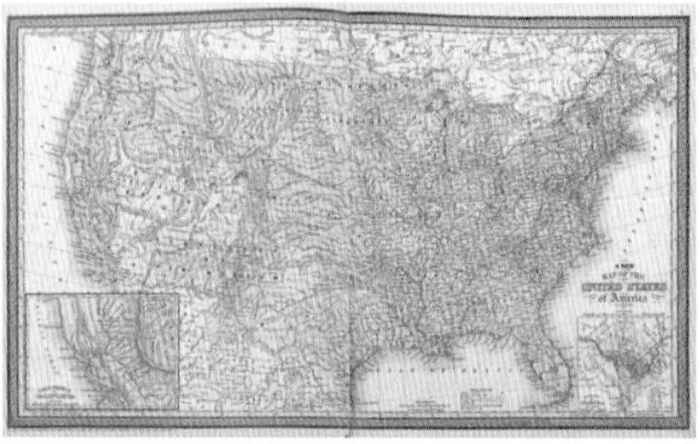

An S. Augustus Mitchell 'New Universal Atlas', comprising 122 maps, 73 hand-coloured, including a double-page map of the United States with an inset of the California gold regions, Thomas Copperthwait, Philadelphia.

This edition was the first to show counties in California and New Mexico.

1852

£2,500-3,000 FRE

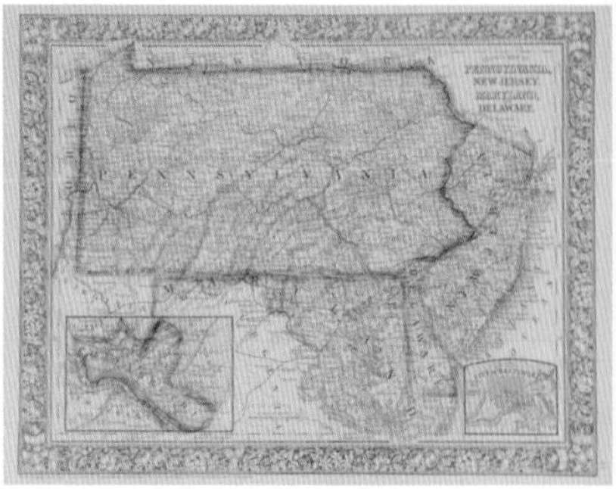

An S. Augustus Mitchell 'Mitchell's New General Atlas', with 84 hand-coloured lithographic maps, Philadelphia.

1864

£700-1,000 FRE

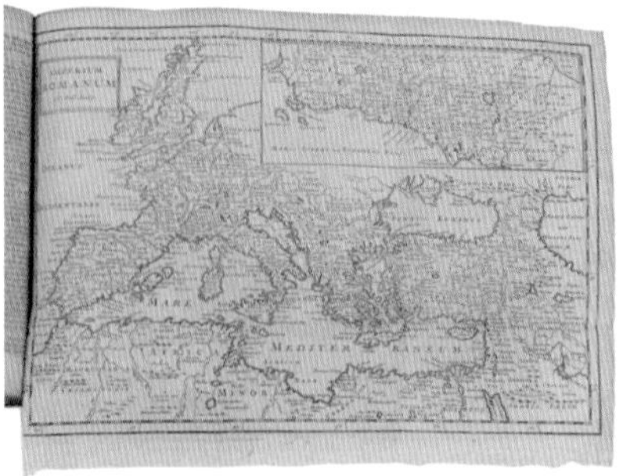

Two volumes of Herman Moll's 'Atlas Geographus', comprising 67 of 68 maps, with plates and tables, damaged.

1711

£1,500-2,000 FRE

A mid-18thC Herman Moll 'Bowles's Atlas Minor', comprising 65 maps, hand-coloured in outline, Carrington Bowles, London.

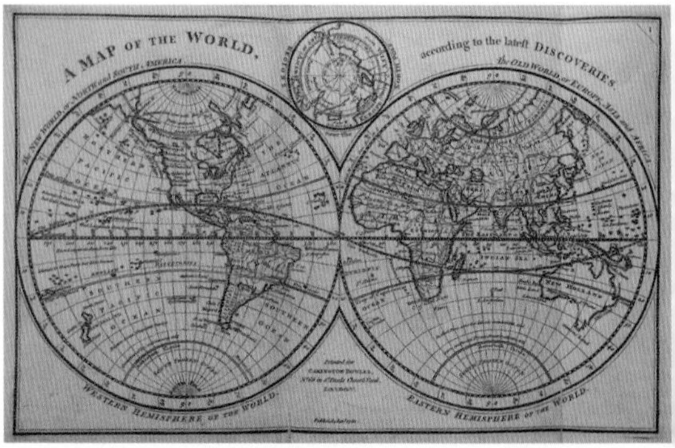

Moll's 'Atlas Minor' was first issued in London in 1729, with later editions appearing as 'Bowles's Atlas Minor.' The world map shows the hypothetical east cost of Australia and Tasmania as joined. The map of North America is described as 'a new map ... according to the newest observations', but does not show the alterations to the boundaries of Carolina in the light of the Treaty of 1763.

£2,000-3,000 L&T

A CLOSER LOOK AT AN ABRAHAM ORTELIUS ATLAS

The Flemish scholar and geographer Abraham Ortelius (1527-1598) produced the highly regarded mapbook 'Theatrum Orbis Terrarum'. As a collection of bound map sheets, it is considered the first true atlas.

Copper printing plates were specifically engraved to produce the fine graphic illustrations. The atlas includes five hand-coloured copper plate engravings and 63 engraved double-page map sheets with vivid hand-coloured copper plate.

This was the leading European atlas of the period, making it an important acquisition for a collector.

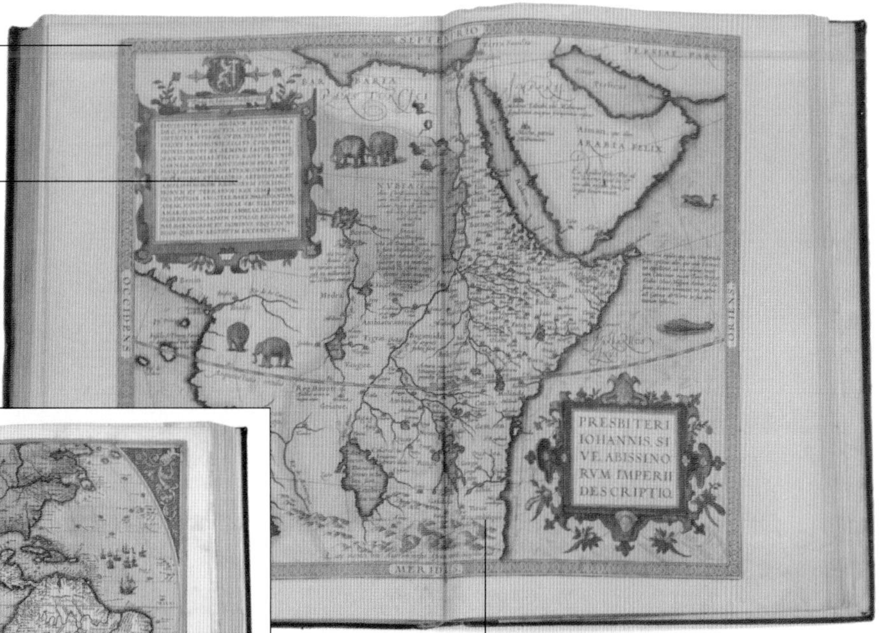

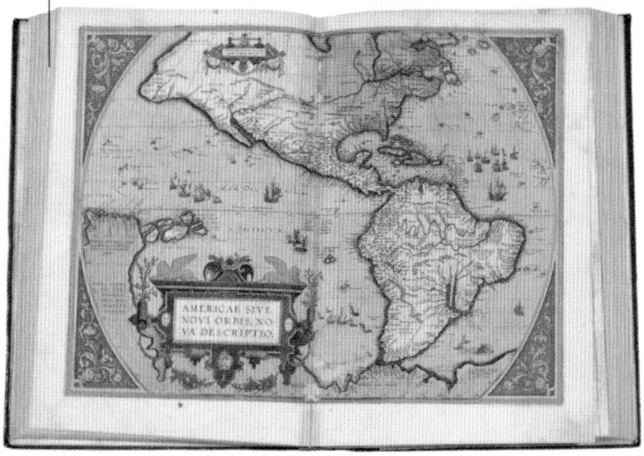

The Theatrum atlas was introduced in 1570 and was published until 1612. More than seven thousand copies were printed in seven different languages. This was an extremely large print run for the period.

An Abraham Ortelius 'Theatrum Orbis Terrarum', comprising 63 double-page, hand-coloured map sheets, bound in from the Latin-language editions of 1603 and 1609, with 18thC engraved harbour map bound in rear.

£22,000-28,000 **FRE**

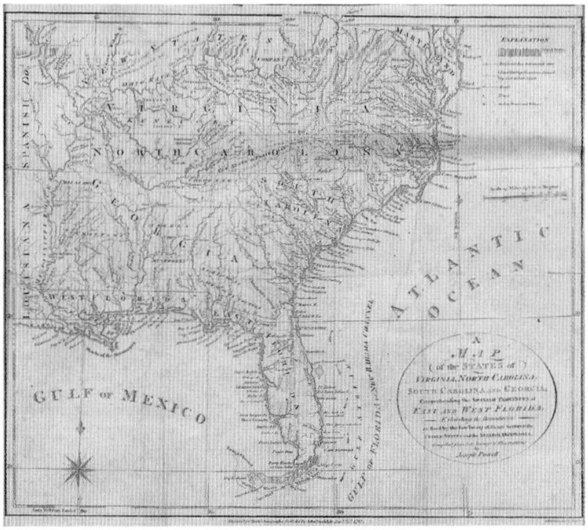

A map entitled 'A map of the States of Virginia, North Carolina, South Carolina and Georgia...from Surveys by Joseph Purcell', engraved by W. Harrison, Jr. and Sr., for 'Morse's Geography,' second edition, 1782, damaged.

1792 *14.75in (37.5cm) wide*

£500-700 **BRU**

A R. Sayer & J. Bennet 'The American Military Pocket Atlas', first edition, with six maps, hand-coloured in outline, damage, London.

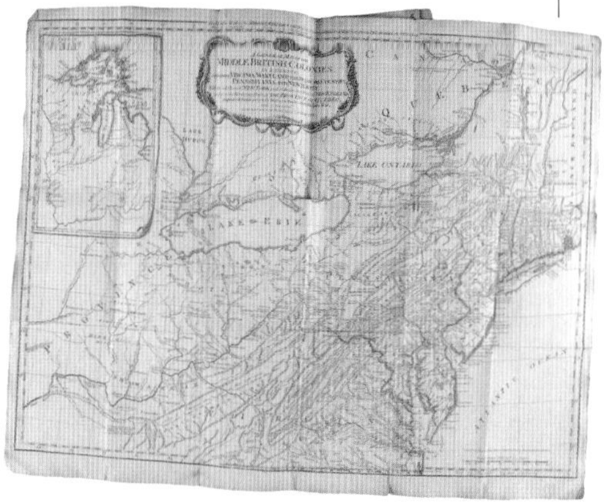

Known as a 'holster' atlas, this map was deliberately designed for mounted officers in the American Revolutionary war. The publishers described it as 'a portable Atlas of North America calculated in its Bulk and Price to suit the Pockets of Officers of all Ranks'. This Baedeker was available for purchase both in London and New York. Such maps were also useful for those following the progress of the war.

1776

£8,000-12,000 **L&T**

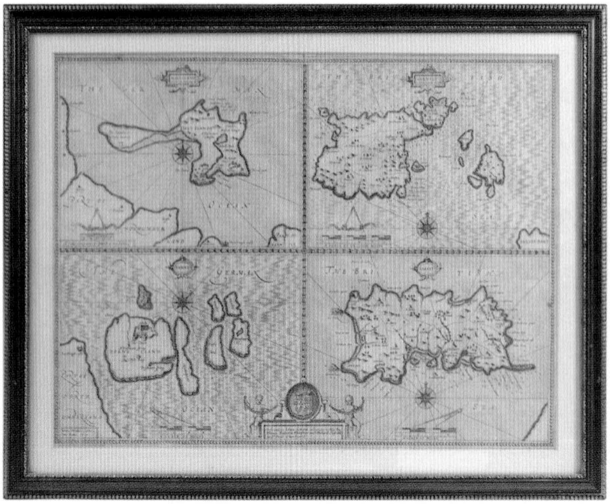

A John Speed 'Map of the Channel Islands', hand-coloured, with a cartouche and scales, mounted in a double glazed frame.

19.75in (50cm) wide

£200-300 **SWO**

A John Speed engraved map of Wiltshire, hand-coloured in outline with 15 coats of arms, with an inset plan of Salisbury, a view of Stonehenge and other features, mounted in a double glazed frame.

19.75in (50cm) wide

£500-700 **SWO**

A John Speed map entitled 'The Kingdom of Persia with the Cheef Citties and Habites Described', with vignettes of Persian society, coloured engraving.

20.5in (52cm) wide

£300-500 **SWO**

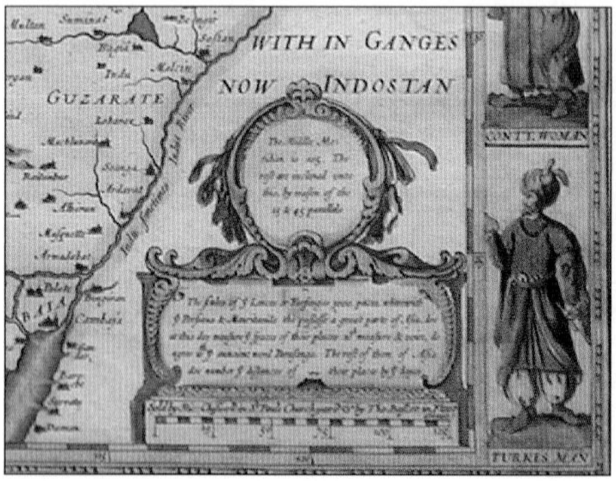

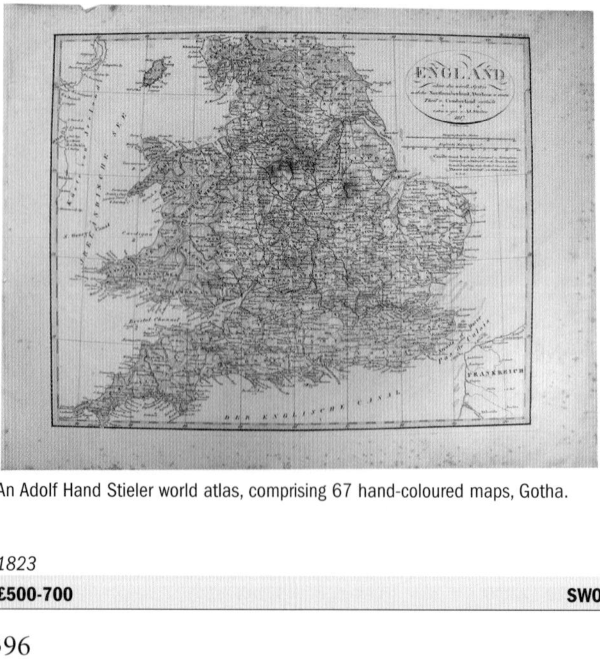

An Adolf Hand Stieler world atlas, comprising 67 hand-coloured maps, Gotha.

1823

£500-700 **SWO**

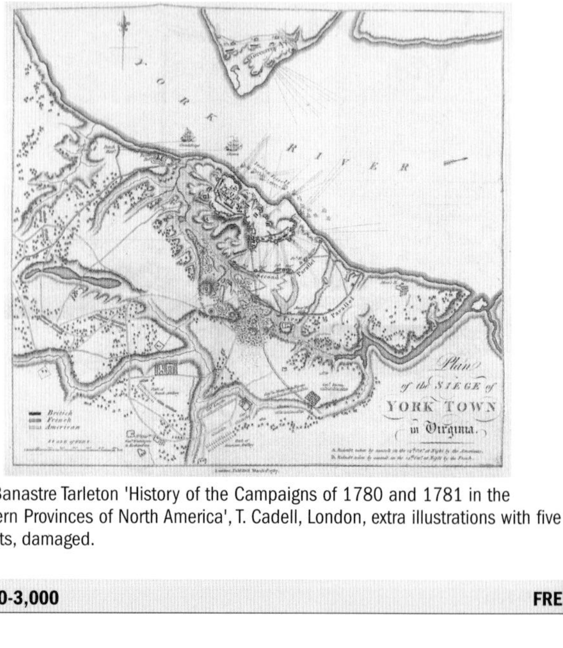

A Sir Banastre Tarleton 'History of the Campaigns of 1780 and 1781 in the Southern Provinces of North America', T. Cadell, London, extra illustrations with five portraits, damaged.

1787

£2,500-3,000 **FRE**

A printed and hand-coloured birth certificate, by John Baumann of Ephrata, Pennsylvania for Peter Ehrlich of Berks County, depicting birds and tulips surrounding a heart with script, dated.

1802 *15in (37.5cm) wide*

£800-1,200 **POOK**

A watercolour and ink on paper birth certificate by Abraham Brubaker of Lancaster County, Pennsylvania for David Roth, with red and yellow fanciful script and tulips, birds and flowers, signed "Abraham Brubaker".

16in (40cm) wide

£1,500-2,000 **POOK**

An ink and watercolour birth certificate, by Georg Burger of Westmoreland County, Pennsylvania for Elisa Singhaas, with eagle and angels surrounding script, signed lower right centre "Georg Burger", dated.

1817 *15.25in (38cm) high*

£800-1,200 **POOK**

An ink and watercolour birth and baptism certificate, attributed to George Peter Deisert, for Samuel Hostatter, unsigned, dated.

1790

£2,000-2,500 **FRE**

An ink-on-paper taufschein, by J.L. Kurtz of Springfield Township, Ohio for Anna Susanna Mayer, with potted flowers and birds surrounding script, dated.

1814 *12.25in (30.5cm) wide*

£400-600 **POOK**

A watercolour taufschein, for Elisabeth Laran of Berks County, Pennsylvania, with central script surrounded by birds and flowers, dated.

1783 *15.75in (39cm) wide*

£280-320 **POOK**

A watercolour on paper fraktur birth certificate, by Daniel Otto of Centre County, Pennsylvania for Magdalena Stober, with central heart enclosing script surrounded by typical flat tulips and buds, within a red painted frame with yellow floral highlights, dated.

1817 *13in (32.5cm) wide*

£3,000-5,000 **POOK**

A watercolour on paper fraktur birth and baptismal certificate, by Henry Young of Pennsylvania for Franklin Bohn, depicting his parents Daniel and Sarah Anna clutching a bouquet, dated.

1855 *11.75in (29cm) high*

£2,500-3,000 **POOK**

A watercolour and ink birth and baptismal certificate, by Henry Young of Union County, Pennsylvania for Maria Amanda, dated.

1850 *14.5in (36cm) high*

£1,200-1,800 **POOK**

A watercolour and ink on paper taufschein, for Joseph Jaekelnorth of Hampton County, South Carolina, unsigned, restored.

1800 *7.75in (19.5cm) high*

£2,000-2,500 **FRE**

One of a pair of ink and watercolour taufsheins, for Elizabeth and Joseph Lang of Northampton County, Pennsylvania, each with central heart with script surrounded by birds, tulips, and vines, dated.

1799 & 1801 15.75in (117.5cm) wide

£2,500-3,000 pair **POOK**

TAUFSCHEIN

- Taufschein are a specialist type of the hand-painted or hand-decorated manuscripts known as 'fraktur' first brought over by mid-European settlers and made in America from the mid-18thC.
- Their purpose was to record birth and baptism dates of children born to families living in America. They are most associated with German migrants living in rural areas in Pennsylvania.
- Local schoolmasters would draw up these records on behalf of families living within their communities using goose quill pens with steel nibs.
- Devotional motifs such as angels and crowns are drawn from the Lutheran religion of the German settlers. These were combined with astrological and natural symbols and pictures.
- English gradually supplanted German as the dominant language for taufschein documents. They became less widespread as the use of printing proliferated in America throughout the 19thC.

An ink and watercolour taufschein, for Jonathan Schmeltzer of Berks County, Pennsylvania, with central script surrounded by blue, red, yellow and green tulip vines and flowers and stylized flowers emerging from pots, dated.

1815 *16in (40cm) high*

£800-1,200 **POOK**

An ink and watercolour taufschein, for Henry Carl Heimbach of Berks County, Pennsylvania, with tulip and floral decoration, dated.

1830 *14in (35cm) wide*

£400-600 **POOK**

An ink and watercolour taufschein, from Dauphin County, Pennsylvania, with angels and an eagle surrounding script, dated.

This example is particularly rich in colour and unusual in design.

1836 *15in (37.5cm) high*

£500-800 **POOK**

A centre-shafted putter by Anderson & Son of Edinburgh, with brass head and hickory shaft.

£700-1,000 L&T

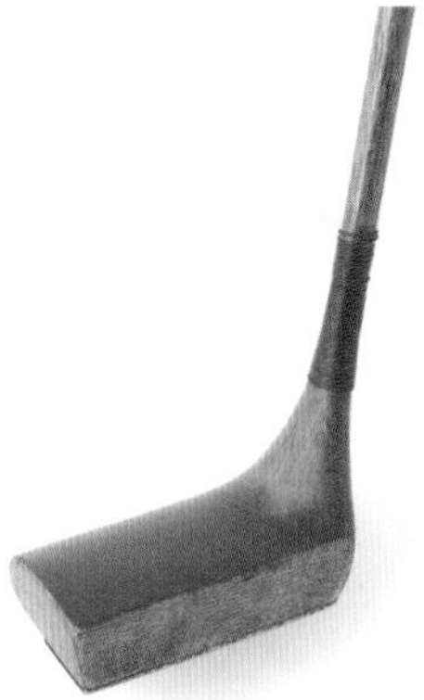

A Gassiat-type putter.

4.25in (11cm) long

£350-450 MSA

A 'Ping Anser' Gary Player putter, by Karsten Co., with brass head, replica signature to underside, stamped.

£1,000-1,500 L&T

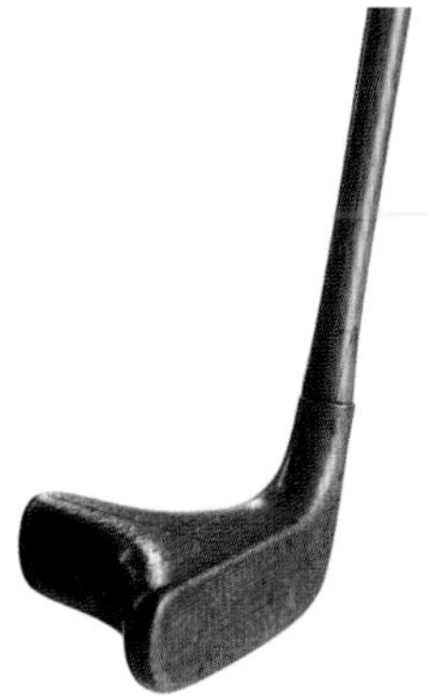

A 'Straight Line' putter, by Fred Saunders, with hickory shaft and alloy head with hatched face, adapted as a walking stick.

£280-320 L&T

A centre-shafted Chicopee putter, by A.G. Spalding & Bros., with dot face and hickory shaft.

£180-220 L&T

An extremely unusual mallet head putter, with beech head, tapered brass sole plate, lead counterweight and hickory shaft.

£2,500-3,000 L&T

A Sunday stick, with scared head formed as a wood, horn insert to sole, lead counterweight and greenheart shaft, stamped "J. Thomson, Felixstowe".

£350-450 L&T

A patent adjustable iron golf club, by Urquhart, the collar stamped "No.1299 URQUHART'S PATENT".

A button near the neck of the club releases the head which can be adjusted for loft.

7.5in (19cm) long

£1,200-1,800 MSA

An adjustable head iron, no. 20642, by Urquhart, hickory shaft.

This model was the first of Urquhart's patent irons and one of only a handful to survive.

c1895

£1,800-2,200 L&T

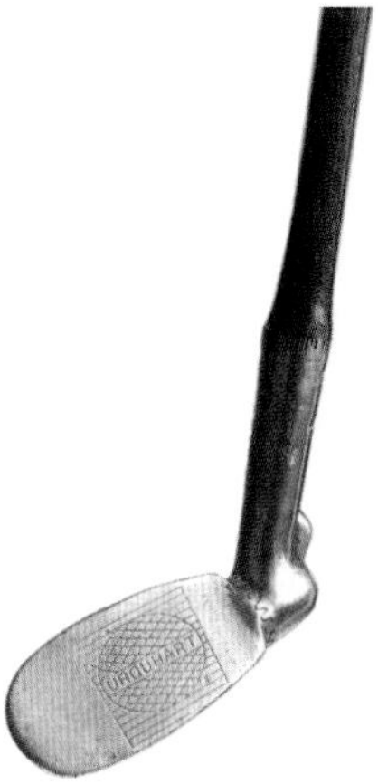

An adjustable head iron, no. 3323, by Urquhart, hickory shaft.

£800-1,200 L&T

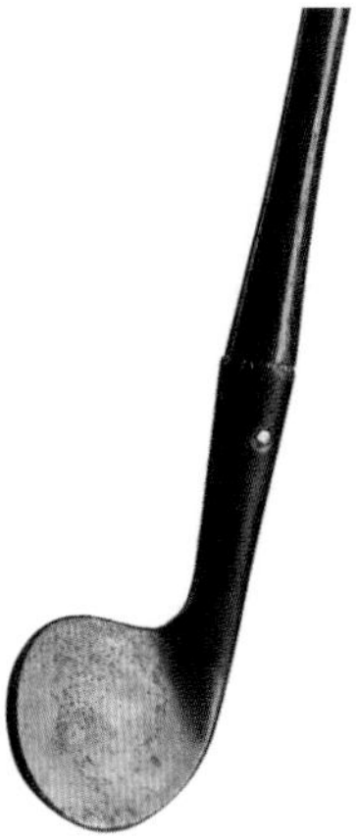

An unnamed smooth-faced rut iron, with rounded head and hickory shaft.

£600-900 L&T

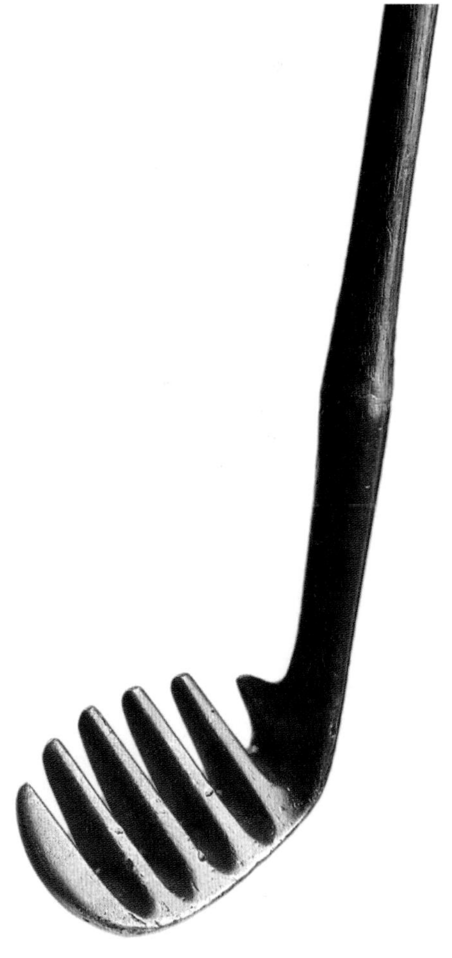

A Brown's patent rake iron, by Winton of Montrose, stamped 'Thistle' model, with hickory shaft, the head consisting of six tines to facilitate its passage through water and rough grass.

c1905

£4,000-6,000 L&T

An unusual brass ball back iron, with cast brass head and hickory shaft.

£3,500-4,500 L&T

A crosshead playclub, by Francis Brewster, patent number 9514, with hickory shaft, stamped "Simplex".

c1895

£2,000-3,000 L&T

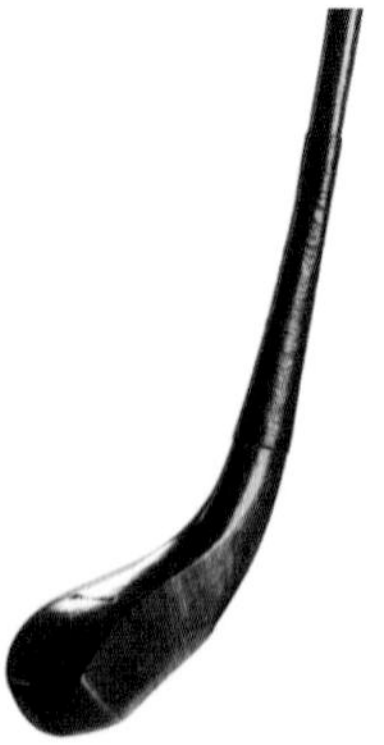

A longnose playclub, by Dunn, with scared head inset with horn, lead counterweight, hickory shaft and wrapped grip.

c1875.

£3,500-4,500 L&T

A playclub by R. Forgan of St. Andrews, with shallow-faced pear and applewood head and unusual ash shaft, stamped "R. Forgan".

c1865

£1,500-2,000 L&T

A playclub, by Tom Morris of St. Andrews, with hickory shaft.

c1875

£2,800-3,200 L&T

A longnose baffing spoon by McEwan of Edinburgh, with hickory shaft.

c1850

£3,000-5,000 L&T

A very early short spoon, by Tom Morris of St. Andrews, with shallow-faced long head and hickory shaft.

c1855

£4,000-6,000 L&T

A longnose spoon, by H. Philp, with scared head inset with horn, lead counterweight, hickory shaft and wrapped smooth leather grip.

£4,000-5,000 L&T

A long nose driver, by G. Forrester of Ely, stamped "G.FORRESTER".

c1875

£3,000-3,500 MSA

A longnose driver, by McEwan of Edinburgh, with scared head inset with horn, lead counterweight, hickory shaft, and leather wrapped grip.

£1,000-1,500 L&T

An extremely unusual combination wood, the brass-framed wooden head with hatched face, with lead counterweight and greenheart shaft.

£5,000-8,000 L&T

An extremely unusual combination wood, with brass-framed fruitwood head, partly gilt, with wooden face and hickory shaft.

£5,000-8,000 L&T

A 'Mammoth Niblick', by Cochranes Ltd of Edinburgh, with hickory shaft and original leather grip, the head stamped "A.W. GAMAGEL HOLBORN".

c1925

£1,000-1,500 MSA

AN 'RL 2 1/2' model Duplex club, by Standard Mills Co., with hickory shaft.

This club was used for a game called 'crolf' which is a hybrid of golf and croquet.

£800-1,200 L&T

A feathery golf ball, with painted finish and several hack marks, traces of stamped initials "T.D."

£1,500-2,000 L&T

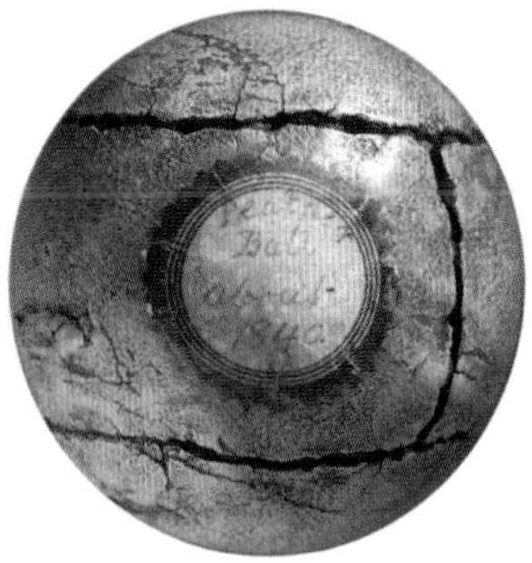

A feathery golf ball, with distinct paper label.

£6,000-8,000 L&T

A feathery golf ball, by J. Gourlay of Musselburgh, in unused condition, stamped "J. Gourlay. 28".

c1840

£6,000-8,000 L&T

A 'Silvertown' gutta ball, with red and black stamp.

c1890

£350-450 L&T

A 'Silver King S' rubber core golf ball.

c1910

£700-1,000 L&T

A 'Colonel' patent golf ball, painted red for winter usage, in original wrapper, with small hairline crack.

£400-600 L&T

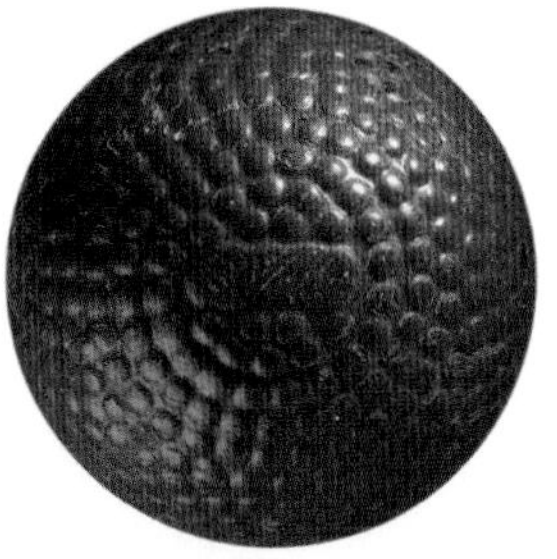

A 'Springvale Kite' bramble pattern rubber core golf ball, painted red.

The Springvale Kite was the first rubber core golf ball used by Tom Morris.

c1905

£600-900 L&T

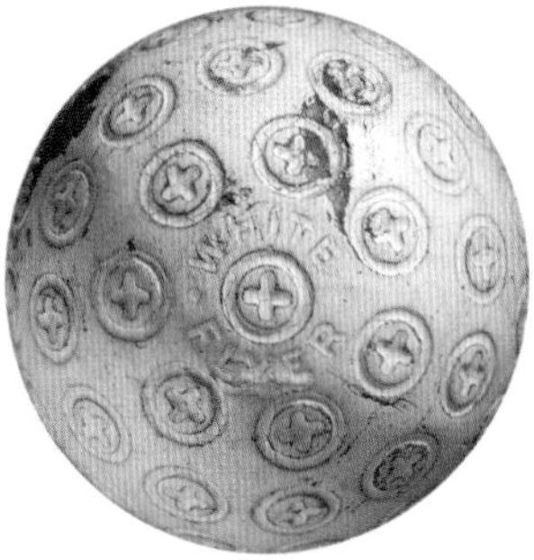

A 'White Flyer' golf ball, by Craig Park Elec. Co. Ltd, with circle and cross dimples.

c1910

£400-600 L&T

A CLOSER LOOK AT A SPALDING GOLF BALL

The presentation case has kept this ball in good condition.

Bobby Jones is remembered by many as the greatest player in the history of the game. He remains the only golfer to have won every major in a single year.

This ball dates from the 1920s, when most golf balls were made from rubber. Feathery and gutta balls are generally more valuable, but the famous signature makes this an exception.

Spalding was the first American manufacturer of golf balls and one of the first to market the modern rubber-cored ball.

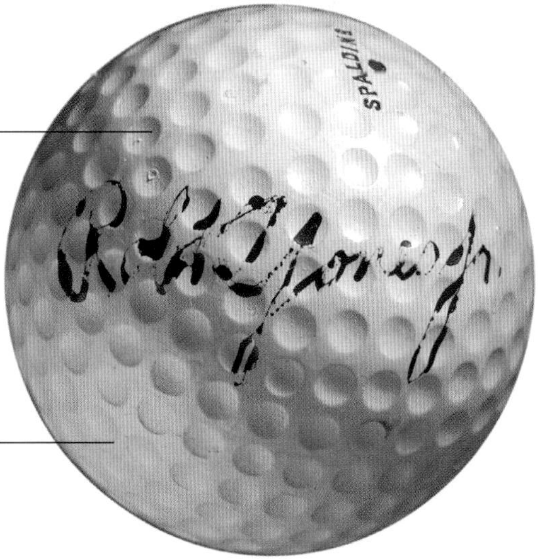

A Spalding golf ball, signed in ink by Bobby Jones, with presentation case.

Provenance*: Obtained from the daughter of a private individual who had worked with and was a good friend of Jones. The father obtained it during a tournament played in Detroit in the early 1940s. Since then it has lived in a sock!*

£6,000-8,000 L&T

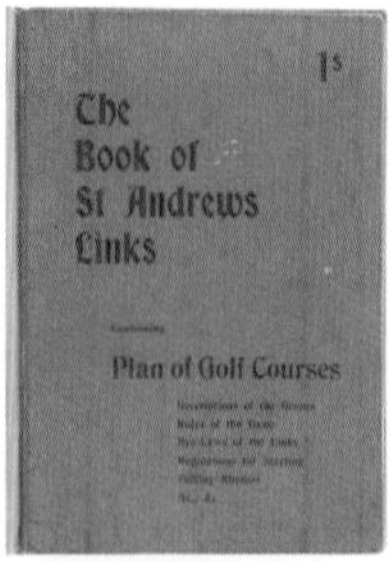

A first edition of "The Book of St. Andrews Links" by Andrew Bennett, published by Innes & Menzies of St. Andrews and Edinburgh, containing plans of golf courses, descriptions of greens and rules of the game, with frontispiece, folding course map and original cloth boards.

1898

£2,500-3,000 L&T

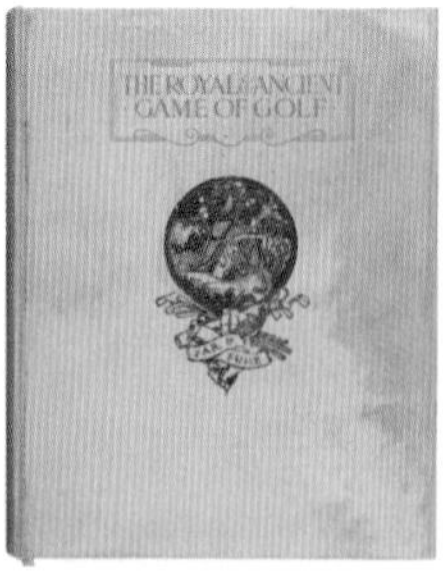

A first large paper edition of "The Royal & Ancient Game of Golf" by Harold H. Hilton & Smith Garden G. Hilton, illustrated with colour plates and photogravures, vellum cover with gilt lettering and tooled pictorial lion emblem, rebound, number 19 in a deluxe edition of 100.

1912

£3,000-4,000 L&T

A first edition of "Aspects of Book Collecting: Collecting Golf Books" by Cecil Hopkinson, published by Constable & Co. of London, with red paper wrappers, cover with black lettering.

This was O.M. Leland's personal copy and has his personal handwritten annotations in the margins.

1938

£2,000-3,000 L&T

A first edition of "The Golf Song Book", edited by Rev. John Kerr, published by John Menzies & Co. of Edinburgh, with green pictorial paper wrappers.

1903

£1,500-2,000 L&T

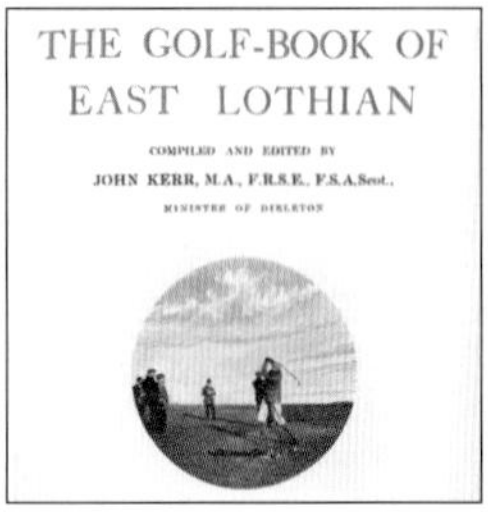

A first edition of "The Golf-Book of East Lothian" by John Kerr, published by T. & A. Constable of Edinburgh, illustrated throughout, including frontispiece with tissue-guard, tan cloth covers with gilt vignette and lettering, from an edition of 500, signed by the author.

1896

£1,500-2,000 L&T

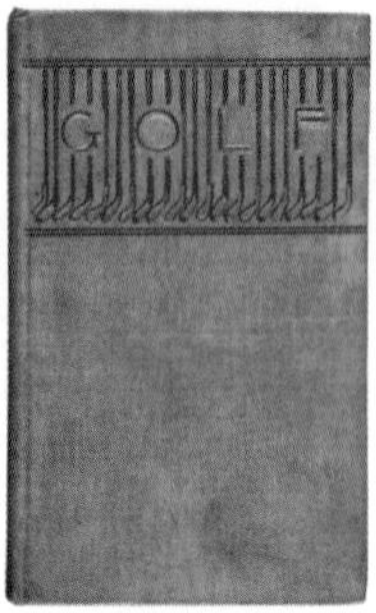

A first edition of "Golf in America: A Practical Manual" by James. P Lee, published by Dodd, Mead & Co. of New York, illustrated with plates from photographs, with original silver and green lettered yellow cloth cover and spine.

c1895

£1,500-2,000 L&T

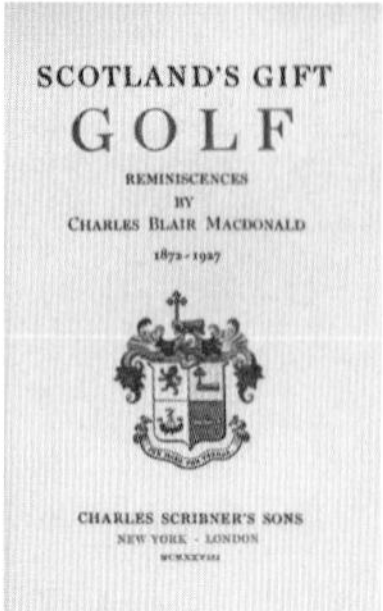

A first edition of "Reminiscences, Scotlands Gift, Golf" by Charles Blair MacDonald, published by Charles Scribner's Sons of London, signed by the author, with colour frontispiece after Gari Melchers, red boards, from a limited edition of 250.

1928

£2,000-3,000 L&T

A copy of "The Actis and Constitutiounis of the realme of Scotland, Maid in Parliamentis by Kingis James the First, Secund, Third, Feird, Fyft and the Tyme of Marie Now Quene of Scottis, Edinburgh", by R. Lepreuik, dated 28th November 1566, rebound in full brown calf, the title page has a woodcut of the Royal Arms of Scotland, signed "Jacobus Balfour" and "Jacobus Makgill", restored.

This is a rare and historic book that includes an early mention of golf relating to the Acts of 1457, 1471 and 1491.

1566

£6,000-8,000 L&T

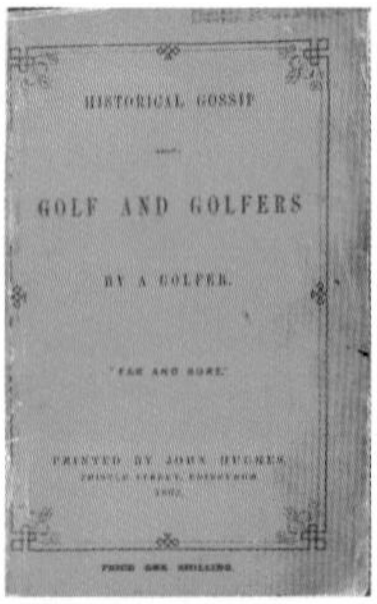

A first edition of "Historical Gossip about Golf and Golfers, by a Golfer" by George Robb, published by John Hughes of Edinburgh, with cloth-lined covers and original green wrappers with black lettering, inscribed "To Gordon Robb Esq. with the author's compliments, September 2/79".

1863

£6,000-8,000 L&T

A first edition of "The Links of Ancient Rome", by Bert Leston Taylor & Payson Sibley Wild, privately printed for the Brothers of the Book of Chicago, illustrated, with cloth boards and gilt lettering to cover, specially bound presentation edition, signed by Bert Leston Taylor and dated "March 1920".

1912

£2,500-3,000 L&T

A photogravure after Douglas Adams, 'The Drive and the Putting Green', signed in pencil and dated "1898" within the plate, published by The British Art Publishers, modern frames.

37in (94cm) wide

£1,500-2,000 **L&T**

A coloured reproduction by Michael Brown, 'Holylake - playing to the Briars', printed by Banks & Co. of Edinburgh.

13in (33cm) wide

£180-220 **L&T**

An oil on canvas by Graham W. Baxter, 'Cruden Bay, October 1998', signed by the artist.

£7,000-10,000 **L&T**

A Life Association of Scotland calendar, decorated with sepia reproductions, after Michael Brown, the cover with a depiction of the perfection bunker at North Berwick Links.

1910

£600-900 **L&T**

A pencil drawing by Craig Campbell, "Seve Ballesteros, British Open Champion, 1984 (1988) 1979", signed and dated 1989.

Educated at Glasgow College of Art, Craig Campbell was considered the outstanding British golf artist of his generation.

17.75in (45cm) high

£300-400 **L&T**

A coloured reproduction by J.W. Williamson, "Robert Tyre Jones Jr. winning the British Open Championship, 1927", published by Currier & Ives Inc.

c1930 *16.5in (42cm) wide*

£400-600 **L&T**

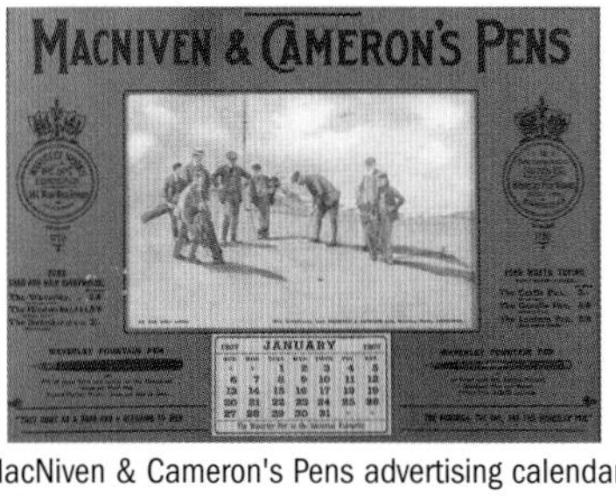

A MacNiven & Cameron's Pens advertising calendar for 1907, incorporating a coloured print of a golfing scene, framed.

1907 *20.25in (51.5cm) wide*

£300-400 **L&T**

A Peek Frean's Biscuits shop display card, entitled "The Heath Robinson Golf Course", with a comical depiction of a miniature golf course, inscribed "Try your skill with it".

11.75in (30cm) wide

£500-600 **L&T**

A silhoutte oil portrait on panel, depicting a golfer and caddy, inscribed "Edward Row, British Open, Muirfield 1912, Winners score 295".

19.75in (50.5cm)

£350-450 **L&T**

A Frank Buckley pottery coffee pot and cover, with transfer-printed and gilt scene of golfers to the reverse, inscribed "Presented to J B Carr, Amateur Champion, Royal Liverpool Golf Club, Hoylake, 28th - 30th May 1953".

6.75in (17cm) high

£700-1,000 **L&T**

A Copeland Late Spode pottery tyg, relief-moulded with a scene of golfers and caddies in a landscape, on a blue and gilt-decorated ground, three foliate scrolled handles.

5.25in (13.5cm) high

£1,000-1,500 **L&T**

An early 20thC Gerz saltglazed stoneware beer jug, relief moulded with golfers and caddies, with ornamental border, impressed marks to the underside.

7.5in (19cm) high

£1,800-2,200 **L&T**

A Lenox pottery tankard, painted with a golfing scene in shades of green, silver rim, printed marks to the underside.

5.75in (14.5cm) high

£1,500-2,000 **L&T**

A Weller Dickensware pottery jug, of ovoid form, incised and polychrome decorated with golfers in a landscape, impressed mark and numbered "374/11" to the underside.

5.75in (14.5cm) high

£800-1,200 **L&T**

An early 20thC Royal Bonn pottery tankard, transfer-printed with golfers putting on a seaside course, blue printed marks to the underside and numbered "1378".

6.25in (16cm) high

£3,000-4,000 **L&T**

A Wood & Wood biscuit barrel, printed and painted with scenes of golfers, with silver-plated rim, lid and swing handle.

4.75in (12cm) high

£800-1,200 **L&T**

A large Royal Doulton Seriesware two-handled vase, entitled "He Hath a Good Judgment Who Relieth Not Wholly on His Own", of tapering circular form, decorated with Crombie golfers, gilt decorated handles.

11in (28cm) high

£7,000-10,000 **L&T**

A large Royal Doulton Seriesware punch bowl, inscribed "He Hath A Good Judgment Who Relieth Not Wholly On His Own" and "All Fools Are Not Knaves But All Knaves Are Fools", decorated with Crombie golfers, on a circular spreading foot.

8in (20.5cm) high

£4,000-6,000 **L&T**

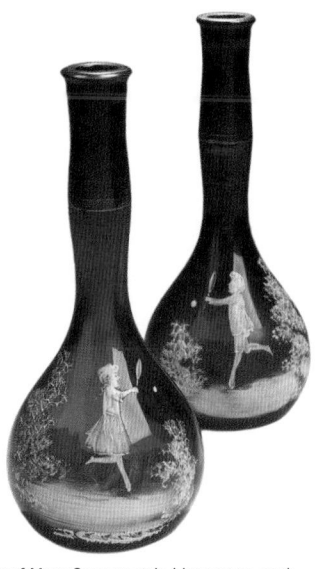

A pair of Mary Gregory-style blue vases, each decorated in white enamel with scenes of a boy and a girl playing tennis, gilt rims.

8in (20.5cm) high

£200-250 **L&T**

A late Victorian tennis trophy, in the form of a dinner gong, the moulded oak base with silver-plated mounts surmounted by crossed tennis racquets with suspended circular gong and beater.

13in (33cm) wide

£200-300 **L&T**

A small silver-cased hand mirror, in the form of a tennis racket, with hallmarks for Birmingham.

1922 *5in (13cm) high*

£200-250 **MSA**

Two from a set of Wimbledon tennis postcards, by E. Trim & Co, including depictions of Jack Crawford, Fred Perry, H. W. Austin and others, all signed in ink and most with embossed roundel.

£1,500-2,000 **SWO**

A pair of spelter figures of footballers, one taking a throw in, the other kicking a ball.

c1910 *taller 12.5in (31cm) high*

£180-220 **SWO**

A Scotland international football cap from the 1927/28 season.

Ths cap was awarded to Tommy Law, on the occasion of Scotland's famous 5-1 victory over England in 1928.

£800-1,200 **L&T**

A Hardy 'The Unique' mahogany and brass salmon fly cabinet, with a recessed handle to the top, the hinged fall-front enclosing ten numbered drawers with ivory handles and labels, containing some 350 salmon flies, on repolished rubber feet.

9.75in (25cm) wide

£3,500-4,500 **L&T**

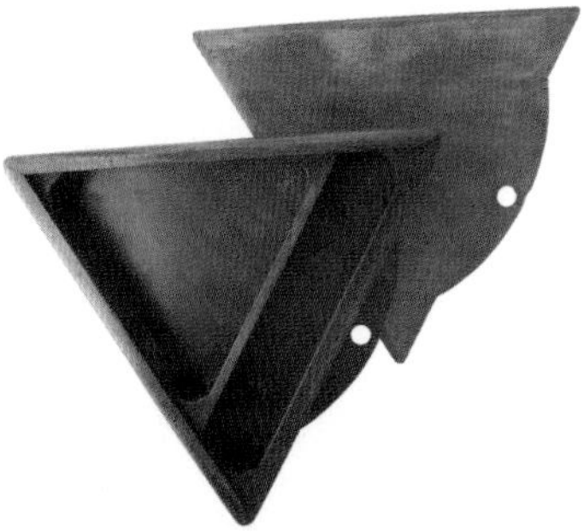

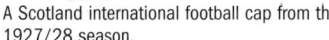

An unusual mahogany snooker ball box, with inbuilt triangle and removable sliding covers.

17.75in (45cm) high

£350-450 **MSA**

THE DECORATIVE ARTS MARKET

International exhibitions devoted to the Arts and Crafts movement together with landmark sales of works by Dr Christopher Dresser and Marie Zimmermann have contributed to a greater awareness and appreciation of late 19th and 20th century decorative arts.

While works by Dresser are regularly seen at auction and in the hands of specialist dealers, Zimmerman's work is seldom seen and so it is perhaps no surprise that an elaborately handcarved wooden box by the artist – perhaps better known for her metalwares – fetched a record price at auction in America. Dresser – a Victorian whose futuristic designs preceded the Modern movement by fifty years – designed everything from toast racks to vases, wallpaper to furniture.

The market for Arts and Crafts furniture continues to improve steadily, and although not at the level it reached in the 1990s it is healthy and improving. This is especially true of rare pieces in good condition which continue to command good prices.

The trend for Modern furnishings has brought an increased demand for Art Deco pieces which has resulted in higher prices.

Cameo and other art glass by makers such as Gallé, Daum, Tiffany and Lalique continue to command good prices, as do pieces by Schneider and Loetz. Again rare items in excellent condition and which are new to market have the upper hand when it comes to desirability.

The work of Hannah Barlow and her peers at Doulton Lambeth continue to attract attention, as do Poole, Carlton Ware and Keith Murray. Work by Clarice Cliff and Susie Cooper can also command a premium, especially if they have a rare shape or pattern. The market for examples by European factories such as Zsolnay, Boch Freres and Goldscheider is also strong.

CARLTON WARE

Part of a Carlton ware 'Melon' shape coffee set, comprising covered coffee pot, milk jug, sugar bowl and six cups and saucers, with 'Awakening' pattern number 3450, designed by Violet Elmer.

c1930 *pot 8.5in (21cm) high*

£1,500-2,000 set **WW**

A large Carlton ware 'Chinaland' ginger jar and cover, pattern number 3530, on a wooden base, with printed and painted marks, minor wear to shoulder.

12.5in (32cm) high

£2,200-2,800 **WW**

A Carlton ware 'Chinaland' vase, designed by Horace Wain and Enoch Boulton, shape number 326 and pattern number 2948, with coloured crown mark.

The full-colour crown backstamp was only ever used with this pattern.

c1925 *6.25in (15.5cm) high*

£1,500-2,000 **WW**

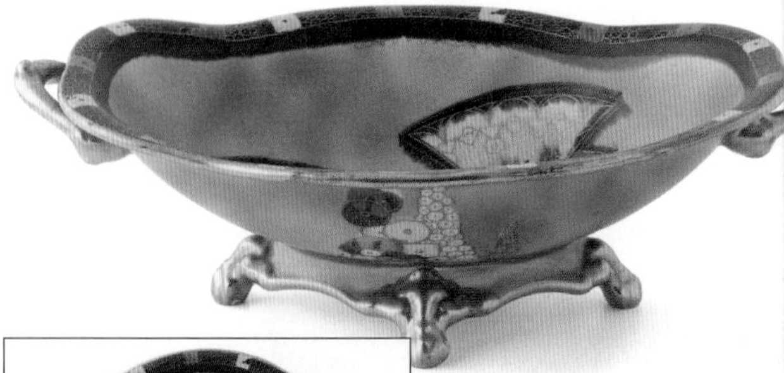

A Carlton ware 'Fan' pedestal bowl, printed and painted in colours and gilt on a matt blue and pink ground, with printed mark.

12.5in (31.5cm) wide

£500-800 **WW**

A Carlton ware 'Fan' footed bowl, pattern number 3558, with printed and painted marks.

10.75in (27cm) diam

£800-1,200 **WW**

A Clarice Cliff Bizarre 'Apples' inkwell and cover, shape number 458.

3.25in (8cm) high

£500-800 **DN**

A Clarice Cliff Bizarre 'Aurea' fern pot, with printed mark.

3in (7.5cm) high

£150-200 **WW**

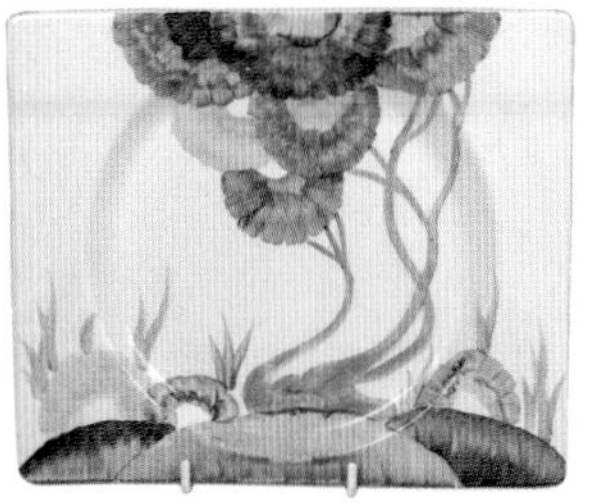

A Clarice Cliff Biarritz 'Aurea' plate, painted in warm colours, with printed marks and facsimile signature.

9.25in (23cm) wide

£150-250 **SWO**

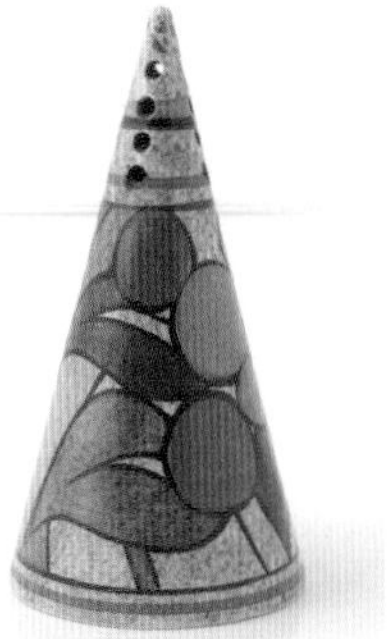

A Clarice Cliff 'Berries' conical sugar sifter, on a café au lait ground, with printed marks.

5.5in (14cm) high

£500-800 **CHEF**

A Clarice Cliff Fantasque Bizarre 'Berries' preserve and cover, shape number 230, with printed mark.

3.25in (8.5cm) high

£300-350 **WW**

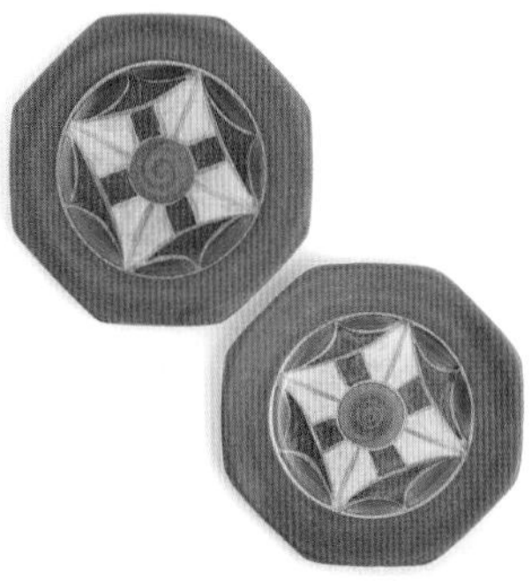

A pair of Clarice Cliff Original Bizarre octagonal plates, with printed gilt marks.

8.75in (22cm) wide

£300-400 **WW**

A Clarice Cliff Fantasque 'Broth' conical teapot and cover, painted with a panel of bubbles on a green, black and orange banded ground, with black printed marks to underside.

c1930 *7in (18cm) high*

£500-700 **ROS**

A Clarice Cliff 'Green Capri' plate, with printed mark.

9in (23cm) diam

£220-280 **WW**

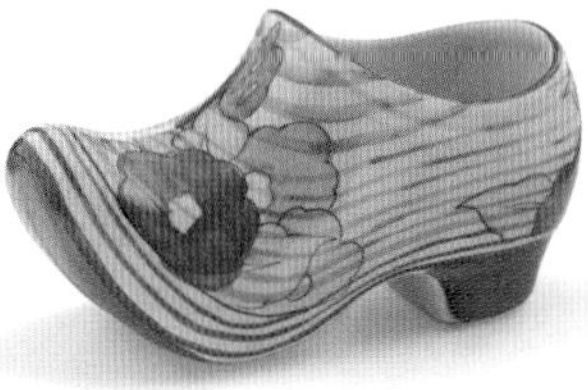

A Clarice Cliff Bizarre 'Orange Capri' clog, with printed mark.

4.5in (11.5cm) wide

£320-380 **WW**

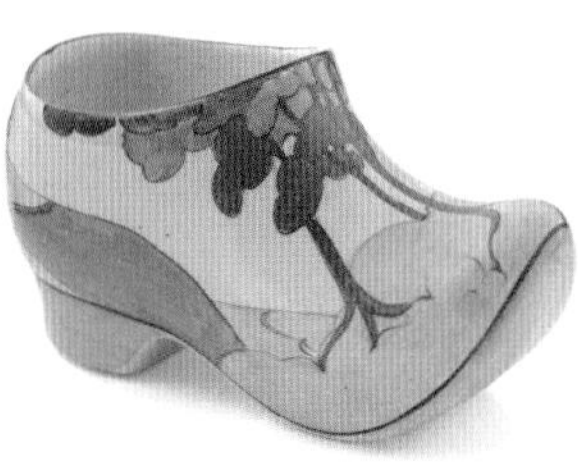

A Clarice Cliff 'Coral Firs' clog.

5.5in (14cm) high

£220-280 **GORL**

A rare Clarice Cliff 'Applique Caravan' octagonal plaque, with painted applique mark.

11in (28cm) wide

£3,500-4,500 **WW**

A Clarice Cliff Fantasque Bizarre 'Coral Firs' bowl, with stepped handles, painted with trees in orange, brown and yellow, with printed factory mark and impressed shape number "515".

5in (12.5cm) high

£500-700 **DN**

A Clarice Cliff 'Orange Roof Cottage' conical salt and pepper, with printed mark, missing tip and minor nicks.

3.25in (8cm) high

£200-250 **WW**

A Clarice Cliff Bizarre conical sugar sifter, in the 'Crepe de Chine' pattern, the white ground with a printed flower design, hand-enamelled in green, yellow and blue, printed factory marks to underside.

5.5in (14cm) high

£350-450 **ROS**

A Clarice Cliff 'Crocus' preserve pot, with painted "Bizarre" mark.

c1930 *3in (8cm) high*

£120-180 **SWO**

A set of three Clarice Cliff 'Crocus' cups and saucers and a side plate, with printed mark.

£180-220 **WW**

A Clarice Cliff Bizarre 'Blue Crocus' preserve and cover, with printed marks, restored finial.

4.25in (11cm) high

£280-320 **WW**

A Clarice Cliff 'Orange Crocus' sugar sifter, with printed mark, minor nick.

5in (13cm) high

£400-600 **WW**

A Clarice Cliff 'Delecia' cauldron, with printed mark.

3in (7.5cm) high

£150-200 **WW**

A Clarice Cliff Bizarre 'Double V' vase, shape number 368, with printed mark.

8.25in (21cm) high

£500-700 **WW**

A rare Clarice Cliff Bizarre 'Football' conical milk jug, with printed mark.

4in (10cm) high

£1,000-1,500 **WW**

A Clarice Cliff Bizarre 'Fragrance' cauldron, with printed mark.

4.25in (11cm) high

£300-500 **WW**

A Clarice Cliff Fantasque Bizarre 'Orange Gardenia' cube inkwell, shape number 458, with printed factory marks.

2.25in (5.5cm) high

£200-300 **WW**

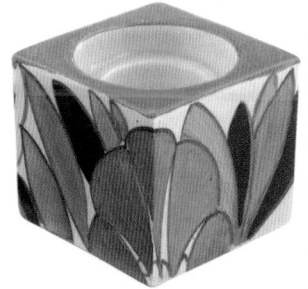

A Clarice Cliff Bizarre 'Gayday' sardine dish and cover, of oblong form, the handle in the form of a sardine, with black printed Newport Pottery mark.

5in (13cm) wide

£500-700 **DNT**

A Clarice Cliff Fantasque Bizarre 'Gibraltar' trumpet vase, shape number 280, with printed mark.

6.25in (16cm) high

£1,500-2,000 **WW**

A Clarice Cliff Fantasque Bizarre 'House and Bridge' orange preserve and cover, with printed mark.

3.25in (8cm) high

£320-380 **WW**

A Clarice Cliff Bizarre 'Blue Japan' plate, with printed mark, faint crack.

9in (23cm) diam

£120-180 **WW**

A Clarice Cliff Bizarre 'Killarney' preserve and cover, shape number 230, with printed mark.

3.5in (9cm) high

£180-220 **WW**

A Clarice Cliff Bizarre 'Applique Lucerne' conical bowl, with printed mark.

6in (15cm) diam

£1,000-1,500 **WW**

A CLOSER LOOK AT A CLARICE CLIFF FANTASQUE BIZARRE VASE

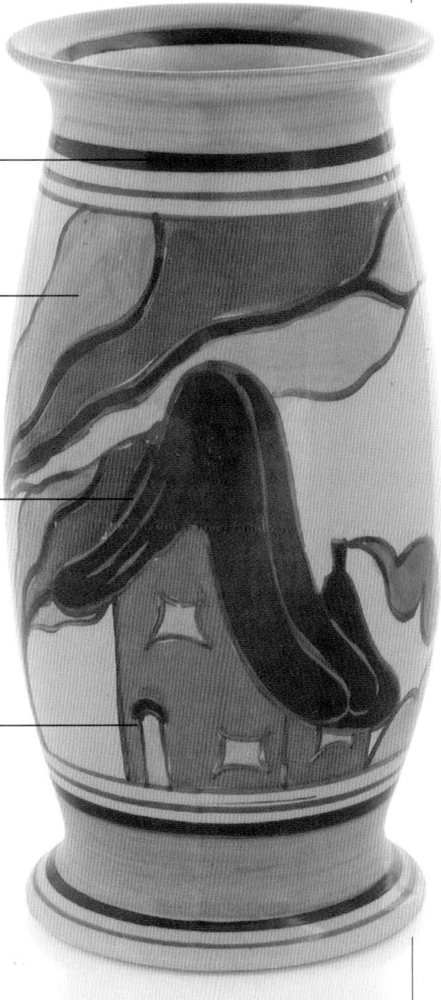

This is a basic shape that was used by A.J. Wilkinson before Clarice Cliff began to design her own range of wares.

At 6in (15.5cm) high, this vase is an ideal size for display. Collectors will often pay a premium for pieces that can be displayed easily and show a designer's work to its best advantage.

Clarice Cliff ceramics are hand-decorated, and collectors will pay close attention to the quality of painting on individual items. The skill of the artist responsible for this particular piece makes it more valuable.

The 'Orange House' pattern is relatively scarce and sought-after by collectors. Produced between 1930-32, it depicts a distorted landscape in bold, unnatural colours, typical of Cliff.

A Clarice Cliff Fantasque Bizarre 'Orange House' vase, shape number 265, with printed mark.

6in (15.5cm) high

£2,200-2,800 **WW**

A Clarice Cliff Bizarre 'Latona Tree' wall charger, with printed and painted marks.

17.75in (45cm) diam

£1,800-2,200 **WW**

A Clarice Cliff Bizarre 'Marguerite' conical sugar caster, pierced above orange and green lines, the base moulded and painted with flowerheads, with printed marks.

5.25in (13.5cm) high

£280-320 **CHEF**

A Clarice Cliff 'Pastel Melon' beehive preserve and cover, with printed mark.

4in (10cm) high

£500-700 **WW**

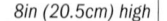

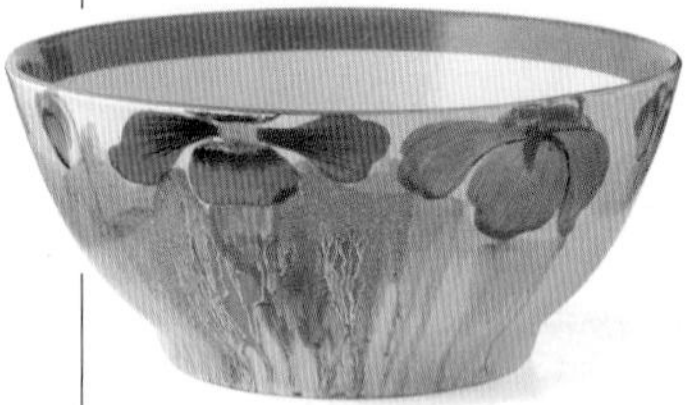

A Clarice Cliff Bizarre 'Delecia Poppy' bowl, painted with poppies in red, yellow and purple, with printed factory mark.

8.75in (22cm) diam

£150-200 **DN**

A Clarice Cliff Bizarre 'Poplar' octagonal bowl, with printed factory marks to underside.

7in (18cm) diam

£220-280 **ROS**

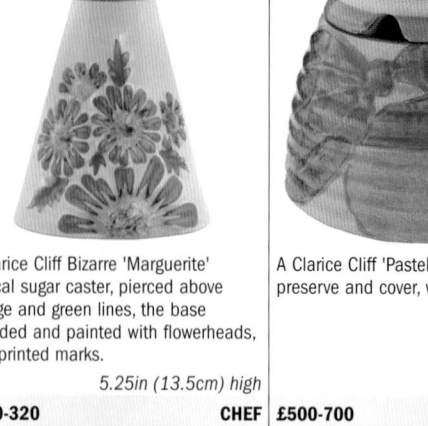

A Clarice Cliff Bizarre 'New Flag' vase, shape number 362, with printed mark, minor restoration to top rim.

8in (20.5cm) high

£400-600 **WW**

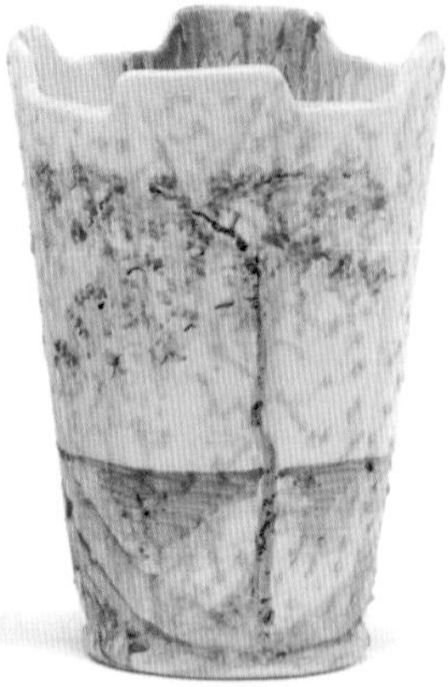

A Clarice Cliff 'Patina' vase.

6in (15cm) high

£400-600 **FRE**

A Clarice Cliff 'Patina Mushroom' vase.

5.5in (14cm) high

£400-600 **FRE**

A Clarice Cliff Bizarre 'Delecia Poppy' Lotus jug, painted with poppies in yellow, red and purple, with printed factory marks.

11.5in (29cm) high

£800-1,200 **DN**

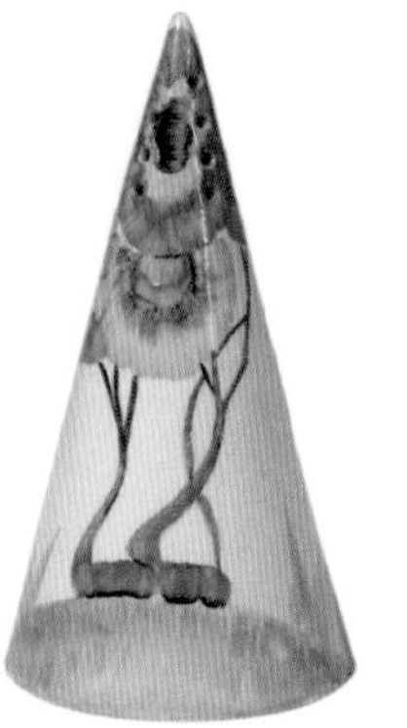

A Clarice Cliff 'Rhodanthe' sugar sifter, with printed marks.

5.25in (13.5cm) high

£250-300 **SWO**

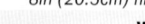

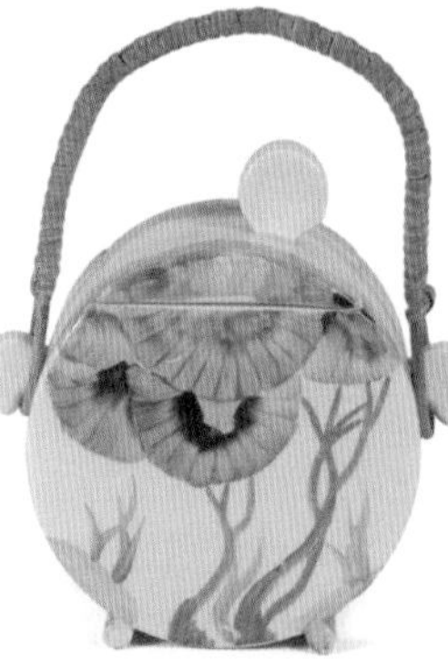

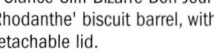

A Clarice Cliff Bizarre Bon Jour 'Rhodanthe' biscuit barrel, with detachable lid.

£400-600 **BIG**

A Clarice Cliff Fantasque Bizarre 'Red Roofs' Isis vase, with printed mark.

10in (25.5cm) high

£1,800-2,200 **WW**

A Clarice Cliff Fantasque Bizarre 'Red Roofs' meiping vase, with printed mark.

12.25in (31cm) high

£2,200-2,800 **WW**

A Clarice Cliff Bizarre 'Red Roofs' vase, shape number 360, with printed marks.

8in (20cm) high

£1,500-2,000 **SWO**

A Clarice Cliff Fantasque Bizarre 'Red Summerhouse' conical sugar basin, with printed mark.

3in (7.5cm) diam

£300-500 **WW**

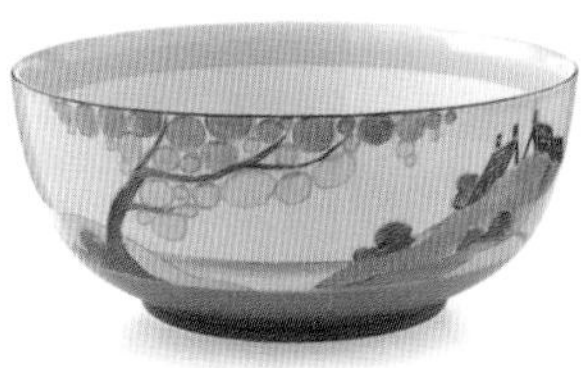

A Clarice Cliff 'Secrets' bowl, printed mark, minor restoration.

8.5in (21.5cm) diam

£180-220 **WW**

A Clarice Cliff Fantasque Bizarre 'Trees and House' Stamford tea set, with printed marks, some damage.

1931

£2,200-2,800 **SWO**

A Clarice Cliff Fantasque 'Umbrellas and Rain' teapot, painted in yellow, orange and blue.

5.25in (13.5cm) high

£280-320 **GORL**

A Clarice Cliff Bizarre 'Woodland' bowl, with printed outline, enamelled blue and purple flowers and a tree.

£280-320 **ROS**

Part of a Clarice Cliff Bizarre 61-piece tea and dinner service, comprising teapot and stand, hot water jug, sugar bowl, milk jug, six tea cups and saucers, and various plates and bowls, with gilt polka dot decoration.

Stand 16.25in (41cm) wide

£1,000-1,500 set **DNT**

A pair of Clarice Cliff teddy bear book ends, on square bases, with printed marks.

6.25in (16cm) high

£1,500-2,000 **WW**

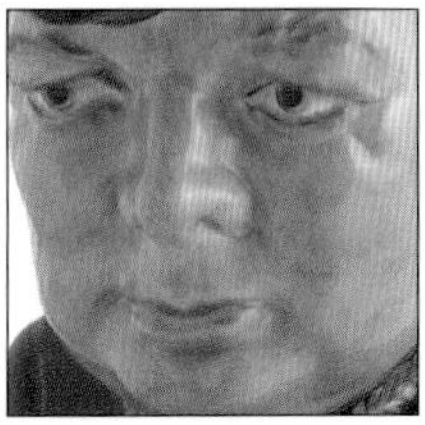

A 'Sir Winston Churchill' Toby jug, designed by Clarice Cliff, modelled seated in navy uniform, with printed marks, chipped.

11.75in (30cm) high

£1,200-1,800 **WW**

WILLIAM DE MORGAN

- A central figure in the British Arts and Crafts movement, William de Morgan (1839-1917) was a stained glass designer before he became interested in ceramics.
- Common motifs in his work include flora and fauna, usually stylized and frequently in grotesque forms. He was inspired by medieval Persian and Moorish design.
- De Morgan experimented with lustre glazes at his pottery at Chelsea, established in 1872. His method for transferring designs to tiles while maintaining the individuality of each one continues to remain a mystery.
- Having originally taken in blanks from other companies to decorate, de Morgan began to produce his own ceramics after he relocated to William Morris' Merton Abbey Workshops in 1882.
- From 1888, de Morgan worked from a pottery at Sands End in Fulham. It was here that he developed the Moonlight and Sunlight series of double- and triple-lustred ceramics.
- Driven from Britain by the damp climate, de Morgan spent the last part of his career in Florence, working for Cantagalli.

A William de Morgan tile panel, of the pattern used for the companionway frieze on Cunard's liner 'Arabia'.

This panel was probably made for an archive or as a spare and was not actually used on the 'Arabia'.

c1890 *34.5in (87.5cm) high*

£12,000-15,000 **PC**

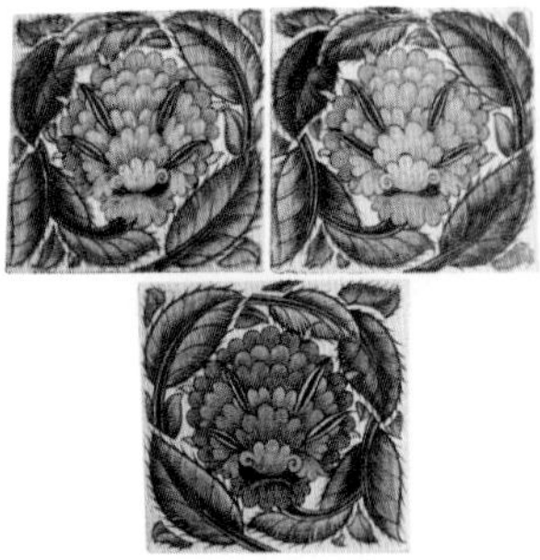

Three William de Morgan 'Cavendish' pattern tiles, the backs impressed with circular "DM 98" mark.

6.25in (16cm) wide

£1,000-1,500 **SWO**

Four William de Morgan 'India' pattern tiles, the backs impressed with circular marks for "Sands End, Fulham Pottery" and rose marks.

These tiles were commissioned by the architect T.E. Colcutt for the companionway frieze on the P&O ship 'India'.

c1895 *9in (23cm) wide*

£2,000-3,000 **SWO**

A William de Morgan 'Peacock' pattern tile.

9in (23cm) wide

£1,500-2,000 **PC**

Three William de Morgan pottery tiles, decorated with chrysanthemums in green, blue and white, impressed with Fulham marks.

c1880 *6in (15cm) wide*

£1,200-1,800 **SWO**

Three matching William de Morgan 'Persian' design tiles, with stylized pattern of fish in a river with flowers and foliage, decorated in shades of turquoise, green and brown, with "Sand's End Pottery" mark.

6in (15cm) wide

£1,500-2,000 **GORL**

A William de Morgan square tile, finely painted in underglaze blue with a bird, with impressed rose head mark.

This tile dates from de Morgan's early Fulham period.

c1890 *6in (15cm) wide*

£1,500-2,000 **LFA**

A William de Morgan circular charger, decorated by Charles Passenger, with a fantastical winged beast reserved on a foliate ground with painted marks for "W. De Morgan & Co. C.P."

c1890 *16in (40cm) diam*

£14,000-18,000 **L&T**

A William de Morgan pottery bowl, painted by Fred Passenger, decorated in ruby lustre with scaly fish to the interior, painted mark "FP".

7.5in (19cm) diam

£1,500-2,000 **WW**

A William de Morgan ovoid vase, with straight neck, painted in Persian style with panels of flowerheads and leaves, with decorator's monogram "JH", restored.

9.25in (23.5cm) high

£600-900 **LFA**

A Doulton Lambeth stoneware vase, decorated by Arthur Barlow, incised with stylized leaves in indigo, amber and green, with ovoid stamp "1873/ABB/944/GHT".

1873 *7.5in (19cm) high*

£600-900 **DRA**

A Doulton Lambeth gourd-shaped stoneware vase, decorated by Arthur Barlow, incised with a zig-zag pattern and covered in indigo and amber glaze, with oval stamp "1875/ABB/718/LG".

1875 *9.5in (24cm) high*

£600-900 **DRA**

A large Doulton Lambeth stoneware vase, decorated with horses by Hannah Barlow, dated.

1881 *16.5in (42cm) high*

£700-1,000 **JN**

A Doulton Lambeth stoneware pitcher, decorated by Hannah Barlow in sgraffito with a mother cat surrounded by kittens, with floriform stamp "HBB/AB/2280/MA/782".

c1890 *6.5in (16cm) high*

£1,500-2,000 **DRA**

An early 20thC Doulton Lambeth shouldered vase, decorated by Hannah Barlow with ponies, everted rim, restored.

15.25in (38.5cm) high

£1,000-1,500 **ROS**

A pair of Doulton Lambeth vases, by Frank A. Butler, with sgraffito foliate scrolling decoration and raised floral medallions, with impressed marks "F.A.B. & A.O." and rosette mark.

1884 *largest 9.25in (23.5cm) high*

£700-1,000 **SWO**

A Doulton Lambeth stoneware bowl, by Frank Butler, decorated in relief with a continuous scrolling frieze on a pale brown ground, the silver rim inscribed "Walton on Thames Regatta 1891", with impressed marks and incised monogram to base.

1891 *7.75in (20cm) diam*

£300-400 **SWO**

A Doulton Lambeth stoneware pitcher, carved by Frank Butler with stylized leaves, pods and whiplash elements, covered in brown and green glaze, with floriform stamp "England/FAB/299".

c1895 *7in (17.5cm) high*

£600-900 **DRA**

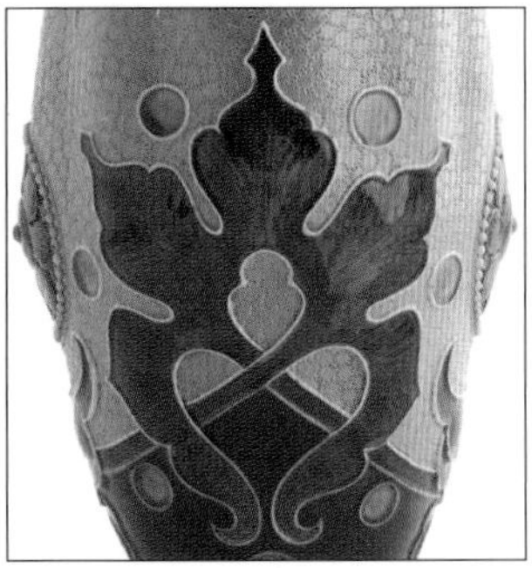

An early 20thC Doulton Lambeth foliate form ewer, by Frank Butler, with shaped rim, enriched with highly stylized foliate fronds and flowers, restored.

12in (30.5cm) high

£280-320 **ROS**

A Doulton Lambeth faience pottery jardinière, by Florence Lewis, painted with panels of flowers on a turquoise ground, with impressed mark and Mortlock paper label to base.

11.5in (29cm) diam

£220-280 **DN**

A Doulton Lambeth stoneware bowl, by Mark V. Marshall, the three feet modelled as cherubs, incised with panels of fish, a squirrel, a kingfisher and a swan, with silver rim by Hukin & Heath, marked and signed, some damage.

1880 *7.75in (20cm) diam*

£1,200-1,800 **WW**

A pair of Doulton Lambeth stoneware vases, by Bessie Newbery, decorated with scrolling flowers and foliage, with impressed marks.

10.75in (27cm) high

£250-300 **WW**

A Doulton Lambeth Carrara ware vase, painted by Kate Rogers with orange and yellow flowers reserved on a cream ground.

£120-150 **DN**

A Doulton Lambeth stoneware pitcher, decorated by George Tinworth in the scroll work style, with hinged silver lid, with oval stamp and artist's cipher.

c1870 *11in (27.5cm) high*

£700-1,000 **DRA**

A Doulton Lambeth stoneware vase, by George Tinworth, with trumpet body and applied mice playing drum and pan pipes, raised on a stepped oval base, with impressed marks and incised monogram.

5in (13cm) high

£2,000-2,500 **DN**

A Doulton Lambeth stoneware menu holder, by George Tinworth, modelled as mice playing a harp and an accordion, raised on an oval base, with incised marks and artist's monogram.

3.75in (9.5cm) high

£1,000-1,500 **DN**

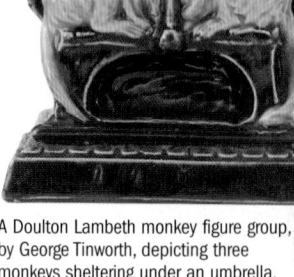

A Doulton Lambeth monkey figure group, by George Tinworth, depicting three monkeys sheltering under an umbrella, incised "Busy", with impressed marks and incised monogram, restored.

4.75in (12cm) high

£1,500-2,000 **DN**

A Doulton Lambeth Silicon ware chess pawn, attributed to George Tinworth, in the form of a seated mouse wearing a peaked cap, on a circular base, with impressed marks.

2.5in (6.5cm) high

£500-700 **DN**

A rectangular stoneware plaque, by George Tinworth, depicting two biblical scenes, inscribed "The Wise and The Foolish", with quotations inscribed to the frame, marked "H.DOULTON LAMBETH, G. TINWORTH SC".

8.5in (21cm) wide

£700-1,000 **SWO**

A Doulton Lambeth stoneware vase, naturalistically painted with bees and wild flowers, with impressed marks and artist's cipher.

11.75in (30cm) high

£350-400 **WW**

A Doulton Lambeth faience vase and cover, with dedicatory inscription to H.R.H. The Prince of Wales and H.R.H. The Duke of York, marked, finial glued.

18in (46cm) high

£220-280 **DN**

A pair of Doulton Lambeth faience vases, of baluster form, decorated with poppies against an orange, crimson and purple background, with "HK" and "MW" monograms, numbered "99".

c1900 *11.5in (29cm) high*

£700-1,000 **SWO**

A Doulton Lambeth stoneware owl jar and cover, with impressed marks, restored.

1883 *7.75in (19.5cm) high*

£1,000-1,500 **WW**

A Doulton Lambeth stoneware clock, the case decorated with winged female masks, garlands, dancing putti and surmounted by two deer.

13.5in (34.5cm) high

£1,800-2,200 **JN**

A Royal Doulton stoneware vase, by Hannah Barlow, incised with a band of horses.

11in (28cm) high

£400-600 **JN**

A Royal Doulton Lambeth stoneware vase, by Hannah Barlow, incised with a central band of ponies, within borders of stylized flowers, with impressed factory mark and incised decorator's initials.

11.25in (28.5cm) high

£600-900 **DN**

A Royal Doulton stoneware vase, by Hannah Barlow, incised with a band of ponies before mountains, the interior glazed in blue, with impressed factory mark and incised artist's initials.

6.25in (16cm) high

£800-1,200 **ROS**

A Royal Doulton vase, decorated by Hannah Barlow, with goats within Art Nouveau brown and blue glazed borders and incised and impressed marks.

1881 *29cm (11.5in) high*

£500-800 **SWO**

A Royal Doulton vase, decorated by Hannah Barlow, with ponies in a mountainous landscape within blue and green glazed borders, with incised and impressed marks.

c1880 *13.5in (34cm) high*

£800-1,200 **SWO**

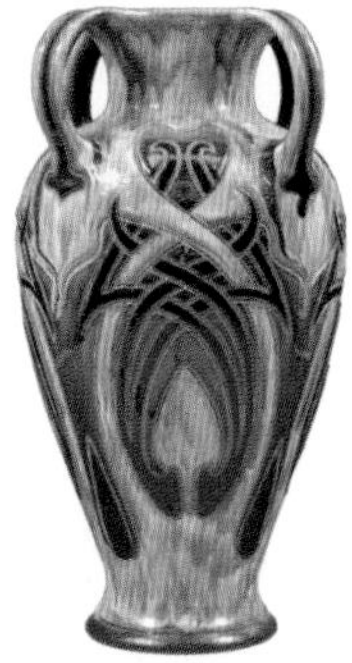

A Royal Doulton four-handled stoneware vase, by Frank Butler, incised and painted in colours, with incised and impressed marks, restored handles.

15.25in (38cm) high

£350-400 **SWO**

A large Royal Doulton stoneware vase, by Vera Huggins, painted in colours and gilt with flowers, with impressed marks and artist's cypher.

15.25in (38.5cm) high

£180-220 **WW**

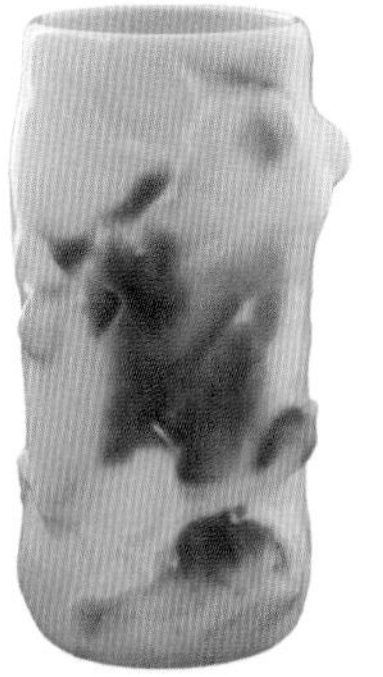

A Royal Doulton cylindrical Jade vase, by Charles Noke, with printed mark and painted signature.

6in (15.5cm) high

£1,000-1,500 **WW**

A rare pair of Royal Doulton 'Lapis' vases, probably by Charles Noke, modelled in low relief with prunus sprays, with printed marks, one with paper retail label.

3.25in (8cm) high

£500-800 **WW**

A pair of Royal Doulton stoneware vases, by Eliza Simmance, tubeline decorated with friezes of fruiting vine, with impressed marks and artist's monogram.

13.5in (34cm) high

£800-1,200 **WW**

A CLOSER LOOK AT A ROYAL DOULTON VASE

This vase was made for Royal Doulton's display at the 1893 World's Columbian Exhibition in Chicago. A demonstrable link with such an important event in the world of decorative arts inevitably increases the value.

The elaborately moulded floral forms surrounding the body of this vase are by Charles Noke. Especially well known for his figures, he was one of Royal Doulton's premier designers.

The quality of the decoration is excellent. It was painted by two of Royal Doulton's best artists, working from an original by Auguste Renoir.

Despite the stapled repair to the base, restoration and damage, the piece remains very desirable.

A Doulton Burslem 'Diana' Vase, modelled by Charles Noke and painted by George White and Fred Hancock with the adoration of Diana the Huntress, flanked by griffin handles, raised on a pedestal foot decorated with mask motifs, with printed marks, some damage and restoration.

c1895 *39.5in (100.5cm) high*

£10,000-15,000 **FRE**

A Royal Doulton jug, commemorating the 100th anniversary of Lord Nelson's death, with a moulded relief portrait and views of the Battle of Trafalgar, inscribed "England expects every man will do his duty".

c1905 *8in (20cm) high*

£350-400 **SWO**

One of a pair of Royal Doulton baluster vases, incised with panels of blue, white and gold enamelled chrysanthemums on a beige textured ground, with stamped marks.

11in (28cm) high

£500-700 pair **DRA**

A Royal Doulton stoneware vase, applied with stylized flower and leaf motifs against a mottled green glazed ground.

£200-300 **DN**

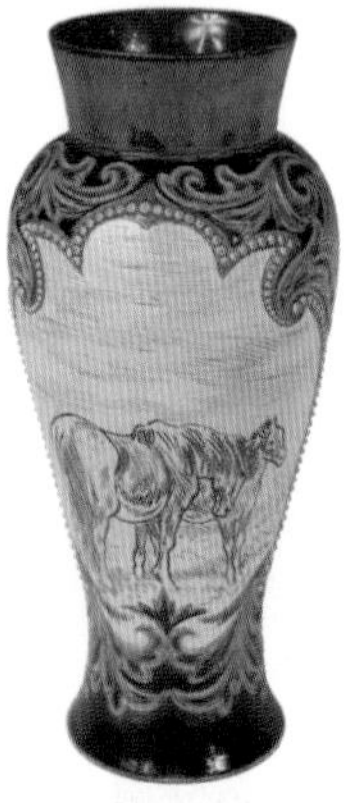

A Royal Doulton vase, decorated with panels of donkeys and ponies within moulded blue and green glazed Art Nouveau borders, with impressed and incised marks, restored.

1881 *11in (28cm) high*

£500-700 **SWO**

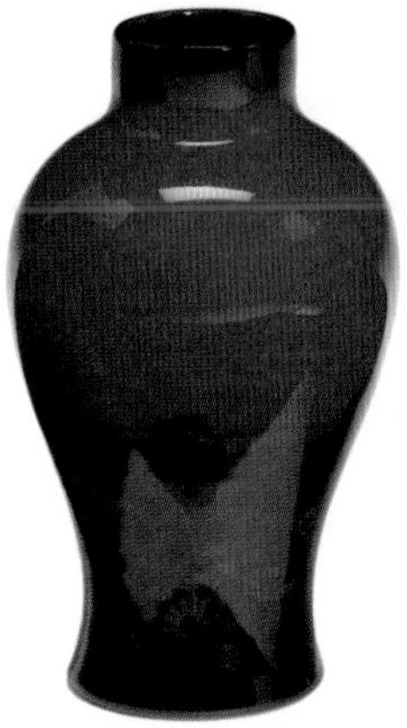

A Royal Doulton flambé baluster vase, glazed in deep red and black, depicting a pastoral scene, with painted artist's monogram "FN" and underglaze black mark.

c1910 *6in (15cm) high*

£80-120 **FRE**

A Royal Doulton veined flambé vase, shape number 1618, with red neck and shoulder trailing into a mottled blue ground body, with black printed factory marks.

c1940 *10in (25.5cm) high*

£100-150 **SWO**

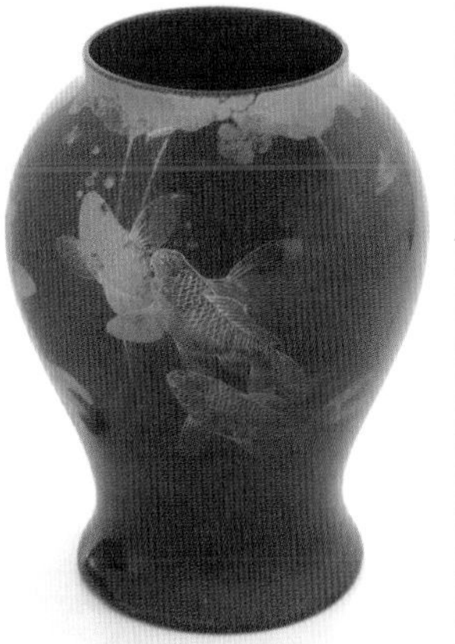

A Royal Doulton flambé baluster vase, decorated with carp, with incised number "1042".

7in (18cm) high

£400-600 **GORL**

A Royal Doulton Lambeth stoneware figure of a water nymph, seated on a globe beside a lizard, the base supported by frogs, painted with glazes, impressed factory marks.

13in (33cm) high

£1,000-1,500 **DN**

A Royal Doulton figure, 'Pierrette' by L. Harradine, model number HN644, with printed and painted marks.

7.5in (18.5cm) high

£700-1,000 **WW**

A large Royal Doulton figure 'The Moor' by Charles Noke, model number HN 2082, with printed and painted marks

17in (42cm) high

£800-1,200 **WW**

A Royal Doulton figure, 'Butterfly Girl', model number HN720, with printed and painted marks, restored arm.

£800-1,200 **WW**

A Royal Doulton figure, 'Master Sweep', model number HN2205.

£220-280 **SWO**

A rare Royal Doulton figure, 'Lady with Rose' by E.W. Light, model number HN52A, with factory printed and inscribed marks, hairline crack.

c1930 *10in (25.5cm) high*

£1,200-1,800 **SWO**

GEORGE JONES

- After working for Minton for a number of years, George Jones established his own pottery at Stoke-on-Trent in 1871 where he worked with his seven sons.
- George Jones majolica wares are very similar to those produced by Minton, although the pink and turquoise glazes used in the interiors are of lighter shades.
- Collectors are attracted to the strong naturalistic designs of Jones' majolica, which feature motifs ranging from trestled strawberry plants to marine scenes watched over by seabird finials.
- More outlandish designs include a cheese dish in the form of a castle turret covered with vines, with a flag blowing in the breeze acting as the finial.
- Often marked with a "GJ" monogram, George Jones majolica can also be identified by the distinctive muddy green underglaze the firm frequently used, although this was imitated by rivals.
- George Jones died in 1893 but his firm continued to operate until 1907 when it was renamed as the Crescent Pottery.

One of a set of three George Jones majolica low round tazze, the blue ground rim moulded with flowerheads, leaves and scrolls, with impressed marks, one with rim crack.

c1870 *8.75in (22cm) diam*

£400-600 **LFA**

A George Jones majolica strawberry set, depicting a bird sitting between two nests, the shaped base with strawberry leaves and flowers in relief, marked.

c1870 *10.75in (27.5cm) wide*

£800-1,200 **JN**

A George Jones majolica dish, moulded with vine leaves and with a fox's head and tail applied to the rim, registration mark.

1869 *10.5in (26cm) wide*

£220-280 **WW**

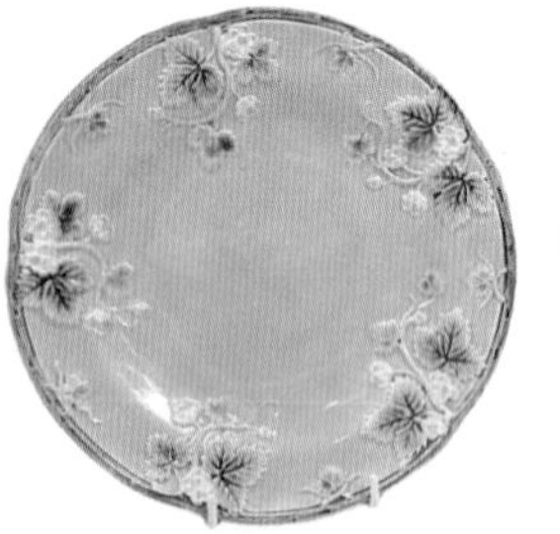

One of a pair of George Jones majolica plates, moulded with strawberry blossom on a light blue ground.

c1870 *8.25in (21cm) wide*

£280-320 pair **SWO**

A George Jones majolica tray, of shaped rectangular form, the centre moulded with a butterfly, bee and dragonfly around a central wheat stem, within a basket weave border.

c1870 *13in (33cm) wide*

£700-1,000 **ROS**

A George Jones majolica cheese dome and stand, moulded with prunus and a wicker fence, with impressed marks.

c1875 *9.75in (25cm) high*

£1,000-1,500 **WW**

A George Jones majolica sardine dish and cover, decorated with panels of fish and foliage, framed by bamboo, the lid decorated with cranes, with impressed marks, crane finial reglued.

c1875 *6in (15cm) diam*

£800-1,200 **SWO**

A George Jones majolica butter dish, with duck handle to cover, the base moulded with fish, seaweed and coral against a light blue ground, damaged.

6in (15cm) wide

£800-1,200 **GORL**

A George Jones majolica part tea service, comprising a teapot and cover, sugar bowl and cover, milk jug and three saucers, each piece moulded with blossoming briars on a deep blue ground, the handles in the form of monkeys, with moulded marks.

c1875 *teapot 6in (15cm) high*

£2,000-2,500 **SWO**

A Minton majolica nut dish, in the form of a squirrel perched on the edge of a leaf nibbling a hazelnut, chipped.

1870 *5.5in (14cm) high*

£280-320 **ROS**

A Minton majolica nut dish, with a partial cover modelled as chestnut leaves and fruit, with impressed mark and date code, some restoration.

1869 *11.25in (28cm) wide*

£500-800 **WW**

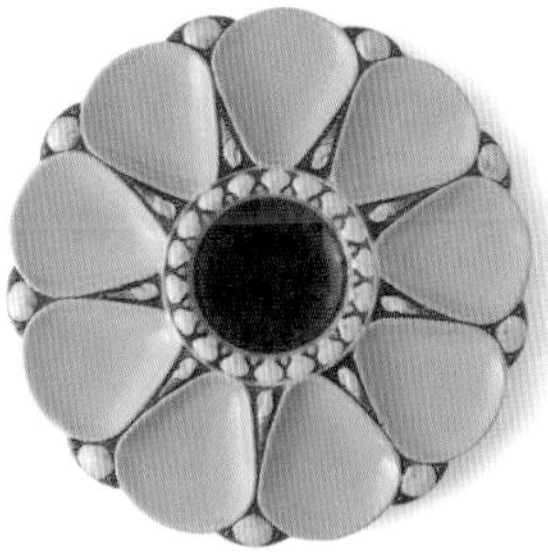

A Minton majolica oyster dish, modelled with nine dished sections within bands of scallop and oyster shells, painted with coloured glazes, with impressed marks and date code.

1867 *9.75in (25cm) diam*

£400-600 **DN**

A Minton majolica comport, modelled as two putti holding a shaped dish, with impressed marks and date code, restored.

1864 *8.75in (22.5cm) high*

£400-600 **SWO**

A Minton majolica four-tier oyster stand, of tapered form with oyster-shell dished sections surmounted by an entwined fish handle, on a revolving base, unmarked, chipped.

c1865 *11in (28cm) high*

£3,000-4,000 **DN**

A Minton majolica twin-handled oval pie dish, cover and liner, modelled in relief with twigs, leaves and berries and animals including hare and pheasant in flight, with impressed factory and date marks.

1874 *14.25in (36cm) wide*

£2,200-2,800 **L&T**

A Minton majolica sweetmeat basket, modelled with two cherubs holding an oval pail, raised on an oval base, impressed mark, restored.

1866 *11.5in (29cm) wide*

£220-280 **WW**

A Minton majolica helmet-shaped salt, painted with coloured glazes, shape number 1571, with impressed marks.

c1855 *3.5in (9cm) wide*

£200-300 **DN**

A rare Minton tortoise teapot and cover, modelled naturalistically with a seashell upon the cover, with moulded and printed marks.

c1895 *8.5in (21.5cm) wide*

£2,000-3,000 **WW**

A Minton majolica box and cover, modelled with a sailor drinking from a tankard and seated on coils of rope, with impressed marks and date code, chipped.

1906 *9.25in (23cm) high*

£1,500-2,000 **WW**

A Minton majolica hexagonal garden seat, decorated with moulded stylized flower and foliate decoration in orange, white and green on a brown ground, with impressed marks.

1871 *20in (51cm) high*

£2,500-3,000 **L&T**

A Brown-Westhead, Moore & Co. novelty majolica desk stand, modelled with a terrier's head flanked by two inkwells and pen tray, in shades of white, brown, green, red and blue, on bun feet, with impressed motto.

11.5in (29cm) wide

£700-1,000 **GORL**

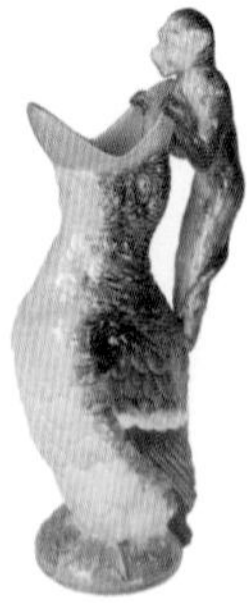

A William Brownfield majolica jug, in the form of a bird with a monkey, with impressed mark and numbers.

c1875 *13.5in (34.5cm)*

£700-1,000 **SWO**

A Joseph Holdcroft majolica teapot and cover, modelled with a boy clambering over a massive coconut, with impressed mark, damaged.

c1880 *7.5in (19cm) high*

£100-200 **WW**

A Royal Worcester majolica shell vase, modelled as a conical shell-formed cup supported on a dolphin and bullrush stem, painted with coloured glazes, with impressed mark, hairline crack to base.

c1865 *4.25in (11cm) high*

£200-300 **DN**

A Joseph Holdcroft majolica strawberry dish, comprising a jug, sugar bowl and two spoons, decorated with coloured glazes and a gold finch surmount, with impressed registration mark, some damage.

c1870 *11.5in (29cm) wide*

£1,000-1,500 **WW**

A Wedgwood majolica part dessert service, comprising a footed stand and three dessert plates with email ombrant centres, with impressed marks and date codes, damaged.

c1875 *8.5in (21.5cm) diam*

£300-500 **DRA**

A Wedgwood majolica vase, decorated with Bacchus masks and vine fruits.

9.25in (23.5cm) high

£150-200 **CA**

A Wedgwood majolica entree dish, of tripartite form, each section modelled as a scallop shell, with central seaweed handle.

15.25in (38.5cm) wide

£1,000-1,500 **ROS**

A Martin Brothers stoneware vase, by Robert Wallace Martin, incised with Classical foliage in shades of ochre, incised "6-1890 R W Martin & Brothers, London & Southall".

1890 *10.25in (26cm) high*

£800-1,200 **WW**

A Martin Brothers stoneware vase, incised with lizards amongst scrolling Classical foliage, in shades of ochre and brown on a blue ground, incised "8-1891 R W Martin & Bros, London & Southall".

1891 *7in (18cm) high*

£1,800-2,200 **WW**

A Martin Brothers stoneware vase, incised with fighting dragons on a brown ground, incised "8-1898, Martin Bros London & Southall", with exhibition paper labels, restored.

1898 *9.75in (24.5cm) high*

£1,500-2,000 **WW**

A Martin Brothers stoneware vase, incised with three grotesque birds amongst wild flowers, dragonflies and insects, incised "1893, Martin Bros, London & Southall", restored.

1893 *10.75in (27cm) high*

£3,500-4,500 **WW**

A large pair of Martin Brothers stoneware vases, by Robert Wallace Martin, incised with large scaly grotesque fish and sea creatures, incised "2-1897, R W Martin & Bros London & Southall".

1897 *13in (33cm) high*

£10,000-15,000 **WW**

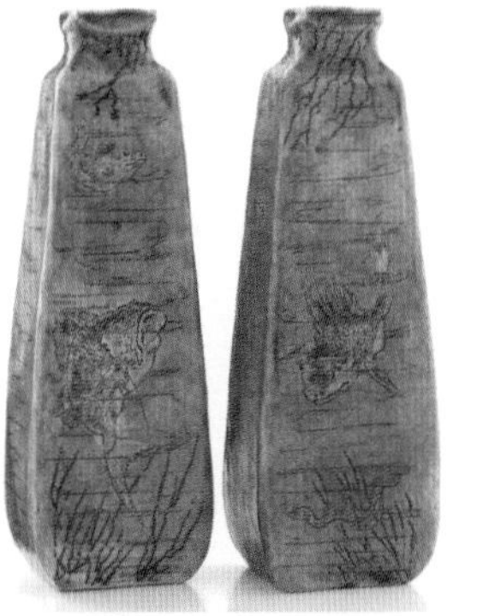

A pair of Martin Brothers stoneware vases, incised with fish, jellyfish and an eel, in shades of ochre and green on a blue ground, incised "10-1903 Martin Bros, London & Southall".

1903 *6in (15.5cm) high*

£3,500-4,500 **WW**

A Martin Brothers stoneware vase, incised with insects flying around wild flowers in green and blue on an ochre ground, incised "2-1905, Martin Bros London & Southall".

1905 *7.25in (18.5cm) high*

£1,500-2,000 **WW**

A Martin Brothers stoneware vase, incised with grotesque fish, in shades of blue and green on a rich blue ground, incised "10 -1911 Martin Bros London & Southall", restored.

1911 *10.5in (26.5cm) high*

£1,000-1,500 **WW**

A Martin Brothers stoneware ewer, by Robert Wallace Martin, deeply incised with stylized foliage, incised "18.8.81 R W Martin, London & Southall".

1881 *9.25in (23.5cm) high*

£1,500-2,000 **WW**

A Martin Brothers stoneware jug, by Robert Wallace Martin, incised with various grotesque fish and shellfish amongst weed, incised "10-88 R W Martin & Bros, London & Southall", restored.

1888 *9.75in (25cm) high*

£2,500-3,000 **WW**

A Martin Brothers stoneware Eskimo jug, by Robert Wallace Martin, covered in a brown and ochre glaze, incised "Martin, London Southall".

This figure may have been produced to commemorate the polar expeditions of the early 20thC.

13in (33cm) high

£8,000-12,000 **WW**

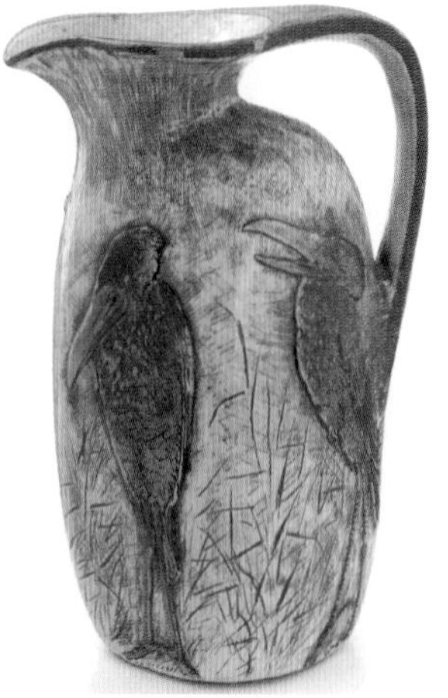

A Martin Brothers stoneware bird jug, carved in low relief with grotesque birds, in shades of green, blue and brown, incised "10-1903 Martin Bros, London & Southall".

1903 *8.75in (22.5cm) high*

£4,000-6,000 **WW**

A Martin Brothers stoneware pitcher, decorated in relief with a face on both sides, incised "Martin Bros. London Southall".

8in (20.5cm) high

£4,000-6,000 **SK**

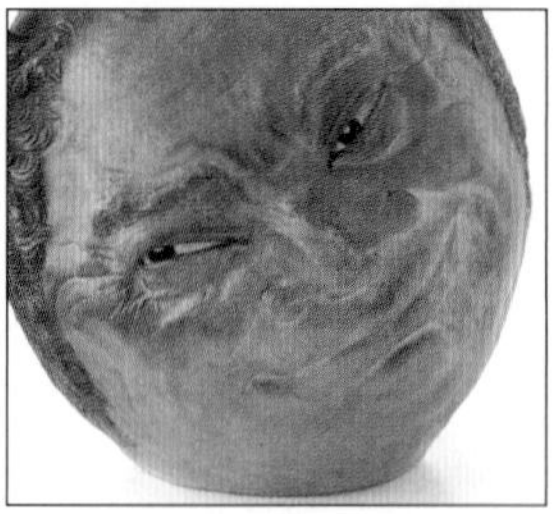

A large Martin Brothers stoneware jug, by Robert Wallace Martin, decorated with smiling faces in shades of brown, incised "R.W.Martin Bros of London & Southall 8.1911".

1911 *8.75in (22cm) high*

£8,000-12,000 **WW**

An unusual Martin Brothers stoneware jug, by Robert Wallace Martin, incised with a smiling face, with over slung handle, incised "10-18 R W Martin & Bros, London & Southall".

7in (18cm) high

£5,000-8,000 **WW**

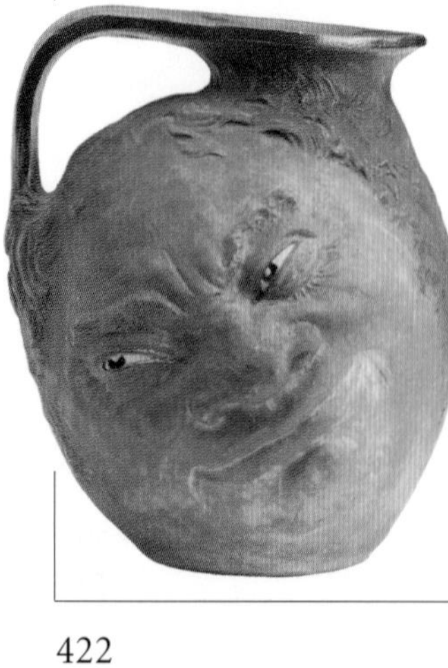

A large Martin Brothers stoneware jug, in dead-matte browns, signed "R.W. Martin & Bros., London & Southall, 4.5.1911, 68".

1911 *9in (22.5cm) high*

£6,000-8,000 **DRA**

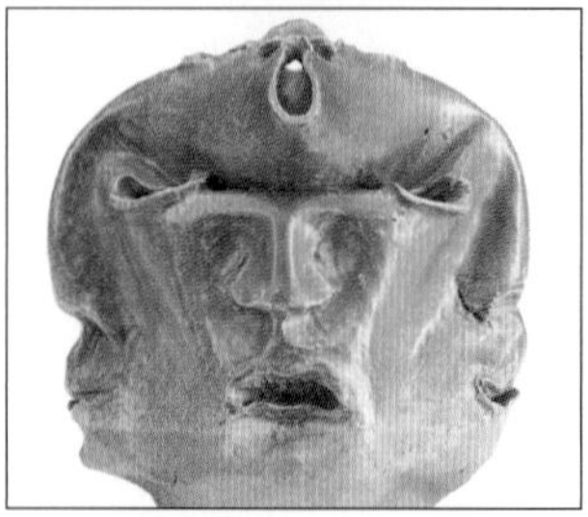

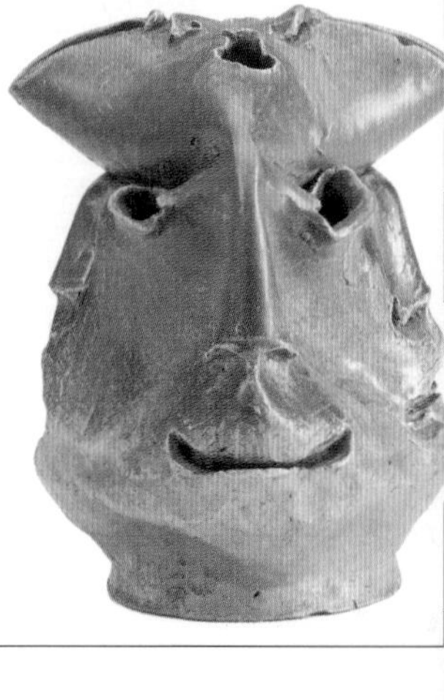

An unusual Martin Brothers sculptural stoneware vessel, pinched, dimpled and carved with four expressive faces covered in brown to amber matte glaze, signed "Martin London".

7in (17.5cm) high

£8,000-12,000 **DRA**

A Martin Brothers stoneware bird, modelled with short beak and large rounded eyes, in shades of brown and ochre, incised "3-1890 Martin Bros London & Southall".

1890 *10.75in (27cm) high*

£24,000-28,000 **WW**

An early Martin Brothers stoneware bird jar and cover, by Robert Wallace Martin, with large webbed claws, incised "R.W.Martin & Bros, London & Southall".

The head and neck of early Martin Brothers birds fit together in only one position. Later birds have a simpler fitting that allows the head to rotate.

c1880 *11.75in (30cm) high*

£30,000-40,000 **WW**

A rare Martin Brothers earthenware bird jar and cover, with broad beak and upright pose, glazed in shades of ochre, incised "RW Martin & Bros, London & Southall".

The Martin Brothers experimented with modelling in earthenware for a short time in the 1890s and examples are uncommon.

11in (28cm) high

£22,000-24,000 **WW**

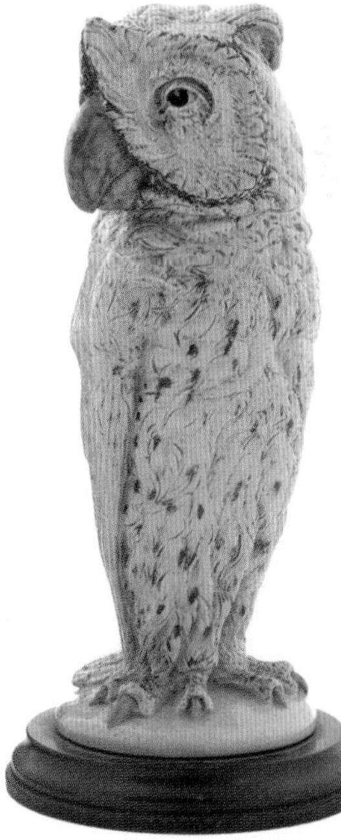

A Martin Brothers stoneware owl jar and cover, by Robert Wallace Martin, on an ebonized wooden base, incised "R.W. Martin & Bros, 3.1.1904 London & Southall".

1904 *11.75in (30cm) high*

£20,000-30,000 **WW**

A Martin Brothers stoneware bird jar and cover, modelled as a standing bird with rueful expression, raised on a turned and ebonized plinth, incised "Martin Bros., London and Southall, 3-1902".

1902 *8.5in (21.5cm) high*

£8,000-12,000 **L&T**

A Martin Brothers stoneware bird jar and cover, modelled with frowning stare, on an ebonized wooden base, incised "Martin Bros, 10-1903, London & Southall", restored.

1903 *8.75in (22cm) high*

£8,000-12,000 **WW**

A Martin Brothers stoneware bird jar and cover, by Robert Wallace Martin, with staring expression over hook nose, incised "R W Martin & Bros, London & Southall 20.6.1904".

1904 *10in (25.5cm) high*

£15,000-20,000 **WW**

A Martin Brothers stoneware bird jar and cover, modelled with broad flat beak and squinting eyes, incised "RW Martin & Bros, London & Southall 19.2.1909", restored.

1909 *9.75in (25cm) high*

£12,000-15,000 **WW**

A Martin Brothers stoneware bird, modelled with sideways glance, covered in a blue glaze, on a wooden base, marked "10-1913 RW Martin, London & Southall".

1913 *8.25in (21cm) high*

£20,000-25,000 **WW**

A CLOSER LOOK AT A MARTIN BROTHERS BIRD GROUP

Martin Brothers birds are extremely popular with collectors and always attract high prices. A set of three birds on a single base is commensurately more desirable.

Only around a dozen similar pieces by the Martin Brothers are known to exist. This rarity, combined with the popularity of these pieces, leads to very high prices.

Each of these birds is excellently modelled. The central figure, with his wings draped around his two companions, has an amusingly avuncular expression.

Robert Wallace Martin had the strongest design experience of the brothers, having studied at Lambeth School of Art and worked as an assistant to Pugin on the Houses of Parliament.

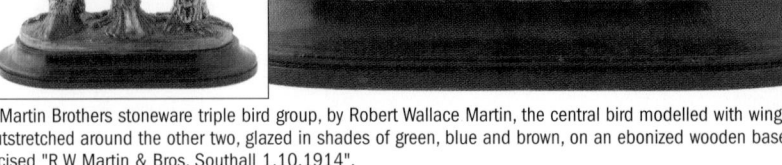

A Martin Brothers stoneware triple bird group, by Robert Wallace Martin, the central bird modelled with wings outstretched around the other two, glazed in shades of green, blue and brown, on an ebonized wooden base, incised "R W Martin & Bros, Southall 1.10.1914".

1914 *7.75in (19.5cm) high*

£40,000-50,000 **WW**

A Martin Brothers stoneware grotesque reptile, unglazed, incised "Martin Bros, London & Southall, 4-1894", chipped.

1894 *5in (13cm) long*

£1,800-2,200 **WW**

A Martin Brothers stoneware grotesque, by Robert Wallace Martin, modelled as a crocodile's head, probably part of a fountain, incised "RWM 1900 Southall".

1900 *4.25in (11cm) high*

£700-1,000 **WW**

A Martin Brothers stoneware grotesque ewer, modelled as a seated creature with gaping mouth, in shades of ochre, restored.

5.5in (14cm) high

£1,500-2,000 **WW**

A Martin Brothers stoneware imp musician, by Robert Wallace Martin, modelled as the conductor, covered in a white glaze, incised "The Imps R W Martin & Bros, London & Southall 4-1906".

1906 *5.75in (14.5cm) high*

£4,000-6,000 **WW**

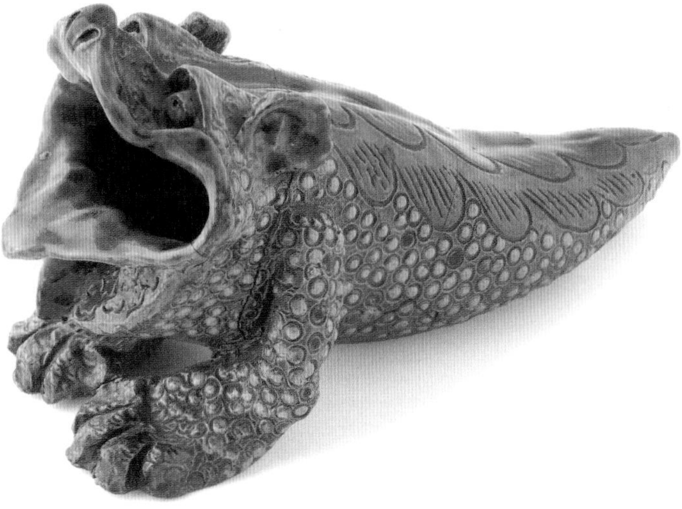

An early Martin Brothers stoneware spoon warmer, by Robert Wallace Martin, modelled as a reptile with gaping mouth, incised "28 R W Martin, London & Southall", firing cracks.

9in (23cm) wide

£5,000-8,000 **WW**

A Martin Brothers stoneware imp musician, by Robert Wallace Martin, modelled as a harp player, covered in a white glaze, incised "R W Martin & Bros, London & Southall 2 1906", restored.

1906 *4.5in (11.5cm) high*

£4,000-6,000 **WW**

A Martin Brothers stoneware imp musician figure, by Robert Wallace Martin, modelled playing the pan pipes, covered in a white glaze, incised "R W Martin & Bros London".

4in (10cm) high

£3,500-4,500 **WW**

A Martin Brothers stoneware imp musician figure, by Robert Wallace Martin, modelled playing the flute, covered in a white glaze, incised "R W Martin & Bros London & Southall 2-1906".

1906 *4.25in (11cm) high*

£4,000-6,000 **WW**

A Martin Brothers stoneware imp musician figure, by Robert Wallace Martin, modelled as a clarinet player, covered in a white glaze, incised "R W Martin London & Southall 3-1906", losses.

1906 *4.25in (11cm) high*

£2,200-2,800 **WW**

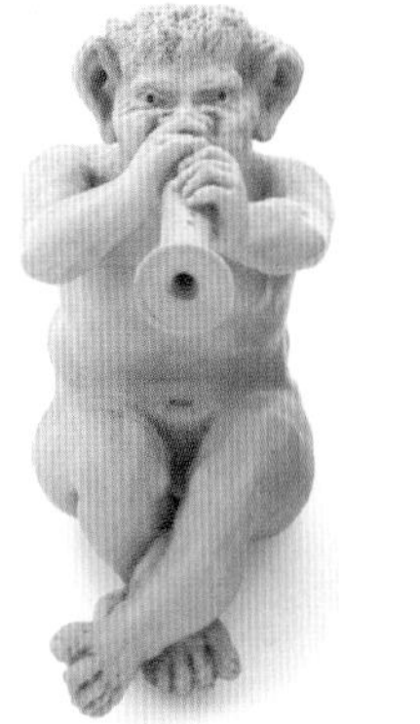

A Martin Brothers stoneware imp musician, by Robert Wallace Martin, modelled as a horn player, covered in a white glaze, incised "Martin Bros London".

4.5in (11.5cm) high

£5,000-8,000 **WW**

THE MARTIN BROTHERS

- The son of a clerk, Robert Wallace Martin (1843-1923) studied at Lambeth School of Art and later enrolled at the Royal Academy of Art.
- After being apprenticed to a sculptor, Robert Martin was employed as an assistant sculptor working on Pugin's designs for the Houses of Parliament.
- Robert Martin founded the Martin Brothers pottery at Lambeth with his brothers Charles, Walter and Edwin in 1873. They relocated to Southall in 1877.
- As the most experienced modeller of the group, Robert Martin was responsible for the majority of the firm's designs, including the famous grotesque birds.
- Martin Brothers pottery is primarily fashioned from stoneware, although the brothers did experiment with earthenware for a short period.
- The brothers enjoyed a degree of success, and counted Queen Victoria among their customers. Favourable press attention helped them to reach a wider audience.
- The pottery eventually closed in 1915 after suffering a series of setbacks including a devastating fire.

A rare Martin Brothers terracotta self portrait plaque, by Robert Wallace Martin, in a wooden frame incised "R W Martin & Bros London & Southall".

c1885 *13in (33cm) wide*

£10,000-15,000 **WW**

A rare Martin Brothers terracotta portrait plaque, of Edwin Martin by Robert Wallace Martin, entitled "Sgrafitto", in a wooden frame, incised to the front "R W Martin Sc Southall Pottery Midd".

13.25in (33.5cm) wide

£10,000-15,000 **WW**

A pair of Martin Brothers stoneware tiles, incised with eels in shades of brown and white on a buff ground, impressed "Martin Brothers London", minor rim nicks.

3in (7.5cm) wide

£700-1,000 **WW**

A Martin Brothers stoneware tile, incised with grotesque scaly fish, in shades of brown and white on a buff ground, impressed "Martin Brothers London", chipped.

3in (7.5cm) wide

£500-800 **WW**

A pair of Martin Brothers stoneware cruets, by Robert Wallace Martin, incised with wild flowers, inscribed "Oil" and "Vinegar", incised "4-1888 R.W.Martin & Bros, London & Southall".

1888 *6in (15.5cm) high*

£1,800-2,200 **WW**

A Martin Brothers stoneware cruet, by Edwin Martin, incised and painted with fish swimming amongst waterweed, incised "8 1890 Martin Bros London & Southall", restored.

1890 *4.25in (11cm) wide*

£700-1,000 **WW**

A Martin Brothers Aesthetic Movement salt-glazed stoneware teapot, incised with stylized daisies, with a gargoyle handle, signed "RW Martin Southall X 6".

8in (20cm) wide

£700-1,000 **DRA**

A Martin Brothers stoneware salad bowl, incised with Classical foliage, inscribed "Vinvm Panis Piper Herba Olevm Sal Ivs Acqu Mel" and incised "9-1898 Martin Brothers, London & Southall".

1898 *10in (25.5cm) diam*

£1,500-2,000 **WW**

A Martin Brothers stoneware jardinière, modelled in low relief with grotesque frogs and reptiles in shades of green on a pale blue ground, incised "12-1908 Martin Bros, London & Southall", restored.

1908 *5in (13cm) high*

£1,000-1,500 **WW**

A Minton encaustic bread plate, designed by A. W. N. Pugin, inlaid with red and blue clays, with stylized wheat ears around a central wheel, the border inscribed "Waste Not Want Not".

This is probably the earliest of Pugin's designs for Herbert Minton.

c1850 *13.5in (34cm)*

£700-1,000 **SWO**

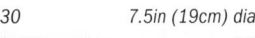

A Minton bone china lustre bowl, printed and painted with a crowing cockerel against a sunrise, with printed mark.

c1930 *7.5in (19cm) diam*

£120-180 **SWO**

A Minton Aesthetic-style porcelain plaque, made for Mortlocks, depicting a semi-clad young lady reclining in a chaise longue, impressed "Minton", with printed and dated Mortlock mark and incised signature.

1876 *20.5in (52cm) high*

£2,000-2,500 **JN**

A pair of Minton cloisonné vases, designed by Dr Christopher Dresser, of twin-handled form, decorated with foliate designs and highlighted in gilt, with impressed marks, some wear.

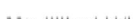

11in (28cm) high

£6,000-9,000 **WW**

A Minton cloisonné vase, designed by Dr Christopher Dresser.

8.25in (21cm) high

£400-600 **WW**

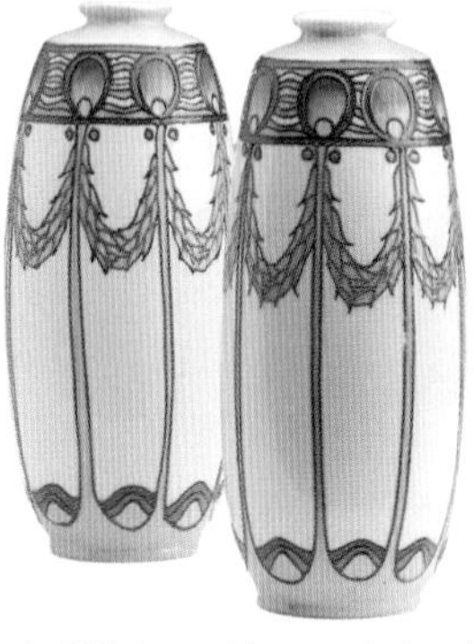

A pair of Minton ovoid vases, designed by Louis Mark Solon, decorated in trailed slip with swags and medallions in bright polychrome, stamped "MINTONS Ltd., No. 1, 3707".

12in (30cm) high

£800-1,200 **DRA**

A Minton two-handled vase, designed by Louis Solon and decorated in trailed slip with swags and medallions in bright polychrome on a red ground, stamped "MINTON Ltd., No. 1, 8503".

11.5in (29cm) high

£500-800 **DRA**

A Minton two-handled vase, decorated in the Art Nouveau style with stylized peacock feathers and swags in squeezebag with yellow, green and red glaze, marked.

12in (30.5cm) high

£500-800 **DRA**

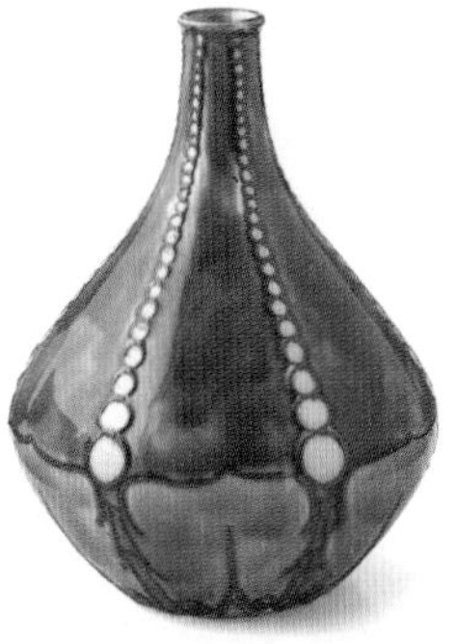

A Minton Secessionist vase, of compressed form, decorated with a stylized band of leaves with tube-lined borders and vertical bands of graduated circles, with printed mark and number.

7in (18cm) high

£220-280 **DN**

A Minton Secessionist jardinière, with stylized leaf and floral motifs, with printed mark "Minton Ltd, Rd No. 616446".

c1900 *8.75in (22cm) high*

£220-280 **SWO**

A Moorcroft Macintyre Florian ware 'Butterfly' vase, decorated with an encircling pattern in shades of blue, with painted initials and printed mark.

c1900 *9.75in (25cm) high*

£800-1,200 **GORL**

A Moorcroft MacIntyre earthenware Florian vase, of tapered form, with piped white on blue 'Poppy' design, signed and numbered "326468".

9.5in (24cm) high

£600-900 **BIG**

A MacIntyre Florian ware baluster vase, with cartouches of poppies and tulips in blue and gilt on a green ground, with printed "MacIntyre" mark, restored.

c1900 *12in (30.5cm) high*

£280-320 **SWO**

A Moorcroft Florian ware jar, decorated with a poppy design, with silver-plated cover, printed mark and painted initials "W M".

c1900

£220-280 **SWO**

A MacIntyre teapot and cover, probably designed by William Moorcroft, of compressed form, decorated with a band of blue flowers, with printed mark, spout restored.

4.75in (12cm) high

£80-120 **DN**

A Moorcroft Macintyre Florian ware coffee can and saucer, decorated with poppies and tulips in shades of blue.

c1900

£120-180 **GORL**

A Moorcroft 'Anenome' pattern pottery vase, impressed "Walter Moorcroft" facsimile signature.

c1945 *10.75in (27cm) high*

£300-500 **SWO**

A Moorcroft 'Anemone' pattern salt-glazed vase, of flared form, with impressed marks and blue signature.

c1930 *8in (20.5cm) high*

£400-600 **SWO**

A Moorcroft 'Banded Peacock Feather' pattern vase, of baluster form with two decorated bands, impressed marks and blue signature.

c1910 *9in (23cm) high*

£1,000-1,500 **SWO**

A Moorcroft 'Bramble' pattern vase, with impressed mark and green monogram.

7.75in (20cm) high

£150-200 **WW**

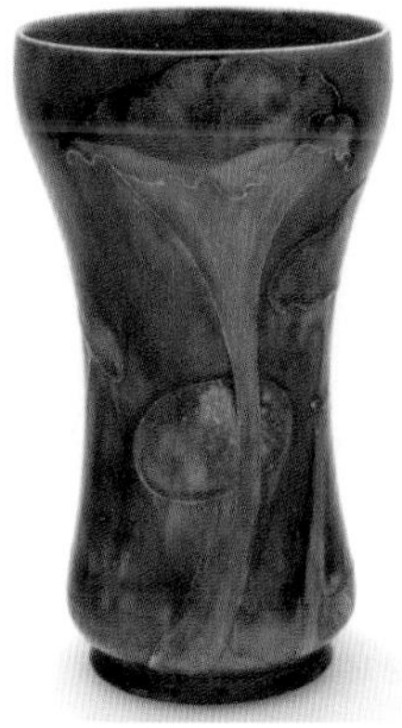

A Moorcroft for Liberty 'Claremont' vase, decorated in shades of green, blue, red and yellow against a turquoise ground, with painted signature and printed mark.

c1910 *8in (20.5cm) high*

£1,500-2,000 **GORL**

A pair of Moorcroft MacIntyre baluster vases, decorated with the 'Cornflower' pattern, with printed marks and green signatures.

12.75in (32.5cm) high

£3,500-4,500 **SWO**

A Moorcroft covered ginger jar, decorated with the 'Dawn' pattern in blues and yellows, with chevron bands to top and bottom.

8in (20.5cm) high

£1,800-2,200 **BRI**

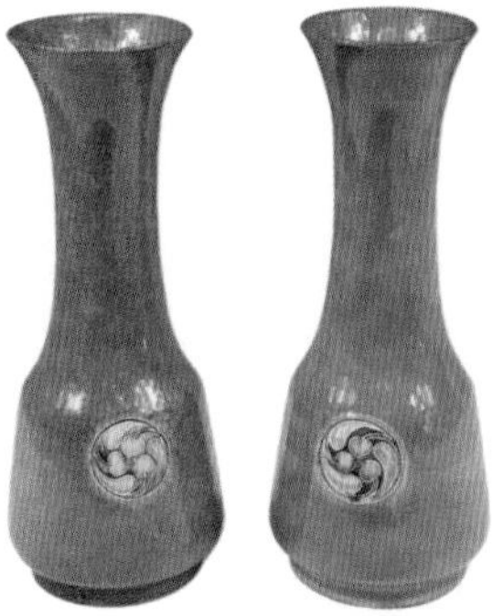

A pair of Moorcroft 'Flamminian' pattern vases, inscribed "Made For Liberty & Co.", with incised signatures.

c1910 *12in (30cm) high*

£400-600 **SWO**

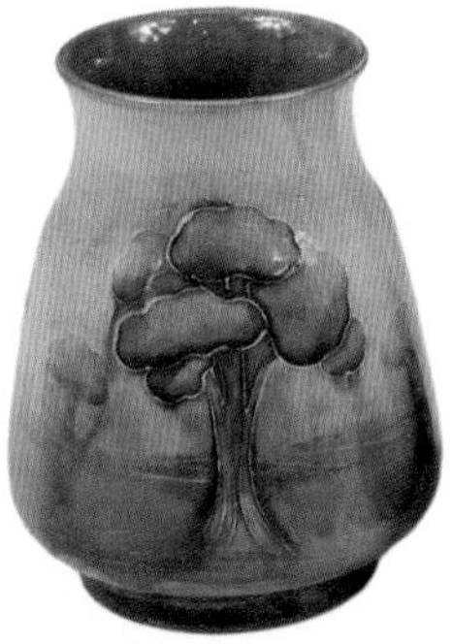

One of a pair of Moorcroft 'Hazeldene' pattern vases, with printed marks "Made For Liberty and Co." and painted signatures.

c1910 *4.75in (12cm) high*

£4,000-5,000 pair **SWO**

A Moorcroft 'Leaf and Blackberry' vase, with painted blue signature.

7.25in (18.5cm) high

£800-1,200 **WW**

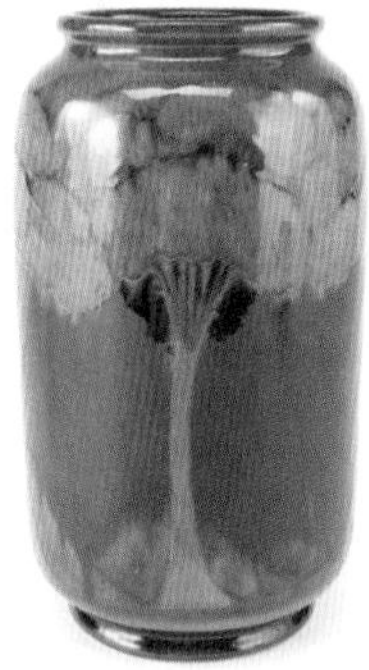

A large Moorcroft 'Moonlit Blue' barrel-shaped vase, with "W. Moorcroft" ink signature, stamped "MADE IN ENGLAND MOORCROFT, M55".

11in (28cm) high

£2,000-2,500 **DRA**

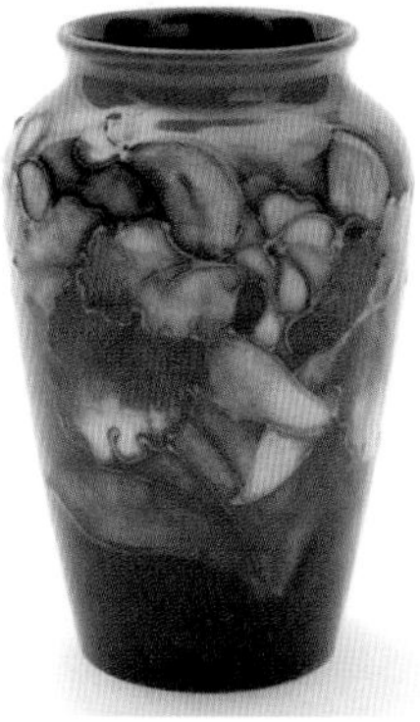

A Moorcroft 'Orchid' posy vase, decorated in shades of blue, green, yellow and red against a blue green ground, with impressed marks.

5in (12.5cm) high

£120-180 **GORL**

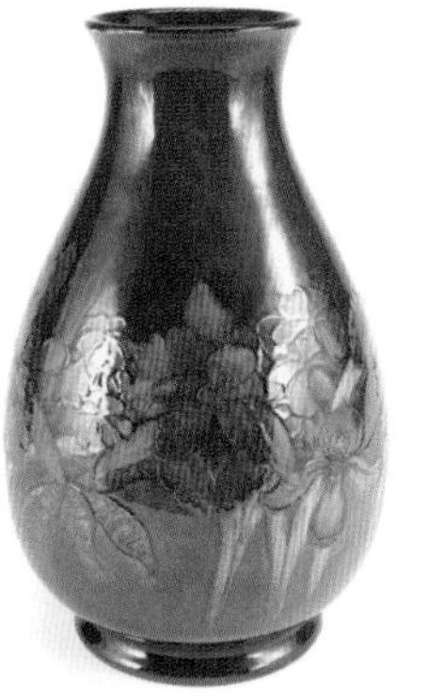

A large Moorcroft bulbous vase, decorated with the 'Orchid' pattern on a deep red ground, with script signature and printed marks.

17.5in (44.5cm) high

£2,000-2,500 **DRA**

A large Moorcroft 'Rain Forest' vase, designed by Sally Tuffin, number three in a limited edition of 150, with impressed and inscribed marks.

1992 *16.5in (42cm) high*

£800-1,200 **SWO**

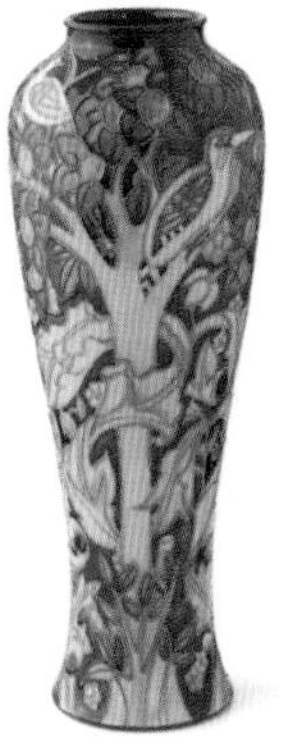

A Moorcroft 'Tree Bark Thief' limited edition vase, with impressed and painted marks, numbered "199" in an edition of 250.

14.25in (36.5cm) high

£400-600 **WW**

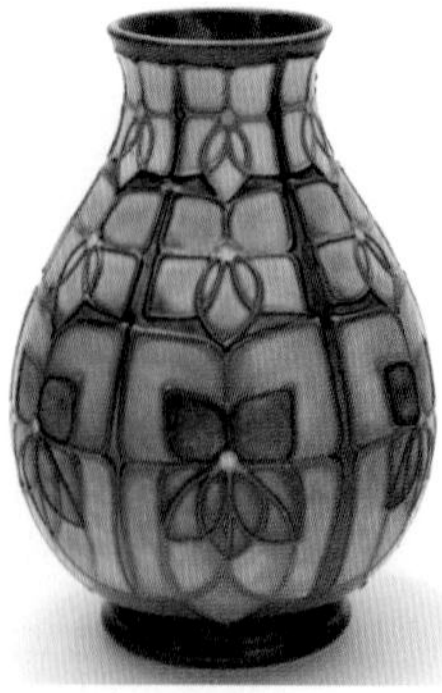

A Moorcroft 'Violet' baluster vase, designed by Sally Tuffin, decorated in shades of green, blue, yellow and pink against a blue green ground.

c1990 *7.5in (19cm) high*

£150-200 **GORL**

A Moorcroft 'Wisteria' flambé vase, of compressed circular form, tubeline decorated against a deep blue ground with flambé glaze, with impressed mark and painted signature "W. Moorcroft".

c1920 *6.75in (17cm) high*

£500-700 **DNT**

A Moorcroft pottery plate, decorated with the 'Freesia' pattern, with painted blue signature.

8.75in (22cm) diam

£150-200 **WW**

A Moorcroft flambé 'Freesia' bowl, with painted blue signature.

10.75in (27cm) diam

£350-400 **WW**

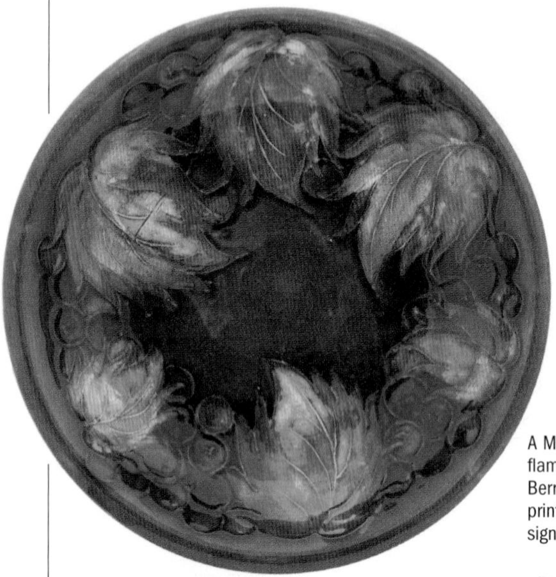

A Moorcroft flambé 'Leaf and Berry' plate, with printed blue signature.

7in (18cm) diam

£280-320 **WW**

A Moorcroft for Liberty Tudric bowl, decorated with the 'Moonlit Blue' pattern in shades of blue and green against a powder blue ground, on a hammered pewter foot, with impressed marks.

7.5in (19cm) diam

£700-1,000 **GORL**

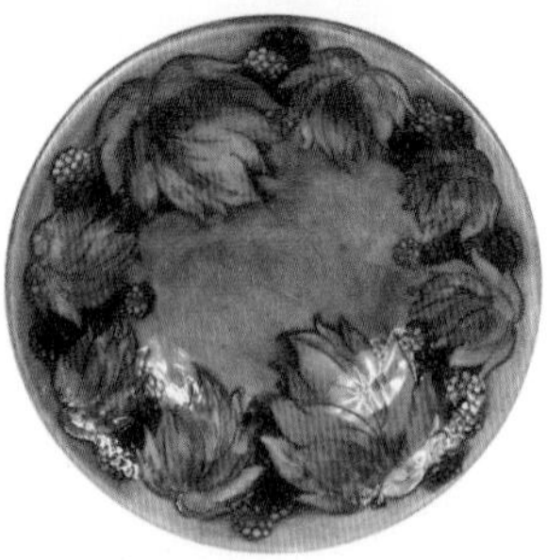

A Moorcroft shallow dish, decorated with the 'Leaf and Berries' pattern on a mottled blue ground, with impressed marks and painted signature to base.

9.5in (24cm) diam

£80-120 **SWO**

A Moorcroft 'Pomegranate' dish, with impressed marks.

4.25in (11cm) diam

£120-180 **WW**

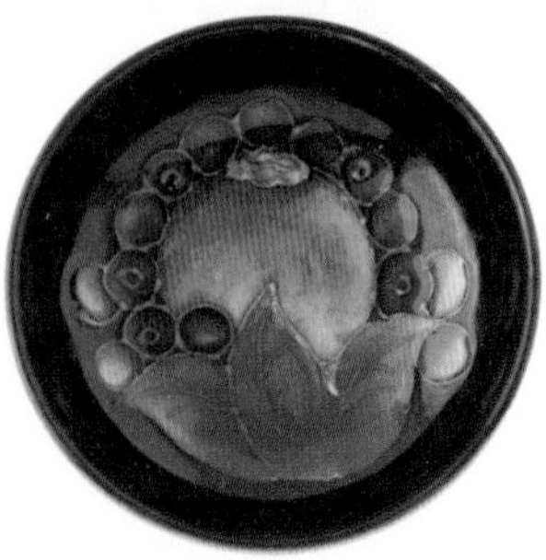

A Moorcroft 'Pomegranate' dish, with original paper label.

4.75in (12cm) diam

£120-180 **WW**

A Moorcroft 'Magnolia' pattern baluster table lamp, on blue ground, stamped "Moorcroft".

10in (25.5cm) high

£150-200 **MAX**

A Pilkington's Royal Lancastrian lustre vase, by Richard Joyce, of bulbous form with slender neck, decorated with fish and seaweed against a green ground, with impressed marks and artist's monogram.

5in (12.5cm) high

£1,000-1,500 **MAX**

A Pilkington's Royal Lancastrian lustre vase, painted by W.S. Mycock with stylized leaf designs in turquoise, with blue impressed marks with incised monogram.

6.75in (17cm) high

£120-180 **SWO**

A tall Pilkington's Royal Lancastrian Secessionist vase, painted by W.S. Mycock, with arabesques and curlicues in feathered bottle green, orange and yellow matte glaze, stamped and signed "WSM".

13in (32.5cm) high

£600-900 **DRA**

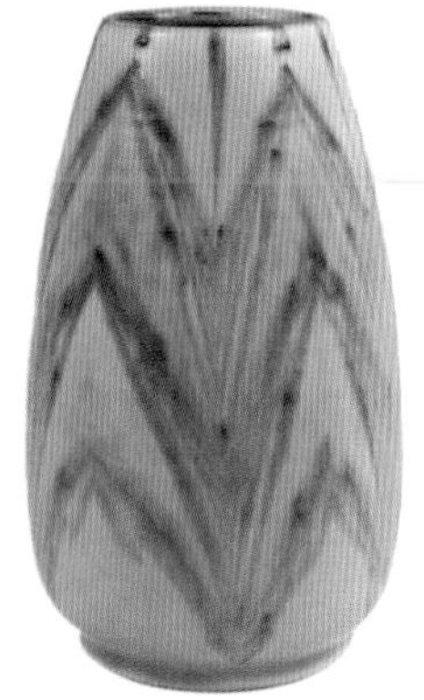

A Pilkington's Royal Lancastrian lustre vase, by Gwladys Rodgers, decorated with green zig-zag patterns, with impressed, incised and painted marks and monogram.

c1930 *8.75in (22cm) high*

£120-180 **SWO**

An early 20thC Pilkington's Royal Lancastrian lustre vase, of shouldered form, decorated in silver lustre with flowering vines on a red ground, the flowers picked out in orange.

8.75in (22cm) high

£700-1,000 **ROS**

A Pilkington's Royal Lancastrian lustre charger, decorated by W.S. Mycock after a design by Walter Crane with a knight charging a dragon, with St George's cross and details in ruby lustre, inscribed "Un chevalier sans peur et sans reproche", with impressed marks and date code.

1907 *19in (48cm) diam*

£500-800 **SWO**

A CLOSER LOOK AT A PILKINGTON'S ROYAL LANCASTRIAN VASE

Richard Joyce was a modeller and decorator who produced a number of designs for Pilkington's celebrated 'Royal Lancastrian' range of wares.

Enthusiasts often collect by designer and Richard Joyce's underwater motifs have a strong following, invariably performing well at auction.

The lustre glaze, based on techniques used in ancient Persia, is particularly well suited to aquatic themes.

The shape of this vase, with its broad shoulders and unobtrusive neck, displays the pattern particularly well.

A Pilkington's Royal Lancastrian lustre vase, by Richard Joyce, decorated with fish and seaweed against a green ground, with marks and artist's monogram.

9in (23cm) high

£1,800-2,200 **MAX**

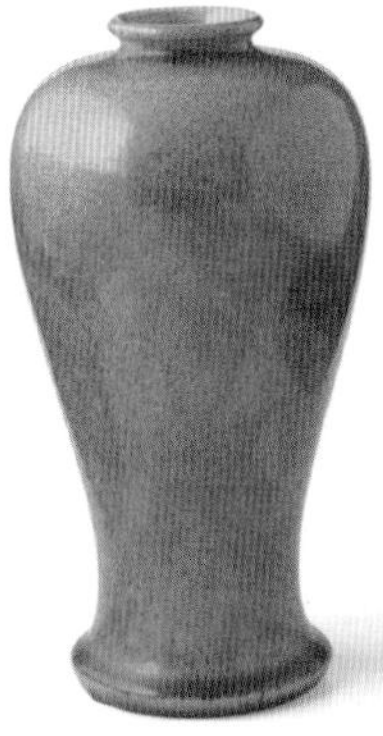

A Pilkington's Royal Lancastrian uranium glazed vase, of ovoid form.

7.5in (19cm) high

£100-150 **DN**

A Pilkington's Royal Lancastrian tile, by Edmund Kent, tubeline decorated with a galleon at sea, with impressed marks.

4in (10cm) wide

£150-200 **WW**

A Pilkington's Royal Lancastrian tile, by Edmund Kent, tubeline-decorated with a galleon at sea, with impressed marks.

4in (10cm) wide

£100-150 **WW**

A Carter, Stabler & Adams Poole 'Sugar and Spice' plate, designed by Olive Bourne, pattern 'CM', with impressed mark and painted marks, restored rim.

10.75in (27cm) diam

£600-900 **WW**

A Carter, Stabler & Adams Poole 'Bluebird' vase, by Ruth Pavely, pattern 'NT', with impressed and painted marks.

10.75in (27cm) high

£350-400 **WW**

A Carter, Stabler & Adams Poole 'Comic Bird' vase, by Truda Rivers, pattern 'ZU', with painted and impressed marks.

8.25in (21cm) high

£400-500 **WW**

A Carter, Stabler & Adams Poole wall plaque, emblematic of 'Summer', with script mark to rear.

14in (36cm) high

£250-300 **SWO**

A rare Carter, Stabler & Adams Poole stoneware figure, 'Piping Boy', designed by Phoebe Stabler, glazed in shades of blue, ochre and buff, with impressed "CSA" mark.

15in (38cm) high

£2,500-3,000 **WW**

A Poole vase, of baluster form, over-painted with stylized birds and flowers, the base signed "H. Blackmore".

13.5in (34.5cm) high

£300-400 **GAZE**

One of a pair of Poole vases, of cylindrical tapering form, decorated with stylized flowers and leaves, with impressed and painted marks.

9.25in (23.5cm) high

£150-250 pair **ROW**

A Poole 'Leaping Gazelle' vase, pattern 'TZ', painted in colours, with impressed and painted marks.

13.5in (34cm) high

£400-500 **WW**

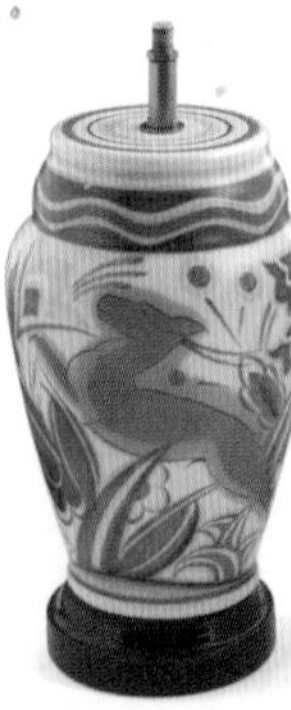

A rare Poole 'Leaping Gazelle' lamp base, painted in colours, on a wooden base.

9.75in (25cm) high

£500-700 **WW**

A rare Poole nursery toys jug, designed by Dora Batty and painted by Ruth Pavely, with impressed and printed marks.

5.25in (13.5cm) high

£400-500 **WW**

A Poole Art Deco vase, by Ruth Pavely, pattern 'KJ', painted with stylized eyebrow motif in shades of mushroom, grey and brown, with impressed and painted marks, restored.

8.5in (21.5cm) wide

£350-400 **WW**

A Poole Art Deco charger, pattern 'SL', with impressed and painted marks, firing crack to well.

15.25in (39cm) diam

£300-400 **WW**

A Poole Art Deco tile, by Edward Bawden, depicting the tea lady from the pottery's tea room.

c1935 6in (15cm) w

£350-400 **JES**

A Poole 'Atlantis' vase, by Beatrice Bolton, with impressed marks.

4in (10cm) high

£200-250 **WW**

A Poole 'Atlantis' vase, by Catherine Connett, with impressed and incised marks.

4in (10cm) high

£300-400 **WW**

A Poole 'Atlantis' vase, by Guy Sydenham, with incised vertical decoration, impressed and incised marks.

8in (20cm) high

£200-250 **SWO**

A Poole 'Atlantis' vase, by Guy Sydenham, of dimpled ovoid form, covered in an orange glaze, with impressed and incised marks.

9.25in (23cm) high

£500-800 **WW**

A Poole 'Sea Urchin' vase, designed by Guy Sydenham, with impressed marks to the base.

4in (10cm) wide

£250-300 **SWO**

A Poole 'Contemporary' vase, pattern 'PKT', with printed and painted marks.

7.75in (20cm) high

£200-250 **WW**

A Poole 'Contemporary' carafe vase, pattern 'YFP', with printed and painted marks.

10.25in (26cm) high

£200-250 **WW**

A Poole 'Delphis' plate, painted with an owl, with printed and painted marks.

10.75in (27cm) diam

£400-600 **WW**

A Royal Crown Derby ewer, of ovoid form, painted with a botanical study in cream on a pink ground, signed "Leroy", with usual cypher and Royal Appointment mark.

1891 *8in (20.5cm) high*

£500-800 **ROS**

A Royal Crown Derby miniature vase, painted with flowers and heightened in gilding.

1896 *4.5in (11.5cm) high*

£80-120 **SWO**

A pair of Royal Crown Derby vases, with narrow necks, scroll handles and gilt floral decoration, the bases with printed and inscribed marks, restored.

c1900 *11.5in (29cm)*

£500-700 **SWO**

A Royal Crown Derby miniature pan and cover, with two handles and loop knop, decorated in the Imari style with flowers and leaves, pattern number 4299, with printed marks in green.

2.75in (7cm) long

£350-400 **LFA**

An unusual Royal Crown Derby miniature rectangular fishing creel, decorated in the Imari style with flowers and leaves, pattern number 6299, with printed marks in green.

1.75in (4.5cm) high

£200-300 **LFA**

A pair of Royal Crown Derby cups and saucers, each painted with an exotic bird and floral studies on a pink ground within gilt borders, signed "Mosely".

1939 *2.25in (6cm) high*

£400-500 **ROS**

ROYAL WORCESTER

A large pair of Royal Worcester vases, painted by Harry Davies, with gilt edged cartouches containing figures and animals in romantic landscapes on a blue ground, shape number 2331, signed.

c1910 *11.5in (29cm) high*

£6,000-9,000 **WW**

A Royal Worcester ovoid vase, painted by Harry Davis in coloured enamels with cattle in an oval gilded cartouche, on a beaded round foot, shape number 2260, signed.

5.5in (14cm) high

£1,000-1,500 **LFA**

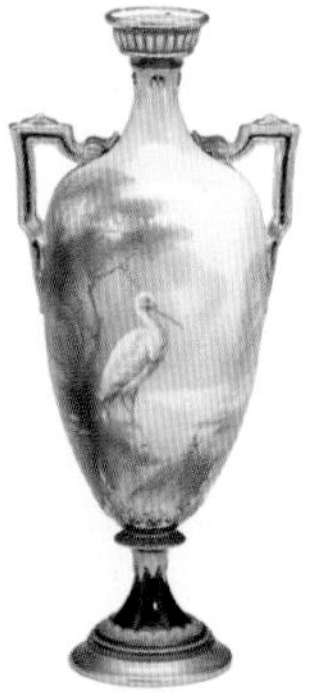

A Royal Worcester porcelain vase, painted by Walter Powell with a stork beside a river, the ovoid sides with twin angular handles, on a socle base, with green printed marks.

10in (25.5cm) high

£500-700 **FRE**

A CLOSER LOOK AT A ROYAL WORCESTER VASE

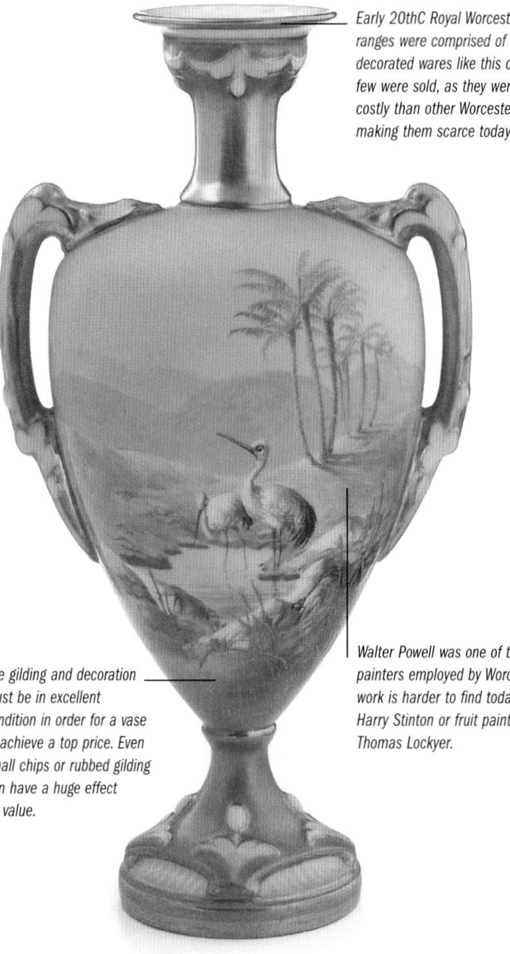

Early 20thC Royal Worcester premium ranges were comprised of artist-decorated wares like this one. Relatively few were sold, as they were far more costly than other Worcester lines, making them scarce today.

Walter Powell was one of the best painters employed by Worcester. His work is harder to find today than that of Harry Stinton or fruit painters such as Thomas Lockyer.

The gilding and decoration must be in excellent condition in order for a vase to achieve a top price. Even small chips or rubbed gilding can have a huge effect on value.

A Royal Worcester two-handled pedestal vase, painted by Walter Powell with storks in a North African landscape, shape number 2248, with puce printed marks and date letter.

1912 *8.25in (21cm) high*

£3,500-4,500 **DN**

A pair of Royal Worcester vases, painted by Harry Stinton with Highland cattle in landscapes, shape number 2330, signed and with printed marks, lacking covers.

c1910 *9.25in (23.5cm) high*

£3,000-5,000 **DN**

LEFT: A Royal Worcester small cylindrical vase, painted by Harry Stinton with highland cattle in a mountainous landscape, the reverse with a rock in a landscape, with pierced gilt rim and foliate scroll feet, signed and with printed marks.

c1910 *6in (15cm) high*

£280-320 **L&T**

RIGHT: A Royal Worcester covered vase, painted by John Stinton with two highland cattle drinking from a stream, the reverse with boulders in a misty landscape, with twin handles, bud finial and gadrooned circular foot, signed and with printed marks.

c1905 *12in (30.5cm) high*

£800-1,200 **L&T**

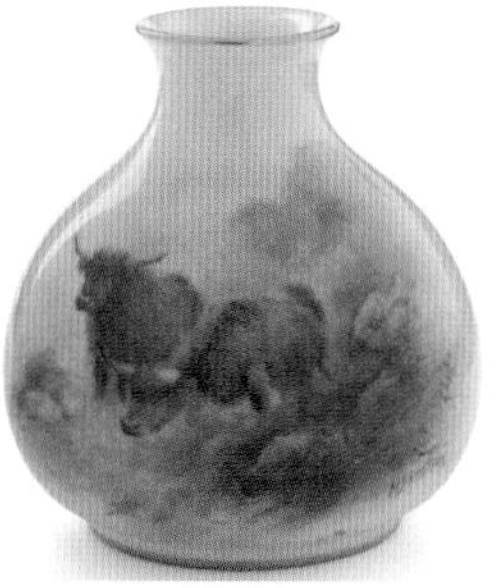

A Royal Worcester globular vase, painted by Harry Stinton with Highland cattle in a landscape, shape number 2491, with puce printed marks and date code.

1915 *2.75in (7cm) high*

£800-1,200 **DN**

A pair of Royal Worcester ovoid vases, painted in coloured enamels by Harry Stinton with Highland cattle in extensive landscapes, signed and with printed marks in puce.

1919

£2,800-3,200 **LFA**

A Royal Worcester ovoid vase and cover, painted in coloured enamels by John Stinton with Highland Cattle in a mountainous landscape, signed and with printed marks.

9.75in (25cm) high

£3,000-4,000 **LFA**

A rare 19thC Royal Worcester vase, with three applied moulded tortoises.

3.5in (9cm) high

£180-220 **BRI**

A Royal Worcester vase, printed and painted with a woman and child before a thatched cottage and rural buildings, the handles with Classical masks, shape number 2363, with printed marks.

1908 *8in (20cm) high*

£400-600 **SWO**

A pair of early 20thC Hadley Worcester porcelain vases, painted with peacocks and foliage, with tall necks, flared rims and twin angular handles, green printed marks.

10in (25.5cm) high

£700-1,000 **FRE**

A large Royal Worcester two-handled vase and cover, painted with a coloured birds within a gilt cartouche on a pale blue ground, pattern number 2010.

17in (43cm) high

£2,500-3,000 **JN**

A Royal Worcester ovoid vase, with pierced reticulated outer shell interspersed with three gilt framed quatrefoils revealing the inner body decorated with rural landscapes, marked.

4in (10cm) high

£400-600 **ROW**

A Royal Worcester vase, decorated in gilt and 'shot enamel' with flowers on a pink ground, with scrolled handles and flared rim.

8in (20.5cm) high

£500-800 **BRI**

A Royal Worcester Chinese-style vase, of square tapering form, painted with figures, with lion ring handles.

11in (28cm) high

£250-300 **BRI**

A large Royal Worcester covered vase, decorated with rich gilt clematis flowers and floral swags on a deep blue ground, with griffin handles, pattern number 1764.

16.5in (42cm) high

£1,000-1,500 **JN**

A rare Grainger Worcester stoneware flagon, of baluster form with loop handle, moulded in relief, with silver-plated hinged cover, incised "G. Grainger, Worcester".

c1850 *8in (20.5cm) high*

£300-500 **LFA**

A Royal Worcester Japanese-style ewer, decorated with gilt, silvered and burnished brown enamel on an incised scale ground, with entwined dragon handle, printed marks and date letter.

1884 *11in (28cm) high*

£250-300 **DN**

A Royal Worcester ewer, painted by John Stinton with Highland cattle, with green printed marks and date code, restored.

1903 *9.75in (25cm) high*

£800-1,200 **DN**

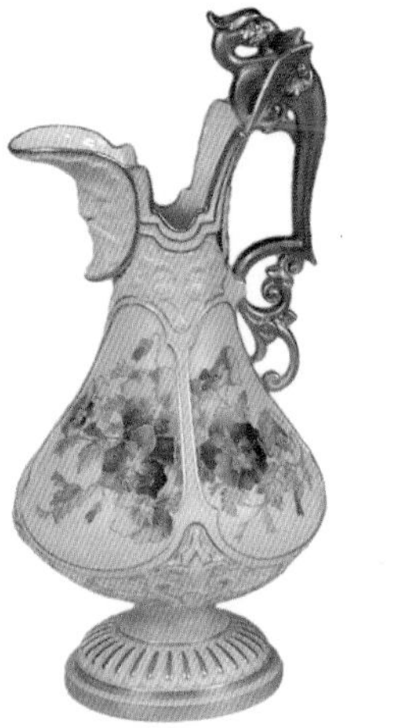

One of a pair of Royal Worcester Renaissance-style ewers, decorated with floral sprays heightened with gilding, with griffin handles and mask spouts, printed and incised factory marks, restored.

1889 *13.5in (34.5cm)*

£700-1,000 pair **SWO**

A large Royal Worcester tusk jug, decorated with roses.

c1900 *11in (28cm) high*

£400-600 **WW**

A Royal Worcester flat back jug, decorated with flowers on a peach ground, with gilt detail.

5.5in (14cm) high

£150-200 **BRI**

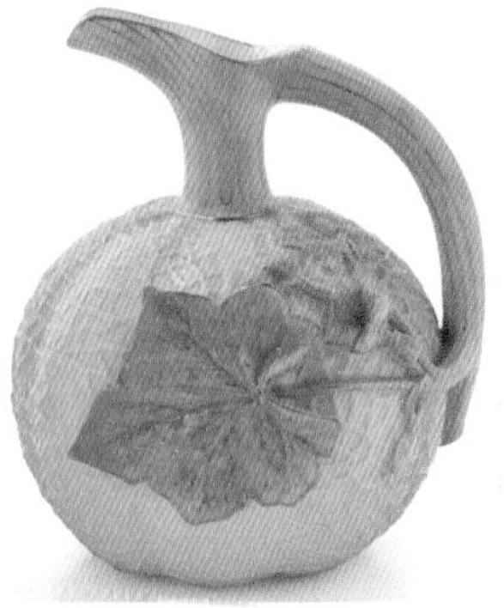

A Royal Worcester jug, naturalistically modelled as a melon, the handle with a flowering branch terminal.

7in (18cm) high

£150-200 **DN**

A 20thC Royal Worcester plate, painted by Frank Rushton with flowers in a garden, signed, with black mark.

10.75in (27.5cm) diam

£400-600 **WW**

A Royal Worcester plate, painted by Richard Sebright with fruit, signed.

c1930 *8.75in (22.5cm) wide*

£800-1,200 **WW**

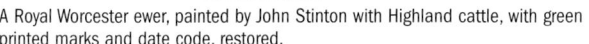

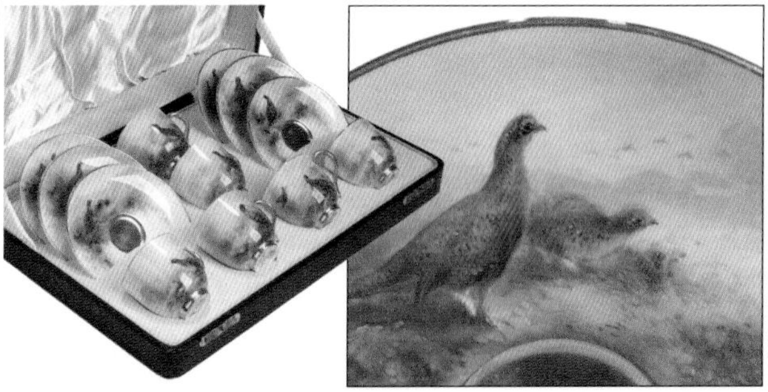

A Royal Worcester boxed coffee set, comprising six coffee cups and six saucers, painted by James Stinton with grouse in a Highland landscape, signed and with printed marks, in a fitted black leather case.

1936

£2,200-2,800 **L&T**

Part of a 19thC Royal Worcester dessert service, comprising two tazzas, two footed dishes, twelve plates, centrally painted with flowers and foliage within gilt turquoise borders, with impressed marks, some damage.

9.25in (23.5cm) wide

£600-900 set **FRE**

A Royal Worcester shell-shaped dish, painted with gilt border and flowers.

9.5in (24cm) wide

£200-300 **JN**

A Royal Worcester commemorative loving cup, painted by Harry Davis with a vignette of Worcester, inscribed "Presented to Mr A. Birbeck on his 42nd birthday by Mr and Miss Dovey. May 20th 1907", with printed marks and date code.

1907 *6.5in (16.5cm) high*

£1,500-2,500 **DN**

A 20thC Royal Worcester teapot and cover, painted by Peter Platt with fruit, with rich gilt borders, spout and handle, black printed mark.

10in (25.5cm) wide

£700-1,000 **DN**

A silver compact, the Royal Worcester porcelain cover painted by Harry Stinton with Highland cattle in a landscape, signed, the mounts with marks for Birmingham.

1927

£400-600 **LFA**

A faceted glass scent bottle, the silver mounted cover with a Royal Worcester plaque painted by James Stinton with a pheasant in a wooded landscape, signed, the mounts with marks for Birmingham.

1928

£220-280 **LFA**

A faceted glass dressing table bottle, the silver mounted cover with a Royal Worcester plaque painted by James Stinton with a pheasant in a wooded landscape, signed, the mounts with marks for Birmingham.

1928

£180-220 **LFA**

A Royal Worcester pedestal urn, painted with flowering thistles, on a tall square tapering pedestal, with printed and impressed marks.

c1900 *13in (32.5cm) high*

£300-400 **SWO**

A pair of Hadley Royal Worcester candelabra, modelled as a young man and lady standing in country dress before tree trunks, on a circular naturalistic base, with printed, impressed and lozenge marks to base.

21in (53.5cm) high

£2,000-2,500 **JN**

A Royal Worcester figure, 'The Fortune Teller', modelled by F.G. Doughty, with black printed mark and script marks.

6in (15cm)

£150-200 **DN**

A Royal Worcester figure, 'Joan', modelled by F.G. Doughty, with puce printed marks and date code.

1932 4.5in (11.5cm) high

£180-220 **DN**

A Royal Worcester 'Months of the Year' figure, 'January', modelled by F.G. Doughty.

7in (18cm) high

£150-200 **GORL**

A Royal Worcester 'Months of the Year' figure, 'February', modelled by F.G. Doughty.

7in (18cm) high

£150-200 **GORL**

A Royal Worcester 'Months of the Year' figure, 'March', modelled by F.G. Doughty.

7in (18cm) high

£150-200 **GORL**

A Royal Worcester 'Months of the Year' figure, 'April', modelled by F.G. Doughty.

7in (18cm) high

£150-200 **GORL**

A Royal Worcester 'Months of the Year' figure, 'May', modelled by F.G. Doughty.

7in (18cm) high

£150-200 **GORL**

A Royal Worcester 'Months of the Year' figure, 'June', modelled by F.G. Doughty.

7in (18cm) high

£150-200 **GORL**

A Royal Worcester 'Months of the Year' figure, 'July', modelled by F.G. Doughty.

7in (18cm) high

£150-200 **GORL**

A Royal Worcester 'Months of the Year' figure, 'August', modelled by F.G. Doughty.

7in (18cm) high

£150-200 **GORL**

A Royal Worcester 'Months of the Year' figure, 'September', modelled by F.G. Doughty.

7in (18cm) high

£150-200 **GORL**

A Royal Worcester 'Months of the Year' figure, 'October', modelled by F.G. Doughty.

7in (18cm) high

£150-200 **GORL**

A Royal Worcester 'Months of the Year' figure, 'November', modelled by F.G. Doughty.

7in (18cm) high

£150-200 **GORL**

A Royal Worcester 'Months of the Year' figure, 'December', modelled by F.G. Doughty.

7in (18cm) high

£150-200 **GORL**

A pair of Royal Worcester 'Down-and-Out Men' menu holders, modelled with their hands in their pockets on grey paved bases, with impressed marks and registration diamonds, damaged.

c1870 *tallest 5.75in (14.5cm)*

£150-200 **DNT**

A Royal Worcester candle extinguisher, in the form of a Chinese Mandarin, modelled with one hand raised and the other holding a fan, with puce printed mark and date code.

1917 *3.5in (9cm) high*

£80-120 **DNT**

A Royal Worcester model of a Shire stallion, by Doris Lindner, model number 105, with black printed marks, restored.

10in (25.5cm) long

£180-220 **DN**

RUSKIN

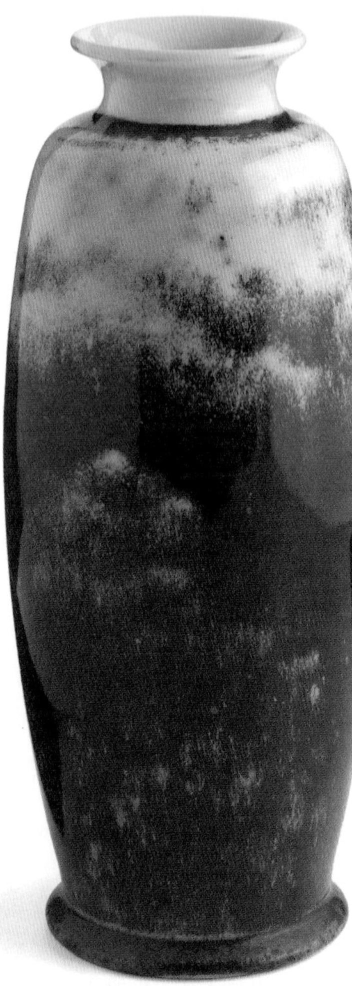

A Ruskin speckled vase, with impressed "Ruskin Pottery 1910" mark.

1910 *11in (28cm) high*

£600-900 **JN**

A Ruskin high-fired bulbous vase, covered in an oxblood glaze with gunmetal spots, stamped "RUSKIN 1913/186".

1913 *7in (17.5cm) high*

£400-600 **DRA**

A Ruskin stoneware ginger jar and cover, covered in a rich mottled blue glaze, with impressed marks.

1919 *7in (18cm) high*

£280-320 **WW**

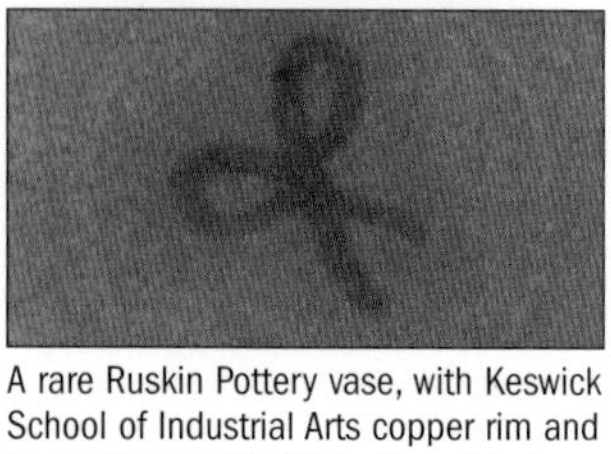

A rare Ruskin Pottery vase, with Keswick School of Industrial Arts copper rim and cover, stamped "KSIA", with painted Ruskin scissor mark.

4in (10cm) high

£500-800 **WW**

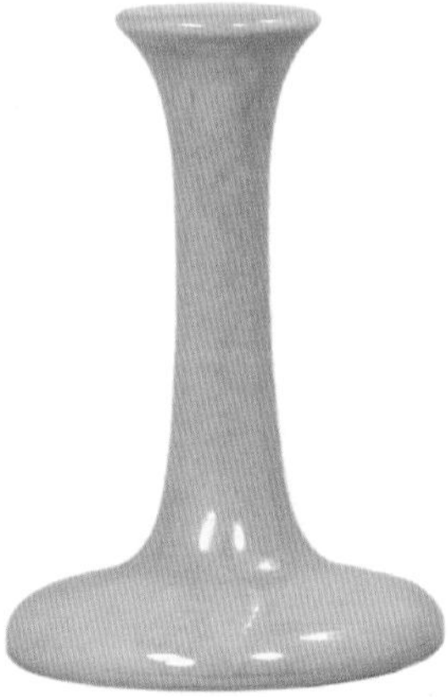

One of a pair of Ruskin earthenware candlesticks, with yellow lustre glaze and low spread bases, impressed marks and dates.

1924 *6in (15cm) high*

£100-150 pair **BIG**

A Wedgwood Fairyland lustre bowl, designed by Daisy Makeig-Jones, with the 'Firbolgs' pattern, printed marks, damaged.

5.25in (13.5cm) diam

£500-800 **WW**

A Wedgwood Fairyland lustre 'Lily Tray' bowl, designed by Daisy Makeig-Jones, with the 'Jumping Faun' pattern, printed factory mark.

9in (23cm) diam

£2,500-3,000 **DN**

A Wedgwood Fairyland lustre Empire bowl, designed by Daisy Makeig-Jones, with the 'Leapfrogging Elves' pattern, printed marks.

5in (13cm) diam

£1,000-1,500 **WW**

A Wedgwood Fairyland lustre octagonal bowl, designed by Daisy Makeig-Jones, with the 'Leapfrogging Elves' pattern on a black lustre ground, printed mark.

8.75in (22.5cm) diam

£2,500-3,000 **WW**

DAISY MAKEIG-JONES

- Susannah Margaretta 'Daisy' Makeig-Jones (1881-1945) spent her Yorkshire childhood immersed in myths and legends.
- Makeig-Jones joined Wedgwood as an apprentice painter and was made designer in 1912. She took inspiration from children's illustrators such as Kay Nielson and Edmund Dulac.
- Her Fairyland range, decorated with magical landscapes and mythological beings, appealed to public nostalgia for a more innocent age following the horrors of WWI.
- Patterns such as 'Candlemas', 'Ghostly Wood' and 'Lahore' contrasted with Wedgwood's traditionalist style but the brilliant colours and sumptuous designs were a huge commercial success.
- The lustre technique uses a mixture of metallic oxide pigments suspended in oil and painted onto the surface of earthenware. When fired, the metal reduces and forms a thin shiny film.
- As production increased, Makeig-Jones took on a supervisory role and stopped decorating her own pieces. She left the factory in 1931 and the production of Fairyland lustre ceased.

A Wedgwood Fairyland lustre bowl, designed by Daisy Makeig-Jones, with the 'Leapfrogging Elves' pattern on a flame ground, printed mark.

5in (13cm) diam

£1,200-1,800 **WW**

A Wedgwood Fairyland lustre bowl, by Daisy Makeig-Jones, with the 'Moorish' and 'Smoke Ribbons' patterns.

7.75in (20cm) diam

£2,000-2,500 **WW**

A Wedgwood Flame Fairyland lustre punch bowl, designed by Daisy Makeig-Jones, with the 'Poplar Trees' pattern, the interior with the 'Woodland Bridge' pattern, with four gilded "MJ" monograms to interior.

9.25in (23.5cm) diam

£4,000-6,000 **GORL**

A Wedgwood Fairyland lustre footed bowl, designed by Daisy Makeig-Jones, with the 'Poplar Trees' pattern, the interior with the 'Woodland Bridge' pattern, with printed and painted factory marks.

11in (28cm) diam

£1,200-1,800 **L&T**

A Wedgwood Flame Fairyland lustre punch bowl, designed by Daisy Makeig-Jones, with the 'Poplar Trees' pattern, the interior with the 'Woodland Bridge' pattern, with four gilded "MJ" monograms to interior.

9.25in (23.5cm) diam

£3,500-4,500 **GORL**

A large Wedgwood Flame Fairyland lustre punch bowl, designed by Daisy Makeig-Jones, with the 'Poplar Trees' pattern, the interior with the 'Woodland Bridge' pattern, with four gilded "MJ" monograms to the interior, painted and printed marks.

11.25in (28.5cm) diam

£4,000-6,000 **CHEF**

A Wedgwood Fairyland lustre bowl, decorated in gilt with magical figures in a landscape, with gilt marks.

c1920 *11in (28cm) diam*

£1,200-1,800 **ISA**

A Wedgwood Fairyland lustre octagon bowl, with printed marks.

c1920 *8.25in (21cm) diam*

£2,200-2,800 **SWO**

A Wedgwood Dragon lustre bowl, decorated with blue and gold dragons on a soufflé blue ground, with gilt marks, damaged.

9.5in (24cm) diam

£250-300 **CHEF**

A pair of Wedgwood Fairyland lustre covered vases, designed by Daisy Makeig-Jones, with the 'Candlemas' pattern, printed marks, chipped.

9in (23cm) high

£3,500-4,500 **WW**

A Wedgwood Fairyland lustre vase, designed by Daisy Makeig-Jones, with the 'Candlemas' pattern, printed mark and paper retail label, missing cover.

7.75in (20cm) high

£500-800 **WW**

A Wedgwood Fairyland lustre covered vase, designed by Daisy Makeig-Jones, of inverted baluster shape, decorated with the 'Candlemas' pattern, with painted and printed marks.

9in (23cm) high

£2,500-3,000 **CHEF**

A Wedgwood Fairyland lustre vase, designed by Daisy Makeig-Jones, with the 'Imps on a Bridge' pattern on a flame lustre ground, with printed mark.

10.75in (27cm) high

£4,000-6,000 **WW**

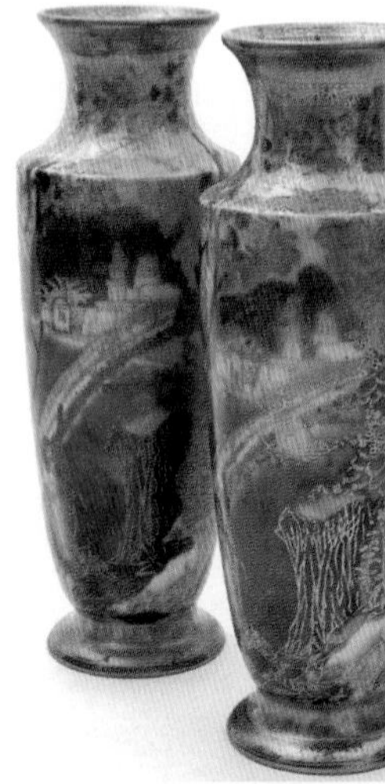

A pair of Wedgwood Fairyland lustre vases, designed by Daisy Makeig-Jones, with the 'Rainbow Bifrost' pattern, restored.

8.5in (21.5cm) high

£400-600 **GORL**

A Wedgwood Moonstone vase, designed by Keith Murray.

11.5in (29cm) high

£200-300 **FRE**

A Wedgwood conical Moonstone vase, designed by Keith Murray, shape number 3753, with banded decoration, printed facsimile signature.

5.5in (14cm) high

£60-90 **CHEF**

A Wedgwood Moonstone charger, designed by Keith Murray, with impressed and printed factory marks, crazed and stained.

14in (35.5cm) diam

£120-180 **DN**

A Wedgwood matte green shoulder vase, designed by Keith Murray, shape number 3805, with printed mark and facsimile signature.

11.75in (30cm) high

£350-450 **WW**

A 20thC Wedgwood English matte green bombé vase, designed by Keith Murray, of near spherical form, moulded with horizontal grooves.

6in (15.5cm) high

£150-200 **ROS**

A Wedgwood deep circular bowl, designed by Keith Murray.

£100-150 **JN**

A rare Wedgwood matte blue vase, designed by Keith Murray, shape number 3820, with printed mark and "KM" monogram.

Keith Murray (1892-1981) was a New Zealand-born architect and glass and ceramic designer. His ceramics, designed for Wedgwood, are known for their bold clean shapes.

7in (18cm) high

£800-1,200 **WW**

A Wedgwood celadon and white vase, designed by Keith Murray, shape number 4217, with printed mark and "KM" monogram.

8.25in (21cm) high

£250-300 **WW**

A Wedgwood pedestal bowl, designed by Norman Wilson, with impressed and printed marks and "NW" monogram.

9.75in (25cm) diam

£700-1,000 **WW**

A Wemyss large round wash basin, boldly painted with pink cabbage roses and leaves beneath a green line rim, with impressed and painted marks and retailer's marks.

15.25in (38.5cm) diam

£300-400 **LFA**

A Wemyss plate, painted with roses, with painted green "Wemyss" signature.

6.75in (17cm) diam

£80-120 **WW**

An early 20thC Wemyss pottery tyg, decorated with roses, with impressed mark, damaged.

9.5in (23.5cm) high

£500-700 **SWO**

A Wemyss tapered slop bucket and cover, with wicker swing handle, boldly painted with pink cabbage roses and leaves, beneath a green line rim, with impressed mark.

11.25in (28.5cm) high

£500-800 **LFA**

A early 20thC Wemyss teapot and cover, painted with cabbage roses, with printed mark, chipped spout.

4.25in (10.5cm) high

£350-450 **SWO**

A small Wemyss pig, painted with full-blown cabbage roses and leaves, with impressed mark.

6.25in (16cm) long

£700-900 **LFA**

A late 19thC Wemyss ovoid jardiniére, of spirally-lobed form, painted with daffodils, with impressed mark, some minor crazing.

6.75in (17cm)

£800-1,200 **DN**

A Wemyss pottery bowl, decorated with pheasants, with impressed "Wemyss" mark.

6in (15cm) diam

£500-700 **WW**

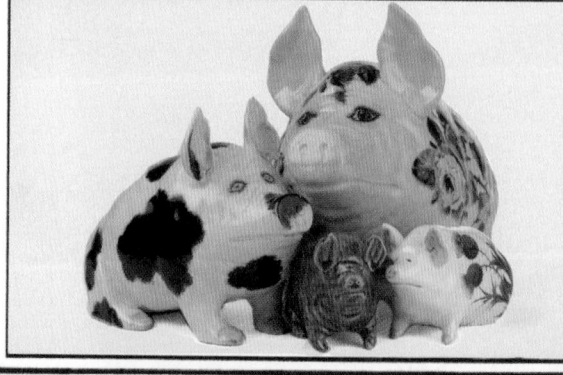

A rare pair of Samuel Alcock & Co. vases.

These are copies of an ancient vase found at Cume in 1885. The design depicts a battle between the Greeks and Amazonians.

8.5in (21.5cm) high

£400-600 **JN**

A C.H. Brannam and William Barrum cameo vase, with narrow neck and bulbous base decorated with birds, flowers, and butterflies in blue overlay, incised "CH" and "WB" monograms, glaze chip at rim.

c1900 *13in (33cm) high*

£350-400 **SK**

A C.H. Brannam sgraffito jug, of tapering shape, decorated with stylized flowers, with incised marks and date.

1902 *8.25in (21cm) high*

£180-220 **GORL**

A pair of Morrisware biscuit jars and covers, designed by G.W. Cartlidge, with tendril handles and tubeline decoration of poppies and oars of wheat, with facsimile signature and printed marks.

7.75in (19.5cm) high

£5,000-7,000 **SWO**

An Ault Pottery vase, designed by Dr Christopher Dresser, modelled with four masks to the shoulder, the tongues forming loop handles, with impressed facsimile signature, chipped.

13in (33cm) high

£3,500-4,500 **WW**

A Christopher Dresser Linthorpe 'Peruvian' earthenware pitcher, decorated in streaked green and brown glazes, with impressed signature.

7in (18cm) high

£300-400 **CHEF**

An exceptional Bernard Moore vase, carved with nasturtium pods and blossoms and covered in a mottled glaze over a brilliant red flambé ground, with stamped marks.

10.5in (26.5cm) high

£2,000-2,500 **DRA**

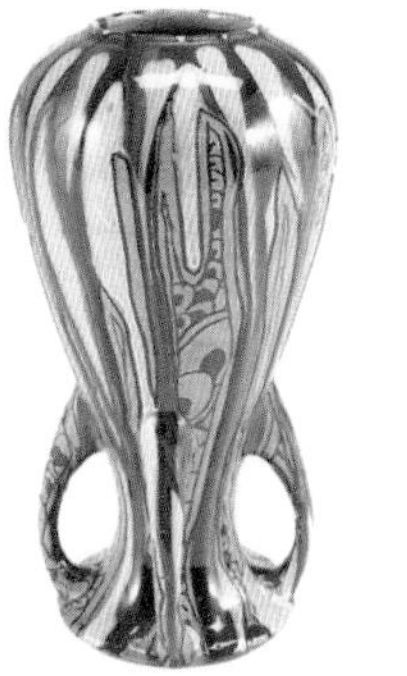

A Foley Faience four-handled vase, designed by Frederick Rhead, painted and carved in an unusual organic design in brown, yellow, green and maroon, with stamped marks.

9.5in (24cm) high

£300-500 **DRA**

A Foley Intarsio Art Nouveau vase, designed by Frederick Rhead, printed and painted with stylized poppies, with printed factory marks.

11in (28cm) high

£350-400 **DN**

An early Bernard Leach circular stoneware charger, painted with Gemini zodiac sign in shades of brown and ochre, with slip-painted "BL" mark and date.

c1925 *15in (38cm) diam*

£2,500-3,000 **L&T**

A Crown Ducal 'Pomegranate' plate, designed by Charlotte Rhead, with printed marks and facsimile signature.

10.5in (26.5cm) diam

£220-280 **WW**

A Wood & Sons Mikado charger, designed by Frederick Rhead, printed in colours, with printed mark.

16.5in (41cm) diam

£600-900 **WW**

A set of two Cube Art Deco teapots, in green and red.

c1920 *largest 8.25in (21cm) high*

£150-200 **JES**

A Crown Devon Orient coffee pot and cover, pattern number 2115, with printed and painted marks.

8.25in (21cm) high

£280-320 **WW**

A teapot and cover, by Sir Edmund Elton, with a platinum craquelure glaze, of dimple form, the spout formed as a beast, with handle to one side, painted signature.

5.75in (14.5cm)

£500-700 **DN**

A scarce William Morris 'Artichoke' tile.

William Morris tiles were made from a particularly fragile biscuit ware and so were easily broken. They are therefore scarce today.

6in (15cm) wide

£700-1,000 **PC**

A William Morris 'Daisy' pattern tile, in blue and yellow, with handwritten "Morris & Co, Daisy" mark.

6in (15cm) wide

£700-1,000 **SWO**

An early Troika wall plaque, modelled in low relief with a geometric design, with painted marks and trident mark.

10.75in (27cm) high

£1,000-1,500 **WW**

A William Morris tile, with the 'Tulip and Trellis' pattern, decorated with yellow flowers, blue stalks and green leaves.

c1865 *6in (15.5cm) wide*

£700-1,000 **SWO**

A Pinder Bourne & Co. Aesthetic Movement jardinière, the frame modelled as bamboo, with impressed marks, restored.

7.75in (20cm) high

£200-300 **WW**

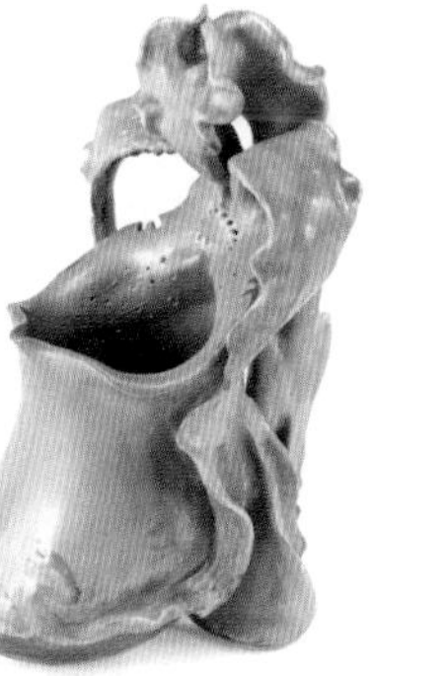

An unusual Amphora vase, designed by Paul Dachsel, in the form of a lady-slipper orchid, and covered in lustred glazes, small chips, reglued near base, stamped "Amphora/ 3417/ II/ 52".

8in (20.5cm) high

£500-800 **DRA**

An Amphora vase, of organic shape, with leaf handles on a textured mother-of-pearl ground, wear to gilding, stamped "crown/ 3898/ 45/ Austria/ Amphora".

10.25in (26cm) high

£220-280 **DRA**

An Amphora vase of organic shape, embossed with waterlilies and lily pads, the stems forming handles, in verdigris and bronze glazes on a mottled ground, restoration, stamped "Austria/ Amphora/ 3850/ 45".

Amphora was Founded in Teplitz, Austria, in 1892. Chiefly known for its earthenware Art Nouveau vases, the company won prizes at all 42 of the expositions it attended between 1893-1907.

19.25in (49cm) high

£800-1,200 **DRA**

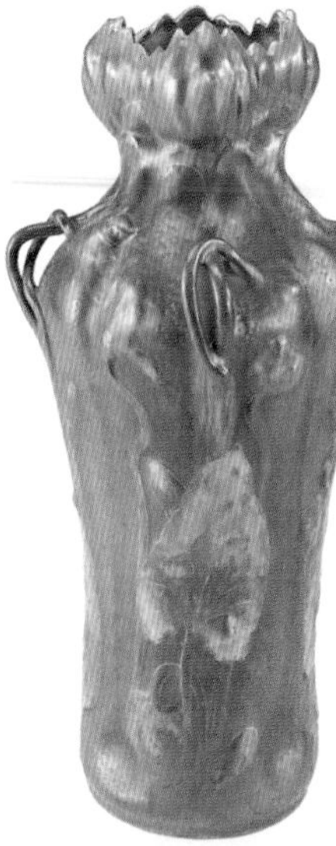

A large Amphora pottery vase, decorated in silver lustre with flowerheads, printed mark.

15.25in (38.5cm) high

£400-600 **WW**

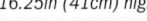

A pair of Amphora pottery slender baluster twin-handled vases, with a crested bird on a tree with foliage and berries, a mottled pale brown ground, factory marks to base.

16.25in (41cm) high

£300-400 **DN**

An Amphora vase, topped by two small handles, enamel-decorated with birds on a branch against a dead matte mottled ground, stamped "Imperial Amphora Made in Austria/Campina".

20.75in (52cm) high

£280-320 **DRA**

An Amphora pottery ovoid two-handled vase, incised with a bird on a branch, printed factory marks.

12in (30.5cm) high

£120-180 **DN**

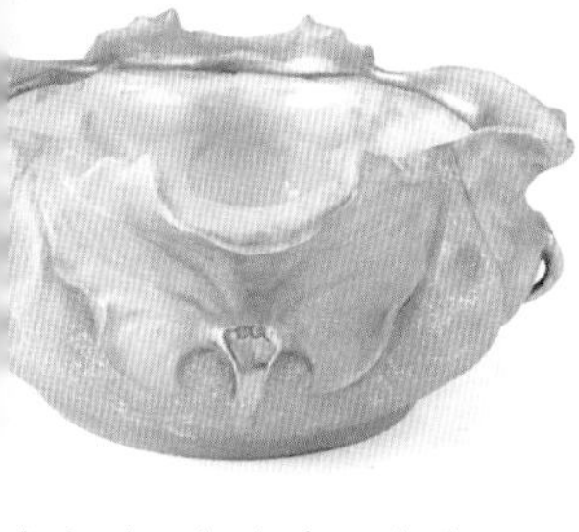

An Amphora bowl, of organic shape, with four large purple and gold lily pads on a green-gold ground, wear to gilding, stamped "crown/ 3869/ 58/ Austria/ Amphora".

10.75in (27.5cm) diam

£220-280 **DRA**

An Amphora table centrepiece bowl, mounted on a central column flanked by supports decorated with mottled cabochons on a stone ground, the inner bowl with lustrous finish, printed mark.

9.5in (24.5cm) high

£120-180 **CHEF**

An Amphora pottery figure of a female tambourine player, seated upon camel, factory impressed marks to the underside, restoration.

c1910 *15.5in (39cm) high*

£300-400 **SWO**

An Amphora rooster figurine, covered in a bronzed glaze, small grinding chip, stamped "Austria Amphora/ 8234 38".

13in (32.5cm) high

£400-600 **DRA**

A rare Art Deco Boch Frères statue by Charles Catteau, with a jazz theme, titled moulded, 'LA DANSE MODERNE' with Josephine Baker stylized dancers and musicians, Catteau signature and BKF signature on front and reverse.

c1925 *14.5in (37cm) wide*

£3,500-4,000 **DD**

A pair of Boch Frères Charles Catteau flattened vases, enamel-decorated in the Art Deco style, with grazing deer on an ivory crackled ground, stamped "D943/Ch. Catteau/KERAMIS MADE IN BELGIUM", some damage.

9.25in (23.5cm) high

£600-900 **DRA**

A large Boch Frères Keramis vase, designed by Charles Catteau, painted with deer, printed mark.

Catteau was the artistic director at Belgian company Boch Frères from 1907. The primitive deer motif is typical of his Deco work during the 1920s-30s.

13.75in (35cm) high

£1,500-2,000 **WW**

A large Boch Frères vase, by Charles Catteau, enamel-decorated in cuerda seca on a crackled ground, blue Boch Frères ink stamp, marked "D.952/Ch. Catteau", impressed "975/K".

12in (30.5cm) high

£400-600 **SDR**

An Art Deco Boch Frères pottery vase, stylized geometric floral vase, titled "Bouquet Stylise" # d1174, designed by Charles Catteau, signed to base.

c1925 *12.5in (32cm) high*

£1,200-1,800 **DD**

A small Art Deco Boch Frères geometric pottery vase, by Charles Catteau, signed on base.

c1925 *6.25in (16cm) wide*

£500-700 **DD**

A pair of Boch Frères crackleware vases in cuerda seca with stylized penguins in black and mint on a white ground, stamped "Made in Belgium/Boch Fes/Alfred/976"

15.25in (38.5cm) high

£2,000-3,000 **SDR**

A large Boch Frères spherical crackleware vase decorated in cuerda seca with stylized penguins, on a white ground, stamped "Made in Belgium/Boch Fes/Alfred/976"

14.5in (37cm) high

£5,000-8,000 **SDR**

An Art Deco Boch Frères pillow vase, decorated in cuerda seca, with deer on a white crackled ground, circular ink stamp.

9in (22.5cm) high

£300-500 **DRA**

A pair of Boch Frères tiles, decorated in cuerda seca with heraldic eagles, light abrasion to surface, a few nicks to edges, stamped "Boch Fres".

8in (20cm) high

£60-90 **DRA**

A CLOSER LOOK AT A DE PORCELEYNE FLES TILE

Joost Thooft bought the struggling Delft factory in 1876 and with artistic advisor Adolf le Comte experimented with new shapes, decorations and glazes, introducing objets d'art, services and tiles to the output.

Spearheaded by Charles Catteau at Boch Frères, stylized animals were a typical decoration at the time and were inspired by a post-WWI interest in primitivism and the Cubist movement.

Cuenca is a cloisonné-like technique where ridges are created in the clay to form pools, which are filled with glaze.

De Porceleyne Fles or 'the Porcelain Jar' applied jar-shaped marks to its wares.

A long horizontal tile by De Porceleyne Fles, decorated in cuenca with a dog hunting a deer in the snow, mounted in Arts and Crafts frame, marked with a bottle and "Delft".

16.5in (42cm) wide

£400-600 **DRA**

A De Porceleyne Fles long tile, decorated in cuenca with a fleet of tall ships, grout on back, no visible mark

16.5in (41cm) wide

£200-300 **DRA**

A De Porceleyne Fles horizontal tile, decorated in cuenca with three tall ships, grout to back obscures mark.

13in (32.5cm) wide

£400-600 **DRA**

A De Porceleyne Fles long tile decorated in cuenca with a fleet of tall ships, marked with a bottle, "TL, Delft".

12.25in (31cm) wide

£80-120 **DRA**

A tall vertical tile by De Porceleyne Fles, decorated in cuenca with a peacock facing right on white brick wall, mounted in Arts and Crafts frame, marked with a bottle, "TL Delft".

tile 13in (33cm) high

£250-300 **DRA**

A De Porceleyne Fles vertical tile, decorated in cuenca with a flamingo facing right, framed, back covered.

tile 12in (30cm) high

£200-300 **DRA**

A rare and large De Porceleyne Fles tile, celebrating the Fiftieth Anniversary of Zeelandia (1900-1950), featuring potters at work, stamped bottle, "TL, Delft".

11.58in (29cm) high

£100-150 **DRA**

Six tiles from the Verzet (WWII Resistance) series, by De Porceleyne Fles, including one pair and two rare ones, "Walcheren Moet Droog", restoration, and "Van't Zwaar Gehavend Nederland", bottle mark, "TL Delft".

each 8in (20.5cm) high

£120-180 **DRA**

A Goldscheider pottery figure of a young girl, from a model by Dakon, impressed factory marks and facsimile signature, small chip to hat.

c1935 *15.25in (39cm) high*

£800-1,200 **SWO**

A Goldscheider pottery figure, by Claire Herzog, model 8483, impressed marks, minor restoration.

14.5in (37cm) high

£800-1,200 **WW**

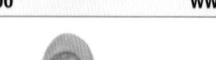

A CLOSER LOOK AT A GOLDSCHEIDER FIGURE

Founded in 1885, Goldscheider became one of the few Austrian companies to focus on Art Deco figures after WWI. It used elaborate moulds that gave its pieces detail which few could match.

Figures were moulded in sections and joined by 'luting' elements together using slip, then cleaning up seams before firing.

Copies can be identified by the visible seams and lack of attention to finish, not found in genuine Goldscheider.

Goldscheider's figures, especially those by Lorenzl and Dakon, epitomize the style of the 1920s flapper, with their cropped hair, high heels, elegant accessories, short hems - and lots of leg.

Pieces were designed to minimize collapse during firing.

An Art Deco Goldscheider figure by Lorenzl, signed "Lorenzl" on the top of the base, maker's mark underneath.

c1930 *17.25in (44cm) high*

£3,000-4,000 **JES**

The 'Butterfly Girl' by Lorenzl, glazed earthenware, modelled as a barefoot dancer in a butterfly dress, the urn marked Lorenzl, the underside with factory mark "Goldscheider Vienne".

c1935 *16in (40.5cm) high*

£1,500-2,000 **SK**

A Goldscheider pottery figure, by Josef Lorenzl, model 7037, impressed marks, original paper label.

14.5in (37cm) high

£500-800 **WW**

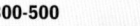

A Goldscheider pottery figure, from a model after Lorenzl, of a reclining nude upon a lozenge-shaped base painted with colours, factory marks to underside.

7.75in (20cm) high

£300-500 **ROS**

A Goldscheider figure of a dancing lady with floral decorated lilac flowering dress, on an oval black base, marked "7855 64 31".

14in (35.5cm) high

£500-800 **BRI**

A pair of Goldscheider pottery figures, modelled as a Chinese woman and man, printed "Goldscheider" mark to underside.

11.75in (30cm) high

£220-280 **ROS**

A Friedrich Goldscheider bust, Vienna, signed "Legegue", numbered "1340, 181" and "8", signed "Reproduction Reserve" and "Friedrich Goldscheider".

c1900 *20in (50cm) high*

£2,000-3,000 **KAU**

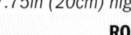

A Goldscheider pottery bust, model 320, impressed number, faint printed mark.

13in (33cm) high

£400-600 **WW**

A 19thC Continental tin glazed majolica wall plaque with intertwined border and Renaissance-style group.

16in (40.5cm) diam

£200-300 **MAX**

A large 19thC Florentine majolica charger, painted with a Classical scene of warriors in a chariot, crack.

24.5in (62cm) diam

£700-900 **SWO**

A large 19thC Continental majolica dish, with serpent scroll handles and dolphin feet, decorated in the Renaissance manner with cherubs, a lake landscape and fortified town.

16in (40cm) wide

£200-300 **MAX**

A large Continental majolica jardinière, decorated with bold female masks and laurel scrolls on a blue background.

16in (40.5cm) diam

£700-1,000 **JN**

A 20thC Moorish-style Italian majolica bottle-form vase, body surmounted by seated lions, above a plinth base, decorated overall with a copper red glaze, underglaze blue rooster mark.

15in (37.5cm) high

£600-900 **FRE**

A Bernhard Bloch majolica wine jug, with a moulded mask of Bacchus and a serpent handle, impressed 'BB'.

The Bernhard Bloch factory, Bohemia (1871-1940), was a major manufacturer of tobacco jars.

c1890 *17in (43cm) high*

£150-200 **SWO**

A late 19thC majolica 'Monkey' teapot, possibly Continental, modelled after the Minton original, indistinctly impressed, repaired.

6.25in (16cm) high

£200-300 **DN**

A 19thC Continental majolica stork vase, modelled holding a frog beside bull rushes, on a moulded oval base, some losses to vase.

24in (61cm) high

£800-1,200 **GORL**

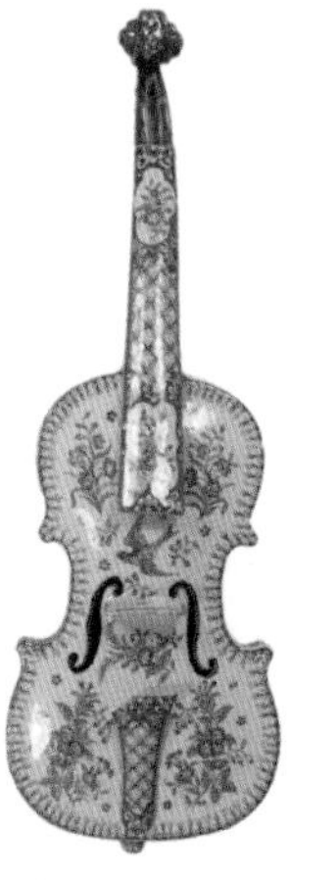

A late 19thC Italian majolica ornamental violin, having with bridge and string retainers, allover decorated with birds, flowers and foliage.

£120-180 **BIG**

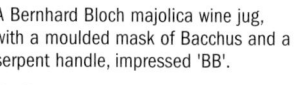

A Theodore Deck plaque, designed by Eugene Gluck, depicting a boar hunt in majolica glazes, mounted in gilded frame, signed "E. Gluck 1866/Th. Deck 1866" and stamped "MAN-RE DE FAYENCES PARIS", restoration and damage.

1866 *28.5in (71cm) wide*

£1,500-2,000 **DRA**

A Meissen model of a bird of prey, by Paul Walther.

1904 *11in (28cm) high*

£2,000-2,500 **DA**

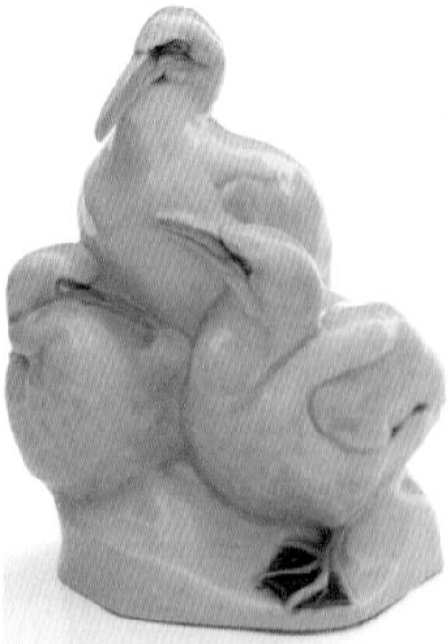

A Meissen group depicting three seagulls, by Paul Walther.

1910 *8.5in (21cm) long*

£2,000-2,500 **DA**

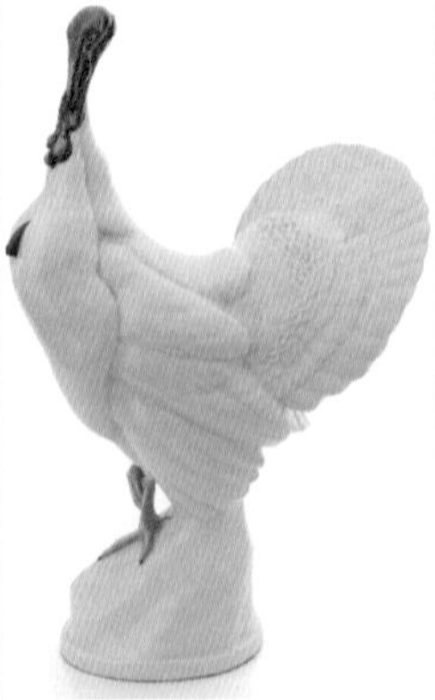

A Meissen model of a turkey, by Paul Walther, impressed "PW 1918".

14.75in (37.5cm) high

£3,000-3,500 **DA**

A Meissen model of a blackbird with grapes, modelled by Paul Walther, with impressed "PW" monogram.

c1920 *13in (33cm) high*

£3,000-3,500 **DA**

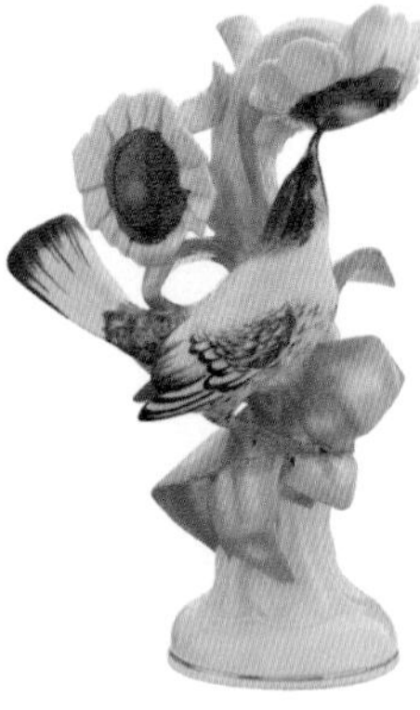

A Meissen group of sunflowers with a blackbird, modelled by Paul Walther, impressed "PW" monogram.

c1920 *11in (28cm) high*

£3,000-3,500 **DA**

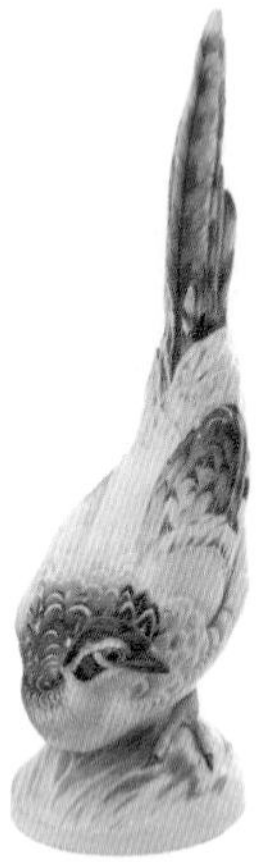

A Meissen model of a pheasant, by Paul Walther, with artist's monogram and signed in red.

1921 *19in (49cm) high*

£5,000-7,000 **DA**

A Meissen model of a cockatoo, by Paul Walther.

1922 *18in (45.5cm) high*

£4,000-6,000 **DA**

A Meissen model of a toucan, by Paul Walther, holding a red pepper in its beak.

1924 *19in (49cm) high*

£7,000-9,000 **DA**

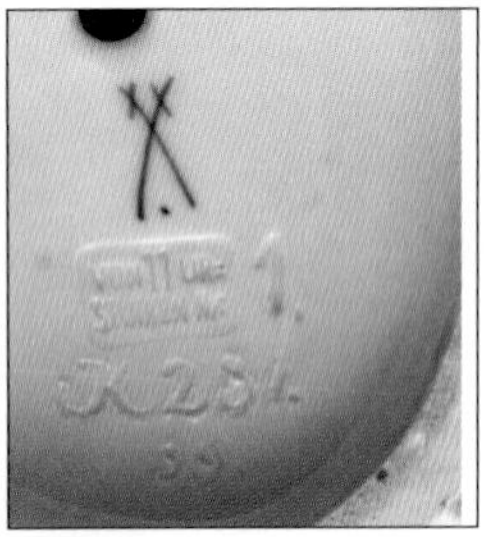

A Meissen model of a cockerel standing on a melon, modelled by Paul Walther, impressed "PW" monogram.

Meissen marked the first 11 models of a new line with numerals identifying them as such. This cockerel is marked with number 1, indicating that it was the first of these cockerels to be made. The modeller would have personally supervised the creation of these first pieces.

1926 *15.5in (39.5cm) high*

£5,000-7,000 **DA**

A Meissen model of two ibis, modelled by M.H. Fritz.

1914 *15in (38cm) high*

£3,000-3,500 **DA**

A pair of Meissen models of golden oriels, each perched on a tree stump and brightly enamelled yellow and black, crossed swords marks.

c1875 *10in (25.5cm) high*

£1,200-1,800 **WW**

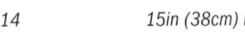

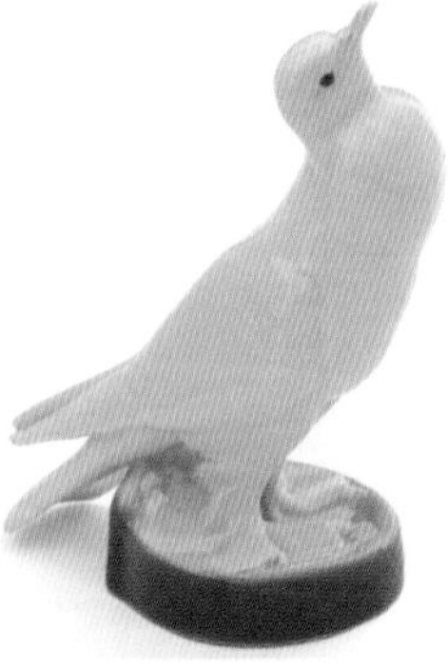

A Meissen model of a feather-footed dove, on a green base.

1905 *7.5in (19cm) high*

£1,500-2,000 **DA**

A Meissen Art Deco model of a badger, modelled by Max Esser, from a series entitled "Reinicke Fuchs" inspired by a German folk tale of the same name, base incised "M. Esser" and signed and dated "M. Esser 1922" in gold.

11in (28cm) high

£2,500-3,500 **DA**

A Meissen model of a goat by Max Esser, base incised "M. Esser" and signed and dated "M. Esser 1923" in gold.

1923 *7.25in (18.5cm) high*

£2,500-3,500 **DA**

An Art Deco Meissen model of a Great Dane, modelled by Max Esser, from a series entitled "Reinicke Fuchs", inspired by a German folk tale of the same name.

This series of models were made and sold in three different forms – in the white, in orange and gold and in polychrome.

1925 *9.75in (25cm) high*

£2,500-3,500 **DA**

A Meissen model of a polar bear, modelled by Otto Jarl.

1903 *20in (51cm) wide*

£4,500-5,500 **DA**

A Meissen group depicting a tiger killing a deer, modelled by Otto Jarl.

Jarl was a freelance artist who worked for Meissen 1903-04. He was inspired in his intricate animal figures by the delicately painted animal figures produced for the 1889 and 1900 World Fairs by Arnold Krog and Carl Liisberg in Copenhagen.

1903

£6,000-8,000 **DA**

A Meissen group depicting two smiling tigers, modelled by Rudolph Lörner.

1912 *14in (35.5cm) wide*

£3,000-4,000 **DA**

A Meissen group depicting a leopard and a panther in battle, on an oval base, modelled by Rudolph Lörner.

1912 *13in (33cm) wide*

£3,500-4,500 **DA**

A Meissen model of a bison, modelled in Boettger stoneware by Elrich Oehme.

1938 *16in (40.5cm) wide*

£1,500-2,000 **DA**

A Meissen model of a seated mandrill, modelled by Otto Pilz.

1907 *9in (23cm) high*

£2,200-2,800 **DA**

A Meissen model of a big cat attacking a zebra, modelled by Otto Pilz.

1911 *12.25in (31cm) high*

£3,000-4,000 **DA**

A Meissen group depicting a pair of llama, first modelled in 1906 by Otto Pilz.

c1925 *14.5in (37cm) wide*

£2,500-3,500 **DA**

A Meissen group of two greyhounds, modelled by Otto Pilz.

9.75in (25cm) high

£3,000-4,000 **DA**

A Meissen model of an oryx, modelled by Paul Walther.

1911 *7.5in (19cm) high*

£3,000-4,000 **DA**

A Meissen model of a Doberman, modelled by Paul Walther.

1912 *6.75in (17cm) high*

£1,500-2,000 **DA**

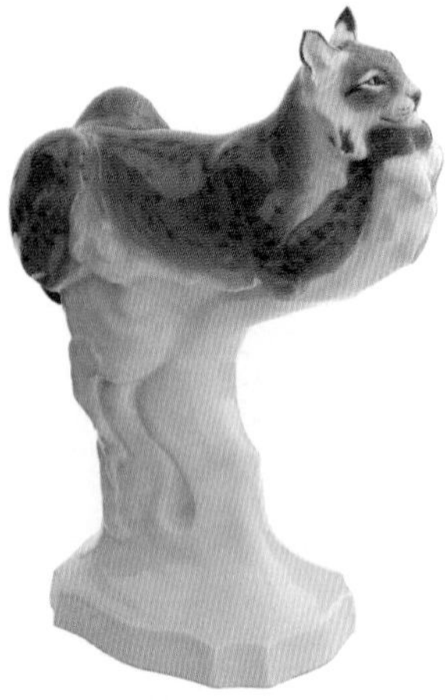

A Meissen model of a lynx perched on a branch, modelled by Paul Walther, with "PW" monogram.

1912 *10.5in (26.5cm) high*

£3,000-4,000 **DA**

A Meissen group depicting a polar bear and cub, modelled by Willy Zugel.

1906 *6in (15cm) high*

£2,500-3,500 **DA**

A Meissen model of an elephant sitting on a multi-coloured dais.

c1914 *7.5in (19cm) high*

£2,500-3,500 **DA**

A Meissen model of a young girl riding a tortoise, modelled by Otto Pilz.

1907 *7in (18cm) wide*

£2,000-2,500 **DA**

An unusual Meissen model of Cupid with two Dachshunds, modelled by Joseph Jakob Ringler.

1899 *6in (15cm) high*

£1,500-2,000 **DA**

A Meissen group depicting a lady and child, modelled by Paul Scheurich.

c1920 *11.5in (29cm) high*

£3,000-3,500 **DA**

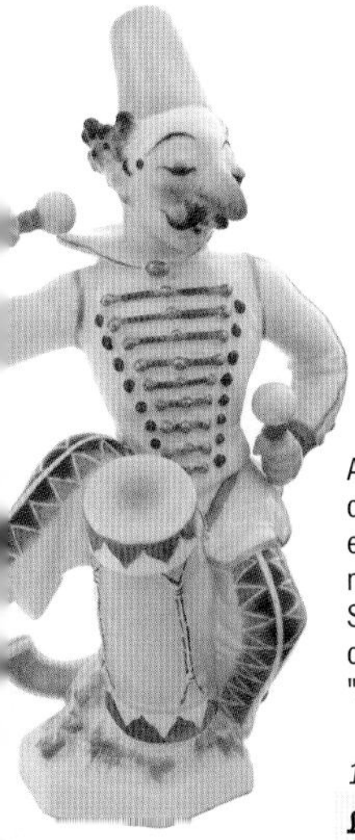

A Meissen model of a clown beating a drum, entitled "Paukenschläger", modelled by Paul Scheurich, from a set of circus performers entitled "Zwergenkapelle".

1938 *6.75in (17cm) high*

£2,000-2,500 **DA**

A Meissen group depicting a centaur and a woman in am embrace, modelled by Martin Wiegend, with Art Nouveau-style motifs in gilt to the base.

1909 *9in (23cm) high*

£3,000-4,000 **DA**

A Meissen group depicting a centaur and a woman grappling, modelled by Martin Wiegend, with Art Nouveau-style motifs in gilt to the base.

1909 *9in (23cm) high*

£3,000-4,000 **DA**

A Meissen group depicting the German folk hero Till Eulenspiegel and his female companion Nele sitting on a wall.

c1900 *13in (33cm) wide*

£3,000-4,000 **DA**

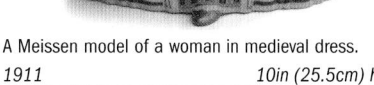

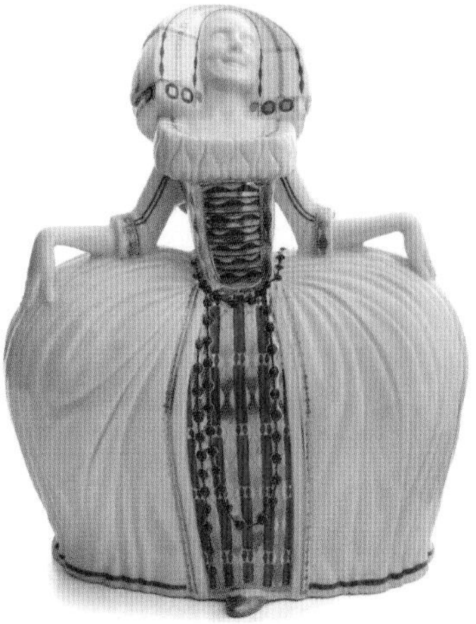

A Meissen model of a woman in medieval dress.

1911 *10in (25.5cm) high*

£3,000-3,500 **DA**

A Meissen model of a woman draped in a black and white robe, modelled by Theodor Eichler.

1913 *9in (23cm) high*

£2,000-2,500 **DA**

A Meissen model of a woman lying on a bed of flowers draped in a diaphanous robe, attended by putti, modelled by Paul Helmig.

1904 *11in (28cm) wide*

£3,000-3,500 **DA**

A Meissen shallow dish, in the form of a pond with water lilies, with an Art Nouveau maiden emerging from waves, possibly modelled by Konrad Hentschel.

1899 *8.5in (21.5cm) wide*

£2,200-2,800 **DA**

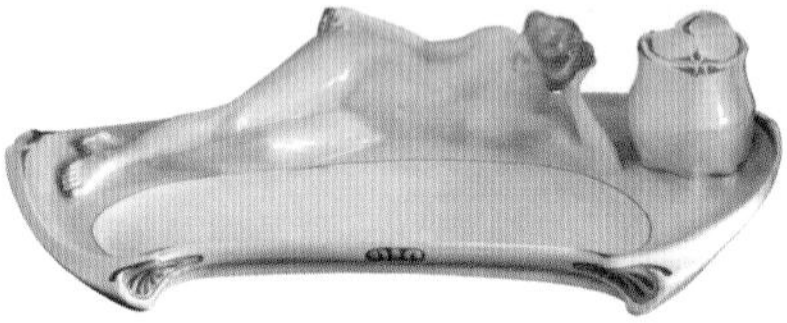

A Meissen Art Nouveau pen tray and inkwell depicting naked woman holding a mirror, modelled by Arthur Lange.

1903 *14.25in (36cm) wide*

£3,000-3,500 **DA**

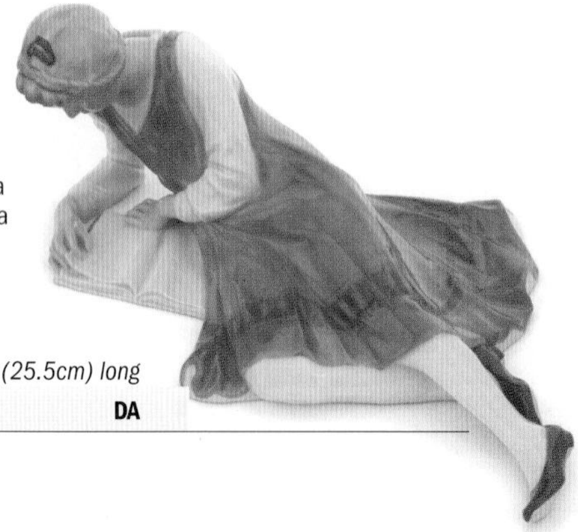

A Meissen model of a reclining girl reading a book, modelled by Richard Langer.

c1905 *10in (25.5cm) long*

£2,500-3,000 **DA**

A CLOSER LOOK AT A MEISSEN FIGURE

Paul Scheurich (1883-1945) was one of the best-known artists of the early 20thC, working for Nymphenberg and KPM, as well as Meissen.

Scheurich conceived the design in 1929 and this model was produced during the 1930s.

This figure is typical of the figures produced in the 1930s by Meissen and other factories, epitomising the Art Deco lifestyle both through costume and extravagant postures.

The 1930s preoccupation with the exotic is reflected in the elaborate ostrich feature fan.

Meissen Art Deco pieces are scarce but both the quality of the design and the manufacture are extremely high. Many pieces were left entirely in the white, and coloured wares are rare.

A Meissen Art Deco painted model entitled "Lady with Fan", modelled by Paul Scheurich, dated "1929".

18.5in (47cm) high

£7,000-9,000 **DA**

A Meissen model of a Balinese woman, first created in 1925 by W. Münch-Khe, modelled in Boettger stoneware.

1953 *10.5in (26.5cm) high*

£1,000-1,500 **DA**

A Meissen plate, by Paul Emile Börner, depicting a naked woman feeding a satyr grapes, decorated in gold and signed.

Paul Börner was employed at the Staatlichen porcelain works at Meissen. Between 1921-28 he developed monumental porcelain figures to decorate the Nikolaikirche in Meissen and the WWI war memorial. He is also famous for casting bells.

c1920 *18in (45.5cm) diam*

£4,000-5,000 **DA**

A Meissen Art Deco plate depicting a lady seated at a writing desk with a parrot, bordered with patterns in black and gold, possibly by Börner.

c1920 *10in (25.5cm) diam*

£2,000-2,500 **DA**

A Meissen white plate, decorated with toucans, painted in Schafferfeurfarben.

c1915 *12in (30.5cm) diam*

£2,200-2,800 **DA**

A Meissen underglaze blue plate depicting a stag in a forest, with a geometric design around the rim.

13.75in (35cm) diam

£1,500-2,000 **DA**

A René Buthaud Art Deco ceramic bowl, signed with artist's monogram.

Buthaud's (1886-1987) simple wares were often decorated with stylized women influenced by the work of Jean Dupas or African art.

c1925 *6in (15cm) diam*

£2,000-2,500 **JES**

An Edouard Cazaux art pottery vase, the bulbous form decorated with scrolls, lines and flowers in blue, green, and brown on white ground, signed "Cazaux".

c1930 *11.5in (29cm) high*

£1,200-1,800 **SK**

An Auguste Delaherche spherical vase, covered in copper and blue crystalline glaze dripping over a dark brown ground, signed "Aug. Delaherche".

6in (15cm) wide

£700-1,000 **DRA**

An Aesthetic Movement faience moon flask and cover, by A.J. Fischer, Budapest, the blue ground reserved with panels of flowers, grasshoppers and florets in enamels and gliding, restoration, stamped mark.

c1880 *13.25in (34cm) high*

£100-150 **SWO**

A Fischer moonflask and cover, Hungary, of circular form enriched with Japanese-style insects among flowering foliage, set on two feet, cover restored.

c1900 *13.5in (34.5cm) high*

£250-350 **ROS**

An Emile Gallé faience cat, the head inset with green marbled glass eyes and painted in grey with flowers, with a pendant brooch bearing a portrait of a dog, the painted mark to the base obliterated.

13.25in (33.5cm) high

£2,800-3,200 **B**

A French Art Deco table lamp, stylized Art Deco floral motif, probably a Clarice Cliff design, signed on base "Grey's Pottery".

c1930 *6in (15cm) high*

£400-500 **DD**

A tall Haviland & Co. red clay vase, decorated by Eugene Chaplet, with applied quatrefoils, covered in green and gold glazes, stamped "H&Co. R.V.1.2, EC", losses.

12.75in (32cm) high

£1,200-1,800 **DRA**

An Art Deco Wiener Werkstatte ceramic box and cover, attributed to Hilda Jesser, printed "Wiener Werkstatte".

c1920 *7.5in (19cm) high*

£500-800 **JES**

An Art Deco Gustavsberg Pottery vase, matte aqua green with silver overlay figural decoration, from the "Argenta" line designed by Wilhelm Kage.

c1930 *8in (20.5cm) high*

£1,000-1,500 **DD**

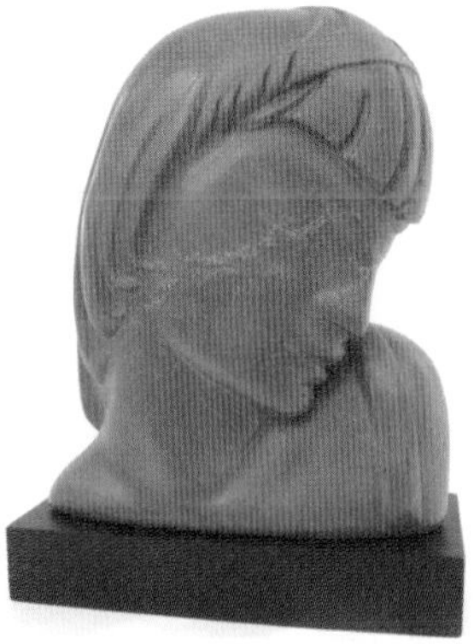

An American Art Deco chalkware sculpture, of a stylized figural Greek bust, signed "Kupur" on back.

c1930 *12in (30.5cm) high*

£700-1,000 **DD**

A tall Max Laueger vase, decorated in squeezebag with branches of pussy willow on a blue ground, glaze flakes, stamped cipher and "MUSTER GESETZL./GESCHTZL/11110".

15.25in (38cm) high

£800-1,200 **DRA**

A Lenci pottery figure of the Madonna, black painted marks and "11-XII-E".

11.5in (29cm) high

£500-800 **DN**

A Lenci figure of a lady and two dogs, inscribed "Torino 25-10-34 XII", reglued.

From the late 1920s, Turin company Lenci (established in 1919) produced ceramic figures in contemporary dress. They are identified by their enlongated limbs, blonde hair and a combination of matte and gloss glazes.

1934 *15.25in (38cm) high*

£3,500-4,500 **SWO**

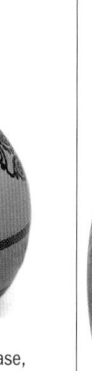

An Emile Lenoble art pottery vase, narrow neck on bulbous body with black stylized decoration on green ground, artist's cipher on base.

c1930 *9.5in (24cm) high*

£1,200-1,800 **SK**

An Art Deco Longwy ceramic stand, retailed through Primavera, printed maker's marks.

c1930 *8in (20.5cm) wide*

£150-200 **JES**

A Longwy Art Deco cloisonné pottery platter, jungle landscape with nudes, signed "Longwy" on the base. 1920s

This piece was inspired by the African art designs of Picasso and made for the Primavera Design Studio at Au Printemps Department store. Stylized female figures were often used to decorate Primavera's wares.

14.5in (37cm) diam

£2,000-3,000 **DD**

A Longwy bowl, with a turquiose rim and handles, centred with stylized peacock motif, marked "Atelier primavera Longwy, France'.

7in (17.5cm) diam

£150-200 **SWO**

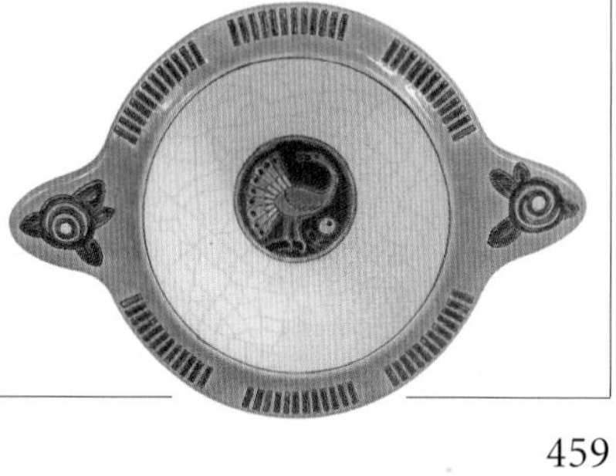

A 20thC French Madoura collector's plate, glazed in white, painted with a Spanish horse rider, the rim with irregular spots, signed "Edition Picasso" and manufacturer's mark.

8.5in (21cm) diam

£800-1,200 **KAU**

A Clement Massier bottle-shaped vase, painted with Art Nouveau flowers in a lustred glaze, restoration around rim, signed "Clement Massier Golfe-Juan".

Established in the Cote D'Azur, the Massier family had been master ceramicists since c1750. Clement (1844-1917) and Delphin (1836-1907) hired technical genius Gaetano Gandolfi in 1859. Rivalry forced Clement to leave the Vallauris factory and establish one in Golfe-Juan. Clement's metallic lustre glazes date from 1887, when he hired Lévy-Dhurmer. The glazes won a gold medal at the 1889 Exposition Universelle de Paris.

11.75in (30cm) high

£250-350 **DRA**

A near pair of Delphin Massier faience garden seats, modelled as flowerheads on pierced base moulded as leaves and painted in colours, one with painted mark "Delphin Massier, Vallauris A. M."

20in (51cm) high

£2,200-2,800 **L&T**

A large Delphin Massier faience jardinière on stand, applied butterflies to the rim, the body with moulded irises, the stand modelled as a peacock amongst reeds, painted marks "Delphin Massier, Vallauris A. M."

Delphin Massier ran the family factory in Vallauris, producing majolica home and garden ware.

52in (132cm) high

£2,200-2,800 **L&T**

An Art Deco Pietro Melandri plate with female figure, Italian.

c1925 *11in (28cm) diam*

£1,000-1,500 **JES**

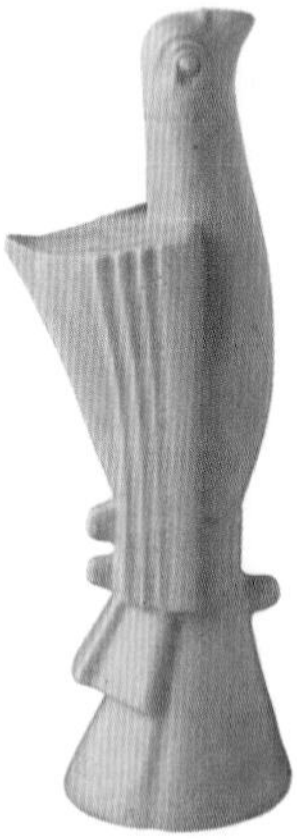

A rare Art Deco bird design sculpture, by Gustav Milkos.

c1925 *15in (38cm) high*

£2,000-3,000 **MOD**

A large Mougin vase, with scalloped rim, partly embossed in a geometric pattern and covered in a bronzed glaze over panels of blue and amber crystalline glaze, stamped "Mougin Nancy 321J".

11in (27.5cm) high

£2,000-3,000 **DRA**

A squat ovoid vase, by Gres Mougin of Nancy, engraved in shallow relief and highlighted in blue, with a stylized landscape containing a Pan figure and naked females.

c1925 *11.5in (29cm) high*

£1,800-2,200 **MOD**

A WMF earthenware box and cover, designed by Christian Neuwirth, with pierced plated mounts, painted in the Secessionist manner with geometric forms, stamped and printed factory marks.

10.5in (27cm) wide

£300-400 **L&T**

A Nippon vase, decorated in Coralene with yellow and orange lilies on a shaded ground, gilt worn, stamped "US Patent 917, Feb 9.1909, Japan".

8.75in (22cm) high

£500-800 **DRA**

A Francesco Nonni Art Deco figure.

c1925 *10.25in (26cm) high*

£2,000-2,500 **JES**

A Wassily Kandinsky cup and saucer, made by St. Petersburg-Leningrad, the cup painted with an abstract composition the saucer with an abstract maritime scene, two manufacturer's marks and dated "1914" and "1921", signed, serial number "856/15-c" and "805/40-I", handle chipped.

saucer 5.5in (14cm) diam

£800-1,200 **KAU**

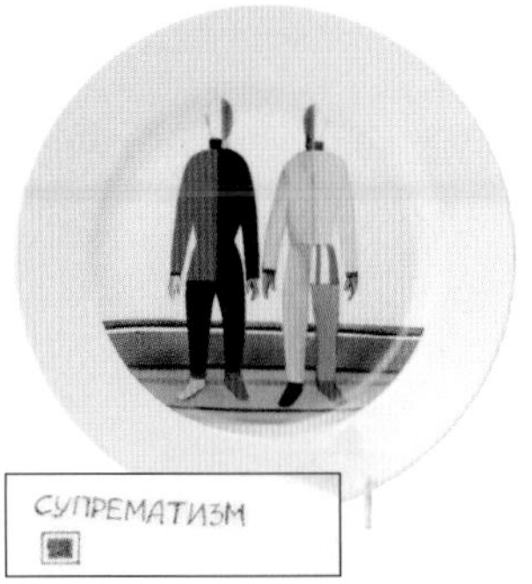

A Kasimir Malewitsch plate, made by St Petersburg-Leningrad, glazed and painted porcelain, depicting two abstract figures, separated into different colour fields, with "VKhUTEMAS" sign, signed and dated.

1923 *9.5in (24cm) diam*

£1,500-2,000 **KAU**

A Primavera Art Deco figure of an ermine, thickly glazed in black and white, impressed marks "13886".

12.5in (31.5cm) high

£1,200-1,800 **L&T**

A Reissner & Kessel porcelain bust, depicting a young lady in a risqué dress, bonnet and cloak, printed "R.S & K" mark.

c1905 *18.25in (45.5cm) high*

£300-500 **SWO**

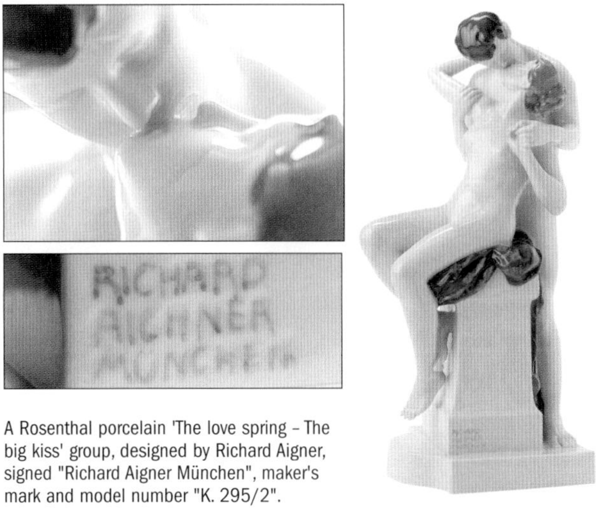

A Rosenthal porcelain 'The love spring – The big kiss' group, designed by Richard Aigner, signed "Richard Aigner München", maker's mark and model number "K. 295/2".

c1913 *15.25in (38cm) high*

£1,800-2,200 **KAU**

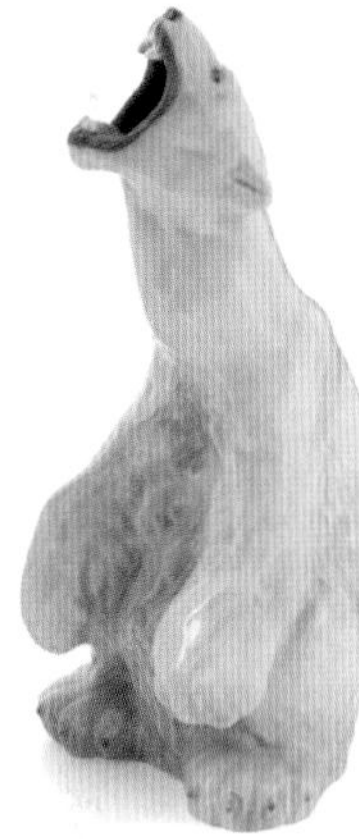

A Royal Copenhagen model of a polar bear, seated on its haunches, printed and painted marks.

12.75in (32.5cm) high

£150-200 **DN**

A pair of Royal Dux figures, a shepherdess with a lamb and a shepherd with a goat, pad mark to bases, goat's ear missing.

Established in 1853, north of Prague, Royal Dux is still in production today.

c1900 *21.25in (54cm) high*

£700-1,000 **SWO**

A Royal Dux figure of a maiden, modelled leaning against rockwork on a large shell base, typically coloured and gilt, impressed pad mark, small chips to shell.

16.5in (42cm) high

£400-600 **DN**

A Royal Dux figure of a maiden, modelled astride a shell holding a lute, typically coloured and gilt, impressed pad mark, damage and losses.

10.25in (26cm) high

£120-180 **DN**

A 20thC art pottery vase by San Marti, redware body decorated in a high gloss deep blue glaze with incised panels decorated with stylized flowers, marked on base.

c1930 *12.25in (31cm) high*

£250-300 **SK**

An Art Deco Royal Dux Pottery figure, in exotic dress, applied pink triangle mark, restored hand.

15.5in (39.5cm) high

£300-500 **WW**

A Viktor Schreckengost figurine of an acrobat on horseback, 'Madam Kitty', in matte yellow, blue and orange on ivory ground, stamped "Viktor Schreckengost" also bears paper label with title.

9.5in (24cm) wide

£2,200-2,800 **SDR**

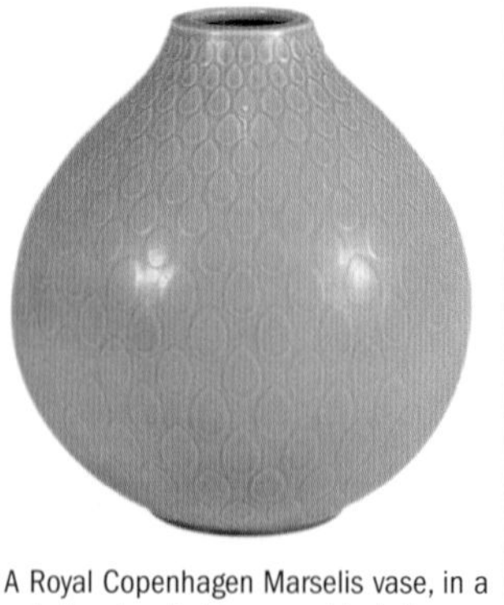

A Royal Copenhagen Marselis vase, in a celadon-dappled tear-moulded glaze, by Nils Thorsson, printed marks.

10.5in (27cm) high

£150-200 **SWO**

A ceramic Italian Art Deco vase and cover, by Tarcisio Tosin, Vicenza, marked with an arrow on the base to represent 'La Freccia'.

1934 *19.75in (50cm) high*

£2,000-3,000 **JES**

A Turn Bohemia porcelain figure of a maiden, by Ernest Wahliss, modelled standing, wearing medieval dress on a plinth base, printed and impressed marks, chips and restoration.

18.25in (46cm) high

£400-600 **DN**

An Essevi 'S.O.S.' figural dish, designed by Sandro Vacchetti, modelled as a fallen skater, painted in colours and raised on a stepped zigzag 'ice' base with opposed dishes, painted marks.

11.5in (29cm) wide

£9,000-11,000 **L&T**

A Zsolnay vase, with a doe amongst reticulated trees covered in purple, gold and green lustred glaze, several firing lines apparently restored in the factory, reglued ear, stamped "Zsolnay Pecs/M6513/A".

18in (45cm) high

£8,000-10,000 **DRA**

An early Zsolnay jardinière, with closed-in rim, enamel-decorated with tulips and whiplash leaves, against a purple lustred ground, raised castle medallion, "644/14".

7in (17.5cm) wide

£2,000-3,000 **DRA**

A pair of Zsolnay pottery plates, with a fruit and vine border surrounding female figures in garden scenes.

c1900

£800-1,200 **FRE**

A late 19thC pair of French 'Japonism' vases, painted with seascape, scenic and chinoiserie reserves on gilt enhanced platinum grounds.

11.5in (29cm) high

£600-900 **FRE**

A French Art Deco Cubist ceramic fish, by the French National Porcelain Factory, Sèvres, marked "DN" for Pate Dure Novelle, a custom ceramic mix, dated 1925.

17in (43cm) wide

£1,000-1,500 **MOD**

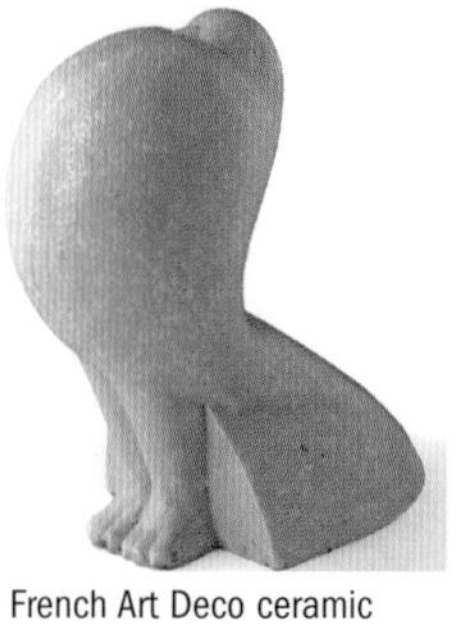

A French Art Deco ceramic model of a pigeon.

c1925 *13.5in (34cm) high*

£800-1,200 **JES**

A Czech Art Deco pottery console set, Cubist designed vase and matching candlestick holders.

c1930 *10in (25.5cm) high*

£1,200-1,800 **DD**

WALL MASKS

- From the 1920s to the 1950s, modern homes throughout Britain, Europe and the US were decorated with brightly coloured, inexpensive wall masks. The style reached a peak in popularity in the 1930s when the main ceramics factories produced innovative yet inexpensive designs, including masks and flying ducks.
- Staffordshire makers Beswick, Cope and Clarice Cliff all produced wall masks reflecting modern interests in fashion and style, which make them so fascinating to collectors today. Most were inexpensive to collect until very recently.
- At the higher end of the market are the unique pieces from Weiner Werkstätte. Goldscheider produced similar masks prior to WWII and these are more common today.
- Unusual models are avidly collected but more common 'Spanish ladies', Viennese style masks, Japanese copies or religious masks do not attract such high prices.

A Goldscheider terracotta wall mask of a dark-skinned young woman with orange curly hair and a yellow veil, model number 8016, small chips.

11.5in (29cm) high

£150-200 **CA**

A Goldscheider terracotta wall mask of a dark-skinned woman in a blue veil, with a black printed mark and inscribed pattern number "7831".

8in (20.5cm) high

£100-150 **CA**

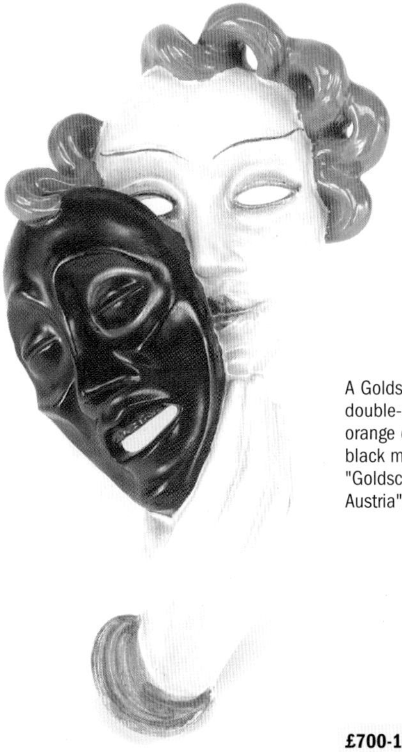

A Goldscheider hanging double-mask of woman with orange curly hair holding a black mask, stamped "Goldscheider/Wien/Made in Austria".

13.75in (35cm) high

£700-1,000 **SDR**

A Goldscheider terracotta wall mask of a black woman with blue hair, modelled with her hand below her neck, repair to one hair ringlet.

Goldscheider (1885-1953), Vienna, was known for its crisp modelling and excellent painting, as well as its use of fine materials. Black masks are scarcer than white models.

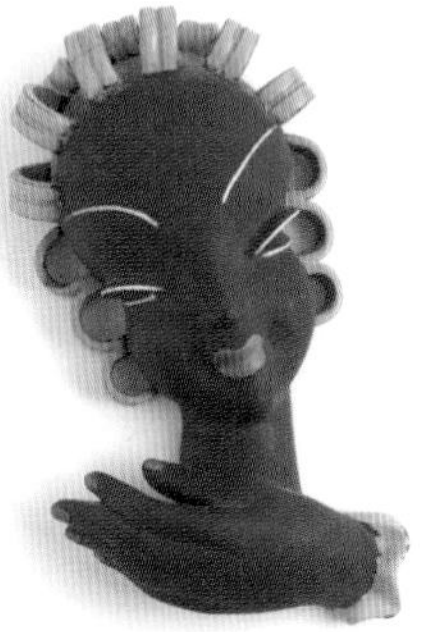

10.5in (26.5cm) high

£120-180 **CA**

A Czech Goldscheider-style terracotta wall mask, of a woman with orange hair and a blue scarf.

11.5in (29cm) high

£100-150 **CA**

A Royal Belvedere Austrian pottery wall mask of a woman, with brown hair, in the Goldscheider style.

11in (28cm) high

£60-80 **CA**

A Czech pottery wall mask, model no.11729, printed and impressed marks.

9.5in (24cm) high

£300-500 **WW**

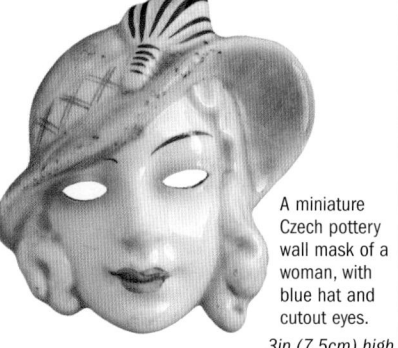

A miniature Czech pottery wall mask of a woman, with blue hat and cutout eyes.

3in (7.5cm) high

£50-80 **CA**

A Czech wall mask of a girl in a blue and green edged bonnet with googly eyes, some restoration.

8.5in (21.5cm) high

£60-100 **CA**

A Beswick pottery wall mask of a woman with blonde hair and a blue beret, model number 197.

6.5in (16.5cm) high

£80-120 **CA**

A small Cope and Co. pottery wall mask of a woman with blonde hair and a green beret.

3in (7.5cm) high

£30-50 **CA**

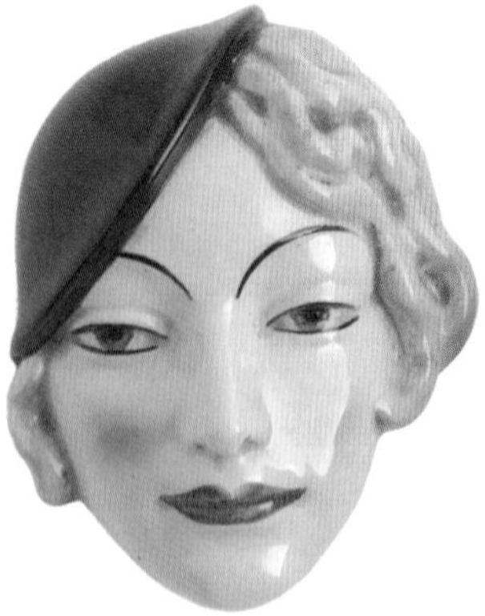

A small Cope and Co. pottery wall mask of a woman with blonde hair and a black beret.

6.5in (16.5cm) high

£40-60 **CA**

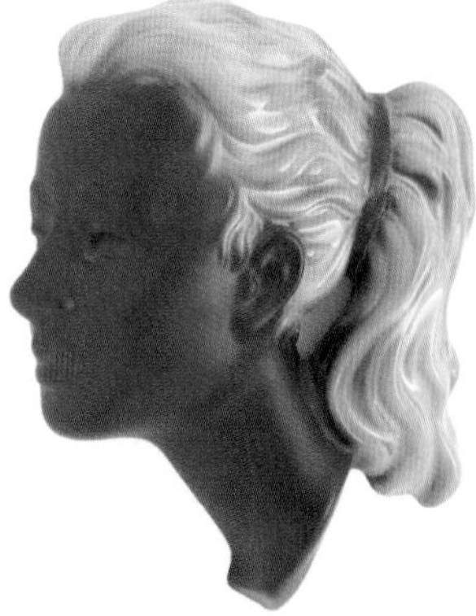

A Corten Dorf pottery wall mask of a woman with light blue hair.

10in (25.5cm) high

£50-80 **CA**

An Essevi pottery wall mask of a girl in a large hat and black eye mask with a monkey on her hand.

10.5in (26.5cm) high

£500-800 **CA**

A Goebels pottery wall mask of a girl with black hair and plaits.

7in (18cm) high

£70-100 **CA**

A Goebels pottery wall mask of a girl with curly hair.

8.5in (21.5cm) high

£80-120 **CA**

A Lancaster & Sons pottery wall mask of a lady with dark hair.

7.25in (18.5cm) high

£40-60 **CA**

A Lenci pottery wall mask, signed "Lenci Made in Italy FV".

11in (28cm) high

£400-500 **WW**

An Art Deco plaster painted wall mask by G. Leonard.

9.5in (24cm) high

£40-60 **CA**

An Art Deco plaster painted wall mask entitled 'Carmen', by Roskelly.

8.5in (21.5cm) high

£30-50 **CA**

A small Austrian 'Felt' pottery wall mask, of a woman in a white hat.

5in (12.5cm) high

£50-80 **CA**

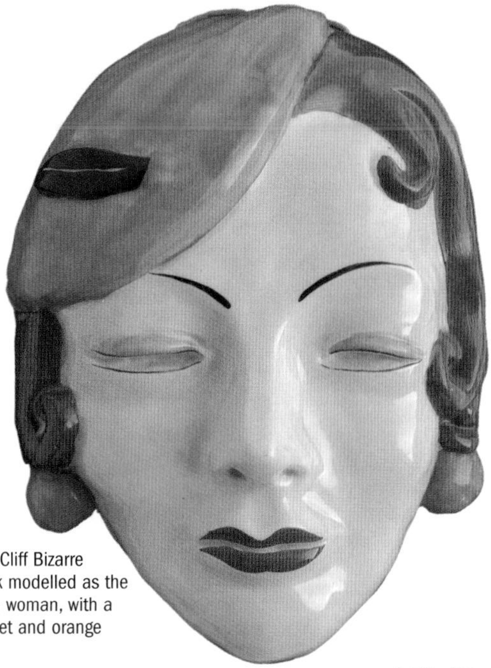

A Clarice Cliff Bizarre wall mask modelled as the head of a woman, with a green beret and orange hair.

8.75in (22cm) high

£600-900 **CA**

A Clarice Cliff 'Jack' pottery wall mask, in Inspiration glaze with yellow hair.

7in (18cm) high

£250-300 **CA**

A Clarice Cliff 'Marlene' wall pocket, with orange headpiece, the back marked "Wilkinson Ltd England".

Cliff's 'Marlene' (after Dietrich) and 'Flora' were available in both bold and pastel colourways and proved highly popular with the public.

7.5in (19cm) high

£200-300 **CA**

A Clarice Cliff Bizarre 'Marlene' wall mask, with yellow and orange headpiece, some restoration.

7in (18cm) high

£150-200 **CA**

A Clarice Cliff 'Pan' pottery wall pocket, modelled in light beige.

9in (23cm) high

£400-600 **CA**

A Clarice Cliff 'Pan' pottery wall pocket, modelled with grey and brown hair.

9in (23cm) high

£400-600 **CA**

A Clarice Cliff 'Pan' pottery wall mask, modelled with green leaves covering blue hair.

9in (23cm) high

£500-800 **CA**

A Clarice Cliff 'Pan' pottery wall mask, modelled with various coloured leaves in green hair.

9in (23cm) high

£500-800 **CA**

A Clarice Cliff 'Pan' pottery wall pocket, modelled with light blue hair and white face, slight retouching to left eye.

9in (23cm) high

£300-500 **CA**

A Clarice Cliff pottery wall pocket, modelled as a woman with a handkerchief and blonde hair.

11in (28cm) high

£200-300 **CA**

A miniature Clarice Cliff wall plaque medallion wall mask, of a woman with a green scarf, with hair line crack.

3in (7.5cm) high

£200-300 **CA**

JOHN BENNETT

- Born in Staffordshire 1840, Bennett trained at the Staffordshire Potteries and worked for Doulton, developing Lambeth faience. His work was exhibited to great acclaim at the 1876 Centennial Exposition in America.
- Bennett relocated to New York in 1877. Initially he imported English biscuit blanks to decorate, eventually establishing his own kilns. He and his team of potters used native clay which gives Bennett ware its characteristic creamy body. His New York work is marked in freehand "J Bennett, N.Y."
- His vigorous, ornate foliate designs, with dark outlines on rich backgrounds, invite comparison with William Morris and William de Morgan. Tiffany & Co. became a major client.
- In 1878, Bennett was employed to run classes in pottery decoration at the Society of Decorative Art but was replaced a year later by Charles Volkmar.
- He moved to West Orange, New Jersey in 1883 and later pieces are marked "East Orange, N.J." Bennett died in 1907.

A rare John Bennett spherical vase, painted with white daisies and butterflies on a turquoise ground, marked in green ink "J. BENNETT/C24/N.Y./JULY 1878/KJ".

1878 *8.25in (20.5cm) high*

£2,500-3,000 **DRA**

A large John Bennett covered jar, painted with branches of yellow dogwood and red roses on a black ground, the interior of the lid with brown-eyed Susans on a golden ground, signed inside vase "J Bennett New York 1881".

1881 *15.5in (39cm) high*

£30,000-35,000 **DRA**

A large John Bennett covered jar, painted with deep purple bearded irises on a cadmium yellow ground, the interior of the lid painted with indigo and green flowers, signed "JB 1881", and "J BENNETT/412 E 24 N.Y. 1881", chipped and restored.

1881 *16in (40cm) high*

£10,000-12,000 **DRA**

A John Bennett covered bottle, painted with white, pink and yellow chrysanthemums with cobalt leaves on a cadmium yellow ground, signed "J. Bennett/N.O.N.Y/6 Nov 1888", restored chip on lid.

13.5in (34cm) high

£2,500-3,000 **DRA**

A rare John Bennett gourd-shaped vase, painted with pink blossoms and green foliage on mottled cobalt ground, signed "J. BENNETT/ 101 LEX AVE/ N.Y."

10.25in (26cm) high

£2,500-3,000 **DRA**

A John Bennett bottle-shaped vase, painted with branches of white dogwood on a teal blue flambé ground, two grinding chips to base, signed "J. Bennett R".

10in (25.5cm) high

£1,000-1,500 **DRA**

A Batchelder 'medieval' tile, with blue and brown engobe decoration of a knight on horseback by a castle, stamped "Batchelder Los Angeles".

7.5in (19cm) wide

£500-700 **DRA**

A Batchelder tile, modelled with a stylized rose in foliage with blue engobe, painted "1674".

8.75in (22cm) high

£200-300 **DRA**

A Batchelder two-piece wall-mounted fountain, modelled with children playing hand flutes, small chips, stamped "Batchelder Los Angeles".

Ernest Batchelder (c1875-1957) founded his tile company in Pasadena, California, in 1909. The factory was very successful and employed 175 workers at the height of production. Batchelder continued making pottery until the early 1950s.

31in (77.5cm) high

£4,000-5,000 **DRA**

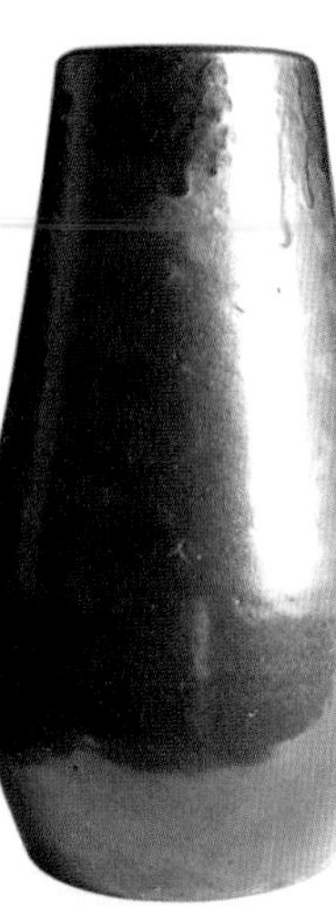

A tall Batchelder tapering vase, covered in a lustred deep plum glaze with bold drips around the top, a few glaze flakes around base, stamped "OLB".

10.5in (26cm) high

£1,200-1,800 **DRA**

A Batchelder tile, modelled with a village and covered in blue and beige matte glaze, mounted in a fine Arts and Crafts frame, stamped "Batchelder Los Angeles".

8in (20cm) high

£280-320 **DRA**

A Batchelder horizontal panel, modelled with three dancing putti against blue engobe glaze, mounted in an Arts and Crafts frame, stamped "BATCHELDER LOS ANGELES".

11.75in (29cm) wide

£800-1,200 **DRA**

CHELSEA KERAMIC ART WORKS

A rare Chelsea Keramic Art Works pillow vase, painted by Hugh Robertson, in barbotine with a white bird, stamped "CHELSEA KERAMIC ART WORKS/ROBERTSON & SONS", artist signed "HCR".

£800-1,200 **DRA**

A pair of pilgrim flasks by Chelsea Keramic Art Works, each with curled feet and angular handles, cold-painted with nasturtium and orange blossoms on a mottled ground, stamped "CHELSEA KERAMIC ART WORKS/ROBERTSON & SONS", glued, chips.

10.5in (26.5cm) high

£500-700 **DRA**

An unusual Chelsea Keramic Art Works ovoid vase with a black and charcoal melt fissure flambé glaze, die-stamped CKAW.

The Chelsea Keramic Art Works was founded in 1872. The company moved location and became the Dedham Pottery in 1895.

5.25in (13.5cm) high

£400-600 **DRA**

A Chelsea Keramic Art Works tall urn of burnished red clay with curled handles, stamped "CKAW", firing split to one handle.

13in (33cm) high

£1,200-1,800 **DRA**

A large Claycraft tile, depicting pirates on the deck of a tall ship, in matte polychrome, mounted in fine Arts and Crafts frame, stamped "Claycraft".

15.75in (39cm) wide

£600-900 **DRA**

A Claycraft three-tile frieze, modelled with a medieval village of thatched-roof cottages and cobblestone streets, stamped "Claycraft".

23.5in (59cm) wide

£600-900 **DRA**

A Claycraft narrow panel, modelled with a pine tree in front of a thatched-roof cottage, covered in dead-matte glazes, mounted in a fine Arts and Crafts frame, unmarked.

tile 12in (30cm) high

£500-700 **DRA**

A Claycraft narrow panel, modelled with a eucalyptus tree against a windmill in a mountainous landscape, covered in dead-matte glazes, mounted in a fine Arts and Crafts frame, unmarked.

tile 16in (40cm) high

£600-900 **DRA**

A Claycraft vertical tile, modelled with a hilly California landscape with tall conifer, covered in an amber and celadon matte glaze, stamped "CLAYCRAFT", chips.

16in (40cm) high

£500-700 **DRA**

A Claycraft pair of wall sconces, each decorated with a mission, in matte polychrome, several chips, stamped "Claycraft".

15in (38cm) high

£700-1,000 **DRA**

A rare Mary Yancey/Claycraft Studios ovoid vase, decorated in squeezebag with a swirled pattern under a thick, mottled blue-green semi-matte glaze, bottom drilled, stamped "Y".

12.75in (32.5cm) high

£600-900 **DRA**

CLIFTON

A Clifton Tirrube baluster vase, delicately painted with a white rose and celadon foliage on bisque-fired ground, incised "Clifton 153".

8in (20cm) high

£150-200 **DRA**

A Clifton Tirrube bottle-shaped vase, painted with an ivory nasturtium and celadon foliage on bisque-fired ground, stamped "CLIFTON 148".

9.5in (24cm) high

£150-200 **DRA**

A Clifton 'Indian' squat vessel, after the Pueblo Viejo tribe of Upper Gila Valley, Arizona, incised "Clifton 240/tribe name", short hairline to rim.

Established in 1905, Clifton is known for two types of ware – the white-bodied 'Crystal Patina' and red clay 'Indian Ware'. By 1914, the company had changed emphasis and was producing tiles.

12.5in (31cm) high

£300-400 **DRA**

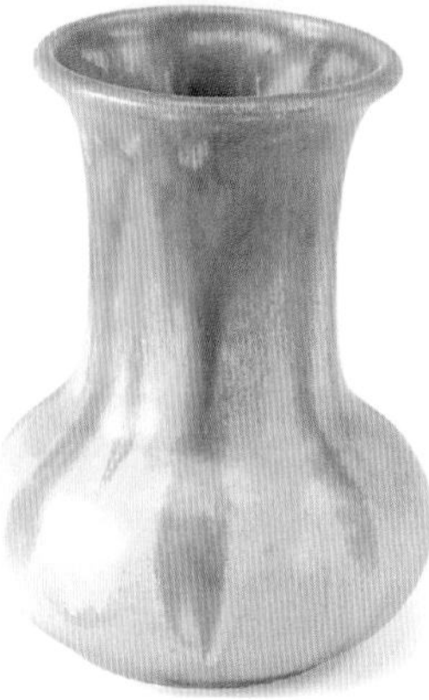

A Clifton Crystal Patina bulbous vase, incised "Clifton 1906".

6.25in (16cm) high

£180-220 **DRA**

A Dedham experimental vase, by Hugh Robertson, covered in a thick, curdled raspberry and amber glaze, incised "Dedham Pottery/BW/HCR", and in ink "DP47D".

8.5in (21.5cm) high

£2,200-2,800 **DRA**

A Dedham experimental vase, by Hugh Robertson, covered in intense volcanic oxblood glaze, Incised "Dedham Pottery HCR", ink "DP/54D; MEUP".

6.5in (19cm) high

£2,000-3,000 **DRA**

A Dedham experimental bulbous vase, by Hugh Robertson, covered in oxblood glaze with a patch of green, incised "Dedham Pottery HCR".

6in (15cm) high

£800-1,200 **DRA**

A Dedham large experimental vase, by Hugh Robertson, covered in a thick, mottled glaze, incised "Dedham Pottery/BW/HCR", and in ink "DP6G".

10.75in (27.5cm) high

£1,200-1,800 **DRA**

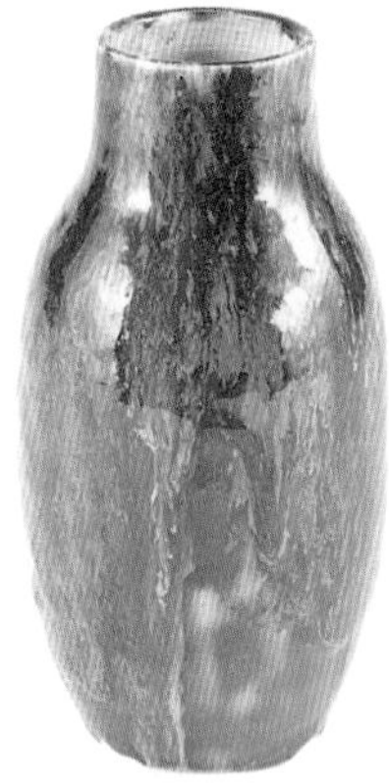

A Dedham experimental vase, by Hugh Robertson, with a thick, curdled glaze, incised "Dedham Pottery/BW/HCR", ink "DP5B".

7.5in (19cm) high

£600-900 **DRA**

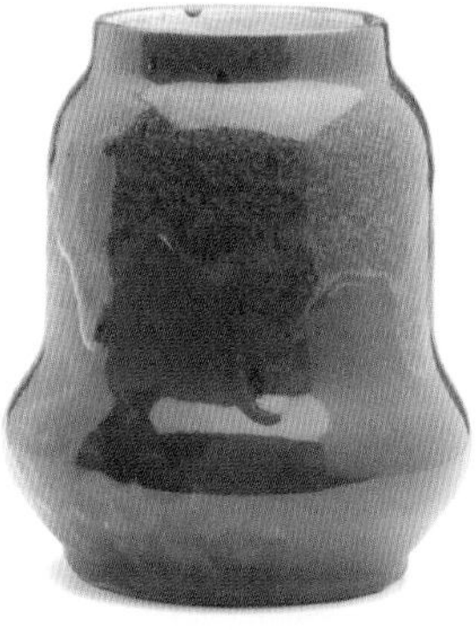

A large Dedham experimental bulbous vase, by Hugh Robertson, covered in a fine, frothy, dripping green glaze, firing line to rim, incised "Dedham Pottery/HCR/B.W", ink "DP8B/#41A".

8in (20cm) high

£700-1,000 **DRA**

A Dedham experimental bulbous vase, by Hugh Robertson, with a thick mottled amber and blue-green glaze, incised "Dedham Pottery", ink "DP88A".

8in (20cm) high

£800-1,200 **DRA**

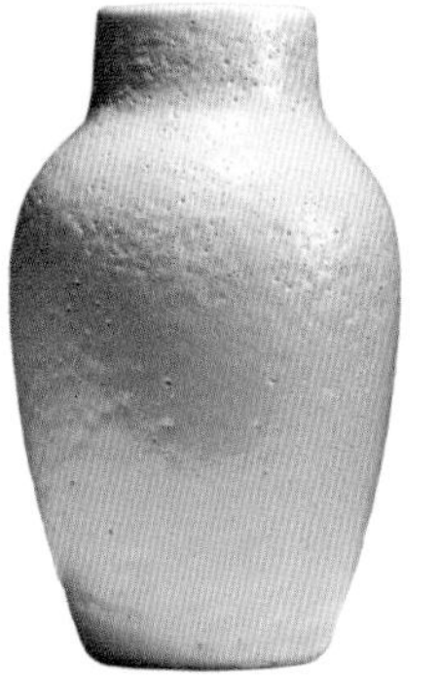

A Dedham experimental vase, by Hugh Robertson, covered in a buff-coloured volcanic glaze, several firing lines, incised "BW/Dedham Pottery/HCR".

10.5in (26cm) high

£600-900 **DRA**

A Dedham crackleware plate, entirely painted in blue and white with poppies and poppy pods, several tight hairlines around rim, ink and rabbit stamps.

8.5in (21.5cm) diam

£180-220 **DRA**

FULPER

- Established in 1805 in Flemington, New Jersey, the Fulper Pottery Co. initially produced simple functional wares.
- Under the direction of the founder's grandson William H. Fulper II and his partner Martin Stangl, a range of art pottery was introduced in 1909. The line, known as 'Vasekraft', was extremely popular and glazes included 'Leopard Skin', 'Mission Matt' and 'Café au Lait'.
- Vessels were cast in moulds and then individually glazed by hand. Colours were rich and subdued.
- The factory had a reputation for pioneering new techniques and experimented with crystalline glazes and original combinations of matt, gloss and flambé glazes.
- One of the most desirable and expensive lines at the time was the 'Famille rose' range. Shapes and colours were inspired by classical Chinese porcelain.
- Most art wares were marked with impressed or printed "Fulper".
- The factory was taken over by Stangl in 1930 and carried on production under the Stangl name until the 1970s when it closed.

A Fulper large baluster vase, in 'Mirror Black' over 'Chinese Blue' crystalline glaze, of hammered texture, vertical mark.

11.75in (29cm) high

£800-1,200 **DRA**

A Fulper tall two-handled urn, in 'Mirror Black-to-Copperdust' crystalline flambé glaze, paper label.

15in (37.5cm) high

£500-600 **DRA**

A Fulper bulbous vase, with 'Mirror Black', frothy ivory and mahogany glaze, ridged body, short line to rim, three restored chips at base, vertical mark.

12.5in (31cm) high

£220-280 **DRA**

A tall Fulper Colonial Ware urn, some burst bubbles to glaze, vertical mark.

8in (20.5cm) high

£400-500 **DRA**

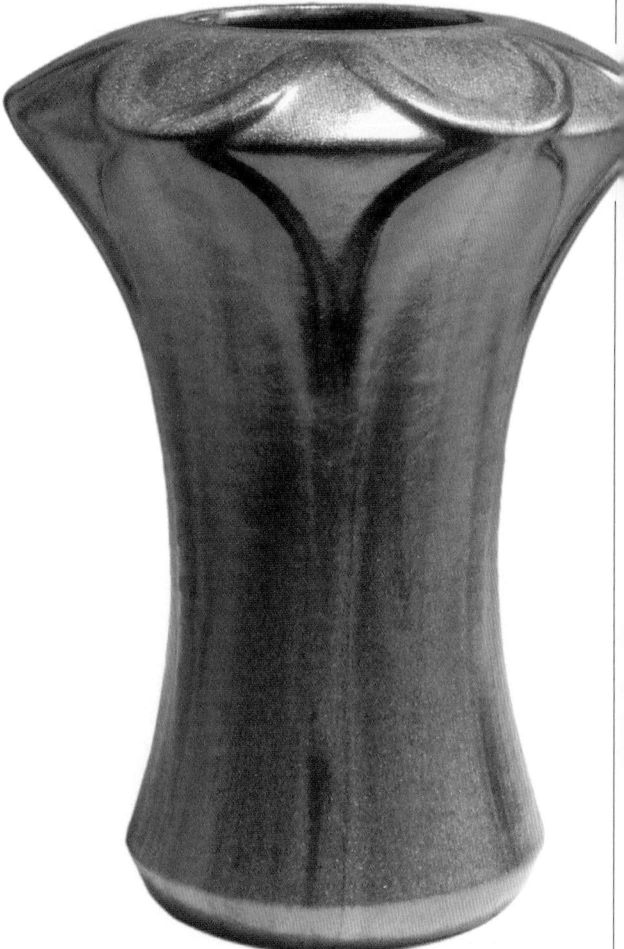

An exceptional Fulper corseted vase, with a fine 'Copperdust' crystalline glaze, modelled with a floriform top and full-height leaves, vertical mark.

11.5in (29cm) high

£4,000-5,000 **DRA**

A Fulper tall baluster vase, covered in an unusual combination of 'Chinese Blue' flambé over 'Cafe-Au-Lait' crystalline base, restored hole on bottom.

15.25in (38cm) high

£400-500 **DRA**

A large Fulper vase, covered in a fine, frothy 'Chinese Blue' flambé glaze, of hammered texture with four small handles, vertical mark.

13in (32.5cm) high

£1,200-1,800 **DRA**

A Fulper large tear-shaped vase covered in 'Chinese Blue' flambé glaze, line from rim, vertical mark.

12in (30.5cm) high

£400-600 **DRA**

A Fulper squat vase, covered in 'Chinese Blue' flambé glaze, opposing hairlines, vertical mark.

10in (25.5cm) wide

£220-280 **DRA**

A Fulper large squat vase, covered in frothy 'Chinese Blue' flambé glaze, unmarked.

10in (25.5cm) wide

£400-600 **DRA**

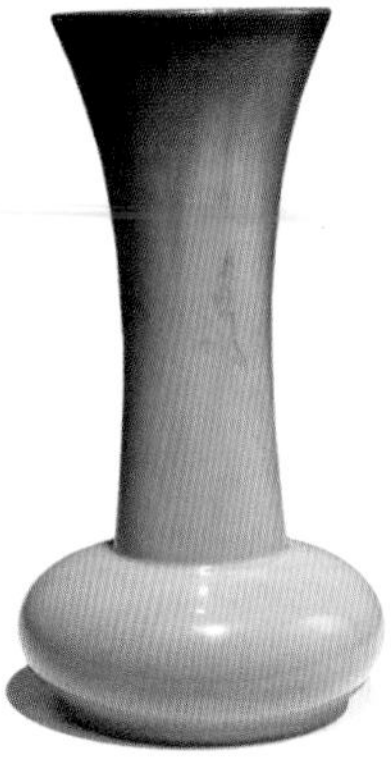

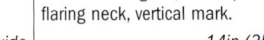

A tall Fulper vase, covered in 'Chinese Blue' flambé glaze, with squat base and flaring neck, vertical mark.

14in (35cm) high

£600-900 **DRA**

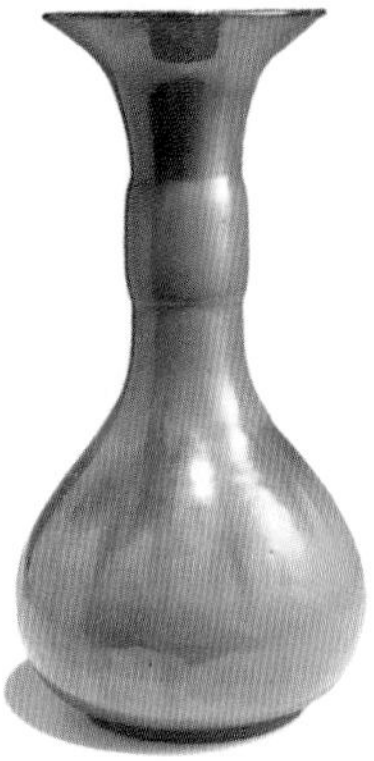

A Fulper tall and fine bulbous vase, covered in 'Chinese Blue-to-Flemington Green' flambé glaze, vertical mark.

15.25in (38cm) high

£280-320 **DRA**

A Fulper tear-shaped bud vase, with a matte cobalt ground covered in a frothy glossy glaze, vertical mark.

5.5in (14cm) high

£220-280 **DRA**

A rare Fulper tall vase, covered in a frothy 'Cucumber' matte crystalline glaze, vertical mark.

16in (40cm) high

£1,000-2,000 **DRA**

A rare Fulper barrel-shaped vase, covered in a frothy 'Cucumber' matte crystalline glaze, vertical mark.

10.5in (26cm) high

£1,200-1,800 **DRA**

A fine, rare and large Fulper melon-shaped vase, covered in a thick, curdled 'Cucumber' crystalline glaze, vertical mark, paper label.

14in (30.5cm) high

£2,800-3,200 **DRA**

A Fulper spherical vase with closed-in rim, covered in a fine frothy 'Flemington Green' flambé glaze, vertical mark.

5.5in (14cm) high

£300-500 **DRA**

A rare Fulper urn, covered in frothy blue, green and butter yellow flambé glaze, restoration to hole on bottom, vertical mark.

14.5in (36cm) high

£400-600 **DRA**

A Fulper faceted vase, with a 'Cat's Eye' base covered in mottled green and blue flambé glaze, restored hole on bottom, small chip to foot ring, vertical mark.

9.75in (24cm) high

£200-300 **DRA**

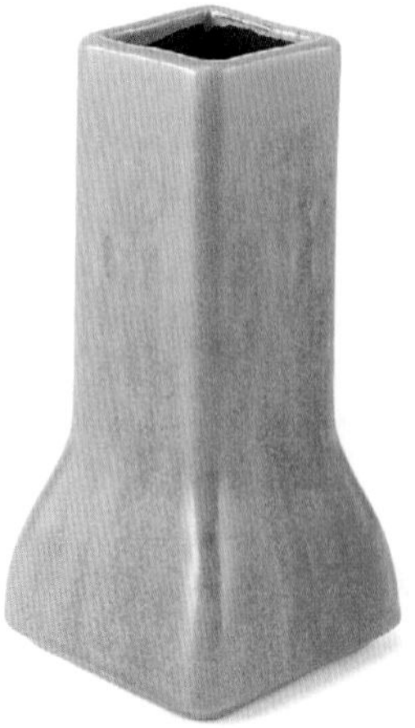

An early Fulper Vasekraft faceted vase, covered in 'Mission Verde' and 'Gunmetal' flambé glaze, early vertical stamp.

The same stoneware body, made from New Jersey clay, was used for the company's functional ceramics.

8.25in (21cm) high

£300-400 **DRA**

A Fulper faceted vase, covered in 'Leopard Skin' crystalline flambé over glossy yellow glaze, with Chinese collar rim, vertical mark.

7.5in (19cm) high

£300-500 **DRA**

A Fulper Vasekraft tapering vase, covered in 'Leopard's Skin' crystalline glaze, with long cut-out buttressed handles, vertical mark.

11in (27.5cm) high

£600-800 **DRA**

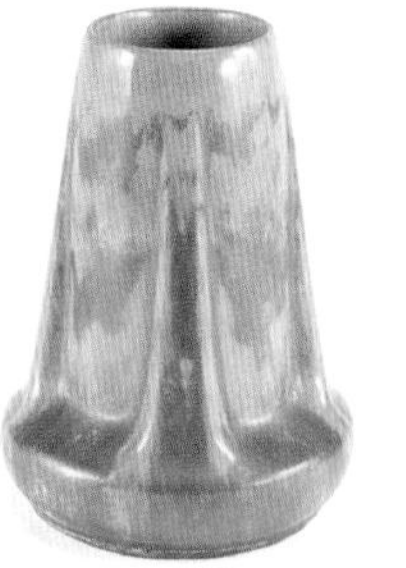

A Fulper buttressed vase, covered in 'Leopard Skin' crystalline glaze, vertical mark.

8.25in (21cm) high

£300-400 **DRA**

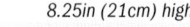

A Fulper/Prang ovoid vase, covered in Leopard's Skin and mauve crystalline flambé glaze, with closed-in rim, stamped "Prang".

Between 1913 and 1924, Fulper produced art pottery for Prang of New York, who retailed the pieces for educational purposes. Pots were generally only marked "Prang" between 1913 and 1916.

8in (20cm) high

£600-800 **DRA**

A Fulper tall urn, covered in 'Moss-to-Rose' flambé glaze, mark obscured by glaze.

11.75in (30cm) high

£180-220 **DRA**

A tall Fulper bullet-shaped vase, covered in a 'Moss-to-Rose' flambé glaze, with ring handles, vertical mark.

12.75in (32.5cm) high

£200-300 **DRA**

A large Fulper baluster vase, covered in frothy 'Moss-to-Rose' flambé glaze, vertical mark.

17in (42.5cm) high

£250-300 **DRA**

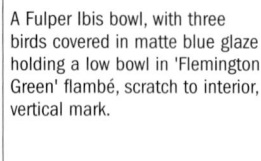

A Fulper baluster bud vase, covered in matte mustard glaze dripped with sheer ivory, minor fleck to base, vertical mark.

9in (23cm) wide.

£200-300 **DRA**

A large Fulper two-handled urn, covered in turquoise crystalline glaze, hammered texture, hairline to rim.

12.25in (31cm) high

£200-300 **DRA**

A fine and large Fulper tear-shaped vase, covered in turquoise crystalline glaze, with ring handles, vertical mark.

12.5in (32cm) high

£300-400 **DRA**

A Fulper Ibis bowl, with three birds covered in matte blue glaze holding a low bowl in 'Flemington Green' flambé, scratch to interior, vertical mark.

11in (28cm) wide

£800-1,200 **DRA**

A Fulper flaring bowl, embossed with fish and waves under a caramel and 'Leopard's Skin' crystalline flambé glaze, the exterior in 'Mission Verde', light abrasion to bottom, vertical mark.

11.25in (28cm) wide

£800-1,200 **DRA**

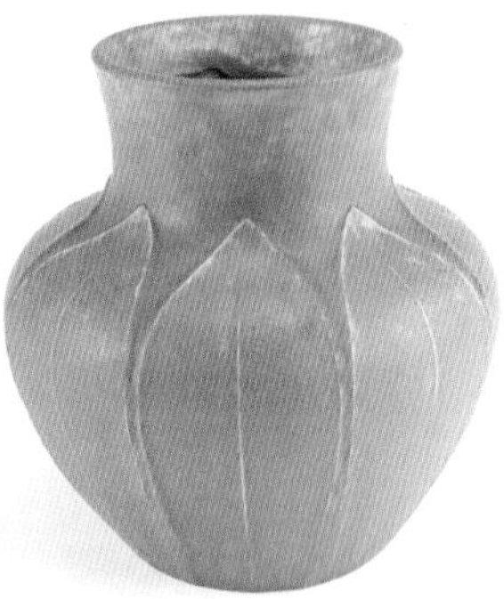

A large Grueby baluster vase by Wilhemina Post, with tooled and applied leaves covered in excellent feathered matte green glaze, circular Grueby Pottery stamp "WP/S".

9in (23cm) high

£2,200-2,800 **DRA**

A Grueby vase decorated by Wilhemina Post, with incised lobes and covered in light green matte glaze, 1/4" chip and minor nick to rim, Grueby Pottery circular stamp, "WP, 119".

6.75in (17cm) high

£800-1,200 **DRA**

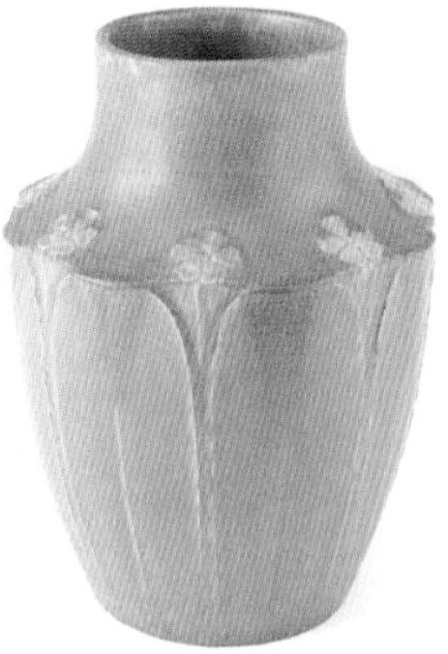

A Grueby vase by Wilhemina Post, with corseted neck, with tooled and applied curled edge leaves, cinquefoils and feathered matte green glaze, Grueby Pottery circular stamp, "WP, 18".

10.5in (26.5cm) high

£3,500-4,000 **DRA**

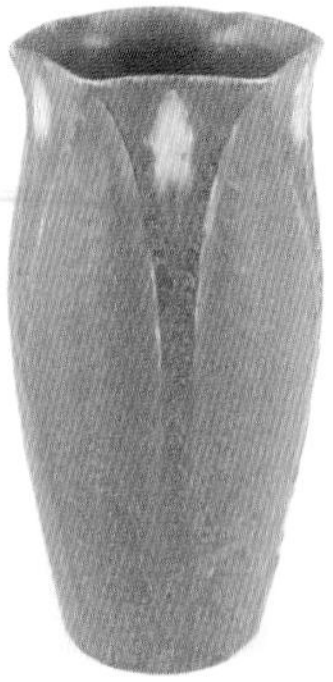

A Grueby Vase by Wilhemina Post, with tooled and applied full-height leaves alternating with yellow buds, leathery matte green glaze, circular stamp "WP", pottery and price paper labels.

8in (20.5cm) high

£2,200-2,800 **DRA**

A rare Grueby spherical vase by Ruth Erickson, with closed-in rim surrounded with tooled and applied full-height green leaves on a blue-grey ground, circular pottery stamp, paper label, incised "RE-D".

4.5in (11cm) wide

£12,000-18,000 **DRA**

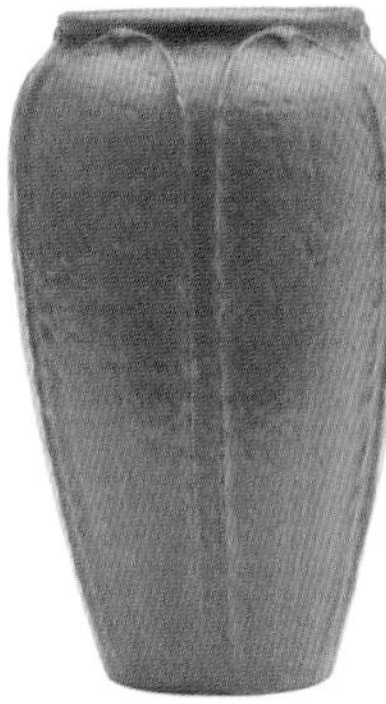

An ovoid Grueby vase, by Ruth Erickson, with full-height tooled and applied leaves covered in an exceptional, veined, oatmealed matte green glaze, a few minor nicks to edges, circular pottery mark, "RE, 9/1"

9in (22.5cm) high

£4,000-5,000 **DRA**

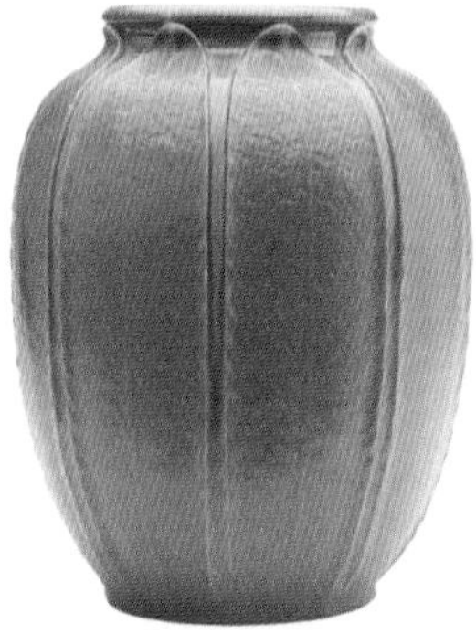

A large Grueby melon-shaped vase, by Ruth Erickson, with full-height tooled and applied covered leaves in a rich, frothy matte green glaze, against a glossier ground, a few small nicks to edges, circular pottery mark, "RE, 10/13".

11in (27.5cm) high

£8,000-12,000 **DRA**

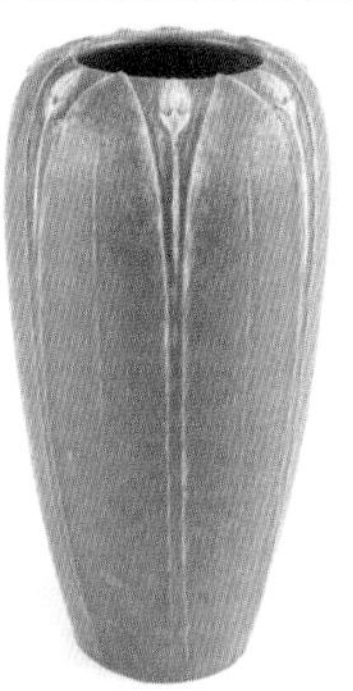

An early Grueby vase by Florence Liley, with closed-in rim and tooled and applied leaves and buds, feathered matte ground, Grueby Faience circular stamp, artist cypher, "23", paper label.

10.75in (27.5cm) high

£4,000-5,000 **DRA**

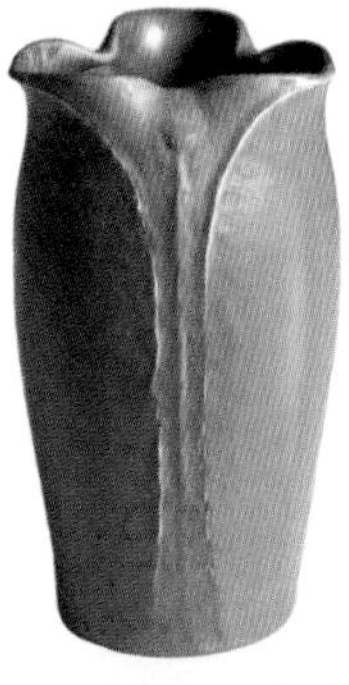

A Grueby three-lobed vase by Gertrude Priest, with tooled and applied full-height leaves alternating with buds, covered in a matte green glaze, stamped Grueby Faience circular mark.

7.75in (19cm) high

£1,200-1,800 **DRA**

A Grueby fine and unusual squat vase by Norma Peirce, with tooled and applied full-height leaves covered in a superior frothy blue-grey matte glaze, Grueby Pottery circular stamp, "139", "P", in triangle, restored chip.

This vase is an unusual form and has an unusual glaze.

8.5in (21.5cm) high

£1,800-2,200 **DRA**

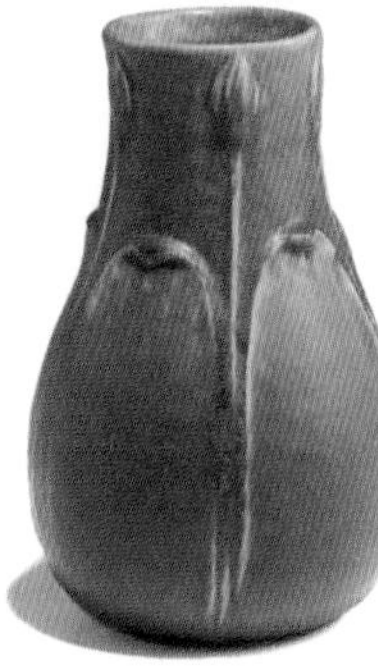

A Grueby vase, with tooled and applied curled leaves alternating with tall buds, covered in a fine, feathered matte green glaze, faint circular stamp.

7.25in (18cm) high

£1,800-2,200 **DRA**

An early Grueby tall vase, with tooled and applied full-height leaves alternating with buds, covered in a good feathered matte green glaze, Grueby Faience circular stamp.

11.5in (29cm) high

£1,800-2,200 **DRA**

A Grueby melon-shaped vase, with tooled and applied full-height leaves alternating with shorter, broader ones, covered in a fine leathery matte green glaze, Grueby Faience circular stamp.

11in (27.5cm) high

£1,800-2,200 **DRA**

A large Grueby bulbous vase covered in a feathered matte green glaze, Grueby Pottery circular stamp "181".

11in (28cm) high

£1,500-2,000 **DRA**

A Grueby ovoid vase covered in a fine, feathered matte green glaze, restoration around base, stabilized tight hairline and a few touch-ups to rim, Grueby circular stamp.

8in (20cm) high

£700-1,000 **DRA**

A fine Grueby bulbous vase with tooled and applied leaves covered in a good matte green glaze, the leaves lighter than the background, small chips to rim, unmarked.

4.5in (11.5cm) high

£800-1,200 **DRA**

A Grueby squat vase, the bulbous base covered with rounded leaves under a fine, veined matte green glaze, circular pottery mark, "EEP".

5in (12.5cm) wide

£4,000-5,000 **DRA**

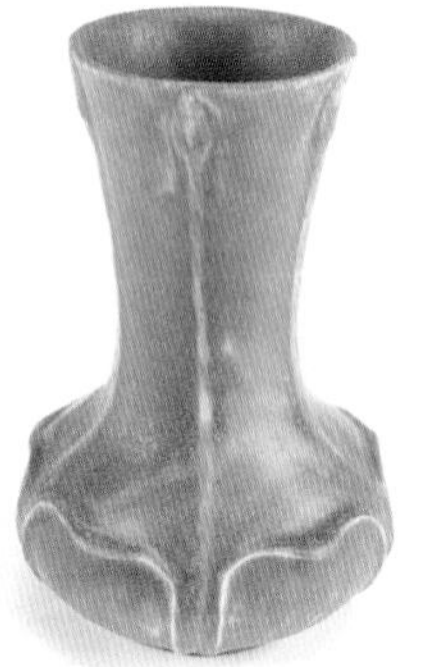

A Grueby bulbous vase with full-height buds alternating with short rounded leaves, covered in feathered matte green glaze. Grueby Pottery circular stamp, "RE", paper label.

6.75in (17cm) high

£1,200-1,800 **DRA**

A Grueby bulbous vase with three-lobed opening with full-height buds alternating with tooled and applied leaves, feathered matte glaze, Grueby Faience circular stamp, clay pimple.

7.5in (19cm) high

£1,500-2,000 **DRA**

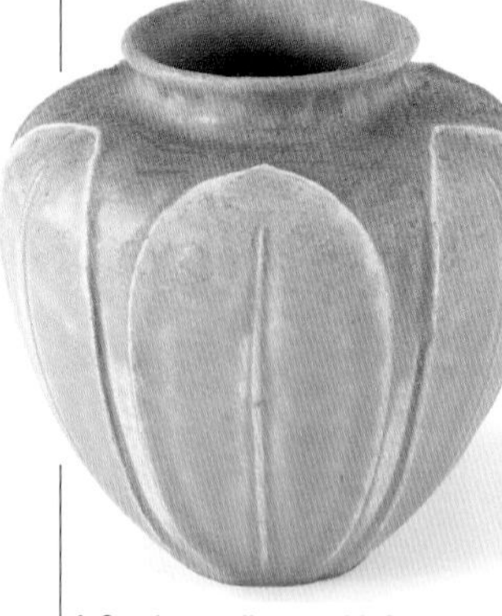

A Grueby small vase with flat shoulder covered with tooled and applied full-height leaves under frothy matte green glaze, circular stamp and paper label, nicks.

4.5in (11.51cm) high

£1,000-1,500 **DRA**

An exceptional Grueby tall gourd-shaped vase with ridged cylindrical neck covered in a superior veined matte green glaze, Grueby Pottery circular stamp, "133", small nick.

This is a rare version of a rare form, beautifully fired.

18.5in (47cm) high

£6,000-9,000 **DRA**

A Grueby vase with flat shoulder covered in feathered matte green glaze, Grueby Pottery circular stamp.

9.5in (24cm) high

£1,000-1,500 **DRA**

A Grueby vase with squat base covered in tooled and applied rounded leaves under an oatmealed matte green glaze, Grueby Faience circular stamp and "X".

4.5in (14cm) high

£700-1,000 **DRA**

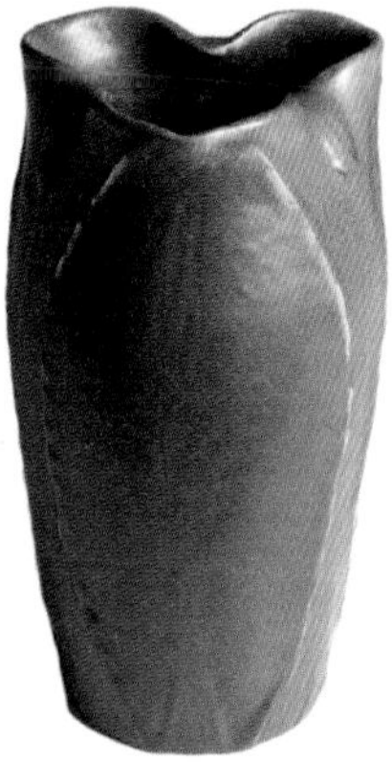

A Grueby trefoil vase, with full-height buds alternating with broad leaves and covered in a feathered matte green glaze, Grueby Faience circular stamp, restoration to several rim chips.

7.5in (19cm) high

£800-1,200 **DRA**

A tall Grueby cylindrical vase, with etched panels, covered in a leathery matte indigo glaze, circular "Grueby Pottery" stamp, "ERT/X", glaze misses, touch-ups, burst bubbles.

11in (27.5cm) high

£600-800 **DRA**

A rare Grueby covered jar by Ruth Erickson with tooled and applied full-height leaves and nicotina blossoms, frothy matte green glaze, Grueby Pottery stamp, "RE", nicks, replaced lid.

5in (13cm) high

£1,200-1,800 **DRA**

A Grueby vessel with a row of stacked full-height leaves covered in leathery matte green glaze, Grueby Faience circular stamp, restoration to chips, nicks.

5.25in (13.5cm) high

£1,000-1,500 **DRA**

A Grueby vessel with three tooled and applied curled leaves alternating with yellow buds, covered in feathered matte green glaze, probable mark covered by glaze, nicks.

4in (10cm) high

£1,500-2,000 **DRA**

An extremely rare oversized Grueby jardinière with tooled and applied full-height leaves alternating with buds and covered in a good curdled matte green glaze, circular Grueby Faience stamp, "129".

Although not the first Arts and Crafts pottery to use it, the Grueby factory is synonymous with matt-decorated art-ware, particularly in green.

19in (48.5cm) wide

£6,000-9,000 **RA**

A Grueby squat vessel, with two rows of tooled and applied leaves covered in a fine, curdled, rich matte green glaze, circular pottery stamp, artist signature.

This vase was owned by Miriam Hubbard Roelofs, daughter of Elbert and Alice Hubbard.

5.5in (14cm) wide

£1,500-2,000 **DRA**

A small Grueby spherical vessel, the top half covered in apple green semi-matte glaze over a bisque body, restoration to small chip at rim, "Grueby Pottery" circular stamp.

3.25in (8cm) high

£150-200 **DRA**

A four-sided Grueby bowl with tooled and applied full-height leaves under a fine, feathered matte green glaze, Grueby Pottery circular stamp, chips, scratches.

6in (15cm) wide

£500-700 **DRA**

A Grueby four-sided bowl with tooled and applied full-height leaves covered in good oatmealed blue-grey glaze, Grueby Pottery circular stamp, glaze lifting.

6in (15cm) wide

£500-700 **DRA**

A Grueby tile, decorated in cuenca with a tall ship on waves in ivory, brown, caramel and green, paper label and "AS".

6in (15cm) high

£800-1,200 **DRA**

A Grueby tile, decorated in cuenca with a tall ship in ivory, mustard and brown, glazed all around on an indigo ground, signed "MCT".

6in (15cm) high

£800-1,200 **DRA**

A Grueby tile, decorated in cuenca with a tall ship on curly waves, in indigo and ivory against blue-grey ground, signed "AS".

6in (15cm) high

£600-900 **DRA**

A Grueby tile, decorated in cuenca with a tall ship in indigo, caramel and light yellow on a blue-grey ground, mounted in a fine Arts & Crafts frame, signed "ZE".

8in (20cm) high

£800-1,200 **DRA**

A Grueby tile, decorated in cuenca with seagulls flying over green waves, mounted in hammered copper footed trivet base, signed "M.C."

4in (10cm) high

£500-700 **DRA**

A Grueby tile, decorated in cuenca with two white bears on a green and blue ground, signed "AS".

6in (15cm) high

£500-700 **DRA**

A Grueby tile decorated in cuenca with a deer under a stylized tree, marked "D.C.", wear, pitting, chip.

4.25in (11cm) wide

£300-400 **DRA**

A rare Grueby tile moulded with a standing wolf in curdled matte green glaze on indigo, matte brown ground, small chip, stamped "B52-L".

6in (15cm) wide

£1,200-1,800 **DRA**

A rare Grueby advertising tile, with half-burnt yellow candle in a green chamberstick against a green ground, the words "GRUEBY TILE", signed "ET".

6.25 (15.5cm) high

£2,500-3,000 **DRA**

A CLOSER LOOK AT A GRUEBY TILE

Grueby is known for the high quality of its matt-decorated artware. The company received a gold medal at the 1900 Paris Exposition.

Grueby, like other Art potters, revisited traditional decorative methods. The Spanish technique of cuenca, originally used in architecture, involves outlining a design in raised lines so that solid pools of coloured glaze form in the spaces.

Grueby favoured shades of green for its art pots, and the colour is also used to a great extent in this tile. The image is at the same time appealingly naturalistic and innovatively abstract.

The tile is exceptionally large, increasing the value.

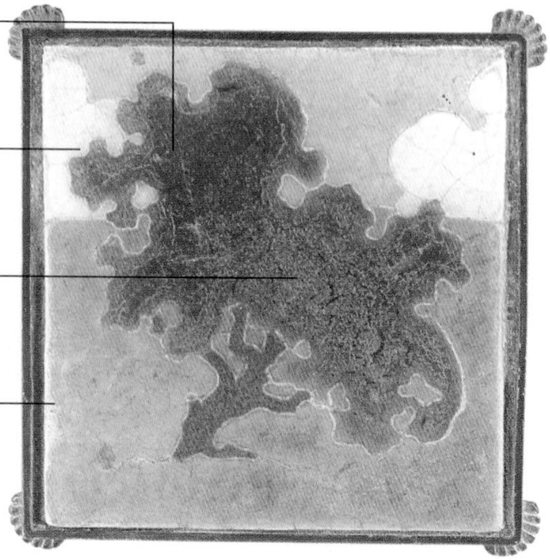

A Grueby/Tiffany Studios tile, decorated in cuenca with an oak tree in greens, mounted in a bronze Tiffany trivet base with four feet, some wear to cuenca walls, small glaze bubble to top left corner, unmarked.

6in (15cm) wide

£2,000-3,000 **DRA**

A Grueby tile decorated in cuenca with a golden tulip and light green leaves on dark green ground, "A.S. 212".

6in (15cm) wide

£2,000-3,000 **DRA**

A rare Grueby diamond-shaped heraldic tile decorated in cuenca with a rampant lion on a shield surrounded by a green laurel wreath on a fine curdled matte brown glaze, chips, unmarked.

8in (20.5cm) wide

£1,800-2,200 **DRA**

A Grueby geometric moulded tile in cruciform pattern with matte green, blue, yellow and pumpkin glazes, light abrasion, chips, unmarked.

8in (20.5cm) wide

£300-400 **DRA**

Three Grueby geometric tiles with central medallion, two covered in matte ochre glaze, one in lavender, stamped "GRUEBY BOSTON", cracks, chips.

Largest 10in (25.5cm) wide

£150-200 **DRA**

Two Grueby geometric floor tiles in cross pattern, one in brown glaze, the other in green, chips to edges, brown tile overfired, unmarked.

8in (20.5cm) wide

£300-400 **DRA**

Two Grueby geometric tiles with medallion centre covered in white, grey and brown glaze, chip to surface of one, other overglazed, unmarked.

8in (20.5cm) wide

£150-200 **DRA**

Ten Grueby tiles covered in matte green glaze, and sixteen Aetco tiles in brown crystalline glaze marked "AETCO".

9in (22.5cm) wide

£180-220 set **DRA**

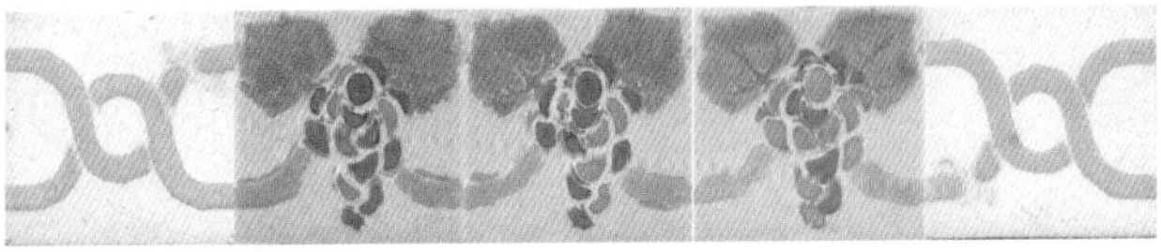

A Grueby frieze of five tiles, with blue grape clusters on beige ground alternating with beige knots on ivory ground, stamped "4085A".

each tile 6in (15cm) wide

£700-1,000 **DRA**

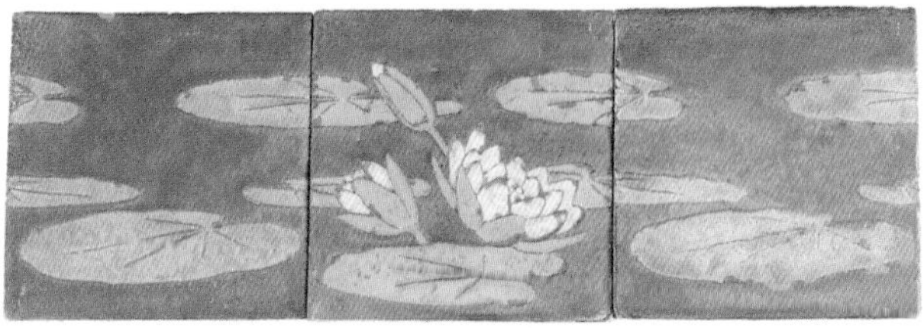

A Grueby three-tile frieze, decorated in cuenca with ivory waterlilies and light green lily pads on dark green ground, stamped "GRUEBY BOSTON", chips to one.

6in (15cm) wide

£2,000-3,000 each **DRA**

A rare and exceptional Grueby 'The Pines' complete frieze of eight tiles, decorated in cuenca with stylized trees in a landscape, artists' initials, restoration.

48in (122cm) wide

£30,000-40,000 **DRA**

A Grueby tile-top table, with one black and mustard floral tile set in new Mission base, unmarked, cracks.

tile 13in (33cm) wide

£400-500 **DRA**

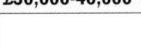

A Grueby Art Deco tile mosaic of twenty-eight tiles, two embossed with blue and white birds, the others in black glossy glaze, stamped with letters, chips.

£120-180 **DRA**

A large Grueby scarab paperweight, covered in mottled blue-green glaze, restoration to several small chips around base, Grueby Faience circular stamp.

4in (10cm) wide

£180-220 **DRA**

A Grueby scarab-shaped paperweight, covered in matte indigo glaze, circular stamp.

4in (10cm) wide

£800-1,200 **DRA**

A Grueby scarab-shaped paperweight, covered in matte ivory glaze, circular stamp.

4in (10cm) wide

£800-1,200 **DRA**

A pair of Grueby hammered copper bookends, possibly by Potters Studio, inset with large Grueby scarab paperweights, covered in matte brown glaze, original dark patina, scarabs marked.

6in (16cm) wide

£1,500-2,000 **DRA**

A rare and large Grueby unglazed vertical panel with three stylized birds on a blooming branch, stamped "30", crack, chip.

24in (61cm) high

£400-600 **DRA**

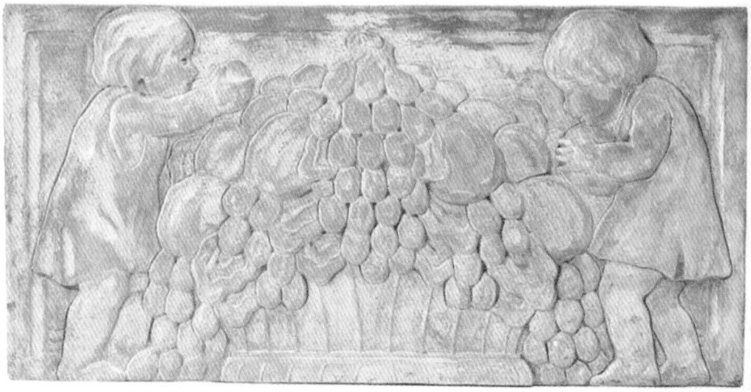

A rare and large Grueby unglazed horizontal panel, with two toddlers grabbing fruit from a large fruit basket, stamped "23".

24in (61cm) wide

£800-1,200 **DRA**

A Marblehead ovoid vase in an unusual purple and blue mottled matte glaze, ship mark.

6.25in (16cm) high

£300-500 **DRA**

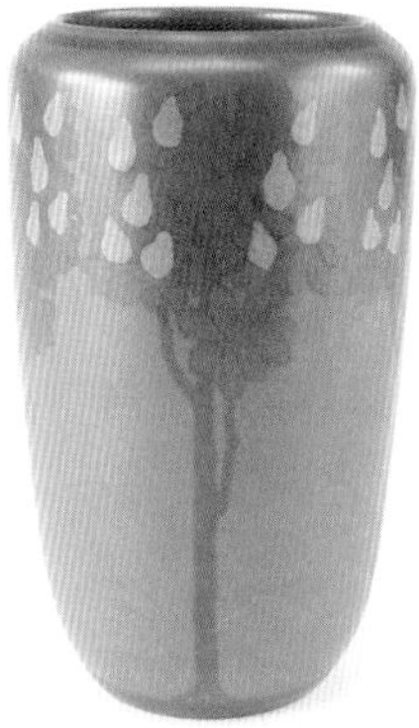

A spectacular large Marblehead vase painted with stylized chestnut trees in green and pale pink with a rich tobacco brown ground, stamped ship mark and paper label, restoration.

11.5in (29cm) high

£2,200-2,800 **DRA**

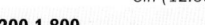

A Marblehead ovoid vase painted with stylized grape vines in green, yellow and blue on grey ground, ship mark, glaze flake inside rim.

7in (18cm) high

£2,000-3,000 **DRA**

An early Arthur Baggs/Marblehead vessel, incised with chestnut leaves covered in matte mustard glaze over a mottled red and green volcanic ground, small firing flaw to side, incised "AB" and early ship mark.

5in (12.5cm) high

£1,200-1,800 **DRA**

A Marblehead ovoid vase, incised with a wreath of grapevines and leaves in purple and green glaze, entirely covered in matte yellow, ship mark.

5.25in (13cm) high

£1,000-1,500 **DRA**

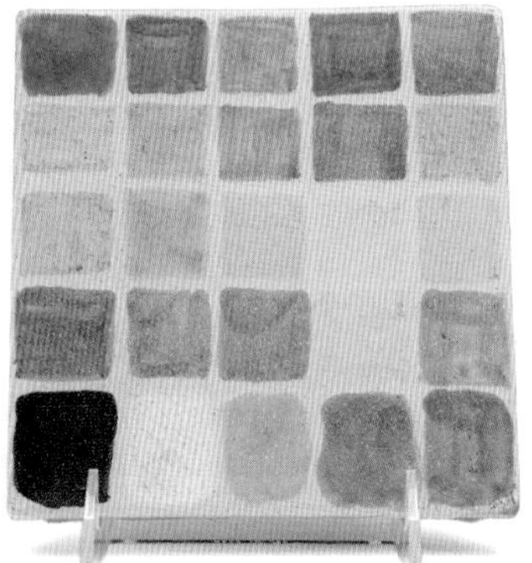

A rare Marblehead glaze sample tile, with twenty-five colours on bright yellow ground, stamped ship mark, chips.

6in (15cm) square

£600-900 **DRA**

A rare Marblehead tile, incised and painted with potted trees in olive green, browns, and blues, stamped ship mark, restoration.

6.25in (16cm) wide

£1,200-1,800 **DRA**

A Marblehead tile, painted with a three-masted tall ship in brown and ivory on a blue and green ground, mounted in an Arts and Crafts frame, stamped ship mark, paper label.

6in (15cm) wide

£500-700 **DRA**

A Marblehead trivet tile, modelled with a blue bird in foliage with red blossoms, mounted in a new Arts and Crafts frame, stamped ship mark and paper label.

trivet 6.25in (15.5cm) high

£1,000-1,500 **DRA**

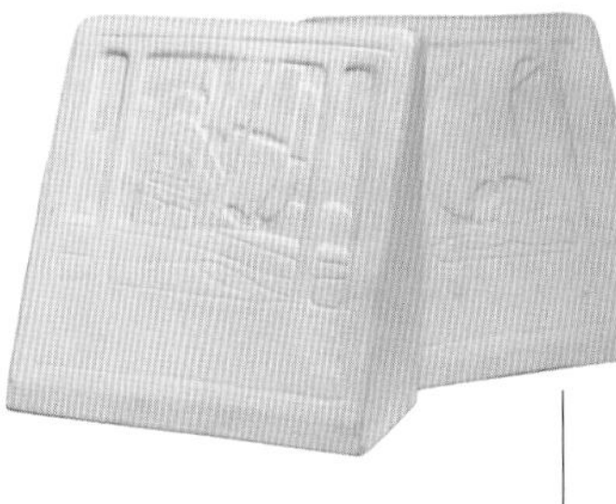

A pair of Marblehead bisque-fired bookends, modelled with ships, ship marks.

6in (15cm) high

£200-300 **DRA**

NEWCOMB COLLEGE

- Founded in 1895 at H. Sophie Newcomb Memorial College in New Orleans, Newcomb pottery was instrumental in training women in ceramic decoration.
- The best student pieces were sold in the gallery shop.
- The enterprise was directed by Ellsworth Woodward (1861-1939) and Mary G. Sheerer (1865-1954). Talented designers and instructors included Sadie Irvine, Harriet Joor, Anna Frances Simpson and Henrietta Bailey.
- Pieces were typically decorated with the flora and fauna of the American South - tobacco plants, cotton plants, lizards and waterfowl were popular motifs.
- Shapes were inspired by Oriental and rustic pottery.
- Early wares were decorated in a distinctive palette of yellow, blue, green and black and were covered with shiny, luminous glazes.
- From 1910, a wider range of softly coloured matte glazes were used to decorate pots.
- Pieces are usually marked with the firm's symbol, an artist's cypher, the potter's mark and a date.
- The quality declined after 1931 and production ceased in 1940.

An early Newcomb College low bowl carved by Henrietta Bailey with large white blossoms and yellow centres on cobalt ground, "NC/HB/ZZ74", line.

1904 *8.5in (21.5cm) wide*

£1,500-2,000 **DRA**

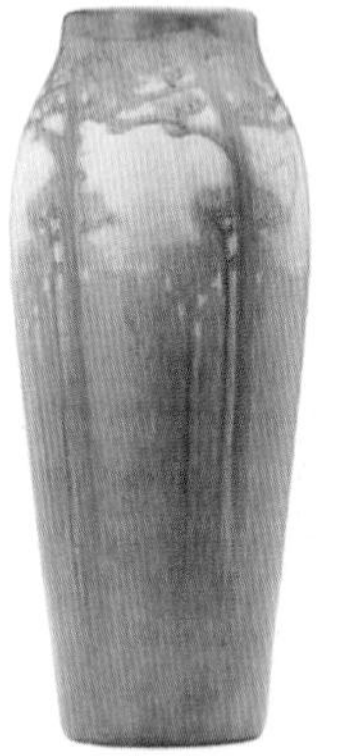

A tall Newcomb College Transitional vase, carved by Henrietta Bailey with tall pines in blue-green on a mottled ground, "NC/JM/HB/DV.28/B".

1910 *11.5in (29cm) high*

£7,000-10,000 **DRA**

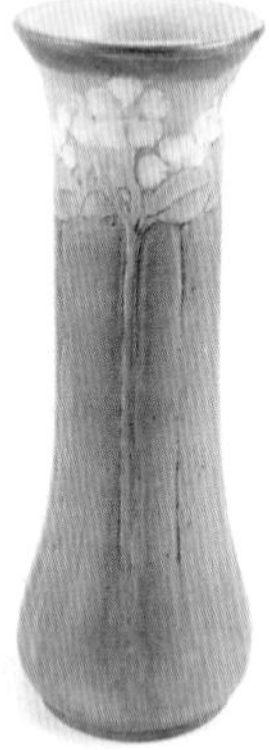

A transitional Newcomb College bulbous vase, carved by May Louise Dunn with yellow cinquefoils, "NC/JM/B/FH51/", artist cypher.

1912 *9in (23cm) high*

£2,000-3,000 **DRA**

A Newcomb College transitional vase, by Sadie Irvine, with white and yellow daffodils on a waxy green ground, "NC/JM/SI/185/GA89".

1913 *4in (10cm) high*

£1,200-1,800 **DRA**

A Newcomb College transitional bulbous vase, carved by Sadie Irvine, with wreaths of quatrefoils on a blue ground, "NC/JM/SI/179/HW69".

1916 *8.5in (21cm) high*

£1,200-1,800 **DRA**

A transitional Newcomb College squat cabinet vase, carved by Sadie Irvine with a landscape of large oak trees with Spanish moss against a yellow sky, "NC/SI/JM/239/IR/58".

1917 *3.5in (9cm) high*

£1,500-2,000 **DRA**

A large Newcomb College vase, deeply carved by Sadie Irvine with live oak trees and Spanish Moss in front of a full moon, "NC/JM/SI/268/KJ66".

1919 *10.5in (26cm) high*

£7,000-10,000 **DRA**

A Newcomb College ovoid vase, carved by Sadie Irvine, with a moonlit landscape of live oak trees and Spanish moss, "NC/JH/SI/SM26".

1930 *5.25in (13cm) high*

£2,000-3,000 **DRA**

A large ovoid Newcomb College vase, carved by Sadie Irvine, with Spanish moss dripping from tall oak trees in front of a full moon, "NC/JH/157/SI/TK33", factory hole to base.

1931 *10in (25.5cm) high*

£2,200-2,800 **DRA**

A Newcomb College cabinet vase, carved by Sadie Irvine, with Spanish moss on live oak trees against a pink sky, "NC/SI/SU37/JH".

1931 *2.75in (7cm) wide*

£1,000-1,500 **DRA**

An early and large Newcomb College vase, incised by Harriet Joor with magnolia blossoms and foliage on a pale blue ground, restoration to two chips at rim, "NC/HJ/0024/JM".

1904 *11.75in (29cm) high*

£10,000-15,000 **DRA**

An early Newcomb College pitcher carved and painted by Marie de Hoa LeBlanc, with a band of violets on a blue ground, "NC/MHLeB/JM/AR43/" paper label, interior crazing.

c1905 *7.5in (19cm) high*

£2,500-3,000 **DRA**

An early Newcomb College pitcher, carved and painted by Sarah Bloom Levy with blue trumpet vines and green leaves on a washed blue ground, "NC/JM/SBL/FF2/SL", line.

1903 *7in (18cm) high*

£2,500-3,000 **DRA**

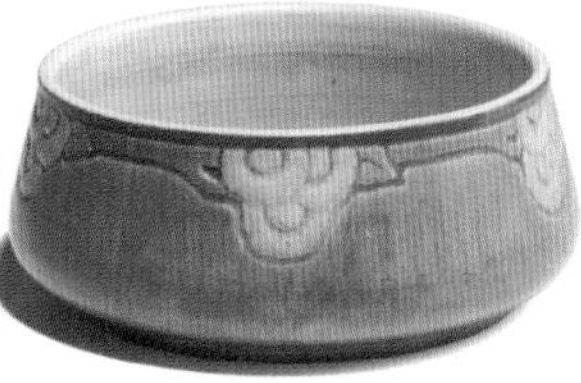

A Newcomb College transitional bowl, carved by Alma Mason, with light blue and yellow daisies on a blue-green ground, marked "NC/JM/AM/FG36".

1912 *7.25in (18cm) wide*

£600-900 **DRA**

A Newcomb College transitional bulbous vase, carved by May Morell, with a wreath of white buds and long green leaves against a blue ground.

1910 *5.5in (14cm) high*

£1,500-2,000 **DRA**

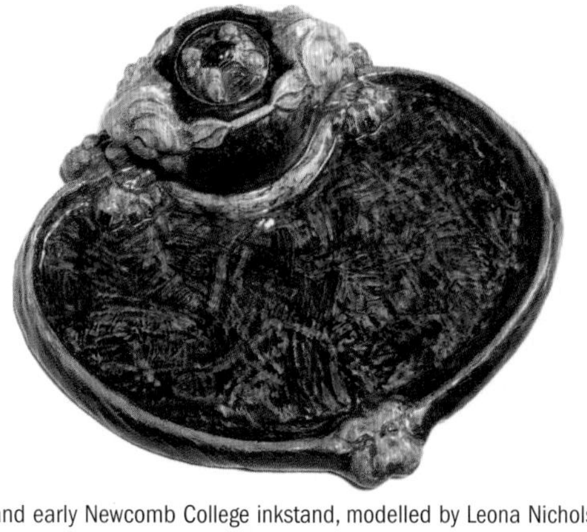

A rare and early Newcomb College inkstand, modelled by Leona Nicholson, with two lion heads flanking the inkwell and one at the front of the tray, marked "NC/LN/BQ89", without liner.

1907 *9in (22.5cm) wide*

£2,000-3,000 **DRA**

An exceptional and early Newcomb College vase, carved by Leona Nicholson, with full-height yellow and light blue blossoms on a stylized cobalt and deep green ground, minor glaze fleck to rim, "NC/JM/LN/CO-26".

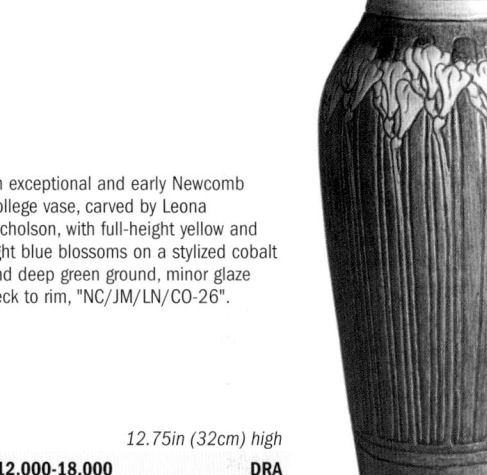

12.75in (32cm) high

£12,000-18,000 **DRA**

An early Newcomb College charger, incised by Charlotte Payne, with clusters of fruit and foliage against an indigo ground, around a stylized cross-section of same fruit in blues and greens, "NC/JM/CP/TT31".

1904 *9.5in (24cm) diam*

£2,200-2,800 **DRA**

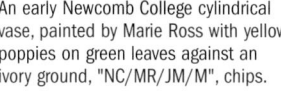

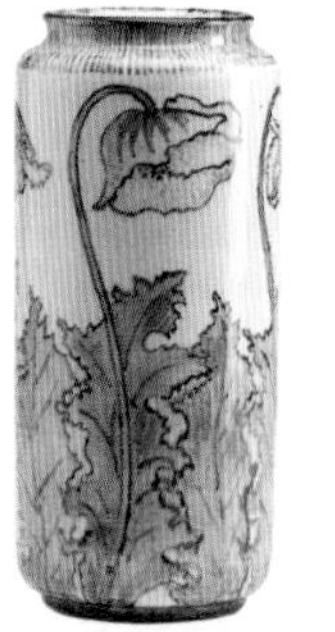

An early Newcomb College cylindrical vase, painted by Marie Ross with yellow poppies on green leaves against an ivory ground, "NC/MR/JM/M", chips.

c1904 *7.75in (19cm) high*

£4,000-5,000 **DRA**

A Newcomb College transitional corseted bud vase, carved by A.F. Simpson, with white and yellow freesia on green leaves, "NC/JM/170/AFS/GI63".

1913 *8in (20cm) high*

£1,500-2,000 **DRA**

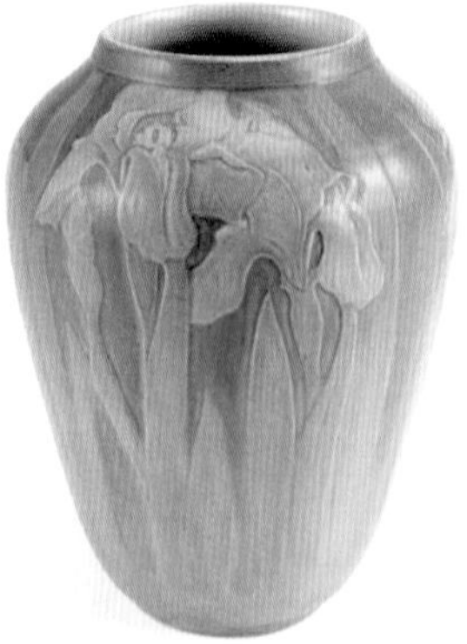

A large Newcomb College vase carved and painted by A.F. Simpson with pink irises on green leaves against a purple and blue ground, "NC/AFS/JM/150/KL36".

1919 *9in (23cm) high*

£5,000-7,000 **DRA**

A Newcomb College low bowl carved by A.F. Simpson with light pink trumpet blossoms on a pink and blue ground, "NC/A.F.S/JZ94/265", line.

1919 *11in (28cm) diam*

£800-1,200 **DRA**

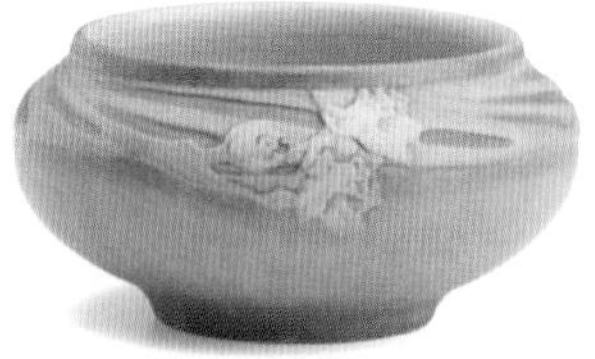

A Newcomb College squat bowl, carved by A.F. Simpson, with a wreath of white and yellow daffodils on blue ground, "NC/JM/AFS/56/KV45".

1920 *6.5in (16cm) wide*

£1,000-1,500 **DRA**

A large Newcomb College bulbous vessel, carved by A.F. Simpson with a richly coloured moonlit scene of live oak trees and Spanish moss,"NC/AFS/LE87/JM/49", short line.

1920 *8.5in (21cm) wide*

£2,800-3,200 **DRA**

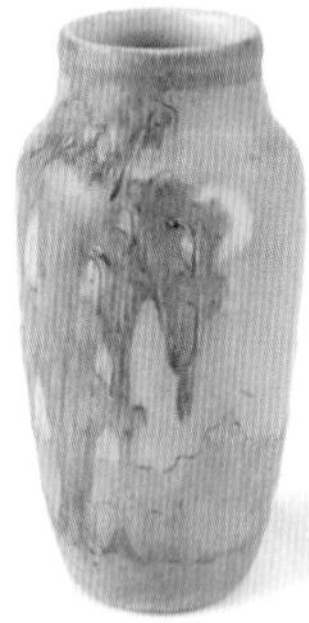

An ovoid Newcomb College vase, carved by A.F. Simpson with tall pine trees and Spanish moss in front of a full moon, "NC/JM/AFS/182/MC2".

1921 *6in (15cm) high*

£1,500-2,000 **DRA**

A Newcomb College corseted bud vase, carved by A.F. Simpson, with white and yellow daffodils on a blue ground, "NC/JM/170/AFS/LU18".

1921 *7.5in (19cm) high*

£1,500-2,000 **DRA**

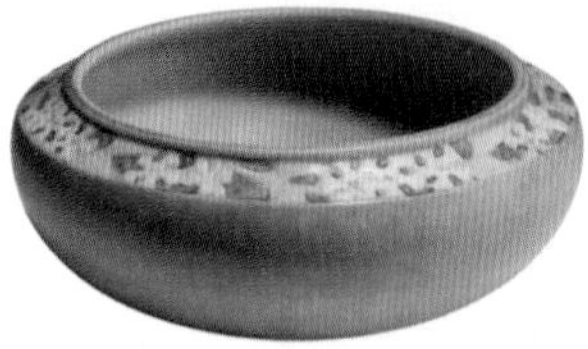

A Newcomb College bowl, carved by A.F. Simpson, with a band of white blossoms on blue ground, marked "NC/AFS/0148/68".

1924 *8.25in (20.5cm) wide*

£800-1,200 **DRA**

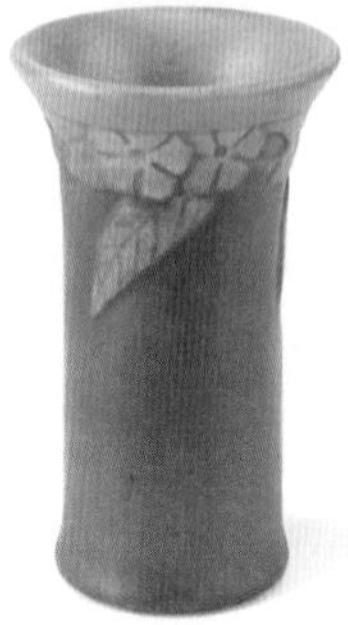

A Newcomb College bud vase, carved by A.F. Simpson with pink cinquefoils on indigo ground, marked, restored.

1928 *4.5in (11.5cm) high*

£300-500 **DRA**

A rare Newcomb College wall pocket, carved by A.F. Simpson, with a band of irises and leaves over a fluted indigo ground, "NC/SG63/AFS", hole, nicks.

1930 *8.25in (20.5cm) high*

£800-1,200 **DRA**

A Newcomb College squat vessel, carved by an unidentified artist, with pink morning glories on a purple ground, "NC/JM/IC25/205".

1916 *5.25in (13cm) high*

£1,200-1,800 **DRA**

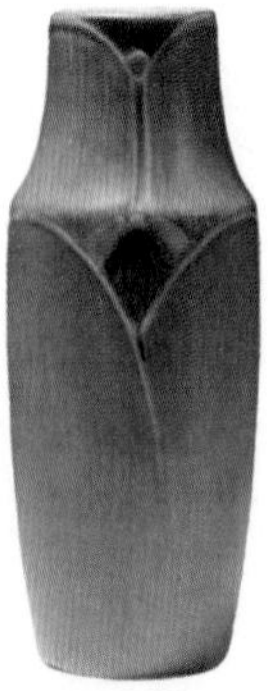

A Newcomb College corseted vase, decorated by an unidentified artist with an Art Deco pattern in blue-green and yellow on a blue and purple ground.

1923 *8.5in (21cm) high*

£1,800-2,200 **DRA**

A Newcomb College cream pitcher, carved by an unidentified artist, 'Ferns', in green and blue matte glaze, "NC/V96/AA", paper label.

c1935 *6in (15cm) wide*

£500-700 **DRA**

A George Ohr corseted vessel with two different ear-shaped handles, covered with mustard yellow, gummetal, and green glaze sponged on a raspberry and grey ground, stamped "G.E. OHR, Biloxi, Miss", restored.

5in (13cm) high

£2,200-2,800 **DRA**

An extremely rare tyg, by George Ohr and Susan Frackelton, with three different ear-shaped handles alternating with three spouts, incised "Health, Wealth, Happiness" stamped "G.E. OHR, Biloxi, Miss.", hand-incised "S. Frackelton 1899".

7in (18cm) high

£7,000-10,000 **DRA**

A George Ohr pitcher with lobed rim and ear-shaped handle, its interior covered in gunmetal crystalline glaze, the exterior with gunmetal brown drips on khaki ground, script signature, restored.

5.5in (14cm) wide

£1,200-1,800 **DRA**

A George Ohr tall corseted Joe Jefferson mug, incised "Here's Your Good Health and Your Family's and May They All Live Long and Prosper, J. Jefferson," covered in olive green and gunmetal mottled glaze, script signature, "18?9" restored.

7.5in (19cm) high

£1,000-1,500 **DRA**

A tall George Ohr pitcher, sponge-painted with three bands in gunmetal brown and green over a glossy amber ground, with gunmetal interior, stamped "GEO. E. OHR, BILOXI, MISS".

8.75in (22cm) high

£3,000-4,000 **DRA**

A small George Ohr column-shaped bud vase, covered in a mottled deep green lustred glaze with melt fissures, stamped "G.E. OHR, Biloxi, Miss".

5in (12.5cm) high

£800-1,200 **DRA**

A tall George Ohr corseted and bulbous vase, the top with folded rim covered in gunmetal brown glaze, the flaring base in mottled green and amber, stamped "G.E. OHR, Biloxi, Miss".

8in (20cm) high

£4,000-5,000 **DRA**

An unusual George Ohr baluster-shaped vase, the top covered in indigo glaze over a green and raspberry mottled base, "G.E. OHR, Biloxi, Miss".

6.75in (17cm) high

£5,000-6,000 **DRA**

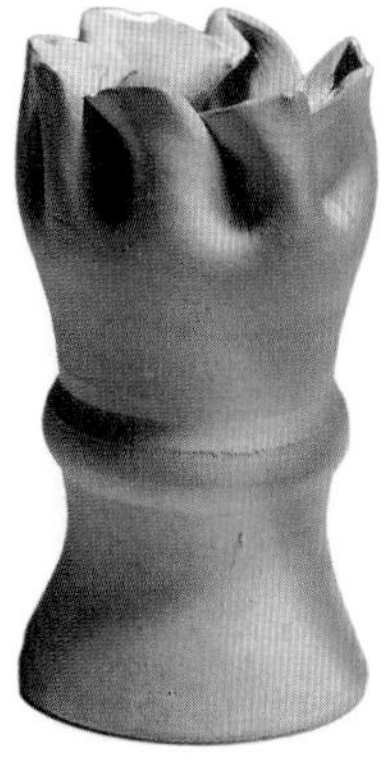

A George Ohr bisque-fired corseted vessel with folded rim, the pale clay showing different reactions to the kiln's fire, script signature.

4.5in (11cm) high

£700-1,000 **DRA**

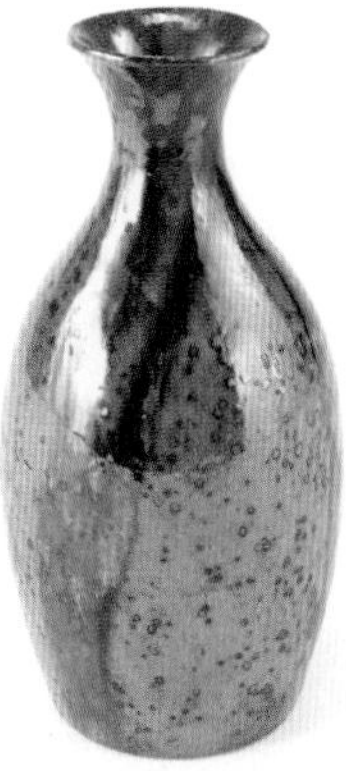

A George Ohr sake bottle-shaped vase with three broad deep brown stripes over an ochre base, entirely speckled with gunmetal glaze, "OHR BILOXI", restored.

6.5in (16.5cm) high

£800-1,200 **DRA**

A George Ohr double gourd-shaped cabinet vase covered in sponged bands of ivory, green, raspberry and indigo glaze, stamped "G.E. OHR, Biloxi, Miss".

4in (10cm) high

£2,000-3,000 **DRA**

A small George Ohr vase with closed-in rim covered in sponged-on gunmetal glaze over green and brown mottled base, script signature.

4in (10cm) high

£700-1,000 **DRA**

A George Ohr corseted vase with randomly folded rim covered in sheer blue-green glaze over blue-green and raspberry mottled base, stamped "BILOXI, MISS. GEO. E. OHR", nicks.

4in (10cm) high

£3,500-4,000 **DRA**

A George Ohr corseted vessel, with four-lobed rim over a deep in-body twist, covered in a fine red, green and blue leathery matte glaze, restoration to rim chips, script signature.

4.5in (11cm) wide

£2,800-3,200 **DRA**

A George Ohr cinched vase with folded top covered in an indigo-speckled raspberry glaze, stamped "G.E. OHR, BILOXI", restoration.

4in (10cm) high

£2,200-2,800 **DRA**

A George Ohr squat vessel with torn rim covered in indigo, green, raspberry and mustard yellow sponged-on glaze, stamped "G.E. OHR, Biloxi, Miss", chip, abraded line.

4.75in (12cm) wide

£1,800-2,200 **DRA**

A George Ohr double gourd vase with closed-in rim, the top covered in gunmetal speckled brown glaze, the base in light and dark green stippled glaze, script signature, restoration.

4.25in (11cm) wide

£700-1,000 **DRA**

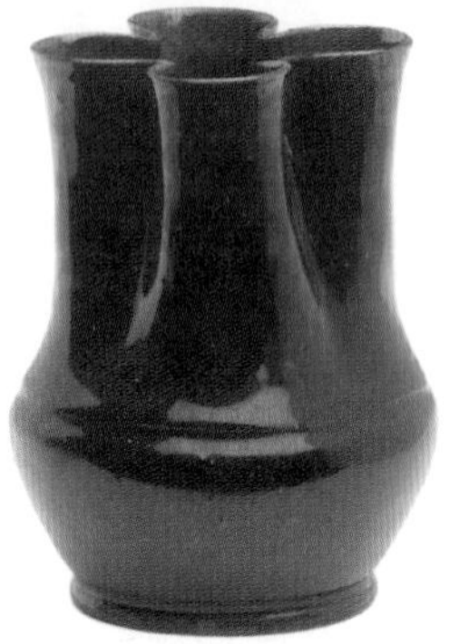

A bulbous George Ohr vase, with four-lobed openings covered in dark green-to-indigo glossy glaze, stamped "G.E. OHR, Biloxi, Miss".

3.75in (9cm) high

£1,800-2,200 **DRA**

A George Ohr pear-shaped vase with folded rim covered in gunmetal glaze, stamped "G.E. OHR, Biloxi, Miss", re-glued chip.

3.75in (9.5cm) high

£800-1,200 **DRA**

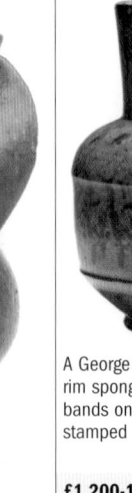

An urn-shaped George Ohr cabinet vase, with bulbous base beneath a pinched and folded rim, covered in black-speckled green glaze, "BILOX, MISS. GEO. E. OHR".

3in (7.5cm) high

£4,500-5,000 **DRA**

A George Ohr bulbous vase, with collar rim sponge-painted in black and brown bands on a speckled green ground, stamped "GEO. E. OHR BILOXI, MISS".

4.5in (11cm) high

£1,200-1,800 **DRA**

A George Ohr vase with bulbous base and deep in-body twist at shoulder, with green, indigo and raspberry sponged-on glaze, stamped "G.E. OHR, Biloxi, Miss".

4.5in (11cm) high

£2,500-3,000 **DRA**

A large vase by George Ohr with pie-crust rim and very deep in-body twist, covered with a band of dripping mustard yellow and cobalt-raspberry glaze sponged on a brown ground, stamped "G.E. OHR, Biloxi, Miss".

5.25in (13.5cm) high

£8,000-12,000 **DRA**

A bulbous George Ohr vessel, with deep in-body twist, covered in gunmetal, brown and green sponged-on speckled glaze, over a buff body, stamped "GEO. E. OHR, BILOXI, MISS".

Provenance: *Passed down through the Ohr family to the current owner.*

3.75in (9cm) wide

£3,500-4,000 **DRA**

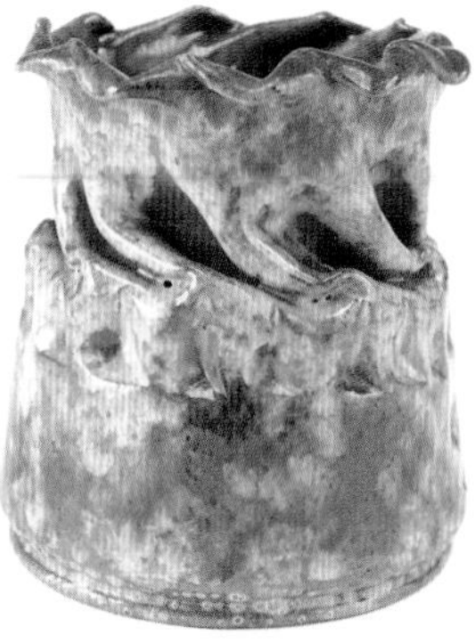

A George Ohr tapering vase with folded rim and deep in-body twist above a checked band, covered in white and raspberry glaze sponged on orange clay body, stamped "G.E. OHR, Biloxi, Miss".

3.25in (8.5cm) high

£4,500-5,000 **DRA**

A George Ohr bulbous vase with lobed rim covered in turquoise, bottle-green and gunmetal sponged-on glaze, complete with original clay price tag for $20, stamped "G.E OHR, Biloxi, Miss", glaze flakes.

3.5in (9cm) high

£4,000-5,000 **DRA**

A George Ohr bulbous footed vase with folded rim covered in bottle green and raspberry mottled glaze, stamped "G.E. OHR, Biloxi, Miss", restored chip.

5in (13cm) high

£2,800-3,200 **DRA**

A CLOSER LOOK AT A GEORGE OHR VESSEL

George Ohr (1857-1918) has been called the first art potter in the US. He finished many of his striking pots with glossy lustrous glazes, sometimes using two different glazes at opposing ends of a piece like on this vase. After c1900, he lost interest in glazes and much of his later work was left unglazed.

The thinly potted shape, favoured by Ohr, makes this vase brittle and susceptible to damage. The piece has, however, been preserved in good condition.

Like this piece, most Ohr pottery is signed with "Geo. E. Ohr", "Miss" and "Biloxi".

The folded and twisted form gives the piece a sculptural quality and exemplifies the distinctive characteristics of Ohr's pottery. His unusual approach and unconventional personality led him to be known as the "Mad Potter of Biloxi".

A large George Ohr vessel with folded rim and deep, folded, protruding base, the top covered in gunmetal glaze, the base in brown-speckled glossy amber, marked "BILOXI, MISS GEO. E. OHR", glaze flake, retouched line.

7.25in (18.5cm) high

£10,000-15,000 **DRA**

A bulbous George Ohr vase, with scalloped rim and floriform dimple on front, covered in a green, gunmetal brown and amber mottled glaze, complete with a hand-written letter by George Ohr with poem and signature by George and his six children, as well as a period newspaper clipping describing a conversation between potter Jules Gabry and Ohr, small nicks to rim of vase, vase marked "G.E. OHR, Biloxi, Miss".

1899 *6in (15cm) wide*

£15,000-20,000 **DRA**

A bulbous George Ohr vase, with corseted neck, covered in gunmetal glaze, stamped "BILOXI, MISS. GEO. E. OHR".

3.75in (9cm) high

£1,200-1,800 **DRA**

A George Ohr squat spherical vessel, with small opening covered in gunmetal speckled bottle-green glaze, signed "OHR Biloxi".

4.25in (10.5cm) wide

£800-1,200 **DRA**

A George Ohr bulbous vase with closed-in rim over a dimpled band, its interior with mottled glaze, the exterior with mottled matte glaze, signed.

4.75in (12cm) high

£3,000-4,000 **DRA**

A George Ohr coupe-shaped vase with folded rim and dimpled band covered in indigo, raspberry, dark and light green mottled glaze, stamped "G.E. OHR, Biloxi, Miss".

4.75in (12cm) high

£4,000-5,000 **DRA**

A George Ohr Footed vase with band at shoulder, its exterior covered in raspberry, indigo and green sponged-on glaze, the interior in green and gunmetal flambé, stamped "G.E. OHR, Biloxi, Miss", fleck.

5.5in (14cm) high

£2,200-2,800 **DRA**

A George Ohr pinched vessel with lobed rim covered in a rare green, turquoise and gunmetal mottled glaze, script signature.

4in (10cm) high

£5,000-6,000 **DRA**

A bulbous George Ohr vessel, with pinched, four-lobed rim, half covered in gunmetal glaze, and half in mirrored green, stamped "G.E. OHR, BILOXI".

4.5in (11cm) wide

£2,500-3,000 **DRA**

A George Ohr bisque-fired dimpled vessel of white clay, script signature, small chip to rim, some firing lines to base.

5.5in (14cm) wide

£1,200-1,800 **DRA**

A George Ohr flaring bowl with closed-in rim, its interior covered in gunmetal crystalline glaze, exterior with gunmetal drips over bright amber ground, script signature.

6.5in (16.5cm) diam

£800-1,200 **DRA**

A George Ohr squat vessel with asymmetrically dimpled and folded rim, covered in brown and green speckled brown glaze, stamped "G.E. OHR, Biloxi, Miss".

5.25in (13.5cm) diam

£2,000-3,000 **DRA**

A George Ohr cabinet vase, with closed-in rim of marbleized clay covered in a sheer mottled green glaze, marked "GEO. E. OHR, BILOXI".

3.5in (9cm) diam

£700-1,000 **DRA**

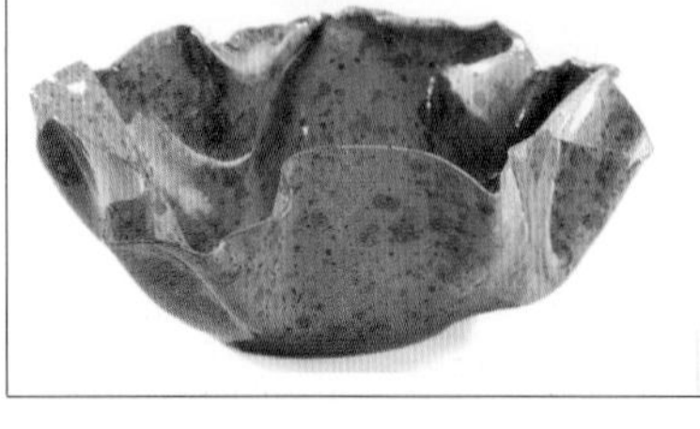

A George Ohr handkerchief bowl, now with brown speckled glaze on green ground, impressed "GEO E OHR/BILOXI, MISS".

8in (20.5cm) diam

£1,200-1,800 **ISA**

An extremely rare George Ohr cottage inkwell novelty, with a tile roof, two arches, and a swinging picket fence, covered in green and amber speckled glaze, short firing line to base, "G.E. OHR BILOXI".

6in (15cm) wide

£3,000-4,000 **DRA**

A large Pewabic vase, covered in a lustred, richly textured flambé glaze, stamped "Pewabic Detroit PP".

19in (47.5cm) high

£8,000-12,000 **DRA**

A Pewabic tall and fine baluster vase covered in green and indigo curdled lustred glaze circular "Pewabic Detroit" stamp and two paper labels, two holes.

12.5in (32cm) high

£800-1,200 **DRA**

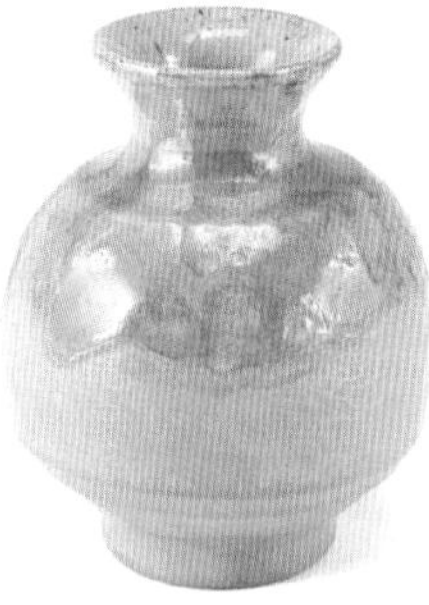

A Pewabic bulbous vase with a crackled blue glaze dripping over lustred celadon, circular "Pewabic Detroit" stamp, chip.

4.75in (12cm) high

£150-200 **DRA**

A Pewabic bottle-shaped vase, covered in green and purple matte lustred glaze, restoration to small rim chip, stamped "Pewabic Detroit".

11in (27.5cm) high

£800-1,200 **DRA**

A Pewabic arched plaque carved with a Virgin Mary with snake at her feet covered in turquoise glaze on a sheer white ground, Pewabic Pottery circular stamp.

4.75in (12cm) high

£150-200 **DRA**

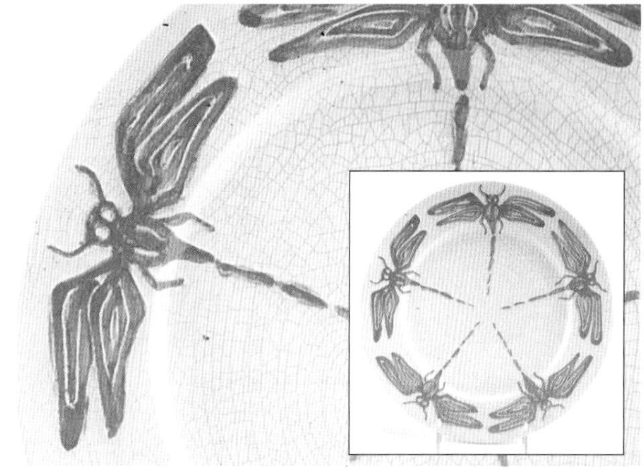

A Pewabic fine and rare plate painted with dragonflies in periwinkle blue on a white crackled ground, stamped "PEWABIC" and paper label, chips.

10.75in (27.5cm) diam

£1,200-1,800 **DRA**

ROOKWOOD

A rare Laura Fry/Cincinnati Pottery Club pitcher decorated by Laura Fry with incised fronds covered in indigo and dark green glaze, stamped "ROOKWOOD 1882", incised "Cincinnati Pottery club", "LAF".

Laura Fry was a member of the Women's Pottery Club of Cincinnati, a china-painting group, along with Clara Chipman Newton and Mary Louise McLaughlin, before joining the first generation of decorators at Rookwood. During her ten-year stay at the pottery, she developed and patented the atomizer for glazing purposes. From Rookwood, she moved on to the Lonhuda Pottery in Steubenville, OH.

7in (18cm) high

£1,000-1,500 **DRA**

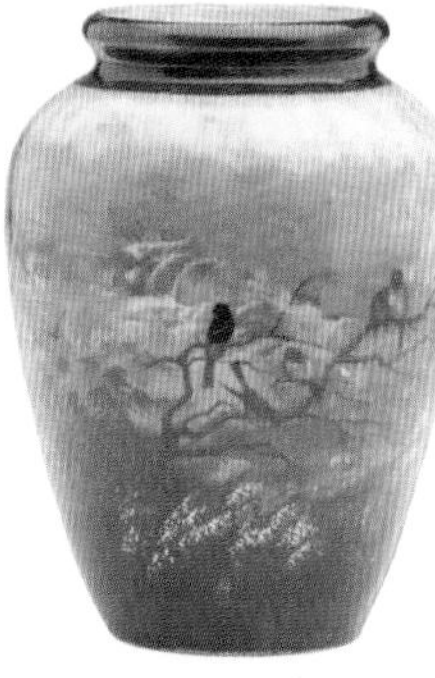

A Rookwood baluster vase, painted in the Limoges style by N.J. Hirschfeld, with birds on tree branches and in flight.

1882 *7.75in (19cm) high*

£300-400 **DRA**

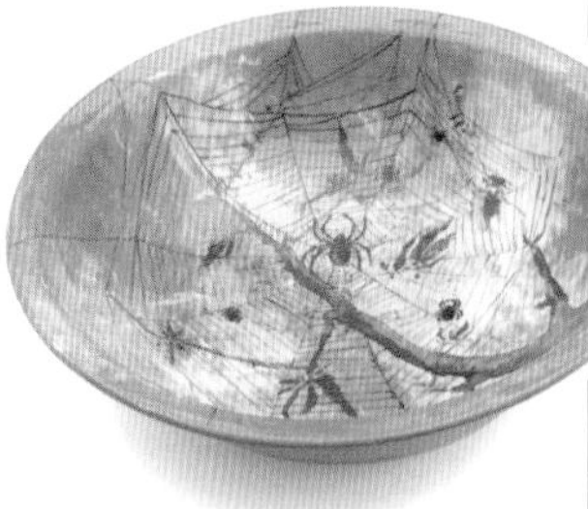

An early Rookwood centre bowl, decorated in the Limoges style by Albert Valentien with spiders in a large web on a branch, stamped "ROOKWOOD 1882", anchor, "A.R.V.", some abrasion to base.

1882 *14.5in (36cm) wide*

£1,200-1,800 **DRA**

ROOKWOOD

- Founded in c1880 in Cincinnati, Ohio, by Maria Longworth Nichols (1849-1932), Rookwood is considered the most powerful and influential pottery in the US.
- From the beginning, the company focused on producing high quality art pottery and employed skilled craftsmen, technicians and artists.
- Early wares were heavily potted, slip-cast or thrown and forms were often Japanese-inspired.
- Japanese ceramicist Kataro Shirayamadani became one of the company's most important designers. Joining in the late 19thC, he stayed with Rookwood until his death in 1948.
- Other notable artists included Matt Daly, Grace Young and Artus Van Briggle, who favoured the use of high-quality matte glazes.
- Developed by Laura Fry, 'Standard' – a clear, glossy glaze – was applied with an atomizer over pots with brown and ochre decoration. Variations on 'Standard' glaze included 'Sea Green' and 'Iris'.
- Portrait decoration was popular. Subjects included Old Masters and Native Americans.
- Pieces are often signed "RP" with a flame.
- The company closed in 1967.

A late 19thC Rookwood pottery vase, by Albert Valentien, decorated with flying insects and fine leaf foliage, incised geometric pattern at shoulder with gilt accents, impressed marks and two paper labels.

c1885 *9in (23cm) high*
£1,500-2,000 **SK**

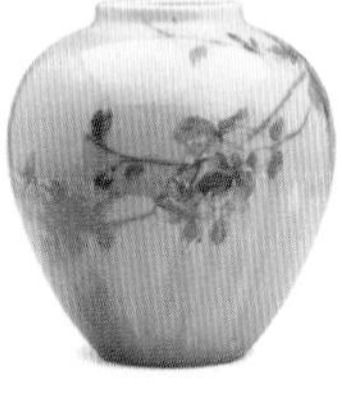

A Rookwood Standard glaze light large ovoid vase, crisply painted by Kataro Shirayamadani, with branches of yellow dogwood on a yellow and amber ground, flame mark, "531F", Japanese cypher, remnants of red crayon museum marks.

This piece was once in the Cincinnati Museum Collection.

1886 *9.25in (23cm) high*
£1,200-1,800 **DRA**

A Rookwood Standard glaze large light urn, finely painted by Matt Daly with branches of yellow dogwood, a gently tooled underglaze design encircling the collar, flame mark, "MAD/L/425/W".

1888 *13in (32.5cm) high*
£1,800-2,200 **DRA**

An early Rookwood Standard glaze vase with floriform rim beautifully painted by Harriet Wilcox, with a branch of yellow roses, flame mark "HEW", grinding marks.

1889 *5.5in (14cm) high*
£200-300 **DRA**

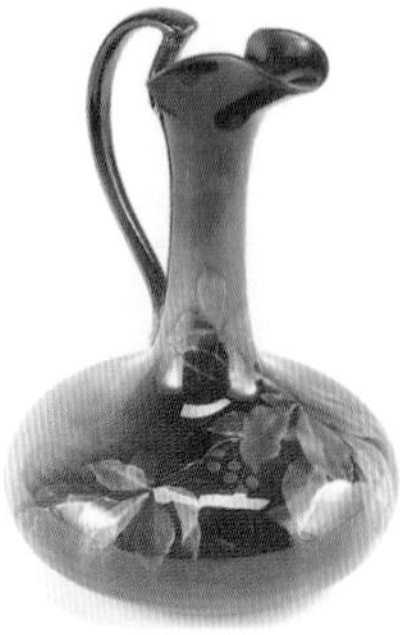

An early Rookwood standard glaze ewer, possibly painted by Grace Young, with gooseberries, reglued handle.

c1890 *7in (18cm) high*
£300-400 **DRA**

A large Rookwood Standard glaze urn, decorated by Matthew Daly, with elaborate silver overlay by Spaulding & Co., flame mark, "581C/W/MAD/ Spaulding & Co. Jewelers, Chicago".

1892 *12.5in (31cm) high*
£1,500-2,000 **DRA**

A Rookwood Standard glaze light ewer painted by A.M. Valentien, with golden chrysanthemums, efflorescence and deep crazing line to handle, flame mark "AMV".

1892 *9.5in (24cm) high*
£180-220 **DRA**

A Rookwood standard glaze bulbous vase, painted by Irene Bishop with yellow wild roses, 1894, flame mark "ICB".

7in (18cm) high
£250-300 **DRA**

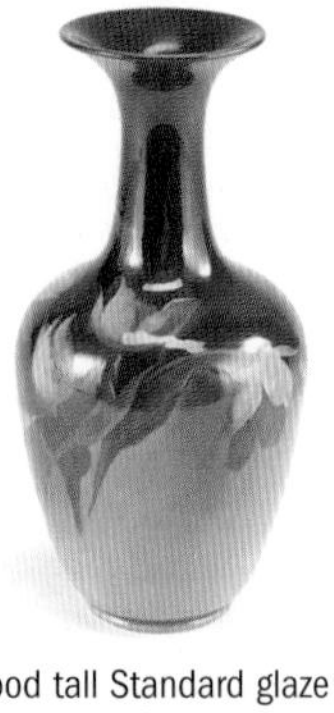

A Rookwood tall Standard glaze vase, painted by Amelia Sprague, with amber tulips, opposing hairlines to top, flame mark, "ABS".

c1895 *11.25in (28.5cm) high*
£200-300 **DRA**

A Rookwood Standard glaze loving cup, decorated by Grace Young with a Native American brave with illegible name, chased silver band and silver medallion, flame mark, "810/GY", titled, Stanley Burt's red mark.

Provenance: *Deaccessioned from the Cincinnati Museum.*

1898 *8in (20cm) wide*

£3,000-5,000 DRA

A Rookwood Standard glaze ewer, by A. Sehon, with golden crocuses, flame mark "A.D.S".

c1899 *5.5in (14cm) high*

£300-400 DRA

A Rookwood Standard glaze squat vase, painted by Elizabeth Brain, with brown nasturtium blossoms, flame mark "EWB".

1900 *3.75in (9.5cm) wide*

£150-200 DRA

A Rookwood rare and fine Standard glaze tall vase, with bronze overlay, decorated by Kataro Shirayamadani with a Japanese scene of fish and sea plants, flame mark, "804C", Japanese cypher.

This piece was once in the Cincinnati Museum Collection.

1898 *12.75in (32cm) high*

£15,000-20,000 DRA

A Rookwood Standard glaze two-handled vase, painted by Olga Reed, with fleshy orchids, flame mark, "804C/O.G.R."

1900 *9.25in (23cm) high*

£800-1,200 DRA

A Rookwood standard glaze ewer by an unidentified artist, with falling maple leaves, flame mark and illegible artist signature

1899 *7in (18cm) high*

£300-500 DRA

A Rookwood Standard glaze two-handled vase, painted by E. Nourse, with yellow orchids, flame mark.

1903 *5.75in (14.5cm) high*

£200-300 DRA

A Rookwood Standard glaze vase, painted by A.D. Sehon with the Native American chief Sitting Bull, flame mark, "I/735D/A.D.S./Sitting Bull".

1901 *7.25in (18cm) high*

£5,000-7,000 DRA

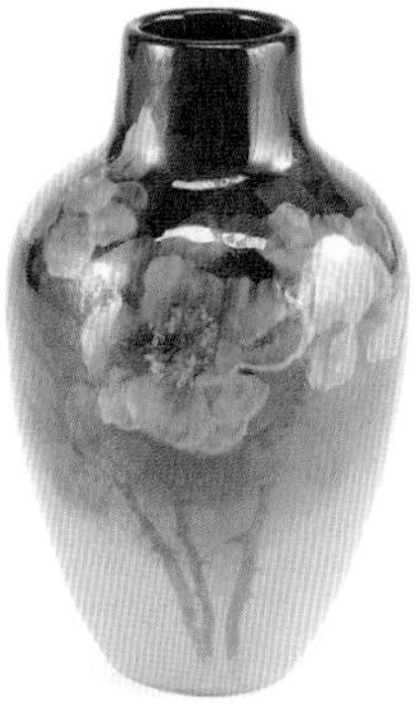

A Rookwood standard glaze bulbous vase painted by Jeanette Swing with large yellow roses, flame mark "JS", some cloudiness.

c1903 *8in (20.5cm) high*

£180-220 DRA

A rare and exceptional Rookwood Standard glaze plaque, by Bruce Horsfall, of a putto with large banana leaves and clusters of fruit, scratches, framed.

Originally part of a mantelpiece from the Probante House in Cincinnati.

plaque 10.5in (26.5cm) wide

£2,000-3,000 DRA

A Rookwood 'Tiger Eye' narrow vase, beautifully painted by Harriet Wilcox, with iris buds, small stilt pull chips to inner footrim, flame mark, "589E/R/HEW".

1894 8.25in (20.5cm) high

£1,000-1,500 DRA

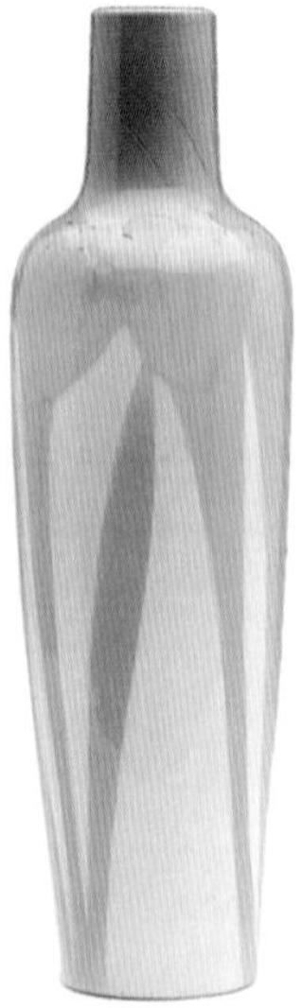

A fine Rookwood Iris glaze tall bottle-shaped vase, beautifully carved and slip-painted with golden tulips and long celadon leaves on white ground, flame mark, "S1656/W".

An original factory label covers the artist signature. It appears to be the work of Sara Sax. There are also traces of the red crayon museum marks.

1900 13.25in (33cm) high

£7,000-10,000 DRA

A Rookwood Iris glaze three-handled cabinet vase painted by Rose Fechheimer, with a branch of white cherry blossoms on lavender ground, flame mark "R.F".

1901 3in (7.5cm) high

£300-400 DRA

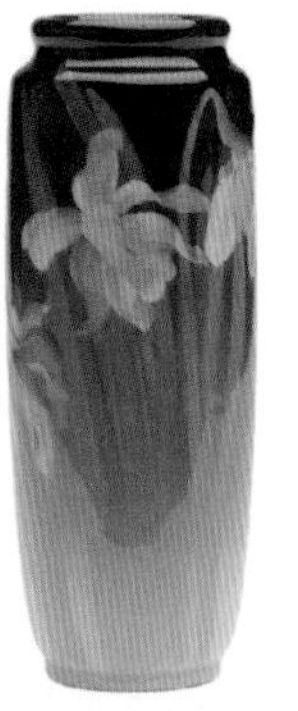

A Rookwood Iris glaze vase, painted by Sara Sax, with white daffodils on a black-to-apricot ground, flame mark, "II/589E", artist cypher.

1902 8.5in (21cm) high

£800-1,200 DRA

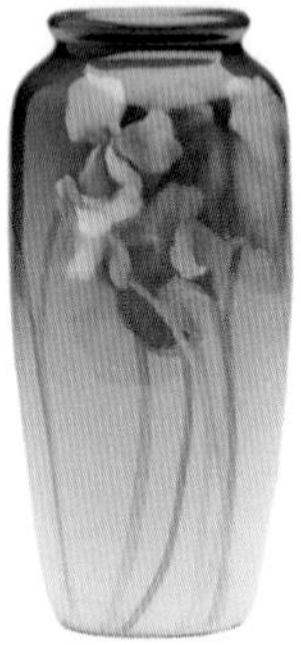

A Rookwood Iris glaze vase, painted by Fred Rothenbusch, with purple violets on a shaded purple ground, seconded mark for scaling around rim, opposing hairlines, flame mark, "III/984E/FR".

1903 6.75in (17cm) high

£500-700 DRA

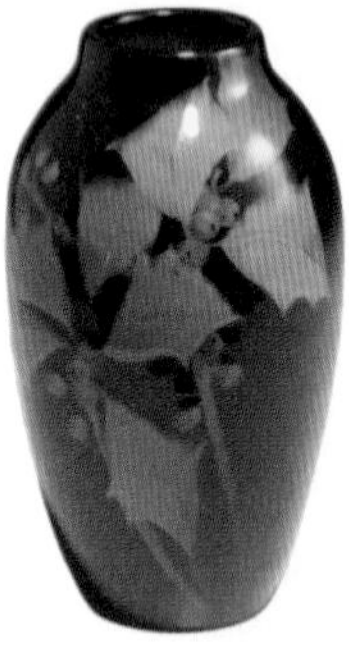

A Rookwood black Iris ovoid vase, painted by Sarah Sax, with a holly branch against black ground, three glaze misses at rim, flame mark, artist cypher.

1906 6.25in (15.5cm) high

£4,000-6,000 DRA

A Rookwood Iris glaze bulbous vase, painted by Clara Lindeman, with a branch of pink apple blossoms on shaded ground, flame mark, "VIII/654C/C.C.L."

1908 5in (12.5cm) high

£600-900 DRA

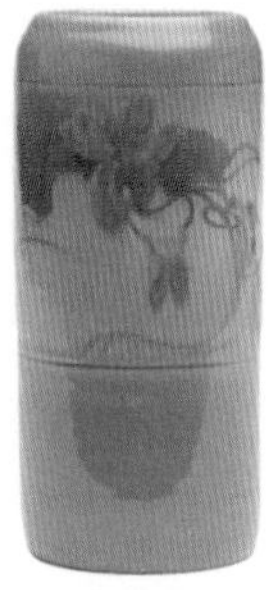

A Rookwood Iris glaze cylindrical vase, painted by Fred Rothenbusch with a band of violets on a yellow and purple ground, flame mark, "IX/952E/FR".

1909 7in (17.5cm) high

£1,500-2,000 DRA

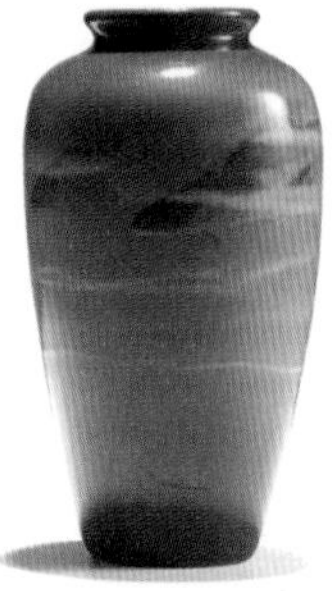

A fine Rookwood Iris glaze vase, decorated by E.T. Hurley, with fish swimming against celadon water, flame mark.

1910 8in (20cm) high

£2,800-3,200 DRA

A large Rookwood Vellum vase, painted by Carl Schmidt, with purple irises on a shaded ground, flame mark "XII/614B", artist cypher, imperfections.

1912 15.5in (39cm) high

£3,500-4,000 DRA

A CLOSER LOOK AT A ROOKWOOD VASE

The clear glossy 'Iris' glaze was developed c1895, under the direction of chemist Stanley G. Burt.

The clarity of the glaze makes possible the display of light shades and an astonishingly sharp and realistic image, in this case an autumnal landscape.

Rookwood is known for employing talented artists, including the highly regarded Carl Schmidt. His painting is extremely well realised and the colours are attractive. The bulk of Rookwood's output features decoration inspired by the natural world.

The "X" in the mark was used to indicate a trial piece and is probably explained in this case by some scaling to the rim and a couple of minor glaze bubbles to the surface.

An exceptional Rookwood tall Iris glaze 'Scenic' vase, painted by Carl Schmidt, with an autumn landscape with brook, flame mark "X/907A/W", some imperfections.

c1910 20in (51cm) high

£25,000-30,000 DRA

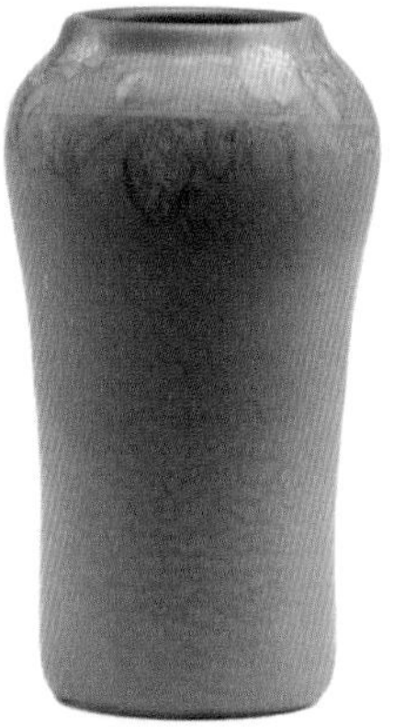

A Rookwood wax matte bulbous vase, painted by Olga G. Reed, with red cherry blossoms on a shaded green-to-raspberry butterfat ground, flame mark, "IV/935E/O.G.R."

1904 *6.25in (15.5cm) high*

£1,200-1,800 **DRA**

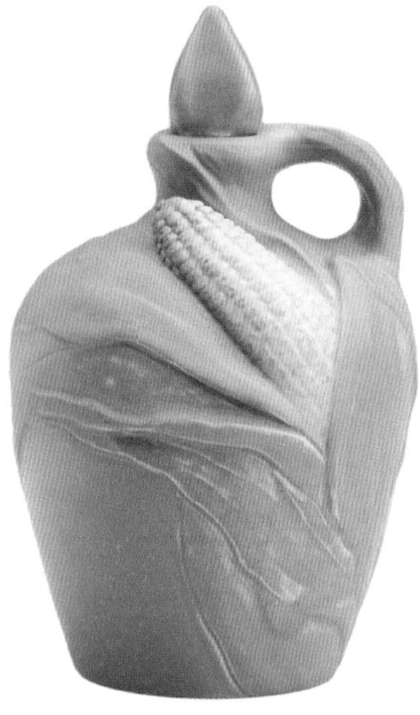

A rare Rookwood carved matte corn jug, by Kataro Shirayamadani, in matte greens and browns, seconded mark for small glaze miss on back, chip to husk, flame mark, "IV/765BZ/X", artist cypher.

1904 *9in (22.5cm) high*

£2,200-2,800 **DRA**

A Rookwood massive garden pot covered in a fine feathered matte green glaze, flame mark.

1905 *15.5in (39cm) high*

£400-600 **DRA**

A Rookwood carved matte squat vessel by Cecil Duell with a band of leaves in blue on a matte green ground, flame mark "VII/214A/CAD", flock.

1907 *8in (20.5cm) wide*

£500-700 **DRA**

A Rookwood fine carved matte vase by unidentified artist "MF", with stylized purple flowers on whiplash green stems on a green ground, flame mark, two small cracks.

1909 *10in (25.5cm) high*

£500-700 **DRA**

A Rookwood painted matte cabinet vase, by William Hentshel, with a branch of red cherry blossoms on black ground, flame mark "WEH".

1910 *3in (7.5cm) wide*

£500-700 **DRA**

A tall Rookwood carved matte tankard, by William Hentschel, with swaying cornflower blossoms in blue on burgundy ground, flame mark.

1912 *11.75in (29cm) high*

£700-1,000 **DRA**

A Rookwood carved matte bulbous vase, by William Hentschel, with stylized geese in flight in greens and browns, dark crazing line to interior only, flame mark, "XIII/1045/WEH".

1913 *5.75in (14cm) high*

£800-1,200 **DRA**

A Rookwood carved matte ovoid vase, by C.S. Todd, with a wreath of red and yellow blossoms on brown and red ground, flame mark "CST".

1914 *6.75in (17cm) high*

£400-500 **DRA**

A Rookwood incised matte vessel, by Sara Sax, with stylized pink and purple flowers on green and brown whiplash stems, against a shaded purple ground, flame mark, "VI/1848/V", artist cypher.

1915 *7in (17.5cm) wide*

£700-1,000 **DRA**

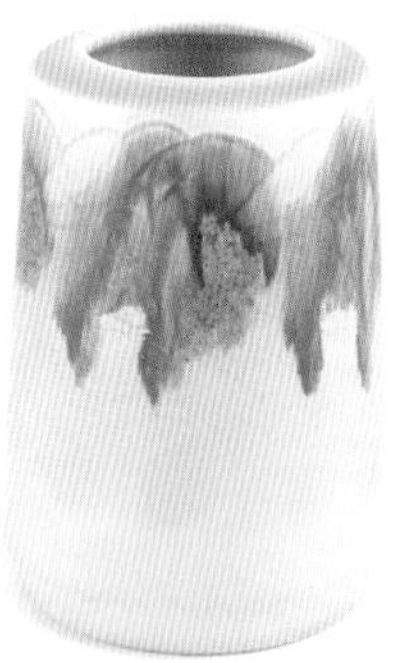

A Rookwood incised matte vase, with closed-in rim painted by Charles Todd, with blue, red and yellow blossoms on a vermilion ground, flame mark "CST".

1919 *5in (14cm) high*

£300-500 **DRA**

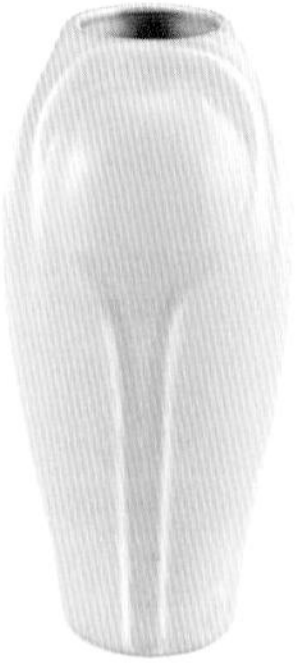

A tall Rookwood production vase with three buttresses covered in a smooth matte amber glaze.

1920 *10in (25.5cm) high*

£300-400 **DRA**

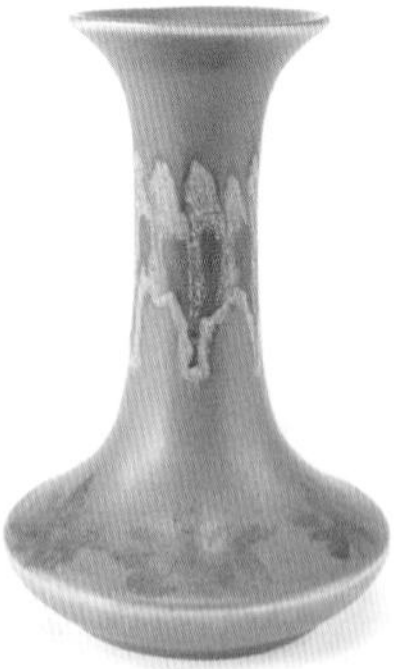

A Rookwood wax matte bottle-shaped vase painted by C.S. Todd, with abstract red flowers and yellow band against a blue-green ground, flame mark "XXI/497/CST".

1921 *7.75in (19.5cm) high*

£800-1,200 **DRA**

A pair of Rookwood rook bookends, designed by William McDonald, in matte indigo glaze, marked.

1926 *5.5in (14cm) wide*

£400-600 **DRA**

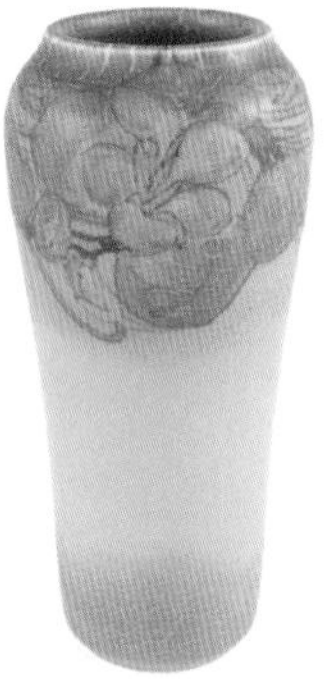

A Rookwood wax matte vase, painted by Sallie Coyne, with pink and yellow nasturtium blossoms on green leaves against a turquoise ground, flame mark "SEC", line.

1927 *9.25in (23.5cm) high*

£300-500 **DRA**

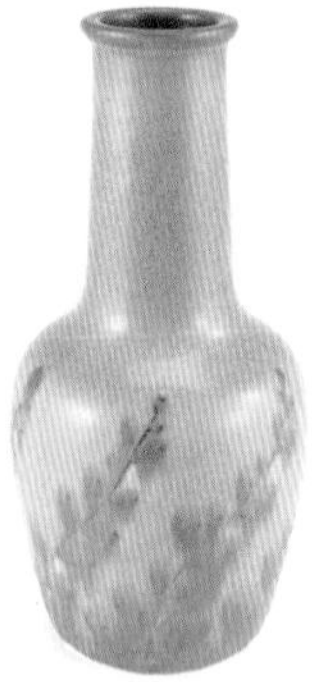

A Rookwood squeeze bag tall vase, by William Hentschel, with branches of brown leaves on a caramel and blue matte ground, flame mark "XXVII/2970/WH".

1927 *12.25in (31cm) high*

£500-700 **DRA**

A Rookwood wax matte bulbous vase painted by unidentified artist, with red hollyhocks in relief on a red and green butterfat ground, flame mark.

1928 *6.75in (17cm) high*

£800-1,200 **DRA**

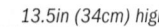

A large Rookwood squeezebag-decorated Art Deco vase, by William Hentschel, with a nude, antelopes and geese, covered in matte brown and white glaze, flame mark, "XXIX/6080/WEH", drilled hole to base.

1929 *13.5in (34cm) high*

£2,800-3,200 **DRA**

A Rookwood wax matte urn painted by Jens Jensen, with large red blossoms and green-brown leaves on a butter yellow ground, flame mark, artist cypher.

1929 *8.5in (21.5cm) high*

£600-900 **DRA**

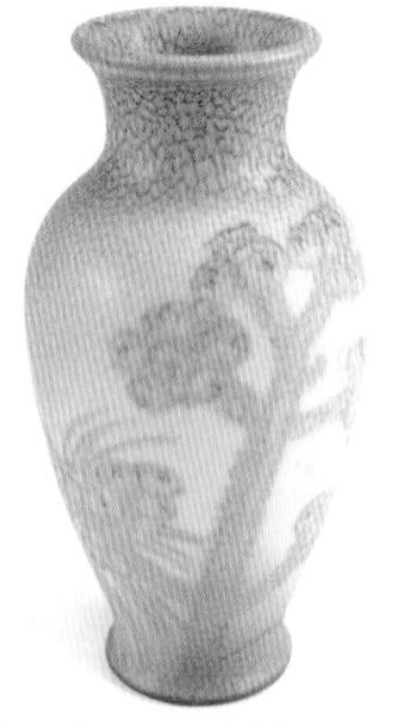

A Rookwood wax matte baluster vase, painted by Kataro Shirayamadani, with tropical plants in orange, red and green on a butterfat ground, flame mark, Japanese cypher.

1935 *7.5in (19cm) high*

£2,000-3,000 **DRA**

A Rookwood carved matte cabinet vase, by A.M. Valentien, modelled with a nude wrapped around the opening and covered in matte purple glaze, flame mark "I/16?Z/A.M.V".

1901 *3.25in (8.5cm) wide*

£800-1,200 **DRA**

A Rookwood Faience tile, modelled with a tall ship in matte glaze, mounted and framed, stamped "ROOKWOOD FAIENCE/12378Y", chips.

8in (20cm) high

£800-1,200 **DRA**

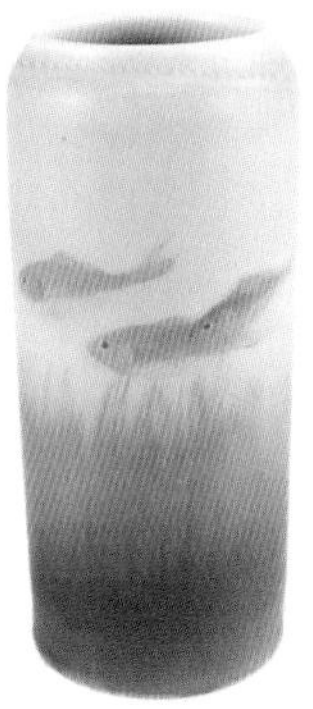

A Rookwood green Vellum cylindrical vase, painted by E.T. Hurley, with swimming fish on a turquoise ground, flame mark "V/952E/E.T.H./V".

1905 *7in (18cm) high*

£3,000-4,000 **DRA**

A Rookwood Vellum vase, painted by E.T. Hurley, with white geese in flight in front of a pink-green sky, flame mark "VI/Ada Dwyer/E.T. Hurley 2-8-06".

1906 *6.25in (15cm) high*

£1,200-1,800 **DRA**

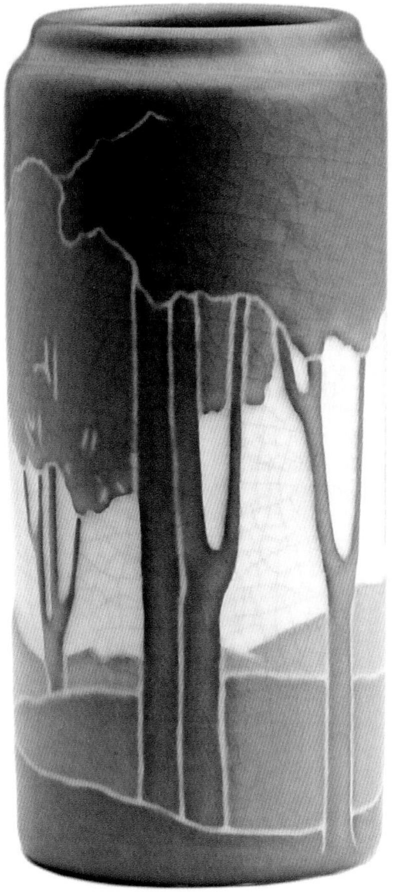

A Rookwood carved Vellum cylindrical vase, decorated by Sarah Sax, with an abstracted landscape of silhouetted trees, flame mark, "VIII/952E", artist cypher, "V".

This piece was part of the Cincinnati Museum Collection.

1908 *7.5in (19cm) high*

£10,000-15,000 **DRA**

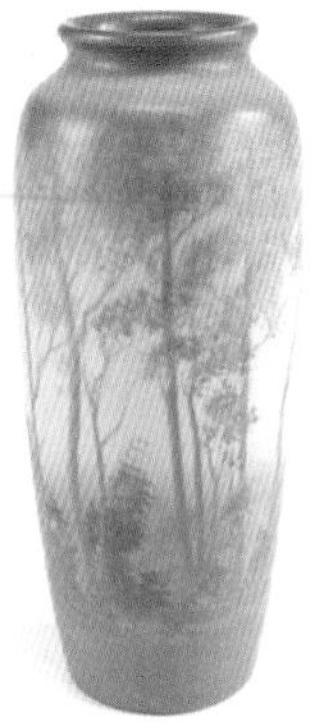

A Rookwood Scenic Vellum vase painted by Ed Diers, with an autumn landscape, flame mark "XVI/904D/V/ED".

1916 *8.75in (22cm) high*

£2,500-3,000 **DRA**

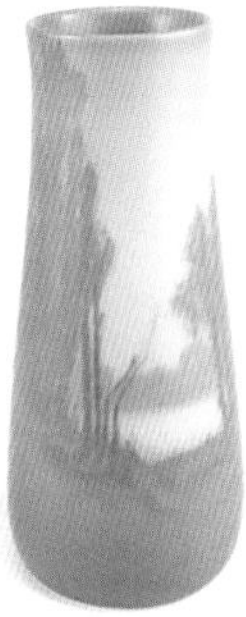

A Rookwood Scenic Vellum bulbous vase, painted by Sallie Coyne, with dark silhouetted trees against an amber river and turquoise sky, flame mark "XVI/950D/V/SEC".

1916 *9.25in (23.5cm) high*

£1,500-2,000 **DRA**

A Rookwood Scenic Vellum baluster vase, finely painted by Sallie Coyne, with a hilly landscape under a pink sky, flame mark, light peppering.

1916 *11in (27.5cm) high*

£800-1,200 **DRA**

A Rookwood Scenic Vellum vase, painted by Sallie Coyne, with a snow-covered forest landscape, flame mark, "XX/2060/V/SEC".

1920 *7.75in (19cm) high*

£2,200-2,800 **DRA**

A tall Rookwood Vellum vase, delicately painted by K. Shirayamadani, with buff-coloured poppies and teal blue wheat stalks, flame mark, "XXI", "951B", "V", Japanese cypher.

1921 12.75in (32cm) high

£7,000-10,000 **DRA**

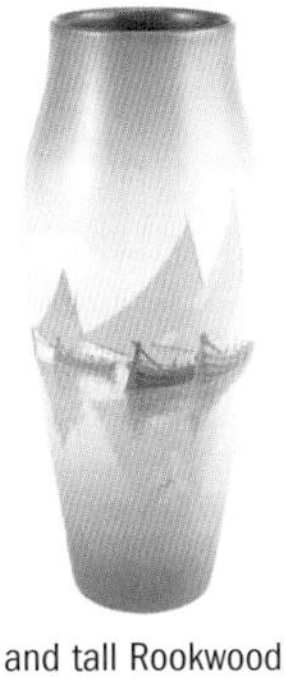

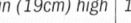

A rare and tall Rookwood Scenic Vellum vase, painted by Carl Schmidt, with fishing boats in a Venetian harbour, flame mark "XXI/30D/V", artist cypher.

1921 *9.75in (25cm) wide*

£3,000-4,000 **DRA**

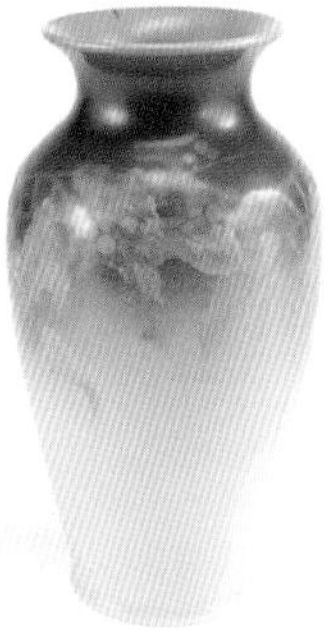

A rare Yellow Vellum Rookwood baluster vase, painted by Lenore Asbury, with red berries and green leaves on an amber ground, flame mark "XXIV/546C/L.A./Y.V".

1924 *9.5in (24cm) high*

£1,800-2,200 **DRA**

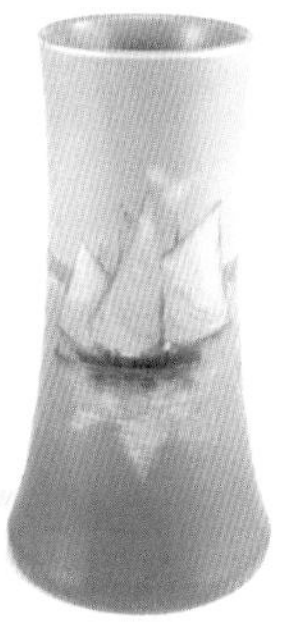

A rare Rookwood Scenic Vellum tapering vase, painted by Arthur Conant, with sailboats, flame mark "XVI/1358D/V", artist cypher.

9.25in (23.5cm) high

£2,500-3,000 **DRA**

A Rookwood scenic vellum plaque, by E.T. Hurley, 'The Tropics', with tall palm trees in silhouette, mounted in original frame, flame mark.

1913 *plaque 8in (20cm) high*

£3,000-4,000 **DRA**

A large and unusual Rookwood scenic vellum plaque, painted by E.T. Hurley, with sheep grazing under apple trees, in original Arts and Crafts frame, flame mark, "XIV/E.T.H."

1914 *plaque 12.25in (30.5cm) wide*

£12,000-18,000 **DRA**

A Rookwood scenic vellum plaque, by Sallie Coyne, with tall trees in a snow-covered landscape, mounted in original frame, flame mark.

1916 *plaque 8.25in (20.5cm) high*

£5,000-7,000 **DRA**

A Rookwood scenic vellum plaque, by Carl Schmidt, with a placid water landscape in turquoises and pinks, mounted in original frame, flame mark.

1916 *plaque 11in (27.5cm) high*

£5,000-7,000 **DRA**

A Rookwood scenic vellum plaque, by Charles McLaughlin, with green and blue trees against a yellow sky, reflected in water, mounted in original frame, flame mark.

1916 *plaque 10.75in (27cm) high*

£4,000-5,000 **DRA**

A Rookwood scenic vellum 'Summer' plaque, by Margaret H. MacDonald, with a lakeside landscape, mounted in original frame with paper label, flame mark, "XVII/V/MHM."

1917 *plaque 8.25in (20.5cm) wide*

£3,000-4,000 **DRA**

A Rookwood scenic vellum 'Winter' plaque, painted by Sallie Coyne, with a snowy landscape in pinks and blues, mounted in original Arts and Crafts frame, flame mark, "XVIII", artist cypher.

1918 *plaque 9.25in (23cm) wide*

£5,000-7,000 **DRA**

A Rookwood scenic vellum plaque, painted by Sara Sax, 'The Road to the River', with a snowy mountain road in browns, blues and greens, mounted in original frame, flame mark "XIX/Sax".

1919 *plaque 12.5in (32cm) high*

£6,000-9,000 **DRA**

A Rookwood scenic vellum plaque by E.T. Hurley, 'A Michigan...', with a pink sky over a landscape of purple mountains and birch trees, mounted in original frame, flame mark.

1920 *plaque 9.5in (24cm) wide*

£4,000-5,000 **DRA**

An exceptional and large Rookwood scenic vellum plaque, painted by Ed Diers with a Venetian scene in mauve and ivory, 'On the Riva.', original frame, "ED", flame mark.

plaque 14.5in (37cm) wide

£8,000-12,000 **DRA**

A Rookwood marine scenic vellum plaque by Carl Schmidt, 'Morning in the Lagoon – Venice', with sailboats in a Venetian harbour, mounted in original frame, flame mark.

plaque 12in (30cm) high

£8,000-12,000 **DRA**

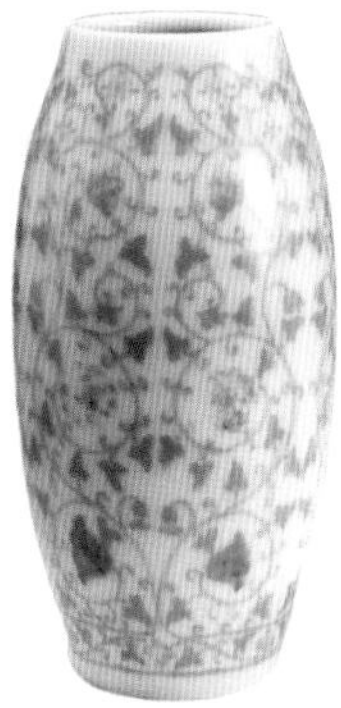

A Rookwood Jewel porcelain ovoid vase, decorated in a Persian floral pattern by Arthur Conant, flame mark, artist cypher.

1921 *6.5in (16cm) high*

£700-1,000 **DRA**

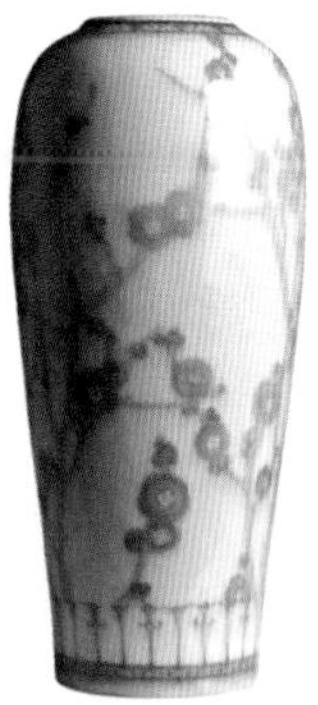

A tall Rookwood Jewel porcelain vase, painted by Lorinda Epply, with branches of plum-coloured cherry blossoms on ivory ground, uncrazed, flame mark.

1922 *12.25in (30.5cm) high*

£1,000-1,500 **DRA**

A Rookwood Jewel porcelain hemispherical vase painted by Lorinda Epply with blossoms on a chartreuse ground, flame mark "XXVI/2254E/LE".

1926 *5.5in (14cm) high*

£300-500 **DRA**

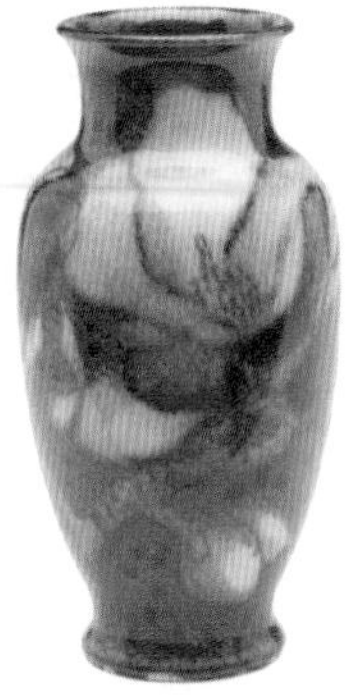

A Rookwood jewel porcelain baluster vase, painted by Jens Jensen, with blossoms on a butterfat brown ground, flame mark, "XXXIII/S", artist cypher.

1933 *7in (17.5cm) high*

£800-1,200 **DRA**

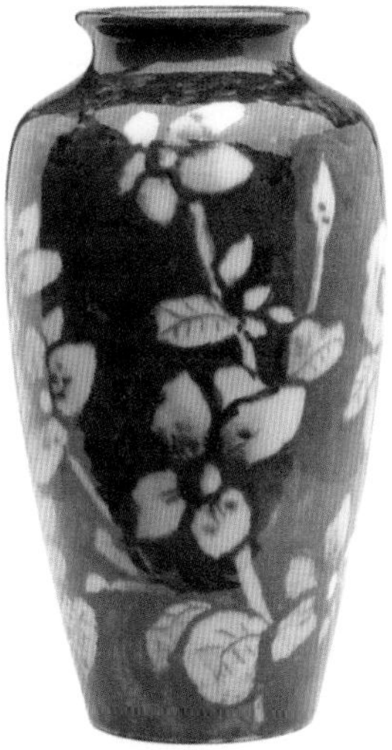

A tall Art Deco Rookwood Jewel porcelain vase, painted by Jens Jensen, with ivory hibiscus blossoms and leaves, on a grey-brown butterfat ground, uncrazed, flame mark, "XXXI/614C", artist cypher.

1931 *12.5in (31cm) high*

£2,500-3,000 **DRA**

A Rookwood jewel porcelain squat vessel, decorated by Jens Jensen, with birds of paradise in ivory on a mottled purple and blue ground, flame mark, artist cypher.

1934 *4.75in (12cm) high*

£1,200-1,800 **DRA**

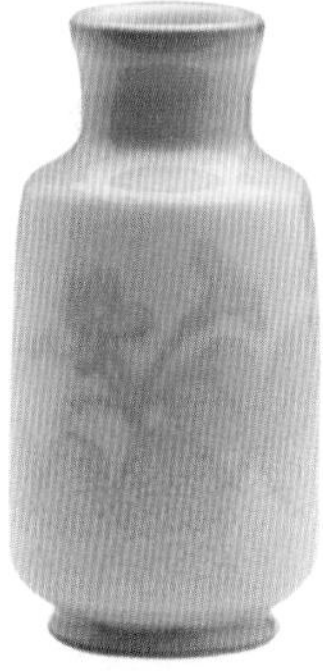

A Rookwood jewel porcelain vase, painted by Kataro Shirayamadani, with pink and yellow flowers on a vermilion ground, uncrazed, flame mark, "XXXIV/S", Japanese cypher.

1934 *6.25in (15.5cm) high*

£1,000-1,500 **DRA**

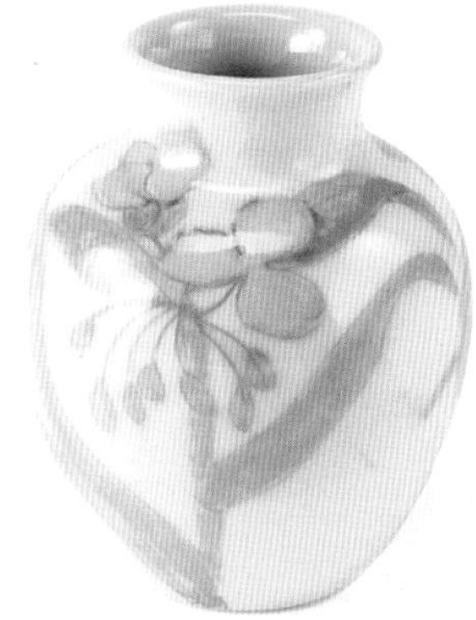

A Rookwood Jewel porcelain vase by Jens Jensen, with blue trefoils on ivory ground, flame mark, artist cypher.

c1945 *5.75in (14.5cm) high*

£700-1,000 **DRA**

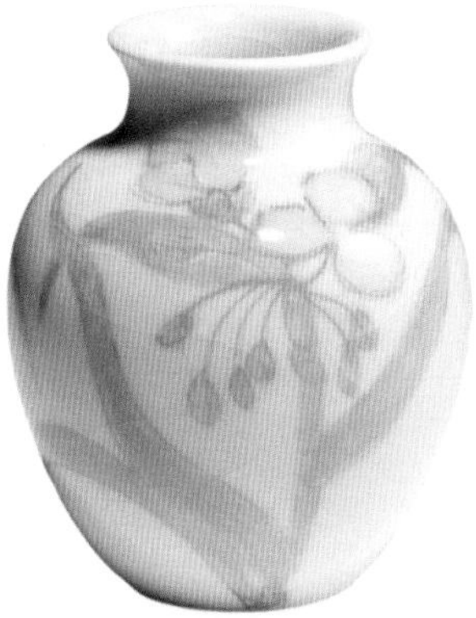

A Rookwood Jewel porcelain vase, by Jens Jensen, with blue trefoils on ivory ground, flame mark, artist cypher.

1945 *5.75in (14cm) high*

£400-600 **DRA**

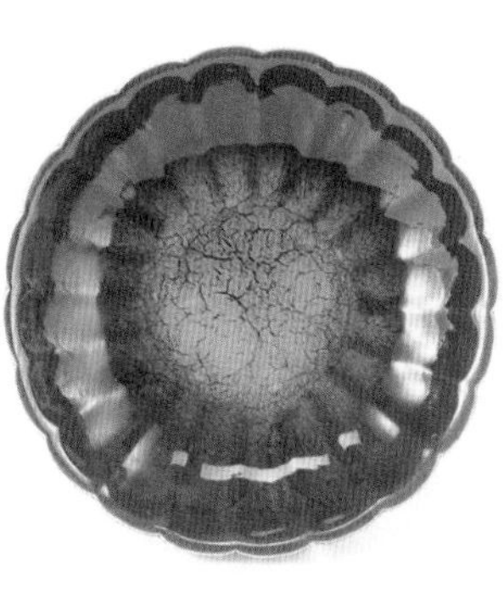

A Rookwood jewel porcelain scalloped bowl, painted by Sarah Sax, with abstract blossoms on a sung plum and blue ground, flame mark "XXVII/2813C", artist cypher.

13.5in (34.5cm) diam

£700-1,000 **DRA**

A Rookwood Jewel porcelain lamp base, painted with purple magnolia on an ivory ground and mounted in its original brass fixture, mark hidden by base.

13.25 (33cm) high

£200-300 **DRA**

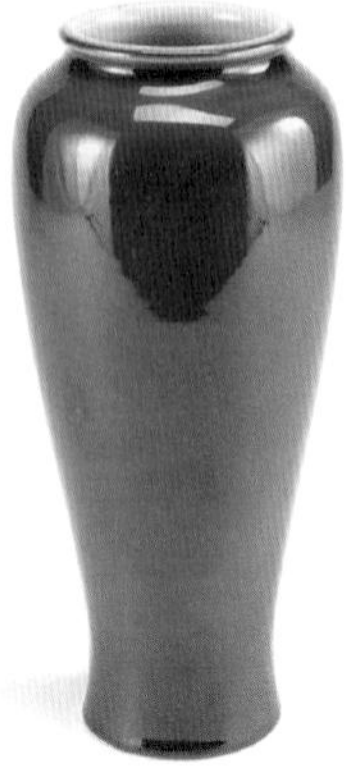

A tall Rookwood porcelain Production baluster vase, with yellow interior and indigo exterior.

1921 *14in (35.5cm) high*

£200-300 **DRA**

A Rookwood Production vase, embossed with blossoms under a fine crystalline blue glaze, flame mark.

1930 *7.25in (18.5cm) high*

£200-300 **DRA**

A Rookwood Production incense burner, in the shape of a mask covered in blue crystalline glaze, flame mark.

1921 *5.5in (14cm) wide*

£200-300 **DRA**

A Rookwood 'Sea Green' two-handled vase, painted by E.T. Hurley, flame mark "77A/E.T.H./G", dated 1898, restored.

7.75in (19.5cm) high

£1,200-1,800 **DRA**

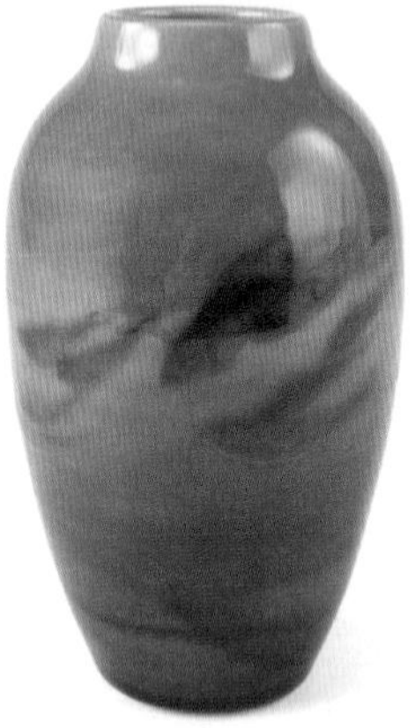

A rare Rookwood 'Sea Green' ovoid vase, painted by E.T. Hurley, with swimming fish, flame mark "II/900C/ETH".

1902 *8in (20.5cm) high*

£2,000-3,000 **DRA**

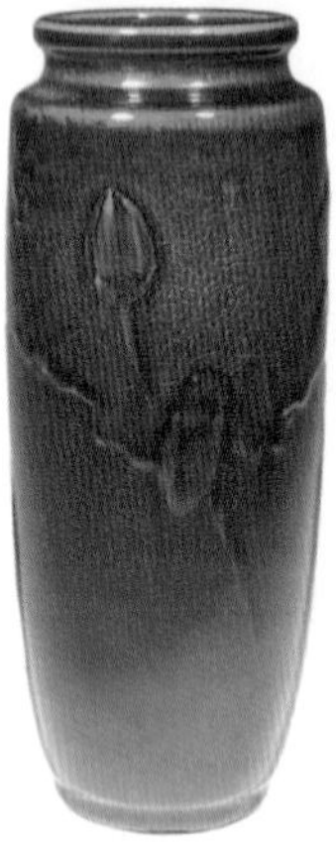

A Rookwood 'Tiger Eye' narrow vase, painted by K. Shirayamadani, with a cicada on a large lily pad, flame mark "589F", Japanese cypher.

1897 *7in (18cm) high*

£800-1,200 **DRA**

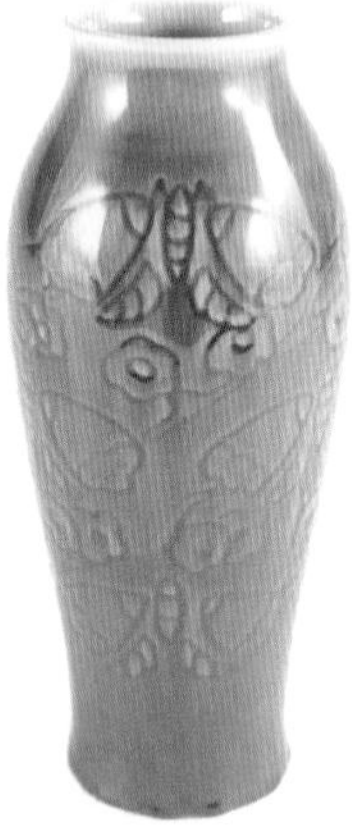

A Rookwood 'Aventurine' vase, carved by Elizabeth Lincoln, with flowers and butterflies under a green crystalline glaze, flame mark "XX/937/LNL".

1920 *9.75in (25cm) high*

£600-900 **DRA**

A Rookwood wax urn, painted by W. Rehm, with blue and yellow pansies against a chevron border, flame mark, artist cypher.

c1929 *8.5in (21.5cm) high*

£600-900 **DRA**

A Rookwood porcelain baluster vase, painted by E.T. Hurley, with red and yellow fish in blue and white waves, uncrazed, flame mark, "XLIV", "6765", "ETH".

1944 *7in (17.5cm) high*

£3,000-4,000 **DRA**

A Rookwood Faience fine tile embossed with a scrub oak tree in green and brown within a beige medallion against a sand ground, stamped "ROOKWOOD FAIENCE", glaze chip.

£1,500-2,000 **DRA**

A large Rookwood Faience frieze of three tiles, depicting in cuenca a thatched roof cottage in a bucolic landscape, covered in matte polychrome glazes, mounted in a new Arts and Crafts frame, back covered, no visible mark.

48in (120cm) wide

£8,000-12,000 **DRA**

ROSEVILLE

- Established in 1890 in Zanesville, Ohio, Roseville concentrated on the production of functional wares. Between 1900 and 1920 the company expanded into fine hand-painted art pottery known as 'Rozane Ware'.
- Pieces were characterized by moulded, painted and incised decoration and often featured flowers, foliage and fruit. Glazes were typically luminous and rich in colour.
- 'Rozane Ware' initially emulated the work of the Rookwood pottery, although it was less expensively produced. From 1905 the company became more imaginative, producing ranges such as 'Fudji', 'Woodland' and 'Della Robbia'.
- The high quality 'Della Robbia' range was designed by the British potter Frederick Hurten Rhead, who held the post of art director from 1904 until his brother Harry G. Rhead took over the post in 1908.
- Small bowls and vases are most common, while hanging baskets, tea sets and wall pockets are harder to come by.
- A great deal of Roseville pottery is unmarked, although over half of all 'Rozane Ware' produced prior to 1907 was marked.
- The pottery ceased production in 1954.

A fine Roseville blue 'Falline' vase, with ribbed base and tapered neck, unmarked.

9.5in (24cm) high

£1,500-2,000 **DRA**

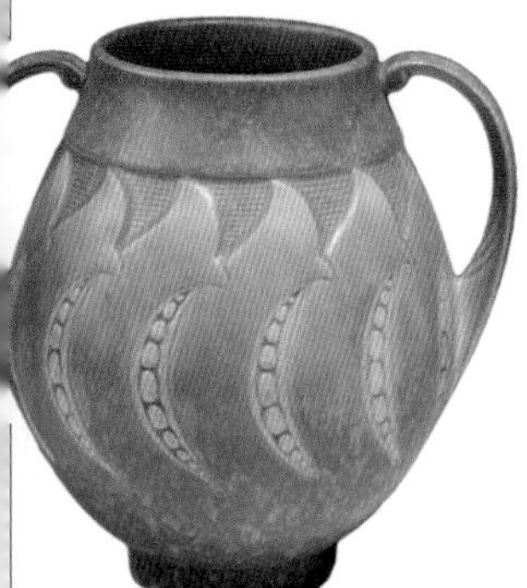

A fine Roseville blue 'Falline' bulbous vase, unmarked.

8.25in (20.5cm) high

£1,000-1,500 **DRA**

A fine and large Roseville blue 'Falline' ovoid vase with stepped rim, foil label.

15.5in (39cm) high

£800-1,200 **DRA**

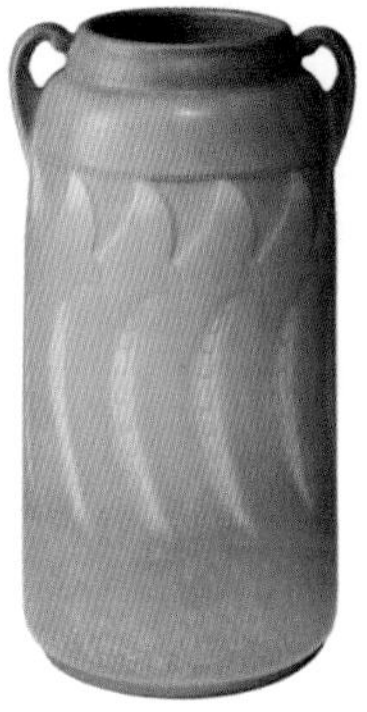

A fine and large Roseville blue 'Falline' slightly tapered vase, unmarked.

14in (35cm) high

£1,500-2,000 **DRA**

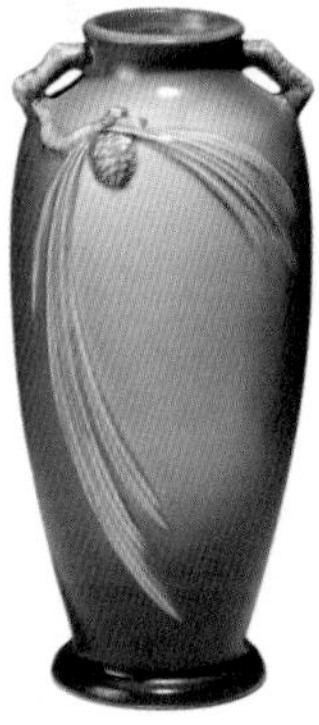

A Roseville blue 'Pine Cone' ovoid vase, impressed mark.

£500-700 **DRA**

A Roseville blue 'Pine Cone' jardiniere and pedestal set, raised mark.

£800-1,200 **DRA**

A rare Roseville blue 'Pine Cone' ewer, raised mark.

£700-1,000 **DRA**

A rare Roseville blue 'Pine Cone' wall pocket, impressed mark.

£800-1,200 **DRA**

A Roseville brown 'Pine Cone' vase, impressed mark.

£700-1,000 **DRA**

A Roseville brown 'Pine Cone' bulbous vase with flaring rim, impressed mark.

£400-600 **DRA**

A Roseville brown 'Pine Cone' bulbous pitcher, impressed mark.

£400-600 **DRA**

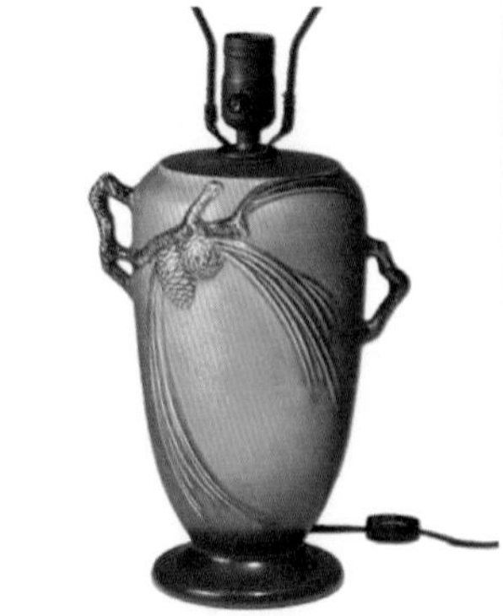

A rare Roseville brown 'Pine Cone' lamp base, no visible mark.

10.5in (26cm) high

£800-1,200 **DRA**

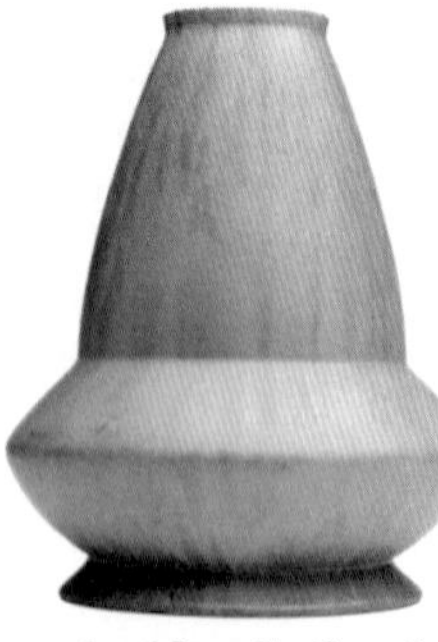

An exceptional Roseville 'Carnelian II' vase, with squat base and tapering neck, covered in a matt rose, green and purple mottled glaze, unmarked.

14.25in (35.5cm) high

£1,500-2,000 **DRA**

A large Roseville pink 'Cherry Blossom' ovoid vase, unmarked.

12.5in (31cm) high

£700-1,000 **DRA**

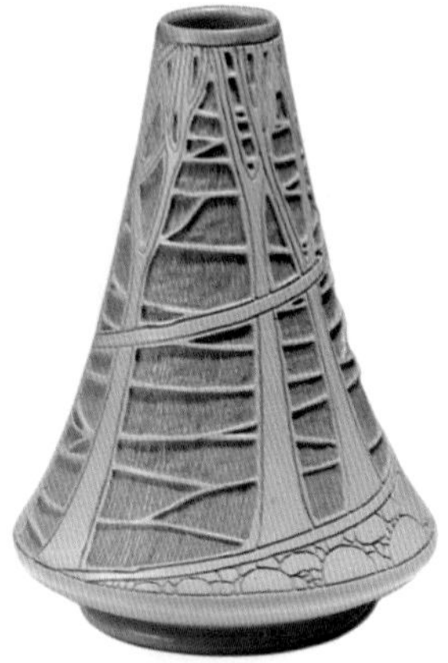

A rare Roseville Della Robbia two-colour tapering vase, incised with a rocky trail through a forest.

10.75in (27cm) high

£1,800-2,200 **DRA**

A Roseville red 'Ferella' flaring vase, unmarked.

6.5in (16cm) wide

£600-800 **DRA**

A Roseville red 'Ferella' two-handled corseted vase, unmarked.

9.5in (24cm) high

£700-1,000 **DRA**

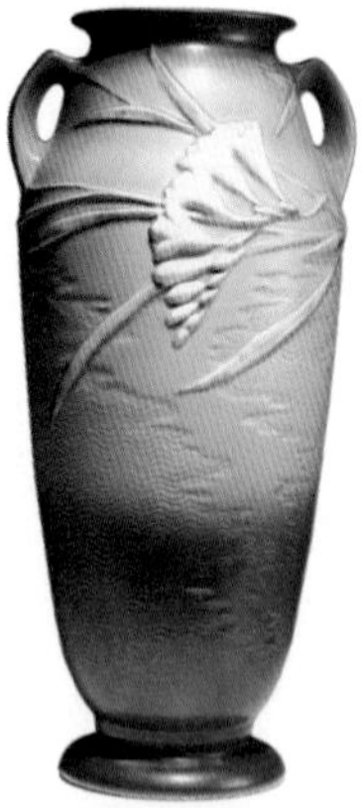

A Roseville green 'Freesia' floor vase, raised mark.

£300-500 **DRA**

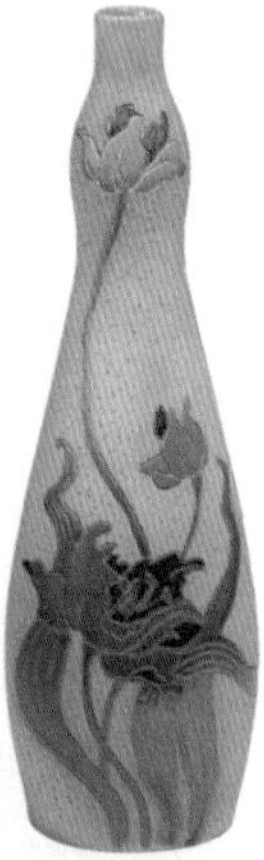

A fine Roseville 'Fudjiyama' gourd-shaped vase, decorated with brown blossoms and green leaves, ink stamp.

11.5in (29cm) high

£500-700 **DRA**

A Roseville 'Fudji' four-sided twisted vase, squeezebag-decorated with poppies, unmarked.

9.75in (24cm) high

£1,000-1,500 **DRA**

A fine Roseville 'Fudji' corseted vase, decorated in squeezebag with stylized floral design, Rozane seal.

10.75in (27cm) high

£1,000-1,500 **DRA**

A fine Roseville 'Fudji' bulbous vase, beautifully decorated in five colours, Rozane seal.

9in (22.5cm) high

£1,000-1,500 **DRA**

A rare Roseville 'Imperial II' bowl, embossed with banded snail-like design around the body, covered in a pale dripping green glaze over a pink ground, unmarked.

7in (17.5cm) wide

£1,500-2,000 **DRA**

A fine Roseville 'Imperial II' flaring vase, covered in a curdled green over orange glaze, unmarked.

8.25in (20.5cm) high

£2,200-2,800 **DRA**

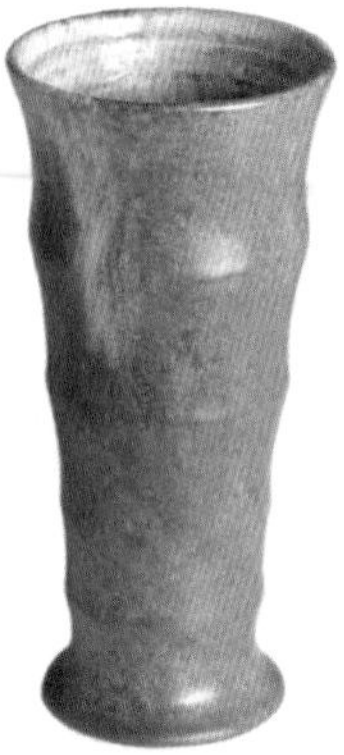

A fine Roseville 'Imperial II' ribbed flaring vase, covered in blue and yellow mottled glaze, exceptional colour, unmarked.

9.25in (23cm) high

£500-700 **DRA**

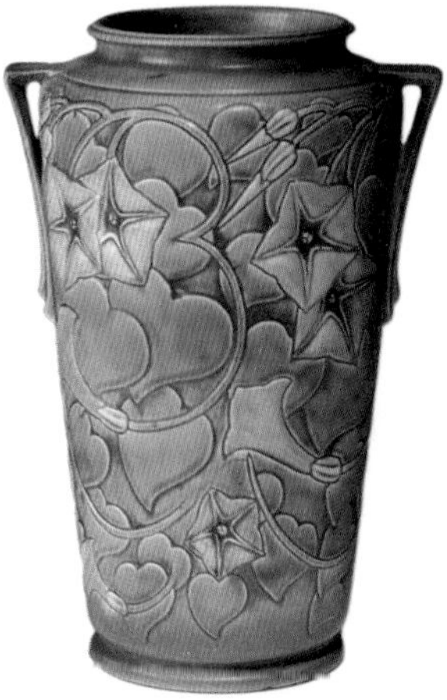

A large Roseville green 'Morning Glory' vase, strong mould and colour, unmarked.

14.5in (36cm) high

£1,000-1,500 **DRA**

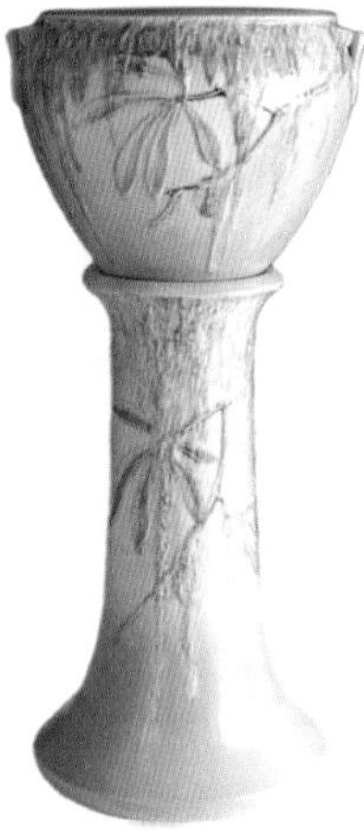

A Roseville blue 'Moss' jardinière and pedestal set, impressed mark.

£600-800 **DRA**

A fine Roseville experimental bulbous vase, embossed with pink and white blossoms on a shaded blue to green ground, experimental numbers in blue ink to underside.

9.25in (23cm) high

£2,000-3,000 **DRA**

A Roseville green panel flaring two-handled vase, "RV" ink mark.

11.5in (29cm) high

£700-1,000 **DRA**

A fine Roseville Sunflower vase with flat shoulder, strong mould, unmarked.

10.25in (25.5cm) high

£1,500-2,000 **DRA**

A fine Roseville Sunflower ovoid vase, unmarked.

10.25in (25.5cm) high

£1,000-1,500 **DRA**

A Roseville Sunflower jardinière, unmarked.

9.5in (24cm) wide

£400-600 **DRA**

An exceptional and large flaring bowl decorated by the Saturday Evening Girls, in cuerda seca with yellow nasturtiums and green leaves on a taupe and yellow ground, "SEG/513/S.G".

The Saturday Evening Girls Club was established in Boston, Massachusetts, in 1906. The idea behind the enterprise was to enable immigrant girls to decorate pottery that could be sold to support them financially. Success was instant and in 1908 the club moved to larger premises and changed its name to the Paul Revere Pottery, after the US revolutionary hero. It closed in 1942.

11.5in (29cm) diam

£10,000-15,000 **DRA**

A Saturday Evening Girls bowl, painted with a hen and chick on a bright orange band against mottled grey ground, opposing hairlines, signed "SEG".

4.25in (10.5cm) wide

£400-500 **DRA**

A small Saturday Evening Girls tapering vessel, painted by Cross with a band of brown tulips and green-yellow leaves on a blue-green ground, "S.E.G.", cross in circle, "2.25".

1925 *3.75in (9.5cm) high*

£800-1,200 **DRA**

A rare Saturday Evening Girls faceted tea caddy, decorated in cuerda seca with a yellow cottage in a hilly verdant lake landscape, missing lid, "SEG 4-14/S.G".

The lids of these caddies are usually missing.

1914 *4.5in (11cm) high*

£2,500-3,000 **DRA**

A rare Saturday Evening Girls tile, decorated in cuerda seca with a night-time scene of a tall ship in a New England bay, with the words, "The Bay Where Lay the Somerset British Man-of-War", signed "AM/S.E.G."

6in (15cm) high

£2,200-2,800 **DRA**

A Saturday Evening Girls three-piece breakfast set, for "Anne", "Her Bowl", "Her Plate", and "Her Pitcher", decorated in cuerda seca, marked "S.E.G.", decorator's mark, "12-16".

bowl 5.5in (14cm) wide

£800-1,200 **DRA**

A Saturday Evening Girls six-piece desk set, with letter rack, perpetual calendar, pencil holder, vase, stamp box, and inkwell, each decorated in cuerda seca on a semi-matt cobalt ground, "S.E.G./AM/12-17", and "S.E.G. Bowl Shop" paper label to calendar.

1917 *letter rack 8in (20cm) wide*

£4,000-6,000 **DRA**

A Paul Revere flaring bowl, decorated in cuerda seca with 'The Midnight Ride of Paul Revere', the interior with a band which reads "A Voice in the Darkness, A Knock at the Door, and a Word That Shall Echo Forever More", signed "PRP/6-41/LS".

1941 *7.25in (18cm) wide*

£4,000-6,000 **DRA**

An exceptional Saturday Evening Girls/Paul Revere large flaring bowl, decorated in cuerda seca with large white geese and green trees in a white, blue and yellow landscape, circular stamp and paper label.

The 'cuerda seca' technique involves drawing a design on a piece in wax and glazing. During firing, the wax acts as a barrier creating flooded areas of bold colour separated by strong outlines.

11.5in (29cm) diam

£10,000-15,000 **DRA**

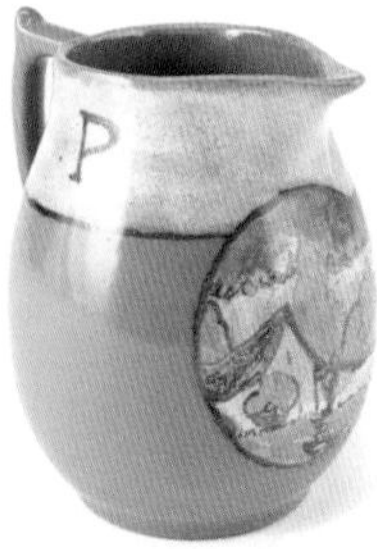

A Paul Revere pitcher painted, with a cottage in a landscape and monogrammed "P" on a white band against a teal green ground, circular stamp, restored spout.

7.5in (19cm) high

£400-600 **DRA**

A Stangl double blue jay, no. 3717, marked.

13in (32.5cm) high

£2,500-3,000 **DRA**

A rare Stangl porcelain single crossbill, no. 3726, marked.

5.5in (14cm) high

£1,800-2,200 **DRA**

A Stangl single white wing crossbill, no. 3753, marked.

3.5in (9cm) high

£1,800-2,200 **DRA**

A rare Stangl fish hawk/osprey, impressed mark.

11in (27.5cm) high

£2,500-3,000 **DRA**

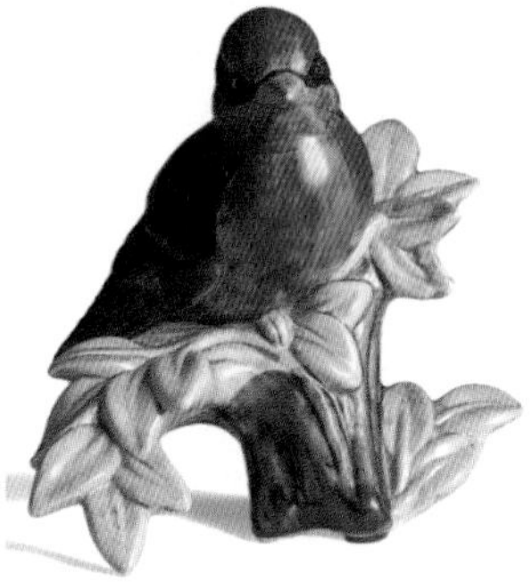

A Stangl vermilion flycatcher, no. 3923, marked.

5.75in (14cm) high

£1,200-1,800 **DRA**

A rare Stangl porcelain robin, no. 3741, marked.

9.5in (24cm) high

£1,800-2,200 **DRA**

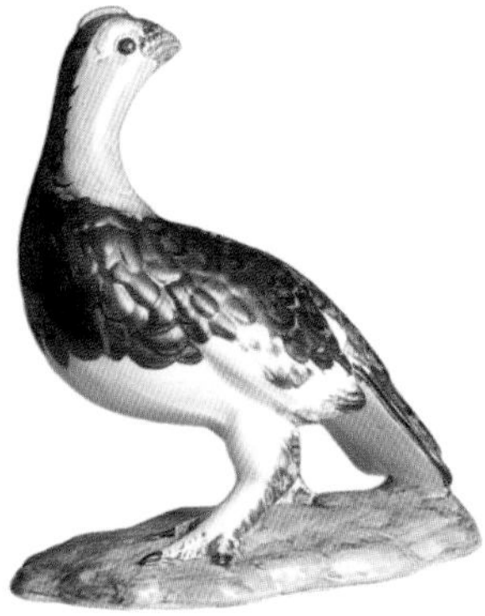

A Stangl willow ptarmigan, no. 3451, marked.

11.25in (28cm) high

£1,800-2,200 **DRA**

A rare Stangl porcelain double red-headed woodpecker, marked.

7.75in (19cm) high

£1,500-2,000 **DRA**

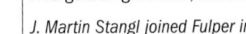

A large Stangl rooster, no. 3435, unmarked.

J. Martin Stangl joined Fulper in 1910, and by 1930 he had acquired the firm. The company continued production under the Stangl name until 1972.

16in (40cm) high

£4,000-5,000 **DRA**

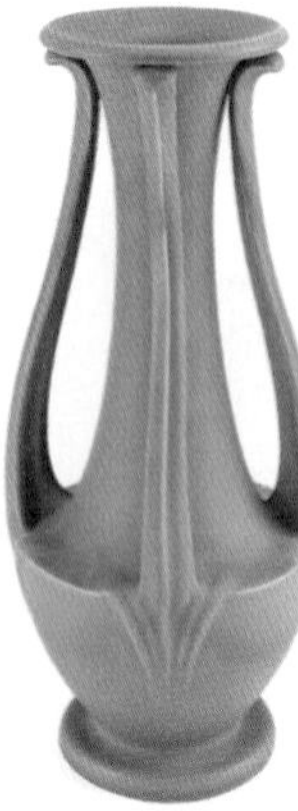

A large Teco vase, of classical shape with four delicate handles, covered in a dark green microcrystalline glaze with charcoaling on the handles, stamped "Teco".

11.5in (29cm) high

£1,800-2,200 **DRA**

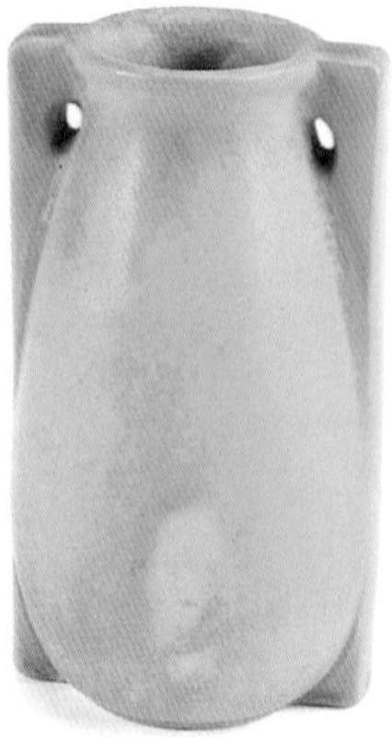

A Teco ovoid vase, with two full-height buttressed handles covered in smooth matt green glaze with charcoaling, stamped "Teco".

5.5in (14cm) high

£600-900 **DRA**

A CLOSER LOOK AT A TECO VASE

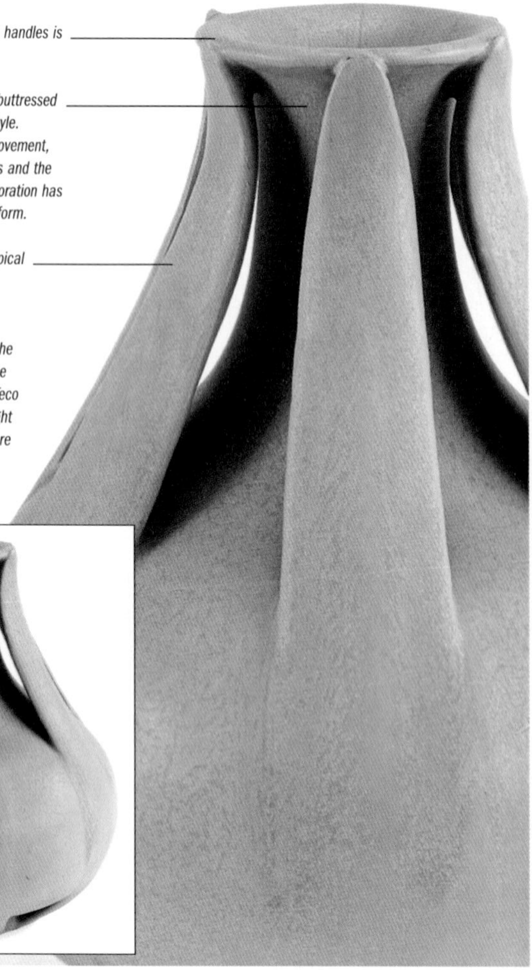

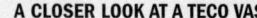

This curvaceous vase with its foliate handles is one of Teco's rarest forms.

The clean, architectural shape and buttressed handles are emblematic of Teco's style. Influenced by the Arts and Crafts movement, contemporary architectural practices and the Midwest Prairie School, surface decoration has been rejected in favour of a strong form.

This vessel is entirely moulded, a typical characteristic of Teco pottery.

Green is by far the most common colour for pieces produced around the turn of the century. Influenced by the popularity of Grueby's green ware, Teco green can be distinguished by a slight greyish finish. New glaze colours were introduced c1910.

A rare Teco bottle-shaped vase with six full-height leaf-shaped buttressed handles, covered in smooth matt green glaze, restoration to chips on tips of four leaves, stamped "Teco 191".

10.25in (26cm) high

£15,000-20,000 **DRA**

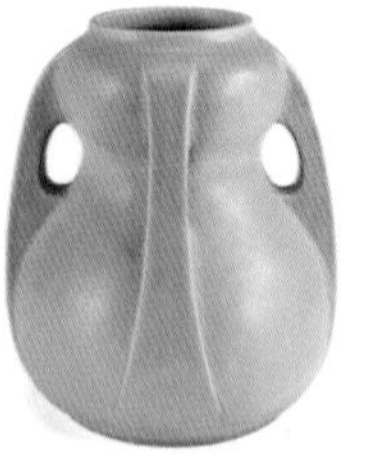

An exceptional Teco double-gourd vase with four buttressed handles covered in smooth matt green glaze with charcoaling along the edges, stamped "Teco", glaze flake and glaze miss.

This example is the largest and rarest version of this form.

12.5in (32cm) high

£10,000-15,000 **DRA**

A Teco three-handled cylindrical cup, with horizontal ridges, covered in smooth matt green glaze, stamped "Teco".

7in (17.5cm) wide

£800-1,200 **DRA**

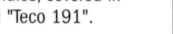

A Teco barrel-shaped ridged vessel, in smooth matt green glaze with charcoaling at the base, stamped "Teco", paper label.

4in (10cm) high

£400-600 **DRA**

A rare Teco spherical jardinière with four buttressed feet, covered in smooth matt green glaze with charcoaling around the buttresses, stamped Teco.

8.5in (21.5cm) diam

£5,000-7,000 **DRA**

A Teco Bulbous vase, with scalloped rim, covered in matt green glaze, stamped "Teco 233".

5in (13cm) high

£400-600 **DRA**

A tall Teco vase, with two buttressed handles, in matt green glaze with charcoaled edges, stamped "Teco", restoration, flaw.

11in (27.5cm) high

£800-1,200 **DRA**

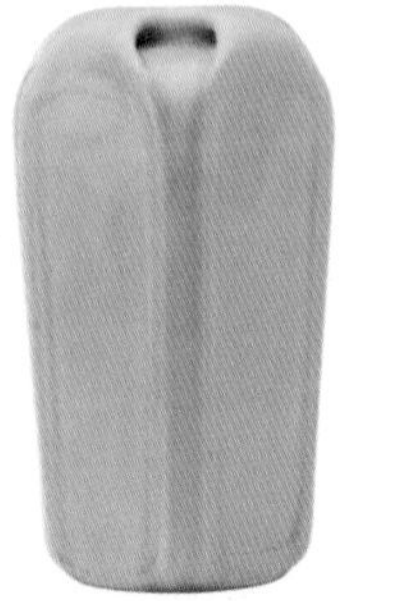

A Teco architectural four-sided vase, with four short buttressed handles at top, covered in matt green glaze, stamped "Teco".

9in (22.5cm) high

£2,000-2,500 **DRA**

A tall Teco Art Nouveau vase, with four buttressed feet, rising to a spherical top, stamped "Teco".

18.5in (47cm) high

£8,000-12,000 **DRA**

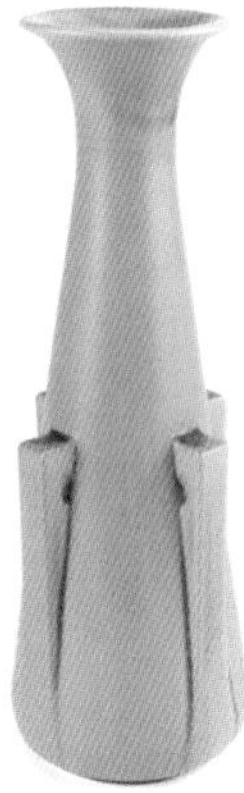

A rare Teco tall vase, with four buttressed handles, in smooth matt green glaze with charcoaling, stamped "Teco", drilled hole.

17.75in (45cm) high

£7,000-10,000 **DRA**

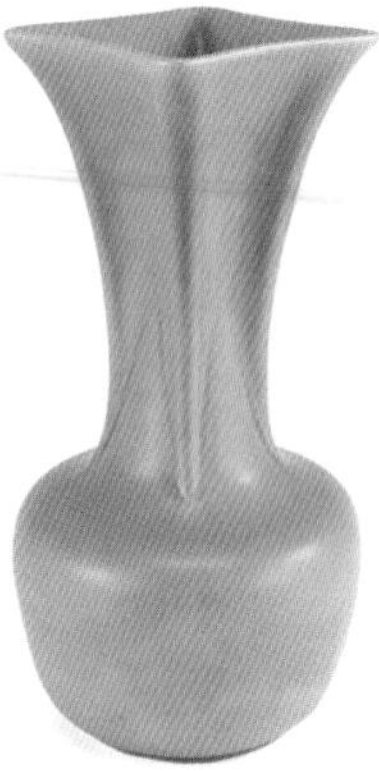

A fine and large Teco vase, with bulbous base and flaring four-sided neck covered in smooth matt green glaze with light charcoaling, stamped "Teco".

16.5in (42cm) high

£4,000-6,000 **DRA**

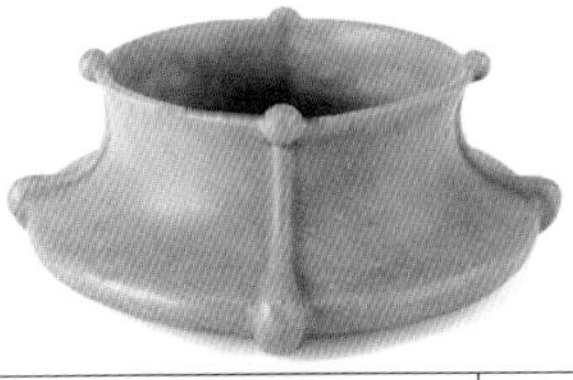

A Teco corseted jardinière, of unusual form with four whiplash buttresses under matt green glaze with charcoaling around the edges, stamped Teco.

9in (23cm) wide

£1,800-2,200 **DRA**

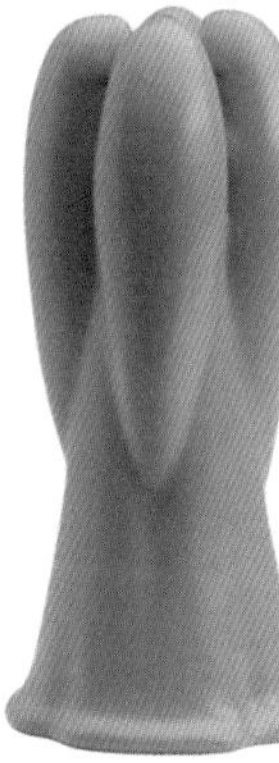

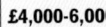

A Teco four-lobed vase, covered in smooth matt blue glaze with green seams, stamped "Toco"

9in (22.5cm) high

£1,000-1,500 **DRA**

A Teco bottle-shaped vase covered in matt yellow glaze, stamped "Teco".

5.5in (14cm) high

£280-320 **DRA**

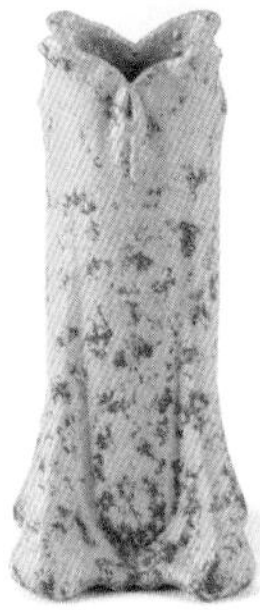

An unusual Teco organic vase, with four buttressed feet, four-lobed rim, covered in a rare deep yellow marbleized glaze, stamped "Teco".

13.5in (34.5cm) high

£1,000-1,500 **DRA**

A small Teco pitcher, covered in smooth matt brown glaze, stamped "Teco 58".

4in (10cm) high

£200-300 **DRA**

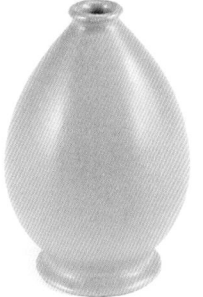

A Teco small ovoid vase, covered in smooth matt brown glaze, stamped "Teco 62".

4.5in (11.5cm) high

£400-500 **DRA**

A Teco flat wall pocket, embossed with pinwheels and covered in matt green glaze, hairline to front corner, stamped "Teco".

6.5in (16.5cm) high

£150-200 **DRA**

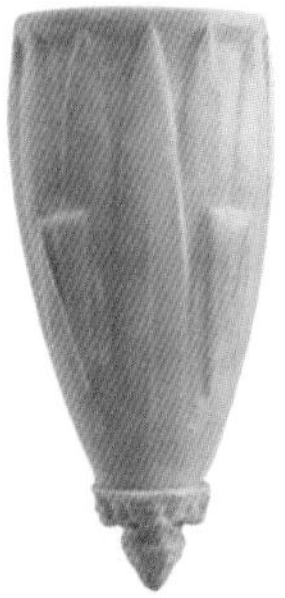

A large Teco wall pocket, embossed with tall slender leaves and covered in smooth matt green glaze, stamped "Teco" with two paper labels, line.

14.5in (36cm) high

£800-1,200 **DRA**

A Van Briggle Squat vase, carved with poppies under Persian Rose glaze, "AA/Van Briggle/III/1903/204".

1903 *4.5in (11.5cm) high*

£1,200-1,800 **DRA**

A bulbous Van Briggle vase, embossed with trefoils under a rich, feathery matt green glaze, some burst glaze bubbles from firing, "AA/Van Briggle/Colo Springs/1906".

1906 *7in (17.5cm) high*

£1,200-1,800 **DRA**

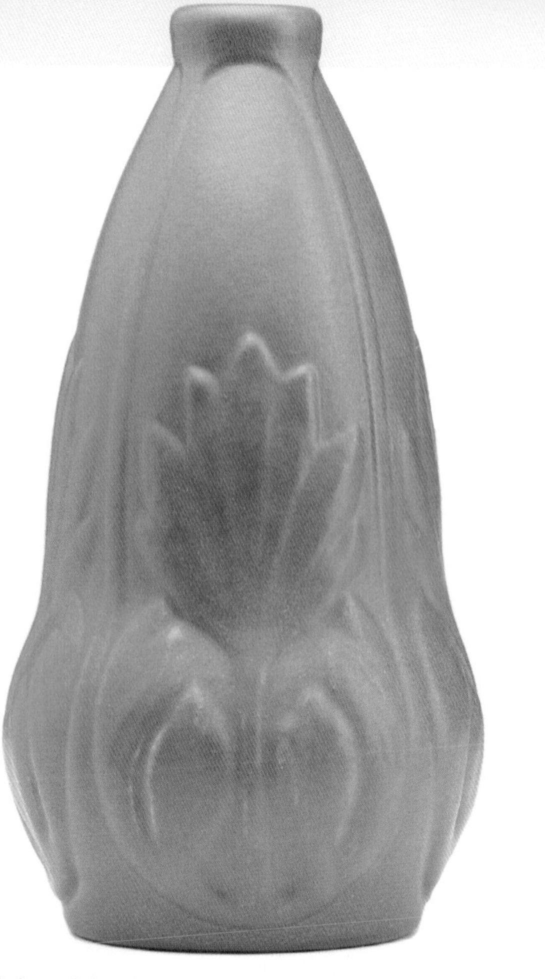

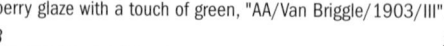

A Van Briggle gourd-shaped vase, embossed with blossoms and leaves under matt raspberry glaze with a touch of green, "AA/Van Briggle/1903/III".

1903 *10in (25cm) high*

£1,800-2,200 **DRA**

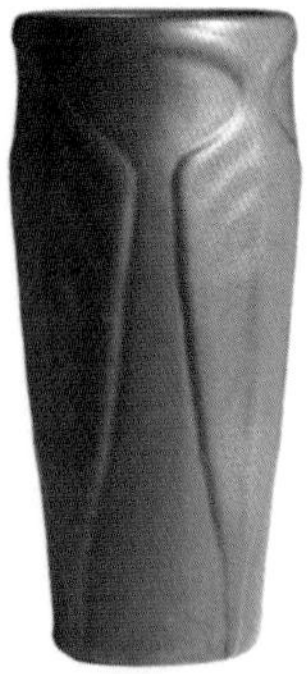

An early Van Briggle vase, modelled with full-height tobacco leaves, covered in mottled yellow over purple ground, "AA/Van Briggle/1906/295".

1906 *8in (20cm) high*

£500-700 **DRA**

A Van Briggle small bulbous vase, with modelled full-height leaves covered in sheer matt blue-grey glaze, mark obscured by glaze.

c1905 *4.5in (11cm) high*

£400-600 **DRA**

A Van Briggle experimental bottle-shaped vase, with copper sheeting over a cut-down neck, "AA/593/Van Briggle/Colorado Springs/1907/6".

The metal was apparently applied when the neck was damaged in production.

1907 *8in (20cm) high*

£1,500-2,000 **DRA**

A bulbous Van Briggle vessel, embossed with spade-shaped leaves and peacock feathers and covered in matt green glaze, "AA Van Briggle/Colo Spgs/151".

c1910 *5in (12.5cm) wide*

£800-1,200 **DRA**

A rare Van Briggle copper-clad cabinet vase, with full-height stylized trefoils and leaves, "AA/Van Briggle/Colo. Spg./310".

c1910 *3in (7.5cm) high*

£700-1,000 **DRA**

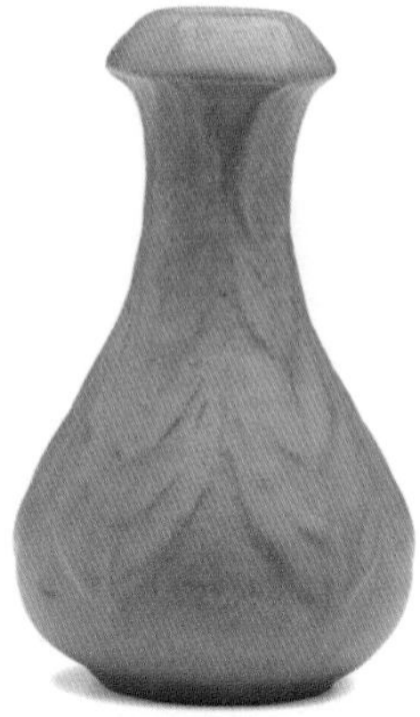

A Van Briggle bottle-shaped vase, embossed with leaf decoration under a rich matt green glaze, "AA/Van Briggle/Colo Spgs/700".

c1910 *6in (15cm) high*

£700-1,000 **DRA**

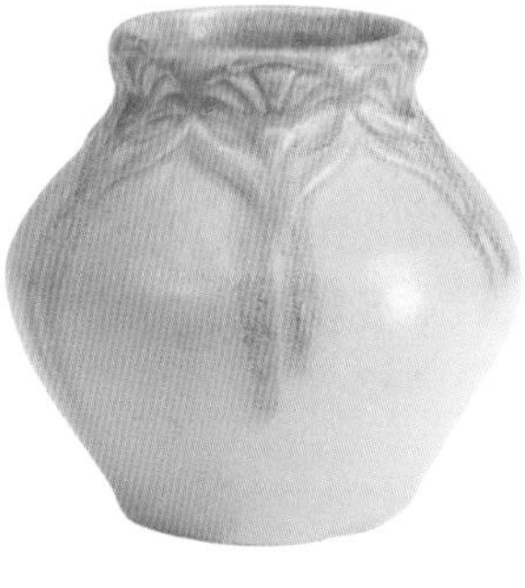

A Van Briggle bulbous vase, crisply embossed with stylized daisies under indigo and turquoise matt glaze, "AA Van Briggle/Colo. Spgs./771".

1908-1911 *4.75in (12cm) wide*

£500-700 **DRA**

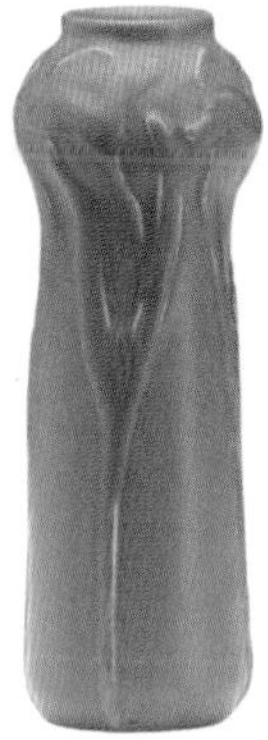

A Van Briggle bulbous vase, embossed with daffodils covered in Persian Rose glaze, "850/AA/1915".

1915 *8.5in (21cm) high*

£400-600 **DRA**

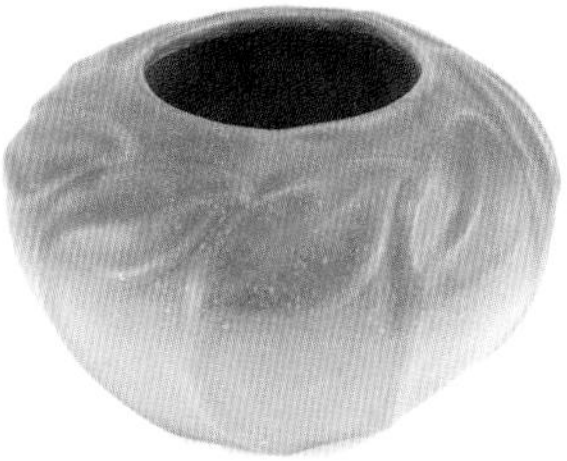

A Van Briggle squat vessel, embossed with leaves on swirling stems under indigo and turquoise matt glaze, "AA/Van Briggle", cracks.

1818 *6.75in (17cm) diam*

£50-70 **DRA**

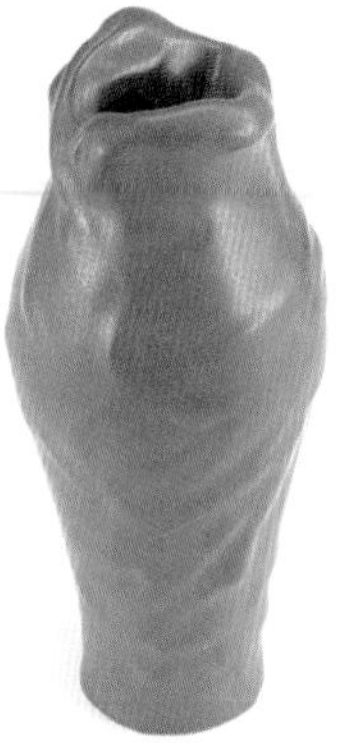

A Van Briggle Lorelei vase, in Persian Rose glaze, body line.

c1925 *9in (23cm) high*

£220-280 **DRA**

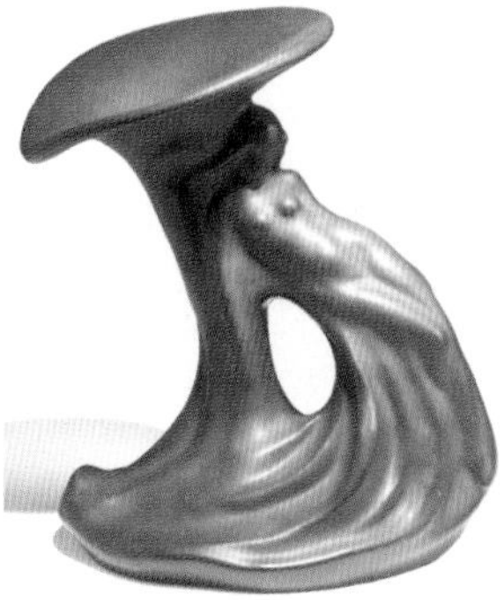

A 1930s Van Briggle 'Lady-of-the-Lily' vase, covered in Persian Rose glaze, "AA Van Briggle/Colo Spgs".

11in (27.5cm) high

£700-1,000 **DRA**

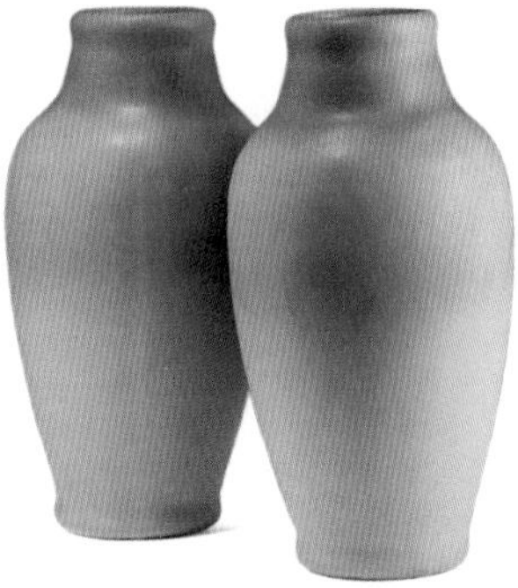

A 1940s Van Briggle pair of baluster vases, covered in blue and turquoise matt glaze, both marked.

10.75in (27cm) high

£400 600 **DRA**

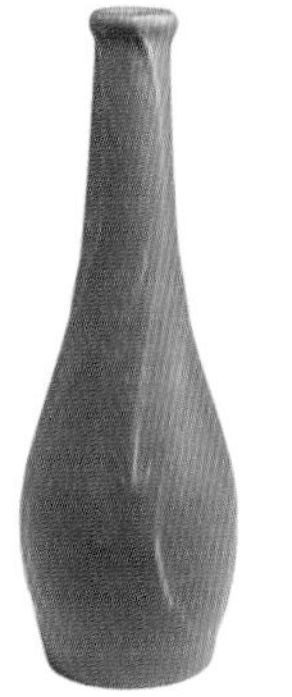

A tall Van Briggle bulbous vase, with sinewy stems, matt green glaze, mark obscured by glaze, chips, fleck.

12in (30cm) high

£500-700 **DRA**

A Van Briggle paperweight, modelled with an amber horned toad on a green base, unmarked.

5in (12.5cm) wide

£600-900 **DRA**

A rare and early Van Briggle straight-sided vessel, embossed with tulips and covered in a fine, frothy brownish-green matt glaze, the red clay showing through, "AA/VAN BRIGGLE/COLORADO SPRINGS/19??/06".

Artus Van Briggle worked for Rookwood before establishing his own pottery in Colorado in 1899. Wares varied from high quality art vases to everyday commercial products. Van Briggle died in 1904 but the factory is still in operation today.

5in (12.5cm) wide

£800-1,200 **DRA**

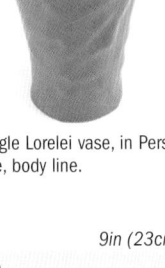

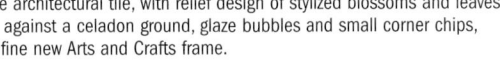

A Van Briggle architectural tile, with relief design of stylized blossoms and leaves, in gunmetal against a celadon ground, glaze bubbles and small corner chips, mounted in fine new Arts and Crafts frame.

tile 6in (15cm) wide

£300-500 **DRA**

A Volkmar/Durant Kilns centre bowl on pedestal, the bowl modelled with scales and the pedestal with three dolphins, both covered in sheer white semi-matt glaze, the red clay showing through, bowl incised "Durant 1919", base "Durant 1917".

Provenance: *From the artist's widow's estate, exhibited at the Art Institute of Chicago, 1953.*

12.5in (31cm) wide

£150-200 **DRA**

A Volkmar/Durant Kilns flaring bowl, with a band of modelled flowers, the exterior covered in blue crackled Persian glaze, the interior in oxblood, wear to footrim, shoulder and rim, incised "Durant 1919".

Provenance: *From the artist's widow's estate.*

1919 *8.75in (22cm) wide*

£200-300 **DRA**

A Volkmar/Durant Kilns plate, with ridged edge, covered in gold lustred crackled glaze, incised "D Volkmar '45".

Provenance: *From the artist's widow's estate.*

10in (25cm) diam

£60-90 **DRA**

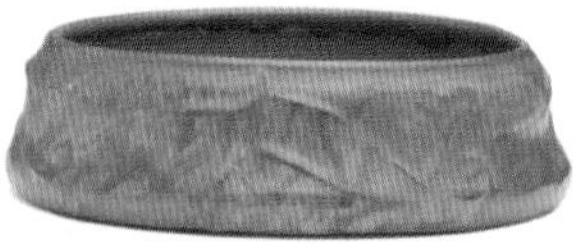

A Volkmar low centre bowl, modelled with leaves and blossoms and covered in a fine, frothy matt green glaze, a few minor nicks to high points, incised "M Zim and V".

11.5in (29cm) wide

£800-1,200 **DRA**

A Charles Volkmar plaque, painted in barbotine with figure and cows along a river, abrasion to surface, signed "Chas Volkmar".

9.5in (24cm) high

£800-1,200 **DRA**

A Charles Volkmar large baluster vase, painted in barbotine, with a cow and calf in a landscape, wear to glaze around rim, stamped "CH", signed "Chas Volkmar".

14.5in (36cm) high

£800-1,200 **DRA**

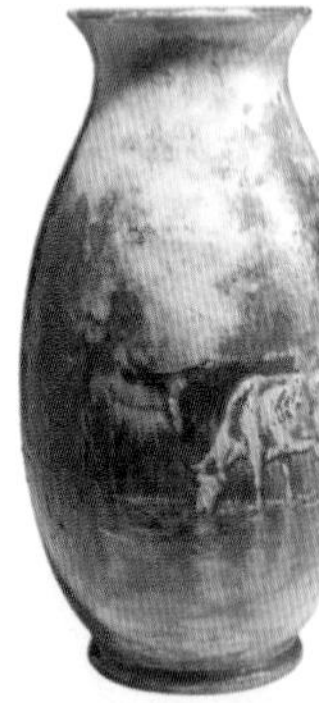

A Charles Volkmar large baluster vase, painted in barbotine, with two cows in a landscape, wear to glaze around rim and base, glaze flake to body, stamped "CH", signed "Chas Volkmar".

14.5in (36cm) high

£800-1,200 **DRA**

WELLER

A rare Weller Camelot vase, unmarked.

Weller marks are inconsistent and many pieces are unmarked.

12in (30.5cm) high

£1,200-1,800 **DRA**

A Weller Dickensware vase, incised and painted by Edwin Pickens, with portrait of Native American, 'Chief Hollow Horn Bear', impressed Dickensware mark, incised artist's initials.

10.25in (25.5cm) high

£700-1,000 **DRA**

A tall Weller Dickensware vase, incised and painted with a 'David Copperfield' street scene, quote on reverse side, impressed mark.

17in (42.5cm) high

£400-500 **DRA**

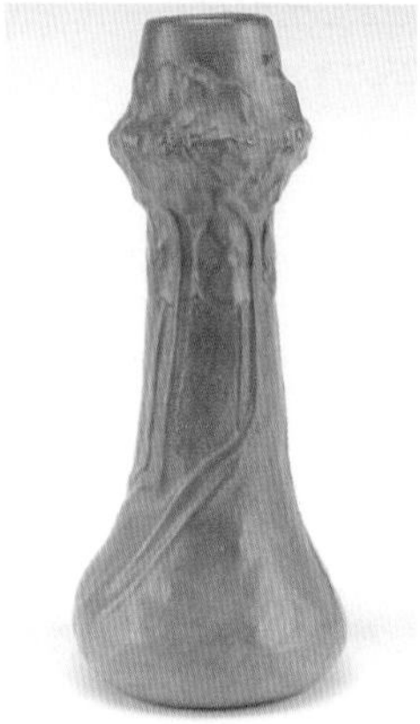

A rare Weller 'Fru Russet' vase, embossed with flowers under a pale blue-grey and green glaze, impressed mark.

14in (35.5cm) high

£1,500-2,000 **DRA**

A Weller 'Fru Russett' bulbous vase, decorated by Pickens, with pink lilies on a curdled pale green ground, impressed mark, artist's mark.

13in (32.5cm) high

£1,800-2,200 **DRA**

An unusual Weller Dickensware corseted vase, with two round handles near neck, finely decorated with female golfer, impressed Dickensware mark, artist's initials "KP".

10.5in (26cm) high

£800-1,200 **DRA**

A Weller 'Jap Birdimal' ewer, decorated by Rhead, in squeezebag with trees and a geisha, incised "Weller Faience Rhead G580", fleck.

10.75in (27.5cm) high

£1,800-2,200 **DRA**

A Weller 'Knifewood' vase, carved with hooded owls in a tree under a crescent moon, unmarked.

8.5in (21.5cm) high

£600-900 **DRA**

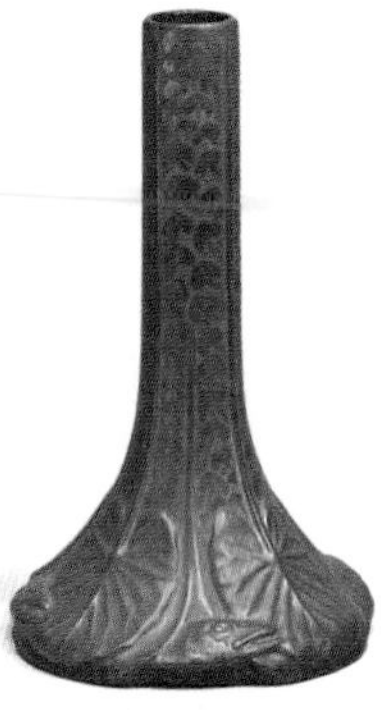

An early 20thC Weller Sicard art pottery lamp base, relief decorated with trailing stems, broad leaves and fish at base, iridescent body, signed Weller at side of base, base chip.

1903-07 14in (35.5cm) high

£1,500-2,000 **SK**

A large and unusual Weller Sicard bulbous vase/lamp base, decorated with seashells and sealife under thick, flowing nacreous purple, red, gold, and green glazes, opposing lines from rim.

15.5in (39cm) high

£800-1,200 **DRA**

A Weller Sicard bulbous twisted vase, decorated with gold clovers on a purple, red, gold, and green ground, signed on body.

5.25in (13cm) high

£500-700 **DRA**

A Weller Sicard 'blown-out' vase, decorated with spade-shaped leaves under a beautiful iridescent threaded gold, purple, and green glaze, signed "Weller Sicard".

4.5in (11cm) high

£400-600 **DRA**

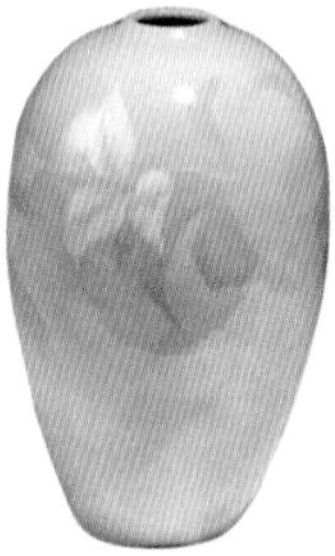

A fine Weller bulbous vase, painted with peach and ivory flowers on a blended pastel ground, marked "Weller" in script.

9.25in (23cm) high

£1,800-2,200 **DRA**

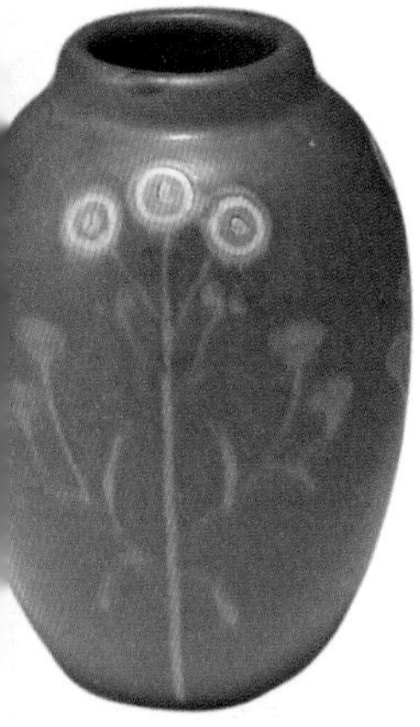

A rare Weller matte vase decorated with small white blossoms on a deep blue ground, impressed "WELLER".

5.25in (13cm) high

£700-1,000 **DRA**

A rare Weller frosted matte vase, with curdled yellow-green glaze over a brown ground, unmarked.

13.5in (34cm) high

£1,000-1,500 **DRA**

A rare Weller Coppertone 'dancing frogs' model, marked in script.

After producing functional wares from 1872 in Fultonham, Ohio, Sam Weller moved his factory to Zanesville in 1889 and started to produce art pottery. The company was dissolved in 1949.

16.5in (41cm) wide

£3,000-5,000 **DRA**

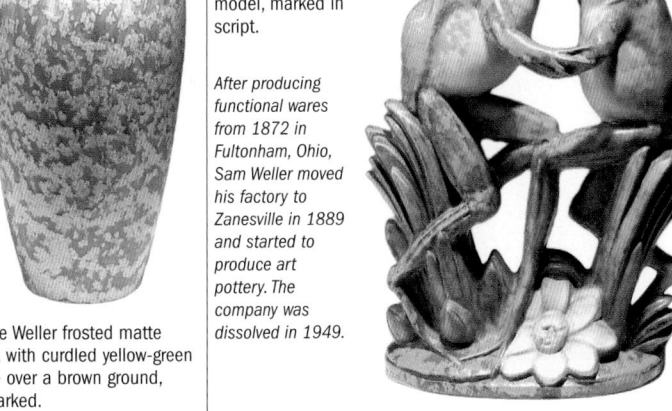

A large Weller Pop-Eye Dog figure, extensive repair, spidering lines through back still visible, marked in script.

10.25in (26cm) high

£250-300 **DRA**

A vertical panel from the American Encaustic Tiling Co., embossed in high relief with a classical figure brandishing a torch, covered in matte yellow glaze with "AETCO" medallion on front, mounted in gilded frame.

18in (45.5cm) high

£800-1,200 **DRA**

Two vertical panels with a man and woman in period garb by American Encaustic Tiling Co., the man playing a lute, over three tiles, the woman a single panel, both covered in sheer glossy burgundy glaze, losses, chips to both, marked.

18in (45.5cm) high

£180-220 **DRA**

An Arequipa tall baluster vase carved with foliate design and covered in sheer green and turquoise glaze, probably from the Solon period, incised "G.B. Arequipa California".

13.5in (34.5cm) high

£1,500-2,000 **DRA**

A massive Burley Winter floor vase, with medallion on both sides, covered in a fine lavender over deep rose glaze, impressed mark.

21in (52.5cm) high

£500-700 **DRA**

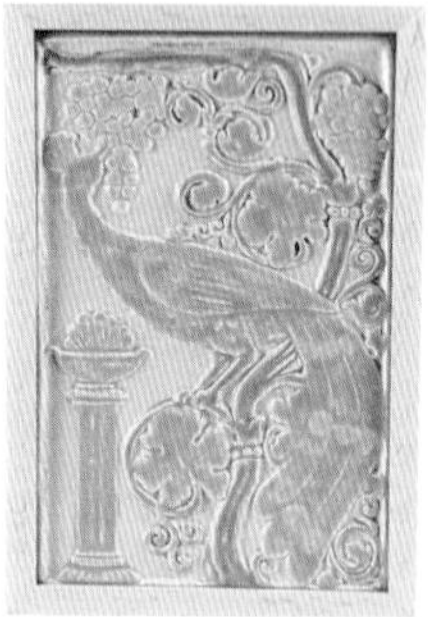

A California vertical art tile, embossed with a peacock perched on a grape vine in matte pastel glazes, mounted in frame covering back.

12in (30.5cm) high

£300-400 **DRA**

A large California Clay Products (CALCO) tile, moulded with tall redwood trees in a mountainous landscape in maroon on a blue-green ground, glaze chip, unmarked.

12.25in (31cm) wide

£1,500-2,000 **DRA**

A California Faience circular trivet, decorated in cuenca with a basket of fruit in matte polychrome glazes, very light wear to rim, stamped "California Faience".

5.25in (13.5cm) diam

£80-120 **DRA**

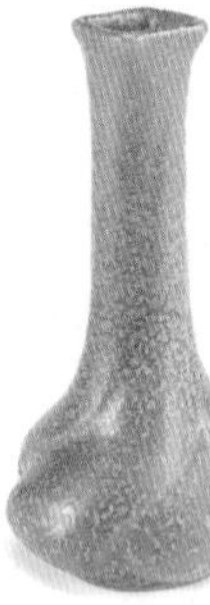

A Chicago Crucible bulbous bud vase covered in a good frothy light green and amber matte glaze, stamped "Chicago Crucible, Chicago".

8in (20.5cm) high

£300-400 **DRA**

A Clewell fine and large copper-clad bulbous vessel, covered in a verdigris patina, two very short scratches, incised "Clewell 167-215".

11.25in (28.5cm) high

£1,200-1,800 **DRA**

A Clewell spherical copper-clad vase, covered in original bronze and verdigris patina, a few minor pock marks, incised "Clewell 471".

9in (23cm) high

£1,200-1,800 **DRA**

A fine Clewell vase, with two curved handles on squat base, etched mark "505-219".

7.5in (19cm) wide

£600-900 **DRA**

An exceptional and rare Clewell/Owens tall vase, embossed with trees under copper overlay, marked "OWENS LOTUS X233".

13.5in (34cm) high

£1,500-2,000 **DRA**

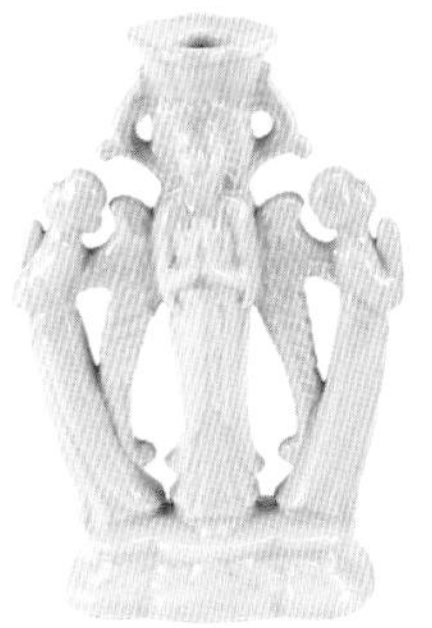

One of a pair of Cowan praying angels candlesticks, covered in mustard crackled glaze, minor nick to rim of one, stamped Cowan.

9in (23cm) high

£200-300 pair **DRA**

A Cowan ovoid vase, in orange lustred glaze, stamped "Cowan".

9in (23cm) high

£40-50 **DRA**

A Cowan King decanter with stopper, by Waylande Gregory, covered in Oriental Red matte glaze, firing line to base, stamped "Cowan", and marked "X-12".

c1930 *12in (30.5cm) high*

£300-500 **DRA**

A Russel Crook large tapering stoneware vase, decorated in cuerda seca, with swimming fish and sea plants, unmarked, burst bubble.

14.75in (37cm) high

£600-900 **DRA**

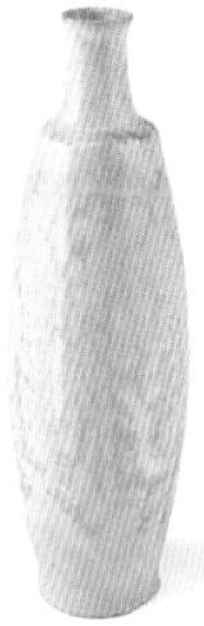

A Dalpayrat porcelain vase covered in a fine, white crystalline glaze, stamped "DALPAYRAT".

9in (23cm) high

£400-500 **DRA**

A Denver 'Denaura' vase with squat top, modelled with nasturtiums under a dark green vellum glaze, a few scratches to top and around rim, stamped "Denver Denaura 1903 USA".

1903 *6.25in (15.5cm) wide*

£1,200-1,800 **DRA**

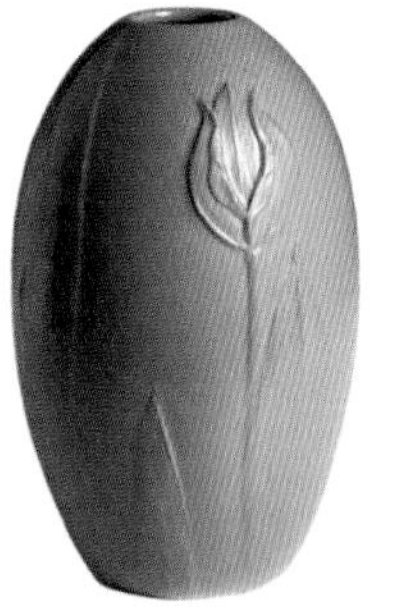

A Denver 'Lonhuda' ovoid vase, modelled with tulips and tall leaves under matte green glaze, minor nick to glaze on leaf, stamped "DENVER/LONHUDA/LF" in shield.

8.5in (21cm) high

£700-1,000 **DRA**

A small decorated Susan Frackelton stoneware dish, with carved poppies and painted butterflies on a grey ground, "SF", nicks, bruise.

4.75in (12cm) high

£800-1,200 **DRA**

An exceptional and large Susan Frackelton salt-glaze stoneware punch bowl, with three-lobed rim and large clusters of applied blue grapes and vines, the interior painted "Love Is the Sweet Wine of Life," and "M.N.C.W.L. 1902."

Susan Frackleton made her salt-glaze pottery in Milwaukee from c1883.

14in (35.5cm) diam

£8,000-12,000 **DRA**

A rare Franklin vertical tile, embossed with a Nordic scene of moose and Canada geese in dark brown silhouette, self-framed in matte green and gunmetal, no visible mark.

13.5in (34.5cm) high

£2,200-2,800 **DRA**

A CLOSER LOOK AT SUSAN FRACKELTON VASE

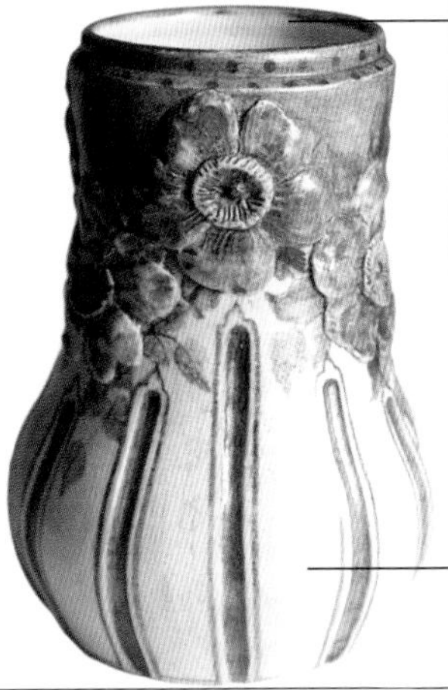

Susan Frackelton, the maker of this vase, was an extremely important American art potter, known for experimenting with new paints and establishing the National League of Mineral Painters. Her Frackleton China Decorating Works (est. 1883) fired up to 2,000 pieces a week.

Salt-glazed stoneware is an unusual medium for American Art Pottery.

The provenance is strong - the piece descended through the Frackleton family.

Artware is marked with an incised "SF" cypher or a Frackleton signature.

A Susan Frackelton salt-glazed stoneware bulbous vase, carved with roses and stems, in semi-matte indigo glaze on creamy ground, signed "SF/IX/988".

6.25in (15.5cm) high

£12,000-18,000 **DRA**

A Hampshire vase, moulded with full-height buds alternating with leaves and covered in a fine green and teal blue mottled matte glaze, stamped "Hampshire Pottery".

6.75in (17cm) high

£300-500 **DRA**

A Hampshire ovoid vase, with full-height leaves covered in a fine blue and green oatmealed glaze, stamped "Hampshire Pottery 98".

7in (17.5cm) high

£400-600 **DRA**

A Hampshire vase, with moulded full-height leaves under a fine curdled blue-green glaze, grinding chips inside footrim, stamped "Hampshire Pottery 129".

6.5in (16cm) wide

£600-900 **DRA**

A Charles Harder red clay plate, painted in the Mexican style with indigo horses and cactus plants, 1928, glaze flaking around rim, some abrasion to surface, incised "C Harder/1928".

8in (20.5cm) diam

£500-700 **SDR**

A Harding Black tile, incised and outlined with two kneeling and praying figures in front of a large stylized sun, one with a sombrero, in matte polychrome glazes, signed and dated.

1945 *5.5in (14cm) wide*

£400-500 **DRA**

A Harding Black tile, incised and outlined with a mission, in matte polychrome glazes, signed and dated.

1945 *5.5in (14cm) wide*

£400-500 **DRA**

A rare Hartford Faience mosaic tile panel, with a hilly landscape and tall trees in matte greens and browns on a blue sky, mounted in its original pine box, stamped "HARTFORD FAIENCE".

box 19.25in (48cm) high

£8,000-12,000 **DRA**

A rare Jervis (Oyster Bay) enamel-decorated mug, with a repeating pattern of a rabbit crouched in front of a full moon, incised "Jervis", chips, lines.

5.25in (13cm) wide

£800-1,200 **DRA**

A Jervis (Oyster Bay) flaring vase, enamel-decorated with green and white mistletoe on a teal-blue ground, short and tight opposing hairlines, incised "Jervis".

6in (15cm) high

£800-1,200 **DRA**

A Jugtown bulbous 'Chinese Burial' stoneware vase, circular stamp "Jugtown Ware", initials, restored hole.

9in (23cm) high

£1,500-2,000 **DRA**

Two Jugtown vases, covered in Chinese Blue mottled glaze, one bulbous with two handles, the other flaring, both with Jugtown Ware stamp.

larger 6.5in (16cm) high

£500-700 **DRA**

A large Jugtown bowl with pie-crust shoulder, covered in frothy white matte glaze with red and turquoise accents, several small chips, circular Jugtown Ware stamp.

11.75in (29cm) wide

£300-500 **DRA**

A Jugtown large baluster vase, covered in a Chinese Blue mottled glaze, small flat chip to base, Jugtown Ware stamp.

8.5in (21cm) high

£800-1,200 **DRA**

A Kenton Hills flaring porcelain vase, painted by William Hentschel, with red magnolia blossoms on a grey ground, stamped "KH Hentschel".

7.25in (18cm) high

£500-700 **DRA**

A Lenox Belleek beer pitcher, with silver hinged lid, and six mugs painted by Sturgis Laurence in the Delft style, with different male characters drinking spirits, each signed "FWR Sturgis Laurence, Trenton NJ, Dec. 8 '94", nick to one.

These were produced just before Laurence joined Rookwood Pottery in 1895.

1894 *pitcher 12in (30cm) high*

£1,200-1,800 **DRA**

A Marblehead/Cowan conical three-handled hanging basket, in indigo and sky blue glazes, Cowan mark, line.

9in (23cm) diam

£70-100 **DRA**

A rare and early bulbous Louise Mclaughlin vase, painted in barbotine with white daisies on a pink ground, incised "LMCL/Cincinnati/1879/butterfly/86/A".

c1879 *6.5in (16.5cm) high*

£500-700 **DRA**

An A.G. Meaders stoneware face jug with six teeth, covered in drizzling bottle-green glaze, incised "A.G. Meaders".

11.75in (30cm) high

£1,000-1,500 **DRA**

An A.G. Meaders stoneware three-opening face jug, with seven teeth, covered in drizzling bottle-green glaze, incised "A.G. Meaders".

11.75in (30cm) high

£1,000-1,500 **DRA**

A Merrimac corseted vessel, with two angular handles, covered in deep green frothy semi-matte glaze with gunmetal, stamped "MERRIMAC' with fish, bruise.

6.25in (17cm) high

£300-500 **DRA**

A Merrimac bottle-shaped vase, covered in a fine feathered light and dark green glaze with brown mottling, restoration to nicks around rim, paper label.

9in (22.5cm) high

£500-700 **DRA**

A Merrimac vase, covered in speckled matte indigo glaze, restoration to small rim chip, stamped "MERRIMAC" with fish.

5.25in (13cm) high

£500-700 **DRA**

A Merrimac ridged and dimpled bulbous vase, covered in matte green glaze, with bubbles toward base, restoration to rim chip, stamped "MERRIMAC" with fish.

4.5in (11cm) high

£300-400 **DRA**

A Moravian rare block inkwell, in the Vicar of Stowe pattern, covered in matte green glaze, the red clay showing through, with copper lid over hinged liner, unmarked, chips.

4.75in (12cm) high

£120-180 **DRA**

One of a pair of Moravian tile bookends with a tall ship covered in ivory and green glaze, mounted on brass brackets, firing chips to edges, no visible marks.

3.75in (9.5cm) wide

£80-120 pair **DRA**

A rare Mueller Mosaic colour chart of thirty-six small sample tiles, marked with colour numbers, "MUELLER MOSAIC CO./TRENTON NJ/COLOR CHART/FAIENCE/PLASTIC/HAND-MADE/FROST-PROOF FOR EXTERIOR OR INTERIOR DECORATION".

6.5in (16.5cm) wide

£250-300 **DRA**

A four-tile frieze, attributed to Herman Mueller, incised with a stylized hilly landscape with puffy trees in matte greens and sky blue, restoration to two tiles, mounted in fine, new Arts and Crafts frame, unmarked.

tiles 24in (60cm) wide

£1,800-2,200 **DRA**

A Niloak Mission ware cordial set, with a stoppered bottle and four tumblers of marbleized clay, paper labels and stamp.

Niloak Pottery produced art pottery in Benton, Arkansas from 1909 to 1946. The most sought after Niloak line is 'Mission Swirl' which was developed by Charles Hyten.

bottle 12in (30cm) high

£500-700 **DRA**

A Norse humidor on three animal feet, incised with an Egyptian-revival pattern of snakes and papyrus in verdigris on bronzed ground, minor flecks to rim and base, stamped "NORSE 84".

8in (20cm) high

£800-1,200 **DRA**

A large Norse squat urn, with four handles turning into embossed foliate branches, under a black bronzed glaze, stamped "Norse 24".

The Norse pottery was opened in 1903 by Thorwald P. A. Sampson and Louis Ipson in Egerton, Wisconsin. It is best known for making replicas of excavated Norse bowls in matte and metallic glazes. The pottery closed in 1913.

9.5in (24cm) high

£600-900 **DRA**

A North Dakota School of Mines squat vessel, carved with repeating owls under a light to dark brown matte glaze, ink stamp "M.O.R. to KSR 34".

5.25in (13cm) wide

£1,000-1,500 **DRA**

A North Dakota School of Mines vase, decorated by Julia Mattson, with a band of leaping bison in matte green on a brown ground, ink stamp "JM 111".

6in (15cm) wide

£800-1,200 **DRA**

A North Dakota School of Mines bulbous vase, decorated by Julia Mattson, with rodeo scenes in olive green and dark brown, circular ink stamp "JM/75".

7in (17.5cm) high

£800-1,200 **DRA**

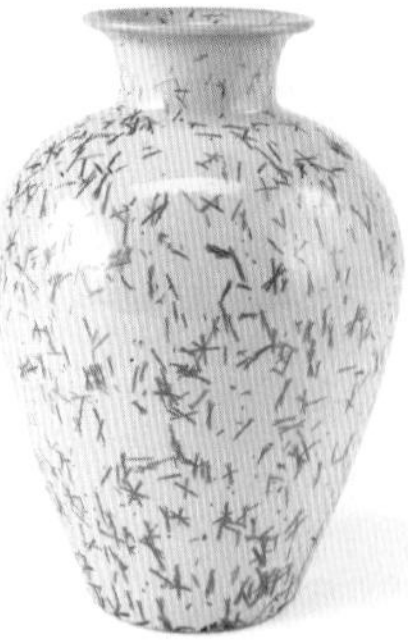

A Norweta baluster vase covered in a cobalt and beige crystalline glaze, stamped "NORWETA".

8in (20.5cm) high

£800-1,200 **DRA**

A tall North Dakota School of Mines vase, painted by Flora Huckfield, with flowers on a soft brown ground, circular mark, "FCH", restoration.

9.5in (24cm) high

£400-600 **DRA**

An Overbeck rare trivet tile carved with a bowl of stylized flowers, covered in indigo, brown, yellow and green semi-matte glaze, carved "OBK", chip, abrasion.

5.5in (14cm) wide

£1,500-2,000 **DRA**

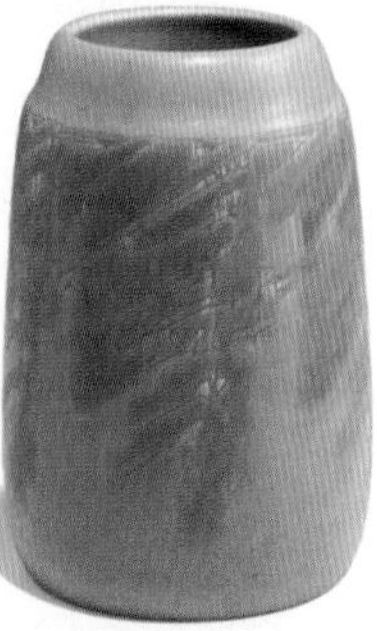

An Overbeck tapered vase, decorated by Elizabeth and Hannah Overbeck, with stylized maple leaves and pods in purple and green on a buff ground, incised "OBK/E/H".

6.75in (17cm) high

£1,800-2,200 **DRA**

An Overbeck bottle-shaped vase, decorated by Elizabeth and Frances Overbeck, with carved stylized pink blossoms and green stems on a matte celadon ground, carved "OBK/E/F".

8.5in (21cm) high

£3,500-4,000 **DRA**

An exceptional Overbeck vase, decorated by Elizabeth and Hannah Overbeck with heavily stylized Queen Anne's Lace blossoms in mottled brown, cherry red and turquoise on a brown and mauve ground, incised "OBK/E/H", restoration, chip.

8.5in (21cm) high

£12,000-18,000 **DRA**

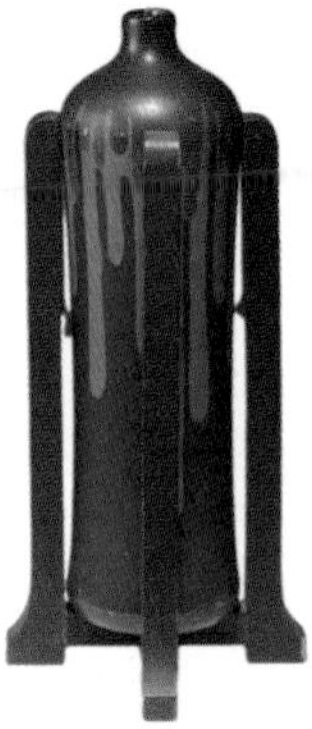

A rare Owens Mission tall bottle-shaped vase, in original oak stand, the vase with dripping red and green glaze on a blue ground, unmarked.

15.25in (38cm) high

£800-1,200 **DRA**

A Rettig-Valentien pilgrim flask, beautifully painted in barbotine with a veiled Oriental woman, incised "R-V 1880", artist-signed "CDV".

1880 *12in (30cm) high*

£700-1,000 **DRA**

A Rhead Santa Barbara low bowl, decorated in squeezebag with white pods on a dead-matte blue-grey ground, glaze bubbles due to overfiring, stamped "Rhead Pottery Santa Barbara".

7.5in (19cm) diam

£2,000-3,000 **DRA**

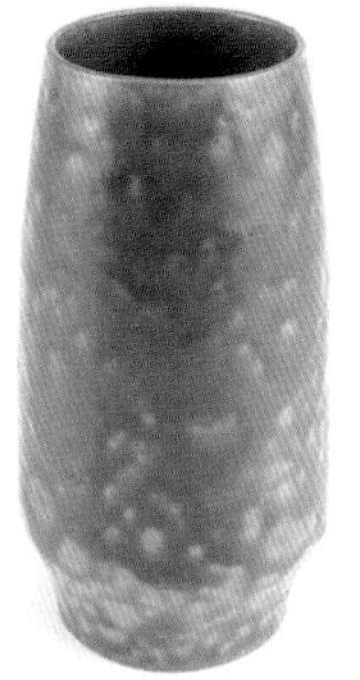

A Frederick Rhead/Santa Barbara tapering vase, covered in green semi-matte mottled glaze over a brown clay ground, potter's mark, chip.

7in (18cm) high

£1,200-1,800 **DRA**

An Adelaide Robineau porcelain squat vessel, covered in beige and celadon crystalline glaze, tight firing line to base, carved "AB 659".

5in (12.5cm) wide

£1,800-2,200 **DRA**

An Adelaide Robineau tapering porcelain vase, covered in a fine purple and celadon crystalline flambé glaze, short line to rim, mostly to interior, carved "AR 1919".

1919 *5in (12.5cm) high*

£2,500-3,000 **DRA**

A San Jose tile, decorated in cuerda seca, with three sombrero-clad men at a cock fight, in glossy polychrome glaze, mounted in a rustic period frame, unmarked.

6in (15cm) wide

£300-400 **DRA**

A Johann von Schwarz vertical Art Nouveau panel, decorated in cuenca with a long-haired maiden with red poppies on a purple ground, marked "XII/Q/1024".

12in (30cm) high

£1,000-1,500 **DRA**

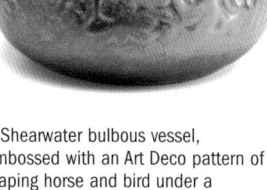

A Shearwater bulbous vessel, embossed with an Art Deco pattern of leaping horse and bird under a turquoise and gunmetal mottled glaze, unmarked.

7in (17.5cm) wide

£700-1,000 **DRA**

An Austrian A. Stuchly tapering vase, embossed with a lady's head with long flowing hair and violets, covered in brown and green matte glaze, signed "A. Stuchly", chip.

12in (30.5cm) high

£250-300 **DRA**

A Teplitz vase by Schwarz with mermaid figure, fish and plants covered in a brown and green bronze-like glaze, several small nicks, stamped "CROWNOAKWARE, Teplitz, Austria, 3776B".

12in (30.5cm) high

£500-700 **DRA**

A Teplitz four-handled faceted vase, enamel-decorated by Paul Dachsel, with lustred irises on a mottled and textured gold ground, purple stamp "TURN TEPLITZ PD/MADE IN AUSTRIA", die-stamped "1 151 12".

9.25in (23cm) high

£220-280 **DRA**

A Tiffany tall textured vase with a blue, green, and grey mottled matte glaze, incised "LCT", circular paper label, etched "P251 Tiffany Favrile".

15in (38cm) high

£4,000-6,000 **DRA**

A six-inch Owens tile, Owens/Tiffany Studios, decorated in cuenca with a cluster of purple grapes below green foliage, mounted in a bronze Tiffany footed trivet base, wear to cuenca walls, unmarked.

£500-700 **DRA**

Two Tiffany bisque-fired bulbous vases of white clay, modelled with leaves and vines, no visible marks.

5.75in (14cm) high

£1,500-2,000 **DRA**

A fine Vance Avon squat vessel, decorated by Rhead with landscape, company and artist's marks.

5.25in (13cm) wide

£600-900 **DRA**

A CLOSER LOOK AT A TIFFANY VASE

Tiffany ceramics are relatively difficult to come by. Made from c1905, they were not as successful as many of the other ranges and by c1917 Tiffany pottery production had largely ceased. It is likely that commercially unsuccessful pieces were destroyed, leaving few on the market today.

Green tints were successfully used from 1906. Designs and glazes were unique and pieces were time consuming to produce.

The arrowroot decoration is typical of the local fauna found in design motifs.

Like this vase, pieces are marked "LCT" and sometimes "Favrile Pottery".

The body is moulded from high-fired white clay.

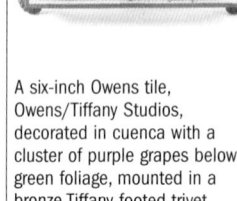

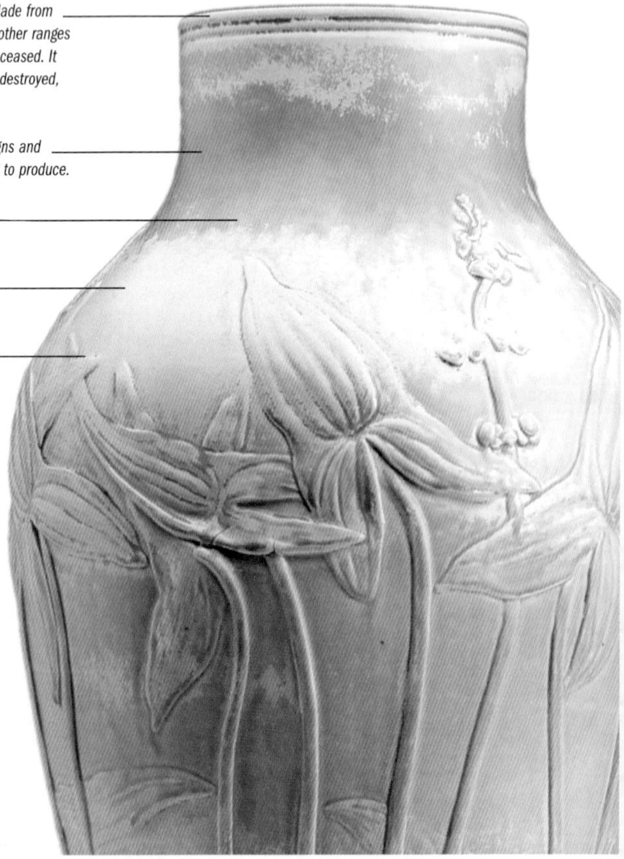

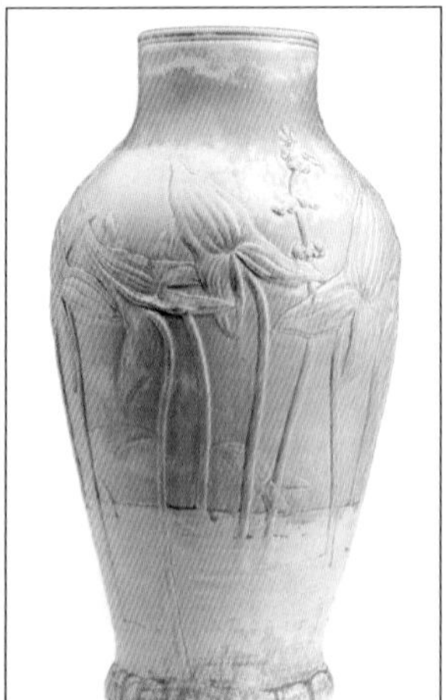

A tall L.C. Tiffany vase, embossed with arrowroot plants, covered in a rich chartreuse and mint green matte crystalline glaze, marked "LCT/P/978/L.C.", "Tiffany - Favrile Pottery", spider line to base, restoration to three areas on rim.

21in (52.5cm) high

£8,000-12,000 **DRA**

A Walrath low bowl, painted with stylized blush blossoms and green leaves on a café-au-lait ground, incised "Walrath Pottery".

7in (17.5cm) wide

£300-400 **DRA**

A W.J. Walley squat vessel, with three twisted handles, covered in a thick, curdled matte green glaze, restoration to half of inner rim, glaze bubbles to top and bottom, stamped "WJW".

9in (22.5cm) wide

£600-900 **DRA**

A tall W.J. Walley ovoid vase, covered in glossy and crystalline green flambé glaze, stamped "WJW".

9.5in (24cm) high

£800-1,200 **DRA**

A T.J. Wheatley large Kendrick-type vase, with rows of repeating leaves under a rich, feathered matte green glaze, small touch-up, minor restoration.

12.5in (31cm) high

£800-1,200 **DRA**

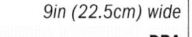

A Walrath matt-painted vase, with orange water lilies on light green lily pads and elongated stems against a rich feathered matte green glaze, short scratch to side, incised "Walrath Pottery".

7.25in (18cm) high

£2,500-3,000 **DRA**

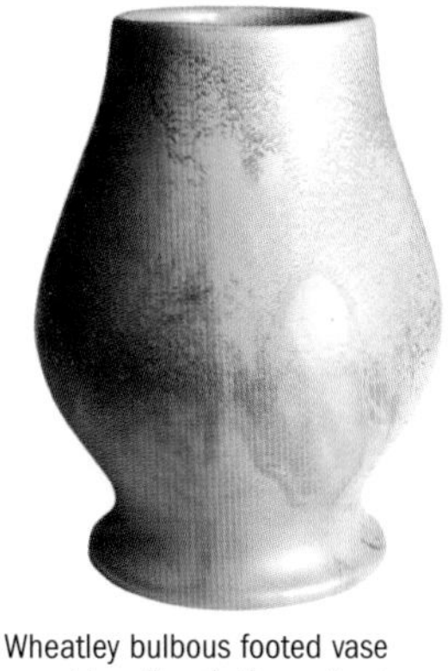

A Wheatley bulbous footed vase covered in a fine, frothy matte green glaze, stamped "WP".

8.5in (21cm) high

£300-400 **DRA**

A Wheatley floor vase, with full-height buttressed handles and tall moulded leaves alternating with buds, covered in a fine, frothy matte green glaze, stamped "WP 623".

19.5in (49cm) high

£1,200-1,800 **DRA**

An Arts and Crafts faceted humidor, embossed with putti playing instruments topped by an acanthus leaf lid, covered in matte green glaze, chips, unmarked.

9.75in (25cm) high

£100-200 **DRA**

A rare pair of American Terra Cotta gargoyle bookends, one animal and one bird, both covered in an unusual light green matte glaze, stamped "AMERICAN TERRA COTTA CHICAGO".

7.25in (18.5cm) high

£600-900 **DRA**

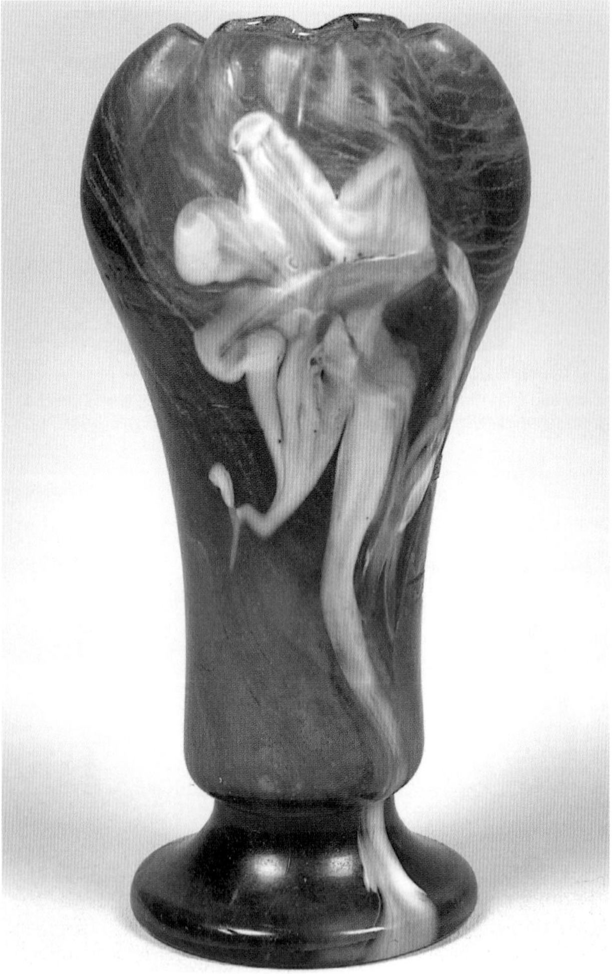

A vase, by Emile Gallé, with a 'Snow Flower', the brown glass with white and brown striae, the front with a cut white 'Snow Flower', an aphorism by Theophile Gautier, signed "Gallé" and "Exp. 1900".

1900 *7.75in (19.5cm) high*

£12,000-14,000 **DOR**

A lily pond cameo glass vase, by Emile Gallé, of tapering cylindrical form with an inverted rim, the yellow and orange glass overlaid in purple, cameo mark "Gallé".

c1900 *4.75in (12cm) high*

£800-1,000 **SWO**

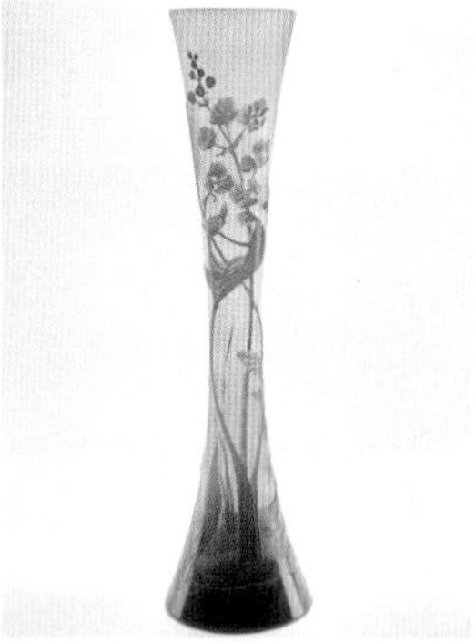

A Gallé vase, the inside overlaid in yellow, the outside in purple, etched decoration of water lilies at a lake with a dragonfly, signed "Gallé".

c1905 *15.5in (39cm) high*

£2,000-3,000 **HERR**

A Gallé vase, the inside overlaid in yellow, the outside in purple, etched decoration of crocus plants, signed "Gallé".

c1905 *8.75in (22cm) high*

£700-1,000 **HERR**

A Gallé vase, with yellow overlay to the inside, the outside overlaid in dark red and pink, etched decoration of phlox blossoms and leaves, signed "Gallé".

c1910 *16.75in (42cm) high*

£5,000-7,000 **HERR**

A Gallé cameo glass vase, clear glass, partly encased red with blue inclusions, light-green and dark-blue on the outside with etched orchid tendrils and tree, frosted ground, signed "Gallé" in relief.

c1915 *15.8in (39.5cm) high*

£3,000-5,000 **DOR**

A Gallé landscape vase, the clear glass underlaid in pink, overlaid in light green and dark brown, etched lake scenery, matted ground, signed "Gallé".

c1915 *11.25in (28cm) high*

£2,000-3,000 **DOR**

A Gallé cameo vase, the clear glass underlaid in yellow and overlaid in red, decorated with etched magnolias, matted ground, the lentil-shaped body with ship-shaped mouth, signed "Gallé".

c1925 *13in (32.5cm) high*

£7,000-9,000 **DOR**

A Gallé vase, with an amber-coloured overlay, shape-blown, decorated with plums in brown, etched, signed "Gallé".

c1925 *13in (32.5cm) high*

£5,000-8,000 **HERR**

A large Gallé cameo vase, with cameo decoration of vines, leaves and flowers, deep amber glass and window pane flowers, signed to side in cameo "Gallé".

15.25in (38.5cm) high

£7,000-9,000 **JDJ**

A Gallé large vase, with cameo cherry blossoms and limbs against a frosted white background, signed on the side in cameo "Gallé".

13.25in (33.5cm) high

£7,000-10,000 **JDJ**

A CLOSER LOOK AT A GALLÉ VASE

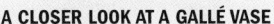

Considered the master of cameo, Gallé used up to five layers of glass, which were cut away to reveal coloured layers beneath, lending the decorative motif a three-dimensional feeling, as seen here.

Both its impressive size and the amount of cut decoration make this a significant and valuable piece, despite slight damage.

Gallé pieces were usually marked and various forms were used. Cameo pieces tend to have a bold signature. After Gallé's death in 1904, a star was added after the signature.

A large Gallé cactus flower vase, with heavy cameo cut leaves and foliage extending down from the lip and window pane cactus flowers, signed to side in cameo "Gallé", fleabite to lip.

16in (40.5cm) high

£19,000-21,000 **JDJ**

A Gallé cameo vase, red floral acid-cut back design of flowers, leaves, stems and tendrils set against a frosted background, signed "Gallé" in cameo.

13.5in (34.5cm) high

£3,000-5,000 **JDJ**

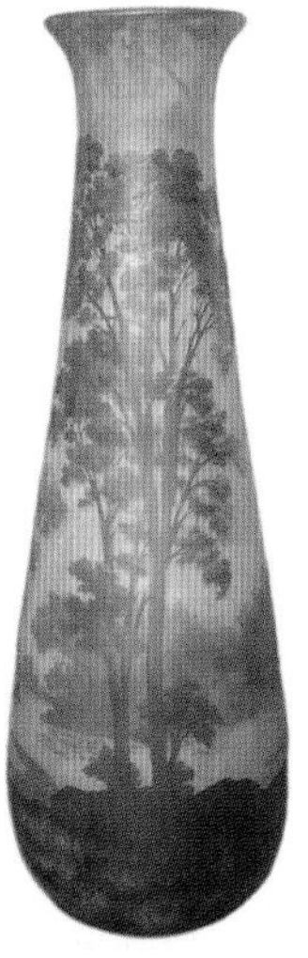

A Gallé cameo glass vase, of tall baluster form with trees in a landscape with distant hills.

16.25in (41cm) high

£1,200-1,800 **BRI**

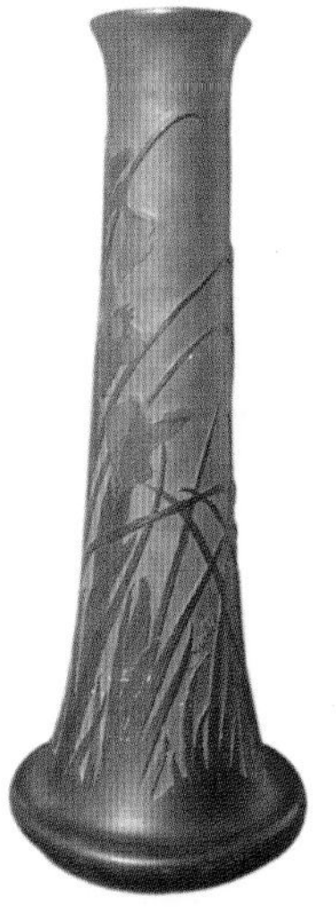

A Gallé cameo glass vase, of tall tapering cylindrical form with flowering iris in pale mauve.

18.5in (47cm) high

£1,200-1,800 **BRI**

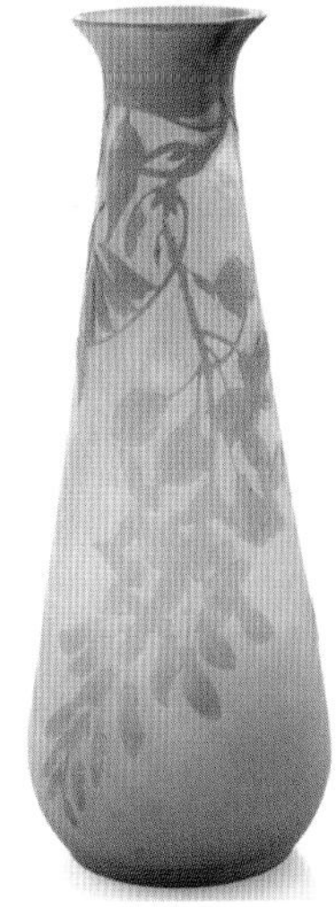

A Gallé cameo glass vase, decorated with sweetpeas in relief, cameo signature.

11.5in (29cm) high

£500-800 **JN**

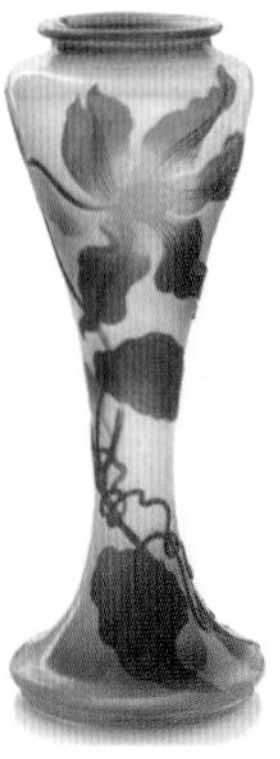

A Gallé cameo glass vase, of baluster shape, acid-etched with a plum-coloured hibiscus design, moulded mark in cameo, chip to neck rim.

9.5in (24cm) high

£300-500 **GORL**

A Gallé red overlay and enamel vase, enamelled with stems, leaves and flowers, against a latticework background, signed on base with engraved flower and "Cristallerie de Gallé Nancy Modele et Décor Depose".

22.25in (56.5cm) high

£10,000-12,000 **JDJ**

A rare vase, by Emile Gallé, painted in gold, depicting the fable 'The Fox and the Crow', with a lentil-shaped body, carried on a Japanese tree, signed in rusty red.

c1880 11.25in (28cm) high

£1,800-2,200 **DOR**

A rare lidded bowl, by Emile Gallé, clear glass with milky, partially dark green powder inclusions, overlaid in light brown and green, polished, etched and cut algae decoration, signed "Gallé 4".

1898 5.5in (14cm) high

£1,200-1,800 **KAU**

A Gallé bowl, clear glass over- and underlaid in yellow and brown, decorated with a river scene, signed "Gallé".

Provenance: *Baron of Glaubitz and Altengabel.*

c1910 9.5in (24cm) high

£400-600 **KAU**

A table lamp, by Emile Gallé, Nancy, cased yellow and red clear glass, continuous almond blossom decoration, marked "Gallé" on stand and shade, wired, chips on rim of shade.

c1900 12in (30cm) high

£4,000-6,000 **KAU**

A rare table lamp, by Emile Gallé, with iris and bats, matte white interior, overlaid in purple and orange-brown, decorated with etched branches of iris and flying bats, brass mountings, signed "Gallé" to foot and shade.

c1900 25.5in (63.5cm) high

£25,000-30,000 **DOR**

A small Gallé table lamp, the clear glass underlaid in yellow, overlaid in red, decorated with etched orchid branches, matted ground, bronze mounting, electrified, signed "Gallé" to shade and foot.

c1910 14.5in (36cm) high

£11,000-14,000 **DOR**

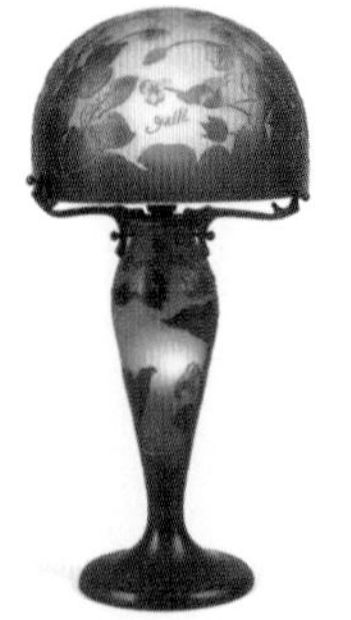

An early 20thC Gallé cameo glass table lamp, the domed shade depicting wild flowers in green with brown foliage, amber ground, shade and base signed "Gallé", small chip.

13.75in (35cm) high

£3,000-5,000 **SK**

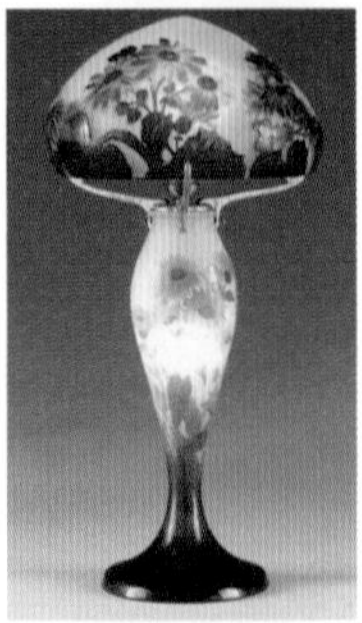

A Gallé table lamp, decorated with flowers and leaves against a shaded yellow background, matching domed shade, base and shade signed in cameo "Gallé", spider replaced.

17.5in (44.5cm) high

£6,000-9,000 **JDJ**

A large Gallé cameo lamp, the purple floral and foliage pattern on camphor-coloured ground, signed "Gallé" in cameo.

27in (68.5cm) high

£5,000-8,000 **JDJ**

DAUM FRÈRES

- The factory at Nancy was operated by the Daum family from 1875, when it came to Jean Daum (1825-85) in payment for a bad debt. It was renamed Verrerie de Nancy and is still in operation today.
- Daum ran it with his sons Jean-Louis (1853-1909) and Jean-Antonin (1864-1931). Upon their father's death, the sons changed the name to Daum Frères. They specialized in overlaid and etched glass in the Art Nouveau style.
- In 1900 Daum cameo glass won a prize at the Paris Exhibition.
- In 1909 Jean-Louis' son, Paul, introduced new designs. Pre-WWI production consisted mainly of cameo glass and acid-etched pieces. Post-1919 the factory focused its attention on large, acid-etched pieces and internal decoration, incorporating metalworked designs by Brandt and Majorelle.
- WWII saw production cease. Paul Daum (1888-1944) was arrested and died in a Nazi concentration camp. The factory reopened in 1946.
- In 1962 the factory became a public company and was renamed Cristallerie Daum.

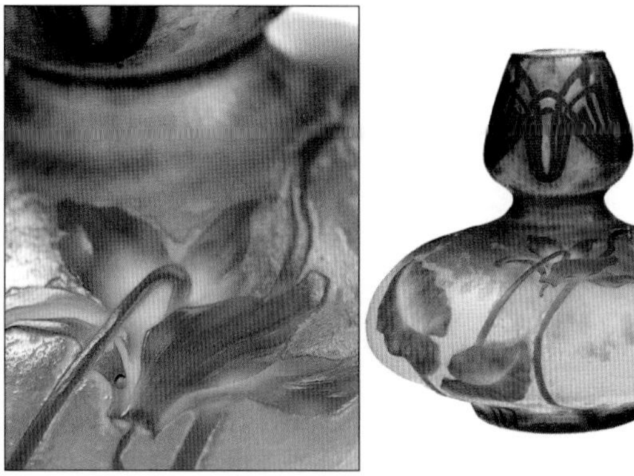

A rare Daum Frères clear glass vase, overlaid in dark purple, etched, cut, bevelled and the inside matted, decorated with cyclamen, the neck with geometrical lines, signed "Daum Nancy" and with cross of Lorraine.

The cross mark reflected the Daum family's pride in the Nancy region.

1898 *6.5in (16cm) high*

£2,500-3,000 **KAU**

A Daum Frères, cameo glass vase with violet decoration, clear glass with white and mottled violet inclusions, frosted ground, signature "Daum Nancy" and cross of Lorraine in relief on wall.

c1900 *4.8in (12cm) high*

£2,000-3,000 **DOR**

A Daum Frères cameo glass vase with violet decoration, clear glass with white and mottled violet inclusions on a frosted ground, with signature "Daum Nancy" and cross of Lorraine on base.

c1900 *4.8in (12cm) high*

£2,000-3,000 **DOR**

A Daum Frères cameo glass vase, in clear and raspberry-red glass, with etched and gilded flower stalk, openwork silver mounting with French silver hallmark, base with remnants of signature in gold "Daum Nancy" with cross of Lorraine.

c1900 *7.5in (18.8cm) high*

£1,200-1,800 **DOR**

A Daum Frères mould-blown, wheel-carved overlay 'Crocus' cabinet vase, the ground finely martelé, etched "Daum Nancy" signature under foot with traces of gilt.

c1900 *6in (15cm) high*

£2,000-3,000 **ISA**

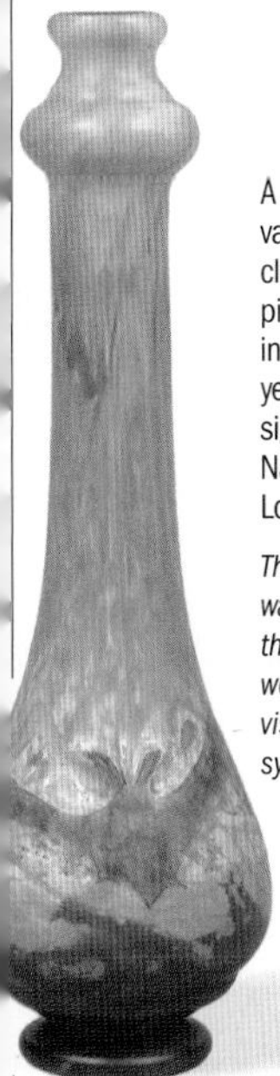

A rare Daum Frères vase with a bat, the clear glass with white, pink and red inclusions, overlaid in yellowish green, cut signature "Daum Nancy" with cross of Lorraine.

The influence of nature was predominant in the Daum brothers work, especially its visual rather than symbolic appeal.

c1905 *12.25in (30.5cm) high*

£23,000-25,000 **DOR**

A Daum Frères glass vase with light blue powdery inclusions, etched decoration of peacock feathers, signed "DAUM NANCY" with cross of Lorraine.

c1905 *10.25in (25.5cm) high*

£3,000-4,000 **HERR**

A Daum Frères glass vase, overlaid in brown, etched decoration of rose hip bushes, on a plate foot, signed "Daum Nancy" with cross of Lorraine.

c1905 *15in (37.5cm) high*

£2,000-2,500 **HERR**

A Daum Frères glass vase, the lower part with inclusions in yellow and pink, etched decoration of magnolia, signed "DAUM NANCY" with cross of Lorraine.

c1905 *11.25in (28cm) high*

£1,500-2,000 **HERR**

A Daum Frères landscape vase, the clear glass with thick orange-red inclusions, overlaid in green, made in the 'Soufflé' or mould-blown technique, etched and cut, signed "Daum Nancy" with cross of Lorraine.

c1910 11.5in (29cm) high

£3,000-4,000 **DOR**

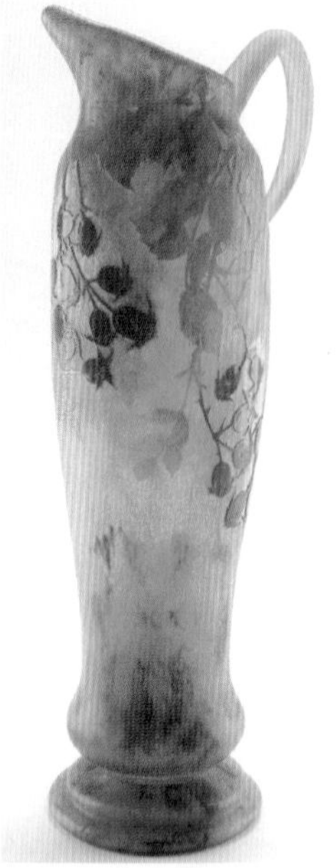

A Daum Frères glass vase, overlaid in pink, yellow-red, light-green, yellow and red, etched rosehip decoration, pointed spout, with one handle, signed "DAUM NANCY" with cross of Lorraine.

c1910 13.5in (34cm) high

£2,000-3,000 **HERR**

A Daum Frères vase, decorated with foxgloves, the clear glass with thick orange and light red inclusions, overlaid in orange-brown and dark brown, with etched foxglove decoration, matted ground, signed "Daum Nancy" with cross of Lorraine.

1913 10.5in (26cm) high

£2,000-4,000 **DOR**

A rare Daum Frères vase with bats, the clear glass with blue inclusions, overlaid in red and brown, decorated with flying bats, with tripod mouth, signed "Daum Nancy" with cross of Lorraine.

c1915 3.5in (9cm) high

£12,000-14,000 **DOR**

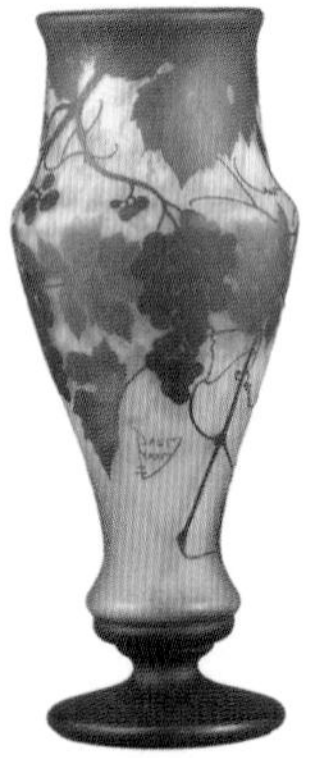

A Daum Frères tapering cylindrical vase, with mottled yellow graduating to lime green overlaid in olive green and brown-black and cut with grape clusters and leaves on vines, signed in cameo "DAUM NANCY" with cross of Lorraine.

c1915 13.75in (35cm) high

£1,800-2,200 **ISA**

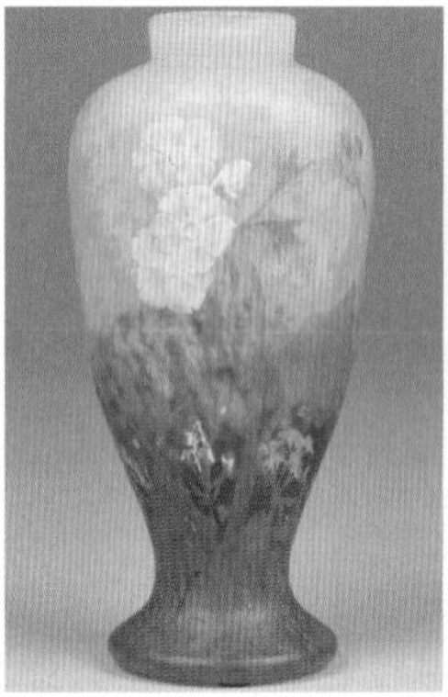

A Daum Frères 'Primula veris' vase, clear glass with single orange and thick ochre inclusions, decorated with primula flowers on a frosted ground, cut signature "Daum Nancy" with cross of Lorraine on wall.

c1920 8.25in (20.5cm) high

£7,000-9,000 **DOR**

A rare Daum Frères snail vase, with two applied snails with frosted glass bodies and carved shell, cameo grape leaves and grape clusters with purple cabochons, signed on base "Daum Nancy" with cross of Lorraine.

10.75in (27.5cm) high

£10,000-12,000 **JDJ**

A Daum Frères cameo glass vase, with white floral decoration and green foliage on a modelled orange and blue background, engraved "Daum Nancy France" with cross of Lorraine.

8in (20cm) high

£5,000-8,000 **JDJ**

A Daum Frères cameo vase, decorated with a lakeland landscape in shades of amethyst against a pale blue and mottled ground, cameo signature "Daum Nancy" with cross of Lorraine.

10.75in (27.5cm)

£1,200-1,800 **DRA**

A Daum Frères cameo glass vase, with tall purple trees against a lake landscape, signed "Daum Nancy".

12.25in (31cm) high

£800-1,200 **DRA**

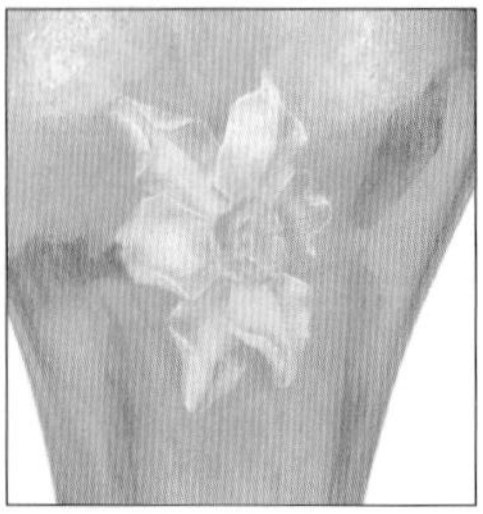

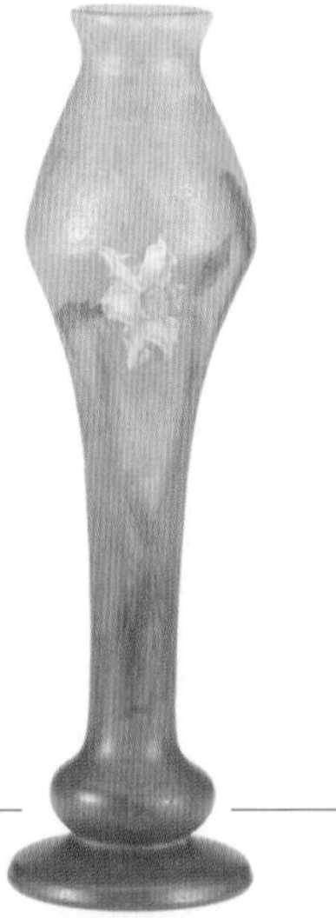

A tall Daum Frères bulbous cameo vase, with white daffodils and green foliage on a mottled white and yellow ground, etched "Daum Nancy".

16in (40cm) high

£4,000-6,000 **DRA**

A large Daum Frères thistle cameo vase, with gold trim and veining on leaves and stems, blue opalescent body, finished with an acid texture, signed on base "Daum Nancy" with the cross of Lorraine.

19in (48cm) high

£4,000-6,000 **JDJ**

A Daum Frères cameo glass vase, with trumpet flowers in shades of red and amber on mottled and martelé finish, red and amber ground, wheel-cut "DAUM NANCY" with cross of Lorraine.

14in (35.5cm) high

£2,000-3,000 **DRA**

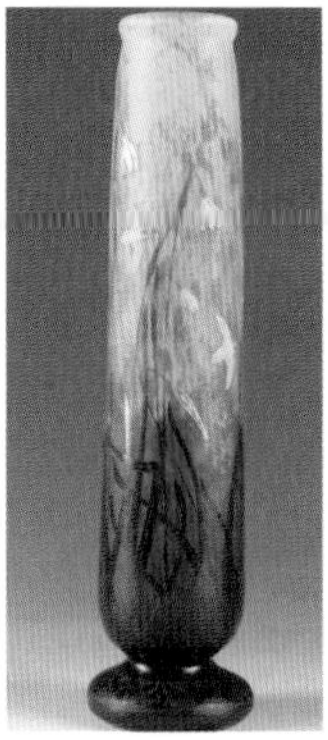

A Daum Frères padded and wheel-carved vase, decorated with brown cameo leaves and stems on a mottled background, 12 wheel-carved padded white flowers and buds.

17.5in (44.5cm) high

£3,000-5,000 **JDJ**

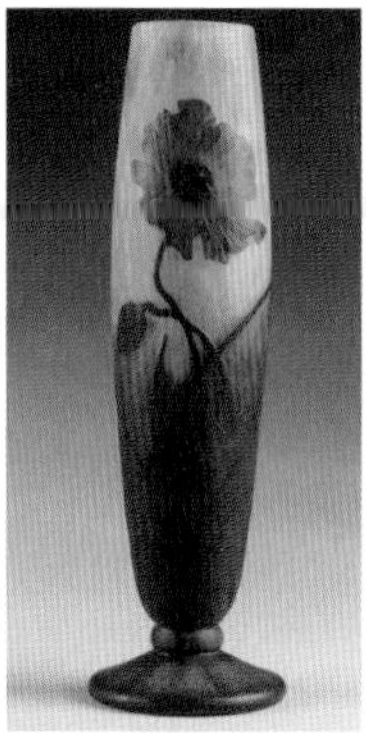

A Daum Frères wheel-carved vase, with poppy decoration on mottled background with engraved "Daum Nancy" signature.

11.5in (29cm) high

£4,000-6,000 **JDJ**

A Daum Frères wheel-carved cameo vase, decorated with wheel-carved daisies, the background internally decorated with a wheel-carved martelé finish behind the cameo carving, signed on foot with carved signature "Daum Nancy" with cross of Lorraine.

A martelé finish is a hammered metal effect background.

15.5in (39.5cm) high

£9,000-11,000 **JDJ**

A Daum Frères squat cameo jardinière, with a silhouetted lake landscape at dusk in brown, yellow, green and red, "Daum Nancy" with the cross of Lorraine.

9.75in (24cm) wide

£1,200-1,800 **DRA**

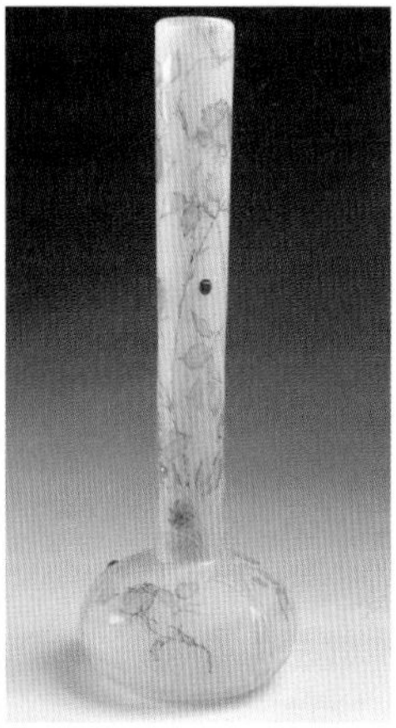

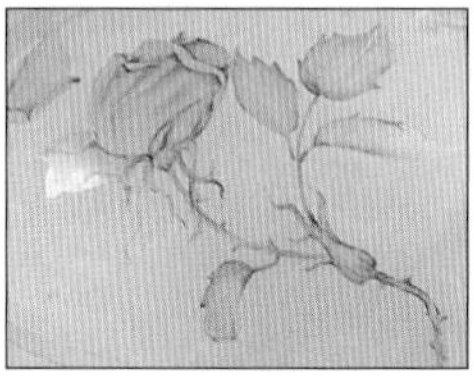

A large Daum Frères cameo vase, carved and enamelled with roses, leaves and stems in panels, with applied cabochons, a cameo and pastel enamelled butterfly and a dragonfly, signed on base "Daum Nancy" with Cross of Lorraine.

24.75in (63cm) high

£8,000-10,000 **JDJ**

A large Daum Frères bumble bee vase, decorated in cameo and enamels with wild orchids and bees against a mottled background, the base with cameo spider webs, the foot with stylized floral design trimmed in gold gilt, signed on base "Daum Nancy" with the cross of Lorraine.

21in (53.5cm) high

£10,000-12,000 **JDJ**

A rare Daum Frères 'Meadow Scene' cameo and enamelled footed vase, with an Oriental poppy and floral pattern, gold gilt to foliage and Art Nouveau decorative design, signed "Daum Nancy" in gilt on base.

6in (15cm) high

£3,000-5,000 **JDJ**

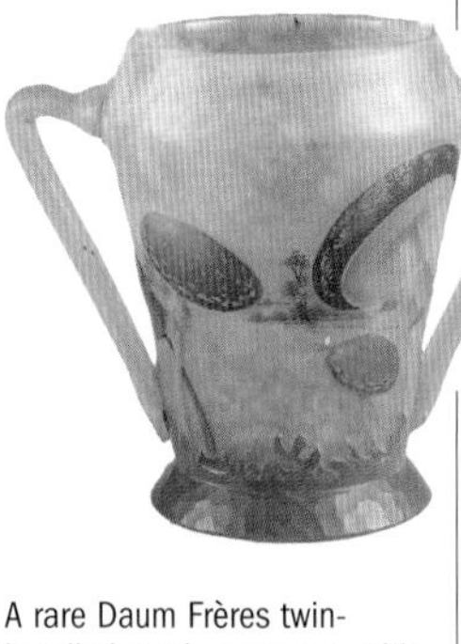

A rare Daum Frères twin-handled mushroom vase, with enamelled and cameo decoration, signed "Daum Nancy" with cross of Lorraine in enamelling on base.

6in (15cm) high

£6,000-9,000 **JDJ**

A Daum Frères centre bowl, with painted swan design, decorated with cameo and enamelled trees, on a blue mottled background, signed "Daum Nancy" in enamel.

Landscape cameo vases usually date from post-WWI. The most elaborate and expensive used up to five layers of colour, a highly skilled task as each colour cools at a different rate. These were then often etched, engraved, carved and enamelled.

9.25in (23.5cm) wide

£8,000-10,000 **JDJ**

A Daum Frères glass vase, partly overlaid in blue, etched decoration of poppies and stars, enamelled in black, etched, gilded, on silver foot, signed "DAUM NANCY" with the cross of Lorraine.

c1895 4.75in (12cm) high

£500-800 **HERR**

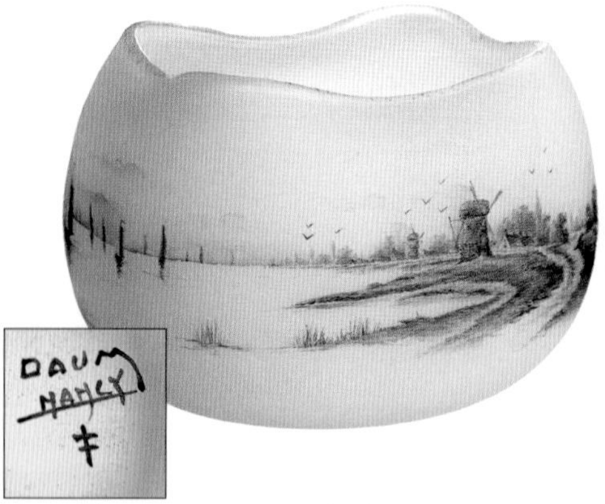

A Daum Frères vase, clear glass with milky white overlay, enamelled, decorated with a Dutch coastal scape with windmills, signed "Daum Nancy" and the cross of Lorraine.

c1900 4.5in (11cm) high

£1,000-1,500 **KAU**

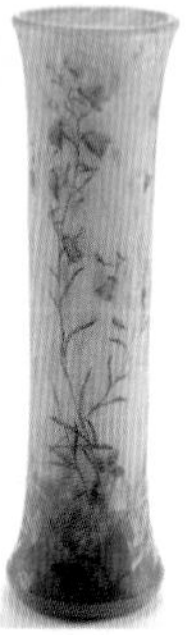

A Daum Frères 'Campanules' glass vase, etched clear glass, powder inclusions in white, blue and rose, etched flower decoration, signed "Daum Nancy" with cross of Lorraine.

1905 19.5in (49cm) high

£4,000-6,000 **HERR**

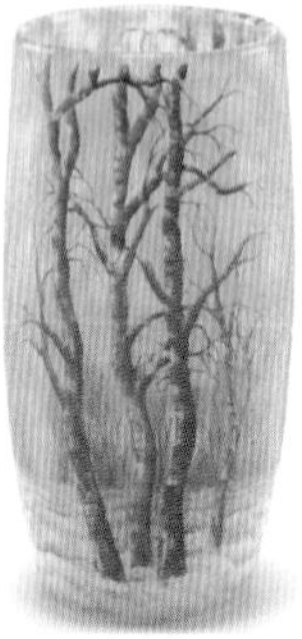

A Daum Frères glass vase, with yellow and orange inclusions, etched decoration of a winter landscape with trees, painted in enamels, signed "Daum Nancy" with cross of Lorraine.

1905 4.75in (12cm) high

£1,200-1,800 **HERR**

A Daum Frères rain scene pillow-form vase, with enamelled decoration, signed "Daum Nancy" with Cross of Lorraine, possible grinding to top rim, minute pinhole flakes to interior rim.

4.75in (12cm) high

£3,000-5,000 **JDJ**

A Daum Frères etched and enamelled glass footed coupe, the upper section decorated with wild flowers, a spider's web and bees, enamelled against a deep violet ground shading to lemon, painted "Daum Nancy" with cross of Lorraine.

8.5in (21.5cm) high

£6,000-9,000 **DRA**

A Daum Frères etched and enamelled glass vase, decorated with blackberries in naturalistic colours on shaded pale green ground, etched signature "Daum Nancy" with cross of Lorraine.

8.25in (21cm) high

£1,500-2,000 **DRA**

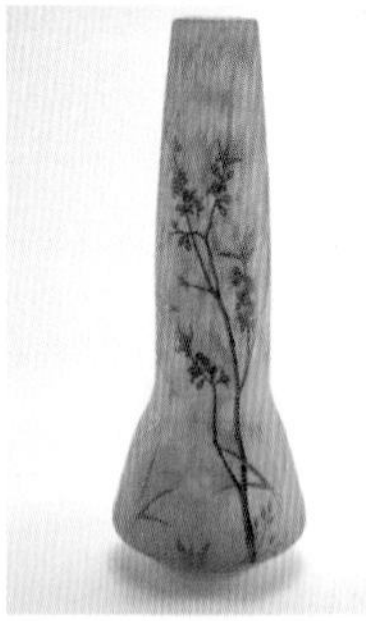

A Daum Frères glass vase, etched decoration and enamels, a long cylindrical neck, signed "Daum Nancy" with cross of Lorraine.

c1905 13in (33cm) high

£2,000-2,500 **HERR**

A Daum Frères iridescent glass vase, etched and gilded with seagulls and a rising sun, and carved with turtles, signed "Daum Nancy" with cross of Lorraine in gold gilt to base, minor imperfections and wear.

7.5in (19cm) high

£5,000-8,000 **JDJ**

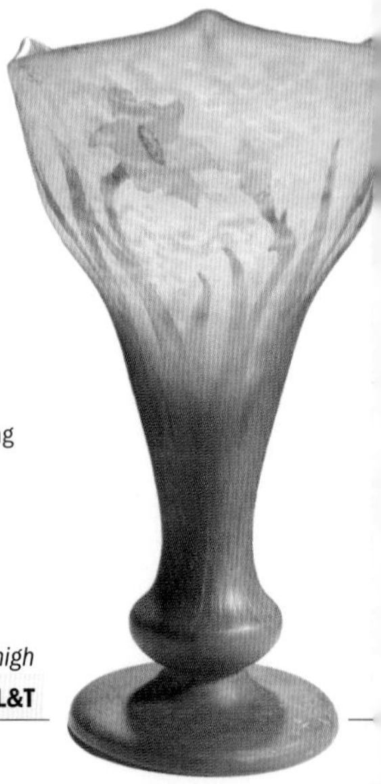

A Daum Frères etched and carved glass vase, of tapering form with applied foot and pulled rim, the frosted glass body with mottled blue and white inclusions, decorated with daffodils, etched mark "Daum, Nancy".

13.75in (35cm) high

£4,000-6,000 **L&T**

A Daum Frères etched and carved glass vase, of slender tapering form with bulbous body and applied foot, the frosted body with mottled grey inclusions decorated with flowering poppies.

16.5in (41.5cm) high

£3,000-5,000 **L&T**

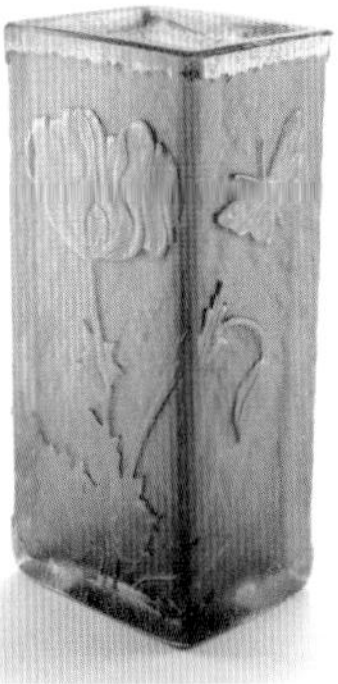

A Daum Frères glass vase, with purple underlay, with etched decoration of poppy seed plants with butterflies, gilded, signed "Daum Nancy" with cross of Lorraine.

c1895 *7.5in (19cm) high*

£600-900 **HERR**

An Daum Frères Art Deco vase, brownish-black transparent glass with cut geometric decoration, with cut signature "Daum Nancy France" and cross of Lorraine on foot rim.

c1925 *5.8in (14.5cm) high*

£700-1,000 **DOR**

A Daum Frères Boudoir lamp, with unusual wooded landscape scene, in enamelled and cameo glass, on mottled amethyst and green background, signed "Daum Nancy".

14in (35.5cm) high

£8,000-10,000 **JDJ**

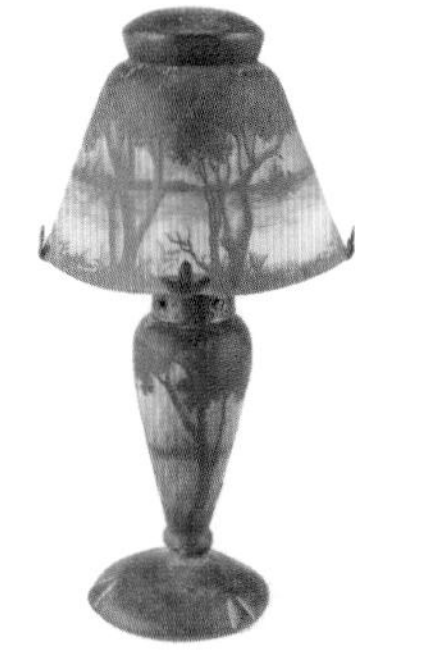

A Daum Frères cameo glass landscape lamp, the shade and base decorated with a wooded lakeland landscape, shade with cameo signature "Daum Nancy" and cross of Lorraine, base with cameo signature and DN monogram.

14in (35.5cm) high

£5,000-8,000 **DRA**

A Daum Frères lampshade, of globular form, with floral decoration, on an iron base.

12in (30.5cm) high

£800-1,000 **FRE**

A Daum Frères table lamp, the clear glass matted in white, etched with stripes and stylized floral decoration, nickel-plated metal mounting, electrified, etched signature "Daum Nancy France" with cross of Lorraine to shade and foot.

c1925 *16.5in (41cm) high*

£6,000-9,000 **DOR**

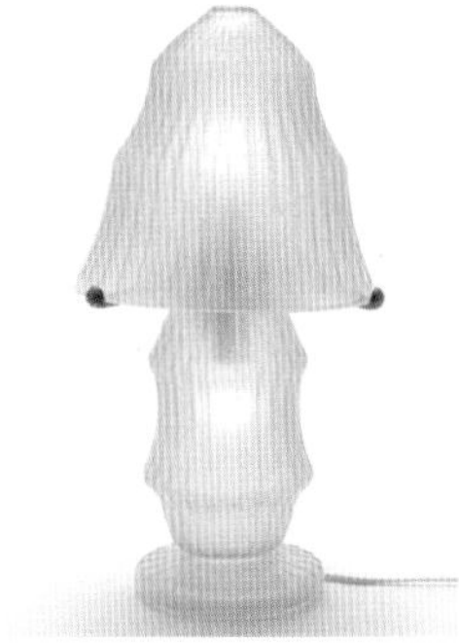

A Daum Frères glass table lamp, ice-glass etched stripe decoration, on a plate foot, a bell-shaped shade, metal fittings with three arms, electrified, signed "DAUM NANCY FRANCE" with Lorraine Cross.

c1925 *17.5in (44cm) high*

£2,000-3,000 **HERR**

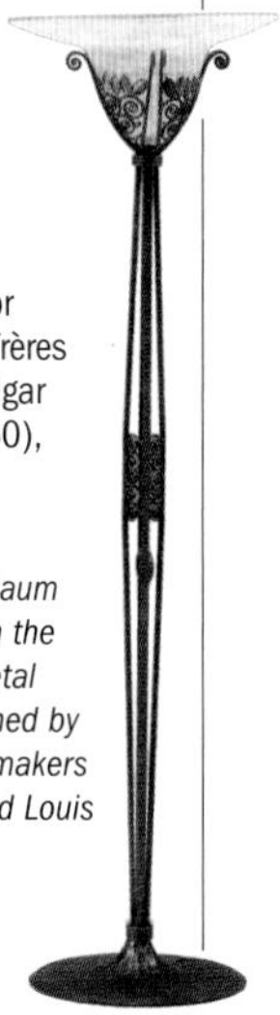

A wrought iron floor lamp, with Daum Frères glass shade, by Edgar Brandt (1880-1960), signed.

Lamps became an important area of Daum Frères production in the 1920s and 30s. Metal mounts were designed by some of the major makers including Brandt and Louis Majorelle.

c1925 *68in (170cm) high*

£8,000-12,000 **FRE**

A Daum Frères ceiling lamp, the clear glass with thick orange powder inclusions, overlaid in green and dark brown, decorated with etched leaves, iron mounting with leaves and helixes, matted ground, signed "Daum Nancy" with cross of Lorraine to shade.

c1905 *18.5in (46cm) high*

£3,000-4,000 **DOR**

A rare Daum Frères perfume bottle, of organic form, with cabochon carved in the shape of an insect, signed "Daum Nancy".

5.5in (14cm) high

£7,000-9,000 **JDJ**

A Daum Frères glass model of a pelican, with frosted beak and feathers, engraved "Daum, France".

8.5in (22cm) high

£70-100 **JN**

A rare 'Davos' vase, designed by René Lalique, in red, olive-green to brown transparent glass, notch decoration in relief, with etched signature "R. Lalique France" on base.

Lalique initially worked as a jewellery maker, but began exhibiting glass in 1912. His factory opened in 1921 and he started to produce glass in the Art Deco style. He exhibited through US department stores in the 1930s, attracting a strong following. The company is still in operation today.

1932 *11.5in (28.5cm) high*

£7,000-9,000 **DOR**

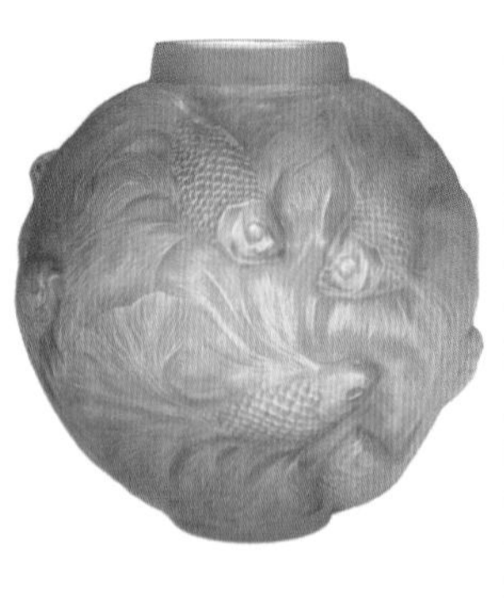

A Lalique clear and frosted glass vase, 'Formose', of spherical form moulded with fish and with blue stained decoration, etched mark "R Lalique, France no. 934".

7in (17.5cm) high

£1,500-2,000 **L&T**

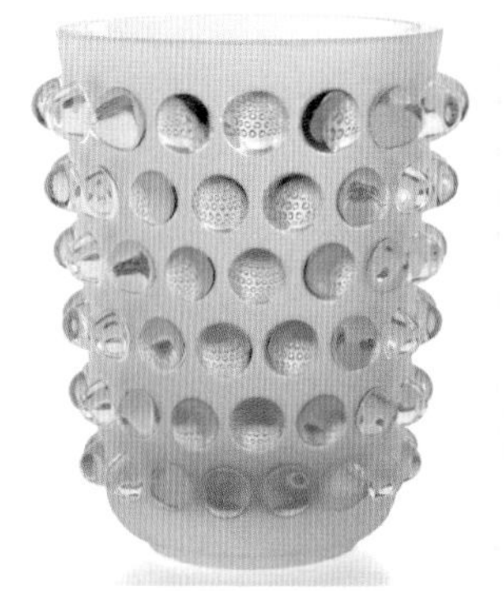

A Lalique frosted glass vase, with bubbles in clear glass, engraved "Lalique France", with original box.

8.5in (22cm) high

£200-300 **JN**

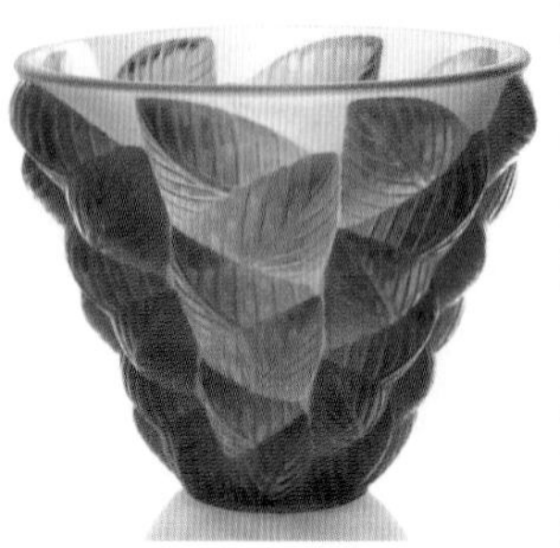

A Lalique clear and frosted grey-brown glass 'Moissac' vase, number 992, with intaglio "R Lalique" mark.

5in (13cm) high

£1,500-2,000 **WW**

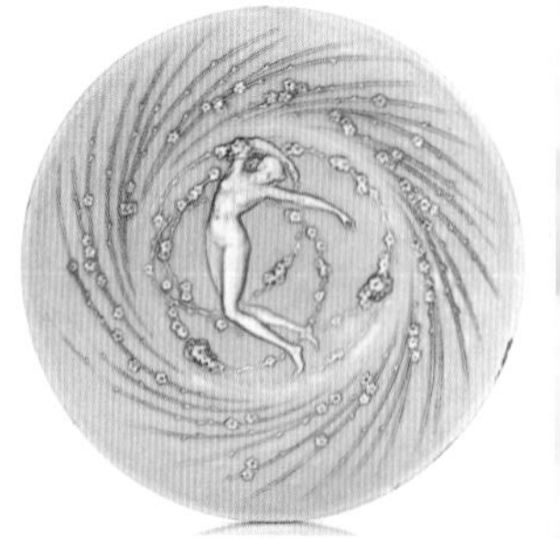

One of a set of twelve Lalique brown-stained glass ice plates, each moulded with a naked young woman amid flower garlands, the rim with spiralling prunus, moulded marks, some engraved "France".

6.75in (17cm) diam

£3,000-5,000 set **LFA**

Two of a set of eight Lalique brown-stained round bowls, each moulded with radiating leaves, moulded marks.

5in (12.5cm) diam

£700-1,000 set **LFA**

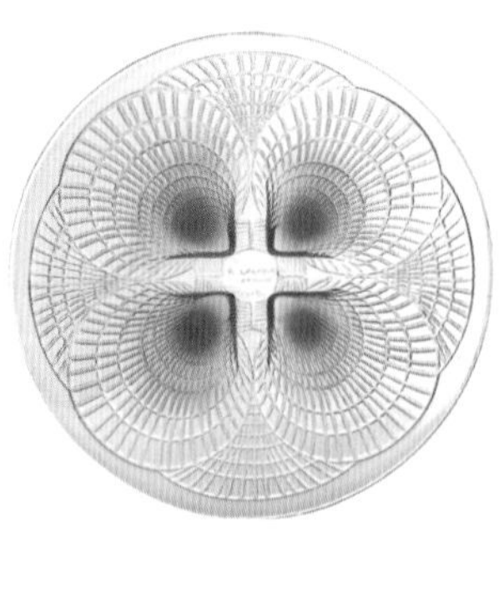

One of a set of eight Lalique opalescent glass round bowls and matching plates, each moulded with overlapping scallop shells, engraved marks and number "3204".

5.25in (13.5cm) diam

£2,200-2,800 set **LFA**

Two of a set of six mid-20thC black 'Alga' plates, black satin polished crystal with aquatic plant motif, signed "Lalique France".

c1950 *7.75in (19.5cm) diam*

£700-1,000 set **SK**

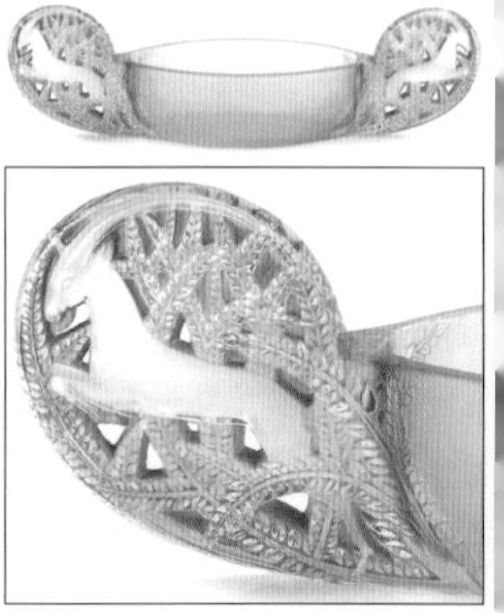

A Lalique clear glass handled bowl, each handle featuring a stylized leaping gazelle on a fern background.

12in (30cm) wide

£1,200-1,800 **WW**

A car mascot, by Persons Majestic Company of Worcester MA, after the Victoire model by Lalique, of clear and frosted yellow glass, moulded as a female head with stylized streaming hair, affixed to a circular chromium-plated metal base, moulded maker's mark, chips.

10.25in (26cm) long

£1,500-2,000 **SK**

A car mascot, after the Victoire model by Lalique, in clear and frosted amethyst glass, modelled as a female head with stylized streaming hair, affixed to a circular chromium-plated metal mount, nicks.

c1935 *10.25in (26cm) long*

£1,500-2,000 **SK**

A CLOSER LOOK AT A LALIQUE CAR MASCOT

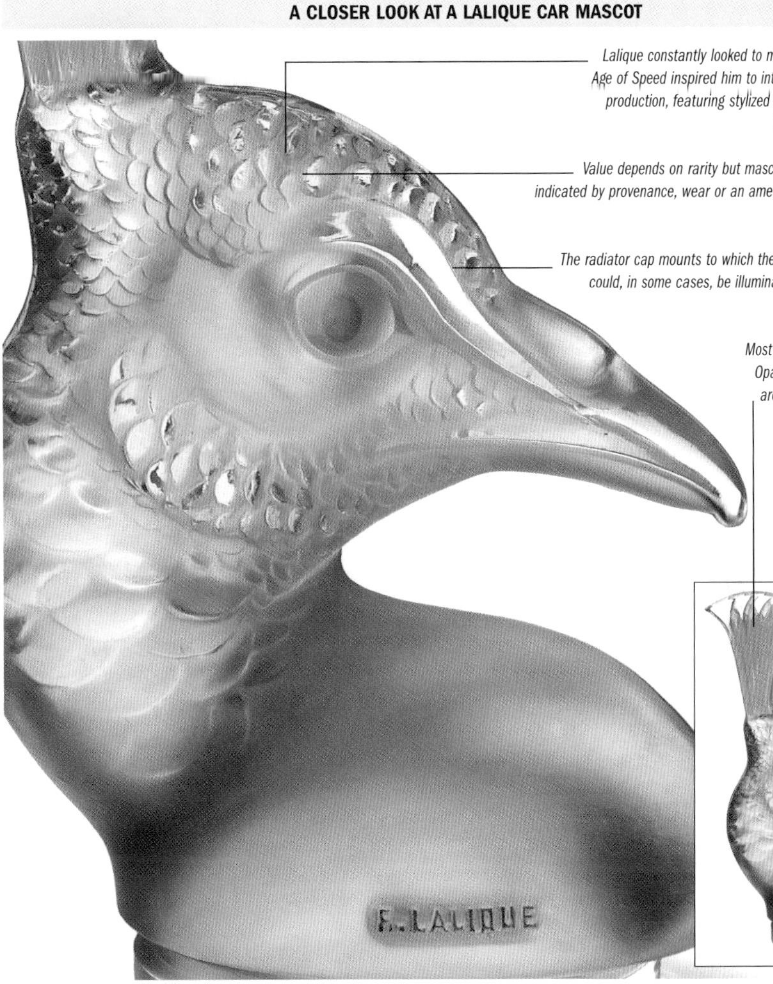

Lalique constantly looked to modernity for influence. The Age of Speed inspired him to introduce 28 car mascots to production, featuring stylized animals or female figures, between 1925 and 1932.

Value depends on rarity but mascots that have been used – indicated by provenance, wear or an amethyst tint from exposure to sun – are preferred.

The radiator cap mounts to which the base of the mascot fitted could, in some cases, be illuminated, lighting up the piece.

Most were made in clear glass. Opalescent or colour mascots are rarer and more valuable.

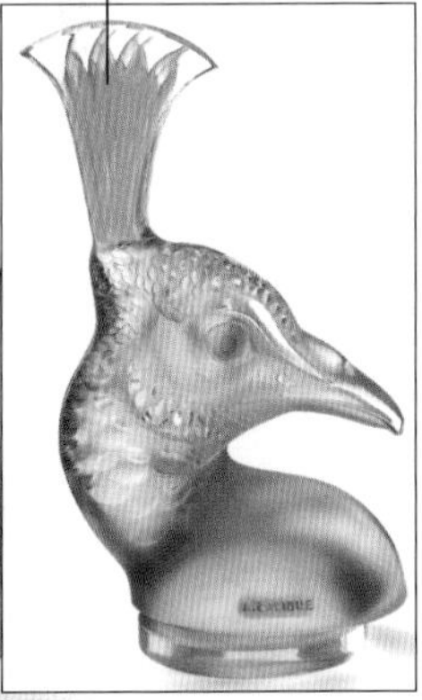

A rare Lalique clear and frosted car mascot, 'Tete de Paon no.1140', intaglio "R Lalique France".

c1930 *7in (18cm) high*

£9,000-11,000 **WW**

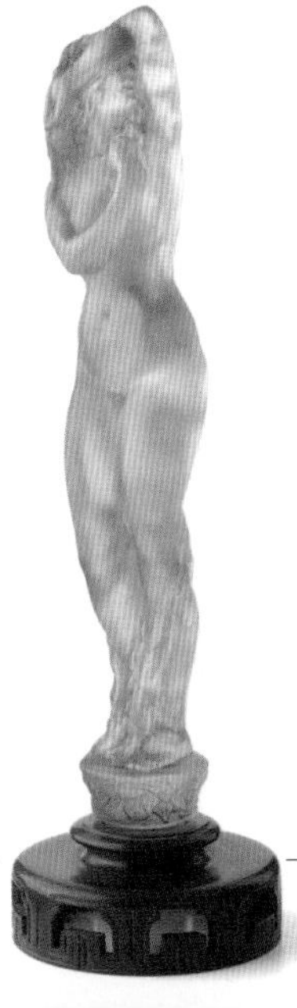

A rare Lalique sepia-stained frosted glass figure, 'Grand Nue avec Socle Lierre' No.836, on ebonized wood base etched "R Lalique, France no.830".

15.5in (39cm) high

£25,000-30,000 **WW**

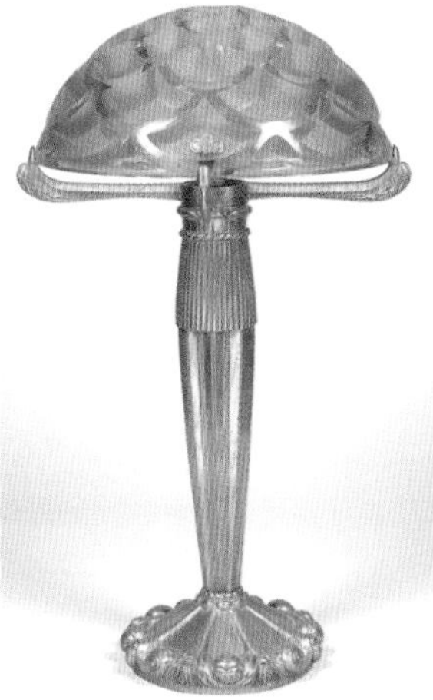

A Lalique table lamp with 'Rinceaux' shade, the clear pressed glass shade decorated with geometrical dents, the silver-plated bronze foot with stylized floral decoration, electrified, shade with signature "R. Lalique France".

c1925 *28in (70cm) high*

£9,000-11,000 **DOR**

A Lalique clear, frosted and opalescent 'Enseparables' glass clock, moulded with opposed budgerigars and raised on a stepped onyx base, moulded mark "R Lalique".

4.5in (11cm) high

£2,000-3,000 **L&T**

An Argy-Rousseau pâte-de-verre vase, decorated with trailing peonies in shades of green, violet, black and orange on shaded purple ground, moulded signature, base moulded "18874".

Joseph-Gabriel Argy-Rousseau (1885-1953) was a ceramicist who began to specialize in pâte-de-verre glass after WWI. He produced a wide range of small, richly decorated pieces at his Paris workshop.

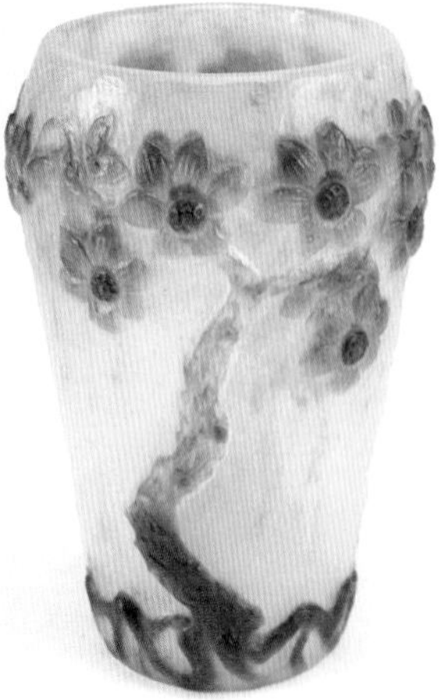

5.75in (14.5cm) high

£5,000-8,000 **DRA**

An Argy-Rousseau pâte-de-verre vase, decorated with thistles in shades of orange, purple and black on shaded black and orange ground, base impressed "FRANCE".

4in (10cm) high

£2,000-3,000 **DRA**

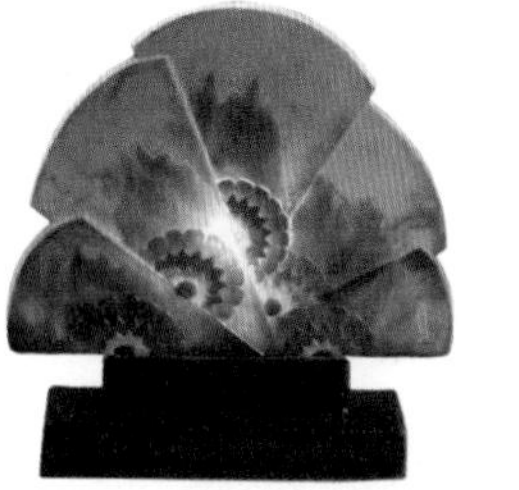

An Argy-Rousseau pâte-de-verre Art Nouveau table-top light sculpture, shaped as a fan, modelled and incised with stylized flowers in blue and green on green ground, mounted on a later wood-grain iron stand, stamped "FRANCE/G. ARGY-ROUSSEAU".

7.75in (19cm) high

£5,000-8,000 **DRA**

An Argy-Rousseau pâte-de-verre Art Nouveau table-top light sculpture, shaped as a fan, modelled and incised with stylized flowers in red and black on a purple ground, mounted on a later wood-grain iron stand, stamped "FRANCE/G. ARGY-ROUSSEAU".

7.75in (19cm) high

£5,000-8,000 **DRA**

An Argy-Rousseau box, decorated with roses, signed "G. Argy Rousseau", with minor roughness to rim of box and base.

3in (7.5cm) high

£2,500-3,000 **JDJ**

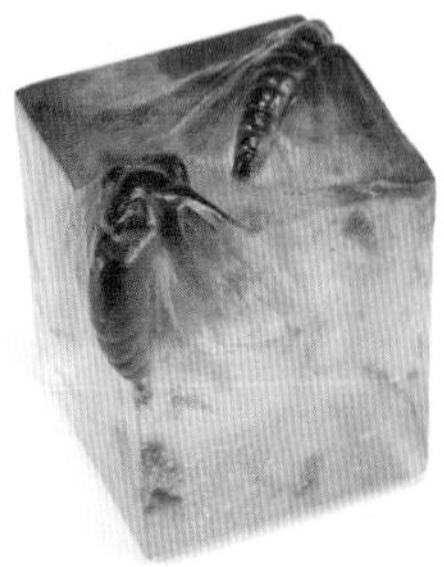

An Argy-Rousseau pâte-de-cristal amber-mottled paperweight, moulded with two black-bodied moths, moulded signature.

2.5in (6.5cm) wide

£2,500-3,000 **DRA**

A CLOSER LOOK AT AN ARGY-ROUSSEAU VASE

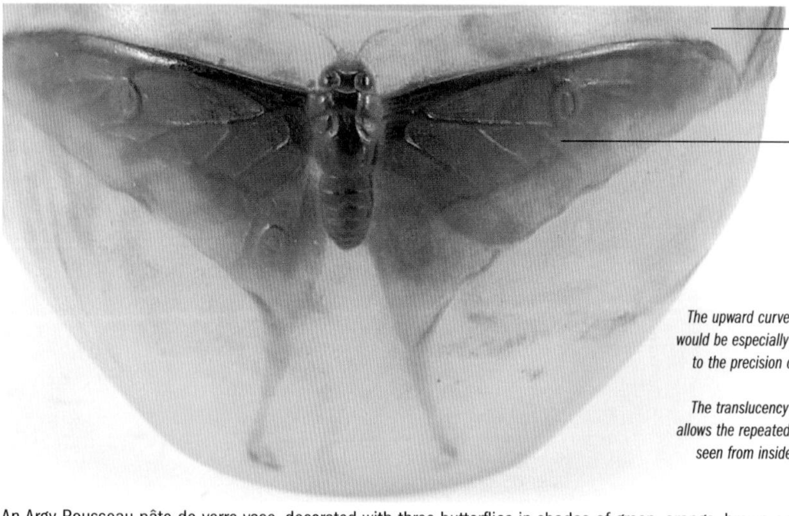

The complexity of the design and precise use of colour here demands highly skilled workmanship and justifies the high price that collectors are willing to pay for a carefully crafted piece, signed by an expert glassmaker.

The butterfly motif represents the natural world reflected in most Art Nouveau design.

The upward curve of the vase would be especially challenging to the precision of the motif.

The translucency of the body allows the repeated motif to be seen from inside, as well as externally.

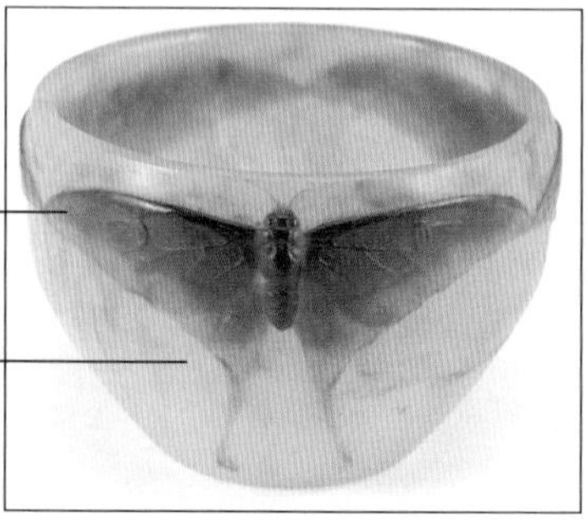

An Argy-Rousseau pâte-de-verre vase, decorated with three butterflies in shades of green, orange, brown and black on pale green mottled ground, moulded signature.

The pâte-de-verre, or glass paste, technique was developed by the Egyptians and revived in France in the late 19thC. A mould is filled with crushed glass, coloured with metal oxides and heated to fuse the glass. It is then hand-finished.

3in (7.5cm) diam

£6,000-9,000 **DRA**

SCHNEIDER & LE VERRE FRANÇAIS

- The Schneider factory was established in c1920 by Ernest (1877-1937) and Charles Schneider (1881-1953) and became a major producer of marvered, bubbled and cameo glass.
- Charles was the main designer but the company also used etched patterns from Gustav Hoffman and Maurice Dufrene in the early 1920s.
- Gallé's artists worked from Schneider's glassworks when the Gallé factory burned down in 1918. During this time Charles Schneider learned the marquetrie-de-verre technique.
- High end, luxury glass was marked "Schneider". Originally cheaper, moulded pieces were marked "Le Verre Français" or "Charder", in an attempt to popularize art glass. However, by 1921, acid-etched cameo vases and lamps were produced under these brands. With their rich range of contrasting colours, developed by the company's chemists Babille and Granger, they were technically more advanced than the earlier ware.
- The relief designs on Schneider cameo vases were flat, unlike the graduated layers of cameo created by Gallé and Daum, and the surface was often partly satin-finished, partly polished. Major designs include simple shapes with stylized, semi-abstract natural motifs such as flowers or spiky patterns.
- Following legal action against a rival, Schneider went bankrupt in 1938. Charles' sons, Charles and Robert, set up a small factory in 1946 called Cristallerie Schneider which ran until the brothers retired in 1981.

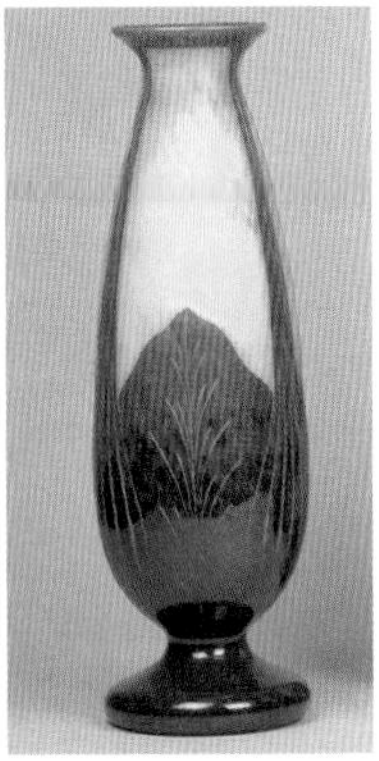

A Schneider floor vase, in clear glass with dense yellow inclusions, outside with red-violet marble-effect, frosted ground, cut signature "Le Verre Francais" on base.

c1925 *22.5in (56cm) high*

£2,200-2,800 **DOR**

A Schneider flared vase, with ball-knop stem and round base, cased red and clear glass with swirling red and blue inclusions, signed "Schneider" on base.

c1925 *11.5in (29.5 cm) high*

£1,000-1,500 **VZ**

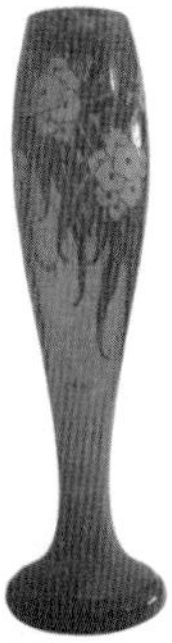

A large Schneider Art Deco cameo glass vase, signed, "Le Verre Francais" on the base, and below the floral design, "Charder".

A grand example of one of the vases in the elite line of glassware designed by Charles Schneider.

c1925 *28in (71cm) high*

£4,000-6,000 **DD**

A Schneider glass vase, clear glass with orange and purple and yellow inclusions, transparent overlay, signed "Schneider".

c1925 *17.75in (44.5cm) high*

£1,000-1,500 **HERR**

A Schneider Art Deco acid-etched geometric vase, signed, "Le Verrer Francais" on the contrasting black pedestal base.

c1925 *9in (23cm) high*

£4,000-6,000 **DD**

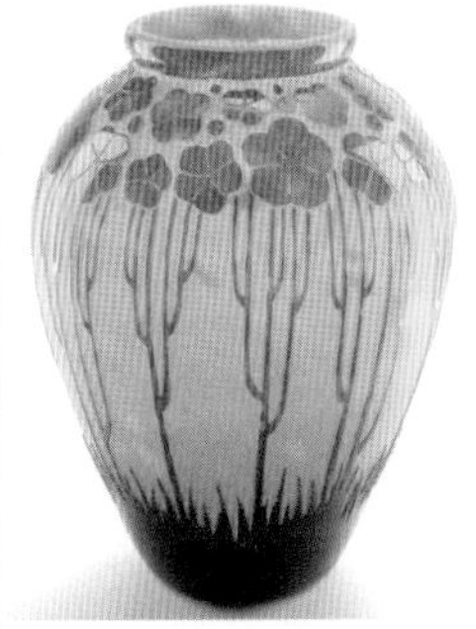

A Schneider glass vase, with orange and yellow inclusions, overlaid in red and brown, etched and polished Caramine decoration, signed "Le Verre Francais".

c1925 *9.25in (23cm) high*

£1,200-1,800 **HERR**

A large Schneider ovoid art glass vase, with green inclusions on a red ground.

18.5in (47cm) high

£600-900 **DN**

A Schneider table lamp, the clear glass with yellow and orange inclusions, overlaid in dark brown, decorated with etched stylized vases with fruit, matted ground, iron mounting, signed "Le Verre Francais" to foot.

c1925 *21.5in (54cm) high*

£4,000-6,000 **DOR**

A Schneider table lamp shade, the clear glass underlaid in yellow, overlaid in orange-blue, with etched geometrical floral decoration, matted ground, the black iron foot decorated with vines.

c1925 *17.5in (43.5cm) high*

£1,200-1,800 **DOR**

A gilt bronze table lamp, by C. Ranc, the frosted shade by Schneider, signed "C. Ranc", shade signed "Schneider".

c1925 *14.8in (37cm) high*

£2,500-3,000 **DOR**

An Art Nouveau footed vase, attributed to Schneider, with etched and enamelled decoration on frosted ground, unmarked.

c1900 *5.25in (13cm) high*

£300-500 **DRA**

A Le Verre Francais cameo glass footed bowl, decorated with brown trumpet-form flowers on mottled and shaded orange and yellow ground, raised on brown, round footed base, signed on base.

10.5in (26.5cm) high

£1,800-2,200 **SK**

A Le Verre Francais Art Deco mottled glass vase, of ovoid form, with a graduating blue body, overlaid in dark amethyst and cut with a stylized geometric motif, etched signature at base.

12in (30.5cm) high

£1,500-2,000 **ISA**

A large Le Verre Francais cameo vase, decorated with flying geese, signed "Le Verre Francais".

17in (43cm) high

£2,000-3,000 **JDJ**

A Le Verre Francais Art Deco glass tall vase, decorated with vertical stylized berried branches in green, mottled orange and brown on frosted ground, applied 'candy cane' signature.

19.5in (49cm) high

£1,800-2,200 **DRA**

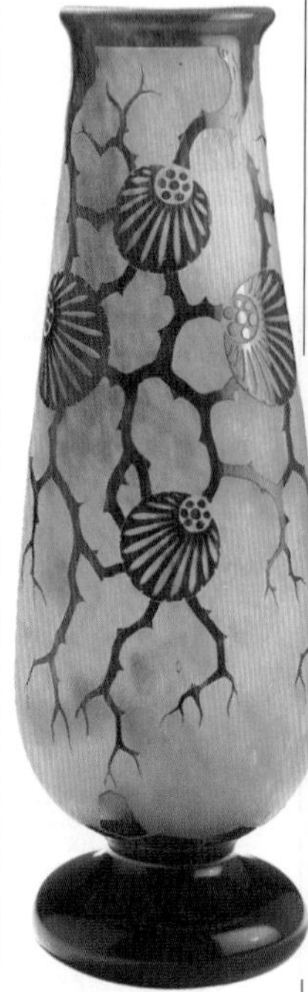

A Le Verre Francais Art Deco glass tall vase, patterned with stylized Japanese blossoms in red over mottled orange ground, engraved "Le Verre Francais".

19in (47.5cm) high

£1,200-1,800 **DRA**

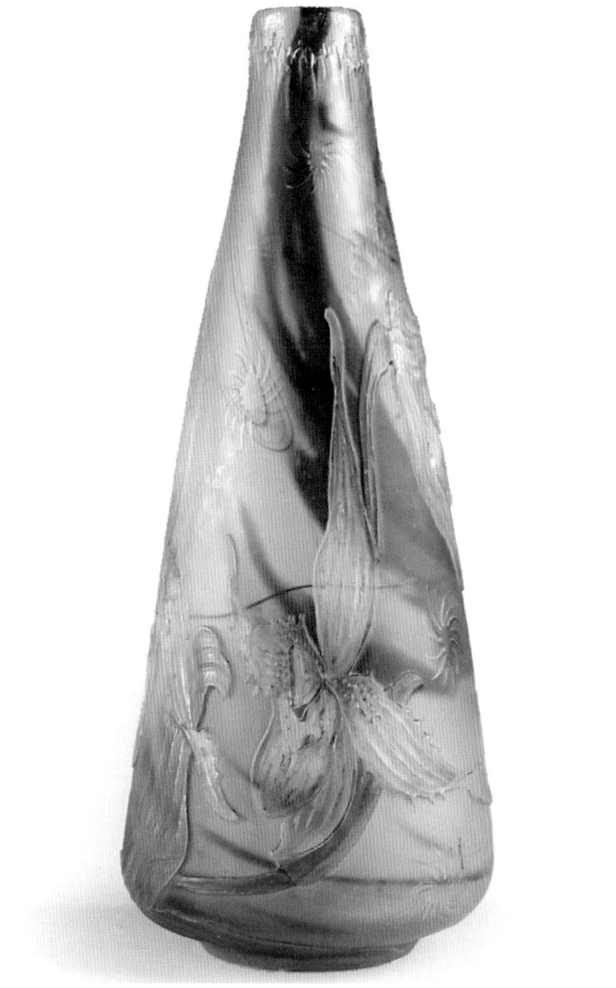

A Burgun Schverer cameo vase, decorated with lady slipper orchids, with internal decoration, signed "BS & Co Verrerie D'Art Delorraine Depose".

12in (30.5cm) high

£8,000-12,000 **JDJ**

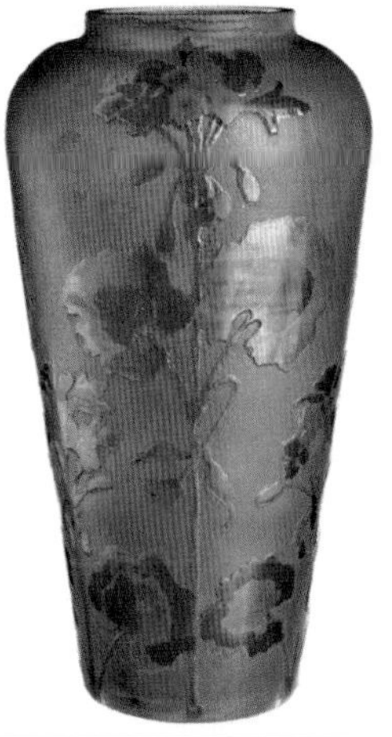

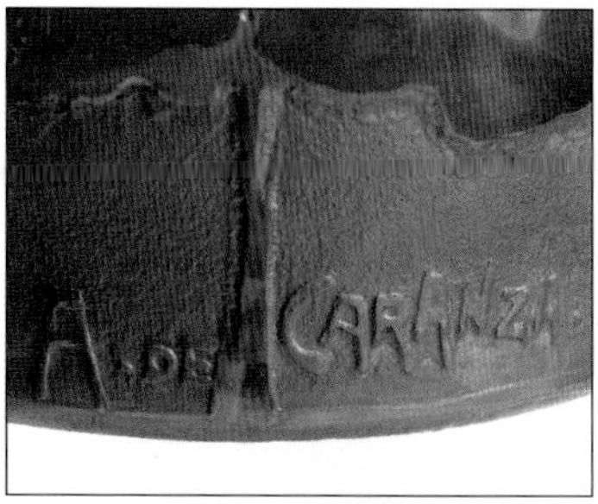

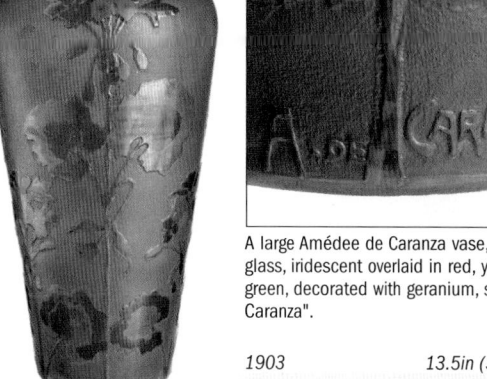

A large Amédee de Caranza vase, in clear glass, iridescent overlaid in red, yellow and green, decorated with geranium, signed "A. de Caranza".

1903 *13.5in (33.5cm) high*

£2,500-3,000 **KAU**

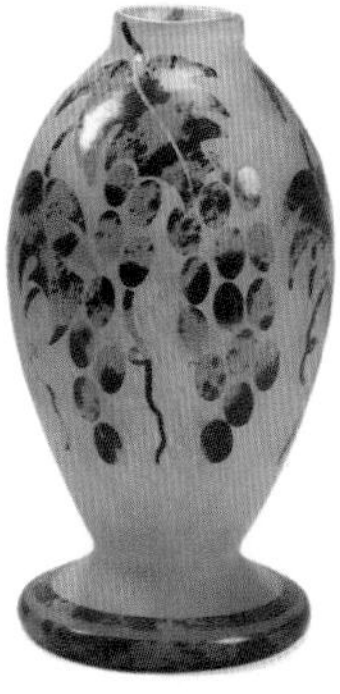

An early 20thC monumental Degue cameo glass vase, cameo-etched decoration of grapes, leaves and tendrils on a peach ground, signed.

The 1920s were a boom time for French glassmakers and many, including Degue, used mechanical production techniques to emulate top designs by Lalique, Daum and other major art glass manufacturers.

19.5in (49.5cm) high

£1,000-1,500 **SK**

A monumental Degue cameo glass vase, decorated with orange sunflowers shaded to brown with a mottled pink ground, signed on side, inscribed "Made in France" to base.

18in (45.5cm) high

£700-1,000 **SK**

A large Degue glass vase, with mottled purple, pink and orange body, dark purple foot and applied handles, signed.

14.25in (36cm) high

£400-600 **SK**

A Degue Art Deco glass tall vase, in mottled blue, with original wrought-iron foot, engraved "Degue".

16.25in (40.5cm) high

£250-300 **DRA**

A French frosted cameo glass bowl, by Legras, with silver band and decorated with fruiting vines.

5.5in (14cm) diam

£200-250 **JN**

A Legras Art Deco glass vase, with peridot-coloured acid-etched decoration, signed at base.

c1925 *8.5in (22cm) high*

£1,200-1,800 **DD**

A Muller Frères owl cameo ewer, decorated with a forest scene, the front of the ewer with a blue cameo tree limb with a dark red cameo owl, with applied clear amber glass handle, signed on base "Muller Croismare".

11in (28cm) high

£6,000-9,000 **JDJ**

A Muller Frères glass and wrought iron table lamp and shade, acid-etched "Muller Fres Luneville".

Founded in 1895, Muller Frères was run by two brothers who had worked for Gallé. Their work is comparable to Schneider in quality and appearance. The factory closed in 1936.

25.25in (64cm) high

£1,500-2,000 **WW**

A Cristalerie de Pantin cameo glass vase, decorated with rose-coloured fuchsia flowers and leaves against an opaque ground, signed on base "Cristallerie de Panton", imperfections.

6.5in (16.5cm) high

£300-500 **SK**

A Cristalerie de Pantin cameo glass vase, decorated with rose-coloured flowers executed in two layers on an opaque ground, signed to the base "Cristallerie de Panton", imperfections.

13.75in (35cm) high

£500-800 **SK**

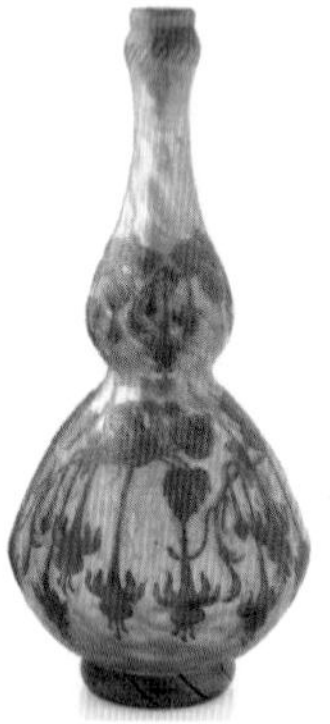

A Cristalerie de Pantin cameo glass vase knopped solifleur vase, iridescent glass body with red cameo overlay of fuchsia flowers etched "cristal de Pantin, Paris".

16.5in (41cm) high

£600-900 **WW**

A latticinio presentation vase, possibly by St Louis, the body in white spiral latticinio glass, the rims decorated in multiple colours, polished pontil, chip at base rim.

10.5in (26.5cm) high

£400-600 **SK**

A Val St.-Lambert glass vase, with abstract iridescent decoration on pale blue ground, paper label, signed "Val St-Lambert/SH".

6.5in (16cm) high

£500-800 **DRA**

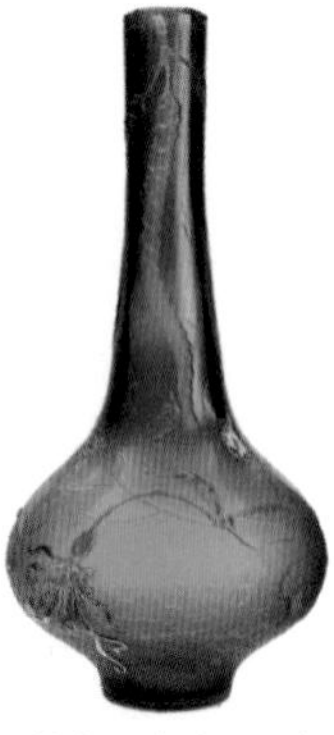

A rare Vallerysthal vase, in dark green glass, enamelled and gilded, decorated with an underwater scene with blossoms and fish, etched, signed "Vallerysthal".

c1900 *10in (25cm) high*

£800-1,200 **KAU**

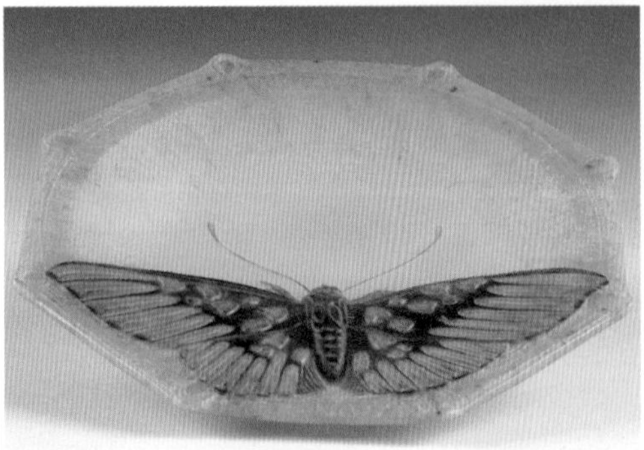

An Amalric Walter butterfly tray, with large butterfly motif, signed "A. Walter Nancy" and artist signed "Berge SC".

8.5in (21.5cm) wide

£6,000-9,000 **JDJ**

A very unusual French coloured glass pansy jug, with deep overlay of flowers.

13in (33cm) high

£280-320 **JN**

A French Art Deco frosted glass clock, moulded with pigeons, acid-etched, chips to base.

6.75in (17cm) high

£200-300 **WW**

A French glass and bronze lamp base, with dogwood blossoms on a purple ground.

13.25in (33cm) high

£400-600 **DRA**

LOETZ

- Described as 'the Austrian Tiffany', Loetz epitomizes iridescent glass in the Art Nouveau style.
- The factory was established in 1840 but became internationally renowned under Max Ritter von Spaun in the 1880s and 1890s. It exhibited at the Chicago World Fair in 1893.
- In 1906, Josef Hoffman (1870-1956) was employed as a freelance designer. He went on to become a major force in the company's designs until 1914.
- The company became insolvent in 1911 but was re-established in 1913 as Loetz-Witwe. It closed in 1948.
- Iridescent pieces, characteristically blue, have a gleaming oil-on-water effect and utilize Art Nouveau motifs such as stylized plants and feathers. 'Phanomen' glass, with its wavy internal decoration, and 'Papillon' which resembled butterfly's wings, are two of the most highly sought-after patterns.

A Loetz-Witwe 'Luna' vase, in a black wooden frame, by Josef Hoffmann for E. Bakalowits Sons, Vienna, with iridescent blue and light green coloured glass.

1899 *15.5in (38.5cm) high*

£8,000-12,000 **DOR**

A Loetz iridescent glass vase, with "Phanomen 2/177" decoration, designed by Leopold Bauer, of shouldered and baluster form with a broad blue and grey glass band.

10.5in (26cm) high

£1,000-1,500 **DN**

A Loetz-Witwe vase, by Josef Hoffmann, Klostermühle, in clear and white opaque glass, with pink etched foliate and geometric decoration.

This piece was designed on commission for the Austrian Museum of Art and Industry.

1912 *10.5in (26cm) high*

£3,000-5,000 **DOR**

A Loetz-Witwe vase, by Michael Powolny (1871-1954) for J. & L. Lobmeyr, Vienna, in grey-green glass with three applied circular medallions and putti.

c1920 *5.5in (13.5cm) high*

£1,000-1,500 **DOR**

A Loetz-Witwe 'Luna' iridescent vase, by Arno Richter, Klostermühle, with encased blue and light-green glass and four applied green drops.

This piece was designed for E. Bakalowits Sons, Vienna.

1901 *4.5in (11.5cm) high*

£2,200-2,800 **DOR**

A Loetz-Witwe 'Luna' iridescent vase by Arno Richter, for E. Bakalowits Sons, Vienna, in blue and light green glass.

1901 *3.5in (9cm) high*

£2,200-2,800 **DOR**

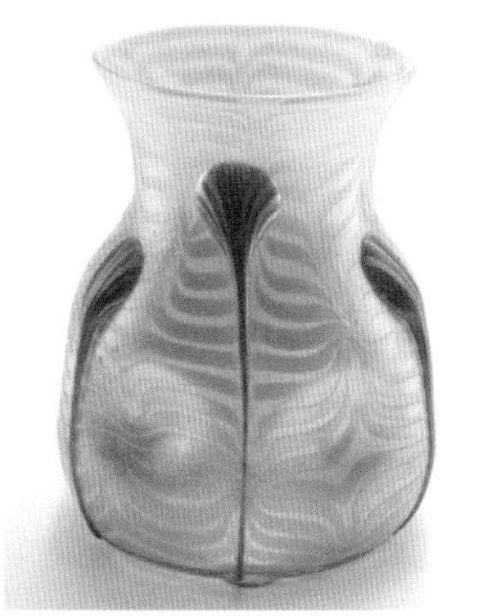

A Loetz-Witwe iridescent vase, with "Phanomen Gre 1/4" decoration and six trailing drops of brown glass, signed "Loetz Austria".

c1900 *7.25in (18cm) high*

£3,000-4,000 **HERR**

A Loetz-Witwe iridescent tulip vase, with green foot and stem, the cup underlaid in silver and decorated with 'creta rusticana', applied leaves.

Developed in 1899, 'creta rusticana' was a knotty, wood-like finish.

c1900 *9.25in (23cm) high*

£600-900 **HERR**

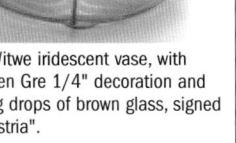

A Loetz-Witwe vase, with overlay and iridescent snake-string decoration, conical shape, signed "CZECH SLOVAKIA".

c1925 *6.5in (16cm) high*

£700-1,000 **HERR**

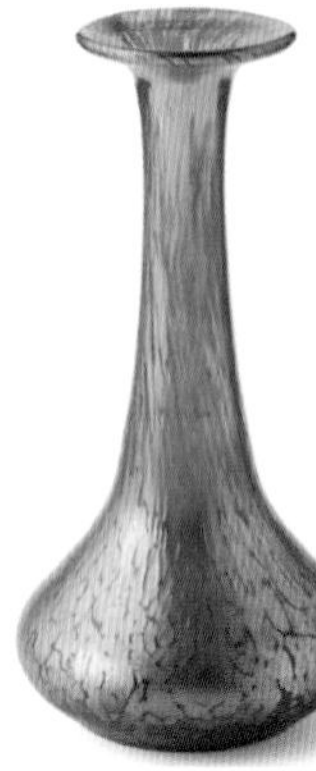

A small Loetz-Witwe green iridescent bulbous vase.

6in (15cm) high

£200-250 **JN**

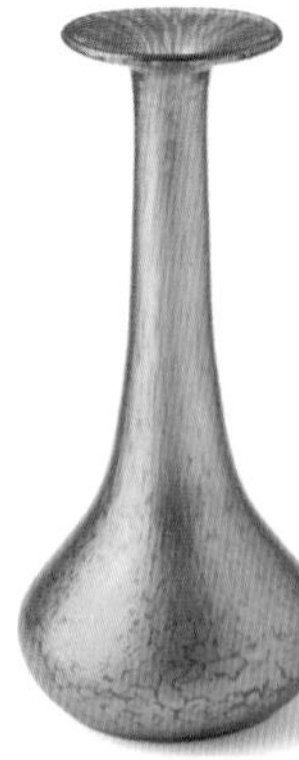

A Loetz-Witwe iridescent glass vase, of tear-shaped form with slender neck and covered overall with a vivid Cobalt Papillon lustrous sheen.

8.75in (22cm) high

£250-350 **DN**

A Loetz-Witwe silver-overlaid iridescent glass vase, of sinuous plant form with engraved silver flowers and leaves against an iridescent green glass ground, unsigned.

8.75in (22cm) high

£800-1,200 **GORL**

A Loetz-Witwe iridescent glass posy vase, of sinuous plant form with engraved silver flowers and leaves against an iridescent green glass ground, unsigned.

8.75in (22cm) high

£600-900 **GORL**

An Art Nouveau glass vase, probably Loetz, with trefoil lip, and lappet decoration in blue and white on red ground, unmarked.

6.75in (17cm) high

£700-1,000 **DRA**

A Loetz-Witwe Art Nouveau glass vase, with applied iridescent handles and blue oil-spot body.

7.5in (19cm) high

£500-800 **DRA**

A pair of Loetz glass vases, in iridescent blue and dimpled green, with green trails, unmarked.

8.5in (21cm) high

£300-500 **WW**

A Loetz squat glass vase, with trefoil rim and dimpled sides decorated with blue swirling bands on gold ground, unmarked.

4.25in (10.5cm) wide

£1,000-1,500 **DRA**

A Loetz-Witwe silver overlay titanium vase, decorated in green and cranberry with sterling silver overlay, marked "Sterling".

8.25in (21cm) high

£3,000-5,000 **JDJ**

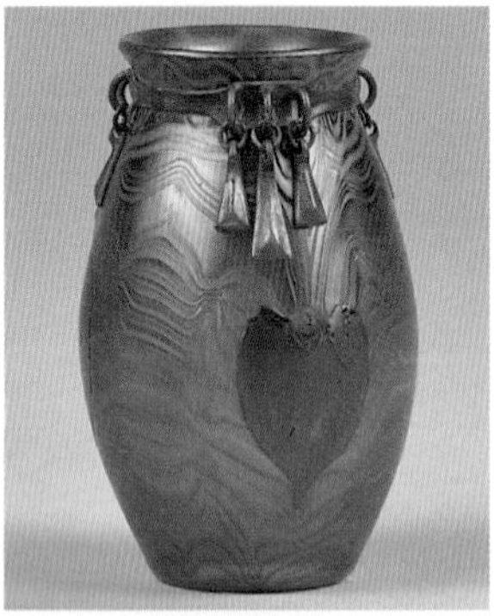

A small Loetz-Witwe vase, with silver mounting, in clear glass with red and green underlay and with two large green hearts, the neck with silver-plated brass ring.

1902 *4in (10cm) high*

£3,000-4,000 **DOR**

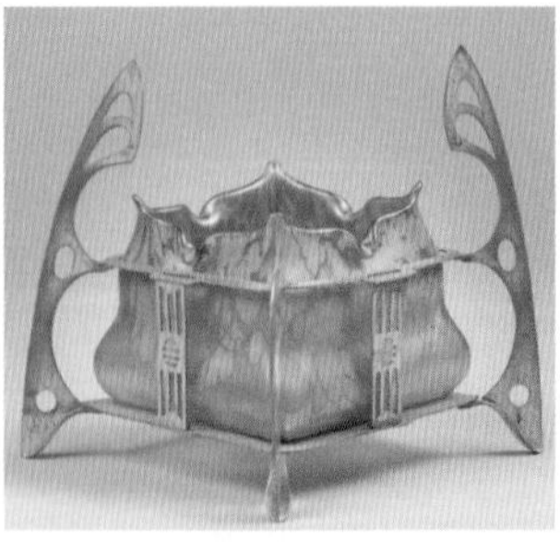

A Loetz-Witwe iridescent gilt-metal mounted vase, in brown glass with silver-yellow fused glass inclusions, the holder by Messrs. Argentor, Vienna.

1902 *10.75in (27cm) high*

£3,000-3,500 **DOR**

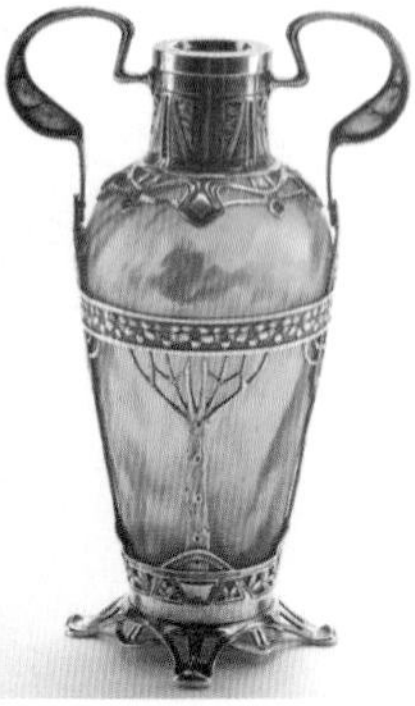

A Loetz-Witwe glass vase, overlaid in green, with open-work silver mounting and two scrolling handles, the enamel, base with four feet, marked "935".

1903 *7.5in (19cm) high*

£800-1,200 **HERR**

A WMF Ikora glass bowl, the cased clear glass with large grey and rust oxide and bubble inclusions in the form of a flower, sulphur-yellow oxide inclusions along rim.

c1930 *16.5in (41cm) diam*

£220-280 **VZ**

A WMF Ikora glass food warmer, opaque-red and clear glass, vertical oxide inclusions with fine bubbles, heating plate chromium-plated nickel silver.

c1930 *5.5in (13.5cm) diam*

£80-120 **VZ**

A WMF Ikora vase, in clear glass, inlays of dark-brown and amber, model number "E690/5027", manufacturer's label.

c1935 *16in (40cm) high*

£1,000-1,500 **HERR**

A WMF Ikora' vase, the short oval body with a flared rim, in opaque white glass with inclusions in various shades of red and green.

This may be a production sample.

c1940 *4.75in (12cm) high*

£70-100 **VZ**

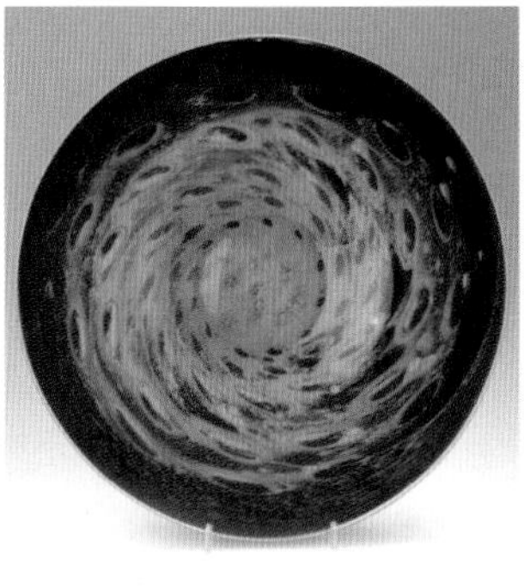

A WMF Lavaluna glass plate, the black and clear glass with swirling oxide inclusions in ochre-grey and blue with sulphur-yellow, bubble inclusions.

c1935 *12.25in (30.5cm) diam*

£150-200 **VZ**

A WMF Myra glass bowl, with vertical ribbing in the form of rosettes, matte petrol iridescence, with delicate craquelure work on rim.

c1930 *9.2in (23cm) diam*

£150-200 **VZ**

A WMF Myra glass vase, honey-coloured with matt gold iridescence, vertical ribbing on body, short neck with flared rim.

c1930 *6.2in (15.5cm)*

£150-200 **VZ**

A WMF Art Nouveau glass, Britannia metal and clear transparent glass with opaque green enamel paint, bowl with continuous wave and berry decoration, ostrich mark.

c1900 *9.75in (24.5cm) high*

£120-180 **KAU**

A WMF vase, by Walter Dexel, the thick clear glass with powder inclusions.

1935 *5.5in (14cm) high*

£180-220 **VZ**

A WMF vase, in cased clear glass with bubbles, sulphur-yellow inclusions and a fine craquelure layer of light-emerald inclusions, chips to base.

c1935 *5.5in (14cm) high*

£180-220 **VZ**

An Austrian Art Nouveau bottle-shaped vase of lustred green and purple glass in elaborate pewter mount, metal stamped "RICESZINN 642".

7in (18cm) high

£300-500 **DRA**

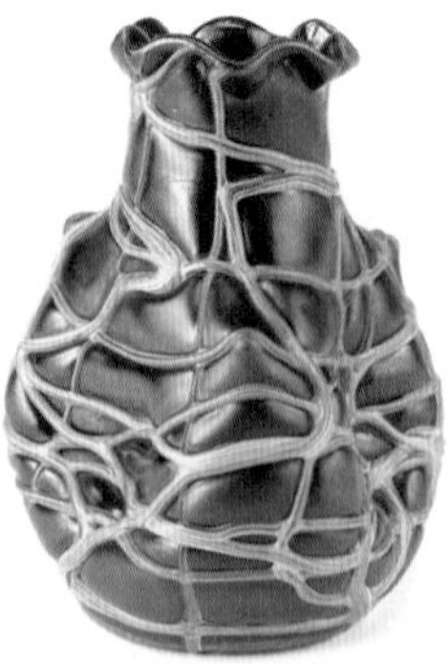

An Art glass vase, attributed to Kralik, of pinched form with threaded iridescent decoration, unmarked.

4.5in (11.5cm) high

£120-180 **DRA**

An Austrian art glass bowl, with scalloped rim and ribbed body, unmarked.

c1900 *10in (25.5cm) diam*

£300-500 **DRA**

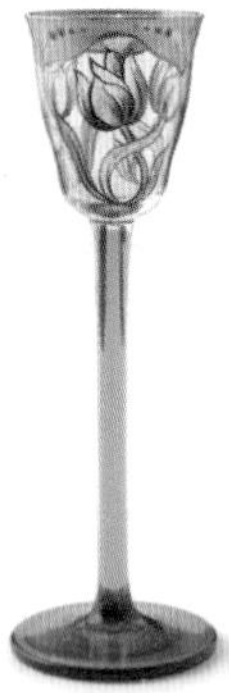

An Austro-Bohemian enamelled wine glass, the clear ogee bowl decorated with tulips beneath a gilt band, on a green glass stem and conical foot.

6.25in (15.5cm) high

£120-180 **DN**

A 1935 Czech art glass decanter set, with cordial glasses, etched and cut crystal with black enamel and canary yellow details.

decanter 9in (23cm) high

£1,200-1,800 **DD**

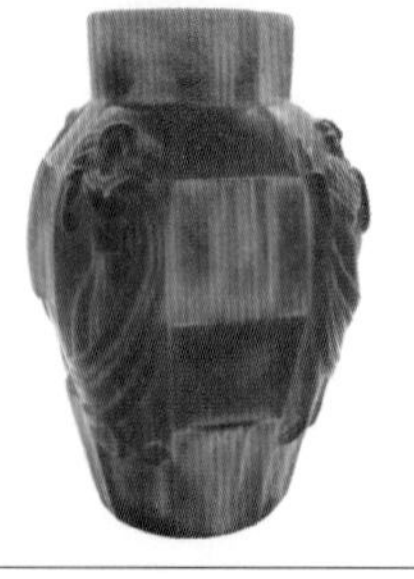

A Czech Art Deco malachite 'Ingrid' moulded glass vase, designed by Curt Schlevogt, Czechoslovakia.

1935 *10in (25.5cm) high*

£500-700 **DD**

A Czech Art Deco glass Cubist decanter set, the crystal decanter with four cordial glasses, etched and cut crystal with black enamel and silvered details.

c1935 *decanter 7in (17.75cm) high*

£1,800-2,200 **DD**

A 20thC Moser blue glass bowl, with etched and gilt decoration depicting the Greeks fighting the Amazons, signed.

12.25in (31cm) long

£300-400 **ROS**

A Moser Art Nouveau glass vase, with cut, applied and enamelled floral and insect decoration, etched signature on body.

4.75in (12cm) diam

£150-200 **DRA**

A Czech Art Deco crystal perfume atomizer, with carved blue enamel decoration.

c1930 *5in (13cm) high*

£150-200 **DD**

A crystal Art Deco perfume atomizer, cut crystal with acid etched red and yellow geometric enamel decoration.

c1930 *3.5in (9cm) high*

£500-700 **DD**

A Tiffany Favrile glass vase, decorated with stylized tendrils in gold on blue ground, engraved "Louis C. Tiffany D2898".

5in (12.5cm) high

£1,500-2,000 **DRA**

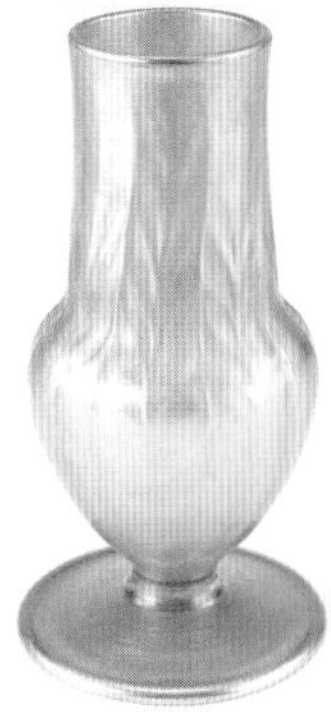

A Tiffany gold Favrile glass footed vase with quilted, swelling body and applied base with folded foot, engraved "L.C. Tiffany Inc. Favrile 1559", paper label.

8in (20.5cm) high

£700-1,000 **DRA**

A CLOSER LOOK AT A TIFFANY FAVRILE VASE

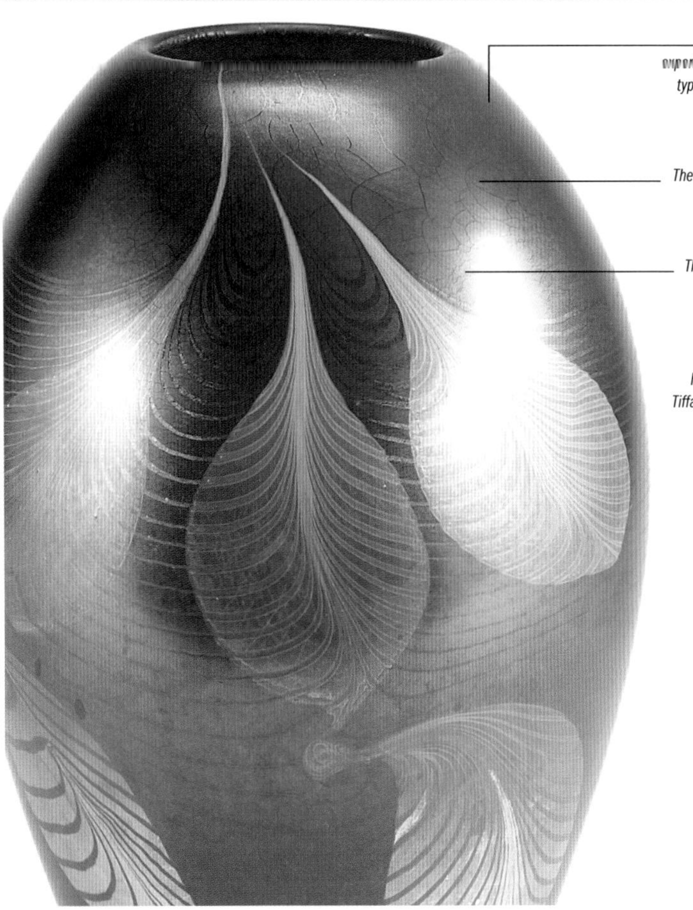

Louis Comfort Tiffany (1848-1933) experimented widely, creating over 5,000 new types of glass. He was probably best known for his 'Favrile' iridescent glass, patented in 1894.
The iridescent effect is achieved by spraying the surface of molten glass with metallic lustres.
The pulled-feather technique, one of many technically demanding decorative motifs Tiffany used, was created by pulling and marvering hot glass onto the surface.
Famed for his innovative plant-like forms, Tiffany chose simpler vase shapes to display his more elaborate finishes.

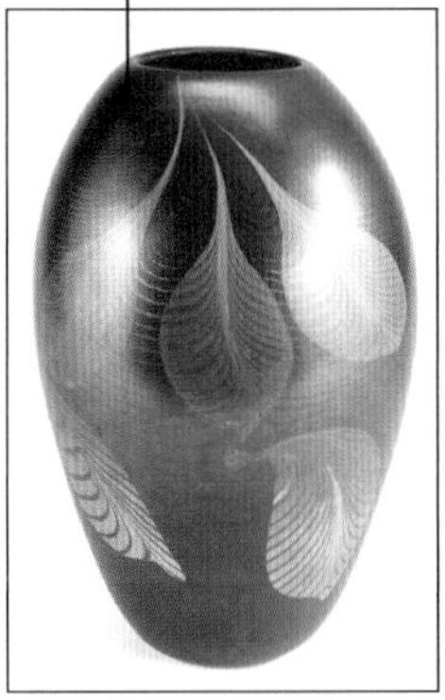

An early Tiffany Favrile glass vase, with green and blue leaves in pulled-feather pattern on a lustred cobalt and indigo ground, etched "Louis C. Tiffany, D259", scratches.

17.75in (45cm) high

£18,000-20,000 **DRA**

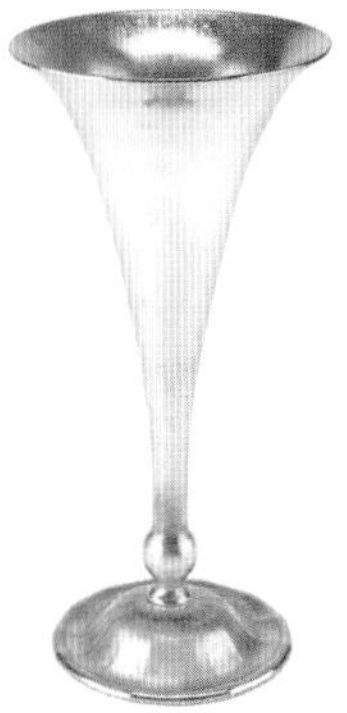

A Tiffany gold Favrile glass trumpet vase, with lower knop and applied ribbed spreading base with folded foot, water staining to interior, engraved "L.C. Tiffany Favrile 9??D".

13.75in (35cm) high

£1,000-1,500 **DRA**

A Tiffany gold Favrile glass trumpet vase, with lower knop and applied ribbed spreading base with folding foot, engraved "L.C. Tiffany Favrile 1534-2692 M".

12.25in (31cm) high

£1,000-1,500 **DRA**

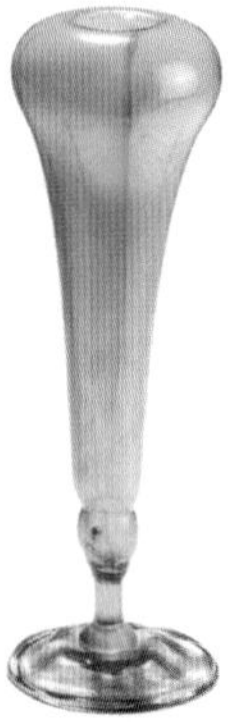

A Tiffany Favrile glass floriform vase, with green pulled-feather decoration on gold and opalescent ground, engraved "L.C.T. W 3270".

9.5in (24cm) high

£1,200-1,800 **DRA**

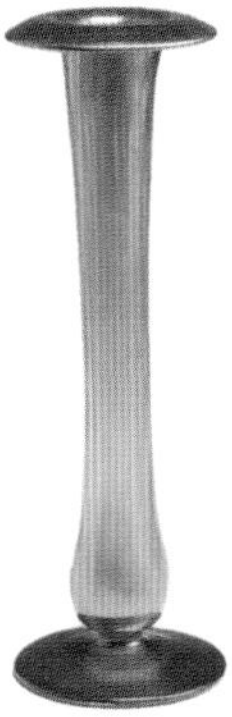

A Tiffany gold Favrile ribbed glass bud vase, with flaring rim, etched "1730 L.C. Tiffany Favrile".

10in (25cm) high

£700-1,000 **DRA**

A L.C. Tiffany favrile glass bud vase, with gold feathers on verre-de-soie ground, etched "L.C. Tiffany Favrile 1502 - 9507L".

10in (25cm) high

£800-1,200 **DRA**

A Tiffany tall bud vase, with a Favrile glass tube in amber feathered pattern in a bronze and brass base with swirls, original patina, "TIFFANY STUDIOS NEW YORK 711".

14in (35cm) high

£1,500-2,000 **DRA**

A Tiffany gold Favrile glass saucier, with applied handle, engraved "L.C. Tiffany - Favrile, 4292E".

5in (13cm) long

£200-300 **DRA**

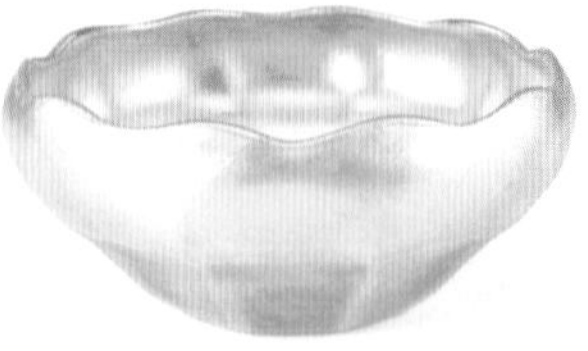

A Tiffany gold Favrile glass scalloped bowl, engraved "LCT Favrile 4479M".

8.25in (21cm) diam

£300-500 **DRA**

A Tiffany Favrile glass footed bowl with diamond quilted centre and pastel glass rim, engraved "L.C. Tiffany Inc. Favrile 1561".

9.5in (24cm) diam

£500-800 **DRA**

A Tiffany gold Favrile glass creamer and salt, creamer engraved "L.C.T. Favrile", salt unmarked.

creamer 2.75in (7cm) high

£250-300 **DRA**

An early Tiffany Favrile glass globe, decorated with gold swirls on green ground, mounted on an Etruscan-style tripod base of the same period, unmarked.

18.5in (46cm) high

£1,500-2,000 **DRA**

A Tiffany lamp, with damascene shade.

15.5in (39.5cm) high

£3,000-4,000 **FRE**

A Tiffany lamp, of lily form with three lights.

11.5in (29cm) high

£2,000-3,000 **FRE**

A Tiffany bronze desk or hanging lamp, with a shell-form shade, stamped "Tiffany Studios New York 797".

11in (28cm) high

£3,000-5,000 **FRE**

A rare Tiffany Favrile glass and metal picture frame, bordered by blue and green panels of Favrile glass in blackened metal mount, impressed with Tiffany Glass and Decoration Company symbol.

10.25in (26cm) high

£4,000-6,000 **DRA**

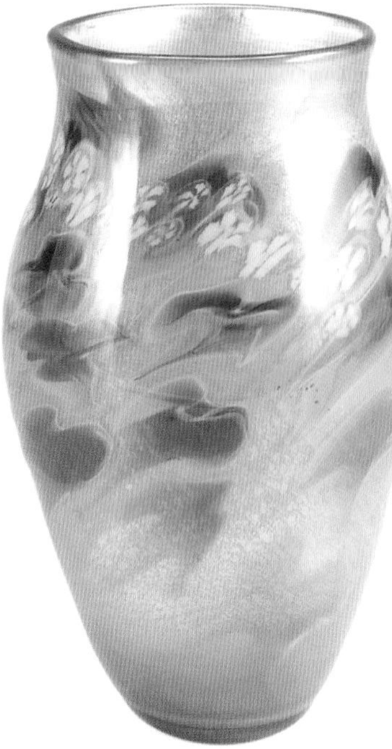

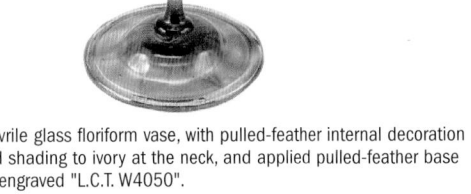

An L.C. Tiffany paperweight vase, with millefiore decoration in ivory and yellow with green leaves on a gold ground, marked "L.C.T./U/5135".

8.25in (21cm) high

£5,000-8,000 **DRA**

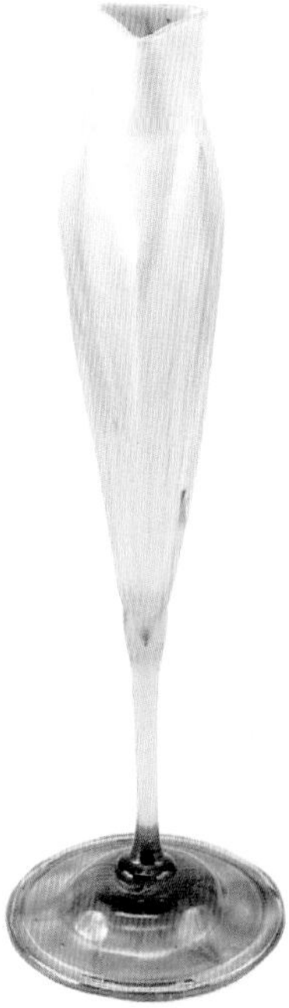

An L.C. Tiffany Favrile glass floriform vase, with pulled-feather internal decoration in green and gold shading to ivory at the neck, and applied pulled-feather base with folded foot, engraved "L.C.T. W4050".

13in (33cm) high

£3,000-5,000 **DRA**

A rare pair of L.C. Tiffany gold Favrile glass candlesticks, the bobeches applied to ribbed stems on ribbed bases with folded feet, engraved "L.C.T. Favrile 1825".

12in (30.5cm) high

£2,500-3,000 **DRA**

A L.C. Tiffany gold Favrile glass covered jar, with two rows of lappets, jar etched "L.C.T. 1681.W", lid etched "M 7891".

9.5in (24cm) high

£10,000-12,000 **DRA**

A Pairpoint Rosaria glass vase, decorated with the Lincoln pattern, with clear glass block base.

c1915 *13.5in (34.5cm) high*

£1,000-1,500 **BRK**

A Pairpoint cobalt twirl vase.

c1925 *10in (25.5cm) high*

£300-500 **BRK**

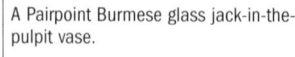

A Pairpoint Burmese glass jack-in-the-pulpit vase.

c1925 *7in (18cm) wide*

£200-300 **BRK**

A Pairpoint Burmese glass vase, with crimped rim.

c1925 *10.25in (26cm) high*

£300-500 **BRK**

A pair of Pairpoint ruby glass cornucopia vases, with paperweight bases.

The paperweight is a device often used by Pairpoint.

c1945 *7.25in (18.5cm) high*

£120-180 **BRK**

A Pairpoint Flambeau glass vase.

This rare range was supposedly made for the Christmas season. Production problems meant that few examples survive. A similar range by Steuben, known as 'Rouge Flambé' is even rarer and more valuable.

c1925 *9in (23cm) high*

£500-800 **BRK**

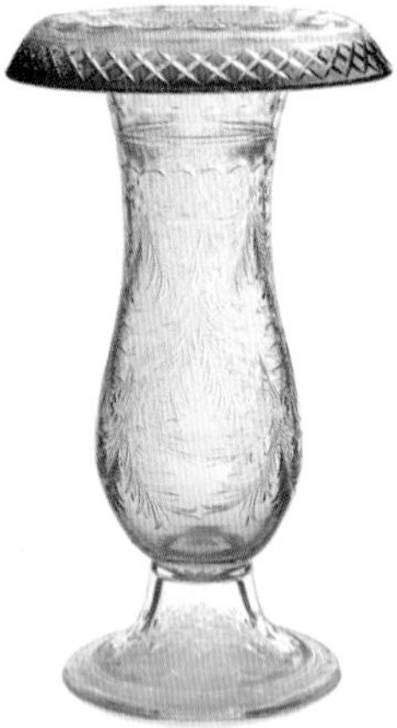

A Pairpoint Darlington pattern glass vase, with everted rim.

12.5in (32cm) high

£500-800 **BRK**

A Pairpoint Fine Arts covered glass vase, with silver-plated mounts including pineapple finial and horned satyr mask handles.

The Fine Arts range was one of Pairpoint's most prestigious lines.

c1925 *13in (33cm) high*

£1,200-1,800 **BRK**

A Pairpoint Fine Arts cut glass dish, on an onyx base and a stand supported by putti, with glass ball.

c1925 *11.75in (30cm) diam*

£1,000-1,500 **BRK**

A Pairpoint Marina blue tazza, cut with the 'Colias' pattern depicting wheat stems and a butterfly caught in a web.

c1915 *8in (20.5cm) wide*

£400-600 **BRK**

A Pairpoint Flambeau glass tazza and candlestick set, with silver overlay, possibly by Rockwell.

c1925 *12in (30.5cm) high*

£2,000-3,000 **BRK**

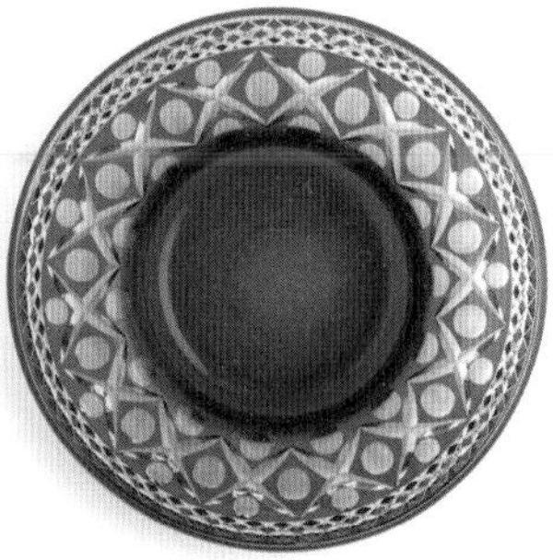

A Pairpoint cobalt blue glass covered tazza, with a pattern of fruiting vines done in silver resist.

c1925 *9.5in (24cm) high*

£250-350 **BRK**

A Pairpoint Amethyst glass covered compote, with Vintage pattern.

c1925 *7in (18cm) wide*

£300-400 **BRK**

A Pairpoint Amethyst glass covered compote, with Vintage pattern.

c1925 *7in (18cm) wide*

£300-400 **BRK**

A Pairpoint Flambeau glass covered bonbon dish.

c1925 *7in (18cm) high*

£800-1,200 **BRK**

A Pairpoint Black Amethyst glass bonbon dish, with upturned foot rim.

c1925 *5.5in (14cm) high*

£100-150 **BRK**

A Pairpoint Black Amethyst glass decanter.

c1925 *10in (25.5cm) high*

£300-400 **BRK**

A pair of Pairpoint Venetti candlesticks, with latticino twist stems and swag design to sconces.

c1915 *10.25in (26cm) high*

£1,500-2,000 **BRK**

A pair of Pairpoint Venetti candlesticks, with looped latticino twist stems.

c1915 *6.5in (16.5cm) high*

£1,200-1,800 **BRK**

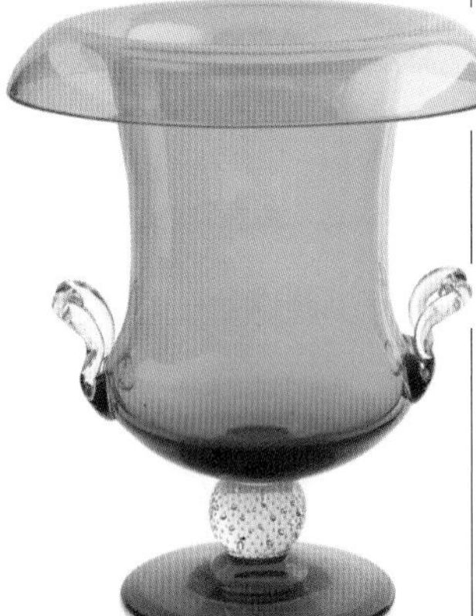

A Pairpoint Marina blue glass two-handled urn.

c1915 *12in (30.5cm) high*

£200-400 **BRK**

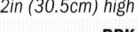

GUNDERSON PAIRPOINT

- As the centre of the American art glass industry, New Bedford attracted master glassblowers from across Europe.
- Robert Gunderson trained at Hadelands Glassworks in Norway. He emigrated to America and became a key player at New Bedford's biggest glassworks.
- When the Pairpoint Corporation ran into financial difficulties in the 1930s, inventor and entrepreneur Isaac Babbit rescued the firm and appointed Gunderson as chief glass blower.
- During this period the plant was known as Gunderson Glassworks, and the glass was shipped with silver labels marked "Gunderson Masterpiece".
- Glass artists such as Ciro Angelini designed original shapes that were retailed through prestigious outlets such as Tiffany & Co.
- During the 1950s Gunderson Pairpoint re-issued classic designs from the Peachblow, Burmese and Rose Amber ranges originally made by Mount Washington.
- Robert Gunderson died in 1952, and the New Bedford factory finally closed in December 1956.

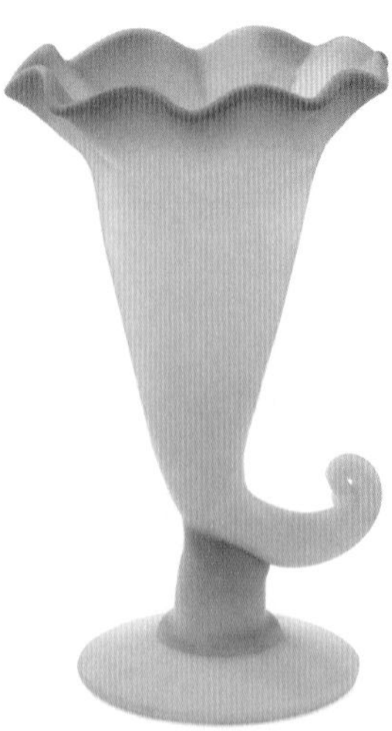

A Gunderson Peachblow glass cornucopia vase.

c1945 *6.75in (17cm) high*

£150-200 **BRK**

A Gunderson Peachblow glass vinegar cruet.

Gunderson glass is heavy in relation to other American 19thC art glass.

c1945 *7.75in (19.5cm) high*

£300-400 **BRK**

A Gunderson Peachblow glass cup and saucer.

c1945 *5in (12.5cm) diam*

£200-250 **BRK**

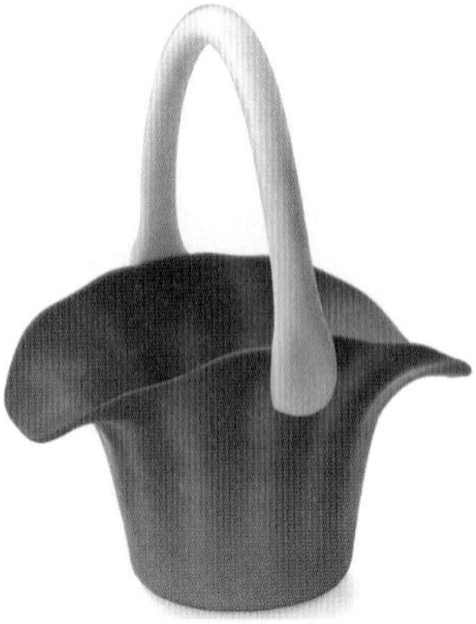

A Gunderson Peachblow glass basket, with applied handle.

c1945 *9.75in (25cm) high*

£500-800 **BRK**

A Gunderson ruby glass pitcher, with clear base and handle.

c1945 *13.5in (34.5cm) high*

£80-120 **BRK**

A Gunderson glass swan, in marina blue.

The influence of Portuguese workers at Gunderson Pairpoint led to Latin-sounding names for some of the colours, such as Marina and Rosaria.

c1945 *9in (23cm) high*

£200-300 **BRK**

A unique pair of Gunderson clear glass candlesticks, by Ciro Angelini, with applied leaves to sconces.

These candlesticks were made by Ciro Angelini for his own house.

c1935 *11.5in (29cm) high*

£1,000-1,500 **BRK**

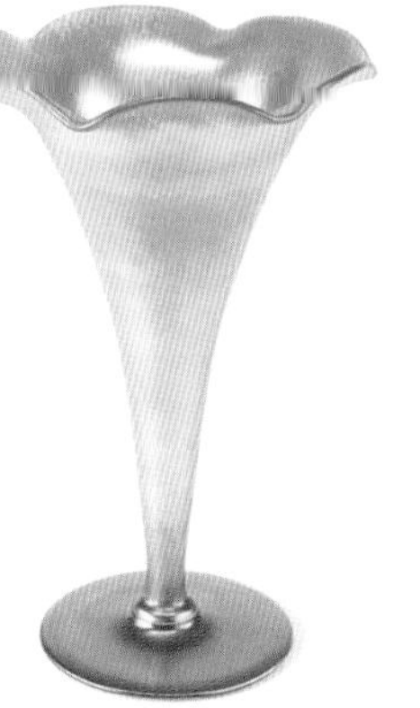

A Steuben Gold Aurene glass trumpet vase, with lily ruffled rim and applied, plain foot, engraved "Aurene 346".

10in (25.5cm) high

£700-900 **DRA**

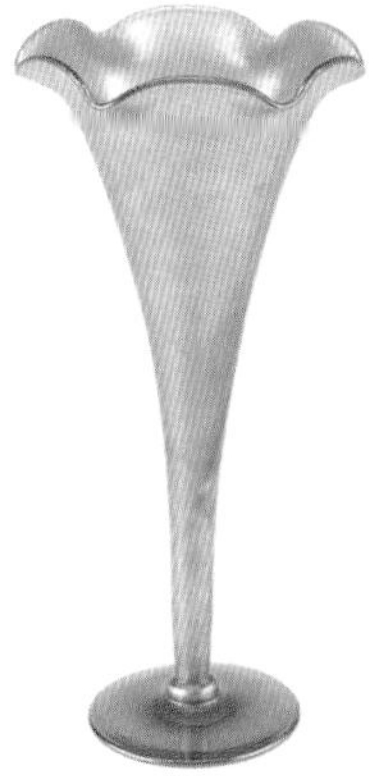

A Steuben Gold Aurene glass trumpet vase, with lily ruffled rim and applied, plain foot, engraved "Aurene 346".

12in (30.5cm) high

£800-1,200 **DRA**

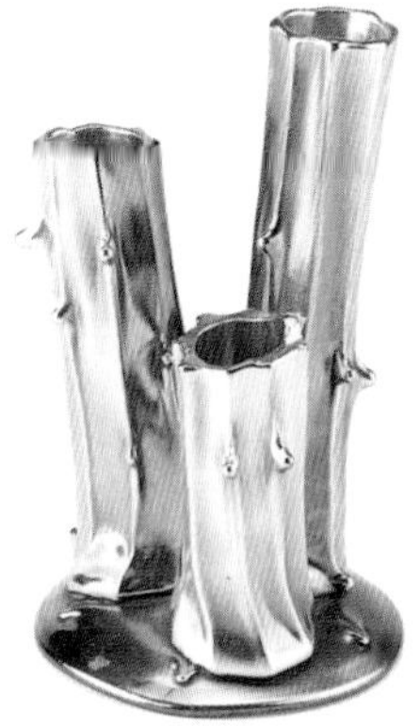

A Steuben Gold Aurene glass rustic tree stump vase, engraved "Steuben Aurene 2749".

6.25in (16cm) high

£300-500 **DRA**

A Steuben Gold Aurene glass vase, engraved "Steuben Aurene".

6.5in (16.5cm) high

£300-500 **DRA**

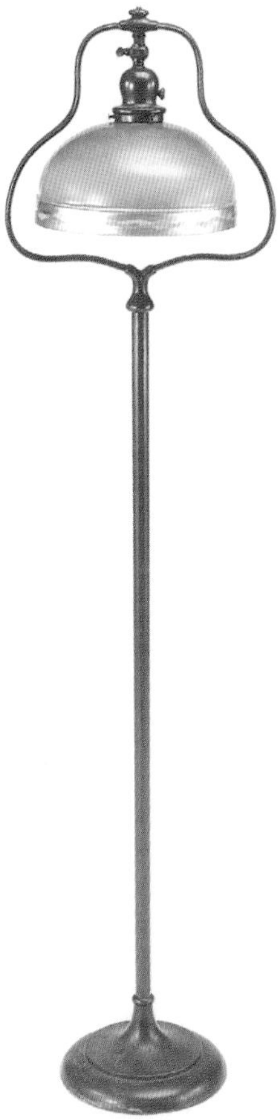

A Steuben/Handel brown Aurene glass domical shade with applied internally decorated intarsia rim and Calcite interior on a Handel bronzed metal harp floor lamp base with plain foot, unmarked.

58in (147.5cm) high

£1,800-2,200 **DRA**

A Steuben Rosaline glass spherical vase with acid-cut back blossoms and branches on pink and frosted ground, original retailer's label.

6.5in (16.5cm) diam

£500-800 **DRA**

A Roycroft/Steuben hammered copper single-socket table lamp, with Steuben gold Aurene flaring ribbed shade, original patina to base, new patina to cap, base stamped orb and cross mark, shade unmarked.

18.5in (47cm) high

£1,500-2,000 **DRA**

A Steuben Calcite shade desk lamp, decorated with millefiore and pulled-feather decorations, gold Aurene interior, on unmarked period bronzed metal harp base, shade with stencilled fleur-de-lys signature.

10.25in (26cm) high

£500-800 **DRA**

A set of six Steuben gold Aurene glass waisted and ribbed lamp shades, stencilled Fleur-De-Lys marks, chips to one.

5.25in (13.5cm) diam

£700-1,000 **DRA**

Three Steuben jade glass perfume bottles, a tall pair with dauber stoppers, and a pale green bottle, stencilled marks and paper label.

tallest 10.25in (25.5cm) high

£700-1,000 **DRA**

A pair of Steuben blue Aurene glass candlesticks, the bobeches on applied spiral twisted stems and plain spreading feet, engraved "Aurene 989".

8in (20.5cm) high

£1,000-1,500 **DRA**

A Durand glass vase, decorated with white swirling pattern on iridescent gold ground, engraved "Durand 1974-15".

Victor Durand Jnr. trained at Baccarat in France before taking over the Vineland Glass Manufacturing Co. in New Jersey, USA. Art glass production ceased when Durand died in 1931.

c1915 *14.25in (35.5cm) high*

£1,200-1,800 **DRA**

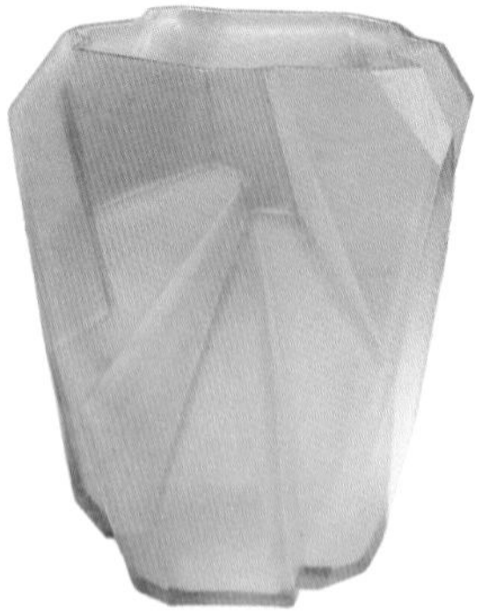

A Consolidated Art Glass Co. 'Rhuba' rhombic pale green glass vase, unmarked.

9.25in (23cm) high

£800-1,200 **DRA**

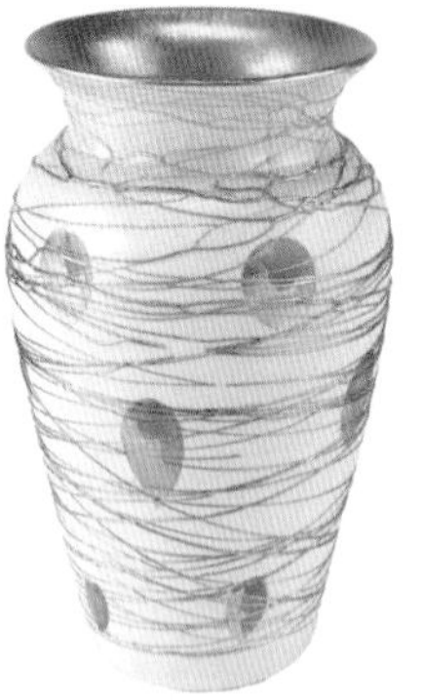

A Durand glass vase with heart-shaped gold and blue leaves and gold threading on a mother-of-pearl ground, marked "DURAND", threading damage.

c1815 *7.75in (19.5cm) high*

£500-800 **DRA**

A Durand iridescent glass vase.

c1925 *6in (15cm) high*

£600-900 **BRK**

A Durand gold iridescent vase, shape number 1978.

c1925 *8.25in (21cm) high*

£500-800 **BRK**

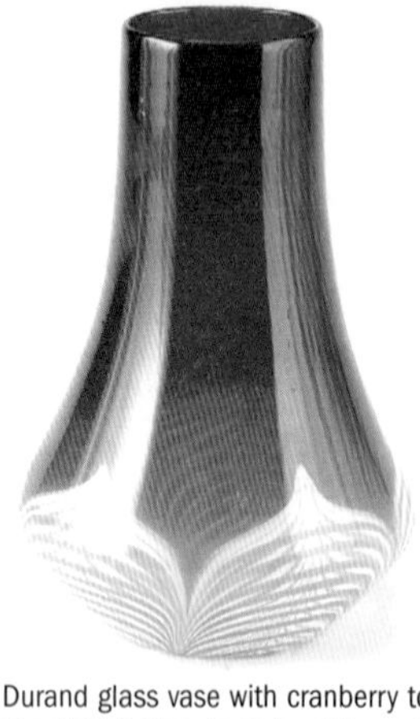

A Durand glass vase with cranberry top and pulled-feather base in white and pink, engraved "Durand 1907", interior water staining.

9.75in (25cm) high

£500-800 **DRA**

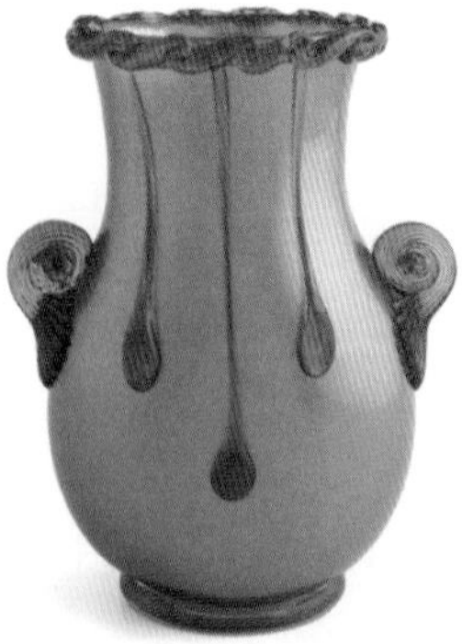

A Farrall Venetian-cut aventurine glass vase.

This vase has been exhibited in the Smithsonian.

8.5in (21.5cm) high

£1,000-1,500 **BRK**

A Fenton Karnak vase.

7.75in (19.5cm) high

£2,000-3,000 **BRK**

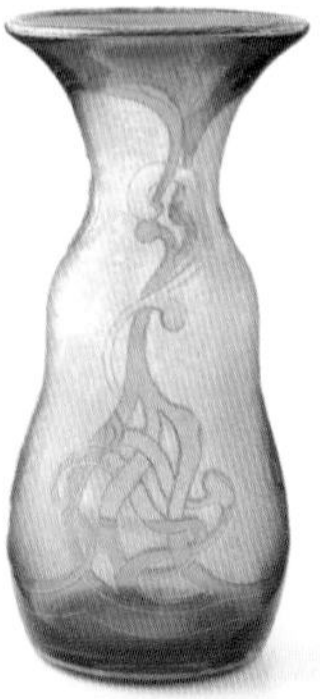

A Honesdale cameo glass vase.

Honesdale bought in blanks from other companies and specialized in decorating.

c1915 *10in (25.5cm) high*

£200-250 **BRK**

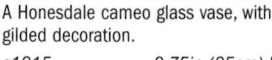

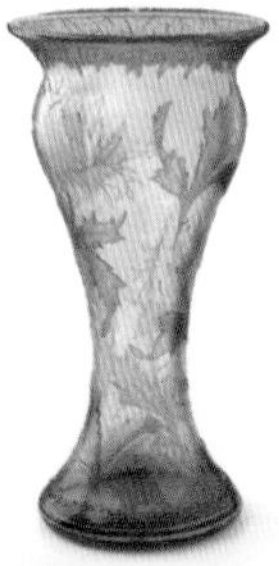

A Honesdale cameo glass vase, with gilded decoration.

c1915 *9.75in (25cm) high*

£800-1,200 **BRK**

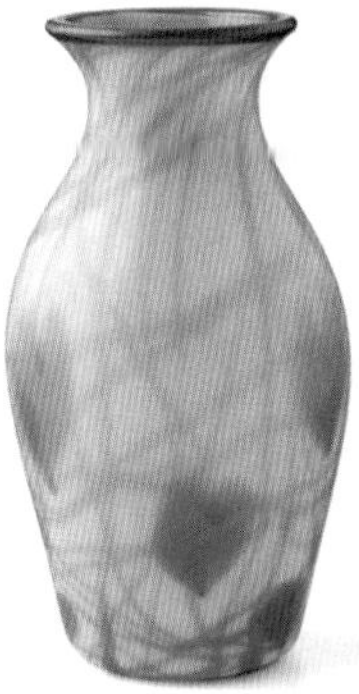

An Imperial Glass Company 'Free Hand' vase.

c1920 8.25in (21cm) high

£400-600 **BRK**

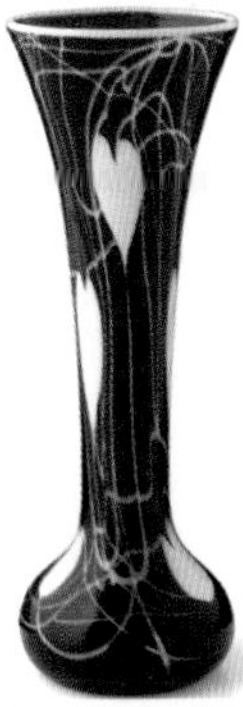

An Imperial Glass Company 'Free Hand' vase, with the heart and vine pattern.

Imperial mainly produced pressed glass. The Free Hand range was the only free-blown line the company made.

c1920 10in (25.5cm) high

£300-500 **BRK**

A Kew Blas iridescent glass bowl.

Kew Blas glass was made by the Union Glass Company of Somerville, MA.

c1895 7.5in (19cm) wide

£400-600 **BRK**

A Kimble Clutha glass vase.

8.25in (21cm) high

£300-400 **BRK**

A lustred Chintz glass vase, by Douglas Nash, with vertical pattern in gold iridescence, on applied foot, engraved "GD 57 NASH".

12in (30.5cm) high

£1,000-1,500 **DRA**

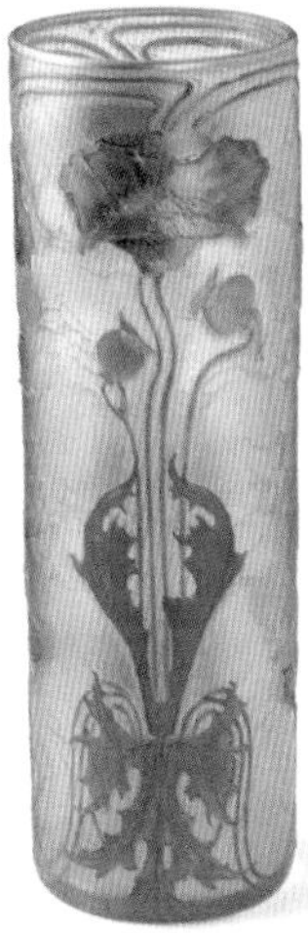

A Mont Joye Art Nouveau cylindrical cameo glass vase, decorated with stylized poppies in shades of green, pale pink and burnished gilt, printed factory mark.

12.5in (31.5cm) high

£600-900 **DN**

A Mount Washington glass vase decorated with flowers in pink and gilt on ivory ground, painted "893/3 W206".

10in (25.5cm) high

£180-220 **DRA**

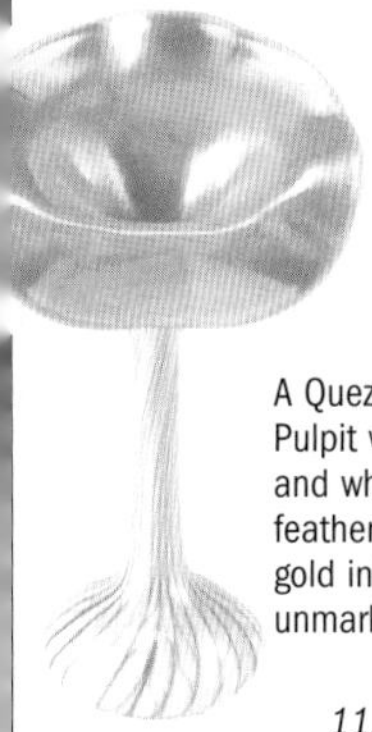

A Quezal Jack-in-the-Pulpit vase with green and white pulled feather pattern and gold interior, unmarked.

11.5in (29cm) high

£600-900 **DRA**

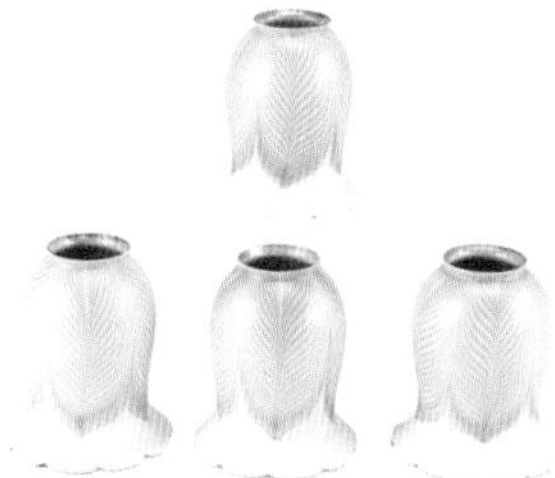

Four Quezal glass shades with green and gold feather pull decoration on ivory ground, with gold interiors, engraved "Quezal".

5.25in (13.5cm) high

£400-600 **DRA**

A Quezal iridescent glass cup and saucer.

c1915 4.5in (11.5cm) diam

£300-500 **BRK**

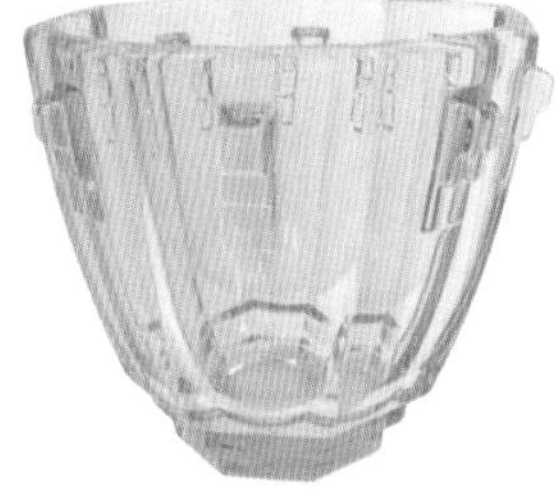

An American Art Deco Skyscraper crystal ice bucket, with repeated stepped design details and base.

7in (18cm) diam

£600-800 **DD**

A Webb cameo vase, with floral and foliage decoration, with a Webb signature butterfly.

10in (25.5cm) high

£2,000-3,000 **JDJ**

An unsigned Webb cameo vase, red background with white floral and foliage design over all.

9.5in (24cm) high

£1,500-2,000 **JDJ**

A Webb Gem Cameo art glass vase, ovoid body of pastel blue, layered white, cameo cut with vines and berries, circular mark "Thomas Webb & Sons Gem Cameo" on base.

6.5in (16.5cm) high

£2,800-3,200 **SK**

A Webb cameo glass bowl, in white over ruby red, decorated with flora and a butterfly, etched mark.

5in (12.5cm) diam

£300-500 **DRA**

A Webb Gem Cameo art glass vase, cameo-cut decoration of raspberry plants, stylized geometric border above, circular mark "Thomas Webb & Sons Gem Cameo" on base.

13.5in (34.5cm) high

£1,800-2,200 **SK**

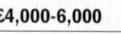

A Webb Gem Cameo art glass vase, made for Mary Morgan by the Woodall team, flared trumpet form overall with geraniums, signed "Thomas Webb & Sons/Gem Cameo."

George Woodall (1850-1925) and his team were highly respected cameo glass designers, known for their technically challenging intricate white cameo on coloured backgrounds.

15in (38cm) high

£4,000-6,000 **SK**

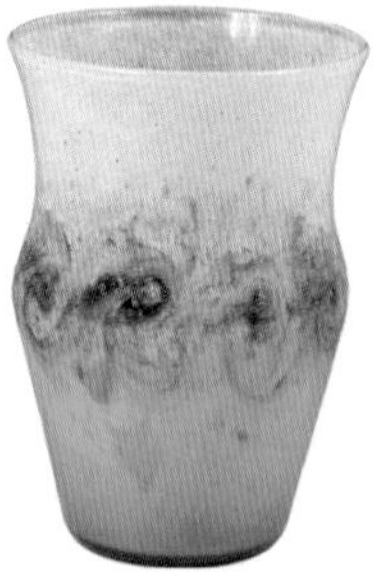

A Monart glass vase, light blue and green with aventurine and whorls.

7.5in (19cm) high

£200-300 **SWO**

A rare Stuart engraved vase, designed by Paul Nash for the 1934 Art in Industry exhibition, engraved with geometric panels of circles and lines, acid-etched mark, original paper label.

8.25in (21cm) high

£2,800-3,200 **WW**

A Stuart cut-glass vase, by Ludwig Kny, of flaring cylindrical form, decorated with seagulls flying over waves, acid-etched mark.

Ludwig Kny, son of the important Bohemian engraver Frederick Kny, joined Stuart & Sons in 1918 as chief designer.

7in (18cm) high

£800-1,200 **WW**

A John Walsh Walsh glass vase, by Clyne Farquharson, cut and etched with foliate sprays and etched signature.

8.25in (21cm) high

£220-280 **WW**

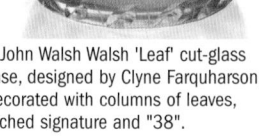

A John Walsh Walsh 'Leaf' cut-glass vase, designed by Clyne Farquharson, decorated with columns of leaves, etched signature and "38".

7.75in (20cm) high

£200-300 **WW**

STAINED GLASS

- Stained glass windows and panels became popular during the early 20thC in British and American homes.
- Stained glass was integrated into the design of the house and positioned to exploit natural light, such as fanlights above front doors, or were set into screens which could be moved into the sunlight.
- Key designers include Tiffany, Mackintosh and Mucha but many firms made panels.
- Major design motifs include: Classical maidens in the Art Nouveau style, typified by Mucha's designs; stylized floral designs, such as Macintosh's famous Glasgow rose; and patriotic icons such as flags.

An Arts and Crafts leaded glass window with stylized blossoms on a wavy, tiled border, in different textures of glass and jewels, mounted in window frame.

This window survived the 1906 San Francisco earthquake and fire.

frame 58in (145cm) wide

£2,000-3,000 **DRA**

An Arts and Crafts leaded glass window with a long-haired maiden swinging on a crescent moon in ambers and blue-greens, mounted in window frame.

frame 31.5in (79cm) high

£2,500-3,000 **DRA**

Three Arts and Crafts leaded glass windows, with stylized blue blossoms and green leaves on Prairie School geometric ground, mounted in window frames.

51.75in (129cm) high

£2,800-3,200 **DRA**

An Arts and Crafts leaded glass door, with stylized floral pattern in greens, pinks and amber.

door 79.25in (198cm) high

£1,500-2,000 **DRA**

Two Arts and Crafts tall leaded glass windows, with green leaves and pink berries on a blue-green ground, mounted in window frames.

frames 65in (162.5cm) high

£1,000-1,500 **DRA**

An Arts & Crafts leaded glass window, with a swag and medallion of Glasgow roses in jewel tones, mounted in window frame.

frame 43in (107.5cm) wide

£180-220 **DRA**

An Arts & Crafts stained-glass window, depicting a landscape with a windmill in slag glass, mounted in its original window sash, breaks to a couple of pieces, unmarked.

sash 48.25in (120.5cm) wide

£500-800 **DRA**

A stained glass window, removed from Princeton University, inscribed with scene of "The Birth of our Nations Flag June 14, 1777".

c1900 *78.5in (196cm) high*

£3,000-5,000 **POOK**

An early 20thC stained and leaded glass window, depicting birds in branches, framed and glazed.

interior 47in (119.5cm) wide

£3,000-5,000 **SK**

An early 20thC stained glass window, inscribed "From the Class of 1917 Commemorating the Surrender of Nassau Hall Princeton January 3 1777 and Students of Revolutionary Times Distinguished Public Life", removed from Princeton University.

78.5in (196cm) high

£5,000-8,000 **POOK**

A 20thC leaded and stained glass window, centred by opalescent white glass lattice with stained decoration depicting mauve flowers, surrounded by a caramel and green slag glass ground, framed and protected by a clear glass pane, cracks.

51.75in (131.5) wide

£300-500 **SK**

A 20thC stained glass window, with a compass design.

27.5in (70cm) wide

£700-1,000 **FRE**

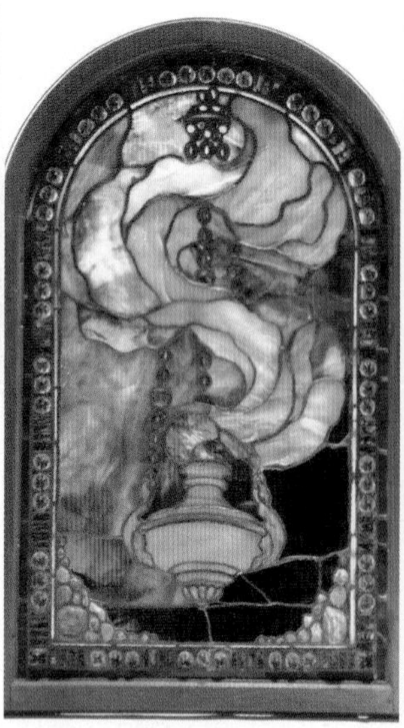

A 20thC stained glass window, attributed to John Lafarge, blown glass, lead, wood, includes chipped jewel and drapery glass.

43in (109cm) high

£5,000-8,000 **FRE**

A demi-lune leaded glass window, in the style of Tiffany, mounted as a light fixture, with peacock and cornucopia in polychrome slag glass, damage, unmarked.

fixture 44in (110cm) wide

£9,000-11,000 **DRA**

A large Dirk van Erp hammered copper 'Milk Can' table lamp, with four mica panels below a vented cap, base with four sockets above four riveted arms.

25.5in (64cm) high

£22,000-28,000 **DRA**

A Dirk van Erp tear-drop shaped hammered copper table lamp, with three sockets and three arms supporting a new mica shade, new patina, stamped "Dirk van Erp/San Francisco".

21in (52.5cm) high

£4,000-6,000 **DRA**

A Dirk van Erp hammered copper and mica lamp, the shade with rolled rim over a three-socket bottle-shaped riveted base, original patina and mica, resoldering, Windmill stamp.

20in (50cm) high

£8,000-12,000 **DRA**

A Dirk van Erp hammered copper and mica 'Bean Pot' boudoir lamp, on a single-socket base, original mica and patina, open box mark, remnant of "D'Arcy Gaw".

12.25in (30.5cm) high

£4,000-5,000 **DRA**

A copper and mica hanging conical fixture with single sconce and four panels, attributed to Dirk van Erp, divided with riveted bars, original mica, patina and on-off switch, unmarked.

9in (22.5cm) high

£1,500-2,000 **DRA**

A Heintz sterling-on-bronze boudoir lamp, with a silver overlay of day lilies on a verdigris patina, pierced shade with new lining, no visible mark.

12in (30cm) high

£800-1,200 **DRA**

A Heintz sterling-on-bronze boudoir lamp, the shade pierced with poppies and lined in mica, on a single-socket base overlaid with poppy on verdigris patina, unmarked.

10in (25cm) high

£800-1,200 **DRA**

A Heintz sterling-on-bronze acid-etched brass-finish boudoir lamp, the shade pierced in a flame pattern, on a single-socket base overlaid with dancing ladies, mica panel lining probably replaced, unmarked.

12.25in (30.5cm) high

£700-1,000 **DRA**

A large and rare Heintz sterling-on-bronze table lamp, the pierced shade lined in beige silk and decorated in a Virginia creeper pattern, the three-socket base with silver overlay and, "HAMS" patent stamp, wear.

20in (50cm) high

£2,800-3,200 **DRA**

A rare Heintz sterling-on-bronze table lamp, the helmet shade inset with 'jewels', over a single-socket trumpet base with an overlay of silver branches, leaves and berries, stamped "Pat. APD 4 1035", cleaning to patina.

14in (35cm) high

£800-1,200 **DRA**

A Heintz sterling-on-bronze table lamp with helmet shade on single-socket harp base, with stylized floral overlay on verdigris patina, some scratches to rim of shade and around base, refelted.

12.5in (32cm) high

£400-500 **DRA**

An exceptional Roycroft hammered copper table lamp, designed by Dard Hunter, with a flaring shade of pumpkin orange and periwinkle blue leaded glass on a brass-washed baluster three-socket base, orb and cross mark, light pitting.

22in (55cm) high

£18,000-22,000 **DRA**

A rare Roycroft hammered copper table lamp, designed by Dard Hunter, with a leaded glass shade over a baluster three-socket base with two riveted rings and handles, orb and cross mark, new patina to heat cap, minor damage.

22.5in (56cm) high

£8,000-12,000 **DRA**

A CLOSER LOOK AT A ROYCROFT TABLE LAMP

The Roycroft Arts and Crafts Community was founded in 1895, in East Aurora, New York by writer-philosopher Elbert Hubbard. Inspired by William Morris, pieces were hand-crafted to a high standard.

Dard Hunter was a prominent Roycrofter. Very few examples of his ceramic work remain, making this piece rare and desirable.

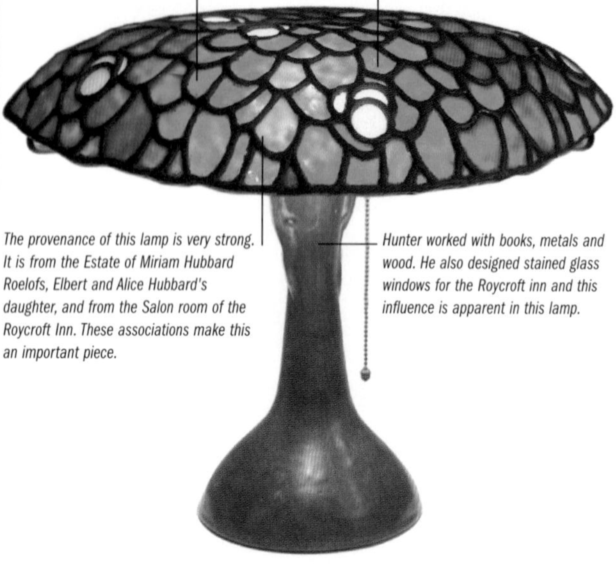

The provenance of this lamp is very strong. It is from the Estate of Miriam Hubbard Roelofs, Elbert and Alice Hubbard's daughter, and from the Salon room of the Roycroft Inn. These associations make this an important piece.

Hunter worked with books, metals and wood. He also designed stained glass windows for the Roycroft inn and this influence is apparent in this lamp.

An extremely rare Roycroft table lamp, designed and executed by Dard Hunter, with a leaded-glass shade decorated with fruit and foliage in yellow and green slag glass, over a glazed ceramic base modelled with salamanders, base marked "DH".

17.25in (43cm) wide

£35,000-40,000 **DRA**

A Roycroft brass-washed hammered copper table lamp, its helmet shade lined in hammered red glass, wear, tilt, later paint or patina on lead, orb and cross mark.

The hammered red glass makes this a rare version of this form.

13.5in (34.5cm) high

£4,000-5,000 **DRA**

A Roycroft hammered copper table lamp, in woodgrain pattern with brass-washed finish, topped by a helmet-shaped shade with mica panels, original finish and mica, orb and cross mark.

14in (35cm) high

£1,500-2,000 **DRA**

An extremely rare Roycroft floor lamp, designed and executed by Dard Hunter and Victor Toothaker, the leaded glass shade with a slag glass pattern of fruit and foliage, over a three-socket, decorated, wrought-iron base, unmarked, damage.

61in (152.5cm) high

£12,000-18,000 **DRA**

A Roycroft cylindrical lantern, designed by Dard Hunter, of bright green and purple leaded glass, topped with an over-hanging circular cap, complete with single-link chain and ceiling cap, unmarked.

16in (40cm) high

£5,000-7,000 **DRA**

A Roycroft hammered copper American Beauty vase made into a table lamp, no visible mark, wear, dents, shortened.

12.5in (32cm) high

£200-300 **DRA**

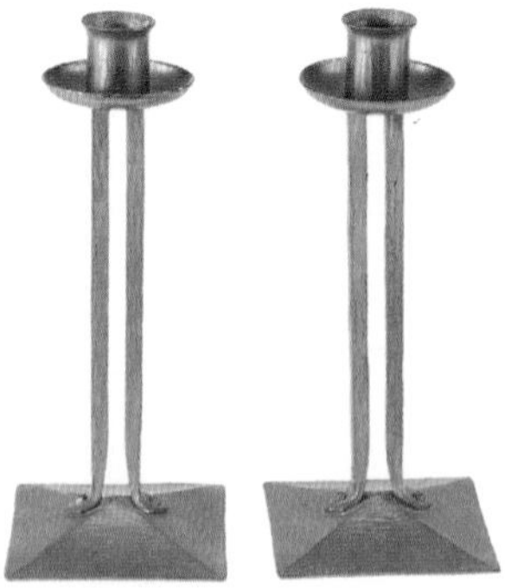

A pair of Roycroft brass-washed hammered copper Princess candlesticks in wood grain pattern, original finish, orb and cross marks.

7.75in (19.5cm) high

£600-800 **DRA**

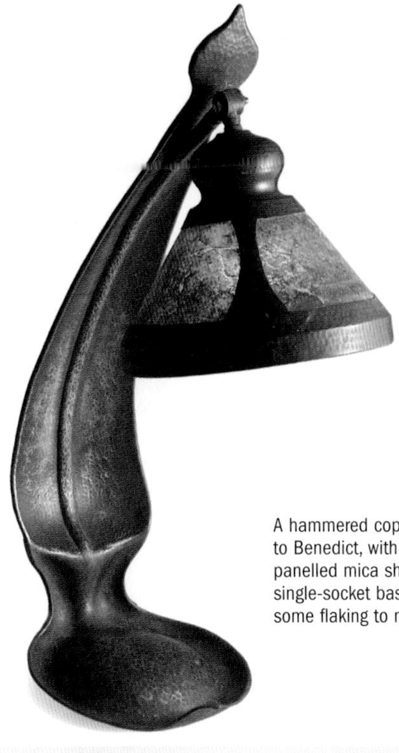

A hammered copper desk lamp, attributed to Benedict, with an adjustable, three-panelled mica shade hanging from a single-socket base, replaced swivel screw, some flaking to mica, unmarked.

23in (57.5cm) high

£7,000-10,000 **DRA**

A W.A.S. Benson copper and brass table lamp, with leaf-applied decoration and a petal tray on a tripod base.

19in (48cm) high

£700-1,000 **SWO**

A hammered copper glass and mother-of-pearl table lamp, in the style of Elizabeth Burton, with faceted lit base and conical shade, single-socket, unmarked, missing two screws, dent.

22.5in (57cm) high

£2,000-2,500 **DRA**

A Hampshire Pottery table lamp, the leaded shade with a brickwork design in green slag glass, relief-decorated base with broad leaves, with two-socket standard.

18in (45.5cm) high

£1,800-2,200 **SK**

A 20thC bat-form bronze hanging ceiling light, the green and black webbed decorated shade by Pallme Konig.

21.5in (55cm) high

£1,500-2,000 **FRE**

A large Onondaga Metal Shops cast and hammered chandelier, with nine copper lanterns hanging from a cut-out iron ring, lined with original yellow glass shades, unmarked.

32in (80cm) high

£18,000-22,000 **DRA**

A Lilian Palmer hammered copper table lamp, with a four-panel mesh shade painted with hollyhocks over a tear-drop shaped, two-socket base in medium-brown patina, unmarked.

21in (52.5cm) high

£6,000-9,000 **DRA**

A Gustav Stickley hammered copper and cast iron two-lantern wall sconce, each with original butter-yellow shade below heart-shaped cut-outs, unmarked.

lanterns 9.75in (24cm) high

£700-1,000 **DRA**

A Gustav Stickley copper chandelier, with four hammered glass lanterns, original patina and glass, stamped mark on ceiling plate.

24in (60cm) high

£8,000-12,000 **DRA**

A rare Gustav Stickley bronze candle sconce, unmarked.

10.5in (26cm) high

£400-500 **DRA**

A Gustav Stickley hammered copper hanging lantern, four-sided with riveted trellis top and overhanging cap, lined in original yellow hammered glass, complete with chain and ceiling plate, unmarked.

9.75in (24cm) high

£1,200-1,800 **DRA**

A pair of Gustav Stickley cedar newel post lamps, with hammered copper lanterns lined in period mica, unmarked, missing screws, mica possibly not original.

29.5in (74cm) high

£3,000-4,000 **DRA**

An Arts and Crafts slag glass table lamp, with a green bronze metal base.

25.5in (65cm) high

£300-400 **FRE**

An early 20thC slag glass and metal overlay lamp, the shade with metal silhouettes of aladdin lamps and the border with "and from the mist of ages gone we gain new light" on four-socket standard and scrolled and riveted base.

23in (58.5cm) high

£1,500-2,000 **SK**

A large Arts and Crafts floor lamp, with green slag glass panels on fringed shade and base, original dark finish, some looseness, unmarked.

69.5in (174cm) high

£1,200-1,800 **DRA**

An Arts and Crafts copper and caramel slag-glass table lamp, with riveted strap hardware, above a three-socket base, original dark patina and sockets, one missing chain ball, unmarked.

24.5in (61cm) high

£700-1,000 **DRA**

An Arts and Crafts lamp, with a conch shell shade on a brass-washed hammered copper base, unmarked.

17in (42.5cm) high

£300-400 **DRA**

An Arts and Crafts brass hall lantern, repoussé-decorated with stylized plant forms, with green leaded glass panels, the whole supported with scrolling bracket.

23.5in (60cm) high

£1,000-1,500 **L&T**

An Arts and Crafts parcel gilt bronze hanging light fixture, with bellflower decoration over eight concave slag glass panels, the rim with dangling glass beads.

25in (63.5cm) high

£800-1,200 **ISA**

A pair of Arts and Crafts-style copper outdoor lanterns, lined in hammered yellow glass, hanging from ceiling plates on chain, replaced parts, unmarked.

14in (35cm) high

£800-1,200 **DRA**

A Tiffany gold Favrile glass candlestick lamp, with ruffled shade, spirally ribbed base and green and white centre, retains original wax candle, engraved "L.C.T".

12.25in (31cm) high

£1,000-1,500 **DRA**

A Tiffany gold Favrile glass desk lamp, with vertically patterned shade and base, ivory interior, engraved "L.C. Tiffany Favrile".

12.75in (32.5cm) high

£2,000-3,000 **DRA**

An unusual Merrimac and Tiffany oil lamp, the Merrimac pottery base with applied leaves and a matte green glaze, fitted with a small oil font topped with a Tiffany 'Favrile' glass shade, chip, shade etched "L.C.T".

12.5in (32cm) high

£2,500-3,000 **DRA**

A Tiffany Studios bronze and Favrile glass table lamp, with original fixtures and on-off switch, base stamped "TIFFANY STUDIOS NEW YORK 9521", shades signed "L.C.T".

13.25in (33.5cm) high

£5,000-6,000 **DRA**

A CLOSER LOOK AT A TIFFANY CHANDELIER

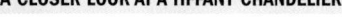

In 1881 Tiffany patented his unique type of iridescent glass, named 'Favrile' which means 'handcrafted' in German. The glass broke with the fashion for decorating pieces with painted designs and was instead sprayed with metallic lustres to create an opalescent and multi-dimensional finish.

As pieces were handmade, no two lamps were identical.

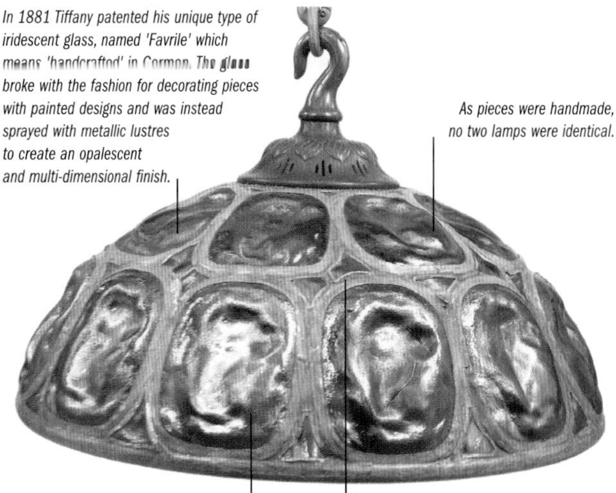

This chandelier was authenticated by the family of the original owners, making the provenance strong and traceable. This is especially important as the shade is unsigned.

Louis Comfort Tiffany had been fascinated by stained glass windows in his youth and by introducing a range of lamps in 1899, he was able to experiment with decorative glass and artificial light while bringing his work to a wider domestic audience. This is an exceptional piece of his work.

An exceptional Tiffany Studios turtle-back hanging chandelier with two rows of glass medallions in lustred blue-green 'Favrile' glass over a six-socket fixture, topped by a vented Lotus bronze cap with hook, no visible signature.

22in (56cm) diam

£60,000-80,000 **DRA**

A Tiffany Studios gold Favrile table lamp, the shade on bronze oil lamp base of urn form, electrified, base impressed "TIFFANY STUDIOS NEW YORK".

15.5in (39.5cm) high

£3,000-4,000 **DRA**

A Tiffany Studios bronze and 'Favrile' glass lily lamp, with three gold iridescent shades, signed, impressed mark and numbered "253" to base.

13.5in (34.5cm) high

£5,000-7,000 **SK**

A Tiffany gold Favrile glass candlestick lamp, with spiral-ribbed base and green pulled feather stem, electrified, shade and base engraved "L.C.T".

11.75in (29cm) high

£1,200-1,800 **DRA**

A Tiffany Favrile damascene glass evergreen-shaped table lamp, with a green and pearl zig-zag pattern, wheel-cut with a butterfly, dragonfly and wasps, single-socket base, etched "L.C.T. Favrile" and "L.C. Tiffany-Favrile" on base.

20in (50cm) high

£1,500-2,000 **DRA**

A Tiffany Studios Favrile leaded glass and gilt bronze table lamp, the shade stamped "Tiffany Studios 1947", the base "Tiffany Studios New York 534".

22.75in (57cm) high

£8,000-12,000 **WW**

A Tiffany Studios bronze acid-etched 'Favrile' glass desk lamp, with an Arabian-pattern glass shade, adjustable socket, shade etched "L.C.T.", base "TIFFANY STUDIOS NEW YORK 637", chips.

base 13in (32.5cm) wide

£2,500-3,000 **DRA**

A Tiffany Studios lamp, with a leaded glass shade in the 'Geranium' pattern with fractured, confetti, and ribbed glass, bronze base, three sockets, base and shade stamped "TIFFANY STUDIOS NEW YORK", shade "1451-1", base "9509", damage.

22.5in (57cm) high

£22,000-28,000 **DRA**

A Tiffany Studios glass and doré table lamp, with three-socket standard on a relief-decorated base, impressed mark "Tiffany Studios New York 1954 no 368", shade stamped "Tiffany Studios New York 1594", cracks.

£12,000-18,000 **SK**

A Tiffany Studios table lamp, with lemon leaf shade of green slag glass on a bronze Secessionist three-socket base with verdigris patina, stamped "TIFFANY STUDIOS NEW YORK 21096", base stamped "TIFFANY STUDIOS NEW YORK 528", damage.

24.5in (62cm) high

£15,000-20,000 **DRA**

A Tiffany Studios leaded glass swirling leaf lamp shade, on a period unmarked bronzed base, rim impressed "TIFFANY STUDIOS NEW YORK 1435-138", damage and new glass.

21.5in (54.5cm) high

£2,200-2,800 **DRA**

A leaded glass and metal table lamp, in the manner of Tiffany Studios, with green mottled leaded glass shade with vine leaf decoration, two-socket standard, unsigned.

18in (45.5cm) high

£3,000-4,000 **SK**

A Tiffany Studios gilt-parcel table lamp in the Venetian pattern, with a mosaic of polychromatic slag glass in gilded leading, filigreed base, three-socket fixture, marked "TIFFANY STUDIOS NEW YORK 515", damage.

20in (51cm) high

£22,000-28,000 **DRA**

A Tiffany Studios hydrangea cone shade, signed with metal tag "Tiffany Studios New York", lower beaded border, accompanied by a large patinated metal lamp base, with Oriental design motif in relief, fitted with six-socket standard, unsigned.

c1940 *33in (84cm) high*

£60,000-90,000 **SK**

A small Tiffany Studios table lamp with a faceted Linenfold glass shade, on a gilt-parcel base, single-socket, "TIFFANY STUDIOS NEW YORK 1940 PAT APPL'D FOR", base stamped "419".

13.5in (34.5cm) high

£3,000-4,000 **DRA**

A Tiffany Studios gilt-parcel desk lamp in geometric patterns, base stamped "TIFFANY STUDIOS NEW YORK 635".

13.5in (34cm) high

£1,200-1,800 **DRA**

A Tiffany Studios gilt-parcel table lamp, with Classical figure sitting and reading on an Aladdin oil lamp base, on green marble foot, stamped "TIFFANY STUDIOS NEW YORK".

11in (28cm) wide

£800-1,200 **DRA**

A Tiffany Studios bronze counterbalance desk lamp base, impressed mark "Tiffany Studios New York 417".

c1900 *16in (40cm) high*

£1,800-2,200 **FRE**

A Tiffany Studios bronze fluted three-socket table lamp base, with embossed hearts, marked "TIFFANY STUDIOS NEW YORK 309", shade caps probably replaced, retouched patina.

16in (40cm) high

£3,000-4,000 **DRA**

A Handel reverse-painted table lamp, with a Japanese scene of pine trees, mountains and a pagoda on a ribbed bronzed metal base with moulded foot.

23.5in (59.5cm) high

£4,000-5,000 **SK**

A Handel reverse-painted table lamp, the acid-etched shade with a moonlit tropical scene with tall ships, over a Classical three-socket bronzed base, shade signed "Handel 6391", base unmarked.

24in (60cm) high

£6,000-9,000 **DRA**

A Handel reverse-painted table lamp, with leaves and vines, the three-socket Chinese urn-shaped bronzed base embossed with chrysanthemums and birds in flight, shade signed "Handel 6955/BD".

23in (57.5cm) high

£1,800-2,200 **DRA**

A Handel table lamp with a reverse-painted shade, depicting a continuous mountain and forest scene, on bronzed metal base, shade painted "HANDEL 5464", base moulded "HANDEL".

19.75in (50cm) high

£4,000-6,000 **DRA**

A reverse-painted table lamp, in the style of Handel, the acid-etched glass shade with a moonlit seashore and farmstead scene, on a bronzed two-socket base, unmarked.

21in (52.5cm) high

£800-1,200 **DRA**

A Handel polychrome slag glass table lamp, with overlay of tall pine trees, on a three-socket gourd-shaped base embossed with trees, complete with converted oil font, base and shade stamped.

24in (61cm) high

£2,200-2,800 **DRA**

A Handel slag glass table lamp, with six-panelled shade, on bronzed metal base, base impressed "HANDEL".

21in (53.5cm) high

£800-1,200 **DRA**

A Handel leaded slag glass table lamp, with faceted geometric shade with a band of caramel glass on a copper-patinated etched base, two sockets, shade stamped "HANDEL", base unmarked.

24in (61cm) high

£1,800-2,200 **DRA**

A Handel caramel slag glass table lamp, with applied bands of red hearts on a three-socket leaf and bud base in the style of Grueby, unmarked.

25.5in (65cm) high

£2,500-3,000 **DRA**

A Handel caramel slag glass table lamp, with metal overlay and green glass border, raised on three-socket trunk form base, unsigned, design number "5339".

25.25in (64cm) high

£2,000-3,000 **SK**

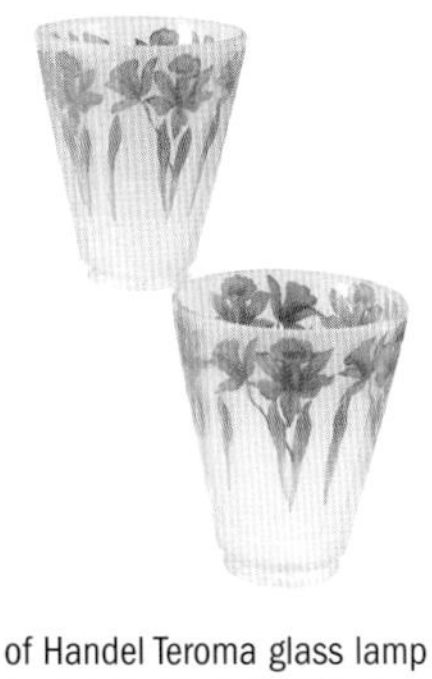

A pair of Handel Teroma glass lamp shades painted with daffodils on frosted ground, with vertical ribbing, painted "Handel 3180", and decorator initials.

5.25in (13.5cm) high

£600-900 **DRA**

A brass and leaded glass floor lamp, possibly by Bigelow and Kennard, with a domed shade in a gridwork of white slag glass, over four sockets and a tripod base.

66in (167.5cm) high

£2,200-2,800 **SK**

A Chicago Mosaic table lamp, with waterlily decoration in pink, white and green slag glass against an amber ground, on a bronze three-socket tree trunk base, chip to one glass panel, hairlines to others, unmarked.

27in (68.5cm) high

£1,800-2,200 **DRA**

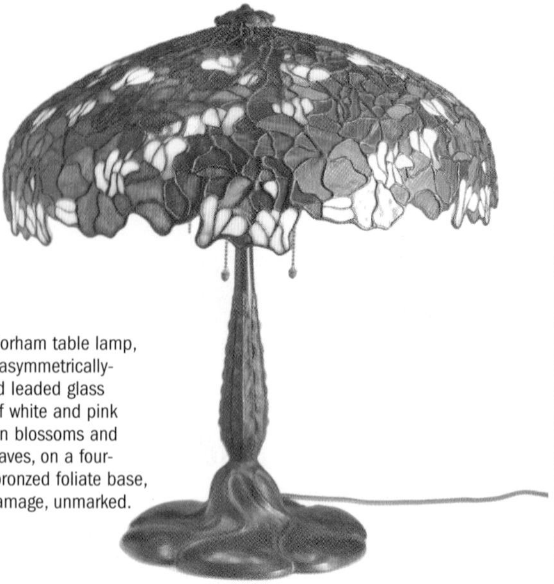

A rare Gorham table lamp, with an asymmetrically-bordered leaded glass shade of white and pink cyclamen blossoms and green leaves, on a four-socket bronzed foliate base, some damage, unmarked.

22.5in (56cm) high

£7,000-10,000 **DRA**

A leaded glass lamp, in the manner of J. A. Whaley of New York, the conical shade with drop apron raised on a patinated metal base.

24in (61cm) high

£1,500-2,000 **SK**

A glass daffodil lamp shade, the shade with a repeating pattern of daffodils, married with a two-socket standard Czechoslovakian pottery base.

25.5in (65cm) high

£3,500-4,000 **SK**

A leaded glass hanging lamp, in olive green and caramel slag glass, three sockets suspended on a heavy chain with ceiling plate.

20.25in (51.5cm) diam

£280-320 **SK**

A Bradley and Hubbard table lamp, with ribbed glass faceted shade reverse-painted with stylized orange blossoms, on a fluted bronzed two-socket base, triangular mark.

22in (55cm) high

£800-1,200 **DRA**

A Jefferson table lamp, with a reverse-painted 'hammered' glass shade, on a ribbed two-socket patinated base, shade signed "2369-R", base and shade stamped "Jefferson".

21.5in (16cm) high

£1,500-2,000 **DRA**

A Moe Bridges of Milwaukee reverse-painted table lamp, decorated in a landscape pattern, raised on two-socket standard, the base with linear decoration, signed on base.

20.5in (52cm) high

£800-1,200 **SK**

A Pairpoint reverse-painted table lamp, decorated with birds and flowers, three-socket standard with centre rod on tripod columnar base in brass finish, unsigned shade, base signed and numbered "D3070".

22in (56cm) high

£2,500-3,000 **SK**

A Pairpoint reverse-painted table lamp, the acid-etched shade with roses and poppies, on a bronzed two-socket base, shade stamped "The Pairpoint Corp'n", base stamped "1915".

22in (55cm) high

£1,200-1,800 **DRA**

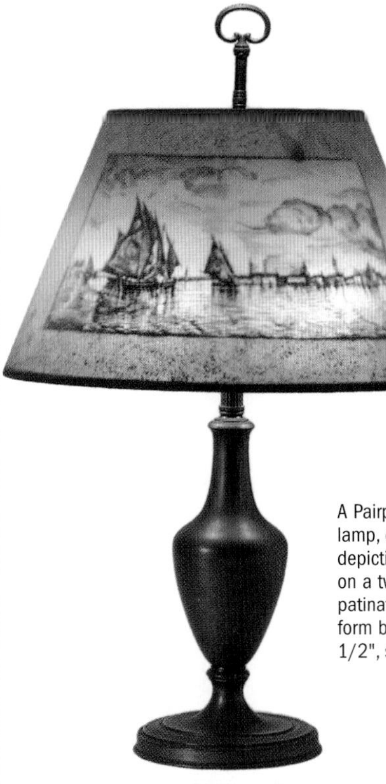

A Pairpoint reverse-painted table lamp, each side of the shade depicting a European harbour scene, on a two-socket standard, with patinated copper finish and baluster-form base, base impressed "D205 1/2", some wear to finish.

25in (63.5cm) high

£2,000-3,000 **SK**

A Pairpoint desk lamp, with puffy glass shade moulded with flowers, on gilt metal base, impressed "Pairpoint Made in USA, D3024" and with paper label, shade stencilled "The Pairpoint Corp.".

This lamp was patented in July 1907.

15.25in (38.5cm) high

£1,200-1,800 **DRA**

An early 20thC reverse-painted table lamp, possibly Pittsburgh, with domed etched glass shade, single-socket standard on weighted brass base, unsigned.

19.25in (49cm) high

£300-500 **SK**

A reverse-painted table lamp, the dome shade with a country village scene, on a two-socket standard and patinated metal Pairpoint base, the base signed "D3053".

20in (51cm) high

£1,000-1,500 **SK**

An early 20thC reverse-painted table lamp, the bell-shaped shade decorated with red poppy plants on an etched ground, two sockets on vasiform body, unsigned, nicks to shade.

20.5in (52cm) high

£200-300 **SK**

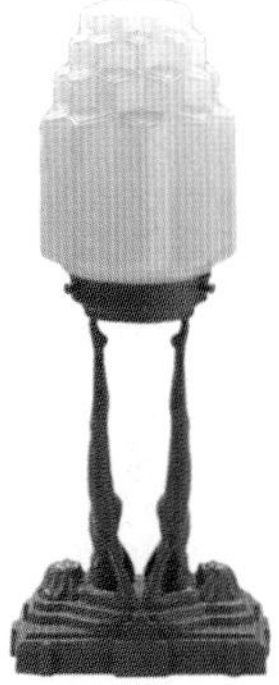

A Frankart Inc. table lamp, with a stepped globe in white glass upheld by the outstretched legs of two female nude figures, with Frankart mark, copyright date and patent number.

19.5in (49.5cm) high

£1,200-1,800 **SK**

A Jugendstil brass and amber-coloured table lamp, the base with floral decoration, with irregular fluted shade and seven semicircular nuggets, electrified.

c1900 *22.75in (57cm) high*

£1,000-1,500 **KAU**

A pair of Art Nouveau cast and gilt-metal candelabra, the five candle sockets with flame-form finial snuffers.

18in (46cm) high

£700-1,000 **SK**

A Canadian amber 'Guardian Angel' miniature lamp, with burner and green glass globe shade, marked "L'ANGE GARDIENI/EXTRA/C. H. BINKS & Co. MONTREAL".

7in (17.5cm) high

£300-400 **WAD**

A Canadian cast iron hanging kitchen lamp, with white shade and smoke bell, font etched with beavers and maple leaves.

27in (69cm) high

£400-600 **WAD**

A 1930s French Art Deco Modernist chandelier, polished nickel with frosted glass tubular shades, attributed to Jacques Adnet.

28in (71cm) high

£6,000-9,000 **DD**

A Degue glass and wrought iron chandelier, with colourless mould-blown and etched glass shade, mounted in a wrought iron frame with vine ornamentation, signed "Degue 534."

c1930 *30in (76cm) high*

£400-600 **SK**

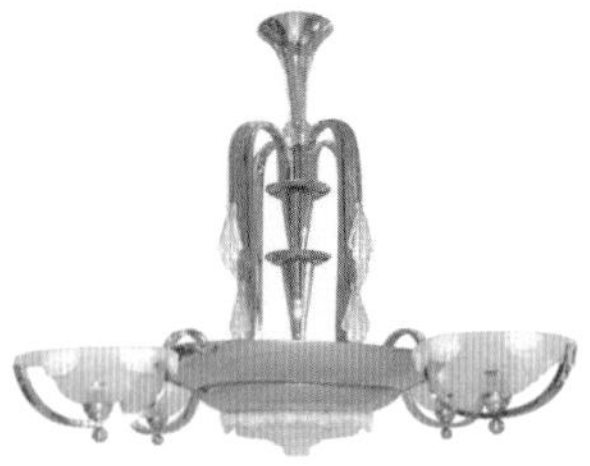

A late 1920s French Jules Leleu Art Deco chandelier, made with Sabino opal glass shades and opal glass drops, copper and chrome mixed metal.

This unique waterfall design was popularized at the 1925 Exposition.

32in (81cm) wide

£4,000-5,000 **DD**

A Muller Frères glass and wrought iron chandelier, the etched glass shades with geometric designs mounted in a wrought iron frame, signed "Muller Frères Luneville."

c1930 *31in (79cm) high*

£600-900 **SK**

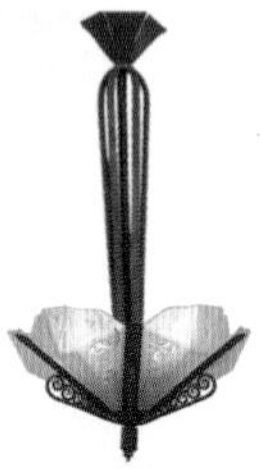

A French Art Deco chandelier, with Muller Frères moulded stepped art glass shades, within a hand-wrought iron frame with, rare square shape.

1920s *32in (81cm) wide*

£4,000-6,000 **DD**

A French Art Deco geometric iron chandelier, with alabaster shades in an iron frame in the manner of Raymond Subes.

c1935 *36in (91cm) high*

£5,000-7,000 **DD**

An Egyptian Revival faceted leaded glass hanging chandelier, with six panels embossed with king's heads over stylized papyrus blossoms on caramel slag glass ground, original bronzed patina, unmarked.

20.75in (52cm) high

£800-1,200 **DRA**

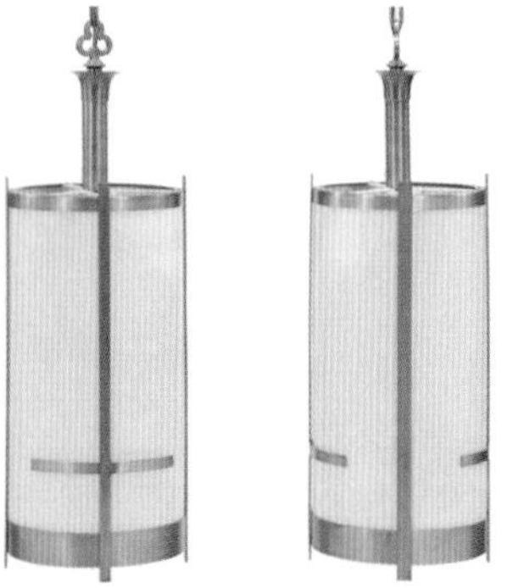

A pair of Art Deco-style brass chandeliers.

37in (94cm) high

£70-100 **FRE**

An American Art Deco chandelier.

c1935 *23in (58.5cm) diam*

£5,000-7,000 **HSD**

A French Art Deco chandelier, with Muller Frères peacocks to the moulded glass globes, supported by wrought iron frame with Paul Kiss-style rosettes, signed.

c1925 *32in (81cm) high*

£4,000-5,000 **DD**

A 1920s French Art Deco table lamp, with Daum moulded lamp shade and wrought-iron base.

18in (45cm) high

£2,000-3,000 **DD**

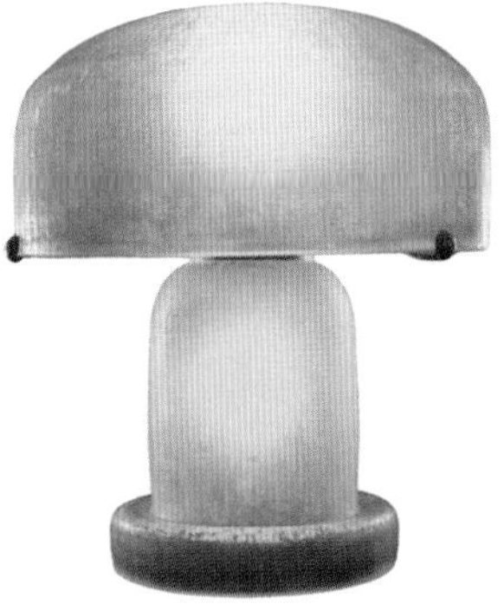

A Daum Art Deco lamp, shade and base signed.

c1925 *18in (46cm) high*

£7,000-10,000 **JES**

A CLOSER LOOK AT AN ADNET LAMP

French architect and designer Jacques Adnet (1900-1984) was highly regarded for his solid, functional designs. Examples of his work are sought after.

The lack of applied ornamentation is typical of his style and reflects his attempts to combine Classical design with Modernism. He described himself as an "innovator and Classicist, a champion of the tradition leading toward the future."

This lamp is especially appealing today as it would sit quite happily within a contemporary space.

The extensive use of chrome, the streamlined design and the ribbed conical uplighter, make this piece an epitome of innovative Art Deco design.

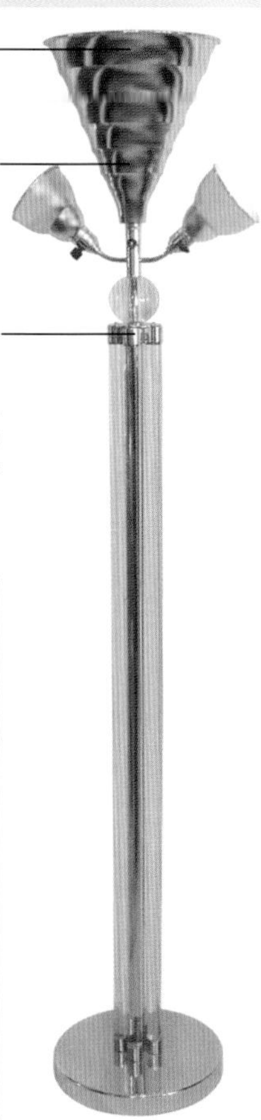

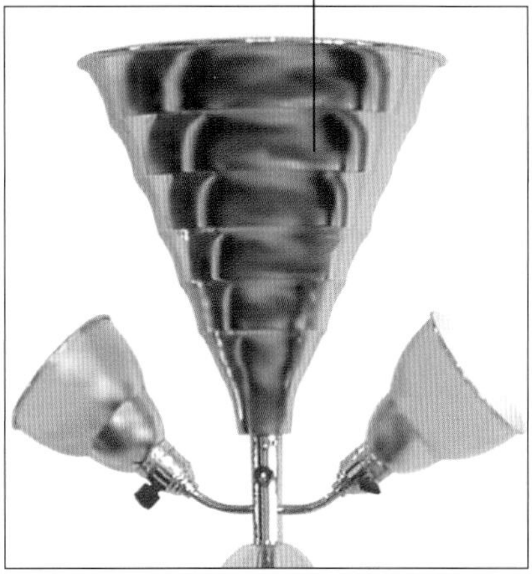

A Jacques Adnet Art Deco Modernist chrome floor lamp, the triple glass rod posts with glass sphere finial, ribbed chrome torchère up-lighter shade and two side beehive down-lights.

c1930 *70.5in (179cm) high*

£7,000-10,000 **DD**

A Durand Egyptian Revival incense lamp with a woman kneeling and holding a vase, topped by a cylindrical glass shade with pulled-feather pattern in gold and green below gold threading, unmarked.

12.5in (31cm) high

£400-500 **DRA**

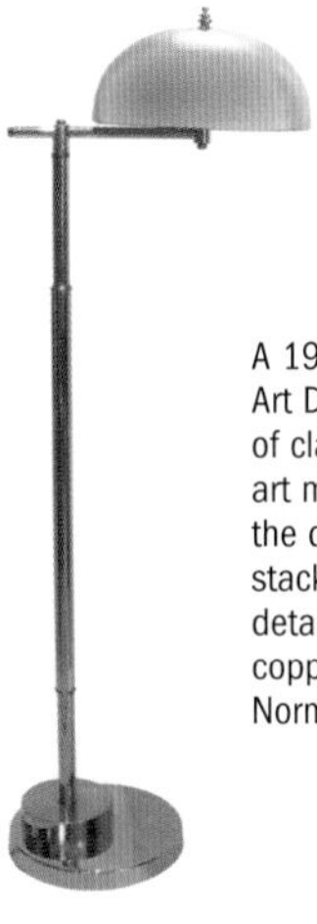

A 1930s American Art Deco floor lamp, of classic streamline art moderne design, the dome shade with stacked disc finial detail, chrome and copper, attributed to Norman Bel Geddes.

53in (134cm) high

£2,000-3,000 **DD**

A Lalique 'Ceylan' opalescent glass vase, no. 905, with blue staining, original light fitting and shade, etched "R Lalique".

9.75in (24.5cm) high

£3,000-4,000 **WW**

An Edward Miller and Company table lamp, the domed shade with caramel marbled glass panels held by a leaf-cast frame, above a tapering divided column cast with fruiting sprigs on spreading base, bears maker's marks.

19.75in (50cm) high

£1,200-1,800 **L&T**

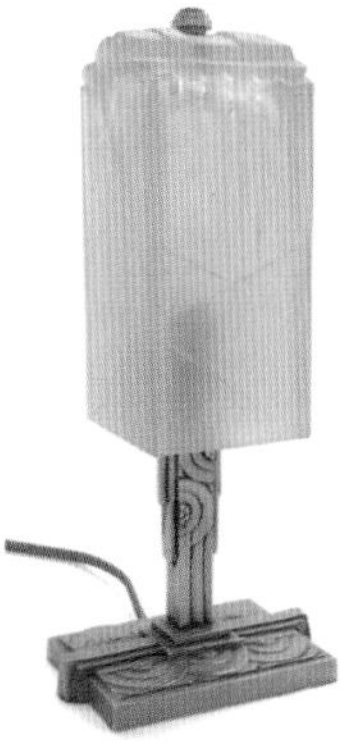

A late 1920s French Art Deco petite table lamp, with a moulded glass shade, on a cast nickel base with a geometric design.

11.25in (28.5cm) high

£1,500-2,000 **DD**

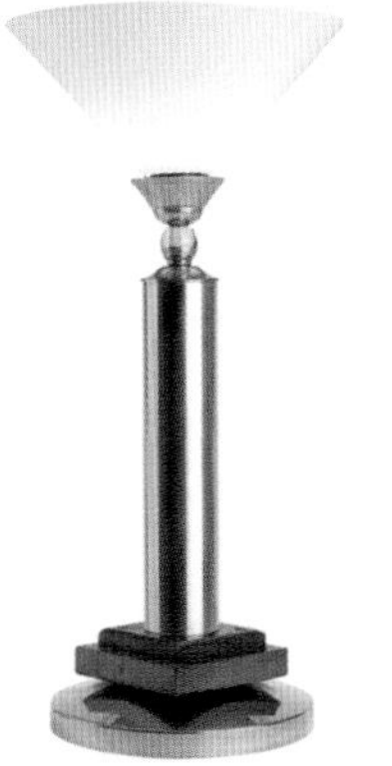

A French Art Deco torchère, with a clear and milky glass shade, above a chromed circular foot and wooden base.

c1930 *28.75in (72cm) high*

£300-400 **KAU**

A pair of French Art Deco table candelabras, of nickel-plated U-shaped design with three bands of streamline detail to base.

c1935 *14in (35cm) high*

£1,500-2,000 **DD**

A pair of Chase Art Deco 'Disc' candlesticks, designed by Ruth Gerth.

These were listed as No.24005 in the Chase catalogue and were originally sold for $4.50 (£2.50) each.

1934 *4.75in (12cm) high*

£200-300 pair **DD**

A pair of Art Deco Chase 'Taurex Uneven' candlesticks, designed by Walter Von Nesson.

No.24004 in the Chase catalogue, these were originally priced at $3.00 (£1.65) each.

1934 *9.75in (25cm) high*

£200-300 **DD**

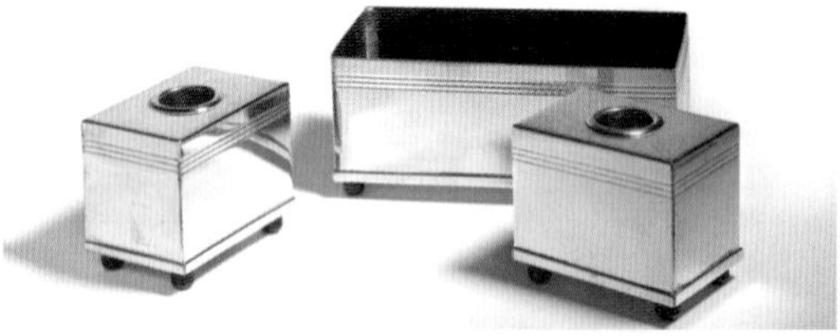

A pair of Art Deco candlesticks with a centrepiece box, marked "The Architex", by Chase USA.

c1935 *6in (15cm) wide*

£300-400 **HSD**

A pair of Art Deco bubble candlesticks in chrome and blue glass, by Chase Corp.

c1945 *2.5in (6.5cm) wide*

£200-300 **HSD**

A pair of aluminium Art Deco candlesticks by Bel Geddes for Kensington.

c1935 *7in (18cm) wide*

£300-400 **HSD**

A Le Verre Francais glass and bronze boudoir lamp, with pomegranate design shade in red over mottled orange, the base applied with pussy willows, original cap, engraved "Le Verre Francais".

11.5in (29cm) high

£1,200-1,800 **DRA**

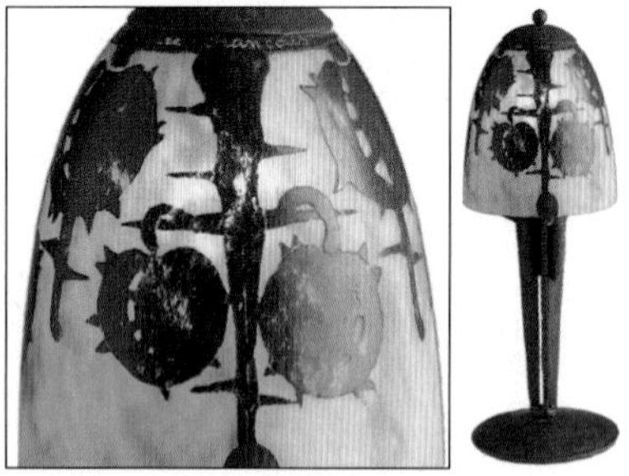

A Japanese skyscraper lamp box.

c1950 *48.75in (124cm) high*

£400-500 **FRE**

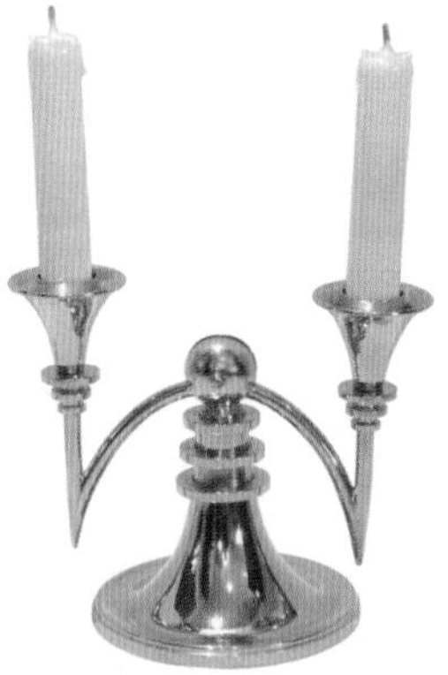

A 1930s French Art Deco Modernist table candelabra, with optional cups for wax candles or illuminated glass candles, triple disc art moderne decoration, nickel plated, electrified.

13in (33cm) high

£1,200-1,800 **DD**

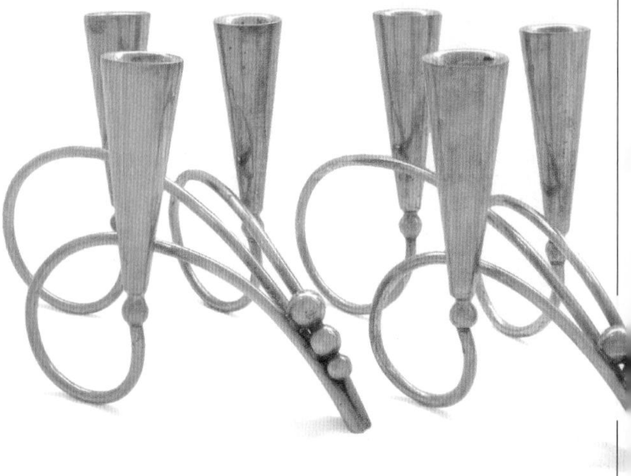

A pair of late 1930s Mexican Art Deco Modernist sterling candelabra.

6.5in (16.5cm) high

£1,200-1,800 **DD**

A mid-19thC Gothic Revival pitch pine wall clock, the twin train fusee movement striking on a steel bell, dial with ivory disc chapters and serrated inlaid border, enclosed within case.

22.5in (57cm) wide

£1,200-1,800 **L&T**

A patinated bronze clock, by W.A.S Benson, cast in low relief with stylized foliage, the enamelled dial with Roman numerals.

8.5in (21.5cm) high

£1,000-1,500 **WW**

A Scottish School Arts and Crafts brass and inlaid wall clock, attributed to Peter Wylie Davidson, repoussé-decorated with a band of flying birds and galleon, inlaid with opalescent roundels.

dial 11.5in (29cm) wide

£1,000-1,500 **L&T**

A Continental Art Nouveau brass clock, with marble, enamel and mixed metal detail.

17in (42.5cm) high

£1,200-1,800 **FRE**

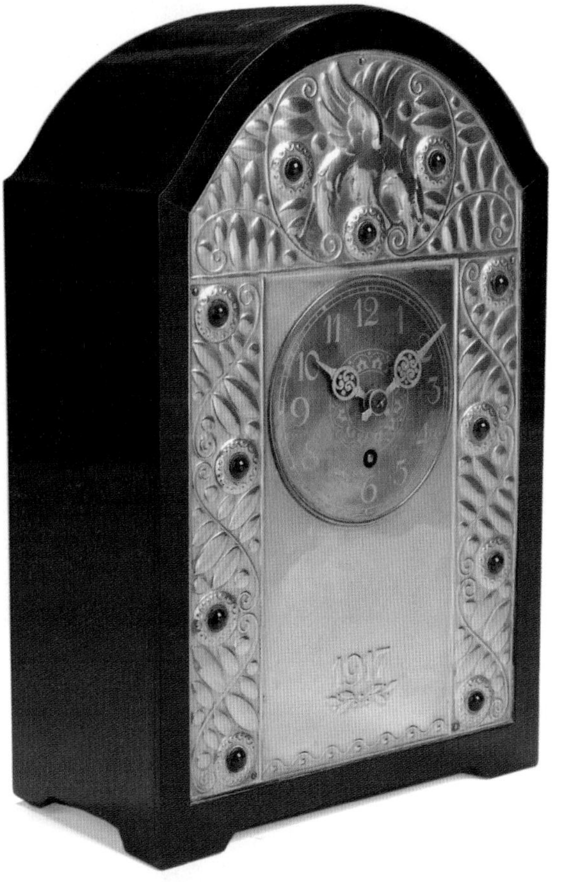

An Austrian Art Nouveau mantel timepiece, in the style of the Weiner Werkstatte, single train movement, copper dial, silvered border repoussé-decorated with flowering foliage with blue cabochons, within an ebonized case, dated.

1917 *12.25in (31cm) high*

£1,500-2,000 **L&T**

An early 20thC longcase clock, from the Darmstadt/Jugendstil School, in the manner of Richard Riemerschmid, hammered copper face and pendant in fruitwood frame.

c1905 *84in (213.5cm) high*

£3,000-5,000 **SK**

An Australian Arts and Crafts silky oak longcase clock, the broken pedestal top with arched glazed door enclosing a domed brass dial, movement unknown.

103in (262cm) high

£2,500-3,000 **BONA**

An Art Deco silver clock with enamelled blue vase and two yellow roses, "Made in France".

c1925 *4in (10cm) wide*

£1,000-1,500 **JES**

An Art Deco enamel on gilded silver clock, with turquoise vase of flowers, easel back, marks for "Turler Zurion".

c1925 *4.25in (11cm) high*

£1,000-1,500 **JES**

An Art Deco spelter and alabaster mantel clock.

18.5in (47cm) wide

£500-800 **WW**

An Art Deco spelter and marble mantel clock, unsigned.

12.75in (32.5cm) wide

£300-500 **WW**

An Art Deco bronze mantel clock, the arched clock flanked with kissing children, on stepped onyx and marble base, unsigned.

9.75in (25cm) high

£300-400 **WW**

A French Art Deco Shagreen mantel clock, with ivory piping and button feet, with silver face, stamped "France/LF".

5.75in (14cm) high

£500-800 **SDR**

An Art Deco Telechron clock, model 4F65, blue glass with Roman numeral dial, on flat chromed metal bar with curvilinear foot, electric movement.

c1935 *7.25in (18.5cm) wide*

£400-600 **SK**

A Modernist / Art Deco clock, black glass on clear glass base, chrome numeral marks, hands and square face holder.

c1935 *9.75in (25cm) wide*

£1,500-2,000 **DD**

A Modernist Art Deco clock, mirrored round face with carved disc numeral marks, stepped chrome base.

c1935 *9.5in (24cm) wide*

£600-900 **DD**

A Gilbert Rohde/Herman Miller Art Deco 'Telechron' electric clock, with burlwood veneer, numbered "4082B".

13in (32.5cm) wide

£1,000-1,500 **SDR**

An Art Deco chrome timepiece, in the form of a tennis racket.

Provenance: *Elton John Sale Lot 1872.*

9in (22.5cm) wide

£500-800 **SWO**

A rare Pierre Fargette French Art Deco mantel clock, with gilded bronze stylized floral decoration, silver sunrays and nude copper relief, on an onyx base, signed on back.

Pierre Fargette was known for his lighting designs which he exhibited at the 1925 Paris Exposition.

c1925 *9in (23cm) wide*

£4,000-6,000 **DD**

A French Art Deco Shutter watch, a Gerard Sandoz design, in sterling with eggshell and black geometric enamel decoration, Swiss movement by Otomato, the ends depress to reveal clock face, 18ct gold numerals.

c1930 *2.75in (7cm) wide*

£4,000-6,000 **DD**

A Rene Lalique Art Deco moulded glass clock, stepped base with bronze painted numerals, signed "R. Lalique" on face.

c1935 *8in (20.5cm) wide*

£4,000-6,000 **DD**

A French Art Deco Ato clock, carved and frosted glass square face, black stepped Bakelite base.

c1935 *7.5in (19cm) wide*

£1,000-1,500 **DD**

A Christopher Dresser silver teapot, manufactured by Hukin and Heath, silver, ivory and enamel, with rush-covered handle, stamped marks "Designed by Dr C Dresser", Birmingham 1878.

Hukin and Heath were the first to commission Dresser after his visit to Japan. This teapot incorporates real Japanese elements with its inlaid Shibayama lid. Dresser produced several tea services in silver for Hukin and Heath, but this teapot is apparently unique. With its luxury materials it is clearly a departure from Dresser's mass-produced wares.

4.25in (10.5cm) high

£40,000-60,000 **L&T**

A Christopher Dresser teapot, manufactured by James Dixon & Sons, silver plate with ebony handle, stamped with facsimile signature 'Chr. Dresser', and marked 'JD & S 2277', design registered 1879.

5in (13cm) high

£60,000-80,000 **L&T**

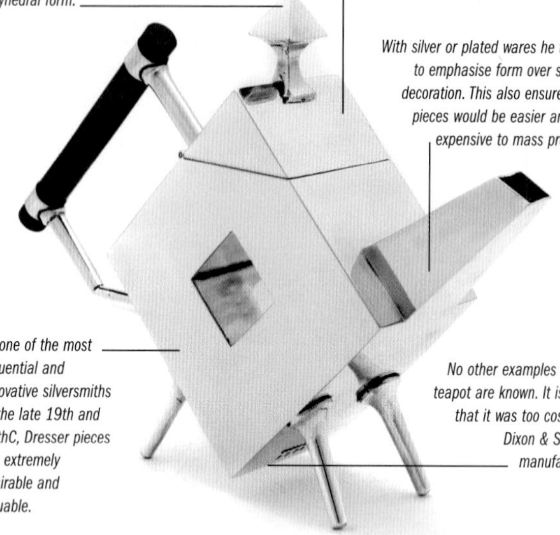

A Christopher Dresser silver plate three piece tea service, manufactured by James Dixon and Sons, with ebony handles, signature and marked "JD & S, 2273".

This set, with its particularly 'modern' look, has been copied by Italian design firm Alessi who have reproduced it as part of their Dresser range.

1880 Teapot 11cm (4.25in) high

£10,000-15,000 **L&T**

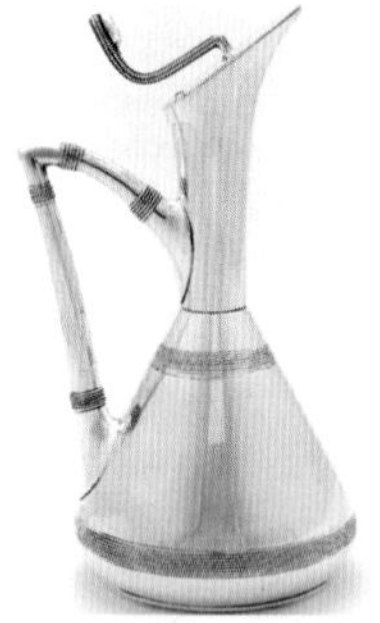

A Christopher Dresser silver plate lidded jug, manufactured by Elkington & Co., stamped marks 'Elkington & Co. 16587'.

c1865 9.5in (24cm) high

£800-1,200 **L&T**

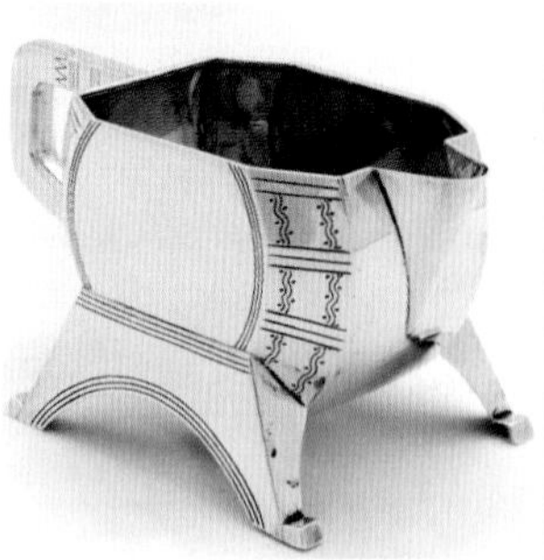

A Christopher Dresser copper and silver plate hot water jug, probably manufactured by Richard Perry, Son & Co., with a hardwood handle, stamped marks "G1 3".

c1880 9.25in (23.5cm) high

£1,000-1,500 **L&T**

A CLOSER LOOK AT A CHRISTOPHER DRESSER TEA POT

The influence of Dresser's 1876 trip to Japan is clearly evident in the design of this teapot. The simplicity of line and lack of ornamentation are based on Japanese precedent, as is the polyhedral form.

This is an extremely original design and is one of his seminal works. Despite being produced over 120 years ago, it still looks 'modern' today.

With silver or plated wares he tended to emphasise form over surface decoration. This also ensured that pieces would be easier and less expensive to mass produce.

As one of the most influential and innovative silversmiths of the late 19th and 20thC, Dresser pieces are extremely desirable and valuable.

No other examples of this teapot are known. It is likely that it was too costly for Dixon & Sons to manufacture.

A Christopher Dresser silver plate teapot, manufactured by James Dixon & Sons, with ebony handle, stamped with facsimile signature "Chr. Dresser" and marked 'J.D. & S. 2274'.

This iconic teapot forms one of a series of 37 radical designs Dresser supplied to James Dixon and Sons from 1879 to 1882.

1879 6.75in (17cm) high

£150,000-200,000 **L&T**

A Christopher Dresser water jug, manufactured by Elkington & Co., silver plate, stamped marks 'Elkington & Co. 17558', with registration mark for 1885.

9.5in (24cm) high

£15,000-20,000 **L&T**

A Christopher Dresser silver and silver gilt milk jug, manufactured by Elkington & Co, stamped marks "Elkington & Co.", Birmingham 1886, registration mark for 1885.

2.5in (6.5cm) high

£5,000-7,000 **L&T**

A four piece Christopher Dresser silver plate and glass cruet set, manufactured by Hukin and Heath, stamped marks "H & H 2592".

6.75in (17cm) high

£1,500-2,000 **L&T**

A Christopher Dresser silver plate and glass decanter, with ebony handle, unmarked.

c1880 *11in (28cm) high*

£2,800-3,200 **L&T**

A Christopher Dresser silver plate and glass lidded decanter, manufactured by Hukin and Heath, with an ebony handle, unmarked.

c1880 *8.5in (21.5cm) high*

£2,000-2,500 **L&T**

A Christopher Dresser silver plate toast rack, manufactured by Hukin and Heath, stamped marks "Designed by Dr C Dresser" and "H & H 2566".

1878

£1,500-2,000 **L&T**

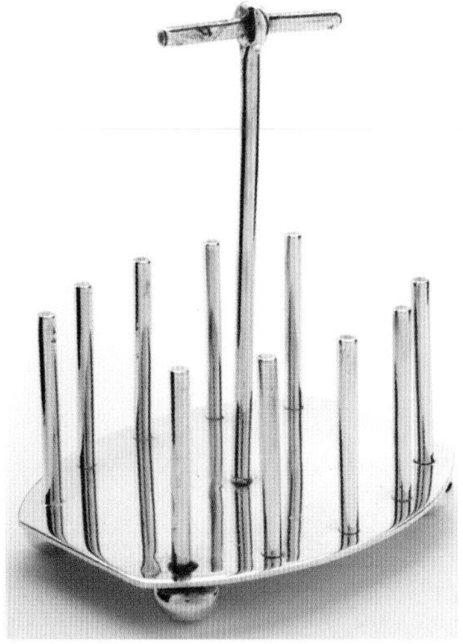

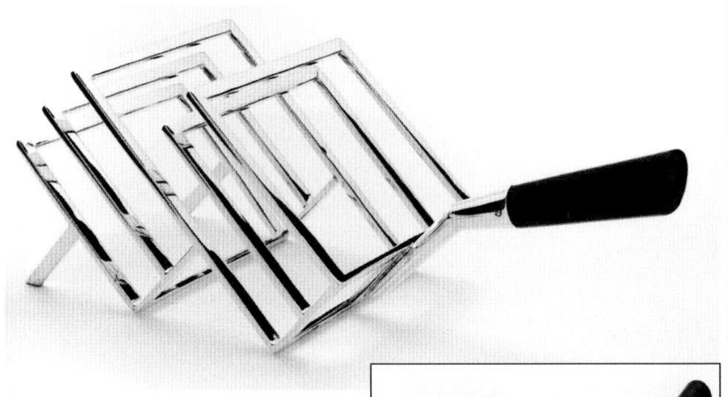

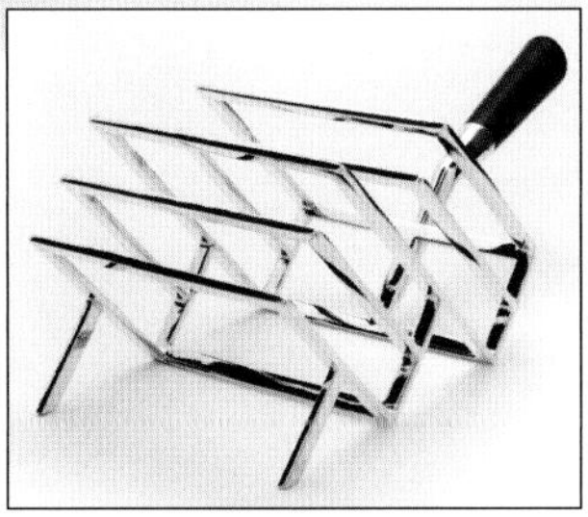

A Christopher Dresser silver plate and ebony toast rack, manufactured by James Dixon & Sons, stamped "Chr. Dresser" and marked "J.D. & S. 963".

c1880 *9.5in (24cm) wide*

£22,000-28,000 **L&T**

A Christopher Dresser silver plate toast rack, manufactured by James Dixon & Sons, stamped "Chr Dresser", and marked "J.D. & S. 67".

c1880 *4.75in (12cm) high*

£6,000-7,000 **L&T**

A Christopher Dresser silver plate spoon warmer, manufactured by Hukin and Heath, with ebony handle, inscribed with the letter "D", stamped marks "H & H 2887".

c1880 *4.75in (12.5cm) high*

£1,000-1,500 **L&T**

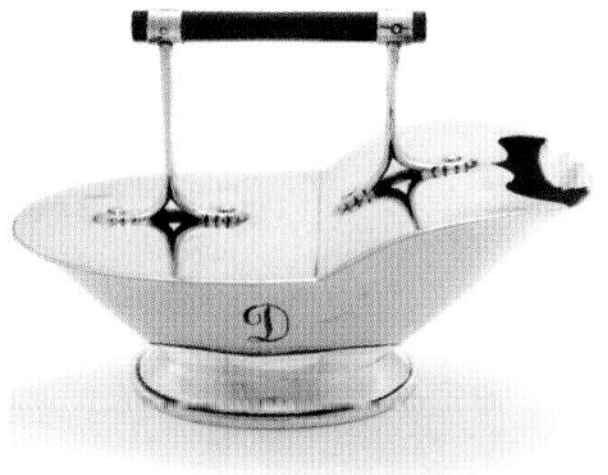

A Christopher Dresser silver plate tureen, cover and ladle manufactured by Hukin and Heath, with ebony handles, stamped marks "Designed by Dr C Dresser" and "H & H 2123".

1880 *12.25in (31cm) wide*

£10,000-15,000 **L&T**

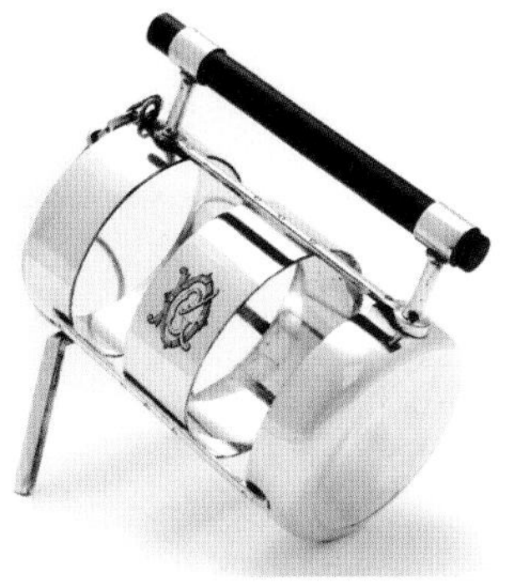

A Christopher Dresser silver plate port cradle, manufactured by Hukin and Heath, with ebony handle, stamped marks "H & H 3128", with registration mark for 1884.

7.25in (18.5cm) high

£2,200-2,800 **L&T**

A Christopher Dresser silver plate sugar bowl, manufactured by Elkington & Co, marks "Elkington & Co. 247".

A drawing of this bowl appears in Dresser's 'Principles of Design' article for 'The Technical Educator'. He explained "the sugar is always collected together, and the dust sugar separates itself from the lumps".

1885 *3.25in (8.5cm) high*

£22,000-28,000 **L&T**

A Christopher Dresser brass chamberstick, manufactured by Perryson & Co., with a wooden handle, stamped "Chr. Dresser's Design", registry mark.

7.5in (19cm) high

£600-900 **DRA**

A rare Jarvie Omicron two-branch candlestick, with conical holders set in spirals, bright finish and original bobeches, incised "Jarvie".

Robert Riddle Jarvie (1865-1941) was an important Chicago metalsmith who founded The Jarvie Shop.

10.75in (27.5cm) high

£4,000-5,000 **DRA**

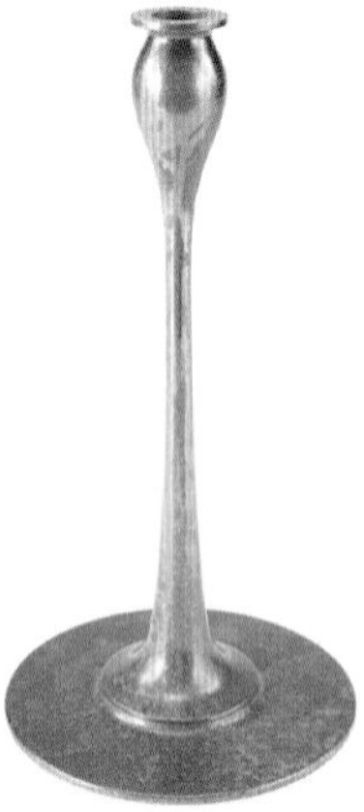

A Jarvie Iota bronze candlestick with bulbous top, missing bobeche.

14in (35.5cm) high

£1,200-1,800 **DRA**

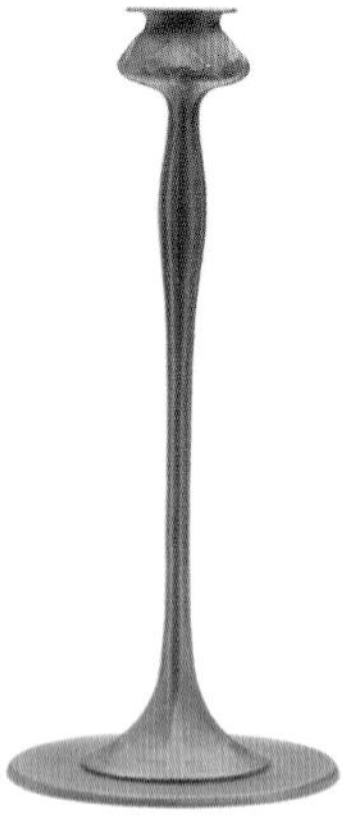

A tall Jarvie candlestick, embossed with spade-shaped leaves on long stems, complete with original bobeche, new patina, unmarked.

13.75in (34cm) high

£1,000-1,500 **DRA**

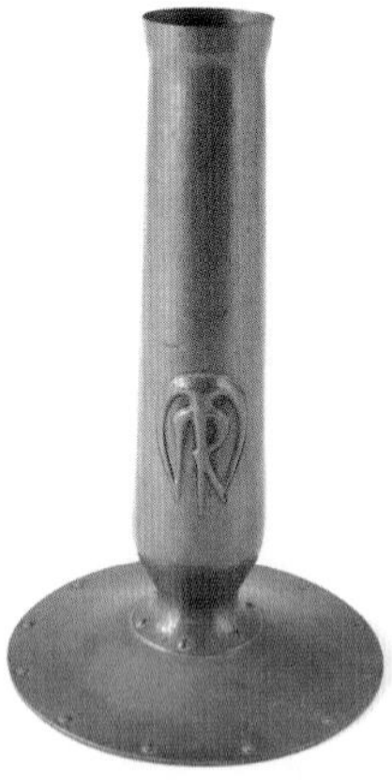

A Jarvie hammered copper bud vase, embossed "RT", with a broad circular riveted base, patina cleaned, incised "Jarvie".

11.5in (29cm) high

£2,500-3,000 **DRA**

A Jarvie hammered copper bowl, with closed-in rim covered in a medium patina, stamped "MADE BY THE JARVIE SHOP", shallow dent and small tear to rim.

6.5in (16.5cm) diam

£250-300 **DRA**

ROYCROFT

A rare Roycroft hammered copper bud vase, in a wood-grain pattern, with four buttressed handles alternating with four silver squares, in the Secessionist style, original patina, orb and cross mark.

8in (20.5cm) high

£3,000-4,000 **DRA**

A Roycroft hammered copper riveted 'shell-casing' vase, with tall cylindrical neck, medium patina, orb and cross mark.

10.25in (28.5cm) high

£1,800-2,200 **DRA**

A Roycroft brass-washed hammered copper tall 'American Beauty' vase, monogrammed "SWW", orb and cross mark, short split and wear to rim.

18.5in (47cm) high

£1,200-1,800 **DRA**

A Roycroft hammered copper card tray, with stitched and textured ground in cruciform pattern with verdigris patina on a medium base, early orb and cross mark.

6.75in (17cm) diam

£800-1,200 **DRA**

A pair of Heintz sterling-on-bronze cylindrical vases, overlaid with daffodils on verdigris patinas, "HAMS" stamps, scratches.

8in (20.5cm) high

£700-1,000 **DRA**

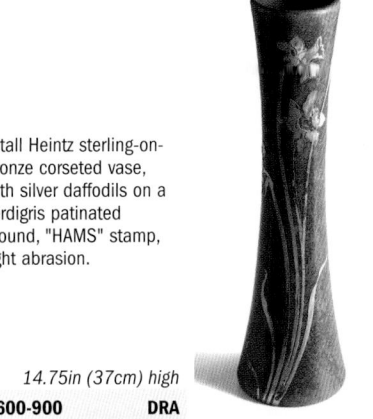

A tall Heintz sterling-on-bronze corseted vase, with silver daffodils on a verdigris patinated ground, "HAMS" stamp, light abrasion.

14.75in (37cm) high

£600-900 **DRA**

A large Heintz sterling-on-bronze urn overlaid with bands of floral decoration on dark bronze patina, "HAMS" with patent, wear, scratches and dent to base.

17in (43cm) high

£150-200 **DRA**

A large Heintz sterling-on-bronze cigar humidor, overlaid with dogs hunting a leaping deer, original dark patina and cedar lining, stamped "HAMS Sterling-on-Bronze", Patent, replaced foot.

10in (25.5cm) wide

£400-600 **DRA**

SAMUEL YELLIN

A pair of early 20thC Samuel Yellin wrought iron andirons, impressed "Samuel Yellin" on base.

28in (71cm) high

£2,800-3,200 **POOK**

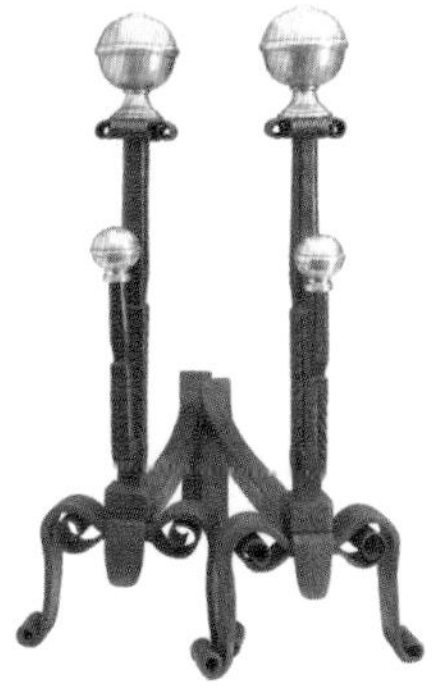

A pair of Samuel Yellin andirons, etched with a geometric leaf pattern and topped by brass balls, stamped "SAMUEL YELLIN".

24in (60cm) high

£1,000-1,500 **DRA**

A large Samuel Yellin wrought-iron triple candelabrum, with whiplash branches over a cruciform base, unmarked.

From the estate of Carl Schoeck, who produced this piece at the Yellin Workshop. Schoeck worked on many significant Yellin commissions, including the Packard Building in Philadelphia and the Bok Tower in Lake Wales, Florida.

c1935 *22in (55cm) high*

£2,200-2,800 **DRA**

A Samuel Yellin wrought-iron hinged door or screen, with rings joined by barbed knots, some wear to black enamel, stamped "33".

25.5in (64cm) high

£600-900 **DRA**

An Arts and Crafts silver and copper caddy, with lid marked for the Artificers' Guild and the base marked for Edward Spencer.

1931 *5in (12.5cm) high*

£1,200-1,800 **VDB**

Two tall Arts Crafts Shop, Buffalo, copper candlesticks, enamelled with blossoms, one with original patina, one with new patina, stamped, chips.

19in (44.5cm) high

£500-700 **DRA**

A Carence Crafters pagoda-shaped brass covered box, acid-etched with wild roses in a copper patina, impressed "CC".

7in (17.5cm) high

£800-1,200 **DRA**

A Chicago School copper and oak match holder, with a Prairie School backplate mounted on a wooden tile, original finish and patina, unmarked.

8in (20cm) square

£400-600 **DRA**

A Scottish Arts and Crafts copper wall plaque, attributed to Margaret Gilmour, with turquoise enamel roundel and repoussé border with Celtic strapwork, unsigned.

20.5in (52cm) diam

£500-700 **L&T**

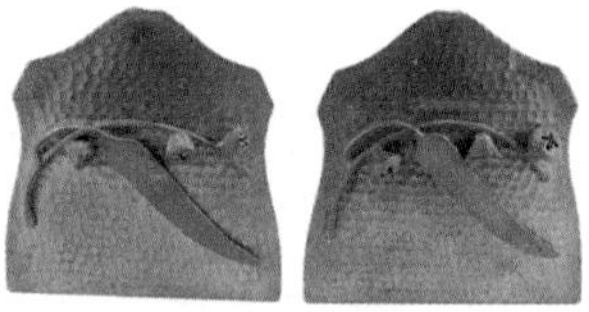

A pair of A. Hairenia hammered copper bookends, with applied eucalyptus branches with verdigris patina, one stamped "A. HAIRENIA/S.F. CAL".

7in (18cm) high

£600-900 **DRA**

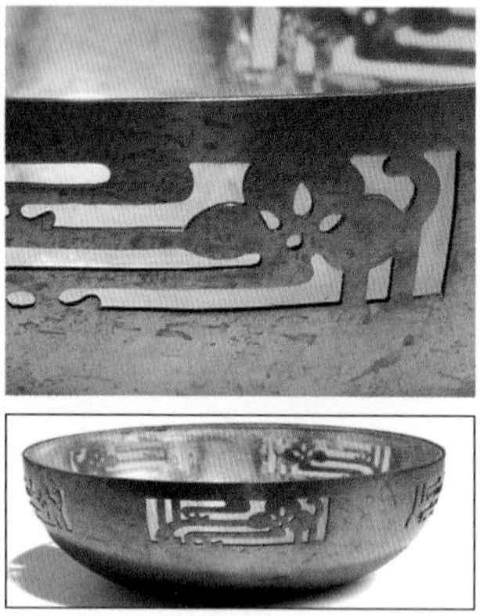

A Handicraft Guild hammered copper low bowl, with cut-out panels of stylized blossoms, lined in clear glass, cleaned patina, stamped "HANDICRAFT GUILD MINNEAPOLIS".

18in (45cm) wide

£1,200-1,800 **DRA**

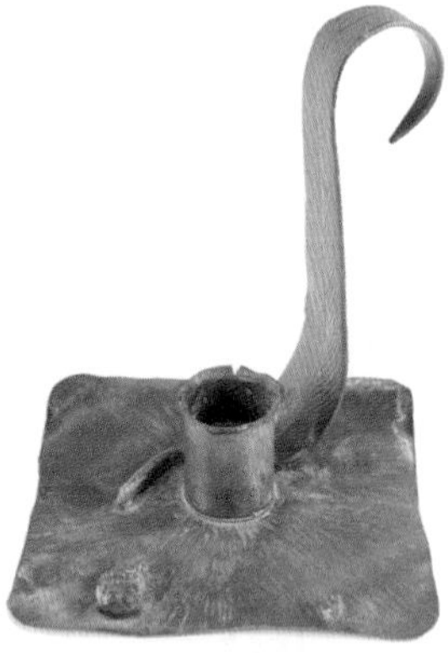

A Jauchen's hammered copper chamberstick, with tall eucalyptus leaf-shaped handle in green patina, stamped "JAUCHEN'S OLDE COPPER SHOP".

5.5in (14cm) high

£400-600 **DRA**

A rare Hans Jauchens copper plaque, embossed with tall trees under a fine dark original patina, incised "H Jauchens/sculptor/special".

24in (60cm) high

£3,000-4,000 **DRA**

An Arts and Crafts copper and silver tobacco jar, by Albert Edward Jones, hallmarked "Birmingham, 1910".

5.75in (14.5cm) high

£1,200-1,800 **VDB**

A rare Karl Kipp hammered copper peasant candlestick, with a four-sided stem in contrasting wood grain pattern, original dark patina, "stamped KK".

6.5in (16.5cm) high

£1,200-1,800 **DRA**

A Liberty & Co. copper mirror, with embossed repoussé flowers and two blue Ruskin roundels.

c1900 *25in (64.5cm) wide*

£1,800–2,200 **PUR**

A John Pearson copper deed box with latch, with carved peacock on the cover and side panels from William de Morgan's tiles, signed "J Pearson 1898".

9.5in (25cm) wide

£700-1,000 **VDB**

A John Pearson copper planter, decorated with three ships at the sides signed "J.Pearson 1894".

Pearson was a leading metalworker at the Guild of Handicrafts.

11.8in (30cm) wide

£3,000-3,500 **VDB**

A John Pearson brown patinated copper charger, with an urn issuing stylized flowers against a spot-hammered ground, inscribed mark to verso "J. Pearson, 1894, 2058".

16.25in (41cm) diam

£1,800-2,200 **B**

A pair of Charles Rohlfs copper and oak chambersticks, with carved feet and tall handles supporting trays, original finish and patina, marked "R 1901".

10in (25cm) high

£1,000-1,500 **DRA**

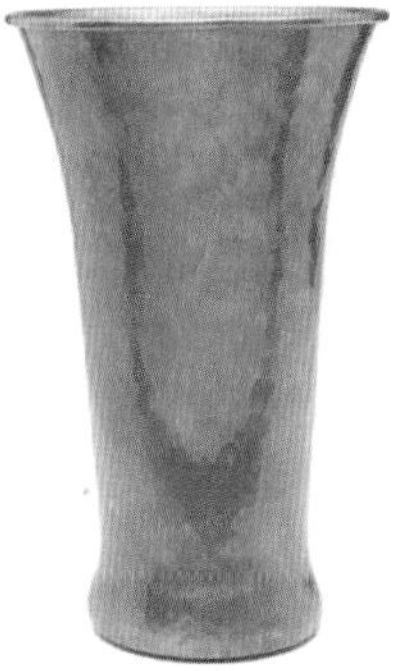

A Gustav Stickley hammered copper flaring vase, with rolled rim, cleaned patina, "Als Ik Kan" stamp.

10.5in (26cm) high

£600-900 **DRA**

A Stickley Brothers hammered copper two-handled jardinière, embossed with a band, stamped "71", patina cleaned.

14.5in (37cm) diam

£500-700 **DRA**

A Stickley Brothers hammered copper two-handled jardinière, for the Mission Inn, Riverside, California, with embossed bell logo, stamped "71", patina cleaned.

16in (40cm) wide

£2,000-3,000 **DRA**

A very large Dirk Van Erp hammered copper vessel, with rolled rim and original dark patina, "2", open box and windmill stamps, scratches.

15.75in (40cm) high

£6,000-8,000 **DRA**

A Dirk van Erp hammered copper baluster vase, with rolled rim, windmill mark, remnants of D'Arcy Gaw, wear to original patina.

9.5in (24cm) high

£1,200-1,800 **DRA**

A large English Arts and Crafts hammered copper charger, embossed with stylized poppy pods, original dark patina, unmarked.

21in (53.5cm) diam

£1,800-2,200 **DRA**

LIBERTY TUDRIC

- Liberty was founded by Arthur Lasenby Liberty in 1875 in London's Regent Street. The fashionable store soon became a favourite source of quality decorative items, many produced in the Arts and Crafts style.
- The Tudric pewter range was introduced from c1900. It was a more affordable alternative to the silver Cymric range, introduced the previous year.
- Many Tudric pieces were designed by Archibald Knox. His work kick-started the Celtic revival.
- For design inspiration, Knox turned to his Manx heritage and Celtic roots. Pieces feature interwoven knots, intricate entrelacs and stylized foliate motifs. Enamel cabochons and semi-precious stones were also used.
- Inspired by traditional manufacture techniques, surfaces were hammered.
- The pewter contained a high proportion of silver. It was fairly easy to mould and took on the luminous quality of silver when polished.

A Liberty & Co. pewter Tudric four branch candelabrum, model no.0530, designed by Archibald Knox, cast with stylised leaves on a pierced base.

c1905 *11in (28cm) high*

£2,800-3,200 SWO

A pair of Liberty & Co. tall pewter Tudric candlesticks, designed by Archibald Knox, stamped "Tudric 0725".

12.75in (32cm) high

£4,000-5,000 DRA

A Liberty pewter Tudric tea service, designed by Archibald Knox, cast with stylized whiplash foliage, stamped factory marks "Tudric 0231", tray stamped "Tudric 0309".

Tray 18in (45.5cm) wide

£800-1,200 L&T

A Liberty pewter Tudric two-handled rose bowl, designed by Archibald Knox, with entrelac Celtic style motifs, impressed "0229" and "RD No. 420290".

12in (30.5cm) wide

£700-1,000 DNT

A Liberty & Co. polished pewter Tudric cedar-lined cigarette box, with enamelled blossoms, marked "0851 TUDRIC".

3.5in (9cm)

£500-700 DRA

A Liberty pewter Tudric cigar box, model no.0236, inset with an enamel landscape panel.

c1905 *7in (17.5cm)*

£700-1,000 SWO

A Liberty pewter Tudric biscuit jar embossed with stylized sunflowers, and a tray with enamelled medallion, both marked.

tray 12.25in (31cm) wide

£1,000-1,500 DRA

A Liberty & Co. pewter Tudric pewter mantel clock, model no.01156, with a hammered finished and a copper and enamelled dial, stamped marks.

7in (17.5cm) high

£800-1,200 SWO

An Arts and Crafts pewter part dressing table set, each item set with a Ruskin cabochon, within engraved borders.

Mirror 17in (43cm) high

£400-500 B

An Elizabeth Copeland silver and enamel box, with stylized enamel flowers and applied wire and silver balls, raised artist's initials "EC".

4in (10cm) wide

£1,500-2,000 **SK**

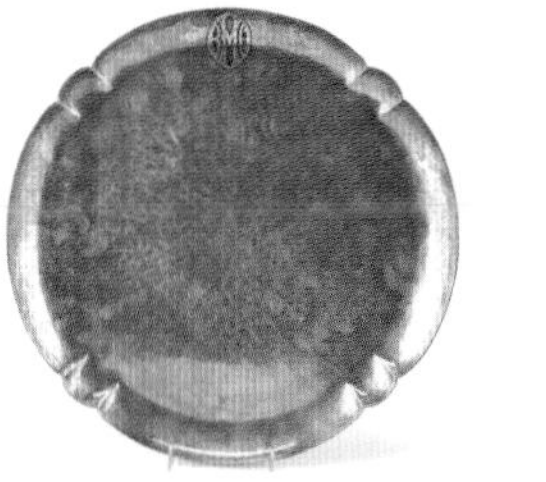

A Fallick Novick hammered sterling silver circular tray, monogrammed "BMH", scratches.

Fallick Novick work in silver is extremely rare.

16in (40.5cm) diam

£800-1,200 **DRA**

An American silver fruit bowl, by C.G. Forrsen and retailed at the Handicraft Shop of the Boston Society of Arts and Crafts.

1907 *9.25in (23.5cm) high*

£300-500 **IHB**

An A.E. Jones three piece silver tea service, with rosette bands and hammered grounds, hallmarked Birmingham.

1912

£350-400 **L&T**

A Liberty & Co. silver box, inset with an enamel plaque by Fleetwood Charles Varley, with a hammered finish and cedar wood lining, signed "Varley".

1911 *8.75in (22cm) wide*

£3,000-5,000 **SWO**

A Petersen Sterling goblet, with grapes to the stem, stamped marks to foot.

Danish silversmith Carl Petersen (1895-1977) was apprenticed to Georg Jensen. He emigrated to Canada in 1929.

11.5cm high (10cm) high

£400-600 **TCF**

A set of Petersen sterling salad servers, with Art Nouveau moulding and stamped marks.

10.25in (26cm) long

£1,000-1,500 **TCF**

An Omar Ramsden silver and enamel pin tray, with lightly hammered sides and an enamel monogram, marked for London.

1927 *4.5in (11.5cm) wide*

£500-700 **GORL**

A Ramsden and Carr silver hinged rectangular box, with enamelled lid decorated with a landscape with castle, hallmarks include "RN & CR".

4.25in (11cm) wide

£1,200-1,800 **DRA**

An Arts and Crafts silver tazza, by John Reilly, with a spot-hammered bowl set on three whiplash supports, foot set with a ruby glass cabochon, stamped "10901" "RD No. 437773", Sheffield.

1904 *5in (13cm) high*

£600-900 **B**

An Arts and Crafts silver plaque, engraved with Mary on a donkey with Joseph at her side, in an ebonized frame.

3in (7.5cm) high

£300-500 **LFA**

A Carence Crafters brass tray, with patinated surface and acid-etched design, signed "Carence Crafters Chicago", with monogram.

9in (23cm) wide

£400-600 **CHI**

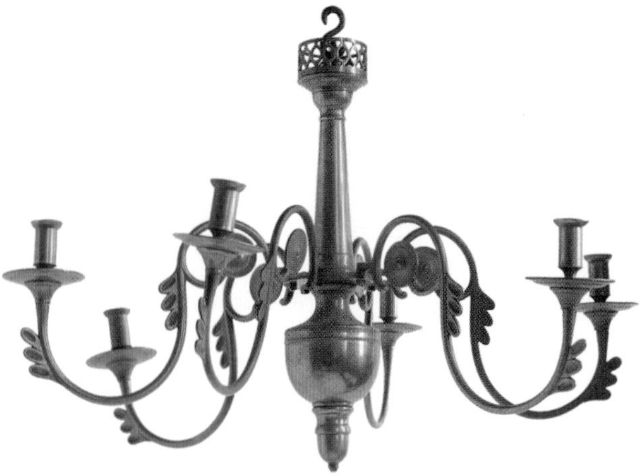

An Arts and Crafts brass chandelier, designed by Ernest Gimson for Robert Weir Schultz, with six scroll shaped branches cast with stiff leaves, one sconce missing.

£1,200-1,800 **LFA**

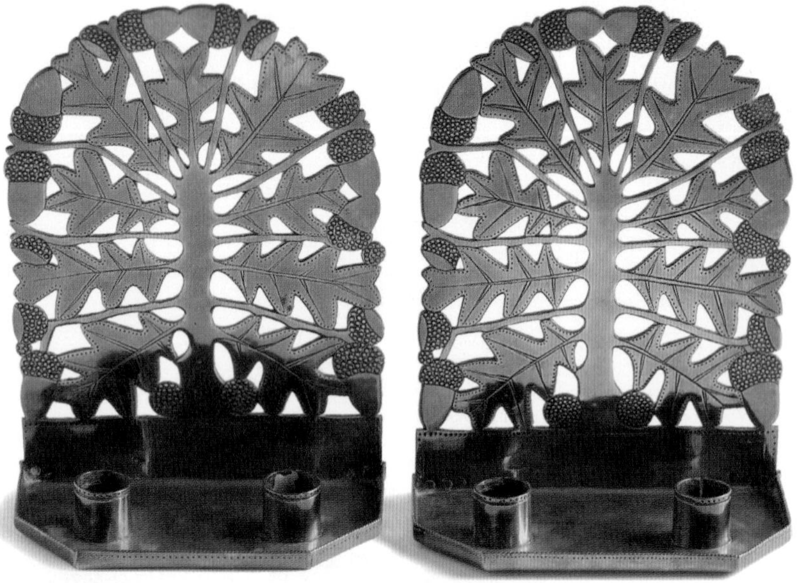

A pair of brass wall sconces, designed by Ernest Gimson and made by Alfred Bucknell, each with two candle sconces, the backplate pierced with a fruiting tree.

9.75in (25cm) high

£12,000-18,000 **LFA**

A single brass Newcomb College candlestick embossed with roses on a stippled background, some lifting of edges and tear to one panel, stamped and dated.

1910 *8.25in (21cm) high*

£200-300 **DRA**

A John Pearson beaten brass jardinière, each side embossed with a central cabochon, on four ball feet, stamped "J Pearson 1895".

6.75in (17cm) high

£30-60 **DNT**

A tall Jessie Preston brass candlestick, with trumpet-shaped shaft, medium patina, triangular stamp.

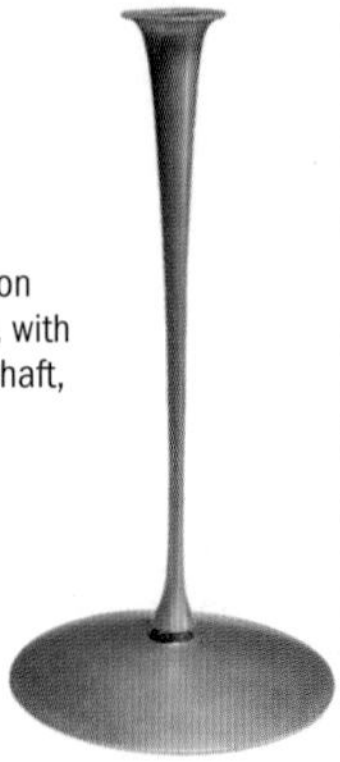

14in (35cm) high

£400-600 **DRA**

An Arts and Crafts wall mirror, within a hammer-beaten brass surround, inset with cabochon enamel panels.

32.75in (83cm) wide

£280-320 **SWO**

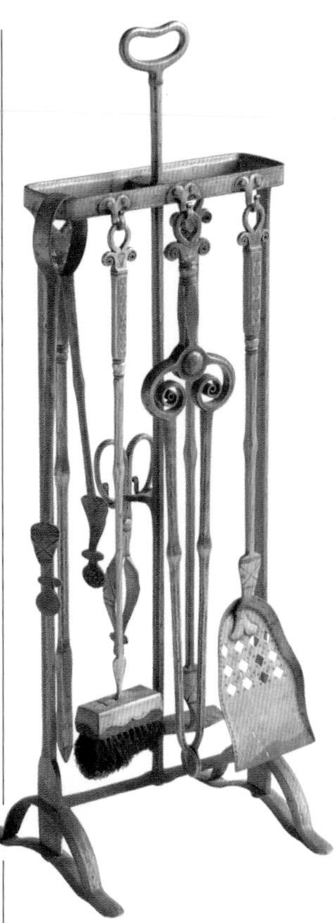

A polished steel set of fire irons on stand, by Ernest Gimson and made by Alfred Bucknell, decorated with engraved geometric designs.

37in (94cm) high

£5,000-7,000 **LFA**

A polished steel pair of fire dogs, by Ernest Gimson and made by Alfred Bucknell, each with a stamped circular disk held by a swan neck, on stylized leaf-shaped feet.

24.25in (61.5cm) high

£4,000-6,000 **LFA**

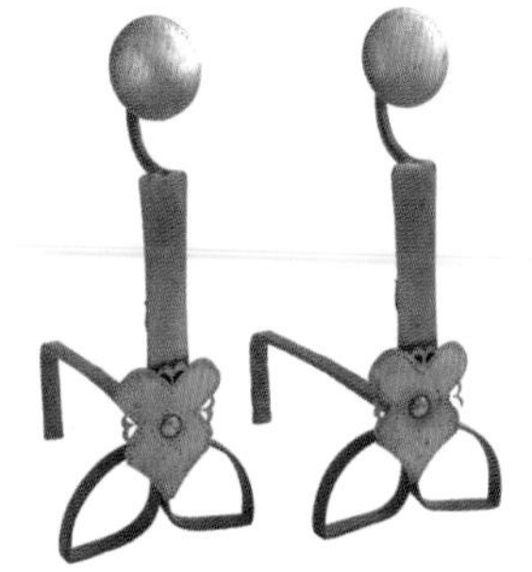

A steel pierced folding fender, by Ernest Gimson, with chamfered finials and bow-shaped cresting with pierced hearts.

52in (132cm) wide

£2,200-2,800 **LFA**

A polished steel fender, by Robert Lorimer, designed for Hallyburton and made by Thomas Hadden, with hinged side panels, twisted stems and ball finials.

1906 *26.5in (66cm) wide*

£2,500-3,500 **WW**

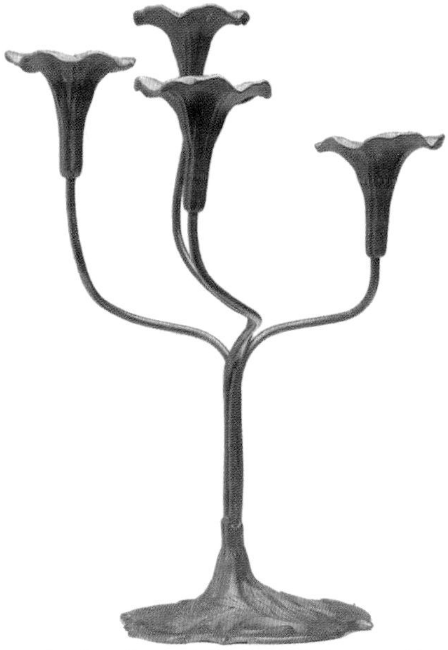

A bronze four-branch candelabra, by Jessie Preston, with trumpet flowers on swirling stems, original patina, "J. Preston Chicago".

18in (45cm) high

£5,000-7,000 **DRA**

An Arts and Crafts burnished steel wall sconce, possibly Artificers Guild, the pierced back plate with hexagonal panels of ball flowers and foliage, stamped to base "481".

12.5in (31cm) high

£1,500-2,000 **WW**

A bronzed doorstop, by Bradley & Hubbard, embossed with a mansion on top of a hill, stamped "B&H".

9.5in (24cm) high

£1,500-2,000 **DRA**

An unusual rutilated metal mirror, by Bradley & Hubbard, with attached candlesticks and coils, stamped "Bradley & Hubbard Mfg. Co.", dents.

18in (45cm) high

£1,000-1,500 **DRA**

An Arts and Crafts silvered hanging light fitting, fitted with coloured glass panels, the base hung with cast flowering thistle and with thistle leaf finial.

38.5in (98cm) high

£1,500-2,000 **L&T**

TIFFANY

- Louis Comfort Tiffany (1848-1933) established Tiffany Studios in 1902. He sold his products through his father's successful shop, Tiffany & Co.
- He had experience as a painter and glassmaker and had previously run an interior decorating company.
- He produced high quality and yet relatively affordable Arts and Crafts metalware and many other decorative items.
- Items tended to be small and practical, ranging from lamp fittings to decorative desk accessories, as well as boxes, bowls and candlesticks.
- Metalwork centred mainly on bronze and was often used in conjunction with glass.
- Pieces were embellished with low-relief patterns. Vine and trellis decoration was particularly popular, as were other designs inspired by Ancient Egypt, Native American motifs and astrological signs.
- The most collectable pieces have a gilt or gilt-doré finish.
- Most pieces are impressed "Tiffany Studios New York".

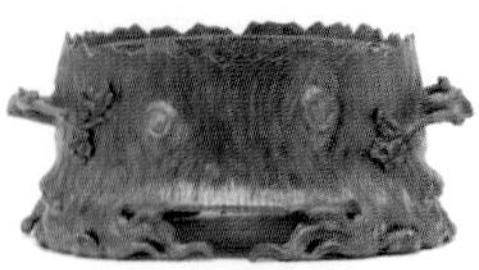

A Tiffany bronze-finished copper bowl, of organic trunk form with silver mounts and liner stamped "Tiffany Studios New York 50".

8in (20.5cm) diam

£1,200-1,800 **FRE**

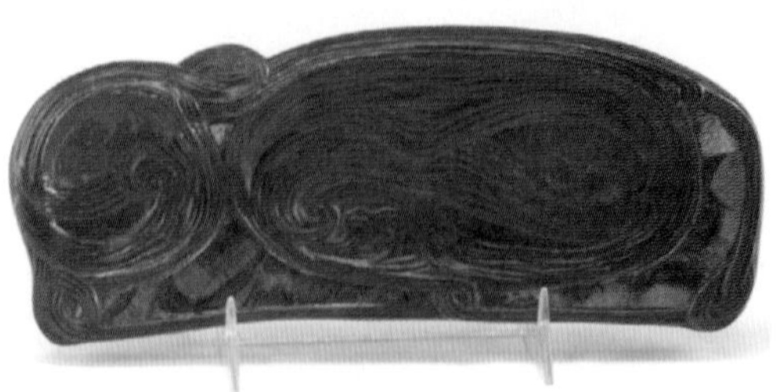

A Tiffany bronze pen tray, with raised swirls below a mosaic of Favrile glass, stamped "Tiffany Studios New York 24336".

8in (20cm) wide

£4,000-5,000 **DRA**

A Tiffany Studios bronze playing card holder, in the 'Pine Needle' pattern, lined in green slag glass and covered in verdigris patina, stamped on divider.

4in (10cm) high

£800-1,200 **DRA**

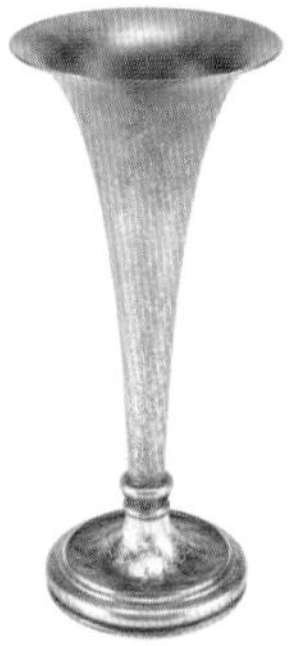

A Tiffany Furnaces gilt bronze and enamel trumpet vase, decorated in peacock blue enamel shading to gold and white, stamped "FAVRILE 165".

13.5in (34.5cm) high

£300-400 **DRA**

A Tiffany Studios bronze ashtray stand, with an acid-etched brass finish, stamped "TIFFANY STUDIOS NEW YORK 1649", wear to patina.

28in (70cm) high

£500-700 **DRA**

A Tiffany Studios picture frame in the 'Zodiac' pattern, covered in a verdris and bronze patina, "TIFFANY STUDIOS NEW YORK 943".

8in (20cm) wide

£800-1,200 **DRA**

A Tiffany Studios gilt-parcel inkwell, in the 'Grape' pattern. with mother-of-pearl dots, complete with glass liner, stamped "TIFFANY STUDIOS NEW YORK 1157", wear.

3.75in (9.5cm) high

£500-700 **DRA**

A Tiffany Studios gilt-parcel jewellery box, in the 'Grapevine' pattern, lined in caramel slag glass, original velvet-lined compartments, "TIFFANY STUDIOS NEW YORK 830".

9.5in (24cm) wide

£800-1,200 **DRA**

A Tiffany Studios gilt-parcel fernary in foliate pattern, acid-etched finish, stamped "TIFFANY STUDIOS NEW YORK 834 459".

11in (27.5cm) wide

£2,800-3,200 **DRA**

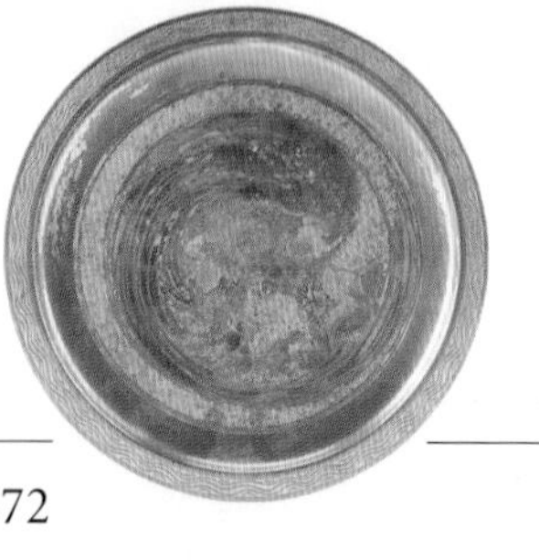

A Tiffany Studios card tray, enamelled with a bird of paradise eating grapes on a gold doré ground, "TIFFANY STUDIOS NEW YORK 2014", wear.

8in (20.5cm) diam

£220-280 **DRA**

A Tiffany Studios twelve-piece desk set, in the 'Mosaic' pattern, comprising perpetual calendar, two letter holders, ink blotter edges, rolling blotter, pen tray, letter opener, paper clip, inkwell with Favrile glass liner, and stamp moistener, all marked "LOUIS C. TIFFANY FURNACES", flakes.

£18,000-22,000 **DRA**

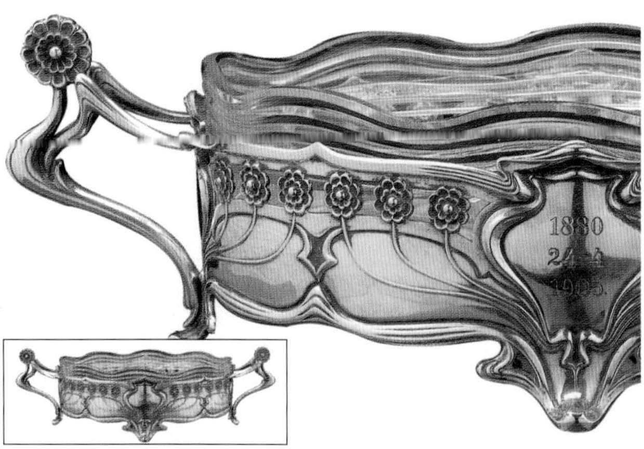

An A. Dragstedt silver and glass jardinière, with an openwork bowl with floral handles, signed "1880 24 - 4 1905", monogram, Copenhagen.

1904 *15.5in (39cm) wide*

£15,000-20,000 **KAU**

A William Hutton and Sons Ltd. silver and enamel photograph frame, embossed with stylized peacock feathers and trailing tendrils, flooded with enamels, London, splitting.

1904 *8.75in (22.5cm) high*

£1,800-2,200 **B**

A pair of Georg Jensen silver cigar lighters, of ornate oil lamp form, with detachable capped nozzles.

5in (12.5cm) wide

£1,000-1,500

A Georg Jensen sterling silver compote, the flared bowl raised on organic-motif support, signed underfoot.

5.25in (13.5cm) high

£1,200-1,800 **ISA**

An A.E. Jones silver triangular box, embossed with pansies, with leaf and berry borders, entwined clasp, slightly worn, Birmingham.

1906 *4.75in (12cm) wide*

£350-450 **B**

A WMF plated Jugendstil bowl, of four-leaf clover shape with a central female figure, WMF mark, some scratches.

c1900 *10.5in (26cm) high*

£500-700 **KAU**

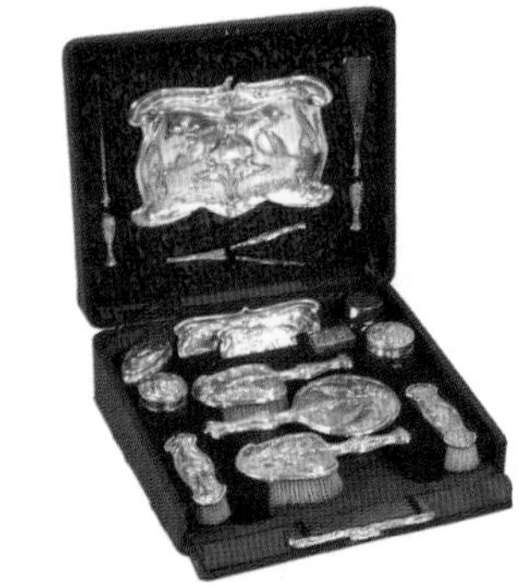

An Art Nouveau 16-piece silver dressing table set, by W** N**, each piece having repoussé back and adorned with Kingfishers and waterlilies, cased, Chester hallmarks.

1906

£800-1,200 **BIG**

ART NOUVEAU SILVER PLATE

An Art Nouveau Moritz Hacker electroplated table lamp, cast as a maiden entwined with whiplash foliage supporting two nautilus shell shades, stamped factory mark.

26.5in (67cm) high

£2,500-3,000 **L&T**

A pair of Art Nouveau WMF electroplated two-handled vases, cast with flowers and trailing tendrils, stamped marks.

5.5in (14cm) high

£200-300 **DNT**

An Art Nouveau WMF electroplate photograph frame, with pierced scrollwork borders cast with a female figure, easel back, impressed marks.

10in (25.5cm) high

£700-1,000 **DNT**

An Art Nouveau electroplated strut dressing-table mirror, elaborately cast with flowering irises.

18in (46cm) high

£2,000-2,500 **L&T**

An 'Embracing Couple' silvered bronze, by Sir Alfred Gilbert R.A., raised on an Art Nouveau stylized leafy base with canted plinth, unsigned.

5.75in (14.5cm) high

£2,000-2,500 **L&T**

An exceptional pair of cast bronze vases, by Francois Raoul Larche, each cast with four female allegorical figures standing amidst relief moulded lilies, inscribed signature and founder's mark "Siot Fondeur Paris".

16in (41cm) high

£8,000-12,000 **ISA**

A French Art Nouveau bronze patinated bust of 'Phryne', cast from a model by Emmanuele Villanis, foundry stamp for H. Hirschwald, Berlin.

c1900 *16.5in (41.5cm) high*

£800-1,000 **SWO**

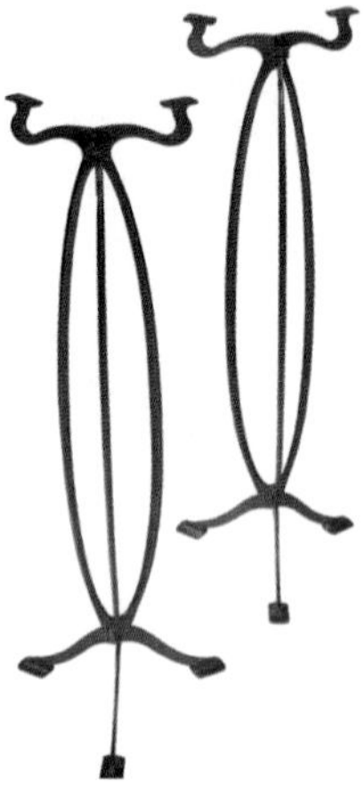

A pair of Art Nouveau bronze stands, each with three whiplash brackets and pad feet.

29.5in (75cm) high

£400-600 **L&T**

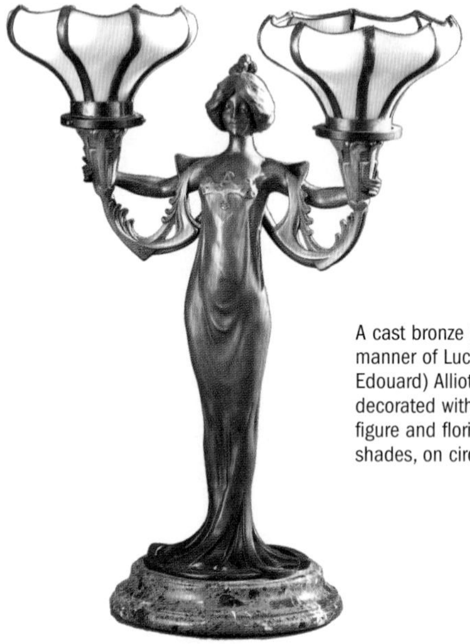

A cast bronze lamp, in the manner of Lucien (Charles Edouard) Alliot, polychrome decorated with female allegorical figure and floriform leaded glass shades, on circular marble base.

19.25in (49cm) high

£2,000-2,500 **ISA**

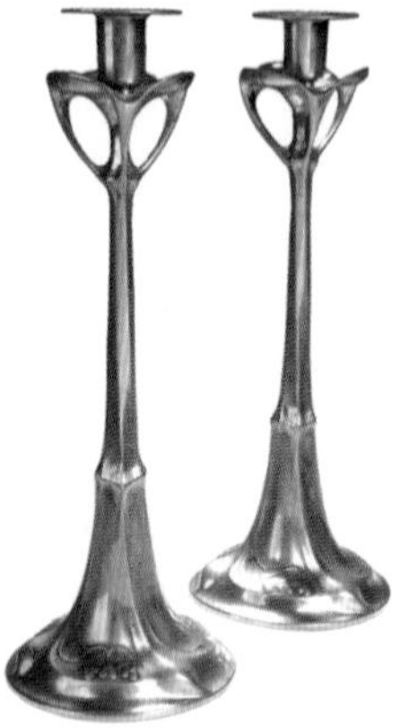

A pair of Kayserzinn pewter candlesticks, designed by Hugo Leven, cast with leafy whiplash foliage, cast factory marks 'Kayserzinn 88/4427'.

(42cm) high

£700-900 **L&T**

A WMF Art Nouveau baluster vase, of naturalistic organic form beneath a shaped rim and set with a figure, on foliate spreading base.

9in (23cm) high

£80-120 **NEA**

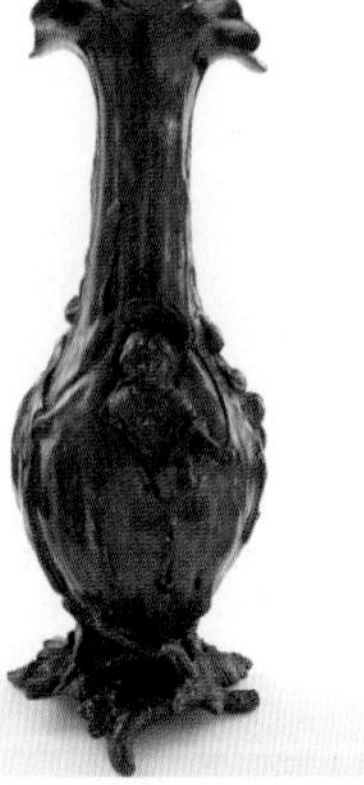

An Art Nouveau copper box, embossed with stylized poppies and scrolling tendrils on riveted tapered feet, with wooden lining, some dents.

7in (18cm) wide

£250-300 **DNT**

A 'Lively Harlequin' silvered bronze, cast from a model by Marcel Bouraine, on a signed marble base, stamped bronze.

15in (38cm) high

£1,500-2,000 **WW**

An Adolf Briitt 'The Sword Dancer' model, signed "A Briitt" with foundry mark for Guss H Noack, Berlin.

c1900 *20in (50cm) high*

£2,000-2,500 **SWO**

An Erte (Romain De Tirtoff) 'Lovers and Idol' cold painted bronze group, inscribed "Chalk and Vermillion, Stevenarts, 288/375".

52cm (20.5in) high

£1,500-2,000 **SWO**

An Art Deco Pierre Le Faguays silver-plated nude and gazelle model, on a stepped black marble base, signed with the LeVerrier foundry mark, and "Fayral".

'Fayral' and 'Guerbe' were the two pseudonyms used by the famous sculptor Pierre Le Faguays. He was best friends with Max Le Verrier, whose foundry made most of, if not all of, Le Faguays' work. His sculptures more typically featured dancers.

c1925 *26.5in (67.5cm) wide*

£2,200-2,800 **DD**

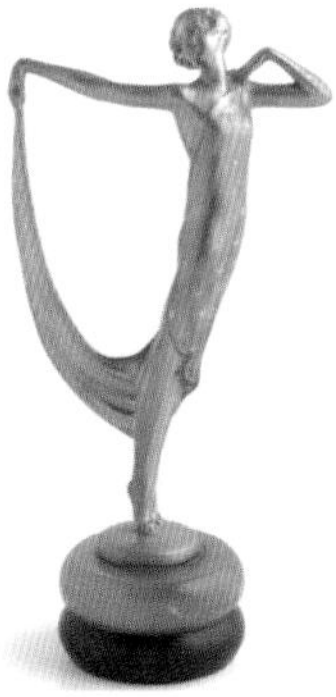

A silvered bronze figure, cast from a model by Josef Lorenzl, on an onyx base, signed in the bronze.

9.5in (24cm) high

£1,500-2,000 **WW**

A bronze figure of a lady, cast from a model by Josef Lorenzl, on onyx base, signed in the bronze "Lorenzl made in Austria".

10.25in (25.5cm) high

£1,200-1,800 **WW**

A silvered bronze figure of a girl, cast from a model by Josef Lorenzl, modelled holding an onyx pot, on an onyx tray base, signed in the bronze.

10.25in (26cm) high

£1,200-1,800 **WW**

An Art Deco patinated figure, in the manner of Ferdinand Preiss, cast as a dancer on stepped black marble base.

19.25in (49cm) high

£2,000-2,500 **L&T**

A patinated bronze 'Seated Fox' figure, cast from a model by Edward Sandoz, signed in the bronze "E S Sandoz".

9.5in (24cm) wide

£7,000-10,000 **WW**

A Phoebe Stabler bronze figure, signed in the bronze.

3.75in (9.5cm) high

£500-700 **WW**

A 20thC Bruno Zach bronze, the full length seated nude with a monkey, Austrian.

17in (43cm) high

£4,000-6,000 **FRE**

A Demetre Chiparus bronze and ivory figure of 'The Hoop Girl', in two piece costume, on a veined black marble base, with engraved "D.H. Chiparus" signature to base.

19in (48.5cm) high

£10,000-15,000 **GORL**

A David Alonzo bronze and ivory figure of a lady in medieval costume, on white onyx stepped base, with engraved signature "D Alonzo".

14in (35.5cm) high

£1,200-1,800 **GORL**

A Demetre Chiparus gilded bronze and ivory 'La Bourrasque' figure, gilded bronze, on a stone socle, unsigned.

c1930 *12.25in (31cm) high*

£4,000-6,000 **DOR**

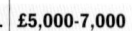

A Gerda Iro Gerdago bronze and ivory dancer, in an enamelled costume, on a silvered stand and green onyx base, engraved with a monogram and "Gerdago".

13.5in (34.5cm) high

£5,000-7,000 **GORL**

A Richard W. Lange Art Deco bronze and ivory parachute lamp, signed with artists name and "RUM".

1925 *33.75in (86cm) high*

£7,000-10,000 **JES**

A Josef Lorenzl silvered bronze and ivory figure, of a lady in exotic head dress and costume, enamelled with flame motifs, on a green onyx base, engraved "Lorenzl".

14.5in (37cm) high

£1,800-2,200 **GORL**

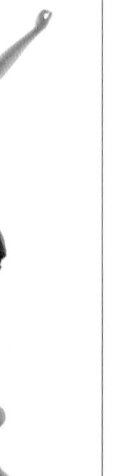

A Paul Philippe 'The Russian Dancer' bronze and ivory figure, on a circular marble base.

16in (40.5cm) high

£3,000-4,000 **GORL**

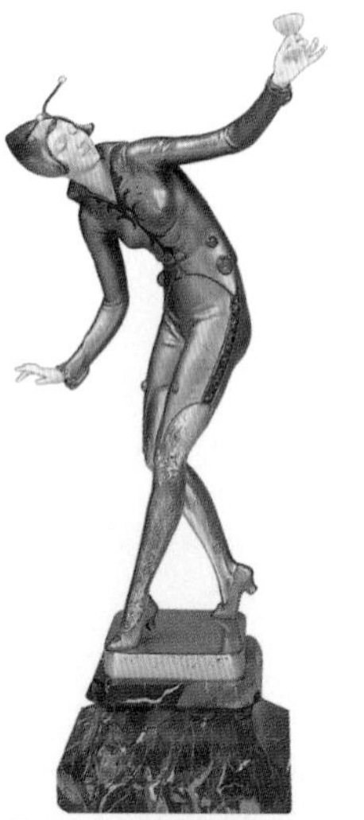

A Ferdinand Preiss 'Champagne-Dancer' bronze figure, enamelled in black, carved ivory, on a marble base, signed in the plinth.

c1930 *16.5in (41.5cm) high*

£6,000-9,000 **DOR**

A Ferdinand Preis bronze and ivory figure of a boy skiing, impressed "200014" and "P.K." for Preiss & Kassler.

Preiss worked extensively in bronze and ivory and is perhaps best known for his models of children and sporting subjects, the two brought together in this figure. His work reflected German pre-war ideals of youth and physical achievement, a fact particularly evident in the works produced during the Berlin Olympics of 1936.

8.75in (22.5cm) high

£6,000-9,000 **SWO**

A Ferdinand Preiss bronze and ivory 'Bat Girl' figure, on a stepped rectangular green onyx base, with engraved signature "F. Preiss".

9.25in (23.5cm) high

£4,000-6,000 **GORL**

A Ferdinand Preiss bronze and ivory figure of 'Aphrodite', on a pink circular marble base, signed "F. Preiss", with foundry stamp.

9in (23cm) high

£2,000-3,000 **GORL**

A Theodor Ullman bronze and ivory figure of a dancing lady, with a floral enamelled dress, on a silver plate oval base engraved "Th Ullman" and with a foundry logo, on concave green onyx base.

9.5in (24cm) high

£2,800-3,200 **GORL**

A German bronze and ivory figure of a dancer, partially painted in gold, with polychrome glass pearls, on a stone socle, unsigned.

c1915 13.25in (33cm) high

£2,000-3,000 **DOR**

ART DECO METAL FIGURES

An American Frankart nymph figural cast metal ashtray, signed.

c1930 9.25in (23.55cm) high

£280-320 **DD**

A pair of American Frankart nymph cast metal bookends, with green paint, on skyscraper bases, signed.

1928 9in (23cm) high

£1,500-2,000 **DD**

An Ernest Trova double walking figure, in stainless steel, fully signed and impressed on the base.

This was originally intended as an edition of nine, however, the edition was not completed.

1927 102.5in (259cm) wide

£30,000-50,000 **ISA**

An Art Deco patinated metal figural lamp, on rectangular marble base.

14.5in (37cm) wide

£500-600 **WW**

A Jean Verschneider (1872-1943) 'Lion Tamer' bronze, with a greenish brown patina, signed "Jean Verschneider L N Paris", foundry seal.

31.5in (79cm) high

£800-1,200 **FRE**

A 19thC bronze group, of a female Bacchante astride a goat, raised on an oval naturalistic base, on a canted rectangular slate plinth.

16.5in (42cm) high

£1,500-2,000 **WW**

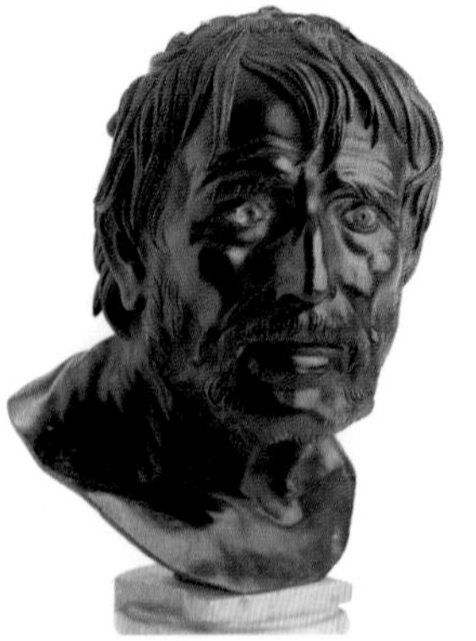

A Seneca bronze bust, possibly 19thC, patinated in black, with inlaid marble eyes, the neck with a three-leave blossom mark, one pupil missing.

17.5in (44cm) high

£1,200-1,800 **KAU**

A 19thC pair of French bronze figures, modelled as two draped seated putti, raised on fluted wood pedestals and square bases.

18.25in (45.5cm) high

£1,800-2,200 **FRE**

An 'Honor Patria' bronze, after Emil Louis Picault, with a dark brown patina.

70in (175cm) high

£3,000-4,000 **FRE**

A second half 19thC bronze figure of the 'Borghese Gladiator', the stump with a Latin inscription, now on an ebonized stand.

The original marble figure was produced in 1611 and was eventually purchased by Napoleon.

31.5in (80cm) high

£2,000-2,500 **SWO**

A Russian equestrian 'Officer on Horseback' bronze, with a dark brown patina, signed, raised on a naturalistic base.

16.5in (41cm) high

£2,200-2,800 **FRE**

A 'Satyr and Nymph' bronze, after Clodin, with a dark brown patina, signed "Clodin", raised on a rouge marble base.

15.5in (39cm) high

£800-1,200 **FRE**

A 'Marsys' bronze, after Antonio del Pollajuolo (1433-1489), with a dark brown patina, raised on a bombé baroque base, the corners cast with mythical figures.

12in (30cm) high

£2,500-3,000 **FRE**

A patinated bronze model of a Greek holding a scroll leaning on a tree stump, on a round base, unsigned.

12.25in (31cm) high

£800-1,200 **DN**

A 'Marcus Aurelius' gilt and patinated bronze, after the antique, raised on marble pedestal base.

15.25in (38cm) high

£2,200-2,800 **FRE**

GEORG JENSEN

- Danish designer Georg Jensen (1866-1935) was one of the most important silversmiths of the 20thC.
- After considering a career as a sculptor, Jensen established his own workshops on Bredgade, a fashionable Copenhagen street, in 1904.
- Working in jewellery and hollowware, his forms are typically simple and elegant. Tea ware often had graceful curves, decorated finials and elongated handles. Jewellery was inspired by nature and incorporated semi-precious stones.
- He adhered to the principles of the Arts and Crafts Movement.
- His delicate hand-hammered finishes draw attention to the qualities of the silver, often in lieu of any other surface decoration.
- Many of the designers hired by Jensen, including Johan Rohde and Sigvard Bernodotte, have also produced work that is very highly regarded today.
- Jensen used many marks over the years and these can help date objects.
- Many of his designs are still produced today and the Georg Jensen company continues to operate.

A Georg Jensen silver lidded dish, with dolphin finial to cover.

c1925 *5in (12.5cm) diam*

£3,000-4,000 **SF**

A Georg Jensen silver muffin dish, with ivory handle.

7in (18cm) diam

£3,000-4,000 **SF**

A Georg Jensen silver bowl, impressed mark "220634 - 0676/3".

1933 *6.5in (16.5cm) wide*

£600-800 **SF**

A Georg Jensen deep bowl, with a folded-in rim.

1933 *4.75in (12cm) diam*

£600-800 **SF**

An Art Deco large Georg Jensen silver table dish.

c1935 *13.25in (33.5cm) diam*

£8,000-12,000 **SF**

A pair of Georg Jensen silver pill boxes, with applied red and blue glass balls.

c1915 *1.5in (4cm) diam*

£800-1,200 **SF**

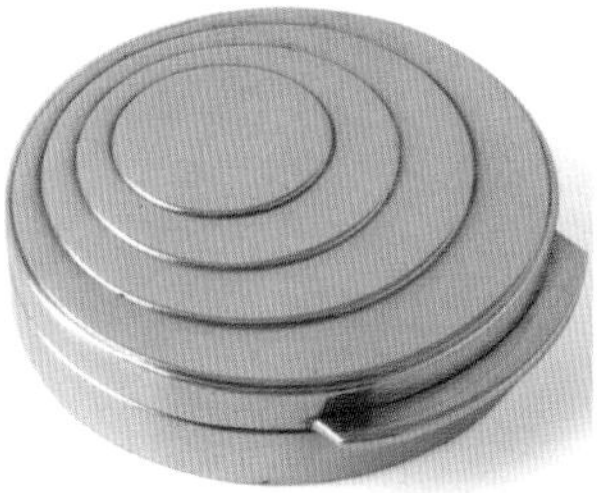

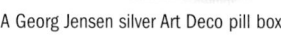

A Georg Jensen silver Art Deco pill box

c1930 *1.75in (4.5cm) diam*

£400-600 **SF**

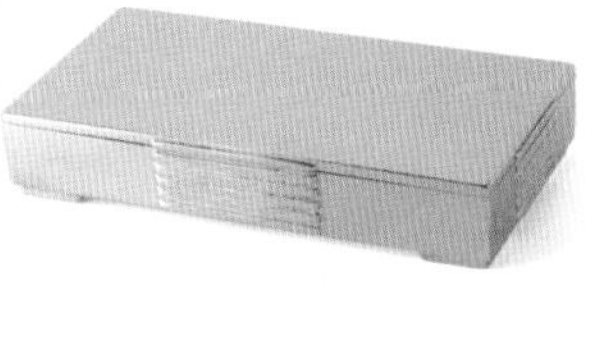

A Georg Jensen silver Art Deco cigar case, designed by Bernadotte.

c1933 *6.5in (16.5cm) wide*

£2,200-2,800 **SF**

A Georg Jensen silver Art Deco ashtray.

5in (12.5cm) diam

£600-800 **SF**

A Georg Jensen silver pin tray.

c1925 *10.25in (26cm) wide*

£1,800-2,200 **SF**

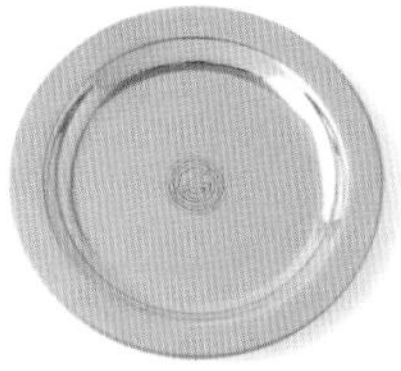

A Georg Jensen monogrammed silver coaster.

c1925 *5in (12.5cm) diam*

£400-500 **SF**

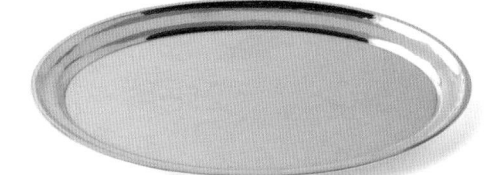

A Georg Jensen shallow silver dish.

c1945 *8.75in (22cm) wide*

£1,200-1,800 **SF**

A Georg Jensen silver teapot.

9.5in (24cm) wide

£4,000-5,000 **SF**

A Georg Jensen three-piece silver tea set, comprising a tall water pot, teapot and sugar bowl.

water pot 7.75in (19.5cm) high

£2,200-2,800 **SF**

A Georg Jensen three-piece silver tea set and tray, comprising a sugar bowl, double-spouted milk bowl and tall coffee pot.

c1935 *14.75in (37.5cm) wide*

£6,000-8,000 **SF**

A pair of Georg Jensen silver candelabra.

c1925

£6,000-9,000 **SF**

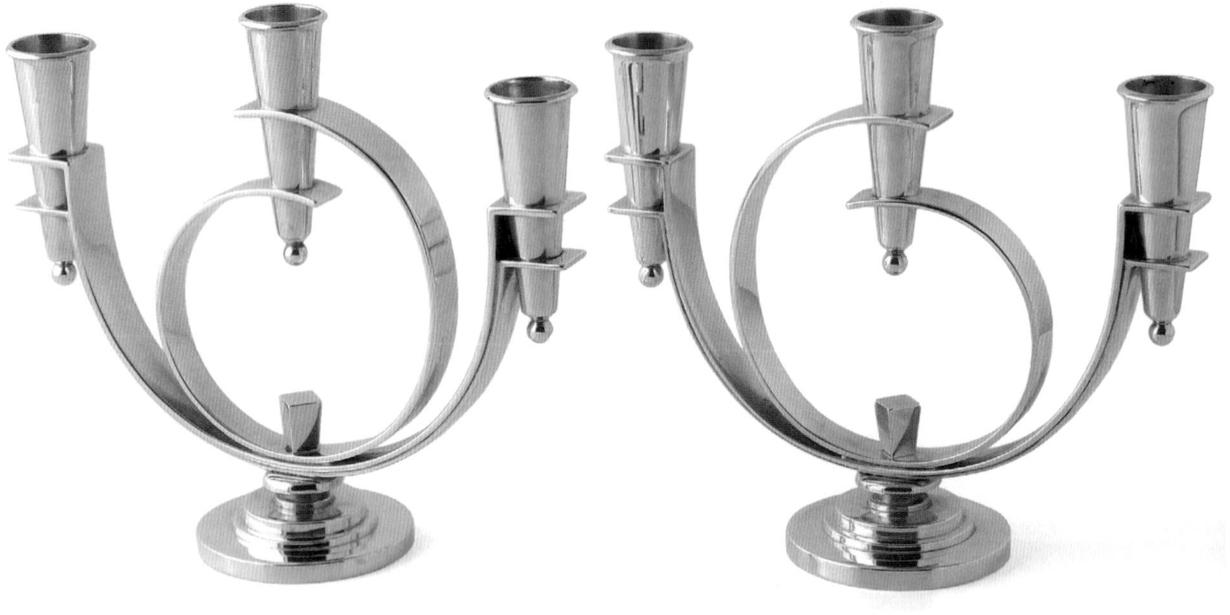

A pair of Art Deco Georg Jensen silver candelabra.

c1935 *6.5in (16.5cm) high*

£10,000-15,000 **SF**

A Georg Jensen companion pair of sterling silver candelabra, by O. Gundlach-Pedersen, 623B, signed, one with rectangular mark, the other with oval mark.

7.5in (19cm) high.

£3,000-5,000 **ISA**

A pair of Georg Jensen 'Pyramid' candlesticks.

5.5in (14cm) diam

£7,000-9,000 **SF**

A Georg Jensen skyscraper condiment set, comprising salt and pepper cruets and a mustard pot with spoon.

c1935

£4,000-5,000 **SF**

A Georg Jensen jug-shaped cocktail shaker, designed by S. Bernadotte, with a covered spout, with banded handle and cap rim and checkered body.

c1925 *5.75in (14.5cm) high*

£3,000-4,000 **SF**

A silver Georg Jensen cover with a stylized loop, fitted to a blue ceramic cup marked "B&G Rjobenmayx Danmark".

c1933 *4.75in (12cm) high*

£1,000-1,500 **SF**

A Charles Boyton Art Deco silver teaset, stamped maker's marks, facsimile signature, London.

1934 *Teapot 4.25in (11cm) high*

£1,200-1,800 **JES**

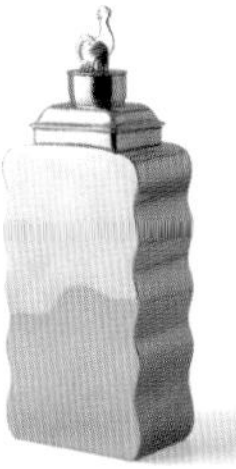

An Arnold Bung silver cocktail shaker.

8in (20.5cm) high

£3,000-4,000 **SF**

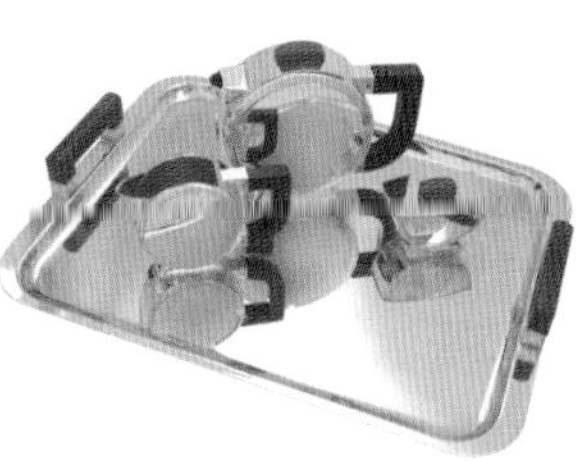

A Christofle Art Deco tea set with tray, silver plated circular design with burl ambonia wood handles.

c1935 *teapot 7in (18cm) high*

£3,000-4,000 **DD**

A French high Art Deco Ravinet d'Enfert silver coffee and tea set, with Cubist details and macassar ebony handles, hallmarked.

Ravinet d'Enfert exhibited at the 1925 Paris Exposition.

1925 *teapot 7in (18cm) high*

£3,000-4,000 **DD**

A rare American Art Deco Lurelle Guild silver-plated coffee set, for International Silver, with ebonized handles, sleek profile and decorative finial.

Guild was one of the first pioneering American industrial designers to translate French Art Deco designs into American everyday products.

12in (30.5cm) high

£3,000-5,000 **DD**

An Art Deco Mappin & Webb silver compote, with concentric linear design inside bowl, stepped base, signed.

1930 *9in (23cm) diam*

£600-800 **DD**

An Art Deco Mappin & Webb silver Martini shaker, with etched linear design, signed "Mappin & Webb, Price's plate, London Sheffield".

c1935 *9in (23cm) high*

£400-500 **DD**

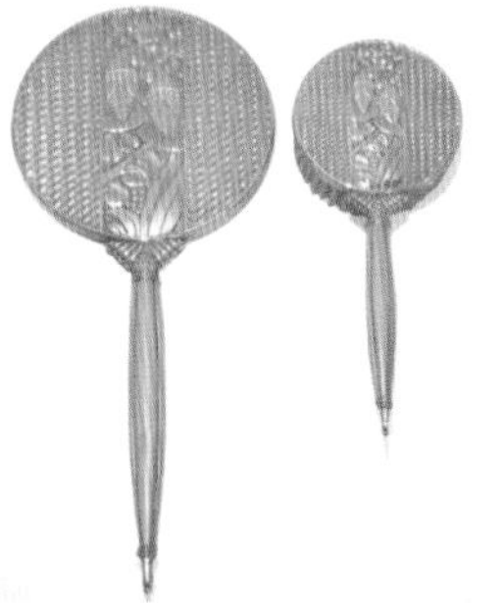

An American Art Deco Napier sterling vanity set, featuring stylized birds and floral design set in basketweave decoration.

c1935 *mirror 14.5in (37cm) long*

£600-800 **DD**

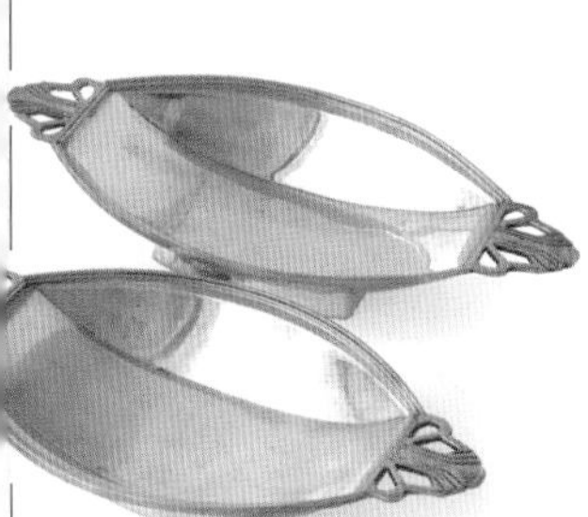

A pair of Art Deco W. Neale Ltd. bon bon dishes, with angular openwork handles, Birmingham.

1936 *8.25in (21cm) wide*

£150-200 **WW**

A Maria Regnier handwrought sterling silver flatware service, each piece with applied and pierced "MS" monogram, impressed signature "MR" and "sterling"

£4,000-5,000 **ISA**

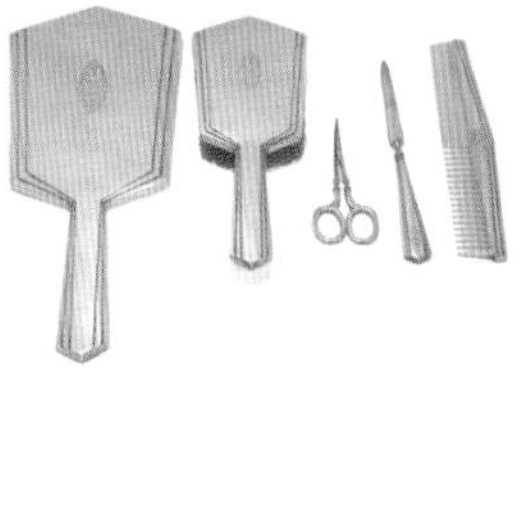

A rare American Art Deco Eliel Saarinen sterling silver 'Skyscraper' vanity set, for International Silver.

This set was exhibited in 1934 at Cranbrook Academy of Art and was part of a larger vanity collection designed for International Silver.

1934 *mirror 11.75in (30cm)*

£1,500-2,000 **DD**

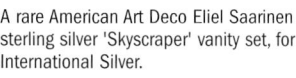

A rare American Art Deco Eliel Saarinen sterling silver mirror, from the 'Skyscraper' vanity set.

1934 *11.75in (30cm) long*

£500-700 **DD**

A rare Art Deco Eliel Saarinen sterling silver set of geometric powder boxes, for International Silver.

5in (13cm) high

£700-1,000 **DD**

A William Spratling Modernist belt buckle, Mexico, sterling, signed.

c1935 *2in (5cm) wide*

£1,500-2,000 **DD**

A CLOSER LOOK AT A LOUIS VUITTON TRAVELLING CASE

Pieces bearing the Louis Vuitton name are extremely sought-after. The company was founded in 1854 in Paris and its success continues today.

The extensive contents - which includes ladies' and gentlemen's vanity items, a fitted manicure set, picture frames, jewellery boxes and other accessories - add considerably to the desirability of this piece.

The famous intertwined "LV" trademark monogram design was developed by Georges Vuitton 1896, in honour of his father Louis Vuitton, to prevent counterfeiting.

The canvas covering was chosen to be durable and stylish, important factors at a time when world travel was becoming more widespread, but was still an expensive luxury.

A rare French Art Deco Louis Vuitton fitted travel trunk, with original canvas cover and 44 gold-trimmed tortoise, sterling and crystal vanity items, all signed "Louis Vuitton, Paris" and monogrammed "VS".

c1925 *24in (61cm) wide*

£12,000-18,000 **DD**

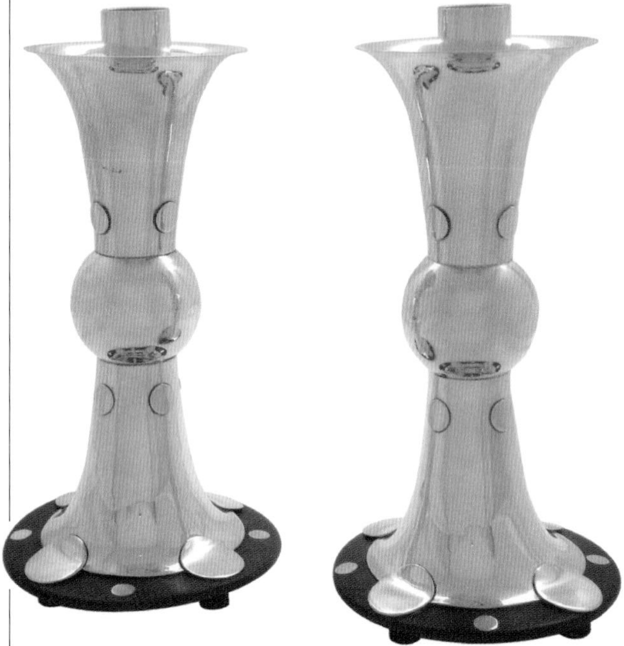

A pair of Art Deco William Spratling 'Fiesta' candlesticks, in sterling with an ebony base, signed on the base, Mexico.

c1940 *8in (20,5cm) high*

£8,000-12,000 **DD**

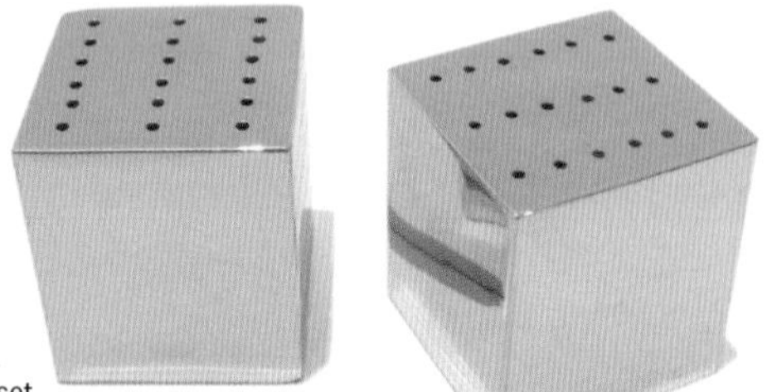

A Russel Wright salt and pepper shaker set.

1930 *1.25in (3cm) wide*

£300-400 **DD**

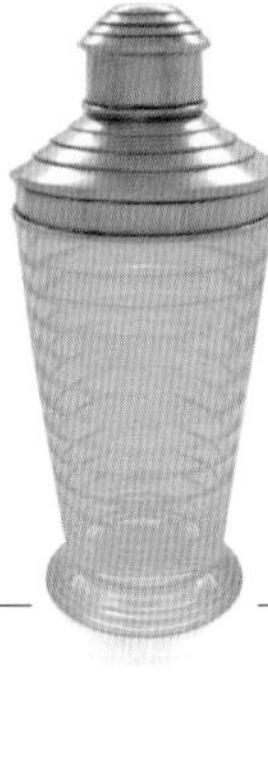

An English Art Deco crystal and silver cocktail shaker, the Hawks crystal shaker with carved linear design and stepped silver-plated shaker top.

c1935 *9in (23cm) high*

£200-250 **DD**

An English Art Deco silver-plated skyscraper cocktail shaker, marked "EPNS".

c1935 *10in (25.5cm) high*

£400-500 **DD**

A French Art Deco cruet set, in silver and crystal.

c1930 *8in (20.5cm) high*

£700-1,000 **DD**

A French Art Deco silver tea set, with stepped skyscraper design details and macassar ebony handles, hallmarked.

c1925 *Tray 20in (51cm) wide*

£3,000-4,000 **DD**

A pair of Belgian silver candelabra.

c1935 *14.5in (5.75in) wide*

£3,000-5,000 **SF**

An unusual Art Deco set of six silver and enamel bottle labels, with makers mark "T&S" Birmingham.

1933 *1.5in (4cm) wide*

£1,000-1,500 **JES**

An English Art Deco cruet set, of angular form, with stamped marks "ALD" Birmingham.

1938 *4.25in (11cm) wide*

£400-600 **WW**

A French silver-plated box, with hinged lid and bakelite handles.

c1935 *10.75in (27.5cm) wide*

£1,800-2,200 **SF**

A French silver dish, with incorporated stand.

c1935 *8.25in (21cm) wide*

£1,200-1,800 **SF**

A late 1930s Art Deco/Modernist sterling centrepiece bowl, with stacked sphere handle design and insert.

17.5in (44.5cm) wide

£1,200-1,800 **DD**

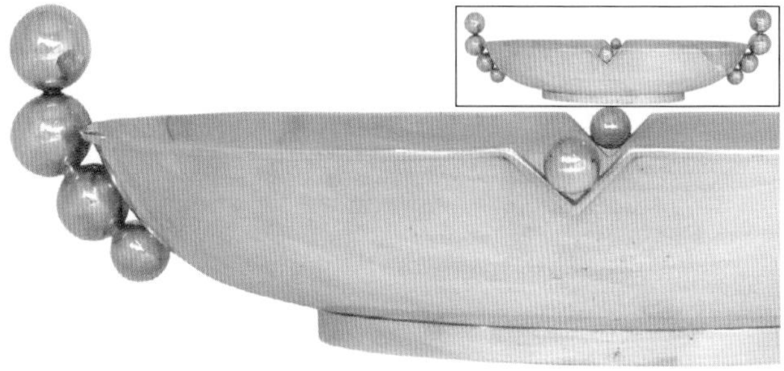

A late 1930s Art Deco/Modernist centrepiece bowl, with stacked sphere handle design and insert, Mexico.

17.5in (44.5cm) diam

£1,200-1,800 **DD**

An Art Deco Folke Arstrom cocktail shaker, designed for Guldsmeds Atchie Bolaget, marked to base "PRIMA NS", Sweden.

1935 *8.75in (22cm) high*

£600-800 **JES**

A Charles Boyton & Son electroplated samovar, of tapering cylindrical form with conical lid, raised on three struts linked by a removable burner, stamped factory marks.

12.5in (32cm) high

£300-500 **L&T**

An Art Deco Christofle silver-plated compote, with Modernist sphere base design, designed by Luc Lanel for the Normandie Ocean Liner.

c1935 *13in (33cm) diam*

£1,800-2,200 **DD**

An Art Deco Dunhill Machine Age aluminium humidor, with maker's marks to lid.

c1930 *4.75in (12cm) high*

£350-450 **JES**

An Art Deco Joseph Rodgers & Sons silver-plated tea set, by an unknown designer, stamped marks.

1935 *7.5in (19cm) high*

£3,000-4,000 **JES**

An Art Deco 'The Cube' tea set, all stamped "The Cube" with trade marks and "Cube teapots Leicester, sole manufacturers in metal T W & S".

The Cube teapot was registered in 1917 by Robert Crawford Johnson. Its unique shape made it easy to clean and store and it became popular with tearooms, cafes and ocean liners. T. Wilkinson & Sons produced this silver plate version under license.

c1920 *4.25in (11cm) high*

£800-1,200 **JES**

An Art Deco silver-plated nickel box, marked "L&MT Co. Fatima".

c1925 *6.25in (16cm) wide*

£100-150 **HSD**

Two Art Deco Lurelle Guild canapé plates and cups, designed for Chase, in polished chrome.

c1935 *8.5in (21.5cm) diam*

£50-80 each **DD**

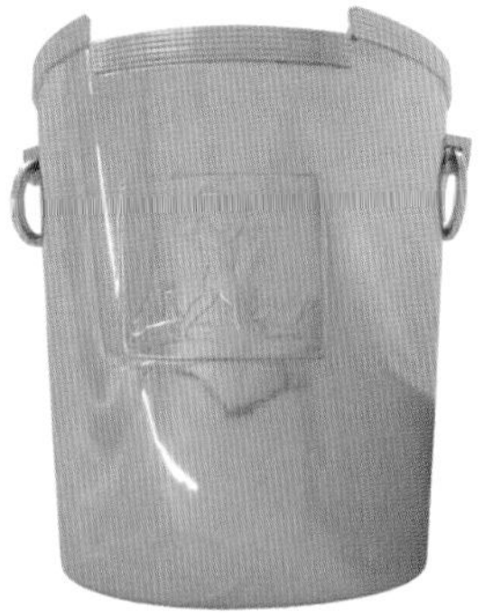

A Rockwell Kent Art Deco wine cooler, designed for Chase, with Bacchus, no.27015 in the Chase catalog.

Rockwell Kent was a noted illustrator and was the youngest artist to be shown at the Metropolitan Museum of Art. This is one of three pieces that Kent designed for Chase, all featuring Bacchus bringing home the grapes.

1934 *9.25in (23.5cm) high*

£700-1,000 **DD**

An Art Deco Walter Von Nesson 'Diplomat' chrome-plated coffee service, designed for Chase, no.17029 from the Chase catalog.

This set was originally priced at $15.00 (£8).

1933 *Coffee pot 8in (20.5cm) high*

£400-500 **DD**

An Art Deco Russel Wright chrome-plated 'Pancake and Corn Set', for Chase, no.28003, on a cobalt blue glass tray rimmed in chrome, with pitcher for melted butter or syrup.

Chase was established in Waterbury, Connecticut in the second half of the 19thC. It later began to experiment with new materials such as chrome and plastics, and produced Art Deco designs from the mid-1920s.

Pitcher 5.25in (13.5cm) high

£300-400 **DD**

An Art Deco Russel Wright 'Liqueur Set', for Chase, with six chrome-plated cordial cups on the cobalt blue glass tray, no.90046 from the Chase catalog.

1934 *tray 6in (15cm) diam*

£300-400 **DD**

An Art Deco style novelty Zeppelin cocktail shaker, attributed to A.J.A Henckels, comprising various measures, a flask and a strainer, stamped "made in Germany", missing pieces.

12.25in (31cm) high

£400-600 **WW**

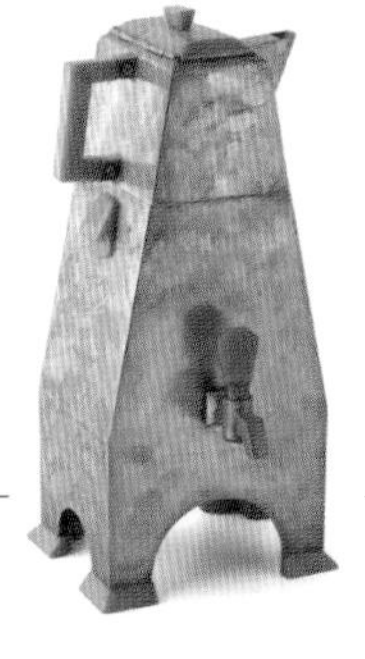

An Art Deco chrome and bakelite teapot and urn, unmarked.

15.5in (39cm) high

£300-400 **WW**

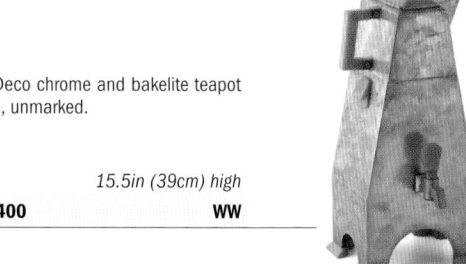

An Art Deco bronze paper knife, by Lucien Bazor, with a female form.

1928 *9.75in (25cm) long*

£400-600 **JES**

An important silver-plated bronze medallion, by Norman Bel Geddes/Medallic Art Company, "Commemorating the Twenty-fifth Anniversary of General Motors 1908-1933", with "Norman Bel Geddes/copyright/1933".

3in (7.5cm) diam

£800-1,200 **SDR**

A bronze sculpture, entitled 'Head of Choun', by William Zorach, with gold patina, inscribed signature "Zorach", and numbered "2/6" on side of neck.

7 in (17.5 cm) high

£2,500-3,000 **FRE**

An Art Deco bronze medal, with figural female nude and lightning bolts.

2.75in (7cm) diam

£120-180 **DD**

An early 1920s French Art Deco wrought iron fire-screen, attributed to Edgar Brandt, with a polished and hammered finish and rose design and stepped fan detail.

The Art Deco Cubist rose design was popularised by Brandt, a leading ironwork designer, in the 1920s.

28.5in (72.5cm) high

£7,000-10,000 **DD**

A rare iron sculpture, by Wilhelm Hunt Diederich, of a stag and hound, in black patina on a replaced marble base, unmarked.

Wilhelm Hunt Diederich (1884-1953) is known for his stylized Art Deco figures and animals in iron and other metals.

Provenance: *This piece was acquired from the artist and descended through the owner's family. It is accompanied by a black and white photograph showing the sculpture in-situ.*

20.5in (52cm) wide

£22,000-28,000 **SDR**

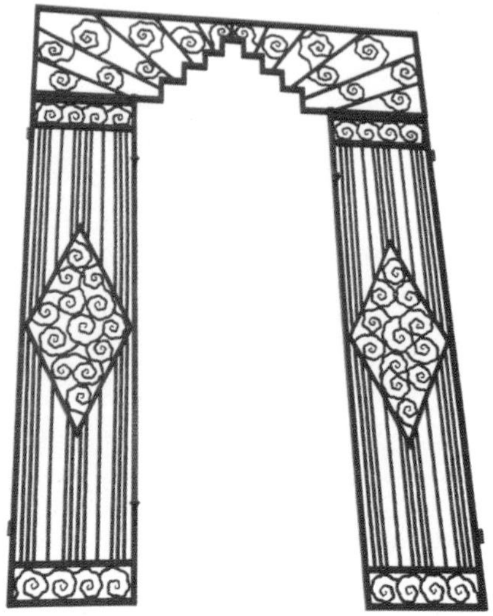

A French Art Deco set of wrought iron sidelight panels, with matching transom, attributed to Paul Kiss, stylized floral design and stepped skyscraper with sun rays.

c1925 *96in (244cm) high*

£12,000-18,000 **DD**

A French Art Deco iron radiator cover, with a Modernist design of rosettes.

25.25in (64cm) wide

£2,000-2,500 **DD**

An American Art Deco aluminum railing insert, removed from an Art Deco cinema in New York City.

c1935 *38in (96.5cm) wide*

£1,800-2,200 **DD**

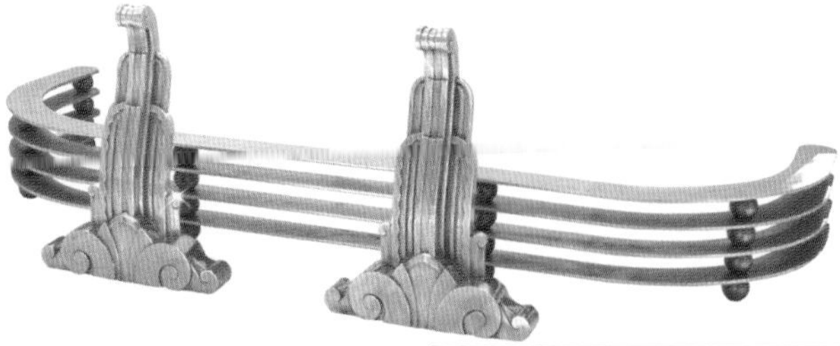

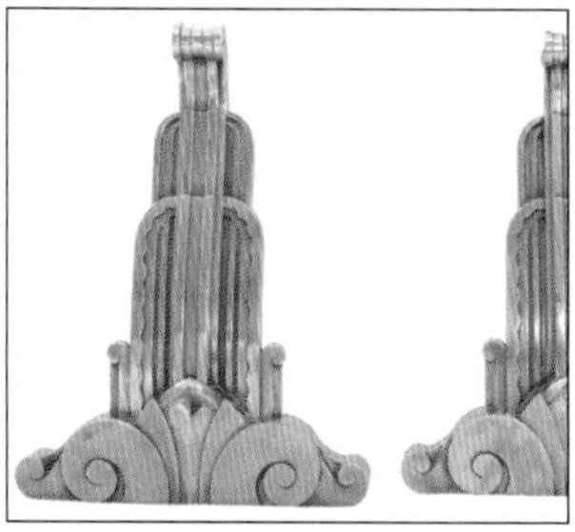

An American Art Deco aluminum fireplace fender and andirons, the streamline fender with bronze spheres, the andirons in polished aluminum and bronze with high Art Deco relief design, a custom commission.

1930 *fender 70in (178cm) wide*

£7,000-10,000 **DD**

A Walter Kantack pewter reflective wall sconce, from the Roxy Theatre, with an Art Deco mask over a large brass basin, unmarked, scratches.

17.25in (44cm) diam

£5,000-7,000 **SDR**

A Walter Kantack pewter mask, with highly stylized hair and features, unmarked, minor dent.

This was probably once part of a wall sconce executed for the Roxy Theatre.

9in (22.5cm) high

£800-1,200 **SDR**

An Art Deco pair of solid brass and wrought iron andirons, one missing nut, brass recently polished, unmarked.

15in (38cm) high

£400-600 **SDR**

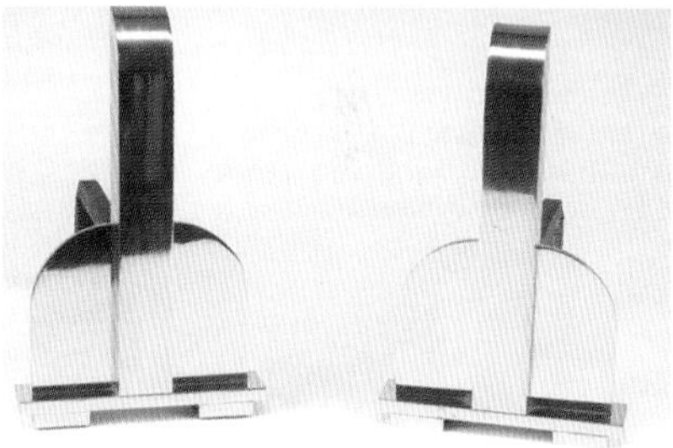

A Wurtenburg Jugendstil brass kettle and stand, hand-hammered with circular tray.

tray 15in (38cm) diam

£80-120 **FRE**

An Art Deco pair of brass and copper bookends, by Walter von Nesson, designed for Chase.

5.25in (13.5cm) wide

£300-400 **HSD**

An Art Deco pair of WMF metal vases, Ikora.

c1925 *12.5in (32cm) high*

£1,500-2,000 **MOD**

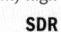

A French Art Deco geometric mixed metals vase, signed "George" and "Jacques Douau Edition D'Art Fabricon Francaise, made in France".

c1925 *10.5in (26.5cm) high*

£300-500 **DD**

An Aesthetic movement amboyna and ebonized cabinet, with four frieze drawers over two mirrored doors and shelves, with strung and parcel-gilt decoration.

72.75in (185cm) wide

£500-700 **SWO**

An Aesthetic movement ebonized and gilt side cabinet, by Edwards & Roberts, with mirrored back, painted panels, three burr wood panelled doors and marquetry cupboards, stamped to the drawer.

68.5in (171cm) high

£2,000-3,000 **SWO**

An Aesthetic movement walnut sideboard, by Gillows, with a mirror plate, two spindle galleried shelves and two doors painted with gilded flower panels, door top stamped "Gillows 9812".

81.5in (204cm) high

£2,500-3,500 **SWO**

An Aesthetic movement mahogany buffet, with a raised shelf on carved angular supports over three panelled doors and a plinth base.

54in (137cm) wide

£400-600 **SWO**

A third quarter 19thC ebonized Aesthetic movement corner cabinet, with vine and griffin-carved dashboard and glazed door, on ring and block turned supports.

69in (175cm) high

£600-900 **FRE**

A late 19thC Gothic Revival oak bureau bookcase, in the manner of Richard Norman Shaw, the sloping fall enclosing a fitted interior, panelled doors with decorative ironwork.

37.75in (96cm) wide

£2,200-2,800 **L&T**

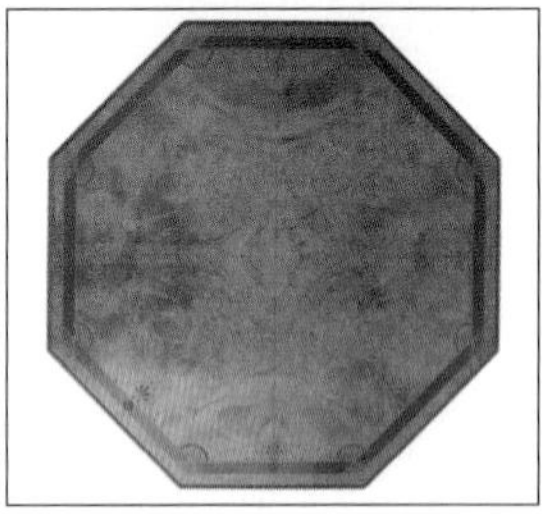

A Victorian burr-walnut Aesthetic movement table, by Druce & Co. of London, on four turned supports and splayed feet.

35in (89cm) high

£400-600 **BRI**

A Victorian Aesthetic movement carved walnut library table, attributed to Campbell Brothers of Chicago, the top over a geometric carved frieze with two drawers.

c1880 *39in (97.5cm) wide*

£800-1,200 **FRE**

Three 19thC Gothic Revival oak ceremonial chairs, in the manner of A. W. Pugin, with upholstered backs enclosed by ogee arched frames carved with leafy borders.

£500-700 **L&T**

A 19thC Gothic Revival oak hall bench, in the manner of Charles Bevan, the arcaded back pierced with quatrefoils.

41.75in (106cm) wide

£800-1,200 **L&T**

A rare early pair of Tiffany Studios Gothic-style chairs, solid quarter-sawn oak, pinned construction, original dark finish, branded "REPRODUCTION BY TIFFANY STUDIOS", reupholstered.

38.25in (97cm) high

£2,200-2,800 **DRA**

An early and rare Gustav Stickley chestnut side chair, with two horizontal back slats, original hard leather seat, unmarked, overcoated finish, damage.

34in (86.5cm) high

£1,000-1,500 **DRA**

Eight Gustav Stickley dining chairs, no 306.5, with tacked-on leather seats, original finish, branded, edge wear, some looseness, replaced leather.

36in (90cm) high

£3,000-4,000 **DRA**

A Gustav Stickley set of four ladderback side chairs, no. 306.5, with rush seats, original finish, red decal, edge roughness, looseness, replaced paper rush.

36in (90cm) high

£700-1,000 **DRA**

A set of six Gustav Stickley V-back side chairs with five vertical slats, re-covered in brown leather, unmarked, refinished.

36in (91.5cm) high

£4,000-6,000 **DRA**

Six early Gustav Stickley dining chairs, covered in original tacked-on hard leather, some paper labels, wear.

armchair 37.5in (95cm) high

£5,000-7,000 **DRA**

A Gustav Stickley V-back office chair, with five back slats and posts mortised through the arms, overcoated original finish, replaced leather, unmarked.

36in (90cm) high

£1,200-1,800 **DRA**

A Gustav Stickley rocker, no. 323, with slatted sides, drop-in seat and back recovered in leather, red decal, minor wear.

37in (94cm) high

£3,000-4,000 **DRA**

A Gustav Stickley rocker, no. 323, with drop-in spring seat, recovered in maroon leather, decal inside back stretcher, refinished.

40in (100cm) high

£1,500-2,000 **DRA**

A Gustav Stickley cube chair, with slats all around and loose cushion covered in vinyl, cleaned original finish, red decal inside back stretcher.

29in (72.5cm) high

£2,000-3,000 **DRA**

A Gustav Stickley lamp table, with tacked-on circular leather top and stacked trumpet cross-stretchers topped with a finial, red decal under top, refinished, replaced leather.

40in (100cm) wide

£1,500-2,000 **DRA**

An early Gustav Stickley lamp table, no. 436, with trumpet-shaped stretchers topped by a finial, red decal under top, wear, damage.

28in (70cm) high

£6,000-9,000 **DRA**

A Gustav Stickley mahogany 'Poppy' tea table, with floriform top and lower shelf, original finish, losses, seam separation, loose, unmarked.

23.5in (59cm) high

£10,000-15,000 **DRA**

A Gustav Stickley library table, no. 624, with hexagonal top over cloud-lift stretchers and faceted finial, paper label, original finish to base, new finish to top.

48in (120cm) wide

£3,000-4,000 **DRA**

A fine and rare Gustav Stickley tea table, with twelve green square Grueby tiles, arched aprons, the stretcher mortised with tenon-and-keys, unmarked, refinished.

c1900 *24in (61cm) wide*

£12,000-18,000 **DRA**

A rare Gustav Stickley spindled three-drawer library table, no. 659, with copper v-pulls, black stamp mark, damage, reglued and refinished.

54in (137cm) wide

£2,200-2,800 **DRA**

A Gustav Stickley two-drawer library table, with cast iron oval pulls and long corbels, decal inside drawer, refinished.

42in (105cm) wide

£1,500-2,000 **DRA**

A Gustav Stickley drop-leaf table with shoe feet and narrow bottom stretcher, refinished, unmarked.

closed 42in (106.5cm) wide

£1,200-1,800 **DRA**

A Gustav Stickley trestle table, with original leather top and tacks, shelf mortised to sides with keyed through-tenons, original finish, red decal, remains of paper label, cracks, stains, warping.

48in (120cm) wide

£2,000-3,000 **DRA**

An extremely rare Gustav Stickley inlaid side table, designed by Harvey Ellis in 1903, with a stylized pewter and copper inlay, red decal, thin shellac overcoat.

This model, illustrated in the January 1904 issue of The Craftsman Magazine, was made in such a small run that only three other surviving examples are known.

30in (91.5cm) wide

£40,000-50,000 **DRA**

A small Gustav Stickley bench, with trestle base, decal on side, paper label, dry original finish with light overcoat, wear.

36in (90cm) wide

£1,800-2,200 DRA

A Warren Hile reproduction of Gustav Stickley director's table.

78in (198cm) wide

£1,500-2,000 DRA

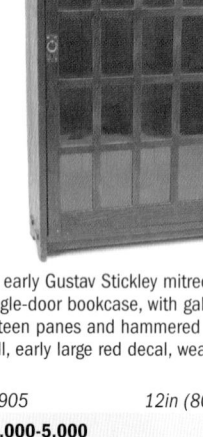

An early Gustav Stickley mitred-mullion single-door bookcase, with gallery top, sixteen panes and hammered copper pull, early large red decal, wear.

c1905 *12in (80cm) wide*

£4,000-5,000 DRA

A Gustav Stickley single-door bookcase, no. 715, with gallery top, copper V-pull, signed inside, skinned finish, missing one glass pane.

35in (89cm) wide

£2,000-3,000 DRA

A Gustav Stickley single door bookcase with sixteen panes, gallery top, and iron hardware, remnant of paper label, red decal inside, skinned finish, wear.

35in (89cm) wide

£1,200-1,800 DRA

A Gustav Stickley two-door bookcase, no. 716, with iron V-pulls, signed inside, skinned original finish, three panes missing.

42.5in (142cm) wide

£2,200-2,800 DRA

A Gustav Stickley two-door bookcase, no. 717, with copper V-pulls and original key, original finish, red decal inside right, remnant of paper label.

56in (140cm) high

£3,000-4,000 DRA

A Gustav Stickley two-door bookcase, no. 719, with 24 panes and V-pulls, original finish, paper label and red decal, rubbed.

60in (150cm) wide

£4,000-5,000 DRA

A Gustav Stickley two-door china cabinet, with gallery top and copper V pulls, branded, paper label, small holes under one shelf.

This piece is in remarkably good condition and has an excellent finish.

39.5in (100.5cm) wide

£5,000-7,000 DRA

A Gustav Stickley single-door china cabinet, with gallery top, sixteen panes, hammered copper V-pull, ghost of paper label, refinished, replaced glass.

58.25in (145.5cm) high

£2,500-3,000 DRA

A rare Gustav Stickley music cabinet, no. 70, with gallery top, the panes backed by yellow hammered glass, two adjustable shelves, and copper V pull, branded mark, wear and some damage.

20in (51cm) wide

£3,000-5,000 DRA

A Gustav Stickley two-door armoire, with panelled doors and sides, hammered copper V-pulls, and interior drawers, clothing hanger and mirror, original finish, paper label on back, veneer lifting.

63.5in (159cm) high

£4,000-5,000 DRA

GUSTAV STICKLEY

- Gustav Stickley, the best known of the five Stickley brothers, started his career in his uncle's chair factory before establishing a company in 1883, in Binghamton, New York, with his brothers. In 1888 he left the company and set up alone. After working on various products, he established the Craftsman Workshops.
- He stuck firmly to the principles behind the Arts and Crafts Movement and sought to produce "simple, strong and comfortable furniture". He promoted his vision through his monthly 'The Craftsman' magazine.
- Early pieces heavily featured chunky evidence of construction such as keyed tenons and hammered hardware. Later furniture was lighter with more subtle structural features. In the last years, designs became simpler still.
- A line of inlaid furniture produced with Harvey Ellis in 1903 is especially sought after today. Spindle furniture is also rare and valuable. Distinctive Stickley features such as overhanging tops, even-arms and arched aprons are desirable. Bedroom furniture is particularly hard to find.
- The joiner's compass mark appears on many pieces made between 1902 and 1916, often with "Als ik kan", Flemish for "As best I can". "Gustav" was added to the "Stickley" signature from 1904 to 1912.
- The firm went bankrupt in 1915.

An early Gustav Stickley chest of drawers, with two-over-three configuration, cast-iron oval pulls, panelled sides and chamfered back, small red decal, wear, chip, rust.

26.5in (67.5cm) wide

£5,000-7,000 **DRA**

A Gustav Stickley dresser with overhanging top, two-over-three drawer configuration, brass-washed V-pulls, large red decal, paper label, skinned original finish, wear and damage.

37in (94cm) wide

£1,500-2,000 **DRA**

A Gustav Stickley chest of drawers in two-over-four configuration, with round wooden knobs, original finish, faint brand and paper label, stains to top, replaced back.

47in (117.5cm) high

£1,500-2,000 **DRA**

A large Gustav Stickley chest of drawers, in two-over-two configuration, with swivel mirror and cast-iron oval pulls, large red decal, wear.

68.25in (173.5cm) wide

£5,000-6,000 **DRA**

A Gustav Stickley chest-of-drawers, with swivelling mirror and panelled sides, red box mark, partial paster, refinished, stains.

48in (120cm) wide

£3,000-4,000 **DRA**

A Gustav Stickley child's dresser, in two-over-two drawer configuration, pivoting mirror flanked by a spindled backsplash, paper label on back, original finish.

52.5in (131cm) high

£1,800-2,200 **DRA**

An early Gustav Stickley desk, with nine drawers and keyed through-tenons, old restored finish.

53in (132.5cm) wide

£2,000-3,000 **DRA**

A Gustav Stickley postcard desk, together with an H-back desk chair, branded, some wear to original finish, staining to desk top, missing upholstery.
desk

40in (100cm) wide

£1,200-1,800 **DRA**

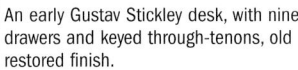

A Gustav Stickley chestnut drop-front desk with plank sides topped by cut-out handles, branded mark, stains, thin original finish, chips.

29in (73.5cm) wide

£700-1,000 **DRA**

A Gustav Stickley magazine stand, with three shelves, branded under lower shelf, refinished, discolouration.

30in (75cm) high

£600-900 **DRA**

A Gustav Stickley music stand with four shelves, tapered posts, and shaped apron, original finish, decal on leg, paper label, losses, stains and seam separation.

39in (97.5cm) high

£1,500-2,000 **DRA**

A Gustav Stickley 'Tree-of-Life' stand, with tapering plank sides carved with stylized trees, original dark finish, unmarked two cracked shelves, seam separation to top, missing parts.

14.25in (36cm) wide

£1,000-1,500 **DRA**

A Gustav Stickley somno cabinet, with hammered pull on drawer, branded in drawer, paper label, refinished, losses, repairs.

34in (85cm) high

£2,500-3,000 **DRA**

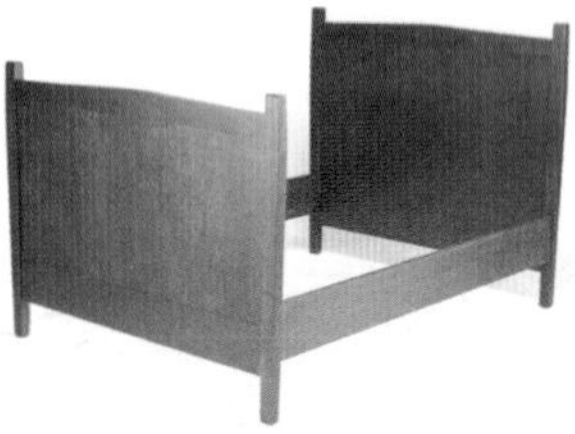

A Gustav Stickley double bed with panelled head and footboard, complete with side rails, red decal, wear.

58.25in (148cm) wide

£2,800-3,200 **DRA**

A rare Gustav Stickley three-piece child's set of two benches and a trestle table, paper labels, new finish with paint remnants, some seam splits and stains.

table 36in (90cm) wide

£1,800-2,200 **DRA**

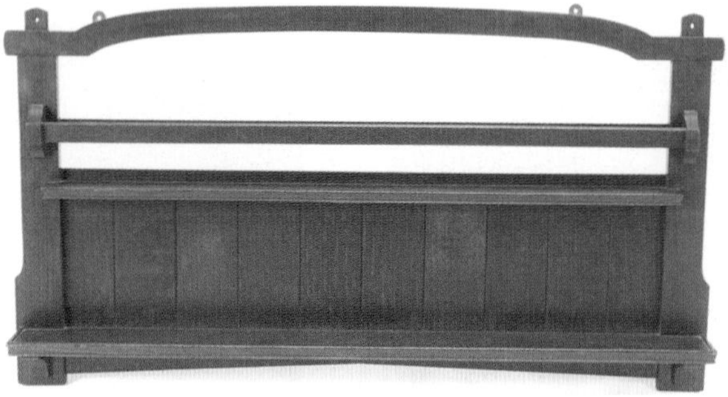

A Gustav Stickley early plate rail, with chamfered board back, unsigned.

45in (114.5cm) wide

£3,000-4,000 **DRA**

An extremely rare and early Gustav Stickley chalet smoker's cabinet, with square bevelled overhanging top and gallery interior, the panelled door and lower shelf mortised with keyed through tenons, unmarked, chips, wear.

1901 *16in (40.5cm) wide*

£18,000-22,000 **DRA**

A Gustav Stickley hammered copper umbrella stand, with riveted strap hardware, new patina, missing drip pan, unmarked.

27in (67.5cm) high

£600-900 **DRA**

A rare Gustav Stickley slatted umbrella stand, no. 100, with three riveted hammered bands to interior and original copper drip pan, large red decal, scratches, stains.

24in (61cm) high

£1,000-1,500 **DRA**

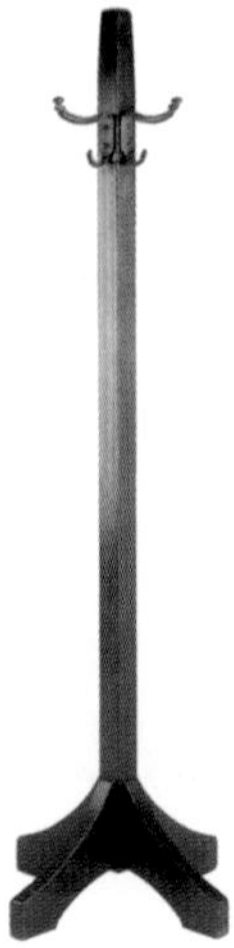

A Gustav Stickley costumer, with tapering post and four iron hooks, original finish with overcoat, unmarked.

72in (180cm) high

£700-1,000 **DRA**

STICKLEY BROTHERS

- Brothers Gustav, Albert and Charles Stickley, established what was to become the Stickley Brothers Company in 1883 to concentrate on selling and producing reproduction furniture. In 1888, the two other Stickley brothers, Leopold and John, joined the firm and Gustav left to set up on his own.
- In 1891, Albert and John moved to Grand Rapids, Michigan, taking the company name with them. The firm they left behind was renamed The Stickley & Brandt Chair Company.
- John left Stickley Brothers in 1900 to establish another company with his brother Leopold, leaving Albert in charge of the company.
- British Arts and Crafts designers had a great influence on Albert and pieces feature cut-out decoration.
- The company is known for its utilitarian furniture as well as its Arts and Crafts designs.
- Pieces are often marked with "Quaint" labels, decals, tags or brands, and "Grand Rapids".
- The company closed c1940.

A set of six Stickley Brothers dining chairs, no. 479 1/2, with vertical back slats and drop-in black vinyl seats, original finish with overcoat, stencilled number.

37.25in (94.5cm) high

£2,000-3,000 **DRA**

A set of six Stickley Brothers dining chairs, with vertical slats and original finish, oilcloth and tacks, Quaint decal, damage.

38.75in (97cm) high

£1,200-1,800 **DRA**

A set of six Stickley Brothers ladder-back side chairs with saddle seats, original finish, Quaint metal tags, wear.

37.5in (95.5cm) high

£1,000-1,500 **DRA**

A Stickley Brothers armchair, with three under-arm slats and drop-in spring cushion, Quaint metal tag, refinished, replaced leather.

34.5in (86cm) high

£800-1,200 **DRA**

A Charles Stickley heavy armchair, with cut-out back slats, the drop-in spring seat recovered in leather, remnant of label, light overcoat to fine original finish, chip.

36.5in (92.5cm) high

£1,500-2,000 **DRA**

A Stickley Brothers oversized armchair, with long paddle arms and fixed back, metal tag, missing cushions, refinished, stains.

36in (91.5cm) high

£800-1,200 **DRA**

A Stickley Brothers mahogany armchair, with drop-in spring seat and five slats under each shaped arm, original finish, recovered in green leather, unmarked.

38in (95cm) high

£800-1,200 **DRA**

A Charles Stickley three-piece parlour set, with loveseat, armchair and rocker, each with cut-outs to centre slats and crest rails, refinished, some stains and discolouration, split, unmarked.

loveseat 59in (150cm) wide

£2,000-3,000 **DRA**

A Stickley Brothers drop-arm three-section settle, with three slats under arms, original finish, stencilled No. "922-3715", wear.

72.5in (184cm) wide

£600-900 **DRA**

A Stickley Brothers dining table, with four-sided base with shoe feet, two leaves, original finish, Quaint metal tag.

48in (122cm) diam

£1,200-1,800 **DRA**

A Stickley Brothers oak dining table, with two leaves, remnant of paper label, original finish, stains, losses, wear.

48in (122cm) diam

£800-1,200 **DRA**

A Stickley Brothers split pedestal dining table, with four leaves, refinished, unmarked.

54in (135cm) diam

£1,200-1,800 **DRA**

A Stickley Brothers round table, with drop leaves and gate legs, shadow of metal tag, original finish, minor chips.

40in (100cm) wide

£1,000-1,500 **DRA**

A Stickley Brothers small drop-leaf table, with shoe feet, remnant of paper label, refinished, some stains to top.

30in (75cm) high

£300-500 **DRA**

A Stickley Brothers small library table, with spindled sides and single blind drawer, shadow of tag, refinished.

30in (75cm) high

£500-700 **DRA**

A Stickley Brothers lamp table, with tacked-on circular leather top, lower shelf, refinished, replaced leather, unmarked.

29in (72.5cm) high

£400-600 **DRA**

A Stickley Brothers lamp table, with leather top and spade-shaped cut-out sides, new finish and leather, unmarked.

30in (75cm) high

£1,200-1,800 **DRA**

A Stickley Brothers lamp table, the four legs mortised through a flush circular top, brass tag and remnant of paper label, refinished, loose, gouges.

24in (61cm) diam

£500-700 **DRA**

A Stickley Brothers mahogany magazine stand, with slatted back and sides, metal tag, refinished.

15.25in (38.5cm) wide

£600-900 **DRA**

A Stickley Brothers magazine stand, with slatted back and sides, Quaint metal tag, refinished, seam separation.

15.5in (38cm) wide

£600-900 **DRA**

L. & J.G. STICKLEY

- After acting as plant manager for his brother Gustav between 1899 and 1901 Leopold Stickley established Onondaga Shops with his brother John George in 1902.
- Based in Fayetteville, not far from Gustav Stickley's workshops, the enterprise was an immediate success.
- The company was renamed "Handcraft" in 1906 and was later renamed L. & J.G. Stickley in 1912.
- Early pieces were inspired by the Arts and Crafts work of Gustav Stickley. Quality was extremely high.
- Innovations included an interlocking post leg design and the use of splines on tabletops to prevent splitting.
- Long corbels with flared ends and hand-hammered copper hardware are characteristic.
- L. & J. G. Stickley were happy to use modern production methods in the construction of furniture.
- A red shop mark was used from 1906 until 1912, when a yellow decal and "The work of L.&.J.G. Stickley" mark were introduced.
- The last Arts and Crafts furniture was produced c1922 and the company turned its attention to reproduction early American furniture, and in recent years, Arts and Crafts pieces.

An early and rare set of four L. & J.G. Stickley/Onondaga Shops dining side chairs, no. 633, with drop-in seats recovered in chocolate brown leather, refinished, unmarked.

39in (97.5cm) high

£1,500-2,000 **DRA**

An L. & J.G. Stickley assembled set of four dining side chairs , two with "The Work of..." decal, two with Handcraft decal, original finish to one, three with overcoat, stains, wear.

36in (91.5cm) high

£1,500-2,000 **DRA**

An L. & J.G. Stickley set of six dining chairs, with drop-in seats re-covered in new leather, remains of decal on one side chair, refinished.

armchair 40in (100cm) high

£2,200-2,800 **DRA**

An extremely rare L. & J.G. Stickley/Onondaga Shops set of six mahogany dining chairs, with tacked-on leather seats, original finish, wear, three with original leather and tacks, unmarked.

41.5in (104cm) high

£2,200-2,800 **DRA**

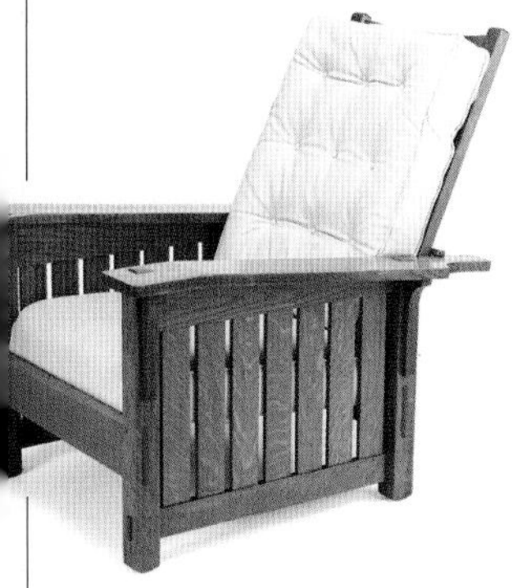

An L. & J.G. Stickley drop-arm slatted Morris chair, no. 410, with slats to floor, handcraft decal, original finish to base, arms refinished, replaced reclining bar.

40in (101.5cm) high

£3,000-5,000 **DRA**

An L. & J.G. Stickley Morris chair, no. 471, with short slats and long corbels under flat arms, "The Work of..." decal, original finish, chips, missing peg, wear.

41in (104cm) high

£2,000-2,500 **DRA**

An L. & J.G. Stickley Morris chair, no. 471, with slats to seat under long flat arms, branded mark on back, recovered in brown leather, refinished.

40in (101.5cm) high

£1,800-2,200 **DRA**

An L. & J.G. Stickley Morris chair, with five slats under flat arms, original finish, handcraft decal inside leg, wear, chip, repair.

41in (102.5cm) high

£2,200-2,800 **DRA**

An L. & J.G. Stickley even-arm settle, no. 222, with vertical slats all around, tall tapering posts, re-covered in medium brown leather, handcraft decal, original finish.

76in (190cm) wide

£4,000-6,000 **DRA**

An L. & J.G. Stickley even-arm settle, with broad side and back slats and drop-in spring cushion, original finish, handcraft decal, wear.

72in (180cm) wide

£1,800-2,200 **DRA**

An L. & J.G. Stickley 'Prairie' loveseat, no. 214, refinished, a few minor chips to edges, wear to top of one arm, branded mark.

62in (157.5cm) wide

£4,000-5,000 **DRA**

A late 20thC L. & J.G. Stickley 'Prairie' settee, by Manlius NY, with cherry wood panels to sides and back and upholstered slip seat, signed with metal tag and Stickley burn mark.

84.5in (214.5cm) wide

£500-700 **SK**

An L. & J.G. Stickley settee, with drop-in spring seat and loose pillow, branded mark, original finish, minor staining, looseness.

78in (198cm) wide

£800-1,200 **DRA**

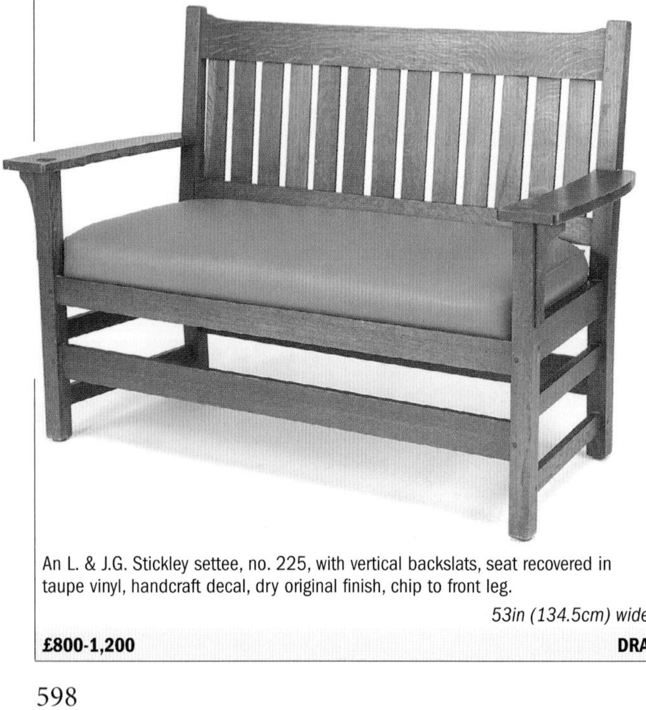

An L. & J.G. Stickley settee, no. 225, with vertical backslats, seat recovered in taupe vinyl, handcraft decal, dry original finish, chip to front leg.

53in (134.5cm) wide

£800-1,200 **DRA**

An L. & J.G. Stickley Trestle table, no. 593, with lower shelf mortised through the sides with two pairs of keyed through tenons, refinished, added castors, unmarked.

48in (122cm) wide

£1,200-1,800 **DRA**

An L. & J.G. Stickley two-drawer library table with hammered copper pulls and long corbels, "The Work of..." decal inside, refinished, two filled holes in top.

53in (135cm) wide

£800-1,200 **DRA**

An L. & J.G. Stickley two-drawer console table, with hammered copper pulls and narrow top, "The Work of..." decal, overcoated original finish, stains and separations to top.

40in (100cm) wide

£800-1,200 **DRA**

LIMBERT

- Charles P. Limbert (1854-1923) established his company in 1894 in Grand Rapids, Michigan. New premises were opened in Holland, Michigan in 1906.
- From the early years of the 20thC, the company began to produce pieces in the Arts and Crafts style.
- Limbert experimented with high quality designs in oak, inspired by the Glasgow and Prairie schools.
- Earlier pieces often had dark finishes and cut-out decoration of hearts, rectangles and squares. Shapes were simple and rectilinear.
- By c1910, Limbert was moving away from Mission furniture and dark leather upholstery and producing pieces with lighter designs and colours.
- The Ebon-Oak range was introduced c1915 and featured fine lines and ebony inlay. By 1918, the Arts and Crafts range had been phased out.
- Pre-1906 labels refer only to "Grand Rapids" while later versions show "Grand Rapids and Holland". A large rectangular branded mark was also used.

A set of four Limbert dining chairs, the vertical back slats with arrow cut-outs, new leather upholstery, cleaned original finish, edge wear, damage, looseness, unmarked.

36in (90cm) high

£800-1,200 **DRA**

Six Limbert dining chairs with arched back stretcher and two vertical back slats, drop-in seats, branded under seat, reupholstered, wear, scratches.

36.5in (91cm) high

£1,200-1,800 **DRA**

A rare Limbert Morris chair, with long flat open arms, covered in tan leather, original finish, branded mark, damage.

36in (91.5cm) high

£1,800-2,200 **DRA**

An oversized Limbert armchair, fixed back, drop-in seat, branded under arm, refinished and reupholstered.

33in (82.5cm) high

£1,200-1,800 **DRA**

Part of a complete Limbert original dining room set, consisting of a china cabinet, sideboard with mirrored back splash, dining table and a set of seven dining chairs, branded marks.

£5,000-7,000 set **DRA**

A Limbert tall-back armchair with drop-in seat re-covered in brown vinyl, overcoated original finish, branded, reglued, crack.

42.75in (108.5cm) high

£300-500 **DRA**

A Limbert Ebon-oak armchair, with geometric inlay and drop-in cushion seat newly re-covered in wool Navajo print, branded under arm, refinished, some looseness.

38in (95cm) high

£700-1,000 **DRA**

A Limbert Ebon-oak three-piece parlour set, consisting of a settee, armchair and rocker, branded marks, new finish, cane and upholstery.

settee 45in (112.5cm) wide

£2,000-3,000 **DRA**

A Brooks Morris chair, no. 20, in the style of Limbert, reupholstered in grey velvet, original finish with overcoat, minor burn marks, replaced parts, unmarked.

40in (101.5cm) high

£2,300-2,800 **DRA**

A Limbert china cabinet, no. 447, the front door with three small panes over one large one, overcoated original finish, branded mark, and stencilled "F447", replaced shelves.

34.25in (87cm) wide

£1,800-2,200 **DRA**

A Limbert china cabinet no 447, with plate rack, three small panes, and three shelves, branded mark, and stencilled "F447", overcoated original finish, replaced shelves.

62in (155cm) high

£1,200-1,800 **DRA**

A Limbert china cabinet, no. 1473, with three small panes and side shelves supported by long corbels, original finish, branded on back, metal store tag, scratches.

57in (142.5cm) high

£3,000-4,000 **DRA**

Part of a complete Limbert original dining room set, consisting of a china cabinet, sideboard with mirrored back splash, dining table and a set of seven dining chairs, branded marks.

cabinet 58.5in (146cm) high

£5,000-7,000 set **DRA**

A Limbert chest of drawers, with pivoting mirror, copper pulls and arched apron, original finish, branded inside drawer, stain, losses.

67in (167.5cm) high

£800-1,200 **DRA**

A Limbert five-drawer tall chest, with original loop hardware and locks, overcoated original finish, branded mark, raised seam.

36in (91.5cm) wide

£1,800-2,200 **DRA**

A Limbert sideboard with plate rack, two small drawers over linen drawer and two cabinet doors, copper hardware, branded mark, top refinished.

45in (114.5cm) wide

£1,800-2,200 **DRA**

A Limbert sideboard, with mirrored and slatted backsplash, original finish, branded in drawer, stencilled "1453" on back, losses, wear.

52.25in (130.5cm) high

£1,200-1,800 **DRA**

Part of a complete Limbert original dining room set, consisting of a china cabinet, sideboard with mirrored back splash, dining table and a set of seven dining chairs, branded marks.

cabinet 58.5in (146cm) high

£5,000-7,000 set **DRA**

A Limbert magazine stand with two shelves, arched aprons, inset top, original finish, branded under bottom shelf, minor wear.

29in (72.5cm) high

£600-900 **DRA**

A Limbert stand, with two shelves, original finish with light overcoat on base, branded under bottom shelf, top refinished, chip.

36in (90cm) wide

£700-1,000 **DRA**

A Limbert plant stand, the rounded square overhanging top on cut-out plank sides, branded under top, refinished.

30in (75cm) high

£1,200-1,800 **DRA**

A Roycroft tabouret, with keyhole cut-outs, carved orb and cross mark, worn original finish, split to top.

15in (38cm) wide

£2,000-2,500 **DRA**

A Roycroft Tabouret from Emerson Hall, Roycroft Campus, with keyhole cut-outs, carved orb and cross mark and "E.050" refinished, reglued, chip, screws added.

Provenance: *From the collection of Charles Hamilton, author of "Roycroft Collectibles".*

15in (38cm) wide

£1,200-1,800 **DRA**

A Roycroft sideboard with mirrored backsplash, with leaded glass cabinet doors, hammered copper hardware, original finish to base, carved orb and cross mark, new finish on top.

60in (150cm) wide

£4,000-6,000 **DRA**

A Roycroft desk with two drawers, bank of four side drawers and pull-out writing surface, original finish, bearing the registry mark from the office at the Roycroft Inn, carved orb and cross mark, die-marked "OF.338", wear and stains.

Provenance: *This desk is from the Estate of Miriam Hubbard Roelofs, Elbert and Alice Hubbard's daughter.*

60in (150cm) wide

£3,000-4,000 **DRA**

A Roycroft tall magazine stand, with five shelves mortised through flaring plank sides with keyed through-tenons, original finish, orb and cross mark, reglued, wear, losses.

63.75in (159cm) high

£3,000-4,000 **DRA**

A Roycroft pine goody box, with patinated hammered metal strap hardware, stamped orb and cross mark on lid, new finish and patina.

23in (57.5cm) wide

£400-600 **DRA**

A Roycroft mahogany child's crib, carved "Mary Moore" to interior, orb and cross mark, worn original finish, missing mattress support.

Carved for Mary Moore, a direct descendant of Elbert Hubbard.

54.5in (136cm) wide

£3,000-4,000 **DRA**

A Roycroft Picture frame, with thin overcoated finish, unmarked.

24.75in (63cm) wide

£400-600 **DRA**

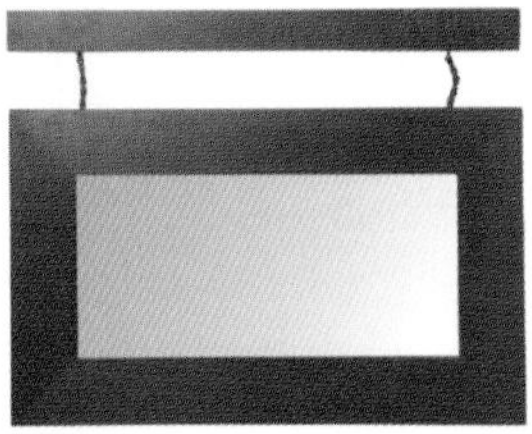

A Roycroft hanging mirror, with broad mouldings, original hanging chain and board, dark original finish, minor chip.

50in (125cm) high

£2,200-2,800 **DRA**

A Lifetime three-door bookcase, with gallery top, keyed through-tenons and copper pulls, original finish, decal inside back, wear, damage.

59in (147.5cm) wide

£2,200-2,800 **DRA**

A rare Lifetime three-door bookcase, with 18 panes, the gallery top and bottom mortised through the sides with keyed through-tenons, original finish,"Paine Furn. Co." label, minor sagging.

59in (147.5cm) wide

£3,000-4,000 **DRA**

A Lifetime double-door bookcase, with eight panes per door, and arched toe-board, original finish, separation to inside back, slight ripple, unmarked.

51in (129.5cm) wide

£1,200-1,800 **DRA**

A Lifetime Puritan single-door bookcase, with mullioned top and long corbels, original finish, paper label on back.

51.5in (129cm) high

£1,000-1,500 **DRA**

A Lifetime single-door bookcase, with copper hardware, through-tenons and panelled sides, original finish, decal inside back.

57.75in (144cm) high

£800-1,200 **DRA**

An Arts & Crafts Morris chair, attributed to Lifetime, with drop-in spring seat and back pillow, refinished, new suede upholstery, unmarked.

40in (101.5cm) high

£700-1,000 **DRA**

A Lifetime large open-arm rocker, newly recovered in medium brown leather, original finish, remnants of paper label, "Paine furniture Co." metal tag.

39in (97.5cm) high

£1,500-2,000 **DRA**

A Lifetime massive rocker and armchair set, with drop-in spring seat and back cushion reupholstered in brown leather, original finish with edge wear, armchair has rot and chips, unmarked.

34in (86.5cm) high

£2,000-3,000 **DRA**

An Arts & Crafts server, attributed to Lifetime, with backsplash, ring pulls and flaring legs, refinished, unmarked.

36in (91.5cm) wide

£600-900 **DRA**

A Lifetime Puritan dining table, complete with four leaves, paper label, refinished, missing castors.

54in (137cm) diam

£1,200-1,800 **DRA**

A Lifetime cellaret, with a single drawer over a cabinet door, original finish, stencilled "47.262" and remnants of paper label on bottom.

29in (72.5cm) high

£800-1,200 **DRA**

An exceptional Charles Rohlfs drop-front desk on pivoting base, with two interior drawers, bookstand, side cabinet with shelves and four drawers on opposite side, elaborately carved with flame finials to top, original finish, original green varnish to drawer interiors, carved "R 1900" and tag "This Piece is Guaranteed to be Made by Charles Rohlfs and is Number 847", two spots reglued, minor chips.

25.75in (65.5cm) wide

£80,000-120,000 **DRA**

A rare Rohlfs chest of six graduated drawers, with wooden bin pulls, the top and bottom mortised through the sides with keyed through-tenons, and faceted pegs all around, original finish, impressed signature and "'07" on front apron, filled-in chip.

1907 *60in (150cm) high*

£6,000-9,000 **DRA**

A Charles Rohlfs fine and rare hanging shelf with rounded and pegged drawer and faceted square pull, fine original ebonized finish, a few scratches to top, stamped "R 1900".

1900 *15in (37.5cm) wide*

£1,500-2,000 **DRA**

A rare Charles Rohlfs hinged desktop box, with copper strap hardware over a heavily carved lid, the central medallion monogrammed "M", the interior divided into compartments and stained green, stamped "R 1901", small chip, some stains to interior.

1901 *12.5in (31cm) wide*

£20,000-25,000 **DRA**

OLD HICKORY

An Old Hickory drop-leaf table with spindled gate-legs and oval oak top, original finish to base, branded on leg, top finish new.

open 49in (122.5cm) long

£1,000-1,500 **DRA**

An Old Hickory barrell-shaped rocker, with split-reed back and seat, and accompanying footstool, original finish, both pieces branded, wear.

rocker 37in (92.5cm) high

£1,200-1,800 **DRA**

An Old Hickory/Paine plant stand with spindled sides, original finish, "Paine Furniture Co." label, stencilled "1207.152", some discolouration and looseness, nails added.

30in (75cm) high

£400-600 **DRA**

A pair of Old Hickory rockers, with split-reed backs and seats, original finish and reed, branded marks, metal "Old Hickory" tags.

32in (80cm) wide

£1,500-2,000 **DRA**

A Brunswick-Balke-Collenver Co. convertible trestle billiard table/settee, complete with cues, rack and balls, original finish, metal tag, new felt and pockets.

70in (175cm) wide

£8,000-12,000 **DRA**

A Byrdcliffe oak chiffonier, the two doors with oil painted landscapes, attributed to Jane Byrd McCall Whitehead.

***Provenance**: This table was at White Pines, the home of founders of the Byrdcliffe colony, Ralph Radcliffe Whitehead and Jane Byrd Whitehead (nee McCall), until 1984.*

1904 *27.25in (68cm) high*

£18,000-22,000 **POOK**

A Byrdcliffe cherry trestle table, designed by Zulma Steele (1881-1979), the top supported by square iris carved legs.

***Provenance**: This table was at White Pines until 1984.*

96.5in (241.5cm) wide

£8,000-12,000 **POOK**

A Dirk van Erp hammered copper three-panel fire screen, with cut-out medallions and ball hinges, some variations in colour to original finish, unmarked.

33in (82.5cm) high

£3,500-4,000 **DRA**

A rare Dirk van Erp hammered copper shelf unit, with open box mark, new patina.

30.25in (75.5cm) wide

£2,200-2,800 **DRA**

A Grand Rapids Furniture Co. magazine stand, flaring slatted sides over four shelves, remnant of paper label, refinished.

16.5in (42cm) wide

£1,000-1,500 **DRA**

A Harden footstool, with slatted sides and loose pillow, overcoated original finish, unmarked.

17.75in (45cm) wide

£300-500 **DRA**

A Harden Morris chair with broad, rounded arms, newly upholstered in aubergine twill, unmarked.

39in (97.5cm) high

£800-1,200 **DRA**

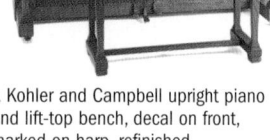

A Kohler and Campbell upright piano and lift-top bench, decal on front, marked on harp, refinished.

piano 63in (157.5cm) wide

£2,000-3,000 **DRA**

A Hert Brothers of New York oak breakfront sideboard, with mirrored panel back carved with patera, back impressed, "Herts Brothers NY, Broadway & 20 St. NY", later brass candelabra.

c1910 *69.5in (174cm) high*

£3,000-4,000 **FRE**

A George Mann Niedecken lamp table with square top and column base, refinished, unmarked.

24.5in (62cm) wide

£3,500-4,000 **DRA**

A Michigan Chair Co. magazine stand, with keyed through-tenons, original finish, paper label under shelf, minor finish loss.

33in (82.5cm) high

£500-700 **DRA**

A Northern Furniture Co. of Sheboygan, WI, china cabinet, with original finish, minor edge chips, unmarked.

63in (157.5cm) high

£800-1,200 **DRA**

A C. S. Paine Company server, with plate rack, "Paine Furniture" metal tag, refinished.

C.S. Paine Company was a Mission Furniture maker, based in Grand Rapids Michigan from 1892-1924.

38in (96.5cm) wide

£1,000-1,500 **DRA**

A Phoenix settee and armchair, carved with dogwood blossoms, overcoat on original finish, seam separation, chips, repairs, unmarked.

settee 57.25in (145.5cm) wide

£1,500-2,000 **DRA**

A Plail Bros. barrel-back armchair, with slats to seat, drop-in spring seat, residue of light overcoat on original finish, slight separation, wear, unmarked.

31.5in (80cm) high

£1,200-1,800 **DRA**

A Shop of the Crafters postcard desk, with gallery top, original finish, paper label, screw holes, edge roughness to legs.

35in (89cm) wide

£800-1,200 **DRA**

A winged-back armchair, attributed to Henry Hobson Richardson, with carved crestrail with acanthus leaves and flowers, original finish, chip, repair, replaced seat decking and cushions.

c1885 *47in (117.5cm) high*

£3,000-5,000 **DRA**

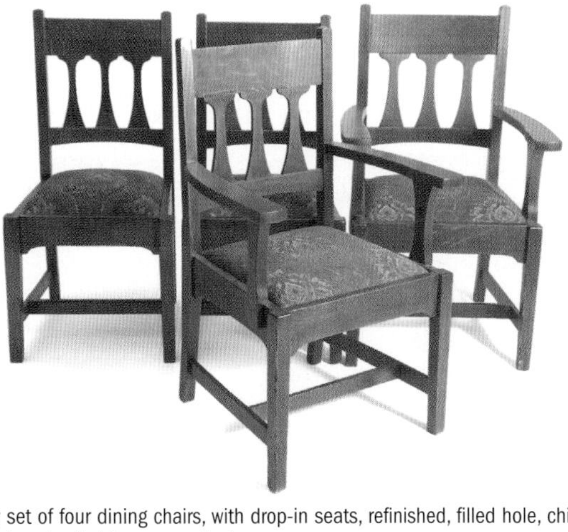

A Tobey set of four dining chairs, with drop-in seats, refinished, filled hole, chip to one, replaced upholstery, unmarked.

39in (97.5cm) high

£300-500 **DRA**

IMPORTANT BRITISH MAKERS

- **Ernest Barnsley (b.1863)** and his brother Sidney, worked with Ernest Gimson in the Cotswolds Pinbury Mill workshop from 1893, before moving to premises in Shapperton. Made from local woods, such as ash, elm, oak and fruitwoods, Sidney Barnsley's output was crafted entirely by his own hands.
- **Ernest Gimson (1863-1919)** was inspired by the work and ideology of William Morris. The Leicester born architect specialized in decorative plaster work and furniture making before establishing the Pinbury Mill workshop.
- **Liberty & Co.** was established by Arthur Lasenby Liberty (1843-1917) in 1875. The store produced and commissioned furniture to meet growing demand for the fashionable Arts and Crafts style. Pieces were produced more economically than the furniture handmade by art guilds. Designs ranged from the very simple to the ornately inlaid.
- **William Morris** is credited as the founding father of the Arts and Crafts Movement. Opposing industrialization and mass-production, he encouraged the use of traditional skills and craftsmanship. The Morris & Co. company produced fine, hand-crafted furniture inspired by country and medieval designs and with construction elements as decorative features. The company closed in 1940.
- **Robert 'Mouseman' Thompson** (1876-1955) produced handcrafted oak furniture, using traditional methods, at his rural Yorkshire workshop. Pieces are signed with a carved mouse.

An Armitage giltwood wall mirror, carved in bold relief with trees in arches, fish in a choppy sea and flowers and leaves, incised monogram to reverse.

32.75in (83cm) high

£10,000-15,000 **LFA**

An Arts and Crafts oak standing bookcase, attributed to the Gimson & Barnsley workshop.

37in (94cm) wide

£3,500-4,000 **LFA**

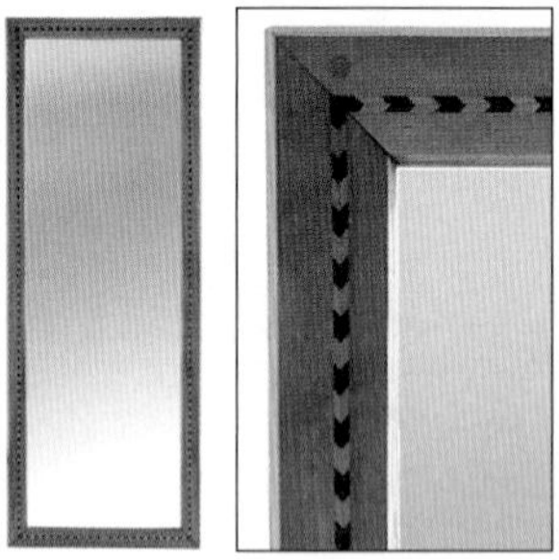

An Edward Barnsley walnut-framed wall mirror, with ebony and herringbone stringing.

48in (122cm) high

£1,800-2,200 **LFA**

An oak log basket, designed by Sidney Barnsley, of lattice form, constructed using mortice and tenon, and wrought iron supports and nails.

22in (56cm) wide

£1,200-1,800 **LFA**

An Arts and Crafts oak chest, of two short and three long drawers, attributed to Sidney Barnsley, with brass stamped ring handles.

38.5in (98cm) wide

£5,000-7,000 **LFA**

An English walnut and fruitwood revolving bookcase, designed by Sidney Barnsley, with visible dovetails and chip carved edges on a flat triform base.

15in (38cm) wide

£7,000-10,000 **LFA**

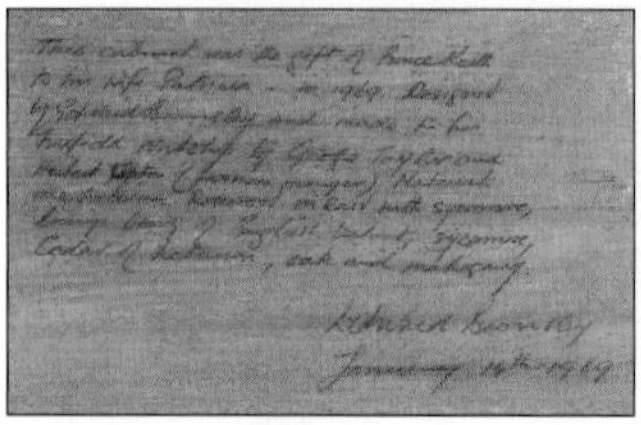

An Edward Barnsley walnut secretaire chest, with a panelled secretaire drawer and diamond ebony inlay, detailed inscription to underside of central drawer "This cabinet was the gift of Bruce Keith to his wife Patricia in 1969. Designed by Edward Barnsley...".

The workshop record shows a retail value for this piece of £848.0s.10d and a build time of 632 hours."

43in (109cm) wide

£15,000-20,000 **LFA**

An oak casket by Sidney H. Barnsley, inlaid with abalone, mother-of-pearl and coromandel, the turned handle opening to a series of drawers and pigeon holes.

21in (53.5cm) wide

£15,000-20,000 **LFA**

An oak coffer designed by Sidney Barnsley, the hinged lid with chip carved edge, shaped front and splayed legs.

48in (122cm) wide

£2,000-3,000 **LFA**

An oak side table by Sidney Barnsley, with lattice back and sides, chip carved supports and downswept feet.

27in (68.5cm) wide

£1,800-2,200 **LFA**

An oak rectangular dining table, by Sidney Barnsley for Robert Weir Schultz, with three plank top, chip carved edge, on square chamfered legs with hay rake and wishbone stretchers.

c1905 *84in (213.5cm) wide*

£40,000-50,000 **LFA**

A walnut escritoire, designed by Ernest Gimson for Robert Weir Schultz, with ebony and holly-inlaid chequer banding, with a drawer above a fall-front enclosing an arrangement of drawers and pigeonholes above a drawer and two panelled cupboard doors, on ebonized trestle base, with stamped brass ring handles.

34in (86.5cm) wide

£35,000-40,000 **LFA**

A walnut casket, designed by Ernest Gimson for Robert Weir Schultz, inlaid with mother-of-pearl, the stepped cover opening to reveal three tiers of trays, with two lug handles.

10in (25.5cm) wide

£18,000-22,000 **LFA**

An oak coffer, designed by Ernest Gimson for Robert Weir Schultz, the plank front carved with Weir Schultz's initials and dated "1903", and with chip carved sides and chamfered stile feet.

30in (76cm) wide

£5,000-7,000 **LFA**

A black stained ash and beech triple back settle, designed by Ernest Gimson for Robert Weir Schultz, with bobbin-turned uprights.

66in (168cm) wide

£800-1,200 **LFA**

An Ernest Gimson oak standing double-sided bookcase, with two glazed doors above two panelled doors, with stepped feet, repeated on the reverse.

24.75in (63cm) wide

£3,500-4,000 **LFA**

An ash six tier open bookcase, with turned uprights, attributed to Ernest Gimson.

26.5in (67.5cm) wide

£2,000-3,000 **LFA**

A high back ash rocking chair, designed by Ernest Gimson for Robert Weir Schultz, with rush seat, on turned legs linked by turned stretchers.

24in (61cm) wide

£1,500-2,000 **LFA**

One of a pair of black stained ash and beech open armchairs, designed by Edward Gimson for Robert Weir Schultz, each with bobbin-turned uprights.

24in (61cm) wide

£6,000-9,000 pair **LFA**

An oak coffer, designed by Ernest Gimson for Robert Weir Schultz, the hinged cover above a plank front with style ends.

57.5in (146cm) wide

£6,000-9,000 **LFA**

A set of six tall-backed dining chairs, attributed to William Birch/High Wycombe, with cut-out crest rails and three with original rush seats, wear, unmarked.

39.5in (99cm) high

£700-1,000 **DRA**

A high back ash open armchair, designed by Ernest Gimson for Robert Weir Schultz, with rush seat on turned legs linked by turned stretchers.

24in (61cm) wide

£1,500-2,000 **LFA**

An ebonized mirror-back display cabinet after E.W. Godwin, with open gallery above central mirror and drawers, cupboards and open shelves.

71.75in (182cm) wide

£2,000-3,000 **L&T**

An oak sideboard, by Peter Heap 'The Rabbitman of Wetwang', with an adzed top and frame, three central drawers flanked by a panelled door either side, with the rabbit signature.

72.25in (183.5cm) wide

£800-1,200 **SWO**

A Liberty & Co. oak 'Thebes' stool, the concave slatted seat above four square supports linked by stretchers enclosing slatted sides.

13.75in (35cm) wide

£1,000-1,500 **L&T**

An oak high barrel back chair, designed by William R. Lethaby for Robert Weir Schultz, with flattened scroll arms, solid seat and shaped seat rail.

53.75in (136.5cm) high

£12,000-18,000 **LFA**

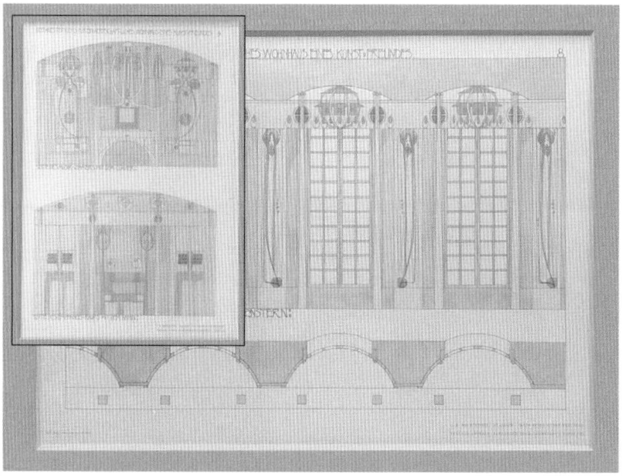

A pair of Charles Rennie Mackintosh architectural drawings, numbers 8 and 9 from the series "Haus Eines Kunst-Freundes," printed by Alexander Koch-Darmstadt, matted and framed.

15.25in (38cm) high

£1,200-1,800 **DRA**

A Liberty & Co. 'Anglo-Moresque' walnut sideboard, with mirrored back and blind fretwork arabesque panelled doors, bears paper label.

74in (188cm) wide

£1,000-1,500 **L&T**

An oak Morris chair, the flat arms with through tenons and short corbel supports over four vertical slats, later hinges, adjustable wood rod, losses.

30.5in (77.5cm) wide

£800-1,200 **SK**

An Australian cedar armchair by Diego Lamaro, "RIPOSO REST HER" banner.

Diego Lamaro studied woodcarving in Rome before moving to Australia c1900. His furniture typically mixes kangaroo and emu with traditional European motifs.

£700-1,000 **SHA**

An Arts and Crafts oak armchair, attributed to E. G. Punnett and manufactured by William Birch, with a central inlaid stylized motif and two rush woven panels, the seat in need of repair.

c1900

£2,500-3,000 **SWO**

An oak and ebony inlaid open armchair, by E.G. Punnett for William Birch, inlaid with a stylized motif and with rush panels and seat.

£2,200-2,800 **SWO**

An oak side cabinet, attributed to Robert Weir Schultz, with one frieze drawer above two pierced and carved panelled doors on square feet, with stamped brass ring handles.

36in (91.5cm) wide

£1,500-2,000 **LFA**

A pair of open oak bookcases, each with six shelves, designed by Sir Giles Gilbert Scott.

These bookshelves were designed for Whitelands College, Fulham, which was built in 1929.

30in (76cm) wide

£700-1,000 **SWO**

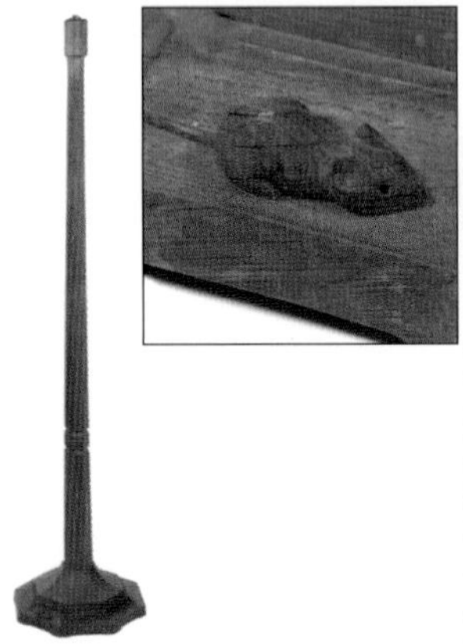

A 'Mouseman' oak standard lamp, by John Thompson, of octagonal form.

54in (137cm) high

£400-600 **B**

An early 20thC oak and pine trestle table, by Whytock and Reid, Edinburgh, in the manner of Robert Lorimer, replaced top.

54.75in (137cm) wide

£1,200-1,800 **L&T**

A Scottish Arts and Crafts hall stand, by Wylie and Lochhead, Glasgow, with a bevelled mirror plate flanked by repoussé-decorated copper panels.

33.5in (85cm) wide

£800-1,200 **L&T**

An early 20thC fruitwood sunburst vitrine, with two glass doors, applied ray pattern in black finish and mullioned glass side panels.

43.75in (111cm) wide

£1,200-1,800 **SK**

An oak Arts and Crafts bookcase, with two glazed doors above two panelled doors with bronze handles and plinth base.

45in (114.5cm) wide

£1,000-1,500 **LFA**

An exceptional Arts and Crafts two-door bookcase, with leaded glass doors and pegged joints, original finish, tight seam separation to top, unmarked.

51.5in (129cm) high

£1,500-2,000 **DRA**

An 20thC English oak cabinet, single door with strapwork handles and copper repoussé inserts, fitted with a clothing pole.

33in (84cm) wide

£180-220 **SK**

An early 20thC Arts and Crafts oak cabinet, four cabinet doors with fitted interior central cabinet door, with shelves.

43in (109cm) wide

£700-1,000 **SK**

A Scottish Arts and Crafts carved oak gun cabinet, with a castellated cornice and a glazed door opening to reveal a baize interior.

49.5in (126cm) wide

£1,000-1,500 **SWO**

An Arts and Crafts oak wardrobe, with two panelled doors carved with stylized fruiting trees bearing inscription "Salve Vale".

43in (109cm) wide

£1,500-2,000 **L&T**

A British Arts and Crafts sideboard, with mirrored backsplash, partially refinished, worn patina on brass pulls, looseness, unmarked.

65.5in (164cm) high

£1,200-1,800 **DRA**

An early 20thC Arts and Craft oak drop-front desk, with drop lid, interior fitted with letter holders and pen tray over two lower shelves.

25.5in (65cm) wide

£250-300 **SK**

A British Arts and Crafts chiffonier, with a single-panel door with hammered copper hardware, original finish, stencilled "no. 3422A", wear, damage.

71in (177.5cm) high

£1,800-2,200 **DRA**

An Arts and Crafts chest of drawers, with pivoting mirror mounted on carved posts, original finish, stains, replaced hardware, unmarked.

65in (162.5cm) high

£1,500-2,000 **DRA**

A British Arts and Crafts wash stand, with turned posts, towel rack, and free-standing shaving mirror, original finish, stencilled model number "5406A", wear.

52in (130cm) high

£700-1,000 **DRA**

An Arts and Crafts oak stool, with a rush seat and pierced heart motifs.

£200-300 **SWO**

A Scottish School laburnum occasional table, with four twin supports linked by flattened stretchers.

33in (84cm) wide

£600-900 **L&T**

An early 20thC oak chair, from Darmstadt/Jugendstil, and Richard Riemerschmid, with two horizontal slats below back rail, minor losses.

c1905 *35.75in (91cm) high*

£1,800-2,200 **SK**

An elm spindle back rocking chair, with flat shaped arms, rush seat, turned legs linked by similar stretchers.

20.5in (52cm) wide

£600-900 **LFA**

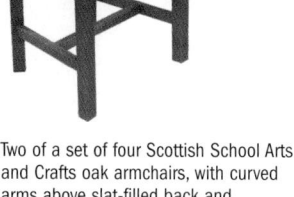

Two of a set of four Scottish School Arts and Crafts oak armchairs, with curved arms above slat-filled back and moulded solid seat.

£400-600 set **L&T**

An important Emile Gallé floral marquetry and parcel gilt-wood centre table, decorated with flowering branches in exotic woods, signed with intertwined "EG" monogram, dated "1887" and "Nanceii".

This table represents a most exceptional transition from the Belle Époque style into Art Nouveau design.

43.25in (110cm) wide

£15,000-20,000 **ISA**

An Emile Gallé burr oak, walnut and marquetry inlaid side cabinet, with a single door inlaid with thistles in specimen woods, carved moth bracket, the base carved with bats, inlaid signature 'Emile Gallé à Nancy'.

36.75in (93cm) wide

£15,000-20,000 **L&T**

An Emile Gallé Art Nouveau inlaid wood fire screen, decorated with a spray of lilies within a carved frame, inlaid signature lower left.

c1895 *22.25in (56.5cm) wide*

£2,200-2,800 **DRA**

An Emile Gallé inlaid wood tray, decorated with a scene of fishing boats, vertical Japanese-style inlaid signature.

c1900 *23.5in (59.5cm) wide*

£600-900 **DRA**

SHAPLAND & PETTER

A Shapland & Petter oak wardrobe and dressing table, each with marquetry panels, the locks stamped "S+PB".

wardrobe 79.5in (202cm) wide

£400-600 **SWO**

An Art Nouveau mahogany desk by Shapland & Petter, with leaded glass panel and slatted sides above top with inset writing surface.

39in (99cm) wide

£1,200-1,800 **L&T**

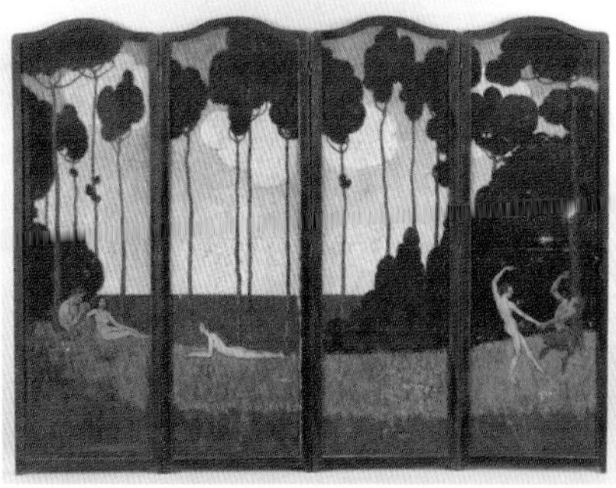

An Elenore Plaisted Abbott 'Rose Valley' four part folding screen, oil on canvas, each panel with wooded landscape and nudes.

c1905 *79in (197.5cm) wide*

£10,000-15,000 **POOK**

A Bill Becker organic-form cherry vanity, top with horizontal tambour slide enclosing fitted interior.

66in (168cm) wide

£1,200-1,800 **FRE**

A Carlo Bugatti corner armchair, inlaid with brass and pewter, with vellum upholstered seat.

£2,500-3,000 **L&T**

An important Art Nouveau marquetry and metal-inlaid carved exotic and fruitwood display cabinet, by Louis Majorelle, with ormolu mounts, the set-back central buffet portion having a pair of brackets supporting two glass shelves above a tambour-fronted cabinet, all flanked by a pair of side cabinets with glazed doors above recessed niches over bowed drawers and moulded cupboard doors.

This architecturally and sculpturally significant example was commissioned by the Gallé family for their Nancy home at rue Pont-Casse.

c1905 *64in (162.5cm) wide*

£25,000-30,000 **IS**

An Art Nouveau mahogany and inlaid bowfront display cabinet, probably designed by G. M. Ellwood for Bath Furniture Makers.

60.25in (153cm) wide

£6,000-9,000 **L&T**

A late 19thC rosewood inverted breakfront mirror-back sideboard, with Florentine-style inlaid decoration, on square tapering legs.

60in (152.5cm) wide

£700-1,000 **SWO**

An Art Nouveau burlwood fitted jewellery box, brass inlaid with panels depicting children's tales.

13in (33cm) wide

£2,800-3,200 **FRE**

An Art Nouveau mahogany and inlaid display cabinet, inlaid with whiplash flowering foliage and fish swimming through waterlilies, locks stamped "Salmon Brothers, London".

50.5in (128cm) wide

£2,200-2,800 **L&T**

An Art Nouveau mahogany display cabinet, with astragal glazed doors and stylized flower inlay in coloured woods, back stamped "R 1796".

46.5in (118cm) wide

£1,500-2,000 **SWO**

EPSTEIN

- Epstein furniture was originally founded in East London by Polish immigrants in the 1890s.
- The firm passed to brothers Harry (1909-93) and Lou Epstein (1911-86) and the pair turned their attention to the production of Art Deco forms from the 1930s until the 1950s.
- Finished to high standards, most pieces were custom-made in veneers of burr maple, sycamore or walnut.
- The design of the famous 'cloud' seat furniture is credited to Epstein and the company also popularized the uniquely British taste in suite furniture.
- Following WWII, Epstein had showrooms in London, Manchester and Glasgow.
- A conservative Art Deco style became the company's trademark after the war and most pieces were made from bleached walnut.
- Art Deco pieces are not signed. From the 1960s, some pieces were labelled "H. & L. Epstein" or "Epstein & Goldman".

A tall Art Deco Epstein cocktail cabinet, with circular moving central section revealing a mirrored display case.

1929 *36.25in (92cm) wide*

£4,000-5,000 **JAZ**

An Art Deco Epstein semi circular cocktail cabinet, in walnut, opens to a mirrored shelved bar.

c1935 *64in (162.5cm) high*

£1,500-2,000 **JAZ**

An Art Deco Epstein maple sideboard, with opening section with mirrored bar and light.

1935 *59.75in (152cm) wide*

£1,000-1,500 **JAZ**

An Art Deco Epstein three front drawer side cabinet, with a large lower shelf.

1930 *42in (107cm) wide*

£600-800 **JAZ**

An Art Deco Epstein table from a table and eight chair set, in burr maple with U-base.

1932 *78in (198cm) wide*

£5,000-7,000 **JAZ**

An Art Deco Epstein walnut table, from a table and six chair set, in an octagonal style.

1935 *72in (183cm) wide*

£4,000-5,000 set **JAZ**

An Art Deco Epstein 'Quartetto' nest of tables, in burr maple with four smaller tables.

c1930 *30in (76cm) diam*

£1,000-1,500 **JAZ**

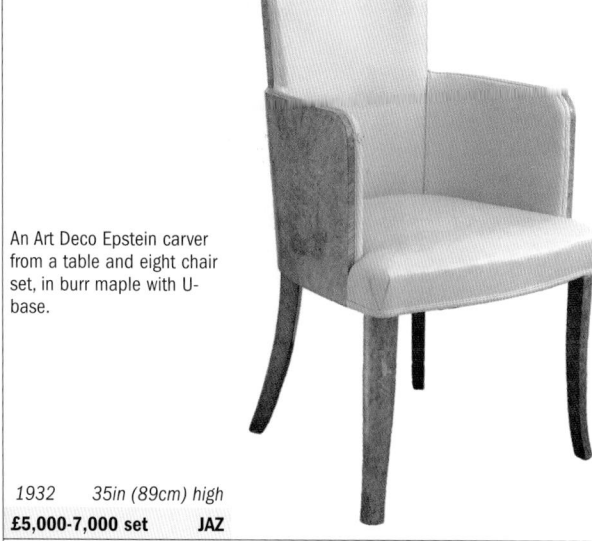

An Art Deco Epstein carver from a table and eight chair set, in burr maple with U-base.

1932 *35in (89cm) high*

£5,000-7,000 set **JAZ**

One of a pair of Art Deco Epstein cloudback carvers, upholstered in a cow patch fabric.

1928 *33.5in (85cm) high*

£4,000-5,000 pair **JAZ**

A walnut carver from an Art Deco table and set of chairs by Epstein, in an octagonal style.

1935 *36.25in (92cm) high*

£4,000-5,000 set **JAZ**

An Art Deco Epstein octagonal-style chair, from a table and six chair set.

1935 *36.25in (92cm) high*

£4,000-5,000 set **JAZ**

An Art Deco Epstein chair from a table and eight chair set, in burr maple with U-base.

1932 *35in (89cm) high*

£5,000-7,000 set **JAZ**

A late 1920s black lacquer and nickel plated steel console, designed by Paul Frankl for Skyscraper.

27in (68.5cm) wide

£3,000-4,000 **MSM**

A Paul Frankl chrome and black lacquer Art Deco console table with black glass top.

1930s *27in (68.5cm) wide*

£5,000-7,000 **AMO**

One of a pair of Paul Frankl 'D' chair, finished in black lacquer with black vinyl upholstery and red piping.

Similar chairs by Frankl are illustrated in his June 1928 article in 'Art & Decoration' and in 'New Backgrounds for a New Age' in 1927.

c1925 *26.5in (67cm) high*

£4,000-6,000 pair **MSM**

A Paul Frankl men's valet, from a 1928 commission by his Skyscraper Furniture Company for the scion of the Texas King Ranch family.

42.5in (108cm) wide

£3,000-4,000 **MSM**

A 1930s Paul Frankl streamline sofa, in black lacquer and black leather with inset nickel plated speed bands.

This is one of the rarest and most striking pieces of Frankl's production furniture.

88in (223.5cm) wide

£6,000-9,000 **MSM**

A Paul Frankl coffee table, one of a kind from the La Jollas Paul Frankl commission, in red and black lacquer with undershelf for storage or magazines.

c1945 *30.5in (77.5cm) wide*

£3,000-4,000 **MSM**

An important Paul Frankl Skyscraper vanity, the mirror supported by a cast aluminum frame, on a moulded wood pedestal plinth, bears firm's metallic label "SKYSCRAPER FURNITURE / Frankl Galleries / 4 East 48th Street, New York".

63.25in (160.5cm) wide

£7,000-10,000 **ISA**

GILBERT ROHDE

- Gilbert Rohde (1894-1944) founded his New York design studio in 1927. He soon became known for his avant-garde ideas and is credited with some of the most stylish and practical furniture ever made.
- Rohde had travelled in Germany and pieces were inspired by the late Bauhaus. His modular and sectional furniture shows the influence of Walter Gropius.
- Pieces were made from natural materials such as American maple. Exotic hardwood was used for veneers and the sparse hardware was usually metal.
- Much of Rohde's work was designed for corporate manufacturers, such as the Herman Miller Furniture Co., Heywood-Wakefield and John Widdicomb.
- Rohde designed innovative children's furniture for Krohler and a range of tubular steel seating furniture for Troy Sunshade Co. in 1933.
- Rohde also contributed designs to New York's World Fair of 1939.
- Furniture is often marked. Some custom furniture bears a paper label.

An Art Deco matte black lacquer console, designed by Gilbert Rohde.

c1930

£2,000-3,000 **MSM**

A Gilbert Rohde coffee table for the Herman Miller Company, listed in their catalogue as '4119', the top with a figured veneer in mahogany, the legs wrapped in fabricoid.

1941 *44in (112cm) wide*

£2,000-2,500 **MSM**

A Gilbert Rohde/Herman Miller pair of East India laurel sofa end tables, each with open storage cubicle and single drawer with horizontal black enamelled wood pull over two shelves, unmarked.

33.5in (85cm) wide

£3,000-4,000 **SDR**

Two Gilbert Rohde/Herman Miller occasional tables, with glass tops supported by a vertical chrome bar, top to smaller one replaced, unmarked.

larger 24.75in (63cm) wide

£1,500-2,000 **SDR**

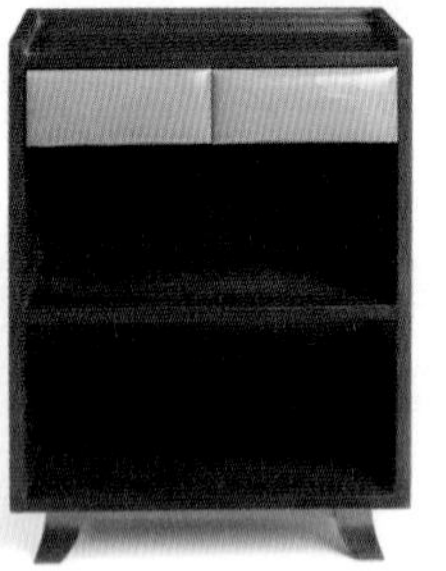

One of a pair of 1940s Gilbert Rohde mahogany and leather end tables.

18in (45.5cm) wide

£2,000-2,500 pair **HSD**

A Gilbert Rohde Art Deco 'cloud' table, in acacia burl with three leatherette-wrapped legs.

c1940 *27in (68.5cm) wide*

£2,000-2,500 **HSD**

A Gilbert Rohde/Herman Miller East India laurel bookcase, with single shelf over two-door cabinet with brushed chrome and black enamelled woods pulls, Herman Miller metal tag and stencilled numbers.

31.5in (80cm) wide

£1,200-1,800 **SDR**

A Gilbert Rohde/Herman Miller East India laurel sideboard, with chrome and black enamelled wood pulls concealing drawers and single shelf, on black plinth base, unmarked.

48in (121cm) wide

£3,500-4,000 **SDR**

An Art Deco chest of drawers in sycamore and mahogany, designed by Gilbert Rohde.

c1935 *43in (109cm) wide*

£4,000-5,000 **HSD**

A Gilbert Rohde/Herman Miller two-door dresser, with three horizontal chrome bands, six concealed drawers, accompanied by a free standing circular mirror on square base, unmarked.

Chest 35.5in (90cm) wide

£3,000-5,000 **SDR**

A pair of Gilbert Rohde/Herman Miller three-drawer chests, with tufted white leatherette, on ebonized wood feet, unmarked.

44.5in (111cm) wide

£1,500-2,000 **SDR**

A Gilbert Rohde/Herman Miller vanity with tall rectangular mirror and demi-lune case, with chrome bands and pulls, two attached drawers and three pivoting drawers, unmarked.

47in (119.5cm) wide

£2,200-2,800 **SDR**

A Gilbert Rohde/Herman Miller 'Paldao' single-pedestal desk, with freeform top containing two blind drawers, tacked-on ochre leatherette to pedestal and leg, marked with stencilled number.

52in (132cm) wide

£1,200-1,800 **SDR**

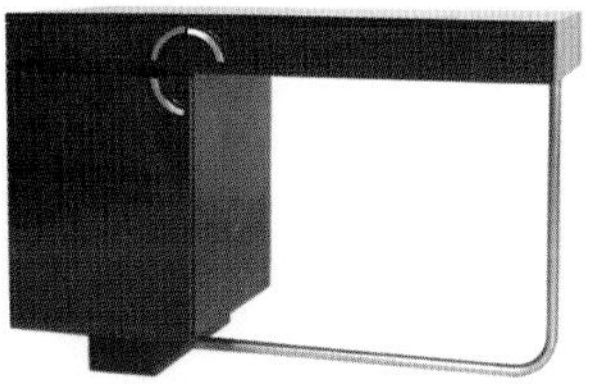

A Gilbert Rohde/Herman Miller East India laurel single-pedestal desk, with cabinet door concealing three additional drawers, chrome pulls, on tubular metal frame, unmarked.

44in (112cm) wide

£3,000-4,000 **SDR**

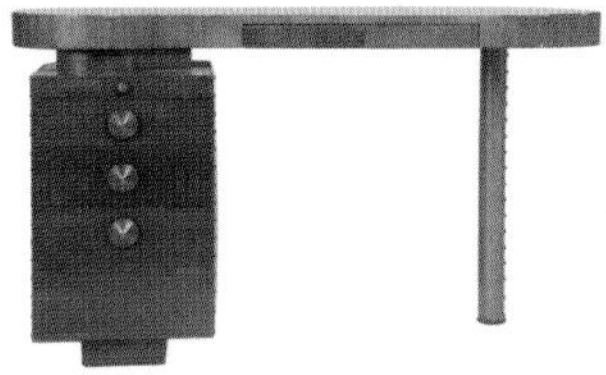

A Gilbert Rohde/Herman Miller single-pedestal 'Paldao' desk, with tacked-on brown leatherette details, and raised kidney-shaped top, carved wood pulls.

52in (130cm) wide

£1,200-1,800 **SDR**

A lounge chair, attributed to Gilbert Rohde, on bent brushed steel, upholstered in charcoal grey fabric, unmarked.

32in (81cm) high

£3,500-3,000 **SDR**

An Art Deco Gilbert Rohde chair.

c1939 *33.5in (85cm) high*

£3,000-4,000 **HSD**

A pair of Gilbert Rohde lounge chairs, for Heywood-Wakefield Co.

This is the 'Female' version of this chair design.

c1934 *25.25in (64cm) wide*

£3,000-4,000 pair **HSD**

A Gilbert Rohde/Herman Miller electric mantel clock, in rosewood with enamelled metal hands and chrome details, minor chip to rear, marked.

16.75in (42.5cm)

£3,000-4,000 **SDR**

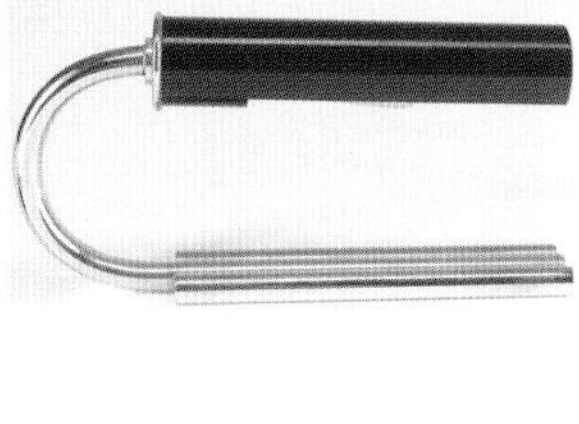

A Gilbert Rohde/Herman Miller desk lamp with black enamelled metal shade on tubular polished chrome base, unmarked.

13.75in (35cm) wide

£800-1,200 **SDR**

An Art Deco Eugene Schoen china cabinet.

c1931 *32in (81.5cm) wide*

£3,000-3,500 **MSM**

A Eugene Schoene three drawer chest, designed for Schmieg Hungate and Kotzian, with cross-hatched parquetry front.

c1935 *45in (114.5cm) wide*

£6,000-8,000 **AMO**

An Art Deco mahogany and bleached mahogany five drawer chest of drawers, designed by Eugene Schoen for Schmieg Hungate and Kotzian.

c1935 *41.5in (10.5.5cm) wide*

£5,000-7,000 **AMO**

A rare pair of Eugene Schoen end tables, constructed by Schmieg & Kotzian, in East Indian rosewood veneer, branded "S.K."

Schmieg & Kotzian were among the most prestigious cabinet makers in New York in the Art Deco period.

14in (35.5cm) wide

£4,000-5,000 **MSM**

A maple Art Deco desk, designed by Eugene Schoen for Schmieg Hungate and Kotzian, marked.

c1935 *45in (114.5cm) wide*

£6,000-8,000 **AMO**

One of a pair of Eugene Schoen red lacquer console tables, designed for Schmieg Hungate and Kotzian, marked.

c1935 *72in (183cm) wide*

£8,000-12,000 pair **AMO**

OTHER ART DECO

One of a pair of Art Deco armchairs by Jacques Adnet.

1932 *28in (71cm) high*

£7,000-10,000 pair **MOD**

A small Art Deco table, attributed to Andre Arbus.

c1945 *18in (45cm) diam*

£3,000-3,500 **MOD**

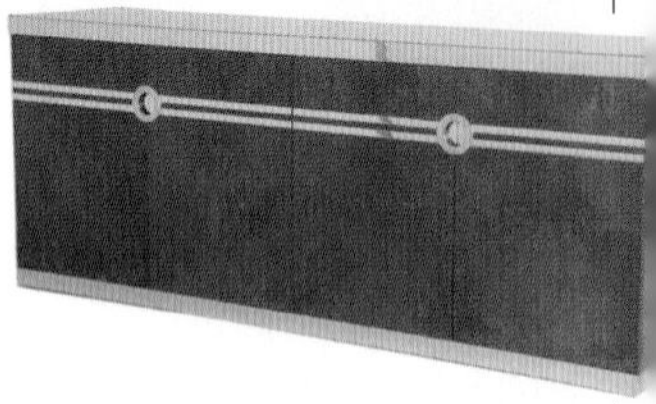

A Pierre Cardin four-door sideboard with burlwood veneer, polished brass and chrome trim, with two interior drawers and two shelves, stamped "Pierre Cardin" in script.

74in (185cm) wide

£1,500-2,000 **SDR**

A J. Cayette nest of three Art Deco tables.

c1925 *26in (66cm) wide*

£5,000-7,000 **MOD**

A Robert Winthrop Chanler three panel screen, painted with two zebras on one side in black and tan on ivory ground, the back with diagonal stripes with silver foil, signed and dated.

Broadway composer Kay Swift and her husband James P. Warburg commissioned Chanler to execute this piece for their New York home. 'Fine & Dandy: The Life and Work of Kay Swift' contains a photo of the screen shown in a 1970s interior. This piece descended through Ms Swift's family.

1928 *Each panel 78in (198cm) wide*

£5,000-7,000 **SDR**

A Chase demi-lune bar, polychrome painted with a jazz orchestra, and chrome rails by Chase, composition signed "Smith", rails marked "Alpha Brass/Chase" with centaur.

50.75in (127cm) wide

£1,500-2,000 **SDR**

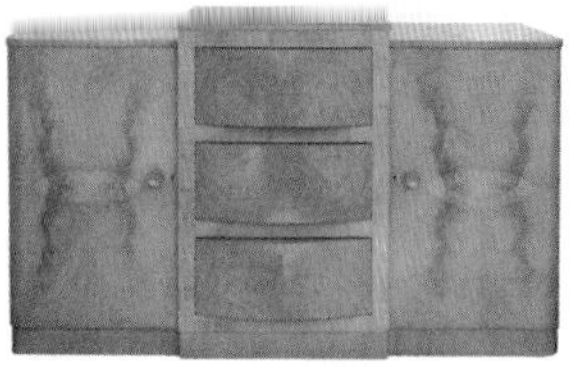

An Art Deco sideboard by M. P. Davis of London, in bleached mahogany with three central drawers and two side cabinets.

1929 *63.75in (162cm) wide*

£700-1,000 **JAZ**

One of a pair of Donald Deskey Art Deco filing cabinets, in black lacquer and rosewood with nickel and bronze fittings.

c1935 *16.5in (42cm) wide*

£8,000-12,000 pair **AMO**

An Art Deco two level coffee table designed by Donald Deskey in nickel and Bakelite.

c1925 *28in (71cm) wide*

£4,000-6,000 **MSM**

An Art Deco Donald Deskey Radio City Music Hall sofa, from the main lounge of the hall at Rockefeller Center, vinyl, fabric and rosewood.

c1930 *72in (183cm) wide*

£8,000-12,000 **MSM**

An Art Deco desk by Donald Deskey for Widdicomb Co.

c1935 *52in (132cm) wide*

£7,000-10,000 **HSD**

A French Art Deco/Modernist three drawer commode, in macassar ebony, of asymmetrical design on a pedestal base, polished Nickel tubular modernist hardware, attributed to La Maison Desny.

La Maison Desny is believed to have been established by two designers, Desnet and René Nauny from whose names the contraction of Desny was derived. The rigorous geometric configurations appear avant-garde even by today's standards.

c1925 *25.5in (65cm) wide*

£6,000-8,000 **DD**

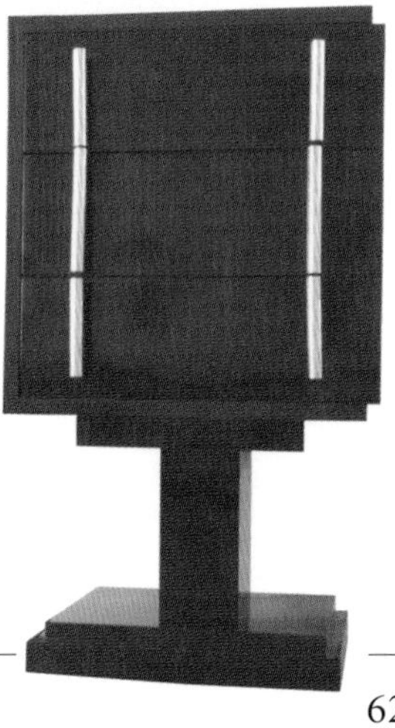

A French Art Deco/Modernist tiered side table, possibly by La Maison Desny, in macassar ebony, with starburst veneer pattern to top, the centre post with curved back panel.

The crisp symmetry and uniformity in the composition of this coupe recalls the interlocking planes and circles found in Russian Constructivism.

c1925 *16in (40.5cm) diam*

£4,000-5,000 **DD**

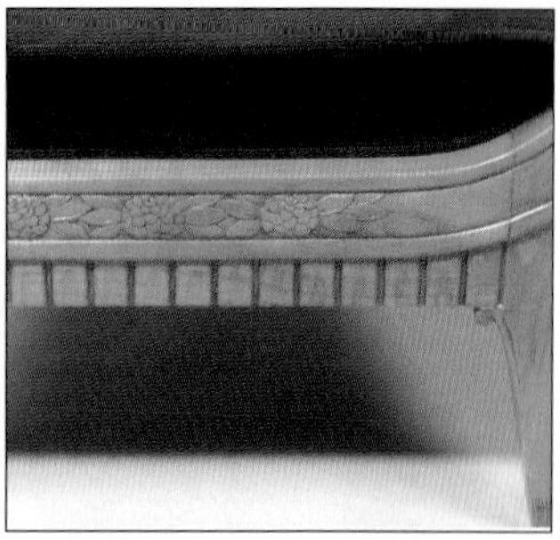

A pair of Art Deco Maurice Dufrene chairs.

c1925 *31in (78.5cm) high*

£7,000-10,000 **MOD**

An Art Deco centre table, by Maurice Dufrene.

c1925 *36in (91.5cm) diam*

£10,000-15,000 **MOD**

Two Art Deco inlaid stands, attributed to Maurice Dufrene, in amboyna wood inlaid with stylized flowers in various fruitwoods and mother-of-pearl.

c1925 *15in (38cm) wide*

£1,200-1,800 **SK**

A French Art Deco occasional chair, by Maurice Dufrene, rosewood frame with scalloped edge back and carved melon style feet.

Maurice Dufrene was the artistic director of La Matrisse Department store and exhibited prolifically during the early 20thC.

c1925 *32in (81cm) high*

£2,000-3,000 **DD**

A black lacquered wood small table, designed by Jean Dunand, the top inset with a gold-fleck lacquer, stamped underneath "JEAN DUNAND LAQUEUR" and "1248", minor imperfections.

c1925 *20.75in (53cm) wide*

£8,000-12,000 **ISA**

A pair of Art Deco American Skyscraper black lacquer and silvered wood end tables.

c1935 *12in (30.5cm) wide*

£4,000-5,000

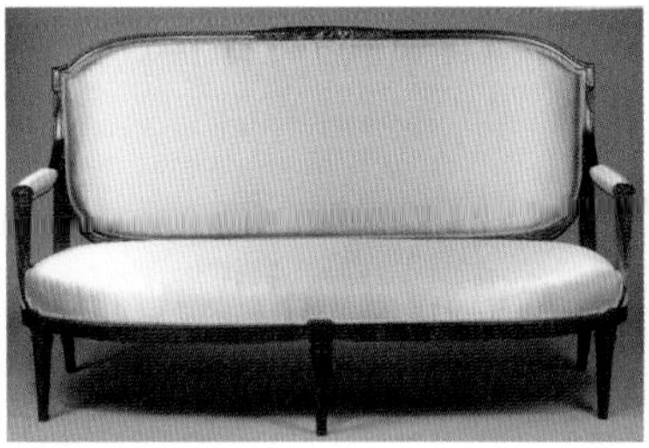

An Art Deco sofa by Paul Follot.

c1925 63in (160cm) wide

£7,000-10,000 MOD

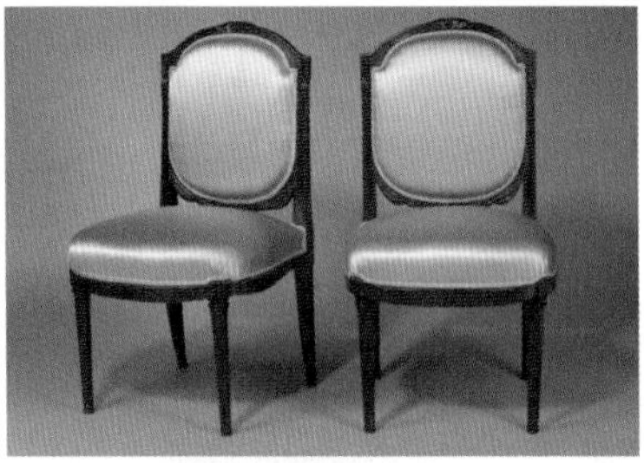

A pair of Art Deco chairs by Paul Follot.

c1925 37in (94cm) high

£4,000-6,000 MOD

A pair of Art Deco chairs by Paul Follot.

c1925 42in (107cm) high

£7,000-10,000 MOD

An Art Deco vanity, designed by Norman Bel Geddes for the Simmons Company.

This is one of the first pieces of American metal case goods. The April 1930 issue of House and Garden Magazine described it as "A practical dressing table...of black enamelled steel with chromium plated base and trimming."

1930 43in (109cm) wide

£1,500-2,000 MSM

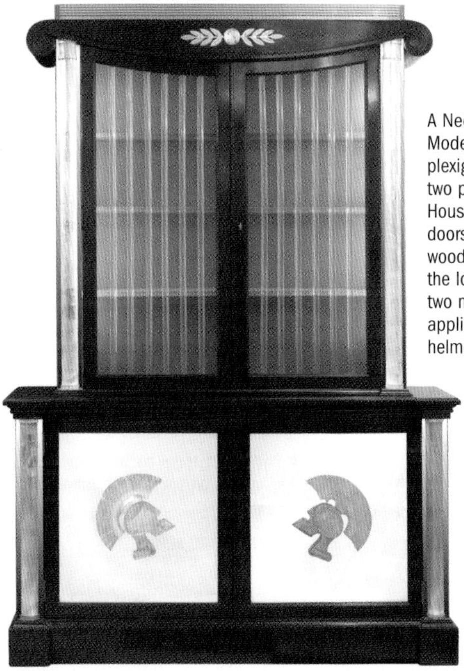

A Neoclassical Art Moderne mahogany and plexiglass bookcase in two parts, by Grosfeld House, with mahogany doors and a lacquered wood shelved interior, the lower section with two mirrored doors with applied plexiglass helmets.

c1935 54in (137cm) wide

£7,000-10,000 HSD

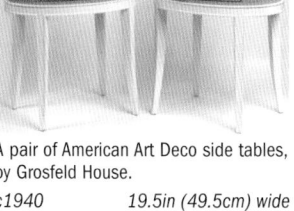

A pair of American Art Deco side tables, by Grosfeld House.

c1940 19.5in (49.5cm) wide

£4,000-5,000 HSD

An Art Deco aluminium inlaid rosewood end table with glass top, custom made by Hammond-Knoll.

c1935 26in (66cm) wide

£4,000-5,000 AMO

An Art Deco side table, by Charles Hardy for Belmet Products of New York.

c1935 20in (51cm) wide

£1,500-2,000 HSD

A rosewood dining room suite designed by Robert Heritage, comprising a dining table and six matching chairs with slatted backs and upholstered seats.

table 56in (142cm) diam

£600-900 set L&T

A CLOSER LOOK AT A JULES LELEU DINING SUITE

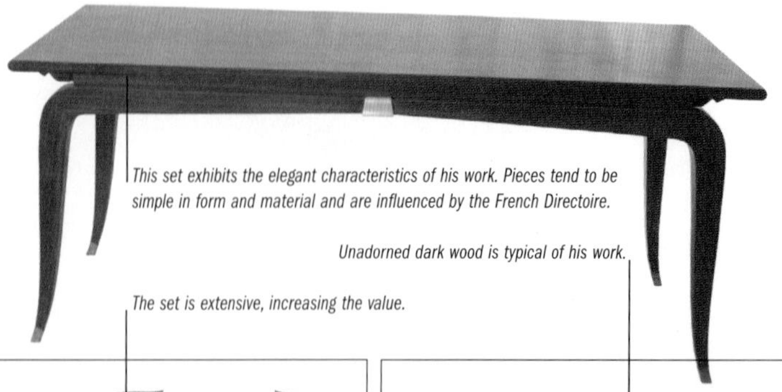

This set exhibits the elegant characteristics of his work. Pieces tend to be simple in form and material and are influenced by the French Directoire.

Unadorned dark wood is typical of his work.

The set is extensive, increasing the value.

Pieces by Jules Leleu (1883-1961) are highly sought after. Trained as a sculptor, his mastery of form is evident in his work.

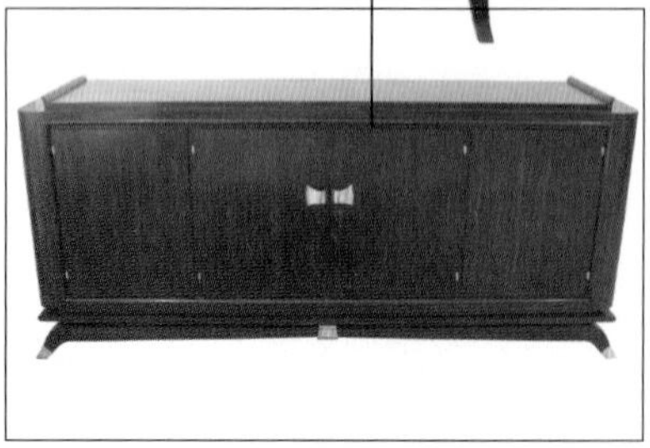

A French Art Deco dining suite by Jules Leleu, comprising dining table with extensions, six side chairs, two arm chairs and matching Credenza, macassar ebony, bronze hardware and sabots.

Leleu is also well known for his design work on Ocean Liners such as 'Ile de France', 'L'Atlantique' and 'The Normandie'.

c1928 *71in (180.5cm) wide*

£40,000-50,000 suite **DD**

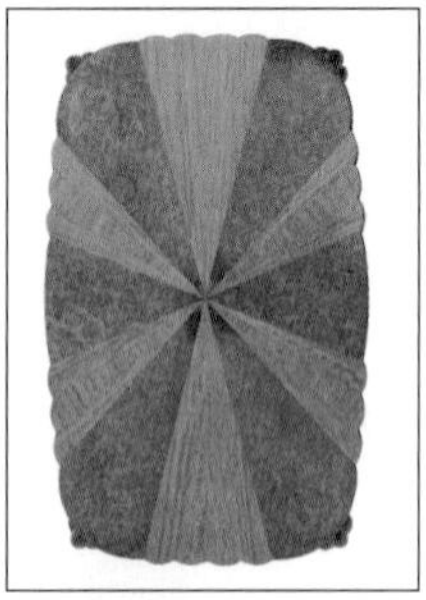

A nest of three Art Deco tables by Hille & Co. in amboyna and satinwood.

1925 *largest 31in (79cm) wide*

£1,500-2,000 **JAZ**

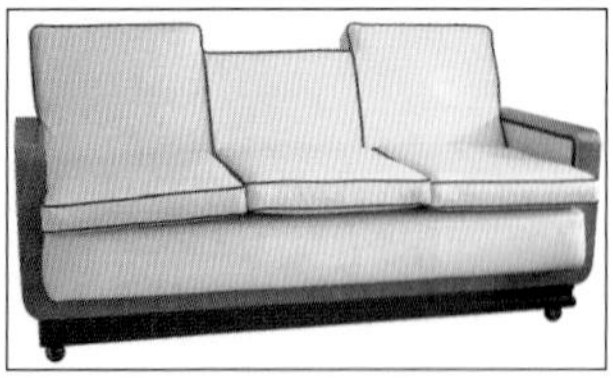

A Hille & Co. three piece suite, in walnut with cream leather upholstery.

1928 *sofa 72.5in (184cm) wide*

£4,000-5,000 suite **JAZ**

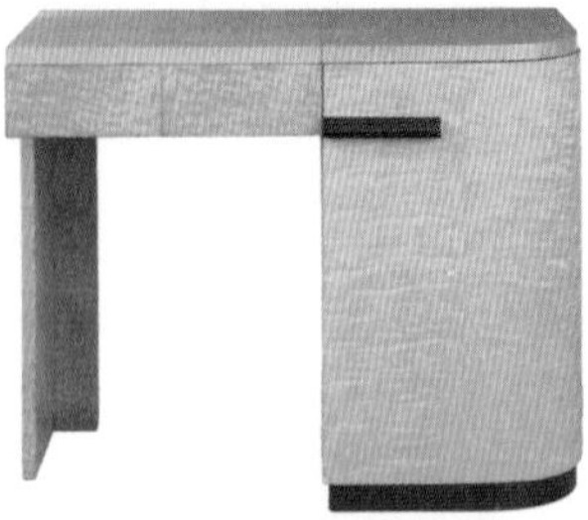

An Art Deco desk dresser by Hille & Co., in sycamore.

1928 *35in (91cm) wide*

£1,000-2,000 **JAZ**

An Art Deco Wolfgang Hoffmann coffee table.

1934

£1,800-2,200 **MSM**

An Art Deco Wolfgang Hoffmann occasional table for the Howell Company, St Charles, Illinois, the lacquered wood top on a chrome steel base.

A similar table was exhibited at the 1933 World's Fair.

1935 *24in (60cm) diam*

£1,200-1,800 **MSM**

A fine Jules Leleu secretary with cabinets flanking a drop-front door and two lower drawers, its base with brass trim and short sabre legs, unmarked.

54.5in (136cm) wide

£3,000-4,000 **SDR**

A four-door sideboard, in the manner of Jules Leleu, with glass top, parquetry door fronts, and star-shaped brass ornamentation, on trestle base with scroll supports, unmarked.

112.25in (280cm) wide

£2,200-2,800 **SDR**

A macassar ebony display cabinet, in the manner of Jules Leleu, with two sliding glass doors and two interior glass shelves, over two-door cabinet, unmarked.

55.5in (139cm) high

£1,500-2,000 **SDR**

A pair of mahogany side chairs, by Louis Majorelle, with arched tops over pierced and upholstered back-rests and seats, on carved tapered square legs.

38in (98cm) high

£700-1,000 **ISA**

A monumental Art Deco Warren McArthur/Albert Chase McCarthy wrought-iron fern stand, for the lobby of the Arizona Biltmore Hotel, scattered oxidation, unmarked.

c1930 *30in (76cm) high*

£1,200-1,800 **SDR**

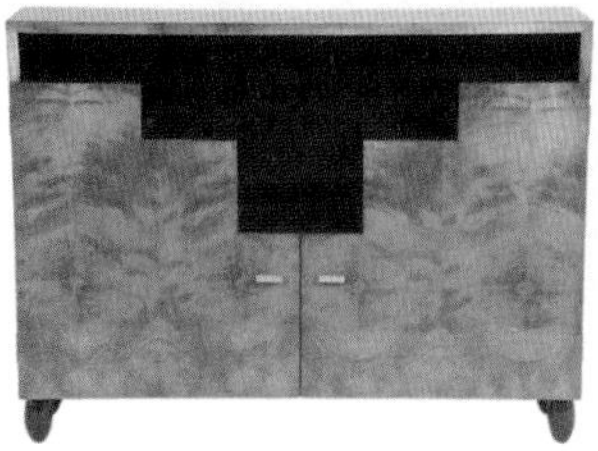

A Modernage stepped cabinet, with burled veneer exterior and two doors mounted on bulbous ebonized legs, with ebonized interior, unmarked.

48in (120cm) wide

£1,200-1,800 **SDR**

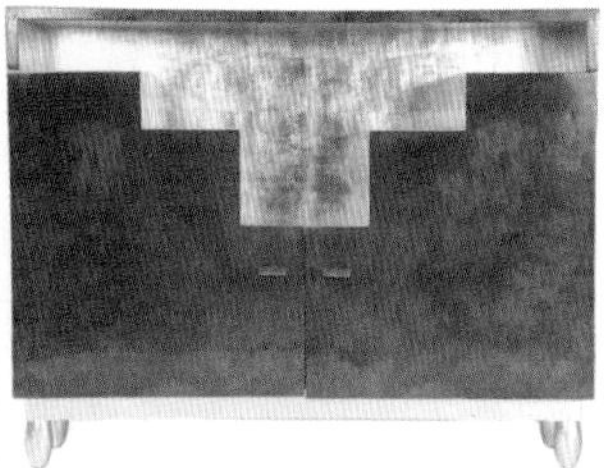

An exceptional Modernage two-door display cabinet, in sycamore veneer, with stepped front and gold leaf interior concealing drawers and shelves, on giltwood base with ovoid feet, unmarked.

48in (120cm) wide

£2,200-2,800 **SDR**

A Jean Royere 'Polar Bear' overstuffed sofa, upholstered in plush navy blue Alpaca wool, on low oak feet, unmarked.

This is one of Royere's most iconic and sought-after designs.

93in (232.5cm) wide

£18,000-22,000 **SDR**

A Schmieg & Kotzian leather, plexiglass and Carpathian burled elm desk.

c1945 *38in (96.5cm) wide*

£5,000-7,000 **HSD**

A Soubrier Art Deco table.

c1930 *27.5in (70cm) diam*

£3,000-3,500 **MOD**

Two Soubrier Art Deco armchairs.

c1930 *31in (78.5cm) high*

£6,000-8,000 **MOD**

An Art Deco Piano by John Strohmenger, London, in burr ample with sunburst sycamore motif on the top.

1928 *55in (140cm) wide*

£6,000-9,000 **JAZ**

A set of six Thonet dining chairs, two arm and four side, each upholstered in muslin, with Thonet paper labels.

armchairs 34in (86.5cm) high

£1,800-2,200 set **SDR**

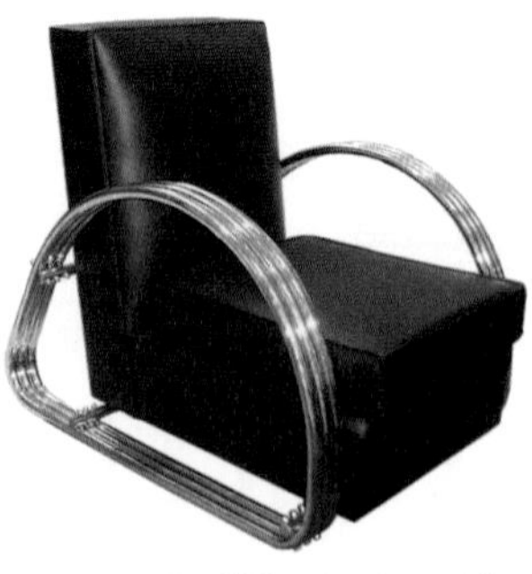

An Art Deco Kem Weber American triple band chair, for Lloyd Manufacturing Company, with machine age triple band arms enclosing a sprung seat and back.

This chair is featured in Lloyd's 1937 and 1938 catalogues.

1937 *27.5in (70cm) wide*

£2,200-2,800 **MSM**

A French Art Deco vanity in the manner of Emile-Jacques Ruhlmann, with circular mirror and inset black marble top, ivory drawer pulls and feet, unmarked.

52.25in (130.5cm) high

£1,500-2,000 **SDR**

A pair of Art Deco beds, each single curvilinear bed frame with hanging shelf compartments.

c1930 *82in (208.5cm) wide*

£800-1,200 pair **SK**

A pair of mirrored cabinets with bevel-edged glass panes, and single drawer over two doors, on tapering legs, unmarked.

35in (87.5cm) wide

£1,500-2,000 **SDR**

An American Art Deco fine tall chest, with inlaid trim, with drop-front parquet panel and pyramidal amber Bakelite pulls, marked "Made in Grand Rapids", stencilled no. on back.

60.5in (153.5cm) wide

£700-1,000 **SDR**

A French Modernist sideboard, in mahogany and walnut with chrome detail.

1925 *65in (165cm) wide*

£1,200-1,800 **JAZ**

A French Art Deco double-pedestal executive desk, covered in parchment with two cabinet doors concealing drawers, on oak cylinder feet, unmarked.

56in (140cm) wide

£1,800-2,200 **SDR**

An Art Deco desk of mixed woods, with sliding tambour doors concealing three drawers, on sculpted wood frame, unmarked.

51.75in (129cm) wide

£600-800 **SDR**

A pair of French Art Deco boudoir chairs, of Cubist angular design with lacquered wood frame, possibly by Eileen Gray, in a re-issue of the original French geometric art deco carved velvet fabric.

c1930 *32in (65cm) high*

£4,000-5,000 **DD**

A pair of Art Deco club chairs re-upholstered in black leather on low wood feet, unmarked.

30.5in (77.5cm) high

£800-1,200 **SDR**

One of a pair of French Art Deco streamline club chairs, in tobacco coloured buffalo hides.

c1935 30.5in (77cm) high

£5,000-6,000 pair **DD**

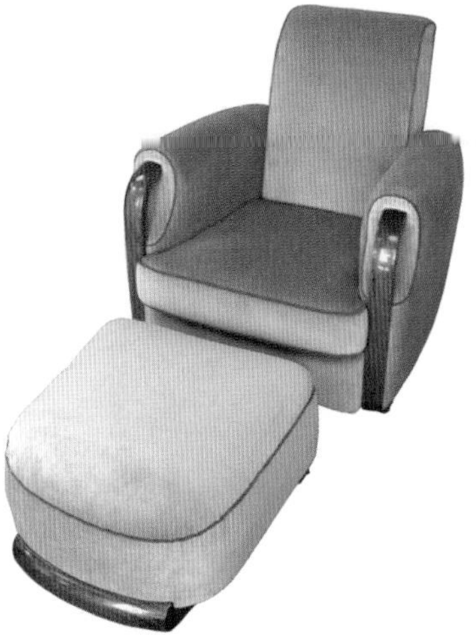

A French Art Deco Dominique club chair with ottoman, mohair velvet upholstery with walnut trim.

c1935 *33in (84cm) high*

£5,000-7,000 **DD**

A pair of club chairs, with loose cushions upholstered in espresso-coloured leather, on tapering hardwood legs, unmarked.

36in (90cm) wide

£1,500-2,000 **SDR**

An Art Deco pair of loveseats, with undulated backs and green velvet upholstery, raised on four tapering, fluted legs, unmarked.

63in (157.5cm) wide

£2,500-3,000 **SDR**

A pair of Art Deco club chairs, upholstered in black knit fabric on rosewood veneer block feet, unmarked.

31.5in (79cm) wide

£1,200-1,800 **SDR**

A pair of Art Deco club chairs, re-upholstered in brown leather with brass studs on chunky Mackmurdo style front feet, unmarked.

30.75in (78cm) high

£1,200-1,800 **SDR**

A pair of French Art Deco chairs.

c1925 *37in (94cm) high*

£3,000-4,000 **MOD**

An English Art Deco chest of drawers with black lacquer banding, in walnut.

c1935 *48in (123cm) wide*

£600-800 **JAZ**

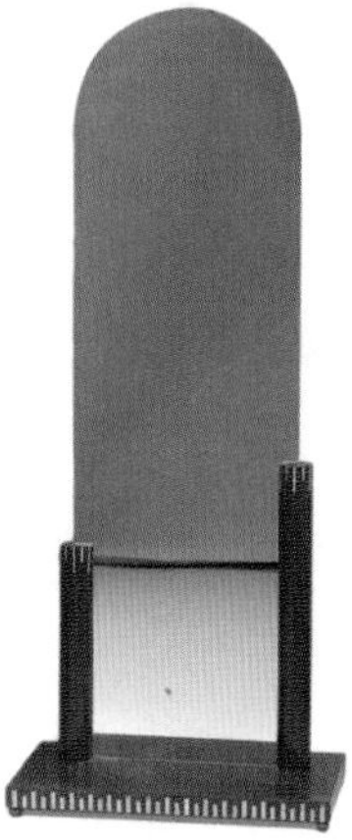

An Art Deco floor mirror, full-length mirror with arched top, asymmetrical rosewood base with geometric ivory inlay.

c1925 *29in (73.5cm) wide*

£800-1,200 **SK**

An Italian Art Deco wall-hanging mirror with parcel-gilt frame, geometric and floral mosaic border, and attached planter.

£300-400 **SDR**

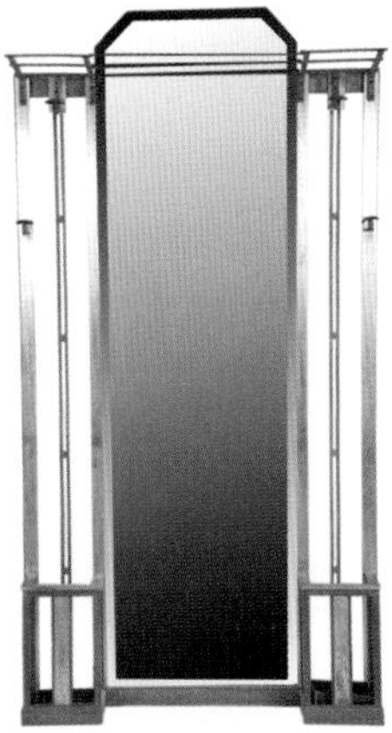

A French Art Deco hall mirror, with aluminum uprights and cast metal inserts, four hooks and two integrated umbrella stands, unmarked.

79in (197.5cm) high

£300-500 **SDR**

A Continental Art Deco cheval mirror, and bedside table with single cabinet drawer.

1930 *43.5in (110cm) wide*

£400-600 **JAZ**

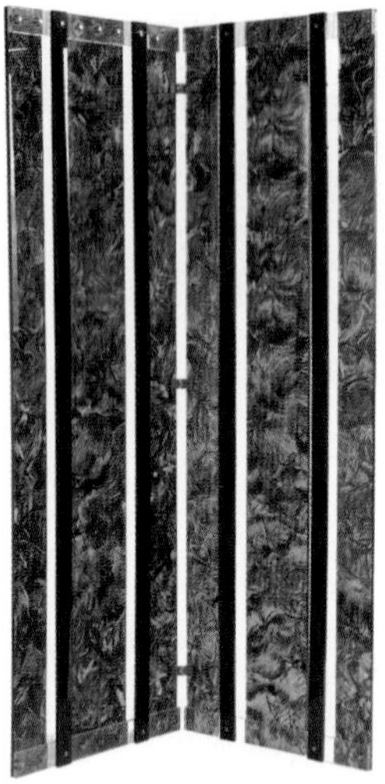

A 20thC two-fold perspex screen, with alternating tortoiseshell and black slats linked by clear supports and chrome hinges.

48in (142cm) wide

£700-1,000 **LFA**

A French Art Deco cushioned low stool, upholstered in Art Deco fabric with rose wood with Zebrano banding.

1928 *18in (46cm) wide*

£300-400 **JAZ**

An American Art Deco cocktail table, of ribbon mahogany with chrome banding.

c1935 *36in (91.5cm) wide*

£3,000-4,000 **HSD**

An Art Deco inlay dining table, the oval top with geometric inlay border and central medallion, on shaped platform base.

c1930 *43.5in (110.5cm) wide*

£800-1,200 **SK**

An Art Deco burl, ebony, and ash inlay dining table, with burlwood oval top with fine ebony inlay decoration raised on four canted legs, accompanied by two conforming leaves.

c1930 *40in (101.5cm) wide*

£600-900 **SK**

A French Art Deco walnut side table, with coromandel crossbanding and ebony lining, quarter veneered top above drawer with tassel handles, on semi-reeded legs.

32in (81cm) wide

£1,200-1,800 **L&T**

A small French Art Deco side table, with octagonal top over ovoid pedestal base, unmarked.

21in (52.5cm) diam

£400-600 **SDR**

A pair of Art Deco lamp tables with circular top and and cruciform bases, unmarked.

28in (70cm) diam

£1,800-2,200 **SDR**

A French Art Deco coffee table with oval top on double-pedestal base with stretcher, unmarked.

44.75in (112cm) wide

£400-600 **SDR**

A large French Art Deco dining table with gilded details, the serrated glass disc legs supporting a black checked top, unmarked.

96.5in (241cm) wide

£10,000-15,000 **SDR**

An American Art Deco mirror and glass rod sidetable.

c1935 *15.5in (39.5cm) diam*

£1,500-2,000 **HSD**

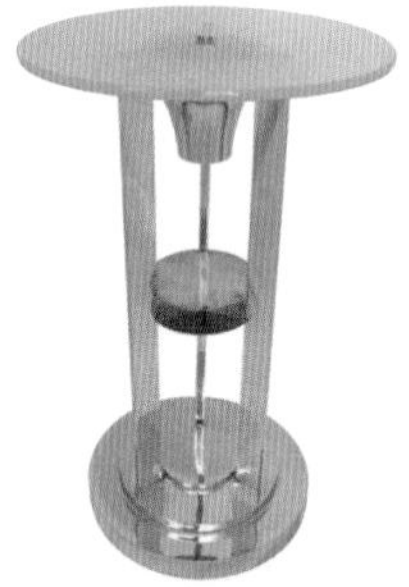

A French Art Deco illuminated streamline cigarette table, frosted glass disc top, chrome stair stepped circular base and supports, copper disc decoration.

c1935 *12in (30.5cm) diam*

£1,500-2,000 **DD**

An Art Deco Skyscraper vanity with rectangular mirror, single drawer and two cabinets, in bird's eye maple veneer with black enamelled trim, unmarked.

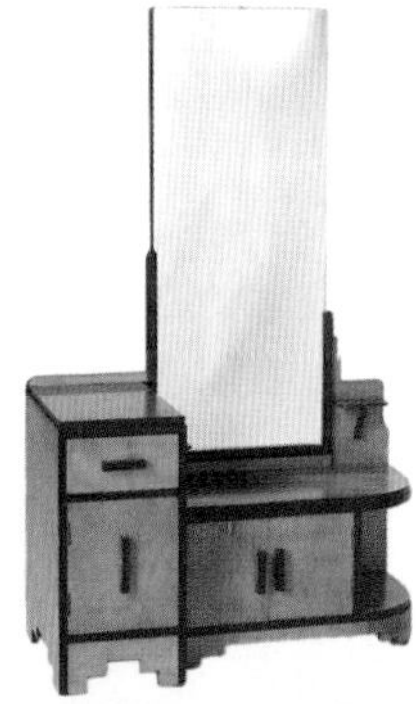

61.25in (155.5cm) high

£300-500 **SDR**

A CLOSER LOOK AT AN ART DECO FRIEZE

Only two such triptych sets are known to exist, making this one rare and valuable.
The great size makes this a substantial piece and increases its appeal.
Work that characterizes the Art Deco period is sought after and the leaping gazelle motif is synonymous with the movement.
This large and unusual plasterwork design evokes the glamorous golden age of cinema. It was originally used as ventilation covers for the radiator rooms of a grand Art Deco movie theatre in Cincinnati, Ohio.

A 1920s American Art Deco carved plaster frieze, with triptych arched 'leaping gazelle' design.

146in (371cm) wide

£7,000-10,000 **DD**

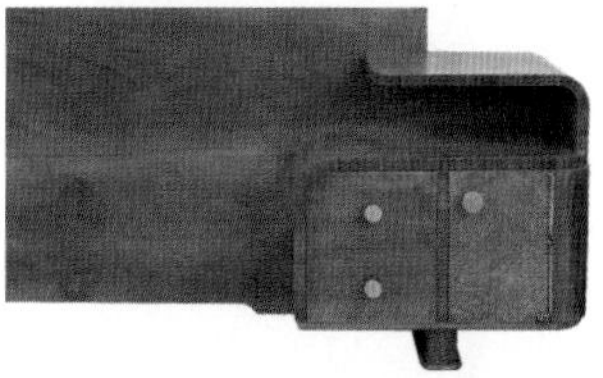

A late 1920s walnut Art Deco Continental headboard, the side tables with drawers.

62in (158cm) wide

£600-900 **JAZ**

A 1940s French Art Deco Cubist bar, in macassar ebony and various exotic wood species, with inlay design featuring stylized New York skyscraper skyline with Empire State building and the Chrysler building.

106in (269cm) wide

£7,000-10,000 **DD**

OTHER DECORATIVE ART FURNITURE

A gilt and gesso cabinet by Max Kuehne, with two glass cabinet doors, with floral decorated gesso panels on a turquoise ground, incised and gilt decoration on surround.

Max Kuehne (1880-1968) trained under William Merritt Chase, a member of The Ten, and Robert Henri, a leading artist of the Ashcan school. He took to making decorative screens, panels and furniture in gesso and silver-leaf when it was difficult to make a living as an artist during the Depression.

72.5in (184cm) wide

£5,000-7,000 **SK**

An early 20thC Longhorn chair and ottoman, with black upholstered seat and back, the ottoman with hinged lid revealing a compartment.

20in (51cm) wide

£200-300 **SK**

A rustic chair and ottoman, the frames constructed from moose antlers, the cushions upholstered in dark brown leather.

46in (115cm) wide

£2,200-2,800 **SDR**

A Morris & Co. 'Bird' pattern jackard loom woollen textile, printed "Morris & Co."

'Bird' was made in three colourways – red, blue and green. It was one of Morris' most popular weaves and is more common than many others.

29x21in (73.5x53.5cm)

£300-500 **PC**

A 'Dove and Rose' textile, designed by William Morris, in hand-woven silk on a wool base.

This fabric is made from silk suggesting it was produced to be hung on walls, typically from brass dado rails. It was expensive to make, so production of this fabric stopped c1905.

48x36in (122x91.5cm)

£2,000-3,000 **PC**

A William Morris-style rug, with pomegranate and fern motif in ochre, coral and shades of green, on a celadon ground.

120x237in (305x602cm)

£1,000-1,500 **DRA**

A Morris & Co. three fold embroidered screen, with panels of various embroidered floral designs, including 'Parrot Tulip' to the centre, in mahogany frame, unmarked.

Provenance: *Mrs Barbara Morris. Other variations also exist of the simple frame with different embroidered panels, with two illustrated in the Morris & Co. catalogue.*

£5,000-8,000 **WW**

A William Morris-style runner with floral vinescroll panel in crimson, black and brown on a teal ground.

31x144in (78.5x366cm)

£300-350 **DRA**

A William Morris-style rug, with floral vinescroll centre panel in shades of blue, coral and ivory within a coral border.

112x142in (284.5x360.5cm)

£600-900 **DRA**

A William Morris-style rug, with leaf and flower vine scroll in shades of green, coral and ivory on a black ground, within cayenne and olive border.

96x120in (244x305cm)

£400-600 **DRA**

A William Morris-style area rug, with olive green, mustard and crimson bud and vine pattern surrounded by an ivory floral border.

172in (430cm) wide

£800-1,200 **DRA**

A William Morris-style runner, with red, yellow and blue buds against a green ground with polychrome geometric border.

120in (300cm) long

£300-500 **DRA**

A William Morris-style runner, with stylized poppy and scroll panel in shades of coral and brown on a celadon ground.

30x259in (76x658cm)

£600-900 **DRA**

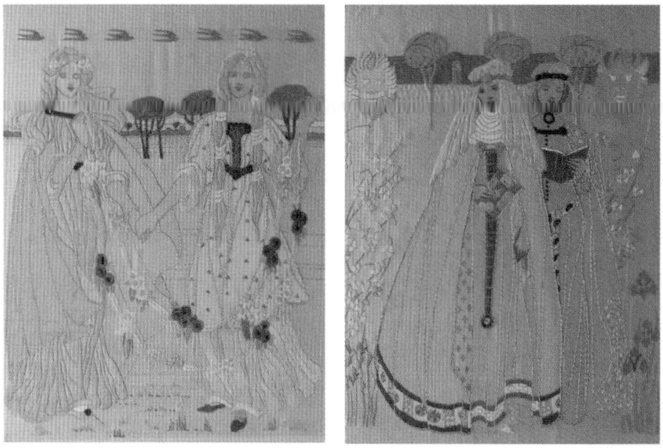

A pair of 19thC framed embroidered pictures, in the manner of William Morris, depicting two women with two images of the devil, with metallic stick on the dresses, reframed.

17in (43cm) high

£500-1,000 each

A Scottish School silkwork panel, in the manner of Ann MacBeth, worked in coloured silks with three maidens in a garden playing musical instruments, with oak frame, carved with entwined fruiting and flowering brambles.

panel 9.5x15in (24x38cm)

£800-1,200 **L&T**

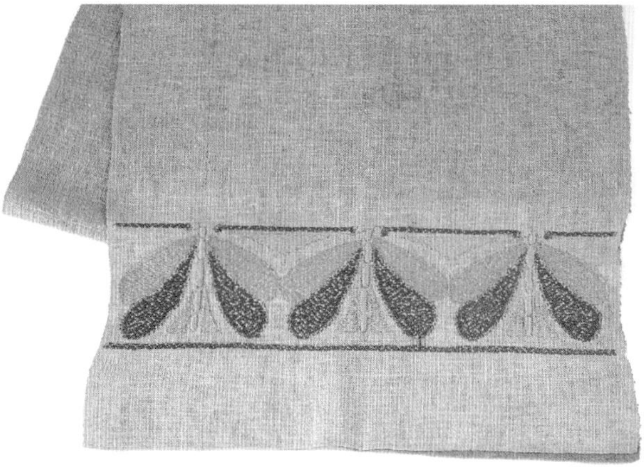

An extremely rare Gustav Stickley embroidered linen, by Newcomb College decorator Harriet Joor, with gold and green dragonflies on a natural linen ground, unmarked.

60x16in (152.5x40.5cm)

£8,000-12,000 **DRA**

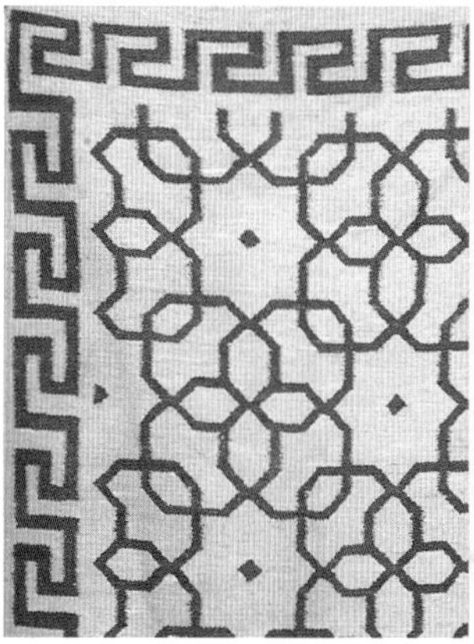

A Gustav Stickley drugget rug, with dark green links and Greek Key pattern on oatmeal ground, two stains, mostly to underside.

6x9in (15x23cm)

£300-500 **DRA**

A Gustav Stickley Indian room-size drugget rug, in the 'Nile' pattern, with a repeated floral pattern in red and black on a natural ground.

174in (435cm) long

£400-600 **DRA**

A pair of Arts and Crafts curtain panels, with large yellow flowers in trees, a few tears, unmarked.

88x48in (223.5x122cm)

£350-450 **DRA**

A pair of French Arts and Crafts woven wool reversible portieres, with gold and purple blossoms and leaves in the Art Nouveau style. A few stains and some discolouration, unmarked.

104x48in (264x122cm)

£350-450 **DRA**

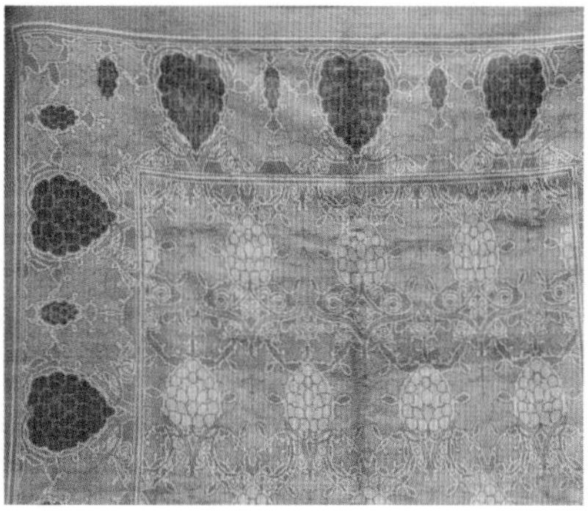

A Turkish Arts and Crafts-style rug, with a centre panel of pomegranate and vinescroll in ivory and shades of green within a crimson pomegranate border.

123x168 (312.5x426.5cm)

£1,200-1,800 **DRA**

A Donald Deskey/Radio City Music Hall Art Deco wool carpet, decorated with a patchwork of musical instruments, marked "RADIO CITY MUSIC HALL" on backing.

1933 *82x46.5in (208x118cm)*

£600-900 **SDR**

A very rare late 1920s Eileen Gray Modernist wool area rug, in pale rose with burgundy, beige and gold, signature stamp and number on back.

77x114in (195.5x289.5cm)

£6,000-8,000 **DD**

A pair of French Art Deco area bedside rugs, with geometric Modernist design, tan field with brown and teal geometric design in wool with original fringe.

c1935 *25x52in (63.5x132cm) each*

£1,000-1,500 pair **DD**

A late 1930s Chinese Art Deco area rug, probably American, in the manner of Nichols Rugs, with a rare nine Dragon design with rainbow cloud border.

Walter Nichols is one of the most famous American makers of Chinese Art Deco rugs. Carpets were densely knotted creating a plush finish.

102x128in (259x325cm)

£6,000-8,000 **DD**

A late 1930s French Modernist area rug, in vivid, brightly coloured wool.

53x76in (134.5x193cm)

£1,200-1,800 **DD**

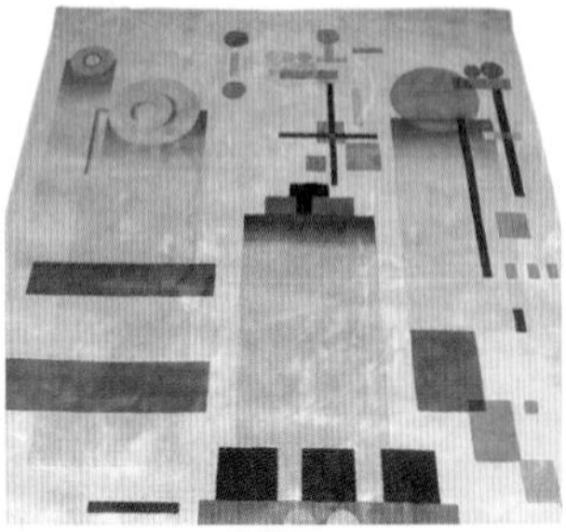

A room size Art Deco rug with geometric pattern in polychrome against a light beige ground, marked "GN" in the pile, minor soiling.

138x106in (350.5x269cm)

£3,500-4,000 **SDR**

An Art Deco wool area rug, with stylized pattern in shades of blue and brown on a taupe ground, with fringed ends, unmarked.

85x53.5in (216x136cm)

£300-400 **SDR**

An Art Deco wool area rug, with geometric pattern in shades of peach, brown, and grey, hole and minor stains, unmarked.

77x54in (195.5x137cm)

£300-500 **SDR**

An Art Deco German textile design, in black and white ink on paper, stamped plate.

c1935 *6.5in (16.5cm) high*

£30-50 **DD**

An Art Deco German textile design, colour stamped plate.

c1935 *9in (23cm) high*

£120-180 **DD**

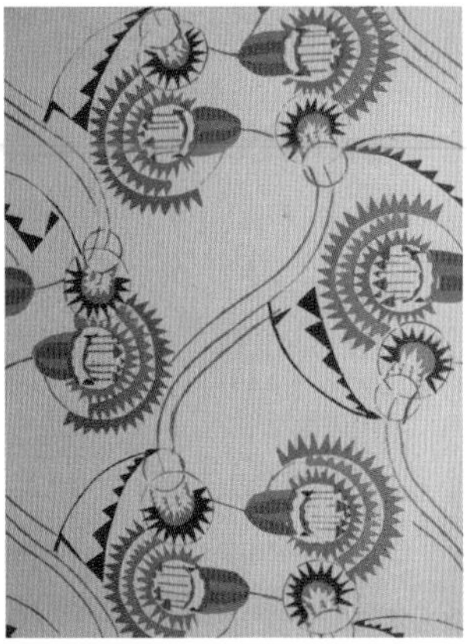

An Art Deco German textile design, colour stamped plate.

c1935 *5.5in (14cm) high*

£30-50 **DD**

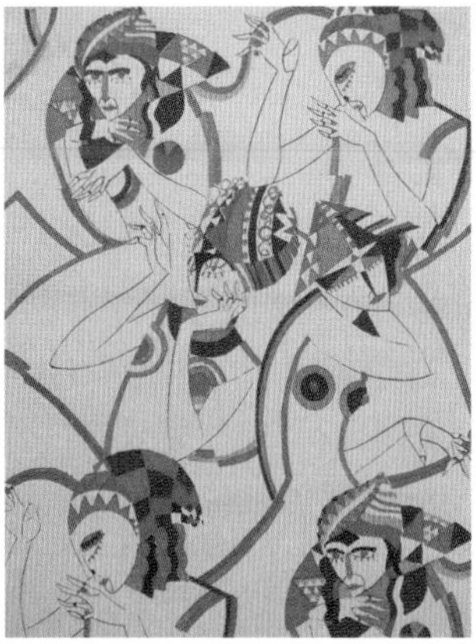

An Art Deco German textile design, colour stamped plate.

c1935 *9.75in (25cm) high*

£100-150 **DD**

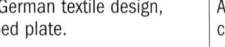

An Art Deco German textile design, colour stamped plate.

1930s *9.25in (23.5cm) high*

£70-100 **DD**

An Art Deco German textile design, colour stamped plate.

c1935 *5.5in (14cm) wide*

£30-50 **DD**

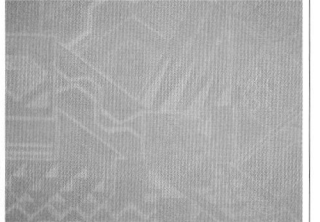

A block-printed Art Deco cotton tapestry by Ruth Reeves, entitled 'The American Scene', for W & J Sloane.

c1930 *83in (211cm) wide*

£4,000-5,000 **AMO**

A French Art Deco upholstery fabric, carved velvet in a Jazz age geometric pattern.

c1935

£220-280 **DD**

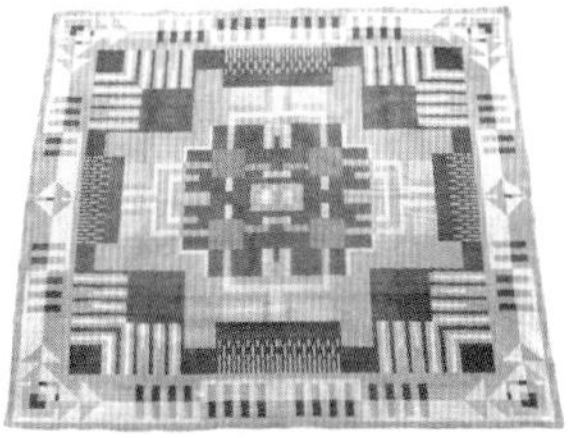

A French Art Deco Modernist divan, chenille texture in a geometric symmetrical pattern.

c1935 *55x55in (140x140cm)*

£700-1,000 **DD**

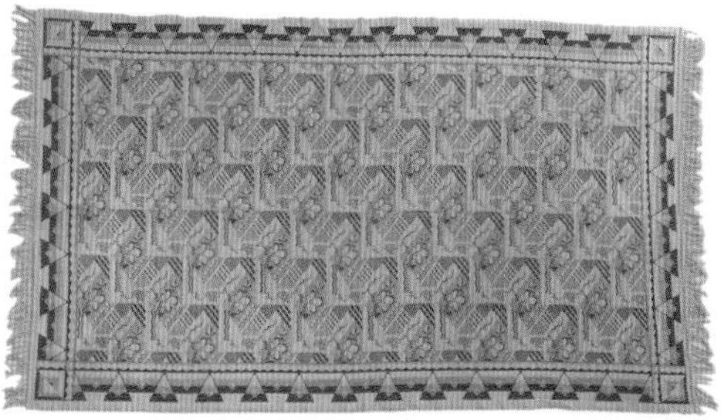

An Art Deco Viennese Secessionist textile throw, in woven cotton with floral and geometric pattern, fringe on ends.

c1935 *54x99in (137x251.5cm)*

£1,200-1,800 **DD**

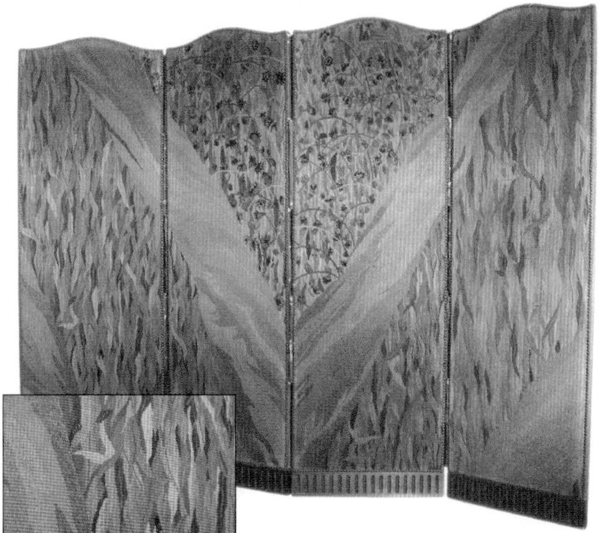

An early European Art Deco woven tapestry screen, hand-stitched in four panels with a stylized tree, poppy and field pattern, brass nail head border, in the manner of Liberty.

1915-1920 *71x94in (180.5x239cm)*

£6,000-8,000 **DD**

THE MODERN MARKET

Mid-century Modern furniture has an optimism and integrity that attracts buyers who might never have considered buying an "antique". Design is very important to people today – from their mobile phones to their trainers the look has to be right.

While the current growth in the Modern market may seem sudden to traditionalists it has been growing steadily over the past few years – gaining admirers who appreciate its values and its style. It may also be that collectors are reaching the point at which they see what attracted their own parents to a particular style.

The Modern furniture produced in Europe and the US after 1945 shows a forward-thinking spirit and an intention to improve on the past that resonates with people today.

Classics by Marcel Breuer, Charles and Ray Eames, Edward Wormley, Wendell Castle and George Nakishima consistently do well at auction. Even modern reproductions or versions of their early work sells well on the secondary market – although not as well as an original. Piero Fornasetti is also a name to watch with more and more people entranced by his combination of classical designs and modern take on form.

Furnishings made at the end of the 20th century are also performing well. While it is still a little early for the work of Ettore Sottsass and the Memphis Group to enjoy a reniassance, work by America's New Hope school head boy Paul Evans continues to increase in value. Also growing is appreciation for the work of Gaetano Pesce, Olivier Mourgue, Joe Colombo, Philippe Starck and Tapio Wirkkala.

The market for studio and art glass – especially examples made on the Venetian island of Murano in the 1950s and 1960s – continues to grow.

– John Sollo, Sollo:Rago Modern Auctions, Lambertville NJ

WENDELL CASTLE

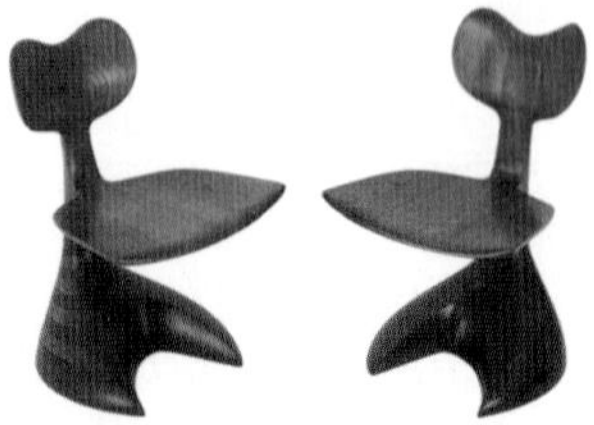

A rare matched pair of early lounge chairs by Wendell Castle, made from stacked oak laminate, signed "W.C. 67" under seat.

1967 *33in (82.5cm) high*

£10,000-12,000 **SDR**

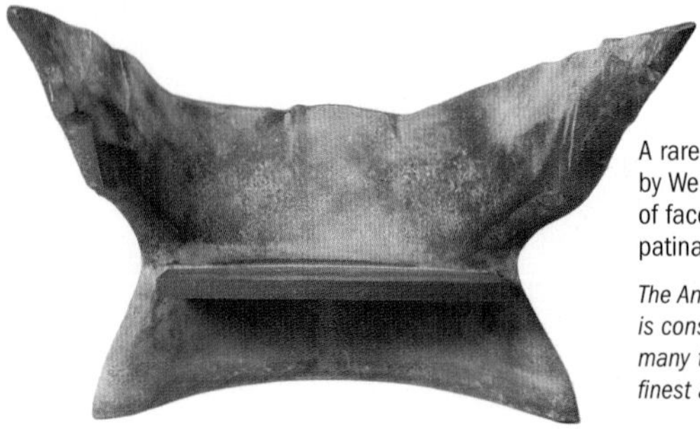

A rare 'Angel Chair' by Wendell Castle, of faceted and patinated bronze.

The Angel Chair series is considered by many to be Castle's finest achievement.

c1990 *63in (157.5cm) wide*

£30,000-40,000 **SDR**

A console table by Wendell Castle, with Caligari-decorated top and ebonized crossbars with metal rings, on exotic wood supports, signed and dated.

1987 *68in (170cm) wide*

£3,000-4,000 **SDR**

An 'Urn Cabinet' by Wendell Castle, the door with abstract polychrome composition concealing drawers and shelves, on large urn supports with turquoise finish, signed "Castle/91".

1991 *71.75in (179cm) high*

£2,500-3,000 **SDR**

A 'Three Beans' wall-hanging mahogany cabinet by Wendell Castle, the single door with painted polychrome composition, concealing interior shelves.

36.5in (91cm) high

£2,000-2,500 **SDR**

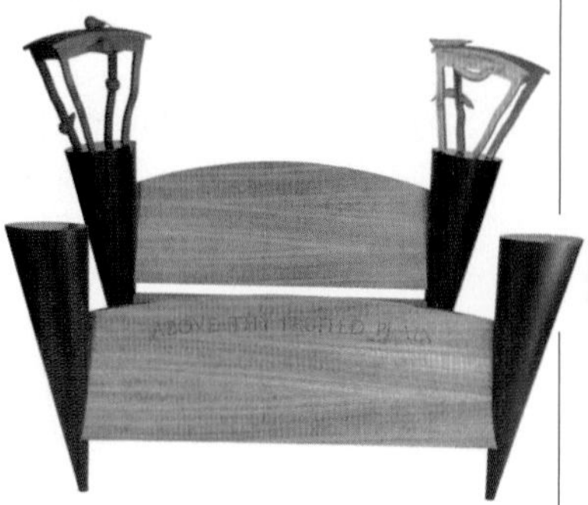

An 'Above Thy Fruited Plain' full-size bed by Wendell Castle, with black enamelled conical posts and lantern-shaped finials to headboard, one carved with pears and inscribed "Pearwood", the other with bananas and "Bananawood".

92.5in (235cm) long

£3,500-4,500 **SDR**

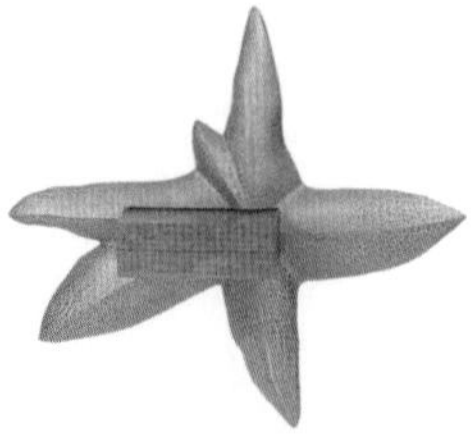

A 'Seventh Heaven' wall cabinet by Wendell Castle, with star-shaped jetulong frame and neon tubing to back, mounted with two-drawer bubinga veneer cabinet, signed "Castle 96".

1996 *68in (170cm) wide*

£6,000-9,000 **SDR**

A 'Caligari' Steinway piano by Wendell Castle, painted with loose indigo brushstrokes in the Abstract Expressionist style on a white ground, with matching bench upholstered in indigo velvet, signed "Wendell Castle/1990".

71in (178cm) wide

£35,000-40,000 **SDR**

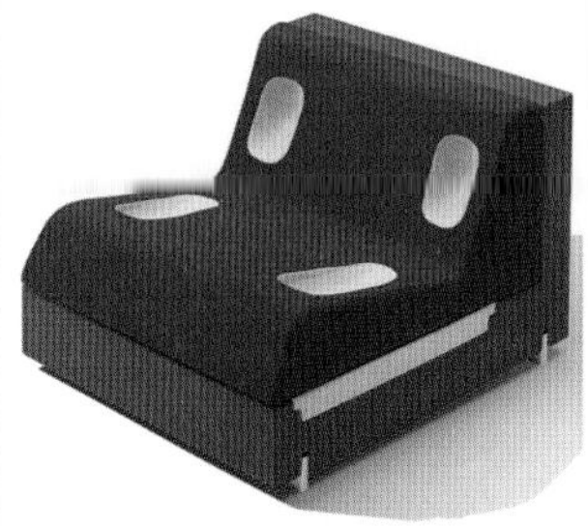

A 'Decompression Space' armchair by Matali Crasset.

2004 *31.5in (80cm) wide*

£800-1,200 **MCP**

An 'Il Capricio di Ugo' armchair by Matali Crasset, with foam seat and tray armrests on a steel frame.

1997 *24.75in (63cm) wide*

£700-1,000 **MCP**

An 'Interface' modular armchair suite by Matali Crasset, with polyurethane coated fabric and brushed stainless steel legs.

This set was designed for the Hi Hotel in Nice.

2003 *22.75in (58cm) wide*

£600-900 **MCP**

A 'Licence to Build' chair and children's game by Matali Crasset, made from high-resilience foam with cotton cover.

2000 *28.25in (72cm) wide*

£1,500-2,000 **MCP**

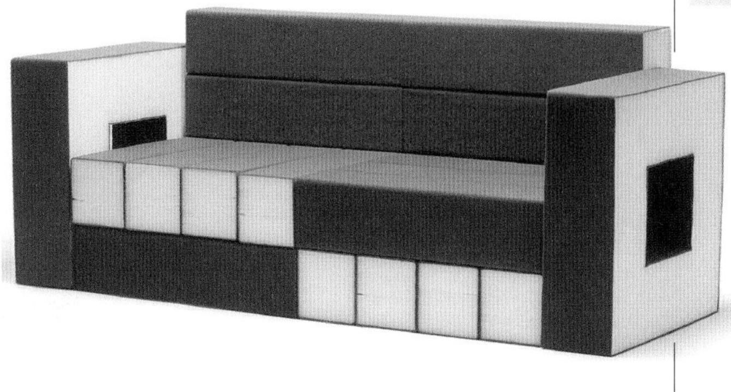

A 'Licence to Build' sofa and children's game by Matali Crasset, made from high-resilience foam with cotton cover.

2000 *28.25in (72cm) wide*

£1,500-2,000 **MCP**

TOM DIXON

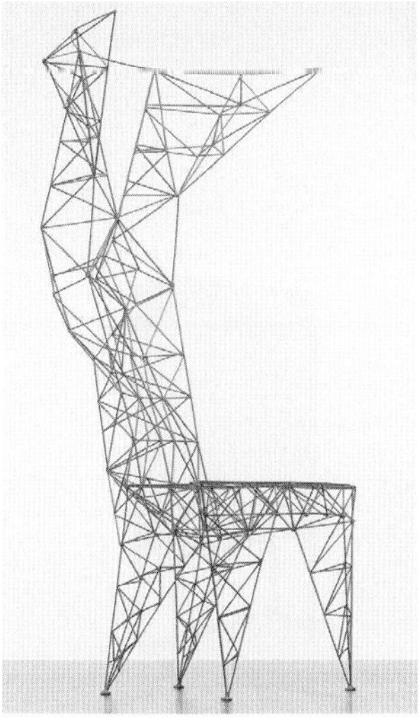

A 'Pylon' chair by Tom Dixon for Cappellini, of iron wire varnished in orange.

26.5in (67cm) wide

£2,500-3,000 **SCP**

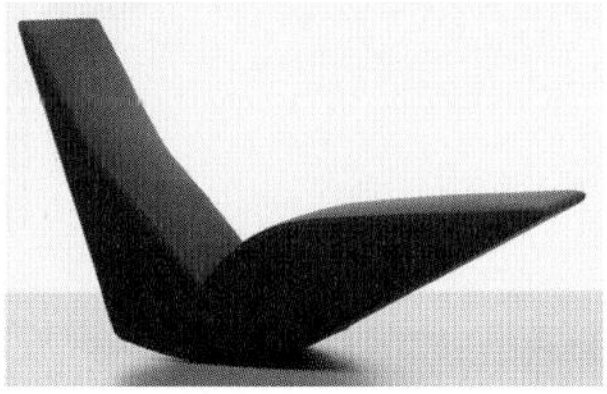

A 'Bird' rocking chair by Tom Dixon for Cappellini, with wooden frame and multi-density foam.

19.75in (50cm) wide

£1,800-2,200 **SCP**

A set of three 'S' chairs by Tom Dixon for Cappellini, with metal frames covered in painted wicker and spotted leather.

16.5in (42cm) wide

£600-900 each **SCP**

An 'S' chair by Tom Dixon for Cappellini, with a metal frame covered in painted wicker.

Tom Dixon is head of design at Habitat, where he has revived historic designs by the likes of Verner Panton.

16.5in (42cm) high

£600-900 **SCP**

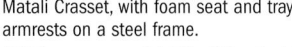

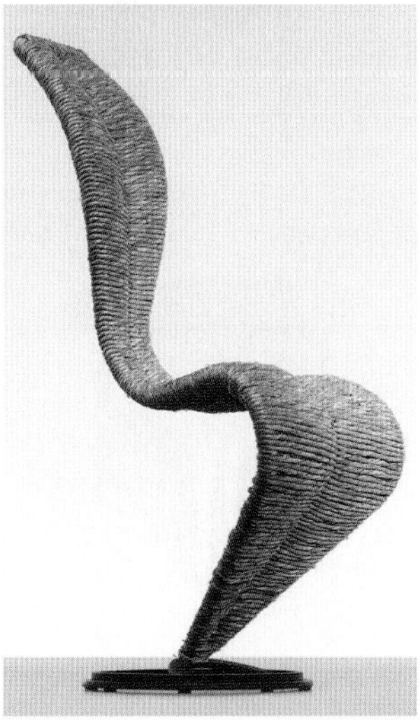

An 'S' chair by Tom Dixon for Cappellini, with a metal frame covered in woven marsh straw.

16.5in (42cm) wide

£800-1,200 **SCP**

A pair of Dunbar armchairs, with original orange fabric upholstery on dark stained tapering legs, marked "Dunbar".

30in (76cm) high

£800-1,200 **SDR**

A pair of Dunbar lounge chairs, with original tufted ochre wool upholstery on dark stained base with tapering legs, marked "Dunbar".

34in (86.5cm) high

£600-900 **SDR**

A Dunbar three-seat sofa, with original brown fabric upholstery on ebonized black legs.

84in (210cm) wide

£2,500-3,000 **SDR**

A large Dunbar 'Janus' ottoman, with original tufted silk tweed upholstery in beige and brown, with brass tag.

32in (81.5cm) wide

£1,200-1,800 **SDR**

A Dunbar 'Dinette' table, with smoked glass top and pedestal base composed of cylinders with a bronzed finish, unmarked.

1970s *36in (90cm) wide*

£1,200-1,800 **SDR**

A Dunbar walnut coffee table, inset with six Tiffany tiles in lustred glazes, on an A base with cruciform stretcher, with metal "Dunbar" tag.

77in (195.5cm) wide

£5,000-6,000 **SDR**

A Dunbar triangular magazine rack, with raised top over two compartments on a dowel leg frame, with brass "Dunbar" tag and paper factory tag.

25in (63.5cm) wide

£1,000-1,500 **SDR**

A Dunbar revolving bookstand, the circular top inset with a dark brown leather panel, the base with open cubicles to each side, with "Dunbar" tag.

36in (91.5cm) diam

£1,200-1,800 **SDR**

A Dunbar party server, with laminate top and drop leaf concealing storage compartments, with "Dunbar" metal tag with paper label.

31.5in (80cm) high

£2,800-3,200 **SDR**

A Dunbar cabinet-on-stand, with two glass doors concealing shelves over a drop-front drawer with natural wood panel and brass knob pulls, with "D" tag.

72in (183cm) high

£800-1,200 **SDR**

A pair of 'DAR' dining chairs by Charles and Ray Eames, in ivory-coloured fibreglass reinforced plastic, with steel rod bases.

24in (61cm) wide

£400-600 **GAZE**

An early 'RAR' shell rocker by Charles and Ray Eames, in salmon-coloured fibreglass, with wooden rockers.

c1950 *24.5in (62cm) wide*

£350-400 **GAZE**

Two of a set of four 'DCR' dining chairs by Charles and Ray Eames, on zinc rod bases.

18in (45.5cm) wide

£600-900 set **GAZE**

A set of four 'Time-Life' armchairs by Charles Eames for Herman Miller, with tufted black leather upholstery and aluminum swivel bases, one with metal Herman Miller tag.

35in (89cm) high

£1,500-2,000 **SDR**

A 'Soft Pad' chair and ottoman by Charles Eames for Herman Miller, upholstered in cordovan brown leather, on polished aluminum swivel bases, with paper label.

chair 38in (95.5cm) high

£1,500-2,000 **SDR**

A 670 lounge chair and 671 ottoman by Charles Eames for Herman Miller, with rosewood-faced moulded plywood frames and black leather upholstery, with original Herman Miller tag label.

chair 32.5in (81cm) high

£1,200-1,800 **SDR**

A dining table by Charles Eames for Herman Miller, with square laminated wood top and flared tapering ebonized wood legs, unmarked.

33.75in (85.5cm) wide

£200-250 **SDR**

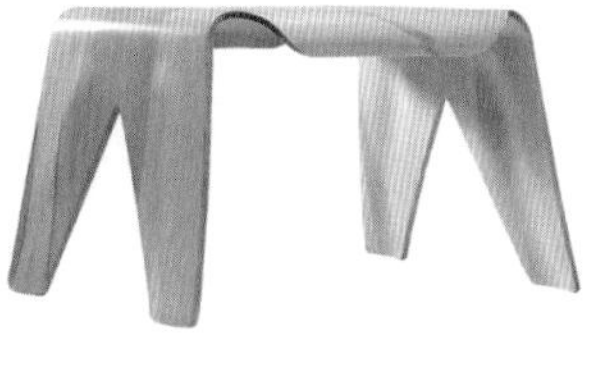

A moulded plywood child's stool by Charles Eames for Herman Miller, unmarked.

10.25in (26cm) wide

£800-1,200 **SDR**

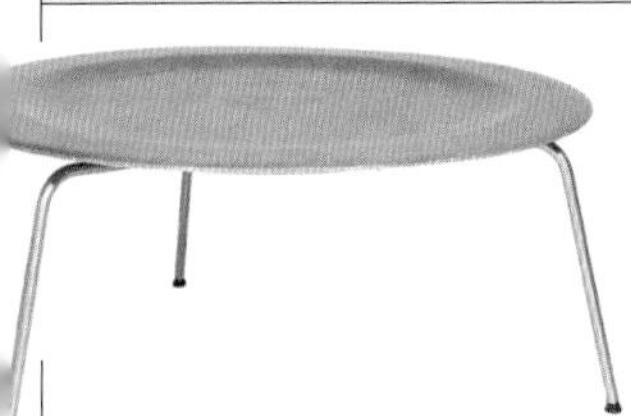

A prototype 'CTM' coffee table by Charles Eames for Herman Miller, with moulded plywood top and polished chrome legs, unmarked.

This is an extremely rare and early version of this iconic Eames design.

34.25in (87cm) diam

£6,000-9,000 **SDR**

An 'ESU-400' unit by Charles Eames for Herman Miller, with four dimpled sliding doors, five drawers, and polychrome side and back panels, unmarked.

48.25in (122.5cm) wide

£4,000-6,000 **SDR**

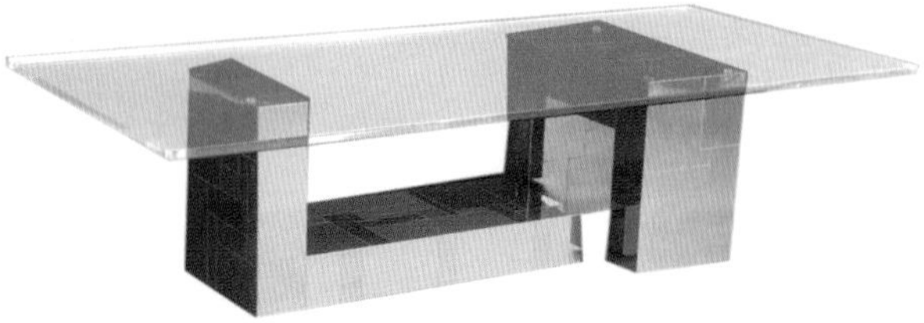

A coffee table by Paul Evans for Directional Furniture, with rectangular plate glass top resting on two geometric elements covered in polished chrome patchwork, marked "An Original Paul Evans".

67.5in (171.5cm) wide

£2,000-2,500 **SDR**

A unique Paul Evans table.

This table mixes two of Evans' signature styles with its wave base and sculpted steel top. It was made by the designer for a close friend.

83in (207.5cm) wide

£15,000-20,000 **SDR**

A sculpted bronze coffee table by Paul Evans, with elliptical glass top on a freeform openwork base, signed "PE 73".

1973 *48in (122cm) wide*

£3,500-4,500 **SDR**

A pair of sculpted bronze drum side tables by Paul Evans, with circular plate glass tops, one marked "P.E./69".

1969 *26in (65cm) diam*

£3,000-4,000 **SDR**

A rare wall cabinet by Paul Evans, with welded steel door in sunburst motif with enamel and bronze finish, with welded signature and date.

32.5in (81cm) wide

£4,000-6,000 **SDR**

A faceted buffet by Paul Evans, in polished chrome with broad white laminate top, plinth base and bi-fold doors concealing shelves, unmarked.

61in (155cm) wide

£18,000-22,000 **SDR**

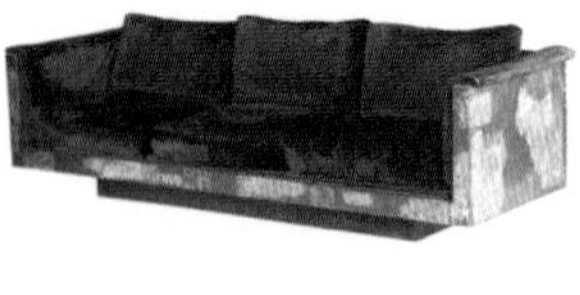

A three-seat cube sofa by Paul Evans, with dark brown velvet upholstery, covered in copper, bronze and pewter patchwork, on a welded steel plinth base, inscribed "PE 70".

92in (233.5cm) wide

£5,000-8,000 **SDR**

A set of six high-back dining chairs by Paul Evans, with decorative chenille upholstery on arched wavy-front sculpted steel bases with gilded highlights.

52.5in (131cm) high

£1,800-2,200 **SDR**

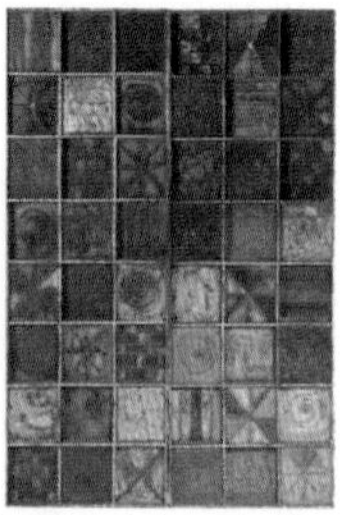

A pair of sculpted doors by Paul Evans, with geometric elements covered in gold and coloured patinas, marked "PE 65D".

1965 *60in (152.5cm) wide*

£6,000-9,000 **SDR**

A steel room divider by Paul Evans, with geometric sculptural elements, covered in treated red, green and purple paint with gold-leaf accents, signed "Paul Evans".

This is an excellent example of Evans' signature 'Sculpture Front' technique.

1967 *96in (244cm) wide*

£40,000-60,000 **SDR**

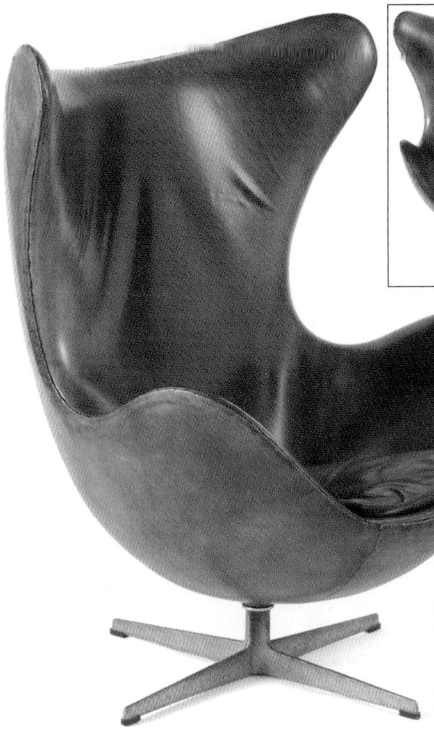
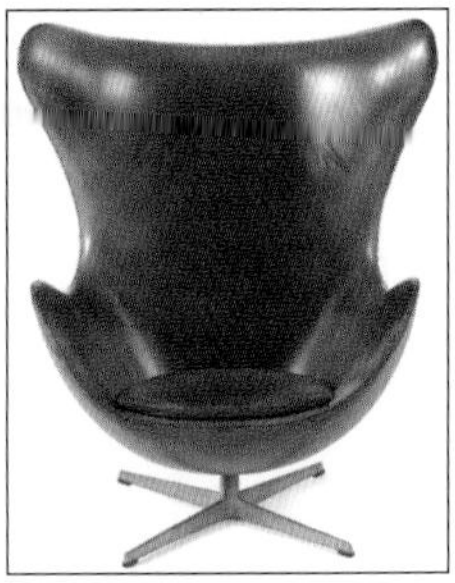

A tan leather egg chair by Arne Jacobsen for Fritz Hansen.

This chair was designed for the SAS hotel in Copenhagen.

1960s

£2,800-3,200 **JN**

One of a pair of 'Swan' chairs by Arne Jacobsen for Fritz Hansen, with grey woollen upholstery on a star-shaped swivel base.

c1960

£1,500-2,000 pair **JN**

A pair of 'Swan' chairs by Arne Jacobsen for Fritz Hansen, with red woollen upholstery, on star-shaped swivel bases, one with Fritz Hansen label.

29.75in (74cm) high

£1,800-2,200 **SDR**

A 'Swan' sofa by Arne Jacobsen for Fritz Hansen, with royal blue woollen upholstery, on an aluminum trestle base with matte finish, with Fritz Hansen label.

57in (142.5cm) wide

£1,200-1,800 **SDR**

An armchair by Arne Jacobsen for Fritz Hansen, with original green finish and orange tweed upholstery, on chrome tubular legs, with remnant of foil label.

29in (73.5cm) high

£700-1,000 **SDR**

FINN JUHL

A 'Chieftain' chair by Finn Juhl, with dark green leather upholstery, unmarked.

38in (95cm) high

£2,200-2,800 **SDR**

A set of four dining chairs by Finn Juhl for Bovirke, the sculptural teak frames with scalloped aprons, with black leather upholstery, unmarked.

32.75in (82cm) high

£500-800 **SDR**

A pair of armchairs by Finn Juhl, with contoured armrests and beige fabric upholstery, on tapering dowel leg frames, unmarked.

32.5in (82.5cm) high

£1,000-1,500 **SDR**

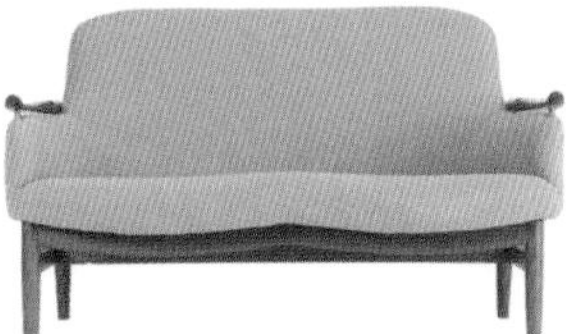

A '#53' settee by Finn Juhl for Niels Vodder, with green bouclé upholstery, scalloped apron and whalebone arms, on tapering legs, with branded mark.

50.5in (128.5cm) wide

£2,500-3,000 **SDR**

A teak coffee table by Finn Juhl, with tray top on tapering dowel legs, and pitched stretchers, marked with stencilled numbers.

61.25in (155.5cm) wide

£1,000-1,500 **SDR**

A '175F' rocking chair and '175GH' stool by Vladimir Kagan, sculpted walnut upholstered with peach-coloured fabric, unmarked.

chair 40.5in (103cm) high

£7,000-10,000 **SDR**

A '175E' armchair and ottoman by Vladimir Kagan for Kagan-Dreyfuss, sculpted walnut frames upholstered with original Jack Lenor Larsen stretch fabric with Larsen tag.

c1965 *chair 36in (90cm) high*

£5,000-8,000 **SDR**

A reclining chair by Vladimir Kagan for Kagan-Dreyfuss, mahogany frame with green velvet upholstery, with branded Kagan-Dreyfuss mark.

41in (102.5cm) wide

£4,000-6,000 **SDR**

A set of four 'VK101' and 'VK102' sling chairs by Vladimir Kagan, with woven beige upholstery on sculpted walnut frames, unmarked.

37in (94cm) high

£2,500-3,000 **SDR**

A floating seat sofa by Vladimir Kagan, upholstered in royal blue velvet on sculptural walnut legs, unmarked.

80in (203cm) wide

£10,000-12,000 **SDR**

A contoured sofa by Vladimir Kagan, with sculpted walnut base, upholstered in olive green ultrasuede, unmarked.

c1955 *93in (236cm) wide*

£8,000-12,000 **SDR**

A curved sofa by Vladimir Kagan, upholstered in textured cream-coloured wool, with ebonized slab legs and central slab support, unmarked.

108in (270cm) wide

£12,000-18,000 **SDR**

A 'Tri-Symmetric' coffee table by Vladimir Kagan , with amoeba-shaped plate glass top on a sculptural walnut base, unmarked.

58in (147.5cm) wide

£3,500-4,500 **SDR**

A workstation by Vladimir Kagan, with three drawers and open storage cubicle, on Lucite plank legs, with studio label.

60in (152.5cm) wide

£3,000-4,000 **SDR**

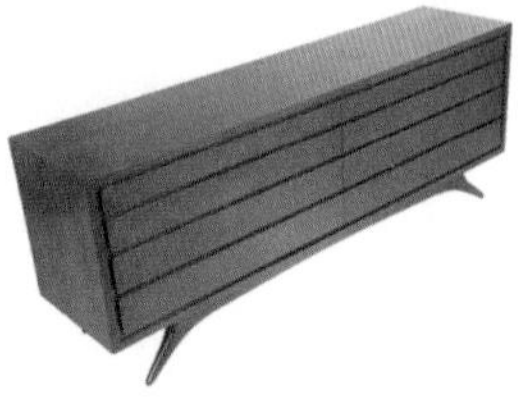

A large chest of drawers by Vladimir Kagan for Kagan-Dreyfuss, with eight graduated drawers and sculpted whalebone base, with branded mark.

84in (210cm) wide

£5,000-6,000 **SDR**

KNOLL

- Hans Knoll was born in Stuttgart in 1914. He established the Hans G. Knoll Furniture Company in New York in 1938. The company's first collection was designed by Jens Risom.
- Hans' wife Florence studied architecture alongside Mies van der Rohe at the Illinois Institute of Technology in Chicago. She went on to contribute many designs to the Knoll catalogue.
- In 1951 Knoll expanded into Europe, opening manufacturing plants in France and Germany.
- Florence Knoll oversaw the creation of Knoll's strong brand identity throughout the 1950s and became president of the company when Hans died in 1955.
- Knoll acquired the rights to Mies van der Rohe's furniture and retained the talents of many leading designers including Eero Saarinen and Harry Bertoia.
- Florence Knoll continued to design for Knoll until her retirement in 1965. Her 'Executive Collection' was first released in 1961.
- The Knoll brand is still recognized as one of the major players in corporate design to this day.

An early credenza by Florence Knoll for Knoll, the grass-lined sliding doors with leather tabs concealing compartments and shelves, on an ebonized base with flaring legs, unmarked.

72in (183cm) wide

£6,000-9,000 **SDR**

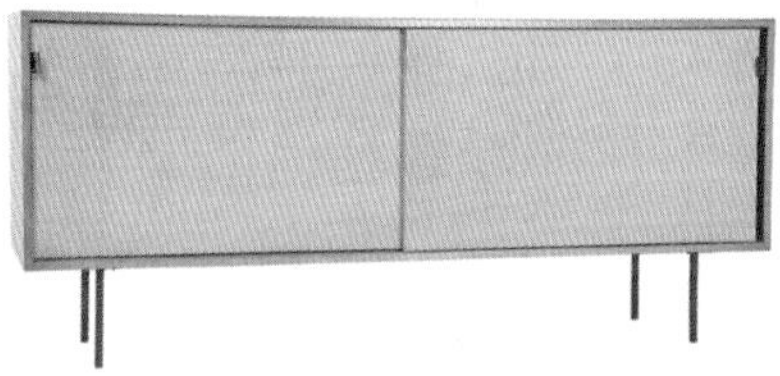

An early credenza by Knoll, the sliding doors with leather tab pulls concealing drawers and shelves, on tubular metal legs, unmarked.

72in (180cm) wide

£700-1,000 **SDR**

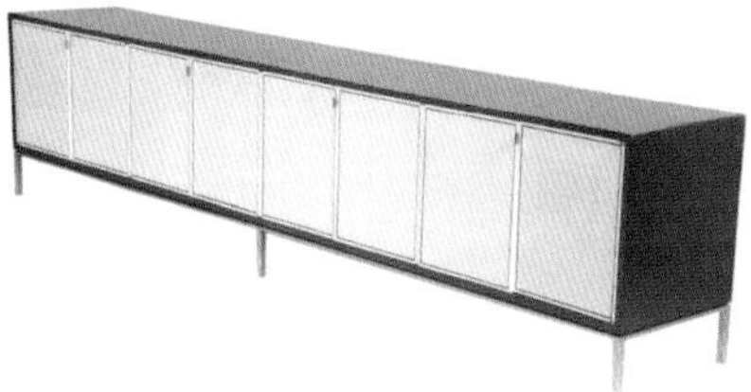

A credenza by Knoll, the eight doors with polished chrome tab pulls and white enamelled fronts, on an angular steel base, unmarked.

107in (267.5cm) wide

£1,800-2,200 **SDR**

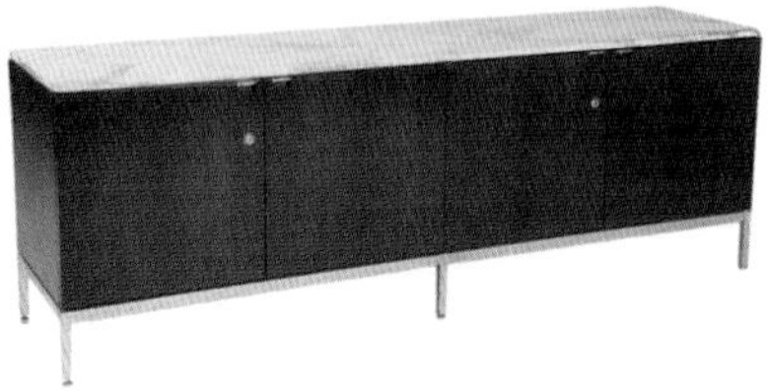

A rosewood credenza by Knoll, with white marble top and doors with recessed pulls concealing interior shelves, on a polished chrome base, inscribed "Knoll" in red.

74in (185cm) wide

£700-1,000 **SDR**

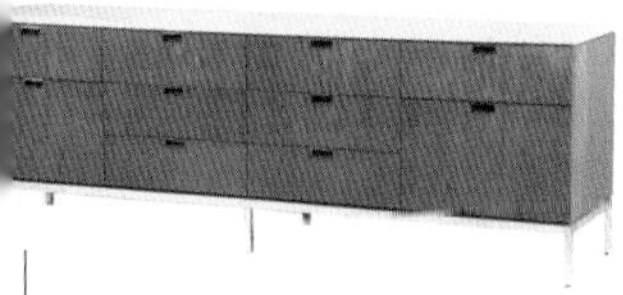

A teak credenza by Florence Knoll for Knoll, with white marble top and ten drawers with recessed pulls, on a polished steel base, with Knoll International label.

75in (190.5cm) wide

£1,500-2,000 **SDR**

An armless sofa by Knoll, with original royal blue ribbed vinyl upholstery, on parallel bar steel frame with brushed and enamelled finish, with Knoll Associates factory tag.

83.5in (212cm) wide

£500-800 **SDR**

A conference table by Florence Knoll for Knoll, with oval teak top on a polished steel pedestal base, with Knoll International label.

77.5in (197cm) wide

£600-900 **SDR**

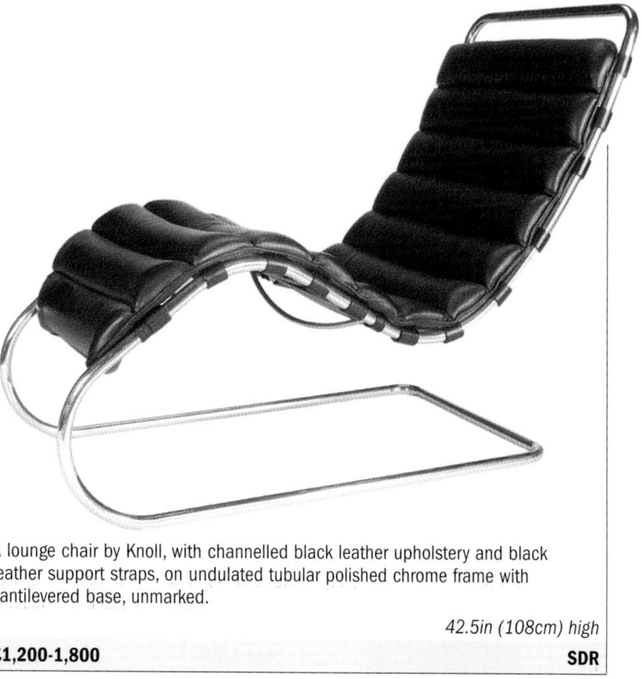

A lounge chair by Knoll, with channelled black leather upholstery and black leather support straps, on undulated tubular polished chrome frame with cantilevered base, unmarked.

42.5in (108cm) high

£1,200-1,800 **SDR**

A bronze coffee table by Philip and Kelvin Laverne, decorated with scenes at a Chinese palace gate, on a faceted pedestal base, signed.

42.25in (105.5cm) wide

£2,200-2,800 **SDR**

A bronze coffee table by Philip and Kelvin Laverne, decorated with flowering vines, the base with cut-out and applied brass elements, signed.

39in (97.5cm) diam

£1,500-2,000 **SDR**

A pewter and bronze coffee table by Philip and Kelvin Laverne, with a pattern of overlapping circular designs, on cylindrical legs with stretchers, unmarked.

40in (101.5cm) wide

£2,800-3,200 **SDR**

A coffee table by Philip and Kelvin Laverne, with a scalloped top incised with verdigris floral branches on a burnished metal ground, unmarked.

54in (137cm) wide

£2,500-3,000 **SDR**

A 'Chan' coffee table by Philip and Kelvin Laverne, the boat-shaped top decorated with an Asian scene in pewter, bronze and enamel paint, on V-shaped legs with trailing leaf motif, signed.

c1955 *53.5in (136cm) wide*

£3,500-4,500 **SDR**

A bronze and pewter coffee table by Philip and Kelvin Laverne, with a scalloped top incised with classical figures in profile, on cylindrical legs with applied ornamentation, signed "Philip Kelvin Laverne".

48in (122cm) wide

£3,000-4,000 **SDR**

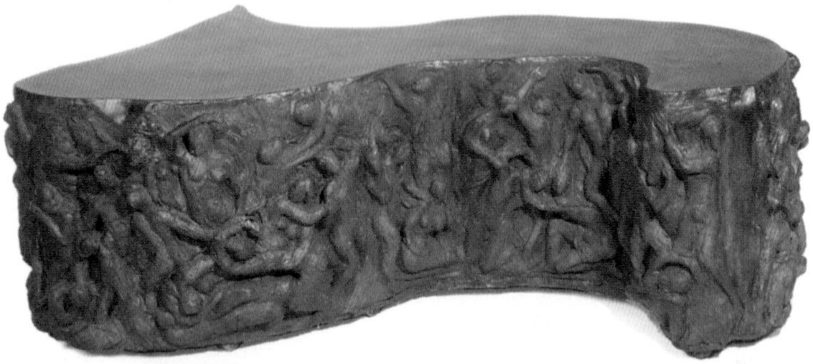

A rare Laverne 'Le Fe Force' freeform coffee table, in patinated bronze, the exterior modelled with figures in high relief, on castors, unmarked.

60in (152.5cm) wide

£18,000-22,000 **SDR**

A pair of low bronze tables by Laverne, decorated with Oriental motifs.

19in (48.5cm) wide

£1,500-2,000 **FRE**

A small side table by Philip and Kelvin Laverne, with circular etched brass top on a faceted copper pedestal base, unmarked.

18.25in (46.5cm) diam

£800-1,200 **SDR**

A small table or stool by Philip and Kelvin Laverne, 'The Kiss', after a sculpture by Constance Brancusi, in cast metal with a verdigris patina, unmarked.

17.5in (44.5cm) wide

£2,500-3,000 **SDR**

A black leather 'MR20' chair by Mies van der Rohe, with tubular steel frame.

21in (53.5cm) wide

£220-280 **GAZE**

A pair of 'Barcelona' chairs by Mies van der Rohe for Knoll, with dark brown leather cushions and brown hard leather strap supports, on polished steel bases, with Knoll Associates factory tags.

30in (75cm) high

£1,500-2,000 **SDR**

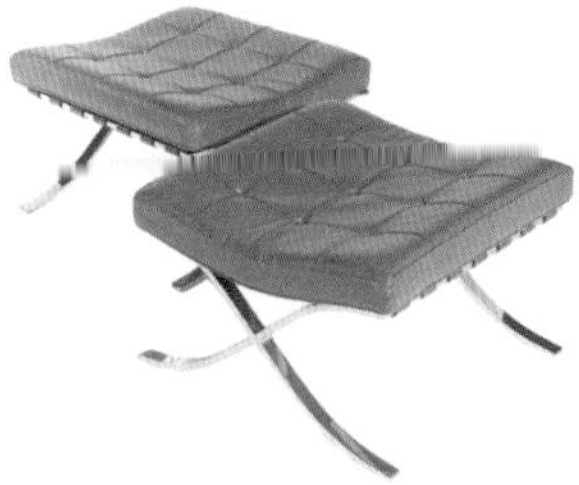

A pair of 'Barcelona' ottomans by Mies van der Rohe for Knoll, with cafe-au-lait leather cushions and support straps, on flat polished steel frames, one with Knoll International tag.

25in (63.5cm) wide

£1,000-1,500 **SDR**

A 'Barcelona' daybed by Mies van der Rohe for Knoll, with tan leather upholstery, on a wooden frame with polished metal legs, cushion with Art Metal/Knoll Associates tag.

73in (185.5cm) long

£2,200-2,800 **SDR**

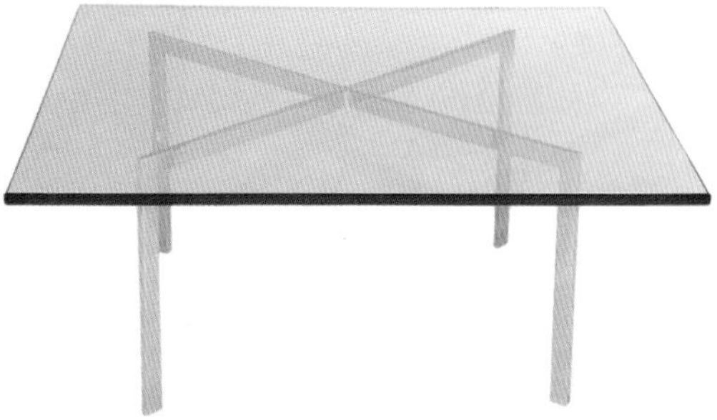

A 'Barcelona' coffee table by Mies van der Rohe for Knoll, with square plate glass top and polished chrome base, unmarked.

40in (100cm) wide

£280-320 **SDR**

GEORGE NAKASHIMA

Two of a set of six 'Conoid' dining chairs by George Nakashima, in solid rosewood with hand-hewn hickory spindles, marked on base with original owner's name.

20.75in (52.5cm) wide

£120,000-150,000 set **SDR**

A 'Conoid' chair by George Nakashima, in Persian walnut with hickory spindles and single board saddle seat, marked "Persian Walnut one-pc. seat".

35.25in (88cm) high

£5,000-6,000 **SDR**

A walnut lounge chair by George Nakashima, with single free-edge writing arm, spindled back and saddle seat, on tapering dowel legs, unmarked.

32.5in (82.5cm) high

£3,500-4,500 **SDR**

A walnut rocker by George Nakashima, with hickory spindles and saddle seat, signed under seat "To Helen & Ezra/George Nakashima/Aug 1973".

1973 *36.25in (90.5cm) high*

£6,000-9,000 **SDR**

A large walnut open-arm sofa by George Nakashima, with slatted back and tapering dowel legs, unmarked.

101in (252.5cm) wide

£7,000-10,000 **SDR**

A sofa by George Nakashima for Widdicomb, with caned pagoda-shaped back and upholstered seat cushion, on tapering plank legs, with branded marks and numbers.

101.5in (254cm) wide

£4,000-6,000 **SDR**

A pair of 'Greenrock' stools by George Nakashima, with upholstered cushions, signed "George Nakashima" in script.

18in (45cm) wide

£7,000-10,000 **SDR**

A 'Minguren' coffee table by George Nakashima, with free-edge Persian walnut top.

67.5in (169cm) wide

£18,000-22,000 **SDR**

A walnut coffee table by George Nakashima, the free-edge English walnut top with single butterfly key and natural occlusions, on black walnut sled base, signed "George Nakashima/Sept. 1983".

1983 *53.5in (136cm) wide*

£18,000-22,000 **SDR**

A cherry 'Slab' coffee table by George Nakashima, the freeform top with fissures and three butterfly keys, with remnant of signature and date.

1956 *61.75in (154cm) wide*

£15,000-20,000 **SDR**

A coffee table by George Nakashima, with figured free-edge top and single rosewood butterfly key, on slab base, marked with original owner's name.

38.75in (97cm) wide

£6,000-8,000 **SDR**

A walnut 'Frenchman's Cove' table by George Nakashima, the bookmatched top with two free-edges, unmarked.

1970 *58in (145cm) wide*

£20,000-25,000 **SDR**

A rare 'Milkhouse' table by George Nakashima, with single large butterfly key, on a plank-leg base with keyed stretcher, unmarked.

The Milkhouse table is one of Nakashima's earliest and most important designs, produced in very limited numbers.

34.25in (87cm) wide

£18,000-22,000 **SDR**

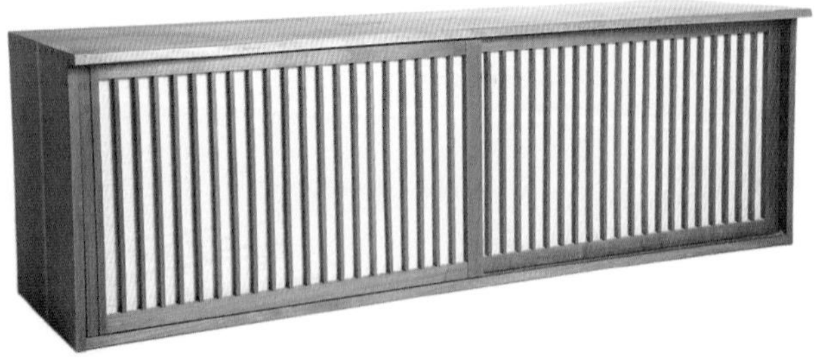

A walnut wall-hanging cabinet by George Nakashima, with free-edge front and grilled sliding doors with grasscloth lining concealing six drawers, unmarked.

c1960 *72in (180cm) wide*

£18,000-22,000 **SDR**

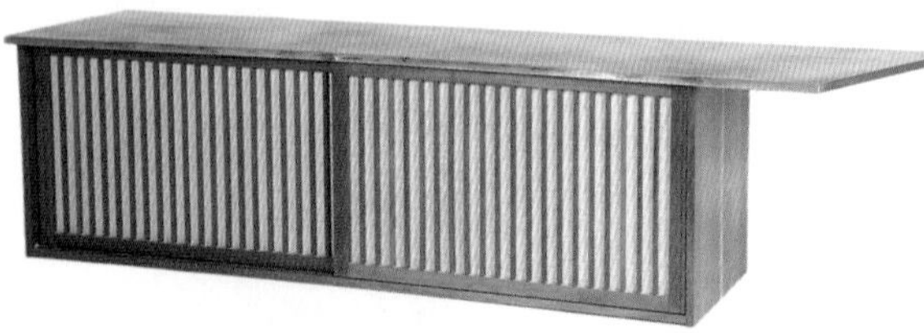

A walnut wall-hanging cabinet by George Nakashima, with overhanging free-edge top and grilled sliding doors with grasscloth lining concealing six drawers, marked with original owner's name.

c1960 *92.5in (231cm) wide*

£20,000-25,000 **SDR**

A walnut and rosewood tea trolley by George Nakashima.

This is a rare Nakashima design produced for an important patron. The only other example belonged to the designer's wife.

£8,000-12,000 **SDR**

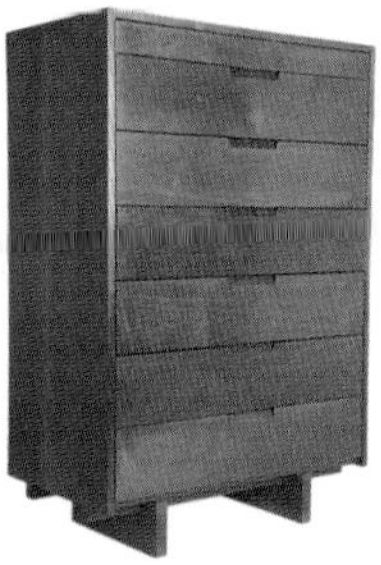

A walnut highboy by George Nakashima, with blind drawer over six larger drawers with recessed horizontal pulls, on trestle base, marked with original owner's name.

52.75in (132cm) high

£12,000-15,000 **SDR**

A free-standing walnut mirror by George Nakashima, with overhanging bevelled top rail and exposed tenons, unmarked.

36in (91.5cm) high

£5,000-8,000 **SDR**

A pair of walnut twin beds by George Nakashima, with slatted headboards and plank mattress supports on tapering legs with exposed joinery, unmarked.

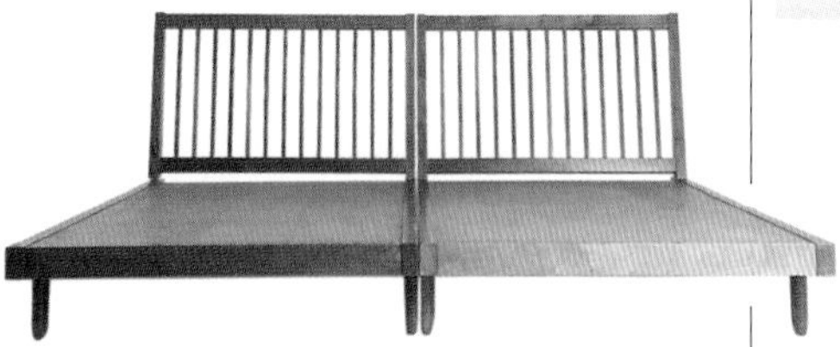

80.75in (202cm) long

£2,000-3,000 **SDR**

GEORGE NELSON

A 'DCW' chair by George Nelson for Herman Miller, with brown slunkskin upholstery, unmarked.

29in (73.5cm) high

£600-900 **SDR**

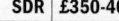

A pair of armchairs by George Nelson, with flat wood armrests and woven fabric upholstery in pink and blue, on black angle iron frames, unmarked.

25.75in (65.5cm) high

£350-400 **SDR**

A 'Sling' sofa by George Nelson for Herman Miller, with dark brown leather upholstery on tubular polished chrome frame, embossed mark.

85.75in (218cm) wide

£1,200-1,800 **SDR**

A 'Coconut' chair by George Nelson for Herman Miller, with coral upholstery on chromed metal base, unmarked.

40in (100cm) wide

£1,500-2,000 **SDR**

A compact upholstered sofa by George Nelson for Herman Miller, covered in mauve fabric.

72in (183cm) long

£500-800 **FRE**

A swag-leg desk by George Nelson for Herman Miller, with gallery top and white laminate surface over three blind drawers, on enamelled metal base, unmarked.

42in (106.5cm) wide

£600-900 **SDR**

An end table with attached lamp by George Nelson for Herman Miller, with two integrated planters with metal inserts and leather-covered surface, on tapering legs.

45in (114.5cm) wide

£180-220 **SDR**

A swag-leg desk by George Nelson for Herman Miller, with gallery top, white laminate surfaces and coloured dividers, on polished legs, with Herman Miller tag.

39in (99cm) wide

£2,800-3,200 **SDR**

A stereo cabinet by George Nelson for Herman Miller, with ebonized finish, single drop-front door and pull-out shelf over storage compartment, on plank legs, unmarked.

56.25in (143cm) wide

£600-900 **SDR**

A bookcase by George Nelson for Herman Miller, with sliding glass doors and interior shelf, resting on a slatted wood bench with ebonized legs, unmarked.

48in (122cm) wide

£350-450 **SDR**

ALBERT PALEY

A monumental 'Amazon Mystery Table' by Albert Paley, of forged and fabricated steel with white marble top, signed "Albert Paley 1992".

1992 *51in (127.5cm) high*

£15,000-20,000 **SDR**

A pedestal dining table by Albert Paley, of forged and fabricated steel with dark charcoal patina and plate glass top, base stamped "Paley 1979".

1979 *60in (150cm) wide*

£10,000-12,000 **SDR**

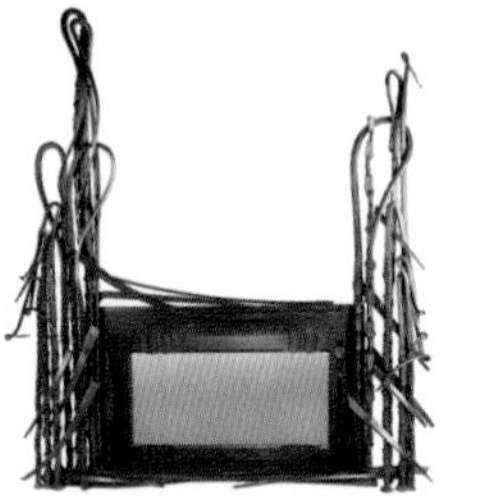

A fireplace surround by Albert Paley, of forged milled steel with charcoal patina.

78in (198cm) wide

£22,000-24,000 **SDR**

A 'Wave Mirror' by Albert Paley, with bevelled steel frame supporting a freeform blonde-wood shelf, stamped "Albert Paley/1992".

1992 *101in (252.5cm) wide*

£12,000-15,000 **SDR**

Two pairs of door handles by Albert Paley, unmarked.

96in (240cm) high

£22,000-24,000 **SDR**

A wing-back bentwood rocker by Gio Ponti, with webbed rubber seat support and red channelled fabric seat pad, unmarked.

40in (101.5cm) high

£3,500-4,500 **SDR**

A rare extension dining table by Gio Ponti, with applied latticework design and cream top.

47in (119.5cm) wide

£10,000-15,000 **SDR**

A rare set of eight dining chairs by Gio Ponti, with applied latticework and yellow herringbone fabric upholstery, on tapered flaring legs.

36.5in (92.5cm) high

£22,000-24,000 **SDR**

A sideboard by Gio Ponti, the top portion with cabinet door and open shelves, the bottom with doors concealing drawers and compartments, marked "Made in Italy".

78.75in (200cm) wide

£12,000-14,000 **SDR**

A six-door sideboard by Gio Ponti, with applied latticework to door fronts, the interior with drawers and shelves, on elegantly tapering legs, unmarked.

98.5in (250cm) wide

£18,000-22,000 **SDR**

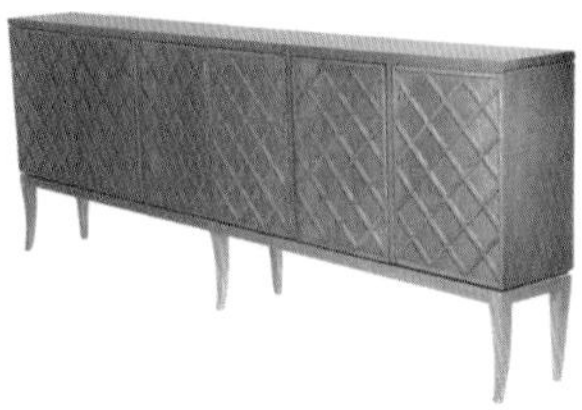

PHILIP LLOYD POWELL

A coffee table by Phillip Lloyd Powell, with circular slate top and shelf, on three chip-carved plank legs with hammered metal hardware, on castors, unmarked.

36.25in (92cm) high

£800-1,200 **SDR**

A set of three walnut nesting tables by Phillip Lloyd Powell, with tapering legs mortised through the tops, unmarked.

17.25in (44cm) high

£1,200-1,800 **SDR**

A 'New Hope' lounge chair and ottoman by Phillip Lloyd Powell, in walnut with black leather upholstered cushions, unmarked.

chair 32.75in (82cm) high

£2,000-3,000 **SDR**

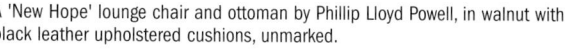

A set of three walnut hexagonal side tables by Phillip Lloyd Powell, with slate tops and exposed pinning, unmarked.

26in (66cm) wide

£1,500-2,000 **SDR**

A walnut credenza by Phillip Lloyd Powell, with dovetailed corners, three sliding linen-covered doors, slate inset to top and overhanging slate shelf, raised on six tapering legs, unmarked.

114in (285cm) wide

£2,200-2,800 **SDR**

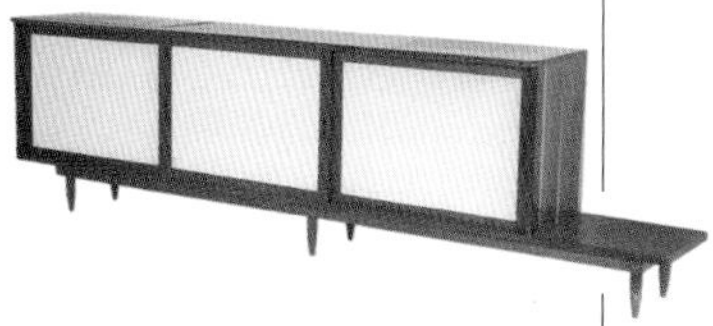

A 'Grasshopper' chair by Eero Saarinen for Knoll, with gold fabric upholstery on laminated bentwood frame, unmarked.

34.5in (86cm) high

£800-1,200 **SDR**

A 'Womb' chair and ottoman by Eero Saarinen for Knoll, marked with Knoll Associates tag.

38.5in (98cm) high

£1,500-2,000 **SDR**

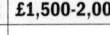

A 'Womb' settee by Eero Saarinen for Knoll, upholstered in white on gold fabric, on tubular brass base, unmarked.

59.5in (151cm) wide

£1,500-2,000 **SDR**

A 'Womb' settee by Eero Saarinen for Knoll, upholstered in charcoal grey leather, on tubular black metal frame, unmarked.

60in (152.5cm) wide

£1,800-2,200 **SDR**

A Pedestal Group dining table by Eero Saarinen for Knoll, with oval white laminate top, accompanied by eight chairs, with burnt orange Naugahyde cushions, on swivel bases, with Knoll Associates labels and factory tags.

Saarinen used pedestal bases to liberate the dining space from what he called the "clutter of legs".

table 77.5in (194cm) wide

£3,500-4,500 **SDR**

KARL SPRINGER

An extension dining table by Karl Springer, with oval bevel-edged top on double-pedestal base, covered in lacquered goatskin, unmarked.

closed 71.5in (179cm) wide

£1,800-2,200 **SDR**

A dining table by Karl Springer, with parquetry top on ivory enamelled wooden base with tusk legs and matte chrome accents, unmarked.

85.5in (214cm) wide

£1,200-1,800 **SDR**

A games table by Karl Springer, with ivory lacquered grasscloth finish and chrome inlay, with removable centre panel revealing a backgammon board and felt-lined storage compartment, unmarked.

48.25in (120.5cm) wide

£1,500-2,000 **SDR**

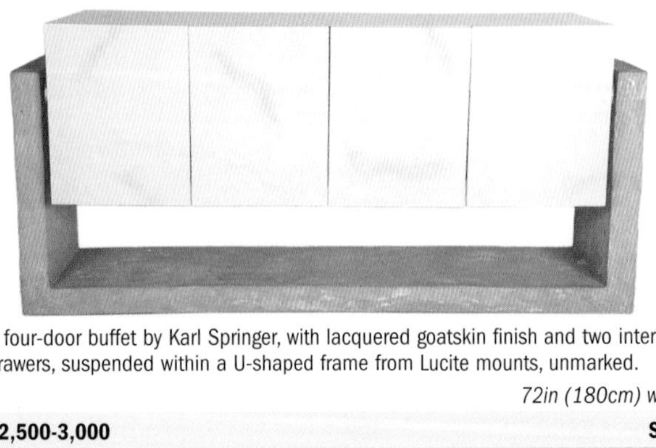

A four-door buffet by Karl Springer, with lacquered goatskin finish and two interior drawers, suspended within a U-shaped frame from Lucite mounts, unmarked.

72in (180cm) wide

£2,500-3,000 **SDR**

A set of six high-back dining chairs by Karl Springer, with metal horn frames, and light silver upholstery, unmarked.

42.75in (107cm) high

£1,800-2,200 **SDR**

A pair of 'Papa Bear' chairs by Hans Wegner, with oatmeal-coloured woollen upholstery and exposed teak armrests, on flaring legs.

38.75in (98.5cm) high

£7,000-10,000 **SDR**

A pair of 'The Chair' sculpted dining chairs by Hans Wegner for Johannes Hansen, unmarked.

29.75in (75.5cm) high

£3,000-4,000 **SDR**

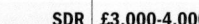

An oak saw back chair by Hans Wegner for Carl Hansen, with leather seat and back.

29in (73.5cm) wide

£500-700 **GAZE**

A teak lounge chair and ottoman by Hans Wegner, with reclining upholstered cushion seat.

c1960 chair *34.5in (87.5cm) high*

£2,500-3,000 **SK**

A 'Shell' side chair by Hans Wegner, with broad seat and back, on dowel-leg frame, with stamped marks with partial factory label.

27in (68.5cm) high

£1,800-2,200 **SDR**

A desk chair by Hans Wegner for Johannes Hansen, with brown leather upholstery and angular polished steel frame, unmarked.

c1975 *30.75in (78cm) high*

£800-1,200 **SDR**

A 'Peter's Table and Chairs' child's set by Hans Wegner, with keyed tenon joints and black "FDB" stamp mark.

Wegner designed this set to mark the birth of Borge Mogensen's son. The "FDB" stamp is for a manufacturing co-op with which Wegner was associated before becoming successful.

c1959 *chairs 19in (48.5cm) high*

£1,000-1,500 **SDR**

An oak, brass and leather 'Valet' chair by Hans Wegner for Johannes Hansen, with branded marks.

37in (92.5cm) high

£2,500-3,000 **FRE**

A rare leather and canvas club chair by Hans Wegner, with matching ottoman, on teak legs.

chair 40in (100cm) high

£2,500-3,000 **SDR**

A rosewood even-arm sofa by Hans Wegner, with blue-green fabric upholstery, unmarked.

75.25in (188cm) wide

£1,800-2,200 **SDR**

A set of four ebonized armchairs by Edward Wormley for Dunbar, with tall backposts, horizontal backslats, tweed drop-in seat cushions and gold Dunbar metal tags.

36in (90cm) high

£1,200-1,800 **SDR**

A lounge chair and ottoman by Edward Wormley for Dunbar, upholstered in camel-coloured brushed fabric, on angled wood base with tapering legs, unmarked.

chair 34in (85cm) wide

£1,000-1,500 **SDR**

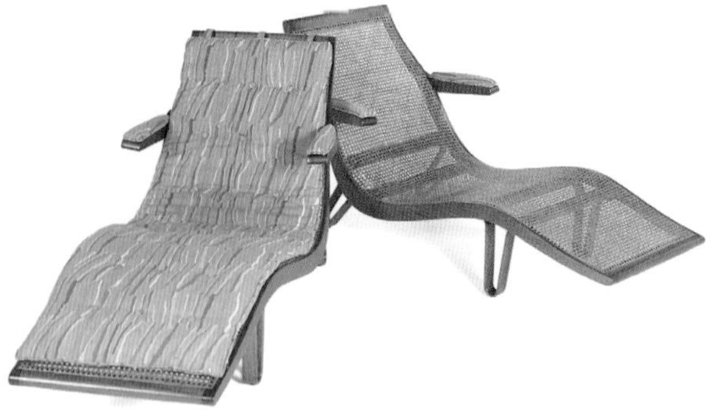

A pair of chaise lounges by Edward Wormley for Dunbar, with curvilinear frames, caning, upholstered armrests and matching cushions, on hairpin legs, unmarked.

48.5in (121cm) wide

£7,000-10,000 **SDR**

A 'Floating' sofa by Edward Wormley for Dunbar, with oatmeal-coloured bouclé upholstery on dark wood frame, unmarked.

90.75in (230.5cm) wide

£1,800-2,200 **SDR**

A '4856' walnut occasional table by Edward Wormley for Dunbar, with inset birch burl panel, brass handle and tripod base, with metal Dunbar tag and paper factory tag.

27in (67.5cm) high

£1,200-1,800 **SDR**

A side table by Edward Wormley for Dunbar, with trapezoidal glass mosaic top on tripod base with Y-shaped stretcher, metal Dunbar tag.

22in (55cm) high

£3,000-4,000 **SDR**

A console table by Edward Wormley for Dunbar, with stylized wave pattern across apron and large shell pedestal base, stencilled "Dunbar".

c1945 *32in (81.5cm) wide*

£1,800-2,200 **SDR**

A three-drawer server by Edward Wormley for Dunbar, with brass hardware and dowel side stretchers, unmarked.

54in (137cm) wide

£1,200-1,800 **SDR**

A sideboard by Edward Wormley for Dunbar, with eight drawers flanking a two-door cabinet with interior glass tray and shelf, over a linen drawer, all with brass hardware, unmarked.

70in (178cm) wide

£2,800-3,200 **SDR**

A teacart by Edward Wormley for Dunbar, with inset glass top flanked by two semi-circular drop leaves, over two removable trays, unmarked.

38.5in (98cm) wide

£400-600 **SDR**

A birch desk chair by Alvar Aalto.

£200-300 **JN**

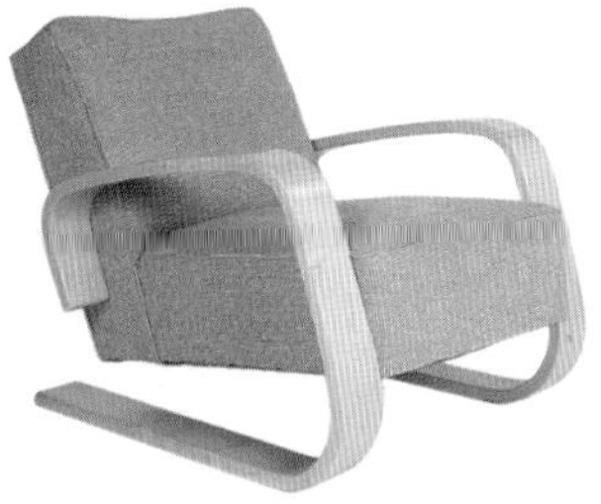

A 'Tank' armchair by Alvar Aalto for Artek, with tweed upholstery in amber and ivory, on cantilevered base, unmarked.

c1945 *29.5in (74cm) high*

£1,200-1,800 **SDR**

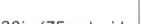

A birch drop-leaf dining table by Alvar Aalto, with bentwood legs and black laminate top, unmarked.

30in (75cm) wide

£700-1,000 **SDR**

A chrome framed chair by Mario Bellini for Vitra, with brown leather upholstery.

27in (68.5cm) wide

£350-450 **GAZE**

A ball chair by Eero Aarnio for Asko.

c1965

£1,500-2,000 **JN**

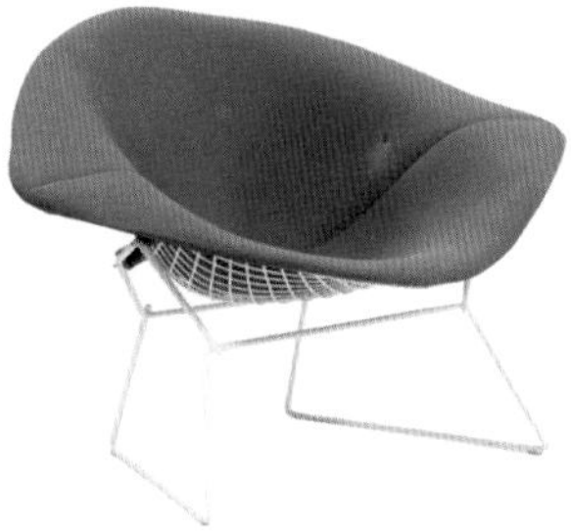

A diamond wire chair by Harry Bertoia, with blue upholstery.

£180-220 **FRE**

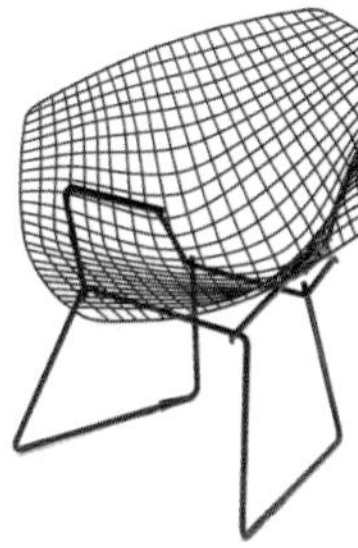

One of a pair of black covered diamond wire chairs by Harry Bertoia.

33.25in (84.5cm) wide

£180-220 pair **GAZE**

A walnut daybed by Samson Berman, with royal blue vinyl cushions and white laminate shelf to one side inset with three tiles in yellow, orange and blue, unmarked.

86.5in (219.5cm) wide

£600-900 **SDR**

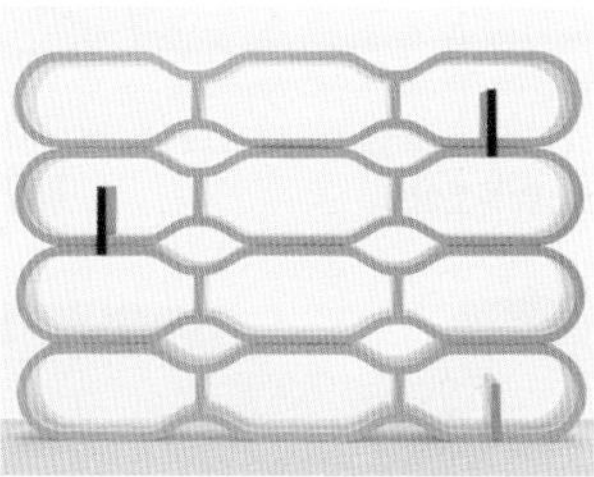

A 'Brick' bookshelf by Ronan & Erwan Bouroullec for Cappellini, comprising stackable honeycomb plywood shelves in white matt lacquer.

118in (300cm) wide

£2,500-3,000 per module **SCP**

A 'Strap' chair by Boym Partners, with polypropylene strapping tape.

£2,200-2,800 **BOY**

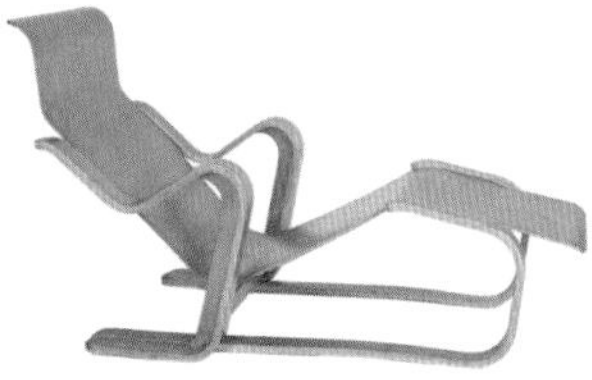

An early laminated plywood chair by Marcel Breuer for Isokon, with undulated seat and Isokon decal.

1935 *45in (112.5cm) wide*

£3,500-4,500 **SDR**

A reproduction 'Wassily' tubular chrome armchair, designed by Marcel Breuer, with clear plastic stringing.

30.75in (78cm) wide

£150-200 **GAZE**

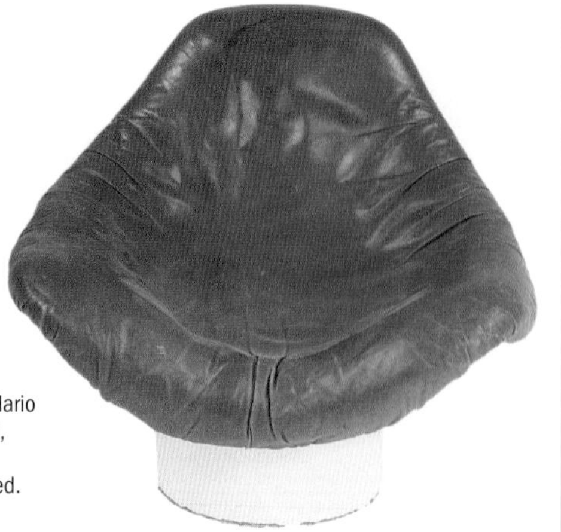

A lounge chair by Mario Bruno for Soronami, with brown leather upholstery, unmarked.

c1975 *40in (100cm) wide*

£800-1,200 **SDR**

A pair of 'Delfino' chairs by Erberto Carboni for Arflex, with tubular metal legs, rubberized seat supports and fabric upholstery.

1954 *32.75in (82cm) high*

£1,500-2,000 **SDR**

A pair of mirrored side tables by James Clark, in peach with clip-corner bevel-edged tops on tapering pedestal shafts with wood-trimmed bases, unmarked.

23.75in (59cm) wide

£1,500-2,000 **SDR**

A lounge chair by Le Corbusier for Cassina, with chrome base, leather seat and Cassina label.

64in (160cm) wide

£600-900 **SDR**

A pair of plank-style armchairs, attributed to Erich Dieckmann, with broad backslats, on angular frames, unmarked.

27.25in (68cm) high

£400-600 **SDR**

A 'Ditzel' chair by Nana Ditzel, with woven wicker barrel seat on tapering dowel leg base, unmarked.

32in (80cm) wide

£180-220 **SDR**

A pair of Coconut-style lounge chairs by A.J. Donahue, with original orange pile upholstery, on ebonized bent plywood frames with flared metal legs, unmarked.

35in (87.5cm) wide

£2,200-2,800 **SDR**

A 'Lamino' easy chair and ottoman by Yngve Ekström.

1956

£600-900 **SCP**

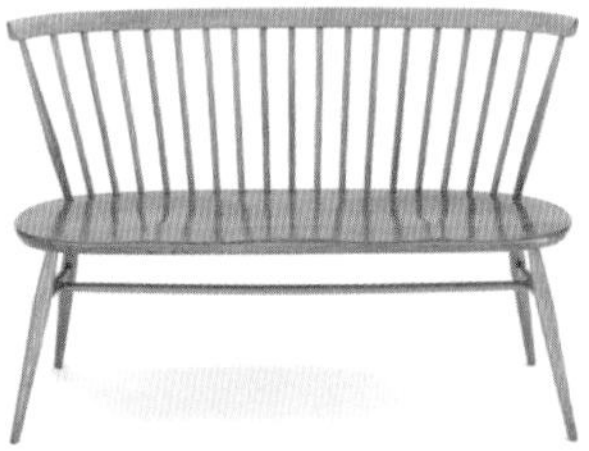

An elm double seat settee by Ercol, with spindle back.

44.25in (112.5cm) wide

£180-220 **GAZE**

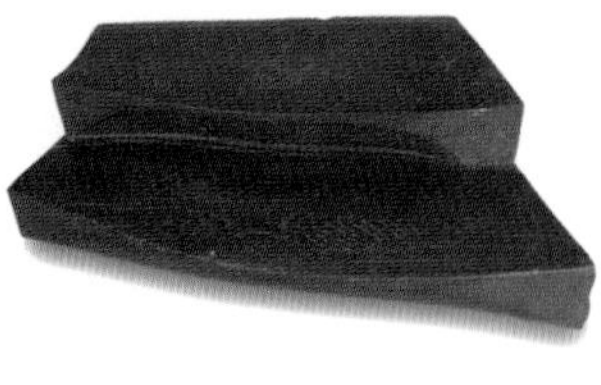

A pair of carved steps by Wharton Esherick, unmarked.

These steps originally led from the living room to the bedroom hall of the Harry Milliken house in Pennsylvania.

c1955 *largest 47.5in (119cm) wide*

£2,800-3,200 **SDR**

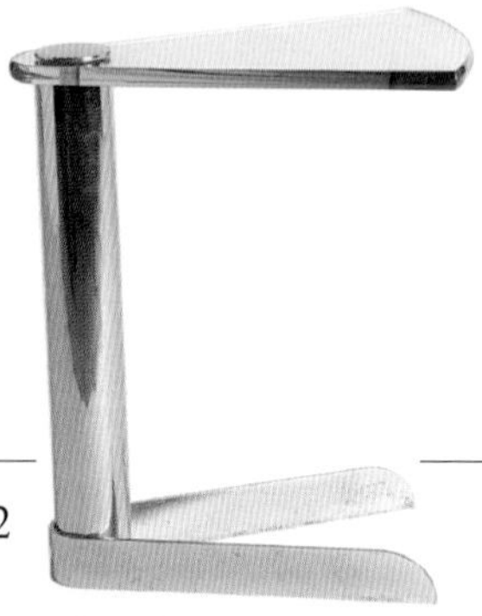

A side table by Fontana Arte, with wedge-shaped plate glass top on cantilevered polished brass base, unmarked.

20.25in (50.5cm) high

£800-1,200 **SDR**

A pair of 'Sesann' chairs by Gianfranco Frattini for Cassina, fully upholstered in black leather on tubular polished chrome frames, with low cylindrical legs, marked for Atelier International.

1970 *40in (100cm) wide*

£1,000-1,500 **SDR**

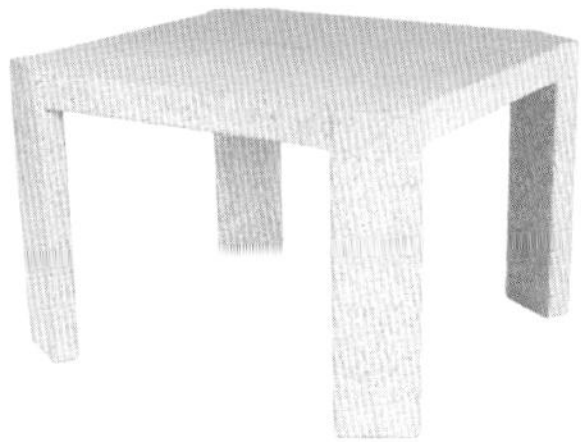

A laminated cork occasional table by Paul Frankl, with clip-corner top and rectangular legs, stencilled number on bottom.

31.75in (79cm) wide

£600-900 **SDR**

A mahogany and cork buffet by Paul Frankl for Johnson Furniture Co., with four drawers, two doors and eight pull-out shelves.

73in (182.5cm) wide

£1,500-2,000 **SDR**

A custom-made 'Hand and Foot' chair by Pedro Friedeberg, of laminated Mexican mahogany, marked "Para Lisa De Pedro Friedeberg".

1966 *34in (85cm) high*

£3,000-4,000 **SDR**

A prototype dining chair by Frank Gehry, of laminated cardboard construction, unmarked.

1979 *35.5in (89cm) high*

£1,800-2,200 **SDR**

A rare coffee table by Greta Magnusson Grossman for Glenn, with three circular tops laminated in primary colours, on black enamelled metal base with ball feet, unmarked.

58in (145cm) wide

£7,000-10,000 **SDR**

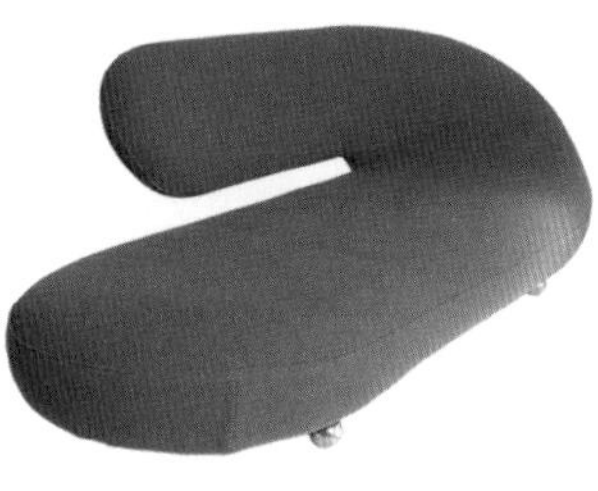

A 'Cleopatra' sofa by Geoffrey Harcourt for Artifort, of upholstered foam and tubular steel, covered in royal blue wool fabric on ball casters, with Artifort label.

74.25in (185.5cm) wide

£400-600 **SDR**

A 'Balzac' armchair by Matthew Hilton, with solid beech frame and elasticated webbing covered in foam with feather cushions and American oak legs.

33.5in (85cm) high

£2,000-2,500 **SCP**

A cocktail cabinet by Heal & Son, with a pair of rosewood veneered doors and a single formica door printed in black and white with sea shells fitted with shelves, bottle racks and a drawer, door folds down to become a serving table.

96.5cm (38in) wide

£400-600 **SWO**

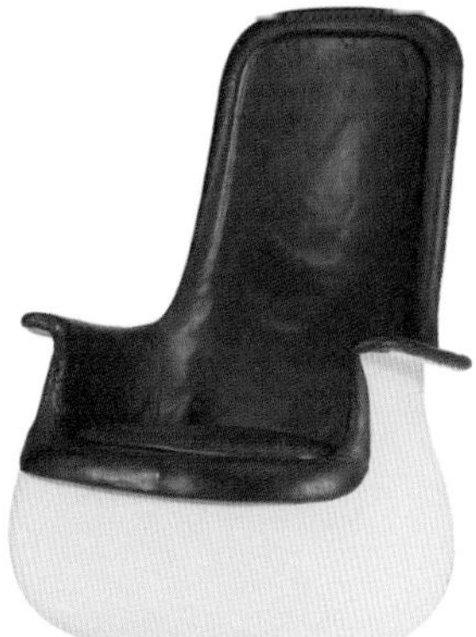

A 'Culbuto' chair by Marc Held for Knoll, upholstered in black leather with white fibreglass shell, unmarked.

44.5in (113cm) high

£1,200-1,800 **SDR**

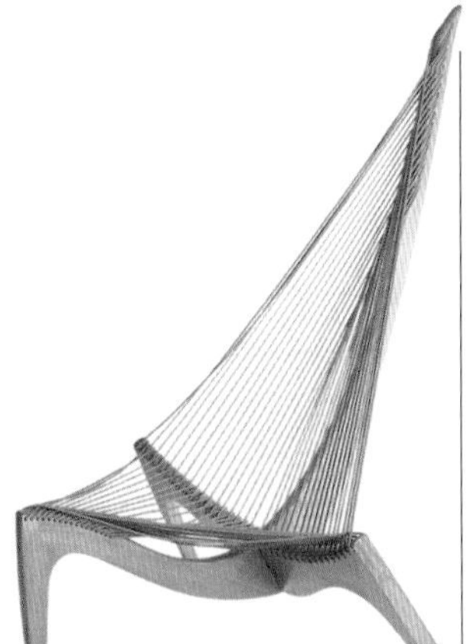

A 'Harp' chair by Jorgen Hovelskov, with birch frame and flag line seat, unmarked.

52.25in (130.5cm) high

£2,200-2,800 **SDR**

A 'Six Inch Cabinet' by Thomas Hucker, in wenge and Synskin with curved shoji-screen back and two rounded doors with bronzed pulls concealing three interior shelves, unmarked.

1992 *75.5in (189cm) high*

£2,000-2,500 **SDR**

A frame-back chair by Thomas Hucker, in rosewood and rolled steel, on disc feet, unmarked.

48in (120cm) wide

£1,000-1,500 **SDR**

A 'Tea Cup Desk' by Michael Hurwitz, with inlaid marble mosaic top, single drawer and ribbed base with cross-slats, unmarked.

1994 *42.5in (106cm) diam*

£4,000-6,000 **SDR**

Two of a set of four stackable 'Jason' chairs, designed by Carl Jacobs for Kandya, in yellow painted beech laminate.

c1955 *20.75in (52.5cm) wide*

£250-300 each **GAZE**

A pair of 'Scissor' chairs by Pierre Jeanneret for Knoll, with chrome struts, blonde-wood frame and plaid wool cushions in black, brown and beige, unmarked.

29in (73.5cm) high

£1,200-1,800 **SDR**

One of a pair of 'Tulip' chairs by Jorgen Kastholm and Fabricus for Alfred Kill, brown leather upholstery over steel frame.

c1965

£1,000-1,500 pair **JN**

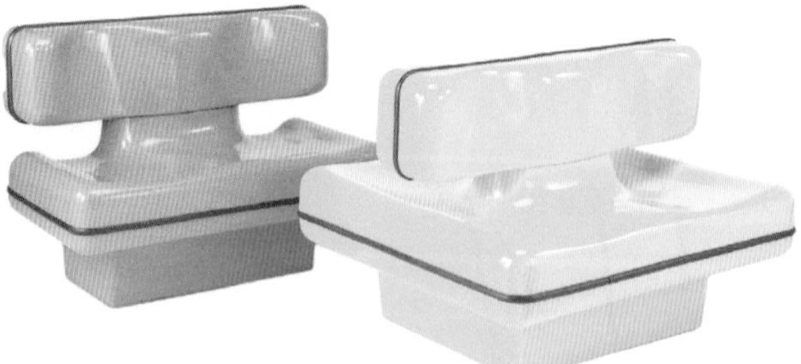

A pair of French cast fibreglass settees by La Defense.

These settees were commissioned for the Neptune Towers in Paris.

c1985 *45in (112.5cm) wide*

£800-1,200 **SDR**

A rare two-seater lounge chair by Walter Lamb, with original webbing, on tubular bronze frame with verdigris patina, unmarked.

48in (120cm) wide

£3,000-4,000 **SDR**

A 'Fibreglass Group' armchair by Erwine & Estelle Laverne, with freeform cutout seat in ivory fibreglass on a steel pedestal base, unmarked.

24in (61cm) wide

£600-900 **SDR**

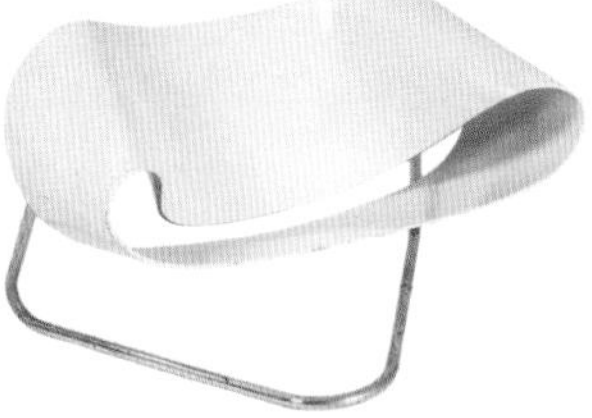

A 'Ribbon' chair by Cesare Leonardi, with ivory moulded fibreglass seat on cantilevered base of tubular chromed steel, unmarked.

36.5in (91cm) wide

£1,800-2,200 **SDR**

Two of a set of four 'Maralunga' chairs by Vico Magistretti for Cassina, with brown leather upholstery on steel frames.

This design featured in Fortune magazine's list of the top design products of 1977.

38.5in (98cm) wide

£1,800-2,200 set **SK**

A walnut slatted bench by Sam Maloof, with contoured seat rail and hand-worked details, on tapering legs, with impressed mark.

1961 *57.5in (146cm) wide*

£10,000-12,000 **SDR**

A walnut pedestal side table by James Martin, with free-edge top and base, carved "James Martin Woodworking."

25.5in (64cm) high

£1,200-1,800 **SDR**

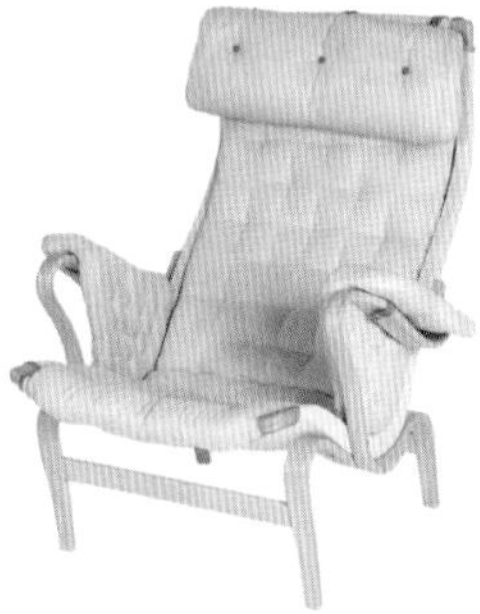

An armchair by Bruno Mathsson for Dux, with fabric upholstery and brown leather straps, branded mark.

38.25in (95.5cm) high

£280-320 **SDR**

A pair of 'PTJ' highchairs by Alphonse Mattia, in mixed woods on tapering dowel legs with stretchers, signed and dated.

1995 *37in (94cm) high*

£800-1,200 **SDR**

A lounge chair by Warren McArthur, with original red upholstery on tubular aluminum frame with curved side rails.

33in (82.5cm) high

£1,200-1,800 **SDR**

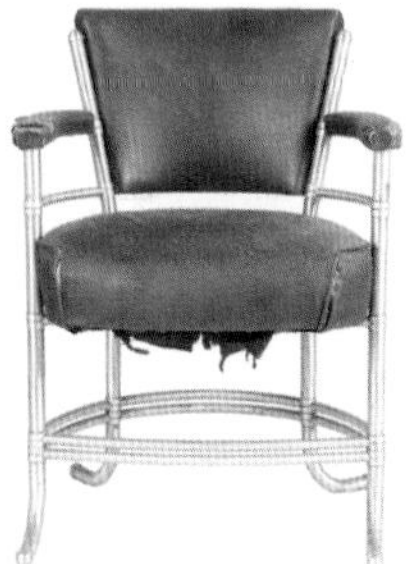

An armchair by Warren McArthur, on tubular aluminum frame with original blue oilcloth upholstery, with McArthur Corporation decal.

31.75in (79cm) high

£1,800-2,200 **SDR**

A card table by Warren McArthur, with original red oilcloth to inset square top, on tubular aluminum base with discs, unmarked.

31.75in (79cm) wide

£600-900 **SDR**

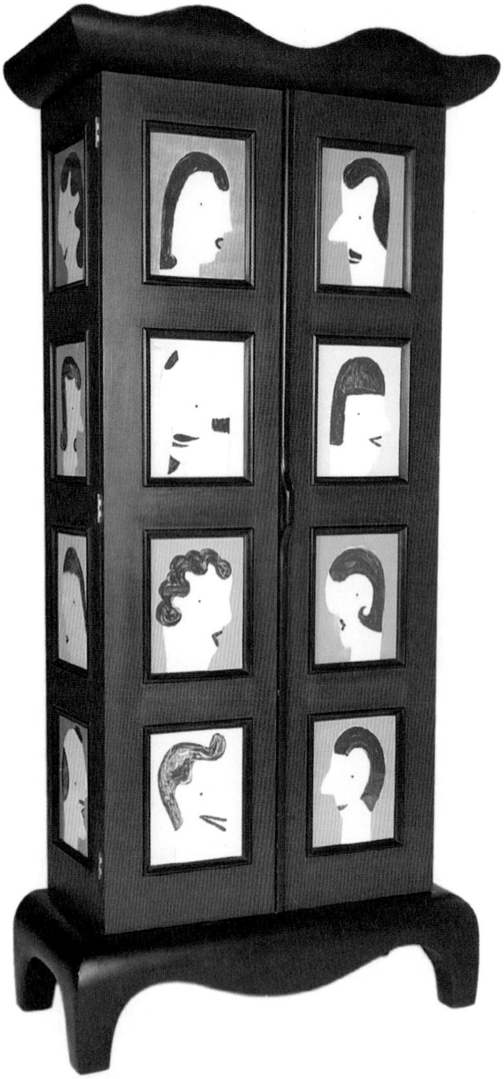

A 'Faces' cabinet by Judy Kensley McKie, with interior shelves, its doors and sides decorated with whimsical portraits of men and women in profile, marked "JHM/1991", with copyright.

1991 *73.25in (183cm) high*

£3,500-4,500 **SDR**

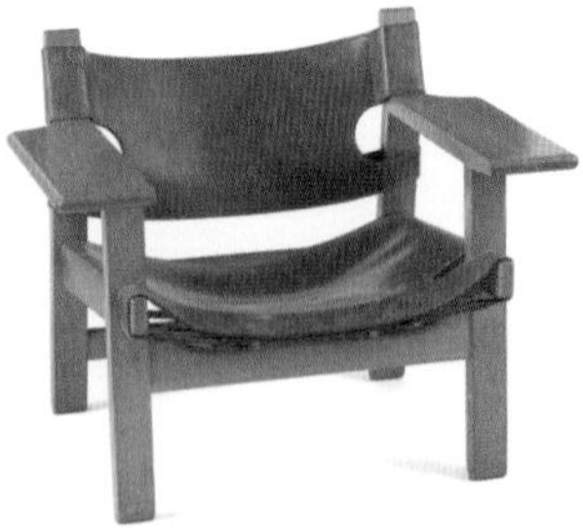

One of a pair of Spanish chairs, by Borge Mogensen for Fredericia.

c1965

£800-1,200 pair **JN**

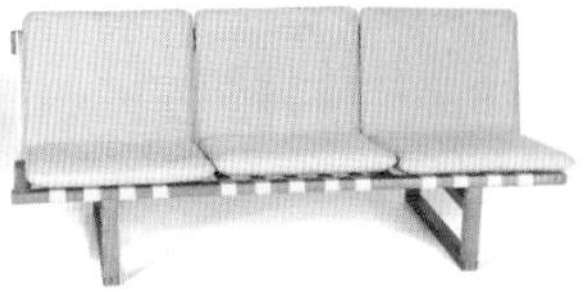

An oak settee by Borge Mogensen, with rubberized set and back supports and six oatmeal fabric cushions, on open rectangular legs, unmarked.

64in (162.5cm) wide

£600-900 **SDR**

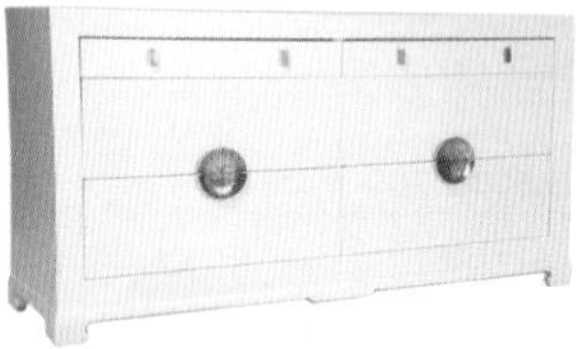

A six-drawer dresser by James Mont, with white finish and polished brass hardware, on bracketed base, unmarked.

64.25in (160.5cm) wide

£2,200-2,800 **SDR**

A gilded metal table in the style of James Mont, with modified egg and dart pattern, red marble top with white striations and arched leg supports, unmarked.

80in (200cm) wide

£1,500-2,000 **SDR**

A 'Thinking Man's Chair' by Jasper Morrison, with varnished metal frame, the arms fitted with trays to hold glasses.

1988 *22.5in (57cm) wide*

£600-900 **SH**

A small armchair by Forrest Myers, with tubular black metal seat and copper panel base, unmarked.

31.5in (79cm) wide

£5,000-6,000 **SDR**

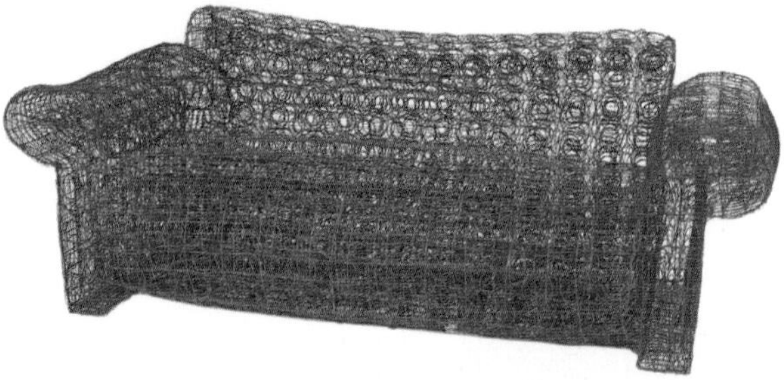

A wire sofa by Forrest Myers, with internal spring supports and rolled armrests, unmarked.

80.5in (201cm) wide

£5,000-6,000 **SDR**

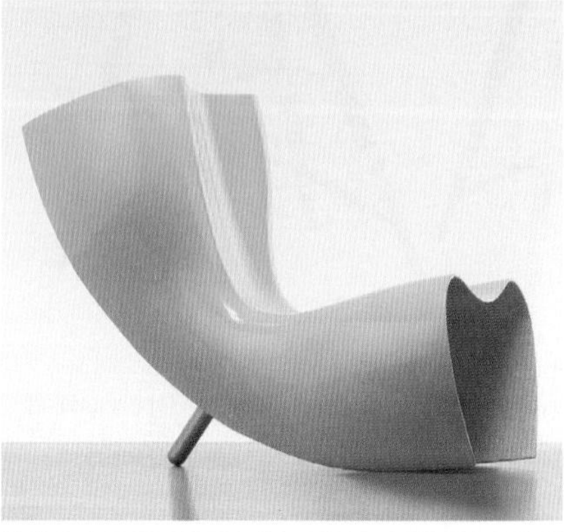

A 'Felt' chair by Marc Newson for Cappellini, in reinforced fibreglass with polished aluminium legs.

This piece has organic lines similar to Newson's celebrated 'Orgone' lounger.

26.5in (67cm) high

£1,800-2,200 **SCP**

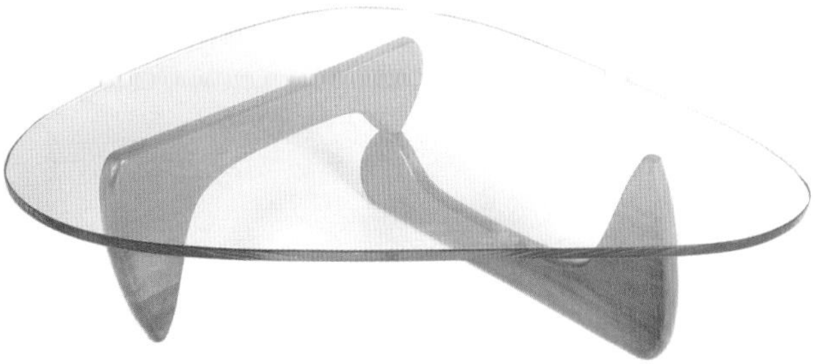

An early 'Boomerang' coffee table by Isamu Noguchi, with folding walnut base and three-sided plate glass top, unmarked.

50.5in (126cm) wide

£1,500-2,000 **SDR**

A rocking stool by Isamu Noguchi, with ebonized seat and base and corseted chrome wire supports, unmarked.

16.25in (40.5cm) high

£1,800-2,200 **SDR**

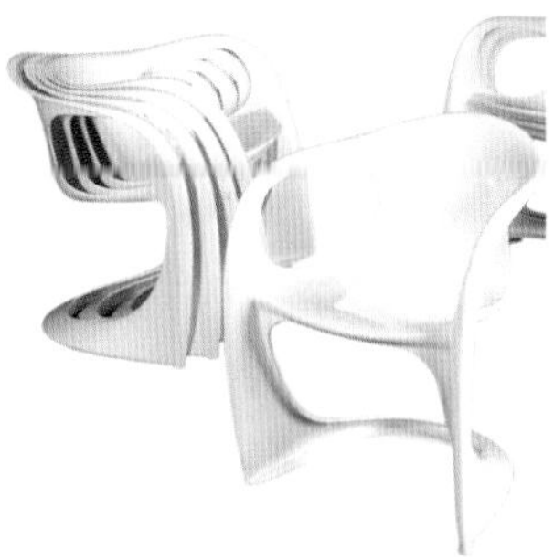

A set of eight moulded plastic armchairs by Verner Panton, with cut-out sides and cantilevered bases, unmarked.

28in (71cm) high

£800-1,200 **SDR**

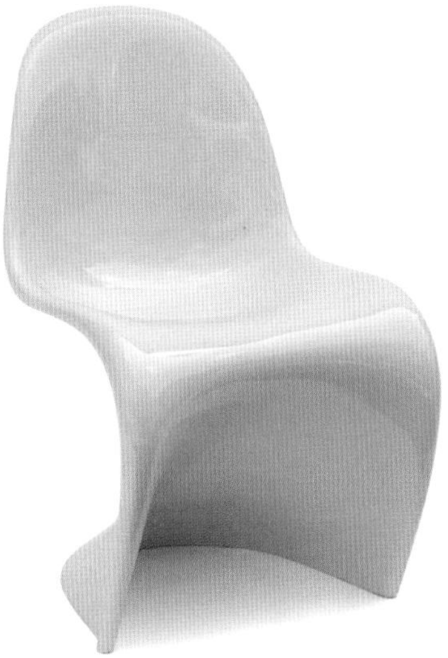

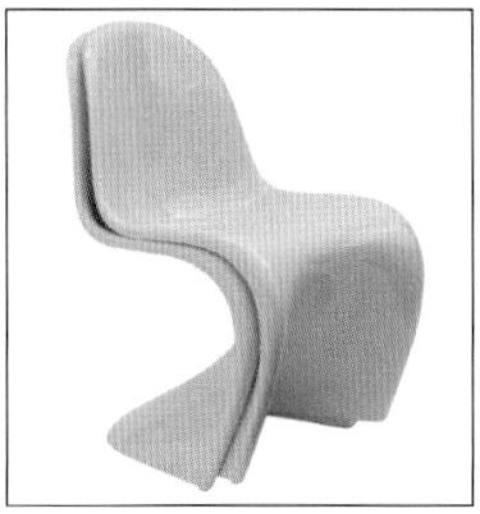

A pair of stackable 'Panton' chairs by Verner Panton, in matte white plastic, with impressed "Verner Panton" mark.

This was the first chair made entirely from one piece of plastic.

19in (48.5cm) wide

£300-400 **GAZE**

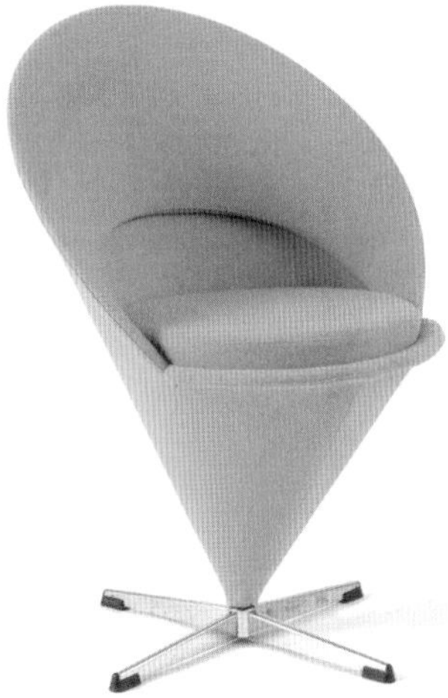

A 'Cone' chair by Vernon Panton.

c1960

£400-500 **JN**

A custom-designed bar by Tommi Parzinger, the four doors with etched brass pulls concealing a mirrored and lacquered interior, unmarked.

74.25in (185.5cm) high

£4,000-6,000 **SDR**

An extension dining table by Tommi Parzinger, with parquetry top on tapering fluted legs with brass-capped feet.

68in (170cm) wide

£1,200-1,800 **SDR**

An ebonized chest-on-stand by Tommi Parzinger for Charak, the single drawer with silver leaf front and chrome pull, on a sabre-leg base, with label.

36in (90cm) high

£2,500-3,000 **SDR**

A rare wardrobe by Charlotte Perriand, with chamfered back and slatted door concealing fitted interior, on cylindrical black metal legs, signed on one tray.

67.75in (172cm) wide

£2,500-3,000 **SDR**

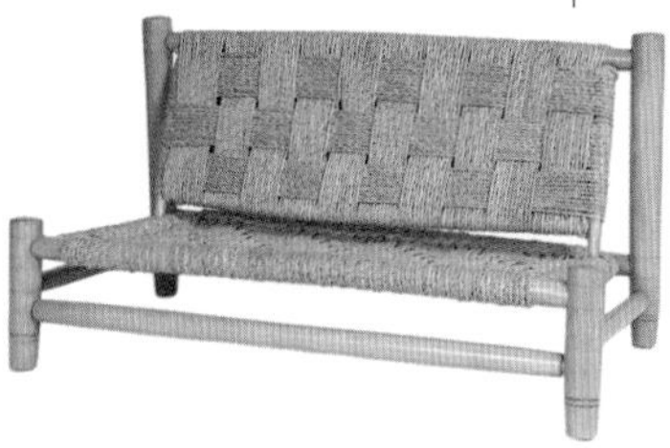

A settee in the manner of Charlotte Perriand, with woven seat and back on thickly-turned wooden frame, unmarked.

49.5in (124cm) wide

£400-600 **SDR**

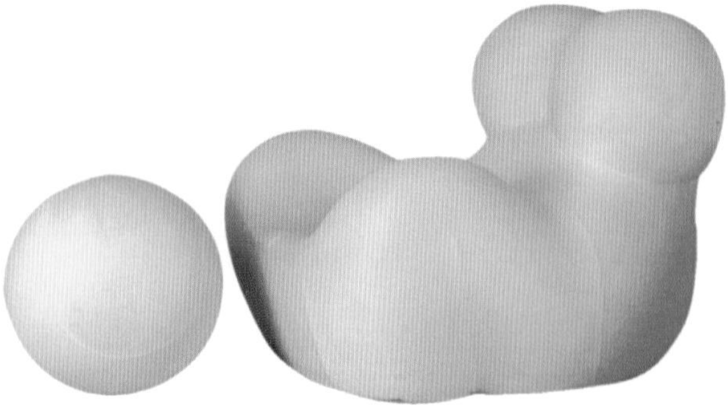

A 'Donna' foam lounge chair and ottoman by Gaetano Pesce for B&B Italia, from the 'UP' series, upholstered in yellow stretch fabric, with label.

£1,200-1,800 **SDR**

A small writing desk by Timothy Philbrick, with low backsplash, single drawer with ivory knob pull and tapering legs, signed "Timothy S. Philbrick/Naragansett R.I./1990".

1990 *30.5in (76cm) high*

£2,000-3,000 **SDR**

A lounge chair by Gio Ponti for Singer & Sons, with orange fabric upholstery, dowel side rails and tapering legs with brass struts, unmarked.

28.5in (71cm) high

£800-1,200 **SDR**

A rare pair of club chairs by Giuseppe Pagano Pogatschnig, with original fabric and finish, unmarked.

Pagano was an important functionalist architect who worked in Turin during the late 1920s.

c1930 *31in (78.5cm) high*

£6,000-9,000 **SDR**

A pair of barrel-back lounge chairs by Harvey Probber, with caning and dark brown vinyl-upholstered seat pads, unmarked.

32.5in (81cm) wide

£1,200-1,800 **SDR**

A wooden and metal wardrobe by Jean Prouvé, with two sliding doors ending in long vertical pulls concealing a fitted interior, with gold enamelled metal panels and feet.

63.25in (160.5cm) high

£12,000-18,000 **SDR**

A metal drinks trolley by John Risley, in the shape of a horse.

33.5in (85cm) wide

£220-280 **FRE**

An extension dining table by T.H. Robsjohn-Gibbings for Widdicomb, with broad rectangular top on turned legs with stretcher, marked with Widdicomb label and Grand Rapids metal tag.

72in (183cm) wide

£1,800-2,200 **SDR**

A table by T. H. Robsjohn-Gibbings, with bookmatched burlwood veneer top, on fluted pedestal base trim, unmarked.

46in (116cm) diam

£3,000-4,000 **SDR**

A set of three nesting tables by T.H. Robsjohn-Gibbings for Widdicomb, with dark brown finish and flaring dowel legs, with Widdicomb decal.

largest 24.25in (61.5cm) high

£500-600 **SDR**

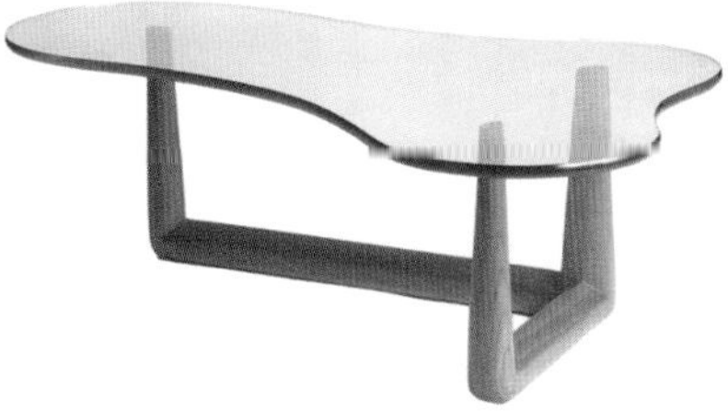

A coffee table by T.H. Robsjohn-Gibbings, with amoeba-shaped glass top on bevelled walnut base with tapering supports, unmarked.

54.5in (138.5cm) wide

£1,200-1,800 **SDR**

A pair of lounge chairs by Gilbert Rohde for Troy Sunshade, with tubular polished chrome frames and slatted metal seat supports, re-upholstered in Knoll fabric, unmarked.

33in (83.5cm) wide

£1,200-1,800 **SDR**

A 'Palladio' desk by Gilbert Rohde, with kidney-shaped top over shaped ends fitted with three drawers on each side, one with a pullout for writing, with domed circular brass pulls.

56in (142cm) wide

£800-1,200 **SK**

A notebook table by Pierre Sala, with legs in the form of pencils.

34.5in (87.5cm) wide

£500-800 **FRE**

A 'Supporto' chair by Fred Scott for Hille, with aluminium frame and foam upholstery.

This chair set a benchmark for ergonomic office furniture design.

21.5in (54.5cm) wide

£150-200 **GAZE**

An upholstered steerhorn chair by Frank Smith.

£600-900 **FRE**

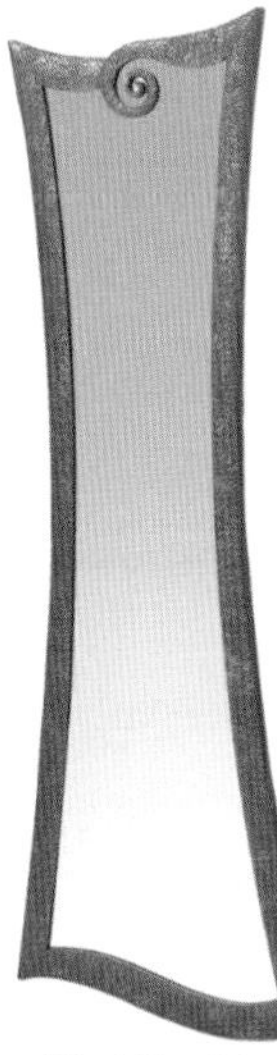

A 'Top Knot (Gloria)' wall-hanging mirror by Rosanne Somerson, with corseted hardwood frame in raspberry and speckled gold finish, unmarked.

1993 *65in (162.5cm) high*

£600-900 **SDR**

A coffee table by Abel Sorenson for Knoll, with boat-shaped walnut top and exposed tenons, on tapering dowel legs, unmarked.

60in (152.5cm) wide

£800-1,200 **SDR**

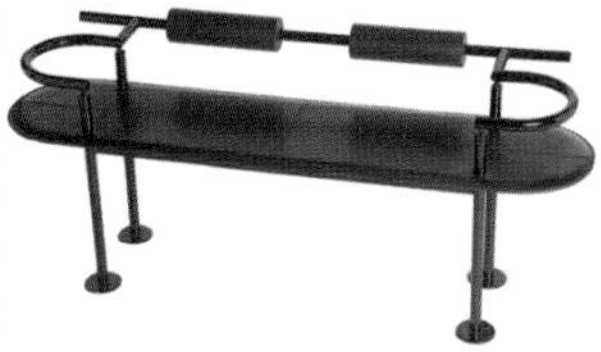

A bench by Ettore Sottsass, with tubular steel frame, hard leather seat and two rubber bolsters in black, unmarked.

59in (147.5cm) wide

£500-800 **SDR**

One of a set of five chairs by Philippe Starck for Aleph, with bentwood backs and cast aluminium rear legs, stamped "Starck/Aleph".

These chairs were designed for the Royalton Hotel in New York.

18.5in (47cm) wide

£1,500-2,000 set **SDR**

A pair of high-back chairs by Philippe Starck, with single arms, white enamelled wooden legs and velvet upholstery with laced trim, unmarked.

From the Paramount Hotel in New York.

54in (135cm) high

£400-600 **SDR**

A set of four wrought-iron side chairs attributed to Raymond Subes, with open-work backs and crimson velvet-upholstered seat pads, on hairpin leg bases, unmarked.

38.75in (97cm) high

£600-900 **SDR**

A small table by Ilmari Tapiovaara, with concave triangular top on three tapering dowel legs, unmarked.

24.5in (61cm) wide

£800-1,200 **SDR**

A sofa by Thema, with pink fabric upholstery on a powder blue enamelled steel frame, with Thema foil label.

72.5in (181cm) wide

£1,800-2,200 **SDR**

A chair by Smokey Tunis, with matte painted finish, chip-carved top and original floral upholstery, signed "Tunis".

The signature "Tunis" is rare.

c1960

£1,200-1,800 **SDR**

A rare carved wood music stand by Smokey Tunis, with crooked spine, two lower shelves and base with castors, painted finish, unmarked.

56.5in (141cm) high

£1,500-2,000 **SDR**

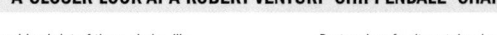

A 'Sheraton' moulded plywood chair by Robert Venturi for Knoll, with ebonized finish, silkscreen-printed decoration and black leather upholstered seat pad, unmarked.

33.25in (84.5cm) high

£1,200-1,800 **SDR**

A table by Robert Venturi for Knoll, with the 'Grandmother's Tablecloth' pattern in printed laminate, the top inset with black laminate, unmarked.

This is a non-production showroom model.

48in (120cm) wide

£1,000-1,500 **SDR**

A CLOSER LOOK AT A ROBERT VENTURI 'CHIPPENDALE' CHAIR

The pierced backslat of these chairs, like their name, is an ironic allusion to Thomas Chippendale, the great 18thC cabinet maker.

Postmodern furniture takes key styles from historic periods and uses them in unexpected ways, often juxtaposing very different ideas in the same piece.

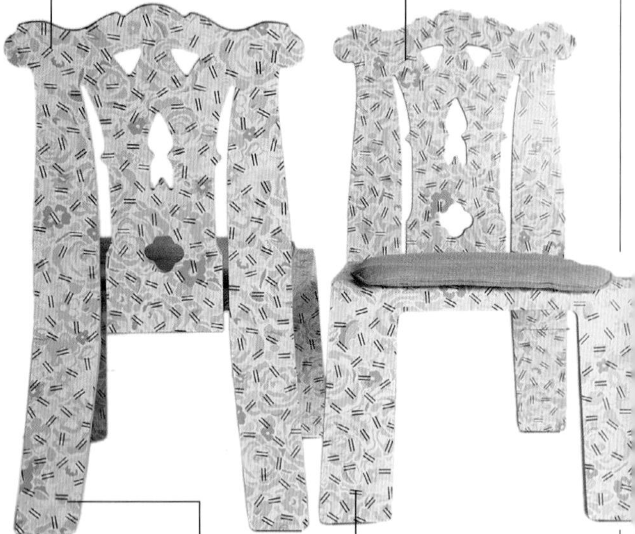

This printed pattern is known as 'Grandmother's Tablecloth' for its similarity to 1950s-style chintz.

The unsuitability of laminated bentwood as a material for reproducing a Chippendale-style chair is a kind of design joke. This humour and irreverence is an important feature of postmodernism.

A pair of 'Chippendale' chairs by Robert Venturi for Knoll, with attached seat pillows covered in original Knoll fabric, unmarked.

37.5in (94cm) high

£3,500-4,500 **SDR**

A rare three-piece coffee table by Betty Woodman, with two pod-shaped ceramic bases covered in volcanic glaze, topped by an amoeba-shaped papier-mâche slab, unmarked.

46.5in (118cm) wide

£2,200-2,800 **SDR**

A rare early dining table by Russel Wright for Heywood Wakefield, with hinged rectangular top and two quilted maple plank supports on a curved base, stencilled mark.

50in (125cm) wide

£600-900 **SDR**

A pair of Italian armchairs in the style of Marco Zanuso, with oval cut-out sides, tapering black legs with brass-capped feet, upholstered in grey vinyl, unmarked.

32in (80cm) high

£500-800 **SDR**

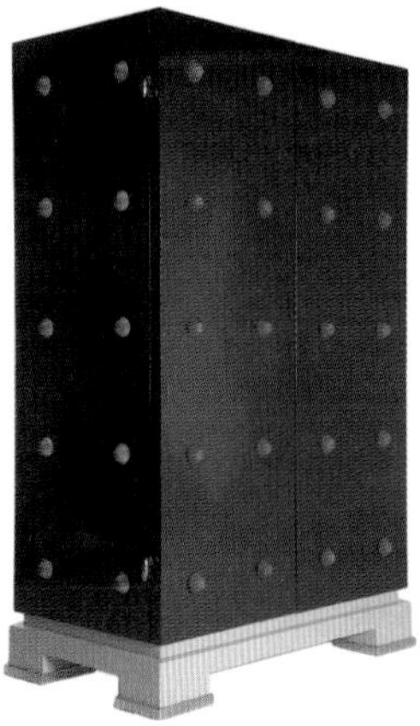

An Italian black lacquered wardrobe, with bronzed shell-studded exterior, silvered metal bullet hinges and two doors concealing a fitted interior, on enamelled metal base with gilt-trimmed bracket feet, unmarked.

c1975 *70in (175cm) high*

£1,800-2,200 **SDR**

A Norwegian 'Desk in a Box', with rosewood veneer case and doors concealing interior shelves, cubicles, and a desk light.

45.25in (115cm) wide

£1,000-1,500 **SDR**

A wooden storage unit, with three shelves and a single drawer, on castered base, unmarked.

c1955 *33.75in (84cm) wide*

£400-500 **SDR**

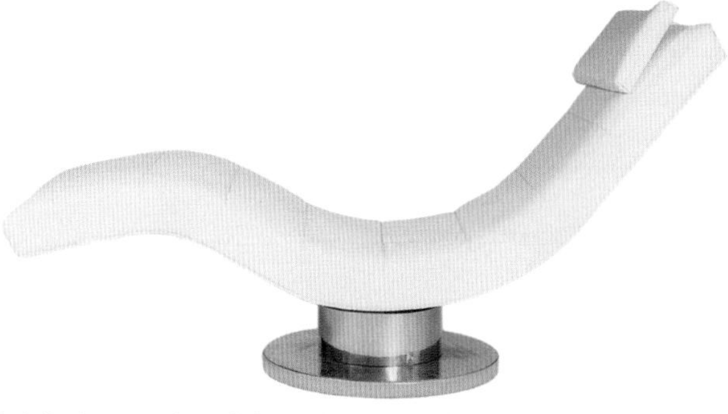

A chaise longue rocker, upholstered in textured white leather, with attached headrest, on a chrome swivel base, unmarked.

c1975 *36.25in (90.5cm) high*

£1,200-1,800 **SDR**

A Pop Art 'Bookchair', re-upholstered in high-quality white and black leather, on an aluminum frame.

48in (120cm) wide

£1,500-2,000 **SDR**

A kidney-shaped sofa, with rolled back and tufted ivory chenille upholstery, on brass-wrapped base, unmarked.

c1975 *75in (187.5cm) wide*

£1,200-1,800 **SDR**

A tall wood-fired totemic vessel by Paul Chaleff, with applied handles, closed-in rim and deep red and matte mustard finish, signed "Paul Chaleff, 1984".

30.5in (77.5cm) high

£600-900 **SDR**

A red clay wood-fired vessel by Paul Chaleff, of bulbous form, with cover and two small handles, unmarked.

1984 *12in (30.5cm) diam*

£1,200-1,800 **SDR**

A large wood-fired vessel, by Paul Chaleff, with hatched surface in iron red, grey and matte mustard finish, signed "Paul Chaleff, 1981".

18in (45.5cm) high

£800-1,200 **SDR**

A large stoneware charger by Paul Chaleff, with a random brush stroke in celadon and gun metal on a white and sand vellum ground, signed "Paul Chaleff."

20in (51cm) diam

£300-400 **SDR**

A stoneware tea set by Paul Chaleff, comprising a spherical teapot with bamboo handle and six cups in assorted glazes, signed "Paul", with chop mark.

largest 10in (25.5cm) high

£350-450 **SDR**

FANTONI

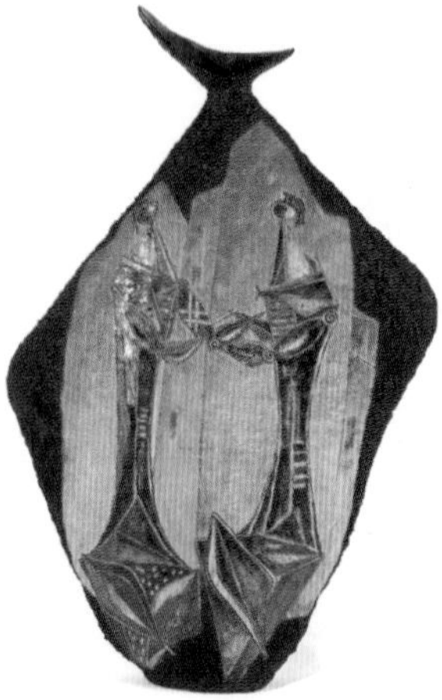

A monumental diamond-shaped flat vase by Fantoni, painted and incised with two stylized Venetian carnival figures on a beige and black ground, signed "Fantoni", restored.

41in (104cm) high

£7,000-10,000 **SDR**

A large ceramic vase by Fantoni, of hammered texture covered in matt white, brick, green and amber glaze, signed "Fantoni/Italy".

16in (40.5cm) high

£500-800 **SDR**

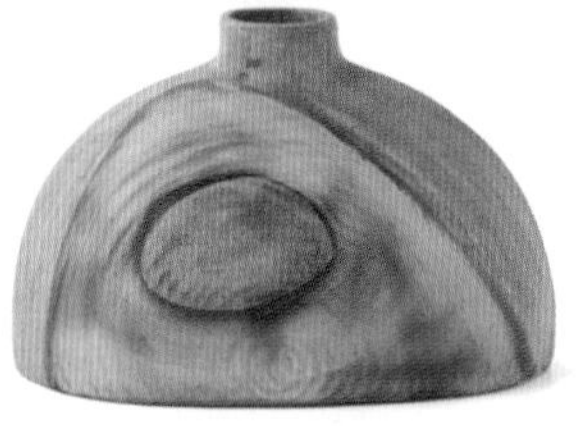

A large and unusual shoulder-shaped vessel by Fantoni, incised with concentric circles and painted in a verdigris and blue matt glaze, signed "Fantoni/Italy".

17in (43cm) wide

£600-900 **SDR**

A whimsical cow figure by Fantoni, decorated with geometric shapes in polychrome glazes, signed "Fantoni/Italy".

7.25in (18cm) wide

£1,200-1,800 **SDR**

A pair of faience figures by Fantoni, depicting Venetian revellers in a Cubist style, covered in bright polychrome glazes, marked "Fantoni Italy".

tallest 15in (38cm) high

£1,500-2,000 **SDR**

A massive two-handled stoppered bottle by Gambone, covered in a thick white glaze over a rich wine-coloured ground, signed "Gambone".

12.25in (30.5cm) high

£2,500-3,000 **SDR**

A large cylindrical stoppered faience vessel by Gambone, painted with dogs and a bird in matt polychrome glaze, signed "Gambone/Italy".

14.5in (37cm) high

£700-1,000 **SDR**

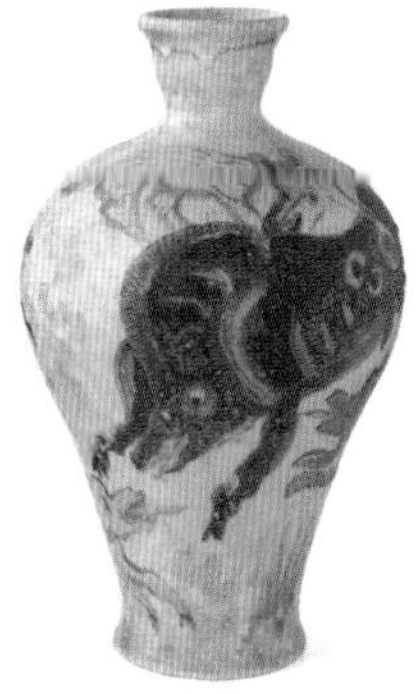

A large baluster faience vase by Gambone, painted with a boar hunt in matt polychrome glaze, marked "Gambone Italy".

16.75in (42.5cm) high

£600-900 **SDR**

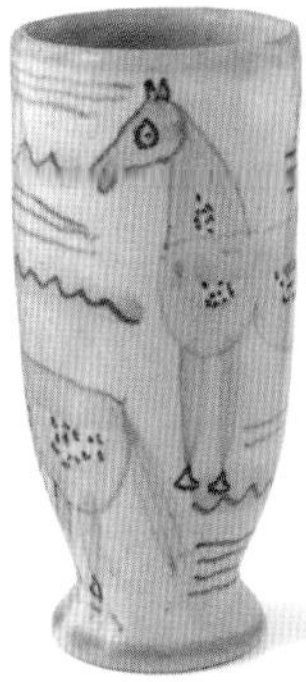

A ceramic vase by Gambone, painted with yellow horses on matt white and green ground, marked "Gambone Italy".

7.75in (19.5cm)

£500-800 **SDR**

A bottle-shaped faience vase by Gambone, painted with Cubist figures in indigo and matt white glaze, marked "Gambone Italy".

11.25in (28.5cm) high

£600-900 **SDR**

A large flaring low bowl by Gambone, painted with an abstract design in gunmetal glaze on a black, beige and gunmetal ground, signed "Gambone Italy".

17.25in (44cm) diam

£600-900 **SDR**

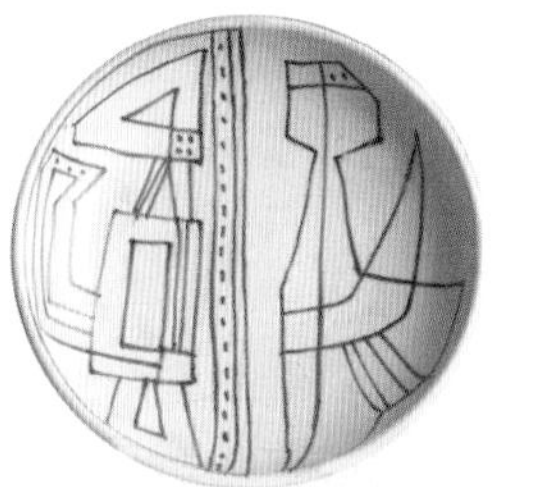

A Gambone charger, the interior decorated with two stylized figures in yellow and brown on a white ground, marked "Gambone/Italy".

9.25in (23cm) wide

£1,000-1,500 **SDR**

A charger by Gambone, with geometric pattern in bright orange, green, manganese and ivory, signed "Gambone/Italy".

9in (22.5cm) diam

£1,000-1,500 **SDR**

A figural floor vessel by Gambone, depicting a man and his dog covered in yellow, aubergine and white glazes, signed "Gambone/Italy", damaged.

33.5in (84cm) high

£1,500-2,000 **SDR**

VIVIKA & OTTO HEINO

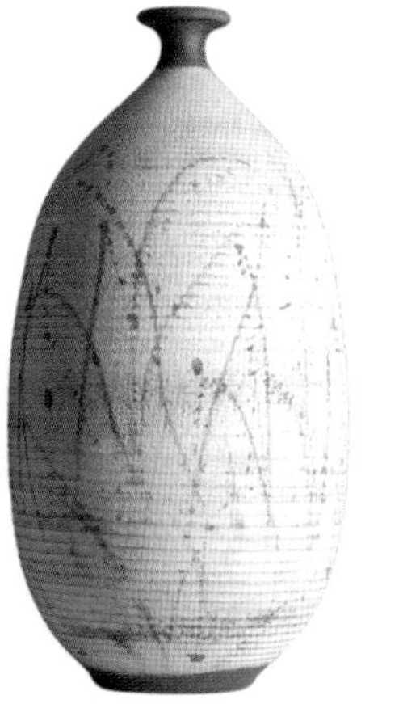

A large bottle-shaped vase by Vivika & Otto Heino, with horizontal throwing ridges and random pattern of brown on a pale ground, signed "Vivika & Otto".

20in (50cm) high

£800-1,200 **SDR**

A large faceted stoneware bowl by Vivika & Otto Heino, with dimples, decorated in sgraffito with dragonflies and plants in white on a mottled blue and ivory matte ground, incised "VIVIKA + OTTO".

13.5in (34cm) wide

£600-900 **SDR**

A large stoneware bowl by Vivika and Otto Heino, incised and moulded with stylized fish under a chocolate brown and white speckled glaze, signed "Vivika + Otto".

16.5in (42cm) diam

£700-1,000 **SDR**

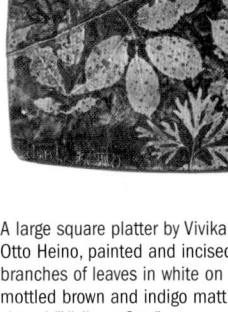

A squat ridged vessel by Vivika and Otto Heino, covered in ivory yellow and brown speckled volcanic glaze, incised "Vivika + Otto".

9in (23cm) diam

£500-800 **SDR**

A large square platter by Vivika and Otto Heino, painted and incised with branches of leaves in white on a mottled brown and indigo matt glaze, signed "Vivika + Otto".

18in (45.5cm) wide

£1,000-1,500 **SDR**

An exceptional stoneware bottle by Bernard Leach, painted with brown fish on a white ground, signed "B.L."

12in (30cm) high

£5,000-8,000 **SDR**

A flat-sided stoneware bottle by Bernard Leach, painted with a stylized pattern in rust on a matte grey quadrant, stamped "B.L." with St. Ives monogram.

7.75in (19.5cm) high

£1,800-2,200 **SDR**

A black pottery vase by Bernard Leach, with incised scratch decoration.

7.5in (19cm) high

£1,500-2,000 **JN**

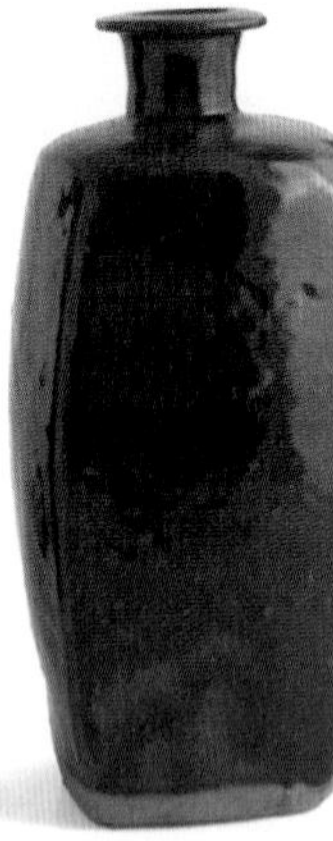

A large brown pottery vase by Bernard Leach.

15in (38cm) high

£1,800-2,200 **JN**

A porcelain stem cup by Bernard Leach, with knife-cut decoration under a pale celadon glaze, impressed "B.L.", with original paper label.

5.25in (13.5cm) high

£400-600 **SWO**

A stoneware bowl by Bernard Leach, decorated with a snail, signed "B.L.", restored.

12in (30.5cm) diam

£1,200-1,800 **SDR**

A red earthenware plate, by Bernard Leach, painted with a yellow and black pulled feather pattern, stamped "B.L.".

9.25in (23.5cm) diam

£1,000-1,500 **SDR**

A brown pottery bulbous vase by Janet Leach.

9in (23cm) high

£400-600 **JN**

A black circular pottery bowl by Janet Leach, with striped decoration.

4.5in (11.5cm) diam

£400-600 **JN**

A 'Corrida' earthenware charger, by Picasso for Madoura, decorated in wax resist with a bull fight in dead-matte gun metal glaze on a semi-matte white ground, marked "Empreinte originale de Picasso".

17in (43cm) diam

£2,200-2,800 **SDR**

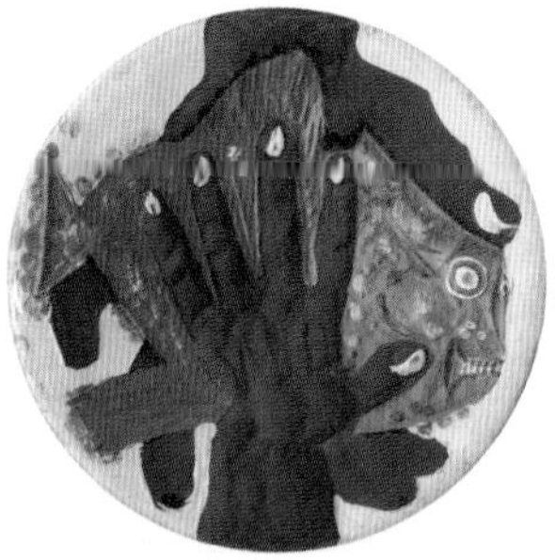

A 'Mains au Poisson' terracotta plate by Picasso for Madoura, moulded with two black hands and a fish in terracotta, green and cobalt, stamped "Empreinte Originale de Picasso/Madoura Plein Feu".

12in (30.5cm) diam

£2,200-2,800 **SDR**

A 'Visage aux Yeux Carrés' earthenware plate by Picasso for Madoura, moulded with a mask face in brown, white and turquoise, stamped "Empreinte Originale de Picasso/Madoura Plein Feu/51/100".

10in (25.5cm) diam

£3,000-4,000 **SDR**

A plate by Picasso for Madoura, moulded with a still life of flowers and fruit in brown, turquoise and yellow on a white ground, stamped "EMPREINTE ORIGINALE DE PICASSO/MADOURA PLEIN FEU".

1956 *10in (25.5cm) diam*

£1,000-1,500 **SDR**

A small faience dish by Picasso for Madoura, decorated in wax resist with a mounted figure in dead-matte black on a glossy white ground, signed "Edition/Picasso/Madoura".

6in (15cm) wide

£600-900 **SDR**

A ceramic vase by Picasso for Madoura, incised and moulded with a prancing goat in black, brown and blue on a white ground, stamped "Empreinte Originale de Picasso/Madoura Plein Feu", restored.

9in (23cm) diam

£4,000-6,000 **SDR**

A white clay pitcher by Picasso for Madoura, painted with a face in green, blue and brown on white, signed "Edition/Picasso/168/500/Madoura".

1969 *12in (30.5cm) high*

£1,500-2,000 **SDR**

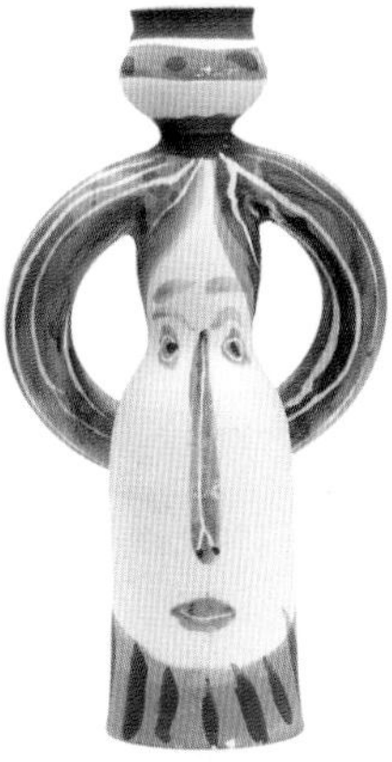

A clay figural vessel by Pablo Picasso for Madoura, depicting a peasant woman with a face painted and incised on her apron, stamped "Madoura/plein feu/D'apres Picasso".

13.75in (35cm) high

£3,000-4,000 **SDR**

A pitcher by Picasso for Madoura, decorated in wax resist with primitive faces and abstract patterns in dead-matte black on a white semi-matte ground, stamped "Edition/Picasso/ Madoura".

6in (15cm) high

£1,000-1,500 **SDR**

A circular pottery stem bowl by Lucie Rie, with black splash rim.

c1955 *4.5in (11.5cm) diam*

£600-900 **JN**

A studio pottery salad bowl by Lucie Rie and Hans Coper, with impressed seals to the base.

6in (15cm) high

£800-1,200 **GAZE**

A circular pottery bowl by Lucie Rie and Hans Coper, with brown interior.

5in (12.5cm) diam

£1,000-1,500 **JN**

A small pottery oval tapering vase by Lucie Rie.

c1955 *3.5in (9cm) high*

£500-800 **JN**

A circular pottery stem bowl by Lucie Rie, with a white ground and brown splash decoration.

c1955 *5in (12.5cm) diam*

£2,000-2,500 **JN**

EDWIN & MARY SCHEIER

An early bulbous vase by Edwin & Mary Scheier, incised with alternating stylized faces and wavy lines, against a gunmetal ground, signed "Scheier/49".

10in (25.5cm) diam

£4,000-5,000 **SDR**

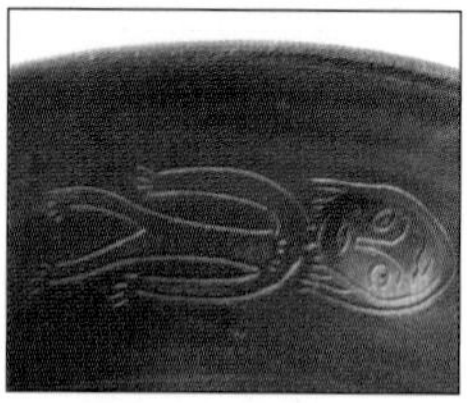

A large chalice by Edwin & Mary Scheier, incised and modelled with female figures covered in bronzed glaze on a gunmetal ground, incised "91 Scheier".

12.5in (32cm) high

£2,200-2,800 **SDR**

A chalice by Edwin & Mary Scheier, modelled and incised with whimsical female figures covered in bronze glaze, incised "Scheier".

9in (23cm) diam

£1,500-2,000 **SDR**

A coupe-shaped vase by Edwin & Mary Scheier, incised with a band of organic abstract designs in bronzed glaze on a stippled celadon glaze, incised "Scheier 1988".

The Scheiers were inspired by Central and South American pottery traditions.

1988 *9in (23cm) diam*

£1,500-2,000 **SDR**

A large bowl by Edwin & Mary Scheier, decorated in wax resist with rowers in ivory and purple matte glaze, signed "Scheier".

14.5in (37cm) diam

£2,800-3,200 **SDR**

EDWIN AND MARY SCHEIER

- Edwin and Mary Scheier met in 1937 at the Big Stone Gap Federal Art Gallery in Virginia. During the Depression they made a living touring with a hand-made puppet show.
- From 1938 the Scheiers were involved with the Federal Art Project in Tennessee, where they were able to use the pottery studio in exchange for watching over the kilns. They travelled the southern states learning about the folk pottery of the region.
- Stopping in Glade Spring, Virginia to change a tyre, the Scheiers noticed deposits of red clay in the ground. They set up a pottery shop in the town, digging their own clay straight from the earth.
- The Scheier's work soon garnered national acclaim, and they were eventually invited to teach at the University of New Hampshire (UNH).
- Their work deals with basic human themes such as birth, coupling and protection and is sometimes incised with simple line drawings by Edwin.
- After retiring from UNH in 1960 the Scheiers travelled to Mexico and eventually settled in Arizona.

A monumental footed floor vase by Edwin & Mary Scheier, embossed with faces, masks and bodies covered in a volcanic bronzed glaze against shaded matte turquoise, signed "Scheier/66".

1966 *22.5in (56cm) high*

£8,000-12,000 **SDR**

An early flaring bowl by Edwin & Mary Scheier, with a band of etched faces around the rim, over a brown to ivory mottled matte brown glaze, incised "Scheier".

c1950 *13in (33cm) diam*

£500-800 **SDR**

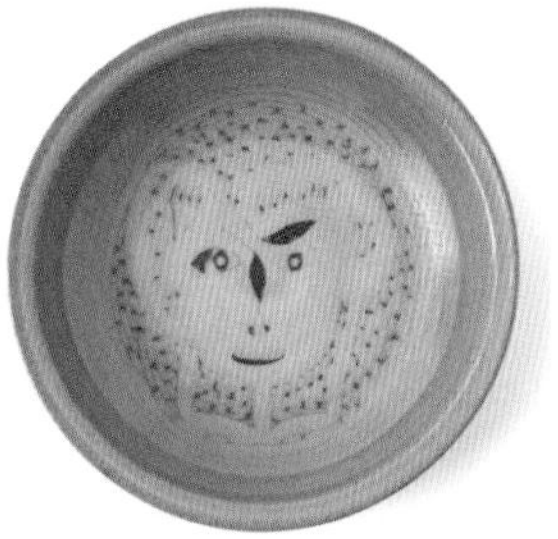

A low bowl by Edwin & Mary Scheier, decorated in wax resist with an expressive face, in ivory and lavender matte glaze, signed "Scheier".

12.75in (32.5cm) diam

£500-700 **SDR**

TOSHIKO TAKAEZU

A spherical stoneware vessel by Toshiko Takaezu, with random indigo brushstrokes on a sand and dark ground, incised "TT".

6.75in (17cm) high

£1,200-1,800 **SDR**

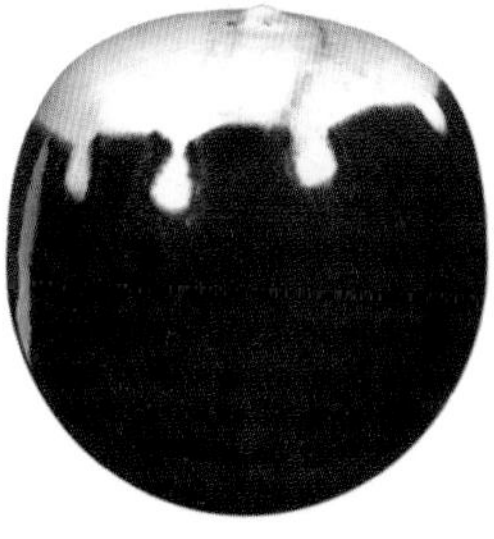

A porcelain 'Moon' pot by Toshiko Takaezu, covered in white and black crackled glossy and matte glaze, incised "TT".

5.5in (14cm) high

£800-1,200 **SDR**

A ridged stoneware vessel by Toshiko Takaezu, with a small opening, covered in a random pattern of frothy matte white glaze on a mottled white and brown ground, marked "TT".

7.25in (18.5cm) high

£1,200-1,800 **SDR**

A low bowl by Toshiko Takaezu, with random pattern in gun-metal and dead-matte white on a cobalt ground, signed "TT".

9.5in (24cm) wide

£800-1,200 **SDR**

A flaring stoneware bowl by Toshiko Takaezu, signed "TT".

14in (35.5cm) diam

£300-500 **SDR**

A tapered vase by Beatrice Wood, covered in uranium red volcanic glaze, signed "Beato".

15.5in (39cm) high

£3,500-4,500 **SDR**

A bottle-shaped bud vase by Beatrice Wood, covered in celadon, blue and purple volcanic glaze, signed "Beato".

8.5in (21.5cm) high

£800-1,200 **SDR**

A cylindrical vase by Beatrice Wood, the exterior with a black volcanic glaze, oxblood-glazed interior, signed "Beato".

9in (23cm) high

£800-1,200 **SDR**

A flaring vase by Beatrice Wood, covered in Persian blue volcanic glaze, signed "Beato".

5.25in (13.5cm) high

£1,200-1,800 **SDR**

A spherical vessel by Beatrice Wood, with a small opening, covered in blue-green mottled volcanic glaze, signed "Beato".

6in (15cm) high

£700-1,000 **SDR**

A chalice by Beatrice Wood, modelled with four couples and covered in celadon volcanic glaze, signed "Beato".

6.5in (16.5cm) high

£1,500-2,000 **SDR**

A chalice by Beatrice Wood, modelled with four figures, covered in oxblood glaze over a sand-coloured volcanic ground, signed "Beato".

9.5in (24cm) high

£2,800-3,200 **SDR**

A ceramic sculpture by Beatrice Wood, 'The Conqueror', depicting a seated female nude surrounded by four male heads, signed "Beato", restored.

9.5in (24cm) high

£2,500-3,000 **SDR**

An important sculpture by Beatrice Wood, with five door-shaped openings occupied by figures alternating between single women and embracing couples, glazed in bright cadmium yellow volcanic glaze against walls of mottled yellow, black and brick, mounted on a pine board.

60in (152.5cm) wide

£10,000-15,000 **SDR**

A partial tea set by Beatrice Wood, comprising two tea pots, a bowl, two trivets and a small footed bowl, all covered in mottled semi-matte blue glaze, signed "Beato".

largest 12in (30.5cm) wide

£1,200-1,800 **SDR**

A large sculptural clay vessel by Rudy Autio, with two flat masks surrounded by four candles and a bird's head, with iron-red finish covered in white, beige and black matte glaze, signed "Autio".

20.5in (52cm) high

£7,000-10,000 **SDR**

A gourd-shaped stoneware vessel by Clyde Burt, with rows of incised bars in yellow, amber and brown, incised "CB".

13in (32.5cm) high

£800-1,200 **SDR**

A tall tapering clay bottle by Clyde Burt, decorated in wax resist with geometric pattern in speckled slate grey glaze, incised "CB", restored.

24.25in (60.5cm) high

£800-1,200 **SDR**

A flaring stoneware vase by Clyde Burt, incised with lines and covered in indigo, white and speckled brown matte glaze, incised "CB".

6.25in (15.5cm) high

£180-220 **SDR**

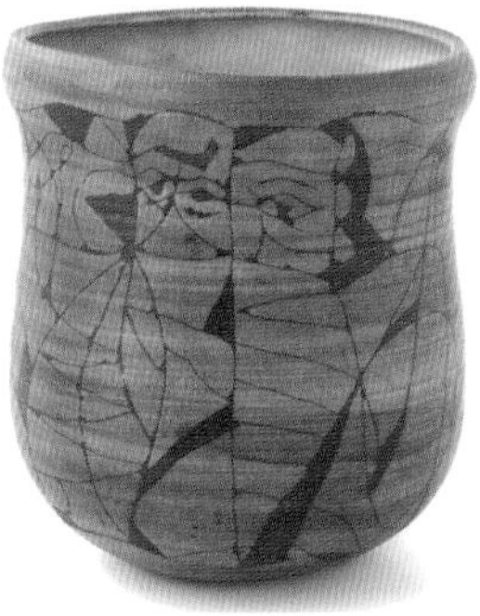

A ceramic vessel by Katherine Pao Yu Choy, decorated in wax resist with an abstract pattern in matte blue on a dark brown ground.

7.5in (19cm) high

£400-600 **SDR**

A red terracotta charger designed by Jean Cocteau, painted with a female profile on a blue and white striped ground, signed and dated with manufacturer's marks.

14in (35.5cm) diam

£1,500-2,000 **SDR**

A ceramic charger by Jean Cocteau, painted with an abstract seaside pattern in black, white and red, signed and dated with manufacturer's marks.

1958 *14in (35.5cm) diam*

£1,200-1,800 **SDR**

A ceramic charger designed by Jean Cocteau, painted in bright yellow and red glazes with a man chasing a woman with a hose, signed and dated with manufacturer's marks.

1958 *12in (30.5cm) diam*

£1,000-1,500 **SDR**

A studio pottery oviform vase by Joanna Constantinides, decorated with a mottled brown and cream glaze, impressed mark.

12.5in (32cm) high

£600-900 **DN**

A round studio pottery dish by Joanna Constantinides, decorated in slip with a stylized sun, impressed mark.

11.75in (30cm) diam

£200-300 **DN**

A large stoneware covered vessel by Ken Ferguson, with incisions around the shoulder, covered in matte mustard and speckled brown glaze, stamped "F".

13in (33cm) high

£700-1,000 **SDR**

An octagonal bulbous vase by Sijigeyosiji Jchino.

5.5in (14cm) high

£180-220 **JN**

A black pottery vase by Sijigeyosiji Jchino.

8in (20.5cm) high

£180-220 **JN**

A ceramic light sconce by Georges Jouve, shaped as a cockerel covered in green majolica glaze, unmarked, small nicks to base.

16.75in (42.5cm) high

£2,800-3,200 **SDR**

A slab-moulded bottle vase by Kanjiro Kawai, with rare sculpted base, decorated in hand-painted underglaze with stylized blossom.

c1940 *9in (22.5cm) high*

£3,000-4,000 **SDR**

A set of six plates by El Lissitzky, with a Constructivist pattern in bright red on dead-matte black, stamped "2864".

7.5in (19cm) diam

£1,200-1,800 **SDR**

A hemispherical stoneware bowl by J. Moller Peterson, covered in light yellow mottled glaze, marked with cipher.

9in (22.5cm) diam

£150-200 **SDR**

A slab-moulded stoneware vase by Kanjiro Kawai, with textured body and underglaze abstract decoration in green, orange, black and brown, unmarked.

c1960 *9in (22.5cm) high*

£5,000-8,000 **SDR**

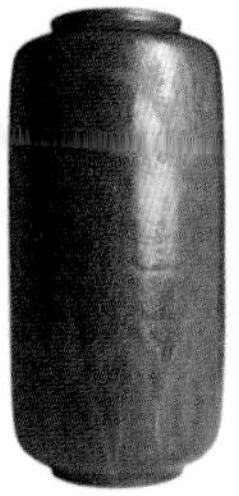

A cylindrical vase by Natzler, covered in a copper microcrystalline glaze with lustred highlights, over a dark brown ground, signed "Natzler" in ink, with typed label "H733".

11in (27.5cm) high

£6,000-9,000 **SDR**

Part of a 17-piece ceramic tea set by Natzler, comprising six cups and saucers, teapot, creamer, sugar bowl, slop bowl and trivet, with black crystalline glaze, signed "Natzler 2-9-31", cups stamped "GON".

teapot 7in (18cm) high

£6,000-9,000 set **SDR**

A large spherical vessel by Polia Pillin, with closed-in rim covered in a glossy sea-green glaze with blue and umber shadings, signed "W+P Pillin".

13in (32.5cm) wide

£800-1,200 **SDR**

A monumental bulbous vase by Gertrude & Otto Natzler, with cupped rim, covered in a blue-green striated volcanic glaze, signed "Natzler" with typed label "K874".

17.5in (44.5cm) high

£25,000-30,000 **SDR**

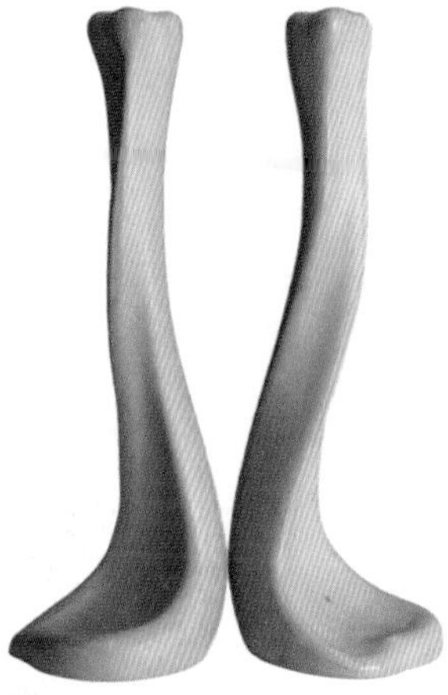

A pair of tall organic terracotta candlesticks by Elsa Peretti for Tiffany & Co., stamped "E. Peretti for Tiffany/Made in Italy".

14.25in (35.5cm) high

£200-300 **SDR**

A spherical vase by Polia Pillin, painted with circus performers on horseback in black, white and brown, signed "Pillin".

8.75in (22cm) high

£600-900 **SDR**

A square charger by Polia Pillin, painted with a woman playing the lute and a child holding a bird, signed "Pillin".

11in (28cm) high

£1,200-1,800 **SDR**

A flaring and footed transfer-decorated cup by Gio Ponti for Richard Ginori, decorated with mounted sportsmen, stamped "Made in Italy, Richard Ginori".

5.5in (14cm) high

£1,500-2,000 **SDR**

A spherical vase by Gio Ponti for Richard Ginori, painted with a stylized bouquet of purple flowers and butterflies on a brown ground, with cipher and marks.

c1935 *11in (28cm) high*

£3,500-4,500 **SDR**

A faience charger by Henry Varnum Poor, decorated in sgraffito with a seated female in yellows, greens and brown on a white ground, signed and dated.

1947 *12.75in (32cm) diam*

£1,200-1,800 **SDR**

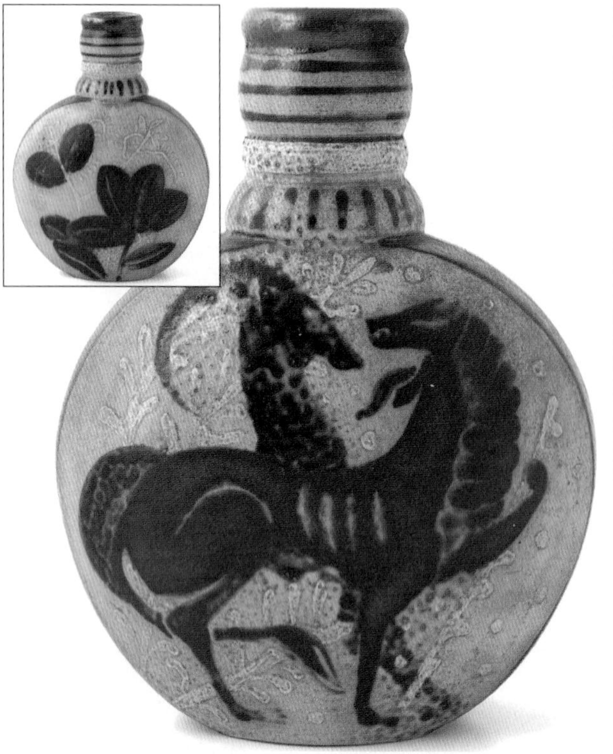

A stoneware bottle-shaped vase by Primavera, painted with a horse and antelope in dark brown and indigo on beige ground, signed "Primavera/France".

12.75in (32.5cm) high

£1,000-1,500 **SDR**

A wood-fired bottle-shaped vessel by Paul Soldner, with random painted and incised decoration in brown and blue on a white and brown volcanic ground, signed "Soldner".

8.5in (21.5cm) high

£280-320 **SDR**

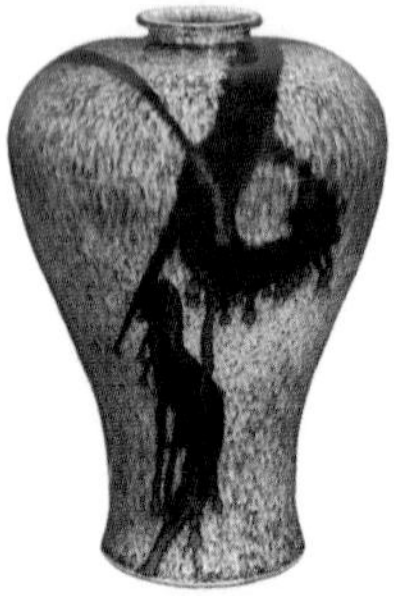

A large baluster vase by Brother Thomas, in dark brown and copper crystalline glaze on a speckled ground, with random strokes, incised "Val Benedictine Monks, Weston, VT".

13.5in (34.5cm) high

£1,200-1,800 **SDR**

A 'Love Plaque' by Troika Pottery, moulded in low relief with lovers in a geometric setting, glazed in shades of blue and red on a white ground, painted "Troika, St Ives", artist cipher.

14.75in (37cm) wide

£1,500-2,000 **WW**

An art pottery bowl by Rima Schulkind , with a cream glaze.

11in (28cm) diam

£350-450 **FRE**

A stoneware centrepiece bowl by David Shaner, covered in a fine matte green and russett mottled glaze, signed "Shaner".

12.25in (30.5cm) wide

£280-320 **SDR**

A large raku charger by Paul Soldner, carved and hand-built of white clay and covered in polychrome matte glazes over an image of a fossilized fish, incised "Soldner".

Soldner was a contemporary of Peter Voulkos.

20in (50cm) diam

£1,200-1,800 **SDR**

A six-piece ceramic totem by Ettore Sottsass for Memphis, with bright polychrome glazes, signed in black ink "Sottsass Flavia Montelupo" and hand-signed in pen "PA/E8 Ettore Sottsass Primo".

In 1965 Ettore Sottsass designed his first Pop Art-inspired ceramic totems, calling them his 'crazy things'. Unapologetically bold and colourful, these objects continue to be sought after by postmodern art and design enthusiasts.

£5,000-6,000 **SDR**

PETER VOULKOS

- Peter Voulkos (1924-2002) was a native of Montana, born in 1924 to Greek migrant parents. He was trained at the California College of Arts and Crafts.
- Along with fellow American ceramicists such as Paul Soldner, Voulkos was a key player in the American Clay Revolution - an artistic movement that developed the status of pottery in America from a craft to a fine art.
- His career has many distinct phases, from early functional pottery through colourful clay work in the 1960s to the wood-fired pieces he produced from c1980.
- Voulkos is best known for his ceramic plates, ice buckets and sculptural 'stacks'. His work is characterized by broken, torn and crudely repaired forms, most frequently in earthy brown tones.
- In the course of his career Voulkos received many awards and citations, including no less than 5 honourary doctorates. He died in Ohio in 2002.

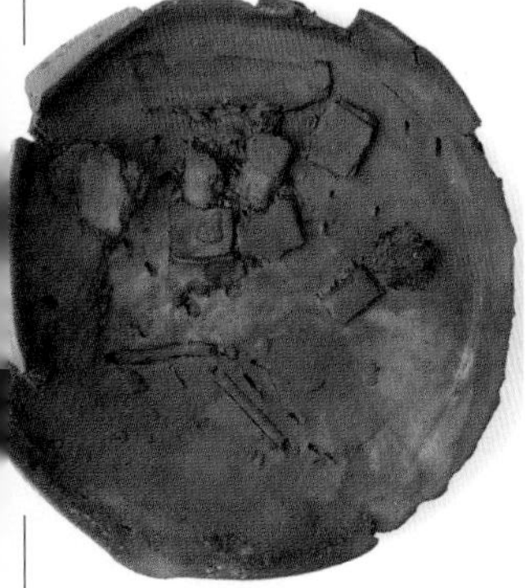

A large charger by Peter Voulkos, with torn rim and applied pieces of clay in an iron-red finish, signed "Voulkos 95".

1995 *21in (53.5cm) wide*

£8,000-12,000 **SDR**

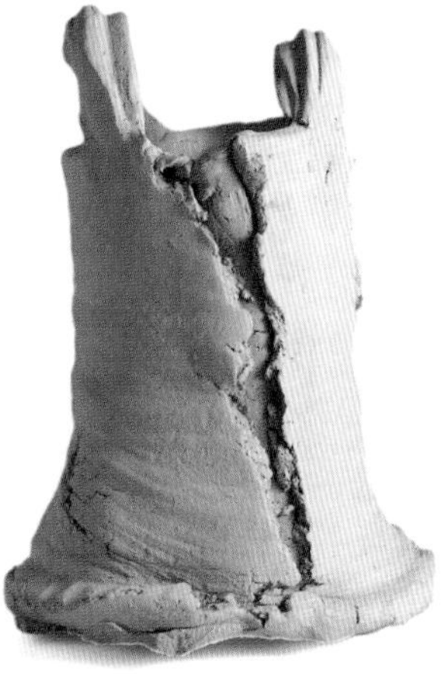

A hand-built two-handled vessel by Peter Voulkos, with horizontal ridges and filled-in tear, unmarked.

14in (35cm) high

£10,000-12,000 **SDR**

A tall brown stoneware totemic vessel by Peter Voulkos, with tears, gouges and incised lines, unmarked.

27.25in (68cm) high

£18,000-22,000 **SDR**

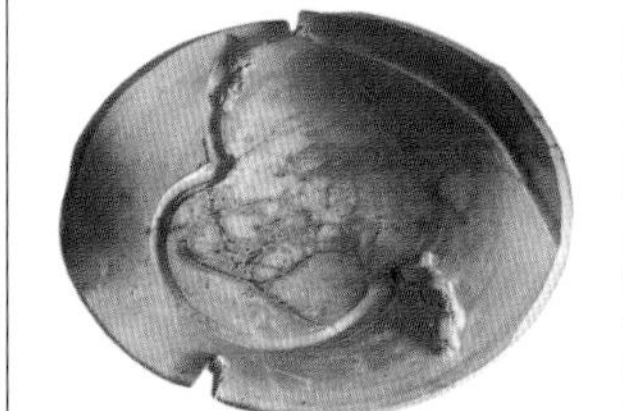

A large stoneware charger by Maria Woo, with tears, incisions and a random pattern in iron oxide and brown, signed "M. Woo".

19.5in (49cm) high

£1,500-2,000 **SDR**

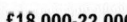

A pillow-shaped pitcher by Betty Woodman, of white clay covered in green, magnesium, yellow and gunmetal majolica glazes, unmarked.

20in (51cm) wide

£4,000-5,000 **SDR**

A tall porcelain vessel by Betty Woodman, with two handles, sponge-painted in green and light blue on a white ground, unmarked.

22in (56cm) high

£800-1,200 **SDR**

A large two-handled stoneware jar, with decorative veining, illegible mark.

14.5in (36cm) wide

£120-180 **SDR**

A bulbous stoneware vase by Robert Zerlin, with random decoration in seafoam green against a violet matte ground, signed "Zerlin".

6.75in (17cm) high

£120-180 **SDR**

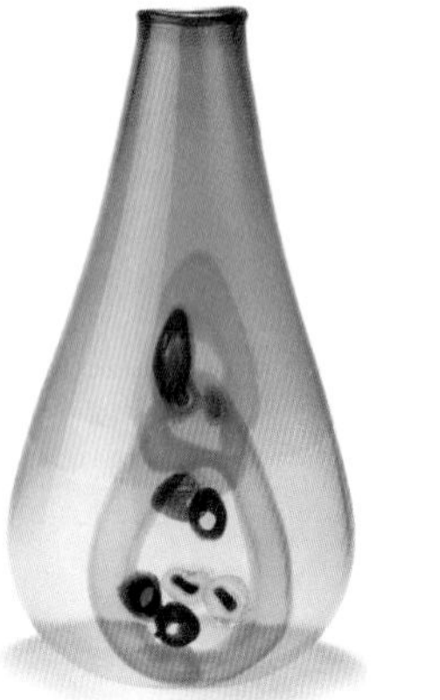

A glass vase by Anzolo Fuga for Arte Vetraria Muranese, with shades of pink and turquoise, decorated with abstract design of blue bands and coloured murrines.

c1960 *17in (42.5cm) high*

£600-900 **VZ**

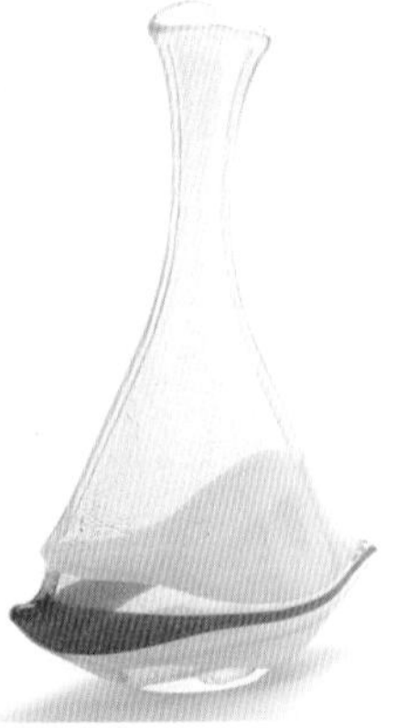

A glass vase by Anzolo Fuga for Arte Vetraria Muranese, with gold inclusions and red and white glass strings, unsigned.

c1955 *19in (47.5cm) high*

£2,800-3,200 **HERR**

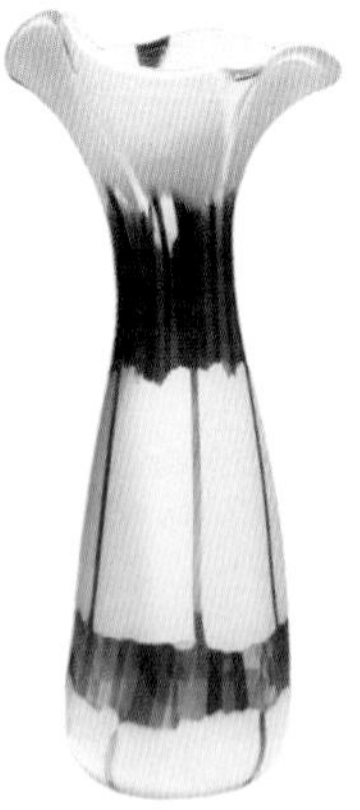

A fine and large patchwork vase by Anzolo Fuga for Arte Vetraria Muranese, with floriform rim and blue, green, yellow and red canes on a lattimo ground, unmarked.

18.75in (47cm) high

£2,800-3,200 **SDR**

A large patchwork vase by Anzolo Fuga for Arte Vetraria Muranese, of elongated gourd-shaped form with blue, red, yellow and green canes on a lattimo ground, unmarked.

16.75in (42cm) high

£2,500-3,000 **SDR**

A large and rare glass bottle by Anzolo Fuga for Arte Vetraria Muranese, with narrow opening, in pink with central band of large free-floating murrines and lavender ribbon.

17in (42.5cm) high

£5,000-6,000 **SDR**

A glass vase by Giorgio Ferro for Arte Vetraria Muranese, thick purple-coloured iridescent glass with two circular apertures.

c1955 *12.75in (32cm) high*

£1,000-1,500 **VZ**

An 'anse volanti' glass vase by Giorgio Ferro for Arte Vetraria Muranese, thick iridescent crimson-coloured glass with handle, unsigned.

c1950 *11.5in (28.5cm) high*

£1,000-1,500 **HERR**

A bowl-shaped glass vase by Aldo Nason for Arte Vetraria Muranese, cased clear and green glass with dense gold particle inclusions.

c1970 *5.4in (13.5cm)*

£320-380 **VZ**

A round glass vase by Giulio Radi for Arte Vetraria Muranese, with inverted rim, amber with light amber dots and gold foil inclusions.

c1950 *5.25in (13cm) high*

£1,000-1,500 **VZ**

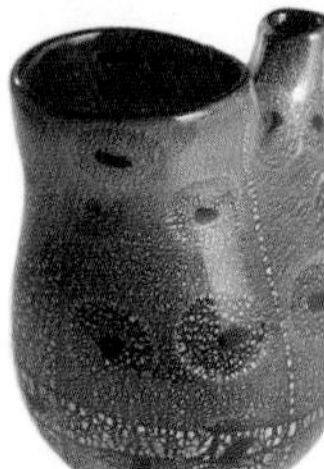

An asymmetric glass vessel by Giulio Radi for Arte Vetraria Muranese, with two openings, in ruby glass with silver foil decoration, unmarked.

7.25in (18cm) high

£1,500-2,000 **SDR**

An 'Athena Cattedrale' bulbous glass vase by Ercole Barovier for Barovier & Toso, with olive opaline and blue lozenge-shaped murrines on a clear ground, unmarked.

11in (28cm) high

£5,000-6,000 **SDR**

An 'Efeso' vase by Ercole Barovier for Barovier & Toso, with blue overlay and air bubble inclusions, signed "Barovier & Toso Milano".

1964 *13.5in (34cm) high*

£1,000-1,500 **HERR**

A 'Graffito Barbarico' ovoid glass vase by Ercole Barovier for Barovier & Toso, with festoon pattern in teal on clear ground, unmarked.

11.5in (29cm) high

£800-1,200 **SDR**

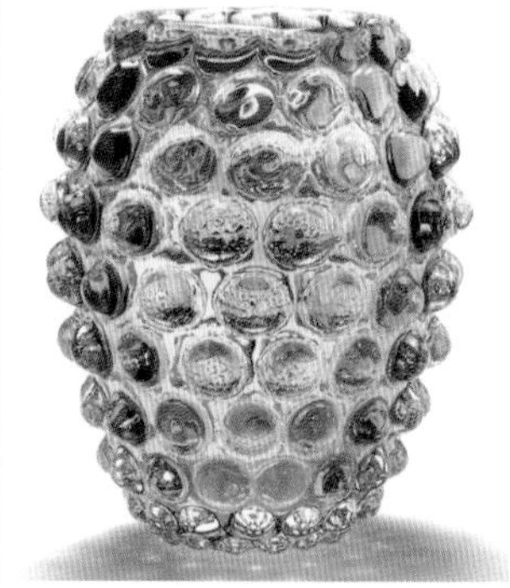

A tall 'Lenti' vase by Ercole Barovier for Barovier & Toso, amber cased glass with hobnail relief decoration, unmarked.

c1940 *6.2in (15.5cm) high*

£120-180 **VZ**

A glass decanter by Christian Dior and Ercole Barovier for Barovier & Toso with a tartan pattern, short neck and blue glass stopper, signed "Christian Dior".

c1965 *9.75in (24.5cm) high*

£3,500-4,500 **HERR**

An 'Intarsia' hemispherical glass bowl by Ercole Barovier for Barovier & Toso, with red triangular tesserae on a smoky glass ground, unmarked.

9.75in (24cm) high

£800-1,200 **SDR**

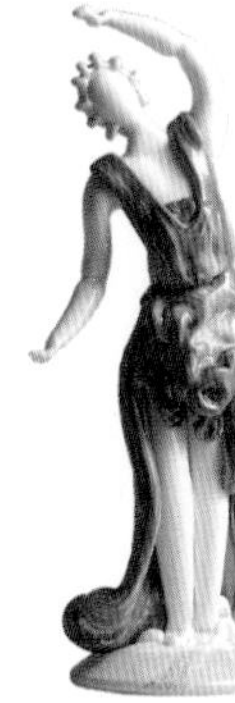

A 'Dancing Woman' figure by Ercole Barovier, white lattimo glass with draped garment in opaque orange and white sprayed with gold, unmarked.

11in (27.5cm) high

£1,500-2,000 **SDR**

A smoky glass vase by Angelo Barovier for Barovier & Co., consisting of three stacked cylinders, the middle one of transparent glass with murrines, unmarked.

c1965 *10in (25.5cm) high*

£600-900 **HERR**

A 'Canne Policrome' tear-shaped glass bottle by Barovier & Toso, lacks stopper, unmarked.

10.75in (27.5cm) high

£350-450 **SDR**

A glass vase by Barovier & Co., with light-green inclusions and air bubbles, of conical shape on a circular stand with four semi-circular bulges, unsigned.

c1935 *6.75in (17cm) high*

£700-1,000 **HERR**

A vase by Barovier & Toso, smoky brown glass of teardrop shape on an oval stand, with triple disc handles and vertical ribbing with aventurine and white bands.

c1960 *11in (28cm) high*

£320-380 **VZ**

A tumbler vase by Antonio da Ros for Vetraria Gino Cenedese, cased clear glass with purplish-black and orange murrines.

c1960 *7in (17.5cm) high*

£4,000-6,000 **VZ**

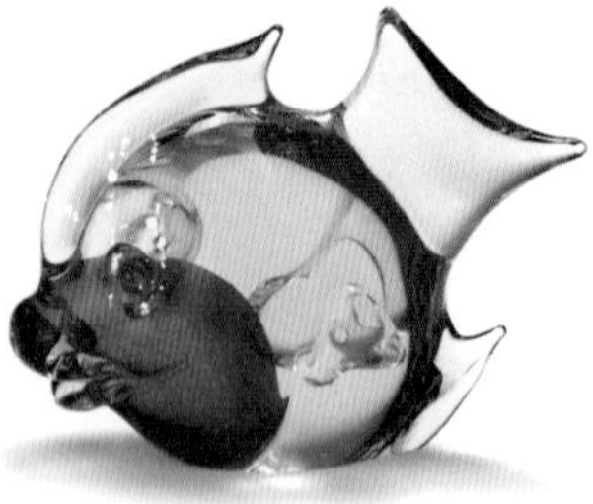

A glass fish by Antonio da Ros for Vetraria Gino Cenedese, purplish-pink glass with pink-red inclusions.

c1960 *3.5in (8.5cm) long*

£150-200 **VZ**

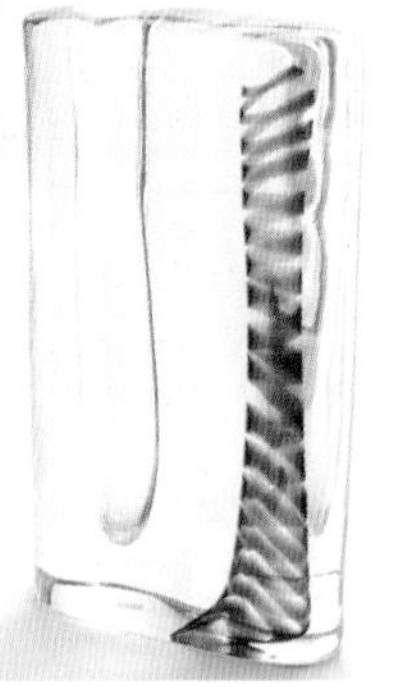

A 'Momento' glass vase by Antonio da Ros for Vetraria Gino Cenedese, clear glass block with brown spiral inclusion, and deep opening to one side.

c1960 *10.75in (27cm) high*

£1,800-2,200 **HERR**

A 'D' vase by Antonio da Ros for Vetraria Gino Cenedese, cased dark orange and light yellow flashed glass.

c1960 *10.25in (26cm)*

£1,500-2,000 **VZ**

A 'Coppa olandese' vase by Antonio da Ros for Vetraria Gino Cenedese, cased dark-blue and flashed leaf-green glass.

c1960 *12in (30.5cm) long*

£1,800-2,200 **VZ**

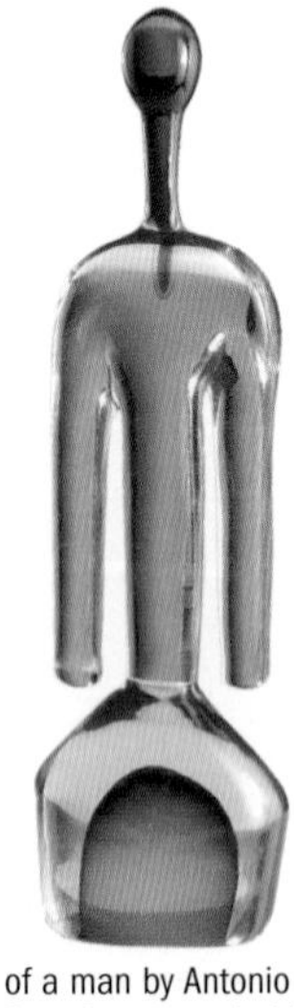

A figure of a man by Antonio da Ros for Vetraria Gino Cenedese, in blue, green and clear sommerso glass, unmarked.

13.25in (33cm) high

£600-900 **SDR**

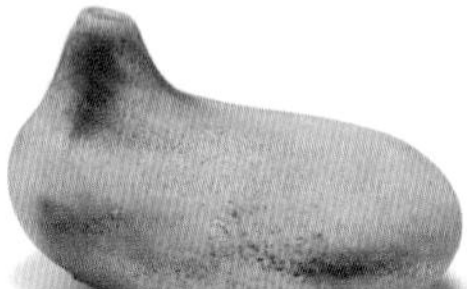

An amorphous vase by Antonio da Ros for Cenedese, clear glass with powder inclusions in turquoise, dark-brown and ochre, etched "Cenedese".

c1980 *8.75in (22cm) long*

£280-320 **VZ**

A wide bowl by Vetraria Gino Cenedese, cased honey-coloured and cherry red-glass, etched "Cenedese".

c1970 *8in (20.5cm) diam*

£800-1,200 **VZ**

A glass flowering cactus by Vetraria Gino Cenedese, light-green glass with diamond-cut pattern and two red flowers, with applied amber glass stand.

c1960 *9.5in (24cm) high*

£320-380 **VZ**

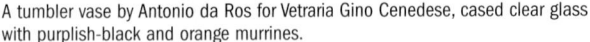

A figure of a man by Vetraria Gino Cenedese, in lavender glass, decorated with green and black features, etched "Cenedese/Murano".

11.25in (28cm) high

£500-800 **SDR**

AURELIANO TOSO

- The Aureliano Toso glassworks was established in 1938 and has received a number of awards for the high quality of its wares.
- Among the most sought-after wares by the Aureliano Toso works are those designed by Dino Martens, a painter who had a long-lived and fruitful association with the company.
- From the mid-1940s to the mid-1960s Martens produced dozens of designs for Aureliano Toso including the 'Oriente' range, which is admired for its combination of decorative techniques.
- Other highly collectable lines by Martens include his richly coloured transparent 'Eldorado' glass and his pastel 'Zanfirico' range, with intricate webbed designs.
- Reproductions of Dino Martens' designs for Aureliano Toso are frequently found, so it is always important to compare a piece with unknown provenance against a known original example. Colour, size and weight can indicate whether it is genuine or not.
- Aureliano Toso continues to operate today, although is now mostly concerned with manufacturing glass for lighting.

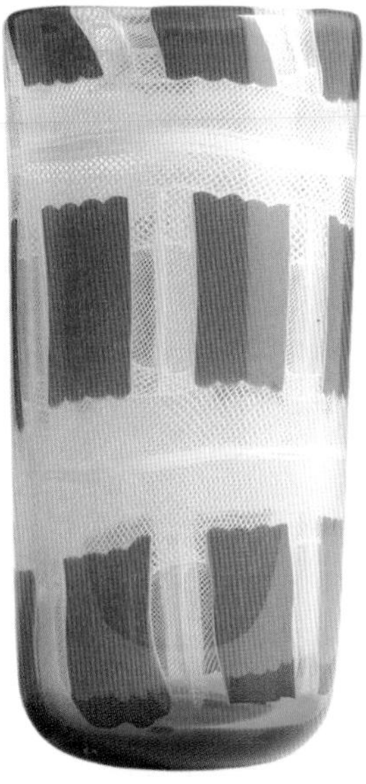

A large cylindrical glass vase by Dino Martens, with white zanfirico rods alternating with rectangular red shapes, shading to dark green at base, unmarked.

12.75in (32.5cm) high

£3,500-4,500 **SDR**

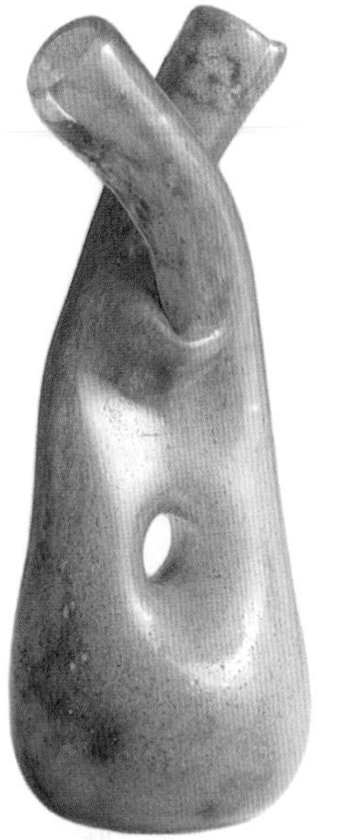

A double-spouted glass vessel by Dino Martens for Aureliano Toso, with hole and melted blue powders, unmarked.

10.75in (27cm) high

£700-1,000 **SDR**

An 'Oriente' jug by Dino Martens for Aureliano Toso, of teardrop shape with narrow inclined neck and loop handle, clear glass with large powder inclusions, spiral and lattice decoration and large murrine.

c1955 *13in (32.5cm) high*

£4,000-6,000 **VZ**

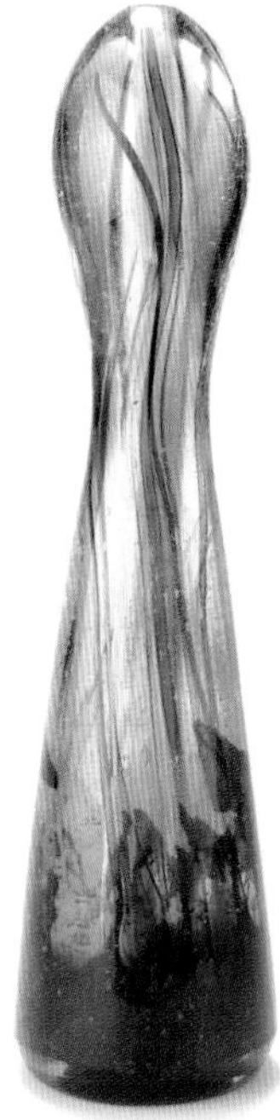

A conical lamp base by Dino Martens for Aureliano Toso, with large green and yellow inclusions, melted oxides, air bubble inclusions and red, green and yellow bands.

c1955 *14.25in (36cm) high*

£800-1,200 **VZ**

A circular bowl by Dino Martens for Aureliano Toso, clear glass with cased opaque-white and dark purple bands spiralling from the centre.

c1955 *7.5in (19cm) diam*

£300-500 **VZ**

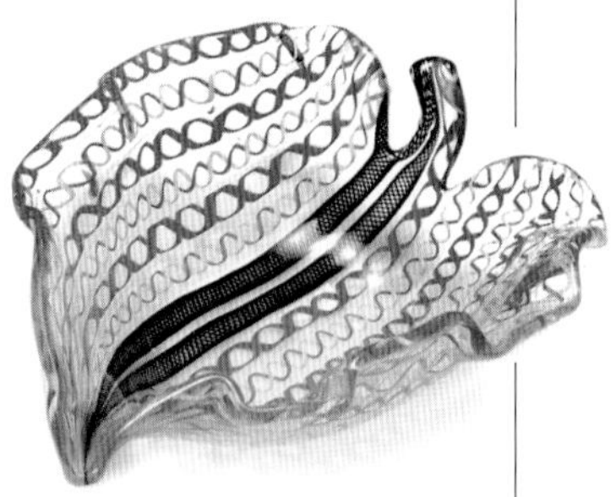

A glass leaf bowl by Dino Martens for Aureliano Toso, clear glass with alternating twisted bands of orange and yellow with a central purple spiral thread.

c1955 *7.5in (19cm) long*

£1,500-2,000 **VZ**

A 'Pezzato' vase by Fulvio Bianconi for Venini, with patchwork of red, blue and green tesserae on a clear glass base, unmarked.

9.25in (23cm) high

£2,200-2,800 **SDR**

A 'Spicchi' pear-shaped glass vase by Fulvio Bianconi for Venini, with vertical panels in clear, yellow, grey and aubergine glass, unmarked.

8.75in (22cm) high

£1,500-2,000 **SDR**

A large thick-walled three-sided vase by Fulvio Bianconi for Venini, with coloured bands cased in clear glass, etched "Venini/Fulvio Bianconi/1992-307".

1992 *12.25in (30.5cm) high*

£1,200-1,800 **SDR**

An 'Arlecchino' figure by Fulvio Bianconi for Venini, with pezzato costume in red, green, blue and clear glass and lattimo details, marked "PV1".

12.5in (31cm) high

£2,200-2,800 **SDR**

A cockerel figure by Fulvio Bianconi for Venini, in lattimo glass with applied polychrome details, on a black base, stamped "Venini/Murano/Italia", restored.

8.5in (21cm) wide

£1,500-2,000 **SDR**

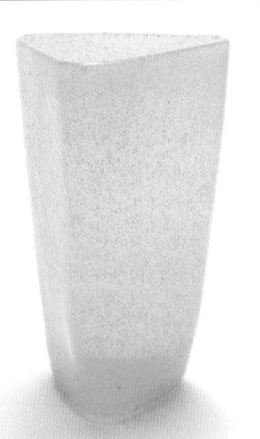

A 'Pulegoso' glass vase by Carlo Scarpa for Venini, with air bubble inclusions, tripod base and rounded corners, signed "Venini Murano".

c1935 *8.75in (22cm) high*

£2,000-2,500 **HERR**

A reissued 'Tessuto' bulbous glass vase by Carlo Scarpa for Venini, with cupped rim, composed of red, white and black fused glass canes, etched "Venini/Italia/84".

1984 *8.5in (21.5cm) high*

£350-450 **SDR**

A glass pillow vase by Carlo Scarpa for Venini, with red overlay and diagonal air bubble inclusions, signed "Venini Murano".

c1955 *7.5in (19cm) high*

£1,200-1,800 **HERR**

A glass vase by Carlo Scarpa for Venini, with diagonal canes in orange and white, signed "Venini Murano".

5.75in (14.5cm) high

£800-1,200 **HERR**

An 'Occhi' glass vase by Tobia Scarpa for Venini, with yellow and olive-brown glass murrines in a checker-board pattern, unmarked.

1960 *13.5in (33.5cm) high*

£1,200-1,800 **HERR**

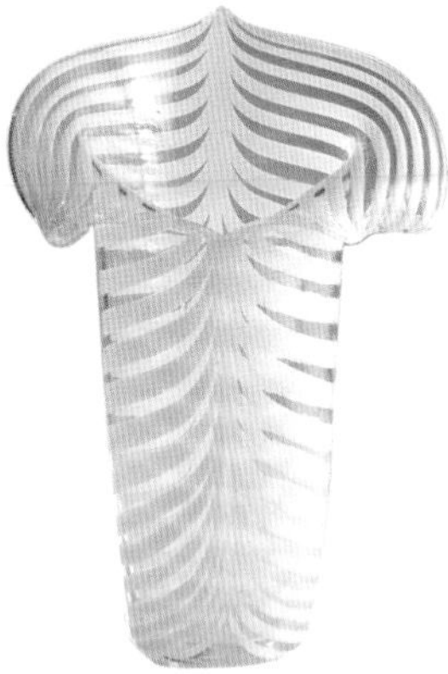

A large 'Calla' glass vase by Tyra Lundgren for Venini, with white fenicio pattern on clear ground, acid-etched stamp "Venini/Murano/Made in Italy".

12.5in (31cm) high

£600-900 **SDR**

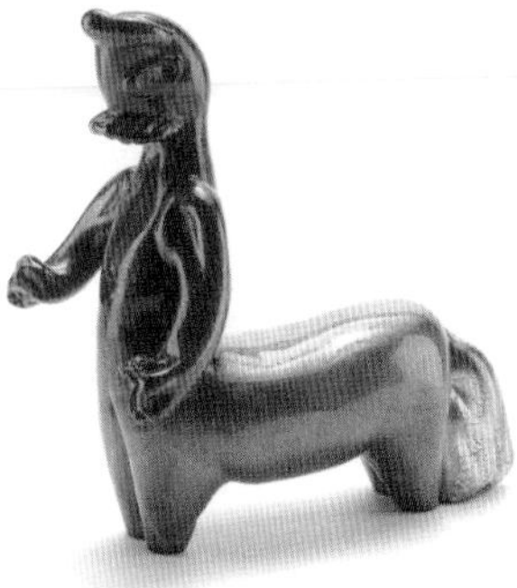

A glass 'Centauro' figure by Mario Romano for Venini, with red and white underlays and gold foil inclusions, signed "Venini Murano".

c1950 *8in (20cm) long*

£1,500-2,000 **HERR**

A cylindrical glass vase by Thomas Stearns for Venini, with spiral decoration in dark red on an orange ground, over a marbleized black base, with paper label.

11in (27.5cm) high

£2,800-3,200 **SDR**

A 'Clessidre' glass hourglass vessel by Paolo Venini for Venini, green and blue blown glass, marked "Venini Murano Italia".

7.5in (19cm) high

£500-600 **SDR**

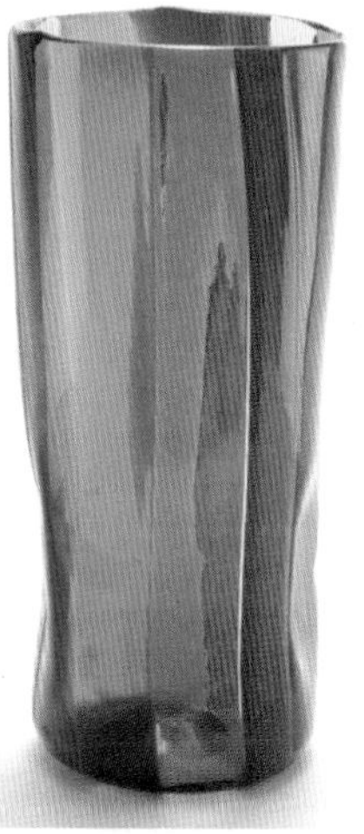

An 'a fasce verticali' cylindrical glass vase by Venini, with vertical amber, blue, red and green glass bands, marked "Venini Murano".

c1950 *9.5in (23.5cm) high*

£1,800-2,200 **HERR**

An 'Inciso' flaring bowl by Venini, of olive green sommerso glass, with circular stamp mark, "Venini Murano".

12in (30cm) wide

£800-1,200 **SDR**

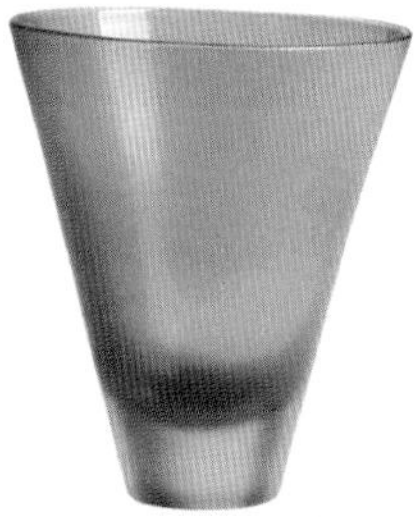

An 'Inciso' flaring vase by Venini, of amber sommerso glass, stamped "Venini Murano".

6.5in (16cm) high

£500-800 **SDR**

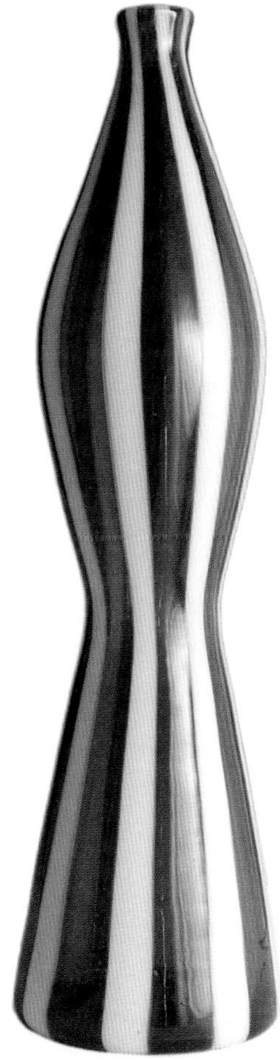

A tall corseted glass vase by Venini, composed of black and white canes, with paper label, marked "658".

16.25in (40.5cm) high

£1,800-2,200 **SDR**

A Harlequin figure by Venini, of white and clear glass canes with applied black details, unmarked.

12.75in (32.5cm) high

£800-1,200 **SDR**

VISTOSI

- The Vistosi dynasty has been important to the glass industry on Murano for centuries – Zuanne Geronimo Gazzabin purchased a furnace there in 1640, long before the family name was changed to Vistosi.
- Guglielmo Vistosi founded the modern Vistosi factory in 1945, during the renaissance of Murano's glass industry that followed a hiatus of more than 100 years.
- Vistosi looked to avant-garde artists and northern European designers for inspiration and the company was among the first Murano factories to develop a distinctive brand.
- Since the 1960s leading artists and architects have worked with Vistosi to develop the company's brand, including Etorre Sottsass, Vico Magistretti and Peter Pelzel.
- As well as architectural glass, Vistosi is known for more playful pieces such as Alessandro Pianon's charming glass birds with applied iron feet.
- Vistosi has traditionally been associated with fine glass lighting as well as art glass. Glass is still produced under the Vistosi name today.

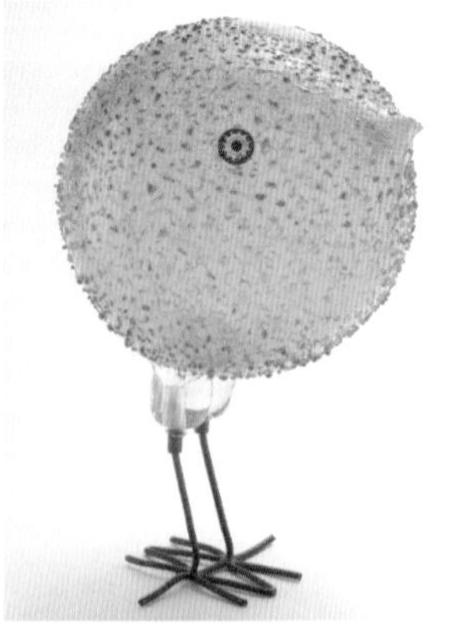

A 'Pulcino' glass bird by Alessandro Pianon for Vetraria Vistosi, orange overlaid glass with copper legs, hammered martelé surface.

1962 *8.75in (22cm) high*

£800-1,200 **HERR**

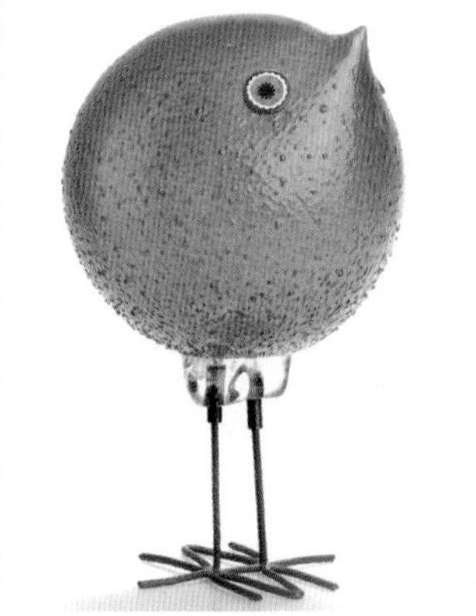

A figure of a bird by Alessandro Pianon for Vetraria Vistosi, orange flashed glass with orange melts, with murrine eyes and hammered martelé surface.

c1960 *8.5in (21.5cm) high*

£1,500-2,000 **VZ**

A glass bird by Alessandro Pianon for Vistosi, with copper legs.

1962 *10.5in (26.5cm) high*

£1,500-2,000 **WW**

A tall glass bottle by Peter Pelzel for Vistosi, with bands of black and cobalt murrines on a blue ground, unmarked.

16in (40.5cm) high

£500-800 **SDR**

A glass bird by Alessandro Pianon for Vetraria Vistosi, turquoise flashed glass with distorted murrine decoration in blue and red, the surface slightly hammered.

c1960 *12.5in (31cm) high*

£1,800-2,200 **VZ**

A limited-edition 'Basilica' sculptural glass vase by Ettore Sottsass for Vistosi, black and dark green glass, etched "E. Sottsass/Vistosi/77" and numbered "31/250".

1977 *9.25in (23.5cm) high*

£600-900 **SDR**

A limited-edition fruit bowl by Ettore Sottsass for Vistosi, of transparent green and opaque white glass, etched "E. Sottsass/Vistosi/77" and numbered "69/250".

1977 *12.5in (32cm) wide*

£600-900 **SDR**

A rare 'Volcano' block glass sculpture by Alfredo Barbini, with four sommerso and battuto craters on a light topaz and clear ground, acid-etched "A.Barbini".

13.75in (35cm) high

£2,000-2,500 **SDR**

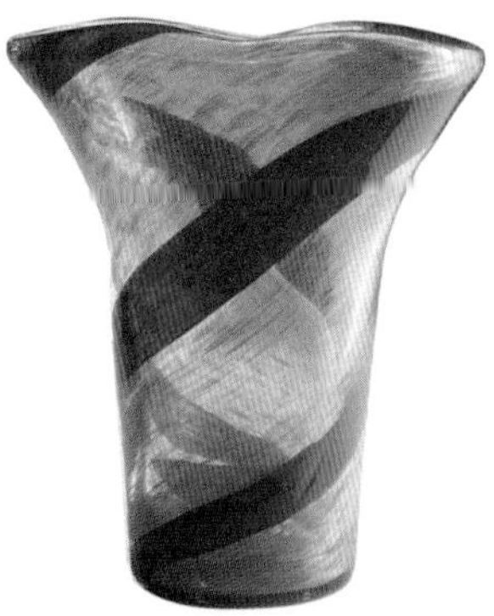

A flaring pillow vase by Fratelli Toso, in aventurine glass with broad orange bands, unmarked.

11in (28cm) high

£350-450 **SDR**

A 'Sassi' glass vase by Luciano Gaspari for Salviati, with small opening and applied bands of black, teal, cobalt, and light grey glass, etched "Salviati/Designer/L. Gaspari".

10.5in (26cm) high

£600-900 **SDR**

A pair of cased glass wall sconces by A.V. Mazzega, in black and white, with A.V. Mazzega and Vetri Murano labels.

14in (35cm) wide

£400-600 **SDR**

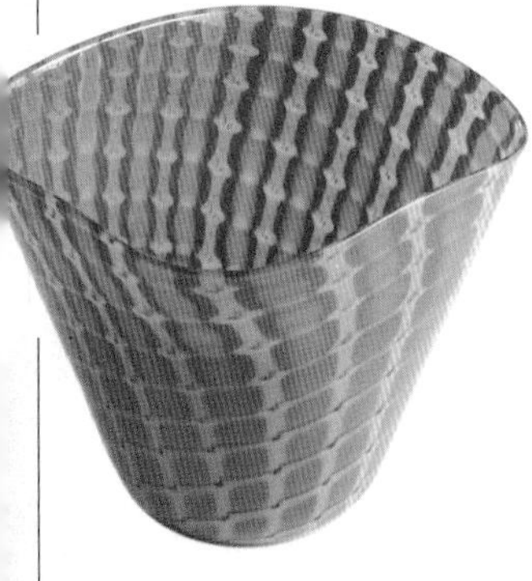

A 'Losanghe' flaring glass vase by Archimede Seguso, with lattice pattern in red, peach, and ivory with brown highlights, unmarked.

8.25in (21cm) high

£700-1,000 **SDR**

A 'Persian Series' five-piece blown glass ensemble by Dale Chihuly, in orange and yellow with blue lips, etched signature and date.

1989 25in (63.5cm) long

£10,000-12,000 **ISA**

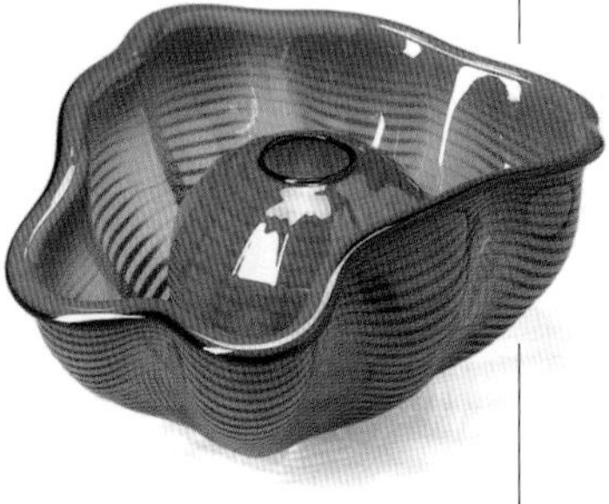

A set of two 'Seaforms' nesting glass vessels by Dale Chihuly, with red bodies and black lip wraps.

4.5in (11.5cm) high

£2,000-2,500 **SK**

A freeform basket by Dale Chihuly, in cobalt blue glass with cadmium red lip wrap, complete with plexiglass presentation box, signed "Chihuly".

1994 7in (17.5cm) high

£2,200-2,800 **SDR**

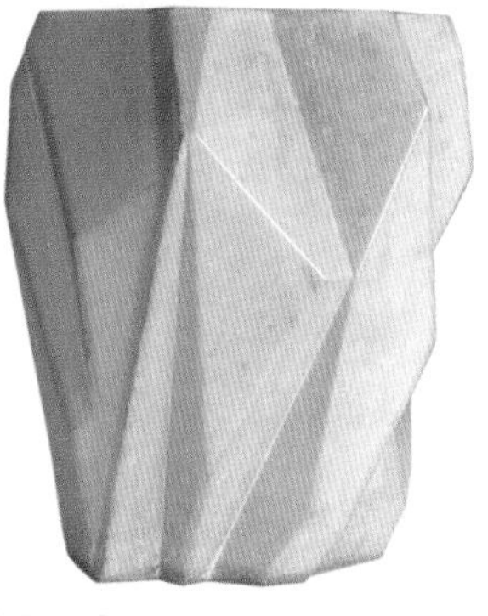

A 'Ruba Rombic' vase by the Consolidated Glass Company, of silvery-grey glass, unmarked.

9.25in (23cm) high

£800-1,200 **SDR**

An 'Air Force' glass sculpture by Kit Karbler and Michael David, large complex vessel with striated colouration and conforming veiled foot, signed.

11in (28cm) high

£800-1,200 **SK**

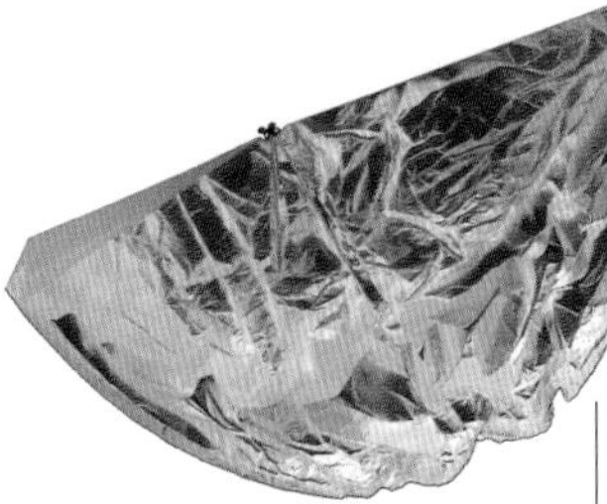

A glass sculpture by Kreg Kallenberger, made of high quality optical glass cast over ceramic fibre.

1986

£7,000-10,000 **JH**

A blue glass bowl by Bertil Vallien for Kosta Boda, inset with spiral glass and gold leaf, engraved marks and numbered 59252.

21.5cm (8.5in) diam

£80-£120 **SWO**

A flaring bowl by Kjell Engman for Kosta Boda, in coral and clear glass with blue veining and chartreuse rim, with etched marks and Kosta Boda label.

10.25in (25.5cm) wide

£250-300 **SDR**

A flattened vase by Ulrica Hydman-Vallien for Kosta Boda, decorated with bands of fish in black and white, on clear ground with bubbles, etched "Kosta Boda Art Coll/Ulrica/HV49463".

10.5in (26cm) high

£400-600 **SDR**

An iridescent glass sculpture by Buxton Kutch, the colourless case with three trapped bubbles in shades of magenta, signed and numbered "2/25" and "981138".

10.25in (26cm) high

£500-800 **SK**

A large pulegoso glass urn by Napoleone Martinuzzi, with ribbon handles, in cobalt with gold foil, unmarked.

This piece is from a series of vessels Martinuzzi designed that were based on ancient forms.

14.5in (36cm) high

£3,000-4,000 **SDR**

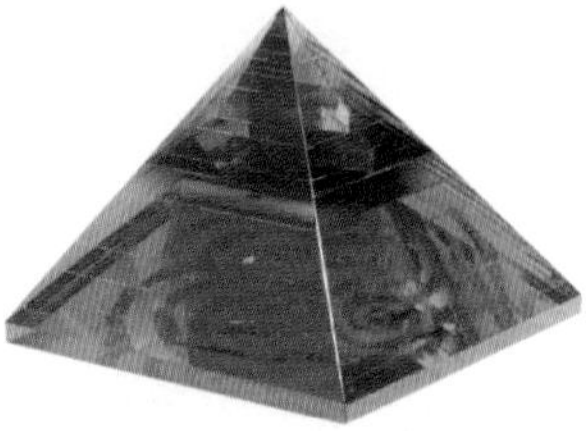

An etched glass pyramid sculpture by Ivo Lill, in green, gold and lavender with satin finish to one side, etched signature and date.

1993 *6.5in (16cm) wide*

£350-450 **SDR**

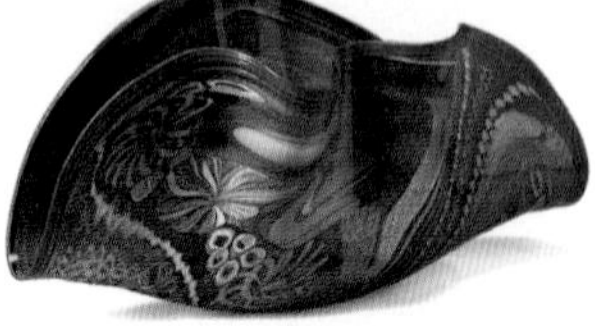

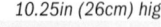

A large sculptural glass vessel by Novak, of clamshell form with complex decoration including millefiori work in multiple colours, signed on base.

22.5in (57cm) wide

£1,200-1,800 **SK**

An 'Ariel' cased glass vase by Ingeborg Lundin for Orrefors, with geometric forms in clear and cobalt, etched "Orrefors/No. 424.E5/Ingeborg Lundin".

8.5in (21cm) high

£600-900 **SDR**

A glass sculpture by Peter VanderLaan, 'Living In My Father's House/Shooting The Pier', of angular form with internal geometric decoration, signed and numbered.

13.25in (33.5cm) high

£1,000-1,500 **SK**

One of a pair of French Art Deco pendant chandeliers by Degue, on a reticulated metal frame with frosted glass shades, complete with ceiling cap.

33in (84cm) high

£1,200-1,800 **SDR**

A sculpted steel hanging light fixture by Paul Evans, with square ceiling plate and square base with four sockets, signed "Paul Evans/69".

1969 *35.5in (89cm) high*

£800-1,200 **SDR**

A red and gold enamelled metal chandelier by Claude Ferre, with three perforated conical shades and floriform frame, unmarked.

18.25in (46.5cm) high

£180-220 **SDR**

A chandelier attributed to Paul Follot, with embossed and faceted bronzed metal frame, and light yellow slag glass panes, complete with ceiling cap.

33.5in (85cm) diam

£280-320 **SDR**

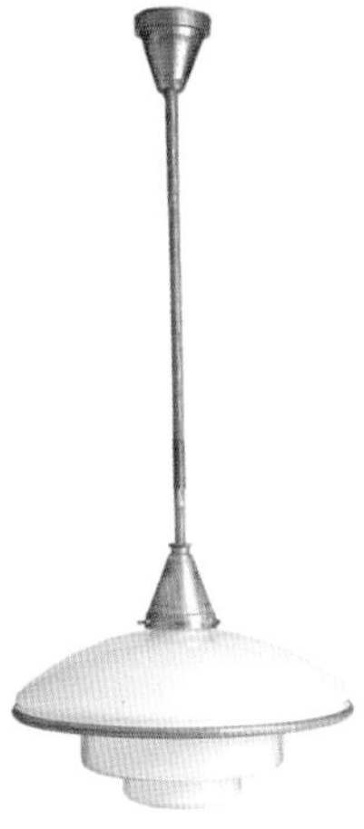

A ceiling lamp by C.F. Otto Mueller for Sistrah-Licht, of cased milk glass with clear glass diffuser and nickel-plated metal fittings.

c1930 *38in (95cm) high*

£600-900 **SDR**

An unusual chandelier probably from Murano, composed of clear and amber glass flowers clustered on a metal frame, unmarked.

26in (66cm) diam

£2,500-3,000 **SDR**

An exceptional chandelier by Verner Panton, in polished chrome and brushed brass with tiered strands of graduated length fitted with spheres, unmarked.

39in (97.5cm) high

£5,000-6,000 **SDR**

A rare chandelier by Tommi Parzinger, in brass with six candlestick fixtures topped by flaring cylindrical shades, draped with strands of glass beads, losses.

42in (105cm) high

£5,000-6,000 **SDR**

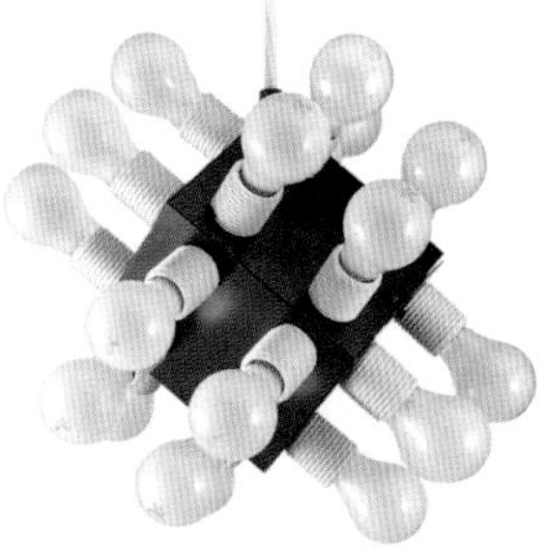

A hanging block-shaped light fixture by Robert Sonneman, with porcelain sockets on a black enamelled metal box, complete with ceiling plate, with Sonneman paper label.

14in (35cm) high

£1,200-1,800 **SDR**

A large twelve-arm brass chandelier by Paavo Tynell for Idman, with flaring opaque yellow glass shades, unmarked.

This chandelier was originally installed in a gentlemen's club in Kuopio, Finland.

c1955 *54.5in (138.5cm) high*

£12,000-18,000 **SDR**

A glass chandelier by Venini, with clear glass bar prisms suspended from a metal frame.

c1965 *18in (45cm) high*

£1,800-2,200 **SDR**

A glass chandelier by Vistosi, with a series of discs in orange and clear blown glass suspended from a tiered frame.

c1965 *22in (55cm) high*

£1,200-1,800 **SDR**

A large 'Wedding' chandelier, with tiers of crystal icicle-style prisms on steel frame, unmarked.

£700-1,000 **SDR**

A French Art Deco hand-forged iron chandelier with reticulated frame and original frosted glass starburst shades, unmarked.

32.5in (82.5cm) long

£220-280 **SDR**

WALL LAMPS

An early and rare 'Bubble' lamp by George Nelson for Howard Miller, with bulbous ribbed shade and adjustable aluminum arm, with Howard Miller decal.

This is an uncommon form from the Bubble lamp line.

c1955 *20in (51cm) high*

£200-300 **SDR**

A pair of lighting fixtures by Verner Panton, in polished chrome and brushed brass, each with six sockets and radiating spokes fitted with spheres, unmarked.

28in (70cm) wide

£1,200-1,800 pair **SDR**

A set of three large 'Sputnik' lighting fixtures, comprising a chandelier and a pair of matching wall sconces, with polished chrome frames and radiating spokes, unmarked.

c1975 *chandelier 45in (112.5cm) high*

£1,000-1,500 **SDR**

A five-arm polished brass wall sconce by Tommi Parzinger for Dorlyn Silversmiths, with etched sunburst motif to backplate, stamped mark.

21.5in (54.5cm)

£280-320 **SDR**

A bronze 'Knife' lamp by Gaetano Pesce, wall-mounted halogen lamp in the shape of a dagger, unmarked.

53.75in (134cm) high

£2,800-3,200 **SDR**

A 'Bookends' illuminated wall sculpture by Edward Zucca, depicting television sets flanked by books, painted poplar wood with plexiglass and lights, unmarked.

1996 *54.75in (137cm) wide*

£2,500-3,000 **SDR**

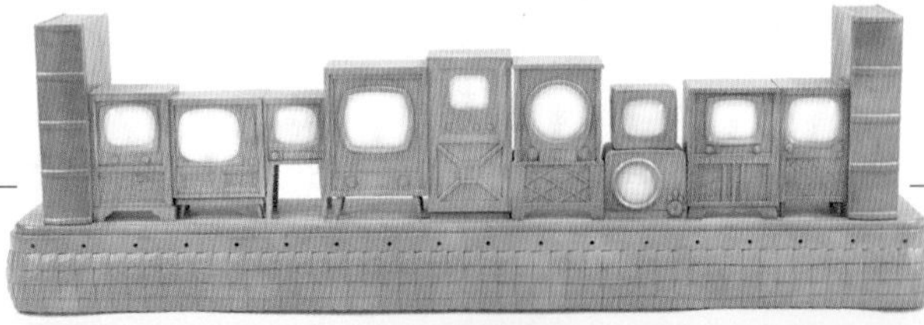

ARREDOLUCE

- Italy's booming post-war economy was a breeding ground for innovative design as consumers demanded more and more stylish products.
- Arredoluce was formed in the 1950s, originally producing chandeliers. The firm quickly rose to international prominence in the field of quality lighting design.
- Acclaimed designers such as Gino Sarfatti – who went on to found Arteluce – helped cement Arredoluce's reputation for innovation and high style.
- The market in vintage Arredoluce lighting has been consistent thanks to its strong architectural appearance and sleek modernity. It holds high appeal for enthusiasts of mid-century design.
- The Triennale lamp is one of Arredoluce's most celebrated designs, representing a triumphant combination of form and function.
- Arredoluce is still active today, exporting lighting systems all over the world from its headquarters in Pescara.

A single-arm floor lamp by Arredoluce, with white enamelled flaring metal shade, enamelled chrome shaft and circular marble base, marked "Made in Italy".

57.5in (144cm) high

£500-800 **SDR**

A 'Triennale' three-arm brass floor lamp by Gino Sarfatti for Arredoluce, the shades and handles enamelled in primary colours, tripod base, stamped "Arredoluce/Made in Italy".

62.25in (158cm) high

£1,800-2,200 **SDR**

A 'Triennale' floor lamp by Arredoluce, the three brass arms with leather-covered handles, with enamelled shades, on a circular marble base, marked "Made in Italy".

60in (152.5cm) high

£2,800-3,200 **SDR**

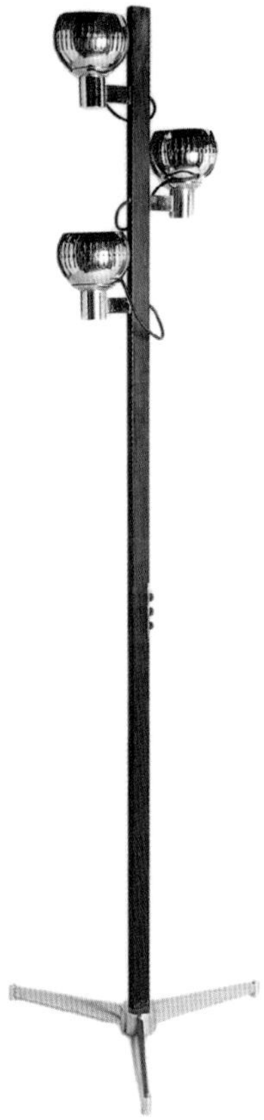

An enamelled metal floor lamp by Arteluce, with three pierced and polished chrome magnetically mounted fixtures, on tripod base, unmarked.

77in (192.5cm) high

£400-600 **SDR**

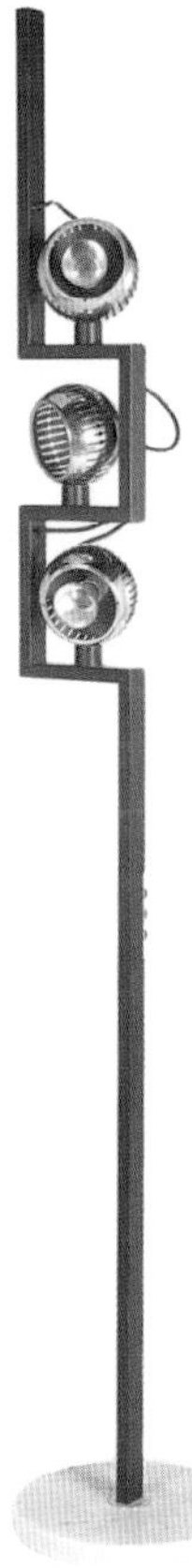

A black metal floor lamp by Arteluce, with three pierced and polished chrome magnetically mounted fixtures in a Greek key frame, on white marble base, unmarked.

79in (197.5cm) high

£1,200-1,800 **SDR**

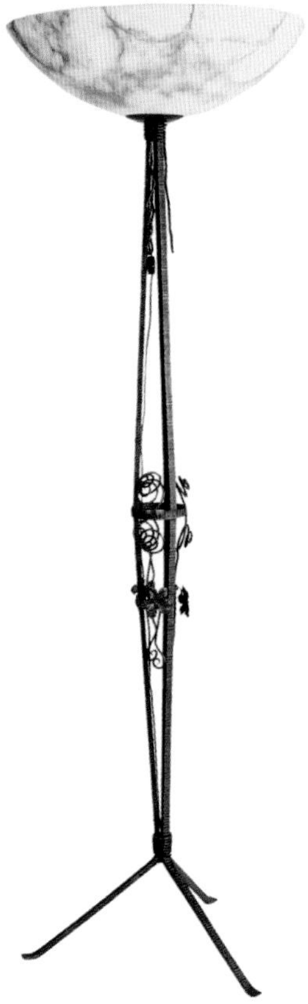

A wrought-iron torchère in the style of Edgar Brandt, with a leaf and coiled vine motif to shaft and tripod base, unmarked.

75in (190.5cm) high

£600-900 **SDR**

An 'Above Thy Fruited Plain' floor lamp by Wendell Castle, with lantern-shaped top carved with pears, unmarked.

64in (160cm) high

£1,800-2,200 **SDR**

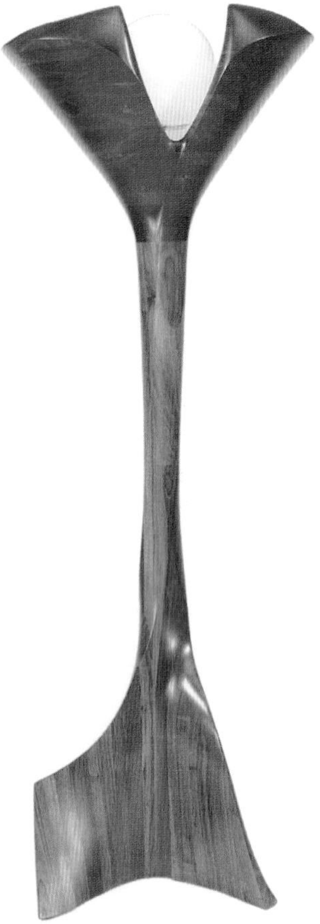

A monumental stack-laminated walnut floor lamp by Wendell Castle, with V-shaped cut-out to flaring top and white glass globe, signed "W.C./70".

1970 *87.5in (219cm) high*

£10,000-12,000 **SDR**

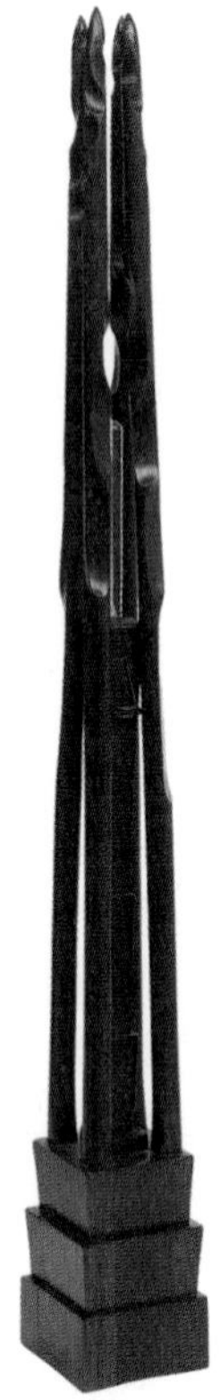

A very rare walnut floor lamp by Wharton Esherick, with four carved and tapering sculptural uprights surrounding a single central socket, on stepped base, with carved signature and date.

1932 *73in (185.5cm) high*

£22,000-28,000 **SDR**

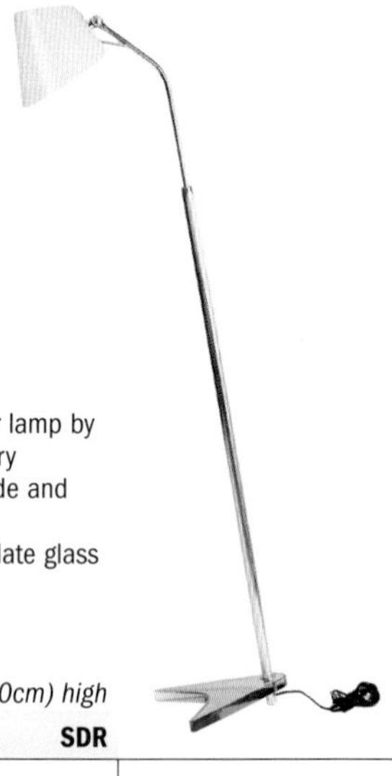

A polished brass floor lamp by Fontana Arte, with ivory enamelled metal shade and adjustable shaft, on boomerang-shaped plate glass base, unmarked.

63in (160cm) high

£1,800-2,200 **SDR**

A 'Grasshopper' floor lamp by Greta Grossman, black enamelled tubular metal with conical shade, unmarked.

51in (127.5cm) high

£500-800 **SDR**

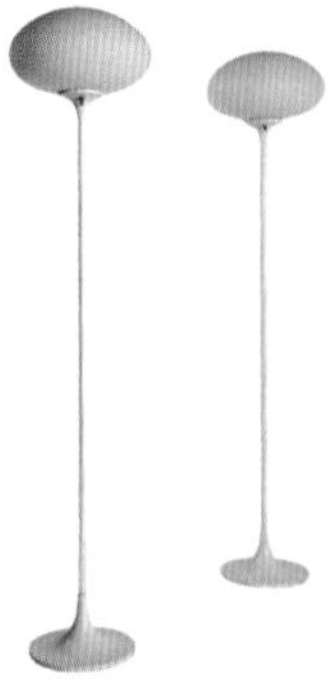

A pair of floor lamps by Laurel, with white enamelled tubular bases and white frosted glass shades, one with a blue paper label.

57in (142.5cm) high

£500-800 **SDR**

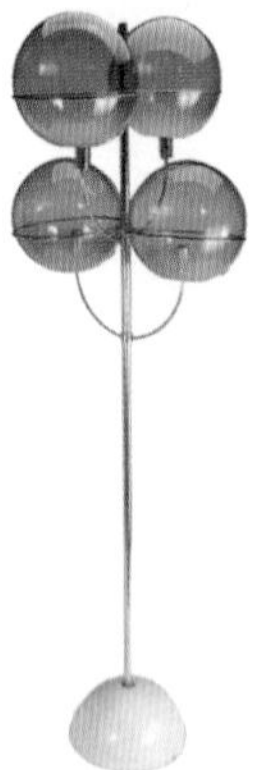

A massive 'Colleoni' four-arm floor lamp by Vico Magistretti for Knoll, with polished chrome frame and four hand-blown Vistosi glass globes, on a white marble base.

102in (259cm) high

£700-1,000 **SDR**

A floor lamp by George Nakashima, of mixed woods including rosewood and walnut, replaced paper panels.

58.5in (146cm) high

£15,000-20,000 **SDR**

A pair of 'Sunrise' candlesticks by Albert Paley, of forged and fabricated steel with brass inserts, stamped and numbered.

Paley designed these candlesticks for the American Ballet Theater.

1993 *21.5in (54cm) high*

£2,200-2,800 **SDR**

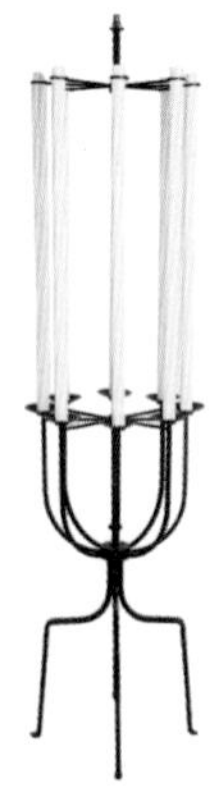

A floor lamp by Tommi Parzinger, with eight tall candlestick fixtures on a black iron base, unmarked.

72in (180cm) high

£1,000-1,500 **SDR**

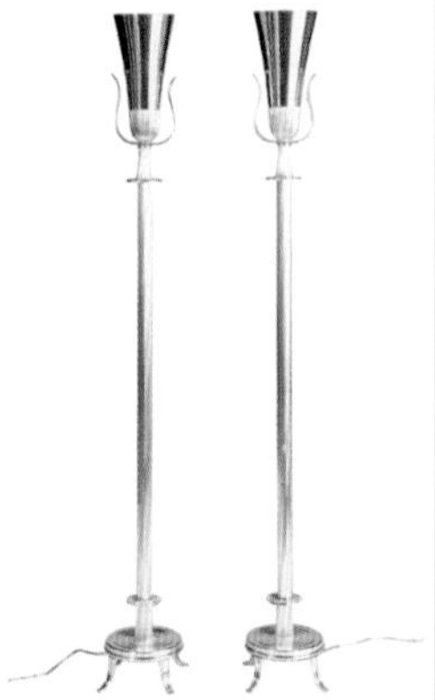

A pair of silvered metal back-lit torcheres by Tommi Parzinger, with ribbed shafts and sabre leg bases, stamped and numbered.

61.5in (156cm) high

£2,800-3,200 **SDR**

A floor lamp by Rispal, with white spherical paper shade suspended from a sculptural walnut frame, unmarked.

65in (157.5cm) high

£1,500-2,000 **SDR**

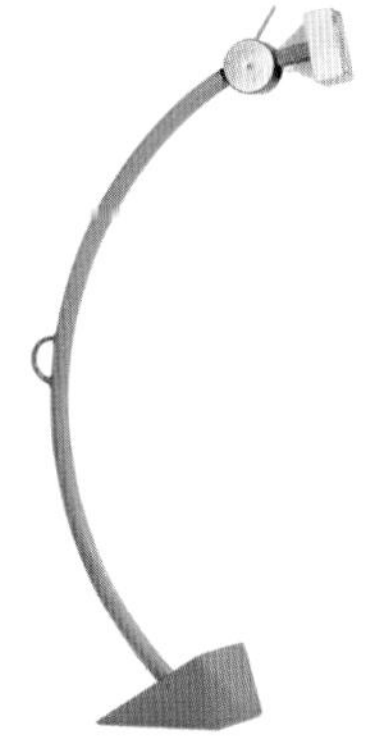

A 'Treetops' lamp by Ettore Sottsass for Memphis.

c1980 71.5in (180.5cm) high

£600-900 **FRE**

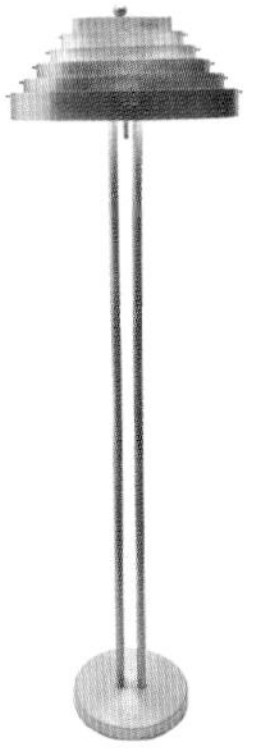

A spun aluminium floor lamp by Kurt Versen, the double shaft topped by an ovoid shade of stepped and riveted strips, remnants of blue paint, unmarked.

58.5in (146cm) high

£1,000-1,500 **SDR**

A spun aluminium torchère by Russel Wright, with trumpet shade, wooden switch and ribbed metal accents to shaft, stamped "Russel Wright/NYC".

65in (162.5cm) high

£180-220 **SDR**

An Italian three-arm floor lamp, in polished chrome with perforated dome shades and black metal handles, on a circular white marble base, stamped "Made in Italy".

60in (152.5cm) high

£700-1,000 **SDR**

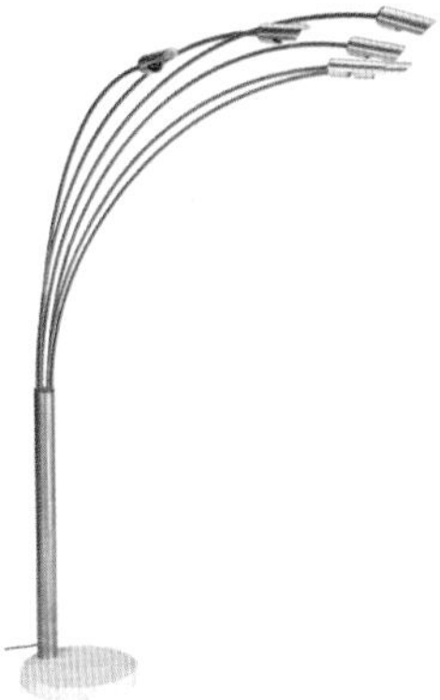

An Italian spray floor lamp, in brass with six overhanging arms and hooded shades, on white marble base, marked "Made in Italy".

83in (211cm) high

£500-800 **SDR**

A modern cylinder lipstick floor lamp, of polished chrome, with moulded plastic reflector shade, unmarked.

64in (160cm) high

£700-1,000 **SDR**

An architectural fin-shaped floor lamp, with red paper covering, bronzed metal final and biomorphic base, unmarked, damaged.

80in (200cm) high

£350-450 **SDR**

A floor lamp by Gilbert Watrous for Heifetz, with single pivoting arm, fibreglass shade and brass handle, magnetically balanced on a black metal tripod base, unmarked.

53in (134.5cm) diam

£1,800-2,200 **SDR**

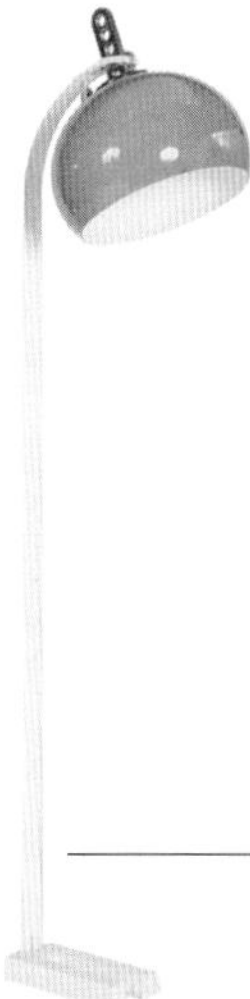

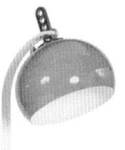

A modern floor lamp, with adjustable orange plastic hemispheric shade, on an arched white enamelled metal base, unmarked.

62in (155cm) high

£120-180 **SDR**

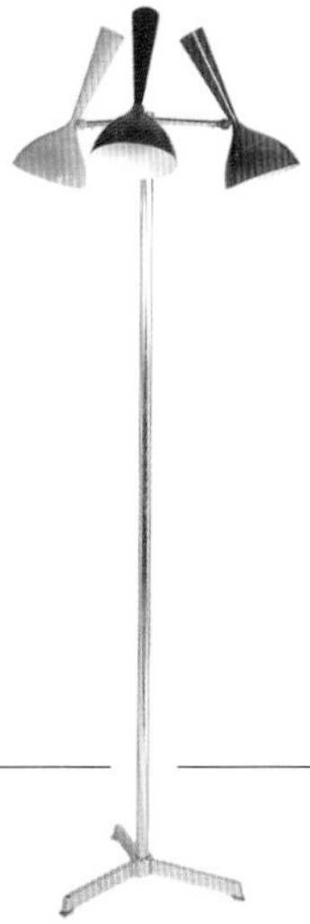

A brass floor lamp, with three enamelled metal shades in red, green, and yellow, unmarked.

75in (187.5cm) high

£1,200-1,800 **SDR**

A table lamp by Franco Albini, with white plastic hemispherical shade and pivoting shaft, on grey metal base, unmarked.

18.25in (46.5cm) high

£500-800 **SDR**

A table lamp by by Gary Knox Bennett, 'A Nite on Lindquist Ridge', stovepipe housing with five flexible black and white shaft fixtures, marked with title and "In Oakland/GKB/Anno 90".

22in (56cm) high

£4,000-6,000 **SDR**

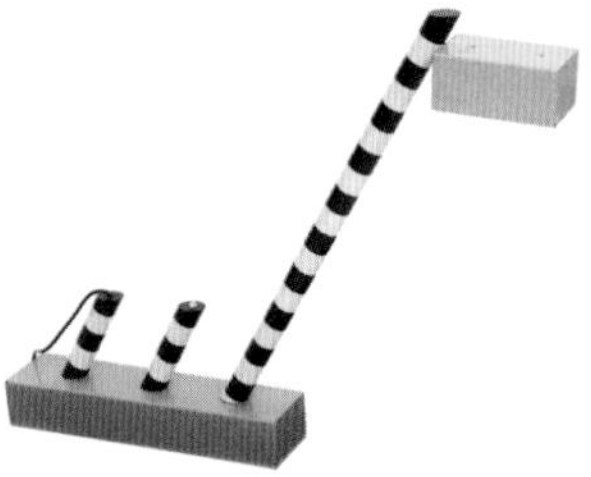

An 'Oceanic' table lamp by Michele De Lucchi for Memphis, in polychrome enamelled metal, unmarked.

1981 *39in (99cm) high*

£600-900 **SDR**

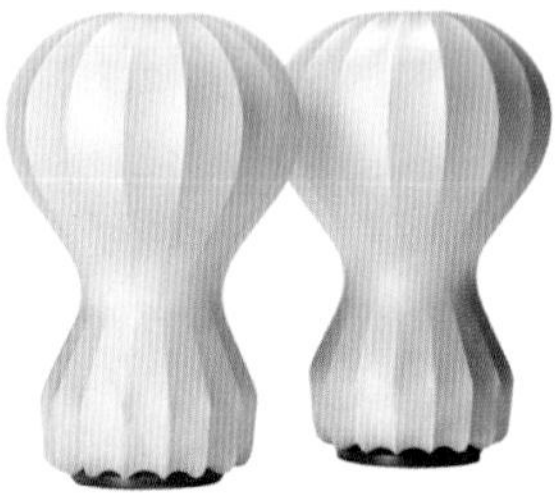

A pair of 'Gatto' table lamps by Achille & Pier Giacomo Castiglioni for Flos, with sprayed-on plastic covering over a corseted wire frame, unmarked.

12in (30.5cm) high

£800-1,200 **SDR**

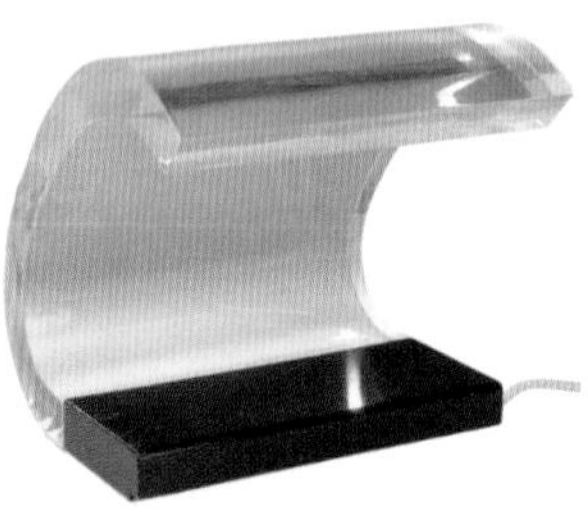

An 'Acrilica' desk lamp by Joe Colombo, with curved overhanging shade on black enamelled metal base, unmarked.

9.25in (23.5cm) high

£1,800-2,200 **SDR**

A desk lamp by Christian Dell, nickel-plated and black enamelled metal, bakelite and wood, stamped "Kaiser Idell".

c1935 *18in (46cm) high*

£500-700 **SK**

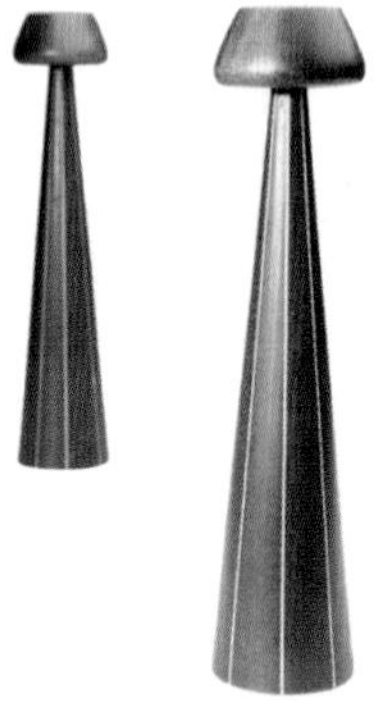

A pair of walnut candlesticks by Paul Evans and Phillip Lloyd Powell, with pewter inlay to flaring bases, marked "Designers Inc. Paul Evans".

13.5in (34.5cm) wide

£800-1,200 **SDR**

A desk lamp by Fontana Arte, in brass and enamelled metal, with adjustable shaft and plate glass base, unmarked.

18.5in (46cm) high

£1,000-1,500 **SDR**

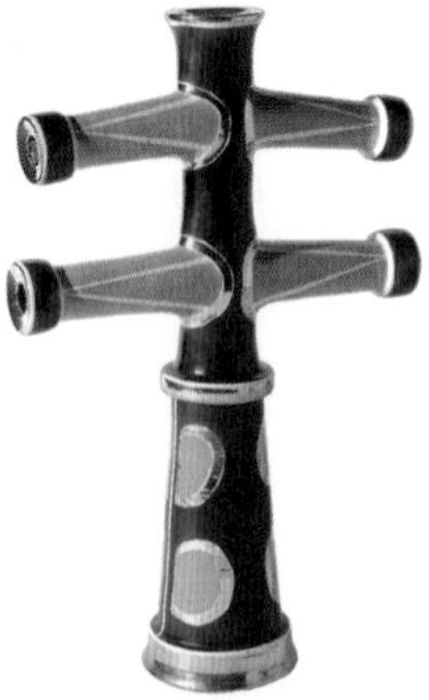

A 'Funk' pottery lamp by Hwa Kwan Hui, with two pairs of arms above a flaring base, painted in bright yellow and gold on a cobalt base, marked in red ink "78.205".

38in (96.5cm) high

£1,800-2,200 **SDR**

A pair of table lamps by Boris Lacroix, with ivory enamelled visor shades and black metal bases, unmarked.

These lamps were commissioned by the Maison du Cambodge at Cité Universitaire in Paris.

19.5in (49.5cm) high

£700-1,000 **SDR**

A table lamp by Ingo Maurer for M Design, injection-moulded in the form of a light bulb, embossed "Design Ingo Maurer".

c1965 *24in (60cm) high*

£400-600 **SDR**

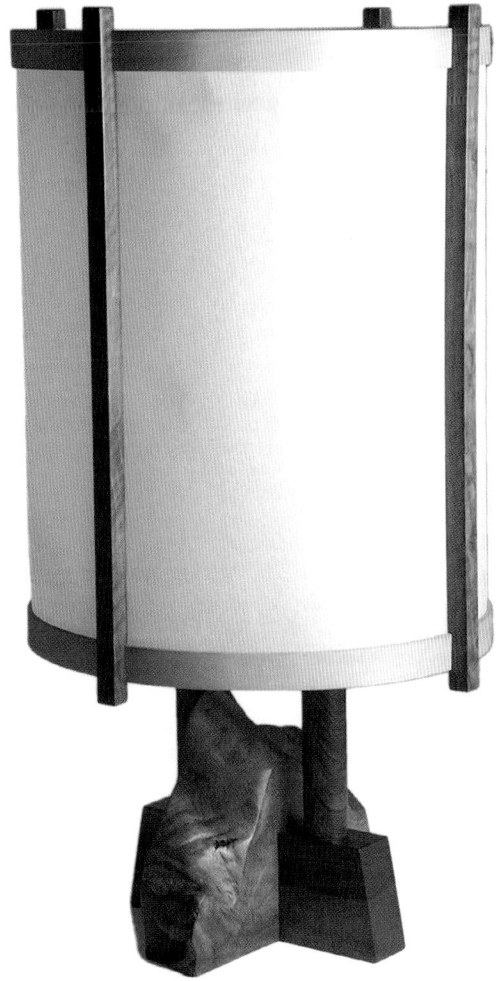

A George Nakashima table lamp, in rosewood and walnut with double-column shaft on cross-plank base, signed "George Nakashima/Dec 1971".

1971 *29.75in (74cm) high*

£8,000-12,000 **SDR**

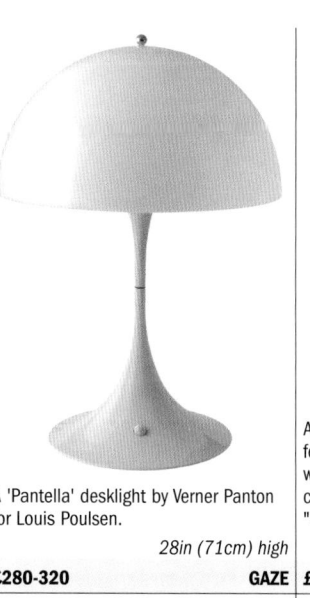

A 'Pantella' desklight by Verner Panton for Louis Poulsen.

28in (71cm) high

£280-320 **GAZE**

A table lamp by T.H. Robsjohn-Gibbings for Hansen, with ecru paper shade and white enamelled metal reflector, on corseted brass tripod base, stamped "Hansen/New York".

21.5in (54.5cm) high

£1,500-2,000 **SDR**

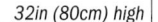

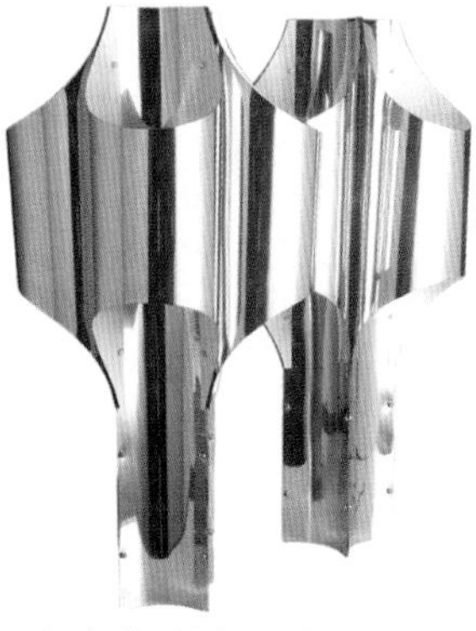

A pair of tall table lamps by Robert Sonneman, of bent and riveted metal with polished chrome exterior, unmarked.

c1975 *32in (80cm) high*

£800-1,200 **SDR**

A 'Tahiti' table lamp by Ettore Sottsass for Memphis, in polychrome enamelled metal on black and white laminate base, unmarked.

1981 *25.5in (65cm) high*

£600-900 **SDR**

A pair of faceted table lamps by Stilux, white plastic and enamelled metal on marble bases, marked "Stilux/Made in Italy".

11in (28cm) high

£400-600 **SDR**

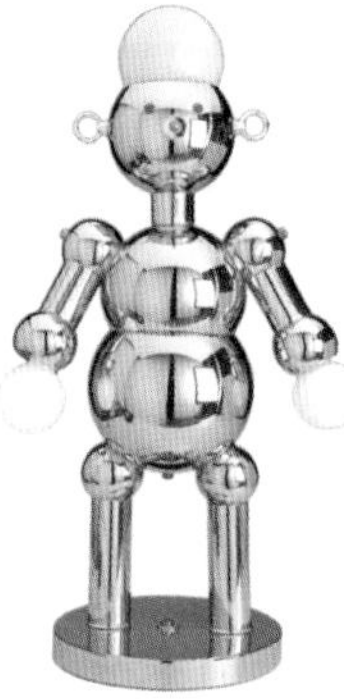

A large figural 'Robot' lamp by Torino, in polished chrome, with remnant of Torino metal tag.

31in (77.5cm) high

£600-900 **SDR**

A pair of polished chrome table lamps, with dome shades and flat discs to tapering shafts, unmarked.

23in (57.5cm) high

£800-1,200 **SDR**

A pair of enamelled metal table lamps with Lucite nubs on splayed legs, unmarked.

12.5in (31cm) high

£1,200-1,800 **SDR**

A sonambient sculpture by Harry Bertoia, with two opposing groups of stainless steel rods arranged in arched configurations, mounted on a square base, unmarked.

24.25in (60.5cm) high

£10,000-12,000 **SDR**

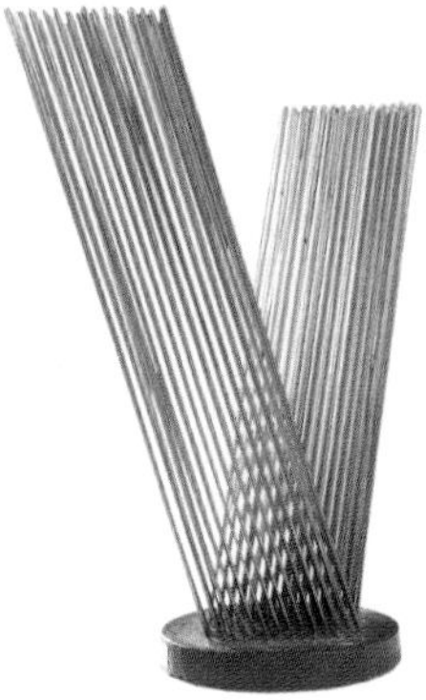

A 'V' sculpture by Harry Bertoia, with two opposing groups of gilded bronze rods mounted on circular bronze base, unmarked.

8in (20cm) high

£1,500-2,000 **SDR**

A sonambient sculpture by Harry Bertoia, comprising 174 beryllium copper and brass rods arranged in diagonal formation on a broad base, unmarked.

c1960 *10in (25.5cm) wide*

£8,000-12,000 **SDR**

A rare pair of 'The Laughing Ones' figural sculptures by Harry Bertoia, one with bronze patina and the other with satin chrome finish, unmarked.

largest 12.25in (30.5cm) high

£2,500-3,000 **SDR**

A large gilded bronze floor sculpture by Harry Bertoia, in the form of a tree, unmarked.

53in (132.5cm) high

£3,500-4,500 **SDR**

PAUL EVANS

An asymmetric wall sculpture by Paul Evans, with sculpted and applied elements covered in blue, green, yellow, and red patinas with gilded highlights, signed "Paul Evans 1978".

1978 *57in (142.5cm) high*

£10,000-12,000 **SDR**

A 'Smiles' room sculpture by Paul Evans, with brazed edges and brass finish around perimeter, unmarked.

This is a rare and early Evans form.

£5,000-6,000 **SDR**

A tall custom-built wine rack by Paul Evans, with polished brass finish, unmarked.

80.5in (201cm) high

£1,000-1,500 **SDR**

A walnut charger by Paul Evans and Phillip Lloyd Powell, with radiating pewter inlay, marked "Designers Inc. Paul Evans".

17.5in (44.5cm) diam

£700-1,000 **SDR**

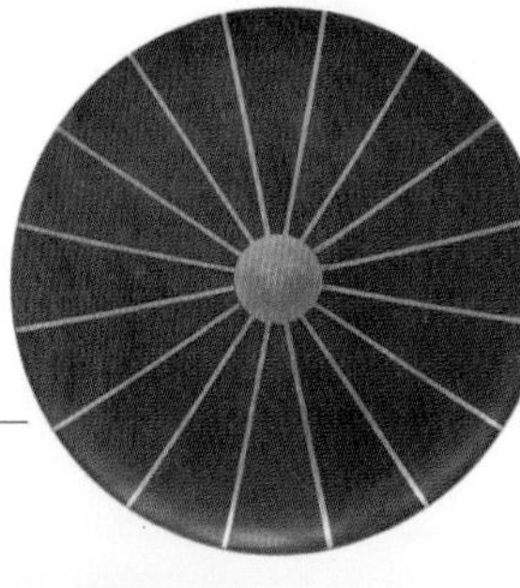

A large ashtray by Paul Evans, with riveted metal patchwork of copper, bronze and pewter patinas, unmarked.

10in (25.5cm) wide

£300-500 **SDR**

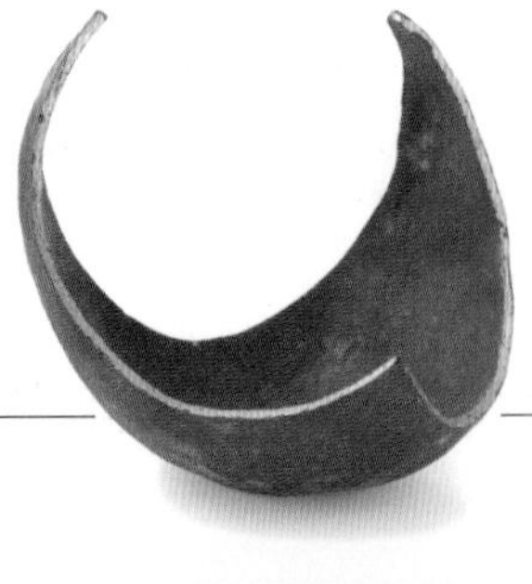

A 'Chimu-Mask' wall sculpture by Klaus Ihlenfeld, in copper and bronze with verdigris patina, stamped "K".

1964 *9.25in (23cm) high*

£600-900 **SDR**

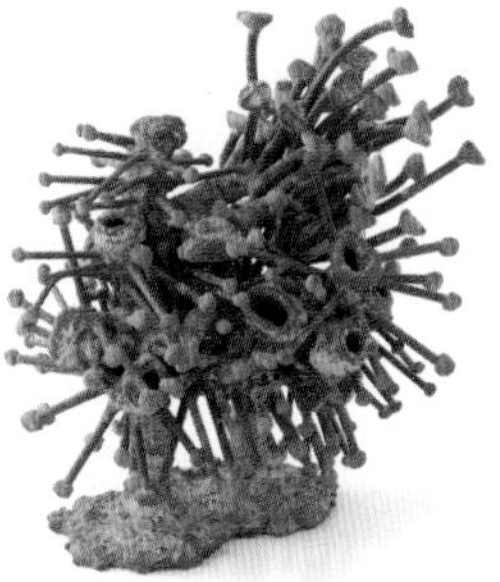

A welded bronze organic sculpture by Klaus Ihlenfeld, with verdigris patina, stamped "KI".

8.25in (21cm) high

£800-1,200 **SDR**

An early 'Flamingo Bird Nest' sculpture by Klaus Ihlenfeld, welded bronze with verdigris patina, stamped "KI".

17in (43cm) long

£1,500-2,000 **SDR**

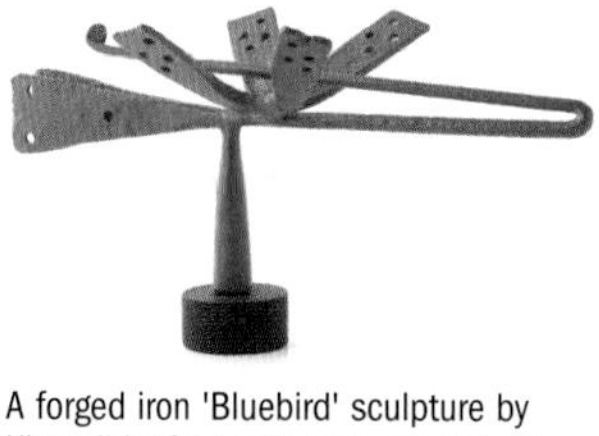

A forged iron 'Bluebird' sculpture by Klaus Ihlenfeld, with blue enamel, on black disc base, marked "KI".

18in (45.5cm) wide

£800-1,200 **SDR**

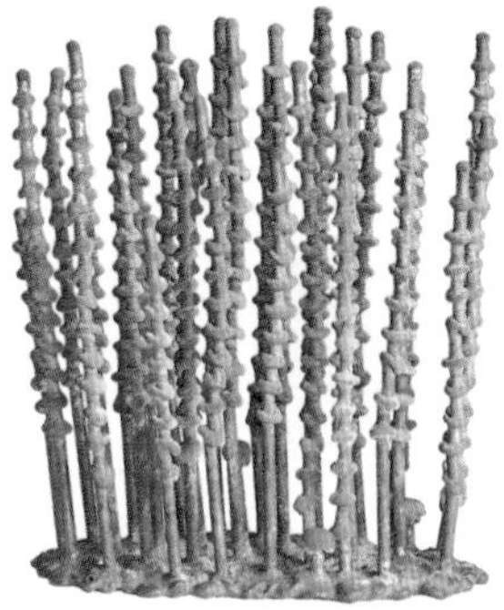

A welded bronze 'Poplars' sculpture by Klaus Ihlenfeld, covered in a verdigris patina, signed "K".

2003 *7in (17.5cm) high*

£1,000-1,500 **SDR**

CURTIS JERE

A wall sculpture by Curtis Jere, comprising burnished metal discs and hemispherical elements welded to a grid-form frame.

47in (117.5cm) wide

£1,200-1,800 **SDR**

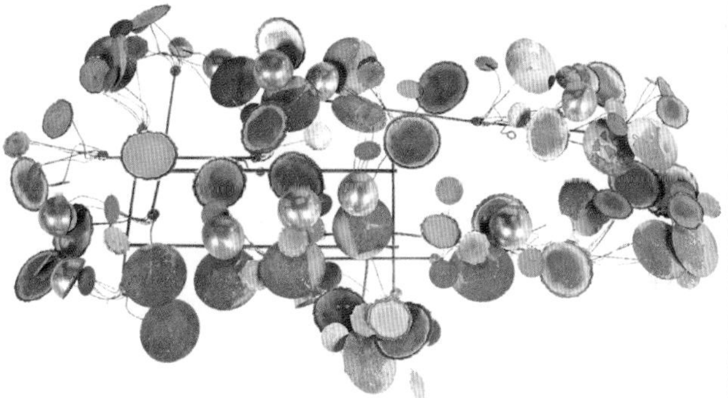

A large starburst wall sculpture by Curtis Jere, of brass-washed metal, signed.

36in (90cm) diam

£1,200-1,800 **SDR**

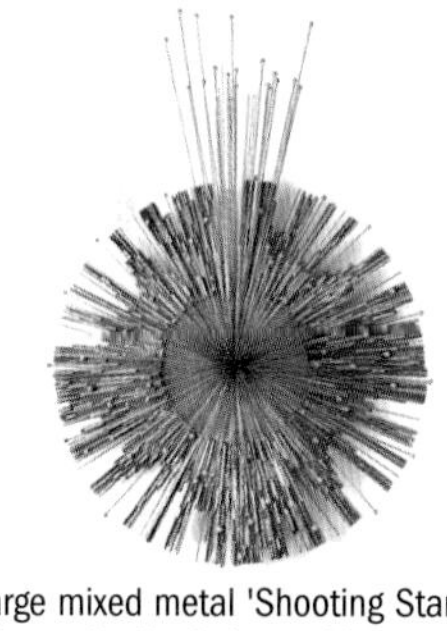

A large mixed metal 'Shooting Star' wall sculpture by Curtis Jere, with a spray of brass rods emanating from the centre, complete with original Artisan House Inc. label.

58in (147.5cm) high

£700-1,000 **SDR**

A coiled wall sculpture by Curtis Jere, with mottled blue-green finish and three tiers of articulated metal rods, signed "C. Jere/1988".

19.25in (49cm) high

£180-220 **SDR**

A large welded metal wall sculpture by Curtis Jere, comprised of overlapping circular and semi-circular elements with brushed finish, signed "C. Jere/1989".

51in (129.5cm) wide

£700-1,000 **SDR**

A welded metal ribbon sculpture by Curtis Jere, on a black enamelled cylinder base, signed "C. Jere".

c1975 *37.5in (95cm) high*

£500-800 **SDR**

A tabletop sculpture by Curtis Jere, comprising red-patinated metal disks on stems, unmarked.

10.25in (25.5cm) high

£1,800-2,200 **SDR**

A pair of 'Infinity' wall mirrors by Curtis Jere, with polished chrome frames.

23.5in (59cm) diam

£1,200-1,800 **SDR**

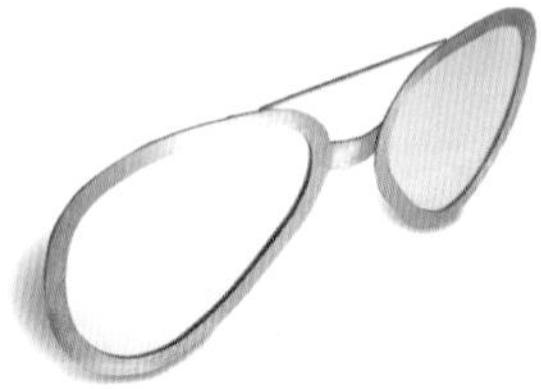

A wall mirror by Curtis Jere, in the form of a pair of aviator glasses, signed and dated.

1980 *31in (77.5cm) wide*

£1,000-1,500 **SDR**

A enamelled metal owl on a branch by Curtis Jere, signed.

13in (32.5cm) wide

£150-200 **SDR**

BRONZE SCULPTURE

A bronze abstract sculpture by Carl Auböck, marked.

14in (35cm) long

£500-800 **SDR**

A 'Moonlight' bronze figure by 'Erté', with blue patina on a black oval base, signed, numbered and dated.

Romain de Tirtoff adopted the pseudonym 'Erté' based on the French pronunciation of his initials.

c1985 *17.75in (45cm) high*

£1,500-2,000 **ISA**

A 'Small Prophet' bronze figure by Mirko Basaldella.

13.25in (33cm) high

£2,200-2,800 **SDR**

A 'Standing Woman' bronze sculpture by Picasso, on a marble base, signed and numbered in the bronze.

9in (23cm) high

£6,000-9,000 **SDR**

A bronze fish sculpture by Nancy Jurs, with dark charcoal patina and verdigris highlights, on an incised cube base, unmarked.

15in (38cm) high

£1,500-2,000 **SDR**

A bronze sculpture by Martel for Susse Frères, depicting a stylized bird, with stamped mark.

13in (32.5cm) high

£2,200-2,800 **SDR**

A maple burl turned wood vessel by Dennis Elliott, with torn rim, signed "Elliott/Big leaf maple burl".

1989 *9in (22.5cm) wide*

£280-320 **SDR**

An intricate vessel by Dennis Elliot, of broad leaf maple burl with torn rim and centre, signed "Elliott/Broad leaf maple burl".

1989 *17in (42.5cm) diam*

£600-900 **SDR**

A large turned wood vessel by Ron Kent, with thin walls and raised foot, signed "Ron Kent/1997".

1997 *18in (45cm) wide*

£700-1,000 **SDR**

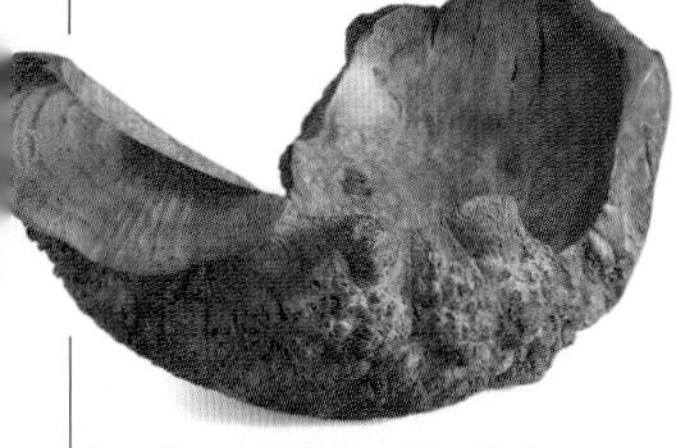

A mulberry burl vessel by Mark Lindquist, signed "1994/#19/Mark Lindquist/Mulberry burl".

1994 *10in (25.5cm) wide*

£800-1,200 **SDR**

A fine turned white pine bowl by Ed Moulthrop, signed "Ed Moulthrop/White pine" with stamped cipher.

11.5in (29cm) diam

£1,500-2,000 **SDR**

A catalpa wood vessel by Philip Moulthrop, with high gloss finish and flaring rim, signed "Philip Moulthrop/Catalpa/894".

9.5in (24cm) wide

£280-320 **SDR**

A manzanita burl vase by Melvin Lindquist, with asymmetrical rim, signed "L/4-79/Manzanita Burl".

1979 *8.5in (21.5cm) high*

£3,000-4,000 **SDR**

A monumental turned maple bowl by Bob Novack, of free-form shape, signed "Maple bowl/Bob Novack".

20in (50cm) high

£1,800-2,200 **SDR**

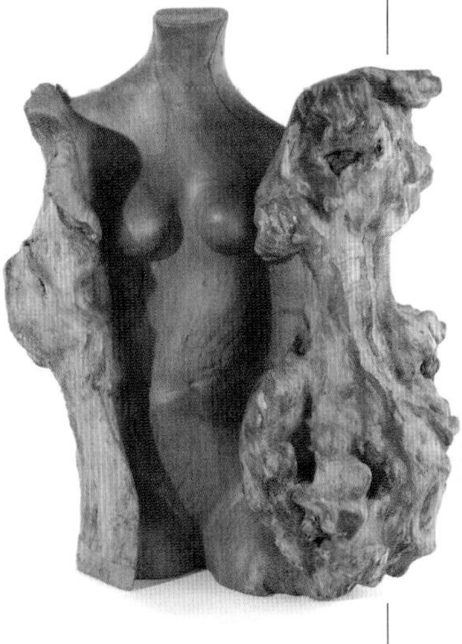

A burlwood sculpture of a torso by Hap Sakwa, with carved signature and date.

1983 *34in (86.5cm) high*

£2,500-3,000 **SDR**

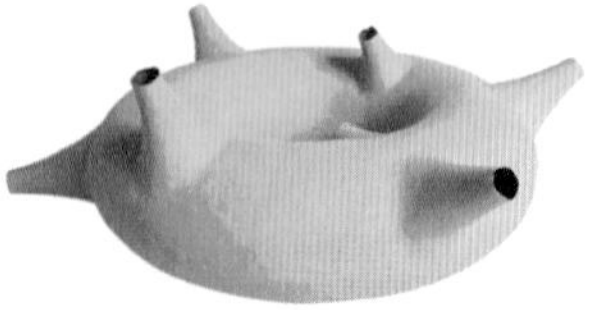

A 'Yellow Vessel' copper sculpture by Jonathan Bonner, with multiple protrusions and painted yellow finish, signed "Jonathan Bonner/1994".

1994 *48in (120cm) diam*

£800-1,200 **SDR**

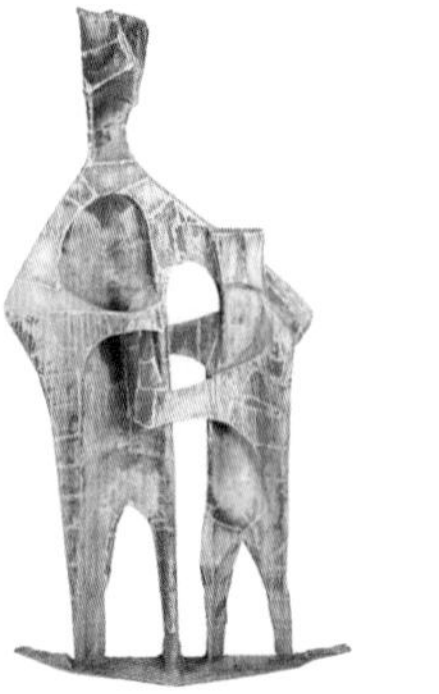

A large welded copper outdoor sculpture by Bernard Brenner, depicting two figures embracing, with verdigris patina.

103.5in (259cm) high

£3,000-4,000 **SDR**

A pewter vase by Bernard Chaudron, made in the Val Davide, Quebec.

c1960 *10.75in (27cm) high*

£100-150 **TCF**

A palm tree sculpture by Gabriella Crespi, with acrylic and brass elements, impressed mark.

c1975 *15in (38cm) high*

£500-800 **SDR**

A solid steel abstract sculpture by Claire Falkenstein, in four pieces, unmarked.

16.5in (42cm) high

£10,000-12,000 **SDR**

An abstract sculpture by Claire Falkenstein, with molten blue glass and curved copper appendages, unmarked.

9in (23cm) high

£4,000-5,000 **SDR**

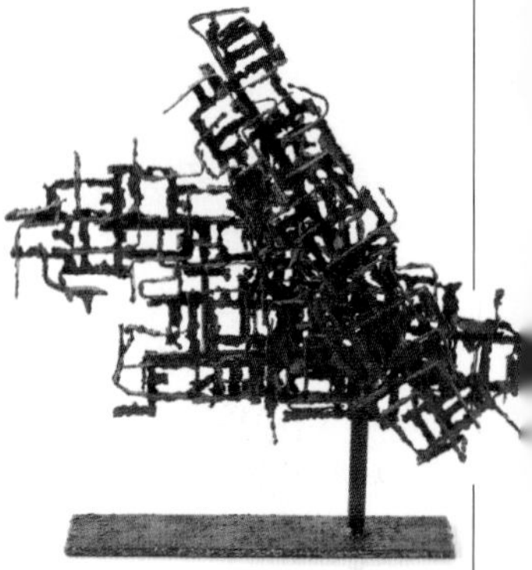

A welded metal abstract sculpture by Fantoni, with grey patina and textured base, stamped "Fantoni/Made in Italy".

15in (38cm) wide

£1,000-1,500 **SDR**

An aluminium 'City Block I' sculpture by LM Foss, composed of geometric shaped blocks, signed and titled with plaque on side.

13.5in (34.5cm) high

£1,000-1,500 **SK**

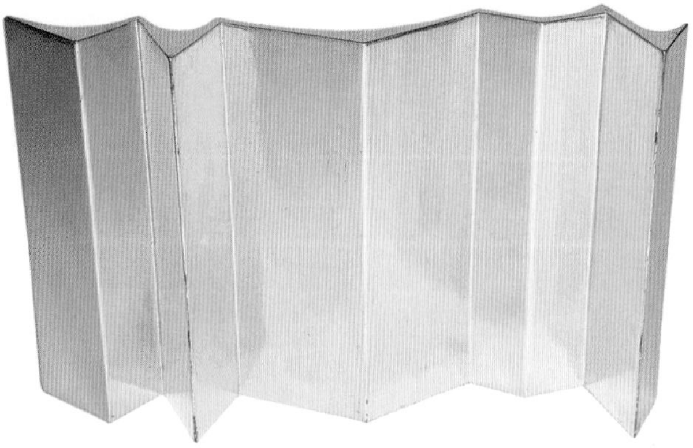

A 'Gold Screen' gold leaf steel sculpture by Mathias Goeritz, initialled "MG" with artist's cipher.

28in (70cm) wide

£15,000-20,000 **SDR**

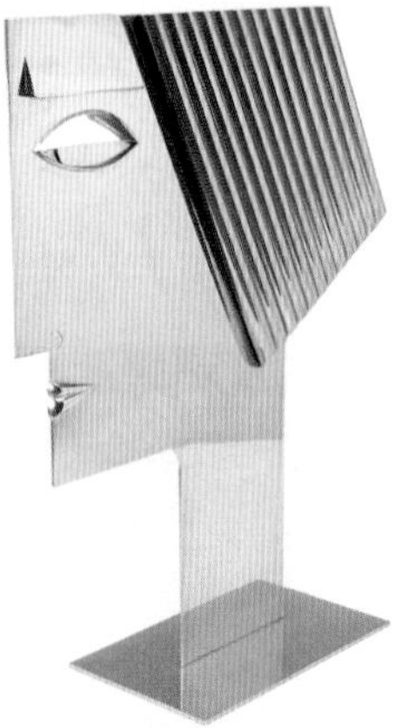

A stylized bust by Franz Hagenauer, with applied and incised angular features, chrome finish, stamped mark.

21.5in (54.5cm) high

£6,000-9,000 **SDR**

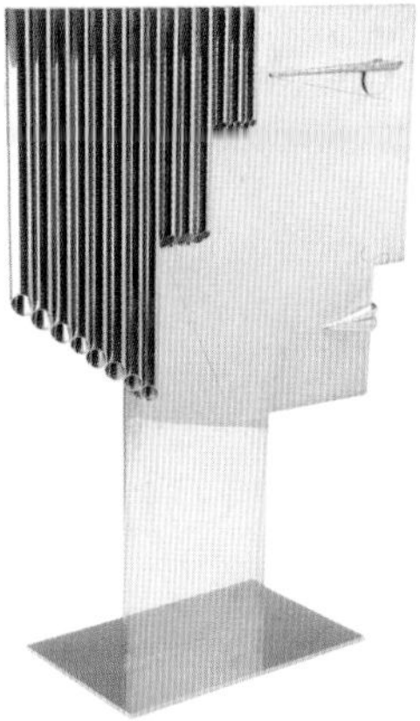

A stylized bust by Franz Hagenauer, with applied and incised angular features, chrome finish, stamped mark.

21.5in (54.5cm) high

£5,000-6,000 **SDR**

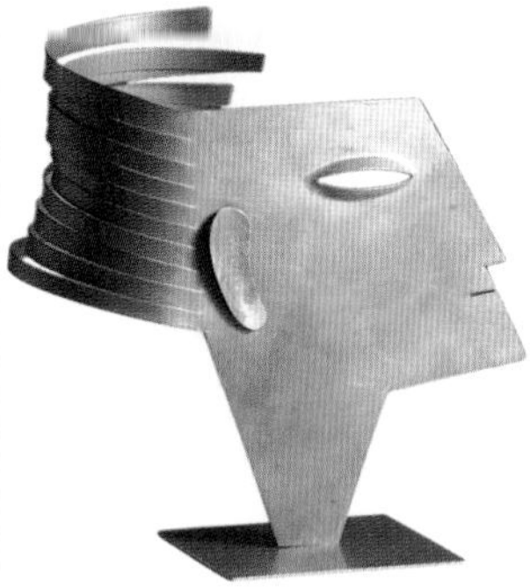

A brass tabletop sculpture in the style of Hagenauer, depicting a male head in profile, base etched "H-207589 HN".

11in (27.5cm) high

£600-900 **SDR**

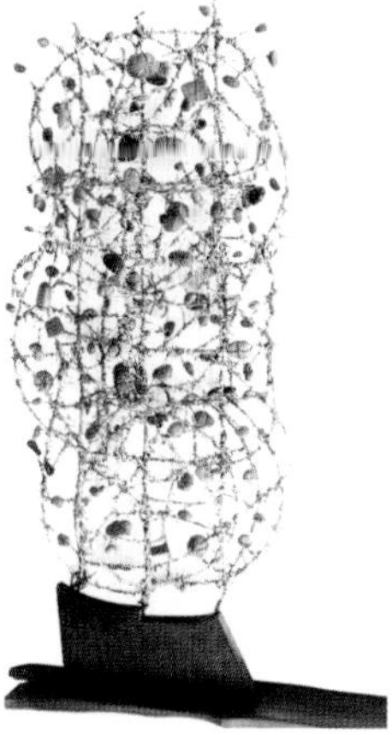

A sculptural room divider by Leonard Nelson, of river rocks and wire frame, on a walnut base, marked "Nelson"

72in (183cm) high

£2,500-3,000 **SDR**

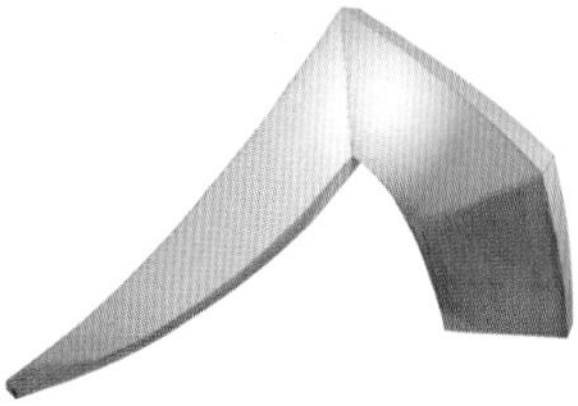

A 'Safe Streets' outdoor sculpture by Christopher Newman, of curved and riveted metal, unmarked.

1975 *109in (272.5cm) wide*

£1,800-2,200 **SDR**

A milled steel 'Sculpture VIII' obelisk by Albert Paley, with cube finial, marked "Albert Paley/1989".

103.5in (263cm) high

£12,000-15,000 **SDR**

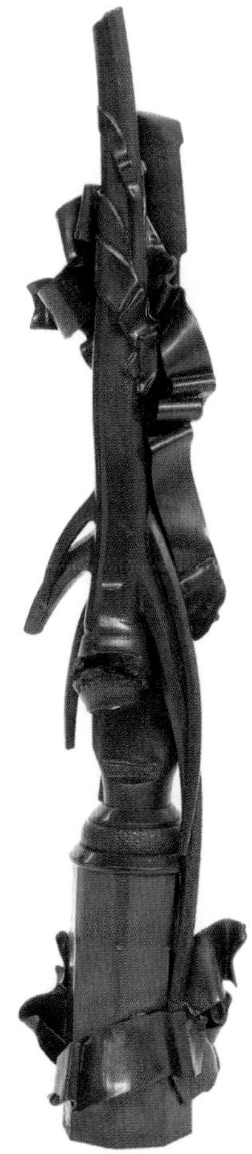

A forged milled steel sculpture by Arthur Paley, with dark charcoal patina, stamped "Paley" and dated.

1990 *41in (104cm) high*

£3,000-4,000 **SDR**

ALBERT PALEY

- Born and raised in Rochester, New York, Albert Paley has forged a successful career as an artist blacksmith and has been among the vanguard of artists to bring this ancient craft to the fore of modern sculpture.
- He was the first metal sculptor to receive the American Institute of Architects' Lifetime Achievement, the highest accolade available to a non-architect.
- Working primarily in milled steel, Paley produces monumental sculpture, architectural furniture and smaller pieces such as paperweights. His work is exhibited in many permanent collections worldwide.
- Paley has completed many prestigious public commissions, including the Portal Gates at the Renwick Gallery of the Smithsonian Institution and 'Synergy', a ceremonial archway in Philadelphia.
- Albert Paley currently holds a chair in Contemporary Crafts at the Rochester Institute of Technology.

A set of four forged milled steel paperweights by Albert Paley, with dark brown patina and rust-coloured flashes, stamped "Paley 1994".

1994 *largest 8.5in (21.5cm) long*

£500-800 **SDR**

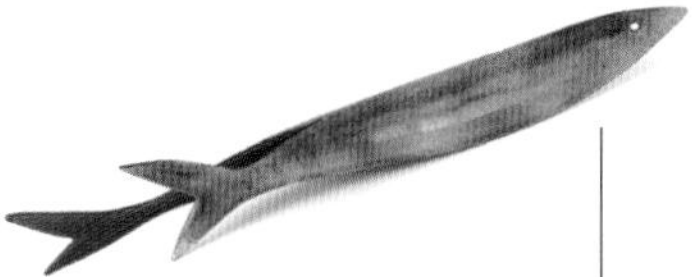

An enamelled metal fish sculpture by Gio Ponti and Paolo De Poli, with molten crimson and gold finish, the interior in cobalt, etched "De Poli".

12.75in (32.5cm) long

£1,200-1,800 **SDR**

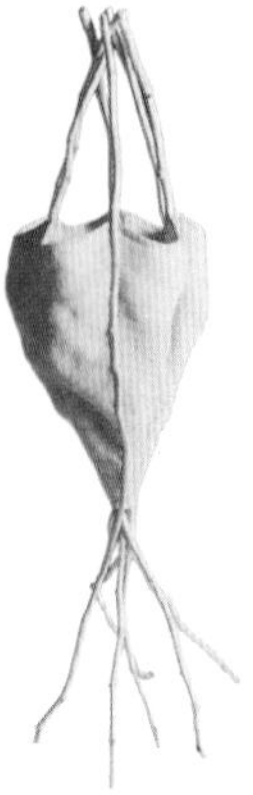

A '3jb Cocoon' basket by Jan Buckman, of twine, waxed linen and hawthorn wood, unmarked.

1997 *15in (37.5cm) high*

£600-900 **SDR**

A 'Geminis' painted cast steel sculpture by Enrique Carbajal.

49.5in (124cm) high

£1,500-2,000 **SDR**

A cast glass 'Tower Box I' sculpture by Tessa Clegg, in red and pearl glass, signed "Tessa Clegg '00".

15.5in (39.5cm) high

£3,000-4,000 **SDR**

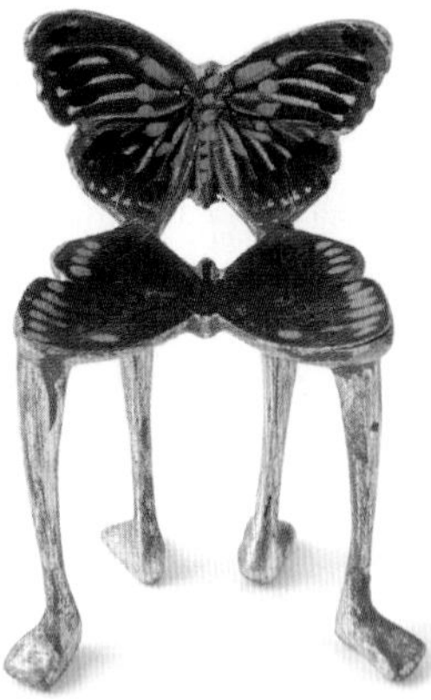

A chair sculpture by Pedro Friedeberg, with butterfly seat and back over human feet, in gold finish with painted paper appliqué, signed "Pedro Friedeberg".

3.75in (9.5cm) high

£600-900 **SDR**

A red clay 'Torsos' sculpture by Nancy Jurs, covered in turquoise, brick red and dark brown matte glazes, signed "Jurs 94".

20in (51cm) high

£700-1,000 **SDR**

A cast paper 'Split Button Model' sculpture by Claes Oldenburg, mounted in a plexiglass case, signed and dated, with cipher.

This piece is from an edition of 100.

1981 *16in (40cm) wide*

£1,200-1,800 **SDR**

An abstract chrome table sculpture by Irving Richards, unmarked.

13.25in (33cm) high

£1,200-1,800 **SDR**

A rare Karl Springer sculpture, with faux-mosaic patchwork finish and brass inlay, on a tall cylindrical base, unmarked.

c1980 *pedestal 60in (150cm) high*

£1,000-1,500 **SDR**

A rare wire wall sculpture by Frederick Weinberg, depicting a team of horses, unmarked.

36in (90cm) wide

£800-1,200 **SDR**

An Edward Zucca 'Primal Television' illuminated sculpture, of painted wood, with rabbit ear aerial, signed and dated.

1994 *14.25in (35.5cm) high*

£600-900 **SDR**

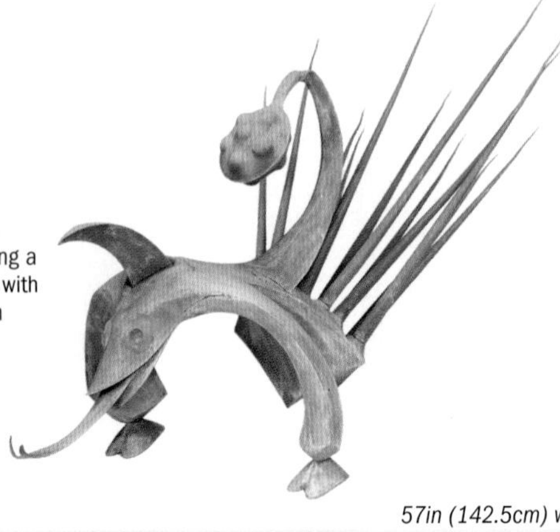

An outdoor metal sculpture, depicting a reptilian creature with spikes, covered in verdigris patina, unmarked.

57in (142.5cm) wide

£800-1,200 **SDR**

EDWARD FIELDS

- Edward Fields pioneered the concept of the 'area rug' in the early 1950s. The more transitory lifestyle many Americans were leading in the post-war years meant that they frequently moved home and abandoned their carpets - rugs provided a portable solution to this problem.
- In partnership with designer Raymond Loewy, Fields introduced a range of five patterned area rugs suitable for covering the floor of a living room. These were 'Heavenly', 'Infinite Star', 'Legend', 'Picnic Basket' and 'Stellar'.
- These rugs became a huge success when they went on sale at Lord and Taylor's on Fifth Avenue. Other interior designers followed suit, but Edward Fields has remained a byword for quality, well-designed rugs, with prestigious commissions including the White House and Air Force One.
- The recent re-issue by Jack Fields, current president of Edward Fields Inc., of Loewy's original five designs has created a resurgence of interest in vintage area rugs.

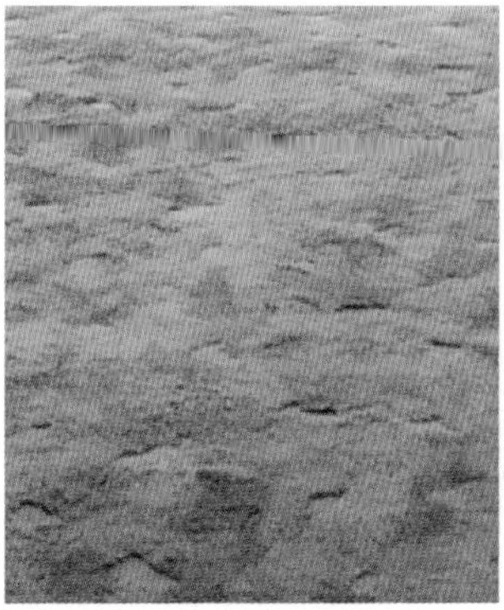

A large rug by Edward Fields, with overall abstract pattern in green, signed and dated on selvage.

1964 *240in (600cm) long*

£800-1,200 **SDR**

A wool area rug by Edward Fields, with geometric design in red, orange and beige, marked on selvage.

1971 *96in (244cm) wide*

£250-300 **SDR**

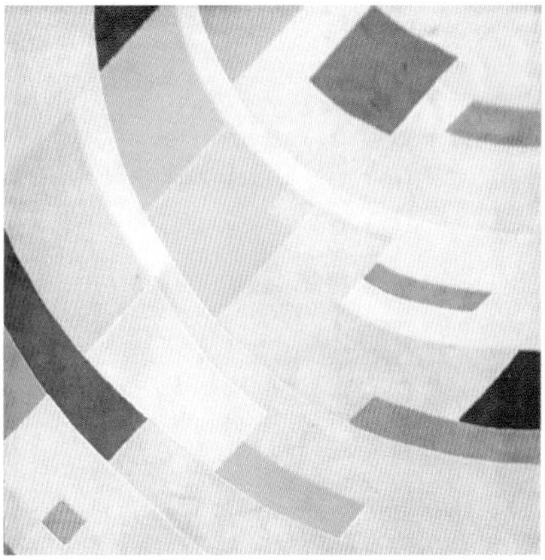

A large area rug by Edward Fields, with geometric patterns in yellow, green, blue and orange, signed on selvage.

216in (540cm) long

£1,000-1,500 **SDR**

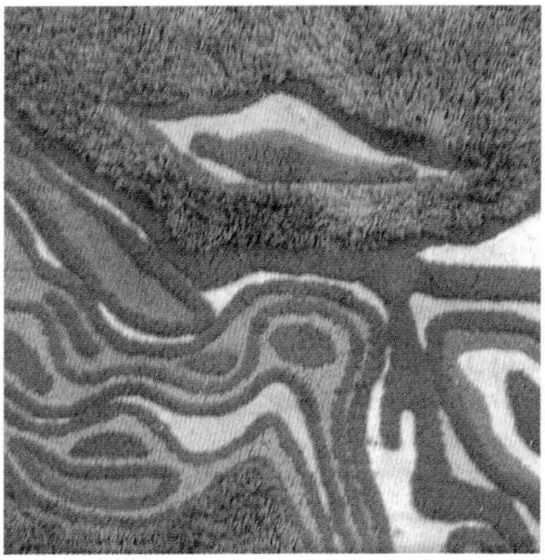

A small area rug by Edward Fields, with half swirl pattern in greens, brown and yellow.

51in (127.5cm) long

£500-800 **SDR**

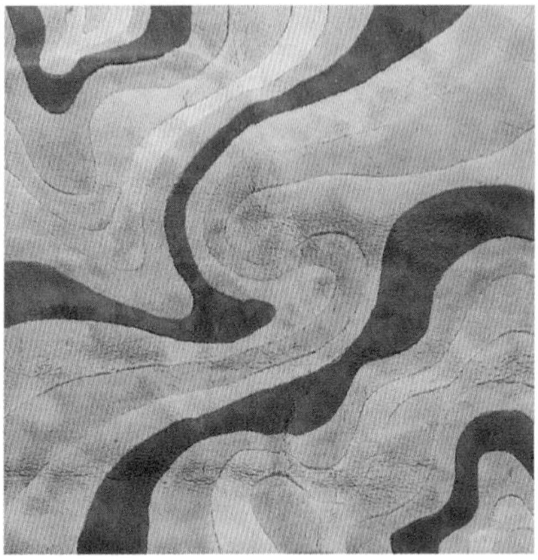

An area rug by Edward Fields, with a swirl pattern, marked on selvage.

80in (200cm) long

£600-900 **SDR**

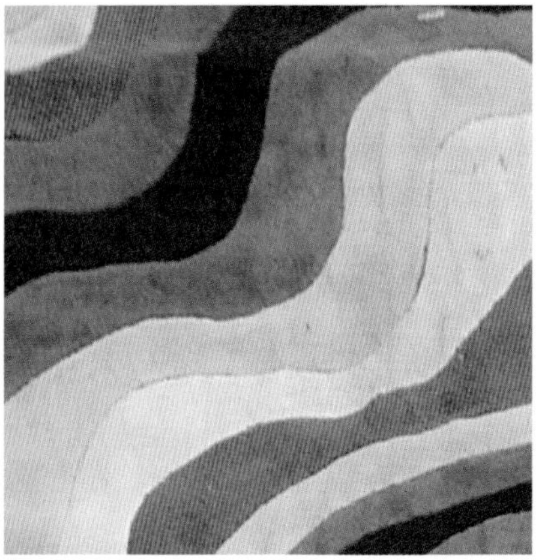

A room-sized rug by Edward Fields, with overall swirl pattern, marked on selvage.

108in (274.5cm) wide

£700-1,000 **SDR**

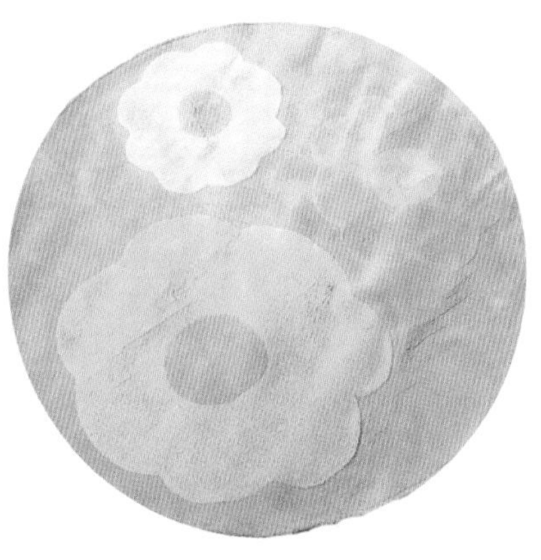

A circular wool area rug by Edward Fields, with Pop Art flowers in yellow and white on a beige ground, signed on selvage.

84in (213.5cm) diam

£500-800 **SDR**

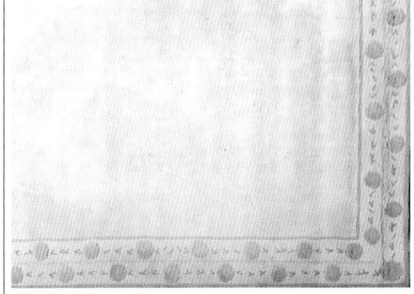

A room-sized woollen area rug by Edward Fields, with floral border in yellow and green on a tan ground, signed on selvage.

140in (355.5cm) wide

£600-900 **SDR**

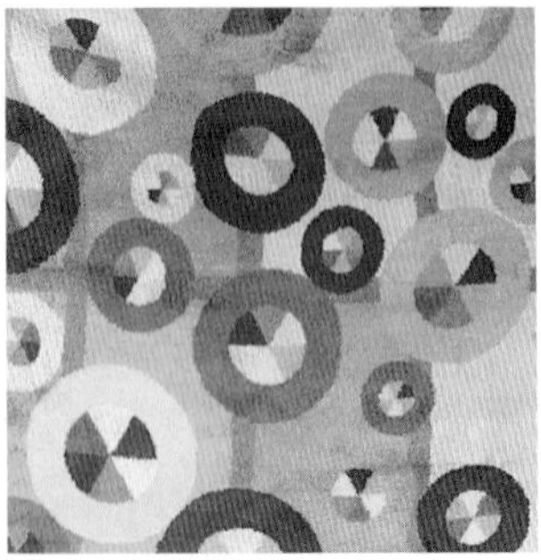

A 'Polo' wool shag rug by Concepts International, with polychrome circles on a gridwork background, label to rear.

119in (297.5cm) long

£700-1,000 **SDR**

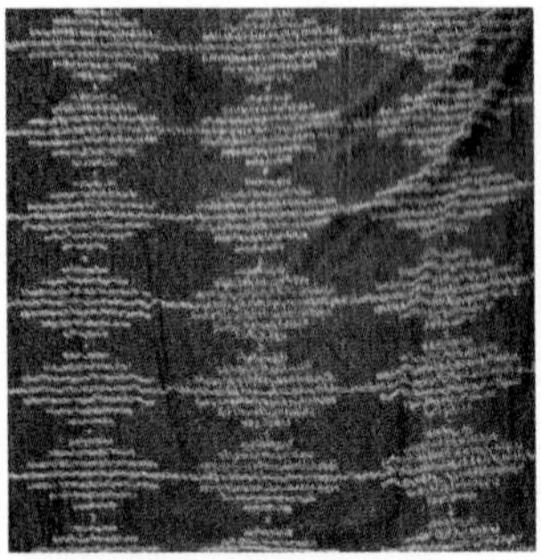

A woven rug by Vibeke Klint, with repeating pattern in orange and yellow on a brown, blue and green ground, unmarked.

139in (353cm) wide

£800-1,200 **SDR**

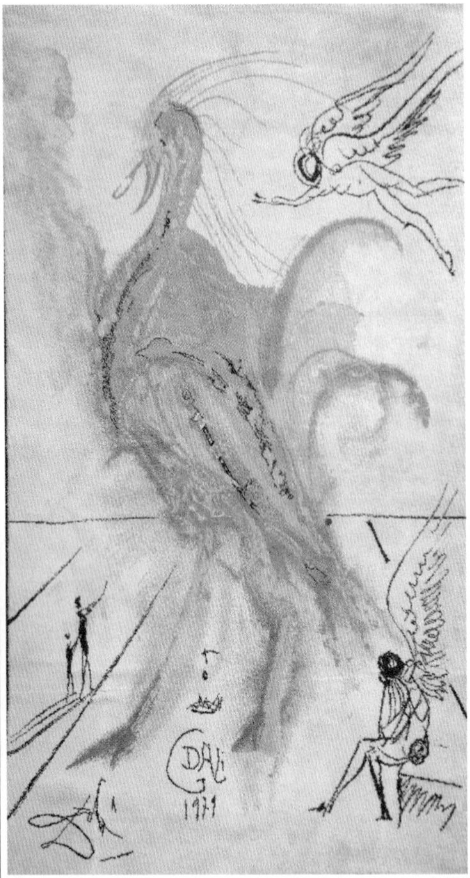

An area rug by Salvador Dali, depicting angels around a large bird, signed and dated.

1979 *108in (274cm) high*

£1,800-2,200 **SDR**

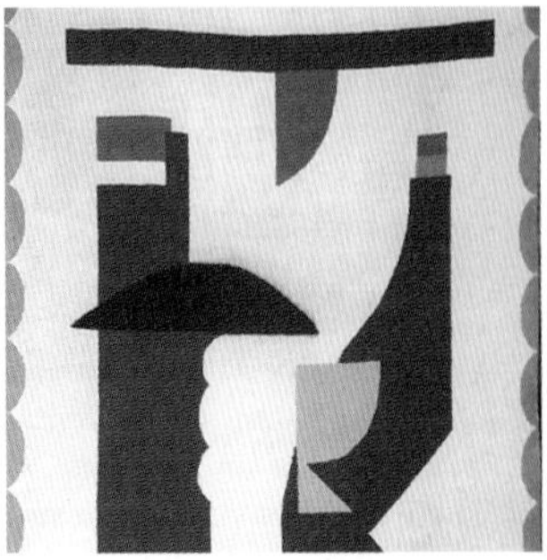

A woollen 'Solidadi: Nude/Torso' area rug by Eileen Gray, featuring an abstract pattern in grey, brown and black on a cream ground, with label.

125in (312.5cm) long

£1,200-1,800 **SDR**

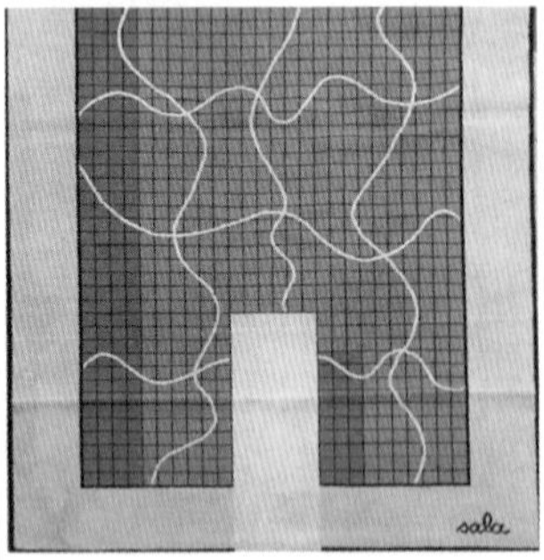

An area rug by Roger Sala, with a swimming pool design, signed.

108in (270cm) long

£200-300 **SDR**

A hand-woven shag rug by Maryann Strengel, with alternating stripes in red, blue and purple.

Strengel was a leading artist of the post-Bauhaus period.

90in (225cm) long

£600-900 **SDR**

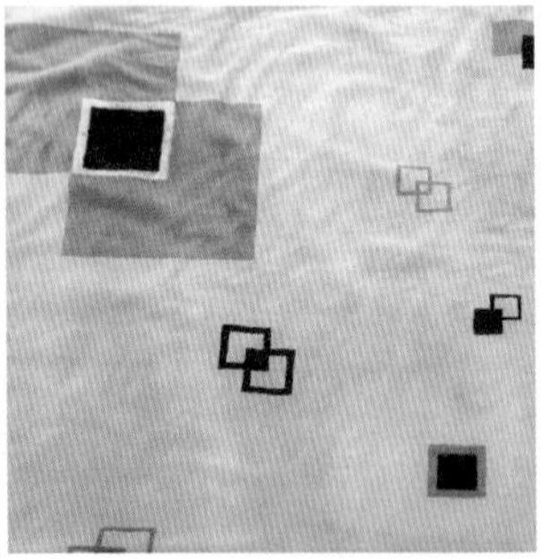

A large woollen rug by Wendy Wahl for V'soske, with black, grey and white squares on a beige ground, manufacturer's label.

18.5in (47cm) high

£400-600 **SDR**

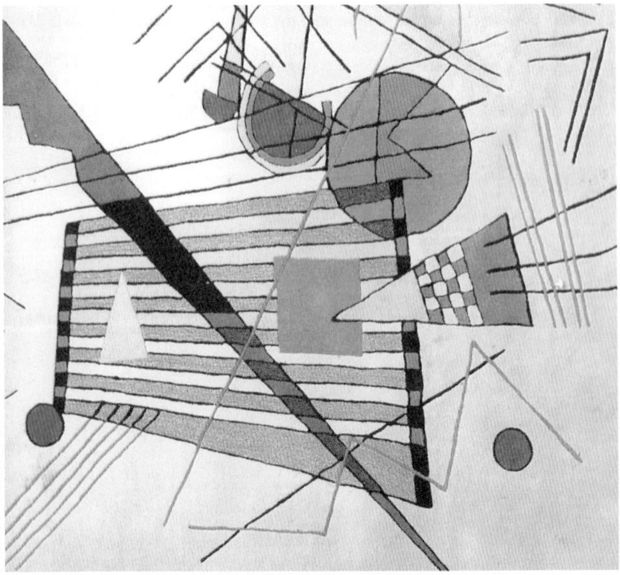

A woollen area rug from the Guggenheim Museum, with geometric design in black, salmon, yellow, and green on a white ground, marked "G".

c1985

£800-1,200 **SDR**

A polychrome 'Sirens' tapestry by Jean van Vlasselaer, woven in the workshop of Royale G. Dewit in Mechlin, Belgium, signed.

80in (200cm) wide

£1,800-2,200 **SDR**

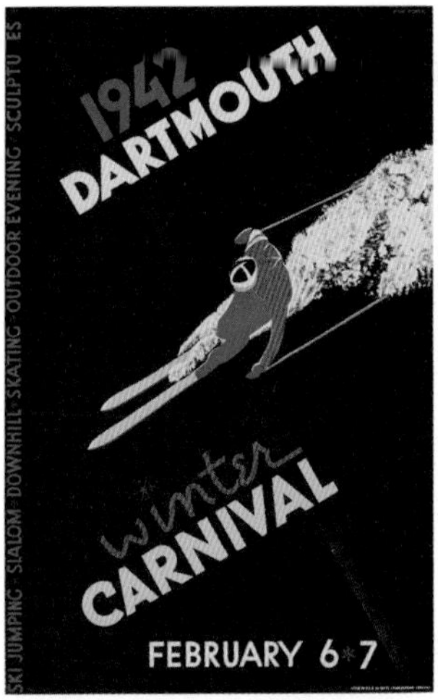

A 'Dartmouth Winter Carnival' poster, by John Bowers, restored losses in top left corner.

c1940 *34in (86.5cm) high*

£2,500-3,000 **SWA**

A 'Scotland by East Coast' poster, by Simon Bussy, McCorquodale, Glasgow, for LNER's Scotland service, with a stylized image of a fawn, previously unseen.

Bussy was connected to the Bloomsbury group of English writers and artists.

1927 *50.5in (128.5cm) wide*

£2,000-2,500 **SWA**

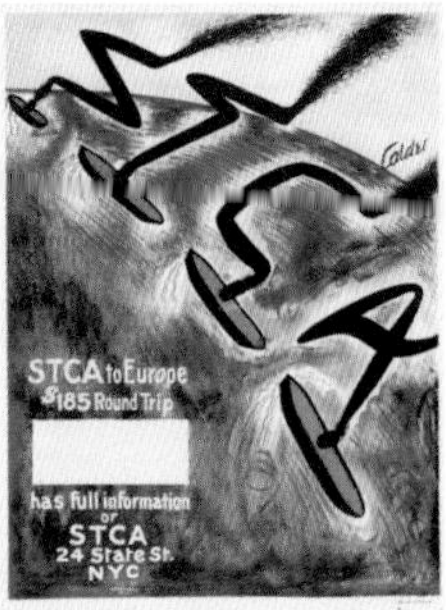

An 'S. T. C. A.' poster, by Alexander Calder, printed by Karl Gut Litho Co., New York.

Before attending art school, Calder received an engineering degree. In 1922 he served as a fireman in the boiler room of a ship, which perhaps served to inspire this design. This is a very early and exceptionally scarce work by the artist.

c1926 *18in (46cm) high*

£800-1,200 **SWA**

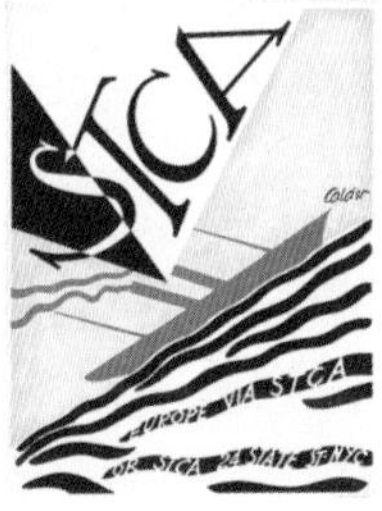

An 'S. T. C. A.' poster, by Alexander Calder, printed by Karl Gut Litho Co., New York.

This extremely scarce poster for a travel agency has an exceptionally Modernist style and may be one of only two commercial advertisements the artist ever designed.

c1926 *18in (46cm) high*

£600-900 **SWA**

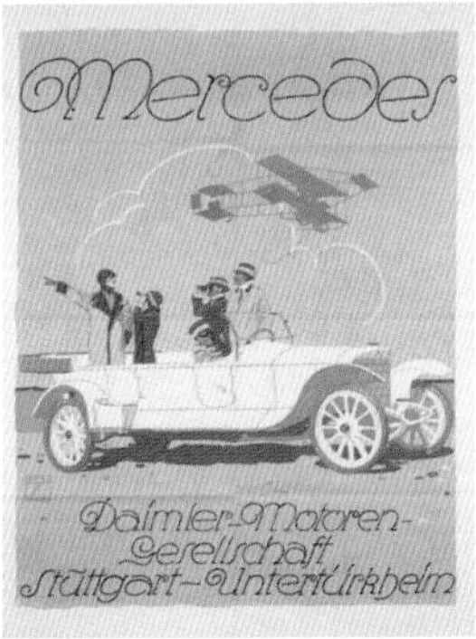

A 'Mercedes' poster, designed by Ludwig Hohlwein, in light pastel tones, with two fashionable couples and a plane flying above.

1914 *43in (107.5cm) high*

£7,000-10,000 **SWA**

An 'Earls Court Motor Show' poster, by E. McKight Kauffer, printed by Baynard Press.

Although he was born in America, McKnight Kauffer spent his most creative years in Great Britain. After producing his first revolutionary poster in 1919 for the Daily Herald, he received commissions from many major clients, including London Transport. He designed 141 posters for them over a span of 20 years. This image, with a photograph inserted in a geometric arrangement and extremely dynamic lettering, is very modernistic and is an archetypal example of the new style in graphic design that emerged in the 1930s.

1937 *39.5in (100.5cm) high*

£1,200-1,800 **SWA**

A 'Greater Power' poster, by Sascha Maurer, printed by Latham Litho, Long Island City, to celebrate the 50th anniversary of the New Haven Railway.

1938 *41.5in (104cm) high*

£1,200-1,800 **SWA**

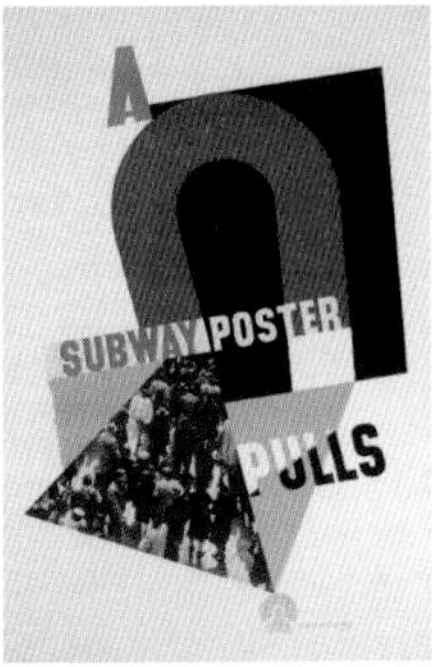

An 'A Subway Poster Pulls' poster, designed by Edward McKnight Kauffer, of photomontage design.

1947 *45in (112.5cm) high*

£4,000-5,000 **SWA**

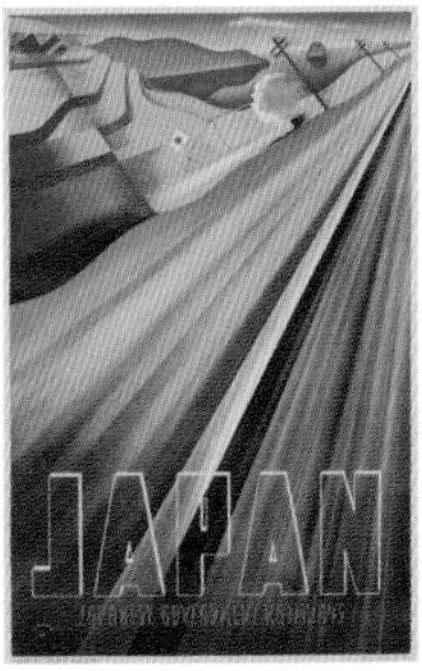

A 'Japan' poster, designed by Munetsugu Satomi, for the Japanese Tourist Board, printed by Seihan Printing Co., Osaka.

1937 *39in (97.5cm) high*

£3,000-4,000 **SWA**

An anonymous small format 'Air France' poster, from a set of six designed by Garetto, Solon, Vinci, Chanove, Koch and Periere.

c1938 *19.5in (49.5cm) high*

£800-1,200 **SWA**

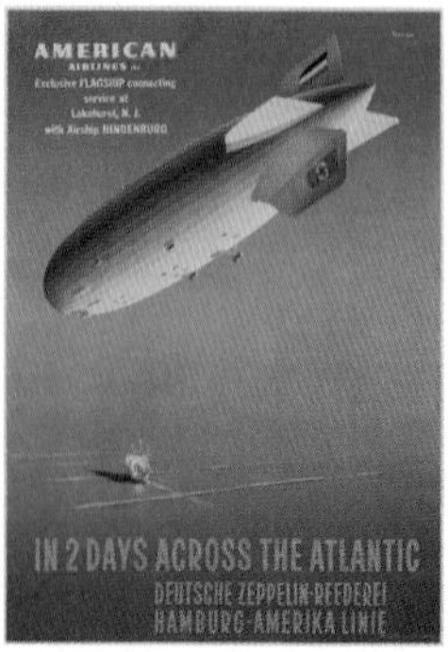

An 'In 2 days across the Atlantic' poster, by Ottomar Anton, printed by Muhlmeister & Johler, Hamburg, depicting the Hindenburg.

This poster appeared in several different languages, but this is the only known copy with an imprint from American Airlines.

c1936 *33in (84cm) high*

£3,500-4,500 **SWA**

A 'North America Express' poster, by Renato Cenni, advertising the trip from Genoa to New York.

c1935 *37in (94cm) high*

£1,800-2,200 **SWA**

A 'New York World's Fair' poster, by Nembhard N. Culin, printed by New York World's Fair 1939 Corporation, New York, depicting fairgoers entering the 'Perisphere' from the 'Trylon' and leaving by the 'Helicline'.

Themed 'The World of Tomorrow,' the fair's main attraction, housed inside the 'Perisphere', was a city of the future called 'Democracity', which visitors could view from revolving balconies. The poster was published two years prior to the fair when the plans were first released to the press. It was not part of the later competition, won by Joseph Binder, for the poster design ultimately chosen to promote the fair.

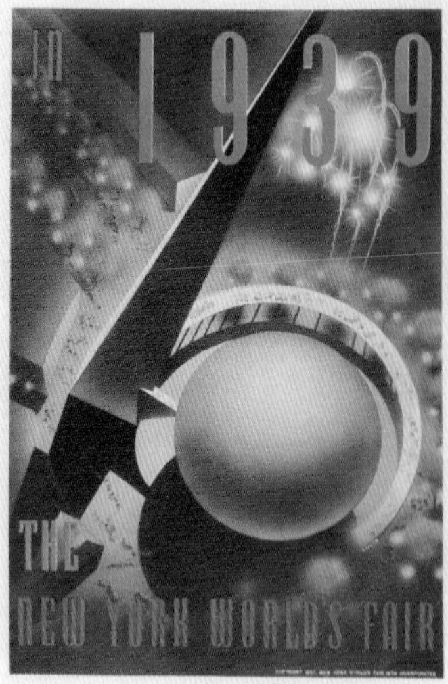

1937 *29in (73.5cm) high*

£2,800-3,200 **SWA**

A 'Zoologischer Garten' poster, designed by Ludwig Hohlwein, printed by G.M.B.H. Munich.

1912 *48.75in (122cm) high*

£15,000-20,000 **SWA**

A 'Beatles' poster, designed by Joachim, in a Pop Art style, with day-glo colours and flowers.

1968 *79in (197.5cm) high*

£800-1,200 **SWA**

An 'XVIII Secession Ausstellung' poster, designed by Gustav Klimt, printed by A. Berger, Vienna, with a provocatively blank space and grey typography.

Advertising a major retrospective exhibition of his own work, Klimt graphically reworks the head of Athena as he first represented her in his famous painting.

1903 *37.25in (93cm) high*

£15,000-20,000 **SWA**

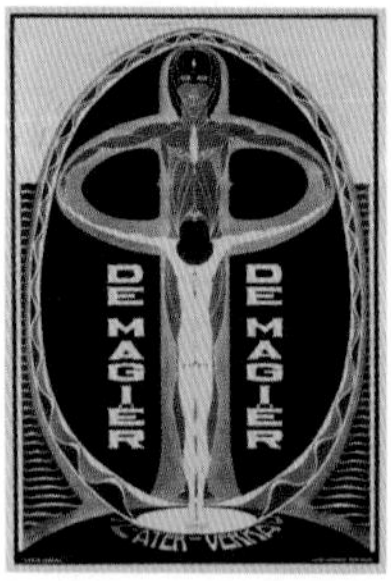

A rare 'De Magier' poster, designed by Chris Lebeau, advertising a theatrical production of G. K. Chesterton's book 'Magic: a Fantastic Comedy' printed by Lankhout, Den Haag.

c1915 *50in (125cm) high*

£4,500-5,500 **SWA**

A 'Monsavon' poster, designed by Charles Loupot, printed by Courbet, Paris, the background in blue airbrush, a woman reaching out of the shower.

1936 *78.5in (196cm) high*

£6,000-9,000 **SWA**

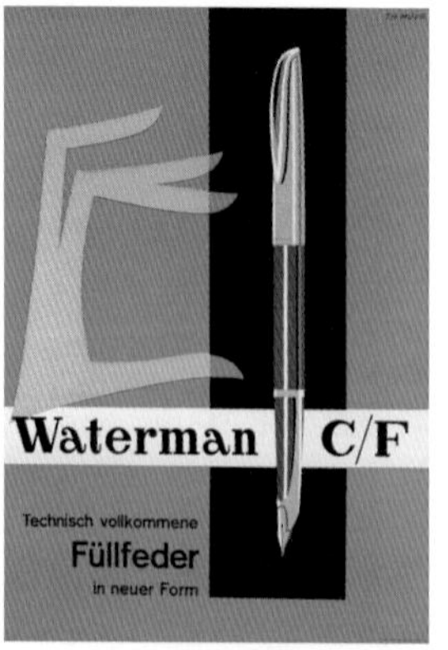

A 'Waterman C/F' poster, designed by Theo Muyr, printed by Bollmann, Zürich.

c1955 *50.5in (126cm) high*

£500-700 **SWA**

A 'World's Fair of San Francisco Bay' poster, by Shawl, Nyeland and Seavey, printed by Schmidt, San Francisco.

Louis Shawl was the first artist to serve on the board of directors of San Francisco's Advertising Club. He later became president of the San Francisco Art Directors' Club.

1937 *34.5in (87.5cm) high*

£2,500-3,000 **SWA**

An anonymous 'Loss of Feeling' poster, advertising the Russian film, featuring a robot and photographic image of the saxophone player.

1935 *34.5in (86cm) high*

£4,000-6,000 **SWA**

A portrait of Ellen F. and her brother George Lemuel Clark, attributed to John Carlin (American 1813-1891), unsigned, oil on canvas.

John Carlin exhibited at the National Academy and many other galleries.

c1850 *48.5in (123cm) high*

£10,000-15,000 **SK**

Thomas Cowperthwaite Eakins, (American 1844-1916), "Study of a Head", oil on board.

6.25in (16cm) high

£18,000-22,000 **FRE**

A portrait of Anna Hoyt, attributed to William Jennys (American 1774-1858), unsigned, oil on canvas.

This Neoclassical portrait is typical of Jennys' early 19thC work. It is full of realism but has sculptural qualities.

29.25in (73.5cm) high

£6,000-9,000 **SK**

Jacob Maentel (American 1763-1863), a pair of watercolour portraits.

10in (25.5cm) high

£3,500-4,500 **POOK**

A portrait of 'Phoebe Frances Ricker in Her Youth', attributed to Samuel Miller of Charlestown, Massachusetts (1807-1853), oil on canvas, unsigned.

35.25in (89.5cm) high

£6,000-9,000 **SK**

A portrait of Abraham Lincoln, attributed to George Frederick Wright (American 1828-1881), oil on canvas, giltwood frame probably original.

c1860 *29in (73.5cm) high*

£12,000-18,000 **SK**

A 19thC American School painting, 'Lady at Piano', oil on canvas, unframed.

45in (112.5cm) high

£7,000-10,000 **FRE**

A 19thC American School oil portrait of two children, on canvas, unsigned.

c1830 *29.75in (75.5cm) wide*

£3,000-4,000 **SK**

An American School portrait of Phoebe Frances Ricker, oil on canvas, unsigned.

Phoebe was the only child of J. C. Ricker, who founded the Amoskeg Fire Department No. 1 in 1859 in Manchester, New Hampshire. Phoebe died at the age of thirteen and her headstone still stands in Valley Cemetery, Manchester.

c1850 *29in (73.5cm) high*

£5,000-7,000 **SK**

Gottfried Lindauer (New Zealand 1839-1926), "Portrait of a Maori Woman in Traditional Dress", oil on canvas.

c1900 *18.5in (47cm) high*

£12,000-18,000 **WEB**

Gottfried Lindauer (New Zealand 1839-1926), "Portrait of a Maori woman in Colonial Dress", oil on canvas.

25.5in (65cm) high

£20,000-25,000 **WEB**

A pair of oil on canvas portraits by Jean Baptiste Greuze (French 1725-1805), depicting the artist's daughters, each signed and dated, in carved giltwood frames.

16.25in (41cm) high

£1,000,000+ **DN**

A painting by George Henry (Scottish 1858-1943), "Two Japanese Girls".

Henry toured Japan in the early 1890s with Edward Atkinson Hornel and his subsequent work was strongly influenced by these trips.

24in (61cm) high

£40,000-50,000 **L&T**

Robert Herdman (Scottish 1829-1888), "Behold Her, Single in the Field"'.

42in (107cm) high

£18,000-22,000 **L&T**

Edward Atkinson Hornel, (Scottish 1864-1933) "The Young Shepherdess".

90cm (35.5in) wide

£12,000-18,000 **L&T**

Robert Gemmell Hutchison (Scottish 1860-1936), "The Village Carnival", signed.

Robert Gemmell Hutchinson was born in Edinburgh and studied art at the Board of Manufacturers' School. This painting would have been executed in the 1880s or 1890s, a period regarded as the high point in his career.

From the Drambuie Collection.

61.5in (156cm) wide

£120,000-180,000 **L&T**

Keeley Halswelle (English 1832-1891), "Newhaven Minstrels".

60in (152cm) wide

£30,000-40,000 **L&T**

William McTaggart (Scottish, 1835-1910), "On the Beach at Carnoustie".

35.5in (90cm) wide

£25,000-30,000 **L&T**

Sir John Lavery (Scottish 1856-1941), "El Embiste", signed and dated "92".

From the Drambuie Collection.

8.5in (22cm) high

£28,000-32,000 **L&T**

Richard Ansdell (Scottish 1815-1885), "The Deer Forest", oil on canvas, signed and dated "1877".

From the Drambuie Collection.

64in (163cm) high

£40,000-60,000 **L&T**

Simon Saint-Jean (French, 1808-1860), "French Partridge at Evening".

37.5in (95cm) wide

£22,000-28,000 **L&T**

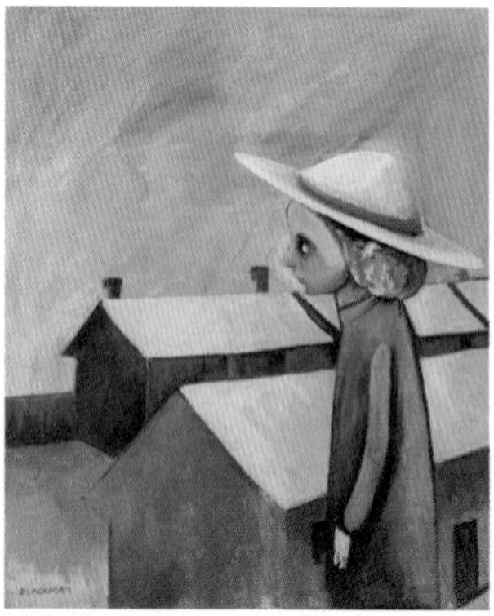

Charles Blackman (Australian 1928-), "Schoolgirl and Buildings", oil on composition board.

c1955 *29.5in (75cm) high*

£30,000-50,000 **DM**

Arthur Beecher Carles (American 1882-1952), "Standing Female Nude", oil on panel, signed, laid down on Masonite.

13in (33cm) high

£30,000-40,000 **FRE**

Arthur Beecher Carles (American 1882-1952), "The Harpist - Edna Phillips Rosenbaum", oil on canvas, accompanied by related photographs of the sitter.

Edna Phillips Rosenbaum became the first woman to occupy a principal position with a major American symphony when she became first harp with the Philadelphia Orchestra in 1930.

30in (76.5cm) high

£30,000-40,000 **FRE**

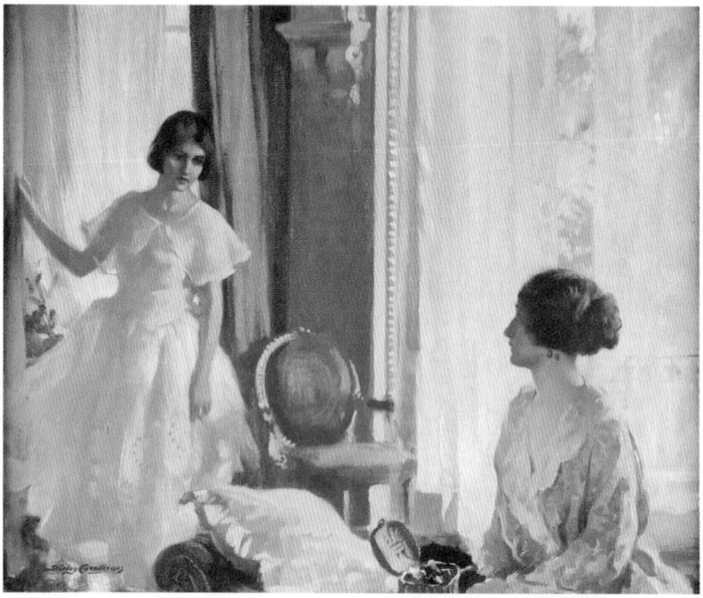

Stanley Cursiter (Scottish 1887-1976), "The Seamstress", signed and dated 1923.

From the Drambuie Collection.

30in (61cm) wide

£60,000-90,000 **L&T**

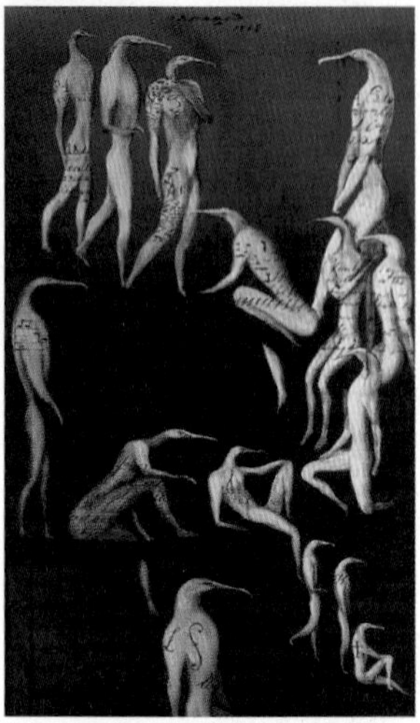

Bill Hammond (New Zealand 1947-), 'Untitled – Bird Study', oil on canvas.

1998 *39.25in (100cm) high*

£50,000-70,000 **WEB**

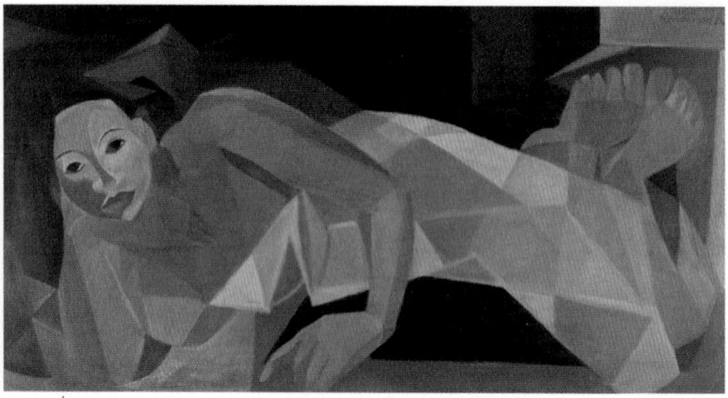

Louise Henderson (New Zealand 1902-1994), "Samoan Woman", oil on canvas.

1954 *39.5in (100.5cm) wide*

£10,000-15,000 **WEB**

Jack Hoggan (Scottish, 1951-), "A Summer Breeze".

Self-taught artist Jack Vettriano was born in Fife as Jack Hoggan. This is an early work by the artist and is very similar to John Singer Sargent's 'A Gust of Wind'.

20in (51cm) high

£6,000-9,000 **L&T**

Edward Atkinson Hornel (Scottish 1864-1933), "Easter Eggs", oil on canvas, signed and dated.

From the Drambuie Collection.

1905 *60in (153cm) high*

£80,000-120,000 **L&T**

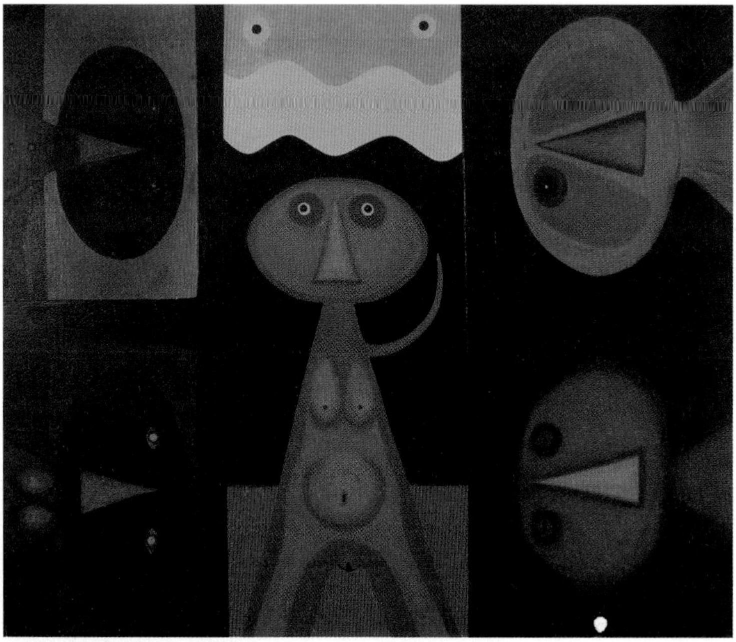

Michael Illingworth (New Zealand 20thC), "Eve Fig in Landscape with Portraits", oil on canvas.

1966 *36in (91.5cm) wide*

£50,000-70,000 **WEB**

A pencil drawing by Norman Lindsay (Australian 1879-1969), untitled study of a woman, inscribed "NL".

15.75in (40cm) high

£5,000-7,000 **SHA**

Norman Lindsay (Australian 1879-1969),"The Soldiers' Admirers", watercolour on paper, signature.

10.75in (27cm) wide

£6,000-9,000 **SHA**

Norman Lindsay (Australian 1879-1969), "The Pool", etching, numbered 31 in an edition of 40, signed.

6in (15cm) high

£2,200-2,800 **SHA**

Violet Oakley (American 1874-1961), "Penn's Vision", oil painting over a printed base, printed inscription, probably a working study for murals in the Pennsylvania State Capitol in Harrisburg.

Violet Oakley was perhaps the greatest female muralist the United States has produced.

54.25in (137.5cm) wide

£8,000-12,000 **FRE**

Michael Smither (New Zealand 1939-), "Sarah with Flowers", oil on board.

1967 *35.5in (90cm) high*

£35,000-45,000 **WEB**

Ruskin Spear (English 1911-1990), "Seated woman with Sardines".

30in (75cm) high

£7,000-10,000 **L&T**

William de la Montagne Cary (American 1840-1922), "Indians on the Plains", oil on board, signed lower left.

1866 *21.5in (54.5cm) wide*

£70,000-100,000 **RENO**

E. Martin Hennings (American 1886-1956), "The Bow and Arrow", oil on canvas, signed lower left.

10in (25.5cm) wide

£40,000-50,000 **RENO**

E. Martin Hennings, "Indian Music", oil on canvas board, signed lower left.

10in (25.5cm) wide

£40,000-50,000 **RENO**

Frank Tenney Johnson (American 1879-1939), "An Unexpected Visitor", oil on canvas, signed lower left.

1929 *30in (76cm) wide*

£100,000-150,000 **RENO**

Frank McCarthy (American 1924-2002), "A Cold Trail", signed lower right, oil on board.

32in (81cm) wide

£30,000-50,000 **RENO**

Peter Rindisbacher (American 1806-1834), Western winter landscape with buffalo and a Native American in snow shoes, signed in lower right margin "P. Rindisbacher".

15.25in (38.5cm) wide

£120,000-180,000 **POOK**

Charles M. Russell (American 1864-1926), "Portrait of a Blackfoot", watercolour, signed and dated.

1900 *9.75in (24cm) high*

£22,000-28,000 **RENO**

Charles M. Russell, "Elk In Lake McDonald", watercolour, signed and dated.

1906 *19.5in (49cm) wide*

£70,000-100,000 **RENO**

CHARLES M. RUSSELL

- Charles Marion Russell (1864-1926) arrived in Montana at the age of 16 with dreams of becoming a cowboy. Whilst working as a night wrangler from 1882, he began to make sketches of the scenes and people that surrounded him.
- He became one of the few 'Western' artists who had lived the majority of his life in the American West. He witnessed the passing of the traditional frontier lifestyle.
- Encouraged by his wife Nancy, he gave up work as a cowboy in the 1890s to become a full-time artist. He worked from a log cabin studio, filled with Western artifacts, from 1903.
- His breakthrough came with an exhibition in New York in 1911, followed by a show in London three years later.
- In his lifetime, he completed more than 4,000 paintings.

Charles M. Russell, "Thurston Held Mona Somewhat Tighter Than He Need To Have Done", watercolour and gouache, signed.

15.5in (39cm) high

£30,000-40,000 **RENO**

A watercolour with ink script letter by Charles M. Russell (American 1864-1926), to 'Friend Thed', second sheet signed lower right.

Theodore Gibson ('friend Thed') dabbled in real estate, managed Great Falls' Park Hotel, and was active in the fight for Native American rights in Montana.

1920 *11in (28cm) high*

£70,000-100,000 **RENO**

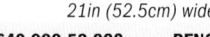

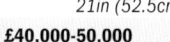

Joseph H. Sharp (American 1859-1953), "The Waterhole, Blackfoot Country", oil on board, signed.

11in (28cm) high

£60,000-90,000 **RENO**

Joseph H. Sharp, "Landscape With Teepee", oil on board, signed.

13.5in (34.5cm) wide

£40,000-60,000 **RENO**

An oil on canvas by Joseph. H. Sharp (American 1859-1953), "Hunting Son", signed lower right.

16in (40.5cm) high

£80,000-120,000 **RENO**

John Mix Stanley (American 1814-1872), "Scene on the Columbia River", oil on canvas.

21in (52.5cm) wide

£40,000-50,000 **RENO**

Howard Terpning (American 1927-), "Winter Blanket", oil on canvas, signed lower left.

30in (76cm) high

£80,000-120,000 **RENO**

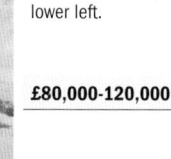

Howard Terpning, "Crows in Yellowstone", oil on canvas, signed lower right.

44in (112cm) high

£180,000-220,000 **RENO**

William Boardman (American 1815-1895), "Squam Lake", signed and dated "Boardman 47", oil on canvas, label from the American Art Union and inscription.

60in (152.5cm) wide

£18,000-22,000 **SK**

Rev. John Thomson of Duddingston (Scottish 1778-1840), "Crichton Castle", oil on canvas.

From the Drambuie Collection.

41in (104cm) wide

£25,000-30,000 **L&T**

John Joseph Enneking (American), "Woodland Stream", oil on canvas, signed and dated "Enneking 97", label from the Ogunquit Museum of American Art and a London canvas stamp on the reverse, framed, restored.

1897 *45in (114.5cm) wide*

£40,000-50,000 **SK**

Edmund Darch Lewis (American 1835-1910), monumental oil on canvas depicting a mountainous Western landscape, signed lower right "Edward Darch Lewis 1865".

69.5in (176.5cm) wide

£25,000-30,000 **POOK**

John Linnell (Scottish 1792-1882), "Storm in Autumn".

From the Drambuie Collection.

52.75in (134cm) wide

£150,000-200,000 **L&T**

CLOSER LOOK AT A J.P. FISK PAINTING

This manufactory produced cotton wadding and batting and suffered one of Pawtucket, Rhode Island's, most destructive fires on September 10, 1870. The incident was sketched by railroad commuter and eyewitness, Boston artist J.P. Fisk.

The work carefully and accurately records the position of the buildings, the steamers and the onlookers in meticulous detail. The scale is large and the image is striking.

Three books relating to the Union Wadding Co. accompany the painting - two ledgers and 'Lamb's Textile Industries of the United States' by E. Everton Foster - increasing the local historical appeal.

The Pawtucket Gazette and Chronicle reported in May 1872, "This beautiful work of art was planned to be exhibited the end of May 1872 in order to raise money to pay for the picture. Photographs of the painting of different sizes will be offered for sale at the festival."

J.P. Fisk (American 19thC), "Union Wadding Co. Fire", Pawtucket, Rhode Island, signed "J.P. Fisk Boston".

c1870 *73.75in (187cm) wide*

£120,000-180,000 **SK**

David Roberts (Scottish 1796-1864), "A View from Calton Hill Looking East Northeast", signed, dated 1863,

From the Drambuie Collection.

30in (75cm) wide

£40,000-60,000 **L&T**

Arthur Fitzwilliam Tait (American 1819-1905), "Steady, Woodcock Shooting", oil on canvas, signed, inscribed and dated "A.F. Tait N.A. 86".

Tait specialized in the depiction of animals.

24in (61cm) wide

£30,000-40,000 **SK**

Walter Emerson Baum (American 1884-1956), "Pennsylvania Winter Landscape with Horse and Sleigh", oil on canvas, signed bottom left.

Walter Emerson Baum was a Pennsylvania Impressionist.

30in (76cm) wide

£12,000-18,000 **FRE**

John E. Berninger (American 1897-1981), oil on canvas depicting a winter landscape with barn, signed lower right "John E. Berninger".

John E. Berninger was a Pennsylvania Impressionist.

30in (76cm) high

£8,000-12,000 **POOK**

Arthur Boyd (Australian 1920-1999), "Wimmera Landscape", oil on composition board.

48in (122cm) wide

£30,000-40,000 **DM**

Arthur Beecher Carles (American 1882-1952), "Notre Dame", oil on canvas.

1907 *39.5in (100.5cm) high*

£25,000-30,000 **FRE**

Alfred Joseph Casson (Canadian 1898-1992), "Graveyard - Carnarvon".

£6,000-9,000 **WAD**

Fern Isabel Coppedge (American 1888-1951), "New Hope - Early Spring", oil on canvas, signed bottom right.

Fern Isabel Coppedge was a Pennsylvania Impressionist.

20in (51cm) wide

£28,000-32,000 **FRE**

Fern Isabel Coppedge (American 1888-1951), "The Old Stone Bridge", oil on canvas, signed bottom centre left, in an original frame by Raymond Vanselous with incised initials and attached business card.

16in (40.5cm) high

£30,000-40,000 **FRE**

Fern Isabel Coppedge, "Hills of Pennsylvania Near New Hope", oil on canvas, signed bottom centre left.

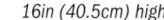

20in (51cm) high

£30,000-50,000 **FRE**

Fern Isabel Coppedge, "A View across a Harbor", oil on canvas, signed bottom right.

20in (51cm) wide

£22,000-28,000 **FRE**

Ray Crooke (Australian 1922-), "Breaking Camp, Laura River", oil on canvas.

59.75in (152cm) wide

£15,000-20,000 **BONA**

Ray Austin Crooke (Australian 1922-), "The Stockyard", oil on paper board, inscribed "R.Crooke".

23.5in (60cm) wide

£3,000-4,000 **SHA**

d'Arcy W. Doyle (Australian 1932-2001), oil on canvas, inscribed "d'Arcy W. Doyle".

23.5in (59.5cm) wide

£4,000-6,000 **SHA**

Russell Drysdale (Australian 1912-1981), "Landscape in the Kimberleys", oil on canvas.

1958 *50in (127cm) wide*

£280,000-320,000 **DM**

Arthur Clifton Goodwin (American 1866-1929), "Boston Street Scene and Wharf View / A Double-Sided Work", oil on panel, each side signed "ACGoodwin".

24in (61cm) wide

£8,000-12,000 **SK**

Aldro Thompson Hibbard (American 1886-1972), "Autumn Landscape at West Townshend, Vermont", oil on canvas, signed "A.T.Hibbard" lower left, with label from Godel & Co., New York.

32in (81cm) wide

£8,000-12,000 **SK**

Paul Henry (Irish 1876-1958), oil on board depicting a western Irish landscape, signed lower right, with label for The Medici Society.

This is a fine example of Henry's late work, completed after a difficult period of domestic problems.

1938 *16in (40.5cm) wide*

£75,000-80,000 **DN**

William Jurian Kaula (American 1871-1953), "Temple Hills", oil on canvas, signed "WILLIAM J. KAULA", label from the Jordan Marsh Company on the reverse, framed.

Renowned for capturing the "illusive gossamer delicacy", Kaula's work often included cloud-filled skies floating above New Hampshire hills. Controlled brushwork captures the fleeting effects of weather and atmosphere.

39.5in (100.5cm) wide

£15,000-20,000 **SK**

Rockwell Kent (American 1882-1971), "Sportsman's Delight, Alternatively Titled Hunter's Delight or Just Shot", oil on canvas, signed and dated "Rockwell Kent 1941 UAA" lower left, label from the Providence Art Club and inscribed "34 Hunter's Delight", in original frame, two corners reworked by the artist.

Rockwell Kent was an artist, craftsman and social activist. His nonconformist views brought him denunciation at the height of his career, but since the 1970s, his work has been the focus of numerous exhibitions and the demand for it has increased.

36in (91.5cm) wide

£70,000-100,000 **SK**

Maud Lewis (Canadian 1903-1970), acrylic and oil on board.

Known as Canada's own 'Grandma Moses', Maud Lewis has become an icon of Canadian folk art.

13.75in (35cm) wide

£2,000-3,000 **BMM**

Doris Lusk (New Zealand 1916-1990), "Landscape - French Bay, Titirangi", oil on board.

36.5in (93cm) wide

£20,000-25,000 **WEB**

Antonio Pietro Martino (American 1902-1989), "Canal Lock", oil on canvas, signed and dated bottom left.

Antonio Pietro Martino was a Philadelphia Impressionist.

1931 *30in (76cm) wide*

£20,000-25,000 **FRE**

Antonio Pietro Martino (American 1902-1989), "Winter Thaw", oil on canvas, signed and dated bottom left.

36in (91.5cm) wide

£18,000-22,000 **FRE**

Antonio Pietro Martino, "A Winter Landscape", oil on canvas, signed and indistinctly dated bottom right.

36in (91.5cm) wide

£12,000-18,000 **FRE**

Arthur Meltzer (American 1893-1989), "The Marsh", oil on canvas, signed lower right "Arthur Meltzer 22", bears "Second Annual Phila. Art Week Association" label verso.

Arthur Meltzer was a Pennsylvania Impressionist.

1922 *24in (60cm) wide*

£10,000-15,000 **POOK**

John Maclauchlan Milne (Scottish 1886-1957), "High Corrie".

19.25in (50cm) wide

£8,000-12,000 **L&T**

Albert Namatjira of the Arrernte (Australian Aboriginal 1902-1959), "Mt Henghlen", watercolour on paper, signed, inscribed with title on backing board, framed and glazed.

Namatjira became famous for his landscapes, different in style to traditional Aboriginal art. He and his wife became the first Aborigines to be granted Australian citizenship.

c1955 *14.25in (36cm) wide*

£8,000-12,000 **SHA**

Sidney Nolan (Australian), "Kelly at Stringybark Creek", oil on composition board.

c1965 *29in (73.5cm) wide*

£40,000-50,000 **DM**

Kenneth Nunamaker (American), "A Winter Panorama", oil on canvas, signed "K. Nunamaker" bottom left.

Kenneth Nunamaker was a Pennsylvania Impressionist.

42in (106.5cm) wide

£15,000-20,000 **FRE**

Roy C. Nuse (American 1890-1957), "Little Neshaminy at Rushland, PA", oil on canvas board, signed with initials bottom left, inscribed and dated verso.

Roy C. Nuse was a Pennsylvania Impressionist.

1940 *12.25in (31cm) wide*

£10,000-15,000 **FRE**

CLOSER LOOK AT A MAXWELL PARRISH PAINTING

Maxfield Parrish (American 1870-1966) is one of the early twentieth century's best known painters. His works are extremely desirable.

His paintings combined romanticism, glowing colours, and the realistic treatment of figures.

His works were so popular that during the 1920s, one out of every four households had a Parrish image in it.

Parrish was inspired by the colour separation processes of new printing technology and adopted a unique painting technique that resulted in a bright and luminous effect. He would lay colours in separate layers of transparent oil, alternating with varnish.

Maxfield Parrish (American 1870-1966), "Winter Dusk", oil on board, signed and dated "Maxfield Parrish 1943", label from Vose Galleries, Boston on the reverse, inscribed "R.W.P FROM M.P MCMXLIII".

11in (28cm) wide

£70,000-100,000 **SK**

Kathleen Letitia (Kate) O'Connor (Australian 1876-1968), "Trees in Tubs, Luxembourg Gardens", oil on canvas, inscribed "K L O'Connor", portrait verso.

26.25in (66.5cm) wide

£18,000-22,000 **SHA**

Sir Robin Philipson (Scottish 1916-1992), "Hillside with Artist".

20.5in (52cm) wide

£10,000-15,000 **L&T**

Edward Willis Redfield (American 1869-1965), "Bridge Over A Canal", oil on canvas, signed and dated "E. W. Redfield 98" bottom left.

Edward Willis Redfield was a Pennsylvania Impressionist.

32in (81cm) wide

£30,000-50,000 **FRE**

Lloyd Rees (Australian 1914-1989), "House By The River Tasmania", pastel on paper, inscribed and dated "L Rees".

1987 *21.5in (54.5cm) wide*

£4,000-5,000 **SHA**

Lloyd Rees (Australian 1816-1989), "Moving Waters", oil on canvas, mounted on hardboard, inscribed "L Rees 74".

29.25in (74cm) wide

£18,000-22,000 **SHA**

Anna Mary Robertson 'Grandma Moses' (American 1860-1961), "March", oil on board, framed and signed "MOSES" lower right, dated, numbered and titled on a Galerie St. Etienne artist's label.

1944 *15in (37.5cm) wide*

£25,000-35,000 **SK**

Hugh Sawrey (Australian 1923-1999), "The Plough Team, Darling Dows, Queensland", oil on canvas, signed.

23.5in (59.5cm) wide

£5,000-7,000 **SHA**

Hugh Sawrey, "Saturday Morning at the Bush Store", oil on canvas, signed "Sawrey".

30.75in (78cm) wide

£5,000-7,000 **SHA**

Walter Elmer Schofield (American 1867-1944), "Berkshire Hills", oil on canvas, signed bottom right.

Walter Elmer Schofield was a Philadelphia Impressionist.

24in (61cm) wide

£20,000-25,000 **FRE**

Walter Elmer Schofield (American 1867-1944), "Village Scene", oil on canvas, signed bottom right.

24in (61cm) wide

£10,000-15,000 **FRE**

Jeffrey Smart (Australian 1921-), "Third Study for The Dividing Line", oil on canvas board.

1978 *19.5in (49.5cm) high*

£25,000-35,000 **DM**

Robert Spencer (American 1879-1931), "The Grey House", oil on canvas, signed and dated, inscribed on stretcher verso, Harer frame with incised signature.

Robert Spencer was a Philadelphia Impressionist.

c1910 *30in (76cm) wide*

£80,000-120,000 **FRE**

Arthur Streeton (Australian 1867-1943), "The Oak Lane", oil on canvas.

1909 *30in (76cm) high*

£35,0000-45,000 **DM**

Marc-Aurelle de Foy Suzor Cote (Canadian 1869-1937), "End of Day".

£25,000-30,000 **WAD**

Grahame Sydney (New Zealand 1948-), "Uplands", oil on linen.

2003 24in (61cm) wide

£12,000-18,000 **WEB**

Tom Thomson (Canadian 1877-1917), "Canoe and Lake, Algonquin Park".

The painting features a canoe which matches descriptions of the artist's own boat. Works by Thomson are considered rare due to his early death at the age of 40.

£180,000-220,000 **WAD**

Frederick Horsman Varley (Canadian 1881-1969), "Don Valley Meadow".

£25,000-30,000 **WAD**

Guy Carleton Wiggins (American 1883-1962), "Morning on the River / An East River View", oil on board, framed and signed "Guy Wiggins N.A." lower right, titled and signed on the reverse.

17.25in (43cm) wide

£12,000-18,000 **SK**

Toss Woollaston (New Zealand 1910-1998), "Evening Landscape with Half Moon", oil on board.

46.5in (118cm) high

£18,000-22,0000 **WEB**

Samuel Finley Morse Badger (American 1873-1919), "Schooner Edward H. Cole", oil on canvas, signed "SFM Badger" and inscribed on the reverse, in moulded giltwood frame, unlined.

32in (81.5cm) wide

£6,000-9,000 **SK**

Chester Charles Harding (American 1792-1866), oil on canvas depicting fishing and sailing vessels, signed lower right "C Harding/Pinxt, 1832,".

36in (91.5cm) wide

£8,000-12,000 **BRU**

J.E. Buttersworth (American 1817-1894), "Schooner Walter Francis", oil on canvas, signed "J.E. Buttersworth", with the Jacob Bell to background.

James Edward Buttersworth's career spanned sixty years. Dedicated to producing portraits of all types of ships at sea, he was born in England and schooled in the tradition of English marine painting.

c1865 *24in (61cm) wide*

£60,000-90,000 **SK**

Antonio Jacobsen (American 1850-1921), "American Screw Steamer", oil on canvas, signed and dated "1889 705 Palisade Av. West Hoboken. NJ".

34.5in (87.5cm) wide

£8,000-12,000 **SK**

Antonio Jacobsen (American 1850-1921), "Excursion Steamer Providence", oil on canvas, signed and dated "A. Jacobsen 1883", restored.

50.25in (127.5cm) wide

£30,000-40,000 **SK**

A 19thC Chinese School oil on linen, "Ship Empress D.R. Lecrew Entering Hong Kong by the Lgemoon Passage", indistinctly signed, in a contemporary moulded wood frame.

1862 *39.5in (99cm) wide*

£15,000-20,000 **SK**

Sunqua (Chinese active 1830-1870), "The Foreign Factories Near the City of Canton", watercolour with gouache on paper, depicting daily life around the hongs, signed "Sunqua".

c1830 *14.5in (36cm) wide*

£28,000-32,000 **SK**

Sam Bough (Scottish 1822-1878), "Peel Harbour", oil on canvas, signed and dated 1875.

From the Drambuie Collection.

48in (122cm) wide

£30,000-40,000 **L&T**

William Bradford (American 1823-1892), "Coastal Rocks, A Sketch", signed "W. Bradford" in lower left corner, in original frame, oil on board.

19.75in (50cm) wide

£12,000-18,000 **SK**

Alfred Thompson Bricher (American 1937-1908), oil on canvas marine scene, possibly off Bailey's Island in Maine, framed and signed "Abricher" lower right, label from Livingston Galleries, New York.

39in (97.5cm) wide

£22,000-28,000 **SK**

He Chung (Chinese 19thC), "Macao, The Praya Grande", oil on canvas, the artist identified on a label verso, titled on a brass tag affixed to the frame, in a period carved wooden frame.

c1850 *31in (77.5cm) wide*

£12,000-18,000 **SK**

Sunqua (Chinese active 1830-1870), 'The City of Macao', watercolour with guache on paper, depicting a view of the Praya Grande from the south, signed "Sunqua".

c1830 *14.5in (36cm) wide*

£6,000-9,000 **SK**

William McTaggart (Scottish 1835-1910), "Natural Harbour, Cockenzie".

From the Drambuie Collection.

37in (94cm) high

£100,000-150,000 **L&T**

A 19thC Chinese School oil on canvas, depicting a view of Whampoa Anchorage and Island, unsigned, with several vessels displaying American, British, and European flags, later gilt gesso frame.

c1810 *23.5in (60cm) wide*

£15,000-20,000 **SK**

A 19thC Chinese School oil on canvas, depicting a view of the Factories at Canton, unsigned, with Dutch and British flags.

The flag of the Netherlands was replaced by the French flag in 1832.

c1830 *23.5in (60cm) wide*

£12,000-18,000 **SK**

Dwight Blaney (American 1865-1944), "A Cove on Ironbound Island", oil on canvas, unframed, signed and dated "D. Blaney 1908".

Blaney's close friend, John Singer Sargent, encouraged him to paint, and Blaney even appears in Sargent's later work. The influence of Monet is seen in many of Blaney's landscapes and seascapes.

34.5in (86cm) wide

£7,000-10,000 **SK**

Dwight Blaney, "View from Ironbound Island to Frenchman Bay", oil on canvas, unframed, signed and dated "D. Blaney 1902" lower left.

1902 *33in (82.5cm) high*

£15,000-20,000 **SK**

Francis Campbell Boileau Cadell (Scottish 1883-1937), "Iona - East Bay".

The artist was part of a group known as 'The Colourists' who were heavily influenced by the Impressionists. He often painted Iona.

From the Drambuie Collection.

30in (76cm) wide

£100,000-150,000 **L&T**

Earl Cunningham (American 1893-1977), "Harbor Scene", oil on board, signed "Earl Cunningham" bottom left.

23.75in (59cm) wide

£4,000-6,000 **FRE**

Arthur Clifton Goodwin (American 1866-1929), oil on canvas depicting a port scene with fishermen attending to a boat, signed "A. C. Goodwin" bottom right.

36in (91.5cm) wide

£5,000-7,000 **FRE**

Emile Albert Gruppe (American 1888-1954), "Boats at Gloucester", oil on canvas, framed, signed "Emile A. Gruppe" lower right, identified on the reverse.

24in (60cm) wide

£8,000-12,000 **SK**

Emile Albert Gruppe (American 1888-1954) "Working on the Nets", oil on canvas, signed "Emile A. Gruppe" lower right, titled and dated, framed, gallery labels.

1966 *30in (75cm) wide*

£7,000-12,000 **SK**

Lawren Stewart Harris (Canadian 1885-1970), "Bylot Island South Shore from Eclipse Sound".

Harris was a founding member of the Group of Seven, a group of Canadian landscape artists inspired by the wilderness paintings of Tom Thomson and the Post-Impressionist movement.

£200,000-250,000 **WAD**

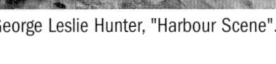

George Leslie Hunter, "Harbour Scene".

10.5in (27cm) high

£12,000-18,000 **L&T**

Harry Leith-Ross (American 1886-1973), "A Gloucester Wharf", oil on canvas, signed lower right "Leith-Ross".

24in (61cm) wide

£10,000-15,000 **POOK**

Colin McCahon (New Zealand 1919-1987), "Muriwai, Necessary Protection and Oaia Island", watercolour, ink and charcoal on paper.

1971 *30.25in (77cm) wide*

£40,000-60,000 **WEB**

John Maclauchlan Milne (Scottish 1886-1957), "Beach Scene, South of France".

From the Drambuie Collection.

18in (46cm) wide

£30,000-40,000 **L&T**

Laurence Sisson (American 1928-), "Coastal Inlet", oil on masonite, signed "L.Sisson" lower right, framed.

63.5in (161cm) wide

£3,000-5,000 **SK**

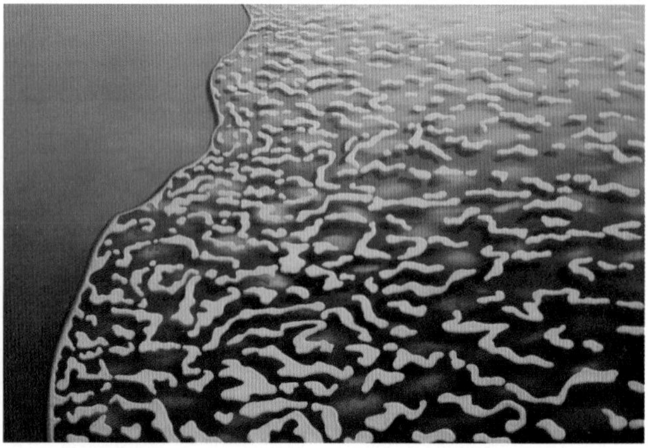

Michael Smither (New Zealand 1939-), "Wave Pool", oil on board.

1975 *71.75in (182.5cm) high*

£30,000-40,000 **WEB**

Bill Sutton (New Zealand 1917-2000), "Land, Sea, Sky Synthesis", oil on board.

1964 *120in (304.5cm) high*

£22,000-28,000 **WEB**

John Whorf (American 1903-1959), "Fisherman", oil on canvas, signed "John Whorf" lower left, framed.

25in (63.5cm) wide

£8,000-12,000 **SK**

John Whorf (American 1903-1959), "Tending to the Sails", oil on canvas, signed "John Whorf" lower left, craquelure, framed.

24in (61cm) wide

£15,000-20,000 **SK**

Francis Campbell Boileau Cadell (Scottish 1883-1937), "Interior – 30 Regent Terrace".

From the Drambuie Collection.

23.55in (60cm) high

£150,000-200,000 **L&T**

Patrick Hockey (Australian 1948-1992), "Moonflowers", acrylic on board.

45.25in (115cm) high

£8,000-12,000 **BONA**

Leslie Hunter (Scottish 1898-1973), "A Still Life of Fruit and Flowers".

From the Drambuie Collection.

22.5in (57cm) high

£70,000-100,000 **L&T**

Kathleen Letitia (Kate) O'Connor (Australian 1876-1968), "My Studio In Paris", oil on board, inscribed "K L O'Connor".

22.75in (58cm) wide

£18,000-22,000 **SHA**

Margaret Olley (Australian 1923-), oil on canvas, "Interior with Still Life".

47.25in (120cm) high

£35,000-45,000 **BONA**

Samuel John Peploe (Scottish 1871-1935), "A Still Life of Pink Roses and Fruit".

Peploe was born in Edinburgh and studied at the Royal Scottish Academy before becoming a member of the 'Scottish Colourists' group. This painting was executed c1919.

From the Drambuie Collection.

18in (46cm) high

£220,000-280,000 **L&T**

Margaret Preston (Australian 1875-1963), "Everlasting Flowers", oil on canvas.

1929 *17.75in (45cm) high*

£30,000-40,000 **DM**

Anne Redpath (Scottish 1895-1965), "Still Life with Round Table".

From the Drambuie Collection.

23.5in (60cm) high

£70,000-100,000 **L&T**

Joseph Stella (American), "Palmette (Lemon)", colour pastel on buff wove paper, signed in pencil, lower right.

17in (45.5cm) high

£6,000-8,000 **SWA**

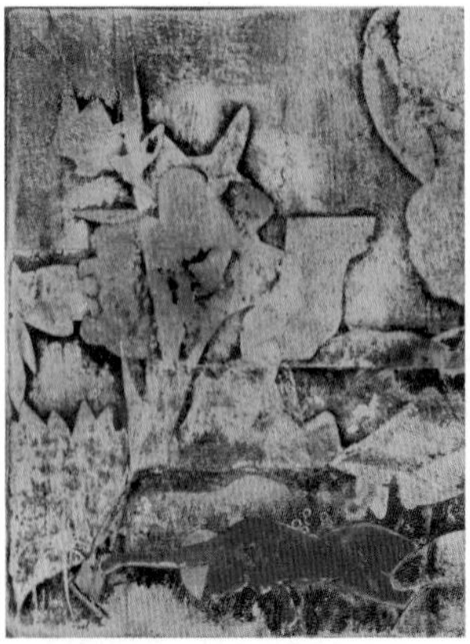

Romare Bearden (American 1914-1988), "Alone (Seul)", acrylic and collage mounted on masonite, signed in pencil, upper right.

9in (23cm) wide

£8,000-12,000 SWA

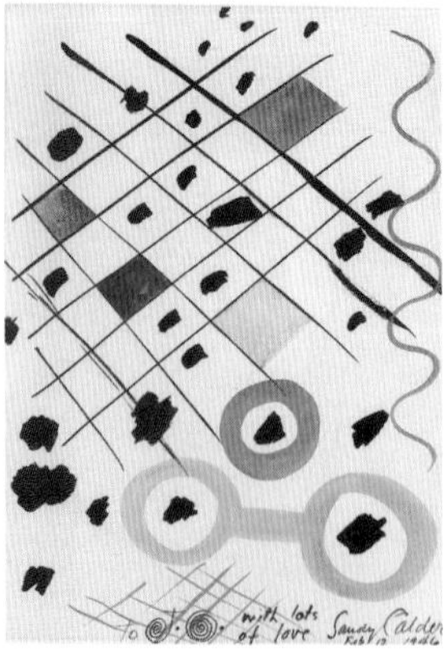

Alexander Calder (American 1898-1976), untitled gouache on paper, inscribed "To J.O. with lots of love Sandy/Calder Feb. 12, 1946".

15.25in (38.5cm) high

£7,000-10,000 SK

A CLOSER LOOK AT A JOHN BRACK PAINTING

John Brack (1920-1999) was one of Australia's leading 20thC artists. He was a member of the 'Antipodean' group that rejected Abstract Expressionism's intolerence of figurative art.

From the 1970s, Brack's work became more surreal. Playing cards, postcards and pencils became common motifs.

The National Gallery of Victoria purchased one of Brack's first paintings "The Barbers Shop". He has since had a number of retrospectives at major galleries such as the National Gallery of Australia.

Paintings are meticulously and precisely painted.

John Brack (Australian 1920-1999), "Assorted, Consorted", oil on canvas.

1989 72in (183cm) high

£180,000-220,000 DM

Philip Clairmont (New Zealand 1949-1984), "Interior with Chair", oil on unstretched canvas.

1978 58.75in (149.5cm) high

£18,000-22,000 WEB

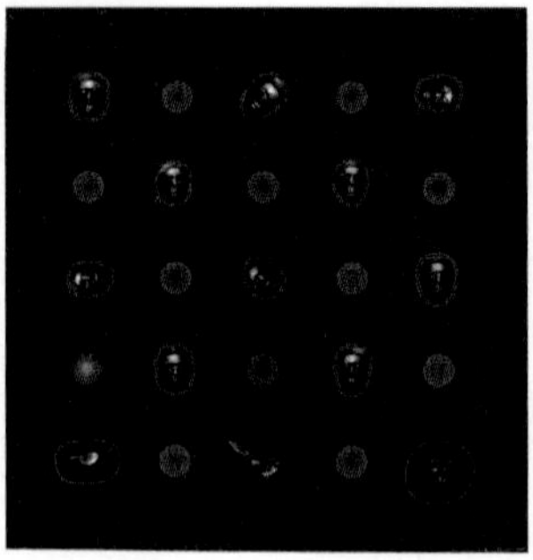

Shane Cotton (New Zealand 1964-), "The Last Laugh", acrylic on canvas.

2002 55.5in (141cm) wide

£20,000-25,000 WEB

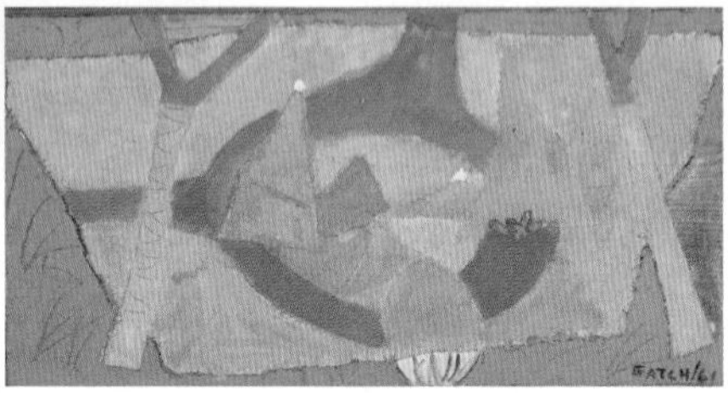

Lee Gatch (American 1902-1968), "Tawney Garden", oil on canvas, incorporating collage on panel with wooden surround, signed and dated "GATCH 61" lower right, inscribed and with artist's stamp.

15in (38cm) wide

£3,000-5,000 FRE

Frances Hodgkins (New Zealand 1869-1947), "Malmains Farm", gouache.

1937 20.5in (53cm) wide

£22,000-28,000 WEB

Henry Bainbridge McCarter (American 1866-1942), "Gwentlands Park, Newham on Severn", oil on board, signed "H. McCARTER" bottom left, signed and dated verso.

40in (100cm) wide

£3,000-5,000 FRE

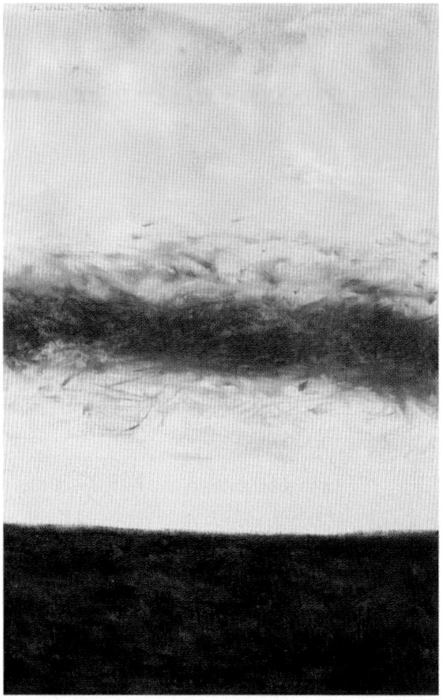

Colin McCahon (New Zealand 1919-1987), "A Poem of Kaipara Flats 17", acrylic, charcoal and watercolour on paper.

1971 *40.75in (103.5cm) high*

£40,000-60,000 **WEB**

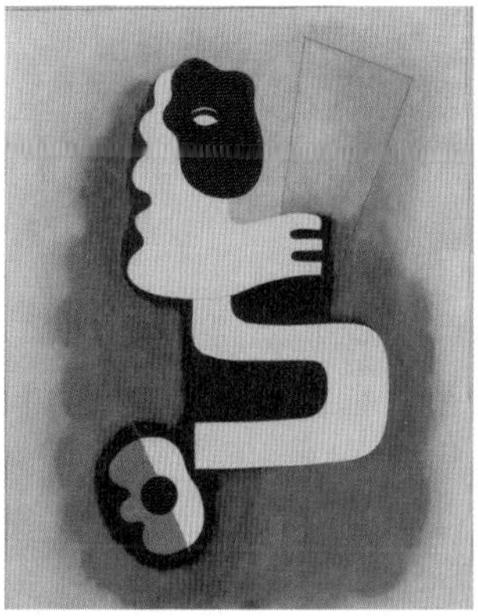

An oil on canvas by Carlos Merida (Guatemalan 1891-1984), "Cancion de Cuna/Song of the Cradle", framed, signed and dated "CARLOS MERIDA 1936" lower centre, incised stamp from Boris Mirski Art Gallery.

1936 *31in (77.5cm) high*

£35,000-45,000 **SK**

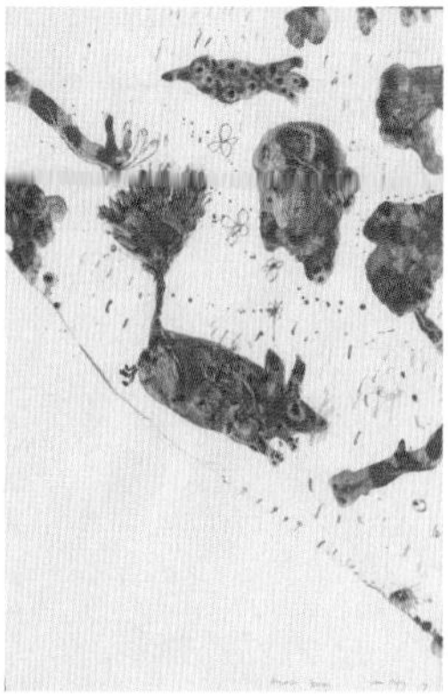

John Henry Olsen (Australian 1928-), "Animals Passing", watercolour on paper, inscribed "Animals Passing John Olsen '79".

29.5in (75cm) high

£4,000-6,000 **SHA**

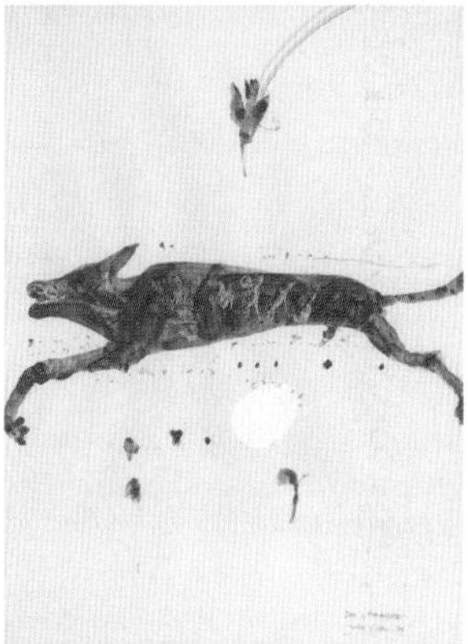

John Henry Olsen, "Dog and Honeyeaters", watercolour on paper, inscribed "Dog and Honeyeaters John Olsen 79".

29.5in (75cm) high

£3,000-5,000 **SHA**

Robert Remsen Vickrey (American 1926-), "Revolving Door", oil on board, signed "Robert Vickrey" lower right, titled on the reverse, framed.

24in (61cm) high

£8,000-12,000 **SK**

Jean-Paul Riopelle (Canadian 1923-2002), "Rouge".

£70,000-100,000 **WAD**

Jean-Paul Riopelle, "Le Cirque".

£80,000-120,000 **WAD**

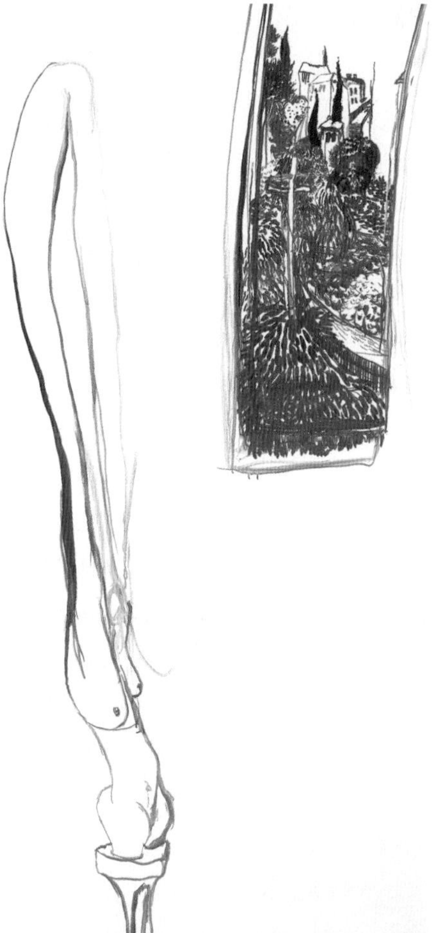

Brett Whiteley (Australian 1939-1992), "Window and Sculpture", oil on board.

Brett Whiteley is one of the best known Australian painters of the 20thC.

1975 *63.75in (162cm) high*

£70,000-100,000 **DM**

Emily Kame Kngwarreye (Australian Aboriginal 1910-1996), "Yam Dreaming", acrylic on linen

£8,000-12,000 **BONA**

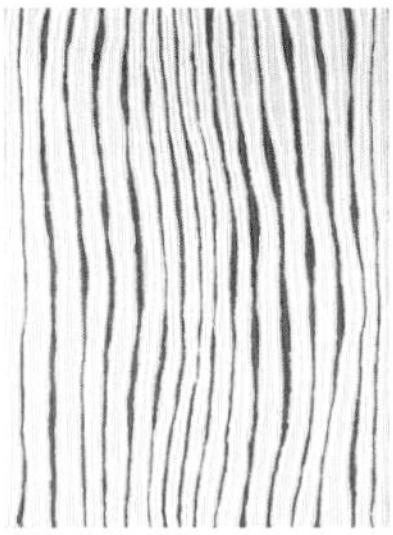

Alice Nampitjinpa of the Pintupi (Australian Aboriginal 1943-), "Tali At Talaapi", synthetic polymer paint on linen, inscribed verso with Ikuntji Arts catalogue number "IK99AN189".

Talaalpi is a swamp east of Walungurru, near Kintore. Here the artist has depicted tali (sandhills) which are located in this area. It is the site of porcupine tjukurrpa (dreaming).

1999 *72.5in (184cm) high*

£4,000-6,000 **SHA**

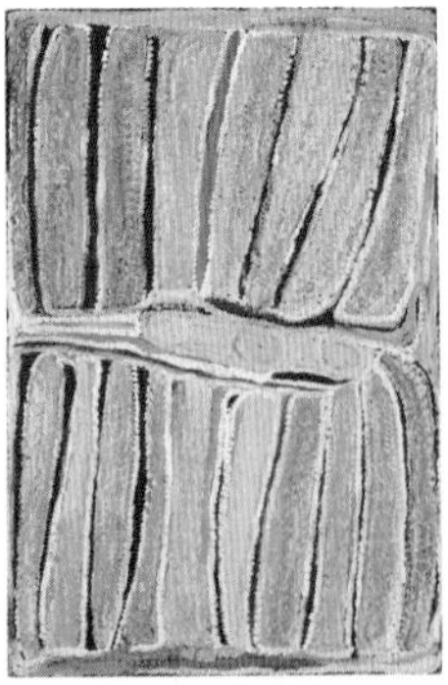

Eubena Nampitjin, Kukatja (Australian Aboriginal, c1920-), "Nyilla", synthetic polymer paint on linen, inscribed verso with artist's name and Warlayirti Artists cat.no.806/99.

This painting depicts some of the Nyilla country around Eubena's birthplace.

1999 *47.25in (120cm) high*

£8,000-12,000 **SHA**

Dorothy Napangardi Robinson of the Walpiri (Australian Aboriginal 1956-), "Karntakurlangu Jukurrpa", synthetic polymer paint on linen, inscribed with artist's details and Gondwana catalogue number.

Karntakurlangu Jukurrpa means 'belonging to women' and the grid illustrates the pathways of the ancestor women as they travelled across country.

2000 *48in (122cm) wide*

£10,000-12,000 **SHA**

Mawukura Jimmy Nerimah of the Walmajarri (Australian Aboriginal 1930-), "Nyimpi", synthetic polymer paint on cotton, signed verso "Jimmy" and inscribed with gallery catalogue numbers.

2001 *40in (101.5cm) wide*

£3,000-4,000 **SHA**

Bobby Barrdjaray Nganjmirra (Australian Aboriginal 1915-1992), "Rock Kangaroo Speared by Mimi".

19.5in (49.5cm) high

£1,200-1,800 **BONA**

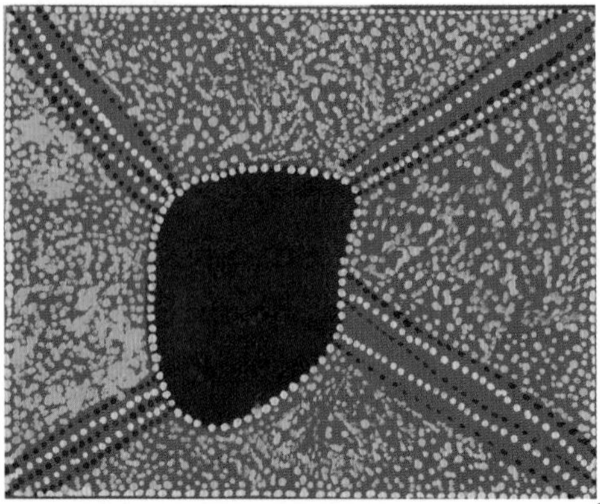

Rover Thomas (Australian Aboriginal 1926-1998), "Crossroads", ochre on canvas.

20in (50.5cm) wide

£2,200-2,800 **BONA**

Kaapa Mbitjana Tjampitjinpa (Australian Aboriginal 1920-1989), synthetic polymer painting on composition board, untitled.

1973 *14.5in (37cm) wide*

£4,000-6,000 **SHA**

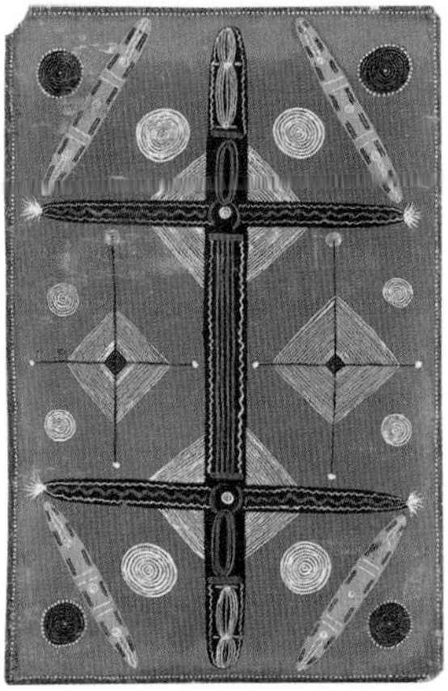

Kaapa Mbitjana Tjampitjinpa, "Children's Corroboree Story", synthetic polymer painting on composition board.

1973 *14.5in (37cm) high*

£4,000-6,000 **SHA**

Ronnie Tjampitjinpa of the Pintupi (Australian Aboriginal c1943-), "Tingari Cycle (Panpanga Site)", synthetic polymer painting on canvas, inscribed verso with artist's name and Papunya Tula catalogue number.

This painting depicts body paint designs associated with the swamp site of Panpanga in Western Australia.

1998 *59.75in (152cm) high*

£7,000-10,000 **SHA**

Ronnie Tjampitjinpa of the Pintupi, "Tingari", synthetic polymer painting on canvas, with Jinta Desert Arts Centre stamp verso with title, inscribed with story, framed.

This piece is accompanied by the original certificate of authenticity including a photo of the artist and the painting.

1996 *75.25in (191cm) high*

£8,000-12,000 **SHA**

RONNIE TJAMPITJINPA

- Ronnie Tjampitjinpa was born c1943 near Muyinnga, and was brought up with the traditional ways of the Pintupi territory.
- In the 1950s, he moved with his family and settled in the Papunya community. Whilst working as a labourer, he became interested in the contemporary art movement emerging in the area and began painting.
- He returned to his traditional lands when the Kintore settlement was established in 1981 and was further inspired to paint, becoming one of Papunya Tula's major artists.
- His paintings follow the Pintupi style of circles connected by lines relating to people, the landscape and Dreamtime.
- His work has featured in many exhibitions and permanent collections are held at The Australian National Gallery and other major galleries.

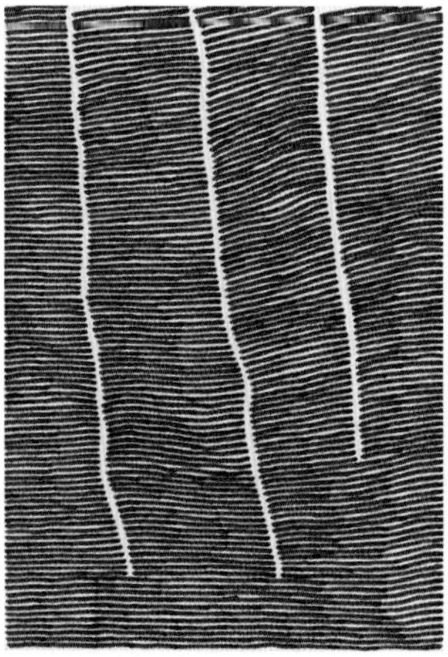

Ronnie Tjampitjinpa of the Pintupi, "Fire Dreaming", acrylic on linen.

£5,000-7,000 **BONA**

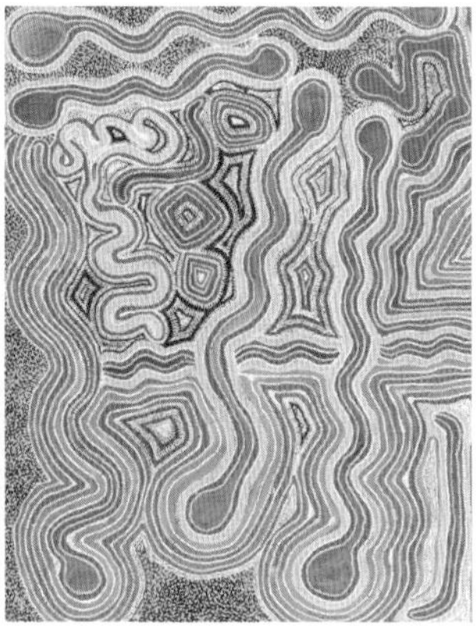

Patrick Oloodoodi Tjungurrayi (Australian Aboriginal 1935-), acrylic on canvas, untitled.

67in (170cm) high

£4,000-5,000 **BONA**

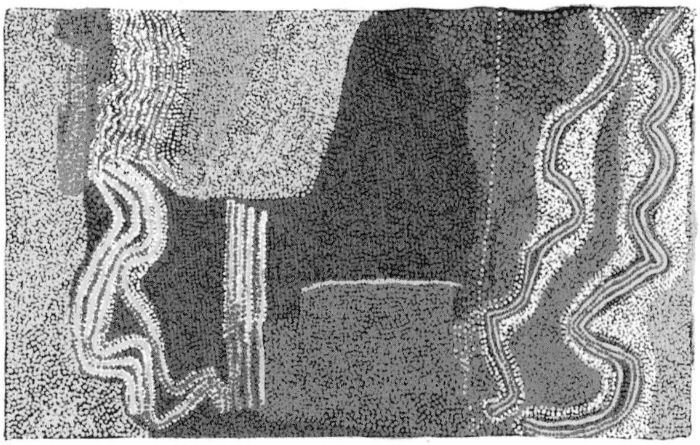

A synthetic polymer painting on canvas, by Tommy Watson of the Pitjantjatjara (Australian Aboriginal 1935-), untitled, inscribed verso with artist's details & Red Sand catalogue number.

Accompanied by an original certificate of authenticity and a suite of images of the artist executing the painting.

2005 *78.75in (200cm) wide*

£18,000-22,000 **SHA**

KEY TO ILLUSTRATIONS

EVERY ANTIQUE ILLUSTRATED in *DK Antiques Price Guide 2007* by Judith Miller has a letter code which identifies the dealer or auction house that sold it. The list below is a key to these codes. In the list, auction houses are shown by the letter Ⓐ and dealers by the letter Ⓓ. Some items may have come from a private collection, in which case the code in the list is accompanied by the letter Ⓟ. Inclusion in this book in no way constitutes or implies a contract or a binding offer on the part of any of our contributors to supply or sell the goods illustrated, or similar items, at the prices stated.

AA Ⓓ
Albert Amor
37 Bury Street, St James's,
London SW1Y 6AU
Tel: 020 7930 2444
www.albertamor.co.uk

AAC Ⓐ
Sanford Alderfer Auction Company
501 Fairgrounds Road,
Hatfield, PA 19440, USA
Tel: 001 215 393 3000
www.alderferauction.com

AMO Ⓓ
Alan Moss
436 Lafayette Street, New York, NY 10003, USA
Tel: 001 212 473 1310

AP Ⓓ
Arte Primitivo
Howard S. Rose Gallery, 3 East 65th Street - Suite 2, New York, NY 10021
Tel: 001 212 570 6999
www.arteprimitivo.com

B Ⓐ
Dreweatt Neate Tunbridge Wells (formerly Bracketts)
Tunbridge Wells Saleroom, The Auction Hall, The Pantiles, Tunbridge Wells, Kent TN2 5QL
Tel: 01892 544500
www.dnfa.com/tunbridgewells

B&I Ⓐ
Burstow & Hewett
Lower Lake, Battle, East Sussex TN33 0AT
Tel: 01424 772374
www.burstowandhewett.co.uk

BEA Ⓐ
Beaussant Lefèvre
32 rue Drouot, 75009 Paris, France
Tel: 00 33 1 47 70 40 00
www.beaussant-lefevre.auction.fr

BIG Ⓐ
Bigwood
The Old School, Tiddington, Stratford-upon-Avon
Warwickshire CV37 7AW
Tel: 01789 269415
www.bigwoodauctioneers.co.uk

BLA Ⓐ
Blanchet et Associés
3 rue Geoffroy Marie, 75009 Paris, France
Tel: 00 33 1 53 34 14 44
blanchet.auction@wanadoo.fr

BLO Ⓐ
Bloomsbury Auctions
Bloomsbury House,
24 Maddox Street, London W1 S1PP
Tel: 020 7495 9494
www.bloomsburyauctions.com

BONA Ⓐ
Bonhams & Goodman
7 Anderson Street,
Double Bay NSW 2028, Australia
Tel: 0061 02 9327 9913
www.bonhamsandgoodman.com.au

BOY Ⓓ
Boym Partners Inc
131 Varick Street, No. 915,
New York, NY 10013, USA
Tel/Fax: 001 212 807 8210
www.boym.com

BRB Ⓓ
Bauman Rare Books
535 Madison Avenue, New York, NY 10022, USA
Tel: 001 212 751 0011
www.baumanrarebooks.com

BRI Ⓐ
Brightwells Fine Art
Fine Art Saleroom, Easters Court, Leominster,
Herefordshire HR6 0DE
Tel: 01568 611122
www.brightwells.co.uk

BRK Ⓓ
Brookside Antiques
44 North Water Street, New Bedford, MA 02740 USA
Tel: 001 508 993 4944
www.brooksideartglass.com

BRU Ⓐ
Brunk Auctions
Post Office Box 2135, Asheville, NC 28802, USA
Tel: 001 828 254 6846
www.brunkauctions.com

CA Ⓐ
Chiswick Auctions
1-5 Colville Road, London W3 8BL
Tel: 020 8992 4442
www.chiswickauctions.co.uk

CHA Ⓓ
Charlotte Marler
Booth 14,1528 West 25th Street,
New York, NY 10010, USA
Tel: 001 212 367 8808
char_marler@hotmail.com

CHEF Ⓐ
Cheffins
Clifton House, 1&2 Clifton Road,
Cambridge, Cambridgeshire CB1 7EA
Tel: 01223 213343
www.cheffins.co.uk

DD Ⓓ
Decodame.com
853 Vanderbilt Beach Road, PMB 8,
Naples, FL 34108, USA
Tel: 001 239 514 6797
www.decodame.com

DJI Ⓓ
Deco Jewels Inc
131 Thompson Street, NY, USA
Tel: 001 212 253 1222
decojewels@earthlink.net

DM Ⓐ
Deutscher-Menzies
1140 Malvern Road, Malvern
VIC 3144, Australia
Tel: 0061 03 9822 1911
www.deutschermenzies.com

DN Ⓐ
Dreweatt Neate
Donnington Priory Salerooms, Donnington,
Newbury, Berkshire RG14 2JE
Tel: 01635 553553
www.dnfa.com/donnington

DNT Ⓓ
Dreweatt Neate Tunbridge Wells (formerly Bracketts)
Auction Hall, The Pantiles,
Tunbridge Wells, Kent TN2 5QL
Tel: 01892 544500
www.dnfa.com/tunbridgewells

DOR Ⓐ
Dorotheum
Palais Dorotheum, A-1010 Vienna,
Dorotheergasse 17, Austria
Tel: 0043 1 515 600
www.dorotheum.com

DRA Ⓐ
David Rago Auctions
333 North Main Street,
Lambertville, NJ 08530, USA
Tel: 001 609 397 9374
www.ragoarts.com

EFI Ⓐ
Esther Fitzgerald Rare Textiles
28 Church Row, London NW3 6UP
Tel: 020 7431 3076
www.estherfitzgerald.co.uk

FRE Ⓐ
Freeman's
1808 Chestnut Street,
Philadelphia, PA 19103, USA
Tel: 001 215 563 9275
www.freemansauction.com

FS Ⓓ
The Frank Steward Collection
P.O. Box 115, Larkspur, Ca. 94977, USA

GAZE Ⓐ
Thos. Wm. Gaze & Son
Diss Auction Rooms, Roydon Road,
Diss, Norfolk, IP22 4LN
Tel: 01379 650306
www.twgaze.com

GORL Ⓐ
Gorringes
15 North Street,
Lewes, East Sussex BN7 2PD
Tel: 01273 472503
www.gorringes.co.uk

H&L Ⓐ
Hampton and Littlewood
The Auction Rooms, Alphin Brook Road,
Alphington,
Exeter, Devon EX2 8TH
Tel: 01392 413100
www.hamptonandlittlewood.co.uk

HAMG Ⓐ
Dreweatt Neate Godalming
(Formerly Hamptons)
Baverstock House, 93 High Street,
Godalming, Surrey GU7 1AL
Tel: 01483 423567
www.dnfa.com/godalming

HERR Ⓐ
Herr Auctions
WG Herr Art & Auction House,
Friesenwall 35, 50672 Cologne, Germany
Tel: 0049 221 25 45 48
www.herr-auktionen.de

HSD Ⓓ
High Style Deco
224 West 18th Street,
New York, NY 10011, USA
Tel: 001 212 647 0035
www.highstyledeco.com

IHB Ⓓ
Imperial Half Bushel
831 N Howard Street,
Baltimore, MD 21201, USA
Tel: 001 410 462 1192
www.imperialhalfbushel.com

ING Ⓓ
Ingram Antiques
669 Mt. Pleasant Road,
Toronto, Canada M4S 2N2
Tel: 001 416 484 4601

ISA Ⓐ
Ivey Selkirk Auctioneers
7447 Forsyth Boulevard, Saint Louis,
MI 63105, USA
Tel: 001 314 726 5515
www.iveyselkirk.com

JDJ Ⓐ
James D Julia Inc
PO Box 830, Fairfield,
ME 04937, USA
Tel: 001 207 453 7125
www.juliaauctions.com

JES Ⓓ
John Jesse
No longer trading

JH Ⓓ
Jeanette Hayhurst Fine Glass
32A Kensington Church St.,
London W8 4HA
Tel: 020 7938 1539

JHOR Ⓓ
Jonathan Horne
66c Kensington Church Street,
London W8 4BY
Tel: 020 7221 5658
www.jonathanhorne.co.uk

JN Ⓐ
John Nicholsons
The Auction Rooms, 'Longfield', Midhurst Road,
Fernhurst, Haslemere, Surrey GU27 3HA
Tel: 01428 653727
www.johnnicholsons.com

KAU Ⓐ
Auktionhaus Kaup
Schloss Sulzburg, Hauptstrasse 62,
79295 Sulzburg, Germany
Tel: 0049 7634 5038 0
www.kaupp.de

KC Ⓓ
Kevin Conru
8a Rue Bodenbroek, B 1000 Brussels, Belgium
Tel: 0032 2 512 7635

L&T Ⓐ
Lyon and Turnbull Ltd.
33 Broughton Place,
Edinburgh, Midlothian EH1 3RR
Tel: 0131 557 8844
www.lyonandturnbull.com

LAN Ⓐ
Lankes
Triftfeldstrasse 1, 95182 Döhlau, Germany
Tel: 0049 92 869 5050
www.lankes-auktionen.de

LFA Ⓐ
Law Fine Art Ltd.
Ash Cottage, Ashmore Green,
Newbury, Berkshire, RG18 9ER
Tel: 01635 860033
www.lawfineart.co.uk

M&D Ⓓ
Myers & Duncan
12 East 86th Street, Suite 239,
New York, NY 10028, USA
Tel: 001 212 472 0115
jmyersprimitives@aol.com

MAX Ⓐ
Maxwells
133A Woodford Road, Woodford, Cheshire SK7 1QD
Tel: 0161 439 5182

MB Ⓓ
Mostly Boxes
93 High St., Eton, Windsor, Berkshire SL4 6AF
Tel: 01753 858 470

MCP Ⓓ
Matali Crasset Productions
26 rue du Buisson Saint Louis,
F-75010 Paris, France
Tel: 00 33 1 42 40 99 89
www.matalicrasset.com

MGL Ⓓ
Mix Gallery
17 South Main Street,
Lambertville, NJ 08530, USA
Tel: 001 609 773 0777
www.mix-gallery.com

MOD Ⓓ
Moderne Gallery
111 North 3rd Street,
Philadelphia, PA 19106, USA
Tel: 001 215 923 8536
www.modernegallery.com

MSG Ⓓ
Morning Star Gallery
513 Canyon Road, Santa Fe,
NM 87501, USA
Tel: 001 505 982 8187
www.morningstargallery.com

MSM Ⓓ
Modernism Gallery
800 Douglas Road, Suite 101,
Coral Gables, FL 33134, USA
Tel: 001 305 442 8743/
001 305 632 4725
www.modernism.com

MUR Ⓐ
Tony Murland Auctions
78 High Street, Needham Market,
Suffolk, IP6 8AW
Tel: 01449 722 992
www.antiquetools.co.uk

MTZ Ⓐ
Auktionshaus Metz
Friedrich-Eber-Anlage 5,
69117 Heidelberg, Germany
Tel: 0049 6221 23571
www.Metz-Auktion.de

NAG Ⓐ
Nagel
Neckarstrasse 189-191,
70190 Stuttgart, Germany
Tel: 0049 711 649 690
www.auction.de

OHA Ⓓ
Owen Hargreaves and Jasmine Dahl
Stall 16 Portobello Antiques Market (Saturdays),
Corsham St, London, N1 6DP
(by appointment)
Tel: 0207 253 2669
www.owenhargreaves.com

PC Ⓟ
Private Collection

PHK ⓅⒸ
Philip Keith Private Collection
www.philipkeith.co.uk

PIA Ⓐ
Piasa
5 rue Drouot, 75009 Paris, France
Tel: 00 33 1 53 34 10 10

POOK Ⓐ
Pook & Pook
463 East Lancaster Avenue,
Downington, PA 19335, USA
Tel: 001 610 269 4040/0695
www.pookandpook.com

R&GM Ⓓ
R & G McPherson Antiques
40 Kensington Church Street,
London W8 4BX
Tel: 020 7937 0812
www.orientalceramics.com

RAC Ⓓ
Race Furniture Ltd
Bourton Industrial Park, Bourton-on-the-Water, Glouchestershire GL54 2HQ
Tel: 01451 821 446
www.racefurniture.com

RAM Ⓓ
Ramona Morris
P.O Box 135, Delaplane, VA 20144, USA
Tel: 001 540 592 3873
rmfineart@earthlink.net

RAON ⓅⒸ
R.A. O'Neil

RDL Ⓐ
David Rago/Nicholas Dawes Lalique Auctions
333 North Main Street, Lambertville, NJ 08530, USA
Tel: 001 609 397 9374
www.ragoarts.com

REL Ⓓ
Rellick 8 Golborne Road, London W10 5NW
Tel: 020 8962 0089

ROS Ⓐ
Rosebery's
74-76 Knight's Hill, West Norwood, London SE27 0JD
Tel: 020 8761 2522
www.roseberys.co.uk

ROW Ⓐ
Rowley Fine Arts
8 Downham Road, Ely, Cambridge, Cambridgeshire CB6 1AH
Tel: 01353 653020
www.rowleyfineart.com

SDR Ⓐ
Sollo:Rago Modern Auctions
333 North Main Street, Lambertville, NJ 08530 USA
Tel: 001 609 397 9374
www.ragoarts.com

SEG Ⓓ
Galerie Segas
34, passage Jouffroy, 75009 Paris, France
Tel: 0033 1 47 70 89 65

SH Ⓓ
Sara Hughes Vintage Compacts, Antiques & Collectables
sara@sneak.freeserve.co.uk
http://mysite.wanadoomembers.co.uk/sara_compacts

SK Ⓐ
Skinner Inc.
The Heritage on the Garden, 63 Park Plaza Boston MA 02116, USA
Tel: 001 617 350 5400
357 Main Street, Bolton, MA 01740, USA
Tel: 001 978 779 6241
www.skinnerinc.com

STE Ⓓ
Stephanie's Antiques
28 West 25th Street, New York NY 10010
Tel: 001 212 633 6563

SWO Ⓐ
Sworders
14 Cambridge Road, Stansted Mountfitchet, Essex CM24 8BZ
Tel: 01279 817 778
www.sworder.co.uk

TA Ⓐ
David Rago Auctions (formerly 333 Auctions)
333 North Main Street, Lambertville, NJ 08530 USA
Tel: 001 609 397 9374
www.ragoarts.com

TB Ⓓ
Trotta-Bono American Indian Art
PO Box 34, Shrub Oak, NY 10588, USA
Tel: 001 914 528 6604

TCF Ⓓ
Cynthia Findlay
Toronto Antiques Centre, 276 King Street West, Toronto, Ontario M5V 1J2, Canada
Tel: 001 416 260 9057
www.cynthiafindlay.com

TFA Ⓓ
Throckmorton Fine Art
145 East 57th Street, 3rd Floor, New York, NY 10022, USA
Tel: 001 212 223 1059
www.throckmorton-nyc.com

TFR Ⓓ
Floyd & Rita's Antiques and Collectables
Toronto Antiques Centre, 276 King Street West, Toronto, Ontario, M5V 1J2 Canada
Tel: 001 416 260 9066
www.floydrita.com

TRIO Ⓓ
Trio
L24, Grays Antique Markets, 58 Davies Street, London, W1K 5LP
Tel: 020 7493 2736
www.trio-london.fsnet.co.uk

TSG Ⓓ
Shand Galleries
Toronto Antiques Centre, 276 King Street West, Toronto, Ontario, M5V 1J2 Canada
Tel: 001 416 260 9056

VEC Ⓐ
Vectis Auctions
Fleck Way, Thornaby, Stockton on Tees, County Durham TS17 9JZ
Tel: 01642 750 616
www.vectis.co.uk

VET Ⓓ
Vetro & Arte Gallery (V&A Gallery)
Calle del Cappeller 3212, Dorsoduro, Venice 30123, Italy
Tel: 0039 041 522 8525
www.venicewebgallery.com

VZ Ⓐ
Von Zezschwitz
Friedrichstrasse 1a, 80801 Munich, Germany
Tel: 0049 89 38 98 930
www.von-zezschwitz.de

W&W Ⓐ
Wallis and Wallis
West Street Auction Galleries, Lewes, East Sussex BN7 2NJ
Tel: 01273 480 208
www.wallisandwallis.co.uk

WAD Ⓐ
Waddington's Auctioneers & Appraisers
111 Bathurst St., Toronto, Ontario M5V 2R1, Canada
Tel: 001 416 504 9100
www.waddingtons.ca

WEB Ⓐ
Webb's
18 Manukau Road, PO Box 99 251, Newmarket, Auckland 1000, New Zealand
Tel: 0064 09 524 6804
www.webbs.co.nz

WDL Ⓐ
Kunst-Auktionshaus Martin Wendl
August-Bebel-Straße 4, 07407 Rudolstadt, Germany
Tel: 0049 3672 4243 50
www.auktionshaus-wendl.de

WJT Ⓓ
Jamieson Tribal Art
Golden Chariot Productions, 468 Wellington West Street, Suite 201, Toronto, Ontario, Canada M5V 1E3
Tel: 001 416 569 1396
www.jamiesontribalart.com

WW Ⓐ
Woolley and Wallis
51-61 Castle Street, Salisbury, Wiltshire SP13SU
Tel: 01722 424 500
www.woolleyandwallis.co.uk

NOTE

For valuations, it is advisable to contact the dealer or auction house in advance to confirm that they will perform this service and whether any charge is involved. Telephone valuations are not possible, so it will be necessary to send details, including a photograph, of the object to the dealer or auction house, along with a stamped addressed envelope for response. While most dealers will be happy to help you, do remember that they are busy people. Please mention *DK Antiques Price Guide 2007* by Judith Miller when making an enquiry.

COLLECTING ON THE INTERNET

The internet has revolutionized the trading of both antiques and collectibles, especially for smaller pieces, such as ceramics and metalware, which are are easily defined, described and photographed. Shipping is also comparatively easy for smaller items. The Internet has provided a cost-effective way of buying and selling, away from the overheads of shops and auction rooms. Around the world, antiques are offered for sale and traded daily, with sites varying from global online marketplaces, such as eBay, to specialist dealers' websites.

When searching online, remember that some people may not know how to accurately describe their item or may use special terminology. General category searches, even though more time consuming, and even deliberately misspelling a name, can yield results. Also, if something looks too good to be true, it probably is. Using this book to get to know your market visually, so that you can tell the difference between a real bargain and something that sounds like one, is a good start.

As you will understand from buying this book, colour photography is vital – look for online listings that include as many images as possible and check them carefully. Be aware that colours can appear differently, even between computer screens.

Always ask the vendor questions about the object, particularly regarding condition. If there is no image, or you want to see another aspect of the object – ask. Most sellers (private or trade) will want to realize the best price for their items so will be more than happy to help – if approached politely and sensibly.

Sellers should describe their item accurately. Include as much detail as possible including maker, size, colour, any other marks, condition, and damage. Always include as many digital photographs as possible. These should be shot in focus and in clear, preferably natural, light. Try to find out likely shipping and packaging costs in advance and aim to include them on your listing, along with methods of payment you will accept. Have the item at hand and be ready to answer questions promptly from potential buyers.

As well as the 'e-hammer' price, you will probably have to pay additional transactional fees such as packing, shipping, and possibly regional or national taxes. It is always best to ask for an estimate for these additional costs before leaving a bid. This will also help you tailor your bid as you will have an idea of the maximum price the item will cost if you are successful.

As well as the well-known online auction sites, such as eBay, there is a host of other online resources for buying and selling, for example fair and auction date listings.

INTERNET RESOURCES

Live Auctioneers
www.liveauctioneers.com
info@liveauctioneers.com
A free service which allows users to search catalogs from selected auction houses in the US and Europe. Through its connection with eBay, users can bid live via the Internet into salerooms as auctions happen. Registered users can also search through an illustrated archive of past catalogs and receive a free newsletter by email.

invaluable.com
www.invaluable.com
sales@invaluable.com
A subscription service which allows users to search selected European auction house catalogs. Also offers an extensive archive for appraisal uses.

The Antiques Trade Gazette
www.atg-online.com
The online version of the UK trade newspaper, comprising British auction and fair listings, news, and events.

Maine Antiques Digest
www.maineantiquesdigest.com
The online version of America's trade newspaper including news, articles, fair and auction listings, and more.

La Gazette du Drouot
www.drouot.com
The online home of the magazine listing all auctions to be held in France at the Hotel de Drouot in Paris and beyond. An online subscription enables you to download the magazine online.

AuctionBytes
www.auctionbytes.com
Auction resource with community forum, news, events, tips, and a weekly newsletter.

Internet Auction List
www.internetauctionlist.com
Auction news, online and offline auction search engines and live chat forums.

Go Antiques/Antiqnet
www.goantiques.com
www.antiqnet.com
An online global aggregator for art, antiques and collectables dealers who showcase their stock online, allowing users to browse and buy.

eBay
www.ebay.co.uk
Undoubtedly the largest of the online auction sites, allowing users to buy and sell in an online marketplace with over 52 million registered users. Collectors should also view eBay Live Auctions (www.ebayliveauctions.com) where traditional auctions are combined with online bidding allowing users to interact with the saleroom.

Tias
www.tias.com
An online global aggregator for art, antiques and collectibles dealers who showcase their stock online, allowing users to browse and buy.

Collectors Online
www.collectorsonline.com
An online global aggregator for art, antiques and collectibles dealers who showcase their stock online, allowing users to browse and buy.

Antiques and The Arts
www.antiquesandthearts.com
Website of Antiques and the Arts weekly newspaper. Calendar of events, auctions, shows, and book reviews.

PayPal
www.paypal.com
An online transaction site, allowing payment to be made and accepted in a secure environment.

BidPay
www.bidpay.com
An online transaction site, allowing payment for goods by Western Union money order, sterling cheque or payment to a US bank account.

KEY TO ADVERTISERS

CLIENT	PAGE NO	CLIENT	PAGE NO
Lyon & Turnbull	106	Skinner	322
Freemans	128	Rogers de Rin	444
Jeanette Hayhurst	223	Rago Arts & Auction Center	591
Dreweatt Neate	262	Dorling Kindersley	617

DIRECTORY OF AUCTIONEERS

THIS IS A LIST OF AUCTIONEERS that conduct regular sales. Auction houses that would like to be included in the next edition should contact us by 1 February 2007.

London

Bloomsbury
Bloomsbury House, 24 Maddox Street, London W1 S1PP
Tel: 020 7495 9494
Fax: 020 7495 9499
www.bloomsbury-book-auct.com

Bonhams
101 New Bond Street, London W1S 1SR
Tel: 020 7629 6602
Fax: 020 7629 8876
info@bonhams.com
www.bonhams.com

Bonhams Knightsbridge
Montpelier Street, Knightsbridge, London SW7 1HH
Tel: 020 7393 3900
Fax: 020 7393 3905
info@bonhams.com
www.bonhams.com

Chiswick Auctions
1 Colville Road, Acton, London W3 8BL
Tel: 020 8992 4442
Fax: 020 8896 0541
www.chiswickauctions.co.uk

Christie's
8 King Street, St. James's London SW1Y 6QT
Tel: 020 7839 9060
Fax: 020 7839 1611
info@christies.com
www.christies.com

Christie's South Kensington
85 Old Brompton Road, SW7 3LD
Tel: 020 7581 7611
Fax: 020 7321 3311
info@christies.com
www.christies.com

Lots Road Galleries
71-73 Lots Road, Chelsea, London SW10 0RN
Tel: 020 7376 6800
Fax: 020 7376 6899
www.lotsroad.com

Rosebery's
74-76 Knights Hill, West Norwood, London SE27 0JD
Tel: 020 8761 2522
Fax: 020 8761 2524
www.roseberys.co.uk

Sotheby's
34-35 New Bond Street, London W1A 2AA
Tel: 020 7293 5000
Fax: 020 7293 5989
www.sothebys.com

Sotheby's Olympia
Hammersmith Road, London W14 8UX
Tel: 020 7293 5555
Fax: 020 7293 6939
www.sothebys.com

Avon

Aldridges of Bath
Newark House, 26-45 Cheltenham Street, Bath, BA2 3EX
Tel: 01225 462830
Fax: 01225 311319

Gardiner Houlgate
9 Leafield Way, Corsham, Bath SN13 9SW
Tel: 01225 812912
Fax: 01225 811777
auctions@gardiner-houlgate.co.uk
www.gardiner-houlgate.co.uk

Bedfordshire

W. & H. Peacock
The Auction Centre, 26 Newnham St, Bedford MK40 3JR
Tel: 01234 266366
www.peacockauction.co.uk
info@peacockauction.co.uk

Berkshire

Dreweatt Neate
Donnington Priory, Donnington, Nr Newbury RG14 2JE
Tel: 01635 553553
Fax: 01635 553599
donnington@dnfa.com
www.dnfa.com

Law Fine Art Ltd.
Ash Cottage, Ashmore Green, Newbury RG18 9ER
Tel: 01635 860033
Fax: 01635 860036
info@lawfineart.co.uk
www.lawfineart.co.uk

Special Auction Services
Kennetholme, Midgham, Nr. Reading RG7 5UX
Tel: 0118 971 2949
Fax: 0118 971 2420
commemorative@aol.com
www.invaluable.com/sas

Buckinghamshire

Dickins Auctioneers
Claydon House Park, Calvert Rd, Middle Claydon MK18 2EZ
Tel: 01296 714 434
Fax: 01296 714492
info@dickins-auctioneers.com
www.dickins-auctioneers.com

Cambridgeshire

Cheffins
Clifton House, 1&2 Clifton Road, Cambridge CB1 7EA
Tel: 01223 213 343
Fax: 01223 271 949
fine.art@cheffins.co.uk
www.cheffins.co.uk

Hyperion Auctions Ltd
Station Road, St. Ives PE27 5BH
Tel: 01480 464140
Fax: 01480 497552
enquiries@hyperionauctions.co.uk
www.hyperionauctions.co.uk

Maxey & Son
Auction Hall, Cattle Market Chase, Wisbech PE13 1RD
Tel: 01945 584609
www.maxeyandson.co.uk

Rowley Fine Art Auctioneers & Valuers
8 Downham Road, Ely CB6 1AH
Tel: 01353 653020
Fax: 01353 653022
mail@rowleyfineart.com
www.rowleyfineart.com

Cheshire

Frank R. Marshall and Co.
Marshall House, Church Hill, Knutsford WA16 6DH
Tel: 01565 653284
Fax: 01565 652341
antiques@frankmarshall.co.uk
www.frankmarshall.co.uk

Maxwells of Wilmslow
133A Woodford Road, Woodford, Cheshire, SK7 1QD
Tel: 01614 395182
www.maxwell-auctioneers.co.uk

Peter Wilson Fine Art Auctioneers
Victoria Gallery, Market Street, Nantwich CW5 5DG
Tel: 01270 623878
Fax: 01270 610508
auctions@peterwilson.co.uk
www.peterwilson.co.uk

Cornwall

W. H. Lane & Son
Jubilee House, Queen Street, Penzance TR18 4DF
Tel: 01736 361447
Fax: 01736 350097
info@whlane.co.uk

David Lay FRICS
The Penzance Auction House Alverton, Penzance TR18 4RE
Tel: 01736 361414
Fax: 01736 360035
david.lays@btopenworld.com

Cumbria

James Thompson
64 Main Street, Kirkby Lonsdale LA6 2AJ
Tel: 01524 271555
Fax: 01524 272939
sales@jthompson-auctioneers.co.uk
www.jthompson-auctioneers.co.uk

Derbyshire

Bamfords Ltd
The Old Picture Palace, 133 Dale Road, Matlock, Derbyshire DE4 3LU
Tel: 01629 574460
www.bamfords-auctions.co.uk

Devon

Hampton & Littlewood
The Auction Rooms, Alphin Brook Road, Alphington, Exeter EX2 8TH
Tel: 01392 413100
Fax: 01392 413110
www.hamptonandlittlewood.co.uk

Dreweatt Neate (formerly Taylor's)
Honiton Saleroom, 205 High Street, Honiton EX14 1LQ
Tel: 01404 42404
Fax: 01404 46510
honiton@dnfa.com
www.dnfa.com/honiton

S. J. Hales Auctioneers
Tracey House, Newton Road, Bovey Tracey, Newton Abbot TQ13 9AZ
Tel: 01626 836 684
Fax: 01626 836 318
info@sjhales.com
www.sjhales.com

Dorset

Cottees Auctions Ltd.
The Market, East Street, Wareham BH20 4NR
Tel: 01929 552826
Fax: 01929 554916
auctions@cottees.fsnet.co.uk
www.auctionsatcottees.co.uk

Dalkeith Auctions Bournemouth
Dalkeith Hall, Dalkeith Steps, Rear of 81 Old Christchurch Road, Bournemouth BH1 1YL
Tel: 01202 292905
Fax: 01202 292931
how@dalkeith-auctions.co.uk.
www.dalkeith-auctions.co.uk

Hy. Duke and Son
Fine Art Salerooms, Weymouth Avenue, Dorchester DT1 1QS
Tel: 01305 265080
Fax: 01305 260101
enquiries@dukes-auctions.com

Wm. Morey and Sons
Unit 3, Pymore Mills Estate, Pymore, Bridport, Dorset, DT6 5PJ
Tel/Fax: 01308 422078
www.wmoreyandsons.co.uk

Onslows
The Coach House, Manor Road, Stourpaine DT11 8TQ
Tel: 01258 488 838
www.onslows.co.uk

Riddetts of Bournemouth
177 Holdenhurst Road, Bournemouth BH8 8DG
Tel: 01202 555686
Fax: 01202 311004
www.riddetts.co.uk

Durham

Vectis Auctions Limited
Fleck Way, Thornaby, Stockton on Tees TS17 9JZ
Tel: 01642 750 616
Fax: 01642 769 478
admin@vectis.co.uk
www.vectis.co.uk

Essex

Chalkwell Auctions Ltd.
The Arlington Rooms, 905 London Road, Leigh-on-Sea SS0 89U
Tel: 01702 710383
www.ridgeweb.co.uk

Cooper Hirst Auctions
The Granary Salerooms, Victoria Road, Chelmsford CM2 6LH
Tel: 01245 260535

Sworders
14 Cambridge Road, Stansted Mountfitchet CM24 8BZ
Tel: 01279 817778
Fax: 01279 817779
www.sworder.co.uk

Gloucestershire

Dreweatt Neate (formerly Bristol Auction Rooms) Bristol Salerooms, St. John's Place, Apsley Road, Clifton, Bristol BS8 2ST
Tel: 0117 973 7201
Fax: 0117 973 5671
bristol@dnfa.com
www.dnfa.com/bristol

Mallams Fine Art Auctioneers and Valuers
26 Grosvenor Street, Cheltenham GL52 2SG
Tel: 01242 235712
Fax: 01242 241943
cheltenham@mallams.co.uk
www.mallams.co.uk/fineart

Moore, Allen & Innocent
The Salerooms, Norcote, Cirencester GL7 5RH
Tel: 01285 646050
Fax: 01285 652862
fineart@mooreallen.co.uk
www.mooreallen.com/cat

Specialised Postcard Auctions
Corinium Gallery, 25 Gloucester Street, Cirencester GL7 2DJ
Tel: 01285 659 057
Fax: 01285 652047

Stroud Auctions Ltd
The Old Barn, Bear of Rodborough, Stroud GL5 5EA
Tel: 01453 873800
info@stroudauctions.com
www.stroudauctions.com

Wotton Auction Rooms Ltd
Tabernacle Road, Wotton-under-Edge GL12 7EB
Tel: 01453 844733
Fax: 01453 845448
www.wottonauctionrooms.co.uk

Hampshire

Andrew Smith & Son
The Auction Rooms, Manor Farm, Itchen Stoke, nr Winchester SO21 9QT
Tel: 01962 735988
Fax: 01962 738879
auctions@andrewsmithandson.com

Jacobs and Hunt Fine Art Auctioneers
Lavant Street, Petersfield GU32 3EF
Tel: 01730 233933
Fax: 01730 262323
auctions@jacobsandhunt.com
www.jacobsandhunt.com

May and Son
Delta Works, Salisbury Road Shipton Bellinger, Hampshire SP9 7UN
Tel: 01980 846000
Fax: 01980 846600
mayandson@enterprise.net

Herefordshire

Brightwells
The Fine Art Saleroom, Easters Court, Leominster HR6 ODE
Tel: 01568 611122
Fax: 01568 610519
fineart@brightwells.com
classiccars@brightwells.com
www.brightwells.com

Hertfordshire

Tring Market Auctions
Brook Street, Tring HP23 5EF
Tel: 01442 826446
Fax: 01442 890927
sales@tringmarketauctions.co.uk
www.tringmarketauctions.co.uk

Isle of Wight

Shanklin Auction Rooms
79 Regent Street, Shanklin PO37 7AP
Tel: 01983 863441
Fax: 01983 863890
shanklin.auction@tesco.net
www.shanklinauctionrooms.co.uk

Ways
The Auction House, Garfield Road, Ryde PO33 2PT
Tel: 01983 562255
Fax: 01983 565108
ways@waysauctionrooms.fsbusiness.co.uk
www.waysauctionrooms.fsbusiness.co.uk

Kent

Dreweatt Neate (formerly Bracketts)
Tunbridge Wells Saleroom, The Auction Hall, The Pantiles, Tunbridge Wells, Kent TN2 5QL
Tel: 01892 544500
Fax: 01892 515191
tunbridgewells@dnfa.com
www.dnfa.com/tunbridgewells

Gorringes
15 The Pantiles, Tunbridge Wells TN2 5TD
Tel: 01892 619 670
Fax: 01892 619 671
auctions@gorringes.co.uk
www.gorringes.co.uk

Lambert and Foster Auction Sale Rooms 102 High Street, Tenterden TN30 6HT
Tel: 01580 762083
Fax: 01580 764317
saleroom@lambertandfoster.co.uk
www.lambertandfoster.co.uk

Mervyn Carey
Twysden Cottage, Benenden, Cranbrook TN17 4LD
Auctions held at The Church Hall, Church Road, Tenterden
Tel: 01580 240283

Parkinson Auctioneers
46 Beaver Road, Ashford TN23 7RP
Tel: 01233 624426
Fax: 01233 665000
www.parkinson-uk.com

Lancashire

Capes Dunn & Co Fine Art
Auctioneers & Valuers, The Auction Galleries, 38 Charles Street, Manchester M1 7DB
Tel: 0161 273 1911
Fax: 0161 273 3474

Leicestershire

Gilding's Auctioneers and Valuers
Roman Way, Market Harborough LE16 7PQ
Tel: 01858 410414
Fax: 01858 432956
www.gildings.co.uk

Tennants Co. (formerly Heathcote Ball & Co) Millhouse, South Street, Oakham, Rutland LE15 6BG
Tel: 01572 724666
Fax: 01572 724422
oakham@tennants-ltd.co.uk
www.tennants.co.uk

Lincolnshire

Eleys Auctioneers
26 Wide Bargate, Boston PE21 6RX
Tel: 01205 361687
Fax: 01205 351091
boston@jameseley.co.uk
www.jameseley.co.uk

Ian H. S. Naylor Auctions
20 St Johns Street, Wainfleet PE24 4DJ
Tel/Fax: 01754 881 210

Marilyn Swain
The Old Barracks, Sandon Road, Grantham NG31 9AS
Tel: 01476 568861
Fax: 01476 576100

John Taylors
The Wool Mart, Kidgate,
Louth LN11 9EZ
Tel: 01507 611107
Fax: 01507 601280
enquiries@johntaylors.com
www.invaluable.com/johntaylors

Merseyside

Cato & Crane & Co
6 Stanhope Street,
Liverpool L8 5RF
Tel: 0151 709 5559
Fax: 0151 707 2454
www.cato-crane.co.uk

Outhwaite and Litherland
Kingsway Galleries, Fontenoy Street,
Liverpool L3 2BE
Tel: 0151 236 6561
Fax: 0151 236 1070
auction@lots.uk.com
www.lots.uk.com

Norfolk

Gaze and Son
Diss Auction Rooms, Roydon Road,
Diss IP22 4LN
Tel: 01379 650306
Fax: 01379 644313
sales@dissauctionrooms.co.uk
www.twgaze.com

Horners Auctions
North Walsham Sale Rooms,
Midland Road,
North Walsham NR28 9JR
Tel: 01692 500603
Fax: 01692 500975
auction@horners.co.uk
www.horners.co.uk

Keys Auctioneers & Valuers
Aylsham Salerooms, Palmers Lane,
Aylsham, Norfolk NR11 6JA
Tel: 01263 733195
www.keysauctions.co.uk

Knights Sporting Auctions
The Thatched Gallery, The Green,
Aldborough, Norwich NR11 7AA
Tel: 01263 768488
Fax: 01263 768788
www.knights.co.uk

Nottinghamshire

Arthur Johnson and Sons (Auctioneers) The Nottingham
Auction Centre, Meadow Lane,
Nottingham NG2 3GY
Tel: 0115 986 9128
Fax: 0115 986 2139
antiques@arthurjohnson.co.uk

Mellors & Kirk Fine Art Auctioneers
Gregory Street, Nottingham,
Nottinghamshire NG7 2NL
Tel: 0115 979 0000
Fax: 0115 978 1111
enquiries@mellors-kirk.com
www.mellors-kirk.co.uk

Dreweatt Neate (formerly Neales)
Nottingham Salerooms,
192 Mansfield Road,
Nottingham NG1 3HU
Tel: 0115 962 4141
Fax: 0115 969 3450
nottingham@dnfa.com
www.dnfa.com/nottingham

John Pye & Sons Auctioneers & Valuers
James Shipstone House,
Radford Road,
Nottingham NG7 7EA
Tel: 0115 970 6060
Fax: 0115 942 0100
ap@johnpye.co.uk
www.johnpye.co.uk

Northgate Auction Rooms Ltd.
17 Northgate, Newark NG24 1EX
Tel: 01636 605905
Fax: 01636 612607
auctions@northgateauction-snewark.co.uk

Peter Young Auctioneers
The Lord Barnby Memorial Hall
Blyth, North Nottinghamshire S81 8HD
Tel: 01777 816 609
Mob: 07801 079818
beaconhillside@btopenworld.com
www.peteryoungauctioneers.co.uk

T Vennett-Smith Auctioneers and Valuers (FSB)
11 Nottingham Road, Gotham,
Nottingham NG11 OHE
Tel: 0115 9830541
Fax: 0115 9830114
info@vennett-smith.com
www.vennett-smith.com

Oxfordshire

Holloway's
49 Parsons Street,
Banbury OX16 5NB
Tel: 01295 817777
Fax: 01295 817701
enquiries@hollowaysauctioneers.co.uk
www.hollowaysauctioneers.co.uk

Jones & Jacob Ltd
Watcombe Manor Saleroom
Ingham Lane, Watlington OX49 5EJ
Tel 01491 612810
Fax 01491 614564
saleroom@jonesandjacob.com
www.jonesandjacob.com

Mallams Fine Art Auctioneers
Bocard House, 24a St. Michael's
Street, Oxford OX1 2EB
Tel: 01865 241358
Fax: 01865 725483
oxford@mallams.co.uk
www.mallams.co.uk/fineart

Mallams Fine Art Auctioneers
Pevensey House, 27 Sheep Street,
Bicester OX26 7JF
Tel: 01869 252901
Fax: 01869 320283
bicester@mallams.co.uk
www.mallams.co.uk/fineart

Soames Country Auctions
Pinnocks Farm Estate, Northmoor,
Witney OX8 1AY
Tel: 01865 300626
soame@email.msn.com
www.soamesauctioneers.co.uk

Shropshire

Halls Fine Art
Welsh Bridge, Shrewsbury SY3 8LA
Tel: 01743 231212
Fax: 01743 271014
FineArt@halls.to
www.hallsgb.com

Mullock & Madeley
The Old Shippon, Wall under
Heywood, Church Stretton SY6 7DS
Tel: 01694 771771
Fax: 01694 771772
info@mullockmadeley.co.uk
www.mullockmadeley.co.uk

Walker Barnett and Hill
Cosford Auction Rooms, Long Lane,
Cosford TF11 8PJ
Tel: 01902 375555
Fax: 01902 375566
wbhauctions@lineone.net
www.walker-barnett-hill.co.uk

Somerset

Clevedon Salerooms
The Auction Centre, Kenn Road,
Kenn, Clevedon,
North Somerset BS21 6TT
Tel: 01934 830 111
Fax: 01934 832 538
info@clevedon-salerooms.com
www.clevedon-salerooms.com

Greenslade Taylor Hunt Fine Art
Magdelene House, Church Square,
Taunton TA1 1SB
Tel: 01823 332525
Fax: 01823 353120
fine.art@gth.net
www.gth.net

Lawrence's Fine Art Auctioneers Ltd.
South Street, Crewkerne TA18 8AB
Tel: 01460 73041
Fax: 01460 74627
enquiries.@lawrences.co.uk
www.lawrences.co.uk

The London Cigarette Card Co. Ltd
Sutton Road, Somerton TA11 6QP
Tel: 01458 273452
Fax: 01458 273515
cards@londoncigcard.co.uk
www.londoncigcard.co.uk

Dreweatt Neate (formerly Wells Auctions)
Wells Auction Rooms
66-68 Southover, Wells BA5 1UH
Tel: 01749 678094
bristol@dnfa.com
www.dnfa.com/bristol

Staffordshire

Hall and Lloyd Auctioneers
South Street, Stafford ST16 2DZ
Tel: 01785 258176

Louis Taylor Fine Art Auctioneers
Britannia House, 10 Town Road,
Hanley, Stoke-on-Trent ST1 2QG
Tel: 01782 214111
Fax: 01782 215283

Potteries Specialist Auctions
271 Waterloo Road, Cobridge,
Stoke-on-Trent ST6 3HR
Tel: 01782 286622
Fax: 01782 213777
enquires@potteriesauctions.com
www.potteriesauctions.com

Richard Winterton Auctioneers and Valuers
School House Auction Rooms,
Hawkins Lane, Burton-on-Trent
DE14 1PT
Tel: 01283 511224

Wintertons
Lichfield Auction Centre, Fradley
Park, Lichfield,
Staffordshire WS13 8NF
Tel: 01543 263256
Fax: 01543 415348
enquiries@wintertons.co.uk
www.wintertons.co.uk

Suffolk

Abbotts Auction Rooms
Campsea Ashe, Nr. Woodbridge
IP13 OPS
Tel: 01728 746323
Fax: 01728 748173
auction.rooms@abbottscountry-wide.co.uk
www.abbottsauctionrooms.co.uk

Durrant's
The Old School House, Peddars
Lane, Beccles Suffolk, NR 34 9UE
Tel: 01502 713490
Fax: 01502 711939
info@durrantsauctionrooms.com
www.durrantsauctionrooms.com

Dyson & Son
The Auction Room, Church Street,
Clare CO10 8PD
Tel: 01787 277 993
Fax: 01787 277 996
info@dyson-auctioneers.co.uk
www.dyson-auctioneers.co.uk

Lacy Scott and Knight Fine Art & Furniture
10 Risbygate Street,
Bury St. Edmunds IP33 3AA
Tel: 01284 748600
Fax: 01284 748620
www.lsk.co.uk
fineart@lsk.co.uk

Neal Sons and Fletcher
26 Church Street, Woodbridge
IP12 1DP
Tel: 01394 382263
Fax: 01394 383030
auctions@nsf.co.uk
www.nsf.co.uk

Tony Murland Auctions
78 High Street, Needham Market,
Suffolk, IP6 8AW
Tel: 01449 722 992
www.antiquetools.co.uk

Surrey

Clarke Gammon Wellers Fine Art Auctioneers
Tel: 01483 880915
Fax: 01483 880918
fine.art@clarkegammon.co.uk
www.clarkegammon.co.uk
www.invaluable.com/clarkegam-monwellers/

Cooper Owen
74 High Street, Egham,
Surrey TW20 9LF
Tel: 01784 434900
auctions@cooperowen.com
www.cooperowen.com

Crows Auction Gallery
Rear of Dorking Halls, Reigate
Road, Dorking RH4 1SG
Tel: 01306 740382
enquiries@crowsauctions.co.uk

Ewbank Auctioneers
Burnt Common Auction Rooms,
London Road, Send,
Woking GU23 7LN
Tel: 01483 223101
Fax: 01483 222171
www.ewbankauctions.co.uk

Dreweatt Neate (formerly Hamptons) Baverstock House, 93
High Street, Godalming GU7 1AL
Tel: 01483 423 567
Fax: 01483 426 392
godalming@dnfa.com
www.dnfa.com/godalming

John Nicholson
The Auction Rooms, Longfield,
Midhurst Road,
Haslemere GU27 3HA
Tel: 01428 653727
auctions@johnnicholsons.com
www.johnnicholsons.com

Lawrences' Auctioneers Limited
Norfolk House, 80 High Street,
Bletchingley RH1 4PA
Tel: 01883 743323
Fax: 01883 744578
www.lawrencesbletchingley.co.uk

Kew Auctions and Antiques Ltd
Richmond Station, Kew Road,
Richmond TW9 2NA
Tel: 020 8948 6677
Fax: 020 8948 2021
kewauctions@hotmail.com

P.F. Windibank Fine Art Auctioneers & Valuers
Dorking Halls, Reigate Road,
Dorking RH4 1SG
Tel: 01306 884556/876280
Fax: 01306 884669
sjw@windibank.co.uk
www.windibank.co.uk

East Sussex

Burstow & Hewett
Lower Lake, Battle,
East Sussex TN33 0AT
Tel: 01424 772374
www.burstowandhewett.co.uk

Gorringes Auction Galleries
Terminus Road,
Bexhill-on-Sea TN39 3LR
Tel: 01424 212994
Fax: 01424 224035
bexhill@gorringes.co.uk
www.gorringes.co.uk

Gorringes Auction Galleries
15 North Street, Lewes BN7 2PD
Tel: 01273 472503
Fax: 01273 479559
clientservices@gorringes.co.uk
www.gorringes.co.uk

Raymond P. Inman
The Auction Galleries, 98A
Coleridge Street, Hove BN3 5 AA
Tel: 01273 774777
Fax: 01273 735660
r.p.inman@talk21.com
www.invaluable.com/raymondinman

Rye Auction Galleries
Rock Channel, Rye TN31 7HL
Tel: 01797 222124

Scarborough Perry Fine Arts
Hove Street, Hove BN3 2GL
Tel: 01273 735266
Fax: 01273 723813
info@gsp.uk.com
www.scarboroughperry.com

Wallis & Wallis
West Street Auction Galleries,
Lewes BN7 2NJ
Tel: 01273 480208
Fax: 01273 476562
auctions@wallisandwallis.co.uk
www.wallisandwallis.co.uk

West Sussex

John Bellman Ltd
New Pound, Wisborough Green,
Billingshurst RH14 0AZ
Tel: 01403 700858
Fax: 01403 700059
enquiries@bellmans.co.uk
www.bellmans.co.uk

Denham's
The Auction Galleries, Warnham,
Nr. Horsham RH12 3RZ
Tel: 01403 255699
Fax: 01403 253837
denhams@lineone.net
www.catalogs.icollector.com/denhams

Rupert Toovey & Co.
Spring Gardens, Washington
RH20 3BS
Tel: 01903 891955
Fax: 01903 891966
auctions@rupert-toovey.com
www.rupert-toovey.com

Worthing Auction Galleries
Fleet House, Teville Gate,
Worthing BN11 1UA
Tel: 01903 205565
Fax: 01903 214365
info@worthing-auctions.co.uk
www.worthing-auctions.co.uk

Tyne and Wear

Anderson and Garland
Anderson House, Crispin Court,
Newbiggin Lane, Westerhope,
Newcastle upon Tyne NE5 1BF
Tel: 0191 430 3000
andersongarland@aol.com
www.andersonandgarland.com

Boldon Auction Galleries
24a Front Street,
East Boldon NE36 0SJ
Tel: 0191 537 2630
Fax: 0191 536 3875
enquiries@boldonauctions.co.uk
www.boldonauctions.co.uk

Corbitts
5 Mosley Street, Newcastle-upon-Tyne NE1 1YE
Tel: 0191 232 7268
Fax: 0191 261 4130
collectors@corbitts.com
www.corbitts.com

Warwickshire

Bigwood Auctioneers Ltd
The Old School, Tiddington,
Stratford-upon-Avon CV37 7AW
Tel: 01789 269415
Fax: 01789 292686
auctions@bigwoodauctioneers.co.uk
www.bigwoodauctioneers.co.uk

Locke and England
18 Guy Street, Leamington Spa
CV32 4RT
Tel: 01926 889100
Fax: 01926 470608
valuers@leauction.co.uk
www.leauction.co.uk

Warwick and Warwick Ltd
Chalon House, Scar Bank,
Millers Road, Warwick CV34 5DB
Tel: 01926 499031
Fax: 01926 491906
info@warwickandwarwick.com
www.warwickandwarwick.com

West Midlands

Biddle & Webb
Ladywood, Middleway,
Birmingham B16 0PP
Tel: 0121 455 8042
Fax: 0121 454 9615
info@biddleandwebb.com
www.biddleandwebb.co.uk

Bonhams
The Old House, Station Road,
Knowle, Solihull B93 0HT
Tel: 01564 776151
Fax: 01564 778069
knowle@bonhams.com
www.bonhams.com

Fellows and Sons
Augusta House, 19 Augusta Street,
Hockley, Birmingham B18 6JA
Tel: 0121 212 2131
Fax: 0121 212 1249
info@fellows.co.uk
www.fellows.co.uk

Wiltshire

Atwell Martin
2 New Road,
Chippenham SN15 1EJ
Tel: 01249 449800
Fax: 01249 447780

Henry Aldridge & Son
Unit 1 Bath Road Business Centre
Bath Road, Devizes,
Wiltshire, SN10 1XA
Tel: 01380 729199
Fax: 01380 730073
andrew@henry-aldridge.co.uk
www.henry-aldridge.co.uk

The Hilditch Auction Rooms
Gloucester Road Trading Estate,
Malmesbury SN16 9JT
Tel: 01666 822577
Fax: 01666 825597
sales@hilditchauctions.co.uk
www.hilditchauctions.co.uk

Woolley & Wallis
Salisbury Salerooms Ltd,
51-61 Castle Street,
Salisbury SP1 3SU
Tel: 01722 424500
Fax: 01722 424508
enquiries@woolleyandwallis.co.uk
www.woolleyandwallis.co.uk

Worcestershire

Andrew Grant Fine Art Auctioneers
St. Marks House, St. Marks Close,
Worcester WR5 3DL
Tel: 01905 357547
Fax: 01905 763942
fine.art@andrew-grant.co.uk
www.andrew-grant.co.uk

Griffiths and Charles
57 Foregate Street,
Worcester WR1 1DZ
Tel: 01906 720160
Fax 01905 745222
rupert@griffiths-charles.co.uk
www.griffiths-charles.co.uk

Philip Laney Fine Art
Malvern Auction Centre,
Portland Road, off Victoria Road,
Malvern WR14 2TA
Tel: 01684 893933
Fax: 01684 577948
philiplaney@aol.com
www.invaluable.com/philiplaney

DIRECTORY OF AUCTIONEERS

Philip Serrell Auctioneers & Valuers
The Malvern Sale Room,
Barnards Green Road,
Malvern WR14 3LW
Tel: 01684 892314
Fax: 01684 569832
serrell.auctions@virgin.net
www.serrell.com

East Yorkshire

Gilbert Baitson
The Edwardian Auction Galleries,
Wiltshire Road, Hull HU4 6PG
Tel: 01482 500500
Fax: 01482 500501
auction@gilbert-baitson.co.uk
www.gilbert-baitson.co.uk

Clegg & Son
68 Aire Street, Goole DN14 5QE
Tel: 01405 763140
gooleoffice@cleggandson.co.uk
www.cleggandson.co.uk

Dee Atkinson & Harrison
Agricultural and Fine Arts,
The Exchange Saleroom,
Driffield YO25 7LJ
Tel: 01377 253151
Fax: 01377 241041
exchange@dee-atkinson-harrison.co.uk
www.dee-atkinson-harrison.co.uk

Hawley's
Albion House, Westgate, North
Cave, East Yorkshire HU15 2NJ
Tel: 01430 470654
Fax: 01430 470655
info@hawleys.info
www.hawleys.info

North Yorkshire

David Duggleby Fine Art
The Vine Street Salerooms,
Scarborough YO11 1XN
Tel: 01723 507111
Fax: 01723 507222
auctions@davidduggleby.com
www.davidduggleby.com

David Duggleby Fine Art
The Paddock Salerooms
Whitby YO21 3DB
Tel: 01947 820 033
Fax: 01947 825 680
auctions@davidduggleby.com
www.davidduggleby.com

Malcolm's No. 1 Auctioneers and Valuers
The Chestnuts, 16 Park Avenue,
Sherburn in Elmet,
Nr. Leeds LS25 6EF
Tel: 01977 684 971
Fax: 01977 681 046
info@malcolmsno1auctions.co.uk
www.malcolmsno1auctions.co.uk

Morphets of Harrogate
6 Albert Street, Harrogate HG1 1JL
Tel: 01423 530030
Fax: 01423 500717
enquiries@morphets.co.uk
www.morphets.co.uk

Tennants
The Auction Centre,
Leyburn DL8 5SG
Tel: 01969 623780 Fax: 01969 624281
www.tennants.co.uk
enquiry@tennants-ltd.co.uk

South Yorkshire

BBR Auctions
Elsecar Heritage Centre,
Nr. Barnsley S74 8AA
Tel: 01226 745156
Fax: 01226 361561
www.bbrauctions.co.uk

A.E. Dowse and Son
Cornwall Galleries, Scotland Street,
Sheffield S3 7DE
Tel: 0114 272 5858
Fax: 0114 249 0550
aedowes@aol.com
www.aedowseandson.com

ELR Auctions Ltd
The Sheffield Saleroom, The Nichols
Bldg., Shalesmoor, Sheffield S3 8UJ
Tel: 0114 281 6161 Fax: 0114 281 6162
elrauctions@btconnect.com
www.elrauctions.com

West Yorkshire

De Romes
12 New John Street, Westgate,
Bradford BD1 2QY
Tel: 01274 734116

Andrew Hartley Fine Arts
Victoria Hall Salerooms,
Little Lane, Ilkley LS29 8EA
Tel: 01943 816363
Fax: 01943 816363
info@andrewhartleyfinearts.co.uk
www.invaluable.com/andrew-hartley

John Walsh & Co. Auctioneers & Valuers
Ashfield House Auction Rooms,
Illingworth Street, Ossett, WF5 8AL.
Tel: 01924 264030
Fax: 01924 267758
valuations@john-walsh.co.uk
www.john-walsh.co.uk

Scotland

Auction Rooms Ltd.
Castle Laurie, Bankside,
Falkirk, Sterlingshire FK2 7XF
Tel: 01324 623000 Fax: 01324 630343
contact@auctionroomsfalkirk.co.uk
www.auctionroomsfalkirk.co.uk

Bonhams
65 George St., Edinburgh,
Midlothian EH2 2JL
Tel: 0131 225 2266
Fax: 0131 220 2547
edinburgh@bonhams.com
www.bonhams.com

Loves Auction Rooms
52-54 Canal Street, Perth,
Perthshire PH2 8LF
Tel: 01738 633337
Fax: 01738 629830

Lyon & Turnbull Ltd.
33 Broughton Place, Edinburgh,
Midlothian EH1 3RR
Tel: 0131 557 8844
Fax: 0131 557 8668
info@lyonandturnbull.com
www.lyonandturnbull.com

Lyon & Turnbull Ltd.
4 Woodside Place, Glasgow,
Lanarkshire G3 7QF
Tel: 0141 353 5070
Fax: 0141 332 2928
info@lyonandturnbull.com
www.lyonandturnbull.com

MDS Auction Co.
15-17 Smeaton Industrial Estate,
Kirkcaldy, Fife KY1 2HE
Tel: 01592 640969 Fax: 01592 640969
sales@scotlandauction.co.uk
www.scotlandauction.co.uk

D.J. Manning Auctioneers
Carriden, Bo'ness,
West Lothian EH51 9SF
Tel: 01506 827693 Fax: 01506 826495
info@djmanning.co.uk
www.djmanning.co.uk

McTear's
Clydeway Business Centre,
8 Elliot Place, Glasgow,
Lanarkshire G3 8EP
Tel: 0141 221 4456
Fax: 0141 204 5035
enquiries@mctears.co.uk
www.mctears.co.uk

Taylor's Auction Rooms
11 Panmure Row, Montrose,
Angus DD10 8HH
Tel: 01674 672775 Fax: 01674 672479
enquiries@scotlandstreasures.co.uk
www.scotlandstreasures.co.uk

Thomson, Roddick & Medcalf Ltd.
44/3 Hardengreen Business Park,
Eskbank, Edinburgh,
Midlothian EH22 3NX
Tel: 0131 454 9090
Fax: 0131 454 9191
www.thomsonroddick.com

Thomson, Roddick & Medcalf Ltd.
Dumfries 60 Whitesands, Dumfries,
Dumfriesshire DG1 2RS
Tel: 01387 279879
www.thomsonroddick.com

Wales

Bonhams
7-8 Park Place, Cardiff,
Glamorgan CF10 3DP
Tel: 02920 727980 Fax: 02920 727989
cardiff@bonhams.com
www.bonhams.com

Bonhams
Napier House,
Spilman Street, Carmarthen,
Carmarthenshire SA31 1JY
Tel: 01267 238231 Fax: 02920 727989
carmarthen@bonhams.com
www.bonhams.com

Evans Bros.
Mart Office, Llanybydder,
Dyfed SA40 9UE
Tel: 01570 480 444
Fax: 01570 480 988
www.evansbros.com

Peter Francis
Curiosity Salerooms,
19 King St., Carmarthen,
Carmarthenshire SA31 1BH
Tel: 01267 233456
Fax: 01267 233458
www.peterfrancis.co.uk

Jones & Llewelyn
Llandeilo Auction Rooms, 21 New
Road, Llandeilo, Dyfed SA19 6DE
Tel: 01558 823430
Fax: 01558 822004
www.jonesllewelyn.freeserve.co.uk

Rogers-Jones & Co.
33 Abergele Road, Colwyn Bay,
Conway LL29 7RU
Tel: 01492 532176
Fax: 01492 533308
www.rogersjones.ukauctioneers.com

Welsh Country Auctions
2 Carmarthen Road, Cross Hands,
Llanelli, Carmarthenshire SA14 6SP
Tel: 01269 844428
Fax: 01269 844428
enquiries@welshcountryauctions.com
www.welshcountryauctions.com

Australia

Bonhams & Goodman
7 Anderson Street, Double Bay
NSW 2028 Australia
Tel: 0061 2 9327 9913
www.bonhamsandgoodman.com.au

Deutscher-Menzies
1140 Malvern Road, Malvern
VIC 3144, Australia
Tel: 0061 3 9822 1911
Fax: 0061 3 9822 1322
www.deutschermenzies.com

Lawson-Menzies
212 Cumberland Street,
Sydney 2000
Tel: 0061 2 9241 3411
Fax: 0061 2 9251 5869
www.lawsonmenzies.com.au

Shapiro
162 Queen Street
Woollahra NSW 2025 Australia
Tel: 0061 2 9326 1588
Fax: 0061 2 9326 1305
info@shapiroauctioneers.com.au

New Zealand

Webb's
18 Manukau Road, PO Box 99
251, Newmarket, Auckland 1000,
New Zealand
Tel: 0064 9 524 6804
www.webbs.co.nz

Specialists who would like to be included in the next edition, or have a change of address or telephone number, should contact us by 1 February 2007.

Readers should contact dealers by telephone before visiting them to avoid a wasted journey.

Antiquities

Ancient Art
85 The Vale, Southgate,
London N14 6AT
Tel: 020 8882 1509
Fax: 020 8886 5235
ancient.art@btinternet.com
www.ancientart.co.uk

David Aaron Ancient Arts & Rare Carpets
22 Berkeley Sq, Mayfair,
London W1J 6EH
Tel: 020 7491 9588

Finch & Co
Suite No 744, 2 Old Brompton Road, London SW7 3DQ
Tel: 020 7413 9937
Fax: 020 7581 4445
www.finch-and-co.co.uk

Helios Gallery
292 Westbourne Grove,
London W11 2PS
Tel/Fax: 07711 955 997
mail@heliosgallery.com
www.heliosgallery.com

John A Pearson
Horton Lodge, Horton Road, Horton, Near Slough, Berkshire SL3 9NU
Tel: 01753 682136

Rupert Wace Ancient Art Limited
14 Old Bond Street,
London W1X 3DB
Tel: 020 7495 1623
rupert.wace@btinternet.com
www.rupertwace.co.uk

Architectural

Pattisons Architectural Antiques
108 London Road, Aston Clinton,
Buckinghamshire HP22 5HS
Tel: 01296 632 300
Fax: 01296 631 329
info@ddd-uk.com
www.ddd-uk.com

D & R Blissett
c/o Coutts & Co, 440 Strand
London WC2R OQS

Joanna Booth
247 King's Road, London SW3 5EL
Tel: 020 7352 8998
Fax: 020 7376 7350
joanna@joannabooth.co.uk
www.joannabooth.co.uk

Drummonds Architectural Antiques
The Kirkpatrick Buildings, 25
London Road, Hindhead,
Surrey GU26 6AB
Tel: 01428 609444 Fax: 01428 609445
info@drummonds-arch.co.uk
www.drummonds-arch.co.uk

LASSCO
St. Michael's, Mark St (off Paul St),
London EC2A 4ER
Tel: 020 7749 9944
Fax: 020 7749 9941
st.michaels@lassco.co.uk
www.lassco.co.uk

Sweerts de Landas
Dunsborough Park, Ripley,
Surrey GU23 6AL
Tel: 01483 225366
garden.ornament@lineone.net
www.sweerts.com

Carpets & Rugs

Atlantic Bay Gallery
5 Sedley Place, London W1R 1HH
Tel: 020 7355 3301
atlanticbaygallery@btinternet.com

C John (Rare Rugs) Ltd.
70 South Audley Street,
London W1K 2RA
Tel: 020 7493 5288
Fax: 020 7409 7030
cjohn@dircon.co.uk
www.cjohn.com

Gallery Yacou
127 Fulham Road, London
SW3 6RT
Tel: 020 7584 2929
galleryyacou@aol.com

Gideon Hatch
1 Port House, Plantation Wharf,
Battersea, London SW11 3TY
Tel: 020 7223 3996
info@gideonhatch.co.uk
www.gideonhatch.co.uk

John Eskenazi Ltd.
15 Old Bond Street,
London W1S 4AX
Tel: 020 7409 3001
john.eskenazi@john-eskenazi.com
www.john-eskenazi.com

Karel Weijand
Lion & Lamb Courtyard, Farnham,
Surrey GU9 7LL
Tel: 01252 726215
carpets@karlweijand.com
www.karkweijand.com

Lindfield Galleries
62 High Street, Lindfield,
West Sussex RH16 2HL
Tel: 01444 483817
david@orientalandantiquerugs.com

Richard Purdon Antique Carpets
158 The Hill, Burford,
Oxfordshire OX18 4QY
Tel: 01993 823777
antiquerugs@richardpurdon.demon.co.uk
www.purdon.com

Wadsworth's
Marehill, Pulborough,
West Sussex RH20 2DY
Tel: 01798 873 555
Fax: 01798 872 333
info@wadsworthsrugs.com
www.wadsworthsrugs.com

Books

Biblion
1/7 Davies Mews,
London W1K 5AB
Tel: 020 7629 1374
www.biblion.com

Boxes

Alan & Kathy Stacey
PO Box 2771 Chapel Lane,
Yeovil, Somerset BA22 7DZ
Tel: 02076 444 049
www.antiqueboxes.uk.com

Mostly Boxes
93 High Street, Eton,
Windsor, Berkshire SL4 6AF
Tel: 01753 858 470
Fax: 01753 857 212

Ceramics

Albert Amor Ltd.
37 Bury Street, St James's,
London SW1Y 6AU
Tel: 020 7930 2444
Fax: 020 7930 9067
info@albertamor.co.uk
www.albertamor.co.uk

Andrew Dando
34 Market Street, Bradford-on-Avon, Wiltshire BA15 1LL
Tel: 01225 422 702
andrew@andrewdando.co.uk
www.andrewdando.co.uk

Brian & Angela Downes
PO Box 431, Chippenham,
Wiltshire SN14 6SZ
Tel/Fax: 01454 238134

Clive & Lynne Jackson
Cheltenham, Gloucestershire
Open by appointment only
Tel: 01242 254 3751
Mob: 07710 239351

Davies Antiques
c/o Cadogan Tate, Unit 6, 6-12
Ponton Road, London SW8 5BA
Tel/Fax: 020 8947 1902
www.antique-meissen.com

E & H Manners
66A Kensington Church Street,
London W8 4BY
Tel: 020 7229 5516
manners@europeanporcelain.com
www.europeanporcelain.com

Garry Atkins
Tel: 020 7727 8737
Fax: 020 7792 9010
garry.atkins@englishpottery.com
www.englishpottery.com

Gillian Neale Antiques
PO Box 247, Aylesbury,
Buckinghamshire HP20 1JZ
Tel: 01296 423754
Fax: 01296 334601
gillianneale@aol.com
www.gilliannealeantiques.co.uk

Hope and Glory Commemorative Ceramics
131A Kensington Church Street,
London W8 7LP
Tel: 020 7727 8424

John Howard at Heritage
Heritage, 6 Market Place,
Woodstock, Oxfordshire OX20 1TA
Tel: 0870 444 0678
Fax: 0870 444 0678
Howards@antiquepottery.co.uk
www.antiquepottery.co.uk

Jonathan Horne Antiques Ltd.
66c Kensington Church Street,
London W8 4BY
Tel: 020 7221 5658
Fax: 020 7792 3090
JH@jonathanhorne.co.uk
www.jonathanhorne.co.uk

Klaber & Klaber
PO Box 9445, London NW3 1WD
Tel: 020 7435 6537
Fax: 020 7435 9459
info@klaber.com
www.klaber.com

Mary Wise and Grosvenor Antiques
58 Kensington Church Street,
London W8 4DB.
Tel: 020 7937 8649
www.wiseantiques.com

Robyn Robb
43 Napier Avenue,
London SW6 3PS
Tel: 020 7731 2878

Roderick Jellicoe
PO. Box No. 50732
London NW6 6XW
Tel: 020 7727 1571
Fax: 020 7624 6471
jellicoe@englishporcelain.com
www.englishporcelain.com

Rogers de Rin
76 Royal Hospital Road, Paradise
Walk, Chelsea, London SW3 4HN
Tel: 020 7352 9007
Tel: 020 7351 9407
rogersderin@rogersderin.co.uk
www.rogersderin.co.uk

Roy W. Bunn Antiques
Tel: 01282 813703
info@roywbunnantiques.co.uk
www.roywbunnantiques.co.uk

Steppes Hill Farm Antiques
Steppes Hill Farm, Stockbury, Sittingbourne, Kent ME9 7RB
Tel: 01795 842205
Fax: 01795 842493
dwabuck@btinternet.com

Stockspring Antiques
114 Kensington Church Street, London W8 4BH
Tel: 020 7727 7995
stockspring@antique-porcelain.co.uk
www.antique-porcelain.co.uk

T C S Brooke
The Grange, 57 Norwich Road, Wroxham, Norfolk NR12 8RX
Tel: 01603 782644

Thrift Cottage Antiques
PO Box 113, Bury St Edmunds, Suffolk IP33 2RQ
Tel: 01284 702470
www.britishporcelain.com

Valerie Main
PO Box 92, Carlisle, Cumbria CA5 7GD
Tel: 01228 711342
valerie.main@btinternet.com

W W Warner Antiques
The Green, High Street, Brasted, Kent TN16 1JL
Tel: 01959 563698

Yvonne Adams Antiques
The Coffee House, 3 & 4 Church Street, Stow on the Wold, Gloucestershire GL54 1BB
Tel: 01451 832 015
antiques@adams.demon.co.uk
www.antiquemeissen.com

Clocks and Watches

Alan Walker
Halfway Manor, Halfway, Nr Newbury, Berkshire RG20 8NR
Tel: 01488 657670
www.alanwalker-barometers.com

Baskerville Antiques
Saddlers House, Saddlers Row, Petworth, West Sussex GU28 0AN
Tel: 01798 342067
Fax: 01798 343956
brianbaskerville@aol.com

Bobinet Ltd.
PO Box 2730, London NW8 9PL
Tel: 020 7266 0783
Fax: 020 7289 5119

David Gibson
PO Box 301, Axminster, Devon EX13 7YJ
Tel: 01297 631179
www.davidgibson.co.uk

Derek and Tina Rayment Antiques
Orchard House, Barton Road, Barton, Nr. Farndon, Cheshire SY14 7HT
Tel: 01829 270429
Fax: 01829 270893
www.antique-barometers.com

Derek Roberts Fine Antique Clocks & Barometers
25 Shipbourne Road, Tonbridge, Kent TN10 3DN
Tel: 01732 358986
Fax: 01732 771842
drclocks@clara.net
www.quallityantiqueclocks.com

G E Marsh (Antique Clocks) Ltd.
32a The Square, Winchester, Hampshire SO23 9EX
Tel: 01962 844443
gem@marshclocks.co.uk
www.marshclocks.co.uk

Jeffrey Formby Antiques
Orchard Cottage, East Street, Moreton-in-Marsh, Gloucestershire GL56 0LQ
Tel: 01608 650558
jeff@formby-clocks.co.uk
www.formby-clocks.co.uk

Jillings Antiques
Croft House, 17 Church Street, Newent, Gloucestershire GL18 1PU
Tel: 01531 822100
Fax: 01531 822666
clocks@jillings.com
www.jillings.com

John Carlton-Smith
17 Ryder Street, London SW1Y 6PY
Tel: 020 7930 6622
Fax: 020 7930 1370
www.fineantiqueclocks.com

Montpellier Clocks
13 Rotunda Terrace, Montpellier Street, Cheltenham, Gloucestershire GL50 1SW
Tel: 01242 242178
info@montpellierclocks.com
www.montpellierclocks.com

Patric Capon
PO Box 581, Bromley, Kent BR1 2WX
Tel: 020-8467 5722
Fax: 020-8295 1475
patric.capon@saqnet.co.uk

Pendulum of Mayfair
51 Maddox Sreet, London W1S 2PJ
Tel: 020 7629 6606
Fax: 020 7629 6616
pendulumclocks@aol.com
www.pendulumofmayfair.co.uk

Raffety & Walwyn Ltd
79 Kensington Church Street, London W8 4BG
Tel: 020 7938 1100
Fax: 020 7938 2519
raffety@globalnet.co.uk
www.raffetyantiqueclocks.com

Somlo Antiques
7 Piccadilly Arcade, London SW1Y 6NH
Tel: 020 7499 6526 Tel: 020 7499 0603
www.somlo.com

Strike One
48A Highbury Hill, London N5 1AP
Tel: 020 7354 2790
www.strikeone.co.uk

The Watch Gallery
129 Fulham Road, London SW3 6RT
Tel: 020 7581 3239
Fax: 020 7584 6497

Weather House Antiques
Foster Clough, Hebden Bridge, West Yorkshire HX7 5QZ
Tel: 01422 882808/886961
kymwalker@btinternet.com

Anthony Woodburn Ltd.
PO Box 2669, Lewes, East Sussex BN7 3JE
Tel: 01273 486666
Fax: 01273 486644
anthonywoodburn@btconnect.com
www.anthonywoodburn.com

Horological Workshops
204 Worplesdon Road, Guildford, Surrey GU2 6UY
Tel: 01483 576496 Fax: 01483 452212
mdtooke@aol.com
www.horologicalworkshops.com

Costume Jewellery and Accessories

Cristobal
26 Church Street, London NW8 8EP
Tel/Fax: 020 7724 7230
steven@cristobal.co.uk
www.cristobal.co.uk

Eclectica
2 Charlton Place, Islington, London N1 8AJ
Tel: 020 7226 5625
www.eclectica.biz

Sara Hughes Vintage Compacts, Antiques & Collectables
sara@sneak.freeserve.co.uk
http://mysite.wanadoo-members.co.uk/sara_compacts

Linda Bee
Grays Antique Market Mews, 1-7 Davies Street, London, W1Y 2LP
Tel: 020 7629 5921
www.graysantiques.com

Lynn & Brian Holmes
By appointment
Tel: 020 7368 6412

Richard Gibbon
neljeweluk@aol.com

Ritzy
7 The Mall Antiques Arcade, 359 Upper Street, London N1 0PD
Tel: 020 7704 0127

Sylvie Spectrum
Stand 372, Grays Antique Markets, 58 Davies Street, London W1K 5LP
Tel: 020 7629 3501
spectrum@grays.clara.net

William Wain at Antiquarius
Stand J6, Antiquarius, 135 King's Road, Chelsea, London SW3 4PW
Tel: 020 7351 4905
w.wain@btopenworld.com

Decorative Arts

Adrian Sassoon
Rutland Gate, London SW7 1BB
Tel: 020 7581 9888
ads@asassoon.demon.co.uk
www.adriansassoon.com

Aesthetics
Stand V2, Antiquarius, 131-141 Kings Road, London SW3 4PW
Tel: 020 7352 0395

Arenski Fine Arts Ltd.
The Coach House, Ledbury Mews North, Notting Hill, London W11 2AF
Tel: 020 7727 8599
arenski@netcomuk.co.uk
www.arenski.com

Art Deco Etc
73 Upper Gloucester Road, Brighton, Sussex BN1 3LQ
Tel: 01273 202 937
Mob: 07971 268 302
johnclark@artdecoetc.co.uk

Art Nouveau Originals c.1900
5 Pierrepont Row Arcade, Camden Passage, Islington, London N1 8EF
Tel: 020 7359 4127

Beth
Stand G043/46
Alfies Antiques Market
13-25 Church Sreet, Marylebone, London NW8 8DT
Tel: 020 7723 5613
Mob: 07776 136 003

Beverley
30 Church Street, Marylebone, London NW8 8EP
Tel: 020 7262 1576

Circa 1900
Shop 17, Georgian Village, Camden Passage, London N1 8DU
Tel: 0771 370 9211
www.circa1900.org

Charles Edwards
19a Rumbold Road (off King's Road), London SW6 2DY
Tel: 020 7736 7172
Fax: 020 7731 7388
charles@charlesedwards.com

Fay Lucas Art Metal
Christie's Fine Art Security, 42 Ponton Road, London, SW8 5BA
Tel: 020 7371 4404
Fax: 020 7371 4404
info@faylucas.com

Gallery 1930 - Susie Cooper Ceramics
18 Church Street, London NW8 8EP
Tel: 020 7723 1555
Fax: 020 7735 8309
gallery1930@aol.com
www.susiecooperceramics.com

H Blairman & Sons Ltd.
119 Mount Street,
London W1K 3NL
Tel: 020 7493 0444
Fax: 020 7495 0766
blairman@atlas.co.uk
www.blairman.co.uk

Halcyon Days Ltd.
14 Brook Street, London W1Y 1AA
Tel: 020 7629 8811
Fax: 020 7406 7901
info@halcyondays.co.uk
www.halcyondays.co.uk

Hall-Bakker at Heritage
6 Market Place, Woodstock,
Oxfordshire, OX20 1TA
Tel: 01993 811 332

Harris Lindsay
67 Jermyn Street,
London SW1Y 6NY
Tel: 020 7839 5767
Fax: 020 7839 5968
www.harrislindsay.com

Keshishian
73 Pimlico Road,
London SW1 W8NE
Tel: 020 7730 8810
Fax: 020 7730 8803

Mike Weedon
7 Camden Passage, Islington,
London N1 8EA
Tel: 020 7226 5319/020 7609 6826
Fax: 020 7700 6387
info@mikeweedonantiques.com
www.mikeweedonantiques.com

Perrault Rago Gallery
333 North Main Street
Lambertville, NJ 08530
Tel: 609.397.1802
fax: 609.397.9377
suzanne@ragoarts.com
www.ragoarts.com

Rainer Zietz Ltd.
1a Prairie Street, London SW8 3PX
Tel: 020 7498 2355
Fax: 020 7720 7745

Richard Gardner Antiques
Swan House, Market Square,
Petworth, West Sussex GU28 0AN
Tel: 01798 343 411
rg@richardgardenerantiques.co.uk
www.richardgardenerantiques.co.uk

Robert Bowman Ltd.
8 Duke Street, St James's,
London SW1Y 6BN
Tel: 020 7839 3100
Fax: 020 7839 3223
info@robertbowman.com
www.robertbowman.com

Rumours
4 The Mall Antiques Arcade, 359
Upper Street, London N1 0PD
Tel: 020 7704 6549

Sladmore Sculpture Gallery Ltd.
32 Bruton Place, Berkeley Square,
London W1X 7AA
Tel: 020 7499 0365
www.sladmore.com

Spencer Swaffer Antiques
30 High Street, Arundel, West
Sussex BN18 9AB
Tel: 01903 882132
Fax: 01903 884564
spencerswaffer@btconnect.com
www.spencerswaffer.com

Style Gallery
10 Camden Passage,
London N1 8ED
Tel: 020 7359 7867
Fax: 020 8361 2357
info@styleantiques.co.uk
www.styleantiques.co.uk

Tadema Gallery
10 Charlton Place, Camden
Passage, London N1 8AJ
Tel: 020 7359 1055
www.tademagallery.com

The Coach House London, Ltd.
185 Westbourne Grove,
London W11 2SB
Tel: 020 7229 8311
arenski@netcomuk.co.uk

The Country Seat
Huntercombe Manor Barn,
nr. Henley on Thames,
Oxfordshire RG9 5RY
Tel: 01491 641349
Fax: 01491 641533
www.thecountryseat.com
www.whitefriarsglass.com

The Design Gallery
5 The Green, Westerham,
Kent TN16 1AS
Tel: 01959 561 234
sales@designgallery.co.uk
www.designgallery.co.uk

The Red House Antiques Centre
Duncombe Place, York, North
Yorkshire YO1 7ED
Tel: 01904 637 000
www.redhouseyork.co.uk

Titus Omega
Tel: 020 7688 1295
info@titusomega.com
www.titusomega.com

Trio
L24, Grays Antique Markets, 58
Davies Street, London, W1K 5LP
Tel: 020 7493 2736
www.trio-london.fsnet.co.uk

Van Den Bosch
Shop 1, Georgian Village,
Camden Passage,
Islington N1 8DU
Tel: 020 7226 4550
info@vandenbosch.co.uk
www.vandenbosch.co.uk

Dolls and Toys

Bébés et Jouets
c/o Lochend Post Office,
165 Restalrig Road, Edinburgh,
Midlothian EH7 6HW
Tel: 0131 332 5650
bebesetjouets@tiscali.co.uk

Collectors Old Toy Shop and Antiques
89 Northgate, Halifax,
West Yorkshire HX1 1XF
Tel: 01422 360434/822148
toysandbanks@aol.com
collectorsoledtoy@aol.com

Sue Pearson Dolls & Teddy Bears
18 Brighton Square, 'The Lanes'
Brighton, East Sussex BN1 1HD
Tel/Fax: 01273 774851
sales@suepearson.co.uk
www.suepearson.co.uk

Victoriana Dolls
101 Portobello Rd,
London W11 2BQ
Tel: 01737 249 525
heather.bond@totalserve.co.uk

Furniture

Adrian Alan
66/67 South Audley Street,
London W1Y 5FE
Tel: 020 7495 2324
Fax: 020 7495 0204
enquries@adrianalan.com
www.adrianalan.com

Alistair Sampson Antiques Ltd.
120 Mount Street,
London W1K 3NN
Tel: 020 7409 1799
info@alistairsampson.com
www.alistairsampson.com

Anthemion
Cartmel, Grange-over-Sands,
Cumbria LA11 6QD
Tel: 015395 36295

Anthony Outred (Antiques) Ltd.
Blanchard, Froxfield,
Nr. Marlborough,
Wiltshire SN8 3LD.
Tel: 020 7730 7948
Fax: 020 7730 9509
antiques@outred.co.uk
www.outred.co.uk

The Antiques Warehouse
25 Lightwood Road, Buxton,
Derbyshire SK17 7BJ
Tel: 01298 72967
Mob: 07947 050 552

Antoine Cheneviere Fine Arts Ltd.
27 Bruton Street, London W1J 6QN
Tel: 020 7491 1007

Antony Preston Antiques Ltd.
The Square, Stow-on-the-Wold,
Cheltenham, Gloucestershire
GL54 1AB
Tel: 01451 831586 Fax: 01451 831596
www.antonypreston.com

Apter Fredericks Ltd.
265-267 Fulham Road,
London SW3 6HY
Tel: 020 7352 2188
Fax: 020 7376 5619
antiques@apter-fredericks.com
www.apter-fredericks.com

Avon Antiques
25, 26, 27 Market Street, Bradford-on-Avon, Wiltshire BA15 1LL
Tel: 01225 862052
www.avon-antiques.co.uk

Baggott Church Street Ltd
Church Street, Stow-on-the-Wold,
Gloucestershire GL54 1BB
Tel: 01451 830 370

Blanchard Ltd
86/88 Pimlico Road,
London SW1W 8PL
Tel: 020 7823 6310
Fax: 020 7823 6303
piers@jwblanchard.com

Brian Rolleston (Antiques) Ltd.
104a Kensington Church Street,
London W8 4BU
Tel: 020 7229 5892

Charles Lumb & Sons Ltd.
2 Montpellier Gardens, Harrogate,
North Yorkshire HG1 2TF
Tel: 01423 503776
Fax: 01423 530074

Chevertons Of Edenbridge Ltd.
71-73 High Street, Edenbridge,
Kent TN8 5AL
Tel: 01732 863196
Fax: 01732 864298
chevertons@msn.com
www.chevertons.com

Christopher Buck Antiques
56-60 Sandgate High Street,
Sandgate, Folkestone,
Kent CT20 3AP
Tel: 01303 221 229
chrisbuck@throwley.freeserve.co.uk

Christopher Hodsoll Ltd.
89-91 Pimlico Road, London
SW1W 8PH
Tel: 020 7730 3370
Fax: 020 7730 1516
info@hodsoll.com
www.hodsoll.com

Country Antiques (Wales) Ltd.
Castle Mill, Kidwelly
Carmarthenshire, SA17 4UU
Tel: 01554 890534
info@welshantiques.com
www.welshantiques.com

David J Hansord (Antiques)
6/7 Castle Hill, Lincoln,
Lincolnshire LN1 3AA
Tel: 01522 530044

David Love
10 Royal Parade, Harrogate,
North Yorkshire HG1 2SZ
Tel: 01423 565797
david.love@btconnect.com

Denzil Grant
Drinkstone House, Drinkstone, Bury
St Edmunds, Suffolk IP30 9TG
Tel: 01449 736576
Fax: 01449 737679
nickygrant@excite.co.uk
www.denzilgrant.com

Didier Aaron (London) Ltd.
21 Ryder Street, London SW1Y 6PX
Tel: 020 7839 4716
Fax: 020 7737 3513
didaaronuk@aol.com
www.didieraaron.com

Douglas Bryan
By appointment only.
Tel: 01580 713103

Elaine Phillips Antiques Ltd.
1 & 2 Royal Parade, Harrogate,
North Yorkshire HG1 2SZ
Tel: 01423 569 745
louise@elainephillipsantiques.wana
doo.co.uk

Freeman & Lloyd
44 Sandgate High Street,
Sandgate, Folkestone,
Kent CT20 3AP
Tel: 01303 248986
Fax: 01303 241353
enquiries@freemanandlloyd.com
www.freemanandlloyd.com

Georgian Antiques
10 Pattison St., Leith Links,
Edinburgh, Midlothian EH6 7HF,
Scotland
Tel: 0131 553 7286
Fax: 0131 553 6299
info@georgianantiques.net
www.georgianantiques.net

Godson & Coles
92 Fulham Road, London SW3 6HR
Tel: 020 7584 2200
Tel: 020 7584 2223
www.godsonandcoles.co.uk

H C Baxter & Sons
40 Drewstead Road,
London SW16 1AB
Tel: 020 8769 5869/5969

H W Keil Ltd.
Tudor House, Broadway,
Worcestershire WR12 7DP
Tel: 01386 852408

Heath Bullocks
8 Meadrow, Godalming,
Surrey GU7 3HN
Tel: 01483 422562
Fax: 01483 426077

Hotspur Ltd.
14 Lowndes Street,
London SW1X 9EX
Tel: 020 7235 1918
Fax: 020 7235 4371
enquiries@hotspurantiques.com

Huntington Antiques Ltd
Church Street, Stow-on-the-Wold,
Gloucestershire GL54 1BE
Tel: 01451 830 842
Fax: 01451 832 211
info@huntington-antiques.com
www.huntington-antiques.com

Jacob Stodel
Flat 53, Macready House, 75
Crawford Street, London W1H 1HS
Tel: 020 7723 3732
jacobstodel@aol.com

James Brett Ltd.
42 St Giles Street, Norwich,
Norfolk NR2 1LW
Tel: 01603 628171

Jeremy Ltd.
29 Lowndes Street,
London SW1X 9HX
Tel: 020 7823 2923
Fax: 020 7245 6197
jeremy@jeremique.co.uk
www.jeremy.ltd.uk

John Bly
By appointment
27 Bury Street, St James's,
London SW1Y 6AL
Tel: 01442 823030
Fax: 01442 890237
Showroom - The Courtyard
Church Square
Tring, Hertfordshire
HP23 5AE
Tel: 07831 888825/6
Fax: 07092 39194
info@johnbly.com
www.johnbly.com

John Hobbs Ltd.
107A Pimlico Road,
London SW1W 8PH
Tel: 020 7730 8369
Fax: 020 7730 8369
www.johnhobbs.co.uk

John King
74 Pimlico Road,
London SW1W 8LS
Tel: 020 7730 0427
Fax: 020 7730 2515
kingj896@aol.com

Lennox Cato Antiques
1 The Square, Church Street,
Edenbridge,
Kent TN8 5BD
Tel: 01732 865 988
cato@lennoxcato.com
www.lennoxcato.com

Lucy Johnson
PO Box 84, Carterton, Burford,
Oxfordshire OX18 4AT
Tel: 07071 881232
Fax: 07071 881233
lucy-johnson@lucy-johnson.com

Mac Humble Antiques
7-9 Woolley Street, Bradford-on-
Avon, Wiltshire BA15 1AD
Tel/Fax: 01225 866329
mac.humble@virgin.net
www.machumbleantiques.co.uk

Michael Foster
118 Fulham Road, London SW3 6HU
Tel: 020 7373 3636
Fax: 020 7373 4042

Michael Norman Antiques Ltd.
61 Holland Road, Hove,
East Sussex BN3 1JN
Tel: 01273 329 253
Fax: 01273 206 556

Norman Adams
8-10 Hans Road, London SW3 1RX
Tel: 020 7589 5266
Fax: .020 7589 1968
www.normanadams.com

Oswald Simpson
The Chapel Maltings, Long Malford,
Suffolk CO10 9HX
Tel: 01787 379287

Owen Humble Antiques
Open by appointment only
Tel: 0191 267 7220

Patrick Sandberg Antiques
150-152 Kensington Church Street,
London W8 4BN
Tel: 020 7229 0373
Fax: 020 7792 3467
psand@antique.net
www.antique.net

Paul Hopwell Antiques
30 High Street, West Haddon,
Northamptonshire NN6 7AP
Tel: 01788 510636
Fax: 01788 510044
PaulHopwell@antiqueoak.co.uk
www.antiqueoak.co.uk

Peter Bunting
Harthill Hall, Alport, Bakewell,
Derbyshire DE45 1LH
Tel: 01629 636203
www.countryoak.co.uk

Peter Foyle Hunwick
The Old Malthouse,
15 Bridge Street, Hungerford,
Berkshire RG17 0EG
Tel/Fax: 01488 682209

Peter Lipitch Ltd.
120 & 124 Fulham Road,
London SW3 6HU
Tel: 020 7373 3328
Fax: 020 7373 8888
lipitcha1@aol.com
www.peterlipitch.com

Phillips of Hitchin (Antiques) Ltd.
The Manor House, Hitchin,
Hertfordshire SG5 1JW
Tel: 01462 432067
Fax: 01462 441368

R G Cave & Sons Ltd.
Walcote House, 17 Broad Street,
Ludlow, Shropshire SY8 1NG
Tel: 01584 873568
Fax: 01584 875050

R N Myers & Son Ltd.
Endsleigh House, High Street,
Gargrave, Skipton,
North Yorkshire BD23 3LX
Tel: 01756 749587
Fax: 01756 749 322
rnmyersson@aol.com

Reindeer Antiques Ltd.
81 Kensington Church Street,
London W8 4BG
Tel: 020 7937 3754
Fax: 020 7937 7199
43 Watling Street, Potterspury,
Northamptonshire NN12 7QD
Tel: 01908 542407
Fax: 01908 542121
www.reindeerantiques.co.uk

Richard Courtney Ltd.
112-114 Fulham Road, South
Kensington, London SW3 6HU
Tel: 020 7370 4020
Fax: 020 7370 4020

Richard J Kingston
Tel: 01491 574535
Fax: 01491 574535

Robert E Hirschhorn
By appointment
London
Tel: 020 7703 7443
hirschhornantiques@macunlimited.net
www.hirschhornantiques.com

Robert Young Antiques
68 Battersea Bridge Road,
London SW11 3AG
Tel: 020 7228 7847
Fax: 020 7585 0489
office@robertyoungantiques.com
www.robertyoungantiques.com

Roderick Butler
Marwood House, Honiton,
Devon EX14 1PY
Tel: 01404 42169

Ronald Phillips Ltd.
26 Bruton Street, London W1J 6LQ
Tel: 020 7493 2341
Fax: 020 7495 0843
advice@ronaldphillips.co.uk

S J Webster-Speakman
By appointment
Tel: 01502 722252

Stair & Company Ltd.
14 Mount Street, London W1Y 5RA
Tel: 020 7499 1784
Fax: 020 7629 1050
stairandcompany@talk21.com

Suffolk House Antiques
High Street, Yoxford, Saxmundham,
Suffolk IP17 3EP
Tel: 01728 668122
Fax: 01728 668122

Oliver Charles Antiques Ltd.
Lombard Street, Petworth,
West Sussex GU28 0AG
Tel: 01798 344443

Thomas Coulborn & Sons
Vesey Manor, 64 Birmingham Road,
Sutton Coldfield,
West Midlands B72 1QP
Tel: 0121 354 3974
Fax: 0121 354 4614
jc@coulborn.com

Tobias Jellinek Antiques
20 Park Road, East Twickenham,
Middlesex TW1 2PX
Tel: 020 8892 6892
Fax: 020 8744 9298
toby@jellinek.com

Turpin's Antiques
17 Bridge Street, Hungerford,
Berkshire RG17 0EG
Tel: 01488 681886
Tel: 01672 870727

W A Pinn & Sons
124 Swan Street, Sible Hedingham,
Essex CO9 3HP
Tel: 01787 461127

W R Harvey & Co (Antiques) Ltd.
86 Corn Street, Witney,
Oxfordshire OX8 7BU
Tel: 01993 706501
Fax: 01993 706601
antiques@wrharvey.co.uk
www.wrharvey.co.uk

Wakelin & Linfield
PO Box 48, Billingshurst,
West Sussex RH14 0YZ
Tel: 01403 700004
Fax: 01403 701173
wakelin_linfield@btinternet.com
www.wakelin-linfield.com

William H Stokes
The Cloisters, 6/8 Dollar Street,
Cirencester, Gloucestershire
GL7 2AJ
Tel: 01285 653907
Fax: 01285 640533

Witney Antiques
96-100 Corn Street, Witney,
Oxfordshire OX28 6BU
Tel: 01993 703902
Fax: 01993 779852
witneyantiques@community.co.uk
www.witneyantiques.com

General

Alfies Antique Market
13-25 Church Street, Marylebone,
London NW8 8DT
Tel: 020 7723 6066
Fax: 020 7724 0999
www.alfiesantiques.com

Antiquarius
131-141 Kings Road
London SW3 4PW
Tel: 020 7351 5353
www.antiquarius.co.uk

Christopher Sykes
The Old Parsonage
Woburn, Milton Keynes,
Buckinghamshire MK17 9QL
Tel: 01525 290259
Fax: 01525 290061

Early Technology
Monkton House, Old
Craighall,Musselburgh,
Midlothian EH21 8SF
Tel: 0131 665 5753
michael.bennett-levy@virgin.net
www.earlytech.com

Grays Antiques Markets
58 Davies St,
London W1K 5LP
Tel: 020 7629 7034
Fax: 020 7499 7034
Email: info@graysantiques.com

Heritage
6 Market Place, Woodstock,
Oxfordshire OX20 1TA
Tel: 01993 811332

Manfred Schotten Antiques
109 High Street, Burford,
Oxfordshire OX18 4RU
Tel: 01993 822302
Fax: 01993 822055
www.schotten.com

Otford Antiques and Collectors Centre
26-28 High Street, Otford,
Sevenoaks, Kent TN14 5PQ
Tel: 01959 522025
Fax: 01959 525858
www.otfordantiques.co.uk

Pantiles Spa Antiques
4-6 Union House,
The Pantiles, Tunbridge Wells,
Kent TN4 8HE
Tel: 01892 541377
Fax: 01435 865660
psa.wells@btinternet.com
www.pantiles-spa-antiques.co.uk

The Ginnel Antiques Centre
Off Parliament Street,
Harrogate, North Yorkshire HG1 2RB
Tel: 01423 508 857

Glass

Andrew Lineham Fine Glass
PO Box 465, Chichester, West
Sussex PO18 8WZ.
Tel: 01243 576 241
Fax: 01243 576 241
Mob: 07767 702 722
andrew@antiquecolouredglass.com
www.antiquecolouredglass.info

Antique Glass at Frank Dux Antiques
33 Belvedere, Lansdown Road
Bath BA1 5HR
Tel: 01225 312367
Fax: 01225 312367
m.hopkins@antique-glass.co.uk
www.antique-glass.co.uk

Christine Bridge Antiques
By appointment only
Tel: 0208 741 5501
Fax: 0208 255 0172
christine@bridge-antiques.com
www.bridge-antiques.com
www.antiqueglass.co.uk

Delomosne & Son Ltd.
Court Close, North Wraxall,
Chippenham, Wiltshire SN14 7AD
Tel: 01225 891505
Fax: 01225 891907
www.delomosne.co.uk

Jeanette Hayhurst Fine Glass
32A Kensington Church St,
London W8 4HA
Tel: 020 7938 1539
www.antiqueglasslondon.com

Mum Had That
info@mumhadthat.com
www.mumhadthat.com

Jewellery

N. Bloom & Son (1912) Ltd.
Tel: 020 7629 5060
www.nbloom.com

J H Bonnar
72 Thistle Street, Edinburgh,
Midlothian EH2 1EN
Tel: 0131 226 2811

Modern

Fragile Design
8 Lakeside, The Custard Factory,
Digbeth, Birmingham, West
Midlands B9 4AA
Tel: 0121 693 1001
www.fragiledesign.com

Francesca Martire
F131-137, Alfies Antique Market,
13 Church Street, Marylebone,
London NW8 8DT
Tel: 020 7724 4802

ISOKON Plus
Turnham Green Terrace Mews,
London W4 1QU
Tel: 020 8994 0636
www.isokonplus.com

John Makepeace
Farrs, Beaminster,
Dorset DT8 3NB
Tel: 01308 862 204
www.johnmakepeace.com

Rennies Seaside Modern
47 The Old High St
Folkestone, Kent CT20 2RN
Tel: 01303 242427
info@rennart.co.uk
www.rennart.co.uk

Twentieth Century Marks
Whitegates, Rectory Rd, Little
Burstead, Nr Billericay,
Essex CM12 9TR
Tel: 01268 411 000
www.20thcenturymarks.co.uk

Oriental and Asian

Millner Manolatos
2 Campden Street, Off Kensington
Church Street, London W8 7EP
Tel: 020 7229 3268
Mob: 07900 248 390
info@millnermanolatos.com
www.millnermanolatos.com

Guest & Gray
1-7 Davies Mews,
London W1K 5AB
Tel: 020 7408 1252
Fax: 020 7499 1445
info@chinese-porcelain-art.com
www.chinese-porcelain-art.com

Ormonde Gallery
156 Portobello Road,
London W11 2EB
Tel: 020 7229 9800

Roger Bradbury
Church Street,
Coltishall, Norwich,
Norfolk NR12 7DJ
Tel: 01603 737 444

R & G McPherson Antiques
40 Kensington Church Street,
London W8 4BX
Tel: 020 7937 0812
Fax: 020 7938 2032
Mob: 07768 432 630
rmcpherson@orientalceramics.com
www.orientalceramics.com

Silver

B. Silverman
4 Campden Street,
Off Kensington Church Street,
London W8 7EP
Tel: 020 7985 0555
Fax: 020 7985 0556
silver@silverman-london.com
www.silverman-london.com

DIRECTORY OF SPECIALISTS

C. & L. Burman
5 Vigo Steet, London W1S 3HF
Tel: 020 7439 6604
Fax: 020 7439 6605

Didier Antiques
58-60 Kensington Church Street,
London W8 4DB
Tel: 020 7938 2537
didier.antiques@virgin.net
www.didierantiques.com

Fay Lucas Artmetal
Christies Fine Art Securities
42 Ponton Road,
London SW8 5BA
Tel: 020 7371 4404
Fax: 020 7371 4404
info@faylucas.com
www.faylucas.com

Gerald Sattin
PO Box 20627,
London NW6 7GA
Tel: 020 8451 3295
Fax: 020 8451 3295
gsattin@compuserve.com

Goodwins Antiques Ltd
15 & 16 Queensferry Street,
Edinburgh EH2 4QW
Tel: 0131 225 4717
Fax: 0131 220 1412

Hannah Antiques
Tel: 01844 351 935
Fax: 07831 800 774

John Bull (Antiques) Ltd.
JB Silverware, 139A New Bond
Street, London W1S 2TN
Tel: 020 7629 1251
Fax: 020 7495 3001
elliot@jbsilverware.co.uk
www.antique-silver.co.uk
www.jbsilverware.co.uk

J. H. Bourdon Smith Ltd
24 Mason's Yard, Duke Street,
St James's, London SW1Y 6BU
Tel: 020 7839 4714
Fax: 020 7839 3951

Marks
49 Curzon Street,
London W1J 7UN
Tel: 020 7499 1788
Fax: 020 7409 3183
marks@marksantiques.com
www.marksantiques.com

Mary Cooke Antiques
12 The Old Power Station,
121 Mortlake High Street,
London SW14 8SN
Tel: 020 8876 5777
Fax: 020 8876 1652
silver@marycooke.co.uk
www.marycooke.co.uk

Nicholas Shaw Antiques
Virginia Cottage, Lombard Street,
Petworth, West Sussex GU28 0AG
Tel: 01798 345 146
Fax: 01798 345 157
silver@nicholas-shaw.com
www.nicholas-shaw.com

Paul Bennett
48a George Street,
London W1U 7DY
Tel: 020 7935 1555
Fax: 020 7224 4858
paulbennett@ukgateway.net
www.paulbennett.ukgateway.net

Payne & Son (Goldsmiths) Ltd
131 High Street
Oxford, Oxfordshire OX1 4DH
Tel: 01865 243 787
Fax: 01865 793 241
silver@payneandson.co.uk
www.payneandson.co.uk

Peter Cameron Antique Silver
PO Box LB739
London W1A 9LB
petercameron@idnet.co.uk

Peter Szuhay
325 Grays Antiques Markets,
58 Davies Street, London W1Y 2LB
Tel: 020 7408 0154
Fax: 020 8993 8864
pgszuhay@aol.com

Sanda Lipton
28a Devonshire Street,
London W1G 6PS
Tel: 020 7431 2688
Fax: 020 7431 3224
sanda@antique-silver.com
www.antique-silver.com

S & J Stodel
Vault 24, London Silver Vaults,
Chancery Lane, London WC2A 1QS
Tel: 020 7405 7009
Fax: 020 7242 6366
stodel@msn.com
www.chinesesilver.com

Shapiro & Company
380 Grays Antiques Markets,
58 Davies Street, London W1K 5LP
Tel: 020 7491 2710

Smith & Robinson
Tel: 020 8994 3783
cwsmith@ukonline.co.uk

Steppes Hill Farm Antiques
Steppes Hill Farm, Stockbury,
Sittingbourne, Kent ME9 7RB
Tel: 01795 842205
Fax: 01795 842493
dwabuck@btinternet.com

The Silver Fund
1 Duke of York Street,
London SW1Y 6JP
Tel: 020 7839 8935
www.thesilverfund.com

Van Den Bosch
1 Georgian Village,
Camden Passage,
Islington, London N1 8DU
Tel: 020 7226 4550
Fax: 020 8348 5410
info@vandenbosch.co.uk
www.vandenbosch.co.uk

Textiles

Antique Textiles and Lighting
34 Belvedere, Lansdowne Road,
Bath, Avon BA1 5HR
Tel: 01225 310 795
Tel: 01225 443884
www.antiquetextilesandlighting.co.uk

Esther Fitzgerald Rare Textiles
28 Church Row, London NW3 6UP
Tel: 020 7431 3076
www.estherfitzgerald.co.uk

Fantiques
Tel: 020 8840 4761
paulajraven@aol.com

Junnaa & Thomi Wroblewski
78 Marylebone High Street, Box 39,
London W1U 5AP
Tel: 020 7499 7793
Fax: 020 7499 7793
junnaa@wroblewski.eu.com
thomi@wroblewski.eu.com

Rellick
8 Golborne Road,
London W10 5NW
Tel: 020 8962 0089

Vintage to Vogue
28 Milsom Street, Bath,
Avon BA1 1DG
Tel: 01225 337 323
www.vintagetovogue.com

Tribal Art

Elms Lesters
Painting Rooms, Flitcroft Street,
London WC2H 8DH
Tel: 020 7836 6747
Fax: 020 7379 0789
gallery@elms-lesters.demon.co.uk
www.elms-lesters.demon.co.uk

Jean-Baptiste Bacquart
www.AfricanAndOceanicArt.com

Michael Graham Stewart
173 New Bond Street
London W1S 4RF
Tel: 020 7495 4001
Fax: 020 7629 4602
www.graham-stewart.com

Owen Hargreaves & Jasmine Dahl
9 Corsham Street
London N1 6DP
Tel: 020 7253 2669
www.owenhargreaves.com

JACKET IMAGES

Front jacket shows: Top row, left to right: 1. Murano 'Sommerso' vase, **£50-70** *Private Collector*. 2. Dayak Tribe Huduk mask. **£5,000-7,000** *Jamieson Tribal Art*. 3. Eames RAR shell rocker, **£400-600** *Gaze & Son*. 4. Loetz vase, **£4,000-6,000** *Sotheby's Picture Library*. 5. Japanese Meiji ivory okimono, **£300-400** Sloanes & Kenyon. Second row: 6. WMF ewer, **£1,200-1,800** *Style Gallery*. 7. Art Deco brooch, **£600-900** *Decodame.com*. 8. English bureau bookcase, **£3,000-4,000** *Sloanes & Kenyon*. 9. Burgun, Schverer & Cie vase, **£10,000-15,000** *Lilian Nassau*. 10. Raymonde Guerbe lamp, **£1,000-1,500** *Herr Auctions*. Third row: 11. Lloyd Kem Weber chair, **£2,200-2,800** *Modernism Gallery*. 12. Art Nouveau candlestick, **£180-220** *The Design Gallery*. 13. Roycroft Dard Hunter lamp, **£15,000-20,000** *David Rago Auctions*. 14. Jno. Bryan clock, **£12,000-18,000** *Derek Roberts*. 15. Rookwood Sally Coyne vase **£200-400** *David Rago Auctions*.

Back jacket shows: 1. Verner Panton cone chair, **£400-600** *John Nicholson*. 2. John Bennett vase **£800-1,200** *David Rago Auctions*. 3. Roycroft lamp, **£3,000-5,000** *David Rago Auctions*. 4. Staffordshire Thomas Mayer plate, **£500-700** *Skinner Inc*.

A

albarello jar An Italian tin-glazed earthenware pharmacy jar.

albumen print Photographic paper that is treated with egg white (albumen) to enable it to hold light sensitive chemicals.

ashet A large plate or dish.

astragal Architectural moulding with a semi-circular section.

aventurine A translucent glass given a sparkling appearance by the incorporation of flecks of oxidised metal. Can also be used as a glaze on ceramics.

B

Bakelite An early synthetic plastic which was patented in 1907.

balance An escape mechanism that is used in clocks without pendulums.

baluster A curved form with a bulbous base and slender neck.

Baroque An ornate and extravagant decorative style which was popular in the 17th and 18thC.

bergère The French term for an upholstered armchair.

bezel The groove or rim on the inside of the cover or lid on vessels such as teapots.

bianco-sopra-bianco A technique involving painting opaque white glaze on to a greyish ground.

boulle A type of marquetry that includes tortoiseshell and metal.

brassing Wear to plating that reveals the underlying base metal.

break-front A term for furniture with a projecting centre section.

broderie anglaise White thread embroidered onto white cloth, used after the 1820s.

C

cabochon A protruding, polished, but not faceted, stone.

cabriole leg A leg with two gentle curves that create an S-shape.

cameo Hardstone, coral or shell that has been carved to show a design in a contrasting colour.

cameo glass Decorative glass made from two or more layers of differently coloured glass, which are then carved or etched to reveal the colour beneath.

caryatid An architectural column in the form of a woman.

cased glass Glass encased with a further layer of glass.

celadon A distinctive grey/green or blue/green glaze.

centre seconds hand A seconds hand that is pivoted at the centre of the dial.

chamfered A surface that has been cut with a slanted edge.

champlevé A type of decoration where enamel is applied to stamped hollows in metal.

chapter ring The ring of hour and minute numbers on a clock dial.

character doll A doll with a face that resembles a real child.

charger A large plate or platter, used for display or serving.

chasing The technique of decorating the surface of silver by punching it with small tools.

chinoiserie Oriental-style lacquered or painted decoration featuring figures and landscapes.

chronometer A timekeeper used for calculating longitude at sea.

clock garniture A matching clock and candelabra set.

cloisonné A decorative technique whereby metal cells are filled with coloured enamels.

commode A decorated low chest of drawers with a curved form.

composition A mixture including wood pulp, plaster and glue and used as a cheap alternative to bisque in the production of dolls.

core forming An early form of glass-making where molten glass is wound around a mud core.

crackle A deliberate crazed glaze effect used on porcelain.

credenza The Italian term for a side cabinet with display shelves at both ends.

crewelwork A wool embroidery technique used on linen.

cricket cage A small box designed to amplify the chirping of a cricket contained therein.

D

daguerreotype An early type of photograph, from c1839 until the 1850s.

davenport A small writing desk. In America, a large parlour sofa.

dentils Small teeth-like blocks that form a border under a cornice.

Deutsche Blumen Floral decoration found on 18thC faience and porcelain.

diecast Objects made by pouring molten metal into a closed metal die or mould.

ding A very small dent in metal.

dovetailing A method of joining two pieces of wood together by interlocking mortises and tenons.

dump A doorstop made from left-over glass, often with decoration.

E

earthenware A type of porous pottery that requires a glaze to make it waterproof.

ebonised Wood that has been dyed black to resemble ebony.

egg and dart A classical moulding that incorporates egg and 'v' shapes used to enrich Neo-classical wares.

enamel Coloured glass paste that is applied to surfaces to create a decorative effect.

escapement The mechanical part of the clock or watch that regulates the transfer of energy from the weights or spring to the movement of the clock or watch.

escutcheon A protective plate, as for a keyhole

F

faïence Earthenware treated with an impervious tin glaze.

fairing A small porcelain figure made in Eastern Germany and given away as prizes or sold inexpensively at fairs.

Fazackerley A style of floral painting found on English delft.

Fazackerley colours The bright enamel colours used to decorate pieces of English delft. The name probably derives from a pair of Liverpool delft mugs, dedicated to Thomas and Catherine Fazackerley, which were destroyed in WWII.

festoon A decorative motif in the form of a garland or chain of fruit, flowers and ribbons suspended on a loop.

figuring A natural pattern created by the grain in the wood.

finial A decorative knob on a terminal or cover of a vessel.

flatware Any type of cutlery.

free blown Glass blown and manipulated into shape without the use of a mould.

fretwork Geometric pierced decoration.

frieze A piece of wood supporting a table top or cornice.

frit Powdered glass added to white clay to produce a soft-paste porcelain. Also describes impurities found in old glass.

fusee A grooved device found in clocks that offsets the force of the spring as it runs down.

G

gadroon A decorative border of flutes or reeds.

gesso A paste mixture applied to timber then carved and gilded.

gnomon The part of a sundial which casts the shadow.

Greek key A Classical motif of interlocking lines.

grosse point A stitch that crosses two warp and two weft threads.

GLOSSARY

guilloché An engraved pattern of interlaced motifs, sometimes with translucent enamels.

H

hard-paste porcelain Porcelain made from kaolin, petuntse and quartz.

harlequin set A set of ceramics or furniture, in which the pieces are similar rather than identical.

hiramakie A Japanese decorative technique whereby a powdered charcoal design is coated with a layer of transparent lacquer.

honey gilding A decorative technique using gold leaf mixed with honey for a reddish tinge.

hotei The Japanese god of contentment and happiness.

I J K

intaglio Cut or engraved decoration on glass.

japanning The process of coating objects with layers of coloured varnish in imitation of lacquer.

knop The knob on lids and covers and also the bulge on the stem of a candlestick or glass.

kovsh A Russian shallow drinking vessel with a handle.

kraak ware Late Ming Chinese blue and white porcelain exported by Dutch traders in ships known as 'carracks.'

L

lacquer An oriental varnish made from tree gum with a gloss finish.

lead glass or crystal A particularly clear type of glass with a high lead oxide content.

lead glaze A clear glaze with a lead based component.

longcase clock A weight-driven, free-standing clock.

lustre An iridescent finish found on pottery and produced using metallic oxides.

M

manganese A mineral used to produce a purple glaze.

maiolica Italian tin-glazed earthenware produced from the 14thC.

marqueterie sur verre A method of decorating glass in which a hot glass shape is pressed onto the surface of a shape.

marquetry A decorative veneer made up from coloured woods.

married A term uses to describe a piece that is composed of parts that were not originally together.

Meiji A period in Japanese history dating from c1868-1912.

Mon A Japanese family crest. A common example is the 16 petal chrysanthemum flower.

movement The entire time-keeping mechanism of a clock or watch.

N O

netsuke A small toggle used to secure pouches and boxes hung on cords through the belt of a kimono.

ogee An S-shaped shallow curve.

okimono A Japanese ornamental carving.

opalescent An opal-like, milky glass with subtle gradations of colour.

opaline glass A translucent white glass made with the addition of oxides and bone ash.

ormolu Bronze gilding used in 18thC and early 19thC France as decorative mounts.

overglaze Enamel or transfer-printed decoration on porcelain that is applied after firing.

ovolo A quarter-circle shaped moulding.

P

parian A semi-matt type of porcelain, made with feldspar, that does not require a glaze.

parquetry A variant of marquetry where veneers are applied in symmetrical designs.

parure A jewellery set usually comprising a matching necklace, pair of earrings, bracelet and a brooch.

paste The mixture of ingredients that make up porcelain. Also a compound of glass used to make imitation gemstones.

patina A surface sheen on objects that is produced over time through polishing and handling.

pavé setting A method of mounting jewels so that each stone is set close to the next.

pearlware English earthenware with a blue tinted glaze, developed by Wedgwood.

penwork Indian ink decoration applied with a pen.

petit point Finely worked embroidery with stitches that cross one warp or weft thread.

pinion A small toothed gear within a clock movement.

piqué A decorative technique where small strips or studs of gold are inlaid onto ivory or tortoiseshell on a pattern and secured in place by heating.

plique-à-jour Technique where enamel is set into an openwork metal frame to create an effect similar to stained glass.

porcelain A mixture of china clay and china stone that becomes hard, translucent and white when fired. Hard-paste porcelain is fired at a higher temperature than soft paste.

pounce pot A small pot for gum dust used to prevent ink from spreading.

press-moulded Ceramics formed by pressing clay into a mould. Pressed glass is made by pouring molten glass into a mould and pressing it with a plunger.

Q R S

repoussé A French term for the raised, 'embossed', decoration on metals such as silver.

sabot The metal 'shoe' on the end of cabriole legs.

sabre leg A leg shaped like the curved blade of a sabre.

scagliola Imitation marble made with plaster.

sgraffito A pattern of scratched decoration that reveals a contrasting colour beneath.

slip A mixture of clay and water used to decorate pottery and to produce slip-cast wares.

soft-paste porcelain Porcelain made from kaolin, powdered glass, soapstone and clay.

splat The central upright in a chair back.

squab A stuffed cushion.

sterling silver A standard of silver where the silver content is 92.5 per cent pure silver.

stretchers The bar between two legs on tables and chairs used to stabilise the structure.

stuff-over seat A chair with an upholstered seat rail.

T

tin-glaze An opaque tin oxide glaze used on earthenware.

transfer printing A method of printing ceramics that involves transferring a design from an inked engraving to a vessel.

transitional The Chinese period around the transition from the Ming to the Qing dynasty.

U V W Y

underglaze Decoration painted on to a biscuit body before glazing.

veneering A technique used in furniture making which involves using fine woods to cover or decorate the surface of less expensive woods.

vermeil Gold-plated silver.

wheel engraving A method of engraving into the surface of glass by holding a rotating wheel of stone or metal against it.

white metal Precious metal that is possibly silver, but not officially marked as such.

yellow metal Precious metal that is possibly gold, but not officially marked as such.

C

G

H

I

J

N

O

P

Q

R

T

INDEX